THE LEGAL ENVIRONMENT OF BUSINESS

9th edition

Roger E. Meiners
UNIVERSITY OF TEXAS AT ARLINGTON

Al H. Ringleb
CONSORTIUM INTERNATIONAL MBA

Frances L. Edwards
CLEMSON UNIVERSITY

THOMSON

WEST

Australia · Canada · Mexico · Singapore · Spain · United Kingdom · United States

THOMSON
WEST

The Legal Environment of Business, Ninth Edition
Roger E. Meiners, Al H. Ringleb, Frances L. Edwards

VP/Editorial Director:
Jack W. Calhoun

Publisher:
Rob Dewey

Acquisitions Editor:
Steve Silverstein

Sr. Developmental Editor:
Jan Lamar

Executive Marketing Manager:
Lisa Lysne

Production Editor:
Robert Dreas

Manager of Technology, Editorial:
Vicky True

Technology Project Editor:
Christine Wittmer

Web Coordinator:
Scott Cook

Manufacturing Coordinator:
Charlene Taylor

Production House:
Argosy Publishing

Printer:
Quebecor World—Versailles
Versailles, Kentucky

Art Director:
Michelle Kunkler

Cover and Internal Designer:
Paul Neff Design

Cover Images:
© Getty Images, Inc.

Library of Congress Control Number:
2004118200

For more information about our products, contact us at:

Thomson Learning Academic
Resource Center 1-800-423-0563

Thomson Higher Education
5191 Natorp Boulevard
Mason, Ohio 45040
USA

Asia (including India)
Thomson Learning
5 Shenton Way
#01-01 UIC Building
Singapore 068808

Australia/New Zealand
Thomson Learning Australia
102 Dodds Street
Southbank, Victoria 3006
Australia

Canada
Thomson Nelson
1120 Birchmount Road
Toronto, Ontario
M1K 5G4
Canada

Latin America
Thomson Learning
Seneca, 53
Colonia Polanco
11560 Mexico
D.F. Mexico

UK/Europe/Middle East/Africa
Thomson Learning
High Holborn House
50/51 Bedford Row
London WC1R 4LR
United Kingdom

Spain (including Portugal)
Thomson Paraninfo
Calle Magallanes, 25
28015 Madrid, Spain

This book is dedicated to
John and Judy Goolsby,
who worked long and hard to build
many things and now give to create
opportunities for the next generation.

BRIEF CONTENTS

Part 3 THE REGULATORY ENVIRONMENT OF BUSINESS 402

Contents

16 *Employment Discrimination* 440

TABLE OF CASES

The principal cases are in bold type. Cases cited or discussed in the text are roman type. References are to pages. Cases cited in principal cases and within other quoted materials are not included.

PREFACE

Courses on the legal and regulatory environment of business provide important background for students preparing for a variety of careers. One faces legal, social, political, and ethical issues in any profession. Most are simple situations that can be handled with common sense, but in many situations ignorance of the principles of law can result in problems.

This textbook presents the legal environment from the perspective of the professional non-lawyer. Few students who take this course will become lawyers, and most will take few additional classes. This course is the opportunity to learn key points of the law from the standpoint of a working professional.

We have received excellent feedback from professors and students who have used the eight previous editions of this book and have pointed out both its shortcomings and its strong points. We have taken these comments into account in preparing this edition to make the book even more helpful and practical as we study the complex legal environment that businesses face in an increasingly international setting.

BASIC ORGANIZATION

A one-semester course in the legal environment of business faces the problem of determining what to cover in such a short time. It is like a physician giving a one-semester course to teach students what they need to know about medicine—so many topics, so little time. There is agreement that the key elements of the legal system must be covered. This is done in Part One of the book, Elements of Law and the Judicial Process. Part Two, Elements of Traditional Business Law, reviews the major areas of the common law (broadly defined) that apply to business. Part Three, The Regulatory Environment of Business, covers the major regulatory laws that managers are likely to face and reviews major points of international business law.

KEY FEATURES

Edited Cases

A primary way to learn law is to read real cases that the courts had to resolve. Each major case presented in the text has the background facts and legal proceedings summarized under the label **Case Background**. Then the court's holding, legal reasoning, and explanation of the law as it applies to the facts at hand are presented from the published opinion in the **Case Decision**. Since most decisions are long, we present only the key portions of the holding. Material that has been deleted is indicated by asterisks (* * *) for lengthy pieces of text and periods (. . .) for shorter amounts.

Finally, **Questions for Analysis** are offered for the reader to consider or for class discussion (answers are provided in the *Instructor's Resource Guide*).

Issue Spotters

About fifty Issue Spotters are scattered throughout the text. Each briefly presents a business situation that requires application of legal elements just covered in the text. These challenges are a way for students to self-test their retention and ability to reason as they apply newly learned principles to practice. They also remind readers that the material learned in this course is practical to everyday issues in business (answers are provided in the *Instructor's Resource Guide*).

International Perspectives

These discuss how similar aspects of the law are handled in other countries. As globalization reaches more businesses, managers must know how to deal with different legal systems and cultures. This feature makes clear that the rules of the game are different in other nations and that managers must be prepared to resolve problems in a complex legal environment.

Cyberlaw

This feature presents short discussions of application of the law to developments arising from the information age. E-commerce and e-mail mean legal issues for the courts to resolve as they apply legal principles to never-before-heard-of ways of doing business, transmitting information, and communicating with friends and strangers.

JurisPrudence?

These add a light touch to the topic at hand by discussing an actual case or unusual legal situation. While law and business are serious, odd things happen that remind us that trouble can come from very unexpected places, that the results of the legal process can be surprising, that scoundrels are among us, and that truth can be stranger than fiction.

Summary

The text of each chapter is summarized in bullet format that provides a quick review of the major points of law and the major rules covered and serves as a self-test of points that will be covered in examinations.

Review and Discussion Questions

The student is first asked to review major terms used in each chapter. (Term meanings are provided in the *Glossary*.) A couple of general questions are asked about major subjects covered in the chapter, followed by *Case Questions*. Several questions in each chapter are answered at http://meiners.westbuslaw.com. We have attempted to keep them short to encourage their use for class discussion or for use as a study tool. *Ethics Questions* pose problems that managers could face. Most chapters have *Internet Assignments* that pose legal environment questions that can be answered by searching materials available on the Internet. These assignments were prepared by Andy

Dorchak, law librarian at Case Western Reserve University. All questions are answered in the *Instructor's Resource Guide*.

Pulling It Together

These case questions at the end of chapters bring together at least one legal issue covered in the chapter and at least one legal issue covered in a previous chapter. We want to keep in mind that when legal matters arise, they often concern more than one area of law. Pulling It Together also serves as a refresher to make sure that concepts covered in previous chapters are not abandoned.

NEW TO THIS EDITION

The tendency in textbooks is to keep packing in more material—adding new information as changes occur. Over the years, this can make books unmanageable. We reduced the coverage of material that students can do without, recognizing that only so many pages and topics can be covered in one class. In paring down the material, we hope to enhance the learning of key concepts.

Our reviewers convinced us that the text needed to be focused more on practical aspects of basic legal rules. Therefore, in this edition, some of the legal detail has been eliminated, such as exceptions that are uncommon or occur in only a few states. We focus on the basic nuts and bolts and use business examples. Half of the major cases in the text are new to this edition. The cases focus on practical situations that students can envision and understand. The holdings are straightforward application of the law to the facts. There is more attention to business law and less focus on legal theory.

The number of chapters is the same, but the orientation is changed. The chapter on alternate dispute resolution was merged with the chapter on the trial process, Chapter 4, with less space devoted to procedure. The chapter on property was divided into two chapters, *Real and Personal Property* and *Intellectual Property*. This allows for more discussion of key areas of the law, especially the rapidly expanding area of intellectual property, which most students particularly enjoy.

Certain chapters have been greatly revised, in order to focus more on application to practical situations. For example, in Chapter 19, *Antitrust Law*, many of the classic antitrust cases were dropped in favor of more modern cases that illustrate application of rules. This approach requires less space and focuses on the key issues in the law. Similarly, Chapter 14, *Employment Relationships*, uses fewer cases on traditional agency matters and more on current employment issues. The key elements are covered in the text, and students will find the cases more readable.

ANCILLARIES

Students and instructors can access the book companion web site at http://meiners.westbuslaw.com. The web site offers answers to selected chapter-ending case problems, online quizzes for each chapter in the text, links to the URLs mentioned in the text, selected case updates, and for instructors, downloadable supplements.

- The *Study Guide* has been revised by text author Roger Meiners. To aid students in their study of the legal environment of business, it includes a chapter summary and outline, multiple-choice and true-false questions, and a test on the key terms included in the chapter. Answers to the questions are included in an appendix at the end of the *Study Guide*.

- The *Instructor's Resource Guide* is revised and expanded. As before, it answers all questions in the book. It also provides a detailed outline of each chapter, summarizing the content of the text, including all cases. The instructor can refer quickly to this guide to remember the points the students have covered in the text. The guide also provides numerous additional summarized cases that the instructor can use to illustrate key points of law. Additional material, such as more discussion of certain points and examples of the law in practice, is provided as lecture and discussion enhancements.

- The updated *Test Bank* has more than 4,000 questions and is available on ExamView, which is a computerized testing software program. Every test question, whether a direct question of information or an application question, is referenced to the main text page. More questions based on fact have been added to test critical thinking ability.

- A set of *Transparency Acetates* and *PowerPoint* slides keyed to the text is available.

New to this edition, *WebTutor ToolBox* is available to those adopters who wish to use it. Preloaded with content and available via a free access code when packaged with this text, *WebTutor ToolBox* pairs all the content of this text's rich Book Companion Web Site with sophisticated course management functionality. You can assign materials (including online quizzes) and have the results flow automatically to your grade book. *WebTutor ToolBox* is ready to use as soon as you log on—or you can customize its preloaded content by uploading images and other resources, adding weblinks, or creating your own practice materials. Students only have access to student resources on the web site. Instructors can enter an access code for password-protected Instructor Resources.

West's Digital Video Library Featuring more than sixty segments on the most important topics in Business Law, West's Digital Video Library helps students make the connection between their textbook and the business world. Four types of clips are represented: 1) **Legal Conflicts in Business** features modern business scenarios; 2) **Ask the Instructor** clips offer concept review; 3) **Drama of the Law** presents classic legal situations; and 4) the newest addition to Digital Video Library, **LawFlix**, features segments from widely recognized modern-day movies. Together these clips bring Business Law to life. Access to West's Digital Video Library is free when bundled with a new text. For more information about this product, visit http://digitalvideolibrary.westbuslaw.com.

Business & Company Resource Center Upon instructor request, the Business & Company Resource Center can be packaged with the text. The Business & Company Resource Center provides access to a dynamic database of global business information, including competitive intelligence, career and investment opportunities, business rankings, company histories, and much more. Unlike other online resources, this comprehensive database offers ever-changing research results, providing accurate and up-to-date company and industry intelligence for thousands of companies!

- Many other West Publishing Company ancillaries are available: Business Law and the Legal Environment Video Library including Court TV® and WestLaw. Please ask your West Representative for the qualification details for these supplements.

Acknowledgments

The authors thank the adopters and reviewers from around the country who sent helpful comments and materials for the ninth edition. Much of the credit for the improvements belongs to them. The reviewers for this edition include:

William N. Bockanic
John Carroll University

Evelyn Boss Cogan
LaSalle University

James G. Frierson
East Tennessee State University

Gamewell Gantt
Idaho State University

Lynda S. Hamilton
Georgia Southern University

S. Jay Sklar
Temple University

Nancy White
Central Michigan University

The authors also extend thanks to the professionals in business, law, and government who assisted in making this textbook as up-to-date and accurate as possible.

Finally, we thank the editors and staff of West Educational Publishing Co. In particular, we thank the sales representatives who continually give us valuable information on the day-to-day perceptions of the textbook—information provided by the instructors and students who are using it. We thank Bob Dreas, whose diligence and determination got us through the production process on schedule. Special thanks also goes to our developmental editor, Jan Lamar, who tolerates us with good humor. The efforts of our publisher, Rob Dewey, and editor, Steve Silverstein, who both manage huge tasks, are much appreciated.

We welcome and encourage comments from the users of this textbook—both students and instructors. By incorporating your comments and suggestions, we can make this text an even better one in the future.

Roger E. Meiners
Al H. Ringleb
Frances L. Edwards

ELEMENTS OF LAW AND THE JUDICIAL PROCESS

PART 1

PART ONE REVIEWS THE MAJOR COMPONENTS of the legal system and provides the framework for understanding the material presented in the other two parts of the book. Just as people in business must understand the elements of accounting, finance, management, and marketing, it is important that they also know how the legal environment plays a critical role in the way business and the economy function. Law changes as the structure of business changes, as social pressures produce changes in political policy that is reflected in the rules under which business operates, as the ethical expectations of business increase, and as the economy becomes more interwoven in international operations.

The chapters in this part review the major components of the legal system: the origins of law, constitutional law, the role of law in society and business, the structure and functioning of the court system and of administrative agencies, and the use of alternative forms of dispute resolution. This serves as a structural background for the rest of the text, which reviews substantive laws that impact business.

Chapter 1

The Modern Environment of Business

Getting full-time employment after college and beginning to build a career are often nerve-wracking. Afraid of being left jobless, some people take less-than-ideal jobs, which sometimes turn out better than expected. On the other hand, some people take what seem to be great jobs, but soon discover otherwise.

It is not uncommon for recruiters to overstate the qualities of a position. A job billed as "character-building" may be one of unending stress. One advertised as having a "team working environment" can mean people jammed in small cubicles. One person reports that while being recruited he was shown a nice office and introduced to his supervisor, whom he liked very much. But when he arrived for work, he was stuck in a back room, the likeable supervisor was gone and replaced by someone he could not stand, and the assignments given were not of the quality discussed.

Suppose that happens to you. Can you sue the recruiter who hired you? Can you sue the company that hired you? Do you have the right to demand a better office? What is your legal status in the situation? These are some of the issues we will explore.

Whether the situation just posed arose intentionally or in the ordinary course of business, the employee probably has little recourse but to keep the job as is, or leave. The employer is unlikely to have violated any legal obligation. But what about the ethical obligation to be honest with current and potential employees? Is overstating the quality of a position unethical, even if it is not in violation of the law? This is another aspect of the modern environment of business.

Because the environment of business is so complex, ethical, legal, social, political, and international issues all impact company operations. As Exhibit 1.1 indicates, whether your field is human resources, banking, advertising, or software development, you must be familiar with a wide range of subjects to have the skills needed to be aware of possible problems and to recognize potential opportunities that someone with a limited view of the world would be likely to miss. This book, which focuses on the legal environment of business, helps to fit one large piece into the complicated puzzle of the modern business world.

The study of the legal environment of business begins with an overview of the nature of law and the legal system. Composed of law from several sources, the legal environment is influenced by the needs and demands of the business community, consumers, and government. This chapter provides an understanding of the functions of law in society, the sources of U.S. law, and the classifications of law. It then considers some major ethical issues that play a large role in the modern environment of business.

Exhibit 1.1

Overview of a Business's Legal Environment

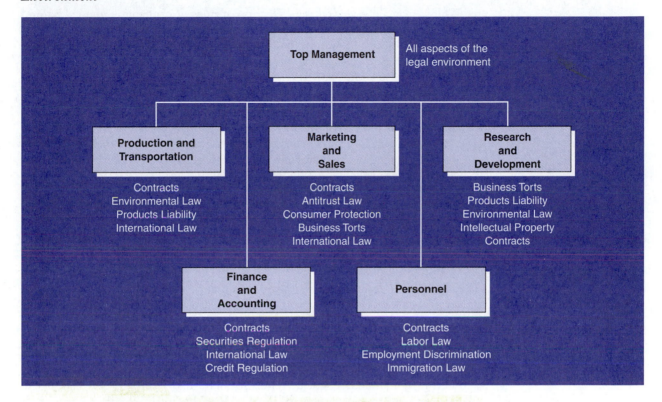

LAW AND THE KEY FUNCTIONS OF THE LEGAL SYSTEM

In the legal environment of business, *law* refers to a code of conduct that defines the behavioral boundaries for business activity. There is no precise definition of law. Law is an abstract term but has long meant the same general thing. According to *Justinian's Institutes*, a summary of Roman law published in 533 in Constantinople, "The commandments of the law are these: live honorably; harm nobody; give everyone his due." A century ago Oliver Wendell Holmes, a legal scholar and Supreme Court justice, offered the following definition:

> Law is a statement of the circumstances, in which the public force is brought to bear . . . through the courts.

In his 1934 book *Growth of Law*, the jurist Benjamin N. Cardozo defined law as follows:

> A principle or rule of conduct so established as to justify a prediction with reasonable certainty that it will be enforced by the courts if its authority is challenged.

Consider these modern definitions from *Black's Law Dictionary*, an authoritative legal dictionary:

1. Law, in its generic sense, is a body of rules of action or conduct prescribed by controlling authority, and having binding legal force.
2. That which must be obeyed and followed by [members of a society] subject to sanctions or legal consequences is a law.

Thus, law may be viewed as a collection of rules or principles intended to limit and direct human behavior. By enforcement, such rules or principles provide a measure of predictability and uniformity to the boundaries of acceptable conduct within a society. Nations have both *formal rules*, that is, what are commonly called laws, and *informal* or *implicit* rules that come from a society's history, customs, commercial practices, and ethics.

Law and the legal system serve several key roles in society. The most important functions include: (1) influencing the behavior of the members of a society, (2) resolving disputes within the society, (3) maintaining important social values, and (4) providing a method for social change. The *International Perspective* feature discusses the efforts in the nation of Chad to develop a legal system that is meaningful to its citizens and attractive to business development. Its experience, which is not unique, reminds us how difficult it is to do business in a country without a workable legal system.

Enhancing Social Stability by Influencing Behavior

The legal system is a major social institution that helps define acceptable behavior and control unacceptable behavior. The law thus limits activities that are detrimental to the "public interest" and encourages beneficial activities. The law restricts business practices that are viewed as outside the ethical and social norms of a society. At the same time, the law can encourage practices that further social and political goals.

The laws in different countries reflect social norms. The business of raising and selling marijuana in Amsterdam (Holland) is legal because the government decided that legalizing marijuana would eliminate the criminal element in the drug trade and make it less likely that people would use harsher drugs that are still illegal, such as cocaine. In the United States, selling marijuana is illegal and can be punished by long prison terms, but the production and sale of alcoholic beverages is legal in most of the country. In Saudi Arabia, people have been executed for being involved in the alcohol business.

Conflict Resolution

The next important function of the law is the resolution of disputes. Disagreements are inevitable, since societies are made up of people with differing desires and social preferences. Karl N. Llewellyn, a legal theorist, states:

> What, then, is this law business about? It is about the fact that our society is honeycombed with disputes. Disputes actual and potential, disputes to be settled and disputes to be prevented; both appealing to law, both making up the business of law. . . . This doing of something about disputes, this doing of it reasonably, is the business of law.

One formal mechanism for the resolution of disputes is the court system, which is used for resolving *private disputes* between members of society and *public disputes* between a person and the government. Our court system is intended to provide a

INTERNATIONAL *Perspective*

Chad: A Third-World Country Tries to Create a Legal System

Chad is in north-central Africa. It is three times the size of California, has a population of eight million people, and has per capita income of about $200 per year.

Chad must develop a legal system more attractive to the world business community and outside investors. No commonly accepted rule of law exists. Chad's citizens do not like to use the court system, because judges often receive orders from the governing authority on how to decide cases. Disputes are often resolved by an unauthorized system of "courts" established by the police and military authorities. Formal law is often in conflict with the customs of various ethnic groups and so is largely ignored. The lack of a predictable legal system is a significant deterrent to the development of the country's commercial base.

To help resolve these difficulties in the legal system, Professor Louis Alcoin recommended the following:

Reform the court system to improve dispute resolution, with emphasis on ensuring that judges are independent of the governing authority.

Establish a separate court to be used only to resolve commercial disputes.

Write and publish the civil and commercial codes.

Reform the areas of enforcing judgments, business registrations, the investment code, property law, government contracts, and banking.

Publish new legislative acts with the understanding that none would take effect until they are published.

In undertaking these legal reforms, include laws that reflect the country's customs and traditions to the extent appropriate.

In the absence of reforms, the country will not overcome the barriers to development that result from the lack of a reliable or respected legal system.

consistent mechanism for resolving disputes. As we will see in Chapter 3, businesses are increasingly turning to conflict resolution processes outside of the courts.

Social Maintenance

A society is shaped by its values and customs. It is not surprising, then, that law plays a crucial role in maintaining the social environment. Honesty and integrity are reflected by the enforceability of contracts; respect for other people and their property is reflected in tort and property law; and some measures of acceptable behavior are reflected in criminal laws. Consider the issue of gay relationships. Until recent years, gay partners could be subject to criminal prosecution for their actions. Now the discussion has turned to whether such relationships can have the same status as traditional marriages. Some contend that legalizing same-sex marriages would be destructive to the structure of society; others argue that it would be stabilizing.

Social Change

The legal system provides a way to bring about changes in "acceptable" behavior. Behavior that was acceptable at one time may not serve society well today, or in the future, as circumstances change. For example, to help alter behavior, laws restrict race discrimination in decisions to hire, promote, or discharge a worker. In the past, race discrimination was an accepted norm of business behavior. Such behavior is no longer acceptable. Social attitudes have changed.

SOURCES OF LAW IN THE UNITED STATES

The most fundamental source of law is the U.S. Constitution, through which other laws are created. The Constitution creates the branches of government—each of which has the ability to make law. Congress—the legislative branch of government—uses its constitutionally granted powers to create what is often referred to as the fourth branch of government, that is, administrative agencies. Similarly, state constitutions determine the structure of government within a state and establish legal procedures and create various rights and restrictions.

Constitutions

A *constitution* is the fundamental law of a nation. It establishes and limits the powers of government. The U.S. Constitution (Appendix C) allocates the powers of government between the states and the federal government. Powers not granted to the federal government are retained by states or are left to the people.

The U.S. Constitution

The U.S. Constitution is the oldest written constitution in force in the world. It sets forth the general organization, powers, and limits of the federal government. Specifically, the Constitution creates the legislative, executive, and judicial branches of the U.S. government.

This division in governmental power is referred to as the *separation of powers*. It arose out of a fear by the founders of this country that too much power might become concentrated in one governmental branch. The separation of powers means that each branch of government has functions to perform that can be checked by the other branches. The government structure that has developed is illustrated in Exhibit 1.2.

The U.S. Constitution is law that is supreme over state or federal laws that go beyond what the Constitution permits. According to Article VI:

> This Constitution, and the Laws of the United States which shall be made in Pursuance thereof; and all Treaties made, or which shall be made, under the Authority of the United States, shall be the supreme Law of the Land; and the Judges in every State shall be bound thereby, any Thing in the Constitution or Laws of any State to the Contrary notwithstanding.

State Constitutions

The powers and structures of all state governments are based on written constitutions. Like the federal government, the state governments are divided into legislative, judicial, and executive branches. The constitutions specify how state officials are chosen and removed, how laws are passed, how the court systems run, and how finances and revenues are paid and collected. Each state constitution is the highest form of law in a state. Some state constitutions, unlike the U.S. Constitution, are very long and are filled with details because amending state constitutions is often much easier than changing the U.S. Constitution.

Legislatures and Statutes

Congress and the state legislatures are the sources of *statutory law*. Statutes or legislation include much of the law that significantly affects business behavior, such as regulations. For example, in 1972, Congress enacted the Clean Water Act. It sets certain standards for water quality for the nation and granted the Environmental Protection Agency the authority to adopt regulations that would make the goals of the statute effective. Similarly at the state level, every state legislature has passed statutes to regulate the insurance industry, usually accomplished with the help of a state insurance commission. Federal courts may review statutes passed by Congress to ensure that they do not violate the U.S. Constitution. The courts in each state may review statutes passed by their legislature to ensure that they do not violate the constitution of the state or of the United States. If a state legislature passes a statute that violates the U.S. Constitution, and a state court does not strike down the statute, the statute may be stricken by a federal court.

United States Congress

Article I, Section 1, of the U.S. Constitution provides that all power to make laws for the federal government is given to Congress, a legislature consisting of a Senate and a House of Representatives. Of the 20,000 pieces of legislation proposed in each session of Congress, fewer than 200 usually reach the House and Senate floors for debate. Many bills are introduced only for political consumption. Of the bills that receive serious consideration, most die in some committee before they reach the full House or Senate for consideration.

State Legislatures

Each state has lawmaking bodies similar to Congress in their functions and procedures. With the exception of Nebraska, all states have a two-part legislature containing a House of Representatives (sometimes called a House of Delegates or an Assembly) and a Senate. The lawmaking process in state legislatures is similar to the procedure followed by the Congress. Note, however, that in some states voters may directly propose or enact legislation through the voting process in referendums or initiatives.

The National Conference of Commissioners on Uniform State Laws works with law professors, the business community, and several legal organizations. For over a century, this organization has proposed "model" laws for consideration by state legislatures. Some are ignored, but others have been widely adopted. An important state law affecting business is the Uniform Commercial Code (UCC). The UCC, discussed in Chapters 11 and 12, is designed to ease the legal relationship between parties involved in commercial transactions by making commercial laws uniform among the various states (and U.S. territories). Another "model" law adopted by most state legislatures is the Uniform Partnership Act, covered in Chapter 13.

Administrative Agencies and Regulations

An administrative agency is created when the legislative or executive branch of the government delegates some of its authority to an agency. Congress (or the state legislature) enacts a law that specifies the duties of the agency. For example, Congress

Exhibit 1.2

*The Government of the
United States*

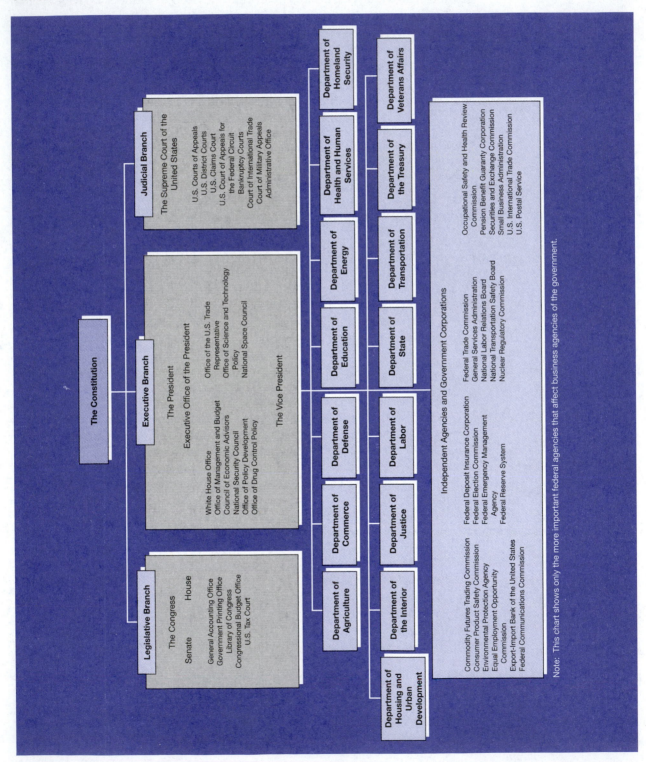

Legislative Branch

The Congress

Senate   House

General Accounting Office
Government Printing Office
Library of Congress
Congressional Budget Office
U.S. Tax Court

The Constitution

Executive Branch

The President

Executive Office of the President

White House Office
Office of Management and Budget
Council of Economic Advisors
National Security Council
Office of Policy Development
Office of Drug Control Policy

Office of the U.S. Trade
Representative
Office of Science and Technology
Policy
National Space Council

The Vice President

Judicial Branch

The Supreme Court of the
United States

U.S. Courts of Appeals
U.S. District Courts
U.S. Claims Court
U.S. Court of Appeals for
the Federal Circuit
Bankruptcy Courts
Court of International Trade
Court of Military Appeals
Administrative Office

Department of Homeland Security

Department of Veterans Affairs

Department of Health and Human Services

Department of the Treasury

Department of Energy

Department of Transportation

Department of Education

Department of State

Department of Defense

Department of Labor

Department of Commerce

Department of Justice

Department of Agriculture

Department of the Interior

Department of Housing and Urban Development

Independent Agencies and Government Corporations

Commodity Futures Trading Commission
Consumer Product Safety Commission
Environmental Protection Agency
Equal Employment Opportunity
Commission
Export-Import Bank of the United States
Federal Communications Commission

Federal Deposit Insurance Corporation
Federal Election Commission
Federal Emergency Management
Agency
Federal Reserve System

Federal Trade Commission
General Services Administration
National Labor Relations Board
National Transportation Safety Board
Nuclear Regulatory Commission

Occupational Safety and Health Review
Commission
Pension Benefit Guaranty Corporation
Securities and Exchange Commission
Small Business Administration
U.S. International Trade Commission
U.S. Postal Service

Note: This chart shows only the more important federal agencies that affect business agencies of the government.

created the Environmental Protection Agency to enact regulations to flesh out the goals of environmental statutes and to be the primary enforcer of those laws. Similarly, all states have created state environmental agencies to help create and enforce state environmental regulation.

With congressional delegation, administrative agencies can exercise broad powers to enact regulations, supervise compliance with those regulations, and adjudicate violations of regulations. Regulations flowing from administrative agencies are among the important sources of law affecting the legal environment of business. The procedures of administrative agencies are discussed in Chapter 5.

The Judiciary and Common Law

The common law—law made and applied by judges as they resolve disputes among private parties—is a major foundation of the legal environment of business. In addition to making the common law, the judiciary interprets and enforces laws enacted by legislative bodies. As we will see, some statutes, such as the antitrust laws, are not precise and require significant court interpretation. The judiciary also reviews actions taken by the executive branch and administrative agencies.

The oldest source of law in the United States, the common law dates to colonial times, when English common law governed most internal legal matters. To maintain social order and to encourage commerce, the colonists retained the common law when the United States became an independent nation.

Case Law

Under the common law, a judge's resolution of a dispute generally follows earlier judicial decisions that resolved similar disputes. For hundreds of years now, the decisions in important cases have been gathered and recorded in books called case reporters. To settle disputes that are similar to past disputes, judges study recorded cases for guidance for their decisions (see Appendix B). A previously decided case provides legal principle, called *precedent*, that can be applied to the facts of a new case under consideration.

To settle unique or novel disputes, judges create new common law. New laws, however, are based on the general principles suggested by many previously recorded decisions. Since common law is state law, there are differences across the states in the interpretation of common-law principles, but the judges in one state often look to cases from other states to help resolve disputes that do not have clearly established principles within a state.

Doctrine of Stare Decisis

The practice of deciding new cases by referencing previous decisions is the foundation of the English and American judicial processes. The use of precedent in deciding present cases forms a doctrine called *stare decisis*, meaning in Latin "to stand on decided cases." Under this doctrine, judges are encouraged (but not forced) to stand by precedents. According to Judge Richard Posner:

> Judge-made rules are the outcome of the practice of decision according to precedent (stare decisis). When a case is decided, the decision is thereafter a precedent, i.e., a reason for deciding a similar case the same way. While a single precedent is a fragile

thing . . . an accumulation of precedents dealing with the same question will create a rule of law having virtually the force of an explicit statutory rule.

Value of Precedent

Stare decisis provides several useful functions. First, consistency in the legal system enhances the ability to plan business decisions. Second, as a rule is applied in many disputes involving similar facts, people will be increasingly confident that the rule will be followed in the resolution of future disputes. Finally, the doctrine creates a more just legal system by neutralizing the prejudices of individual judges. If judges use precedent as the basis for decisions, they are less influenced by their personal biases.

Changes in Society

An advantage of dispute resolution through the common law is its ability to change with the times. As changes occur in technology or in social values, the common law evolves and provides new rules that better fit the new environment. Although most cases are decided on the basis of stare decisis, judges are not prohibited from changing legal principles if conditions warrant. A judge may modify or reverse an existing legal principle. If that decision is appealed to a higher court for review, the higher court may accept the new rule as the one to be followed.

In recent years, there have been rapid changes in the manner in which we can communicate with one another. While the mail dominated in the past, businesses now use faster communications systems to be competitive. E-mail and faxes have often replaced the former method of personally signed documents. The law adapted to accept new communication methods.

JURIS *prudence?*

Creative Common Law

An 18-year-old high school student in California "earned" over $1 million in a stock scam. When the federal authorities busted his operation, charged him with securities fraud, and made him repay his earnings, he was also booted off his high school baseball team.

He then sued his high school for $50 million. The basis of his suit was that he had planned to be a major league baseball player, but now that he could not play on his high school team, he could not perform in front of baseball scouts who would draft him into the pros.

Source: *True Stella Awards*

The Executive

In addition to being the one who signs (or vetoes) bills passed by Congress, the president is another source of law. The president can create law by issuing *executive orders*, requiring federal agencies to do certain things within the president's scope of authority, such as an order to give preference to buying recycled products or to restrict financial transactions by suspected terrorist organizations.

The president can also influence the degree to which administrative agencies undertake their duties and responsibilities. One administration may not pursue environmental, antitrust, or international trade regulation as strongly as another administration. Thus, some industries may face a more hostile legal environment under one administration than under another.

International Sources of Law

Companies doing business in other countries must be as concerned with additional laws. The principal sources of international law affecting business include the laws of individual countries, the laws defined by treaties and trade agreements among countries, and the rules enacted by multinational regional or global entities—such as the World Trade Organization.

Article II, Section 2, of the U.S. Constitution requires approval by two-thirds of the Senate before a treaty (international agreement) agreed to by the president becomes binding on the U.S. Treaties of significance to business include the United Nations Convention on Contracts for the International Sale of Goods (which can govern the sale of goods between parties from different countries), which we discuss in Chapter 11, and the United Nations Convention on the Recognition and Enforcement of Foreign Arbitral Awards (which assists in the enforcement of arbitration clauses in international contracts). Treaties and other laws particular to the international legal environment are discussed in Chapter 21 and at various points in other chapters.

CLASSIFICATIONS OF LAW

The organization of law can be thought of in several ways, such as whether it originated from a constitution, a legislative body, or the judiciary. The more common classification systems, however, classify law on the basis of whether it is: 1) public or private, 2) civil or criminal, or 3) procedural or substantive. Laws may fall into more than one classification. For example, the sale of automobile insurance is affected by private law (a contract between the company and the buyer) and public law (state regulation of insurance, which could result in civil or criminal penalties for insurance sellers who break state law).

Public and Private Law

Some examples of public and private law are provided in Exhibit 1.3. *Public law* is concerned with the legal relationship between members of society—businesses and individuals—and the government. Public law includes statutes enacted by Congress and state legislatures and regulations issued by administrative agencies. It influences the behavior of members of society and brings about social change.

Private law sets forth rules governing the legal relationships among members of society. It helps to resolve disputes and to provide a way for the values and customs of society to influence law. Private law is primarily common law and is enforced primarily through the state court systems. Unlike public law, which at times makes major changes in legal rules, private law tends to be quite stable and changes slowly.

Exhibit 1.3	Public Law	Private Law
Examples of Public and Private Law	Administrative Law	Agency Law
	Antitrust Law	Contract Law
	Bankruptcy Law	Corporation Law
	Constitutional Law	Partnership Law
	Criminal Law	Personal Property
	Environmental Law	Real Property
	Labor Law	Torts
	Securities Regulation	

Civil and Criminal Law

When a legislative body enacts a law, it decides whether the law is to be civil, criminal, or both. Unless a statute is designated as criminal, it is considered civil law. Examples of civil and criminal law are provided in Exhibit 1.4.

Criminal law concerns legal wrongs or crimes committed against the government. As determined by federal or state statute, a crime is classified as a *felony* or a *misdemeanor*. A person found guilty of a criminal offense may be fined, imprisoned, or both. To find a person guilty of a crime, the trial court must find that the evidence presented showed *beyond a reasonable doubt* that the person committed the crime. The severity of punishment depends in part on whether the offense was a felony or a misdemeanor. Generally, those offenses punishable by imprisonment for more than a year are classified as felonies. Misdemeanors are generally less serious crimes, punishable by a fine and/or imprisonment for less than a year.

While criminal laws may be called crimes against the state, most of the cases involve actions against private individuals, not against the government directly. For example, the accounting firm Arthur Andersen was accused of criminal violations for its role in the Enron financial scandal. While those convicted of a criminal offense may be required to pay restitution to the victims of their crimes, the primary purpose of criminal law is not victim compensation, which may be left to civil litigation, but to deter and punish certain behavior.

Civil law is concerned with the rights and responsibilities that exist among members of society or between individuals and the government in noncriminal matters. A person or business found liable for a *civil wrong* may be required to pay money damages to the injured party or to do or refrain from doing a specific act or both. In finding the wrongdoer liable, the jury (or the judge in a nonjury trial) must find that the *preponderance* (majority) *of the evidence* favored the injured party.

Substantive and Procedural Law

Substantive law includes common law and statutory law that define and establish legal rights and regulate behavior. *Procedural law* determines how substantive law is enforced through the courts by determining how a lawsuit begins, what documents need to be filed, which court can hear the case, how the trial proceeds, and so on.

A criminal case, for example, must follow criminal procedural law. The appropriate appellate procedure must be followed when a lower-court decision is appealed to a higher court for review. Similarly, agencies enforcing administrative laws and regulations must follow appropriate procedures. While most of our focus will be on substantive law, it is important to keep in mind that proper procedure must be followed by all participants in the formal legal system. Examples of substantive and procedural law are provided in Exhibit 1.5 on page 16.

	Civil Law	Criminal Law
Exhibit 1.4 *Examples of Civil and Criminal Law*	**Contract Law** Auto Repairs Buying Airline Tickets Forming a Business Sale of Clothing House Insurance **Tort Law** Assault and Battery Defamation Invasion of Privacy Medical Malpractice Trespass	**Misdemeanor Offenses** Assault and Battery (Simple) Disturbing the Peace Larceny (Petit) Public Intoxication Trespass **Felony Offenses** Burglary Homicide Larceny (Grand) Manslaughter Robbery

INTERNATIONAL Perspective

Sources of Law in Japan

An important member of the civil-law family of nations is Japan, which adopted much of the German civil-law legal system in the late 1800s to be more attractive to Western businesses. Like its civil-law counterparts, Japan's basic source of law is its codes. In contrast to common-law systems where many basic laws are developed by judges, civil-law codes are enacted by the government—in Japan, the Diet, or national parliament. The codes arrange categories of law in an orderly and comprehensive way. In Japan, the basic codes are the Civil Code, the Commercial Code, the Penal Code, and procedural codes such as the Code of Criminal Procedure and the Code of Civil Procedure.

To illustrate, under common law, judges have developed rules in tort law imposing liability for intentional and negligent acts. Article 709 of the Japanese Civil Code is quite similar. It states:

A person who violates intentionally or negligently the right of another is bound to make compensation for damages (for injuries to the person, his liberty, or reputation as well as his property) arising therefrom.

The Japanese courts apply codes very strictly. The application of a code provision to a dispute is influenced by past applications, particularly those of the highest courts. Because the Japanese rely more on informal dispute resolution, many parts of the codes have not been litigated. In such situations, Japanese lawyers rely on interpretations of the codes by legal scholars. If no specific code provision applies to a dispute that has arisen, the court may look to traditions in reaching a decision, or it may apply a code provision intended to apply to another type of dispute. Through this process—and the enactment of new code provisions by the Diet—Japan's civil-law legal system adjusts to social, economic, and technological changes.

ETHICS AND BUSINESS

The public image of business has been slipping for decades. According to a poll conducted in 1966, 55 percent of the American people had a "great deal of confidence" in American business executives. In recent years, that percentage has dropped to about 20 percent. Surveys indicate that confidence in business leaders is low—especially with regard to honesty and ethical standards. (Confidence in political leaders and institutions is even lower.)

One possible explanation is that ethical standards have fallen. After all, 75 percent of college students admit to some form of cheating and 79 percent of employees

Exhibit 1.5	Substantive Law	Procedural Law
Examples of Substantive and Procedural Law	Antitrust Law	Administrative Procedure
	Contract Law	Appellate Procedure
	Criminal Law	Civil Procedure
	Environmental Law	Court Orders
	Labor Law	Criminal Procedure
	Securities Regulation	Rules of Evidence

JURIS *prudence?*

Say What?

Michael Price was convicted of two robbery charges in Tulsa, Oklahoma. His lawyer filed an appeal because the trial judge instructed the jury that a defendant is "presumed not guilty" until proven guilty. What the judge should have said is that a defendant is "presumed innocent" until proven guilty. Price's two sixteen-year sentences were overturned, and a new trial was ordered.

Properly charged, the jury in the second trial understood that Price was "presumed innocent" until they found him guilty. Price was found guilty and sentenced to two thirty-year terms.

Source: *Tulsa World* (Ok.)

---

admit to pilfering supplies from their workplace. Unethical (and illegal) behavior is not confined to the top executives at Enron or WorldCom; such instances are noteworthy because of the size of the financial damage done. But such behavior is not new. A study by a professor at Indiana University in 1939 showed that the seventy largest firms in the United States had suffered since their founding an average of fourteen adverse legal decisions for reasons ranging from financial fraud to false advertising.

Whether or not ethics have declined in recent years, it is undeniable that legislation to address issues of corporate dishonesty has mushroomed, accompanied by a cultural expectation that companies will reform themselves. Public anger at real or perceived problems in modern business helps to explain adverse jury attitudes that produce huge verdicts against companies. A survey by the Minority Corporate Counsel Association found anti-business sentiment at an all-time high, regardless of age, race, or sex. The overwhelming majority of people believe that companies hide the truth about the dangers of their products and destroy documents that could get the companies in trouble.

Perceptions of Ethics and Responses

In response to declining public image and real internal problems, most corporations have written codes of ethics. But studies indicate that the development of codes of ethics has done little to improve corporate culture. Professor William Frederick found that corporations with codes of ethics were cited for legal infractions by federal regulatory agencies more frequently than corporations without codes. In corporations making a special effort to improve corporate ethics by placing more people asserted

CYBER *Law*

Online Ethics and Legal Compliance

The evolution of the Internet has meant changes in the law, as we will see at various points in the text. It also means new ethical challenges—but also some opportunities.

Software now allows employers to monitor every keyboard click an employee makes. This is criticized as an invasion of privacy. Is it wrong for an employee to send personal e-mails? Is that really any different from chatting for a few minutes with a co-worker? On the other hand, since employers can be sued for sexual harassment if obscene e-mails are passed around or if pornographic web sites are accessed from company computers, managers have good reason to monitor employees' web site visits and to keep copies of all e-mail transmissions. They can also watch for breaches in security.

Many companies have employees take legal and ethics training online. It is a cost-effective way to make sure employees are informed about employment discrimination, payoffs, conflicts of interest, and other matters that can spell big trouble for businesses. Employees may also be tested online regarding their knowledge of law and ethics. Many employers find online training more effective than gathering people in auditoriums for instruction, where they may tune out the information presented.

to have a socially conscious perspective on their boards of directors, relatively little change in the corporate culture was found.

From Codes to Compliance

Ethics codes matter little unless there is a concerted effort to ensure compliance within an organization. Ethics and legal requirements become blended in compliance codes adopted for an organization. To be effective, such codes require diligent enforcement by management. According to the Department of Justice (DOJ), the existence of an effective corporate *compliance program* is a pivotal factor in the agency's decision whether to prosecute an organization or to recommend leniency to a court when a legal problem arises. DOJ guidelines focus on two critical factors for prosecutors to consider: whether a compliance program is designed to effectively prevent and detect violations, and whether the company in fact enforces its program.

The U.S. Sentencing Guidelines, which list punishment requirements for various crimes, stipulate that a company found guilty of violating a law could have its fines reduced by as much as 95 percent if it is found to have a strong compliance program in place to try to prevent internal wrongdoing and to handle problems appropriately when they do occur. A good ethics/compliance program can also result in a civil proceeding rather than a criminal prosecution of legal violations. Prevention is less costly than a cure. Before we move on to cover specific areas of law in this book, we will first consider the issue of ethics.

Ethics and Morals: Definitions and Applications

When considering standards of behavior, a distinction can be made between morals and ethics. The term *morals* refers to generally accepted standards of right and wrong in a society. The term *ethics* refers to more abstract concepts that might be encountered in the study of the standards of right and wrong in philosophy and theology. For purposes of our practical discussion of business, the terms *morals* and *ethics* are interchangeable.

Putting Ethics into Practice

ISSUE
Spotter

A large chain of stores gives all employees a brief pamphlet called *Business Conduct Guide*. It states that everyone in the company should be "guided by the highest ethical and legal standards." It then gives brief guidance on a number of legal issues. For example:

Antitrust: We must compete vigorously and fairly in the marketplace using our independent judgment to make the best decisions for the Company.

Credit: We must provide accurate disclosure of credit terms and meet all requirements relating to fair credit reporting and equal credit opportunity.

Employees are told to report violations either to their supervisor or to the Chief Financial Officer of the company. Is this likely to be part of an effective ethics/compliance program? Can sales clerks relate to these issues?

Morals and ethics should not be confused with etiquette or good manners. Since statements about either can use terms such as *should* or *ought*, this confusion is tempting. A person may say, "You should not slurp your soup," but that concerns good manners, not moral or ethical behavior. Morals and ethics are more important than etiquette.

Ethics and the Law Compared

Moral and ethical statements should not be confused with rules of law, although the two overlap. The fact that an action is legal does not mean that it is moral and ethical. Suppose management is informed that the company is emitting a toxic pollutant into the atmosphere. The pollutant is not regulated, so no law is being violated. Company scientists believe the pollutant could cause health problems. Should management decide to stop emitting the pollutant? Should it wait until the government makes the emission illegal? Just because emitting the pollutant is legal does not make it ethical.

Questions about legality and morality are not necessarily the same. The court faces this issue in the *Soldano* case. The plaintiff asserts that if the defendant had acted, a life would have been saved. Although the defendant's refusal to act may have been unethical or immoral, the court is asked to decide whether it was illegal.

Soldano v. O'Daniels

California Court of Appeals
141 Cal.App.3d 443, 190 Cal.Rptr. 310 (1983)

CASE BACKGROUND   *Villanueva entered Happy Jack's Saloon, pulled a gun, and threatened to kill Soldano. A patron of Happy Jack's ran across the street to a bar called the Circle Inn, told an employee about the incident at Happy Jack's, and asked the employee to call the police or allow him to make the call. The employee refused. Soldano was killed by Villanueva. Soldano's child (the plaintiff) brought a wrongful death action against the owner of the Circle Inn.*

On the grounds that a person cannot be liable for failure to act, the trial court dismissed the case. The plaintiff appealed, arguing that the case should have been allowed to go to trial.

CASE DECISION   Andreen, Associate Justice.

* * *

Does a business establishment incur liability for wrongful death if it denies use of its telephone to a good samaritan who explains an emergency situation occurring without and wishes to call the police?

* * *

There is a distinction, well rooted in the common law, between action and nonaction. It has found its way into the prestigious *Restatement Second of Torts* (hereafter cited as "*Restatement*"), which provides in section 314:

> The fact that the actor realizes or should realize that action on his part is necessary for another's aid or protection does not of itself impose upon him a duty to take such action.

The distinction between . . . active misconduct [causing] injury and failure to act to prevent [injury] not brought on by the defendant, is founded on "that attitude of extreme individualism so typical of anglo-saxon legal thought."

Defendant argues that the request that its employee call the police is a request that it do something. He points to the *established rule* that one who has not created a peril ordinarily does not have a duty to take affirmative action to assist an imperiled person. It is urged that the alternative request of the patron from Happy Jack's Saloon that he be allowed to use defendant's telephone so that he personally could make the call is again a request that the defendant do something—assist another to give aid. Defendant points out that the Restatement sections which impose liability for negligent interference with a third person giving aid to another do not impose the additional duty to aid the good samaritan.

The refusal of the law to recognize the moral obligation of one to aid another when he is in peril and when such aid may be given without danger and at little cost in effort has been roundly criticized. Prosser describes the case law sanctioning such inaction as a "refus(al) to recognize the moral obligation of common decency and common humanity" and characterizes some of these decisions as "shocking in the extreme. . . . Such decisions are revolting to any moral sense. They have been denounced with vigor by legal writers." A similar rule has been termed "morally questionable" by our Supreme Court. . . . It is time to re-examine the common law rule of nonliability for [nonaction] in the special circumstances of the instant case.

* * *

The employee's conduct displayed a disregard for human life that can be characterized as morally wrong (Footnote 9. The moral right of plaintiff's decedent to have the defendant's bartender permit the telephone call is so apparent that legal philosophers treat such rights as given and requiring no supporting argument. The concept flows from the principle that each member of a community has a right to have each other member treat him with the minimal respect due a fellow human being): he was callously indifferent to the possibility that Darrell Soldano would die as the result of his refusal to allow a person to use the telephone. Under the circumstances before us the bartender's burden was minimal and exposed him to no risk: all he had to do was allow the use of the telephone. It would have cost him or his employer nothing. It could have saved a life. Finding a duty in these circumstances would promote a policy of preventing future harm. A citizen would not be required to summon the police but would be required, in circumstances such as those before us, not to impede another who has chosen to summon aid.

* * *

The words of the Supreme Court on the role of the courts in a common law system are well suited to our obligation here:

The inherent capacity of the common law for growth and change is its most significant feature. Its development has been determined by the social needs of the community which it serves. It is constantly expanding and developing in keeping with advancing civilization and the new conditions and progress of society, and adapting itself to the gradual change of trade, commerce, arts, inventions, and the needs of the country. . . .

In short, as the United States Supreme Court has aptly said, "This flexibility and capacity for growth and adaptation is the peculiar boast and excellence of the common law."

* * *

The possible imposition of liability on the defendant in this case is not a global change in the law. It is but a slight departure from the "morally questionable" rule of nonliability for inaction absent a special relationship. It is one of the predicted "inroads upon the older rule." . . . However small it may be it is a step which should be taken.

continues

We conclude that there are sufficient justiciable issues to permit the case to go to trial and therefore reverse.

CASE NOTE

Note: As later courts have explained, this decision is unique.

QUESTIONS FOR ANALYSIS

1. Under the "established rule" of the common law, the Circle Inn had no duty to provide help. Is the established rule overly broad? Where should the line be drawn?

2. What factors motivated the court to modify the established rule in this case?

Just as legality does not imply morality, illegality does not always imply immorality. The fact that an action is illegal does not necessarily mean it is immoral or unethical. If the speed limit is 65 mph, is it unethical to go 68 mph? The moral status of the civil rights activities of the 1960s is not settled by the fact that some of those activities were illegal. In his *Letter from Birmingham Jail*, Martin Luther King, Jr., said, "I can urge [people] to disobey segregation ordinances, for the [ordinances] are morally wrong."

Laws designed to restrict opportunities for minorities were common until the time of the civil rights movement. The moral force used to oppose those laws was a key reason many of the laws were stricken and segregation was declared illegal. However, some laws remain on the books that restrict economic opportunities. For example, the Davis-Bacon Act, passed in the 1930s, requires building contractors in projects receiving federal money to pay "prevailing wages." In practice, prevailing wages is union scale. The Davis-Bacon Act was passed by northern members of Congress who had strong union support and members of Congress from southern states. Northern all-white unions did not like the competition from building

---

INTERNATIONAL *Perspective*

Does Regulation Improve Business Ethics?

The financial scandals involving Enron and other companies provided strong rationale for expanded securities regulation. The drug trade has resulted in increased control of money transfers. When problems arise, there is usually a call for increased government regulation to prevent future problems.

All nations have regulations and bureaucracy. But the wrong kind of regulation coupled with a corrupt bureaucracy stifles business and reduces economic opportunities for ordinary people. The World Bank report, *Doing Business*, notes that the more regulation a country has, the more corruption it is likely to have, and the lower its standard of living.

The World Bank gives some examples. To start a small business in Indonesia, an entrepreneur must wait an average of six months for permits. In the United Arab Emirates, trying to collect payment from a customer who will not pay requires twenty-seven procedures taking almost two years. In India, bankruptcy procedures take an average of ten years. The countries that regulate business the most include Bolivia, Burkina Faso, Chad, Costa Rica, Guatemala, Mali, Mozambique, Paraguay, the Philippines, and Venezuela. The countries that regulate the least include Australia, Canada, Denmark, Hong Kong, Jamaica, the Netherlands, New Zealand, Singapore, Sweden, and the United Kingdom.

Good regulation requires ethics in government. In many countries, regulation simply provides a legal excuse to collect bribes. The regulations stay as they are because there are political interests that want to keep the system in place—including established business interests that want to be protected against new competitors.

contractors who hired blacks who were willing to do the jobs for lower wages to get out of the rural South. African-Americans were glad to have economic opportunities in the North. Southern politicians did not want blacks to leave the South because it reduced the supply of black farm workers. The effect of the law was to reduce economic opportunities for new entrants into the construction industry, often minorities who would like to compete for government contracts. Can such restrictions on economic competition be justified as moral, even though clearly legal?

Should the courts uphold laws that produce immoral results? In the *Soldano* case we saw a moral problem caused by a legal rule that affects decisions of private citizens. What about statutes that produce immoral results? If the statutes do not violate constitutional rights, the courts tend to leave them alone. Otherwise, judges become legislators. Consider the ethical aspects of the issues raised in the *Stanley* case.

United States v. Stanley
United States Supreme Court
483 U.S. 669, 107 S.Ct. 3054 (1987)

CASE BACKGROUND   *Stanley was an Army sergeant who volunteered in 1958 to participate in a program he was told would test the effectiveness of protective clothing against chemical warfare. The volunteers, unknown to them, were given doses of LSD. The Army wanted to test the effects of that drug. For years afterward, Stanley suffered hallucinations, memory loss, and periods of incoherence; could not work well; and on occasion would "awake from sleep at night and . . . violently beat his wife and children, later being unable to recall the entire incident." Stanley left the Army in 1969 and was divorced. In 1975, the Army contacted him and asked him to cooperate in a study of the long-term effects of LSD on "volunteers" from the 1958 test. That was the first time Stanley knew he had been given the drug.*

Stanley sued the Army for compensation, but the claim was denied. Stanley then filed suit under the Federal Tort Claims Act. The district court ruled for the government because Stanley "was at all times on active duty and participating in a bona fide Army program during the time the alleged negligence occurred. . . . [T]he government is not liable under the Federal Tort Claims Act for injuries to servicemen where the injuries arise out of or are in the court of activity incident to service." The court of appeals upheld this judgment. Stanley appealed.

CASE DECISION   Scalia, Justice.

* * *

. . . [T]he Constitution explicitly conferred upon Congress the power . . . "[t]o make Rules for the Government and Regulation of the land and naval Forces," U.S. Const. Art. I, §8, cl. 14, thus showing that "the Constitution contemplated that the Legislative Branch have plenary control over rights, duties, and responsibilities in the framework of the Military Establishment. . . ."

[The dismissal of Stanley's claim was upheld; he had no case under the Federal Tort Claims Act or under the laws written by Congress concerning the rights of members of the Armed Forces.]

* * *

Justice Brennan . . . dissenting in part.

In experiments designed to test the effects of lysergic acid diethylamide (LSD), the Government of the United States treated thousands of its citizens as though they were laboratory animals, dosing them with this dangerous drug without their consent. One of the victims, James B. Stanley, seeks compensation from the Government officials who injured him. The Court holds that the Constitution provides him with no remedy, solely because his injuries were inflicted while he performed his duties in the Nation's Armed Forces. If our Constitution required this result, the Court's decision, though legally necessary, would expose a tragic flaw in that document. . . .

continues

Before addressing the legal questions presented, it is important to place the Government's conduct in historical context. The medical trials at Nuremberg in 1947 deeply impressed upon the world that experimentation with unknowing human subjects is morally and legally unacceptable. The United States Military Tribunal established the Nuremberg Code as a standard against which to judge German scientists who experimented with human subjects. Its first principle was:

"1. *The voluntary consent of the human subject is absolutely essential.*

"The duty and responsibility for ascertaining the quality of the consent rests upon *each individual* who initiates, directs or engages in the experiment. *It is a personal duty and responsibility which may not be delegated to another with impunity.*" *United States* v. *Brandt* (The Medical Case), 2 Trials of War Criminals Before the Nuremberg Military Tribunals Under Control Council Law No. 10, pp. 181–182 (1949) (emphasis added).

The United States military developed the Code, which applies to all citizens—soldiers as well as civilians. . . .

Having invoked national security to conceal its actions, the Government now argues that the preservation of military discipline requires that Government officials remain free to violate the constitutional rights of soldiers without fear of money damages. What this case and others like it demonstrate, however, is that Government officials (military or civilian) must not be left with such freedom. . . .

* * *

[Brennan argued that Stanley should be allowed to sue the officers who conducted the experiments, but not the U.S. government.]

QUESTIONS FOR ANALYSIS

1. A report issued by Congress expressed outrage at what had happened. Besides express outrage, what else could Congress have done?

2. Brennan would give Stanley the right to sue the people in charge of the experiment but not the right to sue the government. Details of the legal rules aside, is that decision more moral than the one to give Stanley no cause of action?

3. Should the courts be in the business of applying ethical principles rather than enforcing laws held to be constitutional?

SUMMARY

- The modern environment of business means that managers in all firms face a variety of ethical, legal, social, political, and international issues that make business increasingly complex.
- *Law* is a collection of principles and rules that establish, guide, and alter the behavior of members of society. Rules include both the formal rules (law) of society and the informal rules as dictated by customs, traditions, and social ethics.
- Law and the legal system serve important functions in an orderly society. Law helps to define acceptable behavior. To ensure order, the legal system provides a formal means through which disputes can be resolved. The law maintains the important values of a society. Finally, the legal system provides a way to encourage changes in social consciousness.
- Sources of law include the U.S. and state *constitutions*, Congress and the state legislatures, the judiciary, the executive branch (the president at the federal level and the governors at the state level), state and federal administrative agencies, and multiple sources that form the international legal environment of business.
- Judge-made or *common law* is the original source of law in this country. This system encourages judges to use prior decisions—*precedents*—for guidance in deciding new disputes. The doctrine of *stare decisis* helps give consistency to case law.

- Law can be classified on the basis of whether it is public or private, civil or criminal, or substantive or procedural.
- The public image of business and of other institutions has declined. Dishonesty is believed to be more prevalent than it was in years past. To overcome real and perceived problems, the business community is encouraging codes of ethics and firms are enforcing *compliance programs*.
- The terms *ethics* and *morals* are generally interchangeable. These terms should not be confused with statements about etiquette or good manners or with rules of law.

REVIEW AND DISCUSSION QUESTIONS

1. You should be able to define the following terms:

law	substantive law
common law	statute
precedent	ethics
stare decisis	morals
constitution	compliance programs
procedural law	

2. Compare and contrast the following:
   a. Civil law and criminal law
   b. Felony and misdemeanor
   c. Substantive law and procedural law
   d. Preponderance of the evidence and beyond a reasonable doubt
   e. Ethics and etiquette
   f. Ethics and the law

3. Should the common-law maxim "Ignorance of the law is no excuse" apply to an immigrant who does not speak English?

CASE QUESTIONS

4. Consider the following fact situation taken from a judge's decision:
   The crew of an English yacht . . . were cast away in a storm on the high seas . . . and were compelled to put into an open boat belonging to the said yacht. That in this boat they had no supply of water and no supply of food. . . . That on the eighteenth day . . . they . . . suggested that one should be sacrificed to save the rest. . . . That next day . . . they . . . went to the boy . . . put a knife into his throat and killed him then and there; that the three men fed upon the body . . . of the boy for four days; that on the fourth day after the act had been committed the boat was picked up by a passing vessel, and [they] were rescued, still alive. . . . That they were carried to the port of Falmouth, and committed for trial . . . That if the men had not fed upon the body of the boy they would probably not have survived to be so picked up and rescued, but would within the four days have died of famine. That the boy, being in a much weaker condition, was likely to have died before them. . . . The real question in this case [is] whether killing under the conditions set forth . . . be or be not murder. [*Regina* v. *Dudley and Stephens*, 14 Queens Bench Division 273 (1884)] In deciding this case, what factors should the judge take into account?

5. The evidence is clear that smoking is a serious health hazard. Should cigarette manufacturers be liable for the serious illnesses and untimely deaths caused by their products—even though they post a warning on the package and consumers voluntarily assume the health risks by smoking? [*Cipollone* v. *Liggett Group, Inc.*, 505 U.S. 504, 112 S. Ct. 2608 (1992)]

 Check your answer at <u>http://meiners.westbuslaw.com</u>

6. Two eight-year-old boys were seriously injured when riding Honda mini-trail bikes provided by their parents. The boys were riding on public streets and ran a stop sign when they were hit by a truck. One boy was not wearing a helmet. The bikes had clear warning labels on the front stating that they were only for offroad use. The owner's manual was clear that the bikes were not to be used on public streets and that riders should wear helmets. The parents sued Honda. The supreme court of Washington said that there was one basic issue. "Is a manufacturer liable when children are injured while riding one of its mini-trail bikes on a public road in violation of manufacturer and parental warnings?" What do you think the court held? Is it unethical to make products like minibikes that will be used by children? [*Baughn* v. *Honda Motor Co.*, 727 P.2d 655 (Sup. Ct., Wash., 1986)]

7. In 1982, Johnson Controls adopted a "fetal protection policy" that women of childbearing age could not work in the battery-making division of the company. Exposure to lead in the battery operation could cause harm to unborn babies. The company was concerned about possible legal liability for injury suffered by babies of mothers who had worked in the battery division. The Supreme Court held that the company policy was illegal. It was an "excuse for denying women equal employment opportunities." Is the Court forcing the company to be unethical by allowing pregnant women who ignore the warnings to expose their babies to the lead? [*United Auto Workers* v. *Johnson Controls*, 499 U.S. 187 (1991)]

 Check your answer at <u>http://meiners.westbuslaw.com</u>

ETHICS QUESTIONS

8. The federal tax code is riddled with special-interest loopholes. Most of these exist because firms and trade associations lobby Congress and provide campaign support to members of Congress to gain special favors to individual firms or industries. Is it ethical for firms to seek special privilege?

9. Migrant farm workers are at about the bottom of our employment force and quality-of-life standards. They work very hard, do not make much money, and often live in miserable conditions. You run a large vegetable farm operation that hires migrant workers an average of four weeks per year. You pay the going wage rate for the workers, who rent dumps to live in while they work in your area before moving north. Do you have an ethical responsibility to pay more than the market wage so that these workers can live in better conditions? Do you have a responsibility to provide housing to the workers you employ? If you pay above-market rates, your neighbor farmers will be mad at you and point out that—as you know—farm operations run on thin margins as it is, so that higher wages could drive you all out of business. Assuming these to be facts, what responsibilities do you think you have?

10. The ABC Company has been supplying widgets to your XYZ Company for many years. The widgets are needed in the production of gidgets. ABC has always been a fair company to deal with. When problems have arisen, ABC has usually resolved them to your satisfaction. Now the LMN firm from Shanghai has approached you, saying it will provide widgets to you for 30 percent less than you were paying ABC. ABC tells you that there is no way it can cut its prices and, if you cut it off, it will have to pare back production so that fifty people will be fired. Should you stick with ABC to protect American jobs? What other considerations may be involved?

INTERNET ASSIGNMENT

http://uscode.house.gov
http://www4.law.cornell.edu/uscode
http://www.findlaw.com
http://www.uscourts.gov
http://www.ussc.gov

The national agencies of federal judicial administration consist of:

   (a) The Judicial Conference of the United States (28.U.S.C. Section 331),
   (b) The Administrative Office of the U.S. Courts (28 U.S.C. Sections 601–612),
   (c) The Judicial Councils of the Circuits (28 U.S.C. Section 332),
   (d) The Judicial Conference of the Circuits (28 U.S.C. Section 333), and
   (e) The U.S. Sentencing Commission (28 U.S.C. Sections 991-998).

These agencies have a significant impact on the federal legal landscape. For example, recommendations of the Judicial Conference of the United States ordinarily become law with few changes made by the legislature. Understanding the federal courts' operation requires some knowledge of the functions of judicial agencies.

1. Find the U.S. Code section associated with (a)–(c), using the official U.S. government web site.
2. Find the U.S. Code section associated with (d), using the Legal Information Institute web site.
3. Find the U.S. Code section associated with (e), using FindLaw.
4. According to the Federal Judiciary Homepage (FAQs), http://www.uscourts.gov, how many courts of appeals are there?
5. According to the Federal Judiciary Homepage, how many district courts are there?
6. According to the U.S. Sentencing Commission web site (Overview), what two factors do the sentencing guidelines take into account?

Chapter 2 | *The Court Systems*

Folley's Metal Fabrication of California advertises and sells its products in several western states. Its products are all manufactured in California. If a customer in Arizona buys a Folley's product after seeing a Folley's advertisement, and is then injured using it, can that injured customer bring the lawsuit to the Arizona state court systems for resolution? Must the dispute be decided in a California state court because the business is located in that state? Or would such a dispute be decided in the federal court system? Does the law of Arizona or California apply? In any dispute, parties must understand and resolve these questions before they can effectively use our court system.

This chapter provides an overview of the American court system and discusses how a party who has suffered a legal wrong can seek relief in the courts. In their operations, businesses may face disputes with competitors, suppliers, customers, and government agencies. Many problems are resolved by the parties with no serious disruption in business relationships or activities. A significant number, however, require resolution in our court system—through civil litigation.

A business that has a civil dispute going to litigation must first determine (with the help of its attorney), Which court has the power and the authority to decide the case? That is, which court has the jurisdiction to take the case for resolution? Today, many businesses operate in several states—and often in several countries. As a consequence, the choice of the appropriate court may not be clear or the parties may be in a position to choose between appropriate courts.

THE FEDERAL AND STATE COURT SYSTEMS

The federal court system was created in response to the following declaration in the U.S. Constitution:

> The judicial Power of the United States, shall be vested in one supreme Court and in such inferior Courts [courts subordinate to the Supreme Court] as the Congress may from time to time ordain and establish.

After a long period of adjustment, the federal court system developed into a three-level system. It consists of the U.S. district courts, the U.S. courts of appeals, and the U.S. Supreme Court. Each court has its own distinct role within the federal court system. Since the 13 original states had courts before the federal system was created, they have the oldest court systems. Over the years, the two systems have evolved to have many similarities.

Organization of the Court Systems

The state and federal court systems both have lower courts of *original jurisdiction*, where disputes are first brought and tried, and courts of *appellate jurisdiction*, where the decisions of a lower court can be taken for review. In both systems, the courts of original jurisdiction are trial courts. One judge presides. The court's principal function is to determine the facts in the dispute and to apply the appropriate law to those facts in making a decision (judgment). As we discuss in the next chapter, the jury is responsible for deciding the facts in a case; if there is no jury in a case, the judge decides the facts.

Appellate courts are concerned with errors in the application of the law and in the procedural rules applied during the trial court proceeding. Normally three judges review decisions at the intermediate appellate court level. Five or more judges are used in the highest appellate state courts. The basic structure of the American court system is illustrated in Exhibit 2.2. While we focus more on federal courts here, the majority of litigation occurs in state courts.

Federal District Courts

As the trial courts of the federal system, U.S. district courts are the courts of original jurisdiction in the federal system. The district courts are the only courts in the system that use juries. Most cases involving questions of federal law originate in these courts. The geographical boundaries of a district court's jurisdiction will not extend across state lines. Thus, each state has at least one federal district court; the more populated states are divided into two, three, or—as in California, New York, and Texas—four districts. In addition, there are federal district courts in the District of Columbia, Puerto Rico, Guam, and the Virgin Islands.

Federal Appellate Courts

U.S. courts of appeals may review federal district court decisions. Established in 1891, the U.S. courts of appeals are the intermediate-level appellate courts in the federal system. There are now twelve courts of appeals, one for each of the eleven circuits into which the United States is divided and one for the District of Columbia. The division of the states into circuits and the location of the U.S. courts of appeals are presented in Exhibit 2.1.

*The Federal Judicial
Circuits*

As appellate courts, the U.S. courts of appeals exercise only appellate jurisdiction. If either party to the litigation is not satisfied with a federal district court's decision, it has the *right* to appeal to the court of appeals for the circuit in which that district court is located. The Fourth Circuit U.S. Court of Appeals in Richmond, Virginia, for example, will hear appeals only from the federal district courts in the states of Maryland, North Carolina, South Carolina, Virginia, and West Virginia. The one exception is the U.S. government, which does not have the right to appeal a decision involving a criminal dispute.

The U.S. courts of appeals assign three-judge panels to review decisions of the district courts within their circuits. They also review orders of federal administrative agencies when a party appeals the final decision of a regulatory agency. As a practical matter, because it is so difficult to obtain review by the U.S. Supreme Court, the courts of appeals make the final decision in most cases.

Specialized Federal Courts

Although the U.S. Supreme Court, courts of appeals, and district courts are the most visible federal courts, there are a few important courts with limited or special jurisdiction within the federal court system. These courts differ from other federal courts in that their jurisdictions are defined in terms of subject matter rather than by geography.

The most prominent of these courts is the Court of Appeals for the Federal Circuit, created in 1982. Although its territorial jurisdiction is nationwide, its subject-matter jurisdiction is limited to appeals from the U.S. district courts in patent, trademark, and copyright cases and in cases where the United States is a defendant; appeals from the U.S. Claims Court and U.S. Court of International Trade; and the review of administrative rulings of the U.S. Patent and Trademark Office. As in the U.S. courts of appeals, three-judge panels preside over cases before the Court of Appeals for the Federal Circuit.

U.S. Supreme Court

The U.S. Supreme Court is the highest court in the country, as we see in Exhibit 2.2. Created by the U.S. Constitution, the Supreme Court is primarily an appellate review court. Cases reaching the Court are usually heard by nine justices, one of whom is the Chief Justice. The term of the Court begins, by law, on the first Monday in October and continues as long as the business of the Court requires. The Court sits in Washington, D.C.

As an appellate court, the Supreme Court may review appeals from the U.S. district courts, the U.S. courts of appeals, and the highest courts of the states. In rare instances, such as in the case of a dispute between two state governments, the U.S. Supreme Court has *original and exclusive jurisdiction*. Although the Congress may change the Court's appellate jurisdiction, it cannot change the Court's original jurisdiction conferred upon it by the Constitution.

INTERNATIONAL *Perspective*

The French Court System

Like most European countries, France is a civil-law country—its legal system is based on written (code) law rather than on judge-made common law. The structure of the French system appears similar to that of the U.S. federal court system. The French system consists of a supreme court (*cour de cessation*), a court of appeals (*cour d'appel*), and a court of general jurisdiction (*tribunal d'instance*).

The appellate process in France is considerably different from that in the United States. In contrast to the powers held by the U.S. Supreme Court, the *cour de cessation* does not have the authority to pronounce judgment. Rather, it has power either to reject an appeal or to invalidate a decision and return the case to the court of appeals for reconsideration.

In the event the appeal is rejected, the proceedings are finished. If, on the other hand, the decision of the *cour d'appel* is invalidated, that court then reconsiders the case before a five-judge panel. However, the judges are not bound by the higher court's determination of the law as they would be in the United States. They may either accept or reject it. They may also consider new facts.

If the case is then appealed a second time to the *cour de cessation*, the case is heard by a panel of twenty-five judges. If this appeal is rejected, the proceedings end; if the *cour d'appel* decision is invalidated, the case is returned to it for reconsideration. On the second appeal, however, the judges of the *cour d'appel* must follow the higher court's decisions on points of law.

Appellate review is normally obtained by petitioning the court for a *writ of certiorari*. Nearly all appeals to the Supreme Court are at the Court's discretion. The members of the Court determine which cases they wish to review; at least four justices must agree to review a case. If that does not happen, the decision of the lower court becomes final. Although it receives thousands of such petitions each term, the

Exhibit 2.2

The Court Systems

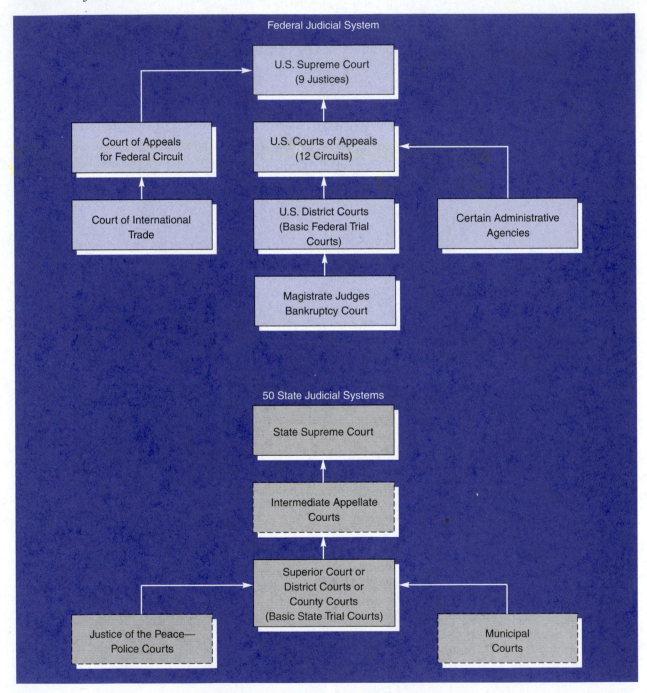

Court accepts less than 200. Most petitions granted involve an issue of constitutional importance or a conflict between the decisions of two or more U.S. courts of appeals.

Despite differences in substantive law, foreign courts are often similar in basic structure, but not in procedure, to those in the United States. *The International Perspective* feature looks at the court system in France.

The State Courts

Although the names and organization differ somewhat from state to state, the state court systems are similar in general framework and jurisdictional authorities. Many are three-level systems and many states have local courts of special or limited jurisdiction.

State Courts of Original Jurisdiction

Each state court system has courts of *original jurisdiction*, or trial courts, where disputes are initially brought and tried. These are often courts of *general jurisdiction* and several courts of *limited* or *special jurisdiction*. The courts of general jurisdiction have authority to decide almost any kind of dispute and are able to grant virtually every type of relief. In many states, the amount in controversy, however, must generally exceed a specific amount, typically $2,000 to $5,000.

The state courts of general jurisdiction, or trial courts, are organized into districts, often on the county level. These district courts have different names in different states, although their jurisdictional limitations are similar. In some states, the courts of general jurisdiction are called superior courts. The same courts in Pennsylvania and Ohio are called the Courts of Common Pleas, and in Oregon, the Circuit Courts. In Kansas, Louisiana, Maine, and other states, the courts of general jurisdiction are called district courts.

Courts of limited or special jurisdiction include municipal courts, justice of the peace courts, and other more specialized courts (such as probate courts, which handle only matters related to wills and trusts). The jurisdiction of the municipal courts is similar to that of the district courts, except the claims they hear typically involve less money. Litigants not satisfied with the decision of the limited-jurisdiction court may appeal to the court of general jurisdiction. On appeal, the parties will get a new trial or, in legal terminology, a *trial de novo*.

Similarly, many states provide *small claims courts*, which have very limited jurisdiction. Restrictions are imposed on the subject matter these courts can hear and the amount in controversy. For example, the amount in controversy in many small claims courts must not exceed $5,000, and the subject matter is limited to debts and contract disputes. Small claims courts are particularly advantageous for collecting small debts because procedure requirements are much less formal and representation by an attorney is not necessary and usually not permitted. Small claims courts are a much faster (and less expensive) forum than the district courts, with disputes generally being heard within a month or two after their filing date.

State Courts of Appellate Jurisdiction

Every judicial system allows the review of trial court decisions by a court with *appellate jurisdiction*. Generally, a party has the right to appeal a judgment to at least one higher court. When a court system contains two levels of appellate courts, appeal usually lies as a matter of right to the first level and at the discretion of the court at the second. The highest appellate court will often limit its review to cases having important legal issues. The most common issues reaching the highest court in a state typically involve the validity of a state law, the state constitution, or a federal law as it is affected by a state law. A party seeking further review from the highest state court may seek review from the U.S. Supreme Court, but that is rarely granted.

Rules of Civil Procedure

From the moment the *plaintiff*—the party who claims to have suffered an injury that the law can remedy—brings an action, a lawsuit is governed by detailed procedural rules. These force the parties to define the issues in the dispute. The rules also control how the parties to the dispute—the plaintiff and the *defendant* (the party who allegedly injured the plaintiff)—present evidence and arguments in support of their positions.

Although the states are free to develop their own procedural rules, most have adopted the *Federal Rules of Civil Procedure* or rules similar to them. The Federal Rules were developed by an advisory committee appointed by the U.S. Supreme Court, became effective in 1938, and have been modified over the years. The Federal Rules govern the procedure of the litigation process, including the pleadings, discovery, trial procedures, and relevant motions. Note that these rules govern only civil litigation; somewhat different procedures are used in criminal and administrative litigation.

The Federal Rules of Civil Procedure are contained in the United States Code, Title 28. In addition to establishing trial procedural rules, Title 28 establishes the organization of the federal courts, judicial agencies, and important rules governing jurisdiction and venue. This chapter concentrates on jurisdiction and the organization of the court system. Chapter 3 examines trial procedures and processes.

JURISDICTION

The literal meaning of the term *jurisdiction* is "the power to speak of the law." A court's jurisdiction defines the limits within which it may declare, expound, administer, or apply the law. The basic limitations imposed upon a court by a constitution and the statutes that created it determine what kinds of disputes it may resolve, depending on who the parties to the dispute are.

When a plaintiff files a lawsuit, the correct court must be chosen to resolve the dispute. While there are a number of courts, the plaintiff's choices are limited to the court or courts having appropriate jurisdiction. The plaintiff must select a court that has both:

1. Subject-matter jurisdiction
2. Personal jurisdiction over a) the person of the defendant or b) the property of the defendant

If a court should rule in a particular case and it is later determined that jurisdiction was lacking, the judgment of that court will be declared null and void upon appeal. Without jurisdiction a court cannot exercise authority.

Subject-Matter Jurisdiction

Subject-matter jurisdiction is created by a constitution or a statute regarding the types of disputes a court can accept to resolve. It might include requirements on the amount in controversy or restrictions on the legal area a court can hear. For example, state statutes might restrict disputes in district (trial) courts to civil cases involving more than $2,000, or they might require that all cases involving wills be heard by a probate court. That is, the state legislature places limitations on the subject-matter jurisdiction of various courts.

JURIS *prudence?*

Being a Judge Makes Me Sick?

A California judicial board fact-finding panel held that Los Angeles judge Patrick Murphy was not entitled to 400 days of paid sick leave he had claimed. Murphy claimed his illnesses included a phobia of sitting in judgment. Apparently to help heal himself, while being paid $130,000 a year as a judge, he enrolled full-time in a medical school in the Caribbean.

Source: *National Law Journal*

Subject-Matter Jurisdiction in the Federal Courts

Under the U.S. Constitution, the federal courts may hear only those cases within the judicial power of the United States. That is, federal courts have the judicial power to hear cases involving a *federal question:*

> The judicial Power shall extend to all Cases . . . arising under this Constitution, the Laws of the United States, and Treaties made, or which shall be made, under their Authority. . . .

This includes cases based on the relationship of the parties involved:

> [The judicial Power shall extend] to all Cases affecting Ambassadors, other public Ministers and Consuls . . . to Controversies between two or more States;—between a State and Citizens of another State;—between Citizens of different States . . . and between a State, or the Citizens thereof, and foreign States, Citizens or Subjects.

When federal jurisdiction is based on the parties involved, most of the litigation is generated (1) by cases in which the United States is a party to the suit or (2) by cases involving citizens of different states. The purpose for allowing federal jurisdiction when a dispute arises between citizens of different states—referred to as *diversity-of-citizenship* jurisdiction—is to provide a neutral forum for handling such disputes.

INTERNATIONAL *Perspective*

London's Commercial Court

When international contracts are signed, the parties can specify how future disputes will be resolved, including the choice of a court. If a court is not agreed upon initially, parties can agree at the time of a dispute where to resolve the matter. The Commercial Court in London has become a popular forum; almost all of its cases involve parties from more than one country.

Formed in 1895, the ten-judge court is often chosen because London is a major business city, most firms have assets in London that the court can easily control, and the judges are all experienced in commercial matters. Each trial is handled by one judge; there is no jury. Trials usually occur within a year and are finished rather quickly; the losing party pays the winner's attorney fees. Since English courts are respected, their judgments are likely to be enforced in other countries, and the remedies used by the court have been innovative and relevant to commercial matters.

State courts might be biased in favor of their own citizens and against "strangers" from other states. To obtain *diversity jurisdiction*, there must be total diversity among the parties. That is, all parties on one side of the lawsuit must have state citizenship different from the parties on the other side of the lawsuit. To establish federal jurisdiction in a diversity case, the parties must also show two things: (1) that they are from different states and (2) that the *amount in controversy* (the sum the plaintiff is suing the defendant for) is more than $75,000. In cases involving questions of federal law, there is no dollar amount requirement.

Personal Jurisdiction

Once it is established that the court has subject-matter jurisdiction, the plaintiff must meet the personal jurisdiction requirements of that court. A court's jurisdictional authority is generally limited to the territorial boundaries of the state in which it is located. Territorial jurisdiction usually does not become an issue unless the defendant is not a resident of the state in which the plaintiff wishes to bring the lawsuit. In such a case, the plaintiff must determine how to bring the defendant—or the defendant's property—before the court.

Jurisdiction over the Person

A court's power over the person of the defendant is referred to as *in personam jurisdiction*. The defendant is served with a *summons*—a notice of the lawsuit (see Exhibit 2.3). That is, after selecting the appropriate court, the plaintiff must properly notify the defendant of the action filed by *service of process*. The summons directs the defendant to appear before the court and to defend against the plaintiff's allegations. The court will issue a *default judgment* against a defendant who fails to appear.

Service of process is usually achieved by *personal service*. The summons is delivered to the defendant by the plaintiff, the plaintiff's attorney, a private process server, or a public official such as a sheriff or a U.S. marshal. If the defendant cannot

Exhibit 2.3

A Typical Summons

**United States District Court
for the
Southern District of California**

Civil Action, File Number **80151**

Elena Gori
Plaintiff

v.   Summons

Tom Eyestone
Defendant

To the above-named Defendant:
You are hereby summoned and required to serve upon *Carol Chapman*, plaintiff's attorney, whose address is *3620 San Felipe, San Diego, California,* an answer to the complaint which is herewith served upon you, within 20 days after service of this summons upon you, exclusive of the day of service. If you fail to do so, judgment by default will be taken against you for the relief demanded in the complaint.

Gloria Hernandez
Clerk of Court

[Seal of the U.S. District Court]
Dated 2/5/06

be located, courts allow the limited use of substituted service, such as publication of the pending lawsuit in a newspaper. The U.S. Supreme Court has emphasized that substituted service must be reasonably calculated to alert the defendant of the action.

Jurisdiction over Out-of-State Defendants

If both parties to a lawsuit are residents of the same state, the courts of the state clearly have jurisdiction over both persons. But if the defendant is a resident of another state, obtaining jurisdiction can be more difficult. The most obvious method for obtaining in personam jurisdiction over nonresident defendants is to serve them with process while they are within the state. The nonresident defendant need only be passing through the state to be legally served with a summons.

While it would seem as if defendants could avoid lawsuits by staying out of state, the court can still often exert jurisdiction. If the defendant committed a wrong (such as causing an automobile accident) within the court's territorial boundaries or has done business within the state, the court can exercise jurisdiction under the authority of the state's *long-arm statute* (see Exhibit 2.4). A long-arm statute is a state law that permits a state's courts to reach beyond the state's boundaries and obtain jurisdiction over nonresident defendants.

Exhibit 2.4

Long-Arm Statute: Revised Statues of Ohio

Sec. 2307.382 Personal Jurisdiction

(A) A court may exercise personal jurisdiction over a person who acts directly or by an agent, as to a cause of action arising from the person's:

(1) Transacting any business in this state;

(2) Contracting to supply services or goods in this state;

(3) Causing tortious injury by an act or omission in this state;

(4) Causing tortious injury in this state by an act or omission outside this state if he regularly does or solicits business, or engages in any other persistent course of conduct, or derives substantial course of conduct, or derives substantial revenue from goods used or consumed or services rendered in this state;

(5) Causing injury in this state to any person by breach of warranty expressly or impliedly made in the sale of goods outside this state when he might reasonably have expected such person to use, consume, or be affected by the goods in this state, provided that he also regularly does or solicits business, or engages in any other persistent course of conduct, or derives substantial revenue from goods used or consumed or services rendered in this state;

(6) Causing tortious injury in this state to any person by an act outside this state, committed with the purpose of injuring persons, when he might reasonably have expected that some person would be injured thereby in this state;

(7) Causing tortious injury to any person by a criminal act, any element of which takes place in this state, which he commits or in the commission of which he is guilty of complicity;

(8) Having an interest in, using, or possessing real property in this state;

(9) Contracting to insure any person, property, or risk located within this state at the time of contracting.

(B) For purposes of this section, a person who enters into an agreement, as a principal, with a sales representative for the solicitation of orders in this state in transacting business in this state. . . .

(C) When jurisdiction over a person is based solely upon this section, only a cause of action arising from acts enumerated in this section may be asserted against him.

The Long Arm of the Internet

Selling goods and services on the Internet allows a seller nationwide sales. When does a web site advertiser become subject to jurisdiction in other states when a buyer or prospective buyer wishes to sue the online seller? As often happens with new areas of law, various courts issued conflicting decisions initially, but the legal standards have become more settled. Some cases help to clarify the law.

In general, personal jurisdiction is appropriate when the defendant has engaged in continuous business in a state. So, for example, Amazon.com, which does active business in every state by selling directly online, is subject to jurisdiction of courts in every state.

However, jurisdiction is not appropriate when the defendant's contact with the forum state is only infor-

mational. Even if the web site is interactive, if it is only informative, no jurisdiction is created (*GTE New Media Serv. Inc.* v. *Bellsouth Corp.*, 199 F.3d 1343, D.C. Cir., 2000). Similarly, if a web site provides information about sales, allows customers to download order forms, and provides an e-mail address for inquiries, that is insufficient to subject the defendant to jurisdiction (*Mink* v. *AAAA Devel. LLC*, 190 F.3d 333, 5th Cir., 1999).

The one area in which the law is still a bit unclear is how much sales activity must occur with residents in a state for the web site seller to become subject to jurisdiction. In one case, when a seller sold one low-cost item to one buyer in a state, that was held not to be active business, especially since the contact was initiated by the buyer.

Jurisdiction over Out-of-State Business Defendants

Long-arm statutes are aimed primarily at nonresident businesses. They give courts a basis for exercising their jurisdiction over nonresident businesses that they may not use when dealing with nonresident private defendants. Do business defendants receive less favorable treatment by courts when it comes to jurisdiction than do private defendants? Juries tend to be more hostile to business defendants, viewing them as potentially powerful and unscrupulous parties, against whom the state's citizens need protection. True or not, courts may exercise jurisdiction over a corporation in the following three situations:

1. The court is located in the state in which the corporation was incorporated.
2. The court is located in the state where the corporation has its headquarters or its main plant.
3. The court is located in a state in which the corporation is doing business.

While the first two points are obvious, the third basis for jurisdiction—doing business in a state—has been subject to constitutional scrutiny by the U.S. Supreme

Can Your Firm Be Reached?

You work for a Florida real estate development firm, Golden Shores. Many of the clients of the firm are people who come to Florida from the New York area to retire or to have a second home. To increase marketing, a colleague suggests sending e-mails to potential clients advertising property for sale and offering a 5 percent discount to any buyers who respond to the e-mail and eventually buy property. New York requires real estate agents who offer property for sale to be registered in the state of New York. Your colleague says that this requirement does not apply to your company, as it is located in Florida and only communicates in New York via e-mail. Further, he claims it does not matter if the state of New York likes the advertisements or not; it cannot come after Golden Shores. Is that right?

Court. In reaching out-of-state corporate defendants, states have relied heavily upon long-arm statutes. As Exhibit 2.4 demonstrates, those statutes often list "transacting business" within the state as a basis for jurisdiction. According to the Supreme Court in *International Shoe Company* v. *Washington* (66 S.Ct. 154, 1945), a state's long-arm statutes must identify certain *minimum contacts* between the corporation and the state where the suit is being filed to qualify as transacting business.

In the following case, the court is asked to consider whether the medical services offered by a physician in Kansas to a Missouri resident provided grounds for Missouri courts to have jurisdiction over the litigation that arose.

Hollinger v. Sifers

Missouri Court of Appeals, Western District
122 S.W.3d 113 (2003)

CASE BACKGROUND *Sifers is a physician in Kansas. He was interviewed on a Kansas City television station about a new weight-reduction surgery known as a "duodenal switch." Hollinger, who wanted weight reduction surgery, saw the program in her Missouri home and contacted Dr. Sifers about the surgery. He saw her in his office and later performed the surgery. After the surgery, Hollinger suffered significant complications. She asserted the problems occurred because Sifers performed a different, more dangerous procedure rather than the one promised.*

Hollinger and her husband sued Sifers and others, in state court in Missouri, for deceptive merchandising practices, fraud, and negligence. Service of process was obtained in Kansas under the Missouri long-arm statute, as Hollinger contended that Sifers was conducting business in Missouri by promoting his medical services in Missouri on television.

Sifers asked the Missouri court to dismiss the suit for lack of personal jurisdiction, contending that he had insufficient minimum contacts with Missouri and that the medical problems were not subject to the long-arm statute. The trial court dismissed the suit for lack of jurisdiction. Hollinger appealed.

CASE DECISION Smart, Judge.

* * *

In order for a non-resident defendant to be subject to the long-arm jurisdiction of this state, two elements must be present: First, the suit must arise out of one of the activities enumerated in Missouri's long-arm statute; and second, the defendant must have sufficient minimum contacts with Missouri to satisfy due process requirements. When a defendant raises the issue of lack of personal jurisdiction, the burden shifts to the plaintiff to make a *prima facie* showing that those two elements exist. . . .

Missouri's long-arm statute provides in relevant part:

Any person or firm, whether or not a citizen or resident of this state, or any corporation, who in person or through an agent does any of the acts enumerated in this section, thereby submits such person, firm, or corporation ... to the jurisdiction of the courts of this state as to any cause of action arising from the doing of any of such acts:

(1) The transaction of any business within this state; . . . .

(3) The commission of a tortious act *within this state* . . . .

To demonstrate that a cause of action "arose out of" an activity covered by the long-arm statute, "a plaintiff must make a *prima facie* showing of the validity of its claim." The Plaintiffs did not need to prove all of the elements that form the basis of their claim, only "that acts contemplated by the statute took place" within the state. Here, Plaintiffs may have made a *prima facie* showing that Defendants fraudulently misrepresented that Dr. Sifers would perform a duodenal switch procedure on Lori and then did not do so. However . . . we conclude they have not shown that the tortious act of fraudulent misrepresentation took place within the State of Missouri.

Where a non-resident defendant is engaged in providing a service, as opposed to providing a product through the stream of commerce, the contact requirements for long-arm jurisdiction are more stringent. Dr. Sifers is licensed only in Kansas, maintains his office

continues

only in Kansas, and treats patients only in Kansas. Assuming for the purpose of the jurisdictional issue that Dr. Sifers misrepresented facts concerning his experience with the duodenal switch, Dr. Sifers' act of appearing on the televised interview is simply too attenuated to act as a basis for jurisdiction under this provision of Missouri's long-arm statute.

While the interview, which was shown in Missouri, acquainted Lori with Dr. Sifers and with his claimed expertise, the interview, standing alone, did not create Lori's agreement to have the procedure done. Indeed, it is clear that the interview merely motivated her to go to his office to discuss the possibility of having the procedure. . . .

All discussions of the proposed procedure and all business and treatment between Dr. Sifers and Lori Hollinger took place in the State of Kansas. The agreement between Lori and Dr. Sifers for the surgery was reached at Dr. Sifers' Kansas office, and the surgery in question was performed in Kansas. Dr. Sifers' alleged fraudulent representation that he would perform the duodenal switch surgery on Lori Hollinger was not made in Missouri. The agreement and consent to treatment were not reached in Missouri, and the alleged wrong that damaged Lori (the surgery for the older procedure) did not occur in Missouri. The commission of the alleged tort, therefore, did not occur "within the State of Missouri," and the long-arm statute cannot extend Missouri's personal jurisdiction to these Defendants.

CONCLUSION

There was no *prima facie* showing that the alleged wrongful actions of Defendants were committed *within the State of Missouri*. For that reason, it is unnecessary to examine Plaintiffs' arguments with regard to sufficient minimum contacts. The judgment is affirmed.

QUESTIONS FOR ANALYSIS

1. Does the dismissal of the suit mean that Hollinger cannot sue Sifers? If she can sue him, what are her options?

2. Suppose Dr. Sifers was also licensed to practice medicine in Missouri and had an office there, but all other facts were the same. Would Missouri courts then have jurisdiction?

Jurisdiction Based upon Power over Property

When a court is unable to obtain jurisdiction over the person of the defendant, it still has authority to establish jurisdiction based on the existence of the defendant's property within the state's boundaries.

In Rem Jurisdiction

In lawsuits based on a dispute over property, a court in the state where the property is located has jurisdiction to resolve claims against that property—whether the property owner is there or not. In such situations, the court is said to have *in rem jurisdiction*. Property in an *in rem* proceeding can include tangible property—real estate and personal property—and intangible property—bank accounts and stocks.

Quasi in Rem Jurisdiction

A court has *quasi in rem* jurisdiction when a defendant's property in a state is attached to secure payment for an unrelated matter. For example, Roth owes AutoBody $3,000 for painting her truck. Unable to collect from Roth, AutoBody sues her. AutoBody cannot serve Roth personally with process because Roth lives in another state. AutoBody discovers that Roth has property in the territorial jurisdiction of the court. AutoBody sues to attach (or seize) Roth's property to satisfy the debt. The court bases its jurisdiction on the fact that Roth owns property in the state. The court is said to have *quasi in rem jurisdiction*, and the decision it renders binds the parties. As in an *in rem* proceeding, the property can be either tangible or intangible.

RELATIONS BETWEEN THE COURT SYSTEMS

The jurisdiction relationships between state and federal court systems are illustrated in Exhibit 2.5. Some disputes can be resolved only in the state courts, some disputes only in the federal courts, and some disputes in either the federal or the state court systems.

Exclusive Jurisdiction

Courts in the federal system have *exclusive jurisdiction* over certain disputes. State courts do not have subject matter jurisdiction over these cases and so may not try them. Congress usually specifies by statute matters over which the federal courts have exclusive jurisdiction. For example, federal courts have exclusive jurisdiction in cases involving federal crimes, bankruptcy, patents, and copyrights.

Similarly, state courts have exclusive jurisdiction over disputes such as divorce, adoption, and other matters controlled by the state government. A state government may confer exclusive jurisdiction on its courts as long as it does not infringe on the supremacy of federal law. If a plaintiff seeks relief for such a state matter in a federal court, the case would be dismissed for lack of jurisdiction. The plaintiff would need to refile the case in the appropriate state court.

With exclusive jurisdiction, the court hearing the case—whether a federal court or a state court—applies its procedural rules and follows its substantive law. If the court with jurisdiction is a state court in California, for example, it follows California procedural rules and applies the laws of the state of California. If the court is a federal court, it follows federal rules of procedure and applies federal law.

Concurrent Jurisdiction

As Exhibit 2.5 illustrates, both the federal and the state court systems have jurisdiction in some disputes. When both systems have the power to hear a case, *concurrent jurisdiction* exists. As Exhibit 2.5 also illustrates, both systems have jurisdiction when either of the following is the case:

1. There is diversity of citizenship and the amount in controversy exceeds $75,000.
2. The dispute involves a federal question and Congress has not conferred exclusive jurisdiction on the federal courts.

Federal Question Jurisdiction

The concurrent jurisdiction of the two court systems is understandable in cases where there is diversity of citizenship. An out-of-state defendant may worry that the state courts in the plaintiff's state might be biased in favor of the plaintiff. The rationale for state courts to exercise jurisdiction in federal question cases has been explained by the Supreme Court. The court has noted that concurrent jurisdiction has long existed.

However, Congress may state "explicitly or implicitly" that state courts do not have jurisdiction over a particular matter of federal law. That is, Congress provides by statute that federal courts have exclusive jurisdiction over an area of law, or Congress provides exclusive jurisdiction "by unmistakable implication from the legislative history, or by a clear incompatibility between state-court jurisdiction and federal interests." In such cases, only the federal court system has jurisdiction over the case. If a plaintiff seeks relief for such a matter in a state court, the case would be dismissed for lack of jurisdiction.

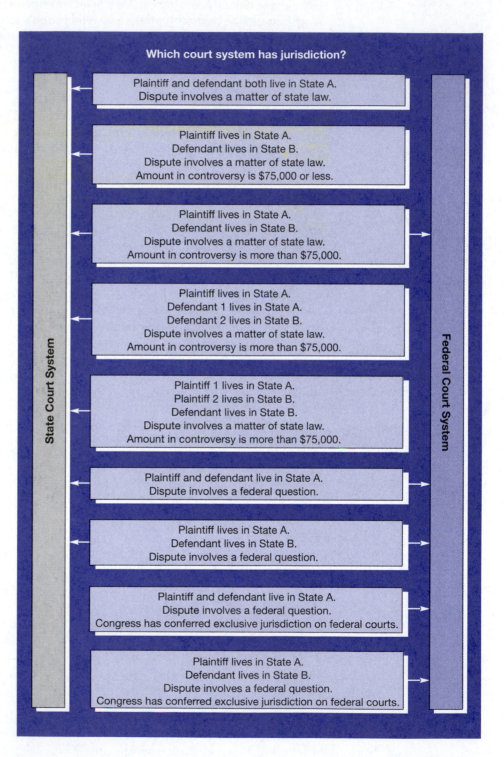

Exhibit 2.5

Jurisdiction Relationships between Court Systems

Which court system has jurisdiction?

State Court System · Federal Court System

Plaintiff and defendant both live in State A.
Dispute involves a matter of state law.

Plaintiff lives in State A.
Defendant lives in State B.
Dispute involves a matter of state law.
Amount in controversy is $75,000 or less.

Plaintiff lives in State A.
Defendant lives in State B.
Dispute involves a matter of state law.
Amount in controversy is more than $75,000.

Plaintiff lives in State A.
Defendant 1 lives in State A.
Defendant 2 lives in State B.
Dispute involves a matter of state law.
Amount in controversy is more than $75,000.

Plaintiff 1 lives in State A.
Plaintiff 2 lives in State B.
Defendant lives in State B.
Dispute involves a matter of state law.
Amount in controversy is more than $75,000.

Plaintiff and defendant live in State A.
Dispute involves a federal question.

Plaintiff lives in State A.
Defendant lives in State B.
Dispute involves a federal question.

Plaintiff and defendant live in State A.
Dispute involves a federal question.
Congress has conferred exclusive jurisdiction on federal courts.

Plaintiff lives in State A.
Defendant lives in State B.
Dispute involves a federal question.
Congress has conferred exclusive jurisdiction on federal courts.

Concurrent Jurisdiction and Removal

When concurrent jurisdiction exists, the plaintiff may bring suit in either the state court or the federal court system. If the plaintiff chooses the state court system, the defendant has the right to have the case removed to a federal court based on diversity of citizenship. This right of removal is intended to protect out-of-state defendants from state courts that might be biased in favor of their own citizens.

A plaintiff considers several issues when deciding which court system best suits her legal needs. For example, the rules of procedure in federal and state courts may be different, and the plaintiff's attorney may be more familiar with (and more successful using) one set of rules than the other. Also, local politics may be an issue for state judges. The plaintiff can do little to prevent the defendant from removing the case to the federal court if the defendant has the right to do so.

Applying the Appropriate Law in Federal Court

When there is diversity of citizenship, and the case is in federal court, the central question becomes, Which body of substantive law should the court apply to resolve the dispute—federal law or state law?

Suppose that Smith and Jones were involved in a dispute and Smith sued Jones in California. If Smith and Jones were both from California, the case would be tried in a California state court, and California law would be applied to resolve the dispute. However, if Smith was from Arizona and Jones was from California (and the amount in controversy exceeded $75,000), the dispute could be decided by a federal court because of diversity of citizenship. If the issue in dispute was governed by statutory law, federal and California courts would apply the same law (the statutory law of California), and the outcomes very likely would be the same. But what would happen if the case involved common-law issues? Would a federal court and a state court hearing similar cases reach different decisions? This is what used to happen in the United States until the Supreme Court decided the landmark 1938 case of *Erie* v. *Tompkins*.

In *Erie* v. *Tompkins*, the Supreme Court overturned an old Supreme Court case, *Swift* v. *Tyson*, and held that except in matters governed by the federal Constitution or by acts of Congress (statutes), federal courts must apply state law. Thus, federal judges must apply both a state's common law and a state's statutory law when deciding diversity-of-citizenship cases. The federal court, however, follows federal procedural law.

Erie Railroad Co. v. Tompkins

United States Supreme Court
304 U.S. 64, 58 S.Ct. 817 (1938)

CASE BACKGROUND *Tompkins was injured on "a dark night" by something protruding from a passing freight train owned by Erie Railroad Company, as Tompkins stood next to the tracks in Pennsylvania. He claimed the accident occurred because of negligent operation of the train. Tompkins was a citizen of Pennsylvania, and Erie was a company incorporated in New York. Tompkins (the plaintiff) brought suit in federal district court.*

continues

Erie argued that the court, in deciding the case, should apply the law of Pennsylvania. Under Pennsylvania common law, Tompkins would be a trespasser, and Erie would not be liable for his injuries. Tompkins argued that because of diversity of citizenship, federal common law should apply. Under federal common law, Erie could be liable for Tompkins's injuries.

The trial court agreed with Tompkins, and the jury awarded him $30,000 in damages. The decision was affirmed by the circuit court of appeals. Erie appealed to the U.S. Supreme Court, arguing that in diversity-of-citizenship cases federal courts must apply the appropriate state statutory and common law.

CASE DECISION   Brandeis, Justice.

* * *

First. *Swift* v. *Tyson*, held that federal courts exercising jurisdiction on the ground of diversity of citizenship need not, in matters of general jurisprudence, apply [the common law] of the State as declared by its highest court; that they are free to exercise an independent judgment as to what the common law of the State is—or should be. . . .

* * *

Second. Experience in applying the doctrine of *Swift* v. *Tyson* had revealed its defects. . . . Diversity of citizenship jurisdiction was conferred [by the Constitution] to prevent discrimination in state courts against those not citizens of the State. *Swift* v. *Tyson* introduced grave discrimination by non-citizens against citizens. It made rights enjoyed under the [state's common law] vary according to whether enforcement was sought in the state or in the federal court. . . . Thus, the doctrine rendered impossible equal protection of

the law. In attempting to promote uniformity of law throughout the United States, the doctrine had prevented uniformity in the administration of the law of the State.

* * *

Third. Except in matters governed by the Federal Constitution or by Acts of Congress, the law to be applied in any case is the law of the State. And whether the law of the State shall be declared by its Legislature in a statute or by its highest court in a decision is not a matter of federal concern. . . . Congress has no power to declare substantive rules of common law applicable in a State. . . . And no clause in the Constitution purports to confer such a power upon the federal courts.

* * *

Fourth. The defendant contended that by the common law of Pennsylvania . . . the only duty owed to the plaintiff was to refrain from wilful or wanton injury. . . . The Circuit Court of Appeals . . . declined to decide the issue of state law. As we hold this was error, the judgment is reversed and the case remanded to it for further proceedings in conformity with our opinion.

Reversed.

CASE NOTE   The concept of federal common law in diversity-of-citizenship cases was ended. Hence, Pennsylvania law applied and Tompkins was a trespasser and Erie was not liable for his injuries.

QUESTIONS FOR ANALYSIS

1. Why had the decision in *Swift* v. *Tyson* prevented uniformity in the administration of state law?

2. After Erie, which court's procedural law must be applied in a diversity-of-citizenship case?

Applying the Appropriate Law in State Court

When a state court hears a case involving incidents that took place in more than one state or entirely in a different state, a conflict-of-law problem may arise. The court determines whether its own law or the law of another state should be applied. To help courts in such situations, states have enacted statutes that provide conflict-of-law rules. Some general *conflict-of-law* rules that affect businesses are presented in Exhibit 2.6.

Conflict-of-law rules vary according to the nature of the dispute. In contract cases, for example, the traditional rule is that the law of the state in which the contract was made determines the interpretation of the contract. In tort cases, the traditional rule is that courts apply the law of the place where the tort occurred. However,

Exhibit 2.6	Substantive Law Issue	Apply State Law from State
Conflict-of-Law Rules Frequently Affecting Businesses	Contract Disagreement	In which contract was formed or in which contract was to be performed or most significantly affected by the contract or designated in the contract
	Liability Issues Arising from Injury	In which injury occurred
	Workers' Compensation	Of employment or in which injury occurred

the rules are not always simple. Courts evaluate the interests of the states involved in a dispute. The state with the most "significant interest" in the case would be the state whose law would be applied.

The states do not all use the same rule, but the rules in all states share important concerns. They try to account for the interests of parties in the fair resolution of the dispute, for the interests of the governments in the effective application of their laws and the policy rationales upon which they are based, and for the benefits that result from the ability of citizens to predict the legal consequences of their actions. The most popular approach is that outlined in the *Restatement (Second) of Conflict of Laws*, which is applied in about half the states. The following case discusses how a court goes about applying the *Restatement*'s approach in conflict-of-law cases.

Hughes v. Wal-Mart Stores, Inc.
United States Court of Appeals, Eighth Circuit
250 F.3d 618 (2001)

CASE BACKGROUND *Hughes bought a gasoline container, made by Rubbermaid, at a Wal-Mart store in Monroe, Louisiana, where he lived. When he poured diesel fuel from the container onto stumps he was burning, the fuel in the container exploded, injuring his daughter, who was playing nearby. Hughes sued Wal-Mart, on behalf of his daughter, in federal court in Arkansas, where Wal-Mart is headquartered. Hughes contended that Wal-Mart was liable for selling a defective product.*

Wal-Mart contended that Louisiana products liability law governed the case. Under Louisiana law, a distributor is not liable unless it knew the product was defective. Hughes contended that Arkansas law should apply to the case. Under Arkansas law, an injured party has a greater chance of recovery from the distributor of a defective product. The federal district court in Arkansas concluded that Louisiana law governed the case and precluded recovery. The court ruled in favor of Wal-Mart. Hughes appealed.

CASE DECISION Hansen, Circuit Judge.

* * *

The Arkansas Supreme Court uses the following five factors to determine which state's law applies to an action: (1) predictability of results; (2) maintenance of interstate and international order; (3) simplification of the judicial task; (4) advancement of the forum's governmental interests; and (5) application of the better rule of law. . . .

* * *

We review de novo the district court's application of the five factors and its choice of law determination. We begin our analysis with the second factor, the maintenance of interstate order, because the first and third factors have no relevance in ascertaining whether Arkansas or Louisiana law should apply to this action. The predictability of results is not implicated when an action arises out of an accident, and the judicial task is not simplified by application of either state's law. A federal district court is faced almost daily with the task of applying some state's law other than that of the forum state, and it is equally capable of resolving the dispute under Louisiana or Arkansas law. . . .

continues

The factor is generally not implicated if the state whose law is to be applied has "sufficient contacts with and interest in the facts and issues being litigated." However, where a state "has little or no contact with a case and 'nearly all of the significant contacts are with a sister state,'" the factor suggests that a state should not apply its own law to the dispute. With these considerations in mind, we agree that the factor points toward an application of Louisiana law because Louisiana has significant, if not all, contacts with the facts relevant to the litigation. The gas container at issue was purchased by a Louisiana resident at a Wal-Mart located in Louisiana, and the injury allegedly involving the product occurred in Louisiana, and the injured party was a Louisiana resident. The only "contact" Arkansas has to the litigation is that the defendant, Wal-Mart, has its principal place of business in the state.

The fact that Wal-Mart is an Arkansas-based corporation leads directly to the fourth factor, Arkansas's interest in the litigation. The district court concluded that Arkansas has little, if any, interest because all the events surrounding Bridgette's injuries occurred in Louisiana. Plaintiffs dispute the district court's conclusion and argue Arkansas has an important governmental interest in having its product liability laws enforced against its own corporate residents when the products they sell to others injure the residents of other states. We agree that a state has at least some interest in protecting nonresidents from tortious acts committed within the state, but even then, courts have recognized that the state's interest is only slight and does not support application of its law to the litigation. . . . Absent some relevant connection between a state and the facts underlying the litigation, we fail to see how any important Arkansas governmental interest is significantly furthered by ensuring that nonresidents are compensated for injuries that occur in another state. The governmental interest factor does not support an application of Arkansas law. . . .

Based on our consideration of the choice-influencing factors, we conclude that the district court was correct in applying Louisiana law to plaintiffs' products liability claims. . . . The judgment of the district court is therefore affirmed.

QUESTIONS FOR ANALYSIS

1. The Louisiana rule was called unfair by the plaintiff because it made recovery against Wal-Mart almost impossible; why did the appeals court not accept that argument?

2. Why is the law not the same in all states? Why did the court not use federal common law to settle this dispute between citizens of different states?

VENUE

A lawsuit must be brought in a court having proper venue. On the basis of fairness, state statutes generally provide that a lawsuit be brought in a court located in the county in which either the plaintiff or the defendant lives. Similarly, the defendant

Juris *prudence?*

Justice Can Have a Bite to It

When West Virginia judge Troisi became irritated with a rude defendant, he stepped down from the bench, took off his robe, and bit the defendant on the nose. A report prepared for the state supreme court found that the judge frequently lost his temper in court. Troisi resigned and pleaded no contest to battery charges. He spent five days in jail and was put on probation. After he was released, he yelled at a court clerk who had testified against him. That violated his probation, so it was back to jail for six months. "Mr. Troisi just doesn't get it," said Judge Recht.

Source: *National Law Journal*

can be sued in a federal court only in a district where either the defendant or the plaintiff lives or where the dispute arose.

Change of Venue

In some controversial or well-publicized cases, defendants request a *change of venue* from the court where the plaintiff filed the case. In such cases, defendants worry that because of the publicity surrounding their case, they will be unable to get a fair trial. Once such fairness requirements are met, the court selected has jurisdiction and venue.

Forum Non Conveniens

Closely related to venue is the doctrine *forum non conveniens* (the forum is not suitable). A party asks the court to dismiss the case and transfer it to another court, even though the original court has jurisdiction, because there is another, more convenient court that could hear the case. When considering the motion, a court considers where the actions related to the case took place, where the witnesses are located, whether the parties will be unfairly burdened by using a particular court, and whether problems of conflicts of law might be avoided by transferring the case.

JUDICIAL OFFICIALS

As the main link between law and society in the judicial system, judges perform several important functions. Obviously, judges resolve disputes. For the system to work well, judges must apply the law evenly and consistently and not be swayed by public opinion. Judges also uphold the dignity of the law and the legal system. It is their responsibility to maintain the legal system's reputation for honesty and impartiality.

 JURIS *prudence?*

The Judge Is in on the Plot, Too!

Teri Tyler filed suit in federal court. Named as defendants, among others, were Bill Clinton, Jimmy Carter, IBM, and NASA. Tyler alleged a "conspiracy involving the defendants to enslave and oppress certain segments of our society. Plaintiff contends she is a cyborg, and that she received most of the information . . . through 'proteus' . . . some silent, telepathic form of communication. . . . Defendants are involved in the 'Iron Mountain Plan,' which provides for the reinstitutionalization of slavery and 'bloodsports' (which she identifies as death-hunting and witch-hunting), and the oppression of political dissidents, herself included."

Tyler contended the defendants had her college dorm room attacked by airplanes and helicopters and that other stu-

dents whispered about her and avoided her socially. "Plaintiff additionally contends that the Gulf War against Iraq was undertaken so that America could restock its sexual slavery camps, which had been depleted."

A U.S. attorney requested the court dismiss Tyler's request for $5.6 billion in damages, the end of the cyborg program run by NASA, and an end to the organ-donor program, among other things. The judge agreed. "A plaintiff asserting fantastic or delusional claims, should not, by payment of a filing fee, obtain a license to consume limited judicial resources and put defendants to effort and expense."

Source: *Tyler* v. *Carter*, 151 F.R.D. 537

Also, judges enhance the legal culture of society by maintaining respect for the law and the legal system.

Federal Judicial Officials

Federal judges are nominated by the president and confirmed by a majority vote in the U.S. Senate. Since the Constitution guarantees federal judges the right to serve "during good behavior," they enjoy a secure lifetime appointment. Judges below the Supreme Court level retire at age 70, but may remain on "senior status" and still hear cases. There are about 1,200 federal judges. According to the Constitution, federal judges may be removed from office only if the Congress impeaches them for treason, bribery, or other high crimes and misdemeanors. The impeachment process includes the actual impeachment (indictment) by the House of Representatives, followed by a trial before the Senate. If at least two-thirds of the senators vote for removal, the judge is removed from office. This happens only rarely—only four federal judges in history have been removed.

While Congress may change the structure of the federal court system, it may not reduce a judge's salary or term of office once an appointment has been made. The writers of the Constitution gave federal judges job security because they wanted to guarantee that judges would be independent and free from the pressure of politics.

State Judicial Officials

State judges are chosen by a variety of methods. They are elected, appointed, or chosen by a method that mixes the election and appointment processes. In several of the states with the mixed system, the state bar association has a committee to recommend qualified attorneys for the bench. The governor then appoints a judge from its list. The judge selected then serves until the next election, at which time the public is asked to vote *for* or *against* him. This system for selecting judges is referred to as the *Missouri System*.

In contrast to the position enjoyed by federal judges, most state judges serve for a fixed term whether they are appointed or elected. Terms range from one year for judges in some Midwestern states to a fourteen-year term for judges in New York. Massachusetts and New Hampshire appoint judges to serve until they reach age seventy; only Rhode Island provides a lifetime term of office.

Some observers claim that appointed judges are of higher average quality than elected judges. Others claim that elected judges work harder than appointed judges. No clear evidence exists that demonstrates that one approach is more effective than another. State supreme court judges are appointed in nine states, elected in twenty-one states, elected by the legislature in three states, and appointed initially then run for retention in seventeen states.

Judicial Immunity

Under the *doctrine of judicial immunity*, a judge is absolutely immune from suit for damages for judicial acts. This immunity applies even when the judge acts maliciously. In the absence of the doctrine, judges could face undue influence on their judicial decisions. As a consequence, judges would lose their ability to be independent decision makers. In addition, judicial immunity protects judges from the burden of defending retaliatory suits by unsuccessful litigants. By protecting judges from such suits, judicial immunity serves to keep judges unconcerned about the relative power of parties who appear in court.

SUMMARY

- Civil litigation involves the use of the law and the legal process to resolve disputes among businesses, individuals, and governments. Litigation through the court systems provides a means of resolving those disputes without the need to resort to force.
- The court system is made up of the *state court systems* and the *federal court system*. Most courts follow the *Federal Rules of Civil Procedure* in governing the important procedural aspects of the litigation process.
- In the study of the court system, the most basic notion is the concept of jurisdiction. The term *jurisdiction* means "the power to speak of the law." A court must have jurisdiction to hear and resolve a dispute. A court's jurisdiction is divided into two basic categories: *subject-matter jurisdiction* and *personal jurisdiction*.
- Subject-matter jurisdiction is a constitutional or statutory limitation on the types of disputes a court can resolve. Typical subject-matter constraints include minimum requirements on the amount in controversy in the dispute and restrictions on the types of disputes the court has authority to resolve.
- The jurisdiction of a court varies according to its position in the court system and the court system it is in. Courts of *original jurisdiction* in the federal and the state court systems are *trial courts*. They have authority to hear virtually any kind of dispute and provide any kind of relief. Courts with appellate jurisdiction have the power to review cases decided by courts below them. Most state court systems and the federal court system have two levels of *appellate courts*. The highest appellate court in the federal system is the U.S. Supreme Court.
- The federal court system has limited subject-matter jurisdiction. The federal courts are limited by the U.S. Constitution to cases involving a *federal question* or *diversity of citizenship* where the amount in controversy exceeds $75,000. The state court systems can hear most disputes, including federal question cases where Congress has not limited jurisdiction to the federal court system.
- In addition to meeting the subject-matter jurisdictional requirements of a court, the parties—the plaintiff and the defendant—must meet personal jurisdictional requirements of the court. A state court's personal jurisdiction is generally limited to the boundaries of its state.
- Personal jurisdiction normally is not an issue unless the defendant is not a resident of the state in which the plaintiff wants to bring the action. Jurisdiction of the court over the defendant is obtained by personal *service of process*. For out-of-state defendants, however, the court may need to exercise jurisdiction under authority of the state's *long-arm statute*. Generally, the plaintiff must show that the out-of-state defendant is transacting business or has some other interest in the state.
- When the court is unable to establish its jurisdiction through personal service on the defendant, the court may be able to establish jurisdiction over property (*in rem jurisdiction*) owned by the defendant that is located within the state.
- The federal courts in diversity-of-citizenship cases must apply the appropriate state common and statutory law.
- In state court cases, when the incident in question took place in another state, the court must look to the forum state's *conflict-of-law* rule to determine what substantive law will apply to resolve the dispute.
- Most U.S. judges are attorneys. It is their responsibility to uphold the legal system's reputation for honesty and impartiality. Federal judges are nominated by

the president and confirmed by the Senate. They enjoy lifetime employment once appointed. State judges are variously appointed and elected, depending upon state procedures.

REVIEW AND DISCUSSION QUESTIONS

1. Terms you should know:

plaintiff	service of process
defendant	*in rem* jurisdiction
jurisdiction	*quasi in rem* jurisdiction
subject-matter jurisdiction	conflict-of-law
personal jurisdiction	venue
appellate jurisdiction	*forum non conveniens*
diversity of citizenship	
summons	

2. Compare and contrast the following:
   a. Service of process and substituted process
   b. Appellate jurisdiction and original jurisdiction
   c. Federal question jurisdiction and diversity-of-citizenship jurisdiction
   d. Jurisdiction over the person and jurisdiction over property

CASE QUESTIONS

3. Smith, a Tennessee resident, was sued in federal court in Arkansas by an Arkansas resident in a contract dispute involving an Illinois corporation. Smith was given his summons to appear in the court in Arkansas while flying on a commercial flight from Memphis to Dallas while the plane was over the state of Arkansas. Did that constitute legal service of summons? [*Grace* v. *MacArthur*, 170 F.Supp. 442 (E.D., Ark., 1959)]

4. Burger King (BK) is headquartered in Miami. Its franchise contracts are governed by Florida law. Rudzewicz had a Michigan franchise that was not doing well. BK terminated the franchise and told Rudzewicz to vacate the restaurant. Rudzewicz refused and kept running the operation. BK filed suit in federal court in Florida, claiming that Rudzewicz was in breach of contract. Rudzewicz claimed that the Florida federal court did not have jurisdiction because he was a Michigan resident and the subject of the case, the restaurant, was in Michigan. The district judge held that under Florida's long-arm statute, the contract Rudzewicz signed made him subject to litigation in Florida. The court of appeals reversed, ruling that fairness did not allow jurisdiction in Florida. What did the Supreme Court hold? [*Burger King* v. *Rudzewicz*, 105 S.Ct. 2174 (1985)]

5. Burlington is a Delaware corporation with its principal place of business in North Carolina. Maples is an Alabama corporation with its principal place of business there. Maples bought machines from BVA, an Arkansas company. Maples made the contract with BVA in Alabama; it sent no employees to Arkansas and it has no operations in Arkansas. Burlington sued Maples, claiming that the machines it bought contained Burlington trade secrets. Can Burlington bring suit against Maples in Arkansas? [*Burlington Industries* v. *Maples Industries*, 97 F.3d 1100 (8th Cir., 1996)]

Check your answer at http://meiners.westbuslaw.com

6. The officers of a Maryland savings and loan that went bankrupt were sued in Maryland state court by depositors who lost money. Among the claims made against the officers was that they violated a federal statute. Before the case came to trial, some depositors filed another suit in federal district court against the same officers, claiming that the federal court had to hear the complaint that the officers violated federal law. The federal trial court dismissed the case, ruling that the state trial court could hear the case and rule on the matters involving possible violations of state law as well as the federal law. Was this correct? [*Tafflin* v. *Levitt*, 110 S.Ct. 792 (1990)]

7. Charlotte Chambers and thirty-four other South Dakota residents chartered a bus in Sioux Falls, South Dakota, from Dakotah Charter, a South Dakota corporation, to attend a Tae Kwon Do tournament in Arkansas. While en route from South Dakota to Arkansas, the bus stopped in Missouri. Chambers fell on the steps in the bus and broke her ankle. She sued, claiming that Dakotah failed to maintain the bus in a safe condition. Dakotah contended that her own carelessness caused her injury. Which law should apply to the case—the law of South Dakota (where the contract was made), Missouri (where the injury occurred), or Arkansas (where the contract was ultimately to be performed)? [*Charlotte Chambers* v. *Dakotah Charter*, 488 N.W.2d 63 (Sup.Ct., S.D., 1992)]

Check your answer at http://meiners.westbuslaw.com

8. Michelle West was born in Georgia in 1972. Her parents were divorced in 1974. Their divorce decree required Michelle's father to pay child support until Michelle turned eighteen. The decree did not require Michelle's father to contribute toward a college education. When Michelle became eighteen, she was living in South Carolina. She applied to and was accepted by a private college in South Carolina. Michelle's father lived in Georgia but worked and paid income taxes in South Carolina. Michelle filed suit in a South Carolina state court against her father, seeking support payments beyond her eighteenth birthday, to help cover the costs of her college education. Under South Carolina law, Michelle's father could be made to contribute to her education. Under Georgia law, Michelle's father would not be responsible for any of her expenses after she turned eighteen. Which law should the court apply in this case? [*West* v. *West*, 419 S.E.2d 804 (Ct.App., S.C., 1992)]

9. Vons, of California, sells meat to fast-food restaurants. Some meat tainted by E. coli bacteria was bought by Washington-state Jack-in-the-Box restaurants. Jack-in-the-Box customers who ate the meat suffered serious illness, and several died. Vons sued the owners of two Jack-in-the-Box franchises in California court, seeking repayment for money it was forced to pay to the food-poisoning victims. Vons claimed that Jack-in-the-Box did not cook the meat properly. The franchise owners responded that the California court did not have personal jurisdiction over them based on insufficient contacts with the state. The owners had assigned their rights to run the restaurants to third parties, who operated the restaurants. Thus, the link between the harms caused by improper cooking and the relationship of the franchise owners to California was too remote. The franchise agreements were signed in California and were governed by California law. The contracts between the Jack-in-the-Box owners and the operators were signed in Washington state. Is there a sufficient connection between the owners and the people actually running the restaurants (the operators) to

the state of California to allow the court to exercise jurisdiction? [*The Vons Companies* v. *Seabest Foods*, 37 Cal.App.4th, 1090 (Ct.App., Cal., 1995)]

 Check your answer at http://meiners.westbuslaw.com

10. An accident in Florida killed three of the four members of a family from Alabama who were riding in their Kia automobile that had been bought in Alabama. Suit was filed in Alabama state court against Kia by the survivor of the accident. Kia requested that the trial be moved to Florida on the ground of *forum non conveniens* because almost all of the witnesses were in Florida. Was that motion accepted? [*Ex parte Kia Motors America, Inc.*, 2003 WL 21040313 (Sup. Ct., Ala., 2003)]

11. Beattey was a resident of Indiana who was attending college in New York. He was driving in the Bahamas on vacation when he was struck by a vehicle driven by an employee of College Centre, a New York–based school with an operation in the Bahamas. Beattey was flown to Florida for treatment of his injuries, but he died by the time the plane landed in Florida. Beattey's parents sued College Centre in a state court in Florida. The accident was the fault of the College Centre driver, so his employer, College Centre, was liable. College Centre argued that the law of the Bahamas should be applied, in which case its liability would be quite limited. The trial court held that Bahamian law would apply. The Beatteys appealed, arguing that New York law should apply because the defendant was a company based in New York. Which law seems most likely to apply? [*Beattey* v. *College Centre of Finger Lakes*, 613 So.2d 52 (Ct.App., Fla., 1992)]

 Check your answer at http://meiners.westbuslaw.com

12. Tracy Prows had a contract with Pinpoint. Under the agreement, Prows worked with companies to develop computer specifications for their needs. Pinpoint would make the computers based on the specifications and sell the computers to Prows at wholesale prices. Prows would resell the computers to the customer at retail prices. Flying J and Prows wrote specifications for computers to meet Flying J's needs. Then Flying J went to Pinpoint and bought directly from the manufacturer, cutting Prows out. Prows sued Pinpoint for breach of contract in Utah court. Prows and Flying J are residents of Utah, and the contract between Prows and Pinpoint was signed in Utah. Pinpoint moved to dismiss the case for improper venue because the contract stated that all claims arising from the contract would be tried in New York, using New York law. What should the Utah court do? The Second Restatement of Conflict of Laws says that when parties specify a particular legal forum, that choice should be honored unless the forum "has no substantial relationship to the parties." [*Prows* v. *Pinpoint Retail Systems*, 868 P.2d 809 (S.Ct., Ut., 1993)]

13. Koh, a California resident, won a judgment in California of $240,000 against Inno-Pacific, a Singapore company, but Inno-Pacific did not pay the judgment. Koh discovered that the company had an interest in some land in Washington state, so he filed suit in Washington to seize the property to satisfy his judgment. The trial court in Washington dismissed the suit because it lacked personal jurisdiction over Inno-Pacific. Koh appealed. On what basis could the Washington court have jurisdiction? Did Koh prevail? [*Koh* v. *Inno-Pacific Holdings, Ltd.*, 54 P.3d 1270 (Ct. App., Wash., 2002)]

14. Colemill Enterprises, a South Carolina company, purchased an airplane from Southeastern Flight Services, a Georgia company. The purchase price includ-

ed a maintenance package that required Southeastern to keep the airplane in top operating condition. Shortly after the purchase, and while carrying Colemill's top executive, the airplane crashed and all passengers and crew were killed. There was evidence that the aircraft had been defectively manufactured and improperly maintained. The airplane was manufactured in Michigan and maintained in Georgia; the crash occurred in South Carolina. In a subsequent wrongful death action brought in Georgia, which state's law will apply? [*Risdon Enterprises, Inc.* v. *Colemill Enterprises*, 324 S.E.2d 738 (Ct.App., Ga., 1984)]

15. Ruth Creech, an Ohio resident, filed an action for malpractice against the City of Faith Hospital and physician McGee, both residents of Tulsa, Oklahoma. The claims arose out of injuries suffered while Creech was a patient at the City of Faith Hospital in Tulsa. Creech had heard of the hospital through the "Expect a Miracle" television program featuring Oral Roberts. Broadcast around the United States, the program invited people to come to the hospital for treatment. The case was tried in federal court in Ohio. The court found for Creech. The hospital and McGee appealed on the ground that the federal court could not exercise jurisdiction over them under the Ohio long-arm statute. They contended that they did not have sufficient minimum contacts with Ohio to confer jurisdiction. Assuming that Ohio's long-arm statute is similar to the one in Exhibit 2.4, was the court's exercise of jurisdiction reasonable? [*Creech* v. *Roberts*, 908 F.2d 75 (6th Cir., 1990)]

ETHICS QUESTION

16. Should judges consider the social consequences of their decisions? What if the case involves an individual who has committed a hideous crime and the judge is being asked to release the individual on a "technicality"?

INTERNET ASSIGNMENT

http://www.uscourts.gov/allinks.html
http://www.findlaw.com/casecode/index.html#federal
http://www.law.villanova.edu/library/researchguides/fedcourtlocator.asp
http://www.law.emory.edu/FEDCTS
http://pacer.psc.uscourts.gov

The Internet can be an important source of federal court opinions. Since 1995, many federal circuit courts have released their opinions via the Internet. District court opinions are increasingly available online.

Search the first four sites, and think about the one you prefer for finding federal court opinions. Are the opinions of the district court closest to your home available via the Internet? If so, when did the service start? Does your circuit court allow keyword searching? Why might PACER, despite its $.07 per page charge, be useful?

Chapter 3

Trials and Resolving Disputes

When Barbara Fong's software company, Gnof, was sued by unhappy stockholders who lost money when stock prices dropped, it is likely that the case was settled out of court. As in other areas of litigation, suits brought by shareholders are almost always settled, which includes suits being dropped. Of all civil cases filed in court, about 90 percent are resolved before a judgment is entered at trial.

Why resolve a suit out of court? Experienced lawyers can make pretty good estimates of the outcome of most cases that go to trial, so they can recommend resolution that heads off costly litigation. Cases that are litigated consume more hours of attorneys' time, are more likely to need expert witnesses, and consume more time of company personnel. Fong would rather concentrate on her business than spend days preparing for a deposition and, later, for possible testimony at trial.

Over the past several decades, the average time required for civil cases to get into court has lengthened, adding to the cost and uncertainty of the litigation process. Criminal cases have priority over civil cases, and court dockets are loaded, so civil litigation may be put off for years. Most judges encourage cases to be settled rather than consume valuable court time. Disputes can be mediated, arbitrated, or negotiated quickly if both parties are interested in doing so. We begin by discussing trial procedure in civil court cases and then move to some of the major forms of alternate dispute resolution.

STRATEGIC CONSIDERATIONS

A distinctive element of our judicial system is that it is an *adversary system of justice*. It requires the parties to represent themselves and to argue their positions before a court. The responsibility for bringing a lawsuit, shaping its issues, and presenting evidence rests upon the parties to the dispute.

Courts play a small role in establishing the facts of a case. Unlike in many countries that use a system of inquiry run by judges, judges in the United States do not investigate the parties or the facts of a case. Instead, the court applies legal rules to the facts that the parties establish. Parties to possible litigation should weigh several factors. Here, we focus on the business perspective.

Business as Plaintiff

Few parties file a lawsuit unless a legally recognized harm has been suffered, but even then an evaluation must be made of the sensibility of filing suit. A key issue for managers to consider, as advised by counsel, is the likelihood of winning an action. Can the necessary parties be located and can the case be proven? If so, would the relief expected from the case make the matter worthwhile? Even if you can win, there is little sense in suing a party that cannot pay a judgment. Furthermore, litigation is public, so what would be the effect of the publicity? Would it send a good or a bad signal to other parties? How much managerial time would be consumed participating in the legal action? Many suits that would probably be successful are never filed.

Business as Defendant

When a party is sued, besides relying on counsel for guidance, many companies have insurance that may come into play. If so, the insurance company may take a command role in the litigation. The question of whether to fight or settle a suit includes several considerations. How will the publicity of litigation affect the company's reputation? Settlements are usually private and avoid bad press. Will settlement help maintain a relationship with a partner or affect relationships with other current and future business partners? Many businesses have disputes that are settled, and the parties continue to do business. What is the cost of settlement compared to the cost of litigation and the expected outcome of a trial? Litigation can consume managerial time and jury verdicts are less predictable than a negotiated settlement.

Litigation or an Alternative?

Trials involving businesses can be costly and uncertain. Some involve complex facts that require extensive evidence, including mountains of business records. Trials often require testimony by managers and high-priced experts, and there is good evidence that juries tend to be less sympathetic to businesses than to individuals.

As we will discuss in this chapter, many suits are settled before litigation resolves a case. Over time, due to the expense, time, and uncertainty of litigation, *alternative dispute resolution (ADR)* has become ever more common. Courts and Congress encourage the use of arbitration, mediation, and negotiation to settle disputes, and parties often find these preferable to litigation. As Exhibit 3.1 illustrates, the various

Exhibit 3.1

*Comparing Disputant
Control under Various
Dispute Resolution
Options*

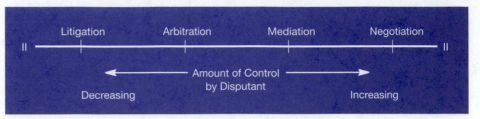

Source: Adapted from Larry Ray, "Emerging Options in Dispute Resolution," *ABA Journal*, June 1989

methods of dispute resolution differ in how the parties may be able to control the outcome. In this chapter we will first discuss litigation, and then the alternatives.

BASIC TRIAL PROCEDURES

The American legal system is an adversary system of justice. That is, the responsibility for bringing a lawsuit, shaping its issues, and presenting convincing evidence rests with the parties to the dispute. This section discusses the major procedural rules governing the civil litigation process. A summary of the stages of a typical civil lawsuit is presented in Exhibit 3.2.

Pleadings Stage

As we discussed in the last chapter, to begin a lawsuit, the plaintiff must determine which court has subject-matter jurisdiction and jurisdiction over the parties to the dispute. The plaintiff gives notice to the defendant by *service of process*, including a *summons*, an example of which is in Exhibit 2.3.

Along with the summons, the plaintiff serves the defendant with the first of the *pleadings*, commonly called the *complaint*. Pleadings are the formal statements made to the court by the parties to a case that list their claims and defenses. The complaint is a statement that sets forth the plaintiff's claim against the defendant. As illustrated in Exhibit 3.3, the complaint contains statements:

- Alleging the essential facts necessary for the court to take jurisdiction
- Of the facts necessary to claim that the plaintiff is entitled to a remedy
- Of the remedy the plaintiff is seeking

Responses to the Complaint

Following the service of the plaintiff's complaint, the defendant must file an answer. If the defendant does not respond, the court will presume the claims of the plaintiff are true and grant the plaintiff's requests. Depending on the circumstances, the defendant may file (1) a motion to dismiss, (2) an answer with or without an affirmative defense, or (3) a counterclaim.

Motion to Dismiss

A *motion to dismiss* by the defendant asks the court to dismiss the case because it does not have jurisdiction over either the subject matter of the dispute or the defendant's person. The defendant may also file a *motion to dismiss for failure to state a claim* or a *demurrer* (some states do not use the term *demurrer*; they use only the term *motion*

Exhibit 3.2

Stages of a Typical Civil Lawsuit

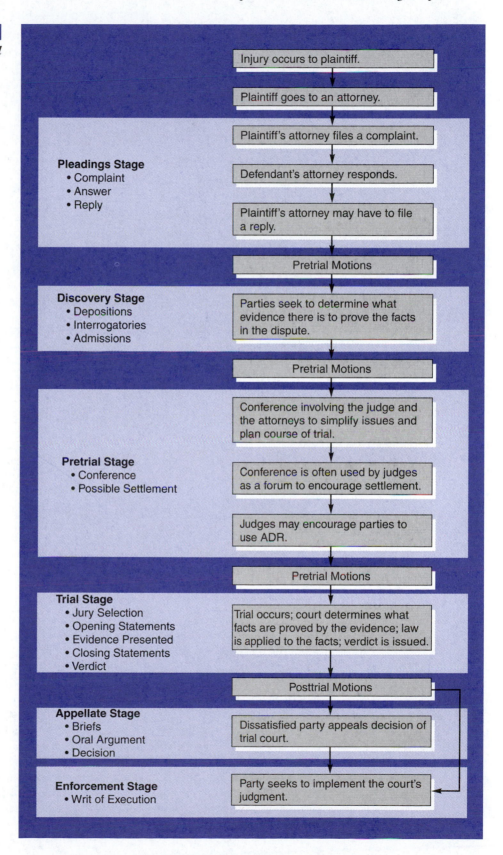

Pleadings Stage
- Complaint
- Answer
- Reply

Discovery Stage
- Depositions
- Interrogatories
- Admissions

Pretrial Stage
- Conference
- Possible Settlement

Trial Stage
- Jury Selection
- Opening Statements
- Evidence Presented
- Closing Statements
- Verdict

Appellate Stage
- Briefs
- Oral Argument
- Decision

Enforcement Stage
- Writ of Execution

Injury occurs to plaintiff.

Plaintiff goes to an attorney.

Plaintiff's attorney files a complaint.

Defendant's attorney responds.

Plaintiff's attorney may have to file a reply.

Pretrial Motions

Parties seek to determine what evidence there is to prove the facts in the dispute.

Pretrial Motions

Conference involving the judge and the attorneys to simplify issues and plan course of trial.

Conference is often used by judges as a forum to encourage settlement.

Judges may encourage parties to use ADR.

Pretrial Motions

Trial occurs; court determines what facts are proved by the evidence; law is applied to the facts; verdict is issued.

Posttrial Motions

Dissatisfied party appeals decision of trial court.

Party seeks to implement the court's judgment.

Exhibit 3.3

*Example of a Typical
Complaint*

United States District Court for the Southern District of California

Civil No. 2–80151

Callie O'Keefe
Plaintiff

v.   Complaint

Morriss, Inc.
Defendant

Comes now the plaintiff and for her cause of action against the defendant alleges and states as follows:

1. The plaintiff is a citizen of the state of California and defendant is a corporation incorporated under the laws of the state of Delaware, having its principal place of business in the state of Massachusetts. There is diversity of citizenship between parties.

2. The amount in controversy, exclusive of interest and costs, exceeds the sum of $75,000.

3. On January 10, 2005, on a public highway called Petty Street in Charlotte, North Carolina, defendant's employee, John Kluttz, negligently drove a motor vehicle owned by defendant against plaintiff who was properly crossing said highway.

4. As a result, plaintiff was hit and knocked down and had her leg broken and was otherwise injured, was prevented from transacting her business, suffered great pain of body and mind, and incurred expenses for medical attention and hospitalization.

5. The costs plaintiff incurred included: $15,000 in medical care, $100,000 in lost business, and $100,000 in pain and suffering.

WHEREFORE, plaintiff demands, judgment against defendent in the sum $215,000 and costs.

by
Carol Akers
Attorney for Plaintiff
5450 Tower of the Americas
San Diego, CA 92138

Dated: 7/19/06

to dismiss). This is an assertion that even if the facts asserted are true, the injury claimed by the plaintiff is one for which the law furnishes no remedy.

Answer

If the defendant's motion to dismiss is denied or if the defendant does not make such a motion, the defendant must file an *answer* with the court. In this pleading, the defendant denies the allegations made by the plaintiff; otherwise a judgment is entered for the plaintiff.

In answering a complaint, the defendant may admit to the plaintiff's allegations but may assert additional facts that should result in the action being dismissed. Called an *affirmative defense*, the defendant admits that he injured the plaintiff but that the additional facts he asserts constitute a defense (a legal excuse) to the plaintiff's complaint. The defendant could admit to being in a car accident involving the plaintiff but could assert that the claim is now barred by the statute of limitations; that is, the plaintiff waited too long to file suit. Other examples of affirmative defenses include self-defense, assumption of risk, contributory negligence, and other defenses we will study later.

Counterclaim

Besides denying the plaintiff's allegations in an answer, the defendant can assert a claim against the plaintiff. The defendant's claim is a *counterclaim* and may be based on the same events that the plaintiff bases the complaint on. The counterclaim is a complaint by the defendant, and the plaintiff must respond to it just as the defendant responded to the original complaint.

Reply

Any new matters raised by the defendant's answer are automatically taken as denied by the plaintiff. When the defendant files a counterclaim, the plaintiff may answer with a *reply*, which is an answer to the counterclaim.

Discovery Stage: Obtaining Information before Trial

After the pleadings, litigation enters the discovery stage. The parties use various legal tools to obtain evidence about the dispute. The attorneys are interested in gathering information from the opposing parties and their witnesses and experts. The process of obtaining information is known as *discovery*. The Federal Rules of Civil Procedure and the corresponding state procedural rules set down the guidelines for the discovery process.

Purpose of Discovery

Discovery serves several functions. Years ago, disputes moved from the pleadings stage directly to the trial stage. As a result, the parties had little information about the specific evidence the other party was going to use. The evidence presented could catch the opposing party by surprise—a "trial by ambush." The discovery process now prevents surprises by giving the parties access to each other's information.

Discovery also preserves evidence of witnesses who might not be available at the time of the trial, as well as the testimony of witnesses whose memory may fade with the passage of time. Finally, by allowing both parties the opportunity to learn what evidence would be available at trial, discovery encourages pretrial settlements. Parties can assess the strengths of both sides and estimate what a reasonable settlement would be. Most cases are settled, but if the case goes to trial, discovery narrows the issues so the trial can focus on the important questions in the case.

Tools of the Discovery Process

The discovery rules offer several ways to get information from an opposing party: depositions, written interrogatories, orders for production of documents, requests for admissions, and orders for a mental or physical examination. According to the Federal Rules of Civil Procedure, a party seeking information must select a discovery tool that is not "unduly burdensome" to the other party. In practice, parties can force out nearly any information related to the legal issues. The opposing party cannot refuse to comply just because of the burden of compliance.

Depositions and Interrogatories   A principal discovery tool is the *deposition*—the sworn in-person testimony of a witness recorded by a court reporter. The person whose deposition is taken, perhaps an eyewitness to an accident or an expert witness expected to provide testimony at trial, is questioned by attorneys from both sides.

The deposition is useful in finding information relevant to the dispute, including leads to other witnesses or documents. It may be used at trial to impeach—challenge—a witness who attempts to change his story at the trial. The deposition of a witness who is unavailable at the time of the trial may be allowed in place of live testimony.

Written interrogatories are questions submitted by a party to a case to the other party, or a witness, or another person with relevant information. The party receiving the interrogatories prepares written answers, usually with the aid of an attorney, and signs them under oath. Although the interrogatories lack the face-to-face spontaneity of a deposition, they can require the party to provide information from her records and files—the kind of information not carried in one's head.

Expert Witnesses   Many trials involving businesses use expert witnesses to help establish facts that are critical to a case, such as the value of lost profits, the costs to a victim of an accident, or the scientific evidence of harm from a product. These witnesses usually have their deposition taken before trial so that the other side knows the essence of their testimony and can prepare questions for trial.

There have been abuses by experts who want to please their clients and overstate the case by inflating damages or asserting harm to exist based on reasoning contrary to general scientific opinion. The Supreme Court has instructed courts to exclude evidence that is not reliable and is contrary to scientific standards. For example, in *Weisgram* v. *Marley Co.* (528 U.S. 440), the Supreme Court held that when expert testimony is critical to a case, but is rejected because it is not scientifically sound, then it is proper to grant summary judgment to the defendant and not allow another trial on the matter. The Court does not want to encourage parties to use hired guns who provide evidence that is not credible.

Orders for the Production of Documents   An order for the production of documents allows a party access to information in the possession of the other party. The kinds of information that are often sought are medical bills, business records, letters, and repair bills. The party seeking the information usually has the right to inspect, examine, and reproduce. Businesses have an obligation to maintain company records in a coherent manner so they may be accessed in case of a lawsuit. Failure to do so may result in sanctions by the court and even a judgment for the opposing party. If a trade secret or other confidential information is involved, a company can get a *protective order* to ensure confidentiality. The court may impose severe sanctions (penalties) on a party found to have violated a protective order.

Requests for Admissions   Either party can serve the other with a written request for an admission of the truth in matters relating to the dispute. Requests are used to settle facts about which there are no real disputes. That eliminates the need to establish such matters at trial. For example, in a contract dispute over the price of a product, one party may ask the other to admit that deliveries were made according to the terms of the contract. If admitted, these facts need not be proven at trial.

Mental and Physical Examinations   When the physical or mental condition of a party is an issue, the court may be asked to order that party to submit to an examination. Because of concerns for privacy, the party requesting the order must show a greater need for the information than in requests for other forms of discovery.

Generally, the party requesting the order specifies the exact type of mental or physical examination desired and the time, the place, and the specialists who are to conduct it.

Sanctions for Failing to Respond to a Discovery Request Under the rules of civil procedure, judges have broad powers to impose sanctions against a party who fails to comply with discovery requirements. If a party fails to comply with the requirements, of, say, a deposition, the requesting party can make a motion to the judge to force compliance. If the party does not comply with a court order, the court may order a *default judgment* granting victory to the other party or find the noncomplying party in *contempt of court* and order the party to jail or impose a fine. For example, one federal judge fined Wal-Mart $18 million for having "a corporate policy" of frustrating discovery and withholding evidence in numerous cases.

Discovery: Impacts on Business

Discovery can impose significant costs on businesses and managers. Businesses can be forced to endure the expense and the disruption of their staff while employees answer questions and produce documents. In one regulatory dispute between Ford Motor and the Federal Trade Commission, it cost Ford $4 million just to copy required documents. The burdens imposed by depositions are heavy when executives have to take time to prepare for and provide a deposition. In disputes involving technical matters or significant detail, the deposition of the manager most knowledgeable about it may take two weeks or more.

It is not uncommon for the chief executive of a corporation to get a subpoena requesting that he appear for a deposition. In most cases, the information sought is in the hands of subordinates. Courts protect executives if the purpose of a deposition is to harass them, but their participation is not uncommon. This expense is one more reason out-of-court settlement is likely. In the following case, the court is confronted with a request for a deposition of a senior executive.

Wauchop v. Domino's Pizza, Inc.
United States District Court, N.D. Indiana
143 F.R.D. 199 (1992)

CASE BACKGROUND *This case was filed as a wrongful death action by the family of a woman killed in a car accident involving a delivery vehicle owned by a Domino's Pizza franchisee. The plaintiffs filed suit against Domino's Pizza; Thomas Monaghan, the president of Domino's; the franchise owner; and the Domino's delivery driver. The plaintiffs charged Domino's with negligence based on its thirty-minute delivery guarantee, claiming the policy caused delivery personnel to drive dangerously.*

The plaintiffs had filed a motion for default judgment against Monaghan because he refused to give a deposition. Monaghan filed a motion for summary judgment.

In this ruling on the motion, the court decides whether Monaghan must attend the deposition.

CASE DECISION Miller, Judge.

* * *

Mr. Monaghan had moved for summary judgment . . . contending that he should not be held personally liable for the accident that forms the basis of this action. His motion is supported by his own written statement, which stated that he was not personally involved in the operation of the franchise, . . . that he never had any dealings with [the driver], and that

continues

his only conduct in relation to the 30-minute guarantee was in his capacity as a corporate director or officer. In his written statement, Mr. Monaghan states that the 30-minute guarantee policy went through corporate channels and was implemented after discussions with franchisees. He also states that the guarantee stresses safe driving. . . .

The plaintiffs planned to test the assertions in Mr. Monaghan's written statement by deposing Mr. Monaghan and other employees of Domino's. Mr. Monaghan, however, has refused to make himself available for deposition for several reasons. Mr. Monaghan's motion to strike the notice of his deposition reiterates the arguments in his summary judgment motion; he claims that he is not personally liable to the plaintiffs because the only allegations against him relate to his implementation of the 30-minute policy in his capacity as a director, shareholder, and chief executive officer of Domino's. He further reiterates that he was never directly involved with [the driver] or with the operation of the franchise. . . .

Mr. Monaghan also claims, surprisingly, that the 30-minute policy is not an issue in this case. He states . . . that no reasonable trier of fact could find that [the driver] was trying to comply with the 30-minute policy when the accident occurred, because at the time of the accident [he] was returning to the store from a pizza delivery. Further, Mr. Monaghan claims that the 30-minute policy could be an issue only if [the driver] was speeding at the time of the accident, and that the only evidence that [he] was speeding is [a passenger's] speculation during his deposition. . . . Finally, Mr. Monaghan argues that he has no knowledge of the policies and procedures of Domino's that cannot be obtained through written discovery or deposition of other Domino's employees.

* * *

The plaintiffs are entitled to take Mr. Monaghan's deposition to inquire into his role in the development of the 30-minute policy, a topic central to the plaintiffs' theory of Mr. Monaghan's liability and central to Mr. Monaghan's written statement. The plaintiffs point to discovery material that lends support to their contention that Mr. Monaghan was directly involved in implementation of Domino's policies. . . .

Under the discovery rules as they exist, Mr. Monaghan has raised no viable impediment to the taking of his deposition. . . . The court cannot avoid the conclusion that Mr. Monaghan is willing to delay and frustrate discovery indefinitely, notwithstanding the previous orders regarding the discovery of the relationship between the 30-minute policy and the accident in this case.

* * *

The court will not enter default against Mr. Monaghan at this time, but will afford him an opportunity to rectify his failure to comply with the court's previous orders relating to discovery. The order found at the conclusion of this memorandum requires Mr. Monaghan to appear in Chicago for his deposition and to pay the plaintiff's fees.

QUESTIONS FOR ANALYSIS

1. Why would Mr. Monaghan and Domino's Pizza not want to give the deposition in this case? Why was his deposition needed?
2. In general, in what situations would the depositions of lower-level employees be sufficient? When would the depositions of higher-level employees be necessary?

Summary Judgment

At the close of discovery, either party may move for a *summary judgment*. The Federal Rules of Civil Procedure state, in Rule 56(c), that summary judgment "shall be rendered . . . if the pleadings, depositions, answers to interrogatories, and admissions on file, together with affidavits, if any, show that there is no genuine issue as to any material fact and that the moving party is entitled to judgment as a matter of law." That is, a party asks the judge to apply the law to the facts and resolve the dispute. If the motion is granted, the case is over or the judgment may apply to only some issues, which are eliminated, and the trial proceeds on the remaining issues.

Pretrial Stage

Either party or the court may request a *pretrial conference*. These commonly held conferences normally involve the attorneys and the judge. The conferences often simplify the issues and plan the course of the trial. To ensure more efficient trials, judges may get the parties to drop certain parts of the case and focus on the key issues. Also at pretrial conferences, judges often encourage the parties to reach an out-of-court settlement.

Trial Stage

After discovery is complete, if there has been no dismissal, summary judgment, or settlement, the dispute is set for *trial*. In many court systems, the trial calendar is quite long. Delays of two or three years before a noncriminal case comes to trial are not uncommon.

The Jury

The Sixth and Seventh Amendments of the U.S. Constitution, as well as state constitutions, provide for the right to a *jury* in certain cases. In criminal cases, there is a right to a jury trial. In the federal court system, this right is guaranteed if the amount in controversy exceeds $20 and a common-law claim. Most state court systems have similar guarantees, although the minimum amount in controversy may be higher. There is no right to a jury trial when a private plaintiff requests an equitable remedy rather than money damages or in civil cases in which the government seeks noncriminal penalties for violating federal law.

Decision to Use a Jury   The right to a jury trial does not have to be exercised. If a jury is not requested, the judge determines the true facts in the dispute and applies the law to resolve it. The judge's temperament, the complexity of the evidence, and the degree to which the emotions of the jury are likely to affect the judgment affect decisions to request a jury trial.

Selection of the Jury   Jury selection begins when the clerk of the court sends a notice instructing citizens to appear for jury duty. The people called are in a jury pool.

Juris *prudence?*

The Dog Ate My Summons

Trying to avoid jury duty is common. The Harris County (Houston, Texas) District Court Clerk compiled the following list of excuses offered by jury duty dodgers:

"I have to feed my bird during the day."

"I take care of three cats during the day."

"I have to pee—a lot."

"I shot holes in my daughter's boyfriend's car."

"My wife killed someone."

"I had something removed from my head this morning."

Source: *National Law Journal*

The process used to select jury members is called *voir dire*. Depending upon the court, either the judge or the attorneys conduct voir dire. The purpose is to determine whether a prospective juror is likely to be so biased that he or she could not reach a fair decision based on the evidence presented. Attorneys are allowed a limited number of challenges that permit them to reject prospective jurors without stating a reason why. Juries traditionally involve a panel of twelve persons, but in many states panels of fewer than twelve—frequently six—are used.

The Trial

Although judges have some freedom to change the structure of a trial, most follow the general order summarized in Exhibit 3.4. Jury and nonjury trials are handled in much the same way, but they have a number of procedural differences. In nonjury trials, the judge may put more limits on the attorneys' opening statements and closing arguments. The following discussion details the steps involved in a typical jury trial.

Opening Statements   After the jurors have been sworn in, both attorneys make *opening statements*. The attorneys tell the jury what the crucial facts are and how they will prove that those facts support their positions. Opening statements are often limited to twenty minutes. The plaintiff's attorney normally presents the first statement.

Presentation of Direct Testimony   Following the opening statement, the plaintiff's attorney calls witnesses. The plaintiff has the burden of proving that his claims are correct. Each witness is first questioned by the plaintiff's attorney on *direct examination*. The defendant's attorney then examines that witness on *cross-examination*. Cross-examination may be followed by *re-direct examination* by the plaintiff's attorney and then by *re-cross-examination* by the defendant's attorney. The judge controls the length and the course of these examinations.

Closing Arguments   Before the case goes to the jury, the attorneys each present a *closing argument*. They summarize the evidence for the jury in a manner most favorable

Exhibit 3.4	Jury Trial	Nonjury Trial
Summaries of Typical Jury and Nonjury Trials	1. The selection of a jury	1. Plaintiff's opening statement
	2. Plaintiff's opening statement	2. Defendant's opening statement
	3. Defendant's opening statement	3. Plaintiff's presentation of direct evidence
	4. Plaintiff's presentation of direct evidence	4. Defendant's presentation of direct evidence
	5. Defendant's presentation of direct evidence	5. Plaintiff's presentation of rebuttal evidence
	6. Plaintiff's presentation of rebuttal evidence	6. Defendant's presentation of rebuttal evidence
	7. Defendant's presentation of rebuttal evidence	7. Defendant's final argument
	8. Opening final argument by the plaintiff	8. Plaintiff's closing argument
	9. Defendant's final argument	9. Judge's deliberation and verdict
	10. Plaintiff's closing argument	
	11. Instructions to the jury	
	12. Jury deliberation and verdict	

to their case. As in the opening statement, the judge limits the amount of time available to the attorneys for their closing arguments.

Instructions to the Jury   Before the jury retires to deliberate and reach a verdict, the judge gives the jury *instructions* (or *charges*). In the instructions, the judge tells the jury the applicable law, summarizes the facts and issues of the dispute, and states which of the parties has the *burden of persuasion*. After the instructions, the jurors are placed in the custody of the *bailiff* or other court official, who sees that they remain together and that there is no misconduct.

Reaching a Verdict   The jury deliberates to reach an agreement and find for either the plaintiff or the defendant. In a civil trial, the parties must prove their contentions to the jury by a *preponderance of the evidence*. If jurors are unable to reach a unanimous decision, the jury is said to be *hung*, and a new trial before a different jury may be necessary. The jury is discharged and a *mistrial* declared.

Because of the cost and delay associated with a new trial, judges are reluctant to allow hung juries. Although many jurisdictions require a unanimous jury decision, some states allow verdicts in civil disputes to be less than unanimous, such as ten of twelve jurors.

After the jury has reached a verdict, the verdict is read in court by the foreman of the jury or by the judge or the clerk of the court. The judgment is then entered. In some cases, the jury deliberates a second time to determine damages to be awarded if they find for the plaintiff.

JURIS *prudence?*

You Got Me There, Counselor!

The editor of the Massachusetts Bar Association's *Lawyers Journal* has a collection of courtroom bloopers by lawyers when questioning parties at trial. Among them:

"Were you present when your picture was taken?"

"Are you qualified to give a urine sample?"

"Did he kill you?"

"Were you alone or by yourself?"

"How many times have you committed suicide?"

Source: *Wall Street Journal*

Motions for a Verdict

The parties may ask the judge to issue a favorable verdict that makes jury deliberation unnecessary. Most common is a *motion for a directed verdict* or a *motion for judgment as a matter of law*. These are the same thing; different jurisdictions use different terms. After the cases have been presented, but before the case goes to the jury, a party requests that the court enter a judgment in its favor because there is not legally sufficient evidence on which a jury could find for the other party. The defense is more likely to prevail on such a motion. That is, the judge holds that the plaintiff failed to provide sufficient grounds, even if what is claimed is true, to be able to win a verdict. The *Carruthers* case illustrates some points of trial procedure, including when such a motion for judgment as a matter of law has been granted and then appealed.

Similarly, after a jury returns a verdict, the losing party may make a *motion for judgment as a matter of law* or a *motion for judgment notwithstanding the verdict*. The judge is asked to hold that there were not legally sufficient grounds to support the jury's verdict and to either overturn the entire verdict or a portion of it.

Carruthers v. BSA Advertising, Inc.
United States Court of Appeals, Eleventh Circuit
357 F.3d 1213 (2004)

CASE BACKGROUND *Jean Carruthers worked for BSA Advertising as art director. When she began to suffer pain in both hands, she visited a physician assigned by BSA. He diagnosed her as suffering from hand strain and restricted the work she could do. BSA fired her and hired a replacement. She sued for disability discrimination in violation of the Americans with Disabilities Act (ADA), contending that BSA fired her because of her disability or a perceived disability.*

The district court set a deadline of 25 July 2002 for all amendments to the pleadings, a deadline of 25 November 2002 for completion of all non-expert discovery, and a trial date for March 2003. Carruthers filed a motion to amend her complaint in January 2003 to add another cause of action, but the district court denied that motion and the case went to trial in March.

At the conclusion of her case, BSA moved for judgment as a matter of law, arguing that Carruthers failed to show that BSA perceived her as having a disability under the ADA. BSA also contended that she had failed to show that she could perform the essential functions of her job. The district court granted BSA's motion. Carruthers appealed.

CASE DECISION Per Curiam.

* * *

On appeal, Carruthers argues that the district court erred in granting BSA's motion for judgment as a matter of law. According to Carruthers, the district court wrongly concluded that her evidence, viewed in the light most favorable to her, failed to establish a case of employment discrimination in violation of the ADA. Specifically, she argues that the district court erred in determining that no reasonable juror could conclude that Carruthers's evidence showed that she was perceived to be disabled or that she was qualified to perform the essential functions of her job with or without a reasonable accommodation.

We review the district court's grant of a motion for judgment as a matter of law *de novo*, considering all the evidence in the light most favorable to the non-moving party. A directed verdict is only proper when the facts and inferences so overwhelmingly favor the verdict that no reasonable juror could reach a contrary decision. However, a mere scintilla of evidence does not create a jury question; instead, there must be a substantial conflict in evidence to support a jury question.

* * *

In order for any ADA claim to succeed, the claimant must show that her condition of impairment rises to the level of a disability. In Carruthers's case, the sole basis of her contention that she was disabled is subsection (C) [that prohibits discrimination against a person who is "regarded as" being disabled]. Under the "regarded as" prong, a person is "disabled" if her employer perceives her as having an ADA-qualifying disability, even if there is no factual basis for that perception. As with actual impairments, however, the perceived impairment must be one that, if real, would limit substantially a major life activity of the individual. . . .

We conclude that no reasonable jury could find that Carruthers's evidence established that BSA perceived her impairment as one that substantially limited the major life activities of working or performing manual tasks. Carruthers herself admitted at trial that BSA's knowledge of her condition was limited to her physician's diagnosis of a bilateral hand strain/sprain and her work restrictions. . . .

Similarly, Carruthers failed to show that BSA perceived her limitations in performing manual tasks as having a permanent or long-term impact and as preventing or severely restricting her from performing activities of central importance to most persons' lives. . . .

Because no reasonable juror could conclude that Carruthers was disabled, the district court did not err in granting BSA's motion for judgment as a matter of law. . . . The judgment of the district court is affirmed.

QUESTIONS FOR ANALYSIS

1. Is the court saying that Carruthers did not suffer any discrimination on the job due to her physical problem?

2. Why does the trial court decide to hold in favor of the defendant instead of allowing the jury to decide the matter?

Remedies in Civil Litigation

A plaintiff brings a civil suit seeking a remedy from the court. A *remedy* is the way a right is enforced or how a violation of a right is compensated or prevented. The remedies awarded by courts in civil disputes are classified as either *equitable remedies* or *monetary damages*. Most cases are for monetary damages, but in some cases a remedy in equity is more appropriate. Exhibit 3.5 summarizes the remedies available in civil litigation.

Exhibit 3.5

Equitable Remedies and Monetary Damages

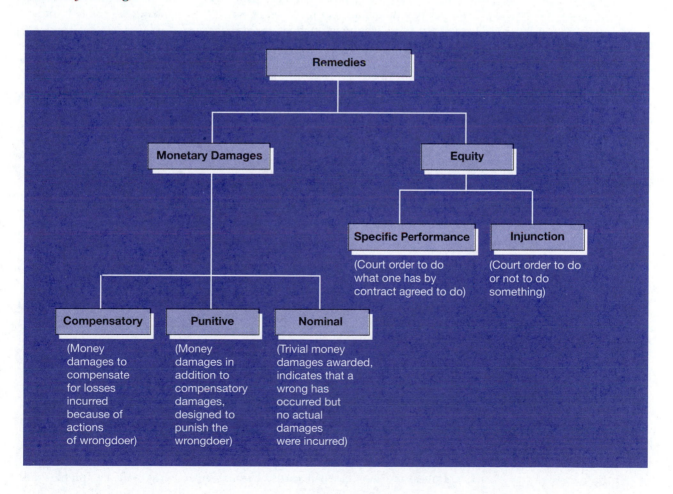

Monetary Damages

If a court finds that a party has suffered a legally recognized harm, monetary damages may be awarded. The general categories of monetary damage awards are compensatory, punitive, and nominal damages.

Compensatory Damages   *Compensatory damages* are intended to give injured parties enough money to restore them to the economic position they were in before the injury or to cover the costs incurred because of the injury. These are the most common monetary damages. Compensatory damages may be awarded for loss of time and money, pain and suffering, injury to reputation, and mental anguish.

Suppose Album Shipping contracts to sell pasta to Camerican International for $200,000. In the event Album does not deliver and Camerican must buy its pasta from another source for $250,000, Camerican is entitled to $50,000 in compensatory damages from Album. It has suffered a net loss of $50,000 in the purchase. In Chapter 10, on contracts, we will review more issues involved in compensatory damages.

Punitive Damages   When the wrongdoer's actions are particularly reprehensible or when the defendant's conduct is willful or malicious, the court may award the injured party *punitive* or *exemplary damages* in addition to compensatory damages. These may be awarded in some tort cases, as we will see in Chapters 7 and 8. Punitive damages are to punish the wrongdoer and discourage others from similar conduct.

An Atlanta jury awarded $4.24 million in compensatory damages to a family whose teenage son was killed when his General Motors pickup truck erupted in flames after being broadsided by a drunk driver. The jury also "sent a message to General Motors" to fix the gasoline tanks it determined were the cause of the death—in the form of an additional $100 million in punitive damages. As we will see in Chapter 4, the Supreme Court has reviewed some of the constitutional issues related to punitive damages.

Nominal Damages   If a plaintiff suffers a legal wrong but has not suffered actual damages to person or property (or the damages are considered trivial by the court), the court may award *nominal damages*. The plaintiff may recover as little as one dollar.

Equitable Remedies

The courts recognize that there are times when monetary damages are not practical or effective. Money may not be relevant, or the defendant may not be solvent yet could do certain things to help rectify a wrong. Using the broad powers of equity that courts have, they have developed *remedies in equity* that can be imposed when remedies at law, such as monetary damages, are inadequate.

Specific Performance   In equity, courts can order *specific performance* as a remedy and require the offending party to do what had been promised. This remedy may apply in contract cases when monetary damages would not be adequate or the subject matter is unique. If the owner of a unique piece of land has a contract to sell the land and then changes her mind, a court may order her to perform as promised and transfer title to the land to the buyer for the promised payment. Specific performance is more likely when the subject matter is land or rare properties, such as art, antiques, or even baseball cards, because such items may be unique and irreplaceable, or because the other party may have incurred substantial expense in expectation of the deal.

JURIS *prudence?*

Why Alabama Courts Are Ranked 48th in the Nation

The state of Alabama sued ExxonMobil, claiming the company underpaid the state for natural gas royalties. An Alabama jury held that Exxon owed the state $64 million in royalties and then tacked on $12 billion in punitive damages. One juror said he voted for that amount because the state needed the money. The U.S. Chamber of Commerce ranks Alabama, West Virginia, and Mississippi courts as the worst in the nation.

Source: *San Francisco Chronicle*

Injunction An injunction is a court order directing a person to do something, to not do something being planned, or to stop doing something. Injunctions can be temporary or permanent. In a *temporary injunction*, the court imposes conditions on the activities of the alleged wrongdoer until the rights of the parties have been determined or the wrongdoer makes changes in the activity to make them acceptable. In a *permanent injunction*, the rights of the parties have been determined and the court found that the activities damage the rights of the injured party and that they cannot be modified to satisfy the court.

Suppose that Amacher decides to store chemical wastes on his farm. His neighbor may ask the court for a temporary injunction stopping Amacher from doing that until the harmful effects on the neighborhood can be determined.

Courts rarely issue injunctions ordering someone to perform personal services. Suppose Dali agreed to paint your portrait, but then refused to do it. A court would not issue an injunction ordering Dali to paint the portrait, because courts do not want to become involved in supervising services, such as making sure that Dali does the job and does it to your satisfaction. Courts also do not want to force people into involuntary servitude—doing work they do not want to do. Monetary damages are more appropriate.

Appellate Stage

The decision in a case may be appealed, as we saw in the *Carruthers* case, if one of the parties believes an *error of law* was made during the trial. The parties cannot appeal the factual determinations made at the trial. However, bases for appeal include failure by the trial judge to admit or exclude certain evidence, improper instructions given to the jury, and the granting or denying of motions to dismiss the case. Appellate courts ensure that the trial court judge correctly applied the law.

Arguments before Appeals Courts

The parties present their arguments to the appellate court through *written briefs* and *oral arguments*, which discuss the law, not the facts in the case. Usually, three judges hear an appeal. The appellate court has authority to review any ruling of law by the trial judge. It has the power to *affirm*, *reverse*, or *modify* the judgment of the trial court. The decision of the appellate court is the one that receives the majority vote of the judges.

JURIS *prudence?*

Shortest Decision by an Appeals Court?

In *Denny* v. *Radar Industries*, the Michigan Court of Appeals disposed of the appeal with this published opinion:

"The appellant has attempted to distinguish the factual situation in this case from that in [an earlier case]. He didn't. We couldn't." Affirmed.

Source: 184 N.W.2d 289 (1970)

Decisions by Appeals Courts

An appellate court's majority decision is referred to as the court's written or *majority opinion*. This opinion gives the legal rationale for the court's decision. It also provides guidance to judges and attorneys for the resolution of similar disputes. A court may also issue a *concurring opinion* (an opinion written by a judge who agrees with the majority decision but for a different reason) or *dissenting opinion* (an opinion written by a judge who disagrees with the decision of the majority). While concurring and dissenting opinions may influence future thinking about the dispute, the majority decision decides the case and has the force of law.

When the appeals court's majority opinion agrees with the trial court's decision, the court has *affirmed* that decision. When the majority opinion disagrees with the trial court, the appellate court's decision *reverses* the trial court's decision. The appellate court may also affirm the decision but *modify* it in some way—for example, by reducing the damages awarded by the trial court. In such situations, the appeals court is likely to *remand* the case—return the case—to the trial court for retrial. The trial court must then retry the case, in part or in whole, taking into account the appellate court's ruling.

Enforcement Stage

After a trial, if no appeal is taken or if no further appeal is available, the *judgment*, or decision, of the court becomes final. The same dispute cannot be considered again in that or any other forum. It is *res judicata*—a thing decided by judgment.

The judgment may be a monetary award to the plaintiff, a declaration of the rights between the parties, or an order prohibiting some activity. When the defendant wins, the judgment generally does not involve an award of money. It states that the defendant is not responsible for the plaintiff's injuries. In some instances, the court may require that the losing party pay the other party's legal expenses, but usually each side is responsible for their own costs.

Enforcing Judgments

When the plaintiff recovers a damage award and the defendant does not pay, the plaintiff can seek a *writ of execution*. The writ is a court order to an official, such as the sheriff, to seize the property of the defendant to satisfy the judgment. Courts may order *garnishment* of a debtor's property, which usually involves an order for a certain amount of the debtor's paycheck to be paid on a regular basis to the judgment winner.

Although obtaining a writ of execution to enforce a judgment may be easy, it is often difficult to collect a judgment. If a party does not have valuable property to seize, or if the losing party flees the jurisdiction taking his property with him, or hides property out of the country, it may be nearly impossible for the plaintiff to collect a judgment. In other cases, the losing party, by stalling or otherwise failing to comply with the writ of execution, makes it difficult and costly for the plaintiff to collect. This is one of the many complexities of the litigation process that cause parties to use alternative forms of dispute resolution.

INTERNATIONAL *Perspective*

German Trial Procedure

The rules governing trial procedures can vary substantially from country to country. In Germany, trials are conducted much differently from trials in the United States. Perhaps most striking to U.S. observers is the fact that judges in Germany play a much more active role in the trial process than do American judges. In Germany, civil procedure is governed by rules called the Zivilprozessordnung (ZPO). Under these rules, the judge holds hearings to gather evidence to help him reach a decision in the case. The trial progresses informally (compared to trials in the U.S.) through these hearings.

In the United States, the role of the judge is usually limited to applying the law to the facts of the case. In Germany, the judge decides the facts of the case and then applies the law to those facts. The judge, not the lawyers, decides which witnesses to call. The judge, not the lawyers, interrogates the witnesses and records their testimony. Judges may ask questions only about the evidence that the parties to the case present themselves. And what is presented is much more limited than what is typically presented at U.S. trials. This is so because German courts protect many more confidential relationships than do U.S. courts.

ARBITRATION

If you have a checking account or a credit card, most likely you have agreed to an arbitration agreement, even though you may not have read the details of the contract when you signed up for the account. Many contracts contain arbitration clauses that obligate the parties to the contract to submit disputes to arbitration, not litigation.

Arbitration is the most widely recognized form of ADR. It is a process similar to litigation in which two or more persons agree to allow a neutral person (or panel) to resolve a dispute. The advantages of using a neutral expert, called an *arbitrator* or *arbiter*, are twofold: (1) because she is mutually agreed upon by the parties, the arbitrator has the trust of both parties, and (2) because the arbitrator is usually an expert in the subject matter, less time is needed to educate her about the dispute. This usually results in a faster resolution of the matter.

In the *Federal Arbitration Act (FAA)*, Congress states in the strongest terms that agreements to arbitrate must be upheld. A "written provision in any . . . contract evidencing a transaction involving commerce to settle by arbitration a controversy thereafter arising out of such contract or transaction . . . shall be valid, irrevocable, and enforceable, save upon such grounds as exist at law or in equity for the revocation of any contract" (9 U.S.C. §2). If a party tries to avoid arbitration, the courts are instructed by the FAA to compel and enforce arbitration.

Similarly, most states have adopted the *Uniform Arbitration Act (UAA)*, which has provisions very similar to those in the FAA. States that have not adopted the UAA have laws that are similar. These laws strongly uphold the integrity of the arbitration process.

There are frequent challenges in court to arbitration awards, but the courts uphold the vast majority of arbitration decisions. As the Supreme Court discusses in the *Waffle House* case, federal agencies are not restricted by private arbitration agreements, most of which are to be upheld.

Equal Employment Opportunity Commission v. Waffle House, Inc.

United States Supreme Court
534 U.S. 279, 122 S.Ct. 754 (2002)

CASE BACKGROUND   *When Eric Baker was hired by Waffle House as a grill operator, he signed an agreement that "any dispute or claim" regarding his employment would be "settled by binding arbitration." This is a standard form signed as a condition of employment for all Waffle House employees. Soon after Baker started working at Waffle House, he suffered a seizure at work and was fired.*

Baker filed a complaint with the Equal Employment Opportunity Commission (EEOC) that he was a victim of discrimination based on his disability, a violation of the Americans with Disabilities Act (ADA), but he did not sue Waffle House. The EEOC investigated and filed suit against Waffle House in federal court, contending that Baker's treatment was a violation of his ADA rights. Waffle House filed a petition under the Federal Arbitration Act (FAA) to stay the EEOC's suit and to compel arbitration. The district court denied the motion. The appeals court reversed, holding that a valid, enforceable arbitration agreement existed between Baker and Waffle House and the EEOC could not file suit in federal court. Noting that different appeals courts had ruled in opposite ways on this matter, the EEOC appealed.

CASE DECISION   Justice Stevens delivered the opinion of the Court.

* * *

The FAA was enacted in 1925, 43 Stat. 883, and then reenacted and codified in 1947 as Title 9 of the United States Code. . . . As we have explained, its "purpose was to reverse the longstanding judicial hostility to arbitration agreements that had existed at English common law and had been adopted by American courts, and to place arbitration agreements on the same footing as other contracts." The FAA broadly provides that a written provision in "a contract evidencing a transaction involving commerce to settle by arbitration a controversy thereafter arising out of such contract . . . shall be valid, irrevocable, and enforceable, save upon such grounds as exist at law or in equity for the revocation of any contract." 9 U.S.C. §2. Employment contracts, except for those covering workers engaged in transportation, are covered by the act.

The FAA provides for stays of proceedings in federal district courts when an issue in the proceeding is referable to arbitration, and for orders compelling arbitration when one party has failed or refused to comply with an arbitration agreement. We have read these provisions to "manifest a 'liberal federal policy favoring arbitration agreements.'" Absent some ambiguity in the agreement, however, it is the language of the contract that defines the scope of disputes subject to arbitration. . . .

The FAA directs courts to place arbitration agreements on equal footing with other contracts, but "does not require parties to arbitrate when they have not agreed to do so." Because the FAA is "at bottom a policy guaranteeing the enforcement of private contractual arrangements," we look first to whether the parties agreed to arbitrate a dispute, not to general policy goals, to determine the scope of the agreement. While ambiguities in the language of the agreement should be resolved in favor of arbitration, we do not override the clear intent of the parties, or reach a result inconsistent with the plain text of the contract, simply because the policy favoring arbitration is implicated. "Arbitration under the [FAA] is a matter of consent, not coercion." Here there is no ambiguity. No one asserts that the EEOC is a party to the contract, or that it agreed to arbitrate its claims. It goes without saying that a contract cannot bind a nonparty. Accordingly, the proarbitration policy goals of the FAA do not require the agency to relinquish its statutory authority if it has not agreed to do so. . . .

We are persuaded that, pursuant to . . . the ADA, whenever the EEOC chooses from among the many charges filed each year to bring an enforcement action in a particular case, the agency may be seeking to vindicate a public interest, not simply provide make-whole relief for the employee, even when it pursues entirely victim-specific relief. To hold otherwise would undermine the detailed enforcement scheme created by Congress simply to give greater effect to an agreement between private parties that does not even contemplate the EEOC's statutory function. . . .

The judgment of the Court of Appeals is reversed, and the case is remanded for further proceedings consistent with this opinion.

QUESTIONS FOR ANALYSIS

1. Since millions of employees have arbitration clauses in their contracts, will this case cause many of them to seek help from the EEOC rather than arbitrate their claims against their employer?

2. Can you think of other matters that this decision may force into litigation rather than require arbitration?

The Arbitration Process

It is common for parties to provide for arbitration of future disputes by inserting an arbitration clause in a contract, such as this standard arbitration clause:

> Any controversy or claim arising out of or relating to this contract, or the breach thereof, shall be settled by arbitration administered by the American Arbitration Association under its Commercial Arbitration Rules, and the judgment on the award rendered by the arbitrator(s) may be entered in any court having jurisdiction thereof.

Similarly, parties to a dispute not already covered by an arbitration clause may agree to submit the dispute to arbitration. A sample submission form from the American Arbitration Association is seen in Exhibit 3.6. Arbitration begins when a party files a *submission* to refer a dispute to arbitration. The time in which a dispute must be filed is usually much shorter than the time in which a lawsuit must be filed. Some commercial arbitration clauses require that cases must be filed within a couple of months of the claim or the right to contest the matter is lost.

Selection of Arbitrators

When a case goes to court, the parties to the case may have no control over who the judge will be. Under arbitration, the parties agree on who the arbitrator will be, or they agree to a selection method under the arbitration rules specified in their arbitration agreement. Most matters are arbitrated by one arbitrator, but panels of three arbitrators are not unusual.

Arbitrators are often attorneys, but that is not a general requirement. Rather, arbitrators are required to be impartial, which means that they must avoid conflicts of interest and should uphold the integrity of the arbitration process as spelled out in codes of ethics for arbitrators. Since arbitration is common in many areas, such as labor disputes, the parties usually insist upon arbitrators with experience in the field. Arbitration associations help ensure the quality of the arbiters, as the associations want to maintain a reputation for quality dispute resolution. Hence, arbitrators often have more expertise in their case area than do most judges, who may hear certain kinds of cases rarely.

Exhibit 3.6

Form Used to Submit a Dispute to Arbitration

American Arbitration Association

_____ **ARBITRATION RULES***
(Enter the name of the applicable rules)

To institute proceedings, please send two copies of this demand *and the arbitration agreement*, with the filing fee as provided in the rules, to the AAA. Send the original demand to the respondent.

DEMAND FOR ARBITRATION   DATE: _____

To: Name _____

Address _____
(of the Party on Whom the Demand Is Made)

City, State _____ ZIP Code _____

Telephone (   ) _____ Fax (   ) _____

Name of Representative (if Known) _____

Representative's Address _____

Name of Firm (if Applicable) _____

City and State _____ ZIP Code _____

Telephone (   ) _____ Fax (   ) _____

The below named claimant, a party to an arbitration agreement contained in a written contract dated _____ and providing for arbitration under the _____ Arbitration Rules of the American Arbitration Association, hereby demands arbitration thereunder.

THE NATURE OF THE DISPUTE:

THE CLAIM OR RELIEF SOUGHT (the Amount, if Any): _____

TYPES OF BUSINESS: Claimant _____ Respondent _____

HEARING LOCALE REQUESTED: _____
(City and State)

DOES THE DISPUTE ARISE OUT OF AN EMPLOYMENT RELATIONSHIP?   ☐ YES   ☐ NO

You are hereby notified that copies of our arbitration agreement and this demand are being filed with the American Arbitration Association at its _____ case management center with a request that it commence administration of the arbitration. Under the rules, you may file an answering statement, within the time frame specified in the rules, after notice from the administrator.

Signed _____ Title _____
(May be Signed by a Representative)

Name of Claimant _____

Address (to Be Used in Connection with This Case) _____

Name of Firm (if Applicable) _____

City and State _____ ZIP Code _____

Telephone (   ) _____ Fax (   ) _____

Name of Representative _____

Representative's Address _____

City and State _____ ZIP Code _____

Telephone (   ) _____ Fax (   ) _____

☐ **MEDIATION is a nonbinding process.** The mediator assists the parties in working out a solution that is acceptable to them. If you wish for the AAA to contact the other parties to ascertain whether they wish to mediate this matter, please check this box or list them on the back (there is no additional administrative fee for this service).

*If you have a question about which rules apply or the address of the nearest case management center, please contact the AAA (1-800-778-7879).

Source: American Arbitration Association (http://www.adr.org)

The Hearing

After the submission and the selection of an arbitrator, a hearing is scheduled. The parties set the rules of the hearing either with or without assistance of the arbitrator and give the arbitrator the power to enforce the hearing rules. The hearing is normally a closed-door proceeding conducted like a trial but without a trial's restrictive procedural rules. For example, the manner in which evidence can be presented in an arbitration hearing is generally less rigid. Since the arbitrator is an expert in the field, he is less likely to be persuaded by improperly presented evidence.

Are There Limits on the Terms of Arbitration?

As a manager at WeLuvPets, you wish to keep down the cost of possible litigation that arises from unhappy former and current employees. You draw up a contract that all new employees must sign as a condition of employment. It says that any and all employment disputes, including claims made under laws against discrimination in employment, will be subject to binding arbitration. It also stipulates that WeLuvPets will choose the arbitrator and that both parties to the dispute will pay one-half of the costs of arbitration. Is the agreement binding on all who sign it? Are all the conditions you put in the arbitration agreement sensible?

ISSUE
Spotter

The Award

After the hearing, the arbitrator reaches a decision, called an *award*, which is usually given within thirty days. The award is usually in writing. However, the arbitrator need not state the legal basis of the decision unless the parties have requested that they be provided (and are willing to pay for that extra work).

The arbitrator makes an award based on an application of law to the evidence presented. Besides deciding if one party owes the other party cash, goods, or something else, the arbitrator decides how the parties will split her fee and the administrative fees. In some arbitration, the arbitrator does not construct an award but chooses between the claims of the two parties. For example, under the rules regarding salary disputes in Major League Baseball, the arbitrator picks either the salary requested by the player or the salary offered by the baseball team.

Arbitrators have wide latitude in making awards. For example, in a case involving a claim by a stockbroker against his former employer, an arbitration panel of the National Association of Securities Dealers ordered the employer to pay $2.7 million in compensatory damages and $25 million in punitive damages. The panel also ordered the company to eliminate "defamatory" materials from the broker's records. The panel held that the employer engaged in "reprehensible conduct" in smearing the broker's name after he was fired. While only a small percentage of arbitration cases involve punitive damages, arbitrators have the authority to order them paid when warranted.

Appealing the Award

Just as parties who lose in court may be dissatisfied, parties who lose in arbitration may want to carry the matter further. Just as attacks on judges are very unlikely to be acceptable, attacks on the integrity of arbitrators are rarely successful.

Furthermore, errors of fact or law by an arbitrator are not reviewable by the courts. According to the Federal Arbitration Act, there are four grounds for overturning an award. These occur when

1. The award was obtained by corruption or fraud.
2. There was evidence of partiality or corruption by an arbitrator.
3. An arbitrator was guilty of serious procedural misconduct, such as refusing to hear relevant evidence, that prejudiced the rights of a party.
4. An arbitrator exceeded his power, and an award was made on a subject not relevant to the proceeding.

Under the doctrine of *res judicata*, the final judgment on the merits of a case by a court prevents an issue from being relitigated. This doctrine also holds to arbitration awards. While this doctrine has certain limitations in arbitration cases (especially in the area of employment rights), in general, an arbitration award is final and the matter cannot be litigated again or appealed.

Voluntary and Compulsory Arbitration

Most arbitration is voluntary. The parties submit their dispute to an arbitrator for a decision rather than go to court. This agreement can occur at the time of a dispute or, more commonly, is a part of a contract that preceded the dispute. Labor contracts (between a union and an employer) and employment contracts often include arbitration requirements. Many commercial contracts include standard terms about arbitration. Most stockbrokers and banks require their customers to sign a contract stating that in the event of a dispute over their account the matter will be arbitrated. Many insurance contracts require arbitration of disputes. Hence, arbitration is a common feature in modern contracts.

Public Sector Employment

Many states require compulsory arbitration for some or all public sector employees. Police officers, firefighters, and public school teachers may not be permitted to strike. Rather, public employees (usually through their unions) and their employer (usually a local government) must arbitrate the terms of employment: wages, hours, and working conditions. When such arbitration is mandatory, legislation usually requires the awards to have a written record and decision so it is clear that the awards are supported by the evidence.

Court-Annexed Arbitration

Some state and federal courts require arbitration as a pretrial requirement. Called *court-annexed arbitration* (or judicial arbitration), these programs are limited to disputes in which the amount in controversy is relatively small. Eligible cases are referred to mandatory pretrial arbitration (or voluntary in some states), which is conducted by an attorney, a retired judge, or, in some court systems, a panel of three attorneys. The procedure employed usually consists of a quasi-judicial hearing leading to a resolution of the dispute.

Either party may reject the decision and insist on a court trial. Relatively few cases submitted to the process, however, proceed to trial, and the dispute is resolved faster than if it waits to get on the court docket. The federal district courts are empowered to use arbitration and other ADR techniques both by the Federal Rules of Civil Procedure and as a part of the court's power to manage cases.

NEGOTIATION

The least formal form of ADR is *negotiation*; it is almost always voluntary and, unlike arbitration, has no mandatory procedure, although there can be legal consequences for lying. Negotiation occurs when parties decide to settle a matter between themselves; the use of lawyers or representatives is not required but is common.

Negotiation has risen in popularity in recent years. For example, Georgia-Pacific Corp. set up an in-house ADR program in the 1990s. After five years of experience, they reported that the program saved the company at least a million dollars a year in litigation expenses by keeping dozens of cases a year out of court. Direct negotiation is the form of ADR that experience has shown to be the most successful. Over 500 major firms have signed a pledge to the CPR Institute for Dispute Resolution to seek ADR. The Institute's experience is that negotiation is generally the cheapest form of ADR and resolves most disputes.

CYBER *Law*

International Arbitration and Mediation of Domain Name Disputes

The global use of domain names means that they must be unique to be effective in the server system. The World Intellectual Property Organization (WIPO), as part of its function to establish international rules for trademarks and other forms of intellectual property, has a domain name dispute resolution service that protects the integrity of country code top-level domains (such as .mx for Mexico) and for generic top-level domains (gTLDs), such as .edu for education.

WIPO, headquartered in Geneva, Switzerland, has a Uniform Domain Name Dispute Resolution Policy (UDRP) that deals with problems such as cybersquatting. Parties can go to the WIPO Arbitration and Mediation Center (http://arbiter.wipo.int) for dispute resolution. Experts from many countries are available to handle disputes. Most are law professors or lawyers who specialize in this area of law. If only one panelist is requested to settle a dispute, the fee for one to five domain names included in a complaint is $1,500; the fee is $3,000 if three panelists are requested. Such resolution has the advantage of global acceptance of the results. Over a thousand disputes a year are submitted to the Center.

Issues in Negotiation

Whenever people bargain for something, they are engaged in negotiation. Many contracts are formed after negotiation. A negotiated settlement of a dispute is usually a contract that, like other contracts, is enforced by the courts. When parties enter into negotiation, it is often with the intention of making a deal, that is, looking forward to forming a contract. The *Red Owl* case in Chapter 10 is a famous example of business negotiations that were not handled properly and resulted in litigation.

Stages of Negotiation

While the steps of negotiation may be much the same in all situations, negotiation in a dispute involves parties at odds with one another. Since the parties to the dispute are unlikely to be experienced negotiators and may be influenced by their anger about what has happened, negotiation to settle a dispute is often handled by an attorney or other experienced person. The negotiator is the agent of the party who authorizes the agent to represent her. The agent works for the party who hired her and must follow her instructions even if she wants to do something the negotiator may think is foolish.

The first stage of negotiation involves studying the issues and planning for negotiation. To do a good job, a party should gather facts and relevant information (not just go on personal opinions), understand the weak points, consider the objectives of negotiation, know the law that would be applied to the situation if litigated, know the alternative routes that can be taken, and decide how to handle the negotiation process, such as whether the parties to the dispute will be present.

Next, the parties must exchange information. At this point, the style of the negotiator plays a role. Some negotiators are combative "tough guys," while others are thoughtful problem solvers in their approach. In either case, the negotiator must know what information to present, such as an offer to settle.

While one negotiation strategy is to state (and mean) that the first offer is the final offer, most negotiators expect to compromise. Some concessions are planned in advance to help get the parties closer to a realistic settlement. Since the courts encourage negotiation, settlement offers presented in negotiation may not be used as evidence in court. If a negotiation is properly run, almost nothing said in the negotiation can be later used in court if the negotiation fails. The fact that a negotiation that fails will not come back to haunt a party in court encourages the integrity of the process. Finally, if an agreement is reached, it is usually spelled out in writing and becomes a contract that can be enforced in court. The courts have a strong policy of enforcing negotiated settlements.

Ethical Duties

Anyone involved in negotiation must be careful not to misrepresent the truth, which can constitute fraud. Fraud that involves lying to someone and misleading them to their detriment can lead to a tort suit, as discussed in Chapters 7 and 8. Misleading someone in contract negotiation can be a breach of contract, which also leads to litigation. Thus, parties to negotiation face legal constraints on their behavior. While all parties to negotiation should be constrained by ethical considerations, attorneys, like other professionals, are bound by codes of ethics or codes of professional responsibility. Attorneys who violate their ethical responsibility may suffer discipline by their bar association.

MEDIATION

Unlike negotiation, where the parties to a dispute or their representatives meet to try to settle a matter, in *mediation* a third party—the *mediator*—is always used to help the parties to a dispute try to reach a solution by coming to an acceptable agreement. Unlike arbitration, where the arbitrator imposes an award on the parties, the mediator cannot impose a decision but can only help resolve a conflict.

The American Arbitration Association suggests the following provision be included in contracts:

> If a dispute arises out of or relates to this contract or the breach thereof and if the dispute cannot be settled through negotiation, the parties agree first to try in good faith

to settle the dispute by mediation administered by the American Arbitration Association under its Commercial Mediation Rules before resorting to arbitration, litigation, or some other dispute-resolution procedure.

Mediation is the most common form of ADR used to resolve disputes that start out in the courts. Many federal and state courts require that mediation be attempted before trial or at least offer the alternative. Surveys indicate that attorneys prefer to go to mediation rather than to arbitration when pressured to go to ADR.

Mediation is also often used to help resolve labor disputes. The Federal Mediation and Conciliation Service was established to help unions and employers bargain to a contract. Mediation is also commonly used to help resolve marital problems and, if not successful, to set the terms of divorce. In such cases, mediation is a voluntary process that helps avoid litigation.

INTERNATIONAL *Perspective*

Global Acceptance of Arbitration

International business contracts usually contain arbitration clauses. Over 100 nations have signed the United Nations Convention on the Recognition and Enforcement of Foreign Arbitral Awards, which binds signatory nations to uphold the validity of arbitration awards. The gap between the formal law and local legal reality has often been large.

Although China signed the Convention, Chinese courts had a reputation for not enforcing arbitration decisions. For example, one non-Chinese company won an award for $4.9 million in arbitration at the Swedish Chamber of Commerce. The Shanghai company that lost did not pay. When the foreign firm sued in court in China to enforce the award, the courts refused to enforce the arbitration decision. China's supreme court has recently held that lower courts in China could not reverse arbitration awards without its permission.

India has also had a reputation as a country where foreign awards are hard to enforce through Indian courts. The government of India adopted the Indian Arbitration Act to encourage the use of arbitration. Indian courts cannot review the merits of foreign arbitration unless the party has substantial proof of bias or the award otherwise violates public policy.

Thousands of international disputes go to arbitration each year. The American Arbitration Association's International Centre for Dispute Resolution handles about 700 cases a year involving billions of dollars in claims. The International Chamber of Commerce's International Court of Arbitration handles a similar number of disputes. The increased acceptance of arbitration by courts around the world facilitates the expansion of global business by helping ensure enforcement of contracts.

The Mediator

Some states do not have requirements about who may serve as a mediator, but most people want a person trained or experienced in mediation, as the results are more likely to be successful. Some states require those offering their services as mediators to be trained professionals. The law in Massachusetts states:

> A "mediator" shall mean a person not a party to a dispute who enters into a written agreement with the parties to assist them in resolving their disputes and has completed at least thirty hours of training in mediation and who either has four years of professional experience as a mediator or is accountable to a dispute resolution organization . . . or one who has been appointed to mediate by a judicial or governmental body. (M.G.L.A. ch. 233 §23C)

The Society of Professionals in Dispute Resolution is an organization that helps to train and govern the credentials of mediators. The Society identifies the skills that a mediator should possess and the steps that should be taken in proper mediation. Those who offer their services as mediators and fail to act in a professional manner may be subject to liability by a party to the dispute unhappy with the outcome.

Mediation Process

A mediator, when agreed upon by both parties, may review the issues to prepare to handle the matter. The mediator explains the process involved and makes clear that she is a neutral party. The mediator collects information, outlines the key issues, listens, asks questions, observes the parties, discusses options, and encourages compromise. If successful, the mediator helps draft an agreement between the parties that settles the dispute. The agreement is an enforceable contract and, therefore, settles the matter.

A standard part of the mediation process is an agreement by the parties to maintain confidentiality. Nothing said in the mediation can be made public or be used in court as evidence if mediation should fail and a suit follows. Regardless of what the parties agree upon, there is a presumption in law that information revealed during negotiation or mediation should not be used in evidence. To encourage honesty in negotiation and mediation, most discussions are privileged, and mediators cannot be required to testify later in court. Some states, including Colorado, have made this a firm rule by statute:

> Mediation proceedings shall be regarded as settlement negotiations, and no admission, representation, or statement made in mediation not otherwise discoverable or obtainable shall be admissible as evidence or subject to discovery. In addition, a mediator shall not be subject to process requiring the disclosure of any matter discussed during mediation proceedings. (Colo. Rev.Stat. 13-22-307)

The possible consequences of violating the confidentiality of mediation proceedings and settlement are made clear in the *Paranzino* case.

Paranzino v. Barnett Bank of South Florida, N.A.

District Court of Appeals of Florida, Fourth District
690 So.2d 725 (1997)

CASE BACKGROUND   *Paranzino claimed that she went to a Barnett bank with $200,000 in cash to obtain two certificates of deposit, each for $100,000. She claimed that she was issued only one certificate for $100,000. She sued the bank for breach of contract. The bank denied having received $200,000 and noted that Paranzino was given a receipt for $100,000 and that her monthly statements reflected that fact for several months before she made her claim. While litigation was pending, the parties and their counsel attended court-ordered mediation and signed a mediation agreement that included a confidentiality statement.*

At mediation, Paranzino was offered $25,000 by Barnett to settle the matter. Paranzino rejected the offer

and called the newspaper, which ran a story about the dispute. The bank then moved the trial court to strike Paranzino's pleadings and for sanctions on the grounds that she and her attorney had breached the confidentiality of the mediation proceedings by disclosing information concerning the settlement offer and by making statements concerning the bank's alleged motivation for making the offer. The trial court granted the bank's motion to strike and dismissed Paranzino's case. She appealed.

CASE DECISION   Shahood, Judge.

* * *

By violating the court-ordered mediation and the confidentiality provision of the Mediation Report and Agreement, the appellant ignored and disregarded the court's authority. The mediation order was entered by the court at appellant's request and the mediation report and agreement signed by all of the parties specifically stated that the mediation proceedings were to be confidential. In addition, the agreement further provided that the mediation was governed by the . . . Florida Rules of Civil Procedure. . . .

In granting appellee's motion, the trial court made the following findings: This court finds that, in the instant case, all parties were aware of the precedent condition of absolute confidentiality regarding the mediation proceedings. The evidence presented revealed that the Plaintiff and her attorney willfully and deliberately disregarded the confidentiality agreement by exposing confidential information, namely the settlement offer, to the media. Indeed, the very basis of court-ordered mediation is that parties can rely upon the confidentiality of all oral or written statements. This was clearly violated with their disclosure of the settlement offer.

In addition, the trial court further based its ruling on strong public policy concerns in finding that appellant's breach of confidentiality violated the parties' confidentiality stipulation, and that the acts of appellant ran "afoul of the statutory language of Fla.Stat. 44.102(3)."

[It] provides in relevant part:

Each party involved in a court-ordered mediation proceeding has a privilege to refuse to disclose, and to prevent any person present at the proceeding from disclosing, communications made during such proceeding . . . all oral or written communications in a mediation proceeding . . . shall be confidential and inadmissible as evidence in any subsequent legal proceeding, unless all parties agree otherwise. . . .

* * *

In this case, the trial court found that the actions of appellant and her attorney "willfully and deliberately disregarded the confidentiality agreement by exposing confidential information, namely the settlement offer, to the media." Such a finding by the court cannot be said to constitute an "abuse of discretion." . . .

We accordingly affirm the order of the trial court striking appellant's pleadings and dismissing the case with prejudice.

Affirmed.

QUESTIONS FOR ANALYSIS

1. Since the mediation was private, not in the courtroom, why did the rules of civil procedure apply?

2. Suppose mediation proceedings were always public. What would be the effect on mediation?

Creative Business Use of Mediation

One party cannot force another party to enter into mediation, but experience indicates that offers to mediate, even though not binding, can resolve many problems and thereby reduce litigation and the bad press that can go with it. For example, Ford Motor has a mediation program through which a mediator can offer solutions to consumers' complaints without costly litigation. Consumers must first discuss complaints with their dealer and local district office. If a problem is not resolved, a complaint may be filed with the Ford Consumer Appeals Boards. The board's decision is binding on Ford and dealers but not on consumers, who retain all legal remedies. Ford has learned that the process, in addition to solving most complaints that reach this level, encourages dealers to be more responsive to consumer problems.

INNOVATIVE FORMS OF ADR

Negotiation, mediation, and arbitration are the oldest and most established forms of ADR, but parties are free to agree upon other forms that allow them to settle

JURIS *prudence?*

Creative Dispute Resolution

The Church of the Immortal Consciousness was headed by Trina Kamp in Tonto Village near Payson, Arizona. The church was the subject of assorted rumors, such as devil worship and baby selling. It sued a Payson couple for slander for supposedly starting the rumors.

At a pretrial hearing to try to mediate the matter, Arizona judge Flournoy allowed Kamp to "channel" testimony from Dr. Pahlvon Duran, a fifteenth-century Englishman who is Kamp's inspiration for the church. While church followers sang Beatles songs, Kamp's voice changed and Duran, speaking through Kamp, said he wanted "to get on with the show." Duran/Kamp explained that the church is about loving and giving and caring. Then Duran had to leave because of an appointment in Russia.

The parties agreed to drop the case. "I believe it's a judge's job to help people settle their differences," said Judge Flournoy. "It was interesting."

Source: *The Arizona Republic*

---

their dispute in a peaceful manner (duels are not legal for settling disputes). Some forms of ADR have been invented by private parties, while others have been implemented by courts and private parties looking for ways to reduce the time and costs of litigation and reduce the burdens imposed on the taxpayer-supported judicial system. The Alternative Dispute Resolution Act of 1998 directs every federal court to implement a dispute resolution program, but Congress has not funded this mandate. Nevertheless, the courts have experience with ADR, as we discuss next.

Minitrial

Despite its name, the *minitrial* is not a trial but a structured settlement process that can blend negotiation, mediation, and arbitration. The parties to the process decide its structure, which varies from case to case, and usually agree to confidentiality. They must agree about the scope of discovery, that is, how much information each side will present. Organizations such as the American Arbitration Association (see http://www.adr.org) have guidelines for conducting minitrials.

Phases of a Minitrial

Unlike in trials, where discovery can consume years of work, minitrial discovery is limited to what is needed for each side to know the key issues involved. The parties trade position papers, key documents, and lists of witnesses and testimony expected.

A hearing, called an information exchange, is held where attorneys summarize the case, usually with executives present who have authority to settle the matter. The rules of evidence do not apply, but the parties are in an adversarial position, making summary arguments for their sides. The executives often understand the matter better by hearing the give-and-take by the attorneys for both sides.

The person hired to help with the matter is usually requested to evaluate the case and give an opinion as to the likely outcome if the case were to go to trial. That opinion often carries great weight with both parties as they consider settlement.

The parties may quit the proceedings at any time, but usually a settlement is negotiated or mediated. The information exchange allows the parties to get to the heart of the matter and bargain over the toughest issue. Even when litigation follows a minitrial, the effect of the minitrial is often to shorten the litigation, because evidence and issues that do not much matter have been reviewed and discarded.

Summary Jury Trial

A *summary jury trial* is the jury equivalent of a minitrial. It generally takes place after discovery has been completed and when it appears that a case will not be settled before trial.

The summary trial begins with the selection of six advisory jurors who do not know that the trial is not binding. Each side is given a short time to summarize its case. Presentations in court generally are limited to evidence admissible at trial, including depositions, discovered documents, expert reports, and other discovery material. Witnesses usually do not participate. After the presentations, the judge gives the jury instructions on the law. The jury then reaches its decision. After the proceeding, a judicial officer (and frequently the jury) meets with the parties to discuss the decision and encourage settlement.

If one or both parties are not satisfied with the result of the summary trial, which usually takes one day, they may still take the dispute to a full trial with no punishment from the court. Nothing learned at the summary trial may be used as evidence at trial. However, the federal court in Ohio reported that of the 200 cases assigned to summary jury trial, 193 settled prior to a full trial. In those summary trial cases that have gone on to a full trial, the trial decision has been consistent with the summary trial decision.

Expanding the Use of ADR

Congress has encouraged the use of ADR, originally in the Federal Arbitration Act and recently in the Judicial Improvements Act and the Administrative Dispute Resolution Act. States have been changing their rules of civil procedure to encourage the use of ADR techniques. The objective is to reduce the costs and delays associated with the state and federal court systems. An executive order issued by the president in 1996 expanded the use of binding arbitration by federal agencies. Many government agency web sites list a variety of ADR processes available as government and business both attempt to reduce the amount of costly traditional court litigation.

SUMMARY

- The American legal system is an adversary system of justice. The responsibility for bringing and presenting a lawsuit rests upon the litigants. The system reflects the belief that truth is best discovered through the presentation of competing ideas.
- Litigation begins with pleadings. The plaintiff must notify the defendant by service of process that a complaint has been filed with a court. The defendant must answer the complaint with a motion to dismiss, a defense, or a counterclaim, or the plaintiff wins by default. The plaintiff may respond to the defendant's answer with a reply.
- Before trial, the discovery process allows both parties to gather legal evidence. Depositions or interrogatories may be taken from both the parties and the witnesses. The discovery process allows both parties to know what the trial is to be about so that few surprises arise. Gathering evidence may cause the parties to settle the case as the likely outcome becomes clear.

- At most trials, the defendant has the right to ask for a jury trial. Attorneys discuss with clients the advisability of a jury trial or a trial where the judge hears and determines the entire matter. When a jury is used, it is the finder of fact.

- At trial, after opening statements by both parties, the plaintiff presents witnesses and evidence to prove the facts of her case. Witnesses are questioned by both sides. After the cases have been stated, either party can request that the judge give a directed verdict to end the case. In most cases, the matter goes to the jury after closing arguments and instructions by the judge. The jury determines the facts of the case and applies the law as explained by the judge.

- The remedies awarded by the courts in resolving civil disputes include monetary damages and equitable relief. Monetary damages include compensatory, punitive, and nominal damages. Equitable remedies include specific performance and injunctions.

- A party unhappy with the result may appeal the decision. The court of appeals reviews the case to determine whether any errors were made in the application of the law to the facts (as they were determined by the judge or jury). The court of appeals may affirm, reverse, or modify the trial court's decision.

- Plaintiffs winning judgments are responsible for attempting to collect the judgment, which is difficult if the defendant leaves the state or has few assets. The plaintiff may have to return to the court to obtain orders to force compliance with the judgment. A writ of execution allows the property of the defendant to be seized to satisfy the judgment.

- Arbitration is the most formal ADR process. A decision to enter into arbitration is a binding contract. The parties who agree to arbitration choose an arbitrator, a neutral party who arbitrates the dispute and issues a binding decision, called an award, much like a judge resolves a case.

- Arbitration hearings are run much like a trial, but the rules of evidence are not as strict. Each side presents its case to the arbitrator and may call witnesses and experts to testify. An arbitrator's award need not be justified in writing. Appeals of awards to the courts are rarely successful because the parties have agreed to be bound by the decision. Unless fraud or other misconduct by the arbitrator can be shown, the courts are unlikely to intervene.

- Arbitration is often a standard part of employment contracts, insurance and commercial sale contracts, and agreements with stockbrokers.

- Negotiation is the least formal form of ADR. The parties deal directly with each other or do so through attorneys or other agents who represent them in confidential discussions to resolve a matter. The parties exchange information, make offers, compromise, and move toward a formal settlement.

- Mediation is a more structured form of negotiation; a neutral mediator helps the parties come to a resolution of a dispute. A mediator must be agreed upon by both parties. A mediator gets the parties to agree on a process, explains the rules, gathers information, outlines key issues, talks to and listens to the parties, suggests options, encourages compromise, and may help draft an enforceable settlement. Mediation is usually confidential.

- Minitrials are a form of mediation in which the parties exchange information, present their arguments before attorneys and executives from both sides, get input from the mediator about likely results, and often then settle. Some courts encourage and supervise minitrials before trial to encourage settlement.

- Summary jury trials are used by some state and federal courts to encourage parties to settle before trial. A brief, nonbinding trial with a jury is held. The decision that results from the summary trial usually leads to a settlement, as the parties have good insight about how the case would be resolved after a regular, more costly, trial.

Review Questions

1. Define the following terms:

pleadings	appeal
complaint	damages
motion	compensatory damages
answer	punitive damages
counterclaim	nominal damages
affirmative defense	equity
deposition	specific performance
interrogatory	injunction
voir dire	dissenting opinion
directed verdict	writ of execution
alternative dispute resolution	mediation
arbitration	minitrial
award	summary jury trial
negotiation	

2. Compare and contrast the following concepts:
   a. Deposition and written interrogatories
   b. Voir dire and challenge for cause
   c. Direct examination and cross-examination
   d. Legal briefs and oral argument
   e. Litigation and arbitration

CASE QUESTIONS

3. Brungart sued for personal injuries she suffered while shopping at a Kmart in Baton Rouge, Louisiana. She alleged that through no fault of her own, a heavy rug fell off a high shelf in the store, hit her on the head, and knocked her to the ground, and another rug fell on her. A manager who came to the scene found the rug display in good order. At trial, Brungart claimed that she had touched and moved only rugs on a lower shelf. According to the store manager, Brungart had told him that she had moved some rugs on the high shelves before her accident. The jury found Brungart 80 percent responsible for her harms and the store 20 percent responsible. Brungart made a motion for judgment notwithstanding the verdict. This can be granted only if "the facts and inferences point so strongly and overwhelmingly in favor of the moving party that reasonable men could not arrive at a contrary verdict." The trial court granted the motion, and Kmart appealed. Should the appeals court uphold the decision of the trial court? [*Brungart* v. *Kmart Corp.* 668 So.2d 1335 (Ct.App., La., 1996)]

4. Bonnie Weisgram died from smoke during a fire in her house. Her son, Chad Weisgram, sued Marley, the maker of a heater, claiming it was defective and caused the fire. At trial, Weisgram offered expert witness testimony to prove that the heater was defective. Marley objected that the testimony was unreliable and therefore inadmissible, but the judge overruled the objections; the jury found for Weisgram. The appeals court held that the testimony of Weisgram's witness was not scientifically sound, and therefore incompetent. The appeals court directed a judgment for Marley, holding that there were no grounds for

a new trial. Weisgram appealed; does he have a good reason for a new trial? [*Weisgram* v. *Marley Co.*, 120 S.Ct. 1011 (2000)]

 Check your answer at http://meiners.westbuslaw.com

5. Hulvey was injured while operating a Caterpillar forklift. He sued Caterpillar for his injuries. Hulvey lost, but the decision was set aside because of juror misconduct. Caterpillar appealed the decision to set aside the verdict of the jury. Hulvey claimed that the verdict should be set aside because one of the jurors (Olmstead) was an attorney, who "swayed" the other jurors with his knowledge of the law. Olmstead made derogatory comments about people who file personal injury suits, noting that despite his claims of pain, Hulvey could sit in a chair at court for long periods of time. Should the appeals court uphold the decision concerning juror misconduct? Should courts inquire into the discussion in the jury room? [*Caterpillar Tractor Co.* v. *Hulvey*, 353 S.E.2d 747 (Sup. Ct., Va., 1987)]

6. Folsom was injured while unloading potatoes at A&P's warehouse. He sued A&P, alleging that the company was responsible for his injuries. At the close of a two-and-one-half-day trial, the jury deliberated thirty-five minutes and found for A&P. Folsom alleged jury misconduct because of short deliberation and moved for a new trial. What result? [*Folsom* v. *Great Atlantic & Pacific Tea Co.*, 521 A.2d 678 (Me. 1987)]

 Check your answer at http://meiners.westbuslaw.com

7. A franchise agreement (contract) between the parent company franchisor and the franchisees who operated 7-Eleven stores said that any dispute between the franchisor and franchisees would be settled by arbitration. A franchisee sued the franchisor in state court, claiming that some actions of the franchisor were in violation of state law concerning franchises. The state supreme court ruled that the issues covered by the state law could be tried in state court and did not have to be submitted to arbitration. What did the U.S. Supreme Court hold about the choice between arbitration and litigation? [*Southland Corp.* v. *Keating*, 465 U.S. 1 (1984)]

8. Chube was a supervisor in a "safety sensitive position" at an Exxon chemical plant. Under company drug policy, employees in such positions were subject to random drug tests. An employee who failed the test could be disciplined or fired. Chube tested positive for cocaine and was fired. He was later sentenced to prison for selling cocaine. Chube's union protested the dismissal, and the case went to arbitration. The arbitrator held that Chube was improperly dismissed, because there was no evidence of drug usage on the job. Hence, Chube must be reinstated in his job (when released from prison) and paid back wages. Exxon appealed to federal court. What result? [*Exxon Corp.* v. *Baton Rouge Oil and Chemical Workers Union*, 77 F.3d 850 (1996)]

 Check your answer at http://meiners.westbuslaw.com

9. An employer and a union disputed what happened at an arbitration hearing. The employer challenged the arbitration award in federal court and subpoenaed the arbitrator to testify about what happened at the arbitration at which he presided. Could the arbitrator be required to testify? [*Main Central Railroad Co.* v. *Brotherhood of Maintenance of Way Employees*, 117 F.R.D. 485 (U.S. Dist. Ct., Me., 1987)]

10. Mediator Hammond assisted in negotiations between a union and a company. After mediation, the union declared that an agreement had been reached. The employer denied that an agreement had been reached and refused to sign the union contract. The union filed an unfair labor practice complaint with the National Labor Relations Board. The company claimed that it had the right to call the mediator as a witness in the unfair labor practice complaint. Could the mediator be called to give testimony in the case? [National *Labor Relations Board v. Joseph Macaluso, Inc.*, 618 F.2d 51 (9th Cir., 1980)]

 Check your answer at http://meiners.westbuslaw.com

11. The Malliks went to arbitration against Fairfield for alleged violations of Ohio's Consumer Sales Practices Act. The Malliks presented their case to an arbitration panel on February 28, 2000. The panel filed a report and award on March 1, 2000, and held for Fairfield. That report stated that either party had thirty days to appeal or the verdict would be the final judgment. Neither party appealed, so the arbitration verdict became the final judgment on March 31. The Malliks filed a notice of appeal in court on April 4. Fairfield moved the trial court to dismiss the appeal on the basis that it was not timely. The Malliks contended that their attorney mailed the notice of appeal on March 30. The trial court dismissed the appeal as not being timely. The Malliks appealed. Can they proceed in court? [*Mallik* v. *Jeff Wyler Fairfield, Inc.*, 2000 WL 1693246 (Ct. App., Ohio, 2000)]

12. Thomas sued his former employer for racial, sexual, and national origin discrimination in violation of two civil rights laws. During pretrial negotiations, the employer offered Thomas his job back "without prejudice," meaning that it would not affect some of his claims in the lawsuit, such as for mental distress, but if he returned to work, he could not claim he was owed back wages from the date from which he could have started working. Thomas refused the offer. The employer asserted that it should have the right to present testimony to the jury about its offer that was rejected. Thomas said that the negotiations were completely confidential and there could be no testimony. Who was right? [*Thomas* v. *Resort Health Related Facility*, 539 F.Supp. 630 (U.S. Dist. Ct., E.D.N.Y., 1982)]

 Check your answer at http://meiners.westbuslaw.com

13. NLO was sued by former employees for injuries they claimed to have suffered on the job. The trial court ordered that a summary jury trial be held and ruled that it would be open to the public. NLO appealed, contending it could not be forced to participate. Is that correct? [*In re NLO, Inc.*, 5 F.3d 154 (6th Cir., 1993)]

14. Lightwave Technologies and Corning Glass Works were involved in extended litigation involving many issues. The parties agreed to hold a minitrial to see whether a settlement could be reached with respect to the antitrust claims Lightwave had made against Corning. Lightwave's attorney told Corning that he had authority to settle the matter. After the minitrial, the parties struck a deal, which Corning presumed was final. Lightwave's president rejected the deal and stated that the attorney did not have authority to bind Lightwave to a deal without his permission. Corning sued to enforce the settlement worked out at the minitrial, because it acted in good faith, presuming that Lightwave's attorney had the authority to settle the matter. Who won? [*Lightwave Technologies* v. *Corning Glass Works*, 725 F.Supp. 198 (U.S.Dist. Ct., S.D.N.Y., 1989)]

ETHICS QUESTION

15. Because litigation is so costly, many firms settle suits that they are quite sure they would win if litigated. It is cheaper to settle for $10,000 or $50,000 than to consume management time and litigation fees. While it is unethical to bring dubious suits that are largely intended to extract a settlement, is it ethical for firms to settle such cases rather than spend additional resources and defeat such suits?

    Another tactic, which is perfectly legal, is for a company to hire opponent law firms as consultants when the firms being to pose major litigation problems for the company. Often, law firms that were leading large areas of litigation against a company, and so had expertise to bring future suits, switched sides when offered hefty consultant fees by the company they were suing. In some instances, as part of settling an existing case, a law firm has taken an extra payment for itself and promised not to take any more cases against the company that it had sued. Are such tactics ethical?

INTERNET ASSIGNMENT

http://www.law.cornell.edu/rules/frcp
http://www.law.cornell.edu/rules/fre
http://www.law.cornell.edu/rules/frcrmp

Rules of court play an important part in legal proceedings. For example, the Federal Rules of Civil Procedure govern both the trial process and the pretrial discovery process, often allowing parties to settle a civil dispute before going to trial. Rules of evidence control what can or cannot be admitted into trial, such as hearsay evidence. Rules of criminal procedure ensure a fair, impartial proceeding. The federal rules can be found in various places on the Internet. (Hint: Legal Information Institute (LII) may be a good place to start, or try an advanced search on Google.)

Using the World Wide Web to find your information (and giving the URL for each source actually used) state, with citation to applicable rule:

1. Which federal rule of civil procedure governs the availability of interrogatories to parties?
2. Which federal rules of evidence deal with hearsay evidence?
3. What is the hearsay evidence rule and what are the first five exceptions to it?
4. What are the four elements of discovery and inspection in the arraignment and preparation of a criminal trial?
5. What are the four elements listed for the (criminal) venue rule dealing with transfer for trial?

http://www.adr.org
http://www.iccwbo.org
http://www.lcia-arbitration.com
http://www.faa.gov/agc/odra/Laufer's%20ADR%20Links.htm
http://www.llrx.com/features/arbitration2.htm

The field of arbitration dispels the myth that everything is available via the Internet for free. Each of the major arbitral associations has a web presence with access to information, rules, and other information. However, arbitral awards themselves are often either confidential or only available via commercial information suppliers (such as *International Legal Materials*, the *International Arbitration Report*, or *Yearbook: Commercial Arbitration*). Find and visit the web sites for the organizations that follow, and browse the available resources.

American Arbitration Association
International Chamber of Commerce
London Court of International Arbitration

Research Guides

Deborah S. Laufer, Esq., Federal ADR Network, *A Guide to ADR Links*
Jean M. Wenger, International Commercial Arbitration, *Locating the Resources*

Chapter 4

The Constitution: Focus on Application to Business

George Washington presided over a convention in Philadelphia in 1787, at which the Constitution of the United States was drafted. The Constitution became effective in March 1789, when it was ratified by the legislatures in nine of the thirteen original states. It is composed of the preamble and seven Articles. The preamble reads:

> We the People of the United States, in Order to form a more perfect Union, establish Justice, insure domestic Tranquility, provide for the common defence, promote the general Welfare, and secure the Blessings of Liberty to ourselves and our Posterity, do ordain and establish this Constitution for the United States of America.

The Articles of the Constitution are:

   I. Composition and powers of Congress
  II. Selection and powers of the president
 III. Creation and powers of the federal judiciary
 IV. Role of the states in the federal system
  V. Methods of amending the Constitution
 VI. Declaring the Constitution to be supreme law of the land
VII. Method for ratifying the Constitution

The Constitution was amended almost immediately. There was concern that there was not enough protection for individual rights. In 1791, the first ten amendments (the *Bill of Rights*) were ratified by the states after having been approved by the First Session of Congress. A proposed amendment must be passed by a two-thirds vote in the House and Senate and then be ratified by three-fourths of the state legislatures. An amendment may be proposed by two-thirds of the state legislatures by calling for a constitutional convention, the results of which must be ratified by three-fourths of the state legislatures, but that has never happened. The Constitution is reprinted in Appendix C.

Some rights are clearly expressed, but much of the Constitution is written in terms that can be interpreted in different ways. Justice Story noted this in 1816 in *Martin* v. *Hunter's Lessee* (14 U.S. 304):

> The constitution unavoidably deals in general language. It did not suit the purposes of the people, in framing this great charter of our liberties, to provide for minute specifications of its powers, or to declare the means by which those powers should be carried into execution. . . . Hence its powers are expressed in general terms, leaving to the legislature, from time to time, to adopt its own means to effectuate legitimate objects, and to mold and model the exercise of its powers, as its own wisdom and the public interest should require.

All citizens are affected by the Constitution. Court rulings about the rights of individuals who are accused of crimes draw the most popular attention. Supreme Court interpretation of the rights of persons accused of crimes and of other constitutionally protected rights changes over time. The Court has reversed itself on major constitutional issues over the years, reading the same words in an opposite manner. Some would say this means the Court is political; but it may reflect changes in technology, social values, economic conditions, and political realities.

THE COMMERCE CLAUSE

While all parts of the Constitution have application to business and to individuals, certain provisions have a particular impact on business. In that respect, perhaps the most important part of the Constitution is Article I, Section 8: "The Congress shall have Power . . . To regulate Commerce with foreign Nations, and among the several States. . . ." Known as the *commerce clause*, these words have been interpreted to give Congress the power to enact most of the federal regulation of business. When combined with the necessary and proper clause, this gives Congress tremendous regulatory power.

The Necessary and Proper Clause

The Constitution lists specific congressional powers (including collecting taxes, regulating commerce, and providing for national defense). At the end of the list, clause 18 of Article I, Section 8, gives Congress power "to make all Laws which shall be necessary and proper for carrying into Execution the foregoing Powers and all other Powers vested by this Constitution in the Government of the United States, or in any Department or Officer thereof." This is the *necessary and proper clause*.

McCulloch v. Maryland

Chief Justice Marshall gave a broad reading to the necessary and proper clause in 1819 in *McCulloch* v. *Maryland* (17 U.S. 316). In that case, the state of Maryland questioned whether Congress had the right to establish a national bank, since banking was not a power of Congress specified in the Constitution. The Supreme Court upheld the constitutionality of the bank under the necessary and proper clause. The Court held that the clause expands the power of Congress:

1st. The clause is placed among the powers of Congress, not among the limitations on those powers.

2nd. Its terms purport to enlarge, not to diminish the powers vested in the government. It purports to be an additional power, not a restriction on those already granted.

Over the years, the Supreme Court has upheld most federal statutes as necessary and proper, even though the subject of the legislation could not have been contemplated when the Constitution was written. For example, the Court upheld a federal statute limiting liability that would arise from nuclear accidents as necessary and proper to achieve the government's objective of encouraging the development of private nuclear power plants.

Federal Supremacy

Another key point made in the *McCulloch* decision is that when the federal government has the power to act under the Constitution, its actions are supreme; that is, they take precedence over the actions of other governments. The state of Maryland argued that even if the federal government had the right to establish a national bank, the state could impose taxes on it, as it did on other banks. The Court struck down the Maryland tax as in violation of Article VI, Paragraph 2, the *supremacy clause*: "The Constitution, and the Laws of the United States . . . shall be the supreme Law of the Land; and the judges in every State shall be bound thereby. . . ." If Congress did not want Maryland to tax a bank created by Congress, Maryland could not do so because, so long as they are constitutional, federal laws are supreme over state laws.

Defining "Commerce among the Several States"

Although most federal regulation of business evolved in the last century, Congress has had broad regulatory powers since the early days of the Republic. In 1824, Chief Justice Marshall established some of the basic guidelines of the commerce clause in *Gibbons* v. *Ogden* (22 U.S. 1). He held that commerce among the states means *interstate commerce*, that is, business that concerns more than one state. Further, Justice Marshall held:

What is this power? It is the power to regulate; that is, to prescribe the rule by which commerce is to be governed. This power, like all others vested in Congress, is complete in itself, may be exercised to its utmost extent, and acknowledges no limitations other than are prescribed in the Constitution.

Power over Interstate Commerce Is Extensive

Just because the effect of a business on interstate commerce is small does not mean that the business is exempt from extensive federal regulation, if Congress so desires. In a landmark case in 1942, *Wickard* v. *Filburn* (317 U.S. 111), the Supreme Court upheld detailed control of the market for wheat. Filburn had a small farm in Ohio.

According to the U.S. Department of Agriculture, which was authorized by Congress set the price of wheat and tell every farmer how much wheat they could grow, Filburn produced 239 bushels of wheat more than he was allowed. He was fined $117 and ordered not to plant more than he was told.

Filburn protested that the law was unconstitutional because he should be free to plant crops on his land and, furthermore, he used the wheat he grew on his farm to feed his chickens and dairy cows, and to make bread for his family, so there was no effect on interstate commerce. The Court held that although Filburn's effect on the market for wheat was "trivial" it was still subject to federal control. The court held that since "home-consumed wheat would have a substantial influence on price and market conditions" Congress could regulate its price and the quantity allowed grown by every farmer. Hence, almost all commerce is defined as interstate commerce.

In the *Katzenbach* v. *McClung* decision, the Court used the commerce clause to extend nondiscrimination requirements of the 1964 Civil Rights Act to local businesses.

Katzenbach v. McClung
United States Supreme Court
379 U.S. 294, 85 S.Ct. 377 (1964)

CASE BACKGROUND   *Ollie's Barbecue was a restaurant in Birmingham, Alabama, owned by McClung. It had 220 seats for white customers. Although most employees were black, black customers were allowed to buy food only at a take-out window. The Department of Justice (Attorney General Katzenbach) sued the restaurant for violating Title II of the 1964 Civil Rights Act, which prohibits racial segregation in places of public accommodation. This includes restaurants that offer "to serve interstate travelers or [if] a substantial portion of the food which it serves . . . has moved in interstate commerce." McClung contended that since his customers were local, not traveling interstate, he should be exempt from the law. The government noted that half of the food McClung bought came from out of state, which was enough to make the business interstate.*

The district court held for McClung and refused to enforce the Act. The government appealed to the Supreme Court.

CASE DECISION   Clark, Justice.

* * *

Much is said about a restaurant business being local but "even if appellee's activity is local and though it may not be regarded as commerce, it may still, whatever its nature, be reached by Congress if it exerts a substan-

tial economic effect on interstate commerce." *Wickard* v. *Filburn.*

This Court has held time and again that this power extends to activities of retail establishments, including restaurants, which directly or indirectly burden or obstruct interstate commerce.

* * *

Confronted as we are with the facts laid before Congress, we must conclude that it had a rational basis for finding that racial discrimination in restaurants had a direct and adverse effect on the free flow of interstate commerce. Insofar as the sections of the Civil Rights Act here relevant are concerned, Congress prohibited discrimination only in those establishments having a close tie to interstate commerce, that is, those, like McClung's, serving food that has come from out of the State. We think in so doing that Congress acted well within its power to protect and foster commerce in extending the coverage of Title II only to those restaurants offering to serve interstate travelers or serving food, a substantial portion of which has moved in interstate commerce.

The absence of direct evidence connecting discriminatory restaurant service with the flow of interstate food, a factor on which the appellees place much reliance, is not, given the evidence as to the effect of

continues

such practices on other aspects of commerce, a crucial matter.

The power of Congress in this field is broad and sweeping; where it keeps within its sphere and violates no express constitutional limitation it has been the rule of this Court, going back almost to the founding days of the Republic, not to interfere. The Civil Rights Act of 1964, as here applied, we find to be plainly appropriate in the resolution of what the Congress found to be a national commercial problem of the first magnitude. We find in it no violation of any express limitations of the Constitution and we therefore declare it valid.

The judgment is therefore reversed.

QUESTIONS FOR ANALYSIS

1. Might the Court have found differently if the restaurant could have shown that all of its food was produced in the state?

2. Suppose evidence showed that when restaurants were required to integrate, they often closed their doors and refused to do more business. Does this go against the argument that the law enhances interstate commerce?

Federal/State Regulatory Relations

The legal environment contains many state and federal laws and regulations. As Exhibit 4.1 illustrates, the responsibility for regulating a particular activity may be the responsibility of a state governing body or a federal governing body, or it may be shared by state and federal governments. Federal environmental regulation, for example, requires the Environmental Protection Agency to set national pollution control standards. Given the federal standards, state environmental regulators must then set specific requirements to be met within a state.

States often legislate on a subject matter on which Congress has legislated. When can state law exist along with federal law? Federal regulation takes precedence over state regulation, so state regulations may not contradict or reduce the standards imposed by federal law. States also may not enact laws that burden interstate commerce by imposing restrictions on businesses from other states.

Exhibit 4.1

State and Federal Regulatory Responsibilities

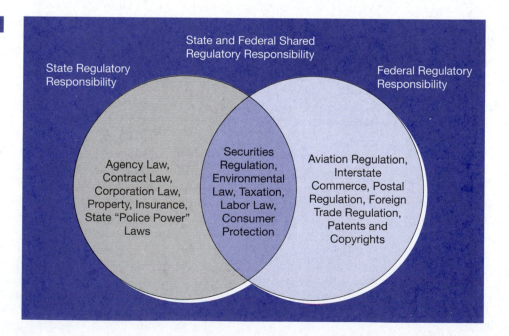

In some areas, such as postal authority, Congress ruled that the states may not regulate at all. States may not pass laws in such areas even if the laws do not contradict federal laws. States may add their own rules to strengthen the impact of a federal rule, so long as the rules do not conflict with the intent of the law and do not impede interstate commerce. For example, states may pass air pollution regulations to apply to their industries that are stricter than the federal air pollution rules. However, unless specifically allowed by Congress, states may not pass rules less strict than the federal rule. In some areas, such as insurance, Congress has authorized states to regulate the business within state borders.

JURIS *prudence?*

Great Constitutional Moments

Arkansas required trucks to have straight mudflaps. Illinois required trucks to have mudguards that "contour the rear wheel, with the inside surface being relatively parallel to the top 90 degrees of the rear and 180 degrees of the whole surface. . . . and must be installed not more than 6 inches from the tire surface . . . and must have a lip or flange on its outer edge of not less than 2 inches." Trucks on interstate highways could be ticketed in either state for having the wrong flap.

The Supreme Court held that the Arkansas flaps were more common and so, "the heavy burden which the Illinois mudguard law places on the interstate movement of trucks and trailers seems to us to pass the permissible limits of safety regulations."

Source: *Bibb* v. *Navajo Freight Lines*, 79 S.Ct. 962

When State Law Impedes Interstate Commerce

In 1911, the Supreme Court, in *Southern Railway Co.* v. *Arizona* (222 U.S. 20), had to consider Arizona regulations that for "safety considerations" required trains to be shorter in Arizona than in other states. The effect of the Arizona requirement was to impede interstate commerce. At the Arizona border, trains had to be shortened.

The Supreme Court struck down the Arizona law. Chief Justice Stone said, "The decisive question is whether in the circumstances the total effect of the law as a safety measure in reducing accidents and casualties is so slight or problematical as not to outweigh the national interest in keeping interstate commerce free from interferences which seriously impede it."

There are many Supreme Court cases in this area. The Supreme Court consistently takes a hard line against state regulations that restrict interstate commerce or are designed to help local businesses at the expense of out-of-state competitors:

- In *Chemical Waste Management* v. *Hunt* (504 U.S. 334), the Court held that it was a violation of the commerce clause for Alabama to impose a higher fee for hazardous waste generated outside the state than it charged for hazardous waste generated within the state when both were disposed at commercial disposal facilities in Alabama.
- In *Morales* v. *Trans World Airlines* (504 U.S. 374), the Court held that the Airline Deregulation Act prohibits the states from regulating airline rates, routes, or services. Therefore, state attorneys general may not sue the airlines under state consumer protection statutes even though they contend that airline fare advertising injured consumers.

- Oklahoma required coal-burning power plants in the state to burn at least 10 percent Oklahoma-mined coal. Wyoming challenged the regulation because it meant less Wyoming coal was sold to Oklahoma. The Court held in *Wyoming v. Oklahoma* (502 U.S. 437) that the Oklahoma law was discriminatory and interfered with interstate commerce.

The states have a legitimate interest in protecting public health, safety, and other public policies. When such goals are the reason for a state law, the regulation chosen must be designed to achieve its legitimate interest with minimal impact on interstate business. The *Hughes* decision concerns small fish but was used by the Court to lay out the principles used to guide evaluation of state regulations that affect interstate commerce.

Hughes v. Oklahoma
United States Supreme Court
441 U.S. 322, 99 S.Ct. 1727 (1979)

CASE BACKGROUND   *To protect minnows that live in state waters, Oklahoma prohibited shipping or selling minnows out of state. Hughes was convicted of transporting minnows from Oklahoma to Texas. He bought the minnows from a dealer licensed to do business in Oklahoma. If the minnows had been captured and sold within the state, it would have been legal. It was illegal to take the fish across the state line. The Oklahoma Supreme Court upheld the statute and Hughes's conviction as constitutional for Oklahoma's interest in protecting its natural resources. Hughes appealed.*

CASE DECISION   Brennan, Justice.

* * *

We turn then to the question whether the burden imposed on interstate commerce in wild game by [the Oklahoma law] is permissible under the general rule articulated in our precedents governing other types of commerce. Under that general rule, we must inquire (1) whether the challenged statute regulates evenhandedly with only "incidental" effects on interstate commerce, or discriminates against interstate commerce either on its face or in practical effect; (2) whether the statute serves a legitimate local purpose; and, if so, (3) whether alternative means could promote this local purpose as well without discriminating against interstate commerce. The burden to show discrimination rests on the party challenging the validity of the statute, but

"when discrimination against commerce . . . is demonstrated, the burden falls on the State to justify it both in terms of the local benefits flowing from the statute and the unavailability of nondiscriminatory alternatives adequate to preserve the local interests at stake." Furthermore, when considering the purpose of a challenged statute, this Court is not bound by "the name, description, or characterization given it by the legislature or the courts of the State," but will determine for itself the practical impact of the law.

[The Oklahoma law] on its face discriminates against interstate commerce. It forbids the transportation of natural minnows out of the State for purposes of sale, and thus "overtly blocks the flow of interstate commerce at the State's borders." Such facial discrimination by itself may be a fatal defect, regardless of the State's purpose, because "the evil of protectionism can reside in legislative means as well as legislative ends." At a minimum such facial discrimination invokes the strictest scrutiny of any purported legitimate local purpose and of the absence of nondiscriminatory alternatives.

Oklahoma argues that [its law] serves a legitimate local purpose in that it is "readily apparent as a conservation measure." The State's interest in maintaining the ecological balance in state waters by avoiding the removal of inordinate numbers of minnows may well qualify as a legitimate local purpose. We consider the States' interests in conservation and protection of wild animals as legitimate local purposes similar to the States' interests in protecting the health and safety of their citizens.

* * *

Far from choosing the least discriminatory alternative, Oklahoma has chosen to "conserve" its minnows in the way that most overtly discriminates against interstate commerce. The State places no limits on the numbers of minnows that can be taken by licensed minnow dealers; nor does it limit in any way how these minnows may be disposed of within the State. Yet it forbids the transportation of any commercially significant number of natural minnows out of the State for sale. [Its law] is certainly not a "last ditch" attempt at conservation after nondiscriminatory alternatives have proved unfeasible. It is rather a choice of the most discriminatory means even though nondiscriminatory alternatives would seem likely to fulfill the State's purported legitimate local purpose more effectively.

[This decision] does not leave the States powerless to protect and conserve wild animal life within their borders. Today's decision makes clear, however, that States may promote this legitimate purpose only in ways consistent with the basic principle that "our economic unit is the Nation," and that when a wild animal "becomes an article of commerce . . . its use cannot be limited to the citizens of one State to the exclusion of citizens of another State."

Reversed.

QUESTIONS FOR ANALYSIS

1. The dissent argued that the burden on commerce from such a regulation was minimal and that more weight should be given to the legitimate interest of protecting natural resources. Where should such a line be drawn?

2. Suppose Oklahoma got other states to agree on a restriction on the shipment of minnows to help other states protect their resources. Would that be a reasonable compromise?

Imitation Not Allowed

The states may not copy federal regulations if such imitation inhibits interstate commerce. Consider the following situation. Congress has long required that timber removed from federal lands in Alaska may not be shipped out of state unless processed in Alaska. Unprocessed logs could not be shipped out of Alaska; they had to be cut into boards first. The state of Alaska imitated the federal rule in 1980, requiring that timber cut on state lands be processed in the state before shipment out of state.

The Supreme Court struck down the state law in *South-Central Timber Development* v. *Wunnicke* (467 U.S. 82). "Although the Commerce Clause is by its text an affirmative grant of power to Congress to regulate interstate and foreign commerce, the Clause has long been recognized as a self-executing limitation on the power of the States to enact laws imposing substantial burdens on such commerce." That is, although Congress could impose such a requirement on timber, the state could not do so, unless authorized by Congress.

THE TAXING POWER

Congress is given the power to "lay and collect Taxes, Duties, Imposts and Excises" by Article I, Section 8, clause 1, of the Constitution. Although this text does not cover tax law (since it is a complex topic requiring specialized courses), keep in mind that taxation is a potent tool of regulation. Taxes can be used for more than raising revenue to pay for government services. They can deter and punish certain behavior. For example, a tax may be tied to a requirement to keep detailed records about goods subject to the tax. This way, goods such as explosives, firearms, drugs, and liquors can be kept under close federal supervision.

Federal Taxation

The Supreme Court rarely questions the constitutionality of federal taxing schemes. In 1937, the Court noted in *Sonzinsky* v. *U.S.* (300 U.S. 506):

> Inquiry into the hidden motives which may move Congress to exercise a power constitutionally conferred upon it is beyond the competency of courts. . . . We are not free to speculate as to the motives which moved Congress to impose it, or as to the extent to which it may operate to restrict the activities taxed.

The Court has upheld taxes on illegal gambling, narcotics, and marijuana. This enhances the ability of the government to prosecute people involved in illegal activities. If the income from such activities is reported, the government has evidence of illegal dealings. If the income is not reported and money is found, then the tax laws have been violated. As the Court held in *U.S.* v. *Kahriger* (345 U.S. 22), "the power of Congress to tax is extensive and sometimes falls with crushing effect on businesses."

State Taxation

Since most commerce is interstate, what can the states tax? The Constitution protects interstate commerce from discriminatory state taxes. As the Court ruled in *Northwestern States Portland Cement Co.* v. *Minnesota* (358 U.S. 450):

> A State cannot impose taxes upon persons passing through the state or coming into it merely for a temporary purpose. . . . Moreover, a State may not lay a tax on the "privilege" of engaging in interstate commerce. . . . Nor may a State impose a tax which discriminates against interstate commerce either by providing a direct commercial advantage to local business . . . or by subjecting interstate commerce to the burden of "multiple taxation." . . . States, under the Commerce Clause, are not allowed "one single tax-dollar worth of direct interference with the free flow of commerce."

Consider the following cases in which the Supreme Court reviewed state taxing schemes to decide whether they interfered with interstate commerce:

- The state of Hawaii imposed a 20 percent tax on all alcoholic beverages except for local products. The Court struck this down (*Baccus Imports* v. *Dias*, 468 U.S. 263), holding that the tax imposed on alcoholic products had to be the same regardless of origin.
- Michigan exempted from state income taxes the retirement benefits paid to state employees. The state taxed all other retirement income, such as retired federal government employees' benefits. The Supreme Court struck this down in *Davis* v. *Michigan Dept. of Treasury* (489 U.S. 803) as discriminatory. State income taxes must apply equally to all retirement benefits.
- In *Quill Corp.* v. *North Dakota* (504 U.S. 298), state sales taxes imposed on out-of-state firms doing mail-order business with North Dakota residents were stricken as a violation of the commerce clause. Mail-order firms that do not have a physical presence in the state may not be taxed.
- Illinois imposes a 5 percent tax on all long-distance calls to or from the state. If a taxpayer can show that another state has billed the call, the Illinois tax is

refunded. This tax was held not to violate the commerce clause in *Goldberg* v. *Sweet* (488 U.S. 252) because it satisfies a four-part test of the constitutionality of state tax schemes. The tax:

1. applies to an activity having a substantial nexus (connection) with the state.
2. is fairly apportioned (to those inside and outside the state).
3. does not discriminate against interstate commerce.
4. is fairly related to services provided by the state.

ISSUE
Spotter

Unconstitutional Business Activity?

Your company, an auto parts maker in Michigan, belongs to the Michigan Industrial Alliance (MIA), a trade association that lobbies on behalf of its members' interests in the state and federal legislatures. The MIA has succeeded in getting influential members of the Michigan legislature to propose legislation that would exempt auto parts produced in Michigan from sales tax, while auto parts brought to Michigan from other states or foreign countries would be subject to the tax. The legislation was designed to encourage auto manufacturers in Michigan to buy more auto parts made in Michigan.

Should your company support this lobbying activity in the legislature? Is it likely to succeed if the bill becomes law?

Apportioning State Tax Burden

The Supreme Court has held that business income may be taxed by the states as long as they use formulas that account for the intrastate share of interstate commerce.

The apportionment issue generates a lot of litigation because firms often have manufacturing and distribution facilities in many states and purchase inputs from many sources. It is difficult to know how to assign the various costs to the different portions of an operation—different accounting techniques produce different results. The federal courts are concerned with whether the tax imposes greater burdens on transactions that cross state lines than on those that occur entirely within a state.

State Taxes May Not Impede Foreign Trade

Although Congress has nearly unlimited taxing power, the states may not interfere with interstate commerce through their taxing schemes. Further, since the Constitution gives Congress the power to regulate international trade, as it does interstate commerce, the states may not interfere with international commerce.

The Supreme Court emphasized that point in *Japan Line, Ltd.* v. *County of Los Angeles* (441 U.S. 434). Several California cities and counties imposed a property tax on cargo-shipping containers owned by Japanese companies. The containers were used only in international commerce on Japanese ships. The California taxes were imposed on the containers in the state during loading and unloading. The Supreme Court held the tax to be unconstitutional. The commerce clause reserves to Congress the power over foreign commerce. Foreign commerce may not be subject to state taxes, or the states could regulate foreign trade.

INTERNATIONAL   *Perspective*

Freedom of Speech

In the United States, there are very few restrictions on what the media may investigate and publish. There is a long tradition of media attempts to uncover bad deeds by public officials. Unless a statement is published about a person that the publisher knew was false and harmful, there is little that the subject of a critical report can do in response. Suits against the media for defamation, or attempts by the government to prevent publication of sensitive material, are rarely successful.

In the rest of the world, there are more restraints on speech. In the United Kingdom, it is quite common for politicians to sue the media successfully for defamation. In many European countries, books asserted to contain hateful material may not be published. In Belgium, journalists must reveal their sources of information.

Hans Tillack, a reporter for a leading German magazine, *Die Stern*, was arrested in Brussels in 2004, all his files were seized, and he was not allowed access to a lawyer. What was he accused of doing? Publishing articles alleging that many members of the European Parliament engage in fraud by collecting pay when they are not working. The rest of the media said little about the matter, but one Danish member of European Parliament said: "The practice of the EU [European Union] is to stop those who reveal fraud, instead of stopping the fraud."

BUSINESS AND FREE SPEECH

The First Amendment restricts congressional control of *freedom of speech:* "Congress shall make no law . . . abridging the freedom of speech. . . ." This right is not absolute. As Justice Holmes said in *Schenck* v. *U.S.* (249 U.S. 47), "The most stringent protection of free speech would not protect a man in falsely shouting fire in a theatre and causing a panic." The Constitution prohibits laws "abridging the freedom of speech," but it does not prohibit all laws restricting communication. For example, as the Supreme Court noted in *Ward* v. *Rock Against Racism* (491 U.S. 781), the City of New York could require a city sound technician to be present to regulate the volume at which music was played at an outdoor concert, but the technician could not control the content of the sound.

Do commercial speech (advertisements) and political statements by corporations (statements about public issues) deserve the same freedoms? In both cases, the parties are trying to convince some people about something—to buy soap or to support a political program. The Constitution does not distinguish between the two kinds of speech, but traditionally there have been more restrictions on commercial speech than on political speech by business.

Business and Political Speech

The Supreme Court has emphasized the right of businesses to speak out on political issues. In 1978, the Court struck down a Massachusetts law that prohibited corporations from making contributions that could influence certain political issues. In *First National Bank of Boston* v. *Bellotti* (535 U.S. 765) the Court noted that "The freedom of speech . . . guaranteed by the Constitution embraces at the least the liberty to discuss publicly and truthfully all matters of public concern without previous restraint or fear of subsequent punishment. . . ."

The Court soon followed this decision with the *Consolidated Edison* decision. In the case, the Court explained the test that restrictions must pass to be allowed to regulate such speech. This is still the key test used today.

Consolidated Edison Company v. Public Service Commission of New York

United States Supreme Court
447 U.S. 530, 100 S.Ct. 2326 (1980)

CASE BACKGROUND   *Consolidated Edison inserted material in favor of nuclear power in the monthly bills sent to its electricity customers. The Public Service Commission of New York ruled that Consolidated Edison could not discuss its opinions on controversial issues of public policy in its bills.*

The New York Court of Appeals upheld the Commission's prohibition. Consolidated Edison appealed. The issue is whether the First Amendment of the Constitution is violated by an order of the Public Service Commission that prohibits the inclusion in electric bills of inserts discussing controversial public policy issues.

CASE DECISION   Powell, Justice.

* * *

The Commission's ban on bill inserts is not, of course, invalid merely because it imposes a limitation upon speech. We must consider whether the State can demonstrate that its regulation is constitutionally permissible. The Commission's arguments require us to consider three theories that might justify the state action. We must determine whether the prohibition is (1) a reasonable time, place, or manner restriction, (2) a permissible subject-matter regulation, or (3) a narrowly tailored means of serving a compelling state interest. . . .

A restriction that regulates only the time, place or manner of speech may be imposed so long as it's reasonable. But when regulation is based on the content of speech, governmental action must be scrutinized more carefully to ensure that communication has not been prohibited "merely because public officials disapprove the speaker's views."

* * *

The Commission does not pretend that its action is unrelated to the content or subject matter of bill inserts. Indeed, it has undertaken to suppress certain bill inserts precisely because they address controversial issues of public policy. The Commission allows inserts that present information to consumers on certain subjects, such as energy conservation measures, but it forbids the use of inserts that discuss public controversies. The Commission . . . justifies its ban on the ground that consumers will benefit from receiving "useful" information, but not from the prohibited information. The Commission's own rationale demonstrates that its action cannot be upheld as a content-neutral time, place, or manner regulation. . . .

The First Amendment's hostility to content-based regulation extends not only to restrictions on particular viewpoints, but also to prohibition of public discussion of an entire topic. . . .

To allow a government the choice of permissible subjects for public debate would be to allow that government control over the search for political truth.

* * *

Where a government restricts the speech of a private person, the state action may be sustained only if the government can show that the regulation is a precisely drawn means of serving a compelling state interest. . . .

Where a single speaker communicates to many listeners, the First Amendment does not permit the government to prohibit speech as intrusive unless the "captive" audience cannot avoid objectionable speech.

Passengers on public transportation or residents of a neighborhood disturbed by the raucous broadcasts from a passing soundtruck may well be unable to escape an unwanted message. But customers who encounter an objectionable billing insert may "effectively avoid further bombardment of their sensibilities simply by averting their eyes." The customer of Consolidated Edison may escape exposure to objectionable material simply by transferring the bill insert from envelope to wastebasket.

* * *

Reversed.

continues

QUESTIONS FOR ANALYSIS

1. Should a distinction be drawn between political speech paid for by private persons and that paid for by customers who may not want the speech? The political inserts in this case were paid for by Con Ed customers who buy electricity.

2. Would you distinguish between speech that addresses issues and corporate political speech that endorses particular candidates for office?

An example of a legitimate restriction comes from *Austin* v. *Michigan Chamber of Commerce* (494 U.S. 652). In that decision, the Supreme Court allowed states to prohibit the use of general corporate money for supporting or opposing political candidates. The compelling government interest that allows this regulation is the desire to eliminate distortions caused by corporate spending for this purpose out of general corporate funds, as opposed to corporate spending for this purpose that comes from corporate money that has been set aside for specific political purposes.

CYBER *Law*

Freedom of Speech on the Net

Georgia passed a statute making it a crime for "any person . . . knowingly to transmit any data through a computer network . . . for the purpose of setting up, maintaining, operating, or exchanging data with an electronic mailbox, home page, or any other electronic information storage bank or point of access to electronic information if such data uses an individual name . . . to falsely identify the person." That is, there could be no anonymous communications.

In *American Civil Liberties Union of Georgia* v. *Miller* (977 F. Supp. 1228), the federal court issued an injunction preventing Georgia from enforcing the statute. Statutes that regulate speech must be narrowly tailored to survive First Amendment challenges. The Georgia statute was too sweeping in its coverage to stand.

Similarly, the Supreme Court, in *Reno* v. *American Civil Liberties Union* (117 S.Ct. 2329), struck down the Communications Decency Act of 1996. While the supposed intent of the law was to restrict pornography for children on the Web, the court held that the act went too far in restricting First Amendment rights; it was like "burning the house to roast the pig."

Business and Commercial Speech

The modern *commercial speech* doctrine first came about as restrictions on advertising were attacked as anticompetitive. Some commercial speech restrictions violated antitrust laws, but almost all such restrictions violated the rights of sellers of legal products and services to inform citizens of the availability and merits of their products and services.

In 1975, in *Bigelow* v. *Virginia* (421 U.S. 809), the Supreme Court reversed the conviction of a Virginia newspaper editor who published ads about the availability of low-cost abortions in New York City. A Virginia law prohibited publications from encouraging abortions. The Court held that speech that is related to legal products or services has value in the marketplace of ideas.

The following year, in *Virginia State Board of Pharmacy* v. *Virginia Citizens Consumer Council* (425 U.S. 748), the Court struck down a Virginia law prohibiting the advertising of prices of prescription drugs. "It is clear . . . that speech does not lose its First Amendment protection because money is spent . . . as in a paid advertisement. . . ." The Board of Pharmacy argued that the restrictions on advertising were needed to protect the public from their ignorance about drugs. The Court rejected that, holding, "that people will perceive their own best interests if only they are well enough informed, and that the best means to that end is to open the channels of communication rather than to close them."

While commercial speech that is not truthful may be regulated (unlike political speech), the Court finds little justification for extensive controls on truthful commercial speech. In the Central Hudson Gas & Electric decision, the Court established a four-part test that must be met to justify restrictions on commercial speech. This is the leading case on this issue.

Central Hudson Gas & Electric Corporation v. Public Service Commission of New York

United States Supreme Court
447 U.S. 557, 100 S.Ct. 2343 (1980)

CASE BACKGROUND *The winter of 1973–74 was difficult because of the Organization of Petroleum Exporting Countries (OPEC) oil embargo and shortages of natural gas. The Public Service Commission of New York ordered electric utilities in New York to end all advertising that "promotes the use of electricity." The order was based on the Commission's finding that New York utilities did not have sufficient capacity to furnish all customer demands for the winter. The Commission declared all promotional advertising contrary to the national policy of conserving energy. It offered to review any proposed advertising that would encourage energy conservation. The New York high court upheld the constitutionality of the Commission's regulation. The utility appealed to the Supreme Court.*

CASE DECISION Powell, Justice.

* * *

The Commission's order restricts only commercial speech, that is, expression related solely to the economic interests of the speaker and its audience. . . . The First Amendment, as applied to the States through the Fourteenth Amendment, protects commercial speech from unwarranted government regulation. Commercial expression not only serves the economic interest of the speaker, but also assists consumers . . . in the fullest possible dissemination of information. In applying the First Amendment to this area, we have rejected the "highly paternalistic" view that government has complete power to suppress or regulate commercial speech. "People will perceive their own best interests if only they are well enough informed and . . . the best means to that end is to open the channels of communication, rather than to close them. . . ." Even when advertising communicates only an incomplete version of the relevant facts, the First Amendment presumes that some accurate information is better than no information at all.

Nevertheless, our decisions have recognized "the 'common-sense' distinction between speech proposing a commercial transaction, which occurs in an area traditionally subject to government regulation and other varieties of speech." . . . The Constitution therefore accords a lesser protection to commercial speech than to other constitutionally guaranteed expression. The protection available for particular commercial expression turns on the nature both of the expression and of the governmental interests served by its regulation.

The First Amendment's concern for commercial speech is based on the informational function of advertising. Consequently, there can be no constitutional objection to the suppression of commercial messages that do not accurately inform the public about lawful activity. The government may ban forms of communication more likely to deceive the public than to inform it, or commercial speech related to illegal activity.

If the communication is neither misleading nor related to unlawful activity, the government's power is more circumscribed.

* * *

In commercial speech cases . . . a four-part analysis has developed. [1] At the outset, we must determine whether the expression is protected by the First Amendment. For commercial speech to come within that provision, it at least must concern lawful activity and not be misleading. [2] Next, we ask whether the asserted governmental interest is substantial. If both inquiries yield positive answers, [3] we must determine whether the regulation directly advances the governmental interest asserted, and [4] whether it is not more extensive than is necessary to serve that interest.

continues

We now apply this four-step analysis for commercial speech to the Commission's arguments in support of its ban on promotional advertising.

The Commission does not claim that the expression at issue either is inaccurate or relates to unlawful activity. . . .

The Commission offers two state interests as justifications for the ban on promotional advertising. The first concerns energy conservation. Any increase in demand for electricity—during peak or off-peak periods—means greater consumption of energy. The Commission argues . . . that the State's interest in conserving energy is sufficient to support suppression of advertising designed to increase consumption of electricity. In view of our country's dependence on energy resources beyond our control, no one can doubt the importance of energy conservation. Plainly, therefore, the state interest asserted is substantial.

* * *

We come finally to the critical inquiry in this case: whether the Commission's complete suppression of speech ordinarily protected by the First Amendment is no more extensive than necessary to further the State's interest in energy conservation. The Commission's order reaches all promotional advertising, regardless of the impact of the touted service on overall energy use. But the energy conservation rationale, as important as it is, cannot justify suppressing information about electric devices or services that would cause no net increase in total energy use. In addition, no showing has been made that a more limited restriction on the content of promotional advertising would not serve adequately the State's interests.

* * *

Reversed.

QUESTIONS FOR ANALYSIS

1. Since the Court found that the state had a substantial interest in the subject in question (electricity conservation), why did it find the ad restrictions to be unconstitutional? What part of the four-part test was not met?

2. Suppose the Commission had said that only advertising designed to promote energy conservation was allowed. Would that have met the Supreme Court test?

The Supreme Court has ruled that First Amendment rights are violated by restrictions on advertising for professional services, such as by lawyers or doctors. In *Shapero* v. *Kentucky Bar Association* (468 U.S. 881), the Court held that the state bar association violated the First Amendment by prohibiting lawyers from soliciting business by sending truthful letters to prospective clients known to face possible legal action. If an attorney engages in misleading or deceptive solicitation practices, the attorney may be punished by the bar for doing so, but the bar may not act as a barrier to truthful commercial speech.

The Court further discussed the regulation of commercial speech in *Board of Trustees of the State University of New York* v. *Fox* (492 U.S. 469). The standard for judging commercial speech regulation is one that is "not necessarily perfect but reasonable" and one "narrowly tailored to achieve the desired objective." The basis of the regulation must be a substantial state interest in controlling an undesirable activity, balanced against the cost imposed by the restrictions. When regulations are challenged, the state bears the burden of justifying restrictions on commercial speech.

Freedom to Criticize

Freedom of speech can mean that a business is criticized. The Supreme Court upheld this right in *Bose Corp.* v. *Consumers Union* (466 U.S. 485). A report in *Consumer Reports* was critical of the quality of a stereo speaker made by Bose. Bose sued, claiming product disparagement.

INTERNATIONAL   *Perspective*

Freedom of Commercial and Political Speech Abroad

Most nations, even democratic countries with a tradition of personal freedom, impose more restrictions on speech than the United States.

Consider incidents involving Internet commercial and political communications. A French court ordered Yahoo! to block French Internet users from having access to auctions selling Nazi artifacts, such as a German uniform from World War II. The court, noting that the sale of such items is illegal in France, ruled that Yahoo! must block access to such products or face a fine of 100,000 francs ($13,000) a day.

Yahoo!, knowing that it is nearly impossible to make such blocks effective, removed such items from its auction site. This would be the equivalent of the U.S. government prohibiting the sale of Osama bin Laden artifacts in the United States.

The highest court of Germany upheld a prison sentence for an Australian citizen who posted information on a web site based in Australia that denies that the Holocaust occurred. Denying the Holocaust is banned as hate speech. The German high court held that it had jurisdiction over this violation of German law. This would be the equivalent of the U.S. Supreme Court upholding a conviction of an Iranian citizen who posted material on an Iranian web site claiming that the World Trade Center terrorist attacks never happened.

The Supreme Court held that for a public figure, such as a corporation selling products, to recover damages for a defamatory falsehood, the trial court must find clear and convincing evidence that there was actual malice in publishing a knowing or reckless falsehood. Since actual malice was not shown in this case, the suit was dismissed.

OTHER KEY PARTS OF THE BILL OF RIGHTS

The Bill of Rights contains the first ten amendments to the Constitution. Some amendments, while providing important rights for citizens, have little special impact on business. Most of the rest of the amendments, numbered eleven through twenty-seven, also have no special impact on business, although we will see that the Fourteenth Amendment has important consequences. No amendment was written specifically to address a business issue. Some just happen to have an impact on the legal environment of business.

Unreasonable Search and Seizure

The Fourth Amendment reads: "The right of the people to be secure in their persons, houses, papers, and effects, against unreasonable searches and seizures, shall not be violated, and no Warrants shall issue, but upon probable cause. . . ." Most cases arising under this amendment are criminal and concern the proper method of search and seizure of suspected criminals and evidence. Searches by government agents to help enforce regulations that may result in criminal charges are subject to limits. In Fourth Amendment cases, key issues are whether proper search and seizure procedures were used by government authorities and whether a person has a constitutionally protected reasonable expectation of privacy.

Limits on Searches and Inspections

If a government inspector shows up at a business to inspect the premises or search company records for some purpose related to the law being enforced by the inspector, does the business have to allow admission? Not without a warrant in many instances, the Supreme Court held in *Marshall* v. *Barlow's* (436 U.S. 307). In that case, an inspector for the Occupational Safety and Health Administration (OSHA) arrived at Barlow's plant in Idaho and asked to search the work areas. Barlow asked the inspector if he had a warrant. Since he did not, Barlow refused admission to the plant. OSHA asked the Court to require businesses to admit inspectors to conduct warrantless searches.

The Court refused, saying that warrantless searches are generally unreasonable and that this rule applies to commercial premises as well as homes. The government argued that if inspectors had to obtain warrants, businesses would have time to hide safety and health defects on worksites. The Court responded:

> We are unconvinced . . . that requiring warrants to inspect will impose serious burdens on the inspection system or the courts, will prevent inspections necessary to enforce the statute, or will make them less effective. In the first place the great majority of businessmen can be expected in normal course to consent to inspection without warrant; the Secretary (of Labor) has not brought to this Court's attention any widespread pattern of refusal.

As the Court predicted, most businesses allow warrantless searches; the requirement to obtain a warrant when demanded is not burdensome nor has much affected law enforcement. Warrantless searches are allowed in cases of "closely regulated" businesses, as the Court discussed in the *Burger* decision. Since the *Burger* decision, more and more businesses have been held to be "closely regulated" and so are subject to warrantless search.

New York v. Burger

United States Supreme Court
482 U.S. 691, 107 S.Ct. 2636 (1987)

CASE BACKGROUND   *Burger ran an automobile junkyard, where cars were dismantled and the parts sold. Because many stolen cars are chopped up for parts, junkyards are licensed and are required to keep records of cars received. A New York statute allowed warrantless inspections of junkyards. Police officers entered Burger's junkyard and asked to see his license and records. Burger told the police that he had neither. The police then searched the place. They found stolen cars and Burger was charged with possession of stolen property.*

At trial, Burger moved to suppress the evidence obtained on the ground that the inspection statute was unconstitutional. The court denied the motion to suppress the evidence. The motion was reversed by the New York Court of Appeals, which held that the statute violated the Fourth Amendment's prohibition of unreasonable searches

and seizures. The decision of the high court of New York was appealed to the Supreme Court to determine whether the statute was unconstitutional.

CASE DECISION   Blackmun, Justice.

* * *

The Court long has recognized that the Fourth Amendment's prohibition on unreasonable searches and seizures is applicable to commercial premises, as well as to private homes. An owner or operator of a business thus has an expectation of privacy in commercial property, which society is prepared to consider to be reasonable. This expectation exists not only with respect to traditional police searches conducted for the gathering of criminal evidence but also with respect to administrative inspections designed to enforce regulatory statutes. An expectation of privacy in commercial premises, however, is different from, and indeed less than, a similar expectation in an individual's home. . . .

Because the owner or operator of commercial premises in a "closely regulated" industry has a reduced expectation of privacy, the warrant and probable-cause requirements, which fulfill the traditional Fourth Amendment standard of reasonableness for a government search, have lessened application in this context. Rather, we conclude that, as in other situations of "special need," where the privacy interests of the owner are weakened and the government interests in regulating particular businesses are concomitantly heightened, a warrantless inspection of commercial premises may well be reasonable within the meaning of the Fourth Amendment.

This warrantless inspection, however, even in the context of a pervasively regulated business, will be deemed to be reasonable only so long as three criteria are met. First, there must be a "substantial" government interest that informs the regulatory scheme pursuant to which the inspection is made. . . .

Second, the warrantless inspections must be "necessary to further the regulatory scheme." . . .

Finally, "the statute's inspection program, in terms of the certainty and regularity of its application, must provide a constitutionally adequate substitute for a warrant." In other words, the regulatory statute must perform the two basic functions of a warrant; it must advise the owner of the commercial premises that the search is being made pursuant to the law and has a properly defined scope, and it must limit the discretion of the inspecting officers.

* * *

The New York regulatory scheme satisfies the three criteria necessary to make reasonable warrantless inspections. . . . First, the State has a substantial interest in regulating the vehicle-dismantling and automobile-junkyard industry because motor vehicle theft has increased in the State and because the problem of theft is associated with this industry. . . .

Second, regulation of the vehicle-dismantling industry reasonably serves the State's substantial interest in eradicating automobile theft. . . .

Third, the statute provides a "constitutionally adequate substitute for a warrant." The statute informs the operator of a vehicle-dismantling business that inspections will be made on a regular basis. Thus, the vehicle dismantler knows that the inspections to which he is subject do not constitute discretionary acts by a government official but are conducted pursuant to statute. . . .

Finally, the "time, place, and scope" of the inspection is limited to place appropriate restraints upon the discretion of the inspecting officers.

* * *

Accordingly, the judgment of the New York Court of Appeals is reversed. . . .

QUESTIONS FOR ANALYSIS

1. Suppose that during such a warrantless search the police found evidence of another crime, such as a stash of cocaine. Should such evidence be allowed to be used?

2. If one goes into the junkyard or other "closely regulated" business, one must accept the possibility of warrantless searches. What businesses are not "closely regulated" and therefore not subject to such searches?

Gathering Evidence

Evidence improperly gathered by law enforcement officials violate Fourth Amendment rights regarding search and seizure and may not be used in court under the *exclusionary rule*. Generally, this means that evidence gathered from a home or business without a warrant was improper and cannot be used. As the *Burger* decision indicates, businesses have fewer constitutional rights in this respect than persons in their homes. The trend is in favor of warrantless searches of regulated businesses, which can include employees.

In *Skinner* v. *Railway Labor Executives' Ass'n* (489 U.S. 602), the Court approved warrantless searches of railroad employees involved in train accidents or safety violations. The searches consist of blood, breath, and urine tests for evidence of alcohol or drugs. These searches do not violate the Fourth Amendment, because they are in a "closely regulated" industry, are based on compelling public interest in safety, and may be used only in specific situations. The employees know they are subject to this requirement, so the limited invasion of privacy is acceptable.

Self-Incrimination

The Fifth Amendment protects individuals against *self-incrimination:* "No person shall be . . . compelled in any criminal case to be a witness against himself." This protection applies to persons, not to corporations. Although corporate executives cannot be made to testify against themselves, business records that might incriminate the corporation (and executives) must be produced, since such records are not protected by the Fifth Amendment.

That corporations are not due the same Fifth Amendment protection as are individuals was noted by the Supreme Court in *Braswell* v. *United States* (487 U.S. 99). Braswell was president and sole shareholder of a corporation. Claiming Fifth Amendment privilege against self-incrimination, he refused to produce company records ordered under a federal grand jury subpoena. The Court rejected this claim, holding that the corporation was an entity not protected by the Fifth Amendment; hence, Braswell had to produce corporate records, even though the records might incriminate him.

Just Compensation

The Fifth Amendment states, ". . . nor shall private property be taken for public use, without just compensation." Termed the *just compensation or takings clause*, it requires governments to pay for property a government requires someone to sell because public officials determine that the property should be used for some specific purpose, such as for the construction of a highway, school, or military base.

While governments have always been required to pay for property taken for public use, what if regulation takes all or most of the value of property? Local governments, where most land-use requirements are determined, have broad powers to change zoning and land-use requirements without paying compensation, even though the value of the land is affected by changes in land-use rules. When new rules reduce property values, must the government compensate property owners?

Cyber
Law

No Right of Privacy in Chat Rooms

An FBI agent monitored online chat rooms to uncover distribution of child pornography. He would enter the chat rooms, so his user name was seen, but he would not participate. Based on the agent's observations, Charbonneau was accused of distributing child pornography to contacts made in the chat room. Charbonneau contended that this method of collecting evidence violated his Fourth Amendment right to a reasonable expectation of privacy.

A federal court held that the evidence collected was good. "The expectation of privacy in E-mail transmissions depends in large part on both the type of E-mail sent and recipient of the E-mail." Messages sent to a chat room, unlike personally addressed E-mails, lose their privacy, so the evidence may be used against him.

Source: *U.S.* v. *Charbonneau* (979 F.Supp. 1177)

Regulatory Takings

A 1987 Supreme Court decision, *Nollan v. California Coastal Commission* (483 U.S. 825), addressed compensation in case of changing land-use rules. The Nollans wanted to tear down their house and build a larger one on their beach property in Ventura, California. The Coastal Commission said that their permit would be granted only if they agreed to allow the public an easement (access) to the private land that was their backyard. The high-tide line determines the lot's oceanside boundary. The Coastal Commission wanted the public to have the right to use what had been the Nollans' backyard—above the high-tide line—along the beach.

The Supreme Court held that the takings clause of the Fifth Amendment had been violated. The state could not tie a rebuilding permit to an easement (land use) that it would have to pay for if it simply imposed the easement. "California is free to advance its 'comprehensive program,' if it wishes, [of increased beach access] by using its power of eminent domain for this 'public purpose,' but if it wants an easement across the Nollans' property, it must pay for it." The *Dolan* decision was the next major decision in this area of law.

Dolan v. City of Tigard
United States Supreme Court
512 U.S. 374, 114 S.Ct. 2309 (1994)

CASE BACKGROUND *Florence Dolan, owner of a plumbing and electric supply store in the business district of Tigard, Oregon, applied for a permit to double the size of her store and to pave the store's gravel parking lot. As a part of its master plan, the city approved Dolan's building permit on the condition that Dolan dedicate about one-sixth of her land to the city. The land would be part of a public recreational greenway in the floodplain along Fanno Creek, which ran next to her property, and would be part of a pedestrian/bicycle pathway. Dolan protested this loss of her property as a condition of getting the building ordinance. The Oregon courts upheld the city's determination; Dolan (petitioner) appealed to the Supreme Court.*

CASE DECISION Rehnquist, Chief Justice.

* * *

Without question, had the city simply required petitioner to dedicate a strip of land along Fanno Creek for public use, rather than conditioning the grant of her permit to redevelop her property on such a dedication, a taking would have occurred [that would have required compensation]. . . .

Under the well-settled doctrine of "unconstitutional conditions," the government may not require a person to give up a constitutional right—here the right to receive just compensation when property is taken for a public use—in exchange for a discretionary benefit conferred by the government where the property sought has little or no relationship to the benefit.

* * *

Because petitioner's property lies within the Central Business District, the Community Development Code already required that petitioner leave 15% of it as open space and the undeveloped floodplain would have nearly satisfied that requirement. But the city demanded more—it not only wanted petitioner not to build in the floodplain, but it also wanted petitioner's property along Fanno Creek for its Greenway system. The city has never said why a public greenway, as opposed to a private one, was required in the interest of flood control. . . .

The city wants to impose a permanent recreational easement upon petitioner's property that borders Fanno Creek. Petitioner would lose all rights to regulate the time in which the public entered onto the Greenway, regardless of any interference it might pose with her retail store. . . .

Cities have long engaged in the commendable task of land use planning, made necessary by increasing

continues

urbanization particularly in metropolitan areas such as Portland. The city's goals of reducing flooding hazards and traffic congestion, and providing for public greenways, are laudable, but there are outer limits to how this may be done. "A strong public desire to improve the public condition [will not] warrant achieving the desire by a shorter cut than the constitutional way of paying for the change."

The judgment of the Supreme Court of Oregon is reversed. . . .

QUESTIONS FOR ANALYSIS

1. The city's action would have reduced the value of Dolan's property by a fraction. Regulatory changes often have such an effect. Could this decision restrict the ability of governments to change building requirements?

2. Is there a difference between a direct taking of property, such as the city's ordering Dolan to give it one of her six acres, and a regulatory taking, such as the city's ordering Dolan to dedicate the use of one acre for public purposes?

Right to Trial

The Sixth Amendment addresses the right of persons to trial by jury in criminal cases. The Seventh Amendment provides for the right to jury trial in common-law cases. Although the law is well established about the constitutional right to jury trial in criminal cases and common-law cases, what about cases in which a business is charged with a violation of a statute that regulates the business? If the charge is criminal, the right to request a jury trial remains. What if the charge is civil?

If the only question at trial arises under a statute that may impose civil penalties (money fines or an injunction), no right to jury trial exists. Since civil penalties are imposed by statute, there is no constitutional right to trial on such matters.

Excessive Fines

The Eighth Amendment is most famous for its restriction on "cruel and unusual punishments," but it also holds that "no excessive fines" may be imposed. As large jury awards have become more common in recent years, defendants have questioned whether the Eighth Amendment offers protection against huge punitive damage awards. As we will see in the *Leatherman* case, the Supreme Court has applied the Eighth Amendment, through the Fourteenth Amendment, to limit excessive punitive damages.

The claim of excessive fines also has been raised in suits that allow the government to press for large damages. For example, when illegal drug dealing occurs on private property, the property may be confiscated. Even if the property is worth a thousand times what the drugs were worth, this has generally been held not to be an excessive fine in violation of the Eighth Amendment, so long as the fines are part of a rational and consistent scheme to deter certain behavior.

A restriction imposed on forfeiture arose in the 1998 Supreme Court case, *U.S. v. Bajakajian* (118 S.Ct. 2028). The Bajakajians were leaving the country with $357,144 in cash. The money was legally earned; they were taking the money to repay relatives who had given them money to start their business. While it was legal to take the money out of the country, the Bajakajians failed to report that they were leaving with more than $10,000. Government agents seized all the money, contending that it could be kept because it was an "instrumentality" of the crime committed. In a five to four vote, the Court held that the forfeiture was an "excessive fine" in violation of the Eighth Amendment as it was grossly disproportional to the seriousness of the offense.

FOURTEENTH AMENDMENT

The Fourteenth Amendment holds, in part, "No State shall . . . deprive any person of life, liberty, or property, without due process of law; nor deny to any person within its jurisdiction the equal protection of the laws." This amendment has been a powerful device for extending federal constitutional guarantees to the states and preventing states from passing laws that diminish federal constitutional protections.

The Fourteenth Amendment, which was passed after the Civil War to prevent the Southern states from passing laws to reinstitute some aspects of slavery, has two key provisions concerning substantive and procedural law: the *due process clause* and the *equal protection clause*. Substantive due process comes into play whenever the courts review the ability of the government to restrict the freedoms of life, liberty, or property. Equal protection comes into play when the courts are called on to review a classification of persons established by a government.

Due Process

In general, due process claims can be stated two different ways. First, due process is violated when the state infringes on fundamental liberty interests without narrowly tailoring that infringement to serve a compelling state interest. Second, due process is offended when state action either shocks the conscience or offends judicial notions of fairness and human dignity.

Suppose a state prohibited all persons from making or selling tobacco products in the state. A challenge to the law could be based on due process. The person claiming he or she should be allowed to make, consume, or sell tobacco products would claim that the Fourteenth Amendment was violated because the substance of the law, not the procedures used to enforce the law, restricted the freedom of all persons in the state without a constitutional rationale. However, when governments restrict the rights of citizens, unless a fundamental constitutional liberty is at stake (would that include access to tobacco products?), the law needs to relate rationally to a legitimate government interest, such as public health, to satisfy due process requirements.

Now suppose a state changed its law to prohibit people under age twenty-five or over age sixty-five from making, consuming, or selling tobacco products. A challenge to the law would be brought by someone under age twenty-five or over age sixty-five claiming that the equal protection clause of the Fourteenth Amendment had been violated. That is, persons in those age groups belong to the class of persons affected by the law, which they claim is constitutionally wrong because it creates a class that suffers a loss of freedom. To uphold such a law that classifies persons, the court must find a valid governmental interest, such as public health because people under twenty-five may have higher addiction rates than older people who have access to tobacco, and to keep down expenditures on health care for people over age sixty-five, who are in the Medicare program. While it may be rational to have age restrictions on access to tobacco, there could be no such rationale for restrictions on tobacco based on race or sex.

While most due process cases involve protection of individual liberties, the constitutional standard also extends to businesses when governments go beyond the discretion they are ordinarily allowed. The *Leatherman* case that follows is an example of due process being applied in a business context. As the Supreme Court notes, when a constitutional issue is at stake, the courts are to review the matter with great care.

Cooper Industries, Inc. v. Leatherman Tool Group, Inc.

United States Supreme Court
532 U.S. 424, 121 S.Ct. 1678 (2001)

CASE BACKGROUND   *Leatherman makes a well-known multifunction tool. Cooper Industries introduced a competitor tool, called the ToolZall, that was a minor modification of the Leatherman product. Cooper used photographs of a slightly modified Leatherman tool in its advertising campaign for the ToolZall. Leatherman sued Cooper Industries for violation of the Trademark Act for passing off—featuring the Leatherman tool rather than its own product in the advertisements, but calling it a ToolZall. Finding that Cooper had committed a tort, the jury awarded Leatherman $50,000 in compensatory damages and $4.5 million in punitive damages. The court of appeals upheld the verdict. Cooper appealed the damage award.*

CASE DECISION   Justice Stevens delivered the opinion of the Court.

* * *

Despite the broad discretion that States possess with respect to the imposition of criminal penalties and punitive damages, the Due Process Clause of the Fourteenth Amendment to the Federal Constitution imposes substantive limits on that discretion. That Clause makes the Eighth Amendment's prohibition against excessive fines and cruel and unusual punishments applicable to the States. The Due Process Clause of its own force also prohibits the States from imposing "grossly excessive" punishments on tortfeasors.

The Court has enforced those limits in cases involving deprivations of life (death is not "a valid penalty under the Eighth and Fourteenth Amendments for one who neither took life, attempted to take life, nor intended to take life"); (sentence of death is "grossly disproportionate" and excessive punishment for the crime of rape); deprivations of liberty (life imprisonment without the possibility of parole for nonviolent felonies is "significantly disproportionate"); and deprivations of property, punitive forfeiture of $357,144 for violating reporting requirement was "grossly disporportional" to the gravity of the offense; ($2 million punitive damages award for failing to advise customers of minor predelivery repairs to new automobiles was "grossly excessive" and therefore unconstitutional).

In these cases, the constitutional violations were predicated on judicial determinations that the punishments were "grossly disproportional to the gravity of . . . defendants' offenses." We have recognized that the relevant constitutional line is "inherently imprecise," rather than one "marked by a simple mathematical formula." But in deciding whether that line has been crossed, we have focused on the same general criteria: the degree of the defendant's reprehensibility or culpability, the relationship between the penalty and the harm to the victim caused by the defendant's actions, and the sanctions imposed in other cases for comparable misconduct. Moreover, and of greatest relevance for the issue we address today, in each of these cases we have engaged in an independent examination of the relevant criteria.

In [an earlier case] we expressly noted that the courts of appeals must review the proportionality determination "*de novo*" and specifically rejected the suggestion of the respondent [Leatherman], who had prevailed in the District Court, that the trial judge's determination of excessiveness should be reviewed only for an abuse of discretion. "The factual findings made by the district courts in conducting the excessiveness inquiry, of course, must be accepted unless clearly erroneous. . . . But the question whether a fine is constitutionally excessive calls for the application of a constitutional standard to the facts of a particular case, and in this context *de novo* review of that question is appropriate."

* * *

Because the Court of Appeals applied a less demanding standard in this case, we vacate the judgment and remand the case for further proceedings consistent with this opinion.

QUESTIONS FOR ANALYSIS

1. What difference does it make if, as the Court says, the court of appeals should review the matter "*de novo*" rather than look for an abuse of discretion by the trial court?

2. Why does the Court say that such determinations are "imprecise"?

JURIS *prudence?*

No Hammer Locks, Ladies

Jerry Hunter was arrested for violating an Oregon law prohibiting women from participating in a "wrestling competition." The Oregon Supreme Court addressed the constitutionality of the law in a 1956 decision:

> The Fourteenth Amendment to the U.S. Constitution does not protect those liberties [to be in a public wrestling match]. . . . The legislature intended that there should be at least one island on the sea of life reserved for man that would be impregnable to the assault of woman. . . . In business . . . in the professions, in politics, as well as in almost every other line of human endeavor, she had matched her wits and prowess with those of mere men, and, we are frank to concede, in many instances had outdone him. . . . is it any wonder that the legislative assembly took advantage of the police power of the state in its decision to halt this ever-increasing feminine encroachment upon what for the ages had been considered strictly as manly arts and privileges?

Source: *State of Oregon* v. *Hunter*, 300 P.2d 455

Equal Protection

The Fourteenth Amendment, as previously noted, says, "No state shall . . . deny . . . the equal protection of the laws." The *equal protection* clause has come to mean that governments must treat people equally. However, equal protection does not extend to all government activities. Some actions by government that discriminate are held to tougher standards than others. Over the years, the equal protection clause of the Fourteenth Amendment has been tied to the due process clause of the Fifth Amendment to strengthen due process requirements, as we see in the *Adarand* case.

Government action that intends to discriminate on the basis of race is held to a standard of strict scrutiny. Hence, government programs that discriminate on the basis of race are not likely to meet a Fourteenth Amendment challenge unless there is a compelling state interest. This meant, of course, that "Jim Crow" laws that discriminated against minorities were stricken as unconstitutional. In more recent years, the issue has been whether governments may intentionally discriminate in favor of certain minorities or disadvantaged individuals. In the *Adarand* case, the Supreme Court held that affirmative action programs would be subject to more strict scrutiny.

Adarand Constructors, Inc. v. Pena

United States Supreme Court
515 U.S. 200, 115 S.Ct. 2097 (1995)

CASE BACKGROUND *The Department of Transportation requires that prime government contractors, such as highway construction firms, hire subcontractors that are certified by the Small Business Administration as being controlled by socially and economically disadvantaged individuals, such as racial minorities. In one highway subcontract for guardrails, Adarand, the low bidder, was passed over by the contractor in favor of a higher-bidding disadvantaged subcontractor. Adarand sued, claiming that the rules used in subcontractor choice violated the equal protection portion of the Due Process Clause. The suit was dismissed by the district court. The appeals court upheld the dismissal. Adarand appealed.*

CASE DECISION O'Connor, Justice.

* * *

continues

Adarand's claim arises under the Fifth Amendment to the Constitution, which provides that "No person shall . . . be deprived of life, liberty, or property, without due process of law." . . . and the Fourteenth Amendment, which provides that "No State shall . . . deny to any person within its jurisdiction the equal protection of the laws." Our cases have accorded varying degrees of significance to the difference in the language of those two Clauses.

* * *

[Previous cases] had established three general propositions with respect to governmental racial classifications. First, skepticism: " 'any preference based on racial or ethnic criteria must necessarily receive a most searching examination.' " . . . Second, consistency: "the standard of review under the Equal Protection Clause is not dependent on the race of those burdened or benefited by a particular classification," that is, all racial classifications reviewable under the Equal Protection Clause must be strictly scrutinized. And third, congruence: "equal protection analysis in the Fifth Amendment area is the same as that under the Fourteenth Amendment." Taken together, these three propositions lead to the conclusion that any person, of whatever race, has the right to demand that any governmental actor subject to the Constitution justify any racial classification subjecting that person to unequal treatment under the strictest judicial scrutiny. . . .

The principle of consistency simply means that whenever the government treats any person unequally because of his or her race, that person has suffered an injury that falls squarely within the language and spirit of the Constitution's guarantee of equal protection. It says nothing about the ultimate validity of any particular law; that determination is the job of the court applying strict scrutiny. The principle of consistency explains the circumstances in which the injury requiring strict scrutiny occurs. The application of strict scrutiny, in turn, determines whether a compelling governmental interest justifies the infliction of that injury.

Consistency does recognize that any individual suffers an injury when he or she is disadvantaged by the government because of his or her race, whatever that race may be.

* * *

Finally, we wish to dispel the notion that strict scrutiny is "strict in theory, but fatal in fact." The unhappy persistence of both the practice and the lingering effects of racial discrimination against minority groups in this country is an unfortunate reality, and government is not disqualified from acting in response to it. . . . When race-based action is necessary to further a compelling interest, such action is within constitutional constraints if it satisfies the "narrow tailoring" test this Court has set out in previous cases.

* * *

Reversed and remanded.

QUESTIONS FOR ANALYSIS

1. The Court appears in this decision to strike down quota systems that would require a certain percentage of state business be given to particular groups. What kind of affirmative action programs might meet the strict scrutiny test?

2. Congress and the office of the president have generally ignored this decision. Few federal set-aside programs have been changed. How can such programs continue in place?

State classifications based on sex are also subject to scrutiny. To be allowed to stand, such laws must substantially relate to important government objectives and provide "exceeding persuasive justification," as the Supreme Court held in the 1996 case, *U.S.* v. *Virginia*. It held that the state of Virginia violated the equal protection clause by excluding women from the Virginia Military Institute.

Subject to less scrutiny under the equal protection clause are economic regulations. For example, in a case in 1988, *Pennell* v. *City of San Jose* (485 U.S. 1), the Supreme Court upheld a rent control ordinance. The claim that the rent control was taken under the Fifth Amendment that violated the equal protection clause was rejected because the controls were "rationally related to a legitimate state interest." Since economic regulations often are not directly intended to be discriminatory on the basis of race or sex, they are more likely to stand judicial review as not in violation of equal protection.

SUMMARY

- The commerce clause and the necessary and proper clause give Congress nearly unlimited discretion to regulate and tax business. Unless a statute specifies that certain businesses are exempt, regulations apply to all, since even local (intrastate) business has been held to affect interstate business.
- States may impose regulations that do not conflict with federal regulations or may impose regulations in areas in which Congress gives them specific regulatory authority, but states may not impose burdens on interstate commerce. Numerous state regulatory and taxing schemes have been limited because they violate the commerce clause of the Constitution.
- The taxing power of the federal government is nearly unlimited. Taxes may be used for purposes other than just to raise revenues. They may be discriminatory or used to regulate and may be punitive in nature. The Supreme Court rarely questions the taxing schemes of Congress. State taxing schemes may not discriminate against interstate or international commerce.
- Commercial speech is afforded a high level of First Amendment protection. Businesses have the right to participate in political discussion whether or not it concerns an issue that directly affects business.
- Restrictions on commercial speech are subject to constitutional guidelines concerning strong public necessity. Truthful speech about lawful activities may be regulated only if the regulation would advance a substantial governmental interest and the regulation is no more extensive than is necessary.
- Since companies have Fourth Amendment guarantees against unreasonable searches and seizures, law enforcement authorities can be required to obtain warrants for most inspections. The main exception is in the case of closely regulated industries. The business sensibility of requiring an inspector to obtain a warrant for a routine inspection is dubious.
- Companies may not withhold documents or testimony requested by prosecutors on the grounds that the evidence might incriminate the company; only individuals may invoke that Fifth Amendment right. Efforts to evade the requirement to testify by holding corporate evidence out of the country will not necessarily work.
- When government agencies prevent property from being used in a legitimate manner because of long, unjustified procedural delays, or if agencies impose rules that substantially change the property value, compensation may be sought under the just compensation clause of the Fifth Amendment.
- The Supreme Court has held that large damage awards (including punitive damages) by juries against businesses do not violate the Eighth Amendment protection against excessive fines, nor do they violate Fourteenth Amendment due process clause protections of fair play and substantial justice.
- The due process clause of the Fourteenth Amendment has been used to extend constitutional protections to matters subject to state regulation. Economic regulations must be shown to be related to a legitimate government interest, such as public safety. The clause is also used to ensure fairness in law enforcement procedures.
- The equal protection clause of the Fourteenth Amendment is used to protect individuals from suffering a loss of freedom from state laws that discriminate against a class of persons when there is no compelling governmental interest in the law, such as public health or safety.

REVIEW AND DISCUSSION QUESTIONS

1. Define the following terms:

   commerce clause   self-incrimination
   interstate commerce   just compensation (takings) clause
   necessary and proper clause   excessive fines
   political speech   due process clause
   commercial speech   equal protection clause

2. Congress requires, via the Internal Revenue Service, that you report to the IRS any income from illegal activities, such as drug dealing. If you report the income, you reveal your illegal activities. If you do not report the income and the dealing is discovered, you can be charged with income tax evasion. Does this violate the Fifth Amendment? If not, why not?

CASE QUESTIONS

3. Many states prohibit their lottery tickets from being sold out of the state, so Pic-A-State would have its agents buy lottery tickets in various states and hold them there; someone in Pennsylvania would buy a claim on the tickets held in the other states. Congress passed a law prohibiting interstate transmission of lottery ticket information to be used for lottery ticket sales. Pic-A-State, which was being put out of business, challenged the law as unconstitutional. Was it correct? [*Pic-A-State Pa. v. Reno*, 76 F.3d 1294 (3rd Cir., 1996)]

4. Plaistow, New Hampshire, passed an ordinance prohibiting truck traffic during late-night hours at a truck terminal loading and unloading facility. It did so to reduce noise and fumes for the benefit of town residents. The truck terminal had been in operation several years. Most of the trucks came five miles from an interstate highway to change loads. The truckers contested the regulation as a restriction on interstate commerce and illegal for regulating an area (interstate trucking) subject to federal regulations. Were the truckers right? [*New Hampshire Motor Transport Assn. v. Town of Plaistow*, 67 F.3d 326 (1st Cir., 1995)]

5. Taylor sold live minnows as fishing bait in Maine. He imported some minnows into Maine from another state in violation of Maine law. He was then indicted under a federal law that makes it illegal to move fish in interstate commerce in violation of state law. Taylor claimed that the indictment should be dismissed because the Maine statute unconstitutionally burdened interstate commerce. Maine argued that it needed the statute to protect the state's fisheries from diseases and undesired varieties of fish. The U.S. Court of Appeals sided with Taylor, and the state of Maine appealed to the Supreme Court. Do the indictment and the statute stand? [*Maine v. Taylor*, 477 U.S. 131 (1986)]

 Check your answer at http://meiners.westbuslaw.com

6. The state of Iowa had a statute limiting to 55 feet the length of trucks on its highways. This made it illegal for commonly used double-trailer trucks 65 feet long to use Iowa highways. The shippers had to either use shorter trucks or go around the state. Iowa justified the regulation on the basis of safety on the highways and because the bigger trucks caused more damage to its highways. Was this regulation constitutional? [*Kassel v. Consolidated Freightways Corp.*, 450 U.S. 662 (1981)]

7. When margarine was invented, it cut into the butter market. The dairy lobby begged Congress for help and got it in the form of a federal tax on margarine of one-quarter of a cent per pound on white margarine and ten cents per pound on yellow margarine. Obviously, since people were used to yellow butter, white margarine was unattractive and less competitive. This discriminatory tax on margarine, especially yellow margarine, was challenged. What result? [*McCray* v. *U.S.*, 195 U.S. 27 (1904)]

 Check your answer at http://meiners.westbuslaw.com

8. Montana imposed a tax on coal that ran as high as 30 percent of its value. The tax generated as much as 20 percent of all state revenues. Since over 90 percent of the coal was shipped to other states, the tax was mostly borne by non-Montanans in higher utility prices. Was this tax constitutional? [*Commonwealth Edison* v. *Montana*, 453 U.S. 609 (1981)]

9. Massachusetts imposed a tax on all milk sold in the state. The tax proceeds, collected by the state, were distributed to dairy farmers in Massachusetts. Milk buyers who bought milk from out-of-state dairies contested the tax as unconstitutional for interfering with interstate commerce. Were they correct? [*West Lynn Creamery* v. *Healy*, 114 S.Ct. 2205 (1994)]

 Check your answer at http://meiners.westbuslaw.com

10. The Mushroom Promotion, Research, and Consumer Information Act mandates that mushroom handlers pay assessments used primarily to fund generic advertisements promoting mushroom sales. United Foods refused to pay the assessment, because it was forced to contribute for advertising it did not care to support, claiming that the Act violates the First Amendment. United Foods wanted to spend its advertising dollars for its own brand of mushrooms. Its administrative appeal to the Department of Agriculture was rejected and the district court upheld that decision, holding that the requirement to pay for advertising is part of a larger regulatory scheme of the mushroom industry. The appeals court reversed, holding that the payments were not part of a comprehensive statutory agricultural marketing program and so could not be justified. The Department of Agriculture appealed. Which position is correct? [*U.S.* v. *United Foods, Inc.*, 121 S.Ct. 2334, Sup. Ct., 2001]

11. The city of Cincinnati, for reasons of the safety and appearance of its streets and sidewalks, would not allow new racks on public property that distributed "commercial handbills" (free newspapers and advertising papers). Regular newspapers were allowed to have racks. The publishers of the free circulars sued the city for violating their First Amendment rights. Did they win? [*Cincinnati* v. *Discovery Network*, 113 S.Ct. 1505 (1993)]

 Check your answer at http://meiners.westbuslaw.com

12. Under the Hazardous Materials Transportation Act, the Secretary of Transportation regulates the transportation of hazardous materials. The regulatory scheme includes warrantless, unannounced inspections of property and records involved in transporting hazardous materials. A propane gas dealer contested the constitutionality of surprise, warrantless inspections of its transport facilities. The government sued to force such inspections. Was that position upheld? [*U.S.* v. *V-1 Oil Co.*, 63 F.3d 909 (9th Cir., 1995)]

13. Albert Wild was served a summons by the Internal Revenue Service to appear and testify about the tax records of Air Conditioning Supply Company, of which

Wild was owner and president. He appeared but refused to produce the records, claiming Fifth Amendment protection against self-incrimination. The IRS wanted to force him to produce the records of the company. Could they do so? [*Wild v. Brewer*, 329 F.2d 924 (9th Cir., 1964)]

14. A church owned land in a rural area that it used as a retreat center and a recreation area for disabled children. A fire in the area destroyed vegetation, allowing flooding to occur. The land was flooded. To protect public safety, the county adopted a temporary ordinance prohibiting any new building in the area until it determined what to do. The church request to rebuild was denied for six years while the county pondered what the building code, if any, should be for the area. The church sued for loss of use of the land. Could it recover under the just compensation clause of the Fifth Amendment? [*First English Evangelical Lutheran Church of Glendale* v. *Los Angeles County*, 482 U.S. 304 (1987)]

15. Curtis Campbell caused an accident in which another person was killed. His insurance company, State Farm, refused to pay claims related to the accident and took the case to trial, where Campbell and State Farm lost. State Farm paid the entire judgment, but Campbell sued the company for bad faith and emotional distress. The jury awarded him $1 million in compensatory damages and $145 million in punitive damages. The Utah supreme court upheld the award. State Farm appealed to the U.S. Supreme Court. Would the punitive damages stand? [*State Farm* v. *Campbell*, 123 S.Ct. 1513 (2003)]

16. The New York City Transit Authority ruled that methadone (a narcotic) users (who are usually recovering from heroin addiction) would not work for it in any job capacity. The district court held that this violated the equal protection clause by unfairly excluding methadone users, even from jobs that were not safety sensitive, such as drivers. The Transit Authority appealed to the Supreme Court. Was there a violation of the equal protection clause? [*New York City Transit Authority* v. *Beazer*, 440 U.S. 568 (1979)]

17. The state of West Virginia imposed a tax on property that was supposed to be in proportion to the value of the property. Taxpayers whose property was assessed at eight to thirty-five times more than comparable neighboring property, so that they were required to pay eight to thirty-five times as much in property tax as were other owners of similar property, sued the state for violation of the equal protection clause. Would such economic regulation be in violation? [*Allegheny Pittsburgh Coal Co.* v. *County Commission of Webster County*, 488 U.S. 336 (1989)]

ETHICS QUESTIONS

18. Many media companies own multiple forms of media—television stations, radio stations, and publishing companies. In some instances, one branch of the company promotes the product of another branch without revealing the connection. For example, the CBS program *60 Minutes* did a favorable lengthy "investigative" feature on a new book, *Against All Enemies*, published by Free Press. Both CBS and Free Press are owned by Viacom. No mention of the corporate link was made on the program. Is that an ethical practice?

19. A firm subject to OSHA inspections requires an OSHA inspector who shows up unexpectedly one day to get a warrant before engaging in the search. The firm owner knows that the inspector is a genuine inspector and that there is no question that the warrant to search will be issued. However, requiring the

inspector to get the warrant takes half a day of the inspector's time (which is paid for by taxpayers). Is it ethical to bar such inspections?

PULLING IT  *Together*

Jurisdiction and Constitutional Law

A Japanese company, Asahi, sold parts to a Taiwanese company that then sold finished products in the United States. One of the products, claimed to be defective, injured a consumer who sued the Taiwanese company in court in California. The company settled the case and then sued Asahi in a California court. The Taiwanese company contended that the part Asahi had sold it in Taiwan was the cause of the defect in the product. Can the Taiwanese company make Asahi appear in court in California? [*Asahi Metal Industry Co.* v. *Superior Court of California*, 480 U.S. 1026 (1987)]

INTERNET ASSIGNMENT

The Supreme Court played a crucial role in the 2000 U.S. presidential election. It also serves as a potential check on the powers of the Congressional and executive branches of government, even during difficult periods of time such as war.

Using FindLaw and/or the official U.S. Supreme Court web site, try to find links to the opinion of the *Bush* v. *Gore* (12/12/00) and pleadings of the Florida election cases. Find the names of two cases during the 2003 term in which the Supreme Court heard cases involving the rights, or lack thereof, of enemy combatants detained by presidential decree.

Chapter 5

Government Agencies and Administrative Process

The Kopczynski family has run a construction company in Washington for many years. Chris, now the head of the company, deals with a more complex set of regulations than his father faced decades ago. Safety and environmental inspectors from assorted federal and state agencies are likely to show up any time at building sites. Permits may be required from the Army Corps of Engineers and the Soil Conservation Service, among others. Local zoning rules and construction codes must be followed. The state requires the company to pay workers' compensation and unemployment insurance taxes, and to file numerous regular and special reports. The IRS requires tax filings on all employees and documentation of work eligibility for every employee. Special labor regulations must be followed on all projects involving government money. Such rules add greatly to the costs and complexity of operations.

Administrative agencies can have a huge impact on the legal environment of all businesses. Regulations concerning worker safety, discrimination, pollution, and many other activities have expanded significantly in recent decades. Some regulations, such as those on transportation, have been reduced, but others arise to deal with new enterprises, such as online businesses. Managers must stay abreast of regulatory developments in their areas if business.

This chapter begins with a discussion of the development of administrative agencies. It then considers the powers delegated to the agencies by Congress, including their legislative, investigative, adjudicatory, and enforcement powers. The last part of the chapter turns to the concept of judicial review—the power of the judicial branch of government to review agencies' actions or decisions.

ADMINISTRATIVE AGENCIES

Administrative agencies are a major part of government. They are the primary tool through which local, state, and federal governments perform regulatory functions. In the words of the Supreme Court in *F.T.C. v. Ruberoid Company* (1952):

> The rise of administration bodies probably has been the most significant legal trend of the last century and perhaps more values today are affected by their decisions than by those of all the courts. . . . They have become a veritable fourth branch of the government. . . .

The first federal agency was the Interstate Commerce Commission (ICC), created in 1887 to regulate railroads. Early in the 1900s, the Federal Trade Commission (FTC), which handles antitrust cases, and the Food and Drug Administration (FDA) were created. During the Great Depression in the 1930s, many agencies were created, such as the Securities and Exchange Commission (SEC) and the Federal Communications Commission (FCC). In the late 1960s and early 1970s, a number of agencies were created, including the Environmental Protection Agency (EPA) and the Equal Employment Opportunity Commission (EEOC). Today, more than fifty independent agencies and the fourteen cabinet departments issue tens of thousands of pages of regulations each year. Exhibit 5.1 is a list of a few agencies and their web site addresses. Almost all agencies can be easily found on the Web.

Creating an Administrative Agency

An *administrative agency* is an authority of the government—other than a legislature or a court—created to administer a particular law. Congress gives an agency power and authority through a *legislative delegation*. It delegates to an agency the power to perform its regulatory purpose, which is to formulate, implement, and enforce policy relevant to its area of authority. A statute delegating those powers to the agency is an *enabling statute*.

Why Create an Agency?

Administrative agencies are created when a problem requires expertise and supervision. By 1970, for example, Congress decided the federal government should address the issue of air quality. But as an institution, Congress has neither the time nor the expertise to determine how such a law might be applied to thousands of different

---

Exhibit 5.1
Selected Federal Administrative Agencies and Web Sites

Commodity Futures Trading Commission (CFTC); *http://www.cftc.gov*
Consumer Product Safety Commission (CPSC); *http://www.cpsc.gov*
Department of Commerce (DoC); *http://www.doc.gov*
Department of Labor (DoL); *http://www.dol.gov*
Equal Employment Opportunity Commission (EEOC); *http://www.eeoc.gov*
Food and Drug Administration (FDA); *http://www.fda.gov*
Federal Trade Commission (FTC); *http://www.ftc.gov*
Health and Human Services (HHS); *http://www.hhs.gov*
Occupational Safety and Health Administration (OSHA); *http://www.osha.gov*
Securities and Exchange Commission (SEC); *http://www.sec.gov*

JURIS *prudence?*

In Case You Don't Know What Kids' PJs Are

The Consumer Product Safety Commission regulates the fabrics used in children's sleepwear. To make sure people know what that means, the commission explains it in a regulation, §1616.2 Definitions:

(a) "Children's sleepwear" means any product of wearing apparel size 7 through size 14, such as nightgowns, pajamas, or similar or related items, such as robes, intended to be worn primarily for sleeping or activities related to sleeping. Underwear and diapers are excluded from this definition.

(b) "Sizes 7 through 14" means the sizes defined as 7 through 14 in Department of Commerce Voluntary Product Standards PS 54-72 and PS 36-70, previously identified as Commercial Standards, CS 153-48, "Body Measurements for the Sizing of Girls' Apparel" and CS 155-50, "Body Measurements for the Sizing of Boys' Apparel," respectively.

Source: *Code of Federal Regulations*

---

sources emitting air pollutants. Congress also lacks the ability to handle law enforcement compliance directly. Hence, when Congress passed the Clean Air Act, it delegated primary responsibility to the Environmental Protection Agency. The EPA has the legislative, investigative, adjudicatory, and enforcement powers to accomplish the task. The EPA can consider technical details more effectively than can Congress and can continuously monitor industry. Congress closely monitors the EPA (and all other agencies) and can change how it operates if not satisfied with the results.

Administrative Law

Administrative law consists of legal rules that define the authority and structure of administrative agencies. The primary sources of *administrative law* include:

1. The enabling statutes of administrative agencies
2. The Administrative Procedures Act
3. Rules issued by administrative agencies
4. Court decisions reviewing the validity of agency actions

The primary structure of administrative law is determined by the *Administrative Procedures Act (APA)*. Enacted by Congress in 1946, the APA defines the procedural rules and formalities for federal agencies. An agency must abide by APA requirements unless Congress specifically imposes different requirements on the agency.

Congress has authority under the commerce clause and the necessary and proper clause in the Constitution to create regulatory agencies and give them powers to enact rules. Agencies are also granted authority to investigate violations of rules the agency creates and to prosecute violators. Although specific powers differ from agency to agency, we can generalize a "typical" administrative agency. A summary of agency regulatory powers is provided in Exhibit 5.2.

Rulemaking

Most agencies are authorized to engage in *rulemaking*. By this process, an agency develops administrative rules and regulatory policy. Agencies use their own terminologies. The Treasury Department, for example, calls its rules "decisions"; other agencies refer to their rules as standards, guidelines, regulations, or opinions.

Types of Rules

The Administrative Procedures Act defines an agency rule as

> The whole or part of an agency statement of general or particular applicability and future effect designed to implement, interpret, or prescribe law or policy describing the organization, procedure, or practice requirements of an agency.

In general, administrative rules are classified as substantive (legislative), interpretative, or procedural.

Substantive or Legislative Rules

Substantive rules or *legislative rules* are administrative laws with the same force of law as statutes enacted by Congress. That is, when an agency issues a substantive rule (regulation) under its grant of authority by Congress, the rule is federal law. Contrary to popular misunderstanding, regulations are not a "lower form" of law than the laws written directly by Congress. Before issuing such rules, an agency is generally required by the APA to provide public notice and the opportunity for interested parties to comment in writing, for the public record.

Interpretative Rules

Interpretative rules are statements issued by an agency to provide its staff and the public with guidance regarding the interpretation of a substantive rule or a congressional statute. Interpretative rules range from informal policy statements to authoritative rulings that are binding on the agency.

In contrast to legislative rules, interpretative rules are exempt from the notice and comment requirements of the APA. As a consequence, an agency may issue interpretative rules without inviting input from interested parties. However, parties affected by rules may challenge an agency's interpretative rule by arguing that it is really a legislative rule. If the challenge is successful, the agency must go through a more complex process to adopt the rule.

Exhibit 5.2 *Administrative Agencies: Summary of Regulatory Powers*	**Regulartory Power**	**Definition**	**Advantages of Agencies**
	Legislative or Rulemaking Power	Develop rules to implement the agency's regulatory policies	Uses experts to consider technical details.
	Investigative Power	Obtain needed information to ensure that the statute and agency rules are observed	Can monitor regulated industries continuously— whether or not there has been a violation.
	Adjudicatory Power	Resolve disputes and violations through a judicial type of proceeding	Can bring actions quickly and enjoy flexibility and informality in their procedures.
	Enforcement Power	Impose sanctions to encourage compliance with statutes, an agency's rules, and an agency's adjudicatory outcomes	Flexibility to impose sanctions: fines, prohibitions, restrictions on licenses, and threat of public exposure.

Procedural Rules

Procedural rules detail an agency's structure and describe its method of operation and its internal practices. The power to enact such rules is authorized by the agency's enabling statute. Once procedural rules are issued, the agency is bound by them. A challenge to an agency decision is usually upheld if the challenging party can show that the agency did not comply with its own procedural rules in reaching a decision.

Rulemaking Procedure

Substantive rules are usually the most important. An agency lays out the requirements of how a statute is to be applied in practice—what regulations will have to be followed. Proposed rules are drafted by agency staff, reviewed internally, and approved by the head of the agency.

After the rule is approved, and published in the *Federal Register* for public inspection, interested parties may submit written comments about the rule. The public comment period is usually 60 to 90 days, after which the agency reviews the comments and finalizes the rule. Most comments are contributed by trade associations and other professional organizations that assist members of an affected industry. These comments, which tend to be technical, are important because they form the basis of most legal challenges to rules. Submitting the comments is proof that the agency was on notice of alleged defects in a rule.

Some statutes require that rulemaking must be "on the record." In these cases, statute requires an agency to hold hearings, at which witnesses appear to testify about the proposed rule. This is done for only a small fraction of all rules issued. In any case, once the agency issues the final rule, it may be appealed to the agency itself, after which appeal is made to the U.S. Court of Appeals. The appeals court ensures that the agency has not exceeded its authority or violated proper procedure, as we see in the *Public Citizen* case.

Public Citizen, Inc. v. Mineta

United States Court of Appeals, Second Circuit
340 F.3d 39 (2003)

CASE BACKGROUND *The National Highway Traffic Safety Administration (NHTSA), a part of the Department of Transportation, was authorized by Congress in 1966 to "prescribe motor vehicle safety standards" in order "to reduce traffic accidents and deaths." NHTSA has issued motor vehicle safety regulations since then. Final approval of regulations is by the Secretary of Transportation (Mineta in this case).*

Congress held hearings about tire safety in 2000 and, in the TREAD Act, ordered a regulation written to deal with the problem of significantly underinflated tires. In 2001, NHTSA issued a preliminary rule to require the installation of tire pressure monitoring systems (TPMS) in new vehicles. In 2002, the final rule was adopted. It permitted automakers the choice to install TPMS that

would inform drivers when one tire on a vehicle was 30 percent underinflated, but would not inform drivers when two or more tires were underinflated, or install a more costly TPMS that would inform a driver when one or more tires are 25 percent underinflated. This rule was challenged by several nonprofit advocacy groups as being contrary to the intent of Congress in dealing with the safety issue involved. The groups petitioned the court for review.

CASE DECISION Sack, Circuit Judge.

* * *

The petitioners' principal arguments are that the agency's adoption of a one-tire, 30 percent standard is contrary to the intent of the TREAD Act and, in light of the relative shortcomings of indirect systems, arbitrary and capricious. We agree on both counts.

The TREAD Act does not speak in terms of types of TPMSs. . . . It says only that "the Secretary of Transportation shall complete a rulemaking for a regulation to require a warning system in new motor vehicles to indicate to the operator when *a* tire is significantly under-inflated." TREAD Act § 13 (emphasis added).

The petitioners argue that the rule's one-tire, 30 percent standard fails to satisfy this minimum statutory requirement by permitting automakers to install currently available indirect systems, even though such systems do not warn drivers when two tires on the same side or the same axle of the vehicle are significantly under-inflated, or when all four tires are significantly under-inflated.

We think that, in light of the language and purpose of the TREAD Act, the petitioners' construction is clearly right and the agency's construction is clearly wrong. Section 13 requires warning systems that indicate "when *a* tire is significantly under inflated." TREAD Act § 13 (emphasis added). The TREAD Act's "*a* tire" plainly means one tire, two tires, three tires, or all four tires, under the elementary rule of statutory construction that the singular ("a tire") includes the plural ("tires").

* * *

The judiciary is the final authority on issues of statutory construction and must reject administrative constructions which are contrary to clear congressional intent. We conclude that the agency's reading of section 13 of the TREAD Act—which permits the agency to adopt a one-tire TPMS standard—is contrary to the unambiguously expressed intent of Congress.

Moreover, even if the Final Rule were not contrary to the intent of the TREAD Act, we would conclude that the agency's adoption of the one-tire, 30 percent standard option was arbitrary and capricious. In light of the administrative record, which documents the relative shortcomings of currently available . . . systems, it was unreasonable for NHTSA to adopt standards that allow automakers to install such systems in new motor vehicles.

* * *

We grant the petition for review, vacate the rule, and remand to the agency for further rulemaking proceedings consistent with this opinion.

QUESTIONS FOR ANALYSIS

1. What right would a group called "Public Citizen" have to challenge a vehicle safety regulation?
2. NHTSA defended the one-tire option as consistent with current technology and as less expensive than the four-tire option; why should that have not been sufficient justification for the rule?

ENFORCING RULES

The main job of most agencies is to enforce laws written by Congress or by the agencies under the authority granted them by Congress. Enforcement means that agencies must gather information and investigate. Agencies have various ways of doing this.

Investigative Powers

Information about compliance with federal laws is obtained in three basic ways:

1. Regulated businesses are required to self-report.
2. Direct observation determines if a business is following the law.
3. Agency subpoena power is used to require a business to produce documents.

Requiring Monitoring and Self-Reporting

Agencies may require businesses to monitor their own behavior. Those subject to a regulation can be required to report certain information to an agency at set times, such as monthly, or when certain events (often a violation) occur. The Clean Air

Act, for example, requires businesses to monitor air pollution emissions and report the data to the Environmental Protection Agency:

> The Administrator may require any person who owns or operates any emission source . . . to (A) establish and maintain such records, (B) make such reports, (C) install, use, and maintain such monitoring equipment or methods, (D) sample such emissions, and (E) provide such other information as the Administrator may reasonably require. . . .

CYBER *Law*

Do Old Regulations Apply to New Forms of Competition?

The growth of Internet-related technology raises tricky issues for regulators. If a new form of technology competes with existing regulated firms, and the new technology is not covered in the regulations that govern existing competitors, are the new competitors covered?

Bandwidth expansion allows Internet telephony and video—new forms of communication not covered by existing regulations. Existing firms want the new competitors to be subject to rules so that they cannot expand so quickly. Even if the regulators agree with existing competitors, the way the laws were written, and the regulations that implement the statutes, they did not envision the new inventions.

In many cases, if regulation is to be maintained, Congress will have to act. Such actions—as in the case of the Communications Decency Act of 1996, which was unanimously struck down by the Supreme Court as unconstitutional—indicate that Congress must not act too hastily or be defeated in its intent to control a new medium.

Reporting information of violations can lead to punishment. If, for example, the information reported indicates that a firm has emitted too much pollution, the EPA can impose a fine. Businesses have contested fines resulting from mandatory self-reporting of violations, arguing that reporting of self-incriminating evidence violates the Fifth Amendment. However, as pointed out in Chapter 4, the Supreme Court has ruled that the self-incrimination privilege of the Fifth Amendment does not provide strong protection for corporations. Failing to report violations or reporting false information almost always leads to heavier penalties than when a party volunteers violations.

Direct Observation by Agencies

Agencies also acquire information by *direct observation*. Examples include on-the-spot worksite safety inspections by OSHA inspectors and testing by the EPA for excessive air pollution emissions. As discussed in Chapter 4, the Supreme Court has imposed limits on warrantless searches by administrative agencies, but the warrants are simple to obtain. However, no warrant is required if an agency's evidence is obtained from an "open-field" observation, that is, if the evidence is gathered by an inspector by observations from areas where the public has access.

In *Dow Chemical Co.* v. *U.S.* (476 U.S. 227), the Supreme Court held it was legal for the EPA to fly over a Dow facility and take photographs for evidence of regulatory violations. Since the airspace over the facility was open to the public, there was no improper search in violation of the Fourth Amendment by this method of observation.

Agency Subpoena Power

An agency may also obtain information by issuing a *subpoena*, a legal instrument that directs the person receiving it to appear at a specified time and place to testify or to produce documents. The Clean Air Act provides an example of a congressional authorization of the power to issue subpoenas and the procedure for enforcing them:

> For purposes of obtaining information . . . the Administrator may issue subpoenas for the attendance and testimony of witnesses and the production of relevant papers, books, and documents, and he may administer oaths. . . . In case of . . . refusal to obey a subpoena served upon any person . . . , the district court . . . shall have jurisdiction to issue an order requiring such person to appear and give testimony before the Administrator . . . and any failure to obey such an order may be punished by such court as a contempt thereof.

Unless the request for information by the agency is vague, or if the burden imposed on the business outweighs the possible benefits to the agency, a business must comply with the subpoena. If a business asserts that the information requested by a subpoena deserves confidential treatment, an agency usually respects the request or the business may seek a court order providing protection.

Enforcement Power

Congress grants agencies many enforcement tools. The EPA, for example, can ensure compliance with air pollution control requirements by seeking civil and criminal penalties and injunctions, if necessary.

In addition to having the authority to sue in federal court to seek civil and criminal penalties, agencies have authority to impose other sanctions. Consider the examples offered by the APA in its definition of *sanction:*

1. Prohibition, requirement, limitation, or other condition affecting the freedom of a person
2. Withholding of relief
3. Imposition of a penalty or fine
4. Destruction, taking, seizing, or withholding of property
5. Assessment of damages, reimbursement, restitution, compensation, costs, charges, or fees
6. Requirement, revocation, or suspension of a license
7. Taking other compulsory or restrictive action

Enforcement methods vary among agencies. Most rely on a mix of formal and informal ways to obtain compliance with regulatory requirements. Our discussion focuses on agency procedures, but when an agency brings criminal charges against a party, it works with the Department of Justice (the Attorney General), which usually handles the prosecution of criminal cases that are heard in federal court.

Informal Agency Procedures

Agencies rely heavily on *informal procedures* that allow leeway in forcing compliance. Since informal procedures generally require less time and cost than formal procedures, agencies prefer to use them when possible.

Informal procedures include tests and inspections, processing applications and permits, negotiations, settlements, and advice in the form of advisory opinions.

Publicity, or the threat of it, can also be considered an informal procedure for an agency to get industry compliance with its rules.

In some cases, agencies may act on the spot. For example, an OSHA inspector, upon finding a situation that endangers workers, may order immediate changes. Many such incidents are handled this way rather than involving formal procedures. Similarly, manufacturers "voluntarily" withdraw products from the shelves and destroy them when a problem is discovered that would likely result in formal action by an agency.

Review of Informal Procedure Decisions   A business unhappy with an agency sanction resulting from informal procedures may seek review. The decision is first reviewed by the agency head. If dissatisfied with the agency's final decision, parties may seek review by the federal court. In reviewing agency procedures, the courts are generally most concerned with whether the agency procedure was fair and the decision was consistent with the legislative intent of Congress.

Formal Agency Procedures

Among the *formal procedures* used by most regulatory agencies are quasi-judicial powers, especially adjudicatory hearings. How hearings are conducted is dictated by the APA. In some instances, an agency's enabling statute may require procedures that differ somewhat from those provided by the APA.

Adjudicatory Hearings   An *adjudicatory hearing* is a formal agency process under APA rules, which are similar to those followed in a trial. As Exhibit 5.3 illustrates, an adjudicatory hearing is initiated by the agency filing a complaint. The business

Exhibit 5.3

Formal Agency Procedure: Adjudicatory Hearing

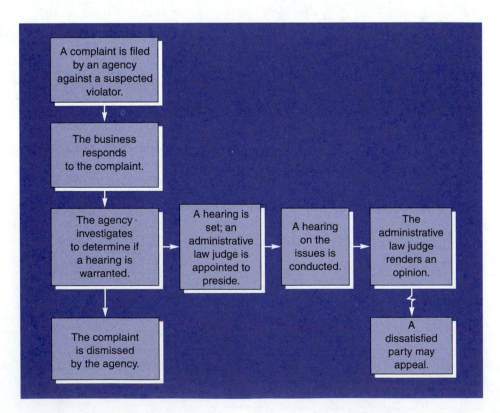

Does It Make Sense to Contest a Regulatory Order

ISSUE
Spotter

The Department of Labor contends that your firm has not been counting overtime work by employees properly. Labor demands the firm pay some back wages to employees to correct the calculation, pay a $1,000 fine, and promise not to violate the law concerning overtime work again. The matter can be settled quietly by accepting the Labor offer. One senior manager thinks Labor is wrong and the matter should be contested. He suggests not only contesting the finding of Labor in this particular case, but contesting the validity of the regulation enforcing the overtime provisions of the Fair Labor Standards Act as written by the Department of Labor.

Would it make sense to contest Labor's administrative decision? What are the pros and cons of a challenge?

must respond to the complaint that alleges violation of the law enforced by the agency. If the matter is not settled by negotiation, a hearing may be necessary.

An *administrative law judge (ALJ)* from the agency presides over the hearing. The ALJ is a civil service employee of the agency, usually a staff attorney. The agency is represented by its counsel, who presents the agency's evidence in support of the complaint; the business presents its evidence. Witnesses may be cross-examined, but the procedure is less formal than a court trial. The hearing must meet the due process guarantees of the Constitution, but there is no right to a jury trial since these are not criminal or common-law causes.

After a hearing, the ALJ issues a written decision. If the business does not object to the decision, the agency normally adopts the decision. If the business is dissatisfied with the ALJ's decision and seeks review, the agency head (commissioners or administrator) reviews the decision. If the business is dissatisfied after this final agency review, it may then proceed to the federal courts for further review.

INTERNATIONAL Perspective

Administrative Agencies in Japan

One of the most worrisome areas of Japanese legal culture for foreign companies is the body of administrative "law" known as "administrative guidance" (*gyosei shido*). This includes all procedural tools Japanese agencies can use to exert regulatory authority over businesses. An administrative agency, for example, may issue guidance by direction (*shiji*), request (*yobo*), warning (*keikoku*), encouragement (*kansho*), or suggestion (*kankoku*).

The power basis of administrative guidance is in the government's control of foreign trade. In theory, businesses are not forced to comply with guidance. But a business that ignores a suggestion might find that its quota of imported materials has been reduced, that it is being denied government financing for expansion, or that some other sanction is imposed.

The Foreign Exchange Control and Foreign Investment Acts, for example, require that any agreement involving expenditures abroad must be approved by the Foreign Investment Council. A business that has not complied with an agency's request that a pollution control device be installed might find that a contract requiring expenditures abroad has not been approved.

The Japanese judiciary has taken a hands-off policy toward administrative guidance. As long as the agency action is within its discretion, the action will not be reviewed unfavorably even if it is abusive. This gives Japanese administrative agencies considerably more power than U.S. agencies.

JUDICIAL REVIEW

The APA sets the procedural requirements for a party seeking court of appeals review of an agency decision. Most appeals concern the legitimacy of regulations and whether a penalty issued by an agency for a violation was justified. That appeal is referred to as *judicial review*, an external check on agency power. This ensures that agencies follow required procedures, do not go beyond the authority granted them by Congress, can justify their actions, and respect constitutional rights.

When Judicial Review Can Occur

Before a court accepts an appeal to review an agency's action, the party making the request must satisfy procedural requirements. Without such requirements, the courts could intrude into areas of agency responsibility and would be flooded with more cases. The most important of these procedural requirements are summarized in Exhibit 5.4.

Jurisdiction

As in any lawsuit, the party challenging an agency action must select a court that has authority to hear the case. Most regulatory statutes declare which court has *jurisdiction* to review agency actions. Suppose, for example, that the EPA enacts a new regulation. The Clean Air Act states the following:

> A petition for review of an action of the Administrator in promulgating any national ambient air quality standard . . . may be filed only in the United States Court of Appeals for the District of Columbia.

Reviewability

An agency action that is challenged must be *reviewable* by the courts. Administrative agencies must follow required procedure rules or risk being found by the reviewing

Exhibit 5.4	Procedural Requirement	Definition
Judicial Review of Agency Actions: Procedural Requirements	Jurisdiction	The complaining party may seek judicial review only in courts that have power to hear the case. Most statutes specify which courts have jurisdiction to hear appeals of agency actions.
	Reviewability	An appellate court has the ability to reconsider an agency decision to determine whether correction or modification is needed.
	Standing	A party seeking judicial review must demonstrate that it incurred an injury recognized by law as a result of the agency's action.
	Ripeness	There can be no judicial review until the agency's decision is final so that the court will have the final issues in the case before it and not hypothetical questions or unresolved disputes.
	Exhaustion	This is a "gatekeeping" device, requiring that a party seeking judicial review must have sought relief through all possible agency appeal processes before seeking review by the courts.

courts to have acted arbitrarily. Further, agencies may not exceed their regulatory objectives or risk being found to have violated the duties they were assigned by Congress. For these reasons, the APA authorizes the courts to review most agency actions. However, judicial review is not available if (1) judicial review is prohibited by statute or (2) the agency action is committed to agency discretion.

Review Prohibited by Statute   Just as Congress may specify in a statute which court has jurisdiction for judicial review, it can prohibit certain judicial review. Consider, for example, the following statutory provision regarding the authority of the Secretary of Veteran Affairs:

> The decisions of the Secretary on any question of law or fact under any law administered by the Department of Veterans Affairs providing benefits for veterans and their dependents or survivors shall be final and no other official or any court of the United States shall have the power or jurisdiction to review any decision.

JURIS *prudence?*

Regulators Protecting Consumers?

Like most countries, Japan has regulations claimed to protect consumers that appear to do the opposite.

Japan's antitrust "watchdog," the Fair Trade Commission, does not allow retailers to give discounts below the listed price on CDs, books, or magazines. Discount coupons may not be issued because they might "confuse" consumers. One Japanese retailer tried to import small plastic food contain-ers from Thailand. The customs agency required every carton to be opened and the containers and their lids tested to make sure they worked. Now the company buys containers made in Japan. They do not have to be tested and cost consumers three to four times as much as the "untrustworthy" imports.

Source: *The Wall Street Journal*

Thus, a party may not seek review of an administrative decision from the Department of Veteran Affairs in court. Congress can include such an exception in a statute as long as the exception does not violate constitutional rights.

Agency Action Committed to Agency Discretion   In addition to statutory exceptions to judicial review, there are also exceptions for actions committed to agency discretion for practical reasons. Some agency actions require speed, flexibility, and secrecy in decision making. For example, decisions affecting the national defense and foreign policy have been found to be committed to agency discretion and therefore nonreviewable. Such agency actions cannot be challenged through the courts.

Standing

A party seeking to challenge an agency action in court must have *standing* to seek judicial review. Section 2 of Article III of the Constitution limits the judicial power to *actual cases or controversies*. Federal courts cannot hear complaints from parties who have no direct stake in a real dispute or who raise only hypothetical questions. Administrative law generally restricts the right of review to parties who can show an injury recognized by law as being entitled to protection.

The U.S. Supreme Court addressed the standing issue in *Lujan* v. *Defenders of Wildlife* (504 U.S. 555). In that case, environmental groups argued that U.S. aid to Egypt to build dams on the Nile River endangered the rare Nile crocodile. Plaintiffs asserted that the agencies providing the aid should comply with the Endangered Species Act. The Court refused to hear the challenge because the plaintiffs lacked standing—they had suffered no "injury in fact." Concern about crocodiles in Egypt was too remote. Disagreement with an agency's policy is not the same as showing a concrete injury to the complaining party resulting from the policy.

Ripeness

The *ripeness doctrine* concerns whether an agency action is final so as to allow judicial review. That is, agency decisions that are not finalized are not ripe for review because they could be changed. According to the Supreme Court in *Abbott Labs* v. *Gardner* (387 U.S. 136), the doctrine is designed "to protect agencies from judicial interference until an administrative decision has been formalized and its effects felt in a concrete way by the challenging parties."

Exhaustion

The *exhaustion doctrine* requires a party to complete all agency appeals procedures before turning to a court for review. That is, parties may not go to the courts until they have exhausted all agency review procedures regarding a new rule or a disciplinary action. An action must be considered final by an agency before proceeding to court.

Scope of Judicial Review

When all procedural requirements have been met, the court of appeals can review an agency action. The court's *scope of review* determines how far it can go in examining the action. The scope of review depends on whether the issue before it involves a question of substantive law, statutory interpretation, or procedure. Each imposes different requirements on the reviewing court.

Review of Substantive Determination

A court's review of an agency's substantive determination generally gets the lowest scope of judicial review. As a rule, the courts yield to the agency's judgment in technical and scientific matters in working out the details of regulations. The courts generally will not find that an agency's actions or decisions are *arbitrary, capricious, or an abuse of discretion* if the following are true:

1. The agency has sufficiently explained the facts and its policy concerns.
2. Those facts have some basis in the agency's record.
3. On the basis of those facts and concerns, a reasonable person could reach the same judgments the agency has reached.

We saw an example of a court review of an agency regulation in the *Public Citizen* case.

Review of Statutory Interpretation

A court's review of an agency's statutory interpretation is given a greater scope of review. In contrast to the technical judgments required of the agency in implementing a statute, the courts have responsibility for the interpretation of the meaning of statutes enacted by Congress. That is, the courts determine whether an agency has gone beyond the authority it was granted by Congress. Although the courts give great weight to the interpretation of a statute by the agency responsible for its implementation, they will reject that interpretation if it does not comply with interpretations by established principles of statutory construction.

Review of Procedural Requirements

The court's review of an agency's procedural requirements is provided the most intense scope of review. The court is responsible for ensuring that the agency has not acted unfairly or in disregard of statutorily prescribed procedures. The courts are regarded as the authority on procedural fair play.

CONTROLS ON AGENCIES

In addition to having checks imposed on them by judicial review, agencies are checked by Congress. Since it delegates powers to an agency, Congress may revoke those powers. This section discusses various measures that Congress uses or has considered using in providing those checks.

Direct Controls on Agencies

Public awareness and concern about the costs and effectiveness of regulation, as well as pressure from special interest groups, prompts responses from Congress. The most immediate control mechanism enjoyed by Congress is the ability to control agency activity through the budget process. The president, appointing top agency officials, helps control agency agendas. In addition, members of Congress have proposed bills calling for, among other things, mandatory *cost-benefit analysis*.

Agency Appropriations and Executive Orders

Administrative agencies depend on public funding to support their activities. Congress requires agencies to report on programs and activities on a regular basis, and congressional committees frequently hold oversight hearings. Administrative agencies submit budget requests annually for review by the president and by Congress. The president or Congress can recommend cuts in an agency's budget if either is opposed to some of the agency's activities. The final budget, which is very detailed, is agreed upon by the House, the Senate, and the president. Through budget appropriations, Congress can mandate that an agency address specific issues. In the *Public Citizen* case, we saw that Congress ordered a new regulation on tire safety. Congress can also prohibit an agency from working on other specific issues. Budget control gives the president, and especially Congress, the ability to control details of agency regulatory policy.

Presidents have used Executive Orders to instruct administrative agencies to undertake certain tasks. Presidents issue several dozen Executive Orders each year (see http://www.nara.gov/fedreg/eo.html). Many are trivial, but some have major policy implications, such as President Johnson's order that affirmative action programs in hiring are required of all companies that contract with the federal government. Congress can pass legislation to undo an Executive Order, or it may be challenged and stricken by the courts as an abuse of executive power, but it remains a strong tool for the president to allocate agency resources.

Cost-Benefit and Risk Analysis

Mandatory cost-benefit analysis requires agencies to weigh the costs and benefits of new regulations. When the costs exceed the benefits derived from a regulation, the regulation is more easily challenged for reasonableness. The same holds true for risk-assessment requirements that estimate the risk reduction achieved by regulations that affect health and safety.

The Data Quality Act, passed in 2000 and enforced by the Office of Management and Budget (OMB), requires agencies to ensure the quality of the analysis done to support regulations. If scientific, technical, and economic information standards are not met, affected parties may challenge a regulation for not being supported by adequate analysis. OMB, reviewing proposed regulations, can also send a proposed regulation back to an agency for not having met sufficiently strong scientific standards.

Indirect Controls on Agencies

Congress has passed several laws that can have the effect of indirectly controlling the power of administrative agencies. Through those acts, which include the Freedom of Information Act, the Privacy Act, and the Government in the Sunshine Act, Congress made it easier for parties outside an agency to obtain information in the possession of the agency.

Freedom of Information Act

The *Freedom of Information Act (FOIA)* makes most documents held by federal agencies available to the public. Unless the document falls within certain exempted categories, it must be released upon a request by a citizen. Exempted are trade secrets, documents related to national security, and documents that would, if disclosed, invade personal privacy.

Privacy Act

The *Privacy Act* is intended to give citizens more control over what information is collected about them and how that information is used. It requires that unless an exception applies, notice and prior consent are required before an agency can disclose information that concerns and identifies an individual. Individuals are given the right to access agency records and to request amendments to correct inaccuracies. The Act provides that individuals can enforce their rights in federal district courts.

Government in the Sunshine Act

Congress enacted the *Government in the Sunshine Act* to limit secret meetings by agencies. Under the Act, the public is entitled to at least one week's notice of the time, place, and subject matter of any agency meeting. The agency must specify whether the meeting is to be open or closed to the public. An agency action taken at a meeting in violation of the Act is not invalid because of the violation; some other basis for overturning an agency action would have to be established. A court may grant an injunction against future violations of the Act.

The Act lists situations in which meetings may be closed. An open meeting is not required, for example, when the meeting might concern matters to be kept secret in the interest of national defense or disclosure of trade secrets or protected financial information.

SUMMARY

- Administrative agencies are created by Congress and granted legislative, investigative, adjudicatory, and enforcement powers.
- The first federal agency was the Interstate Commerce Commission, established by Congress in 1887 to regulate railroads. The most significant growth periods of agencies took place during the Great Depression of the 1930s and the "social reform" era of the 1960s and 1970s.
- Administrative law consists of legal rules defining the authority and structure of administrative agencies, specifying procedural requirements, and defining the roles of government bodies (particularly the courts) in their relationship with agencies. The primary administrative law is the Administrative Procedures Act (APA).
- Administrative regulations are classified as legislative (substantive), which are major regulations issued under grants of power from Congress; interpretative, which help to explain legislative regulations and statutes; and procedural, which detail the steps an agency uses in its rulemaking procedures and enforcement.
- Agencies may require businesses that are subject to regulation to volunteer information related to the regulations on a regular basis, including reporting violations.
- Agencies may also watch for violations, including inspecting business property, and can gather information that is provided when requested or may be forced from a business by use of subpoena.
- Agencies perform regulatory responsibilities by the use of informal and formal procedures. Informal procedures, which consist of tests and inspections, are not subject to the procedural requirements of the APA. Formal procedures, which include adjudicatory hearings, must meet the APA's procedural requirements.
- Agencies may issue fines, citations, or other penalties to rule violators. The violators can accept a penalty or contest it at an agency hearing before an administrative law judge, whose decision can be reviewed by the head of an agency and then by the federal courts of appeals. Criminal charges by an agency must be filed in federal court.
- Judicial review imposes a check on agency actions. To obtain review, the party challenging the action must meet the procedural requirements of jurisdiction, reviewability, standing, ripeness, and exhaustion.
- Congress provides direct and indirect checks on the administrative agencies. The direct checks provided by Congress include control over agency appropriations, reporting requirements, sunset laws, and cost-benefit analysis. Indirect checks include such acts as the Freedom of Information Act, the Privacy Act, and the Government in the Sunshine Act.

REVIEW AND DISCUSSION QUESTIONS

1. Define the following terms and concepts:

   enabling statute   judicial review
   rulemaking   standing
   substantive rules   ripeness
   interpretative rules   exhaustion
   procedural rules

2. What advantages does an agency have over the judicial system in monitoring business behavior?
3. Congress gives some regulatory agencies it creates very general mandates. Congress may say something to the effect of "go regulate the environment in the public interest." The agencies then devise regulations to execute the "intent" of Congress. Should Congress be more specific when it creates agencies?

CASE QUESTIONS

4. Ohio Cast Products was cited by the Occupational Safety and Health Administration (OSHA) for overexposing a worker to silica in the atmosphere at the workstation. Ohio Cast agreed that the air sample taken at the workstation was accurate, but the company contended that OSHA's interpretation of the law requiring workers to be protected from breathing too much silica was not reasonable. OSHA measured all dust, including silica, that workers were exposed to; Ohio Cast contended that only silica should have been measured, not other dusts in the atmosphere, and therefore OSHA's interpretation of the law was not reasonable. The Occupational Safety and Health Review Commission upheld the citation and $8,000 fine; Ohio Cast appealed. Does OSHA have the authority to measure dust besides silica dust, which is the focus of the regulation? [*Ohio Cast Products, Inc.* v. *Occupational Safety & Health Review Comm.*, 246 F.3d 791 (6th Cir., 2001)]
5. Prison inmates sentenced to die by lethal injection sued the Food and Drug Administration for refusing to take action against the makers and users of the drugs used for lethal injection. That is, the prisoners claimed that the drugs violated FDA standards and thus should be subject to an enforcement action to prevent violations of FDA rules. The FDA claimed that it did not have to review drugs or undertake enforcement actions that it did not think necessary. The prisoners claimed that the FDA had to hold all drugs to the same standards and that enforcement action had to be taken. Were the prisoners correct? [*Heckler* v. *Chaney*, 470 U.S. 821, 105 S.Ct. 1649 (1985)]

 Check your answer at http://meiners.westbuslaw.com

6. Dewey owned a mine in Wisconsin. He refused to allow agents of the Department of Labor to inspect the mine without a search warrant. The Department of Labor wanted to determine whether violations discovered in a previous search had been corrected. The Federal Mine Safety and Health Act authorizes a specific number of warrantless inspections, but it does not dictate the procedures that inspectors must follow. Did the warrantless search violate Dewey's Fourth Amendment rights? [*Donovan* v. *Dewey*, 452 U.S. 594, 101 S.Ct. 2534 (1981)]
7. The U.S. Department of Transportation (DOT) adopted a regulation that would require new cars to have either air bags or automatic seat belts (the kind that strap you to the seat when you get in the car). The carmakers protested that this would be too expensive and would not work. In 1981, DOT, under new leadership, repealed the regulation, saying that since it had evidence that people would unhook the seat belts, the regulation was not effective. Car insurance companies sued DOT, claiming that the agency could not repeal the regulation. The court of appeals held that since the repeal was not based on sufficient

evidence, the regulation must be reimposed. What did the Supreme Court have to say? [*Motor Vehicle Manufacturers Assn.* v. *State Farm*, 463 U.S. 29, 103 S.Ct. 2856 (1983)]

 Check your answer at <u>http://meiners.westbuslaw.com</u>

8. OSHA issued a directive establishing a "Cooperative Compliance Program" directed at workplaces with worse-than-average safety records. Companies that "volunteer" to comply with the requirements of the directive will be removed from the "primary inspection list" and have a much lower chance of inspection. The Chamber of Commerce petitioned for review, contending that OSHA should have published the directive for public comment as it does for most new rules before they are issued. OSHA contended that the directive was not a rule subject to public comment and inspection before publication. Is that correct? [*Chamber of Commerce* v. *Dept. of Labor*, 174 F.3d 206 (D.C. Cir., 1999)]

9. The EPA proposed expensive new pollution control regulations for coal-burning electricity plants. After receiving comments in the public review period from those who opposed the higher electricity prices that would result from the pollution controls, and informal feedback from members of Congress, the EPA published its final regulations, which were not as strict as originally proposed. Some environmental groups sued, claiming the EPA had been influenced by informal comments and that such comments to agency heads are illegal or should be in the public record. Did the regulation stand? [*Sierra Club* v. *Costle*, 657 F.2d 298 (D.C. Cir., 1981)]

 Check your answer at <u>http://meiners.westbuslaw.com</u>

10. The Sierra Club sued the Secretary of the Interior for allowing the lease of federal land to be used for a ski resort (after studying the issue and deciding such use was appropriate). The club claimed that the change in the use of the land would adversely change the area's aesthetics and ecology. The court of appeals held that the club did not have standing to sue. Was that correct? [*Sierra Club* v. *Morton*, 405 U.S. 727, 92 S.Ct. 1361 (1972)]

11. Under the Immigration Reform and Control Act of 1986, an alien illegally present in the United States who wanted to get permission to reside in the country permanently had to apply for temporary resident status by showing that he had a continuous physical presence in the country for a certain time period. The Immigration and Naturalization Service issued regulations concerning "continuous physical presence" and other terms of the statute. Class actions were filed on behalf of aliens who would not be eligible for legalization under the regulations issued. Could the suits go forward? [*Reno* v. *Catholic Social Services*, 509 U.S. 43, 113 S.Ct. 2485 (1993)]

 Check your answer at <u>http://meiners.westbuslaw.com</u>

12. A freedom of information request was filed with the Nuclear Regulatory Commission for information about nuclear plant operations that had been provided voluntarily by the plants to the commission on the agreement that the information be kept confidential, even though it did not involve trade secrets. The commission refused to release the information, claiming it would injure its working relationship with the plant operators. Was this a proper reason to refuse the information request? [*Critical Mass Energy Project* v. *Nuclear Regulatory Comm.*, 731 F.2d 554 (D.C. Cir., 1990)]

ETHICS QUESTIONS

13. Most regulatory matters are settled informally; only a small number result in litigation. When a company is in a dispute with a federal agency, it knows that if it does not reach a settlement, there can be costly litigation. From the perspective of the government agency, the litigation is costless—the taxpayers foot the bill. Agencies know that the threat of costly litigation enhances their chance of extracting a settlement from the company. Should the government use this leverage to extract more in a settlement than it knows it would be likely to get in a court-resolved dispute?

14. Suppose you are an administrator at the Environmental Protection Agency. It has been reported that a plant in a small town is in violation of the environmental laws. If you enforce the laws' requirements, the plant will be forced to shut down. The plant is the major source of employment for the town, and its closure would impose severe economic hardships. Should that fact play a role in regulatory enforcement?

15. The Environmental Protection Agency requires your company to self-report pollution discharges daily. It is your job to make those reports. The reports could be easily fudged if the company exceeded its designated limits. Excessive discharges would cost the company $25,000 for each day its limit is exceeded. One morning, your superior forgot to start the pollution control device, and the designated amount of pollution was exceeded. Your superior strongly implies that you should fudge the figures. You are worried that if you don't, you might be fired. Should you report the correct figures to the EPA? Would your answer be different if you knew whether or not the excessive pollution caused any damage?

INTERNET ASSIGNMENT

http://www.gpoaccess.gov
http://firstgov.gov
http://www.infoctr.edu/fwl
http://www.nass.org/acr/internet.html

Federal agencies, and the regulations they impose, often have a significant effect upon industry and commerce. The Internet exercises for other chapters will address agencies, such as the Securities and Exchange Commerce, which impact particular industries. Agencies, pursuant to their Congressional mandates, promulgate regulations that are proposed and first published in the *Federal Register*, then later incorporated into the *Code of Federal Regulations*. Information about federal agencies is published annually in the *United States Government Manual*. The U.S. Government Printing Office has offered its electronic resource, GPO Access, for many years. More recently, the U.S. government has launched its official web port, FirstGov, which includes an A-Z Agency Index. The Federal Web Locator is still useful for linking federal agencies. Information exclusively about the administrative law of individual states can be found at the web site of the National Association of Secretaries of State.

Find the federal agency of your choice using the Federal Web Locator. Using the *U.S. Government Manual*, find the statute by which the agency was created.

Give the URL for the administrative code of the state in which you live, if available.

ELEMENTS OF TRADITIONAL BUSINESS LAW

PART 2

COMMON-LAW RULES EVOLVED OVER CENTURIES as judges and juries responded to changes in business and social norms. The common law is the traditional basis of private legal relationships that dominate the business legal environment. While the common law evolved differently than the major codes of other nations, the basic elements of how private relationships are governed are similar around the world. Over the years, the common law has been modified and codified in various statutes and regulations.

These chapters review the core topics of what traditionally has been called business law. This part of the law concerns the rights and obligations of parties to each other in business formation and in various working relationships.

Contracts, especially those formed in domestic and in international sales of goods, are a key part of business relationships. To make contracts work, credit is often extended and various forms of negotiable instruments are often used. We begin by studying tort law—the common-law obligations and rights we have to protect the sanctity of each others' person and property. We also study the law of property itself—physical property and, of rapidly growing importance, intellectual property.

Chapter 6 | *Elements of Torts*

Involvement in litigation is distressing to most business operators, but fear of tort suit may be the worst of all. Other areas of law are more predictable and more likely to be within control. Tort suits tend to arise from unexpected instances that involve momentary carelessness or bad behavior. Talk on your cellphone to a customer while making a delivery and you might cause an accident by running a stop sign. Your slipup makes you responsible for damages that could be catastrophic. Leave a wet spot on the floor of your store and you could be responsible for a customer who falls and breaks a hip. Become furious at the stupid mistakes of an employee that cause you to lose valuable business and you might do something foolish that results in a rash of suits for your actions.

The biggest jury verdict in history was a tort case. In 1984, Pennzoil agreed to buy a large share of Getty Oil. Texaco, knowing of the agreement, offered more money for Getty and got Getty's owners to refuse Pennzoil's offer in favor of Texaco's. Pennzoil then sued Texaco for the common-law tort of inducement of breach of contract. A Houston jury awarded Pennzoil $10.5 billion in damages. Texaco did not have that much cash and could not raise it, so a settlement of about one-third the verdict was agreed upon. While the dollars in that case are huge, the point we see in many tort cases is the same—juries often place a high value on the enforcement of legal rights.

Like other parts of the common law, the law of torts evolves through case decisions that reflect social values, community standards, and the way we deal with each other in the current environment. In recent years, tort law has become a major issue for business; tort liability is a significant expense, and some claim that tort judgments bear little relation to reality.

THE SCOPE OF TORT LAW

Tort has many definitions. The word is derived from the Latin *tortus* (twisted) and means "wrong" in French. Although the word faded from common use years ago, it has acquired meaning in the law. A *tort* is generally defined as a civil wrong, other than a breach of contract, for which the law provides a remedy. Tort is a breach of a duty owed to another that causes harm. That is, liability is imposed for conduct that unreasonably interferes with the interests of another.

Role of Tort Law

Many accidents result in personal injury and property damage. To have a legal action in tort, the injury suffered by a person or property must legally be the consequence of the actions of another. In a tort action, the party whose interests have been injured sues the party allegedly responsible.

As discussed in Chapter 1, one act may result in both a criminal case and a tort case. For example, O.J. Simpson was tried by the state of California for murder but found not guilty. In a tort suit that followed, based on the same incident, he was held responsible for assault and battery. The criminal case is brought by the government against the alleged wrongdoer for violating a rule imposed by the legislature. The victim of the crime is a witness in a criminal case. The criminal case does not provide compensation to the injured party. The victim is the plaintiff in the tort suit, hiring an attorney to sue for compensation for injuries wrongfully inflicted by the defendant (the accused criminal in the criminal case). In practice, it is not common for there to be both a criminal case and a tort case evolving from the same incident, since most criminals do not have enough assets to be worth suing in tort.

While most criminal acts involve a tort, most torts do not involve criminal acts. The rules vary from state to state, but the principles are similar across the states. Tort law is private law. It is intended, as the Alaska Supreme Court has said, to place an injured party "as nearly as possible in the position he would have occupied had it not been for the defendant's tort." In a small percentage of tort suits, punitive damages are awarded in addition to compensation for injury. Punitive damages are intended to punish the defendant (financially) for malicious behavior and to send a message that such behavior will not be tolerated.

Business and Torts

As we are about to review, torts are classified on the basis of how harm is inflicted: negligently, intentionally, or without fault (strict liability). Regardless of how a tort is classified, businesses become involved in a tort action in one of three ways: (1) a person is harmed by the actions of a business or its employees, (2) a person is harmed by a product manufactured or distributed by the business, or (3) a business is harmed by the wrongful actions of another business or person. The principles of tort law covered in this chapter are applicable to persons in everyday life, but the focus is on business applications. Chapter 7 discusses torts that are peculiar to business. Chapter 8 discusses torts that are particular to property.

TORTS BASED ON NEGLIGENCE

Torts based on *negligence* protect individuals from harm from others' unintentional but legally careless conduct. As a general rule, we have a duty to conduct ourselves in all activities so as to not create an unreasonable risk of harm or injury to others. Persons and businesses that do not exercise due care in their conduct will be liable for negligence in a wide range of torts if the following elements can be shown by an injured party:

1. The wrongdoer owed a duty to the injured party (often known as the duty of ordinary care).
2. The duty of care owed to the injured party was breached through some act or omission on the part of the wrongdoer (often this breach itself is termed "negligence").
3. There is a causal connection between the wrongdoer's negligent conduct and the resulting harm to the injured party.
4. The injured party suffered actual harm or damage recognized as actionable by law as a result of the negligent conduct.

Negligence is conduct—an act or omission (failure to act)—by a person (or business) that results in harm to another to whom the person owes a duty of care. In contrast to an intentional tort, in negligence the harmful results of a person's conduct are not based on an intended invasion of another person's rights or interests. If the person's conduct creates an *unreasonable risk of harm* to others, such conduct may be termed negligent even though there was no intent to cause harm. Thus, the person who intentionally runs over another person while driving has committed the intentional tort of battery. A person who unintentionally runs over another while driving carelessly may have committed a tort of battery based on negligence.

INTERNATIONAL   *Perspective*

Tort Liability in France

In France, as in other code nations, a wrongdoer's liability is established in the Civil Code. In general, the Civil Code makes a wrongdoer liable for damages that result from his or her negligence. In particular, the Civil Code specifically permits recovery for economic loss arising from negligent conduct (quasi-delit). The only limitations on damages are that they must be the immediate and direct consequence of the tort.

The wrongdoer's liability, however, is conditioned on finding the specific elements of the tort. The tort must be defined in the Civil Code, which is more restrictive than the general common-law standards.

First, the harm, either physical or economic, must be specific and certain. Second, there must be a finding of fault on the part of the negligent party. The U.S. doctrine of strict liability in tort is not present to any significant extent in the French system. Third, there must be a finding of causality, and the courts use the notion of proximate cause. Finally, the extent of the harm and the recoverable loss is determined by a judge and not by a jury.

Duty of Care

In determining whether a person's conduct is negligent, that is, violates the duty of care in any given situation, the law applies a standard of reasonableness. The standard is usually stated as *ordinary care* or *due care* as measured against the conduct of a hypothetical person—the *reasonable person.*

The reasonable person represents a standard of how persons in the relevant community ought to behave. If the person is a skilled professional, such as a doctor, financial consultant, or executive, the standard is that of a reasonably skilled, competent, and experienced person who is a qualified member of that profession. In determining whether a person's conduct was negligent, the question is, What would a reasonable qualified person have done under the same or similar circumstances? If the conduct was not that of a reasonable person in the eyes of the jury or the judge, the person has failed the reasonableness test and has acted negligently.

The reasonableness standard or the reasonable person standard is a theoretical concept in law. It describes a person who acts in a reasonable manner under the circumstances. Although the law does not require perfection, errors in judgment must be reasonable or excusable under the circumstances, or negligence will be found. The *Bethlehem Steel* decision indicates how negligence applies to parties responsible for providing accurate financial information.

Bethlehem Steel Corp. v. Ernst & Whinney

Supreme Court of Tennessee (1991)
822 S.W.2d 592

CASE BACKGROUND   *Ernst & Whinney, an accounting firm, prepared an audited financial report for E. L. Jackson Manufacturing. Ernst knew that Jackson needed the report for Bethlehem to show that Jackson's finances were strong enough so that Bethlehem would sell it steel on credit. The report overstated the financial status of Jackson, which went into bankruptcy owing Bethlehem money. Bethlehem sued Ernst for damages resulting from negligent preparation of its audit report. The jury awarded Bethlehem $400,000 in damages, but the judge set aside the verdict and ordered a new trial. The court of appeals reversed the order setting aside the damages and affirmed the grant of a new trial. Parties appealed.*

CASE DECISION   Reid, Chief Justice.

* * *

In fairness, accountants should not be liable in circumstances where they are unaware of the use to which their opinions will be put. Instead, their liability should be commensurate with those persons or classes of persons who they know will rely on their work. With such knowledge the auditor can, through purchase of liability insurance, setting fees, and adopting other protective measures appropriate to the risk, prepare accordingly.

A majority of jurisdictions have adopted the rule set forth in §552 of the *Restatement (Second) of Torts* (1977), which provides, in part:

(1) One who, in the course of his business, profession or employment, or in any other transaction in which he has a pecuniary interest, supplies false information for the guidance of others in their business transactions, is subject to liability for pecuniary loss caused to them by their justifiable reliance upon the information, if he fails to exercise reasonable care or competence in obtaining or communicating the information.

(2). . . the liability stated in Subsection (1) is limited to loss suffered

(a) by the person or one of a limited group of persons for whose benefit and guidance he intends to supply the information or knows that the recipient intends to supply it; and

(b) through reliance upon it in a transaction that he intends the information to influence or knows that the recipient so intends or in a substantially similar transaction.

* * *

Tennessee has adopted the *Restatement (Second) of Torts* §552 as the guiding principle in negligent misrepresentation actions against other professionals and business persons. . . . This Court held that a subcontractor, despite lack of privity, may pursue an action against a construction manager based on negligent misrepresentation. . . . Another case . . . found that an attorney may be liable to a third party for negligence even if no attorney-client relationship was intended. The . . . Court recognized, as follows, that the Restatement principles could extend to all professions. . . .

continues

This Court adopted the principles later approved by the American Law Institute in *Restatement (Second) of Torts*, §552 (1977) in connection with the liability of business or professional persons who negligently supply false information for the guidance of others in their business transactions. These principles, of course, could apply to attorneys as well as to land surveyors, accountants, or title companies.

The conclusion is that Section 552 of the Restatement is the appropriate standard for actions by third parties against accountants based on negligent misrepresentation in this state.

* * *

The judgment of the Court of Appeals is affirmed, and the case is remanded for a new trial consistent with this opinion. Costs are adjudged one-half to the appellant and one-half to the appellee.

QUESTIONS FOR ANALYSIS

1. How does a court determine whether an accountant or other professional has exercised reasonable care in the preparation of work?

2. In some states, only parties that have a direct contractual relationship with an accountant (or other professional) may sue if they suffer a loss because of negligence in preparation of professional work. That is, Bethlehem could not have recovered in those states. Does it make sense that liability for negligence should apply only if the professional has a direct relationship with the party using its work?

Causation

A basic element of a tort in negligence is a *causation* between one party's act and another's injury. For a party to have caused an injury to another and be held negligent, the act must have been the cause in fact and the proximate cause of the other's injury.

Cause in Fact

Cause in fact is established by evidence showing that a person's conduct is the actual cause of an event because the event would not have occurred without it. Courts express this in the form of a rule commonly referred to as the *but for* or *sine qua non* rule. That is, the injury would not have occurred *but for* the conduct of the tortfeasor. A hotel's failure to install a proper fire escape, for example, is not the cause in fact of the death of a person who suffocated in bed from smoke. The person would have died regardless of whether the hotel had a proper fire escape.

Proximate Cause

In many jurisdictions, the injured party must prove that the defendant's act was not only the cause in fact of the injury but also the proximate cause of the injury. *Proximate cause* limits liability to consequences that bear a reasonable relationship to the negligent conduct. Consequences that are too remote or too far removed from negligent conduct will not result in liability.

A person's act may set off a chain of events and injuries that were not *foreseeable*. The principal cause in fact of the Great Chicago Fire of 1871 that destroyed much of the city may have been Mrs. O'Leary's negligent conduct of leaving an oil lamp in the barn for her cow to kick, but no court would hold her liable for the full consequences of her initial act. The chain of events must be foreseeable, as the high court of New York discusses in the famous *Palsgraf* decision.

Palsgraf v. Long Island Railroad Company

Court of Appeals of New York
248 N.Y. 339, 162 N.E. 99 (1928)

CASE BACKGROUND *Helen Palsgraf was waiting on a platform to catch a train. As another train began to leave the station, a man carrying a package ran to catch it. He jumped on the train, but looked like he might fall off. A guard, holding the door open for him on the train, reached to help him, while another guard, standing on the platform, pushed the man from behind. The man dropped the package onto the rails. The package contained fireworks that exploded. The shock from the explosion caused scales located on the platform to fall, striking the plaintiff and injuring her seriously.*

Palsgraf sued the railroad for the negligence of its employees during this event. The jury found in her favor, and the appellate division affirmed the jury's decision. The defendant appealed.

CASE DECISION Cardozo, Chief Justice.

* * *

The conduct of defendant's guard . . . was not wrong in its relation to the plaintiff, standing far away. Relative to her it was not negligence at all. Negligence is not actionable unless it involves the invasion of a legally protected interest, the violation of a right. "Proof of negligence in the air, so to speak, will not do." "Negligence is the absence of care, according to the circumstances." The plaintiff, as she stood upon the platform of the station, might claim to be protected against intentional invasion of her bodily security. Such invasion is not charged. She might claim to be protected against unintentional invasion by conduct involving . . . an unreasonable hazard that such invasion would ensue. . . . If no hazard was apparent to the eye of ordinary vigilance, an act innocent and harmless . . . with reference to her did not take to itself the quality of a tort because it happened to be a wrong, though apparently not one involving the risk of bodily insecurity, with reference to someone else. "In every instance, before negligence can be predicated of a given act, back of the act must be sought and found a duty to the individual complaining, the observance of which would have averted or avoided the injury. The ideas of negligence and duty are strictly correlative."

* * *

The argument for the plaintiff is built upon the shifting meanings of such words as "wrong" and "wrongful" and shares their instability. What the plaintiff must show is a "wrong" to herself; i.e., a violation of her own right, and not merely a wrong to someone else, nor conduct "wrongful" because unsocial. . . .

The range of reasonable apprehension is at times a question for the court, and at times, if varying inferences are possible, a question for the jury. Here, by concession, there was nothing in the situation to suggest to the most cautious mind that the parcel wrapped in newspaper would spread wreckage through the station. If the guard had thrown it down knowingly and willfully, he would not have threatened the plaintiff's safety, so far as appearances could warn him. His conduct would not have involved, even then, an unreasonable probability of invasion of her bodily security. Liability can be no greater where the act is inadvertent. . . .

Negligence is not a tort unless it results in the commission of a wrong, and the commission of a wrong imports the violation of a right, in this case, we are told, the right to be protected against interference with one's bodily security. But bodily security is protected, not against all forms of interference or aggression, but only against some. One who seeks redress at law does not make out a cause of action by showing without more than that there has been damage to his person. If the harm was not willful, he must show that the act as to him had possibilities of danger so many and apparent as to entitle him to be protected against the doing of it though the harm was unintended.

* * *

The judgment of the Appellate Division and that of the Trial Term should be reversed, and the complaint dismissed, with costs in all courts.

QUESTIONS FOR ANALYSIS

1. For the plaintiff to recover, what is the court requiring that she demonstrate?

2. Why did the plaintiff sue the railroad company? Could she have made a better case against the owner of the fireworks?

Most courts stand by *Palsgraf* today. Various state supreme courts have restated the proposition. The Missouri court has held that the duty owed by the plaintiff to the defendant "is generally measured by whether or not a reasonably prudent person would have anticipated danger and provided against it. . . ." The New Mexico court explained: "A duty to the individual is closely intertwined with the foreseeability of injury to *that individual* resulting from an activity conducted with less than reasonable care. . . ." And the Texas court stated that "before liability will be imposed, there must be sufficient evidence indicating that the defendant knew of or should have known that harm would eventually befall a victim."

Intervening Conduct

One issue in determining proximate cause is the possibility of *intervening conduct*. If the causal connection between a person's act and the resulting harm to another is broken by an intervening act or event, there is a *superseding cause*. If the causal relationship between the defendant's act and resulting harm is in fact broken by the intervening act, which was unforeseeable under the circumstances, the defendant will likely not be liable.

Suppose Himarios Construction has dug a ditch across a public sidewalk to lay some pipe. When the workers quit for the night, they negligently leave the ditch uncovered and do not place any warnings. That night, if Hamilton intentionally shoves Yandle into the ditch and Yandle is hurt, Hamilton's act is intervening conduct that relieves Himarios of liability. However, suppose Yandle had accidentally fallen into the ditch at night and was drowning because it was filled with rainwater. Frierson dives into the ditch to save Yandle, and Frierson drowns; Himarios Construction will be liable to Yandle and Frierson. Because *danger invites rescue*, the common law holds the negligent party responsible for the losses suffered by those who attempt to save people who are in danger as the result of the torts of others.

Substantial Factor

Proximate cause has been criticized as difficult to understand and apply. The California Supreme Court, in *Mitchell* v. *Gonzales* (819 P.2d 872), joined some other states in replacing the *proximate cause rule* in negligence actions in favor of the *legal cause rule*, which uses the *substantial factor test*.

The substantial factor test, which was developed by the *Restatement (Second) of Torts* and is believed to be clearer to juries, says: "A legal cause of injury is a cause which is a substantial factor in bringing about the injury." That is, as the Pennsylvania Supreme Court has explained, the jury is asked to determine whether a defendant's conduct "has such an effect in producing the harm as to lead reasonable men to regard

ISSUE
Spotter

When Is a Liability Release Effective?

You help run a resort that in the winter offers snowtubing. Patrons pay to slide down a snow hill on an inflated tube. Since they can fall off and get hurt, you have them sign a liability release that says they will not sue the resort if they get hurt while snowtubing. Is such a release sufficient? What if they claim the injury was due to the negligence of the resort? Will the liability release protect your company against successful litigation that could bankrupt the resort?

it as a cause, using that word in the popular sense." As Exhibit 6.1 indicates on page 148, defendants could be liable even if their negligent behavior was only one factor contributing to an injury, so long as it was found to be a substantial factor.

Defenses to a Negligence Action

Even if an injured party has established the required elements of negligence, the party may be denied compensation if the defendant establishes a *valid defense*. As a general rule, any defense to an intentional tort is also available in a negligence action. In addition, other defenses are available to defendants in negligence actions, including assumption of risk and comparative negligence.

Assumption of Risk

An injured party who voluntarily assumed the risk of harm arising from the negligent or reckless conduct of another may not be allowed to recover compensation for such harm. Such action by the injured party is called *assumption of risk* and creates a defense for the negligent defendant. The defense requires that the injured party knew or should have known of the risk and that the risk was voluntarily assumed. Thus, spectators at sporting events such as baseball games assume the risk for injuries that result from the usual playing of the game and the reaction of the crowd.

Assumption of risk is an affirmative defense as we see in the *Lilya* case. It must be specifically raised by the defendant to take advantage of it. When established, assumption of risk usually bars the plaintiff from recovery, even if the defendant was negligent.

Lilya v. Greater Gulf State Fair, Inc.

Supreme Court of Alabama
855 So.2d 1049 (2003)

CASE BACKGROUND *John Lilya attended a fair on property owned by Gulf State Fair. He decided to ride a mechanical bull. He paid $5 to ride the bull and signed a "Participant Agreement, Release, and Acknowledgment of Risk." The form stated that the rider accepted the possibility of paralysis and death and that the rider would not sue the operator even for "negligent acts or omissions." Lilya fell off the bull, got back on, but fell again and broke his neck.*

Lilya sued Gulf State Fair for negligence in its operation for failure to keep the fair in a reasonably safe condition. The trial court granted summary judgment for the fair. Lilya appealed.

CASE DECISION Houston, Justice.

* * *

Gulf State Fair would owe Lilya, its invitee, the duty to use reasonable care . . . .

If there is a dangerous condition on the premises that is not "open and obvious," the premises owner has a duty "to give sufficient warning so that, by the use of ordinary care, the danger can be avoided."

Here, the only evidence of danger stemming from the mechanical bull ride is the most open and obvious characteristic of the ride: the possibility of falling off the mechanical bull. Lilya was aware that the two riders who had ridden the mechanical bull immediately before he rode it had fallen off. He noticed the thick floor mat, and he knew that the mat was there to protect riders when they fell. Also, he signed a release that explicitly stated, among other things, 1) that riding the mechanical bull involved inherent risks, 2) that injury was a possibility, 3) that the risks included "falling off or being thrown from the bull which could result in musculoskeletal injuries including head, neck, and back injuries," and 4) that Lilya understood the risks and rode voluntarily.

continues

Additionally, the very name of the ride—"Rolling Thunder"—hanging on a banner above the ride, gives a somewhat graphic indication of what is the very nature of bull riding: an extermely turbulent ride the challenge of which is to *hang on and not fall off*. . . .

"One who takes part in such a sport accepts the dangers that inhere in it so far as they are obvious and necessary. . . ."

Affirmed.

QUESTIONS FOR ANALYSIS

1. Do you think Lilya fully appreciated the risk involved? Does it make sense that someone would spend $5 to risk being paralyzed or killed?

2. Was the ride operator negligent in its operation of the bull?

Comparative Negligence

Under *comparative negligence* (which replaced an old rule called contributory negligence), damages are reduced by the percentage of the injuries caused by the plaintiff's own negligence.

For example, in *Wassell* v. *Adams* (865 F.2d 849), a woman opened the door to her hotel room in the middle of the night after she heard a knock on it. She was assaulted by an unknown person. The jury found both the hotel and the woman to be negligent. The hotel was held responsible for 3 percent of the injury that occurred; the woman was 97 percent responsible. When the negligence is compared this way, the damages are allocated by percent of responsibility. Here, the damages were $850,000, so the woman recovered three percent of that sum from the hotel; she was responsible for the rest. Many states have adopted a rule that if the plaintiff is 50 percent or more responsible, no recovery is allowed.

Exhibit 6.1

Elements of Negligence

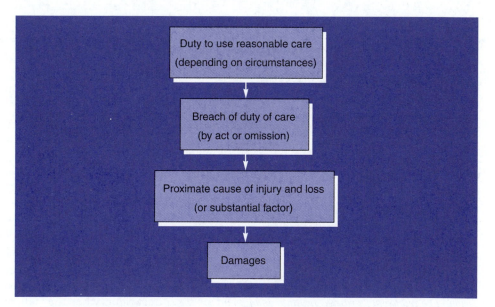

- Duty to use reasonable care (depending on circumstances)
- Breach of duty of care (by act or omission)
- Proximate cause of injury and loss (or substantial factor)
- Damages

INTENTIONAL TORTS AGAINST PERSONS

Some tort liability is based on the intent of a defendant to interfere with the protected interests of a plaintiff. *Intentional torts* are classified on the basis of the interests the law seeks to protect: personal rights and property rights. We first review intentional torts against persons and then look at intentional torts against property. The law imposes a greater degree of responsibility on *tortfeasors* (persons who commit torts) for intentional acts that harm protected interests than for unintentional or negligent acts. As Justice Holmes said, it is the difference between kicking a dog and tripping over a dog. In both cases, the dog gets kicked, but one case is intentional, while the other case is careless.

Establishing Intent

Several elements establish the legal requirement of *intent*. First is the state of mind of the defendant, which means that the person knew what he was doing. Second is that the person knew, or should have known, the possible consequences of his act. Third is knowing that certain results are likely to occur.

While these elements are tied together, there may be legal differences between act, intent, and motive. To be liable, a defendant must have acted. That is, there must have been voluntary actions. An act is to be distinguished from its consequences. Intent is the fact of doing an act, such as firing a gun. The motive—why the person wanted to fire the gun—is legally distinct. If Donna fires a gun into a crowd of people, that is a wrongful act for which she may be held liable regardless of her motives. For her to say that she had no bad motive—that when she fired the gun she really wished no one would be hurt—does not relieve her of liability. Under tort law, she acted voluntarily. She is presumed to have intended the consequences of her act, or should have known what the consequences could be, and so is responsible for them.

Intentional torts are based on *willful* acts that invade protected interests. Intentional torts occur when a jury finds that, under the circumstances, a reasonable person would have known that harmful consequences were likely to follow from the act. Intent matters much less than the act of invading the interests of another person. Even in cases in which the defendant did not have a bad motive (i.e., was playing a trick), if the tortfeasor intended to commit the act that inflicted injury on another, the willful intent would be present for tort liability. Next we review the major categories of torts.

Assault

Assault is intentional conduct directed at a person that places the person in fear of immediate bodily harm or offensive contact. The protected interest is freedom from fear of harmful or offensive contact. Actual contact with the body is not necessary. For example, pointing a gun or swinging a club at a person can constitute an assault. The requirement of "fear" is satisfied if a reasonable person under the same or similar circumstances would have apprehension of bodily harm or offensive contact. An essential element of this tort is that the person in danger of harm or injury must know of the danger of suffering a battery and be apprehensive of its threat. If, for example, a person points a gun at another while the other person is sleeping, there is no assault since there was no fear of harm while sleeping.

Battery

Battery is an unlawful touching—intentional physical contact without consent. The protected interest is freedom from unpermitted contact with one's person. Even if the contact does not cause actual physical harm, it is unlawful if it would offend a reasonable person's sense of dignity. This is the case in many batteries that occur in the workplace that involve inappropriate sexual contact. There may be no physical battering, but the contact is impermissible. The following case involves serious physical harm when a loan collection effort went bad.

Nelson v. Carroll
Court of Appeals of Maryland
735 A.2d 1096, 355 Md. 593 (1999)

CASE BACKGROUND   *Carroll loaned Nelson $8,000. Nelson had repaid $4,200. Carroll, seeking the rest of the money, found Nelson at a nightclub in Baltimore and demanded repayment. Nelson offered $2,300. Carroll, who admitted to being "a little tipsy," pulled out a gun and hit Nelson on the side of the head and then shot him. Carroll was sentenced to seven years in prison for criminal assault. Nelson, who suffered serious health problems from the shooting, sued Carroll for battery. Carroll did not deny that the incident happened; his defense was that the shooting was an accident. The lower court held for Carroll; Nelson appealed.*

CASE DECISION   Chasanow, Judge.

* * *

Our task . . . is to determine whether, considering the essential elements of a tort claim for battery, there is any dispute over material facts from which a jury could conclude that Carroll had not committed a battery when he shot Nelson. Since the only disputed fact relates to whether Carroll shot Nelson accidentally as he was striking him, we need only address the narrow question of whether, under the facts of this case, the defense that the shot was fired accidentally is capable of exonerating Carroll of liability.

A battery occurs when one intends a harmful or offensive contact with another without that person's consent. See *Restatement (Second) of Torts* §13 & cmt. d (1965). "The act in question must be some positive or affirmative action on the part of the defendant." A battery may occur through a defendant's direct or indirect contact with the plaintiff. In this case, Carroll unquestionably committed a battery when he struck Nelson on the side of his head with his handgun. Likewise, an indirect contact, such as occurs when a bullet strikes a victim, may constitute a battery. "It is enough that the defendant sets a force in motion which ultimately produces the result. . . ." Prosser & Keeton, *The Law of Torts* §9, at 40 (5th ed. 1984). Thus, if we assume the element of intent was present, Carroll also committed a battery when he discharged his handgun, striking Nelson with a bullet. . . .

Carroll's defense that he accidentally discharged the handgun requires us to examine the "intent" require-

ment for the tort of battery. It is universally understood that some form of intent is required for battery. See *Restatement (Second) of Torts* §13 (1965) ["An actor is subject to liability to another for battery if . . . he acts *intending* to cause a harmful or offensive contact. . . ." (Emphasis added)]. It is also clear, however, that the intent required is not a specific intent to cause the type of harm that occurred. . . .

On the other hand, a purely accidental touching, or one caused by mere inadvertence, is not enough to establish the intent requirement for battery. . . .

The intent element of battery requires not a specific desire to bring about a certain result, but rather a general intent to unlawfully invade another's physical well-being through a harmful or offensive contact or an apprehension of such a contact. . . .

Thus, innocent conduct that accidentally or inadvertently results in a harmful or offensive contact with another will not give rise to liability, but one will be liable for such contact if it comes about as a result of the actor's volitional conduct where there is an intent to invade the other person's legally protected interests. . . .

* * *

The law imposes upon Carroll the responsibility for losses associated with his wrongful actions. It is of no import that he may not have intended to actually shoot Nelson since the uncontested facts demonstrate that he did intend to invade Nelson's legally protected interests in not being physically harmed or assaulted. He violated those interests by committing an assault and battery when he threatened Nelson with the handgun and struck Nelson on the head.

* * *

[Judgment reversed; case remanded for further proceedings consistent with this opinion.]

QUESTIONS FOR ANALYSIS
1. Was there also an assault in this case, or only a battery? Did it matter that Carroll was drunk?
2. Since Carroll was convicted of the crime of assault, why was he not automatically found liable in tort for the same action?

Assault and Battery

Assault and battery are often the same, although they are separate offenses in some states. The principal distinction is the difference between the requirements of apprehension of an offensive physical contact for an assault and of actual physical contact for a battery. The two torts may exist without each other. An individual may strike another who is asleep, for example, thus committing battery but not assault. On the other hand, an individual may shoot at another and miss, thereby creating an assault but no battery. In common discussion, and in some states, the term *assault* is used to cover assault and battery.

Defenses

There are situations in which assault and battery are permitted. A person accused of a tort may have a *defense*—a legally recognized justification for the actions—that relieves a person of liability. Common defenses are consent, privilege, self-defense, and defense of others and of property. These defenses can be used in any tort but are most common in cases of assault and battery.

Consent occurs when the injured party gave permission to the alleged wrongdoer to interfere with a personal right. Consent may be either expressed or implied by words or conduct. An example of consent in battery includes voluntary participation in a contact sport such as boxing or football.

A *privilege* can give immunity from liability. It can excuse what would have been a tort had the defendant not acted to further an interest of social importance that deserves protection. For example, breaking into a burning store to save someone trapped inside would not be a tort of trespass because of the privilege to save someone.

Self-defense is a privilege based on the need to allow people who are attacked to take steps to protect themselves. The force allowed is that which a reasonable person may have used under the circumstances. A person may take a life to protect his own life, but the measures used in self-defense should be no more than are needed to provide protection. If an attacker has been stopped and made helpless, a person has no right to inflict a beating at that point.

Similarly, *in defense of others* or *in defense of property*, one may use force reasonable under the circumstances. If someone is being threatened with an attack, other persons have a privilege to defend the victim by using force. We have the right to defend our property—to keep others from stealing or abusing it—but again, the force used must be reasonable under the circumstances. Since the law places a higher value on human life than on property, it is unlikely that killing or inflicting serious bodily

ISSUE
Spotter

Dealing with Aggressive Unions

You work for a large construction company that faces disputes with unions. One union tactic is to send a number of union supporters to apply for job openings when the company advertises for workers. The applicants talk to other applicants about joining the union, tie up management time by applying for jobs they do not really want, and, when they have been hired, they begin union-organizing activity. The head of your company has told the union people to stay away, but they send so-called job applicants anyway. One day, knowing that a number of people in line to apply for construction work are in fact union organizers, not serious job applicants, your boss says she wants to lock the doors to the building to hold those people inside until the police can arrive to arrest them for trespassing. Is that a legally defensible move?

injury on someone invading property will be allowed. It is not reasonable to shoot a person stealing a DVD player from a store.

False Imprisonment

The tort of *false imprisonment* (or *false arrest*) is the intentional holding or detaining of a person in violation of a protected interest in freedom from restraint of movement. The detention need not be physical; verbal restraints, such as threats, may be the basis of an action for false imprisonment. Businesses face false imprisonment suits from the detention of suspected shoplifters. It is not uncommon for a suspected shoplifter who is innocent to sue the business for false imprisonment.

Defense

As a result of business lobbying, most states have antishoplifting statutes, which provide businesses with an affirmative defense to a charge of false imprisonment for detaining a shoplifter. The store must have reasonable cause to believe the person has shoplifted, and the person must be delayed for a reasonable time and in a reasonable manner. That defense failed Kmart in the following case.

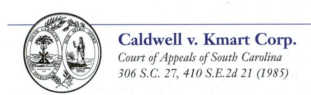

Caldwell v. Kmart Corp.

Court of Appeals of South Carolina
306 S.C. 27, 410 S.E.2d 21 (1985)

CASE BACKGROUND   *A store security employee watched Patricia Caldwell while she shopped at Kmart. Caldwell carried a large purse and was seen studying small items. At times, she bent down out of sight of the guard, who thought she was putting things in her purse. When she left the store, the guard approached her in the parking lot and said he thought she had store merchandise in her purse. Caldwell opened her purse, and although the guard saw no store merchandise in it, he asked her to come back into the store. Caldwell and the guard walked around the store for about fifteen minutes to the areas where Caldwell had been shopping. The guard said six or seven times that he had seen Caldwell put things in her purse. Caldwell left the store when another employee said she could go. She sued Kmart for false imprisonment. The jury awarded her $75,000 in damages plus $100,000 in punitive damages. Kmart appealed.*

CASE DECISION   Cureton, Judge.

* * *

False imprisonment is defined as a deprivation of a person's liberty without justification. To establish a cause of action, the evidence must demonstrate (1) the

defendant restrained the plaintiff, (2) the restraint was intentional, and (3) the restraint was unlawful.

* * *

Caldwell's counsel conceded at oral argument that the initial stop in the parking lot was probably justified but asserted the actions of the guard in walking Caldwell through the store and continuing to accuse her of taking merchandise were not justified as part of a reasonable investigation. We think these facts created an issue for the jury to resolve and the trial judge properly denied the motions of Kmart for directed verdict, judgment notwithstanding the verdict, and new trial based upon the weight of the evidence.

During the course of the trial Caldwell sought to introduce portions of the Kmart loss prevention manual into evidence. The portion in question dealt with shoplifting arrests. Kmart argued the manual was not relevant because the [shoplifting defense] statute, and not the manual, governed the standard by which its conduct was to be judged. The court admitted the manual into evidence. We find no abuse of discretion.

Evidence is relevant when it logically tends to prove or disprove a material issue in dispute. One of the material issues in dispute was the reasonableness of Kmart's actions in investigating the suspected shoplifting. The manual contained guidelines for employees in making shoplifting arrests. For example, it stated as a basic step that before making an apprehension the employee "must see the shoplifter take our property." It also stated the employee should watch the suspected shoplifter continuously and only apprehend the person after he has had an opportunity to pay and is outside the store. Any apprehension should be made in the presence of a witness. Further, any interrogation should be done in privacy in the Loss Prevention Office.

While each case must be dealt with on its own facts, the loss prevention manual was relevant on the material issue of the reasonableness of Kmart's actions.

* * *

The jury awarded Caldwell $75,000 actual damages and $100,000 punitive damages in the false imprisonment claim. Kmart contends the amount of the

verdict necessarily demonstrates the jury was motivated by caprice, passion, and/or other considerations not supported by the evidence.

* * *

Although this is undoubtedly a large verdict, we are not convinced it was motivated by caprice, passion, prejudice, or other improper considerations. Affirmed.

QUESTIONS FOR ANALYSIS

1. Kmart argued that it was not reasonable for the jury to find that fifteen minutes spent in the store discussing the matter was false imprisonment. Would you agree that if the time is short and there is no force there should be no tort action?

2. When arguing for damages, Caldwell's attorney told the jury that Kmart was worth $5 billion. Should the worth of the defendant be taken into consideration in damage estimation?

Infliction of Emotional Distress

The *tort of infliction of emotional distress* (*mental distress*) involves conduct that is so outrageous it creates severe mental or emotional distress in another person. The protected interest is peace of mind. This cause of action protects us from conduct that goes way beyond the bounds of decency, but not from annoying behavior, petty insults, or bad language. Many states also provide compensation to third parties based on emotional distress. For example, a Louisiana court provided compensation for emotional distress to a woman who found that her comatose husband had suffered rat bites while in bed at a hospital where he was being treated.

Bill collectors, landlords, and insurance adjusters are often involved in emotional-distress suits. Badgering, late-night phone calls, profanity, threats, and name-calling lay the groundwork for potential emotional-distress suits. Employers have been

ISSUE *Spotter*

What Duty Is Owed to the Elderly and Their Heirs?

Your company runs assisted care facilities. Most of your clients are elderly people in poor health. Most of your clients die within two years of entering a facility. Unfortunately, some of the clients never have visitors. They seem to have no relationships with any family members, but you know that legally they have heirs. If they provide no information about who to contact in the event of an emergency or death, their body is cremated. You have heard of instances when after a death, a family member suddenly appears and is irate that the family was not contacted. Suits for emotional distress, negligence, and other torts have been filed. How should you handle this matter to cover your legal obligations? What is your ethical obligation?

sued more often in recent years for the distress suffered by employees who have been subjected to extreme statements or harassment at work. The *Monsanto* case is an example of an employee subjected to profane treatment.

White v. Monsanto Company

Supreme Court of Louisiana
585 So.2d 1205 (1991)

CASE BACKGROUND   *Irma White, a church-going woman in her late forties with grown children, worked at a Monsanto refinery. She and other employees were waiting for equipment so they could transfer a chemical from a large container into smaller ones. Shop rules required employees to clean up an area while waiting for equipment. White did cleanup work, but the other employees did nothing. Supervisor McDermott saw that the group was idle and yelled at the workers, cursing them and threatening to fire them. The tirade lasted about a minute, and McDermott left the area.*

White was upset and experienced pain in her chest, pounding in her head, and difficulty breathing. She went to McDermott's office to discuss the incident. McDermott said he apologized to her; she said he did not. White went to the company nurse, who suggested that she see a doctor. White had chest pains, shortness of breath, and cold, clammy hands. Fearing a heart attack, the doctor admitted White to the hospital for three days for observation. A heart attack was ruled out, and the diagnosis was acute anxiety reaction—a panic attack.

White returned to work. She was paid her regular pay while on sick leave. Her medical bills of $3,200 were paid by the company's medical benefits program. White became upset thinking or dreaming about the incident and was prescribed medicine.

White sued Monsanto and McDermott, alleging that McDermott's conduct inflicted mental anguish and emotional distress. The jury awarded White $60,000. The court of appeal affirmed. Defendants appealed.

CASE DECISION   Hall, Justice.

* * *

One who by extreme and outrageous conduct intentionally causes severe emotional distress to another is subject to liability for such emotional distress, and if bodily harm to the other results from it, for such bodily harm.

Thus, in order to recover for intentional infliction of emotional distress, a plaintiff must establish (1) that the conduct of the defendant was extreme and outrageous; (2) that the emotional distress suffered by the plaintiff was severe; and (3) that the defendant desired to inflict severe emotional distress or knew that severe emotional distress would be certain or substantially certain to result from his conduct.

The conduct must be so outrageous in character, and so extreme in degree, as to go beyond all possible bounds of decency, and to be regarded as atrocious and utterly intolerable in a civilized community. Liability does not extend to mere insults, indignities, threats, annoyances, petty oppressions, or other trivialities. Persons must necessarily be expected to be hardened to a certain amount of rough language, and to occasional acts that are definitely inconsiderate and unkind. Not every verbal encounter may be converted into a tort; on the contrary, "some safety valve must be left through which irascible tempers may blow off relatively harmless steam." . . .

Liability can arise only when the actor desired to inflict severe emotional distress or where he knows that such distress is certain or substantially certain to result from his conduct. . . . The conduct must be intended or calculated to cause severe emotional distress and not just some lesser degree of fright, humiliation, embarrassment, worry, or the like.

Applying these precepts of law to the facts of the instant case, we find that plaintiff has failed to establish her right to recover from the defendants for an intentional tort.

The one-minute outburst of profanity directed at three employees by a supervisor in the course of dressing them down for not working as he thought they should does not amount to such extreme and outrageous conduct as to give rise to recovery for intentional infliction of emotional distress. . . . Such conduct, although crude, rough and uncalled for, was not tortious. . . . The brief, isolated instance of improper behavior by the supervisor who lost his temper was the kind of unpleasant experience persons must expect to endure from time to time. The conduct was not more than a person of ordinary sensibilities can be expected to endure. The tirade was directed to all three employees and not just to plaintiff specifically. . . .

The duty here was to not engage in extreme or outrageous conduct intended or calculated to cause severe emotional distress. The duty was not breached because the conduct was not extreme or outrageous to a degree calculated to cause severe emotional distress to a person of ordinary sensibilities and the supervisor did not intend to inflict emotional distress of a severe nature, nor did he believe such a result was substantially certain to follow from his conduct.

For the reasons expressed in this opinion, the judgments of the district court and court of appeal are reversed, and judgment is rendered in favor of defendants dismissing plaintiff's suit, at plaintiff's cost.

QUESTIONS FOR ANALYSIS

1. Would it have made any difference if White had suffered a heart attack? What if she had suffered no physical distress, but only mental distress?

2. Should men and women be held to different standards in such matters? More women than men are likely to be upset by such instances. Should courts take into account differences in sensitivities?

Invasion of Privacy

The concept behind the tort of *invasion of privacy* is a person's right to solitude and to be free from unwarranted public exposure. The tort may be committed in a number of ways:

1. The use of a person's name or picture without permission (which can make advertisers and marketing companies liable)
2. The intrusion into a person's solitude (illegal wiretapping or searches of a residence; harassment by unwanted and continual telephoning)
3. The placing of a person in a false light (publishing of a story with serious misinformation)
4. The public exposure of facts that are private in nature (such as public disclosure of a person's drug use or debts)

While we often think of invasion-of-privacy cases involving the rich and famous, in fact most such cases come about from more ordinary situations, as the *Pachowitz* case illustrates.

Pachowitz v. LeDoux
Court of Appeals of Wisconsin
666 N.W.2d 88 (2003)

CASE BACKGROUND *Katherina LeDoux was a volunteer emergency medical technician (EMT) for the Tess Corners Volunteer Fire Department. Julie Pachowitz's husband called for an ambulance for his wife. LeDoux was on the team that took Pachowitz to the hospital for a possible drug overdose. LeDoux did not know Pachowitz but realized that she knew her close friend, Sally Slocomb, and that both Pachowitz and Slocomb worked at an area hospital. Thinking that she might be able to help Pachowitz, LeDoux called Slocomb to tell her* *of Pachowitz's hospitalization. Slocomb then told people at the hospital where she and Pachowitz worked about Pachowitz's problem.*

Pachowitz sued LeDoux for invasion of privacy. The court awarded her $3,000. Under Wisconsin's fee shifting statute, the trial court also awarded Pachowitz $30,460 in attorney fees. LeDoux appealed.

CASE DECISION Nettesheim, P.J.

* * *

In order to establish a cause of action for invasion of privacy . . . a plaintiff must prove: (1) a public disclosure of facts regarding the plaintiff; (2) the facts disclosed are private facts; (3) the private matter made public is one which would be highly offensive to a reasonable person of ordinary sensibilities; and (4) the defendant acted either unreasonably or recklessly as to whether there was a legitimate public interest in the matter, or with actual knowledge that none existed. . . .

LeDoux advised but one person, Slocomb, about the SMT call . . . Slocomb, not LeDoux, . . . publicized the information to the staff at [the hospital]. . . . Appellants contend that LeDoux did not communicate Pachowitz's private information to the public at large or to so many persons that the matter must be regarded as substantially certain to become one of public knowledge. . . .

We conclude that disclosure of private information to one person or to a small group does not, as a matter of law in all cases, fail to satisfy the publicity element of an invasion of privacy claim. Rather, whether such a disclosure satisfies the publicity element of an invasion of privacy claim depends upon the particular facts of the case and the nature of plaintiff's relationship to the audience who received the information.

Here, the facts established that LeDoux disclosed Pachowitz's private information to Slocomb, who LeDoux knew was one of Pachowitz's fellow employees at [the hospital]. Pachowitz's husband's request to the EMTs that Pschowitz be transported to a different hospital . . . supports an inference that Pachowitz wanted to avoid disclosure of her need for emergency medical care to her fellow employees. . . . we conclude that the question of LeDoux's liability was for a jury.

Affirmed.

QUESTIONS FOR ANALYSIS

1. Since this was a small community, and Pachowitz worked in a hospital, was it likely that the story of her hospitalization was going to go unnoticed and so remain secret?

2. Are attorney fees of $30,000, added to the damages of $3,000, fair for LeDoux to pay, besides paying for her own attorney?

Defenses

In addition to common-law protection, some states have statutes to recognize a right to privacy. In either case, the right to privacy is largely waived when a person becomes a public figure, such as an entertainer, a politician, or a sports personality. In addition, the publication of information about an individual taken from public files and records does not constitute an invasion of privacy.

JURIS *prudence?*

Teaching Torts in Law School

Denise DiFede was attending a class on torts at Pace University's law school. She alleged that her professor used her as a tort demonstration by pulling her chair away from her as she prepared to sit down. She fell and injured her back.

Claiming the incident was "outrageous, shocking and intolerable, exceeding all reasonable bounds of decency," she sued the school for $5 million.

Source: *Reuters*

Defamation

The tort of *defamation* is an intentional false communication that injures a person's reputation or good name. If the defamatory communication was spoken, *slander* is the tort. If the communication was in the form of a printing, a writing, a picture, or a radio or television broadcast, the tort is *libel*. The elements that must be shown to exist for both torts to be actionable are:

1. Making a false or defamatory statement about another person
2. Publishing or communicating the statement to a third person
3. Causing harm to the person about whom the statement was made

Some statements are considered *defamation per se*. That is, they are presumed by law to be harmful to the person to whom they were directed and therefore require no proof of harm or injury. Statements, for example, that a person has committed a crime or has engaged in shady business activities can be defamatory per se.

ISSUE
Spotter

Is It Safe to Say Good Things About a Good Employee?

Jeff was a good employee. He was laid off three years ago when business conditions forced the company to release 20 percent of the workforce. Since then, he has worked for another firm, but you know he has been looking for a better job. Jeff has listed you as a reference. A company interested in hiring Jeff has asked for a letter of recommendation. Your firm generally does not provide such letters because of the possibility of being sued. But you feel that you can write a positive letter about Jeff, which would help a good person who was a loyal employee. Should you write the letter? Can there be a downside to writing a positive letter?

Workplace Defamation

Most defamation suits come about from former employees suing for negative statements made about them by their ex-boss. As a result, many companies have a policy of providing no information about job performance, good or bad, about current or past employees to outsiders who inquire about performance. When managers talk about the negative aspects of an employee's performance, they must remember that if the information is spread to those who do not have a business reason to know the information, then the company is more likely to be exposed to tort liability. In the *Gray* case we see where an employer was protected because of the right a firm has to share negative information for business purposes.

Gray v. AT&T Corp.
United States Court of Appeals, Eighth Circuit
357 F.3d 763 (2004)

CASE BACKGROUND *Gray worked for AT&T. She missed five weeks work due to a non-work-related injury. Under company rules, she filed forms to have the medical reason for her absence verified. Because of inconsistencies in the forms she filed, AT&T would not certify her absence as legitimate. She appealed that decision and the company investigated. A doctor she listed as having seen her had no record of her ever visiting his office. AT&T investigated further and fired Gray for misconduct for falsifying records.*

Gray applied for unemployment benefits from the state. AT&T provided information about why Gray was fired to Gates McDonald & Co., which handled the processing of unemployment claims for AT&T. Gray sued AT&T for defamation by publishing statements that she committed disability fraud against the company. She contended that the statements were published to managers within AT&T and to Gates McDonald. The district court granted summary judgment in favor of AT&T; Gray appealed.

continues

CASE DECISION   Riley, Circuit Judge.

* * *

Under Missouri law, to establish a prima facie case for defamation, a claimant must establish six elements: "1) publication, 2) of a defamatory statement, 3) that identifies the [claimant], 4) that is false, 5) that is published with the requisite degree of fault, and 6) damages the [claimant's] reputation."

Under Missouri law, a person publishes a defamatory statement by communicating the defamatory matter to a third person. However, "communications between officers of the same corporation in the due and regular course of the corporate business, or between different offices of the same corporation are not publications to third persons.". . .

Gray contends the intra-corporate immunity rule does not apply to [AT&T managers who saw the materials about the reason for her dismissal]. We disagree. . . . AT&T managers . . . were part of the team investigating Gray's conduct. . . . [They were all] informed of the basis for Gray's termination during a team meeting, which occurred in the regular course of AT&T's business.

* * *

Gray principally contends publication occurred when her file was transferred to Gates McDonald. This communication apparently occurred after Gray filed an unemployment benefits claim. AT&T forwarded the reason for Gray's termination to Gates McDonald to process Gray's claim. Gates McDonald had a contractual duty to process and respond to Gray's unemployment claim, necessitating AT&T's disclosure of the grounds for Gray's termination.

For many years, the law of libel and slander has recognized a general exemption to the publication rule for corporate communications to necessary third parties authorized to act on behalf of the corporation. . . .

Corporations . . . often rely on outside companies to perform many of their complicated regulatory compliance duties, imposed by a host of laws and regulations. We believe Missouri would apply a similar "need to know" concept for communications between the separate corporations under the facts of Gray's claim.

AT&T's communications of allegedly defamatory statements occurred in the regular course of its business, among persons having a need to know in order to perform their employment duties. No publication, as recognized by Missouri law, occurred. We affirm for the reasons stated.

QUESTIONS FOR ANALYSIS

1. What evidence do fired employees have to provide to establish defamation?

2. AT&T managers had the information about the reason for the termination. Would the company have any right to share the information with other employees?

Defenses

Truth and privilege are defenses to an action for defamation. If the statement that caused harm to a person's reputation is in fact the truth, some states hold that truth is a complete defense regardless of the purpose or intent in publishing the statement. *Truth* is an important defense in a defamation suit.

Depending on the circumstances, three privileges—absolute, conditional, and constitutional—may be used as a defense to a defamation action. *Absolute privilege* is an immunity applied in those situations where public policy favors complete freedom of speech. For example, state legislators in legislative sessions, participants in judicial proceedings, and government executives in the discharge of their duties have absolute immunity from liability resulting from their statements.

A *conditional privilege* eliminates liability when the false statement was published in good faith and with proper motives, such as a legitimate business purpose. Businesses have a privilege to communicate information believed to be true.

CYBER *Law*

Tort Liability for Internet Servers

Internet users will do things that are illegal or violate the rights of others. Are the Internet servers liable? In general, no, so long as they were not aware of, or had no reason to be aware of, the improper activity occurring on their system.

In *Zeran* v. *America Online* (129 F.3d 327), a federal appeals court held that America Online (AOL) cannot be sued for tort liability for a defamatory message that an AOL user sent. The sender may be liable, but AOL was not.

However, in *Marobie-FL, Inc. v. Natl. Assn. of Fire Equipment Distributors* (983 F.Supp. 1167), a federal court held that the improper use (infringement) of copyrighted clip art that was distributed by a web page owner could result in liability if the server was aware of the infringement and took no steps to prevent distribution of the infringed material. It was to be determined at trial if the server "monitored, controlled, or had the ability to monitor or control the contents of [the violating web page]."

Individuals have a conditional privilege to publish defamatory matter to protect their legitimate interests, such as to defend their reputation against defamation by another.

As discussed in Chapter 4, the First Amendment to the Constitution guarantees freedom of speech and freedom of press. This *constitutional privilege* protects members of the press who publish "opinion" material about public officials, public figures, or persons of legitimate public interest. This privilege is lost only if the statement was made with *actual malice*, that is, the false statement was made with reckless disregard for the truth.

INTERNATIONAL *Perspective*

Libel in Foreign Courts

Many countries do not have constitutional freedom of speech. The news media in the United States can communicate defamatory material about public officials or persons of legitimate public interest as long as the material is provided without actual malice. In the United Kingdom, the news media do not have this extensive privilege. Plaintiffs need show only that the defamatory statement was communicated and that their reputation was damaged. To avoid liability, a defendant must demonstrate that the statements made were true or that they had been made either in court or in Parliament.

As a result of this difference in the law of defamation, a number of U.S. communications companies, including *Time*, NBC, and Dow Jones, have found themselves in foreign courts (especially in the U.K.) defending against defamation suits. Although the broadcasts in question may have originated in the United States and may have been republished in the foreign country without the consent of the U.S. company, the company will not be relieved of liability on that basis alone.

SUMMARY

- Tort law concerns legal wrongs inflicted by one party on another by interfering with an interest protected by common law. Tort law changes over time as social values, technology, and business practices change. The primary purpose of tort law is to compensate the injured party and to put the burden on the tortfeasor to return the injured party to his original position.
- Tort liability for negligence arises when the duty of ordinary care—the care expected of a reasonable person under the circumstances—to another person is breached, usually by an act that is the proximate cause (or substantial factor) of harm to the other person.
- Defenses raised in tort lawsuits include that of truth in defamation cases; consent—that the plaintiff had approved of the interference that led to injury; privilege—that the defendant had a right to take the actions now challenged, including self-defense in case of assault; inflicting injury on another to defend someone else being attacked; and physically defending property. Force used should be no more than is reasonable under the circumstances. The law places a higher value on human life than on property. In negligence cases, defenses also include assumption of the risk by the plaintiff and negligence by the plaintiff, which may be compared to the negligence of the defendant.
- Intentional torts are based on willful misconduct that invades a right of another and causes injury. The rights can be the rights of persons to be safe and secure in their person or in their property. Wrongdoers will be expected to pay damages to compensate for injuries.
- Intentional interference with personal rights includes assault—when a person is placed in fear of bodily harm or offensive contact; battery—unlawful physical contact without consent; false imprisonment—detaining someone within boundaries against his or her will; emotional distress—caused by outrageous conduct; invasion of privacy—a violation of a person's right to be free from unwanted exposure; defamation—false communication that injures a person's reputation, including slander and libel; and malicious prosecution—unjustified use of the law to injure another.

REVIEW AND DISCUSSION QUESTIONS

1. Define the following terms:

tort	false imprisonment
negligence	emotional distress
proximate cause	invasion of privacy
comparative negligence	defamation
assault	slander
battery	libel
consent	malicious prosecution
privilege	

2. Are most accidents and injuries covered by tort law?

CASE QUESTIONS

3. Milo Vacanti took his CD player to Master Electronics for repairs. Vacanti presumed that the repairs would be covered by warranty, but he did not discuss the matter with the staff at Master. When he returned to pick up the player after it had been repaired, he was presented a bill, which he refused to pay. He grabbed the player and started to leave the store. Two employees yelled at him and then scuffled with him to get the player back. Vacanti claimed he suffered injuries to his hand, ribs, neck, and lip. He sued for assault and battery, presenting medical bills for $3,150. Did he win? [*Vacanti* v. *Master Electronics*, 514 N.W.2d 319 (Sup. Ct., Neb., 1994)]

4. Ahron Leichtman, an antismoking advocate, was invited to appear on a radio talk show in Cincinnati to discuss smoking on the day of the Great American Smokeout. While he was in the studio, another talk show host lit a cigar and repeatedly blew smoke in Leichtman's face. Leichtman sued the radio station for battery and for invasion of privacy. Did he have a case? [*Leichtman* v. *WLW Jacor Comm.*, 634 N.E.2d 697 (Ct. App., Ohio, 1994)]

5. Charlotte Newsom worked as a cashier at a store. One day she was told to report to the manager's office, where she was accused by two security staff members of stealing $500. She denied stealing the money. The meeting lasted two hours. The security staff asserted to have evidence of theft, although Newsom constantly denied the claim. Whenever Newsom stated that she wanted to leave, the staff told her she would be arrested for theft if she left. Finally, Newsom wrote a statement about the matter, denying the charge. She was fired on the spot and left the store. Did she have a case for false imprisonment? [*Newsom* v. *Thalhimer Brothers*, 901 S.Wd.2d 365 (West. Dist. Ct. App., Tenn., 1994)]

 Check your answer at http://meiners.westbuslaw.com

6. Sharpe worked as a courier for FedEx. She was sent to a hospital for a routine, random drug test that the hospital ran for FedEx. The test came back positive for cocaine and Sharpe was fired. She contended that the hospital was negligent by violating federal regulations concerning the proper standards for collecting and handling urine specimens that resulted in a false reading of her specimen. The hospital defended that it owed no duty of care to Sharpe; its obligation was to FedEx. The trial and appeals court agreed and dismissed the suit. Sharpe appealed to the high court of Pennsylvania. Does the hospital owe her a duty of reasonable care in this instance? [*Sharpe* v. *St. Luke's Hospital*, 821 A.2d 1215 (Sup. Ct., Pa., 2003)]

7. A patron at a casino in Nevada got into a fight with another customer. The bouncer went to throw out the patron and got into a fight with him. The bouncer took the patron to a back room to photograph him (they keep photos of troublemakers), which resulted in another fight in which the patron suffered significant injury to his arm. What torts could the patron bring against the casino? [*Cerminara* v. *California Hotel and Casino*, 760 P.2d 108 (Sup. Ct., Nev., 1988)]

 Check your answer at http://meiners.westbuslaw.com

8. Jerry Katz, a politician, stated that he would not raise taxes if elected. The local newspaper supported Katz, who won the election. At his first board meeting, Katz moved to raise taxes. His actions prompted an editorial that began, "Jerry Katz is a liar. He has lied to us in the past, and he will lie to us in the future." Katz sued the newspaper. What would that action be, and what would be the likely result? [*Costello* v. *Capital Cities Communications*, 505 N.E.2d 701 (App. Ct., Ill., 1987)]

9. After Scarfo quit working for Ginsberg, she claimed that he subjected her to unwelcome sexual conduct and sued him for battery, emotional distress, and invasion of privacy. The Florida supreme court was asked by a federal court if Scarfo could in fact have a claim for invasion of privacy under Florida law. Florida uses the same categories of invasion of privacy as discussed in the chapter. Does Scarfo have a claim? [*Allstate Insurance* v. *Ginsberg*, 863 So.2d 156 (Sup. Ct., Fla., 2003)]

 Check your answer at http://meiners.westbuslaw.com

10. Kelly-Springfield (K-S) agreed to sell some land to D'Ambro. The deal was to be completed on a specified date, but D'Ambro failed to make any payment by the due date. K-S then began talking to other parties who had expressed an interest in the property. D'Ambro filed suits in state and federal court, claiming that K-S failed to live up to the sale agreement, and demanded damages or that K-S be required to sell the property to D'Ambro. Because of the litigation, the interested parties backed away from the K-S property. What action can K-S bring against D'Ambro? [*Kelly-Springfield Tire Co.* v. *D'Ambro*, 596 A.2d 867 (Super. Ct., Pa., 1991)]

11. Huggins's identity was stolen by an unknown person, who used it to obtain credit cards from various banks in Huggins's name. Huggins suffered the grief of dealing with creditors dunning him for payments that were not due and all the other problems of cleaning up the identity theft. He sued the banks and credit card companies for negligence for issuing credit cards without more verification of the identity of the applicant and for failing to adopt other policies to prevent successful identity theft. Do the banks have a duty to protect potential victims of identity theft from imposter fraud? [*Huggins* v. *Citibank, N.A.*, 585 S.E.2d 275 (Sup. Ct., S.C., 2003)]

12. Unknown to him, Greg Gazelle's wife bounced ten checks for $860 at a grocery store from their joint checking account. Gazelle's wife had signed his name to the checks. After trying unsuccessfully to collect, the store filed a criminal complaint against Gazelle, who was arrested and spent a week in jail. Charges were dropped when it was discovered that he had not written the checks. Did Gazelle have a tort action for malicious prosecution against the store? [*Winn-Dixie Stores* v. *Gazelle*, 523 So.2d 648 (First Dist. Ct. App., Fla., 1988)]

13. Dun & Bradstreet, a company that reports on the credit history of businesses, incorrectly stated that Greenmoss Builders had once gone bankrupt when in fact it had not. Greenmoss claimed it lost business because of the incorrect report, which was sent to prospective customers. Greenmoss sued for damages for defamation and won. Dun & Bradstreet said that since there was no "actual malice" in what was said, it could not be held liable. What did the U.S. Supreme Court say? [*Dun & Bradstreet* v. *Greenmoss Builders*, 472 U.S. 749, 105 S.Ct. 2939 (1985)]

14. Tomato growers in Tennessee bought a product called Frostguard from a California company. The company claimed the product would protect tomatoes from the harmful effects of frost. The growers applied Frostguard as direct-

ed but suffered substantial crop losses as a result of a frost. They sued the maker of Frostguard for negligence in advertising. Could they win such a tort action? [*Ritter* v. *Custom Chemicides*, 912 S.W.2d 128 (Sup. Ct., Tenn., 1995)]

ETHICS QUESTIONS

15. Businesses have become more aggressive at suing publications that report negative news about them or make negative comments. A cigarette company sued CBS for interviewing a disgruntled former executive; an infomercial producer sued *Forbes* for $420 million for a negative article about infomercials, and ABC paid $15 million and made on-the-air apologies to settle a suit by two tobacco companies for $10 billion for a report about "spiking" cigarettes with nicotine. It has been claimed that such suits are primarily to scare the media from negative reporting. Since the suits have possible merit, there is no malicious prosecution, but the use of the law seems to be mostly strategic—to discourage the media from being critical of company practices. Is this a defensible business tactic?

16. An employee at the supermarket you manage mopped one of the aisles in the store and placed signs at the ends of the aisles to warn people not to use the aisle until the floor dried. One customer walked around the sign, slipped, fell, and suffered serious injuries. Her lawyer comes to you with the following story. He says he is going to sue the store for negligence that led to her injuries. However, he says he doubts he can win, since case law in the state makes it clear that the sign is considered a reasonable warning so that contributory negligence by the customer would eliminate liability of the store. This means the customer will get nothing, but one can never be completely sure. The worst part is that the customer has no insurance, has incurred large hospital bills, cannot work for several months, and has no source of support. The lawyer makes the following deal. He will forgo any fee for the case and will sue only for an amount equal to the medical costs incurred and the wages lost if you will agree to testify there was no sign in place to warn that the floor was wet. The payment will be made by the insurance company. This will not affect your position with the insurance company, and you will save attorney's fees. Should you make such a deal? What if you knew that the law in most states would provide an award because their law held that warning signs were not sufficient and a complete physical barrier had to be in place?

PULLING IT *Together*

Tort Law and Employment

Pamela Thigpen hired Huntley Johnson to represent her in a lawsuit. Soon after, Johnson hired her to work for him, which she did for 14 months. During her employment, Johnson "engaged in conversations with Thigpen that were sexually explicit, demeaning and vulgar." Besides talking about having sex with her, Johnson left a nude picture of himself on her desk and engaged in "unwelcomed physical contact, including repeated touching of Thigpen's breasts, running a pencil up Thigpen's thigh" and other incidents. What tort actions would Thigpen be most likely to have against Johnson? If there are torts, are they based on negligence or are they intentional torts? [*Johnson* v. *Thigpen*, 788 So.2nd 410 (Ct. App., Fla., 2001)]

INTERNET ASSIGNMENT

Through an ongoing business relationship with the local chamber of commerce, Sunrise Renewal, a commercial redevelopment company, became aware that the owner of a downtown warehouse was interested in selling ten acres of land near the heart of the city. The land had great potential for a restaurant and entertainment complex. To try to acquire the land, Sunrise held a meeting of its board of directors, which consisted of local civic and business leaders, including Joseph Landmark of Landmark Hotel, Inc. At the meeting, a majority of the board authorized the purchase of the property. Sunrise's president then met with the property owner and the two shook hands on the deal. At the office the next day, Sunrise's president sent the owner a letter of intent to purchase the property and later sent a formal contract. Sunrise's president then lined up contractors for the renovation work and secured contracts with three major tenants. Naturally, Sunrise's president kept all of the members of the board up-to-date on his business activities.

However, when construction was only weeks away, the property owner backed out of the deal because he had received a better offer from Landmark. After unsuccessfully attempting to resolve this matter out of court, Sunrise sued both the property owner and Landmark. One of the claims Sunrise alleged against Landmark was for tortious interference with contract. What elements would Sunrise have to prove in order to prevail on this claim? What key factors would make Landmark's conduct particularly culpable? Could Landmark successfully raise the defense of "fair competition"? For answers to these questions, see the case of *Fred Siegel Co. L.P.A., et al.* v. *Arter & Hadden, et al.*, 85 Ohio St.3d 171 (1999), #1997–1998, on the Internet.

Chapter 7 | *Business Torts*

There is no such thing as a "business tort," but many torts involve businesses as defendants, and some torts, in practice, involve only businesses. This chapter focuses on the areas of tort law that are of particular concern to business. About 5 percent of all civil suits are tort actions, but the money involved in some tort cases draws attention to this area of law. Consider some statistics about tort cases:

- Plaintiffs win about 52 percent of personal injury suits and 41 percent of product defect suits.
- The median award in product liability suits has been about $400,000.
- The median award in personal injury suits is over $60,000.
- Ten percent of personal injury suit awards are for over $1 million.
- The average jury award for a rape on business property is $1.8 million.
- The median jury award for paraplegia is $6.5 million.

Defendants who expect to be found liable usually settle out of court. Since little information is available about such settlements, the magnitude of tort litigation is not known. However, a number of products (including ladders) and services (e.g., baby delivery) are estimated to cost about 20 percent to 30 percent more because of expected liability claims.

TORT LAW AND BUSINESS

As seen in Chapter 6, there are several categories of intentional torts. Those torts occur when the tortfeasor is found to have intended to invade a protected interest and the tortfeasor knew, or should have known, of the consequences of the act that resulted in an injury.

Other torts are based on negligence, which is carelessness in a legal sense. When we fail to act the way we are obligated to behave and, as a result, others suffer an injury, we can be held liable. Persons in business are presumed to have a level of expertise that holds them to a higher level of care than is expected of a nonprofessional in the same situation.

While businesses may be defendants in suits for assault, such actions are not as peculiar to business as are the tort actions covered in this chapter. These actions mostly involve only business, and are the cases that most concern business, and tend to be big-dollar cases. As we will see, many suits involve both claims of intentional tort and claims of negligence. Plaintiffs make as many claims in one case as they can. As we will study later in the chapter, other cases involve strict liability in tort.

Costs of Tort Litigation

Each year about one-half million lawsuits involving tort claims are filed in our nation's court systems, most in state courts. As Exhibit 7.1 illustrates, compensation for injured parties—the main purpose of tort law—accounts for less than half of the total cost. The costs of tort litigation, both the process itself and the damages paid, have prompted concern about the ability of the court system to effectively and efficiently compensate innocent parties who are injured.

The cost of the tort system is difficult to calculate. Estimates of the costs are as high as $250 billion per year. Business organizations have lobbied Congress to impose federal statutory limits on tort damages. They claim that many of the awards are excessive or unjustified and that the cost is making American business less

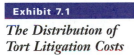

Exhibit 7.1

The Distribution of Tort Litigation Costs

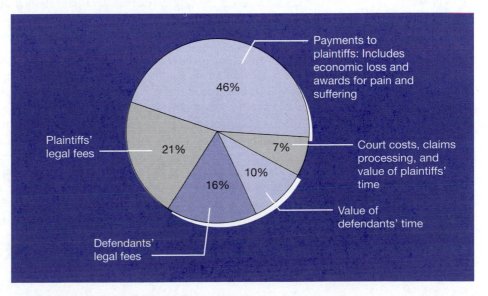

Payments to plaintiffs: Includes economic loss and awards for pain and suffering — 46%

Plaintiffs' legal fees — 21%

Defendants' legal fees — 16%

Value of defendants' time — 10%

Court costs, claims processing, and value of plaintiffs' time — 7%

Source: Institute for Civil Justice, RAND Corporation

competitive in international markets, since most nations have fewer tort cases and less generous damage awards. We next look at some areas of tort law that tend to be peculiar to business and, in the case of product liability, involve massive sums of dollars.

Misrepresentation

When a person suffers an injury (most injuries we study here are financial, not physical) due to deliberate deception, there may be a tort of *fraud, misrepresentation, fraudulent misrepresentation,* or *deceit.* When this issue arises in a business relationship, there is often a breach of contract or some other tort issue present. Misrepresentation is a broad concept and may be held to be an intentional tort or to be a tort based on negligence.

Intentional Misrepresentation or Fraud

When misrepresentation is an intentional tort, there must be proof, as the House of Lords expressed in a famous case in 1889, "that a false representation has been made (1) knowingly, or (2) without belief in its truth, or (3) recklessly, careless whether it be true or false" (*Derry* v. *Peek,* 14 A.C. 337 at 374). While misrepresentation is a common-law rule subject to different interpretations in different jurisdictions, as the law has evolved the following key elements have generally been agreed upon to establish fraud or intentional misrepresentation.

1. A material misrepresentation of a fact: false important information was passed.
2. *Scienter* or intent to defraud: the defendant knew there was a misrepresentation of information being passed.
3. Intent to induce reliance: the defendant wanted the plaintiff to believe the falsehood.
4. Justifiable reliance by the plaintiff on the misinformation: the plaintiff had good reason to believe the misrepresentation offered by the defendant.
5. Relationship between the parties: the plaintiff and defendant were engaged in some relationship that created a legal obligation.
6. Causation: a logical link existed between reliance on the misstatement and the losses that were then suffered by the plaintiff.
7. Damages: losses were suffered by the plaintiff due to reliance on the fraud.

As with other torts, the relationship of the parties can be significant in determining whether legal responsibility is created. If a stranger walking down the street tells you to invest all of your money in Fly-by-Night Company stock, you will not have a cause of action against the stranger when all of your money is lost when the company collapses, because there is no justification to believe a stranger about such a decision, nor is there a business relationship—it was just friendly, stupid advice. But if your stockbroker tells you to invest all of your money in Fly-by-Night Company stock and tells you it is a safe, sure investment, when she knows it is a highly risky venture and she is getting kickbacks for sending clients to invest in the stock, then your reliance may be justified and she and her employing company may well be responsible for your losses when the company goes broke.

Negligent Misrepresentation

A tort action for misrepresentation can occur due to negligence of the other party, which almost only occurs when there is a business or professional relationship. For example, if an attorney fails to file some documents on time and a case is lost due to that careless error, there was not intent to do harm, but there was negligence that caused a loss. Instances in which there is a reliance on information or services provided by professionals who fail to meet the duty of care expected of a professional are the basis of most negligent misrepresentation actions. The *Squish La Fish* case discusses such an instance.

Squish La Fish, Inc. v. Thomco Specialty Products, Inc.
United States Court of Appeals, Eleventh Circuit
149 F.3d 1288 (1998)

CASE BACKGROUND *Squish La Fish holds a patent on a plastic device called "Tuna Squeeze" that squeezes oil and water from cans of tuna. A distributor ordered two million units. Squish hired ProPack to affix each Tuna Squeeze to preprinted cardboard "point of purchase" cards for display in stores. ProPack brought in Thomco to advise it as to the kind of adhesive to use to make the Tuna Squeeze stick to the cardboard. The Thomco representative recommended a 3M adhesive called Extra High Tack Adhesive Transfer and said that the adhesive would easily wash off of the Tuna Squeeze in warm water. ProPack and Squish relied on Thomco's advice.*

After 8,600 units had been produced, it was discovered that the adhesive would not wash off of the Tuna Squeeze and the distributor was not happy with the results. The adhesive was replaced with two-sided tape, but the distributor wanted a guarantee that the product would be delivered on time and that there would not be adhesive problems. Squish could not make the promise because there were problems finding a good adhesive. The distributor canceled the contract.

Squish sued Thomco for negligent misrepresentation. The district court granted summary judgment for Thomco; Squish appealed.

CASE DECISION Cohill, Senior District Judge.

* * *

The Georgia Supreme Court adopted the "negligent misrepresentation exception" from the *Restatement (Second) of Torts* §522 (1977). Under this now well-established . . . rule,

> One who supplies information during the course of his business, profession, employment, or in any transaction in which he has a pecuniary interest has a duty of reasonable care and competence to parties who rely upon the information in circumstances in which the maker was manifestly aware of the use to which the information was to be put and intended that it be so used. This liability is limited to a foreseeable person or limited class of persons for whom the information was intended, either directly or indirectly.

The elements of this cause of action have recently been formulated as follows: (1) the negligent supply of false information to foreseeable persons, known or unknown; (2) such persons' reasonable reliance upon that false information; and (3) economic injury approximately resulting from such reliance.

* * *

We find that the district court committed an error of law when it failed to acknowledge that Squish La Fish's indirect reliance, through ProPack, on Thomco's alleged representations concerning the . . . adhesive, were sufficient to bring the company within the negligent misrepresentation . . . rule. . . .

Applying the three-part test for negligent misrepresentation to the facts before the district court, it is clear that Squish La Fish, as the manufacturer of the product being affixed by Thomco's adhesive, was a foreseeable user of Thomco's representations concerning that adhesive. The parties dispute the remaining two prongs of the analysis: whether any false information was conveyed about the adhesive's removability, and whether Squish La Fish indirectly relied upon any such information. The record shows that disputed issues of material fact remain for trial as to both issues.

* * *

Reversed and remanded.

continues

QUESTIONS FOR ANALYSIS

1. Why did Squish not sue Thomco for breach of contract instead of the tort of negligent misrepresentation?

2. Would Thomco have a good defense that ProPack and Squish should have had the sense to try the adhesive to make sure it worked properly before putting it into production?

Interference with Contractual Relations

One of the more common business torts is *intentional interference with contractual relations*. The basis of the claim is that the injured business's contractual relations were wrongfully interfered with by another party. The elements of this tort are

1. the existence of a contractual relationship between the injured business and another party
2. that was known to the wrongdoer, who
3. intentionally interfered with that relationship.

When a wrongdoer intentionally causes another party to break a good contract, the motive does not matter. The point is that breaking the contract is done to benefit the tortfeasor. This causes injury to the party who suffers the breach of contract. The party who suffers the breach may sue both the party who breached the contract for breach and the wrongdoer for the tort of interference with the contract. The *Seminole* case discusses the elements of this kind of tort.

Seminole Tribe of Florida v. Times Publishing Company, Inc.

District Court of Appeals of Florida, Fourth District
780 So.2d 310 (2001)

CASE BACKGROUND *Goldstein and Testerman, reporters for the St. Petersburg Times, investigated business activities of the Seminole Tribe of Florida. The reporters made phone and written inquiries to employees and agents of the Tribe, asking for confidential and proprietary documents and information. Promising to protect the identity of anyone who gave information, the reporters received internal Tribe documents. They used these as the basis for a three-day series in the newspaper that implied mismanagement and self-dealing in various Tribe operations, including its gambling casinos. The documents used contained sales data, Tribe financial information, and information about potential business opportunities. The Tribe sued the reporters and the newspaper for intentional and unjustified interference with business relationship between the Tribe and its employees, agents, and other parties. The trial court dismissed the suit. The Tribe appealed.*

CASE DECISION Gross, Justice.

* * *

The elements of tortious interference with a contract or business relationship are: (1) the existence of a business relationship between the plaintiff and a third person, not necessarily evidenced by an enforceable contract, under which the plaintiff has legal rights; (2) the defendant's knowledge of the relationship; (3) an intentional and unjustified interference with the relationship by the defendant which induces or otherwise causes the third person not to perform; and (4) damage to the plaintiff resulting from the third person's failure to perform.

The primary issue we address in this case is whether the reporters' conduct was improper or unjustified within the confines of the tort of interference. . . .

Section 767 of the Restatement sets forth a nonexhaustive list of factors to be weighed against each other and balanced in arriving at a judgment concerning the propriety of a defendant's conduct:

> In determining whether an actor's conduct in intentionally interfering with a contract or a prospective contractual relation of another is improper or not, consideration is given to the following factors:
>
> (a) the nature of the actor's conduct,
>
> (b) the actor's motive,
>
> (c) the interests of the other with which the actor's conduct interferes,
>
> (d) the interests sought to be advanced by the actor,
>
> (e) the social interests in protecting the freedom of action of the actor and the contractual interests of the other,
>
> (f) the proximity or remoteness of the actor's conduct to the interference and
>
> (g) the relation of the parties.

Restatement (Second) of Torts §767 (1979).

We focus first on the "nature" of the reporters' conduct. The reporters' actions were not designed to terminate the ongoing relationship between the Tribe and its employees and agents. Unlike a traditional model for interference, where an employee is induced to end his relationship with his employer, the claim here is only that the reporters solicited isolated acts of disloyalty which affected the "quality" of that relationship. In Florida cases concerned with tortious interference of an existing employment relationship, the plaintiff typically demonstrates that the relationship was terminated or blocked in order to state a claim.

The reporters' conduct in this case is not the type of conduct at which the tort is usually directed. The reporters did not undertake to influence the Tribe's employees and agents not to "deal with" the tribe. The reporters did not resort to methods tortious in themselves, such as defamation, bribery, "physical violence, fraudulent misrepresentation and threats" and intimidation. Restatement (Second) of Torts §767 (1979).

* * *

Affirmed.

QUESTIONS FOR ANALYSIS

1. Would not the paper and the reporters be fully protected from such suit by the First Amendment freedom of speech?

2. Would the result have been the same if the reporters had worked for a competitor casino?

Interference with Prospective Advantage

Similar to the tort of interference with contractual rights is the tort of *interference with prospective advantage* (also called interference with prospective economic advantage and interference with prospective contractual relationship). Businesses devise countless schemes to attract customers, but it is a tort when a business attempts to improve its place in the market by interfering with another's business in an unreasonable and improper manner. An employee of Elaine's Hot Threads, for example, cannot be positioned at the entrance of Runners Sportswear to tell customers to go to Elaine's. Such conduct is predatory behavior. If the behavior of the defendant is merely competitive and not predatory in nature—for example, the defendant is so effective in advertising that customers are drawn from the losing business—the courts do not find improper interference.

While we normally think of business loss from such behavior being caused by one business to another, the source of the loss can also be due to manipulation of the government for private benefit. Since business interaction with government is constant, political actors can abuse the public process for political or personal ends and thereby cause harm to a business. In such cases, the taxpayers, who support the government, can end up liable, as the *City of Seattle* case illustrates.

Pleas v. City of Seattle
Supreme Court of Washington
774 P.2d 1158 (1989)

CASE BACKGROUND   *Parkridge, a partnership, bought property in Seattle to build a sixty-unit apartment building. That use of the land was consistent with Seattle zoning regulations. People who lived in the area formed a group to oppose the construction. Parkridge then began a ten-year battle with the city to be allowed to build. When Parkridge was finally allowed to build, it sued the city for interference with business expectancy. The trial court held for Parkridge and awarded it damages of $970,000, which included lost profits, loss of favorable financing, increased construction costs, costs of compliance with city regulations that were imposed inappropriately, and attorney fees. The city appealed and the court of appeals reversed in its favor. Parkridge appealed.*

CASE DECISION   Utter, Justice.

* * *

We believe that the right balance has been struck by our colleagues on the Oregon Supreme Court. . . . That court . . . redefined the tort as "wrongful interference with the economic relationships." Thus a cause of action for tortious interference arises from either the defendant's pursuit of an improper objective of harming the plaintiff or the use of wrongful means that in fact cause injury to plaintiff's contractual or business relationships. A claim for tortious interference is established "when interference resulting in injury to another is wrongful by some measure beyond the fact of the interference itself." . . .

Interference can be "wrongful" by reason of a statute or other regulation, or a recognized rule of common law, or an established standard of trade or profession. Therefore, plaintiff must show not only that the defendant intentionally interfered with his business

relationship, but also that the defendant had a "duty of non-interference; i.e., that he interfered for an improper purpose . . . or . . . used improper means. . . ."

In the present case, Parkridge alleges both improper motives and improper means of interference. The improper motives arise from the City officials' apparent desire to gain the favor of a politically active and potentially influential group opposing the Parkridge project. The improper means arise from the City's actions in refusing to grant necessary permits and arbitrarily delaying the project. . . .

There is ample evidence to support the trial court's finding that the City's action in this decade-long episode were sufficiently improper or wrongful so as to support a claim for tortious interference even under our new formulation of this tort. Parkridge was required to show that the City's conduct was not only intentional but wrongful, and it has done so; the burden then shifted to the City to show that its conduct was either privileged or justified. The City has failed to produce persuasive evidence that its conduct comes under either category. . . .

Municipal liability for the flagrant abuse of power by officials who intentionally interfere with the development rights of property owners cannot be avoided simply by labeling such actions "political." . . .

We reverse the decision by the Court of Appeals and remand to the King County Superior Court.

QUESTIONS FOR ANALYSIS
1. Can governments be sued for torts in the same way as private parties are sued?
2. The appeals court held that there was no tort because what happened was just normal politics. What would be the general result of such a ruling?

PRODUCT LIABILITY

Product liability is a general term applied to an area of the law that is primarily tort law but also involves some contract law and statutory law. This concerns the liability that producers and sellers of goods have to those injured by a product. Since some cases involve thousands of people and billions of dollars, product liability gets considerable attention and is controversial. Major companies have been bankrupted by product liability decisions. The primary political issue is whether the law has become so tough in assigning liability to producers that the legislature should intervene and set limits on liability. The evolution of product liability law in the past century reflects how the law changes as technology and expectations about safety and responsibility changed.

Consumer Products and Negligence

In the nineteenth century, the rule was that a manufacturer was liable for injuries caused by defects in its products to parties with whom the manufacturer had a contractual relationship regarding the product. The term *privity of contract* refers to the relationship that exists between contracting parties. It is essential to a contract case that privity exist between the parties. Since consumers rarely bought products directly from manufacturers, there often was no privity between consumer and producer. Producers were effectively isolated from liability for most product-related injuries.

INTERNATIONAL *Perspective*

Is Japan Really Different?

Some politicians want legislation to restrict tort litigation. Japan is often cited as an example of where there is less litigation and fewer lawyers. This is supposed to make Japan more competitive than the United States, where tort cases are claimed to be out of control.

The United States has twenty-five times more lawyers per person than Japan because the government of Japan allows only between 300 and 500 new attorneys each year. However, Japanese universities produce 50 percent more legal specialists per person than do American universities. These Japanese "nonlawyers" do all legal work except represent clients in court for a fee. Although the nonlawyers are not called lawyers, they are paid to do what Americans call legal work.

A study of fatal traffic accidents in Japan by American and Japanese law professors found that the American and Japanese tort systems are not all that different. The systems are organized very differently, but the results are much the same. Japanese plaintiffs win a higher percentage of tort liability suits than do American plaintiffs. Payments to Japanese plaintiffs are close to those given to American plaintiffs in similar suits. A close examination makes the actual operation of the two tort systems look more alike than is often claimed.

Rule of Caveat Emptor

Parties injured by defective products who did not have privity of contract with the manufacturer operated under the rule of *caveat emptor*, which means "let the buyer beware." According to the U.S. Supreme Court, the rule of caveat emptor "requires that the buyer examine, judge, and test [the product] for himself." Thus, a consumer without privity took the risk that a product was safe. If a product was not safe and there was an injury, the burden fell on the consumer.

Negligence in Tort

The privity rule often left innocent injured consumers without any remedy. In response to the harsh result the rule could impose, the courts began to recognize exceptions. Then, in 1916, in the famous *MacPherson* decision, New York struck down the privity rule and held a manufacturer liable in tort for negligence for a product-related injury. This case is still good law today.

MacPherson v. Buick Motor Company
Court of Appeals of New York
217 N.Y. 382, 111 N.E. 1050 (1916)

CASE BACKGROUND *Buick produced cars and sold them to dealers. MacPherson bought a new Buick from a dealer in New York. The wheels on MacPherson's Buick were made by another company for Buick. Soon after he bought the car, one of the wheels collapsed, causing an accident that injured MacPherson, who sued Buick. His suit against Buick traditionally would have been barred because of lack of privity; that is, Buick sold the car to the dealer, who in turn sold it to MacPherson. The dealer had privity with MacPherson but was not responsible for the defect. Nevertheless, the lower courts ruled for MacPherson, finding Buick liable in tort for injuries caused by the defect. Buick appealed to the highest court in New York.*

CASE DECISION Cardozo, Justice.

* * *

One of the wheels was made of defective wood, and its spokes crumbled into fragments. The wheel was not made by the defendant; it was bought from another manufacturer. There is evidence, however, that its defects could have been discovered by reasonable inspection, and that inspection was omitted. There is no claim that Buick knew of the defect and willfully concealed it. . . . The charge is one, not of fraud, but of negligence. The question to be determined is whether the defendant owed a duty of care and vigilance to anyone but the immediate purchaser.

* * *

If the nature of a thing is such that it is reasonably certain to place life and limb in peril when negligently made, it is then a thing of danger. Its nature gives warning of the consequences to be expected. If to the element of danger there is added knowledge that the thing will be used by persons other than the purchaser, and used without new tests, then, irrespective of contract, the manufacturer of this thing of danger is under a duty to make it carefully. That is as far as we are required to go for the decision of this case. There must be knowledge of a danger, not merely possible, but

probable. It is possible to use almost anything in a way that will make it dangerous if defective. That is not enough to charge the manufacturer with a duty independent of his contract. Whether a given thing is dangerous may be sometimes a question for the court and sometimes a question for the jury. There must also be knowledge that in the usual course of events the danger will be shared by others than the buyer. Such knowledge may often be inferred from the nature of the transaction. But it is possible that even the knowledge of the danger and of the use will not always be enough. The proximity or remoteness of the relation is a factor to be considered. We are dealing now with the liability of the manufacturer of the finished product, who puts it on the market to be used without inspection by his customers. If he is negligent, where danger is to be foreseen, a liability will follow.

* * *

We think the defendant was not absolved from a duty of inspection because it bought the wheels from a reputable manufacturer. It was not merely a dealer in automobiles. It was a manufacturer of automobiles. It was responsible for the finished product. It was not at liberty to put the finished product on the market without subjecting the component parts to ordinary and simple tests. Under the charge of the trial judge nothing more was required of it. The obligation to inspect must vary with the nature of the thing to be inspected. The more probable the danger the greater the need of caution.

* * *

The judgment should be affirmed.

QUESTIONS FOR ANALYSIS

1. Buick argued that it should not be liable because it did not make the wheels. Why not make the injured party sue the producer of the defective part?
2. Buick argued that this was the only wheel out of 60,000 sold that had been shown defective. Should 1/60,000 be sufficient to establish negligence?

Manufacturers must produce products using proper care to eliminate foreseeable harm, or risk being found negligent in tort if a consumer is injured by a defective product. The rule originating with *MacPherson* and adopted in every state provides that

> The manufacturer of a product is liable in the production and sale of a product for negligence, if the product may reasonably be expected to inflict harm on the user if the product is defective.

When liability is based on negligence, a manufacturer is required to exercise *reasonable care* under the circumstances in the production of its product. Liability may be imposed on a manufacturer for negligence in the preparation of the product—for failing to inspect or test the materials, for below-normal-quality workmanship, or for failing to discover possible defects. Defects must be revealed even if the manufacturer becomes aware of them after the sale of the product. Reasonable care must also be taken in presenting the product to the public—through advertisements or other promotions—to avoid *misrepresentation*. If a causal connection can be established between the failure of the manufacturer to exercise reasonable care in any of these areas and an injury suffered by a consumer, liability for damages may be imposed on the manufacturer.

JURIS *prudence?*

Well, It Didn't Look Safe to Me!

Robert Jones of Adel, Georgia, bought Liquid Fire drain cleaner. Thinking that the bottle the product came in did not look safe enough, he poured the contents into another container. That container leaked, causing Liquid Fire to run onto his legs and resulting in "extensive, excruciating burns." Jones sued Liquid Fire because its container, which did not leak, did not appear to be safe.

Source: *Atlanta Constitution*

Consumer Products and Strict Liability

Negligence in tort did not resolve some product-related injury cases. Injured parties had a hard time showing that manufacturers had not exercised reasonable care in the production of their product. The *strict liability* doctrine resolved this by holding manufacturers liable to consumers injured by defective products even though the manufacturer exercised all reasonable care. Thus, the injured party is not required to attack the reasonableness of the conduct of the manufacturer, but rather focuses on problems with the product.

Strict liability was first applied to product-related injuries through a warranty theory under contract law. Later, the adoption of strict liability in tort by the American Law Institute in the authoritative *Restatement (Second) of Torts* helped spur the adoption of strict liability in tort. We now have a mix of contract law and tort law applying to products.

Product Liability under Contract Law

Strict liability under contract law is based on the relationship between the injured party and the manufacturer because of the existence of a *warranty*. Warranty is based upon a manufacturer's assurance that a product will meet certain quality and performance standards. Such warranties may be either express or implied.

Strict Liability Based on Implied Warranty

The first major application of the doctrine of strict liability for defective consumer products was in the area of food and drink. For example, in a 1913 case from Washington State, *Mazetti* v. *Armour* (135 P. 633), the court held: "a manufacturer of food products . . . impliedly warrants his goods when dispensed in original packages." Consumer injury caused by defective food or drink is a breach of *implied warranty* of safety, and the manufacturer is strictly liable for the injury.

The Supreme Court of New Jersey later extended implied warranty of safety to other consumer products. In *Henningsen* v. *Bloomfield Motors, Inc.* (161 A.2d 69), the New Jersey court held the manufacturer of an automobile strictly liable to the purchaser's wife (who was driving the car when the brakes failed and an accident occurred) for her injuries on the basis of an implied warranty of safety.

Understanding Product Problems

Your company makes products that are involved in consumer injuries and deaths at various times. What would you suggest doing with respect to managing the information about defects so that the company can better understand its products' problems and address them more quickly?

ISSUE
Spotter

Strict Liability Based on Express Warranty

Strict liability under contract law is also applied in cases in which a manufacturer makes an *express warranty* about its product to consumers. Manufacturers often advertise quality or performance characteristics of their products. When such claims become part of the bargain between a manufacturer and a consumer, the manufacturer is held to have a duty of performance as to that representation.

Strict liability based on express warranty does not require that injured consumers have purchased the product directly from the manufacturer. As the decision in *Baxter* v. *Ford Motor Company* illustrates, the courts have long allowed the consumer to sue the manufacturer, not the retail dealer. Injured consumers are not required to prove fault because the law requires manufacturers to guarantee the truthfulness of their representations. *Misrepresentation* about a product may be the basis for strict liability in tort.

Baxter v. Ford Motor Company

Supreme Court of Washington
168 Wash. 456, 12 P.2d 409 (1932)

CASE BACKGROUND   *Baxter purchased a new Model A from a Ford dealer in May 1930. Printed material from Ford, distributed by the dealer, stated that the windshield was "Triple Shatter-Proof Car's Glass." This was advertised by Ford as a safety feature. In October 1930, as Baxter was driving the car, a pebble from a passing car hit the windshield, causing a small piece of glass to fly into Baxter's left eye, resulting in its loss.*

Baxter sued Ford because the windshield was not shatter-proof glass. The trial court did not allow the advertising to be admitted in evidence, held there was no privity of contract between the parties, and entered judgment for Ford. Baxter appealed.

CASE DECISION   Herman, Justice.

* * *

In the case at bar the automobile was represented by the manufacturer as having a windshield of non-shatterable glass "so made that it will not fly or shatter under the hardest impact." An ordinary person would be unable to discover by the usual and customary examination of the automobile whether glass which would not fly or shatter was used in the windshield. In that respect the purchaser was in a position similar to that of the consumer of a wrongly labeled drug, who has bought the same from a retailer, and who has relied upon the manufacturer's representation that the label correctly set forth the contents of the container. For many years it has been held that, under such circumstances, the manufacturer is liable to the consumer, even though the consumer purchased from a third person the commodity causing the damage.

* * *

Since the rule of caveat emptor was first formulated, vast changes have taken place. . . . It would be unjust to recognize a rule that would permit manufacturers

of goods to create a demand for their products by representing that they possess qualities which they, in fact, do not possess, and then, because there is no privity of contract existing between the consumer and the manufacturer, deny the consumer the right to recover if damages result from the absence of those qualities, when such absence is not readily noticeable. . . .

The nature of nonshatterable glass is such that the falsity of the representations with reference to the glass would not be readily detected by a person of ordinary experience and reasonable prudence. Baxter, under the circumstances shown in this case, had the right to rely upon the representations made by Ford Motor Company relative to qualities possessed by its products, even though there was no privity of contract between Baxter and Ford Motor Company.

* * *

The trial court erred in taking the case from the jury and entering judgment for respondent Ford Motor Company. It was for the jury to determine, under proper instructions, whether the failure of respondent Ford Motor Company to equip the windshield with glass which did not fly or shatter was the proximate cause of appellant's injury. . . .

Reversed, with directions to grant a new trial with reference to respondent Ford Motor Company. . . .

QUESTIONS FOR ANALYSIS
1. Ford claims there was no contract upon which Baxter could base his claim, because the purchase documents said nothing about shatter-proof glass. Does that argument have merit? Would Baxter have bought the car anyway had he known that it did not have shatter-proof glass?
2. Suppose a passenger riding in Baxter's car was injured by the flying glass. Would the passenger have had a claim against Ford on the basis of express warranty in contract?

Strict Liability in Tort

Strict liability is still imposed under contract law. However, the courts can be faced with the difficulty of determining what constituted a warranty. Manufacturers often try to limit liability by writing a restricted warranty. In response to such difficulties, the courts simplified the legal basis for injured plaintiffs by adopting the rule of *strict liability in tort*. The Supreme Court of California was the first court to adopt a general rule of strict liability in tort in product injury cases.

Greenman v. Yuba Power Products, Inc.

Supreme Court of California
59 Cal.2d 57, 27 Cal.Rptr. 697, 377 P.2d 897 (1963)

CASE BACKGROUND *Greenman's wife bought him a Shopsmith—a power tool that could be used as a saw, drill, and wood lathe. Greenman had studied material about the product and asked his wife to buy it. Two years later, while Greenman was using the machine, a piece of wood suddenly flew out of the machine and struck him on the forehead, inflicting serious injuries.*

Greenman sued the manufacturer, Shopsmith, and the retail dealer, Yuba Power, alleging breaches of warranties and negligence. The verdict in Greenman's favor against Shopsmith was appealed.

CASE DECISION Traynor, Justice.

* * *

Plaintiff introduced substantial evidence that his injuries were caused by defective design and construction of the Shopsmith. His expert witnesses testified that inadequate set screws were used to hold parts of the machine together so that normal vibration caused the tailstock of the lathe to move away from the piece of wood being turned permitting it to fly out of the lathe. They also testified that there were other more positive ways of fastening the parts of the machine together, the use of which would have prevented the accident.

* * *

A manufacturer is strictly liable in tort when an article he places on the market, knowing that it is to be used without inspection for defects, proves to have a defect that causes injury to a human being. Recognized first in the case of unwholesome food products, such liability has now been extended to a variety of other products that create as great or greater hazards if defective.

* * *

The purpose of such liability is to insure that the costs of injuries resulting from defective products are borne by the manufacturers that put such products on the market rather than by the injured persons who are powerless to protect themselves. Sales warranties serve this purpose fitfully at best. . . . Implicit in the machine's presence on the market, however, was a representation that it would safely do the jobs for which it was built. Under these circumstances, it should not be controlling whether plaintiff selected the machine because of the statements in the brochure, or because of the machine's own appearance of excellence that belied the defect lurking beneath the surface, or because he merely assumed that it would safely do the jobs it was built to do. It should not be controlling whether the details of the sales from manufacturer to retailer and from retailer to Greenman's wife were such that one or more of the implied warranties of the sales act arose. "The remedies of injured consumers ought not to be made to depend upon the intricacies of the law of sales." To establish the manufacturer's liability it was sufficient that plaintiff proved that he was injured while using the Shopsmith in a way it was intended to be used as a result of a defect in design and manufacture of which plaintiff was not aware that made the Shopsmith unsafe for its intended use.

* * *

The judgment is affirmed.

QUESTIONS FOR ANALYSIS
1. Why did the court move to strict liability in tort rather than hold that strict liability could be imposed on the basis of implied warranty in contract?
2. Would strict liability be imposed on the manufacturer if a friend of Greenman's had used the machine and was hurt while using it?

Section 402A The principal author of the *Restatement (Second) of Torts*, the American Law Institute, adopted a strict liability in tort rule in product injury cases similar to that imposed in *Greenman*. This helped bring about nationwide acceptance of the strict liability in tort rule. The *Restatement*'s strict liability in tort rule is found in Section 402A:

(1) One who sells any product in a defective condition unreasonably dangerous to the user or consumer or to his property is subject to liability for physical harm thereby caused to the ultimate user or consumer, or to his property, if

    (a) the seller is engaged in the business of selling such a product, and

    (b) it is expected to and does reach the user or consumer without substantial change in the condition in which it is sold.

(2) The rule stated in Subsection (1) applies although

    (a) the seller has exercised all possible care in the preparation and sale of his product, and

    (b) the user or consumer has not bought the product from or entered into any contractual relation with the seller.

Major Applications of Strict Liability

Exhibit 7.2 outlines the chain of events needed to establish strict liability in tort. The application of strict liability in tort covers three primary areas: (1) the manufacturer failed to warn the consumer of risks of use or of known hazards in certain uses of the product, (2) the product is poorly designed (as opposed to being defectively manufactured), or (3) the product produces latent injuries (injuries that occur years after the consumer has used the product).

Failure to Warn   A manufacturer's *failure to warn* consumers of dangers involved in the use of a product, or to instruct consumers about proper procedures in using a product, has long been actionable. In recent years courts have expanded the range of what may constitute failure to warn that can result in strict liability. *Morales* v. *American Honda Motor Co.* illustrates failure to warn.

Exhibit 7.2

Elements of Strict Liability

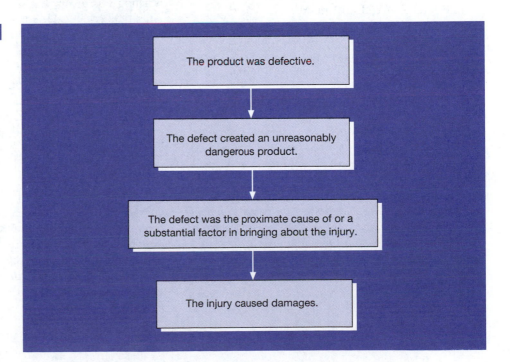

The product was defective.

The defect created an unreasonably dangerous product.

The defect was the proximate cause of or a substantial factor in bringing about the injury.

The injury caused damages.

Morales v. American Honda Motor Co.
United States Courts of Appeals, Sixth Circuit
71 F.3d 531 (1995)

CASE BACKGROUND *Nine-year-old Gary Thompson drove his Honda Z50R motorcycle into the path of a pickup truck as he left an unpaved farm road and drove onto a paved public road in Kentucky. The driver of the pickup was not at fault because her view was limited by bales of hay and she had the right-of-way. Gary suffered permanent brain damage. Medical expenses were over $320,000. Gary's mother, who brought suit on his behalf, had bought him the cycle. The owner's manual stated that the cycle was "designed for junior riders." The small cycle, which could go up to 40 mph, was not for use on public roads: "It is illegal to ride this motorcycle on public streets. . . . It must be ridden only in off-road areas where such activities are permitted. If it becomes necessary to cross a public roadway, remember to get off the motorcycle and push it across."*

On the cycle was a bold-printed warning:

IMPORTANT NOTICE
THIS VEHICLE IS DESIGNED AND MANU-
FACTURED FOR OFF-THE-ROAD USE ONLY.
IT DOES NOT CONFORM TO FEDERAL
MOTOR VEHICLE SAFETY STANDARDS AND
OPERATION IN PUBLIC STREETS, ROADS,
OR HIGHWAYS IS ILLEGAL.
REMEMBER
—PRESERVE NATURE—RIDE SAFELY—
ALWAYS WEAR A HELMET—READ OWNER'S
MANUAL CAREFULLY BEFORE RIDING.

Gary's mother said she told Gary the safety rules many times, including on the day he was hit. Among her claims was that the "warnings were inadequate, because Honda did not explain the potential consequences of a child riding this motorcycle on the road in terms a child could understand."

The district court granted Honda's motion for summary judgment, ruling that "even if the owner's manual contained a stronger and more explicit statement warning the rider that a car could hit him if he rode on the road, no reasonable jury could find that Gary would have followed that warning." Gary's mother appealed.

CASE DECISION Holschuh, District Judge.

* * *

With respect to failure to warn, the character of warnings that accompany the product is generally an evidentiary consideration in deciding whether a product is unreasonably unsafe. . . .

Kentucky's highest court held that a product was unreasonably unsafe if there was a failure to provide adequate warnings to the ultimate user. Under Kentucky law, the duty to warn extends to the dangers likely to result from foreseeable misuse of a product. Further, the . . . court held that in the absence of an adequate warning, the defendant cannot shift to the plaintiff the burden of proving that he would not have misused the product regardless.

The . . . court noted that the fact that reasonable minds could differ as to the adequacy of the warnings made the issue of negligence a jury question.

* * *

A factual question is presented as to whether the warnings given with the motorcycle constituted a substantial factor in contributing to the cause of the accident. The only warning that Honda gave was that it was illegal to ride this motorcycle on public roads. No warning was given that specifically pointed out [specific] dangers. . . . Honda cannot shift to plaintiff the burden of proving that the product would not have been misused had the product contained stronger warnings. A factual question is raised as to whether Honda's failure to give adequate warnings, admitted for the purpose of the summary judgment motion, was a substantial factor in causing the accident. This is properly a jury question that precludes the entry of summary judgment by the trial court.

* * *

In this case, there is sufficient evidence which, when viewed in the light most favorable to plaintiff, would permit the reasonable inference that Honda's alleged design defect and/or failure to warn was a substantial factor in bringing about Gary's harm. Accordingly, we vacate the district court's grant of summary judgment and remand for further proceedings consistent with this decision. . . .

QUESTIONS FOR ANALYSIS

1. Knowing that nine-year-olds are not likely to pay attention to warnings, is there any way Honda could avoid liability regardless of how many warnings were given?

2. Gary's mother argued that the cycle was defective because it did not have a red flag on a flexible pole that would stand up at about six feet to make the cycle more visible to drivers. Is that evidence of an unreasonably dangerous product?

Manufacturers must warn of possible dangers in the use, storage, and handling of their products. For example, although household cleansers are dangerous and not intended for consumption, manufacturers know that adults often leave such products in places where children might get them. Thus, liability may be imposed for not warning people sufficiently of such dangers and for not taking steps to reduce possible tragedies, such as by using containers that are not attractive to children, using hard-to-remove caps, and putting danger labels or symbols on the containers. How far does the failure-to-warn liability in tort extend? The outside limits of the application are illustrated by the following cases:

- A Pennsylvania court found a gun manufacturer that failed to warn users of damage to hearing from long-term exposure to gunfire was liable for injuries.
- The Supreme Court of Alaska upheld a verdict against a diet food producer that failed to provide adequate warnings about using the adult diet food as baby food. Because the food was safe for dieting adults but not for infants, the company should have stated so on its product.
- The high court of New York held liable the producer of a commercial pizza dough roller machine for injuries suffered by a worker who stuck his hands in the machine when he tried to clean it. Although the machine had a safety switch to be used when cleaning the machine, the worker had turned off the switch so he could stick his hands in the machine. The manufacturer failed to warn when it did not clearly explain the dangers of turning off the switch.
- The Eleventh Circuit Court of Appeals held that warnings printed on a bottle of Campho-Phenique, an external medicine, stating "Keep out of reach of children," "For external use," and "in case of ingestion—seek medical help and call poison center" were not strong enough. A four-year-old child drank the medicine and suffered severe injuries. The suit proceeded on the basis of failure to warn.
- A jury in a federal court ordered Johnson & Johnson to pay $8.85 million to a man who had a liver transplant because years of drinking alcohol and taking Tylenol had destroyed his liver. J&J had not warned Tylenol users that liver damage could occur to regular drinkers who took regular doses of Tylenol.

Design Defects   Unlike defective product cases, *design defect* cases are not concerned with a product that has been poorly manufactured and causes an injury. Rather, such cases focus on the determination of whether an injury to users could have been prevented by designing the product differently. In that regard, consider the following design defect cases:

- In a Washington State case, a worker received $750,000 for the loss of a leg. While repairing a machine, coworkers had removed a metal plate from the top of the machine. When they finished, the workers failed to replace the metal plate and covered the machine with cardboard. The plaintiff later walked on what he thought was the metal plate, as was customary, and fell into the machine. The court held that a design defect had allowed the machine to be able to run when the metal plate was removed.

- A restaurant employee was seriously burned when he tried to retrieve something that fell out of his shirt pocket and into a commercial French fryer machine. The D.C. Circuit Court of Appeals held that a jury could find that a safer alternative design of the machine was possible, in which case it could impose liability.
- A child pushed the emergency stop button on an escalator, causing a person to fall and be injured. The Seventh Circuit Court of Appeals ruled that it was a design defect both to make the button red, because that color is attractive to children, and to place the button so that it was accessible to children.
- In an Eleventh Circuit Court of Appeals case, the plaintiff was injured when he took his riding mower up a hill that was too steep; the mower rolled over, and the plaintiff was cut by the whirring blades. The court held that there was technology that would have shut off the mower automatically when it came off the ground or when the rider let go of the controls. Because such technology was not included in the product's design, the manufacturer was strictly liable for the plaintiff's injuries.

The court in the *Sufix* case reviews a jury finding of producer responsibility for a defective product and considers the justification for punitive damages.

Sufix, U.S.A., Inc. v. Cook

Court of Appeals of Kentucky
128 S.W.3d 838 (2004)

CASE BACKGROUND *Sufix makes plastic string—the cutting element in weed trimmers—as well as the heads that hold the string. In 1998, the company sold a new trimmer head, called Pro-Edge, that has pivoting metal blades, instead of string, to cut thicker weeds. Cook's employer, a real estate developer, bought a trimmer for Cook to use on the property. The first time Cook used the trimmer he felt it vibrate oddly and strike his leg. The trimmer head had shattered and his right leg suffered a deep cut through muscles, tendons, and nerves. Cook had two surgeries but did not regain full use of his leg; he is in constant pain and can only walk short distances. He is occupationally disabled.*

Cook sued Sufix, contending the company was grossly negligent for not discovering a defect in the design of the trimmer head. The jury agreed and awarded him $2.8 million compensatory damages and $3 million punitive damages. Sufix appealed.

CASE DECISION Knopf, Judge.

* * *

As originally designed and produced, the Pro-Edge employed a plastic cap to attach the metal blades to the trimmer shaft. Cook introduced expert testimony to the effect that the plastic cap was not strong enough to withstand the normal forces generated by the spinning blades and in particular that the cap had a tendency to fail at the points where the blades were knocked back against the cap when they struck objects too hard to cut, an occurrence likely in ordinary use. . . .

In addition to this evidence of defect, Cook offered testimony by several experts that Sufix could and should have discovered the defect in the course of testing prior to the release of the product, but that its testing had been grossly inadequate. Indeed, Sufix could not document any testing, its president could not recall whether impact tests had been made. . . . There was also evidence that Sufix produced a stronger metal-capped version for distribution in Italy, where the plastic version was rejected, a rejection that should have put Sufix on notice that the plastic version was unsound. . . . Cook presented evidence that soon after the release of the product Sufix received notice from customers of product failures but inadequately investigated those complaints.

* * *

Several courts have held that a manufacturer's failure to test for defects that pose a risk of serious injury and that are susceptible to adequate prerelease testing can amount to a conscious or reckless disregard for the rights and safety of others and thus can justify an award of punitive damages. We agree. . . .

In sum, not only did Sufix market an unreasonably dangerous product, but there was substantial evidence that it did so without conducting the rudimentary tests that would have revealed the danger and prevented Cook's disabling injury. The jury's verdict finding Sufix grossly negligent and liable for punitive damages was not palpably or flagrantly against that evidence. Nor was the three million dollar punitive damage award excessive. It doubled Cook's compensatory damages, which is a penalty both comparable cases and Supreme Court precedent indicate a manufacturer who cavalierly subjects the public to an unreasonable risk of catastrophic injury should expect. Accordingly, we affirm. . . .

QUESTIONS FOR ANALYSIS

1. Why did Cook argue that Sufix was grossly negligent rather than argue for liability based on strict liability only?

2. Would Sufix have been responsible for compensatory and punitive damages if it could have shown that it had properly tested the product before releasing it for sale?

New Directions in Products Liability

As we saw earlier, the American Law Institute's (ALI) definition of strict liability in Section 402A became the leading rule adopted by courts dealing with product injury cases. Experience with the rule in cases the courts have handled over the years has led to the ALI writing a new standard for product defect cases in its *Restatement (Third) of Torts*. State supreme courts are beginning to review the traditional rule of strict liability and some are adopting the new rule, as we see in the *Wright* case. The Iowa high court discusses why it supports changing the definition of when there is a cause of action in product defect cases. This development in tort law is in its early stages, but is likely to indicate how the law will progress in other states too.

Wright v. Brooke Group Limited
Supreme Court of Iowa
642 N.W.2d 159 (2002)

CASE BACKGROUND *Robert and DeAnn Wright sued the major cigarette makers in federal court, contending that the couple had been injured by Robert's cigarette smoking. Knowing that Iowa products liability law was in a state of transition, the district court asked the Iowa supreme court to clarify the rule for product defect cases in Iowa. As the decision indicates, the court did not address the specifics of the liability of cigarette makers, but, in answering the questions from the district court, took the opportunity to spell out the new rule, as some other state high courts have done recently.*

CASE DECISION Ternus, Justice.

* * *

The Products Restatement demonstrates a recognition that strict liability is appropriate in manufacturing defect cases, but negligence principles are more suitable for other defective product cases. Accordingly, it "establishes separate standards of liability for manufacturing defects, design defects, and defects based on inadequate instructions or warnings." Products Restatement §§ comment *a*, at 14. . . . The "unreasonably dangerous" element of section 402A has been eliminated and has been replaced with a multi-faceted

continues

definition of defective product. This definition is set out in section 2:

> A product is defective when, at the time of sale or distribution, it contains a manufacturing defect, is defective in design, or is defective because of inadequate instructions or warning. A product:
> (a) contains a manufacturing defect when the product departs from its intended design even though all possible care was exercised in the preparation and marketing of the product;
> (b) is defective in design when the foreseeable risks of harm posed by the product could have been reduced or avoided by the adoption of a reasonable alternative design by the seller or other distributor, or a predecessor in the commercial chain of distribution, and the omission of the alternative design renders the product not reasonably safe;
> (c) is defective because of inadequate instructions or warnings when the foreseeable risks of harm posed by the product could have been reduced or avoided by the provision of reasonable instructions or warnings by the seller or other distributor, or a predecessor in the commercial chain of distribution, and the omission of the instructions or warnings renders the product not reasonably safe. Products Restatement §§ 2, at 14.

The commentators give the following explanation for the analytical framework adopted in the Products Restatement:

> In contrast to manufacturing defects, design defects and defects based on inadequate instructions or warnings are predicated on a different concept of responsibility. In the first place, such defects cannot be determined by reference to the manufacturer's own design or marketing standards because those standards are the very ones that the plaintiffs attack as unreasonable. Some sort of independent assessment of advantages and disadvantages, to which some attach the label 'risk-utility balancing,' is necessary. Products are not generically defective merely because they are dangerous. Many product-related accident costs can

be eliminated only by excessively sacrificing product features that make products useful and desirable. Thus, the various trade-offs need to be considered in determining whether accident costs are more fairly and efficiently borne by accident victims, on the one hand, or, on the other hand, by consumers generally through the mechanism of higher product prices attributable to liability costs imposed by the courts on product sellers. Products Restatement § 2 comment a, at 15-16. . . .

In addition, the Products Restatement does not place a conventional label, such as negligence or strict liability, on design defect cases.

The rules in this Section and in other provisions of this Chapter define the bases of tort liability for harm caused by product defects existing at the time of sale or other distribution. The rules are stated functionally rather than in terms of traditional doctrinal categories. . . . As long as these requisites are met, doctrinal tort categories such as negligence or strict liability may be utilized in bringing the claim. . . .

In summary, we now adopt Restatement (Third) of Torts; Product Liability sections 1 and 2 for product defect cases. Under these sections, a plaintiff seeking to recover damages on the basis of a design defect must prove "the foreseeable risks of harm posed by the product could have been reduced or avoided by the adoption of a reasonable alternative design by the seller or other distributor, or a predecessor in the commercial chain of distribution, and the omission of the of the alternative design renders the product not reasonably safe."

* * *

QUESTIONS FOR ANALYSIS

1. Suppose the *Sufix* case had been tried under this rule. Would the result have been the same?

2. In this case, a smoker claimed that cigarette makers should be liable for his health problems. Apply the rule; does it seem to make the producers liable?

Unknown Hazards   The largest dollar volume and number of product liability cases are based on *unknown hazards* or latent defects—dangers that were not known or not fully appreciated at the time the product was manufactured. Since the hazard associated with the product may not be learned for years, neither the producer nor the consumer may be able to prevent injury.

Billions of dollars have been awarded in thousands of suits (often joined as class actions) involving the health effects of asbestos, injuries caused by IUDs, and damage caused by drug side effects that did not appear for years. The single largest area of litigation for unknown hazard has involved asbestos. Companies in the asbestos industry, of which dozens have filed for bankruptcy-court protection, have devoted $50 billion to help resolve litigation, which has been proceeding for more than thirty years. Although more than 300,000 plaintiffs have agreed to settlements, many more have not reached resolution.

A Way to Reduce the Damage?

Your company makes large machines used by businesses and consumers. Regardless of the quality of the construction of the machines, accidents happen that kill or injure people. Is there a strategy the company can adopt to reduce the costs of dealing with the litigation that results?

ISSUE
Spotter

Market Share Liability

A new development in product liability arose in a California Supreme Court case, *Sindell* v. *Abbott Laboratories* (607 P.2d 924). The case pioneered the notion of *market share liability* or *enterprise liability*. This arose in response to suits filed involving the daughters of women who had taken DES (diethylstilbestrol) during pregnancy. DES is responsible for cancer in the reproductive systems of (now adult) daughters of women who took DES before it was banned. Because DES was produced by many companies and was taken decades ago, plaintiffs could not identify the manufacturer of the drug taken by their mothers. The California court allowed plaintiffs to sue all drug manufacturers who marketed DES and said that those manufacturers would share liability according to their share of the market for the drug.

JURIS *prudence?*

It's Nerf Basketball for Ivy League

Cornell student Darren Traub was playing pickup basketball when he tried to dunk the ball, which he had never been able to do. He ran at the hoop, his hand hit the rim, and he fell down and hurt both wrists. He sued the university and the hoop maker for negligence and strict liability, contending that the rigid rims caused or enhanced his injuries.

The defendants claimed that Traub assumed the risk inherent in playing basketball with a rigid hoop, noting that "what goes up must come down." Judge Pooler disagreed and held that the suit would go forward. The danger that occurs "when a player's fingers, hands, and wrists come into contact with a rigid basketball hoop," which can make a controlled landing difficult, is not well known, so Traub may not have assumed the risk.

Source: *Traub* v. *Cornell*, 1998 WL 187401

Joint and Several Liability

The Wisconsin Supreme Court addressed the same question in *Collins* v. *Eli Lilly*. It rejected the market share liability terminology but held that plaintiffs could sue any or all manufacturers and that the manufacturers could bring in other manufacturers as defendants so they would share the liability. This is the more traditional *joint and several liability* rule, which has been abolished in some states, that allows any defendant to be held responsible for all damages. In mass tort cases such as DES and asbestos, where numerous producers are involved, in practice the litigation tends to look like market share liability, but that terminology has not been adopted by any other states.

Collins v. Eli Lilly Co.

Wisconsin Supreme Court
116 Wis.2d 166, 342 N.W.2d 37 (1984)

CASE BACKGROUND   *Collins was born in 1958. Her mother had taken DES (diethylstilbestrol) during pregnancy, as prescribed, to prevent miscarriage. DES was banned in 1971 when its cancer risks to adult women whose mothers had taken the drug during pregnancy with their daughter(s) became known. Collins had cancer surgery in 1975. Like at least 1,000 other victims, she attributed the cancer to the DES taken by her mother and sued a dozen producers of DES. Under tort law as it existed, Collins would be unlikely to recover damages because of the lack of ability to prove which specific drug company had produced the pills her mother consumed. The Supreme Court of Wisconsin had to decide how to handle this kind of case.*

CASE DECISION   Callow, Justice.

* * *

Although the defendants in this case may not have acted in concert under the concert of action theory, all participated in either gaining approval of DES for use in pregnancy or in producing or marketing DES in subsequent years. Each defendant contributed to the risk of injury to the public and, consequently, the risk of injury to individual plaintiffs such as Therese Collins. Thus each defendant shares, in some measure, a degree of culpability in producing or marketing what the FDA, many scientists, and medical researchers ultimately concluded was a drug with possibly harmful side effects. Moreover, as between the injured plaintiff and the possibly responsible drug company, the drug company is in a better position to absorb the cost of the injury. The drug company can either insure itself against liability,

absorb the damage award, or pass the cost along to the consuming public as a cost of doing business. We conclude that it is better to have drug companies or consumers share the cost of the injury than to place the burden solely on the innocent plaintiff. Finally, the cost of damages awards will act as an incentive for drug companies to test adequately the drugs they place on the market for general medical use.

* * *

Thus, the plaintiff need commence suit against only one defendant and allege the following elements: that the plaintiff's mother took DES; that DES caused the plaintiff's subsequent injuries; that the defendant produced or marketed the type of DES taken by the plaintiff's mother; and that the defendant's conduct in producing or marketing the DES constituted a breach of a legally recognized duty to the plaintiff. In the situation where the plaintiff cannot allege and prove what type of DES the mother took, as to the third element the plaintiff need only allege and prove that the defendant drug company produced or marketed the drug DES for use in preventing miscarriages during pregnancy.

* * *

At the trial of this case the plaintiff will have to prove each of these elements to the satisfaction of the trier of fact. . . . Remanded for trial and further proceedings consistent with this opinion. . . .

QUESTIONS FOR ANALYSIS

1. Why would Collins be allowed to sue for something that occurred thirty years before?

2. Compare this ruling to that of the Supreme Court of California, which held that the major drug companies would pay the damages on a proportionate share according to their share of the drug market in question. Are these different in impact?

Defenses in Product Liability Suits

Strict liability and the rule of negligence hold manufacturers to a high standard of product safety. This does not mean absolute liability. Manufacturers are not liable if the consumer has engaged in improper activity that increases the risk of injury. Most courts recognize product misuse and assumption of risk as defenses in product-related injury cases. Some other defenses to tort actions were discussed in Chapter 6. The rules vary somewhat from state to state, and regulations may also affect liability.

Product Misuse If it can be shown that the product was misused, combined with another product to make it dangerous, used in some improper and unforeseen manner, or not maintained properly, the negligence of the consumer may preclude recovery for damages. As we saw before, the courts compare the negligence the plaintiff contributes to a situation to the fault of the defendant.

In one case, the court barred recovery by plaintiffs who were injured when the blowout of a fairly new tire was shown to be caused by plaintiff overinflating the tires. The court noted, "To hold otherwise would be to convert a strict liability cause of action into one of absolute liability." In another case, drunkenness by a consumer was held to have led to product misuse that resulted in injury.

Assumption of Risk As we saw in the last chapter, one may consent to assume risk. Playing contact sports and engaging in many other activities that can lead to injury are voluntary choices that include a chance of injury. Certain consumer products are unavoidably dangerous such that, so long as the risks are understood, consumers are presumed to accept the bad with the good. Medicinal drugs are understood to be inherently dangerous. Most have known side effects about which physicians and consumers should be informed, but we must accept the fact that given the current state of scientific knowledge, these beneficial products cannot be made safer.

Another class of goods, which are more controversial, are products such as tobacco and alcohol that inflict well-known undesirable side effects. If a person smokes cigarettes for forty years and contracts lung cancer, should the cigarette producer be liable? If a person drinks large quantities of alcohol for years and develops cirrhosis of the liver, should the liquor industry be liable? In general, the courts have said no; the persons using the cigarettes and alcohol know of the risks involved and should bear the costs. It is not hard to imagine the impact on the liquor and cigarette industries if they were held liable for health problems believed to be associated with the use of their products.

Sophisticated Purchaser The *sophisticated purchaser* or *knowledgeable purchaser* defense usually applies in business settings. It has long been held that there is no need for the producers of obviously dangerous products, such as knives, to warn consumers of the dangers of knives, but what about products that are not obviously dangerous and that are used in the workplace? A sophisticated purchaser is one who by experience and expertise is aware of the possible hazards associated with a product and has an obligation to inform his employees and customers of potential hazards.

INTERNATIONAL Perspective

Strict Liability Goes Global

The United States has always had the toughest product liability standards in the world. U.S. manufacturers have claimed this puts them at a competitive disadvantage. But as Europe and Japan move to a strict liability standard, the fact that American producers are used to meeting high quality standards may enhance their global competitiveness.

As Professors Hurd and Zollers discuss in an article in the *American Business Law Journal*, the European Union (EU) is forcing product liability law to be adopted in Europe. The standard is one of strict liability for injuries caused by defective consumer goods. Similarly, Japan has introduced strict liability through its civil code. As in other areas of law, common standards enhance worldwide product acceptance.

The major difference between the United States and other countries is not the strict liability standard for products but the incentives to litigate. There are fewer damages to sue for in many countries because they have social programs that care for injured consumers. Juries are rarely used outside of the United States; judges in other countries tend to give smaller judgments than similar cases might produce here. The United States is the only major country that allows the contingency fee in litigation, which allows attorneys to carry most of the risk of litigation. Most countries also use the "loser pays" rule that requires the losing party to cover the attorney fees for the winning party; this discourages suits with a small chance of victory. Further, most countries do not allow class action suits and reject ideas such as market-share liability.

A company that constantly buys inputs for use in manufacturing does not need to be fully informed at each purchase about all dangers. The supplier has a duty to inform the user of all known dangers, but once the communication has been made, unless something new comes to the attention of the supplier, the supplier does not need to constantly repeat warnings.

For example, in *Akin v. Ashland Chemical Co.* (10th Cir., 156 F.3d 1030), employees at Tinker Air Force Base in Oklahoma sued several suppliers of chemicals to the Air Force for toxic tort arising out of exposure to chemicals. The appeals court upheld the dismissal of the case. "Because of the wealth of research available, the ability of the Air Force to conduct studies, and its extremely knowledgeable staff, we find that the Air Force easily qualifies as a 'knowledgeable purchaser' that should have known the risks involved with low-level chemical exposure. Employees of the Air Force are also deemed to possess the necessary level of sophistication, so that defendants had no duty to warn the Air Force or its employees of the potential hazards."

Statutory Limits on Liability

Various laws are specifically designed to limit potential tort liability:

- Worker compensation statutes usually make that program the exclusive remedy for injured workers, unless an intentional tort was involved.
- Federal regulations that prescribe maximum allowable radiation exposure levels set the standard of care upon which liability is based.
- As government contractors, manufacturers of products made to government specifications are generally immune from product liability.
- Products that must follow federal regulations regarding label requirements, including warnings of possible injuries, are not subject to common-law failure-to-warn actions.

- State laws may specify limits on liability, such as Colorado's statutory limits on the liability of ski resorts for injuries suffered by skiers.

Ultrahazardous Activity

Long before the development of strict liability for defective products, the common law had developed a rule of strict liability for injuries resulting from *ultrahazardous activity*. This rule, which is in effect in most states, goes back to the 1868 British case, *Rylands* v. *Fletcher*. The *Restatement of Torts* defines such activity as one that "necessarily involves a risk of serious harm to the person, land or chattels of another which cannot be eliminated by the exercise of the utmost care" and "is not a matter of common usage."

This rule has applied to such things as blasting with explosives, allowing chemicals to seep into water supplies, crop dusting, and transporting chemicals in a city. Actually, most of these activities are not all that uncommon, but they are ultrahazardous. The party in charge of such acts is generally responsible for whatever happens. For instance, in *Old Island Fumigation, Inc.* v. *Barbee* (604 So.2d 1246), Old Island fumigated two of the three buildings in a condominium complex. Old Island was told that the third building was sealed from the other two, but, in fact, it was not, and residents of the third building were made ill. Even though the opening that let the fumes into the third building was a mistake made by the architect or contractor who built the buildings, the court of appeals held against Old Island. Because fumigation is an ultrahazardous activity, Old Island was liable for injuries "regardless of the level of care exercised in carrying out this activity." The negligence of other parties is irrelevant to the imposition of liability in such cases.

Does Product Liability Need Reform?

Manufacturers are pushing for statutes that would limit strict liability for producers. They claim that liability costs make America less competitive in world markets. The annual cost to the economy is said to be in the hundreds of billions of dollars, consuming as much as 2.5 percent of GDP, compared to about as little as 0.5 percent of GDP in some other developed nations. The threat of liability forces good products off the market in the United States and results in less research for new products. Liability insurance in the United States often costs more than what it costs for similar businesses in Canada, Japan, or Europe because, in the United States, liability awards are higher and liability suits are easier to bring.

Organized opposition to the proposed legislation mostly comes from trial lawyers associations, which assert that liability is a reflection of our society's belief that if you injure people, you should pay for the costs of their injuries.

A Middle Ground?

Trial lawyers argue for no changes in the product liability system. Business groups want to limit damages, limit the bases for liability, and return some product cases to the rule of negligence instead of strict liability. Many states passed laws to restrict liability and to put caps on damages. Some of these laws have been struck down as unconstitutional, but caps on damages for "pain and suffering" have been upheld in California, Florida, Illinois, Indiana, Maryland, and several other states.

Perhaps a middle ground is provided by the prestigious American Law Institute, which produced a report by leading legal scholars recommending liability reform. Among the recommendations:

- Awards for pain and suffering would be for severely injured plaintiffs only.
- Juries would be given a scale setting dollar amounts for specific injuries to determine damages.
- Payment received by a plaintiff from private insurance would offset jury awards to prevent double collection.
- Compliance with government standards would be a strong defense in a lawsuit and provide a bar against punitive damages.
- Defendants would pay the legal fees of successful plaintiffs.

Summary

- Misrepresentation, or fraud, is a general category of tort that can be intentional or based on negligence. When intentional, it must be shown that there was an intent to provide misleading information to convince someone to do something they would not have otherwise, and that the party had good reason to rely on the deceit, which was then the cause of a loss suffered. Most negligent misrepresentation occurs in a professional setting, when a party suffers a loss due to failure to live up to the standard of care expected of a person in the field of expertise in question.
- The tort of interference with contractual relations occurs when ongoing contractual deals are wrongfully and knowingly interfered with by another party who wants the existing contract to be broken.
- Interference with prospective advantage (or prospective economic advantage) is an unreasonable interference in another party's business dealings so as to prevent an ongoing relationship from succeeding.
- The rule of negligence in tort dominated product liability the first half of this century. Still good law, it requires producers to take the care of a reasonable person when making products to prevent foreseeable injury. The reasonable person is held to the skill of an expert in the industry.
- Strict liability for defective products began in contract law based on implied warranty inferred by the courts from a review of the parties' dealings or based on express warranty about the quality of a product. The Uniform Commercial Code also imposes liability for products that are warranted to be merchantable or have guaranteed quality.
- Strict liability in tort became widely accepted after the 1963 *Greenman* decision in California. Section 402A of the *Restatement (Second) of Torts* imposes strict liability on the manufacturer when a "product in a defective condition unreasonably dangerous to the user or consumer or to his property" is sold. Unlike negligence, it does not matter how much care was used in the preparation of the product prior to sale. Besides a flaw in the product, common reasons for the imposition of strict liability are failure to warn of hazards in using the product and defects in the design of the product that make it less safe than it should be.
- Many strict liability suits have concerned unknown hazards, such as those associated with asbestos, where the danger did not become known until many years later. When claims of thousands of persons exceed all funds of defendants, the claims may be joined together for settlement. When many companies have made the same product, they may be held joint and severally liable, potentially requiring all producers to pay compensation.

- A defense that may be raised in product liability suits is negligence by the user, which can include product misuse. There also can be assumption of risk by the consumer, especially for products such as medicinal drugs that are beneficial but have unavoidable side effects and products such as tobacco and alcohol that are legal but have known bad effects. Producers do not have to constantly warn sophisticated buyers, such as producers, about all dangers in products. Statutes and regulations can also limit the liability of producers.
- Strict liability in tort has long been imposed on those who engage in ultrahazardous activities, such as using explosives, and on those who handle unusually dangerous substances, such as toxic chemicals. If the party involved in the ultrahazardous activity causes an injury to an innocent party, regardless of the degree of care taken to prevent harm, liability is imposed.

REVIEW AND DISCUSSION QUESTIONS

1. Define the following terms:

   intentional interference with contractual relations
   interference with prospective advantage
   caveat emptor
   strict liability
   implied warranty

   express warranty
   failure to warn
   design defect
   unknown hazards
   market share liability
   sophisticated purchaser

2. Refer to §402A of the *Restatement (Second) of Torts:* What does "the seller is engaged in the business of selling such a product" mean? Who is excluded by this? What does "it is expected to and does reach the user or consumer without substantial change in the condition in which it is sold" mean? What situations does this cover? What is the difference between the idea that the rule applies although "the seller has exercised all possible care in the preparation and sale of his product" and the rule of negligence? What does "the user or consumer has not bought the product from or entered into any contractual relation with the seller" mean?

CASE QUESTIONS

3. CMI provided inspection services of fiber optic cable for telephone company Caprock. When CMI's contract with Caprock ended, Caprock refused to rehire CMI and instead hired five other companies to do the inspection work. Caprock told CMI employees that CMI's work with Caprock was ending but that they might apply for work with the five other companies if they wanted to continue doing inspection work for Caprock. One hundred fifty employees of CMI quit and went to work for the five competitor firms. CMI sued Caprock for interference with business expectancy. Did it have a case? [*Construction Management and Inspection, Inc.* v. *Caprock Communications Corp.*, 301 F.3d 939 (8th Cir., 2002)]

4. The buyers of residential property mistakenly believed that the 3.5 acres of land included the well attached to the house, which they later found out was not on the property. The previous owner and the real estate agent had pointed out the well, but had not stated that it was on the property. The buyers did not examine the existing survey of the property, nor did they order a new survey done,

either of which would have shown that the well was not on the property. Did the buyers have a basis for a suit for fraud? [*Crawford* v. *Williams*, 375 S.E.2d 223 (Sup. Ct., Ga., 1989)]

5. Fourteen "disciples" of self-proclaimed yoga guru Amrit Desai worked for Desai at his large "retreat center for holistic health and education," some for as long as twenty years. The disciples had given Desai much of their wealth and worked for him for very low wages as they attempted to follow his teachings of poverty and chastity. They sued Desai for fraud when they allegedly discovered that Desai had huge quantities of cash and assorted sexual relations over many years. Could this be the basis for a fraud action to recover for lost wages and donations? [*Dushkin* v. *Desai*, 18 F.Supp.2d 117 (D. Mass., 1998)]

 Check your answer at http://meiners.westbuslaw.com

6. Dorothy Zimmerman owned a condo at Winding Lake II. Shortly after moving in, she began to experience difficulties with cold, dampness, and mildew on various interior walls. The builder's efforts to remedy the situation proved fruitless. Zimmerman and other occupants stationed themselves in front of the sales office to the condo complex and proceeded to walk about carrying signs and talking to passersby. One sign read: "Open House, See Mildew, Feel Dampness, No Extra Charge." Several prospective buyers left the project without visiting the sales office. No new units were sold during the time in which the occupants picketed. The company sued Zimmerman and others who participated. What will be the action alleged and what will be the result? [*Zimmerman* v. *D.C.A. at Welleby, Inc.*, 505 So.2d 1371 (Dist. Ct. App., 4th Dist., Fla., 1987)]

7. Florida land developer Lehigh would show prospective buyers Lehigh Acres and have the buyers stay at its motel. Competitor Azar would watch for the buyers, contact them at the motel, tell them that under federal law they had three days to cancel any contract with Lehigh, and then show them less expensive property that he was selling. Lehigh wanted a court order to keep Azar away from its customers because Azar was interfering with business relationships. Will the court tell Azar to stay away? [*Azar* v. *Lehigh Corp.*, 364 So.2d 860 (Dist. Ct. App., 2d Dist., Fla., 1978)]

 Check your answer at http://meiners.westbuslaw.com

8. Joe Washington was shot in the head during a robbery at a dry cleaning store at a strip mall in Dallas. Security at the mall consisted of security guards a few hours per week hired by the mall owner. Washington sued the mall owner for failure to provide sufficient security. The dry cleaning store had been robbed ten times before the robbery in question. Does Washington have a case against the mall owner? [*Washington* v. *RTC*, 68 F.3d 935 (5th Cir., 1995)]

9. Many crimes involve the use of cheap handguns. Producers and sellers of such handguns know that some of these guns will be used in crimes by the purchaser of the gun or by a criminal who steals the gun. Could the producers and retailers of such handguns be held liable for the injuries suffered by persons shot during a crime? That is, could such a producer be held strictly liable or negligent for selling a "defective" product in that one of its known end uses is crime? [See *Patterson* v. *Rohm Gesellschaft*, 608 F.Supp. 1206 (N.D.Tex., 1985)]

Check your answer at http://meiners.westbuslaw.com

10. A five-year-old boy was killed when riding in the front seat of a car, without a seatbelt, when an accident occurred that caused the airbag to deploy. The jury

found that the airbag was "overly aggressive" and so held the car maker liable. Hyundai appealed, contending that the cause of death was the failure to have the boy in a seatbelt as required by state law. Should that defense have been allowed? [*Connelly* v. *Hyundai Motor Co.*, 351 F.3d 535 (1st Cir., 2003)]

11. A four-year-old child used a Bic lighter to start a house fire that killed a two-year-old. The lighter had a warning: "KEEP OUT OF REACH OF CHILDREN." The dead child's parents sued Bic for strict liability due to inadequate warning and because the lighter was unreasonably dangerous. What was the result? [*Todd* v. *Societe Bic*, 21 F.3d 1402 (7th Cir., 1994)]

 Check your answer at <u>http://meiners.westbuslaw.com</u>

12. Two experienced welders were working inside a barge. A gas hose leading to the welding torch developed a leak that the workers apparently could not smell because of "nasal fatigue" from having inhaled so much gas. One worker lit a cigarette, igniting the gas, killing both workers. The workers' heirs sued the gas and gas hose producers in strict liability. Was either company liable? [*Little* v. *Liquid Air Corp.*, 37 F.3d 1069 (5th Cir., 1994)]

13. An infant was given St. Joseph Aspirin for Children. The infant had the flu, and the aspirin triggered Reye's syndrome, leaving the child quadriplegic, blind, and profoundly mentally retarded. The product contained a warning, approved by the Food and Drug Administration, about the dangers of giving aspirin to children with the flu or chicken pox, but the child's guardian in the Los Angeles area could read only Spanish. The product was advertised in Spanish, but the warning was not published in Spanish. Was strict liability imposed for failure of duty to warn? [*Ramirez* v. *Plough, Inc.*, 25 Cal.Rptr.2d 97 (Sup. Ct., Cal., 1993)]

14. Brandon Branco, an experienced BMX (bicycle motorcross) racer, suffered severe injuries when he crashed at Kearny Moto Park's BMX course in San Diego. He had complied with all safety rules and claimed that the park was negligent in its design of one jump. His expert witness testified that the jump (two hills in a row) required a very high degree of expertise not likely to be had by most riders at the park. Given that everyone had the chance to observe the jump and other riders successfully go over it, could there be negligence? [*Branco* v. *Kearny Moto Park*, 43 Cal. Rptr.2d 392 (Ct. App., 4th Dist., Cal., 1995)]

15. A three-year-old child turned on the hot water in a bathtub. His eleven-month-old sister climbed into the tub and was severely burned before being rescued by her mother. The child died from the burns. The mother sued the hot water tank maker for installing a thermostat that allowed the water to reach 170 degrees, which was the industry standard. Is that a design defect? [*Williams* v. *Briggs Co.*, 62 F.3d 703 (5th Cir., 1995)]

16. Ralph Fisher died from brain cancer apparently caused by exposure on the job to polychlorinated biphenyls (PCBs) that Monsanto manufactured and sold to Fisher's employer, Westinghouse, which used PCBs in making electrical transformers. PCBs were known to be highly toxic. Fisher's estate claimed that Monsanto should be held liable either for negligence or in strict liability for failure to warn Fisher of the dangers involved. What defense would Monsanto have? [*Fisher* v. *Monsanto*, 863 F.Supp. 285 (W.D., Va., 1994)]

17. Residents and businesses in a Pennsylvania town sued the owners and operators of a nuclear power plant (Three Mile Island) for personal injuries and for loss of business they claim they suffered because of an accident at the nuclear plant that released radiation into the atmosphere. What defense would the power plant have? [*In re TMI*, 67 F.3d 1103 (3rd Cir., 1995)]

ETHICS QUESTION

18. Various industries have lobbied for legislative restrictions on tort liability. For instance, the nuclear power industry has long been protected by a statute that limits its upper-dollar liability in the event of a serious accident that is much lower than the potential losses from such an accident. Also, the industry cannot be held liable in tort for radiation releases so long as federal guidelines are not exceeded. Many companies in other industries would like similar protection. Is it ethical to seek statutory limits on liability? Is it ethical for legislators to grant such protection? What limits would be acceptable?

PULLING IT  *Together*

Multiple Torts

Curtis Cole was head of the financial department at a paper mill owned by Mead. He attended a business meeting in Atlanta with several people he supervised. Two employees, Brenda Chandler and Pola Buckley, reported to the human resources manager that Cole made several sexually inappropriate jokes or comments. After an investigation that included interviews with all parties involved, Mead fired Cole for sexual harassment. Cole contended that the allegations by Buckley and Chandler were false. He also claimed that Mead injured him because, among other things, prospective employers had to be informed of why he was fired from Mead. Cole sued Chandler, Buckley, and Mead. What are the various torts he could claim against those parties?

[*Cole* v. *Chandler*, 752 A.2d 1189 (Sup. Jud. Ct., Maine, 2000)]

INTERNET ASSIGNMENT

http://www.mdd.uscourts.gov

On May 13, 2004, a fire occurred at the Health Food Store (HFS) in Silver Springs, Maryland. Fire investigators determined that the only appliance plugged into the wall at the point of origin of the fire was an ionizer which HFS had purchased in (and used since) 1996. HFS filed a claim with its insurance company. The insurance company brought a products liability suit against the manufacturer of the ionizer to recover the insurance proceeds. Which six facts must the plaintiff establish in order to prevail? Can a defect be inferred in this case? See *Hartford Casualty Insurance Company* v. *Marpac Corporation*, Civil No. JFM-01-918, United States District Court for the District of Maryland (April 2, 2002).

Chapter 8

Real and Personal Property

> Humpty Dumpty sat on a wall
> Humpty Dumpty had a great fall
> All the King's horses
> And all the King's men
> Couldn't put Humpty together again
>
> Nursery rhyme dating to 1600s

What was Humpty's legal capacity on the wall? Was he sitting on his own wall? Was he pushed from the wall? Was the wall the property of another person? Was he a guest who was permitted to be on the wall or did he ignore his host's notice to stay away from the wall? Did he have a legal right to be on the property where the wall was located, or was he a trespasser? Who is responsible for the costs of Mr. Dumpty's health care or, if the fall was fatal, is the property owner liable to his heirs? Little children need not think about these issues, but property owners have good reasons to be concerned about the safety of people who are on their property. Shoppers who fall and suffer injuries on business property often sue business owners.

Here we begin our study of the law of property—the oldest part of the common law—focusing primarily on its application to business. Property refers to an aggregate of rights that are guaranteed and protected by the government. That includes things visible and invisible, tangible and intangible— things that have value. This chapter focuses on real property: things that are immovable, such as land; and personal property: things that are movable, such as furniture and clothing (traditionally called *chattel*). We consider ownership of property, in the many forms it can take, the legal basis for controls on private property imposed by governments and the liability that may rest with property owners when accidents happen on their property.

REAL PROPERTY

Real property refers to land; things under the land, such as oil and minerals; and things solidly attached to the land, such as buildings and trees. At law, *property* is a legally protected expectation of being able to use a thing for one's advantage. That is, it is not physical existence of property that matters so much as the right to use property for one's purposes. If someone has a right to use a piece of land however she likes, or if she has a right to use the land for certain purposes, her expectations about the land change because of her legal interest in it. For example, if you have land that is found to contain a rare plant protected under the Endangered Species Act (discussed in Chapter 17), how you may use the land will be limited by regulations concerning protection for the plant.

The review of tort law was concerned mostly with personal interests protected by the law. *Property interests* differ from personal interests in that property refers to physical things, such as land and objects, in which one can have a recognized interest against other persons. That is, a person has the right to deny others the use of the "things" in which he has an interest. As we will see, tort law is often used to protect interests in property.

Historial Origins

Some of the terms that describe the law regarding real property appear a bit peculiar because the terms and concepts come from the common law as developed in England from the twelfth to the sixteenth centuries. While some terms are old, the substance of the law has changed greatly over the years. As we will see, the common law has been modified by statutory law, although many of the statutes primarily provide procedures for enforcing common-law property rules. Next we look at some of the traditional elements of property law.

Deeds and Titles

Ownership of land is evidenced by various documents. The deed and the title are among the most important. A *deed* is the primary way to transfer ownership interests in property. Deeds are in writing and transfer title from the current property owner to the new owner. They identify the original owner(s), describe the land, identify the new owner(s), and state that ownership is being transferred, possibly subject to certain conditions.

Different types of deeds are used in different states and for different purposes. Here we mention only a few of the most common. A *quitclaim deed* is a deed of conveyance that passes whatever interests the grantor had in the property. This might not provide any assurance of good title to the property; it may only terminate the interest of the previous possessor of the property. The rights conveyed by such a deed vary from state to state. In contrast, a *warranty deed* is a deed that explicitly promises that a good, clear title to the property is being conveyed by the grantor.

The *title*, which comes from receipt of a valid deed, is the means by which the owner of property has legal possession of the property. It is the formal right of ownership. A clear title means that no other persons can claim ownership. Titles may be held by one or more persons or by a business. Titles to land are recorded by state officials, usually at the county level. Title recording provides a public record of who owns what and of limitations or claims on titles, such as the claim that mortgage lenders often hold on real estate.

Fee Simple

The law often refers to one's interest or legal rights in real property as an *estate*. According to the *Property Restatement*, an estate is "an interest in land which (a) is or may become possessory and (b) is ownership measured in terms of duration." That is, one may have possession of land now or may have the right to take possession of land at some point in the future. There are time limits on the length of ownership. Ownership may be for life, which is uncertain in length, but one cannot take property to the grave—one's interests in an estate must pass to other persons.

The most common form of real property ownership is *fee simple* or *fee simple absolute*. Fee simple means the right to exclusive possession of a particular piece of land for an indefinite time as well as the right to dispose of the land as the owner pleases. Most real estate in the United States is in fee simple, meaning it may be inherited, transferred to others, or sold in part or in whole and, in general, is the strongest form of real property control.

Traditionally, ownership in fee simple was said to extend to the skies, but air travel limited that concept. Ownership is also said to extend "to the center of the earth," meaning fee simple ownership includes the right to minerals and oil under the land. Those assets, like other features of land, can be sold or rented separately from the main piece of property. Subsurface *mineral rights* are often legally separated from ownership of the surface land.

Forms of Ownership

Most property is held in the name of more than one person. It may also be in the name of a business. While we commonly use the word "tenant" to mean a person who rents property, at law the word "tenant" has a broader meaning. It refers to one who possesses lands by any kind of right or title, whether in fee simple or for a limited period of time. When we consider the ownership of property, different forms of tenancy are commonly used.

A *tenancy in common* is a form of ownership in which each tenant (owner) has an undivided interest in the property. Suppose Tweedledee and Tweedledum each contribute half the money to buy a piece of property they own equally. They are said to have a tenancy in common. If Tweedledee dies, her interest in the property passes to her estate or to the heirs she has named; it does not go to Tweedledum.

It is usual for married couples or partners to own property in the form of a *joint tenancy*. This is a purchase of property by two or more persons who have the same interest in the undivided possession of property. The primary difference from the tenancy in common is that in a joint tenancy there is a right of survivorship, which means that if one owner dies, the ownership rights pass to the other owner.

The law places few restrictions on the forms used to hold property. For example, one may grant a *life estate* in a piece of property that gives a person the right to be a *tenant for life*. This may be done so that a family member has the right to occupy a piece of property until their death, at which point title to the property passes to the heirs who have been named by the owner of the property.

Evolving Property Law: Condominiums

While property law is old in origin, it adapts to changes in society. Condominiums were not seen much before the 1960s, but the fee simple estate applies to such living arrangements. Each living space in a building may be owned in fee simple (with numerous conditions attached), yet the land the building sits on, as well as common areas such as elevators and lobbies, is held in common (for the benefit of the condo owners) by another person or business. To help adapt property law to such arrangements, all states have statutes that simplified the legal process of having condos and other modern living arrangements consistent with traditional property law.

Servitudes

Servitudes are limitations or requirements about the use of property. Servitudes attach to the estate or property itself and impose certain use limits on the owner of the property. The most important forms of servitudes are easements and covenants.

Easements

An *easement* is a right to enter land owned by another and make certain use of it or to take something from land. An easement is not ownership of an estate but a "burden" on another person's estate. The document that creates an easement is much like a deed: it explains the use of certain property that is conveyed from the property owner to the easement owner.

Positive easements allow the easement holder to go on the estate for certain purposes. A negative easement would be giving up a right that the owner of an estate would normally have, such as agreeing with the Nature Conservancy to preserve and protect certain rare plants that exist on the property. One may also give or sell someone the right to remove valuable things from one's estate, such as oil, mineral, or trees; this right may be referred to as a *profit*.

Unless the easement is for a set time, it will be attached permanently to the property. As with ownership arrangements, parties are generally free to agree upon any kind of easement they wish. Almost all homes have easements for utilities and for public sidewalks. Once an easement is granted, the property owner may not interfere with it unless the easement holder agrees. That is, the sidewalk may not be

---

INTERNATIONAL *Perspective*

Insecure Property Rights

In the United States, property ownership is clear. Land is owned by a private party or by the government. There are few disputes over title to land and no one would think of building a house on land unless clear title was assured. But in much of the world, rights to property are muddled and highly political. Hernando de Soto, head of a think tank in Peru, did a study of land ownership in several nations. He found that most farmers do not own the land they farm and city dwellers do not own the land under their houses.

In the Philippines, only one-third of agricultural land has clear title and only 43 percent of dwellings have clear title. In Peru, 81 percent of farmed land is not owned; only half the urban dwellings are on titled land. The poorest nation in the Western Hemisphere is Haiti, where 97 percent of farm land is not owned and 68 percent of urban dwellings are in the "informal" sector. In Egypt, 92 percent of urban dwellings are on "unowned" land, as are 83 percent of all farms.

De Soto attributes the persistence of poverty in such countries to the inability of most people to have the chance to capitalize on the value they have put into their farms and houses. Without secure property rights, economic progress may be enjoyed mostly by the minority who live in the formal economy that we recognize and is critical to global commerce.

Source: *The Mystery of Capital* (Basic Books)

blocked or removed, and if a gas line needs to be dug up for repair, the gas company has the right, doing as little damage as possible, to dig up the yard to get to the pipe.

Easements are often sold to a neighbor who needs the use of someone else's property. If Ben buys twenty acres in the woods and the property is behind Nancy's land, which faces the road, to have access to his property Ben must get an easement from Nancy to build a road across her property. It is obviously a good idea to get needed easements to property settled before buying such property.

Adverse Possession

Peculiar forms of property use or possession are called *easement by prescription* and *adverse possession*. This is what is called a hostile use of another person's land; that is, someone who has no right to occupy or use an estate does so without permission. The use may be in the form of an easement, such as driving across another's property regularly, or may be actual possession, such as building a house and living on another's property. In such cases, the user of the property may obtain a legally recognized easement, such as the right to continue driving across the land, or may even obtain title to the land on which the house is built, so long as taxes have been paid.

The general conditions needed for adverse possession are that it must be

1. Actual: the adverse user in fact uses or possesses the property in question.
2. Open: the use or possession must be visible so that the owner is on notice.
3. Hostile: the use or possession is without permission of the owner.
4. Exclusive: the use or possession is not shared with others who also have no right to use the property.
5. Continuous: the use or possession must go on without major interruption for as much time as required by law to obtain the easement by prescription or title by adverse possession.

All states have rules, called *statutes of limitation*, for the number of years the adverse possession must occur before it becomes a legally protected possession. State law varies on the time required, from five to twenty years. Issues involving easement and adverse possession are seen in the *Hickerson* case.

Hickerson v. Bender
Court of Appeals of Minnesota
500 N.W.2d 169 (1993)

CASE BACKGROUND *The Fagans owned two lots in a subdivision on Gull Lake, Minnesota. They sold one lot in 1955 to the Beckers. The deed for that lot included an easement "for the purpose of ingress to and egress from Gull Lake over the easterly Fifteen (15) feet" of the lot that the Fagans kept, "on condition that this easement shall perpetually benefit all of the property heretofore and now owned by the grantors . . . the present and future owners of any part of such property so owned by the grantors being entitled to share equally in this ease-* *ment." The Beckers sold the property with the easement. In 1990, Hickerson owned it. Nothing had been built on the lot.*

The Fagans sold their lot to the Benders in 1958, who immediately built a home. The deed from Fagan to Bender did not mention the easement. The Benders' garage and concrete patio, various trees, and a retaining wall blocked the easement. Hickerson sued the Benders, claiming the easement was valid. Testimony at trial indicated that before Hickerson bought the property, previous owners had walked on the easement in 1967 and in about 1977.

The trial court held that the easement had been extinguished by abandonment and adverse possession before Hickerson bought the property, so Hickerson no longer had an easement. Hickerson appealed.

CASE DECISION   Harten, Judge.

* * *

Did the trial court err in determining that the easement was extinguished by both abandonment and adverse possession?

* * *

1. Abandonment. Abandonment of an easement is generally a question of fact.

To have the effect of divesting title and reinvesting the same in the grantor of the easement, the abandonment must amount to something more than mere [nonuse], for there must appear to have been an intentional relinquishment of the rights granted. . . . This intention need not appear by express declaration, but may be shown by acts and conduct clearly inconsistent with an intention to continue the use of the property for the purposes for which it was acquired.

* * *

Here, the trial court determined that the Hickersons' predecessors' acquiescence to the Benders' improvements was evidence of intent to abandon. . . . The failure of the easement holders to object to the Benders' obstruction to the easement is "conduct clearly inconsistent" with the use of the easement.

* * *

2. Adverse Possession. The trial court also concluded that the easement was extinguished by adverse possession. To extinguish an easement by adverse possession, the possessor must prove, by clear and convincing evidence, an exclusive, actual, hostile, open, and continuous possession for the statutory fifteen year period. Adverse possession must be "inconsistent with continuance of the easement." The trial court's factual findings satisfy the elements of adverse possession.

The Hickersons argue that the improvements were not "open, notorious, and hostile" because the improvements may not have been visible to their predecessors in title from adjoining Green Gables Road. We construe "open," however, to mean visible from the surroundings, or visible to one seeking to exercise his rights. . . . Hickersons' argument is refuted by the trial court's finding that "the improvements were obvious obstructions of which anyone who claimed rights adverse to the interest of the Benders would have been aware." . . . The improvements here are also not consistent with continued use of the easement. The trial court's findings support the conclusion that the Benders extinguished the easement by adverse possession.

The trial court's findings support the determination that the easement was extinguished by abandonment and adverse possession.

Affirmed.

QUESTIONS FOR ANALYSIS

1. Why was walking on the easement now and then not enough to keep it good?

2. Should the prior owners be liable to Hickerson, since they passed him a deed that claimed to have an important easement?

Covenants

A *covenant,* or a *covenant running with the land,* is not a legal interest in an estate but may be thought of as a contract with an estate. Most often, covenants are restrictions that attach to the deed when a home is sold. Of course, only people can bind property to promises. Estates cannot form promises, but the agreement made in a covenant "runs" with the land. That is, the covenant is a binding obligation that goes with property when it is transferred to a new owner, who must abide by the covenant.

Most covenants impose a benefit on an estate; otherwise, why would many people agree to them? The most common forms are residential subdivision covenants; for example, only single-family homes are allowed, every home must be at least 2,000 square feet, no prefabricated homes allowed, no dog kennels allowed, no businesses may operate from a home, and homes must be painted pastel colors. Such covenants ensure certain attributes to a subdivision that the owners of the homes think desirable. Covenants in conflict with public policy are not enforceable. For example, years ago some covenants prohibited the sale of homes to members of racial minorities.

Landlord and Tenants

When we rent property, it is called a *leasehold*. The property may be owned in fee simple by the landlord, but that is not necessary to create a leasehold with a tenant. A *tenant* is a party with possessory rights for a fixed time period or at will as agreed upon. That is, the lease gives the tenant certain rights to occupy and use the property. The tenant has possession of the estate; the landlord has the right to reclaim the estate after the lease ends. Unless prohibited by the leasehold, the tenant may lease all or a portion of the property to a subtenant.

JURIS *prudence?*

The Tenants Who Would Not Go Away

Teeman rented an apartment in New York in 1968. She subleased the apartment to the Levys in 1977, renewable year-by-year, intending to return to the city after she had helped her ailing parents. Teeman told the Levys in 1985 that the lease would not be renewed and that she was returning. The Levys refused to vacate and began a series of lawsuits, court motions, and appeals to keep control of the apartment.

The Levys ignored court orders to vacate. Finally, in late 1999, an appeals court upheld the Levys' ejection, calling their many legal tactics "abject nonsense couched as legal argument." The court ordered them to pay Teeman's legal fees and $8,000 in sanctions to the Lawyers' Fund for Client Protection because of their "reprehensible" actions.

Source: *Levy v. Carol Management Corp.*, 698 N.Y.S.2d 226 (1999)

Leases

A *lease* is an agreement that creates a leasehold out of an estate and contains conditions, such as how much rent is to be paid and what restrictions have been placed on the use of the property. All leases are subject to a large body of statutory and common law that sets boundaries on what is legal in a leasehold and on how a dispute about any issue is to be resolved.

Many states have adopted all or part of the Uniform Residential Landlord and Tenant Act, a statute designed to modernize and clarify standard terms of leases. Although state laws may require certain terms, in general, the courts want leases to:

1. Identify the parties
2. Describe the premises (address or legal description of the property) being leased
3. State how long the lease is to be in effect
4. State how much rent is to be paid

Note that a lease does not have to end at a specific date but can go from month to month. Most leases also specify who is responsible for utility bills, tell when and where the rent is to be paid, note the terms of a damage deposit, and state the tenants' responsibility for wear and tear of the property.

Rights of a Tenant

A tenant has a legal interest in the property rented and has the right of possession during the term of the lease. Other parties may be kept out of the property, including the landlord, with some exceptions. The landlord has a privilege to enter the premises to make needed repairs. Leases often state that the landlord has the right to enter the property to inspect it or to show it to future tenants, but there is no general right to pop in anytime the landlord wants.

If a landlord fails to make essential repairs in a timely manner, such as keep the air conditioning working during the summer, or otherwise allows the premises to be uninhabitable, there may be "constructive eviction." We see an example of constructive eviction in the *Barton* case, which involves a typical lease of property for business purposes. In such cases, the landlord has broken the lease, and the tenant has the right to terminate the tenancy, leave, and, in some cases, sue to recover costs incurred by the untimely move.

Barton v. Mitchell Co.

District Court of Appeals, Florida
507 So.2d 148 (1987)

CASE BACKGROUND   *Barton leased premises for five years from the Mitchell Company to operate a store selling patio furniture. Two years into the lease, Mitchell leased an adjacent space in the shopping center to Body Electric, an exercise studio. Loud music, shouts, and yells accompanied the operation of Body Electric during business hours. The volume of the noise hurt Barton's business. She lost customers and salespersons because of the noise. She repeatedly complained to the landlord, who made promises but did nothing for eight months, at which point Barton vacated the premises.*

Mitchell sued Barton for breaking the lease. The trial court awarded Mitchell $18,930, the balance of the rent due for the remainder of the lease. Barton appealed.

CASE DECISION   Walden, Judge.

* * *

The landlord says that it has no responsibility for the inability of Ms. Barton to operate her business on account of the noise and vibration coming from the adjacent tenant's premises because of paragraph 20 of the lease:

> Landlord shall not be liable to Tenant or any other person for any damage or injury caused to any person or property by reason of the failure of Landlord to

perform any of its covenants or agreements hereunder, . . . or for any damage arising from acts or negligence of other tenants or occupants of the Shopping Center. Tenant agrees to indemnify and save harmless the Landlord from and against any and all loss, damage, claim, demand, liability or expense by reason of any damage or injury to property or person which may be claimed to have arisen as a result of or in connection with the occupancy or use of said Premises by Tenant.

We disagree with the landlord's interpretation because here no one is seeking to sue or impose liability or collect damages from the landlord.

As we view it, the dispositive lease proviso is paragraph 40 entitled Quiet Enjoyment:

> Tenant, upon paying the rents and performing all of the terms on its part to be performed, shall peaceably and quietly enjoy the Demised Premises subject nevertheless, to the terms of this lease and to any mortgage, ground lease or agreements to which this lease is subordinated or specifically not subordinated as provided in Article 29(b) hereof.

When there is a constructive eviction such constitutes a breach of the covenant of quiet enjoyment. A constructive eviction occurs when a tenant is essentially deprived of the beneficial enjoyment of the leased

continues

premises where they are rendered unsuitable for occupancy for the purposes for which they are leased.

Since this was a large shopping center, we assume, we hope correctly, that all leases were similar. In paragraph 11 of the printed lease, it was stated that, "nor shall tenant maintain any loud speaker device or any noise making device in such manner as to be audible to anyone not within the premises."

Thus, from our overview, we hold, according to the mentioned authorities, that Ms. Barton was constructively evicted from the premises at the time of her departure and, therefore, has no responsibility for rent thereafter. Here, the landlord was advised of the difficulty. The landlord acknowledged responsibility and agreed to remedy the situation and had the means to

do so. The terms of the lease with reference to noise could have been enforced against Body Electric. The walls could have been insulated. Yet the landlord did nothing. Despite the damage to her business, Ms. Barton waited a reasonable time for the landlord to act.

The judgment on appeal is REVERSED.

QUESTIONS FOR ANALYSIS

1. Suppose Mitchell had installed sound insulation on the wall but the thumping in the exercise studio still created a somewhat unpleasant environment. Could Barton have left then?

2. Since Barton lost business and had to bear the cost of moving, should she have been able to recover damages from Mitchell?

INTERNATIONAL *Perspective*

Global Aspects of Being a Landlord

Property owners in the United States who lease property know of the difficulties that can be encountered when a tenant must be evicted. But such matters are relative. A study of experiences around the world shows the United States to have one of the quickest legal systems in dealing with tenants who must be sued to force them to vacate.

The data, posted by the International Institute for Corporate Governance at Yale University (*http://iicg.som.yale.edu*), shows that it takes an average of six days to complete service of process on a tenant in the United States. It takes an average of thirty-three days to get the matter resolved in court, and ten more days to obtain enforcement, for a total of forty-nine days to go through the legal process for eviction. While the process moves a few days faster in Australia and Canada, the average total time required around the world is eight and one-half months.

In general, poor countries are more likely to have less efficient judicial enforcement of property law. In Thailand and

Bulgaria, it takes about two years to complete the legal process of eviction, but it also takes that long in Italy.

The least efficient enforcement systems were found in countries of socialist legal origin and of German legal origin, which took about a year on average. The most efficient systems were found in countries of English legal origin, which took an average of half that time.

The operation of rental markets is significantly impacted by the on-the-ground rules that determine how the real estate markets will work in practice. Americans are often shocked by the complexity of land transactions in other countries; this data may indicate why landowners in other countries must go to extremes to try to reduce the likelihood of legal action involving renters.

Source: International Institute for Corporate Governance, Yale University

---

Duties of a Tenant

A tenant has the right to use the property but not to abuse it by making changes that will affect the property beyond the lease term. Abuse can come from negligence—careless failure to prevent damage from problems such as a leaking pipe, or careless damage by a tenant—or take the form of *waste*—intentional destruction or the removal of valuable property, such as trees, from the premises. A tenant may not be a nuisance to neighbors and may not engage in illegal activities on the premises.

PUBLIC CONTROL OF REAL PROPERTY

Many statutes modify the common law. Some statutes make property law operate more smoothly by providing offices for the registration of titles to private property, for listing loans taken out against property, and for noting claims made against property (often called *liens*) that are filed by people who assert they are owed money by the property owner, such as for failure to pay for putting a new roof on a house. Governments also have strong powers over the use of private property. Most important are the power of eminent domain and the broad police powers that include such things as control of property by zoning rules. That is what we review next.

Eminent Domain

Governments at all levels may use tax dollars to buy private property, or they may use their power of *eminent domain* to condemn property to force the sale of property or the granting of an easement. Eminent domain is the power to take private property for public use without the consent of the owner. As the U.S. Supreme Court noted in 1875 in *Kohl* v. *U.S.* (91 U.S. 367), "The right of eminent domain always was a right at common law. It was not a right in equity, nor was it even the creature of a statute. The . . . right itself was superior to any statute." That is, it comes from the right of the government as sovereign to control property for its purposes.

The Fifth Amendment to the Constitution states that "private property" shall not "be taken for public use, without just compensation." The same rule applies to state and local governments, which are allowed to force a private property owner to give up title to part or all of his land or to force a property owner to give an easement on the land for some public purpose. These governments must, however, offer compensation, which is generally determined by statutes that allow "fair market value" to be paid for the property interests taken by the government.

While governments have long condemned property to use it for building a school, a road, or some other public purpose, a major issue has arisen in recent years over the use of eminent domain to benefit a private party. When a business wishes to locate in a particular place, it may face the problem that some property owners may refuse to sell or will sell only at very high prices. To encourage business location, governments, especially at the local level, have used their power of eminent domain to allow a private party to get specific property at fair market value and not have to bargain with current property owners. It has also been claimed that poor people facing possible property condemnation are more often subject to such practices, as they have less political clout than wealthier landowners. The Michigan high court reviewed this matter in the *Hathcock* case.

County of Wayne v. Hathcock

Supreme Court of Michigan
684 N.W.2d 765 (2004)

CASE BACKGROUND   *Wayne County wished to help develop a private business park next to the Detroit Airport. The county contended the park would generate thousands of jobs and tens of millions in tax revenues. The county acquired over 1,000 acres for the development, but did not obtain parcels owned by nineteen different owners that were scattered around the 1,000 acres. The county commission used eminent domain power to condemn their*

continues

land. The property owners would be paid the fair market value of their land under the Uniform Condemnation Procedures Act. The matter went to court, the primary issue being if Wayne County had the right to condemn private property for the purpose of putting it into a private business park.

The county court found that the county did not abuse its discretion in determining that condemnation was necessary and served a public purpose. The appeals court affirmed. The landowners appealed.

CASE DECISION   Young, Justice.

* * *

We are presented again with a clash of two bedrock principles of our legal tradition: the sacrosanct right of individuals to dominion over their private property, on the one hand and, on the other, the state's authority to condemn private property for the commonweal.

* * *

Wayne County, as a public corporation, is authorized by [Michigan statute] to condemn property, albeit subject to other constitutional and statutory limitations. . . .

In this case, Wayne County has condemned the defendants' real properties for the following purposes: "(1) the creation of jobs for its citizens, (2) the stimulation of private investment and redevelopment in the county to insure a healthy and growing tax base so that the county can fund and deliver critical public services, (3) stemming the tide of disinvestment and population loss, and (4) supporting development opportunities which would otherwise remain unrealized." . . .

The pursuit of the goals cited above is within the scope of Wayne County's powers, and each goal certainly advances a "public purpose." A "public purpose" has been defined as that which "has for its objective the promotion of the public health, safety, morals, general welfare, security, prosperity, and contentment of all the inhabitants or residents within the municipal corporation, the sovereign powers of which are used to promote such public purpose." . . .

That is not to say, of course, that the exercise of eminent domain in this case passes constitutional muster. . . .

The question presented here is a fairly discrete one: are the condemnation of defendants' properties and the subsequent transfer or those properties to private entities . . . consistent with the common understanding of

"public use" . . . ? For the reasons stated below, we answer that question in the negative. . . .

The transfer of condemned property to a private entity, seen through . . . the law at the time of ratification of our [Michigan] Constitution, would be appropriate in one of three contexts: (1) where "public necessity of the extreme sort" requires collective action; (2) where the property remains subject to public oversight after transfer to a private entity; and (3) where the property is selected because of "facts of independent public significance," rather than the interests of the private entity to which the property is eventually transferred. . . .

The exercise of eminent domain at issue here—the condemnation of defendant's properties . . . and the subsequent transfer of those properties to private entities—implicates none of the saving elements noted by our . . . eminent domain jurisprudence.

The . . . business and technology park is certainly not an enterprise "whose very *existence* depends on the use of land that can be assembled only by the coordination central government alone is capable of achieving." To the contrary, the landscape of our country is flecked with shopping centers, office parks, clusters of hotels, and centers of entertainment and commerce. . . .

Second, the [business park] is not subject to public oversight. . . . Rather, plaintiff intends for the private entities purchasing defendants' properties to pursue their own financial welfare. . . .

Finally, there is nothing about the *act* of condemning defendants' properties that serves the public good in this case. The only public benefits cited by plaintiff arise after the lands are acquired by the government and put to private use. . . .

Every business, every productive unit in society, does . . . contribute in some way to the commonweal. To justify the exercise of eminent domain solely on the basis of the fact that the use of that property by a private entity seeking its own profit might contribute to the economy's health is to render impotent our constitutional limitations on the government's power of eminent domain. . . .

Therefore, the decisions of the lower courts are reversed and this matter is remanded for entry of an order of summary disposition in defendants' favor.

QUESTIONS FOR ANALYSIS

1. Since the business park would generate significant tax revenues for public purposes, why did that not create sufficient basis for public purpose justification for the use of eminent domain?

2. Why did the developer of the business park not buy the land directly since the landowners were to be paid fair market value anyway?

Police Powers

Eminent domain is government taking of land, but government also controls private land use by regulation. Except for environmental regulations, most land regulation is done at the state and local level. This is generally called the *police power* to regulate behavior to protect or promote the "general welfare." While the general welfare usually means health or safety, in practice it means very general power to control private use of property.

A key issue is often not whether or not there is such a power to regulate but whether government must provide compensation when land use controls reduce property values. No one questions that when the government takes property by eminent domain it must pay for the property. But in general, even when the government greatly reduces the value of property by regulation, compensation might not be due. As we saw in Chapter 4, the Supreme Court has declared that when almost all value of property is destroyed by regulation, it is protected by the Fifth Amendment rule of just compensation. But when regulation causes property to lose a lot of its value, compensation is rarely provided, so long as the government can show a rational reason for the police power that caused the economic damage and show that there was no violation of due process with respect to the injured property owner.

Would Tighter Leases Help?

ISSUE *Spotter*

As manager of an apartment complex, you know that a non-trivial number of tenants not only make a mess that is not covered by their damage deposit, but some stop paying rent so they must be evicted. You win the eviction battles, but they incur some legal fees and, since the tenants do not have resources and often leave town, you lose the rent for a couple months too. What can you do to reduce your losses? Can you write leases that will be more effective at making the tenants pay?

Zoning: A Police Power

Governments have long mandated controls on land use. Over 200 years ago regulation stated that dangerous businesses such as gunpowder factories and stinky businesses such as slaughterhouses must be located away from residential areas. In more recent times, *zoning* has become the primary method of local land control. Zoning rules commonly limit building height and size, require green areas, set population density limits, decide what kinds of buildings and businesses can be built where, and set numerous rules about the quality and type of construction that must be used. So long as such regulations do not violate a provision of the Constitution, such as free speech, or violate due process rules, the zoning rules are likely to be upheld. Next we turn to the issues that arise when private parties become involved in tort actions involving property.

Torts against Property

Some wrongs do not harm people but do harm their property or property interests. Property refers to *real property*, such as land; *personal property*, a person's possessions; and *intellectual property*, such as trade secrets. We discuss intellectual property in Chapter 9; here we review the torts that interfere with the right to enjoy and control one's property. Tort actions that may be initiated for intentional violations of the property rights of another include trespass to land, nuisance, trespass to personal property, conversion, and misappropriation.

Trespass to Land

The tort of *trespass to land* is an unauthorized intrusion by a person or a thing on land belonging to another. If the intruder intended to be on another's property, it is irrelevant if the intruder mistakenly thought she owned the land or had permission to be on it. It is not necessary for the property owner to demonstrate actual injury to the property. For example, shooting a gun across another's property may be a trespass to land despite the fact that no physical damage occurs. Land owners have a right of peaceful enjoyment of their property. If, however, a person enters another's property to protect it from damage or to help someone on the property who is in danger, that is a defense against the tort of trespass to land.

The original idea of possession of land included dominion over a space "from the center of the earth to the heavens." A trespass could be committed on, beneath, or above the surface of the land. That rule is much more relaxed today. An airplane flying over a property owner's airspace does not create an action in trespass so long as it is flying at a reasonable altitude.

Nuisance (Private and Public)

The common law of torts recognizes two kinds of nuisance: private nuisance and public nuisance. A *private nuisance* is an activity that substantially and unreasonably interferes with the use and enjoyment of land. The interference may be physical, such as vibration, the destruction of crops, or the throwing of objects upon the land. The interference may cause discomfort or a health risk from pollution, odors, excessive noise, dust, or noxious fumes. A nuisance may include offensive conditions on neighboring land that injures the occupants' mental peace through the problems those conditions create or threaten to create, or simply through their offensive nature. Most people would find, for example, that the use of the house next door for drug deals is upsetting to their mental peace while in their own houses.

Common-law nuisance actions have been useful for challenging environmental damage. In fact, nuisance actions have challenged virtually every major industrial activity that causes some form of pollution, as we will see in Chapter 17. As the *Pendoley* decision shows, even legitimate businesses may be shut down as a result of nuisance.

Pendoley v. Ferreira
Supreme Judicial Court of Massachusetts, Essex (1963)
345 Mass. 309, 187 N.E.2d 142

CASE IN BACKGROUND   *The Ferreiras started a pig farm in 1949 on twenty-five acres. By 1960, the farm had 850 pigs, 225 piglets, and 10 employees. When the farm was started, the area was sprinkled with residences. By 1960, at least thirty new homes had been built within smelling distance of the farm. Pendoley and other homeowners joined to sue Ferreira for damages for nuisance from the smell of the pig operation and requested an injunction to force the farm to be closed. Trial court awarded nine homeowners an average of $300 each in damages and enjoined the Ferreiras "from operating their piggery . . . in such an unreasonable manner as to cause a stench to emanate therefrom which materially interferes with the reasonable enjoyment of the property of a large number of people living in the vicinity." Ferreira appealed for reversal of the trial court decision; Pendoley appealed for a stronger injunction against the farm operation. (Note that the court had appointed a master [an expert] to gather information about the matter to assist it in its findings.)*

CASE DECISION   Cutter, Justice.

* * *

The master's conclusion that a nuisance exists is consistent with common knowledge that the offensive odors of a piggery with a large number of pigs ordinarily cannot be confined to a small area, here twenty-five acres. These owners of residences within a distance to which substantial piggery odors carry are entitled to specific relief against the frequently recurrent smells which interfere substantially with the enjoyment of their property "to the discomfort and annoyance of a large number of residents." . . .

It can hardly be contended that damages alone will be adequate compensation for the affront to the senses of a large group of homeowners and their families from the nauseating piggery odors. In the circumstances established by the master's report, there exists a substantial, unreasonable interference with the proper enjoyment of their residences which calls for explicit injunctive relief.

* * *

Upon the facts appearing in the master's report, the Ferreiras cannot be expected to correct the offensiveness of the piggery. The master has found that the piggery is very well operated. Substantial and effective improvement can hardly be expected in such a piggery. The Ferreiras' difficulty lies in the inherently offensive aspects of any piggery in a residential neighborhood and in the material discomfort which piggeries cause to others.

. . . we think that the plaintiffs are entitled to have the offensive operation terminated entirely within a reasonable time. Due consideration, however, must be given to the Ferreiras' economic interest in an orderly, rather than a hurried, liquidation of their pigs, and to affording them opportunity to find new premises. Accordingly, a permanent injunction against any operation of the piggery is to be granted, but the final decree is to provide (a) a reasonable opportunity for the Ferreiras to dispose of, or to move, the pigs, structures, and equipment, and (b) that the injunction is to take effect completely only at a specified future date, with provisions for the protection of the plaintiffs in the interim in some practicable manner. . . .

So ordered.

QUESTIONS FOR ANALYSIS
1. The court said that due consideration must be given to the losses the Ferreiras would incur from having to move their legitimate business operation, but then ordered them out within one year. Was this really consideration?

2. A defense raised in nuisance cases such as this one is that the plaintiffs were "coming to the nuisance." That is, since the owners all knew that the pig farm was there when they built their homes, they should not be able to claim a nuisance, unlike if the pig farm had come later. Could this defense have applied here?

A *public nuisance* is an unreasonable interference with a right held in common by the general public. A public nuisance usually involves interference with the public health and welfare. For example, an illegal gambling establishment, bad odors, and the obstruction of a highway would be grounds for a public nuisance action. In addition to having the common law, states have statutes that define various activities as being public nuisances.

Whether an action creates a private or a public nuisance depends upon who is affected by it. The pollution of a well by a factory, for example, is a private nuisance if it interferes only with the rights of landowners living next to the plant. The suit will be brought by those landowners against the owners of the plant. However, if the pollution hurts the public water supply, it is a public nuisance. In such circumstances, the legal representative of the community, such as the county attorney, will bring the action on behalf of the citizens against the polluters.

Trespass to Personal Property

The intentional and wrongful interference with possession of personal property of another without consent is a *trespass to personal property*. An important element in this tort is that someone has interfered with the right of the owner to exclusive possession and enjoyment of personal property. Liability usually occurs when the trespasser damages the property or deprives the owner of the use of the property for a time. However, if the interference with the personal property of another is warranted, there is a defense to the trespass. Many states have statutes that allow motel operators to hold the personal property of guests who have not paid their bills.

ISSUE
Spotter

Protecting Company Property

At your office, employees often walk out with assorted supplies. Pencils and paper clips are cheap, but the cost of pens, staplers, reams of paper, and more expensive items can quickly add up. Multiply this amount by the number of employees, and losses can be significant. Can a company have a policy informing employees that taking supplies is theft of company property and will make them subject to dismissal? Does the company need to notify the employees that it is theft, or should they know? How should these losses be handled? As you think about this, remember that theft by employees causes larger losses than theft by non-employees.

Conversion

The tort of *conversion* is an intentional and unlawful control or appropriation of the personal property of another. In contrast to trespass on personal property, conversion requires that the control or appropriation so seriously interferes with the owner's right of control that it justifies payment for the property. Several factors are considered in determining whether the interference warrants a finding of conversion: the extent of dominion or control, the duration of the interference, the damage to the property, and the inconvenience and expense to the owner. As with trespass to land, mistake is not a defense to conversion.

Generally, one who wrongfully acquires possession of another's personal property—by theft, duress, or fraud—is said to have committed the tort of conversion. In most court systems, a bona fide purchaser (a good-faith purchaser who thought the seller was the rightful owner of the property) is liable for conversion if the property was purchased from a thief.

Misappropriation

Some forms of intellectual property, including trademarks and trade secrets (valuable information that is protected from revelation to others), are protected by tort law from *misappropriation* or *theft* by others. We will discuss intellectual property in detail in Chapter 9 and will see that some statutes specify the damages that may be had when such property is taken by others without permission. As with other forms of property, owners may sue those who invade their property rights for damages and may ask a court to issue an injunction against further unauthorized use of the property. Next we turn to a common tort action filed against property owners.

JURIS *prudence?*

Good Trees Might Not Make Good Neighbors

Bloomquist's one-story home sits on a lot on a hill below Dowdell's home. Both overlook the Atlantic Ocean. Bloomquist asked the zoning board to grant him a zoning variance to allow him to build a second story addition on his home. Since the addition would have blocked Dowdell's view of the ocean, he opposed the zoning variance, and it was denied.

Bloomquist then planted a row of forty-foot-high trees on his property in front of Dowdell's home. The trees blocked Dowdell's view of the ocean, so he sued, contending that the trees were a nuisance that created a "spite fence" in violation of state law. The trial court held for Dowdell and ordered Bloomquist to remove the trees.

Bloomquist appealed to the supreme court of Rhode Island. It affirmed the decision, holding that the trees were a malicious nuisance that blocked Dowdell's view and light. Six-foot-high vegetation is the most that would be allowed.

Source: *Dowdell* v. *Bloomquist*, 847 A.2d 828 (2004)

TORTS AGAINST PROPERTY OWNERS

Remember Humpty Dumpty? Did he have a cause of action against the wall owner? It depends on several factors. Was Humpty invited to sit on the wall or was he a trespasser? If he was committing a trespass by sitting on the wall, then the owner of the wall owed him no duty of care, other than not to take steps that could cause him to suffer an injury. If Humpty had been invited to a party, and during the party decided to sit on the wall, then the property owner would not be liable to Humpty unless the owner was aware of some danger about sitting on the wall and failed to tell Humpty about it.

Premises Liability

There are many cases involving slip-and-fall. The customer of a business, presumed by law to be invited to be on the premises in order to shop, suffers an injury due to slipping on a wet or icy spot. The general rule is that the owner of the property has a duty to keep the premises reasonably safe under the circumstances. For example, if it is raining and water seeps into the front of the store, the property owner has a duty to try to limit the slips that could occur by mopping the area, putting down an extra doormat and perhaps a warning sign, but customers are also expected to use common sense in such conditions. If a danger is obvious, people have a duty to protect themselves from it. What if the danger is not so obvious? If a patron is injured, will the property owner be liable? That issue is discussed in the *Fairmont Hotel* case.

Schmid v. Fairmont Hotel Company-Chicago
Appellate Court of Illinois
803 N.E.2d 166 (2003)

CASE BACKGROUND   *After Schmid piloted a plane for Lufthansa Airlines from Frankfurt to Chicago, he checked into the Fairmont Hotel for the night. In the morning he went into the bathroom, turned on the light, and received an electrical shock. He fell backward, striking the edge of the door frame with his head, neck, and shoulder. The injury prevented him from working as a pilot. He sued Fairmont and Maron Electric, an independent contractor that provided Fairmont with electrical services and materials, for negligence. The jury found Fairmont liable and Maron not liable. Fairmont appealed.*

CASE DECISION   Gordon, Justice.

* * *

In premises liability cases, including those where a guest suffered injury while on hotel premises, Illinois courts determine whether a duty of care exists by considering the common law duty factors of (1) reasonable foreseeability of the injury; (2) likelihood of the injury; (3) magnitude of the burden on the defendant of guarding against the injury; and (4) consequences of placing the burden on the defendant. The innkeeper-guest relationship imposes on an innkeeper a duty to exercise "ordinary" care in protecting its guests from injury. . . .

We begin our discussion by noting that reasonable foreseeability is an elusive concept, but not so that it ignores common sense. It has been explained in terms that "the creation of a legal duty requires more than a

mere possibility of occurrence. . . . 'No one can be expected to guard against harm from events which are not reasonably to be anticipated at all, or are so unlikely to occur that the risk, although recognizable, would commonly be disregarded.' " . . . Fairmont argues that the evidence, viewed in the light most favorable to the plaintiff, nevertheless established that plaintiff's injury was not reasonably foreseeable; rather it was "highly extraordinary" or "tragically bizarre" or "unique." . . .

Plaintiff . . . overextends the meaning of the duty of ordinary care. A duty of ordinary care is not absolute: "when a person has no reason to suspect injury, he is not required to look for it." . . .

We do not believe that it would have been reasonable for Fairmont to anticipate the danger of an electric shock to plaintiff at the light switch. As previously stated, in determining foreseeability, the focus is on the defendant—how much it knew or should have known of the possibility of the injury to the plaintiff. In this case, the testimony of Fairmont's employees established that they did not have any reason to anticipate that plaintiff would receive an electric shock at the light switch. . . .

Reversed.

QUESTIONS FOR ANALYSIS
1. Suppose Schmid was the third guest to have been shocked by a light switch. Would that change the result?
2. Schmid is left injured and unemployed as a result of being shocked in the hotel. Is it fair that he should have to bear the cost with no compensation?

Premises liability may also occur when a business does not provide sufficient security to help prevent crimes from occurring on its property. For instance, in 1995 Supreme Court of Connecticut case, *Stewart* v. *Federated Department Stores* (662 A.2d 753), the court upheld a $1.5 million verdict in favor of the heirs of a woman who was robbed and murdered in the parking garage of a Bloomingdale's department store. The store was found negligent for not having a security guard on duty. The store was in a high-crime area and other customers had been robbed in the garage. *Ann M.*, the leading California case on this subject, discusses the duty of a property owner.

Ann M. v. Pacific Plaza Shopping Center

Supreme Court of California
6 Cal.4th 666, 863 P.2d 207 (1993)

CASE BACKGROUND *Ann M. was working alone at a San Diego photo-processing store in Pacific Plaza, a strip mall with twenty-five stores. After she opened the store for business at 8 a.m., a man armed with a knife entered the store, raped her, robbed the store, and fled (he was not caught). Ann M. sued the shopping center for negligence for failing to provide adequate security to protect her from an unreasonable risk of harm. Ann M. contended that the security patrols that drove through the mall area four times a day were inadequate; she claimed that there should have been more continuous patrols of the mall because transients in the area posed a threat. Several purse snatchings had taken place at the mall or in the area. The trial court granted Pacific Plaza summary judgment, holding that it did not violate its duty of care to Ann M. The appeals court affirmed. Ann M. appealed to the California Supreme Court.*

CASE DECISION Panelli, Associate Justice.

* * *

It is now well established that California law requires landowners to maintain land in their possession and control in a reasonably safe condition. In the case of a landlord, this general duty of maintenance, which is owed to tenants and patrons, has been held to include the duty to take reasonable steps to secure common areas against foreseeable criminal acts of third parties that are likely to occur in the absence of such precautionary measures.

* * *

We turn to the heart of the case: whether Pacific Plaza had reasonable cause to anticipate that criminal conduct such as rape would occur in the shopping center premises unless it provided security patrols in the common areas. For, as frequently recognized, a duty to take affirmative action to control the wrongful acts of a third party will be imposed only where such conduct can be reasonably anticipated.

In this, as in other areas of tort law, foreseeability is a crucial factor in determining the existence of duty. . . .

Unfortunately, random, violent crime is endemic in today's society. It is difficult, if not impossible, to envision any locale open to the public where the occurrence of violent crime seems improbable. . . .

While there may be circumstances where the hiring of security guards will be required to satisfy a landowner's duty of care, such action will rarely, if ever, be found to be a "minimal burden." The monetary costs of security guards are not insignificant. Moreover, the obligation to provide patrols adequate to deter criminal conduct is not well defined. "No one really knows why people commit crime, hence no one really knows what is 'adequate' deterrence in any given situation." Finally, the social costs of imposing a duty on landowners to hire private police forces are also not insignificant. For these reasons, we conclude that a high degree of foreseeability is required in order to find that the scope of a landlord's duty of care includes the hiring of security guards. We further conclude that the requisite degree of foreseeability rarely, if ever, can be proven in the absence of prior similar incidents of violent crime on the landowner's premises. To hold otherwise would be to impose an unfair burden upon landlords and, in effect, would force landlords to become the insurers of public safety, contrary to well established policy in this state.

Turning to the facts of the case before us, we conclude that violent criminal assaults were not sufficiently foreseeable to impose a duty upon Pacific Plaza to provide security guards in the common areas. . . .

The judgment of the Court of Appeal is affirmed.

CASE NOTE Ann M. also filed a workers' compensation claim against her employer and was awarded benefits. Since such benefits are by state law an exclusive remedy, Ann M. dropped her employer as a defendant in this suit.

QUESTIONS FOR ANALYSIS

1. Ann M. argued that a robbery and purse snatchings in the mall were sufficient warning of danger. Is that correct, or are more serious crimes necessary to establish danger?

continues

2. The owner of Pacific Plaza had told mall tenants that because of the expense of full-time security, rents would have to be increased. Instead, the tenants paid for a security service to drive by several times a day. Should responsibility for security be in the control of the tenants or the landlord?

ISSUE Spotter

Protecting Customers' Kids

As a manager of a department store, you know that it is not uncommon for kids to run around in the store with little adult supervision. Some kids have been hurt when they run into display cabinets. The edges of the cabinets are sharp and hard. Kids have gashed themselves, requiring trips to the emergency room for stitches. While most customers have not asserted that the store should be liable for the uncontrolled behavior of their kids, some have. Given that this happens at least several times a year, should the store take extra steps to protect itself from possible liability? What sort of steps could be taken?

SUMMARY

- Property law is the oldest part of the common law. It focuses on real property, which is land, houses, and things attached to the land; and personal property, which is movable property such as furniture, books, and cars. The owners of property have legal interests or rights in property. Property rights are limited by common law and by statutes that restrict the use of property.
- Written deeds are used to transfer ownership interests in real property. Many forms of deeds exist that provide different levels of assurances of the quality of ownership rights being provided. Titles to property, which constitute the formal right of ownership, are passed by deeds.
- The strongest form of ownership of real property is fee simple, which is how most real estate in the United States is held. When more than one party owns real estate, it is often held in a tenancy in common, where the parties have an undivided interest that passes to their heirs on death, or it may be in a joint tenancy, which is also an undivided interest but the other owner has a right of survivorship. Few restrictions are placed on the forms of ownership people choose to use.
- Servitudes are restrictions or requirements imposed on the use of property, most commonly easements and covenants. Such legal rights are held to run with the land, as they usually stay in place when title to property passes. Most easements grant the right to another party to enter property for some purpose, such as to have access to power lines. Covenants are often used in real estate developments to impose requirements on the design of houses and characteristics of the property that must be maintained.
- Real estate may be leased to tenants for any terms the parties agree on so long as it does not conflict with state law. Any details not covered in a lease fall under state landlord-tenant law. The parties have obligations. Tenants may not abuse the property and landlords must make certain key repairs in a timely manner and not invade the privacy of the tenants.

- Governments have the power of eminent domain. It allows them to condemn private property and take it for public use, so long as fair market value compensation is paid to the owners. Destruction of substantial property value by regulations such as zoning is generally not compensable. A controversial form of eminent domain in recent years is the use of eminent domain to turn the property over to a private party for profitable use.

- Intentional torts against property include trespass, the unauthorized intrusion on the land of another, and nuisance, a substantial and unreasonable interference with the right of persons to use and enjoy their property. A nuisance may be private, in which case a property owner sues, or public, when many people suffer from the interference and a public attorney acts on their behalf.

- Other intentional torts include trespass to personal property, which is wrongful interference with the right of persons to use their property in a lawful manner, and conversion, which is the unlawful appropriation (theft) of the personal property of another person.

- Property owners may be sued for premises liability by those they have invited to come on their property, such as store customers. If the property owner has been negligent in maintaining the condition of the property and that negligence violates the duty of ordinary care that results in an injury, liability may be imposed. Liability may arise from failure of a property owner to provide reasonable security against criminal attacks.

REVIEW AND DISCUSSION QUESTIONS

1. Define the following terms:

trespass	premises liability
private nuisance	eminent domain
public nuisance	title
conversion	deed
covenant	easement
adverse possession	leasehold

2. A century ago, the common law regarding landlords and tenants held the tenant responsible for major repairs to residences, such as roof repairs. Over the years, the common law changed to put such responsibility on the landlords. Why did the law evolve in that direction? What factors may have brought about the change?

CASE QUESTIONS

3. The Eagles owned 100 acres of mountain land in Virginia. Their neighbor, White, claimed ownership of 919 acres, including 103 acres that the Eagles wanted to buy but White did not want to sell. The Eagles did research about title to White's land and discovered that title to the 103-acre parcel had never been issued to anyone in the history of Virginia and that White had never paid taxes on the land. The land was declared to be "waste and unappropriated." Who gets the land, the Eagles or White? [*Black* v. *Eagle*, 445 S.E.2d 662 (Sup. Ct., Va., 1994)]

4. When David married Jean, he was sole owner of the property in question in this case. In 1967, he wrote a document saying that David and Jean give a life

estate in the property to David's parents and "at their death said property will return in fee simple to [David and Jean], their heirs and assigns." David and Jean divorced in 1980; the divorce divided their property but made no mention of the property in question here. David married Laura in 1984; David died in 1992, leaving his property to Laura. Jean sued Laura, claiming that the 1967 document gave her fee simple one-half interest in the property, subject to the life estate. Does Jean own half of the property in question? [*Wilson* v. *Butts*, 1995 WL 705294 (Ct. of Civ. App., Ala., 1995)]

5. MMI bought property in Dayton, Ohio. BancOhio gave MMI a mortgage to assist in the purchase. Later, MMI was bankrupt and defaulted on the mortgage. As provided by the mortgage, BancOhio attempted to sell the property. The property suffered looting, arson, and vandalism. The city declared the property a public nuisance and ordered the property owners to clean up the problem. Since BancOhio was the only party related to the property with money, the city held it responsible. Could the mortgage holder be liable? [*Hausman* v. *City of Dayton*, 653 N.E.2d 1190 (Ohio Sup. Ct., 1995)]

 Check your answer at <u>http://meiners.westbuslaw.com</u>

6. Peterson operated a private golf course in Sioux Falls, South Dakota. In 1964, Peterson sold property adjoining the golf course, including a restaurant and parking lot, to AL. The parking lot was used by the golfers on Peterson's golf course and by restaurant patrons. In 1978, AL sold the property containing the parking lot to VBC. Peterson had always maintained the parking lot. In 1992, VBC demanded Peterson pay rent for the use of the parking lot by the golfers. Peterson sued, claiming title to the parking lot by adverse possession. Is Peterson right? [*Peterson* v. *Beck*, 537 N.W.2d 375 (Sup. Ct., S.D., 1995)]

7. The Causbys owned a chicken farm near Greensboro, North Carolina. The farm was located in the path of the flyway to a military landing strip 2,000 feet away during World War II. Bombers, transports, and fighter aircraft used the field, often flying just above treetops over the Causby farm. Chickens died of fright and quit laying eggs; the value of the chicken operation dropped to zero. The peace of the Causbys in their home was also disturbed. The Causbys sued the U.S. government. The Court of Claims held that the United States had taken an easement over the property and that the value of the easement and value of the property destroyed was $2,000. Did the judgment stand? [*U.S.* v. *Causby*, 66 S.Ct. 1062 (1946)]

 Check your answer at <u>http://meiners.westbuslaw.com</u>

8. Baxter rented a house from Milheim in Denver for a term of one year. As Milheim knew, Baxter intended to live in the house and rent rooms to boarders. When Baxter moved in, she discovered that the house next door, also owned and leased by Milheim, was a house of ill repute, "where immoral men and women were constantly meeting for immoral purposes . . . she was greatly annoyed by the vulgar and indecent conduct of the tenants." Baxter moved out after two weeks and sued Milheim for the income she lost as a result of not being able to rent rooms. A jury awarded her $2,180. Milheim appealed, claiming that Baxter had no reason to break the lease. Who is correct? [*Milheim* v. *Baxter*, 103 P. 376 (Sup. Ct., Colo., 1909)]

9. While Rouse was looking at new cars at a dealership, he gave his car keys to a sales rep so that his car could be examined for its trade-in value. When Rouse decided to leave without buying, the keys were hidden from him—supposedly lost—for about a half hour. The sales rep thought this was a joke. Rouse sued

and was awarded $5,000 in punitive damages. What was the tort claimed? Would the damages be allowed on appeal? [*Russell-Vaughn Ford* v. *Rouse*, 206 So.2d 371 (Sup. Ct., Ala., 1968)]

 Check your answer at http://meiners.westbuslaw.com

10. The basement of the Girone home was flooded with raw sewage that overflowed from a city sewer line. Walking across the odorous floor, Mrs. Girone slipped and fell, breaking her hip. She sued the city for negligent maintenance of the sewage line and for trespass. The city contended she was negligent for not being more careful walking on the slippery floor. Who won? [*City of Winder* v. *Girone*, 462 S.E.2d 704 (Sup. Ct., Ga., 1995)]

11. Members of Earth First! demonstrated in a forest against logging. Several protestors chained themselves to logging machinery owned by a private company. Logging operations had to be ceased for a day because of the protest and occupation of machinery (which was not damaged). What cause of action does the logging company have against the protesters? [*Huffman and Wright Logging Co.* v. *Wade*, 857 P.2d 101 (Sup.Ct., Ore., 1993)]

 Check your answer at http://meiners.westbuslaw.com

12. McKenzie lived next to a gas station run by Yommer. Unknown to Yommer, a gas storage tank developed a leak, polluting McKenzie's well water, making the water unfit for drinking or bathing. Yommer replaced the storage tank, but the problem with McKenzie's water persisted, and McKenzie sued. What tort was claimed? What, if any, is the basis for liability? [*Yommer* v. *McKenzie*, 257 A.2d 138 (Ct.App., Md., 1969)]

13. Strahs, age 84, slipped on an icy spot in the parking lot of a drugstore, fell, and broke her hip. She sued the drugstore and the company that was under contract to keep the parking lot plowed for snow. While it had been plowed, there were icy spots remaining in the parking lot. Did she have a good case against either of those parties? [*Strahs* v. *Tovar's Snowplowing, Inc.*, 2004 WL 1348985 (Ct. App., Ill., 2004)]

14. Chamblee rented an apartment from Grayco. One day, when walking from her apartment to her car, she left the sidewalk, cut across the grass, and tripped over an exposed drainage pipe and suffered injuries. She sued Grayco for negligence in premises liability. Does she have a case? [*Chamblee* v. *Grayco*, 596 S.E.2d 683 (Ct. App., Ga., 2004)]

15. Allen slipped and fell on a grape that was on the floor at a grocery store. No one saw the accident and no one is sure how the grape ended up on the floor. The manager claimed that the area had been recently checked to make sure it was clean. A jury awarded Allen $10,000 for her injuries. The store appealed. Does the verdict hold? [*Brookshire Food Stores* v. *Allen*, 93 S.W.3d 897 (Ct. App., Tx., 2002)]

ETHICS QUESTIONS

16. In the *Hathcock* case the Michigan high court said that eminent domain may not be used by governments to obtain property at fair market value in order for it to then be sold at the same price to a for-profit firm for business purposes. That is not the rule in all states. In many jurisdictions, the courts have held that it is a proper function of government to take property for such use since the new use will create a higher level of economic activity than the old use. Is such

taking ethical? Is it ethical for one property holder to refuse to sell when all around have agreed to sell to enable new development?

17. A real estate development sells houses with a covenant that prohibits the sale to buyers under the age of fifty-five so as to discourage children from living in the area. The covenant may even prohibit children from being permanent residents of the area; they can come as visitors but not residents. Is that sort of restriction ethically acceptable?

PULLING IT  *Together*

Property and Constitutional Law

Barber erected a sign on his property facing Interstate 20 in west Texas. The sign said "Just Say NO to Searches" and gave a phone number. Callers received information about a citizen's constitutional rights regarding police searches of automobiles. The Texas Department of Transportation sent Barber a letter telling him that the sign violated the Highway Beautification Act and that he must remove the sign or obtain a permit from the Department to have a sign that complies with Department regulations. The trial court ordered Barber to remove the sign and to pay the Department's attorney's fees. He appealed.

[*Barber* v. *Texas Department of Transportation*, 49 SW3d 12 (Ct. App., Tex., 2001)]

INTERNET ASSIGNMENT

http://www.invisible-web.net
http://lawyers.findlaw.com
http://www.martindale.com

Information, often part of databases, accessible via the Internet but not picked up by search engines, is often said to be part of the "invisible" or "deep" web. Such databases may also offer advanced search features, such as limiting a search by location. Two major directories of attorneys, *West's Legal Directory* and *Martindale-Hubbell Law Directory*, are available in searchable databases on the Internet. Use each database to find attorneys in your area who specialize in real estate transactions. Noting the differences in the practice areas covered by each database, which database may be better if your issue involved a zoning problem? How about a problem with a property lease?

Chapter 9 | *Intellectual Property*

Many people receive spam offering software at very low prices. Suppose you accept such an offer and, by doing so, save quite a bit of money buying software that you install on the fourteen computers at your company. Where did that software come from? Do you have proper licensing? Not likely. This can be a poor move if the authorities charge you with illegal use of software that was pirated, or illegally copied. While students might not worry much about getting caught with illegal software, getting caught is a serious problem for a business, possibly involving fines and the cost of legal defense, as well as the likely possible public exposure of the company's illegal act and damage to its reputation.

Reputation, how others view you—also called goodwill—is one part of intellectual property. *Intellectual property* is created by intellectual effort, not by physical labor. It is often called *intangible property* because it may be invisible, impossible to hold, and harder to value than the physical property we discussed in Chapter 8. For many firms, intellectual property is far more valuable than the real property owned by the company. In this information-age economy, intellectual property is more important than it was in the agriculture-based economy in which land was the most important asset.

In this chapter, we will look at the four major forms of intellectual property:

- Trademarks
- Copyrights
- Patents
- Trade secrets

The common law has a long tradition of providing protection for intellectual property, and the Constitution expresses its importance: Article I, Section 8, authorizes Congress "To promote the Progress of Science and useful Arts, by securing for limited Times to Authors and Inventors the exclusive Right to their respective Writings and Discoveries." Today, the Commissioner of Patents and Trademarks annually issues about 190,000 patents—half to Americans and half to foreigners—and annually registers more than 150,000 new trademarks and more than 600,000 copyrights.

Just as the common law protects real property, it also works with various statutes to protect intellectual property by allowing property owners to sue in case of *infringement*. That is, wrongful, unauthorized use of intellectual property in violation of the owner's rights is the basis for a tort action. When intellectual property is infringed upon, damages may be awarded to the property holder and an injunction against further unauthorized use may be issued. This protection has been enhanced by various statutes. How important is protection of intellectual property? The U.S. government estimates that counterfeit and fraudulent use of intellectual property costs business tens of billions of dollars a year.

TRADEMARKS

A *trademark* is a commercial symbol—a design, logo, phrase, distinctive mark, name, or word—that a manufacturer prints on its goods so they can be readily identified in the marketplace. We often recognize them as brand names, such as Nike. Other producers may not imitate genuine trademarks. Since companies spend large sums so consumers will recognize and trust their products, the common law has long recognized the right to protect this property. This common-law protection was made a part of federal law by the *Lanham Act*. Federal trademark law allows trademarks to be registered if they are distinctive and nonfunctional. As long as the owner continues to use and protect the trademark, the trademark's exclusive use can be perpetual.

Traditionally, trademark protection was created by priority of use. The first person to use a symbol in a business or geographic area has the right to stop others

JURIS *prudence?*

Don't Step on His Estate's Velvet Shoes

A bar in Houston was named Velvet Elvis, which was also a trademark. Among its decorations was a large black velvet portrait of the king of rock and roll, Elvis Presley. The bar was advertised as a "monument to the excesses of American culture."

Unamused, Elvis Presley Enterprises of Memphis sued, demanding that the owner remove the name Elvis and commercial representations of Presley. It contended that the decorations are trademark infringements and violate the Presley Enterprise publicity rights to Elvis, just as it requires Elvis impersonators to obtain licenses.

Velvet Elvis won round one in federal court. The judge held that customers would not be misled into thinking that the club was associated with Elvis Presley Enterprises. Presley won round two when the appeals court reversed in its favor and issued an injunction against the use of the mark "The Velvet Elvis." There was a likelihood of confusion, especially since Presley runs an Elvis-theme nightclub in Memphis and has considered expanding.

Sources: *National Law Journal* and *Elvis Presley Enterprises* v. *Capece*, 141 F.3d 188

from using the same or very similar trade symbol in that business or area. The Lanham Act allows a person to register a symbol with the Patent and Trademark Office in Washington, D.C. The Trademark Revision Act allows nationwide claim to a mark from the moment it is registered, so long as sincere intent exists to use the symbol in commerce.

The advantages of registration of trademarks with the U.S. Patent and Trademark Office, rather than relying only on common-law protection of trademarks, include

1. Nationwide notice of the trademark owner's claim
2. Legal presumption of the registrant's ownership of the mark in event of dispute
3. Federal court jurisdiction, if desired
4. Forming the basis for obtaining registration in other nations
5. Filing the registration with U.S. Customs Service to help prevent importation of foreign goods that infringe on the trademark

Registration

The registration process, which can be done online, includes payment of a fee ($335 for each class of goods using a mark), submission of a copy of the mark (a specimen), a description of the goods that will use the mark, and a declaration that to the best of the applicant's knowledge the mark does not conflict with other marks (see *http://www.uspto.gov*).

The applicant is responsible for doing a search of existing trademarks to make sure there is no confusion on infringement with existing marks. A trademark examiner reviews the request to make sure the mark does not conflict with existing marks, is not descriptive, and does not claim too much coverage. That is, if you are trademarking a word for a brand of perfume, you cannot register the word *perfume*, because that is the generic term for that product. If the word *Charlie* is registered as a trademark for perfume, other people may be allowed to use the word in other contexts, such as Charlie's Motel.

Registration is good for ten years, after which it must be renewed. You can make sure people know a mark is protected by stating "Registered in U.S. Patent and Trademark Office" or using the circle-R (®). You also see the symbol "TM," which puts people on notice but is not specified in the Lanham Act. However, lack of notice that a mark is a trademark does not mean the owner of the mark is not due legal protection for the mark. International protection of trademarks is encouraged by the International Bureau of the World Intellectual Property Organization via the Madrid Protocol (*http://www.wipo.int/madrid*).

Classifications of Trademarks

Trademarks are classified as arbitrary and fanciful, suggestive, descriptive, or generic (see Exhibit 9.1).

Arbitrary and fanciful are most favored by the courts because they are inherently distinctive (fanciful), such as made-up names like *Exxon*, or they are names not related to the product (arbitrary), such as *Black and White* for a Scotch whiskey and *Apple* for computers.

Suggestive marks hint at the product, such as *Chicken of the Sea* for canned tuna. They are due legal protection, but establishing that can be more difficult than if the mark is arbitrary and fanciful.

Exhibit 9.1	Arbitrary and Fanciful	Suggestive	Descriptive	Generic (No Longer Trademarks)
Types of Trademarks	Polaroid	Orange Crush	Raisin Bran	Trampoline
	Lexus	Roach Motel	Holiday Inn	Nylon
	Virginia Slims	Dairy Queen	Musky (Perfume)	Thermos
	Ivory (Soap)	Passion (Perfume)	Yellow Pages	Shredded Wheat
	Clorox	Coppertone	After Tan	Zipper

Descriptive marks are not as favored by the law and must be shown to have acquired customer recognition to be allowed protection. Examples of successful descriptive marks are *Bufferin* for aspirin with acid buffering and *Holiday Inn* for hotels.

Generic marks are words that are common and do not refer to products from a specific producer. Some words that were once trademarks have been lost to become generic or unprotected marks: *thermos* for vacuum-insulated bottles, *aspirin* for acetyl-salicylic acid, and *escalator* for moving stairways.

Most colleges have trademarks for their name or a distinctive use of letters in their name and for their sports team name and mascot. Collegiate Licensing is a licensing agent for many universities and the manufacturers that make clothing and various items with university logos. This allows colleges to collect royalties from and control the use of their trademarks so that the trademarks are not used in ways the colleges do not approve.

Extent of Coverage

Trademarks, service marks, and other marks cannot claim too much. For example, if you go to the Trademark Office web site, *http://www.uspto.gov*, and search for the trademark Nike Shox, you will see that Nike claims that combination of two words for watches and sports bags, among other goods. The listing shows the address of the company in Beaverton, Oregon, and gives the serial number assigned to Nike

CYBER Law

Who Owns What Domain Name?

Network Solutions Inc. (NSI), now VeriSign, was chosen years ago by the National Science Foundation to be in charge of issuing and controlling domain names, such as *http://www.swlearning.com/blaw/bus-law.html*. Only one entity can have that name so that the Web is not confounded by multiple persons claiming the same domain name. Delta.com now links one to Delta Airlines, but Delta, the faucet maker, beat the airline to the name and, since Delta faucet is a genuine business, it could claim the name. The airline was Delta-air.com until the airline bought the name Delta.com. First come, first served among legitimate users.

Cybersquatters have grabbed control of many names, since registration of a domain name is cheap. The long-distance phone company Sprint claimed mci.com, knowing it would block its competitor MCI. That was not fair under the rules, so NSI turned mci.com over to MCI. Some cybersquatters have registered many names on the expectation that they would later be desired.

A cybersquatter named Toeppen registered many trademarks as his domain names. Such registrations are not challenged initially. Panavision, a movie equipment maker, sued Toeppen when he demanded $13,000 to sell the company panavision.com and panaflex.com, another of its trademarks. Like most trademark holders, Panavision won the case, but many companies simply paid to have the rights to the name transferred rather than go to the cost and time of litigating the matter.

Shox (78406612), as well as other serial numbers that indicate other registrations by Nike. It also notes that the trademark is live.

Trademarks that are dead or abandoned are listed. For example, Shox was once claimed for "edible film strips in coffee, tea, mint, citrus, soda, candy and ice cream flavors" by a California company, but the company no longer claims the mark, so the mark is listed as dead. Other marks are listed that once used the word "Shox" but are now dead, such as a water purification unit produced by an Alabama company.

The term Shox is used for other products, so Nike does not claim wide ownership of the term. For example, Shox is the trademark for the Louisville Ladder Group that makes plastic supports for ladders; it is also a mark for the Entempo Sdn Bhd Corporation of Malaysia, which uses it for "cushioning and protecting disk drives and sensitive electronic and electromechanical devices." While Nike Shox may be the most famous use of the term *Shox*, other companies use the word "Shox" as their mark, or part of their mark, for other lines of products.

Trademark protection applies to a wide range of creative property other than the names of products. Trademark law applies to titles of movies, advertising slogans, titles of comic books, and fictional characters, such as Batman. This allows the producers of highly popular movies and cartoon characters to license use of the names, such as Lord of the Rings, which shows up in toys and premiums at fast-food restaurants. The extent of trademark protection depends on how well known the mark is and whether a similar mark would be confused with the original mark in nonrelated markets. Firms must be protective of their trademarks, or they can lose them, but, as the *Harley-Davidson* case indicates, a challenge to a user can result in consideration of the validity of a trademark.

Harley-Davidson, Inc. v. Grottanelli

United States Court of Appeals, Second Circuit
164 F.3d 806 (1999)

CASE BACKGROUND *Grottanelli runs The Hog Farm, a motorcycle repair shop in western New York. He used the word "hog" in connection with events he sponsored and products he sold. He also used variants of Harley's bar-and-shield trademark logo.*

Harley sued to enjoin Grottanelli from using the word "hog" in reference to his service and products and from using a logo that incorporates a part of Harley's bar-and-shield logo. The district court held in Harley's favor. Grottanelli appealed.

CASE DECISION Newman, Circuit Judge.

* * *

The word "Hog" Applied to Motorcycles

Public use of the word "hog". In the late 1960s and early 1970s, the word "hog" was used by motorcycle enthusiasts to refer to motorcycles generally and to large motorcycles in particular. The word was used that way in the press at least as early as 1965, and frequently

thereafter, prior to the 1980s when Harley first attempted to make trademark use of the term. Several dictionaries include a definition of "hog" as a motorcycle, especially a large one. The October 1975 issue of Street Chopper contained an article entitled "Honda Hog," indicating that the word "hog" was generic as to motorcycles and needed a tradename adjective. . . .

* * *

Harley-Davidson's use of the word "hog". In 1981, Harley-Davidson's new owners recognized that the term "hog" had financial value and began using the term in connection with its merchandise, accessories, advertising, and promotions. In 1983, it formed the Harley Owners' Group, pointedly using the acronym "H.O.G." In 1987, it registered the acronym in conjunction with various logos. It subsequently registered the mark "HOG" for motorcycles. That registration lists Harley-Davidson's first use as occurring in 1990.

Grottanelli's use of the word "hog". Grottanelli opened a motorcycle repair shop under the name "The Hog Farm" in 1969. Since that time his shop has been located at various sites in western New York. At some point after 1981, Grottanelli also began using the word "hog" in connection with events and merchandise. He has sponsored an event alternatively known as "Hog Holidays" and "Hog Farm Holidays," and sold products such as "Hog Wash" engine degreaser and a "Hog Trivia" board game.

The Bar-and-Shield Logo

Harley-Davidson's use of the logo. Since approximately 1909, Harley-Davidson has used variations of its bar-and-shield logo—a shield traversed across the middle by a horizontal bar. The words "Motor" and "Cycles" (or sometimes "Company") appear at the chief and base of the shield, respectively, and the name "Harley-Davidson" appears on the horizontal bar. Variations of the bar-and-shield logo were registered with the United States Patent and Trademark Office in 1982 and thereafter.

Grottanelli's use of the logo. By 1979, Grottanelli had begun using variants of Harley-Davidson's bar-and-shield logo. His 1979 advertisements include a hand-drawn copy of the bar-and-shield logo, with the name "Harley-Davidson" displayed on the horizontal bar. Since 1982, in response to letters of protest from Harley-Davidson, Grottanelli has replaced the words "Harley-Davidson" on the horizontal bar of his logo with the words "American-Made." He has also placed a banner at the bottom of his logo with the words "UNAUTHORIZED DEALER."

* * *

The District Court . . . enjoined Grottanelli from making various trademark uses of the word "hog." Harley-Davidson acknowledged at oral argument that its . . . claim fails if "hog" is generic as applied to large motorcycles. No manufacturer can take out of the language a word, even a slang term, that has generic meaning as to a category of products and appropriate it for its own trademark use. . . .

We have observed that newspaper and magazine use of a word in a generic sense is "a strong indication of the general public's perception" that the word is generic. In this case, media use of "hog" to mean a large motorcycle began as early as 1935 and continued thereafter.

* * *

For all of these reasons, Harley-Davidson may not prohibit Grottanelli from using "hog" to identify his motorcycle products and services. Like any other manufacturer with a product identified by a word that is generic, Harley-Davidson will have to rely on all or a portion of its tradename (or other protectable marks) to identify its brand of motorcycles, e.g., "Harley Hogs."

Bar-and-Shield Logo

Parody defense. Grottanelli admits that his use of his bar-and-shield logo "purposefully suggests an association with Harley," but argues that his use is a protectable parody. We have accorded considerable leeway to parodists whose expressive works aim their parodic commentary at a trademark or a trademarked product, but have not hesitated to prevent a manufacturer from using an alleged parody of a competitor's mark to sell a competing product. Grottanelli uses his bar-and-shield logo on the signage of his business, in his newsletter, and on T-shirts. The signage on his business is, in effect, trademark use for a competing service, since Harley-Davidson offers motorcycle repair service through its authorized dealers, and Grottanelli's placement of his bar-and-shield logo on his newsletter and T-shirts promotes his repair and parts business. In this context, parodic use is sharply limited.

* * *

Disclaimer defense. Grottanelli gains no protection by coyly adding to his version of the bar-and-shield logo the wording "UNAUTHORIZED DEALER."

* * *

For all of these reasons, Grottanelli was properly enjoined from using his current bar-and-shield logo and any mark that so resembles Harley-Davidson's trademarked logo as to be likely to cause confusion.

Conclusion

The judgment of the District Court is affirmed to the extent it enjoined Grottanelli's use of his bar-and-shield logo and reversed to the extent that it enjoined his use of the word "hog." No costs.

QUESTIONS FOR ANALYSIS

1. Since Grottanelli was using the word "hog" commercially before Harley-Davidson used it commercially, could he not sue Harley for infringement on his trademark?

2. Since "hog" is generic, does that mean it cannot be a trademark for, say, a brand of perfume?

Counterfeiting

Counterfeiting of trademarks means the copying or imitating of a mark without authority to do so. It usually means the passing off of goods as if they were original. Hence, marks owned by universities, Major League Baseball, and well-known companies such as Nike and Disney must be protected by their owners. Levi's has seized millions of pairs of counterfeit pants. Not only are profits lost to counterfeiters, but also, since counterfeit goods are usually low quality, consumers might think the trademarks do not represent quality, and the reputation of the owner can suffer.

Note that even if people are told that the counterfeit goods are counterfeit—so that no one is being fooled—the trademark has still been counterfeited. For example, Ferrari makes very expensive cars with distinctive body designs. Ferrari sued companies that made fiberglass imitations of its car bodies that could be placed on car frames. Even though everyone knew the bodies were not Ferrari, and there was a name other than Ferrari on the bodies, the distinctive design of Ferrari was held to be a trademark that could be protected against imitations.

Trade Dress

A commercial symbol also protected by trademark law and the Lanham Act is *trade dress*, which has been given more attention in recent years, although it is often not registered. Trade dress concerns the "look and feel" of products and of service establishments. This includes the size, shape, color, texture, graphics, and even certain sales techniques of products. This has been applied to many products such as teddy bears, luggage, greeting cards, romance novels, and folding tables.

ISSUE
Spotter

Knock Off the Knock-Offs?

Your company makes high-dollar leather products, such as purses, briefcases, and carrying bags. The company has a well-known logo that is on all the products. Knock-off versions of the product are produced in China and sold by street vendors in the United States and in stores in other countries. At times, the imitation products end up in stores in the United States. What steps can you take to protect your trademark? Should you ignore it, since customers generally know the real thing from the knock-off?

The Supreme Court supported a trade dress claim in *Two Pesos* v. *Taco Cabana* (112 S.Ct. 2753). One Mexican-style restaurant could not copy its competitor's decor, which included distinctive exterior decorations and interior design. Trade dress that is "inherently distinctive" is protected under the Lanham Act and by common-law principles concerning unfair competition.

The Supreme Court further refined the standards for trade dress in *Wal-Mart Stores* v. *Samara Brothers* (120 S.Ct. 1339). The Court held that Wal-Mart had not infringed on Samara's designs of children's clothing when it had produced its own clothing with designs similar to those sold by Samara. To receive protection, trade dress must be distinctive and must have *secondary meaning*. That is, the primary significance of the mark or trade dress is to identify the source of the product, rather than the product itself. A design, such as children's clothing, is not inherently distinctive so as to earn protection under the Lanham Act unless it is identifiable by consumers as to the source. Samara did not have that level of recognition.

JURIS *prudence?*

Chicken Beats Stuffing Out of Barney

The creator and owner of Barney describes the stuffed character as "a purple, highly stylized 'Tyrannosaurus Rex' type dinosaur character with a friendly mien, a swath of green down his chest and stomach, and green spots on his back." Ted Giannoulas, otherwise known as The Chicken, appears at baseball and basketball games. The Chicken uses a character with "a rounded purple body with an oversized, rounded head, a swatch of contrasting color down the chest and stomach, a strip of white around the mouth resembling teeth, and a friendly, smiling demeanor." The crowd knew the purple character was a spoof on Barney. The Chicken would attack Barney and engage in assorted skits with the "putative Barney."

Barney's owners sued the Chicken for trademark infringement, false description, unfair competition, and dilution of trademark. The federal court dismissed the suit with prejudice, holding that "Although plaintiff does not appreciate defendants' intent, there is no doubt that parody is intended. Defendants' act is not an effort to confuse consumers, but rather to amuse."

Source: *Lyons Partnership, L.P.* v. *Giannoulas*, 14 F.Supp.2d 947

Other Marks

The Lanham Act also recognizes service marks. These marks, denoted by "SM," apply to services rather than to goods, but the law is the same as it is for trademarks. Service marks apply to services such as advertising, insurance, hotels, restaurants, and entertainment. For example, the International Silk Association uses the motto "Only silk is silk." That is a service mark. "Burger King" is a trademark. The phrase "Home of the Whopper" is a service mark that is owned by Burger King.

A *certification mark* is any word, symbol, device, or any combination of these that is used, or intended to be used, in commerce to certify regional or other geographic origin ("Made in Montana"). It may also signify the type of material used, mode of manufacture, quality, accuracy, or other characteristics of someone's goods or services, or that the work was performed by members of a union ("Union Made in the USA") or another organization.

A trademark or service mark that is used in commerce by members of a cooperative, an association, or other collective group or organization is a *collective mark*. This includes a mark that indicates membership in a union, an association, or other organization.

Trade Names

A *trade name* is the name of a company or a business. Some products, such as Coca-Cola, have the same trademark as the trade name of their producer. Trade names cannot be registered under the Lanham Act, but they are protected by the common law. About one-half of the states allow trade names to be registered, but the rule is that trade name protection belongs to the first to use the name in a given area of business. The general rule is that the first to use the name in a particular business in a geographic area has the ownership right to the name.

Protection applies to the areas in which the name has meaning; national protection of the name cannot be claimed unless there might be confusion. For example, because Coca-Cola operates and is known worldwide, no one may use the trade name in any business, such as by opening a Coca-Cola Motel. Even though

Coca-Cola is not in the motel business, its name is protected in all uses. Because the name Coca-Cola has tremendous goodwill value, the company could license its use to motel operators. Usage of the good name of the company is thus prohibited without the company's permission. For example, Rollerblade, Inc., has been careful to protect its name from becoming the generic term for in-line skates.

Goodwill

It is the reputation of a firm that gives value to trademarks and other such forms of intellectual property. This is a prized asset of many firms. The trademarks Coke and Coca-Cola are far more valuable assets than the real property owned by the Coca-Cola Company. When firms have created such value—gained the trust of many customers—it is called goodwill.

Goodwill is the benefit or advantage of having an established business and secured customers. When a business is sold, the real property assets, such as buildings and equipment, can be evaluated precisely, as they can be replicated in the market. However, the sale price must also take into account the value of the goodwill that a business has established. Two businesses may have identical physical operations, but perhaps only one has an excellent reputation and strong customer base—that is goodwill, and it is a major intangible asset. It is often closely tied to trademark or brand name. When a trademark or other form of intellectual property suffers an injury, damage estimates must include the loss of profits due to damage to the trade name, or goodwill, of the firm.

COPYRIGHT

Copyrights are rights of literary property as recognized by law. They are intangible assets that are held by the author or owner for a certain time period. More than 600,000 items are copyrighted each year. About half are books and other written works; the other half are musical compositions. Copyrights existed for many years at common law and were supplemented by federal statutes. Copyrights are easy to obtain and the legal protection is strong.

The Copyright Act of 1976 (amended several times since) created statutory protection for all copyrightable works. It protects an original expression automatically from the time it is fixed in expression—printed, sung, used in a computer, or whatever form expression takes. The length of copyright protection depends on when the work was produced, as Congress has changed the terms of protection numerous times. Most copyrighted materials in the United States now have the same protection term, the life of the author plus seventy years, as is the case in the European Union. For works for hire, such as material written by employees of a company, the copyright is 95 years from the date of publication.

The Copyright Act gives a copyright owner five exclusive rights over copyrighted works:

1. The right to reproduce the work
2. The right to publish or distribute the work
3. The right to display the work in public
4. The right to perform the work in public
5. The right to prepare derivative works based on the original work

The 1990 amendment added what are called moral rights, which include the right of the author to have proper attribution of authorship and to prevent unauthorized changes in or destruction of an artist's work.

Copyrighted work must be original. You cannot copyright a 200-year-old song, because you did not create it; the song is in the public domain and may be used, performed, or reproduced by anyone. The Supreme Court noted that copyrighted works must be original in *Feist Publications* v. *Rural Telephone Service Co.* (111 S.Ct. 1282), in which one company copied the white-page telephone listings of another company. The Court ruled that there is nothing original in listing telephone user names, addresses, and phone numbers alphabetically; it is "devoid of even the slightest trace of creativity." Public facts not presented in an original manner cannot obtain copyright protection. There must be an original element in the work.

Registration

Copyright registration is simple (see *http://www.copyright.gov*). Fill out a registration form from the Copyright Office in Washington, D.C.; send two copies of the copyrighted work; and pay a $30 fee. The Copyright Office simply records the registration; it does not check to make sure that the material is in fact original or that all the information provided is accurate. That is, unlike patents, copyrights are not issued by the government; it is only a registration process. Registration provides important evidence of copyright ownership in event of an infringement suit. A notice of copyright consists of the circle-C (©), the year of first publication, and the name of the copyright owner. Notice is not required but is encouraged by the Copyright Act because it helps provide proof of ownership in case of a dispute.

Infringement and Fair Use

We have all made copies of copyrighted works without getting permission. Is that illegal infringement? Not if the copying is considered *fair use*. The Copyright Act allows use of original material "for purposes such as criticism, comment, news reporting, teaching, . . . scholarship, or research." If copying is not authorized or fair use, it is infringement. When considering whether a use is fair, the courts apply four factors:

1. The purpose and character of the copying (for commercial use or for nonprofit educational use)
2. The nature of the copyrighted work
3. The extent of the copying
4. The effect of the copying on the market for the work

In the 1984 Supreme Court case, *Sony Corp.* v. *Universal City Studios*, 104 S.Ct. 774, the fact that VCR owners may copy copyrighted television programs for personal use was held to be covered by the fair-use exception. However, it is not proper for publishers to publish works in manners not anticipated by original contracts with authors. In *New York Times Co.* v. *Tasini* (121 S.Ct. 2381) the Supreme Court held that it was copyright infringement for electronic databases, such as Lexis/Nexis, to publish previously published stories online if the print versions bore copyrights. Since the authors had agreed to paper publication, "reprinting" in electronic media without permission of the authors was infringement. In the *NXIVM* case we see a discussion of some of the factors courts look at when considering infringement.

NXIVM Corp. v. The Ross Institute
United States Court of Appeals, Second Circuit
364 F.3d 471 (2004)

CASE BACKGROUND *NXIVM provides a manual for subscribers to a training program called "Executive Success." The publication has a copyright notice and participants sign a non-disclosure agreement not to release the manual or other proprietary information. NXIVM asserts to have developed a novel method called "Rational Inquiry" to improve communications and decisionmaking.*

Defendant Ross runs web sites in connection to his work as a "cult deprogrammer." The web sites provide public information about controversial groups. Ross was sent the NXIVM manual by defendant Franco, a NXIVM participant. Ross asked defendants Hochman and Martin to write a report on NXIVM. Their critique, posted on Ross's web sites, analyzed NXIVM. It noted that the manual was copyrighted but quoted it extensively in the critique.

NXIVM sued Ross and the others for copyright infringement. It requested that the trial court issue a preliminary injunction ordering Ross to remove all copyrighted information from his web sites. The trial court denied the injunction, finding no likelihood of NXIVM's success on the merits because defendants' fair use defense was likely to succeed. NXIVM appealed.

CASE DECISION Walker, Chief Judge.

* * *

To demonstrate a likelihood of success on the merits of its copyright claim, NXIVM must establish that it owns a valid copyright and that defendants have engaged in unauthorized copying. Defendants can defeat this *prima facie* showing of infringement, however, by demonstrating that their copying is protected by the fair use doctrine. . . .

We turn to the four-factor test for fair use.

1. The "purpose and character" inquiry

The court's function, in inquiring into "the purpose and character of the use" is to see . . . Whether the new work . . . adds something new, with a further purpose or different character, altering the first with new expression, meaning, or message. . . . the websites' use of quotations from the manual to support their critical analyses of the seminars is transformative. . . . Where the defendants' use is for the purposes of "crit-

icism, comment . . . scholarship, or research," factor one will normally tilt in the defendants' favor. . . .

[However] to the extent that Ross, Martin, or Hochman knew that his access to the manuscript was unauthorized or was derived from a violation of law or breach of duty, this consideration weights in favor of plaintiffs. . . .

We find that even if the bad faith subfactor weighs in plaintiffs' favor, the first factor still favors defendants in light of the transformative nature of the secondary use as criticism. . . .

2. The "nature of the copyrighted work" inquiry

The parties do not dispute that because the copyrighted work is unpublished, the district court properly found the second factor, "the nature of the copyrighted work," to favor plaintiffs. . . .

3. The "amount and substantiality" inquiry

Consideration of the third factor, "the amount and substantiality of the portion used in relation to the copyrighted work as a whole has both a quantitative and a qualitative component." This factor favors copyright holders where the portion used by the alleged infringer is a significant percentage of the copyrighted work, or where the portion used is "essentially the heart of" the copyrighted work.

The district court found that this factor was "at best, neutral," because: (1) defendants copied from only 17 pages of a manual 500 pages long; (2) the "heart" of the work for which plaintiffs were seeking protection, the actual process or idea of "Rational Inquiry," is not copyrightable expression; and (3), in any event, this "heart" could not be summed up in the 17 pages that were copied. . . .

Finally, we agree with the district court that, in order to do the research and analysis necessary to support their critical commentary, it was reasonably necessary for defendants to quote liberally from NXIVM's manual. Accordingly, we find that the third factor does not favor plaintiffs.

4. The "market" inquiry

This factor weighs heavily in defendants' favor. It is plain that, as a general matter, criticisms of a seminar or organization cannot substitute for the seminar or organization itself or hijack its market. To be sure, some may read defendants' materials and decide not to attend plaintiffs' seminars. Indeed, the record reflects that soon after the dissemination of defendants' material, actress Goldie Hawn cancelled a visit with NXIVM's leader, Keith Raniere. But that sort of harm, as the district court properly recognized, is not cognizable under the Copyright Act. . . . .

Affirmed.

QUESTIONS FOR ANALYSIS

1. Defendants clearly copied, and made available to the public, multiple pages of a copyrighted work. What one factor was the key to their defense?

2. Another claim by NXIVM was trademark infringement. The court held there was no valid claim for that—why not?

ISSUE *Spotter*

Fair Sharing of Information?

Your company makes electrical components for jet engines. The engineers who do the designing subscribe to a number of electrical engineering journals. The subscriptions are quite expensive, so they order one subscription of each journal and make copies of articles to give to all the engineers who might be interested. Is this copying fair use since it is for educational purposes, or could it be copyright infringement that could lead to trouble? How should this practice be handled?

PATENTS

A *patent* is a grant from the government to an inventor for "the right to exclude others from making, using, offering for sale, or selling" the invention for twenty years after the inventor files a patent application. Unlike other forms of intellectual property that have common-law roots, patents are purely statute based. According to patent law, a person who "invents or discovers any new and useful process, machine, manufacture, or composition of matter, or any new and useful improvement thereof, may obtain a patent." A *process* generally means an industrial or technical process, act, or method. *Manufacture* refers to articles that are made by manufacturing, and *composition of matter* relates to chemical compositions and other mixtures of ingredients. For something to be *useful* means the invention must have a use and be operative, not just be a theory.

Key conditions for an invention to be patented are originality and novelty. The statute states that an invention cannot be patented if "(a) the invention was known or used by others in this country, or patented or described in a printed publication in this or a foreign country, before the invention thereof by the applicant for patent," or "(b) the invention was patented or described in a printed publication in this or a foreign country or in public use of no sale in the country more than one year prior to the application for patent in the United States." That means that even if the inventor is the first to describe the invention or to show it in public, if a patent application is not filed within one year of publication, the right to a patent is lost.

A major advantage of patents is the strong protection provided. For the life of the patent, its owner has the right to exclude all others from making or using the patented invention. For example, Polaroid won a billion-dollar judgment against Kodak for infringement on its instant camera and film patents. However, the patent process has drawbacks. The application process is technical, expensive, and time-consuming. The approval process usually takes about two years, and about half of all patent applications are approved.

INTERNATIONAL *Perspective*

A Gradual Move to Uniform Patents

The World Intellectual Property Organization (WIPO) helps protect intellectual property.

Most developed nations belong to WIPO. They have agreed to a Patent Law Treaty to grant and enforce patents lasting twenty years from the time the patent request is filed in one of the countries. The U.S. Patent Office changed its rules to comply with this system.

An inventor should file a patent application in the United States as soon as possible to establish proof of being the first to invent. Then a Patent Cooperation Treaty application is filed to help establish patent priority around the world. An international searching authority, such as the European Patent Office (EPO), is paid to search for relevant prior art (see *http://ep.espacenet.com*). That is, existing patents that cover the patent application, so an application can be amended or withdrawn so as not to infringe on existing patents. The patent application can be reviewed by the U.S. Patent Office or the EPO. After a patent is issued, there is a strong presumption in other countries that it is valid, but application must still be made in other countries for local patent protection.

Patents issued by the EPO are good in most European nations; patents issued in the United States, Canada, or Mexico are good in all of North America (under the North American Fair Trade Agreement). Patent standards in Japan are becoming more like those of the United States and Europe. Patents in South America, Africa, and the Middle East are often hard to obtain and mean little. This is not a cheap process. The average cost of obtaining a patent is $50,000 in Europe, $15,000 in Japan, and $10,000 in the United States.

For more on international patent applications, see *http://pctgazette.wipo.int*.

Eighteen months after a patent application is made, which contains all the details, it is made public. That means competitors can gain a lot of valuable information even before a patent is issued. As a result, inventors prefer to use trade secrets for some innovations. More than 100 years ago, the Coca-Cola company decided to keep the formula for Coke a secret. Had it obtained a patent instead, the formula could have been used by anyone after about 1907. Some firms use a combination of trade secrets and patents to protect their innovations.

The Federal Circuit Court of Appeals has primary responsibility for reviewing patent cases. Patents may be stricken when challenged if the court determines that the patent office did not apply the proper standards when issuing a patent. If the court upholds a patent that is challenged, then the patent holder has a good chance of recovering damages from a party accused of infringing on the patent. In the *Nystrom* case the court discusses the kind of issues that must be considered when reviewing patent validity.

Nystrom v. Trex Company, Inc.
United States Court of Appeals, Federal Circuit
374 F.3d 1105 (2004)

CASE BACKGROUND *Nystrom runs a two-truck, two-man lumber yard. He received patent number 5,474,831 (the '831 patent). It is for "A board for use in constructing a flooring surface for exterior use [such as a deck] . . . manufactured to have a . . . convex top surface* which sheds water and at the same time is comfortable to walk on. . . ." Nystrom sued Trex for infringing the '831 patent. Trex is a large manufacturer of exterior decking planks made from composites of wood fibers and recycled plastic. A key part of their defense was that their planks are *not cut from logs. The district court held key parts of the patent invalid and dismissed Nystrom's claim. He appealed.*

CASE DECISION   Linn, Circuit Judge.

* * *

The district court construed the word "board" in independent claim 1 to mean a "piece of elongated construction material made from wood cut from a log.". . .

Nystrom argues that "board" in claim 1 is not limited to conventional wood boards that are cut from a log. He argues that the claim language "board" does not contain a description of the material from which the board is composed and the claim should not be so limited. . . .

Trex responds that the ordinary meaning of "board" is a piece of sawn lumber. . . .

In construing claims, the analytical focus must begin and remain centered on the language of the claims themselves. . . . The ordinary and customary meaning may be determined by reviewing a variety of sources, including the claims themselves; dictionaries and treatises; and the written descriptions, drawings, and prosecution history. . . .

While some dictionaries define "board" solely in reference to its material composition, not all dictionaries are so constrained. . . .

An examination of the written description and other claims of the '831 patent reveals that Nystrom did not disclaim boards made from materials other than logs. Indeed, in the written description, Nystom described the invention as "a decking board" . . . . This is consistent with the ordinary and customary meaning and supports a broader construction than that adopted by the district court. . . .

In light of our prior construction of "board" as encompassing materials made not only from wood but from other rigid materials as well, we find no reason to limit the phrase "manufacturer to have" in claim 1 to woodworking techniques. . . . As used in the claim [it] means that the convex top surface is shaped by manufacturing. This claim means exactly what it says, and the district court erred in limiting it to the manufacturing steps used to shape wood. . . .

In light of the foregoing . . . construction of the claim terms . . . the district court's grant of summary judgment of non-infringement cannot stand and is hereby reversed.

QUESTIONS FOR ANALYSIS

1. What is the rationale for requiring that all the details of a patent be revealed to the public?
2. Should the court take into account the commercial success of a patented product when considering a challenge to a patent?

TRADE SECRETS

Coca-Cola has kept a valuable secret for more than 100 years—the formula for Coke. Businesses have many *trade secrets*. Tort law protects such information. The *Restatement (2d) of Torts* defines such information as follows: "A trade secret may consist of any formula, pattern, device, or compilation of information which is used in one's business, and which gives him an opportunity to obtain an advantage over competitors who do not know or use it." Information such as the Coke formula could have been patented. Other proprietary information, such as computer software, could be copyrighted, but firms may prefer to keep the information secret. Some information may not be eligible for patent or copyright protection but is still a valuable secret.

Information is a trade secret if

1. It is not known by the competition.
2. The business would lose its advantage if the competition were to obtain it.
3. The owner has taken reasonable steps to protect the secret from disclosure.

If the owner of a trade secret has taken reasonable steps to protect secret information and it is stolen by a competitor, either by the abuse of confidence of an employee or by trespass, electronic surveillance, or bribery, the courts can provide relief to the injured business in the form of damages and an injunction against further use of the secret.

Generally, businesses with trade secrets protect themselves by having employees agree in their employment contracts not to divulge those secrets. The classic example of a theft of a trade secret involves an employee who steals a secret and then uses it in direct competition with the former employer or sells it to a competitor for personal gain. The *Harvey Barnett* case presents a trade secret situation that is common when such matters are litigated.

Harvey Barnett, Inc. v. Shidler

United States Court of Appeals, Tenth Circuit
338 F.3d 1125 (2003)

CASE BACKGROUND *Barnett developed the Infant Swimming Research program (ISR), which is claimed to be a scientific approach to pediatric drowning prevention. It uses a particular method and a set of procedures for teaching infants as young as six months old how to survive in water. ISR-certified instructors teach survival skills to infants in private lessons, ten minutes a day, five days a week, for about a month.*

Defendants are former ISR instructors who left Harvey Barnett and started a competitor company, Infant Aquatic Survival (IAS). While they worked at Barnett, defendants signed a non-disclosure and confidentiality agreement and another agreement promising to maintain confidentiality of information. Barnett sued for misappropriation of trade secrets, breach of contract, unjust enrichment, unfair competition, and deceptive trade practices. The district court held the ISR program was not a trade secret so dismissed the suit. Barnett appealed.

CASE DECISION Lucero, Circuit Judge.

* * *

Colorado has adopted the Uniform Trade Secrets Act, which defines a trade secret as "any scientific or technical information, design, process, procedure, formula, [or] improvement . . . which is secret and of value." In order "to be a 'trade secret' the owner thereof must have taken measures to prevent the secret from becoming available to persons other than those selected by the owner to have access thereto for limited purposes." Trade-secret status is a question of fact.

Factors considered in determining whether a trade secret exists include:

(1) the extent to which the information is known outside the business; (2) the extent to which it is known to those inside the business, i.e., by the employees; (3) the precautions taken by the holder of the trade secret to guard the secrecy of the information; (4) the savings effected and the value to the holder in having the information as against competitors; (5) the amount of effort or money expended in obtaining and developing the information; and (6) the amount of time and expense it would take for others to acquire and duplicate the information.

In [an earlier case] we held . . . that information can be a trade secret notwithstanding the fact that some of its components are well-known. "A trade secret can exist in a combination of characteristics and components each of which, by itself, is in the public domain, but the unified process, design and operation of which, in unique combination, affords a competitive advantage and is a protectable secret." . . .

Based on our review of the evidence, we conclude that ISR has raised genuine issues of material fact as to the contested factors. ISR submitted evidence that its program is unique. . . . ISR further submitted evidence showing that, through franchise agreements and license agreements, it has taken precautions to guard the secrecy of its program. . . .

In sum, we reverse the district court's decision granting summary judgment in favor of defendants on ISR's claim of misappropriation of trade secrets, and on its claim of breach of contract, and we remand for further proceedings consistent with this opinion.

QUESTIONS FOR ANALYSIS
1. Suppose there was no trade secret. Could there still be a violation of the confidentiality claim?

2. If all aspects of the swim program are in the public domain, how could the program be considered a secret?

ISSUE
Spotter

Protecting Valuable Information

At many companies, employees carry valuable information in their heads. At a sales-based organization, sales representatives know many of the clients and their volume of purchases of various products. If the representatives leave to go to work for a competitor, that information, which can be a trade secret, is carried out the door with them. If you are a manager in such a company, what steps can you take to try to prevent the exploitation of such information when the sales representatives leave?

Economic Espionage

While trade secrets are based on common law and generally enforced by tort litigation claiming misappropriation or other violations of a secret or secrecy agreement, in some cases the government will intervene. The Economic Espionage Act of 1996 contains a provision concerning theft of commercial trade secret: "Whoever, with intent to convert a trade secret, that is related to or included in a product that is produced for or placed in interstate or foreign commerce to the economic benefit of anyone other than the owner thereof, and intending or knowing that the offense will injure any owner of that trade secret" is subject to prosecution. Punishment for an individual can be as high as ten years in prison, and fines up to $5 million may be levied against firms.

SUMMARY

- Intellectual property is usually intangible property, that is, legally protected property created mostly by mental effort. The scope of interests in intellectual property is determined by a mix of common law and statutory law that restricts infringement or appropriation by others.
- Trademarks are designs, logos, distinctive marks, or words that manufacturers put on their goods for identification by consumers. At common law, the first producer to use a mark in a given area establishes priority of use. Under the Lanham Act, marks may be registered with the Patent and Trademark Office. Rights to a mark continue for as long as the mark is used and protected.
- The strongest trademarks are arbitrary and fanciful, which includes made-up words or real words applied to a product not related to the word as commonly used. Suggestive marks that hint at the kind of product are also provided strong protection. Less protection is available for descriptive marks, where the mark implies the good. Generic marks are words that were once protected trademarks but were lost as a result of lack of protection and common usage.
- Counterfeiting of marks is prohibited. The same is true of trade dress, which is trademark law applied to the look and feel of a product, such as a distinctive color or design. Service marks are the same as trademarks but apply to services

instead of goods. Trade names are business names and are protected in the relevant market in which the business is recognized.

- Copyrights allow exclusive control over original written works, musical compositions, art, and photography. Control extends to reproduction, publication, displays, performances, or derived works. While copyright exists at common law, registration under the Copyright Act provides clear evidence of ownership and is good for seventy years plus the life of the creator.

- While copyright ownership is based on the common law, the Copyright Act specifies a fair use defense to avoid a charge of infringement. The factors the courts consider in ruling on fair use include: (1) the purpose and character of the copying; (2) the nature of the copyrighted work; (3) the extent of the copying; and (4) the effect of copying on the market for the original work.

- Patents are exclusive statutory grants to protect an invention, design, or process that is genuine, useful, novel, and not obvious. Protection runs for twenty years from the time of patent application, which reveals to the public all details about the innovation.

- Trade secrets are formulas, patterns, devices, or compilation of information used in business that gives an economic advantage over competitors who do not have the information. They are protected by tort law from theft. Trade secret owners must take reasonable steps to protect the information from disclosure, including employee agreements not to reveal the information.

REVIEW AND DISCUSSION QUESTIONS

1. Define the following terms:

intellectual property	trade dress
intangible property	trade name
goodwill	copyright
infringement	fair use
counterfeiting	patent
trademark	trade secret

2. Garden Company sells wheelbarrows under the name Garden Wheelbarrow. Its sales are not doing well around the country. In an effort to achieve greater standing in the industry, Garden claims the trademark "Wheelbarrow's Wheelbarrows" for its wheelbarrows. If no one else has used that mark before, can Garden claim it?

CASE QUESTIONS

3. U.S. Search, LLC sued U.S. Search.com, Inc. claiming infridgement of its trademark. U.S. Search, LLC claimed first use of U.S. Search. It had not registered the mark, but filed a request with the Trademark Office for registration and also sued, demanding that U.S. Search.com, Inc. not be allowed to have continued use of its registered mark 1-800-US Search. The Trademark Office would not register the mark and the district court held against U.S. Search, LLC, so it appealed. Does it have a good case against U.S. Search.com and 1-800-US Search? [*U.S. Search, LCC v. U.S. Search.Com Inc.*, 300 F.3d 517 (4th Cir., 2002)]

4. Kassbaum, professionally known as Nick St. Nicholas, was a member of the rock band Steppenwolf from 1968 to 1971. He filed a complaint in federal court seeking a declaration that he is not barred from referring to himself as "a former member of Steppenwolf." At the request of Steppenwolf Productions, the district court dismissed his complaint. Kassbaum appealed. Can he refer to himself in that manner? [*Kassbaum* v. *Steppenwolf Productions, Inc.*, 236 F.3d 487 (9th Cir., 2000)]

5. Bruce, a freelance photographer, took a photo of Bill Clinton in 1992 as he was shaking hands with a Secret Service agent. Bruce cosigned the photo to a photo stock agency, which allowed the tabloid *World News* to use the photo. *World News* used the photo by superimposing a "space alien" in place of the agent. The photo was used numerous times in publications and on t-shirts, showing Clinton shaking hands with the alien. Bruce was paid a total of $1,775 in licensing fees. He sued, contending that he was owed much more. Given the sales of t-shirts and other uses of the photo, the district court awarded Bruce $20,142 in damages, plus interest. Bruce appealed, contending that he was due another $359,000. Assuming Bruce's case is upheld, how would his damages be estimated in such a case? [*Bruce* v. *Weekly World News, Inc.*, 310 F.3d 25 (1st Cir., 2002)]

 Check your answer at http://meiners.westbuslaw.com

6. GSI is a steel fabricator—a contractor that makes steel components for various construction projects. Scott Marshall used to work for GSI as an estimator—he determined how much GSI could bid on a project and still earn a profit. Scott asked his brother, Alan, to write a program to help him with estimates. Alan did so and was not paid for his work. Scott used the program while he worked at GSI. When Scott left GSI, he and Alan tried to market a new version of the program to sell to project estimators. GSI sued, contending that the key elements of the bid estimation process in the program were stolen from GSI by Scott, and so constituted a trade secret. The trial court enjoined the brothers from marketing the program; they appealed. [*Marshall* v. *Gipson Steel, Inc.*, 806 So.2d 266 (Supp. Ct., Miss., 2002)]

7. Origins Natural Resources owns the trademark "Origins." It has been used on a few clothing items over the years, but is primarily used on a successful line of cosmetics that are sold nationally. Origins filed for an injunction barring Kotler from using the trademark "Natural Origins" on a line of upscale women's clothing, contending that it was infringement and diluted the value of the "Origins" trademark. Should Origins receive the injunction? [*Origins Natural Resources, Inc.* v. *Kotler*, 2001 WL 492429 (S.D. N.Y., 2001)]

Check your answer at http://meiners.westbuslaw.com

8. Bouchat is an amateur artist. When he heard that Baltimore was to obtain a football team, the Ravens, he designed a possible logo for the team and faxed his design to the team. Soon after, the Ravens unveiled their logo, a raven holding a shield, which Bouchat believed was his design. He contacted a lawyer, who obtained copyright registration for Bouchat's design and then sued the Ravens for infringement. The jury found that the shield design was Bouchat's. The trial judge refused to overturn the verdict. Does the verdict stand? [*Bouchat* v. *Baltimore Ravens, Inc.*, 241 F.3d 350 (4th Cir., 2001)]

9. Hormel is the maker of SPAM luncheon meat, trademarked since 1937. SPAM is a distinctive, widely recognized name. Over $5 billion worth of SPAM has

been sold over the years. Hormel sued Jim Henson Productions for trademark infringement for using a Muppet character "Spa'am" in its *Muppet Treasure Island* movie. "Spa'am is the high priest of a tribe of wild boars that worships Miss Piggy as its Queen Sha Ka La Ka La. . . . Henson hopes to poke a little fun at Hormel's famous luncheon meat by associating its processed, gelatinous block with a humorously wild beast." The district court denied Hormel's request for an injunction against the name Spa'am. Did Hormel win on appeal? [*Hormel Foods* v. *Jim Henson Productions*, 73 F.3d 497 (2nd Cir., 1996)]

 Check your answer at http://meiners.westbuslaw.com

10. The Self-Realization Fellowship Church sued a competitor, the Ananda Church of Self-Realization, for trade name and trademark infringement. The district court refused to issue an injunction against the use of the term *Self-Realization* and ordered the trademark registration to be invalidated. Did this decision stand on appeal? [*Self-Realization Fellowship Church* v. *Ananda Church of Self-Realization*, 59 F.3d 902 (9th Cir., 1995)]

11. Qualitex makes press pads used in dry cleaning and laundry establishments. It is well known in the industry and always made its products in a special shade of green gold. A competitor, Jacobson, began to use a similar shade on its own press pads. Qualitex registered its color as a trademark and sued Jacobson for trademark infringement for using the same color in its products. Does Qualitex have a good claim? [*Qualitex Co.* v. *Jacobson Products Co.*, 115 S.Ct. 1300 (1995)]

 Check your answer at http://meiners.westbuslaw.com

12. Scientists employed by Texaco routinely photocopied articles in scientific journals to enhance their knowledge in their areas of specialization. Publishers of the journals sued Texaco, claiming that such copying infringes their copyrights. Texaco defended by saying that this was fair use. Who wins? [*American Geophysical Union* v. *Texaco Inc.*, 37 F.3d 881 (2d Cir., 1994), order amended and superseded 60 F.3d 913 (2d Cir., 1994)]

13. An American company imported video game cartridges from China that were pirated from the copyrighted originals made by Nintendo. The pirated copies also were sold with the Nintendo name on them. What laws have been violated, and what are the damages? [*Nintendo of America* v. *Dragon Pacific Intl.*, 40 F.3d 1007 (9th Cir., 1994)]

14. United States Gypsum developed a new putty to use on walls and ceilings to cover cracks. A key ingredient in the compound was a silicon product made by another company. The patent application did not list that as an ingredient in the putty. When a competitor started to make and sell the same putty and the two companies ended up in court, could USG win for patent infringement? [*United States Gypsum Co.* v. *National Gypsum Co.*, 74 F.3d 1209 (Fed. Cir., 1996)]

15. Defendant flew his plane over a chemical plant being built by duPont and took numerous photos of the construction. Although the plant was guarded on the ground from outsiders, it was not guarded from aerial inspection. The photographs revealed a lot about secret processes. Defendant said that if duPont cared, it would have covered the construction site. Does duPont have a legitimate trade secret action against the photographer? [*E. I. duPont deNemours & Co.* v. *Christopher*, 431 F.2d 1012 (5th Cir., 1970)]

16. Metro Traffic sold traffic reports to radio stations in the Los Angeles area. Its reporters had an employment contract that could be ended anytime but said that the employee could not work for a competitor in the LA area for two years

because of the "confidential and proprietary" information learned at Metro. Station KFWB was a client. It let its contract with Metro expire in favor of working with Shadow Traffic, which also produced traffic reports. Shadow hired several of Metro's reporters. Metro sued Shadow and its former employees for use of trade secrets. The trial court ruled for Shadow and the employees. Did the appeals court agree? [*Metro Traffic Control v. Shadow Traffic Network*, 27 Cal.Rptr.2d 573 (Cal. Ct. App., Sec. Div., 1994)]

ETHICS QUESTION

17. Poor countries assert that patented drugs are too expensive for most of their people to afford. The issue became especially noteworthy over drugs for AIDS sufferers in Africa. Monthly drug expenses are above average total income levels. Countries have been changing their drug laws to eliminate patent rights in certain cases. Do drug companies have an ethical duty to sell their products for the lowest possible price? Should countries abolish patent protection for drugs?

PULLING IT  *Together*

Torts and Intellectual Property

Landham played the role of "Billy, the Native American Tracker," in the 1987 Fox film called *Predator* starring Arnold Schwarzenegger. In 1995, Fox licensed to Galoob Toys the right to produce and market a line of its "Micro Machine" toys based on *Predator*. One of three sets of toys contained a "Billy" action figure. It is 1.5 inches tall and bears no personal resemblance to Landham. He sued Galoob and Fox for false endorsement under the Lanham Act and for violating his right of publicity (a part of the right to privacy). The district court dismissed the suit. Landham appealed. Does he have a suit in tort for the violation of his right of publicity and/or a suit for trademark infringement?

[*Landham v. Lewis Galoob Toys, Inc.*, 227 F.3d 619 (6th Cir., 2000)]

INTERNET EXERCISES

http://www.patents.com
http://www.uspto.gov
http://www.loc.gov

Many legal web sites are primarily marketing devices. An exception is the *patents.com* Intellectual Property Law Web Server. This site gives lucid explanations of many aspects of intellectual property.

1. What U.S. Code section requires that a patent owner mark goods embodying a patent with the patent number?
2. What organization administers international patent applications filed under the Patent Cooperation Treaty?
3. What four tests must an invention pass in order to be patentable?

The United States Patent and Trademark Office administers the laws relating to patents and trademarks and advises the secretary of commerce, the president, and the administration on patent, trademark, and copyright protection, as well as trade-related aspects of intellectual property. It provides searchable databases for patents and trademarks.

4. What is the trademark (word mark) associated with registration number 78046114? Who applied for it?
5. What is the phone number for the Patent and Trademark Depository Library in Austin, Texas?
6. What is the field code for primary examiner in the Patent Full Text and Image Database?

The Library of Congress, among its many services, hosts the Copyright Office. This office has publications, application forms for copyright registration, links to copyright law, and an online catalog of copyright records since 1978.

7. According to the Copyright Office at the Library of Congress, what are the two principal international copyright conventions?
8. Where can one find a summary of the Digital Millennium Copyright Act?

Chapter 10 | *Contracts*

Acustomer sends an inquiry by e-mail to your electronics distribution company. The customer asks if there is a quantity discount for ordering more than ten flat-screen thirty-inch Samsung LCD television sets. The customer service representative responds that yes, there is a 5 percent discount off the list price of $249.99 per television for orders of ten or more. The customer immediately responds by e-mail: "Great, I will take ten of the thirty-inch flat-screen Samsung LCD televisions at $249.99 each, less the 5 percent discount." The customer gives a credit card number and also offers to send a check. The sales rep who receives this response notices that the previous rep accidentally typed $249.99 instead of the correct price of $2,499.99 per television. The second rep sends a message to the customer apologizing for the mistake and notes the correct price, offering it with a 5 percent discount. The customer demands the televisions at $249.99, less 5 percent, noting that the sets were offered to him at that price, in writing, and he accepted that price in writing. "We have a contract," he says. Is there a contract? Do questions and responses by e-mail count as "writing"? Does your company have to absorb the loss? Can you tell the customer there was no contract, or must you offer an alternative special deal?

Pricing mistakes are only one issue that can arise in the daily business of making contracts with customers and suppliers. Whether it is buying gas at the pump with a credit card, a meal at a drive-through window, or a tuxedo that needs alterations, the transactions are all contracts.

The *law of contracts* evolved in commerce over the centuries. There are specific rules that involve the creation of a contract. The *freedom of contract*, which is a hallmark of the law, means that there are also responsibilities imposed on parties who commit to binding relationships. Next we study the key elements of the creation of contracts and the rights and duties that accompany common-law contracts.

CONTRACT LAW

Contract law is primarily state common law. It has developed through decades of judicial opinions that have resolved virtually every kind of contract dispute. When English courts began to resolve contract disputes in the early 1800s, they made express reference to the law merchant (*lex mercatoria*), which were commercial rules that merchants devised over centuries of doing business across national boundaries. Hence, contract law reflects real business experience. Today, the *Restatement (2d) of Contracts* is an authoritative document that provides a summary of the common law of contract as we know it.

Contract law that comes from the courts is modified by various statutes. Of particular importance is Article 2 of the *Uniform Commercial Code (UCC)*, a statute adopted by the states that applies to sales of goods. The UCC was designed to promote uniformity of the laws relating to commercial sales of goods. The next chapter studies the role of that law.

Definition of a Contract

Sir William Blackstone, a famous English jurist, defined a *contract* as "an agreement, upon sufficient consideration, to do or not to do a particular thing." Modern definitions center on a *promise*—the element common to all contracts. Section I of the *Restatement (2d) of Contracts* defines a contract as "a promise or a set of promises for the breach of which the law gives a remedy, or the performance of which the law in some way recognizes as a duty." It defines a promise as "a manifestation of the intention [of a party] to act or refrain from acting in a specified manner."

A contract, then, is the legal relationship that consists of the rights and duties of the agreeing parties growing out of promises. Contract law governs the enforceability of that relationship.

Not all promises are enforceable contracts. A promise may be either binding (contractual) or nonbinding (noncontractual). For a promise to be binding, and enforceable, it must meet the essential requirements of a contract. If a party fails to perform a nonbinding promise, contract law will not provide a remedy. This makes clear the need to meet the requirements of a contract when parties want their exchange of promises to be legally binding.

Contracts may be created by formal writing or oral discussions, or they may be inferred by the actions of the parties. A contract is an *express contract* if there is a written or oral expression of intent by the parties to enter into a legally binding agreement. A contract is an *implied contract* if it arises from the actions rather than the expressions of the parties. That is, given the way the parties have acted with respect to each other, the court infers that a contract exists. The essence of a contract is illustrated in Exhibit 10.1, regardless of whether the contract is express or implied.

Sources of Contract Law

Contract law is part of the common law that has evolved for hundreds of years. Since contract law is primarily judge-made law at the state level, there are some differences in contract rules across the states, but the basic rules are similar in all states. Unlike common-law countries, many countries rely on code law for their basic legal framework. Most of these countries have civil codes that contain the elements of contract law. Both evolved from the way business was done in practice. As we will

Exhibit 10.1

Essence of a Contract

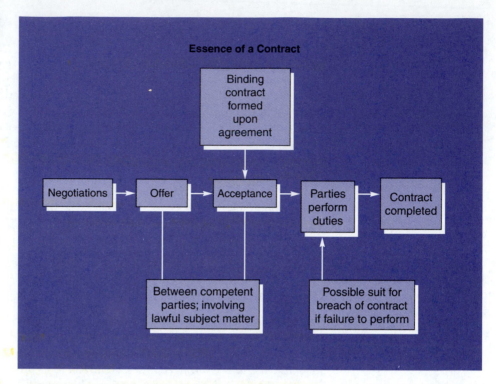

Essence of a Contract

study in the next chapter, there is code law for some contracts in the United States. The Uniform Commercial Code governs many contracts for the sale of goods in the United States. It is similar to the civil codes that govern contract law in non-common-law nations. But we begin by focusing on the common law of contracts.

ELEMENTS OF A CONTRACT

A contract provides parties with reasonable confidence that bargained-for exchanges will be enforceable. This section discusses the basic elements necessary for a bargain between two or more parties to form a valid contract. While many contracts consist of standardized forms, the basic elements of a contract are constant: agreement, consideration, legal capacity to contract, lawful subject matter, and genuine consent to the contract (see Exhibit 10.2). In addition, compliance with the Statute of Frauds may be necessary.

Offer and Acceptance

The essence of a contract is a legally binding agreement, that is, a mutual understanding between the parties as to the substance of the contract. This agreement between the parties is reached through a process of *offer* and *acceptance*.

The Offer

An *offer* is a promise to do something or to refrain from doing some specific thing. As defined in the *Restatement (2d) of Contracts*, "An offer is the manifestation of willingness to enter into a bargain, so made as to justify another person in understanding that his assent to that bargain is invited and will conclude it." The party making an offer is called the *offeror* or *offerer*; the *offeree* is the party to whom the offer is made.

Exhibit 10.2		
Key Elements of a	A.	Offer and Acceptance: An Agreement
Contract	B.	Consideration
	C.	Contractual Capacity
	D.	Legality
	E.	Genuine Consent

You offer to obligate yourself to a contract. You offer to sell your car to someone for $5,000. Since the offeror is allowing the offeree the opportunity to create a binding promise by making a valid acceptance of the offer, the offeror controls the terms of the offer made. To be an effective offer, three requirements must be met:

1. There must be a clear intent by the offeror to become contractually bound.
2. The basic terms and conditions of the offer must be clear and certain.
3. The offer must be properly communicated.

Manifestation of Intent   In making an offer, the offeror must have the intent to be bound to the contract, and that intent must be clearly expressed or manifested. *Preliminary negotiations* are not offers but are invitations to negotiate or to make an offer. Dickering with a salesperson about the price of a car is negotiation, not an offer.

A person's intent is tested by an objective standard. The court decides from the evidence whether a reasonable person familiar with the business being transacted would be justified in believing an offer had been made. If, under the circumstances, the court decides that intent was lacking, a contract could not be formed. For example, if Marie says, "I would like to sell my car for $5,000," there is no offer to sell that allows Tara to form a contract by saying, "Sold. I will pay you $5,000."

Many things that are stated as being for sale are not regarded as definite offers that can be accepted to create a contract. For example, when a jacket worn by Elvis Presley is put on the auction block, unless otherwise stated, it is an invitation for people to submit offers on the jacket. If no offers are high enough, the owner of the jacket can withdraw it.

Similarly, most advertisements are regarded as invitations for others to submit offers to buy. If a catalog lists a particular model of laser printers for $499.99 each, it is most likely that if you order one the order will be accepted and a contract formed. But the seller listing the printers for sale can reject such offers to buy, as such lists are usually considered to be requests for offers to buy, rather than offers themselves. No seller wants to give up profitable sales, but if sales projections are off and inventory is not adequate, offers by customers to buy will be rejected, unless they are willing to wait for the next shipment of goods from China.

Definite Terms and Conditions   Not every tiny detail of an offer must be present for it to be a valid offer. If you order a computer by mail order, the contract does not have to say the computer will be properly packed for shipment; that is presumed. Under the common-law rule, terms of an offer must be sufficient so that each party's promises are reasonably certain. An offer that has unclear major terms, or is missing important terms, cannot be the basis for a contract. Sometimes the courts supply missing terms if they are minor, so that the offer does not fail for *indefiniteness*. That prevents a party from backing out of a contract after the fact, claiming that there never was an offer because some trivial point was not clear.

JURIS *prudence?*

Listener Beware

The band Creed had to defend itself in court in Chicago when an unhappy fan sued the band because it gave, in his opinion, a crummy concert. Judge Peter Flynn held for Creed: "You can't bring a lawsuit against a band for sucking."

Trying a new angle of attack, an attorney filed a class action for breach of contract on behalf of 172 named plaintiffs. They claimed they were defrauded because they paid $75 for tickets to a concert that was billed as presenting full sets by Limp Bizkit, Linkin Park, and Metallica. Limp Bizkit left the stage after 17 minutes, so it failed to deliver the full set as promised, claimed the plaintiffs.

Source: *National Law Journal*

Communication of the Offer   Exhibit 10.3 summarizes the timing of communication of offer and acceptance. An acceptance requires *knowledge of the offer* by the offeree. The case of a person who captures a fugitive and later learns of a reward is an example of an offer failing for lack of communication. Because the communication of the offer occurred after the act of acceptance (capturing the fugitive), a proper acceptance did not take place. A contract cannot be formed by accepting an unknown offer.

Terminating an Offer

Termination of an offer can occur by the action of the parties or by the operation of law. The parties can *terminate* an offer by withdrawing it (by the offeror) or rejecting it (by the offeree) or through lapse of time (by the inaction of the offeree).

An *option contract* is different because it is a binding promise to keep an offer open for a specified period of time. For example, one may pay $100 to have an option to buy a house for $100,000 any time in the next five days. The offer to sell the house may not be withdrawn during that time.

Termination by the Parties   Offerors can terminate most offers by withdrawing an offer before it has been accepted by the offeree. The withdrawal of the offer by the offeror is a *revocation*. To be effective, the revocation must be communicated to the offeree. Generally, the offeror may revoke the offer anytime before acceptance. An offer can also state that it must be accepted within a designated time period. The expiration of that time period terminates the offer.

After an offer has been made, the offeree can create a contract by accepting the offer or can terminate the offer by rejecting it. One important form of rejection is

Exhibit 10.3			
Legal Effect of Offer and Acceptance Communications	**Communication**	**Time Effective**	**Legal Effect**
	By Offeror		
	1. Offer	When received by offeree	Offeree has the power to accept
	2. Revocation	When received by offeree	Ends offeree's power to accept
	By Offeree		
	1. Rejection	When received by offeror	Terminates the offer
	2. Counteroffer	When received by offeror	Terminates the offer
	3. Acceptance	When sent by offeree	Forms a contract

a *counteroffer*—a proposal by the offeree to change the terms of the original offer. For example, if Warisch offers to buy Kohl's old laptop computer for $500 and Kohl says that he will sell it for $600, a counteroffer has been made. The original offer by Warisch is terminated by the counteroffer. That is, by making a counteroffer, Kohl became the offeror and Warisch became the offeree.

Finally, an offer may terminate through *lapse of time*. If an offer does not state a specific period for acceptance, the passage of a reasonable length of time after the offer has been made will terminate it. What is reasonable depends upon the circumstances. An offer to buy stock in a company at a set price terminates through lapse of time very quickly, while an offer to sell a building expires after a longer time. It depends on the normal practices of the businesses involved.

Termination by the Operation of Law   An offer that terminates by operation of law through *intervening illegality* occurs when a court decision or legislation makes an offer illegal after it has been made. Suppose Horace Grant starts a business that offers to sell Powerball lottery tickets from other states to people in South Carolina. South Carolina enacts a law forbidding the sale of lottery tickets from other states in the state. Grant's offer to sell Powerball tickets in South Carolina is terminated by an intervening illegality.

An offer also terminates by law if the *subject matter is destroyed*. Suppose Espinoza offers to sell Washburn her car. Before Washburn accepts Espinoza's offer, the car is wrecked in an accident. The offer terminated when the accident occurred.

The *mental or physical incapacity or death of the offeror or the offeree* also terminates an offer by operation of law. An offer is terminated by mental or physical disability because the person does not have the mental capacity to enter into a contract, or physical limitations, such as a severe injury, may make a party unable to perform a contract that requires certain skills or abilities. Similarly, an offeror or offeree who dies cannot execute a contract. If you agree to buy a home from a seller who dies before the transaction is completed, the deal is off, as the home now belongs to the estate or heirs, who did not agree to the sale.

The Acceptance

In contract law, *acceptance* is an offeree's expression of assent or agreement to the terms of an offer. In most contracts, this means the offeree accepts by making a promise in exchange for the original promise. To be effective, an acceptance must be unconditional, unequivocal, and properly communicated. A supposed acceptance that lacks one of these elements will generally not bring about a binding contract.

Generally, contracts are called *bilateral contracts* when there is an exchange of promises. For example, you say to a friend, "I will sell you my car for $2,000"; he responds, "Fine, I will pay that." In some states, certain contracts are referred to as *unilateral contracts* when there is acceptance by *performance*. For example, your neighbor says to you, "I will pay you $30 to mow my lawn." You say nothing in response, but the next day you mow the lawn—so the offer was accepted by performance. Such contracts are valid whether they are called unilateral or bilateral.

Must Be Unconditional   An offeree must accept an offer as presented by an offeror. In effect, the acceptance must be the *mirror image* of the offer. The common-law rule is that a supposed acceptance that adds conditions to the original offer is a counteroffer. By changing the terms of the offer, there is not unconditional acceptance; the offeree rejects the offer. This is a key issue in the *Ardente* case.

Ardente v. Horan
Supreme Court of Rhode Island
366 A.2d 162 (1976)

CASE BACKGROUND *The Horans offered to sell their house in Newport, Rhode Island. Ardente offered to pay $250,000 for the property. His offer was communicated to the Horans through his attorney. The Horans indicated, in a reply through their attorney, that the bid was acceptable. The Horans' attorney prepared a sale contract and sent it to Ardente for his signature.*

Ardente's lawyer returned the signed contract, with a check for $20,000, and a letter stating "My clients are concerned that the following items remain with the real estate: (a) dining room set and tapestry wall covering in the dining room; (b) fireplace fixtures throughout; (c) the sun parlor furniture. I would appreciate your confirming that these items are a part of the transaction, as they would be difficult to replace."

The Horans did not agree to include those items in the sale, so they refused to sign the contract and returned the check to Ardente. He sued the Horans for performance of the contract. The trial judge held that Ardente's letter was a counteroffer, so there was no contract. Ardente appealed.

CASE DECISION Doris, Justice.

* * *

The general rule is that where, as here, there is an offer to form a bilateral contract, the offeree must communicate his acceptance to the offeror before any contractual obligation can come into being. A mere mental intent to accept the offer, no matter how carefully formed, is not sufficient. The acceptance must be transmitted to the offeror in some overt manner.

* * *

To be effective, an acceptance must be definite and unequivocal. "An offeror is entitled to know in clear terms whether the offeree accepts his proposal. It is not enough that the words of a reply justify a probable inference of assent." The acceptance may not impose additional conditions on the offer, nor may it add limitations. "An acceptance which is equivocal or upon condition or with a limitation is a counteroffer and requires acceptance by the original offeror before a contractual relationship can exist."

* * *

In making our decision we recognize that, as one text states, "The question whether a communication by an offeree is a conditional acceptance or counter-offer is not always easy to answer. It must be determined by the same common-sense process of interpretation that must be applied in so many other cases." In our opinion the language used in plaintiff's letter . . . is not consistent with an absolute acceptance accompanied by a request for a gratuitous benefit. We interpret the letter to impose a condition on plaintiff's acceptance of defendants' offer. The letter does not unequivocally state that even without the enumerated items plaintiff is willing to complete the contract. In fact, the letter seeks "confirmation" that the listed items "are a part of the transaction." Thus, far from being an independent, collateral request, the sale of the items in question is explicitly referred to as a part of the real estate transaction. Moreover, the letter goes on to stress the difficulty of finding replacements for these items. This is a further indication that plaintiff did not view the inclusion of the listed items as merely collateral or incidental to the real estate transaction.

A review of the relevant case law discloses that those cases in which an acceptance was found valid despite an accompanying conditional term generally involved a more definite expression of acceptance than the one in the case at bar.

Accordingly, we hold that since the plaintiff's letter of acceptance . . . was conditional, it operated as a rejection of the defendants' offer and no contractual obligation was created.

The plaintiff's appeal is denied and dismissed. . . .

QUESTIONS FOR ANALYSIS

1. Since the letter that mentioned the additional items was separate from the contact document, which Ardente signed, why does the contract not stand alone as a valid contract?

2. Why does Ardente not have the right to take the contract as written, assuming he withdraws the other requests for the various items mentioned in the letter?

Must Be Unequivocal   Acceptance must be unequivocal or definite. Suppose an offeree receives an offer to buy a car for $10,000. If the offeree says "I see" or "What a good idea," either expression fails the unequivocal test. There is no acceptance.

While the words "I accept" are a clear indication of an offeree's acceptance, any words or conduct expressing the offeree's intent to accept an offer is an effective acceptance. When negotiations take place, however, much is expressed in words and conduct that is not a complete rejection or a clear acceptance. In such cases, the courts look at the offeree's expressions to determine whether a reasonable person would consider them as an acceptance of the offer.

As a general rule, silence is not considered acceptance for the simple reason that it is not unequivocal. It could mean either yes or no to the offeree. However, the past business dealings of the offeror and the offeree may allow silence by the offeree to be acceptance. For example, if a company has serviced a copier for a customer every month for several years, there does not need to be an express statement every month that copier service is desired.

Must Be Properly Communicated   The final requirement of acceptance is that it is properly communicated. Three factors can be important in meeting this requirement: (1) the method of acceptance, (2) the timeliness of acceptance, and (3), in some cases, performance as acceptance. Exhibit 10.4 summarizes the elements of offer and acceptance.

The general rule in communicating an acceptance is that any reasonable method is adequate. Problems arise when the offeror authorizes one way to communicate acceptance but the offeree uses another. If, for example, the offeror requires that acceptance be made by a signed letter, a response by telephone will not create an acceptance. If no method of acceptance is specified, the offeree may use any reasonable means to communicate. The safest approach is to use the method used by the offeror in communicating the offer.

The timeliness of acceptance is important, especially when the value of goods or services being offered changes rapidly. To deal with time problems, the courts created the general rule that if the method of acceptance is reasonable under the circumstances, the acceptance is effective when it is sent.

In some circumstances, an offeror has attempted to revoke an offer before receiving the offeree's acceptance. This led to the *mailbox rule*, which states that acceptance is effective when it is mailed (sent) and revocation is effective when it is received by the offeree. For example, the offeror sends the offer June 1, and the offer is received by the offeree on June 3. The offeror sends a revocation of the offer on June 2, and

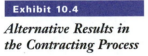

Exhibit 10.4

Alternative Results in the Contracting Process

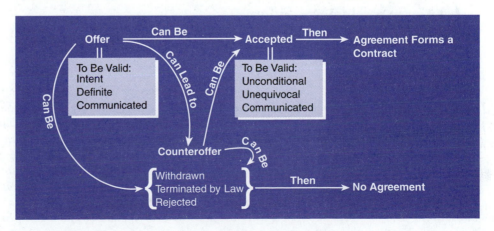

the revocation is received by the offeree on June 4. If the offeree had sent an acceptance to the offeror on June 3 and the acceptance had reached the offeror on June 5, would there be a valid acceptance? Applying the mailbox rule, the answer is yes, since the acceptance is effective upon being sent by the offeree (June 3), while the revocation is effective upon receipt (June 4).

Consideration

Consideration is something of value or something bargained for in exchange for a promise. That is, both parties to a contract get something and give up something. It is the element of a contract that keeps it from being a gift. If consideration is absent, neither party can enforce the promise or agreement.

The traditional rule is that an exchange is consideration if it creates a legal detriment to the *promisee* (the party to whom a promise is made) or a legal benefit to the *promisor* (the party making a promise). A *legal detriment* is an act, or a promise to act, or the refraining from an action, such as giving up a legal right. For example, if you are hit by a careless driver and accept an out-of-court settlement of $20,000, you give up the right to sue in court for damages. A *legal benefit* to the promisor exists when the promisor acquires some legal right through the promisee's act, promise to act, or refraining from doing some act.

Consideration requires either a legal detriment to the promisee or a legal benefit to the promisor, although both usually occur at the same time. Suppose Shaftel buys a watch from SwissWatch for $100. Shaftel suffers a legal detriment (gives up the right to keep $100) in exchange for a benefit (the watch). SwissWatch suffers a legal detriment (gives up the watch) in exchange for a benefit ($100). As the following famous case illustrates, courts use this *detriment-benefit test* to determine whether there is consideration for a contract.

Adequacy of Consideration

For the most part, courts do not inquire into the *adequacy of consideration* given in a contract. The bargaining is the responsibility of the parties to the contract. Even if one party bargains poorly and the values of the items to be exchanged are very unequal, the courts generally do not interfere. Courts support contracts that are bargained for, even if the consideration is not related to market value, as the *Hamer* case explained.

Hamer v. Sidway
Court of Appeals of New York, Second Division
124 N.Y. 538, 27 N.E. 256 (1891)

CASE BACKGROUND   *William E. Story was the uncle of William E. Story II. At a birthday party, Story promised his sixteen-year-old nephew that he would pay him $5,000 if he would refrain from "drinking, using tobacco, swearing, and playing cards or billiards for money" until he was twenty-one years old. Upon turning 21, the nephew wrote to the uncle, telling him that he had performed his part of the agreement and wished to be awarded the $5,000. The uncle wrote a letter to the nephew stating, "Your letter . . . came to hand all right,*

saying that you had lived up to the promise made to me several years ago. I have no doubt but you have, [and] you shall have five thousand dollars, as I promised you."

Two years later the uncle died, without having paid the nephew the $5,000. The executor of the Story estate refused to pay the $5,000, stating that while there had been an agreement, there was no consideration by the nephew for the money. Here the court reviews the agreement and discusses the element of consideration as a part of the contract.

CASE DECISION   Parker, Judge.

* * *

The defendant contends that the contract was without consideration to support it, and therefore invalid. He asserts that the nephew, by refraining from the use of liquor and tobacco, was not harmed, but benefited; that that which he did was best for him to do, independently of his uncle's promise, and insists that it follows that, unless the promisor was benefited, the contract was without consideration, a contention which, if well founded, would seem to leave open for controversy in many cases whether that which the promisee did or omitted to do was in fact of such benefit to him as to leave no consideration to support the enforcement of the promisor's agreement. Such a rule could not be tolerated, and is without foundation in the law. We have defined "consideration" as follows: "A valuable consideration, in the sense of the law, may consist either in some right, interest, profit, or benefit accruing to the one party, or some forbearance, detriment, loss, or responsibility given, suffered, or undertaken by the other."

Courts "will not ask whether the thing which forms the consideration does in fact benefit the promisee . . . , or is of any substantial value to any one. It is enough that something is promised, done, forborne, or suffered by the party to whom the promise is made as consideration for the promise made to him. In general a waiver of any legal right at the request of another party is a sufficient consideration for a promise. Any damage, or suspension or forbearance of a right will be sufficient to sustain a promise. . . . 'Consideration' means not so much that one party is profiting as that the other abandons some legal right in the present, or limits his legal freedom of action in the future, as an inducement for the promise of the first."

Now, applying this rule to the facts before us, the nephew used tobacco, occasionally drank liquor, and he had a legal right to do so. That right he abandoned for a period of years upon the strength of the promise of his uncle that for such forbearance he would give him $5,000. We need not speculate on the effort which may have been required to give up the use of those stimulants. It is sufficient that he restricted his lawful freedom of the action within certain prescribed limits upon the faith of his uncle's agreement, and now, having fully performed the conditions imposed, it is of no moment whether such performance actually proved a benefit to the promisor [the uncle], and the court will not inquire into it; but, were it a proper subject of inquiry, we see nothing in this record that would permit a determination that the uncle was not benefited in a legal sense.

* * *

QUESTIONS FOR ANALYSIS

1. What was the consideration in this case?
2. Was it important that the activities the nephew refrained from did not harm but benefited him?
3. What detriment did the nephew incur?

Preexisting Duty and Past Consideration

Consideration is a present *detriment* to the promisee and a present benefit to the promisor. An obligation that existed before a new agreement (*preexisting duty*) does not constitute consideration. The reason is that the promisee has not incurred a detriment if there was already an obligation to perform; without a detriment, there can be no consideration.

Consider a professional baseball player who is unhappy with his contract because similar players are now making more money than he is. Suppose his team wants to make him happy and will give him a salary increase. An agreement to provide the increase, given an existing contract, would not be supported by consideration by the athlete. Since only the team would be incurring a detriment, the pay increase would be a gift, not a bargain. The athlete had already agreed to perform for the club at the original contract amount (past consideration). To provide new consideration, the team will require the player to agree to a contract extension. The team's detriment is the additional salary, and the athlete's detriment is the additional time he agrees to play for the team at the new salary.

JURIS *prudence?*

My Lawyer Should Be Responsible for My Breach of Contract!

Latrell Sprewell, a $10-million-a-year-plus basketball player for the Golden State Warriors, was kicked off the team and had his contract torn up for physically attacking his coach twice. First Sprewell sued the National Basketball Association, claiming they could not suspend him from playing. A federal judge threw the case out. Sprewell than sued his agent for not including a term in his contract with Golden State that would have made the team pay him regardless of his personal conduct.

Source: *The Wall Street Journal*

Enforceable Promises without Consideration

Circumstances exist where consideration for a promise is not required by the courts for the promise to be enforceable. The doctrine used by the courts is called *promissory estoppel* (or *detrimental reliance*). The rationale for the doctrine is that it will avoid an injustice due to the promisee's reasonable reliance on the promisor's promise.

Under the doctrine, the promisor is *estopped* (prevented) from denying a promise. The *Restatement (2d) of Contracts* explains promissory estoppel this way: "A promise which the promisor should reasonably expect to induce action or forbearance on the part of the promisee . . . and which does induce such action or forbearance is binding if injustice can be avoided only by enforcement of the promise."

We see an application of this doctrine in the *Hinson* case.

Hinson v. N&W Construction Company, Inc.

Court of Appeals of Mississippi
— S.2d — (2004 WL 1445102)

CASE BACKGROUND   *N&W Construction prepared a bid to submit to the Mississippi Job Corps Center (MJCC) to build a kitchen facility at a training center. In preparing the bid, N&W received oral bids from several plumbing contractors. One of them, Hinson, quoted $92,000 as his bid for the plumbing job. The next-lowest plumbing subcontractor bid was $139,000. N&W used Hinson's lower plumbing bid in preparing its general contracting bid for the whole project to MJCC.*

N&W was the low bidder for the construction job, and it was awarded the MJCC contract. N&W notified Hinson that he was needed to do the plumbing work, as construction on the project was beginning. Hinson failed to sign and return the plumbing subcontract, and he refused the job. N&W had to hire the next-lowest bidder and pay an additional $47,000 to get the plumbing work done.

N&W sued Hinson on the basis of promissory estoppel. The trial court granted summary judgment to N&W and awarded $47,000 in damages. Hinson appealed.

CASE DECISION   Irving, Justice.

* * *

The doctrine of promissory estoppel has been stated as follows:

> An estoppel may arise from the making of a promise, even though without consideration, if it was intended that the promise should be relied upon and in fact it was relied upon, and if a refusal to enforce it would be virtually to sanction the perpetuation of fraud or would result in other injustice.

A review of the undisputed facts of this case and the evidence submitted by the parties to N&M's motion for summary judgment . . . clearly indicate that the circuit court correctly granted N&W's motion for summary judgment on the theory of promissory estoppel. . . .

Hinson admits that he provided a verbal quote to N&W in the amount of $92,000 for plumbing work on the building. . . .

Hinson testified that he reviewed the plans and specifications for the building, worked on his quote for approximately a week, and was satisfied with his price of $92,000. . . .

Moreover, Hinson does not dispute that N&W used his quote for the plumbing work in its bid for the building contract. . . . Hinson later explained . . . that he refused to do the plumbing work. . . . "I just had a lot of other jobs going." . . .

Affirmed.

QUESTIONS FOR ANALYSIS

1. Since Hinson did not sign a contract and never received any payment from N&W, should Hinson be responsible? Why did N&W not get an agreement in writing?

2. Since the next bid was 50 percent higher than Hinson's, isn't it likely that Hinson's bid was poorly done and he would have suffered a big loss had he done the work?

This is not a rule imposed lightly by the courts. Promissory estoppel also arises in some cases of promises to charities. Suppose an art museum is raising $50 million for an expansion. It collects promises from various donors, but none of the money is collected until there are enough promises to make the project feasible and construction begins. Once that happens, if a donor backs out, the courts may rule that promissory estoppel applies and the gift must be made. The building contract was entered into on reliance of the donation being made.

Capacity to Contract

One essential element of a contract is *contractual capacity*, or legal ability, to create a contract. The term *capacity* refers to a party's ability to perform legally valid acts, acquire legal rights, and incur legal liabilities. Generally, minors, intoxicated persons, and the insane have limited capacity to contract. A party claiming incapacity has the burden of proving it.

Most individuals have complete capacity to contract. If a person, perhaps as a result of mental disability, does not have capacity to contract, the contract entered into is not enforceable. If a person has *partial capacity*, the contract is enforceable unless the person with partial capacity exercises the right to disaffirm the contract. Contracts created by those with partial capacity are voidable.

Void and Voidable Contracts

If a contract does not exist at law, that is, it cannot be enforced, it is a *void contract*. For example, if someone tries to make a contract with a person who is legally considered to be insane, the contract is void. It does not exist. A contract is also void if it concerns an illegal subject matter, such as a contract to sell cocaine. Disputes over such matters will not be accepted by the courts.

A *voidable contract* is made when one party to the contract has the right to avoid a legal obligation. As we discuss below, this is the case with some contracts entered into by minors or persons with limited mental ability. If a person is so intoxicated when he makes a contract that he does not know what he is doing, then, not having had the capacity to contract, he may later have the right to have the contract declared voidable. A contract is also voidable if there is fraud involved in making the contract. The victim of the fraud can accept the contract, or not.

Minors

A *minor* is a person under the legal age of majority. The traditional age of majority was twenty-one, but all states have statutes that set the age at eighteen for most contracts and younger for some. The general rule is that a minor may enter into contracts but the contracts are voidable at the option of the minor. A company that enters into a contract with a minor—knowingly or unknowingly—may find itself with relatively few rights if the minor disaffirms the contract. If a minor disaffirms a contract after receiving benefits, such as a sixteen-year-old buying a car on credit and driving it for six months, *restitution* must be paid for the value of the benefit received, provided the minor is able to do so.

After a minor reaches the age of majority, most states provide that the person may *ratify* contracts made while a minor. Ratification may be expressed through words, writing, or implied by conduct, such as continued use of an automobile. The right to disaffirm extinguishes after a reasonable time. There are some contracts that minors may not disaffirm. Enlistment contracts to join the Army and marriage contracts are classic examples of *nonvoidable contracts*. Further, some states have statues that do not allows minors to disaffirm certain contracts, such as for insurance, educational loans, medical care loans, and bank account agreements.

INTERNATIONAL *Perspective*

Problems Enforcing Contracts

A study by the World Bank looked at the problem of enforcing a contract in countries around the world. Lack of both effective contract law and honest, efficient judicial enforcement in poor countries discourage foreign firms from investing in those countries or doing business there.

The authors of the study assumed a case in which one business refused to pay another business money that it owed for a transaction, and suit had to be brought to enforce the contract. The study examined the following variables in a selection of different countries: (1) the number of procedures mandated by law that is required to file a contract case and take it through the court system; (2) the average number of days to complete the legal process from service of process to trial and enforcement; and (3) the cost of a legal action as a percent of the value of the debt that is in dispute.

Country	Number of Procedures	Time (days)	Cost (percentage of debt)
China	25	241	25.5
India	40	425	43.1
Mexico	37	421	20.0
United Kingdom	14	288	15.7
United States	17	250	7.5
Guatemala	37	1,459	14.5
Canada	17	346	12.0

The United States is no paragon of efficiency, but the cost of legal action is relatively low, as a fraction of average income. If contract enforcement is too long, too costly, or too complex, ordinary people are unlikely to be able to integrate it into the modern economy.

Source: *http://rru.worldbank.org/doingbusiness*

Legality

For a contract to be valid, its subject matter must be *lawful*. The contract will be illegal and unenforceable if its subject matter violates a state or federal statute, or the common law, or is contrary to public policy. The terms *illegal bargain* and *illegal agreement* rather than illegal contract may be more proper because contract by definition refers to a legal and enforceable agreement.

Illegal Agreements

Promises that violate the law are illegal agreements that the courts will not recognize as enforceable contracts, regardless of the intent of the parties. Statutes prohibit a variety of activities, so attempts to contract for such activities violate the statutes. Deals to trade in prohibited drugs, such as cocaine, are illegal agreements, as are other contracts to engage in criminal activities. State law strictly controls some activities, such as gambling and the sale of alcoholic beverages. Hence, gambling contracts are often illegal and the person who won an illegal wager cannot seek help from the courts. Some states have limits on interest rates that can be charged on certain loans; attempts to charge rates above the maximum allowed is called *usury* and is illegal. When a court is asked to enforce a contract and it finds it to be in violation of law, the court may strike the entire bargain as unenforceable or only strike the part of the bargain that concerns illegal subject matter.

Unenforceable Contracts

Some contracts were legal and enforceable when they were made, but a change in the law makes them unenforceable. For example, suppose a company agreed to sell a shipload of wheat to the government of Iran. While the shipment was under way, the U.S. government declared that no U.S. firms may trade with Iran. The contract at that point becomes *unenforceable* under U.S. contract law, even if it is seen as legal in Iran. The seller must end the effort to sell the goods or face prosecution for trying to fulfill a contract about a matter that is now illegal.

Contracts Contrary to Public Policy

Some contracts are unenforceable because their subject matter is *contrary to public policy*. A contract that conflicts with the law is contrary to public policy, but some contracts that may not violate any particular statute yet may have a negative impact on public welfare. Some contracts that courts have held to be contrary to public policy are exculpatory agreements, unconscionable contracts, contracts with public servants, and contracts in restraint of trade.

Exculpatory Agreements   An *exculpatory agreement* releases one party from the consequences brought about by wrongful acts or negligence. An example of an exculpatory agreement is an employment contract with a clause stating that the employee will not hold the employer liable for any harm to her caused by the employer while on the job. With such a clause, the employer is no longer concerned about being sued for intentional torts or criminal acts. Such clauses generally violate public policy and are not enforceable.

Unconscionable Contracts   The courts usually do not concern themselves with the fairness of a bargain struck by contracting parties. But in some cases, if a contract is grossly unfair to an innocent party, the courts, in equity, will not enforce it. Such contracts are called *unconscionable contracts* and occur when one of the parties, being in a strong position, takes advantage of the other party. The stronger party convinces the other party to enter into a contract contrary to his well-being. Such agreements may violate public policy and not be enforceable.

JURIS *prudence?*

Speaking of Unconscionable Actions . . .

Because of a dispute, Chambers Cable television company dropped the ABC affiliate station that carried, among other programs, *Monday Night Football*. Cable subscriber Phillip Schlenker of Novato, California, sued for breach of contract. He argued that the company claimed that it would carry all major networks, but it no longer did, depriving him of watching *Monday Night Football*.

Being "forced" to go to a bar to drink during five games, Schlenker ran up a $75 bar tab, which the court awarded him in damages, plus attorney fees. After all, "You cannot sit in a tavern and watch a game without buying something from the bar," said Schlenker. The Federal Communications Commission reported that the case appeared to be precedent setting.

Source: *Gannett News Service*

Contracts with Public Servants   A contract to influence a public servant to violate the duty the government employee owes to the public is contrary to public policy. For example, if a lobbyist contracts to pay a legislator if a certain bill is passed, the contract would be unenforceable. It also violates public policy to pay regulators or police officials to give special favors.

Contracts in Restraint of Trade   Contracts that restrain trade or unreasonably restrict competition are considered contrary to public policy and are not enforced by the courts. Part of the common law on this subject became part of modern antitrust law, discussed later in the text.

Even if a contract does not violate a statute, it still may be an unenforceable restraint of trade. A *covenant not to compete*, for example, may be a restraint of trade if it does not meet certain guidelines. A covenant not to compete typically arises in contracts for the sale of a business and for employment. The employee (or seller) agrees not to compete with the employer (or buyer). If the covenant is limited to a reasonable time and territory, courts generally find it enforceable, but the rules vary quite a bit from state to state. Contracts between businesses often restrict the parties from interfering with other existing business relationships that become known by virtue of the parties now working together, as in the *General Commercial* case.

General Commercial Packaging, Inc. v. TPS Package Engineering, Inc.

United States Court of Appeals, Ninth Circuit
126 F.3d 1131 (1997)

CASE BACKGROUND   *General Commercial provides packing services for businesses in Florida and California. Its longtime customer, Disney, hired it to package materials for shipment to EuroDisneyland. General Commercial hired TPS as a subcontractor to help with that work.*

To protect its business with Disney, General Commercial required TPS to sign a contract that included a clause that TPS would not deal directly with Disney during the contract or for one year afterward. If TPS worked with Disney without permission, it would pay

General Commercial 25 percent of its revenues from that business. TPS ignored the provision and began working directly for Disney.

General Commercial sued for breach of contract. The district court held that the contract violated California's prohibition against contracts in restraint of trade. General Commercial appealed.

CASE DECISION   Per Curium.

* * *

Under California law, "every contract by which anyone is restrained from engaging in a lawful profession, trade, or business of any kind is to that extent void." Cal.Bus. & Prof.Code §16600. Although TPS raised no objection to the clause which precluded it from dealing directly with Disney—thereby cementing a highly profitable subcontracting relationship with General Commercial—it now claims that section 16600 renders its promise void. TPS reads section 16600 to nullify "every part of every contract that restricts a person from pursuing, in whole or in part, any trade, business or profession." The contract it signed, TPS concludes, is invalid because it prohibits TPS from infiltrating Disney's corner of the packing and shipping market.

We [previously] rejected this strict interpretation of section 16600. . . . Section 16600 does not impair General Commercial's contract with TPS unless it entirely precludes TPS from pursuing its trade or business.

* * *

General Commercial's contract with TPS is therefore valid unless it "completely restrain[s]" TPS from plying its trade or business. . . . In considering this question, we recognize that a contract does not have to impair a party's access to every potential customer to contravene section 16600. Because most businesses cannot succeed with only a handful of customers, a contract can effectively destroy a signatory's ability to conduct a trade or business by placing a substantial segment of the market off limits. This explains why courts have been less tolerant of contracts that prohibit employees from soliciting all of their former employers' customers, and of wholesale covenants not to compete.

TPS has never disputed General Commercial's claim that the contract "does not prohibit TPS from engaging in the crating and packing business." Nor could it. The agreement only precludes TPS from dealing with Disney and those other firms which General Commercial "has introduced to and contracted with TPS to perform packing and crating subcontracting services." Apart from Disney, TPS was not barred from soliciting work from any firm with which it had a prior relationship. The contract thus only limits TPS's access to a narrow segment of the packing and shipping market.

The district court's order granting TPS's motion for summary judgment on Count I of its complaint is reversed. The breach of contract claim is remanded to the district court for consideration of any remaining defenses which TPS may have raised.

* * *

QUESTIONS FOR ANALYSIS

1. Would a large firm be able to use contract terms as existed in this contract to limit a company that contracts with it not to deal with competitors?

2. Under a rule of reason, what kinds of restrictions that extend beyond the immediate matter of the contract itself could be imposed on the other party to a contract?

Reality and Genuineness of Consent

Freedom of contract is based on the right of individuals to enter into the bargains of their choice. The courts assume that if a person entered into a contract, there was a desire to do so and the other party may rely on the bargain. Under some circumstances, however, a person may enter into an agreement without knowledge of key information surrounding the transaction. Without knowledge, there is no *reality of consent* or *genuine consent* by the parties, and the contract is void or voidable depending on the circumstances. It is often said that there must be a *meeting of the minds* for there to be consent to the contract.

A *unilateral mistake* occurs when one party to a contract enters into it with false information or accidentally makes an error in a calculation or other significant matter. If, for example, a buyer simply thinks something that is not true, but was not misled by the seller, then there is unlikely to be grounds for avoiding the contract. If a mistake is obvious, such as a contract to buy a house that says the price is $20,000, when the buyer knows it should be $200,000, the contract cannot be enforced at the lower price because of the simple mistake made in typing the contract. In general, if the other party should have known of the error, it cannot be enforced to allow one to profit from a simple error.

A famous case from 1887 in Michigan, *Sherwood* v. *Walker* (33 N.W. 919), illustrates the effect of *mutual mistake*. A cow, Rose 2d of Aberlone, was sold for one-tenth of what she would have been worth had she not been believed to be sterile. After the sale, when she was found to be pregnant, the seller wanted to void the contract but the buyer refused. The high court of Michigan held the transaction was void because the parties thought they bargained for a sterile cow, not a more valuable breeding cow, so the deal was made under false assumptions. In any contract, parties take certain risks, but they do not take risks about presumed facts affecting the substance of their bargain.

Statutory Exceptions

In some circumstances, reality or genuine consent is governed by statute. Some statutes deal with high-pressure selling techniques by door-to-door salespeople. These "home solicitation" statutes allow contracts to be voided if the buyer entered into the contract under extreme pressure by a salesperson. For example, the Federal Trade Commission's Cooling-Off Rule allows purchasers of door-to-door sales with a value over $25 to void the contract in writing within three business days.

Fraud and Misrepresentation

A person who "agrees" to a contract due to *fraud*, *misrepresentation*, *duress*, or *undue influence* has the right to disaffirm the contract because there was not genuine consent. Duress and undue influence are not common in contractual matters, but contracts formed under either are voidable. Duress occurs when someone is "forced" to sign a contract; that is, the contract is made because of a threat that gave no easy way out. In the case of undue influence, a person enters into a contract because they are so dominated by another person, or have so much trust in the other person, that they are subject to improper persuasion. This happens sometimes to elderly people who have to rely on a "trusted" caretaker.

Fraud   A contract induced by fraud may be rescinded. If the contract is rescinded before any losses are incurred, then there is not likely to be a cause of action for damages. As we saw in Chapter 7, it is possible that the person who committed the fraud may be sued in tort. If there is a tort, then the injured party may also sue for punitive damages. To establish common-law fraud, the injured party must show that:

1. There was a *misstatement* of an important or *material* fact; that is, false information was presented as fact in the making of the contract. The misstatement must be about a key fact relevant to the contract. Unimportant or unrelated misstatements, such as claiming that Abraham Lincoln was president during World War I, cannot be the basis of fraud. Hyping a product—such as by saying "This is the most fun computer game ever invented" or "Now is the best time to buy"—is not sufficient to indicate an intent to defraud.
2. There must be *scienter* or intent to defraud; that is, the party wanted to mislead the other party and intentionally deceived him. Scienter means that the court finds that there is something rotten about the deal (has a bad scent) about which the seller could not be ignorant.
3. The seller must know, or have reason to know, that the statement she is making is false. If you sell your car, which you bought used, and you believe that

the mileage is correct, when in fact the odometer had been turned back by the person who owned it before you, then you do not know you are not telling the truth.

4. The recipient of the false information must justifiably rely on that information in making the decision to go ahead with the deal. If a seller tells you false information intending to deceive you, but you are not fooled and you go ahead with the deal anyway, there is no fraud. Similarly, if you believe information that you should know to be false, such as a claim that the engine in a car is made out of gold, there is no justifiable reliance.

5. There must be *privity* between the parties; that is, they must have been in a contractual arrangement. A third party observing fraud cannot sue.

6. There must be *proximate cause*. The fact that there was false information that caused the contract to be formed must be related to losses that were suffered for there to be a cause of action for damages.

7. There must be *damages* that were caused by the fraud. That is, even if there is fraud in the making of a contract, if there are no damages that result, there should be no award.

Are You Due a Commission?

ISSUE *Spotter*

You work in commercial real estate. You have a contract to sell a dry cleaning business. Your contract with the seller lasts six months. It says that if the seller sells the business to anyone you brought as a contact within one year after the expiration of your contract as a real estate agent for the seller, you are owed a commission. The business does not sell and your contract as an agent for the seller ends. Eighteen months later you see that the seller sold the business to a buyer that you had brought to the seller when you were the seller's agent. Do you have a claim for a commission? Has the seller committed fraud against you?

Misrepresentation   In practice, misrepresentation and fraud are quite similar and often occur together. But there can be misrepresentation that does not reach the level of fraud. Misrepresentation requires a false statement to significantly influence the making of a contract. A false statement can be made in innocent ignorance or can be intentional. If a false statement is made innocently, the contract may be voidable if the misstatement was material, or key, to the decision to make the contract and the value of the contract. If the misrepresentation of a material fact is intentional, then there is fraud that will be grounds for rescinding a contract. However, there are unlikely to be damages in the case of innocent misrepresentation. The *Johnson* case discusses fraud and misrepresentation in a case involving the sale of a house.

Johnson v. Davis
Supreme Court of Florida
480 So.2d 625 (1985)

CASE BACKGROUND   *The Davises entered into a contract to buy the Johnsons' home. The contract required* *a $5,000 deposit payment and an additional $26,000 deposit within five days. A clause in the contract stated:*

continues

"Buyer shall have the right to obtain a written report from a licensed roofer stating that the roof is in water-tight condition. In the event repairs are required . . . seller shall pay for said repairs which shall be performed by a licensed roofing contractor."

Before paying the $26,000, the Davises noticed water damage. Johnson said that was from a window problem that had been corrected and that there had never been any problems with the roof. The $26,000 payment was made, and the Johnsons moved out. A couple days later, the Davises saw water coming into the house during a rain storm. Roofers hired by Johnson said the problem could be fixed for $1,000. Roofers hired by Davis said the roof was defective and needed $15,000 in repairs. The Davises sued for breach of contract, fraud, and misrepresentation, and sought rescission of the contract and return of their deposit. Johnson counterclaimed to keep the deposit as damages. The district court and the court of appeals held for the Davises. The Johnsons appealed.

CASE DECISION   Adkins, Justice.

* * *

We also agree with the district court's conclusions under a theory of fraud and find that the Johnsons' statements to the Davises regarding the condition of the roof constituted a fraudulent misrepresentation entitling respondents to the return of their $26,000 deposit payment. In the state of Florida, relief for a fraudulent misrepresentation may be granted only when the following elements are present: (1) a false statement concerning a material fact; (2) the representor's knowledge that the representation is false; (3) an intention that the representation induce another to act on it; and, (4) consequent injury by the party acting in reliance on the representation. . . .

The record reflects that the statement made by the Johnsons was a false representation of material fact, made with knowledge of its falsity, upon which the Davises relied to their detriment as evidenced by the $26,000 paid to the Johnsons. . . .

The fact that the false statements as to the quality of the roof were made after the signing of the purchase and sales agreement does not excuse the seller from liability when the misrepresentations were made prior to the execution of the contract by conveyance of the property. It would be contrary to all notions of fairness and justice for this Court to place its stamp of approval on an affirmative misrepresentation by a wrongdoer just because it was made after the signing of the executory contract when all of the necessary elements for actionable fraud are present. Furthermore, the Davises' reliance on the truth of the Johnsons' representation was justified . . . "a recipient may rely on the truth of a representation, even though its falsity could have been ascertained had he made an investigation, unless he knows the representation to be false or its falsity is obvious to him." . . .

That is, where failure to disclose a material fact is calculated to induce a false belief, the distinction between concealment and affirmative representations is tenuous. Both proceed from the same motives and are attended with the same consequences; both are violative of the principles of fair dealing and good faith; both are calculated to produce the same result; and, in fact, both essentially have the same effect.

* * *

Accordingly, we hold that where the seller of a home knows of facts materially affecting the value of the property which are not readily observable and are not known to the buyer, the seller is under a duty to disclose them to the buyer. This duty is equally applicable to all forms of real property, new and used. . . .

Affirmed.

QUESTIONS FOR ANALYSIS

1. The dissent argued that, since the Johnsons were not experts on roofs and had only agreed to pay for repairs if the Davises ordered an inspection, at most Johnson should be responsible for the cost of repairs as the contract stated. The contract did not allow the Davises to back out if there were found to be roof problems. Is that reasonable?

2. When there is conflicting testimony as to who said what about the roof, should that allow the matter to rise to the level of fraud?

Contracts in Writing and the Statute of Frauds

In contract law, the general rule is that contracts do not have to be in writing to be enforceable. Written contracts are a good idea because they are difficult to deny and courts prefer written documents over conflicting oral claims. Some contracts, however, must be evidenced by a writing to be enforceable. Such contracts are subject to the

Digital Signatures and Contracts

CYBER *Law*

The Electronic Signatures in Global and National Commerce Act (E-Sign) became part of federal law in 2000. It is based on the Uniform Electronic Transactions Act, which had been adopted by most states. The purpose of E-Sign is to leave the substance of contract law unchanged, but to be neutral about the use of technology in creating contracts.

E-Sign removes obstacles to the use of electronic media in contract formation. It states that a valid signature includes any "electronic sound, symbol, or process, attached to or logically associated with a contract or other record and executed or adopted by a person with the intent to sign the record." The impact of the law on consumer transactions is minimal because there are few problems related to consumer purchases on the Internet. The primary impact of the law is in internal business record keeping, such as employee timesheets, business-to-business (B2B) transactions that tend to be more complex than consumer transactions, and business-to-government dealings, such as compliance with regulatory procedures over the Internet.

As in the days when written signatures dominated contracts, the authenticity of a "signature" is still critical. Signatures include such things as the PIN number used at an ATM machine. The law does not dictate the technology that must be used for a signature to be accepted as genuine, since such technology continues to evolve. A study by the Federal Trade Commission and the Department of Commerce about the effect of E-Sign found the law to be well received as it helps to provide a "bright line" for electronic signatures that will be found to be legally effective.

Statute of Frauds, which evolved from a 1677 English statute called "An Act for the Prevention of Frauds and Perjuries." The purpose is to prevent parties from committing fraud by claiming that a contract existed when in fact it did not. To reduce such fraud, the statute requires that for certain contracts to be enforceable, they must be in writing.

Virtually every state has a statute similar to the English act. Most states have five types of contracts that are covered by the Statute of Frauds and that must therefore be evidenced by a writing to be enforced by a court in the event of a dispute:

1. Contracts for the sale of real property (land)
2. Contracts that cannot be performed within one year
3. Promises to pay the debt of another
4. Promises by an administrator to personally pay estate debts
5. Promises made in consideration of marriage

Sufficiency of the Writing

For a writing to be *sufficient* under the Statute of Frauds, it must set out the material terms of the contract and be signed by at least the defendant. Courts usually require the writing to contain the names of the parties, the consideration offered by the parties, the subject matter of the contract, and other material terms.

However, confirmations, invoices, e-mails, sales orders, and even checks may satisfy the sufficiency of the writing requirement. Without a necessary writing, the alleged contract is unlikely to be enforced.

Parol Evidence Rule

A contract is often preceded by negotiations. The parties may exchange letters or other communications before signing the actual contract. Parties may omit from

Liars' Contest?

the final contract some terms agreed upon in negotiations. In a subsequent lawsuit, the parties may disagree about those terms.

The *parol evidence rule* restricts the use of evidence in a lawsuit when the evidence is contrary to the terms of a written contract. Oral evidence cannot contradict, change, or add terms to a written contract. Oral or parol evidence may be introduced when the written contract is incomplete or ambiguous; when it proves fraud, mistake, or misrepresentation; or when the parol evidence explains the written instrument through previous trade usage or course of dealing. The parol evidence rule is also a part of the law of sales under the UCC.

PERFORMANCE, DISCHARGE, AND BREACH OF CONTRACTS

Eventually contracts come to an end. When the obligations of a contract have been *performed*, the contract is terminated or *discharged*. Just as there are rules to govern the creation of contracts, there are rules to govern the performance and discharge of contracts. Many of the various ways in which a contract can be discharged are summarized in Exhibit 10.5.

Performance

Most contracts come to an end by the complete *performance* of the parties' obligations under the contract. Contracts may be for one sale or for a long-term provision of a service. Suppose IBM contracts for Microsoft to design a software program especially for use by IBM on some of its computers. When the program specified in the contract has been delivered, and IBM has paid for a program that works properly, the contract is terminated. Both parties completed their part of the bargain. If a contract is to be completed over time, such as for Night Staff to clean the offices in BigBank's office building for two years, once Night Staff has done the cleaning for two years and BigBank has paid, the contract terminates. No further legal obligation is owed by either party.

Substantial Performance

Suppose, in the example above, that Microsoft delivers the program to IBM on time but a couple of minor bugs in the program are discovered. Has Microsoft performed

Exhibit 10.5

Discharge of a Contract and Its Effect on the Parties

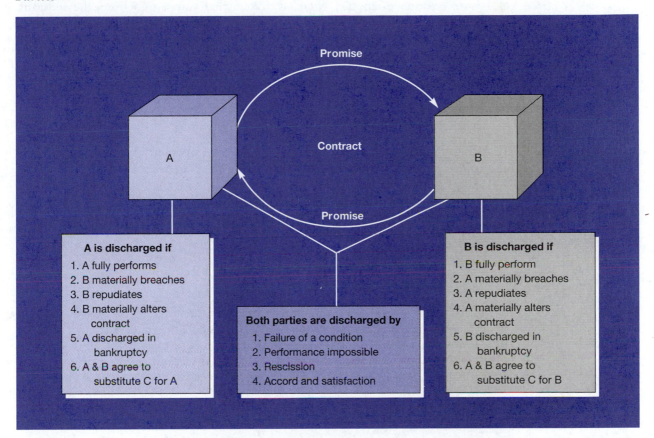

its obligation so that IBM must pay, or is there a lack of performance such that IBM may refuse or can sue Microsoft for breach of contract? In most contracts, *substantial performance* means that the contract basically has been properly fulfilled and payments must be made. The parties are expected to act in *good faith*. Refusing to pay when almost all of the contract was properly completed would not be acceptable. IBM could delay final payment to Microsoft until the bugs were worked out, but there is no justification for IBM to rescind the agreement for lack of performance by Microsoft. Of course, if IBM incurs costs due to the bugs, Microsoft is liable for those damages. The difference between a breach where there has been substantial performance and a *material breach* of contract can be a judgment call, so if a party wants to make sure things will be done according to strict specifications, that must be made clear in the contract.

Assignment and Delegation

A contract may end up being performed by another party. A transfer of contract rights to a third party is *assignment*; a transfer of contractual duties to a third party is a *delegation*. Many contracts are for services (duties) that cannot be assigned. Shaquille O'Neal cannot, without approval, delegate his duty to play for the Miami Heat to any other person. If a dentist has agreed to cap your teeth, you cannot assign your right to have your teeth capped to someone else. However, many contracts are capable of being assigned or delegated to third parties.

For example, if IBM contracted with Microsoft to develop some software for IBM, unless prohibited in the contract, Microsoft may delegate some of the software creation to another company. When that company delivers the software, Microsoft can then integrate it into the final product it delivers to IBM. As another example, if Night Staff has contracted to provide cleaning services for BigBank for two years, it may assign the contract to another cleaning company. Night Staff may be liable for any problems that arise due to poor performance by the other company, but such assignments are not uncommon.

Third-Party Beneficiaries

A *third-party beneficiary* is a party who is not part of an original contract who acquires rights under the contract. This happens mostly in credit contracts. For example, suppose Sting loans Marilyn $5,000. In consideration for the loan, Marilyn promises to pay $5,000 to P. Diddy, to whom Sting already owes $5,000. If Marilyn fails to pay P. Diddy, he may sue Marilyn to collect the $5,000, even though P. Diddy and Marilyn did not enter into a contract. P. Diddy is a third-party beneficiary of the contract between Sting and Marilyn.

Discharge by Breach

When a party to a contract does not perform as the contract requires, there is a *breach of contract*. Similarly, if one party prevents or hinders the other party to a contract from performing her duties, then a breach occurs. The party injured by the breach may be entitled to a remedy (discussed in the next section). To determine the remedy that may be provided, the court will look to determine the extent of the breach.

Material Breach

If the performance provided by a party is substantially less than the requirements of the contract, there is a *material breach*. Suppose Microsoft fails to deliver the program to IBM on time or that it delivers seriously defective software. As a result, IBM cannot deliver its computers because it has no software or bad software. IBM would have a cause of action against the breaching party, Microsoft, for damages. It would be discharged from its performance promised under the contract. It would not have to accept delivery of the wrong version of the program or accept the correct version if it arrived too late to be useful.

Anticipatory Breach

Before the performance of a contract takes place, an *anticipatory breach*, or *repudiation*, occurs if one party indicates inability or lack of desire to perform the contract. Sometimes the breaching party will not volunteer that it is going to breach, but the fact that the contract will not be performed becomes clear. If Microsoft was scheduled to ship the program to IBM by August 1, but IBM learns on July 25 that all copies of the program were destroyed in a fire at Microsoft, IBM does not have to wait until August 1 to look for replacements because it knows Microsoft cannot deliver on time.

The doctrine of anticipatory breach discharges the duties of the nonbreaching party under the contract and allows the nonbreaching party to sue for damages incurred from the repudiation. However, until the nonbreaching party treats the expression not to perform as a repudiation, the breaching party may retract the repudiation, and the duties of the contract will be reinstated.

Discharge by Agreement of the Parties

Just as parties have the freedom to contract, they also have the freedom to agree to modify or to terminate their obligations under the contract. *Discharge by agreement* between the parties can take various forms. Among the most important are rescission, novation, and accord and satisfaction.

Rescission

A mutual *rescission* occurs when both parties agree that their contractual relationship should be terminated without performance. A rescission discharges completely the obligations of both parties under the contract. For example, Avon contracted with Sears to sell cosmetics at Sears stores. Sears decided to cancel the deal and paid Avon $20 million to agree to terminate the arrangement. The parties agreed to rescind—cancel—the contract.

Novation

In a *novation*, all the parties agree to discharge one party from the contract and create a new contract with another party who becomes responsible for the discharged party's performance. Suppose, for example, Greenwood Mills has a contract to provide L. L. Bean with pullover sweaters for five years. Greenwood wants to turn the job over to Beasley Textiles. If Bean agrees that Beasley will perform Greenwood's obligations, the new agreement will be called a novation. That agreement releases Greenwood and replaces it with Beasley.

ISSUE
Spotter

Do You Have to Bear the Loss?

At the start of the chapter, we posed the problem of the sales rep who e-mailed the wrong price information to a customer, who replied that he wanted the LCD televisions for the misquoted price of $249.99 that should have been $2,499.99. All the terms of the contract were in place except for the misquoted price. Is there a contract, or can the seller tell the customer there is no deal without facing the likelihood of successful litigation against the sales company?

Accord and Satisfaction

Another way parties may agree to discharge their duties to one another under a contract is through *accord and satisfaction*. An *accord* is an agreement by the parties to give and accept some performance different from that originally bargained for. *Satisfaction* is the actual performance of the new obligation. The original obligation is discharged when the new consideration is provided.

Suppose Spielberg owes DiCaprio $1,000. If Spielberg offers to direct a movie for DiCaprio in place of paying him the $1,000, and DiCaprio accepts, then there is an accord. If Spielberg then directs a movie for DiCaprio, there is accord and satisfaction. The new consideration discharges the original claim. Had Spielberg failed to direct a movie, then DiCaprio could still have sued him for the $1,000 because there was no satisfaction of the accord.

Discharge by Impossibility, Impracticability, or Frustration

The doctrine of *discharge by legal impossibility* is used to end the obligations of parties to a contract when an event occurs that makes performance impossible. *Impossibility* occurs when a party who was to provide services dies or is incapacitated, a law is passed making performance of the contract illegal, or the subject matter of the contract is destroyed (the factory where Microsoft programs are made burns down). Impossibility discharges the obligations of the parties to the contract.

An extension of impossibility is *impracticability* or *frustration*. The *Restatement (2d) of Contracts* holds, at §262, that impracticability may be applied because of "extreme or unreasonable difficulty, expense, injury or loss. . . ." The term means more than unexpected difficulty and cost. The concept may be applied to wartime shortages, crop failures, or loss of needed supplies due to international embargos. Courts generally expect at least part performance even if full performance is excused by impracticability. Frustration may also terminate a contract, as discussed in the *Pocono Springs* case.

Pocono Springs Civic Association, Inc. v. Rovinsky

Commonwealth Court of Pennsylvania
845 S.2d 200 (2004)

CASE BACKGROUND   *Pocono Springs Estates is a real estate development. Rovinksy owns a lot in Pocono Springs. A covenant to deeds in Pocono Springs requires all property owners to pay dues to the Civic Association. Pocono sued Rovinsky for failure to pay his dues for four years. Pocono requested $2,375 in dues plus attorney fees. Rovinsky did not deny that the dues had not been paid, but claimed that he should not be held responsible because of the doctrine of frustration. He contended that he should not have to pay the dues because the lot was not fit for residential use. The trial court granted summary judgment in favor of Pocono, granting $4,080 for dues and legal fees. Rovinsky appealed.*

CASE DECISION   McCloskey, Senior Judge.

* * *

Landowner submitted an affidavit in which he stated that in 1969 he was invited to a free dinner seminar which involved the sale of land in Northeastern Pennsylvania. He and his wife attended the seminar and decided to purchase land for the purpose of building a retirement home. However, in 1970, after purchasing the land, he learned that he could not build on it. . . . He stated that he has attempted unsuccessfully over the years to sell the lot or even give it away, but he could not as the lot is useless. . . .

Landowner alleges that the trial court erred in granting summary judgment because he had established facts sufficient to bring a claim of frustration of purpose before a jury.

Our Pennsylvania Supreme Court has discussed frustration of purpose, explaining:

There is in the law the doctrine of 'frustration,' which holds that under the implied condition of the continuance of a contract's subject matter, the contract is dissolved when the subject mater is no longer available. 'When people enter into a contract which is dependent for the possibility of its performance on the continual availability of a specific thing, and that availability comes to an end by reason of circumstances beyond the control of the parties, the contract is prima facie regarded as dissolved.' . . .

The trial court noted that there was a problem with Landowner's claim that the doctrine of frustration applied, stating:

In this instance, this Court finds that the affirmative defense of frustration is not available. . . . [Landowner] has not plead anything that this lot is worthless, but only that it is not able to have the type of septic system that he envisioned. . . .

Landowner purchased land that contained a covenant regarding payment of dues to a landowners association. Landowner is obligated to pay dues and in exchange is entitled to use certain facilities for which he pays dues for. As such, the terms of the contract are easily completed. Landowner may consider himself "frustrated" that he cannot build on the land in the way in which he envisioned. However, this does not frustrate either party's ability to fulfill the contract. . . .

Affirmed.

QUESTIONS FOR ANALYSIS

1. Rovinsky indicates that he was cheated in the land deal, claiming that the lot is useless. Does that make sense?

2. Suppose the land requires an unusual and expensive septic system for it to be used for a residence. Should that be a reason for frustration?

REMEDIES

Parties to contracts usually perform their obligations as required. Still, thousands of contract disputes must be resolved every year. In the resolution of such disputes, there is a basic premise that after a breach, innocent parties should be placed in an economic position they would have enjoyed had the contract been performed. If, however, the circumstances are such that the legal remedy of monetary damages is inadequate, the court may grant the injured party an appropriate equitable remedy. The types of remedies available to the parties are presented in Exhibit 10.6.

INTERNATIONAL *Perspective*

Contracting with the Japanese

A typical U.S. view is that a contract defines the rights and responsibilities of the parties and seeks to cover all possible contingencies. The traditional Japanese view is that a contract is secondary in a business transaction; the basis of business is an ongoing relationship, with both parties committed to the pursuit of similar objectives. Consequently, relationships, not contracts, are negotiated in Japan.

The specific details of a Japanese contract are seldom negotiated. Documents are usually brief and flexible. This is important to accommodate the evolving relationship between the parties. Contracts are often viewed as tentative agreements to be redefined as circumstances between the parties change. Long legal agreements drafted by one side are viewed with suspicion. The relationship should take precedence over formal rights and obligations. Practical problems can be resolved by compromise. Reflecting this belief, the Japanese often include a good-faith clause in contracts with Westerners. The clause states that disputes are to be resolved through good-faith discussions among the parties. This desire to establish and maintain mutual trust as a basis for a business relationship may account for the longer time it takes to negotiate an agreement.

Japanese contract-negotiating teams are often larger than American teams. Members of the Japanese group may excuse themselves during a session so they can discuss an issue among themselves. They work for a consensus within the team and the company. As a rule, negotiations proceed slowly. The Japanese do not appear to operate with the urgency typical of Americans. The Japanese take the time they need until they are sure of a decision and have reached consensus that should be the basis of a lasting relationship.

	Monetary Damages	Equitable Remedies
Exhibit 10.6 *Contract Remedies*	Compensatory Damages Liquidated Damages Nominal Damages Special Damages	Specific Performance Injunction Restitution Reformation

Damages

The remedy usually granted for breach of contract is monetary damages. The party who suffered from a breach seeks a money judgment for the thing contracted for, for lost profit, and for any other damages incurred. A variety of damage awards is available to the courts, including compensatory, expectancy, liquidated, nominal, and special damages. The *economic loss rule* states that when a breach of contract causes only economic losses, not physical or mental harm to persons, there may be no tort suit. However, punitive damages may be awarded if there is a tort related to the breach of contract.

In general, the rule is that *damages* should put the party who suffered from the breach of contract in the same economic position as if the contract had been performed. That is, there can be a claim for losses suffered and for any gains (profits) prevented, less any cost savings incurred.

Calculating Damages

Suppose Microsoft and IBM contract for Microsoft to develop a special program over two years that will only be used on IBM computers. IBM agrees to pay $50 million for the exclusive rights to the program. As work progresses, Microsoft gives IBM $2 million worth of specialized software. After six months, IBM decides the software will have little value in the future, so rather than go forward with a deal, it cancels the contract. Microsoft could sue for damages to be compensated: the $2 million worth of software given to IBM and the costs incurred at Microsoft due to work on the project. Assume these costs total $8.1 million. Microsoft could also sue for the $12 million in profit it expected to make from the project. Microsoft might recover $22.1 million, plus interest.

Was IBM foolish to breach? Not if it decided that the whole project was foolish. Better to breach and pay the $22.1 million than spend $50 million. This is referred to as *efficient breach*. Also note that if the work Microsoft did on the software for IBM has alternative use with market value, then it may not be able to recover all costs it incurred in development from IBM. It is also unlikely to recover all expected profits.

Liquidated Damages

Liquidated damages are damages specified in the contract to be paid in the event of breach. Liquidated damages are not allowed if the court finds that they are so excessive that they actually impose a *penalty*. That is, the damages specified in the contract must be related to actual losses that could be suffered. For example, if an office building is supposed to be completed by May 15 for occupancy, the contract may require the builder to pay liquidated damages of $500 per day after May 15 until the building is ready. But the contract could not call for "damages" of $1 million per day; that would be a penalty, which is not allowed because it is against public policy.

Nominal Damages

When a plaintiff has suffered a breach of contract but has not suffered an actual loss, a court may award *nominal damages*. The amount of recovery to the injured party may be as little as a dollar, but attorney fees and court costs may also be awarded. Such awards can be important because proof of breach may be related to other legal issues.

Punitive Damages

Punitive or *exemplary damages* are usually awarded when the wrongdoer's conduct has been willful or malicious. They punish the wrongdoer by allowing the plaintiff to receive relief beyond compensatory or expectancy damages. Punitive damages are intended to discourage the wrongdoer and others from similar conduct in the future. Punitive damages are not awarded in contract actions; the basis for these damages is a tort related to the breach, such as fraud.

Mitigation of Damages

When a breach of contract does occur, the injured party is required to take reasonable efforts to *mitigate*, or lessen, the losses that may be incurred. If Microsoft fails to deliver promised software to IBM, IBM must take steps to get a replacement, if possible. The injured party may not recover for losses that could have been avoided. In the *Copenhaver* case, the plaintiff avoided the loss but attempted to recover damages as though he had not.

Copenhaver v. Berryman

Texas Court of Civil Appeals
602 S.W.2d 540 (1980)

CASE BACKGROUND   *Berryman owned an apartment complex. He contracted for Copenhaver to own and operate the laundry facilities in the complex. With four years remaining on a five-year contract, Berryman terminated the contract and removed Copenhaver's machines on March 10. By September 10, Copenhaver had put the equipment into use in other locations.*

Copenhaver sued, claiming that he was entitled to run the facility for the length of the contract. If he had been allowed to do so, he would have earned a net profit of $13,886.58. The trial court awarded Copenhaver $3,525.84 for the damages suffered from March to September. Copenhaver appealed the decision.

CASE DECISION   Ney, Chief Justice.

* * *

While the defendant is liable for the pecuniary loss sustained by the party injured by the breach, the party so injured must exercise, as a general rule, reasonable efforts in an attempt to minimize his damages. As stated by our Supreme Court:

> Where a party is entitled to the benefits of a contract and can save himself from the damages resulting from its breach at a trifling expense or with reasonable exertions, it is his duty to incur such expense and make such exertions.

Although the injured party has a duty to minimize his loss, the burden of proof as to the extent to which the damages were or could have been mitigated lies with the party who has breached the contract.

* * *

We are of the opinion that there is evidence in the record to support the finding of fact that the plaintiffs suffered no damage from September 10, 1977, to the date of trial. After September 10, all of the equipment

continues

was in use in other locations. There is also some evidence . . . that plaintiffs were generating at least as much income, if not more, from the operation of the machines in question after September 10, 1977. . . .

The testimony concerning the plaintiff's over-all business is vague, speculative, and conclusory. The only evidence we can find to substantiate this contention is some general testimony to the effect that plaintiffs acquired some 14 to 15 new locations after the breach. Plaintiffs admitted they did not even know where the machines in question were ultimately placed. Nor, did the plaintiffs introduce evidence from which it could be reasonably concluded that they would have expanded to each new location even had defendants not breached the contract in question and that defendants' breach somehow limited their expansion.

We are of the opinion that the trial judge could reach no reasonable conclusion other than to find plain-tiffs had not proved they were damaged beyond the six-month period, after which the machines were in use in other locations.

* * *

The judgment of the trial court is affirmed.

QUESTIONS FOR ANALYSIS

1. How did the plaintiff mitigate the losses stemming from the defendant's breach in this case?

2. Suppose the plaintiff had not been able to move the machines into other locations. How would he have then mitigated the losses?

3. What is the purpose of this mitigation of losses rule?

No

Equitable Remedies

If money damages are inadequate to compensate for the injury caused by a breach of contract or do not resolve the problem properly, *equitable remedies* such as specific performance or an injunction may be available. These remedies are available to injured parties only at the discretion of the court. They generally will not be granted where an adequate damage remedy exists or where enforcement would impose a great burden to the defendant.

Specific Performance

Specific performance is an order by the court requiring the party who created the wrong to perform the obligations she promised in the contract. The remedy is granted for breach of a contract when the payment of money damages is inadequate. Contracts for the sale of a particular piece of real property (land) or of a unique good, such as a piece of art, are the types of contract where specific performance may be granted by the courts. Recall in the *Ardente* case that there was no claim of money damages because the price had been agreed upon; the demand was for specific performance—the right to buy the house at the agreed-upon price. Courts will not order people to perform personal service—do some particular job—because it would be involuntary servitude. Damages would be imposed in such cases.

Injunction

As with the remedy of specific performance, the remedy of injunction is allowed when the payment of damages does not offer a satisfactory substitute for the performance promised. An *injunction* is an order by the court that requires a party to do or to refrain from doing certain acts. Suppose a partnership agreement stated that a partner who quits to go into business for herself will not compete against the partnership for three years. If a partner quits the partnership to start a new competing firm, the payment of damages may be an inadequate remedy for the partnership. The court, through the granting of an injunction, may order the departed partner to not compete with the partnership.

Restitution

The remedy of *restitution* may be used to prevent unjust enrichment. That is, if one party has unjustly enriched himself (received a benefit not paid for) at the expense of another party, the court can order payment to be made or the goods involved to be returned. Closely related to this is the idea of quasi contract.

Quasi Contracts

A *quasi contract* is not a contract. The courts created the concept of quasi contract to give relief to innocent parties, or to prevent injustice, even though no true contract exists. In the words of New York's highest court in *Bradkin* v. *Leverton*, 309 N.Y.S.2d 192:

> Quasi contracts are not contracts at all. . . . The contract is a mere fiction, a form imposed in order to adapt the case to a given remedy. . . . Briefly stated, a quasi-contractual obligation is one imposed by law where there has been no agreement or expression of assent, by word or act, on the part of either party involved. The law creates it, regardless of the intention of the parties, to assure a just and equitable result.

A quasi contract, also called *quantum meruit*, is used by the courts to avoid injustice. Something of value has been provided but there was no contract—such as a doctor providing emergency medical assistance to an injured child without first getting permission of the parents—or a contract was not completed. For example, in *Burke* v. *McKee* (304 P.2d 307), the Oklahoma Supreme Court ordered a contractor paid for work he had completed. The contractor had promised to clear eighty acres of land. He quit when he finished half the work, due to a dispute with the landowner. The owner refused to pay unless he finished all the work. The court ordered the contractor be paid the value of his work done to the point at which he quit. The landowner was not to get the value of the work for nothing, as that would be *unjust enrichment*, and he could hire another contractor to finish the job at no higher cost.

SUMMARY

- Basic to the law of contracts is freedom of contract. Every business has the freedom to enter into most contracts they desire. Because of public policy goals, state and federal laws place some restrictions on the kinds of contracts businesses can enter into.
- Contract law is basically common or judge-made law. The *Restatement of Contracts* is an authoritative document providing a summary of the common law of contract. Additional contract law is provided by the Uniform Commercial Code.
- A contract is a promise or set of promises that creates an agreement between parties. It creates legal rights and duties enforceable under the law.

- Contracts may be classified as express or implied; bilateral or unilateral; executory or executed; valid, void, voidable, or unenforceable contracts; and quasi contracts. A contract may fall into several categories; for example, a contract may be express, bilateral, executed, and valid.
- Under the common law, enforceable contracts have several elements in common:

    1. There must be an agreement (offer and acceptance).
    2. The parties to a contract must provide consideration.
    3. The parties must have the legal capacity to contract.
    4. The subject matter of the contract must be legal.
    5. The consent of the parties must be genuine.

- Some contracts must be in writing to fulfill requirements of the Statute of Frauds. They include contracts for the sale of land and real property, contracts that cannot be completed within one year, promises to pay the debt of another, and contracts for goods over $500 under the UCC.
- Contracts may be discharged—or terminated—in several ways: by performance, through a breach by one or both of the parties to the contract, by the failure of a condition precedent or the occurrence of an express condition subsequent, by the impossibility of performance, by operation of law, or by mutual agreement of the parties.
- In the event of a breach of contract, the injured party may ask the court for relief. To a reasonable extent, the injured party has the responsibility to minimize losses from the breach. For the remaining, the courts can award monetary damages or provide equitable relief.

REVIEW AND DISCUSSION QUESTIONS

1. Define the following terms and expressions:

offer	mutual mistake
acceptance	parol evidence rule
consideration	discharge
breach of contract	impossibility
promissory estoppel	damages
legal capacity	mitigation of damages
unconscionable contract	

2. Mr. Jones walks into a grocery store, puts fifty cents down on the counter, and says, "A Coke please." Under contract law, what has just occurred? If the grocery store owner hands him a Coke and takes the fifty cents, what type of contract has been agreed upon?

CASE QUESTIONS

3. Three armed men robbed the First State Bank of Kentucky of more than $30,000. The Kentucky Bankers Association provided and advertised a reward of $500 for the arrest and conviction of the bank robbers. The robbers were later captured and convicted. The arresting officers and the employees of the bank who provided important information leading to the arrest have all claimed the reward.

Is there a contract between these parties and the Bankers Association? [*Denney v. Reppert*, 432 S.W.2d 647 (Ct. App., Ky., 1968)]

4. Barry hired Anglin to produce engineering drawings for work it was doing at a brewery. Anglin said it would charge "street" rates for the work, which meant $35 an hour for regular work, $40 an hour for overtime work, and $45 an hour for his time. Barry gave Anglin a "purchase order" for the work, but no rate was specified. Barry paid bills for two months but then quit paying. Barry insisted that the work be done but constantly complained about the rates and did not pay bills for four months. Anglin sued for $98,618, the amount it was due for work at the "street" rate. Barry claimed there was no contract because there was no meeting of the minds about the rate to be paid. Who prevails? [*Anglin v. Barry*, 912 S.W.2d 633 (Ct. App., Mo., 1995)]

5. Houston Lighting & Power Company sent a brochure that the company "will offer to subdivision developers . . . [of] single family dwellings" underground residential electrical service without construction charge. The brochure also stated, "At Company option certain lots adjacent to overhead distribution facilities will be served from the overhead distribution," that "Developer will provide required easements . . . and install conduit to Company's specifications," and other specifics. A mobile home park developer stated that he was willing to do what was required and demanded the underground service be installed to the mobile home sites. The company refused. The developer claimed that he had accepted an offer; the company claimed the brochure was merely an invitation to discuss the matter. Who was right? [*Edmunds* v. *Houston Lighting & Power*, 472 S.W.2d 797 (Ct. Civ. App., Tx., 1971)]

Check your answer at <u>http://meiners.westbuslaw.com</u>

6. Cantu was a teacher for the San Benito School District. August 18, right before the start of the schoolyear, she hand-delivered a letter of resignation, effective August 17, and requested that her final paycheck be sent to an address fifty miles away. The superintendent received the letter on August 20 and immediately wrote and mailed a letter accepting the resignation. On August 21, Cantu hand-delivered a letter withdrawing her resignation. She was given a copy of the letter that had been mailed the day before and was told she would not be rehired. Was her resignation effective or not? [*Cantu* v. *Central Education Agency*, 884 S.W.2d 565 (Ct. App., Tx., 1994)]

7. At the end of a two-year lease, landlord and tenant discussed a new lease. The tenant sent a letter to the landlord stating that it would pay rent of $1,800 per month and that "all other terms and conditions of the [original] lease including, taxes, insurance, utilities, etc., shall remain the same." The letter also said that it was to be advised "by confirmation letter if the terms of the two-year lease extension are acceptable to [the lessor]." The lessor never responded. The tenant paid rent for a couple months, then moved out. The landlord sued for breach, claiming there was an oral agreement evidenced by the letter from the tenant; the tenant claimed there was no contract. Who is correct and why? [*Valiant Steel* v. *Roadway Express*, 421 S.E.2d 773 (Ct. App., Ga., 1992)]

Check your answer at <u>http://meiners.westbuslaw.com</u>

8. Mary Lowe, in the presence of her son David and Allen Amdahl, wrote: "January 26, 1987. I Mary Lowe in the presence of David Lowe received from Allen Amdahl $1.00 in cash binding the sale of my farm (of 880 acres) for the amount

of $210,000 with final payment due Nov. 1, 1989. Terms of Agreement have been mutually agreed to by both parties. Contract drawn up as soon as possible." She signed this statement, and David Lowe witnessed it. Amdahl wrote on the back of the paper a payment schedule between then and November 1989 but did not sign the paper. When he returned with a formal contract, Lowe refused to sign. Amdahl sued. Was there an enforceable contract? [*Amdahl* v. *Lowe*, 471 N.W.2d 770 (Sup. Ct., N.D., 1991)]

9. Rose, a minor, purchased a new car from Sheehan Buick for $5,000. Rose later, while still a minor, elected to disaffirm the purchase and notified Sheehan of her decision. She also requested a full refund of the purchase price. Sheehan refused, and Rose brought an action to invalidate the contract and to seek a refund of the purchase price. What will be the likely result? [*Rose* v. *Sheehan Buick, Inc.*, 204 So.2d 903 (Fla.App., 1967)]

Check your answer at http://meiners.westbuslaw.com

10. To help in a fund-raising drive for a hospital, Burt executed a pledge for $100,000 that provided, "In consideration of and to induce the subscription of others, I promise to pay to Mount Sinai Hospital of Greater Miami, Inc. the sum of $100,000 in ten installments." Burt made two installment payments of $10,000 each before his death. The hospital filed a claim for the unpaid balance against his estate. Is this a contract for which the estate is now liable? [*Mount Sinai Hospital* v. *Jordan*, 290 So.2d 484 (Sup. Ct., Fla., 1974)]

11. Smith contracted to build a gymnasium for Limestone College. About the time the building was finished, an "extraordinarily heavy rainfall" caused the sewer system to back up into the gymnasium, doing damage that cost Smith $37,000 to repair. Smith billed the city sewer system for the work done. The city refused to pay, claiming there was no contract. Smith claimed an implied contract existed; was he right? [*Stanley Smith & Sons* v. *Limestone College*, 322 S.E.2d 474 (Ct. App., S.C., 1984)]

12. A contract stated: "Contractor shall transport in the Contractor's trucks such tonnage of beets as may be loaded by the Company from piles at the beet receiving stations of the Company, and unload said beets at such factory . . . as may be designated by the company. The term of this contract shall be from October 1, 1980, until February 15, 1981." Contractor was to be paid solely on the basis of the amount of beets he hauled. The company had identical contracts with other independent truckers. After two months, company told contractor that his services were no longer needed even though there were more beets to haul. Contractor sued, claiming he had the right under the contract to haul beets with the other truckers who may be there until all beets had been hauled or until February 15. Was he right? [*De Los Santos* v. *Great Western Sugar*, 348 N.W.2d 842 (Sup. Ct., Neb., 1984)]

13. By oral contract, Olson sold Wilson thirty head of cattle for slaughter. Wilson sent Olson a check for $9,373 "in full payment of . . . cattle, 30 head. . . ." Olson claimed that he was promised 35 cents per pound, which would have been $10,725. Wilson said that it promised to pay based on "grade and yield," a common industry practice. Olson cashed the check and sued for the difference in price. Could he collect? [*Olson* v. *Wilson & Co.*, 58 N.W.2d 381 (Sup. Ct., Iowa, 1953)]

14. A builder constructed a house according to plans provided by the owner. The contract specified that only Reading brand pipe was to be used in the plumbing. After the house was completed, the owner discovered that another brand

of pipe had been used. The owner refused final payment and demanded that the pipe be replaced with Reading pipe, which would have involved major reconstruction. Evidence at trial was that the two brands of pipe were of the same general quality. Did the owner have to make final payment, or did the pipe have to be replaced? [*Jacob & Youngs* v. *Kent*, 129 N.E. 889 (Ct. App., N.Y., 1921)]

15. Lewis Cudd had a life insurance policy that named his mother as beneficiary. During World War II, his ship was missing and "presumed lost" by the Navy, which issued a "Certificate of Presumptive Death." The insurance company paid Mrs. Cudd the value of the policy. Later it was discovered that Lewis was a prisoner of war; Lewis returned home after the war. The life insurance company sued to recover the insurance benefits. On what basis did it recover? [*Pilot Life* v. *Cudd*, 36 S.E.2d 860 (Sup. Ct., S.C., 1945)]

16. GE contracted to provide kitchen appliances for an apartment complex for $93,500. Several months later, GE discovered that a mathematical error had been made in the bid and that the bid should have been for an additional $30,150. GE demanded rescission of the contract. Did it get it? [*General Electric Supply* v. *Republic Construction*, 272 P.2d 201 (Sup. Ct., Ore., 1954)]

17. Employer Engelcke Manufacturing asked one of its employees, Eaton, to design electronic plans for Whizball, a game it planned to produce and sell. Eaton said he thought he could do the job after work for about $1,500. During the next year, the project became more complicated, and Eaton devoted substantially more time to it than had been expected. Engelcke said it would pay him for his work. When the project was mostly done, Engelcke fired Eaton and refused to pay him because the electronic plans were not completed. Engelcke claimed Eaton breached an express contract and that it got nothing of value. Was there a contract? Could there be damages? [*Eaton* v. *Englecke Manufacturing, Inc.*, 681 P.2d 1312 (Ct. App., Wash., 1984)]

18. Transatlantic agreed to ship a load of wheat from the United States to Iran for $305,842. While the ship was enroute, a war caused the Suez Canal to be closed. Transatlantic had to turn around and sail all the way around Africa to get to Iran. It sued for the additional $44,000 it cost to go the extra distance. Could it collect? [*Transatlantic Financing* v. *U.S.*, 363 F.2d 312 (D.C.Cir., 1966)]

PULLING IT  *Together*

Tort and Contract Law

Barry and Sandra Erlich hired Menezes to build their "dream house" on an ocean-view lot in California. They moved into the house in December 1990. Two months later, in the rainy season, "the house leaked from every conceivable location." Walls were so saturated that the plaster fell off, most windows leaked, and there was three inches of water in the living room. Despite various repair efforts by Menezes, water continued to leak in all parts of the house. Another contractor and an engineer found serious defects in the roof, walls, windows, and waterproofing, as well as structural problems with the walls, roof, and foundation. The Erlichs sued Menezes and testified that the problems with their house made them sick. Barry Erlich said that the distress worsened his heart condition, forcing him to resign from his job. Sandra was afraid the house might collapse on the family, especially in an earthquake. Their suit sought recovery on several theories: breach of contract, fraud, negligent misrepresentation, negligent construction, emotional distress, and pain and suffering. Which of their tort and contract claims would seem most likely to stand?

[*Erlich* v. *Menezes*, 87 Cal.Rptr.2d 886 (Sup. Ct., Calif., 1999)]

Ethics Question

19. You would probably not think of paying $1,000 for a $300 refrigerator, but it happens, especially when low-income people with little education sign contracts to buy appliances or furniture on time payments. Since many of these contracts have high interest rates and numerous penalties for late payments, a buyer can wind up paying many times the market value of the goods if the contract is carried to completion. Because many low-income customers do not make payments on time or quit making payments, some businesses justify the exorbitant terms because the high returns from some customers offset the high default rate from others. Is this an ethical selling practice? Is there another way to handle the situation?

Internet Assignment

For over five years, a local appliance vendor has been purchasing various large and small household appliances for resale from several wholesale distributors, one of whom was the All Appliance Company (AAC). For the first three years of their relationship, this vendor and AAC signed formal, written, bimonthly contracts covering all terms of purchase, shipment, delivery, and payment. Thereafter, they dealt informally by telephone under the same terms and conditions. This was not a problem until the vendor began experiencing financial difficulties. Without knowledge of the vendor's problems, AAC shipped its regular monthly shipment of appliances to the vendor's facility. Stuck with $40,000 in merchandise it could not afford, the vendor defaulted on its payment obligations, and AAC sued.

Did these parties have a legally binding oral contract under which AAC could recover? What would be the most relevant evidence to show that a valid contract existed? Under what alternative theory might AAC prevail? For answers to these questions, find the U.S. 9th Circuit Court of Appeals case, #99-55004, *Cable & Computer Technology, Inc.* v. *Lockheed Sanders, Inc.*, *http://www.findlaw.com*.

Chapter 11 | *Domestic and International Sales*

As a food broker, you execute orders that retailers place with food processors. You specialize in knowing who has what and how to get it delivered in a timely fashion by trucking companies you trust. Mostly you rely on reputation, rather than contracts, in your dealing with vendors. You know many of the sellers, buyers, and truckers, and they know you. There is little time for formal contracting. Most of the work is done informally on the phone and by e-mail.

There are few transaction costs and no need for lawyers drawing up contracts. If you sent a contract to a client you have dealt with for a long time, the client would probably wonder what was up. But things can go wrong with this approach. For example, a truck makes a delivery in July from Cleveland to Phoenix and arrives Friday night. The buyer thought the load would arrive on Monday, so it sits over the weekend. A half-million dollars worth of food is spoiled. Who is responsible for the bill? Did the trucker promise to cover such losses? As the broker, you bought and resold the food, picking up a commission in the middle, so are you stuck, or will the buyer suffer the loss? If you have a contract with each party, what does it say? What if you do not have a contract?

These are the types of questions addressed in this chapter on the sale of goods under the *Uniform Commercial Code (UCC)*. *Article 2* of the UCC governs the law of commercial sales. Since buying and selling goods is the primary activity of many commercial enterprises, it is not surprising that the law of sales is an important part of the legal environment of business. This chapter provides an overview of the law of sales in Article 2 of the UCC. It considers the nature of sales contracts under the UCC and the requirements the UCC places upon merchants. The chapter then examines some key aspects of international commercial sales.

INTRODUCTION TO THE UCC

The Uniform Commercial Code is the law that governs many contracts for the sale of goods. That is, the UCC does not apply to the sale of services, real estate, or professional services. Like the common law of contract, commercial law is primarily state, not federal, law.

History of Commercial Law

Commercial rules governing trade—"codes"—existed more than 2,000 years ago in Greece. Over a thousand years later, in medieval Europe, merchants developed a set of rules governing trade issues such as sales, payment, insurance, and shipping. These rules were known as the *lex mercatoria* or *law merchant*. The law merchant was international law that applied to transactions in different countries. For example, a fourteenth-century merchant who sold woolen cloth would be likely to use the same contract rules if the sale took place in London, England; Marseilles, France; or Prague, Bohemia. Merchants themselves, rather than governments, generally enforced this law.

By the eighteenth century, judges in England decided to incorporate the customary law merchant into the common law of England to resolve contract disputes. From that point forward, commercial law became a matter of national law. As the economy developed during the nineteenth century, so too did commercial law. As new technologies—railroads, steam ships, telegraphs—emerged, commercial law was modified to accommodate the changing needs of merchants.

In the early part of the twentieth century, each state in the United States had a different, but related, set of commercial laws. At the same time, companies were better able to do business in many states and international trade increased. One of the costs of doing business in different states was dealing with the different rules of commercial law. By the 1940s, some legal scholars and people in business decided that it would be efficient to have a more consistent set of rules governing commercial transactions.

In 1942, two groups, the National Conference of Commissioners on Uniform State Laws and the American Law Institute, began drafting a commercial law. After ten years of work, under the direction of law professors Karl Llewellyn and Soia Mentchikov, the groups presented the Uniform Commercial Code to the states. Every state has adopted most of the UCC, although Louisiana has not adopted Article 2. Over the years, the UCC has been modified to reflect changes in the way businesses operate. Exhibit 11.1 notes the major sections of the UCC.

Application of the UCC

We refer here, except when noted otherwise, to the "model" UCC and cite specific sections (§) of it. The UCC states that its purpose is "to simplify, clarify and modernize the law governing commercial transactions" (§1-102).

This chapter primarily concerns Article 2 of the UCC, which deals with the sale of goods. When does the UCC apply, rather than the common law of contracts? The UCC applies when "the item involved is movable and is not money or an investment security" (§2-102). Examples of movable goods include wristwatches, computers, and airplanes. Land is not movable, nor are houses or most other buildings. Article 2 covers the sale of *goods*, not services, so, for example, if you contract with

Exhibit 11.1	Article Number and Title	Coverage
The Articles of the Uniform Commercial Code	**1: General Provisions**	Purpose of the UCC; general guidance and definitions
	2: Sale of Goods	Applies to sale of goods (and leases of goods)
	3: Negotiable Instruments	Use of checks, promissory notes, and other financial instruments
	4: Bank Deposits and Collections	Rights and duties of banks and their clients
	5: Letters of Credit	Guaranteed payment by a bank that extends credit on behalf of client
	6: Bulk Transfers	Sale of large part of a company's material
	7: Warehouse Receipts, Bills of Lading, and Other Documents of Title	Papers proving ownership of goods being shipped
	8: Investment Securities	Rights and duties related to stock or other ownership interests
	9: Secured Transactions	Sales in which seller holds a financial interest in goods sold

a lawyer to represent you, that would be under the common law of contracts, as are contracts that deal with intangible property, such as bank accounts, stocks, and copyrights.

Despite all the lawyers who draft contracts and all the business students who have taken courses such as this one, many contracts fail to state what law governs a contract. Also, there may be more than one contract in place at the same time. These issues may not matter unless there is a dispute, at which point it can make a difference if the UCC or the common law governs.

Suppose, as often happens, a contract is for a mix of goods and services and the contract does not specify common law or UCC. Which law governs a dispute? The rule is to look to whether goods or services dominate the contract. If the contract is for $180,000 total and, in breaking it down, the court sees that $70,000 covers the costs of goods and $100,000 is for services such as installation and maintenance, then the value of the services dominate, so the common law governs. In the *i.LAN* case we see a court determining which law governs a dispute over the sale and use of commercial software.

i.LAN Systems, Inc. v. NetScout Service Level Corp.

United States District Court, District of Massachusetts
183 F.Supp.2d 328 (2002)

CASE BACKGROUND   *NextPoint sells sophisticated software that monitors networks. It signed a detailed Value Added Reseller (VAR) agreement in 1998, whereby i.LAN agreed to resell NextPoint's software to customers. i.LAN claims that in the 1999 purchase agreement, for $85,231.42, it bought an unlimited right to rent, not sell, NextPoint's software, including upgrades and support to i.LAN's customers. NextPoint contended i.LAN did not have all those rights to the software. i.LAN claimed its position was supported by the 1999 purchase order. NextPoint claimed the VAR agreement and the clickwrap*

license in the software produce a different resolution of the dispute. Both parties moved for summary judgment.

CASE DECISION   Young, Chief Judge.

* * *

Three contracts might govern this dispute: the 1998 VAR agreement, the 1999 purchase order, and the clickwrap license agreement to which i.LAN necessarily agreed to when it installed the software at issue. The key question for purposes of this memorandum is how the 1998 and 1999 agreements affect the clickwrap license agreement.

The clickwrap license agreement states that it does not affect existing or subsequent written agreements or purchase orders. . . . The natural reading is that to the extent the 1998 VAR agreement and the 1999 purchase order are silent, the clickwrap license agreement fills the void.

Two bodies of contract law might govern the clickwrap license agreement: Massachusetts common law and the Uniform Commercial Code as adopted by Massachusetts. Article 2 of the UCC applies to "transactions in goods," UCC §2-102, but "unless the context otherwise requires, 'contract' and 'agreement' are limited to those relating to the present or future *sale* of goods." Indeed, the title of Article 2 is "Sales," and the definition of "goods" assumes a sale. . . . The purchase of software might seem like an ordinary contract for the sale of goods, but in fact the purchaser merely obtains a *license* to use the software; never is there a "passing of title from the seller to the buyer for a price," §2-106(1). So is the purchase of software a transaction in goods? Despite Article 2's requirement of a *sale*, courts in Massachusetts have assumed . . . that Article 2 govern software *licenses.*

. . . i.LAN argues that the UCC should govern the 1999 purchase order and clickwrap license agreement. NextPoint does not disagree with the idea that the UCC might apply to software purchases in general, but under NextPoint's theory of the case, the 1998 VAR agreement is most important to this dispute, and that agreement predominately concerns *services*, rather than the sale of goods. NextPoint, therefore, argues that the UCC should not govern any part of this dispute.

. . . Admittedly, the UCC technically does not govern software licenses, and very likely does not govern the 1998 VAR agreement, but with respect to the 1999 transaction, the UCC best fulfills the parties' reasonable expectations. . . . Software licenses are entered into every day, and business persons reasonably expect that *some* law will govern them. For the time being, Article 2's familiar provisions . . . better fulfill those expectations than would the common law.

* * *

The Court will enforce NextPoint's clickwrap license agreement. . . . The UCC "shall be liberally construed and applied to promote its underlying purposes and policies," which include "the continued expansion of commercial practices through custom, usage and agreement of the parties." UCC §1-102. "Money now, terms later" is a practical way to form contracts, especially with purchasers of software. . . . To be sure, shrinkwrap and clickwrap license agreements share the defect of any standardized contract . . . but that is not the issue in this case. The only issue before the Court is whether clickwrap license agreements are an appropriate way to form contracts, and the Court holds they are. In short, i.LAN explicitly accepted the clickwrap license agreement when it clicked on the box stating "I agree." . . .

The clickwrap license agreement specifically was intended to fill any gaps left by the 1999 purchase order. "There is a long tradition in contract law of reading contracts sensibly; contract—certainly business contracts of the kind involved here—are not parlor games but the means of getting the world's work done." The only sensible interpretation of the 1999 purchase order is that it did not affect the limitations of liability found in the parties' prior and subsequent agreements. . . .

If i.LAN were to prevail on any of its . . . claims, it would be entitled to recover no more than the amount it paid for the software license at issue, to wit, $85,231.42.

QUESTIONS FOR ANALYSIS

1. Since software is copyrighted, and copyrights are intangible, why would the sale of copyrighted software be the sale of a good rather than the sale of a service?

2. While the judge does not say how the outcomes of the case could be different if the common law or the UCC applied, what differences do you suppose could occur?

Goods, Merchants, Sales, and Titles under the UCC

Goods

The UCC defines *goods* as "all things (including specially manufactured things) which are movable at the time of identification to the contract for sale," §2-105(1). In other words, the subject matter of a sales contract is not considered a good under Article 2 unless it is movable and tangible. A good is *movable* if it can be carried from one location to another. So real estate does not come under Article 2. A good is *tangible* when it has a physical existence—that is, it can be seen and touched. Thus, services and intangible interests—such as stocks, bank accounts, patents, and copyrights, which are called intangible forms of personal property—are not goods under Article 2. A contract involving such items would be governed by the common law of contracts or possibly by another part of the UCC.

Merchants

Section §1-203 holds all parties who enter into an Article 2 sales contract to a standard of *good-faith*, or honest, dealing. Good-faith dealing is defined by UCC §1-201 as "honesty in fact in the conduct or transaction incurred." Article 2 places a higher duty of conduct on merchants, who are treated differently from other parties because they possess more business expertise. A merchant is recognized by §2-104 as a person who

1. Regularly deals in goods of the kind involved in the transaction,
2. By occupation presents himself as having knowledge or skill specialized to the transaction, or
3. Employs an agent who holds herself out as having particular knowledge or skill about the goods involved.

Sales

Article 2 applies to contracts for the *sale* of goods. A sale occurs when there is a "passing of title from the seller to the buyer for a price," §2-106(1). Hence, the sale must involve the *title* to goods being passed. The title represents the legal rights to ownership of a thing, such as a car or a computer. If legal title does not pass, there has not been a sale under the UCC. Article 2 does not apply to the lease of goods, such as the lease of a car, but most states have adopted Article 2A, a new Code article dealing with certain leases of personal property.

Titles

How do we determine who holds title to goods? We look to UCC §2-401. A person may hold legal title to a good if (1) the good exists, and (2) the good has been identified (such as by the serial number on a car) to the contract, meaning that the seller has specified which goods are being sold to the buyer. If these conditions hold, §2-401 allows title to be passed however the parties see fit. For example, the UCC would allow title to pass in any of the following situations, if that is what the parties desire, as determined by contract language, custom, or past practices between the parties:

- When the goods arrive for shipment at a port
- When the goods arrive at the buyer's warehouse
- When the goods leave the seller's warehouse
- When the goods are halfway between the seller's factory and the buyer's warehouse

If the parties should disagree about whether or not title passed, or they failed to specify when title passed, then the courts look to §2-401, which states that

(1) title passes to the buyer when the seller completes all her obligations regarding delivery of the goods; or (2) title passes to the buyer when the seller delivers the title documents, if the goods did not have to be moved.

If a seller "sells" stolen goods, then good title does not pass to the buyer. For example, if someone steals a computer from a university and sells the computer to a buyer who does not know it is stolen, and then the university finds the stolen property, it gets it back. A thief has no title, or void title, and so cannot pass good title.

FORMING A SALES CONTRACT

Contracts are governed by the common law of contracts unless the UCC changes or modifies the rule. The UCC tends to reduce the formality of contract law. The UCC recognizes that most business deals are not highly formal and UCC rules are used to "fill the gap" when a contract is silent on an issue. This section considers the effect of UCC Article 2 on general contract principles. As you read the section, keep in mind the basic differences between the UCC and the common law of contracts, some of which are outlined in Exhibit 11.2.

Intent to Contract

As we discussed in the last chapter, under the common law, a contract cannot be formed until the offer is clearly accepted. Article 2 relaxes this rule; §2-204 provides that a contract "may be made in any manner sufficient to show agreement" between the parties. For example, suppose a buyer and seller have been doing business together for months. The seller delivers various amounts of restaurant supplies to the buyer's restaurant based on orders given by phone and e-mail. Prices are often not discussed or known to the buyer, who pays the invoice by mail. Under the UCC, a contract has been formed by the conduct of the parties. It does not matter that the moment of contract formation is uncertain.

An Indefinite Offer

Under Article 2, if parties intended to enter into an agreement on the basis of the offer, a contract exists. This can be the case even though some of the offer's major terms—such as price, delivery, or payment terms—are omitted or are left open for later determination. UCC 2-204(3) states that a contract does not fail for indefiniteness "if the parties have intended to make a contract and there is a reasonably certain basis for giving an appropriate remedy." When terms are left open by the parties, Article 2 provides rules for determining the terms.

Merchant's Firm Offer

Article 2 modifies the contract rules governing when an offer may be revoked. Under the common law, an offer can be revoked anytime before acceptance. The main common-law exception is the option contract, under which the offeree gives consideration for the offeror's promise to keep the offer open for a stated time period. Section 2-205 provides another exception: If a merchant-offeror gives assurances in a signed writing that the offer will remain open for a given period, the merchant's *firm offer* is irrevocable. More important, the merchant's firm offer is irrevocable without the need for consideration. If the period is not stated in the offer, the offer stays open for a reasonable time not to exceed three months.

Exhibit 11.2

Offer and Acceptance:
Comparing the UCC
and the Common Law
of Contracts

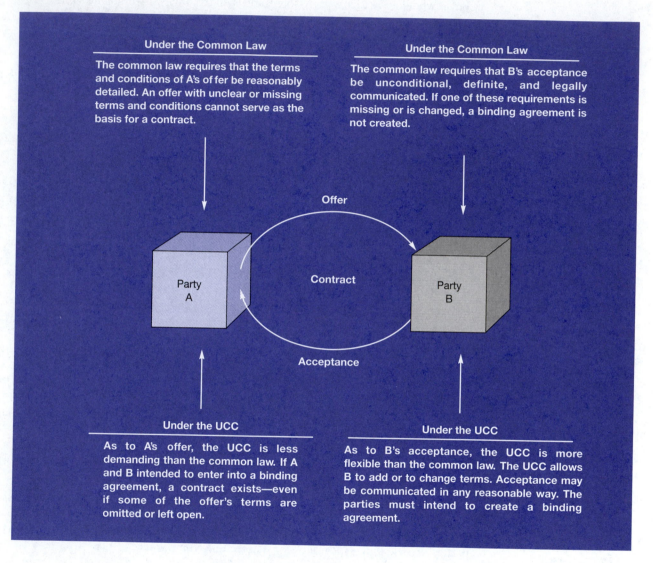

Under the Common Law

The common law requires that the terms and conditions of A's offer be reasonably detailed. An offer with unclear or missing terms and conditions cannot serve as the basis for a contract.

Under the Common Law

The common law requires that B's acceptance be unconditional, definite, and legally communicated. If one of these requirements is missing or is changed, a binding agreement is not created.

Offer

Contract

Party A

Party B

Acceptance

Under the UCC

As to A's offer, the UCC is less demanding than the common law. If A and B intended to enter into a binding agreement, a contract exists—even if some of the offer's terms are omitted or left open.

Under the UCC

As to B's acceptance, the UCC is more flexible than the common law. The UCC allows B to add or to change terms. Acceptance may be communicated in any reasonable way. The parties must intend to create a binding agreement.

Acceptance

Article 2 modifies the common-law rules for acceptance in several important ways. To bring the rules of acceptance more in line with business practices, the UCC provides greater flexibility in the way acceptance can be communicated. If the offeror does not clearly demand a particular method of acceptance, §2-206 holds that a contract is formed when the offer is accepted in any reasonable manner under the circumstances. This flexibility allows the legal rules governing acceptance to adapt to new methods of communication, such as the Internet.

The UCC provides that an acceptance may be valid even if the offeree includes additional terms or changes existing terms in an offer. Under the common law, an acceptance cannot deviate from the terms of the offer without being considered either a rejection or a counteroffer. Article 2 makes an acceptance valid when the parties intend to form a contract—even though the offeree's acceptance contains different terms from those in the offer.

INTERNATIONAL   *Perspective*

How to Assure Foreign Buyers of Product Quality

Reputation in business is critical for a company to be accepted into commerce. When a firm is unknown, especially when it moves into foreign markets, it needs to demonstrate that its goods are of a quality worthy of consideration.

One way to make this demonstration is by obtaining certification from a private organization that has global acceptance as a measure of quality assurance. For many buyers, such certification is much better information than a statement by the company itself, or a government agency promoting the company, that its goods are of high quality.

Many companies seek certification from the International Organization for Standardization (ISO), headquartered in Geneva, Switzerland. The ISO is a network of national standards institutes in 130 countries that coordinates the system and sets standards. ISO certification is required by many firms before they will even consider buying goods from a supplier.

Firms apply for ISO certification, are visited by a certified registrar, and follow a complex procedure to document and organize production procedures. Firms are audited for compliance to ensure that they follow their own proper procedures. See *http://www.iso.ch/iso/en/ISOOnline.frontpage* for more details. ISO does not tell firms how to implement all aspects of the program; rather, firms must demonstrate that they know and follow quality-assurance procedures.

Conflicting Terms

It is not uncommon for an offeror to send an offer on a standard company form that lists standard terms, such as when payment is due. The offeree may accept the offer but send acceptance on its own standard form that does not contain all the terms that were stated in the offer. UCC §2-207(1) states that in such cases there is a valid acceptance. However, the contract is based on the offeror's terms. The different terms contained in the acceptance become a part of the contract only if the offeror accepts the terms posed by the offeree in acceptance.

Contract Modification

Under the common law, contract modifications must be supported by new consideration to be binding on the parties. The UCC §2-209 makes a significant change in the common-law rule by providing that the parties need not provide new consideration to modify an existing sales contract. A modification to a sales contract, however, must meet the UCC's test of good-faith dealing and usually must be in writing.

Statute of Frauds

Article 2 §2-201 provides a *statute of frauds* provision. The basic rule is that a contract for the sale of goods for $500 or more is not enforceable unless it is in writing and signed by the party against whom enforcement is sought. Compared to the common law, the UCC relaxes the requirements for the sufficiency of a writing to satisfy the Statute of Frauds.

Under Article 2, the writing need not specify every material term in the contract. The key element is that there is some basis for believing that the parties made a contract for the sale of goods. For example, suppose a buyer sends a letter to a seller indicating an intent to buy shipping cartons. Later, because other sellers offer lower prices, the buyer wants to get out of the deal. If the buyer indicated an intent to enter into an agreement by writing and signing the letter, the writing is "sufficient" under Article 2 to be binding. The letter must be signed by the buyer, since the seller is seeking enforcement against the buyer.

Failure to Respond to a Writing

The UCC recognizes that it is not uncommon in business for contract writings to be incomplete. This is especially the case when parties discuss a deal, and one sends a writing to confirm what was discussed, but the other party does not send a written reply. However, even when there is a failure to respond to a writing signed by the other party, there may be a good contract.

Section 2-201(2) states: "Between merchants if within a reasonable time a writing in confirmation of the contract and sufficient against the sender is received and the party receiving it has reason to know its contents, it satisfies the [writing] requirements . . . against such party unless written notice of objection to its contents is given within ten days after it is received." This only applies to contracts between merchants; the writing must be complete as to essential terms; and the writing must be sent soon (and received) after the contract has been formed.

Parol Evidence

Since the UCC is more generous than common-law contract law in presuming contracts to exist when terms are not all set, oral testimony is more likely to be needed to clarify disputes over terms of a contract subject to the UCC. Section 2-202 states that written documents may not be contradicted by oral testimony, but that such testimony may be used to explain customary trade dealings or the meaning of certain terms. Parol evidence may not be used "if the court finds the writing to have been intended also as a complete and exclusive statement of the terms of the agreement." In the *Pevar* case we see a court dealing with problems of parol evidence and conflicting forms.

Leonard Pevar Co. v. Evans Products Co.

United States District Court, District of Delaware
524 F.Supp. 546 (1981)

CASE BACKGROUND   *Pevar called various companies for price quotations for medium density overlay plywood to be used in construction. Evans was one company called, and it gave the lowest quote. There was conflicting testimony about what the phone conversation covered. Pevar claims it ordered plywood and Evans accepted the order on the phone, creating an oral contract of sale.*

Evans denied accepting the order on the phone and contends the contract was created when it sent its standard order form to Pevar after the phone call. The form specified the price, quantity, and shipping instructions. The boilerplate language stated that the sale was contingent on Pevar's acceptance of all terms in that document, which greatly limited the buyer's remedies.

Pevar accepted the goods and paid for them. When the plywood turned out to have problems and Evans would do nothing, Pevar sued for breach of warranty. Evans defended the action and both parties moved for summary judgment.

CASE DECISION   Latchum, Chief Judge.

* * *

Evans contends that if Pevar and Evans entered into an oral contract, it would be unenforceable because it would be in violation of the statute of frauds. Section 2-201 generally provides that an oral contract for the sale of goods in excess of $500 is unenforceable. Section 2-201(2), however, provides an exception. If a written confirmation is sent to the receiving party, and the receiving party does not object to the confirmation within ten days, then the oral agreement may be enforceable. The Court finds that Pevar's written purchase order constituted a confirmatory memorandum and Evans' acknowledgment failed to provide sufficient notice of objection to Pevar's confirmation. The acknowledgment did not deny expressly the existence of the purported contract; rather, it merely asserted additional terms. Thus, the statute of frauds will not bar Pevar from proving the existence and terms of the contract. . . .

This case presents a classic example of the "battle of the forms," and its solution is to be derived by reference to section 2-207 of the Uniform Commercial Code which is specifically designed to resolve such disputes. . . .

Section 2-207 was intended to eliminate the "ribbon matching" or "mirror" rule of common law, under which the terms of an acceptance or confirmation were required to be identical to the terms of the offer or oral agreement, respectively. . . . Section 2-207 recognizes that a buyer and seller can enter into a contract by one of three methods. First, the parties may agree orally and thereafter send confirmatory memoranda. §2-207(1). Second, the parties, without oral agreement, may exchange writings which do not contain identical terms, but nevertheless constitute a seasonable acceptance. §2-207(1). Third, the conduct of the parties may recognize the existence of a contract, despite the previous failure to agree orally or in writing. §2-207(3).

A. Oral agreement followed by confirmation.

In the present case, paragraphs [in] Evans' acknowledgment, which disclaimed warranties and limited liability, may include terms not in the original agreement. Generally, these types of clauses "materially alter" the agreement. Nevertheless, the question of a material alteration rests upon the facts of each case. If the trier of fact determines that the acknowledgment includes additional terms which do not materially alter the oral agreement, then the terms will be incorporated into the agreement. If they materially alter it, however, the terms will not be included in the agreement, and the standardized "gap filler" provisions of Article Two will provide the terms of the contract. If the facts reveal that no oral agreement was created, then §2-207(1) may still apply, but in a different manner.

B. Written documents not containing identical terms.

The second situation in which §2-207(1) may apply is where the parties have not entered into an oral agreement but have exchanged writings which do not contain identical terms. If the Court determines that Pevar and Evans did not orally agree prior to the exchange of documents, then this second situation may apply. In such a case, both Pevar and Evans agree that Pevar's purchase order constituted an offer to purchase. The parties, however, disagree with the characterization of Evans' acknowledgment and Pevar's acceptance of and payment for the shipped goods. Evans contends that the terms disclaiming warranties and limiting liability in the acknowledgment constituted a counteroffer which Pevar accepted by receiving and paying for the goods. Evans argues that . . . it effectively rejected and terminated Pevar's offer [on the phone], and initiated a counteroffer; and when Pevar received and paid for the goods, it accepted the terms of the counteroffer. . . .

The drafters of the Code, however, intended to change the common law in an attempt to conform contract law to modern day business transactions. They believed that businessmen rarely read the terms on the back of standardized forms and that the common law, therefore, unduly rewarded the party who sent the last form prior to the shipping of the goods. The Code disfavors any attempt by one party to unilaterally impose conditions that would create hardship on another party. Thus, before a counteroffer is accepted, the counterofferee must expressly assent to the new terms. . . .

An order will be entered in accordance with this Memorandum Opinion.

QUESTIONS FOR ANALYSIS

1. Based on the court's discussion of the formation of a contract, do you think there was a contract here?

2. Based on the discussion of the options, what would you think the final opinion of the judge was likely to be and what remedy, if any, would there be for Pevar?

Filling the Gaps

As the court noted in the *i.LAN* case, courts try to make sense out of contracts to keep commerce going. This is especially true under the UCC, which fills in parts of sales contracts that are left open, are unclear, or otherwise must be settled to make a contract complete. This handles the reality of business dealings where contracts are often not complete or circumstances force changes to occur. The UCC instructs the courts how to resolve uncertain terms.

In §1-205, the Code states that when parties have had regular dealings, their previous conduct will be looked to as the basis for resolving the current situation. Further, the courts will look to *trade usage*—the regular practice and methods of dealings in a given trade—to resolve an unsettled transaction. In addition, the UCC addresses several common areas of contractual disputes, a few of which are reviewed here.

Price

While price is usually specified, in some contracts it is not clear or is to be set over time as the parties work together. If price is unclear when a contract is found to exist, §2-305 directs the courts to determine "a reasonable price." Reasonable price may or may not be "fair market value," depending on the past dealings and conduct of the parties. If the price referred to in the contract relies on benchmarks, such as "the price of wheat on August 15" or "cost plus 10 percent," disputes may arise as to whether the price of wheat included delivery or the "cost" was determined in good faith. In such cases, the courts attempt to determine what the parties intended when they formed the contract and what would be the most reasonable method, given usual business practices, to determine the price to fulfill the contract.

Quantity

The UCC generally requires that a contract specify the quantity to be bought. However, §2-306(1) recognizes requirements contracts and output contracts where the quantities may not be clear. A *requirements contract* is one in which a seller agrees to provide all of a certain good that a buyer needs. For example, Goodyear may agree to provide Ford all of the tires it needs to install on all new models of the Ford Explorer it produces next year. Ford is not certain how many that will be, but Goodyear says it will produce whatever is required. An *output contract* is when a buyer agrees to take all of the output of a certain seller. If The Gap wants to push a hot line of shoes made by Avia, it could agree to take all that Avia can produce next year.

ISSUE *Spotter*

Gouge the Wholesaler

Your chain of six gas stations has a requirements contract with a gasoline wholesaler. The wholesaler promised to deliver to you all the gasoline you need for two years at a price of $1.13 per gallon. After several months, because the price of oil has shot up, the wholesaler is losing thirty cents on every gallon he delivers to you. You are making so much money on every gallon you sell, that you begin to order more tanker loads and resell it to other gas stations. This practice may be unethical, but does it violate the requirements contract?

In both cases, the law imposes a duty to act in good faith. The buyer and seller are expected to act in a reasonable manner, given the customs of their industry.

Delivery Terms

Most sales contracts specify how goods are to be delivered and who is responsible for the cost of transportation. At some point, responsibility for transportation and control of the goods switches from the seller to the buyer. Sections 2-319 to 2-324 detail the definition of delivery terms, such as "free on board" (F.O.B.), often used in contracts. If delivery is not specified, the UCC fills the gap so long as a contract exists. Section 2-309 states that the time for delivery is to be a "reasonable time." What is reasonable depends, of course, on factors such as trade custom, the apparent intentions of the parties, and the availability of transportation services as we see in the *Earle* case. If the parties do not state what is to determine the time of delivery, §2-311 states that "specifications or arrangements relating to shipment are at the seller's option." Section 2-308 presumes that delivery is to be at the seller's place of business. When the seller turns goods over to a shipping company, §2-504 holds that it has a duty to assure that the carrier is competent and that all parties understand who bears the risk of loss at various points before the buyer gets possession of the goods.

In re Earle Industries, Inc.
United States District Court, Eastern District of Pennsylvania
88 B.R. 52, 7 UCC Rep.Serv.2d 691 (1988)

CASE BACKGROUND *In October, Earle, a custom equipment maker, offered to build equipment for CE for $17,800. Earle told CE that the work usually took about ten weeks. In a letter dated November 18, CE stated "Please proceed with fabrication of this order at once" and included a purchase order for $17,800, creating a contract for sale of the equipment under the UCC. The letter stated that CE needed the equipment "in the first week of January" and said "Let us know if there is any problem with that delivery date." Earle responded with a letter that repeated the price and stated that the equipment would be shipped at the end of January. Included was a standard clause that delivery was on a "best efforts" basis. Delays could be caused by accidents, default by suppliers, or other problems, so there would be no specific delivery date guarantee. It also stated that in the event of cancellation, the buyer would be responsible for expenses incurred by Earle.*

When the equipment had not been delivered by the end of January, CE canceled the order. Earle billed CE $4,000 to cover labor and material to date. The equipment was unique and could not be resold by Earle. CE refused to pay, contending that Earle breached the contract

by not delivering by the end of January; Earle contended that CE was liable for costs incurred. When Earle went into bankruptcy, it sought recovery of the $4,000.

CASE DECISION Fox, Bankruptcy Judge.

* * *

The issue then is the disposition of the proposed delivery date requested by CE in its November 18, 1985 letter. UCC §2-207(b) states that proposed additional terms in an acceptance:

. . . are to be construed as proposals for addition to the contract. Between merchants such terms become part of the contract unless:

    (1) the offer expressly limits acceptance to the terms of the offer;

    (2) they materially alter it; or

    (3) notification of objection to them has already been given or is given within a reasonable time after notice of them is received.

In the case at bar, Earle notified CE within a matter of days that it objected to the delivery date in CE's

continues

acceptance by returning an acknowledgment which not only stated that the equipment would be shipped "end of January," but also provided that Earle could not guarantee a delivery date. Under UCC §2-207(b)(3), this objection prevented CE's proposed delivery date from becoming part of the contract.

Thus no deadline ever became part of the contract. In such circumstances under UCC §2-309(a), a reasonable time for delivery must be implied. A reasonable time for delivery must be implied from the totality of the circumstances including trade usage, course of dealings, and the conduct of the parties in the transaction at issue.

Since no evidence was presented about a course of dealings between the parties or trade usage, I can only infer a reasonable time period from the conduct of the parties. The evidence, though thin, suggested that Earle believed production would take approximately 10 weeks. CE, by its conduct, appeared to accept this general time frame. CE presented no evidence at trial that it had informed or otherwise made known to Earle that ten weeks or any shorter period was an absolute deadline or that it had some urgent need for the equipment. Under these circumstances "approximately ten weeks" appears to be a reasonable time to apply to the contract.

Given the generally understood meaning of "approximately 10 weeks," CE was not entitled to cancel the contract on virtually the first day after ten weeks had expired. CE presented no evidence that it had any legitimate reason to expect performance no later than the end of January, 1986, or that it had communicated to Earle any such expectation at the time Earle rejected its proposed additional term. CE's early cancellation thus constituted a breach of contract.

* * *

[CE will pay Earle $4,000 for the costs incurred working on the equipment.]

QUESTIONS FOR ANALYSIS

1. Since CE told Earle it wanted the equipment the first week in January, why was that date not binding?

2. What kind of "trade usage" would courts look for in such instances?

PERFORMANCE AND OBLIGATIONS

Once a buyer and a seller have formed a contract for the sale of goods, both parties must perform their obligations under that contract or risk being found in breach. The general duties and obligations assumed by each party to a contract for the sale of goods include those specified by the contract, imposed by the UCC, and, where necessary, provided by trade custom.

Seller's Rights and Obligations

The seller's basic obligation under the UCC is to transfer and deliver conforming goods to the buyer. The seller must be concerned about the appropriate manner and timeliness of delivery, the place of tender, and the quality of tender. The proper tender of goods to, and their acceptance by, the buyer entitles the seller to be paid according to the contract.

Under the common law, a doctrine developed called the *perfect tender rule*. The seller's tender of delivery was supposed to conform to the terms of the agreement. In practice, so long as there is substantial performance by the seller, it is likely that contract obligations have been met. The UCC expects parties to meet obligations but provides greater flexibility. UCC §2-601 states: "if the goods or the tender of delivery fail in any respect to conform to the contract, the buyer may: (a) reject the whole; (b) accept the whole; or (c) accept any commercial unit or units and reject the rest." This modifies the common-law rule by allowing the buyer to accept less than the entire shipment. The rationale for the rule is that buyers are entitled to receive the goods they have bargained and paid for—and not something less.

On the other hand, allowing a buyer to reject a shipment when the problems are slight would allow the buyer to escape payment obligations. This is a problem particularly when the market price of the goods is falling. The buyer finds some minor nonconformity, cancels the contract, and purchases the goods at a lower price from another seller. Article 2's policy of enforcing contracts when performance is reasonable discourages such behavior.

Right to Cure by the Seller

UCC §2-508 provides some opportunities for a seller to *cure* an improper tender of goods that has been rejected by the buyer. After the buyer has rejected a shipment as not conforming to the contract, the seller may cure the defective tender or delivery if

1. The time for the seller's performance under the contract has not yet passed.
2. The seller notifies the buyer in a timely manner of an intent to cure the defect.
3. The seller properly repairs or replaces the defective goods within the time allowed for his performance.

In the following case, the buyer rejected nonconforming goods and provided the seller with an extended period in which to cure the improper tender.

Ramirez v. Autosport
Supreme Court of New Jersey
88 N.J. 277, 440 A.2d 1345 (1982)

CASE BACKGROUND *On July 20, 1978, Mr. and Mrs. Ramirez bought a van from Autosport. The van cost $14,100, and Autosport gave the Ramirezes $4,700 for their old van as a trade-in. The Ramirezes agreed to turn in their old van immediately and to take delivery of the new van on August 3. On August 3, the Ramirezes tendered payment. However, the new van was not ready: it had paint scratches, missing electric and sewer hookups, and damaged hubcaps. Autosport agreed to cure the problems. After repeated phone calls from the buyers, Autosport promised delivery on August 14.*

On the 14th, the van was still not ready. This time, the repainted surfaces were not dry, and the seat cushions were wet. A third delivery date was set for September 1, but the van was still not ready for delivery. Finally, in October, the Ramirezes returned with their attorney and canceled the contract. They also demanded the return of their old van, but Autosport had sold it to another customer.

The Ramirezes sued Autosport for rescission of the contract and recovery of the value of their old van.

Autosport counterclaimed for breach of contract. The trial court found for the Ramirezes. Autosport appealed.

CASE DECISION Pollock, Judge.

* * *

Section 2-601 states that goods conform to a contract "when they are in accordance with the obligations under the contract." Section 2-601 authorizes a buyer to reject goods if they "or the tender of delivery fail in any respect to conform to the contract." The Code, however, mitigates the harshness of the perfect tender rule and balances the interests of buyer and seller. The Code achieves that result through its provisions for revocation of acceptance and cure.

* * *

Underlying the Code provisions is the recognition of the revolutionary change in business practices in this century. The purchase of goods is no longer a simple transaction in which a buyer purchases individually-

continues

made goods from a seller in a face-to-face transaction. Our economy depends on a complex system for the manufacture, distribution, and sale of goods, a system in which manufacturers and consumers rarely meet. Faceless manufacturers mass-produce goods for unknown consumers who purchase those goods from merchants exercising little or no control over the quality of their production. In an age of assembly lines, we are accustomed to cars with scratches, television sets without knobs and other products with all kinds of defects. Buyers no longer expect a "perfect tender." If a merchant sells defective goods, the reasonable expectation of the parties is that the buyer will return those goods and that the seller will repair or replace them.

Recognizing this commercial reality, the Code permits a seller to cure imperfect tenders. Should the seller fail to cure the defects, whether substantial or not, the balance shifts again in favor of the buyer, who has the right to cancel or seek damages. In general, economic considerations would induce sellers to cure minor defects. Assuming the seller does not cure, however, the buyer should be permitted to exercise his remedies under [the UCC]. The Code remedies for consumers are to be liberally construed, and the buyer should have the option of cancelling if the seller does not provide conforming goods.

To summarize, the UCC preserves the perfect tender rule to the extent of permitting a buyer to reject goods for any nonconformity. Nonetheless, that rejection does not automatically terminate the contract. A seller may still effect a cure and preclude unfair rejection and cancellation by the buyer.

The trial court found that Mr. and Mrs. Ramirez had rejected the van within a reasonable time under [UCC] 2-602. . . . Although the Ramirezes gave Autosport ample time to correct the defects, Autosport did not demonstrate that the van conformed to the contract on September 1. In fact, on that date, when Mr. and Mrs. Ramirez returned at Autosport's invitation, all they received was discourtesy.

* * *

Affirmed.

QUESTIONS FOR ANALYSIS

1. What is the underlying purpose of the seller's right to cure? Was that purpose met in this case?

2. The judge asserts that "Buyers no longer expect a 'perfect tender.'" Are these notions still valid, given the movement of many firms to total quality management? How would you expect the total quality movement to be reflected in future UCC decisions regarding defective products?

Buyer's Rights and Obligations

In general, a buyer's obligations begin when the seller tenders delivery of goods that conform to the sales contract. The buyer is required by §2-507 to accept conforming goods and to pay for them according to the contract. The decision by the buyer to accept or reject the goods determines how the seller will continue to perform. If the buyer accepts the goods, the seller awaits payment. If the buyer rejects the goods as nonconforming, the seller may need to remedy the problem or may have to sue for breach of contract.

Buyer's Right of Inspection

Unless the parties have otherwise agreed, under §2-513 the buyer has a right to inspect the goods before accepting them. Inspection allows the buyer to verify that the goods received are those the seller had agreed to deliver. The buyer must pay for any expenses associated with an inspection. However, the expenses can be recovered from the seller as damages if the goods do not conform to the contract.

Buyer's Right of Rejection

According to §2-601 and §2-602, a buyer who receives goods that are nonconforming may reject them as a breach of contract and withhold payment. The buyer may also cancel the contract and recover from the seller any prepayments made. The buyer must notify the seller of a rejection in a timely manner to allow the seller to either cure the nonconformity, if realistic, or reclaim the goods.

Installment Contracts

An *installment contract* is one contract that provides for delivery in two or more separate lots. Under §2-612 each lot is to be accepted and paid for separately. In an installment contract, a buyer can reject an installment—but "only if the nonconformity substantially impairs the value of that installment and cannot be cured." The entire installment contract is breached only when one or more nonconforming installment "substantially" impairs the value of the "whole contract." If the buyer subsequently accepts a nonconforming installment and fails to notify the seller of cancellation, the contract is reinstated.

Buyer's Duty of Acceptance

When the seller has properly tendered conforming goods, the buyer has a duty to accept them. That is, under §2-606 and §2-607, the buyer has a duty to become the owner of goods properly tendered by the seller. If the goods are nonconforming but have been accepted under §2-608, the buyer may later revoke acceptance only if the nonconformity "substantially impairs" the value of the goods. Of course, if the buyer accepts nonconforming goods, they must be paid for.

Obligation of Payment

Unless otherwise agreed, §2-507 requires payment when and where the buyer receives the goods. Even when the contract calls for the seller to deliver the goods to a transportation company for shipment to the buyer, the buyer's payment for the goods is not due until the goods are received. Payment upon receipt gives the buyer a chance to inspect the goods before paying for them. The *Hoover* case discusses several issues that can arise when a problem occurs in delivered goods. The case illustrates the seriousness of specialized language in a sales contract.

Hoover Universal, Inc. v. Brockway Imco, Inc.

United States Court of Appeals, Fourth Circuit
809 F.2d 1039 (1987)

CASE BACKGROUND   *Hoover was interested in buying a process for making plastic bottles known as ORB VI, which Imco developed and patented. After various trips, inspections, and discussions, including being given all materials related to the machines, production, and cost of operation, Hoover paid $3.5 million for eleven machines. Both parties failed to notice that an error in the handouts overstated the bottles that would be produced by about 20 percent.*

Paragraph 2(d) of the contract stated: "Since Hoover has reviewed the Business and will inspect the Purchased Assets and become familiar with and satisfy itself concerning the same, with the exception of specific representations and warranties set forth in Paragraph 10 hereinafter, Imco makes no representation or warranty to Hoover with respect to the financial condition or prospects of the business, or the merchantability, condition or workmanship of the purchased assets or any part thereof . . . , the absence of any defects therein, whether latent or patent. . . .

continues

Hoover shall be responsible, and assumes all risk and liability, for the consequences of its purchase, ownership, use and possession of the Purchased Assets and the conduct of the Business after closing by or on behalf of Hoover."

When Hoover began to operate the machinery, the error in the handouts on the rate of production was discovered; Hoover sued for breach of warranty and fraud, claiming that the data in the handout was part of the agreement. The trial court held that the comprehensive nature of the written agreement barred both claims. Hoover appealed.

CASE DECISION   Hall, Circuit Judge.

* * *

As the district court implicitly recognized, any effort by Hoover to prove that the handout was part of the basis of the bargain would have inevitably foundered on the barrier raised by the existence of a detailed written contract. . . .

Its reference . . . to a "merged contract" and to the fact that any liability would have to be discovered "within the four corners of the instrument" leave no doubt that the court found the Asset Purchase Agreement to be a "complete and exclusive statement" of the agreement between Hoover and Imco. In light of the detailed nature of the contract, including the well-drafted merger clause, we can see no error in that conclusion.

It follows, therefore, that [the UCC] precludes any effort by Hoover to establish through the handout a warranty relating to the ORB VI cavitation capacity even in the unlikely eventuality that the warranty could be construed as a consistent additional term. . . .

Hoover argues that the [production] capacity described in the handout was a substantial motivating factor in its decision to buy the ORB VI. Its detrimental reliance on that misrepresentation established, in

Hoover's view, a prima facie case of either actual or constructive fraud.

* * *

A seller who misrepresents a material fact in connection with a sale may be liable for fraud in the inducement. However, in circumstances where a prudent buyer would have conducted an investigation and, thereby, discovered the seller's misstatement, a buyer who fails to make such an investigation may not assert fraud based on the factual misrepresentation. A buyer who fails to conduct a proper investigation may still recover if the seller's conduct intentionally diverts the buyer from engaging in a reasonable inquiry.

As the district court recognized in its opinion, Hoover not only should have made a prudent investigation, it expressly agreed in paragraph 2(d) of the contract that it would "inspect" and "become familiar" with the ORB VI. It is undisputed that a timely investigation would have revealed the error in the handout. Furthermore, Hoover alleged no conduct by Imco that could reasonably be construed as an effort to forestall further inquiry by Hoover.

Hoover's clear failure to fulfill the duty of inspection imposed by both the operation of law and contract precludes its effort to assert reliance on Imco's prior statement.

* * *

Affirmed.

QUESTIONS FOR ANALYSIS

1. The contract did not specify the productive capacity of the machines, so why did the court not integrate into the contract the handout that stated the production ability?

2. If the contract had not contained the disclaimer paragraph, would the result have been different?

SALES WARRANTIES

Broadly speaking, a *warranty* is a statement or representation made by a seller that the goods being sold conform to certain standards of quality, safety, performance, and title. If the goods do not conform to the standards created by the warranty, the seller can be held liable in damages for breach of warranty. Article 2 provides five types of warranties (which are summarized in Exhibit 11.3).

Warranty of Title

Under §2-312, a seller warrants that good title is being transferred to the buyer and that goods will be delivered free of any claims against them, such as liens, unless

Exhibit 11.3		
Summary of Warranties under the UCC	**Warranty of Title** §2-312	Seller is the rightful owner of the goods, the goods are free of any liens, and there are no infringements.
	Express Warranty §2-313	Seller's promise as to quality, safety, or performance. May be created by the seller's statements, description, or models.
	Implied Warranties	Imposed on the seller by the UCC:
	Merchantability §2-314	Requires that the goods are reasonably fit, and safe for the purposes they are being sold for; also applies to packaging and labeling.
	Fitness for a Particular Purpose §2-315	If the buyer relies on the seller's skill or judgment in selecting goods for a particular purpose, the goods must be able to perform that purpose.

those have been revealed to the buyer. As the UCC explains in its official comments, the purpose of this is that a buyer gets "a good, clean title" and that the buyer "will not be exposed to a lawsuit in order to protect it." This means that a seller is responsible to the buyer if the seller innocently sells a good that does not have good title, such as a stolen property.

Warranty of title also means that the seller warrants that goods being sold are free of any claim of infringement. If a seller has infringed on a trademark, copyright, or patent owned by a third party, the seller is responsible for expenses incurred by a buyer who is ignorant of the infringement as a result of the infringement. For example, a department store was sued by a producer because the store was selling goods that infringed on the producer's trademarks. The department store sued its supplier for violating the trademarks and was awarded damages to cover all costs incurred.

Express Warranties

An *express warranty* is created by a seller's promise or guarantee as to the quality, safety, performance, or durability of goods being sold. During negotiations, a seller may help induce a buyer to purchase goods by making representations about the goods that become warranties. Section 2-313 lists three circumstances where an express warranty may be created:

1. A seller provides a sample or model of the good that the buyer relies upon as evidence of what the goods will be like,
2. A seller describes attributes about the goods to the buyer, or
3. A seller makes specific oral or written statements or promises to the buyer about the goods that are a part of the basis of the bargain.

Statements about goods are more likely to be held to be express warranties when the claims are specific, not general statements about "how nice" the goods are or other general happy talk (puffery). Similarly, an express warranty is created if statements are made about attributes of the goods that are not obvious, such as claims about the quality of steel used in production of a good, or it is a case in which the buyer has good reason to rely on the expertise of the seller. Obviously, when statements are made in writing, they are more likely to be held to be express warranties. It does not matter that a seller does not intend to create an express warranty by making claims about a product; if it is reasonable that the buyer rely on the seller's claims, then they are likely to be express warranties. This is particularly the case for goods sold to consumers.

Implied Warranties

An *implied warranty* is a quality and safety standard that is imposed by Article 2. This part of the UCC has important implications, for it establishes a standard similar to that imposed by product liability law in tort. Implied warranties exist at law. Unlike express warranties, which are based on representations made by the seller, implied warranties are automatically imposed on sellers unless they specifically disclaim them.

Implied Warranty of Merchantability

Section 2-314 states that unless the parties to the contract expressly agree otherwise, an *implied warranty of merchantability* accompanies every sale by a merchant. This provision of the UCC applies to sellers who are merchants of the goods of the kind in question. That is, it applies to those who routinely deal in such goods or offer their expertise to others about such goods, such as jewelers selling jewelry and restaurants serving food and drink.

Merchantable means that the good "must be of a quality comparable to that generally acceptable in that line or trade." That is, industry standards must be met. Obviously, for such things as jet engines, industry standards are very high and any seller must offer products of current standards. If the product is a common one, such as bushels of #2 winter wheat, the quality must be average; one cannot pass off a load of bottom-of-the-silo, moldy, rat-dropping-infested wheat. Further, the goods must be able to do the tasks expected of the goods in question. If the goods are one-ton trucks, they must be able to carry the loads expected of such trucks. Also, goods must be adequately packaged and labeled and be in conformance with claims made on labels or sales materials.

ISSUE
Spotter

How Much Advice Should Retailers Give?

At self-service "home center" stores where you can buy plumbing, electrical, and other supplies, the employees usually try to be helpful in giving advice. You explain the problem and they point you to the supplies you need to fix the problem. Can the retailers be setting themselves up to be sued for breach of implied warranty of fitness for a particular purpose? That is, if you go into the store, tell an employee what is wrong with your sink—or at least what you think is wrong—and the employee advises you to change a fitting and shows you what to buy, and the result is you flood your kitchen, could you have a suit against the retailer for the damages you suffered? Is it a good idea for store employees to give a lot of advice?

Implied Warranty of Fitness for a Particular Purpose

In some situations, a buyer orders a good with a special use in mind. Section 2-315 is more demanding about a seller who had reason to know the buyer's particular purpose for purchasing certain goods. If the buyer relies on the seller's skill or judgment to select the goods for that purpose, an implied warranty that the goods are suited for that purpose is created.

The buyer is required to demonstrate "actual reliance" on the seller's expertise. The buyer must also show that the seller had "reason to know" of the buyer's purpose. Suppose that Flodden needs to paint a metal barn. She tells the paint store salesperson what she needs. She is concerned about chipping and peeling and asks for a recommendation. The salesperson recommends Pittura Exterior. If Flodden buys Pittura based on the salesperson's recommendation and the paint chips and peels the next year, there is a breach of implied warranty of fitness for a particular purpose.

Warranty Disclaimers

The warranty requirements imposed on sellers by the UCC are a form of strict liability under contract law. Because it is a tough standard, sellers may wish to reduce their liability by issuing *disclaimers*. If a seller has made an express warranty, the courts do not want to see disclaimers that are inconsistent with the promises made in the warranty. Under §2-316, boilerplate language that attempts to dismiss an express warranty is not allowed when the disclaimer is inconsistent with the warranty. The parol evidence rule generally prevents oral promises that have been made from being a part of the warranty, when the oral statement contradicts the written warranty. The *Hoover* case is an example of language in a technical sales contract that disclaimed warranties.

Disclaimers of implied warranties of merchantability and of fitness for a particular purpose are permitted if the disclaimer uses the word "merchantability" and the disclaimer is conspicuous. Under UCC §1-201, conspicuous means that it is written so that a reasonable person would notice it, such as written in all capital letters or in a different color than the rest of the text. Further, a seller is more likely held to have disclaimed warranties if there is a conspicuous notice that the goods are being sold "as is." As the *Lee* case indicates, disclaimers mean consumers should beware.

Lee v. R&K Marine, Inc.
Court of Appeals of North Carolina
598 S.E.2d 683 (2004)

CASE BACKGROUND   *In late 1998, Lee bought a new boat from R&K Marine. Lee signed a standard purchase agreement. On the agreement, all in capital letters, it stated: "EXCEPT TO THE EXTENT REQUIRED BY STATE LAW, SELLER EXPRESSLY DISCLAIMS ALL WARRANTIES, EXPRESS OR IMPLIED, INCLUDING ANY IMPLIED WARRANTY OF MERCHANTABILITY OR FITNESS FOR A PARTICULAR PURPOSE." Three years later, Lee took the boat in for repairs, when cracks and extensive deterioration were discovered in the hull. An appraiser determined that the problems were due to defects in manufacturing and the boat was a complete loss. The manufacturer had gone out of business and was bankrupt, so Lee sued the retailer who sold him the boat, claiming breach of warranties of merchantability and fitness for a particular purpose. Defendant was granted summary judgment. Lee appealed.*

CASE DECISION   Tyson, Judge.

* * *

[UCC § 2-316(2)] provides, "to exclude or modify the implied warranty of merchantability or any part of it, the language must mention merchantability and in case of a writing must be conspicuous, and to exclude or modify any implied warranty of fitness the exclusion must be by a writing and conspicuous." [UCC § 1-201(10)] defines the term "conspicuous" as:

> A term or clause is conspicuous when it is so written that a reasonable person against whom it is to operate ought to have noticed it. A printed heading in capitals (as: NONNEGOTIABLE BILL OF LADING) is conspicuous. Language in the body of a form is "conspicuous" if it is in larger or other contrasting type or color. . . .

continues

The disclaimer here met all the requirements and was conspicuous. Defendant effectively disclaimed any and all warranties of merchantability and fitness for a particular purpose. The trial court did not err in granting defendant's motion for summary judgment on plaintiff's breach of warranty claim.

QUESTIONS FOR ANALYSIS

1. There was no evidence that the retailer knew that the boat was junk, but suppose that could have been shown. How might that have changed the case?

2. Would there be any reason to sue the boat manufacturer?

Juris *prudence?*

Does It Come with a Warranty?

The inventor of the Quadro Tracker said that the device could locate drugs, bombs, and just about anything else whether behind walls, inside cars, on persons, or out in fields. A brochure claimed that it could even detect drugs in a person's bloodstream just by being pointed at a person. An MIT physics professor said that the chances of the Quadro Tracker's working were slim to zero and that there are many hoaxes involving such incredible devices.

Nevertheless, dozens of law enforcement agencies and schools bought the device, also called the Positive Molecular Locator, for prices ranging from $400 to $8,000. Over 1,000 of the plastic boxes were sold, taking in more than $1 million, before a federal judge issued an injunction banning the sale or distribution of the product. An FBI agent said, "The only thing this accurately detects is your checkbook."

Sources: *The Herald* (Rock Hill, S.C.) and *The Atlanta Journal and Constitution*

REMEDIES AND DAMAGES

When a buyer or seller breaches a contract for the sale of goods, the UCC provides the nonbreaching party with a number of remedies. Those remedies are intended to place the nonbreaching party in the same position as if the contract had been performed according to its terms. In applying its remedies, §1-106 of the UCC directs the courts to interpret the remedies liberally.

Seller's Remedies

The buyer may default on contractual obligations by rejecting a tender of goods that conforms to the contract, wrongfully revoking an acceptance, repudiating the contract, failing to make a payment, or failing to complete some other performance required by the contract. In each of these situations, the UCC provides the seller with remedies. As Exhibit 11.4 indicates, the seller is not restricted to any one remedy in particular. Rather, §2-703 states that the seller may use several remedies at the same time.

The remedies available to the seller depend on whether the buyer breached before or after receiving the goods (see Exhibit 11.4). When the buyer breaches before receiving the goods, the seller may elect to cancel the contract, resell or salvage (recycle) the goods, or withhold or stop delivery. If the buyer breaches after receiving the goods, the remedies available to the seller depend upon whether the seller reclaims the goods. If unable to reclaim the goods, the seller may sue the buyer to recover the purchase price and any resulting incidental damages. If the goods are reclaimed by the seller, the seller may use any of the same remedies available had the buyer's breach occurred before receiving the goods.

Exhibit 11.4	Status of the Goods	Seller's Rights and Remedies
Summary of Seller's Rights and Remedies	**Buyer breaches before receiving the goods.**	**The seller may** 1. Cancel the contract 2. Identify the goods; minimize losses if necessary by completing manufacture or by stopping production and salvaging the goods 3. Withhold delivery or, if needed, stop delivery 4. Resell the goods in a commercially reasonable manner 5. Sue the buyer to recover the price loss suffered by having to resell the goods and any resulting damages
	Buyer breaches after receiving the goods.	**The seller may** 1. If the buyer does not pay, sue to recover the purchase price and resulting incidental damages 2. If the buyer wrongfully rejects the goods or revokes an acceptance, the remedies depend on the following: a. If the seller reclaims the goods, the remedies are the same as if the buyer had breached before receiving the goods. b. If the seller does not reclaim the goods, the seller can sue to recover the purchase price and any resulting damages.

Seller's Damages

When reclaiming and reselling the goods does not fully compensate the seller for the buyer's breach, damages are the proper remedy. UCC's damage measures are designed to put the seller in as good a position as if the buyer had performed contractual obligations. The seller is also allowed to seek incidental damages. Under §2-710, such costs may include expenses associated with stopping delivery, transporting and taking care of the goods after the breach, returning or reselling the goods, and taking any other necessary action.

Buyer's Remedies

A seller usually breaches a sales contract in one of the following ways:

1. The seller repudiates the contract before tendering the goods.
2. The seller fails to make a scheduled delivery on time.
3. The seller delivers nonconforming goods.

The buyer's remedies vary somewhat depending on the type of breach by the seller. In any case, the buyer may respond by canceling the contract, arranging to obtain the goods from another supplier, and suing the nonperforming seller for damages. The buyer's rights and remedies are summarized in Exhibit 11.5.

Buyer's Damages

Like the seller's damage provisions, the buyer's damage provisions under the UCC are designed to put the buyer in as good a position as if the seller had performed according to the contract. The terminology for damages is a bit different under the UCC than in the common law, so we consider the primary types of damages specified in the UCC.

Exhibit 11.5	Status of the Goods	Buyer's Rights and Remedies
Summary of Buyer's Rights and Remedies	**Seller repudiates the contract before delivery.**	**The buyer may** 1. Cancel the contract 2. Obtain goods from another supplier 3. Sue the seller for damages and to recover advance payments
	Seller fails to deliver.	**The buyer may** 1. Cancel the contract 2. Obtain goods from another supplier 3. Sue the seller for damages
	Seller delivers nonconforming goods; buyer rejects.	**The buyer may** 1. Cancel the contract 2. Obtain goods from another supplier if goods are rejected 3. Sue the seller for damages 4. Sell rejected goods to recover advance payments 5. If no advance payment, store or reship goods
	Seller delivers noncomforming goods; buyer accepts.	**The buyer may** 1. Deduct damages from price of goods 2. Sue the seller for damages 3. Sue for breach of warranty

Cover   When a seller fails to deliver goods, either by being too late to be useful or because the goods are nonconforming, the buyer is entitled to buy substitute goods and recover the price difference. This is referred to as *cover* in §2-712 of the UCC. The cover price is what is paid for the substitute goods, or the market price may be used to measure the damages. Of course, if similar goods are available at the same or a lower price, then the breaching seller does not have to provide cover. The UCC does not permit overcompensation for losses by requiring the seller to pay the full cost of substitute goods.

Incidental Damages   When the buyer properly rejects a delivery (or does not receive the goods), incidental damages, under §2-710, include the reasonable costs of inspecting, receiving, transporting, and taking care of the goods while they remain in her possession. If there was no delivery at all, or if delivery is late, §2-715 states that the buyer's incidental damages include all reasonable costs or direct expenses associated with the delay in receiving the goods or in tracking down substitute goods.

Consequential Damages   Consequential damages are foreseeable damages that result from the seller's breach. They differ from incidental damages in that consequential damages may result from the buyer's relations with parties other than the seller. That is, the breach may cause the buyer to lose sales and, most important, profits. The *Mississippi Chemical* case illustrates issues that arise regarding damages.

Mississippi Chemical Corp. v. Dresser-Rand Co.

United States Court of Appeals, Fifth Circuit
287 F.3d 359 (2002)

CASE BACKGROUND   *Dresser specially designed and sold Mississippi Chemical (MCC) a gas compressor train (system) for producing ammonia (used in making fertilizer). It consisted of both a high-pressure compressor and a low-pressure compressor. The contract contained an express warranty guaranteeing that the system would be free from defects and would meet technical specifications. As an exclusive remedy, Dresser offered promptly to repair and replace any defect at its expense.*

The high-pressure compressor broke the first year and had to be shipped out for repair. Two years later, the low-pressure compressor began to have problems. It had to be repaired. Then the high-pressure compressor had to be repaired again. MCC sued for breach of express warranty and for breach of the implied warranties of merchantability and fitness for a particular purpose.

The jury found for MCC, holding that the exclusive "repair and replacement" remedy had failed, so it was liable for all breaches of warranty. It awarded MCC $4.42 million in damages for lost profits for when the machine malfunctioned. Dresser appealed.

CASE DECISION   Jolly, Circuit Judge.

* * *

To "repair or replace" represents the exclusive remedy for a breach of the express warranty. Under the . . . UCC, "backing up" an express warranty with an exclusive promise to repair or replace the good in question is permissible. But if the repair or replacement remedy fails its essential purpose, then the buyer may seek any alternative remedy provided in the Code. Under Section 719, the buyer *first* must seek repair or replacement to remedy a breach of an express warranty, and only if the seller fails to meet this promise (in UCC speak, the repair or replacement remedy fails its essential purpose), may the buyer bring a contract action.

. . . The cause of action based on the express warranty did not accrue . . . until the promise to repair or replace the compressor . . . failed its essential purpose.

* * *

MCC's damage calculation—which was accepted in whole by the jury—consisted of a three-step process.

First, MCC computed the profit per unit of ammonia during each of the three malfunctioning periods. Second, it estimated the quantity of ammonia lost in each malfunctioning period because of the reduction in the speed of the compressor train. Finally, it multiplied the profit per unit by the number of units lost to come up with the total amount of damages (i.e., lost profits) caused by the malfunctioning compressor train. . . .

In the event of a breach of warranty, a buyer may seek direct, incidental, and consequential damages. §2-714. Here, the jury was only instructed on—and presumably only awarded—consequential damages. . . .

> Under the . . . UCC, "consequential damages" include:
> (a) Any loss resulting from general or particular requirements and needs of which the seller at the time of contracting had reason to know and which could not reasonably be prevented by cover or otherwise; and
> (b) Injury to person or property proximately resulting from any breach of warranty. . . .

Foreseeability requires that the breaching party, at the time of contracting, have reason to know that such "lost profits" were possible. . . .

From the evidence, a reasonable jury could draw the conclusion that the lost profits from the lost production of ammonia were "reasonably foreseeable."

We now turn to the "cover" requirement necessary for the recovery of "lost profits." Dresser argues that MCC's damages should be limited to the value of the substitute ammonia it secured to replace the diminished production by the compressor train. Under Section 715(2) consequential damages are restricted to those damages "which could not be prevented by cover or otherwise." This "cover" requirement imposes on the buyer a duty to mitigate his damages. When dealing with lost profits, this duty means that a buyer "cannot recover for losses he reasonably could have prevented." . . .

To recognize that "cover," as argued by Dresser, is not mitigation of lost profits in this case, one must understand that the substitute sources of ammonia—

continues

that is, ammonia from inventory—represented a profit opportunity for MCC. . . . Because MCC had to make up for the lost ammonia production by dipping into its own inventory, it had fewer units of ammonia. . . .

Affirmed.

QUESTIONS FOR ANALYSIS

1. Why did MCC not sue for incidental damages too? What would they have been?

2. How might Dresser have written the warranty to have avoided this result?

INTERNATIONAL SALES

As global commerce has expanded rapidly in recent decades, businesses have had to deal with the laws and customs of more countries. Litigation everywhere is costly, and people are often suspicious about the fairness of legal rules and procedures in other nations. So there are strong reasons to give business partners around the world reasons to believe that we will all play by the same "rules of the game" and that those who will serve as "referees" to disputes are qualified and impartial. Effective legal rules substantially reduce the cost of doing international business. While we discuss other aspects of international law in detail in Chapter 21, here we focus on how the law of the international sale of goods has been developing.

General Principles

Parties who make contracts for the sale of goods that cross international boundaries are generally free, given limits set by various nations' domestic laws, to choose the law they want to apply to their contract. That is, if a company in Kansas is buying toys from Bangladesh, the two parties can specify the law that governs their contract. They can specify that the Uniform Commercial Code of Kansas will govern the contract and that disputes will be resolved by the arbitration rules of the International Chamber of Commerce. If the parties do not specify how contract disputes are to be resolved, there are conflict-of-law rules that determine what law will be used to resolve a dispute, and what court system or arbitrator will resolve the matter. Most people would prefer to control their legal destiny, so most contracts for the sale of goods specify what law governs the contract and where disputes must be resolved. Alternatively, as we see next, many are now governed by a common set of rules.

United Nations Convention on Contracts for the International Sale of Goods

The *Convention on Contracts for the International Sale of Goods (CISG)* was adopted by the United Nations in an effort to have a commercial code that most parties would think unbiased to particular national interests. It has been ratified by most major nations, including the United States. Since CISG is a treaty adopted by Congress, it prevails over state laws such as the UCC. Contracts for the sale of goods that fall under the coverage of the CISG between a party in the United States and in another nation that adopted the CISG are resolved by the CISG. Hence, if an auto parts company in the United States buys parts from a German company, the contract is automatically governed by the CISG—unless the parties specify that they want to exclude application of the CISG, or some parts of it, and choose another law to govern.

Sales Covered by the CISG

The CISG applies to contracts for commercial sale of goods made by parties who have *places of business* in different countries that have ratified the CISG. It does not matter what the citizenship of the parties is; it is the location of the businesses that matters. Unlike the UCC, which applies to goods sold to the consuming public, contracts under the CISG only apply to commercial sales or sales between merchants. Even among merchants, certain sales are excluded from the CISG:

- Auction sales
- Consumer goods bought for personal or household use
- Contracts that are primarily for the supply of labor or of other services

Certain goods are excluded from the CISG:

- Electricity
- Ships and aircraft
- Securities such as stocks, negotiable instruments, and money

Again, parties to contracts that would normally be covered by the CISG can pick another law to govern their contract for the sale of goods, if they so desire.

Similarities to UCC

The CISG is not greatly different from the UCC or the commercial civil codes used in most nations. It is based on the business reality that many deals are not based on detailed contracts that account for all possibilities. It instructs judges to look at the plain meaning of words and to look for consistency.

Formality   Contracts need not be formal; the CISG states that "A contract of sale need not be concluded in or evidenced by writing and is not subject to any other requirements as to form. It may be proved by any means, including witnesses." Judges are told to look at the circumstances of past dealings, such as the negotiations, the practices of the parties in dealing with each other, and "any practices which they have established between themselves." However, if parties to a contract made under the CISG desire, they can insert a statement that judges are not to consider parol evidence and should not look beyond the words in the contract.

ISSUE *Spotter*

What Law Applies, and Where, to Your Contract?

Your store buys interesting articles from around the world. You try to track down unusual items that are not found in major retail chains. So you are in international commerce. You have a line of credit at a bank. It makes payments to the sellers once the goods have been accepted in the United States. But what if something goes wrong? You accept a shipment of bamboo furniture from Borneo. It looks great, the bill is paid, but three months later the furniture falls apart due to low humidity. You complain and get the runaround. The contract said nothing about jurisdiction or law. Can you sue? Where? What are you likely to do? What can you do to minimize such problems?

Offers Advertisements under the CISG are not offers that can be accepted to form a contract; they are only offers to enter into negotiations. However, offers made to "one or more specific persons" are valid offers to make a contract. Offers become effective when they reach the offeree, but can be revoked any time before acceptance is communicated.

Much like the UCC, the CISG holds that an offer "is sufficiently definite if it indicates the goods and expressly or implicitly fixes or makes provision for determining the quantity and price." When a contract does not expressly include the price, the parties are held "to have impliedly made reference to the price generally charged at the time of the conclusion of the contract for such goods sold under comparable circumstances in the trade concerned." Similarly, if there is uncertainty over a term, the courts will look to the practices "in the particular trade concerned." For example, in one case, the parties argued about what was meant by "chicken." One party claimed it meant young fryers, but the court found that industry practice meant any size cooking chicken.

Acceptance Acceptance of an offer must be made within the time stated in the offer, or, if not stated, within a reasonable time. Acceptance can be sent by any reasonable means. Any statement or conduct by the offeree to indicate acceptance is sufficient to form the contract. The acceptance is effective when it is received by the offeror, so an offer may be withdrawn up to the point the offeror receives acceptance. As with the UCC and common law, silence is normally not acceptance, but many contracts are formed by performance without stating that there will be performance. For example, if an offeror sends an order asking for 500 boxes of fried grasshoppers, the acceptance occurs when the requested act is performed.

Battle of the Forms It is common in business for orders (offers) to be sent that are accepted by the seller (offeree) returning a different standard form. When a dispute arises, the contract is based upon two forms with different terms. The CISG holds that if the differences are "material" then the second form is a counteroffer, not an acceptance, so there was no contract. Terms that are not "material" are a part of the contract unless specifically rejected by the offeror. In this sense, the CISG is less flexible than the UCC and more like the common law of contracts. Under the UCC, courts are more likely to fill in material terms than they are under the CISG.

Duties of the Parties The obligations that parties to a contract have under the CISG are very similar to those under the UCC. The seller must fulfill the obligation to deliver the goods with good title according to the terms specified, given reasonable commercial practices. If there is a problem, the buyer must notify the seller of defects "within as short a period as is practicable" after delivery. The seller may cure any defects in the delivered goods, so long as it is not costly to the buyer. If the goods are delivered properly, the buyer must take delivery and pay the price specified.

Remedies In the event of a breach of contract, parties are expected to behave in a reasonable manner and give the breaching party a notice of the alleged breach and an opportunity to cure the defect. In this sense, the CISG is like German commercial law, which requires a Nachfrist notice—a notice of the problem and a chance to perform properly—be given to the nonconforming party before suit for breach is filed. As under the common law and the UCC, if there is a failure to perform, there is an obligation to try to minimize the damages—make the best out of a bad situation so that the waste is minimized. If damages must be paid, they are usually the difference between the contract price and the value or cost incurred at the time of the breach. The *Chicago Prime* case reviews many of these issues.

Chicago Prime Packers, Inc. v. Northam Food Trading Co.
United States District Court, Northern District of Illinois, Eastern Division
320 F.Supp.2d 702 (2004)

CASE BACKGROUND *Chicago Prime is a Colorado company. Northam is a Canadian company. Both are meat product wholesalers. Chicago contracted to sell Northam 40,500 pounds of government-inspected fresh, blast-frozen pork back ribs. The price agreed on was $178,200; payment is due within seven days of shipment. The order confirmation contained a product description, price, date, and location of pickup. It did not include an inspection term. Neither party signed the invoice, but do not deny its accuracy.*

Chicago's role in the transaction was as middleman. It bought the ribs from Brookfield, a meat processor. Northam's trucking agent picked up the ribs from Brookfield's cold-storage facility. The trucker signed for the meat, acknowledging that it was "in apparent good order." It delivered the meat to Northam's customer, Beacon, which accepted the meat but noted that some boxes were gouged and the meat in those boxes showed signs of freezer burns. Chicago paid Brookfield for the meat and requested payment from Northam.

As Beacon processed the meat a week later, it thought it looked bad and contacted the inspector from the U.S. Department of Agriculture (USDA). The inspection process took over two weeks. The meat was condemned by USDA and destroyed. Beacon refused to pay Northam. Northam refused to pay Chicago Prime, which sued for payment.

CASE DECISION Brown, United States Magistrate Judge.

* * *

This court previously determined that the transaction between Chicago Prime and Northam was governed by the Convention on the International Sale of Goods ("CISG"), a self-executing agreement between the United States and other signatories, including Canada. Because there is virtually no American caselaw under the CISG, courts look to its language and to the

"general principles" upon which it is based. The Convention directs that its interpretation be informed by its "international character and . . . the need to promote uniformity in its application and the observance of good faith in international trade." Case law interpreting analogous provisions of Article 2 of the Uniform Commercial Code ("UCC"} may also inform the court where the language of the relevant CISG provisions tracks that of the UCC. However, UCC caselaw "is not *per se* applicable."

Under the CISG, "the seller must deliver goods which are of the quantity, quality and description required by the contract," and "the goods do not conform with the contract unless the. . . are fit for the purposes for which goods of the same description would ordinarily be used." CISG, Art. 36.

> Turning to the buyer's obligations, Article 38 provides:
> (1) The buyer must examine the goods, or cause them to be examined, within as short a period as is practicable in the circumstances.
> (2) If the contract involves carriage of the goods, examination may be deferred until after the goods have arrived at their destination. . . .

Furthermore, Article 39 provides:

> (1) The buyer loses the right to rely on a lack of conformity of the goods if he does not give notice to the seller specifying the nature of the lack of conformity within a reasonable time after he has discovered it or ought to have discovered it. . . .

1. Northam has failed to prove that the ribs were nonconforming at the time of transfer. . . .

Even though the rib boxes were labeled with Brookfield establishment numbers, the evidence showed that Beacon had purchased and received other loads of ribs originating from Brookfield [before this load]

continues

Furthermore, some of the ribs examined by [USDA] were stacked both horizontally and vertically. Brookfield packages its loin back ribs only horizontally. . . .

Northam has failed to carry its burden of demonstrating that the ribs that are the subject of this lawsuit were spoiled at the time [the trucking company] took possession of them. . . .

2. Northam failed to prove that it examined the ribs, or caused them to be examined, within as short a period as is practicable under the circumstances. . . .

When an issue is not addressed by the contract, the provisions of the CISG govern. Because the contract at issue did not contain an inspection provision, the requirement under the CISG that the buyer examine the goods, or cause them to be examined, "within as short a period as is practicable in the circumstances" is controlling. Decisions under the CISG indicate that the buyer bears the burden of proving that the goods were inspected within a reasonable time. . . .

Northam did not present any testimony or evidence as to why the ribs or a portion of the ribs were not and could not have been examined by Northam, Beacon, or someone acting on their behalf when the shipment was delivered to Beacon. . . .

3. Northam also failed to prove that it gave notice to Chicago Price of the alleged lack of conformity within a reasonable time after it ought to have discovered the alleged lack of conformity.

Article 39 of the CISG states that "a buyer loses the right to rely on a lack of conformity of the goods if he does not give notice to the seller specifying the nature of the lack of conformity within a reasonable time after he has discovered it or ought to have discovered it. . . .

Because this court has found that Northam failed to examine the shipment of ribs in as short a period of time as is practicable, it follows that Northam also failed to give notice within a reasonable time after it should have discovered the alleged non-conformity. . . .

CISG, Art. 74 . . . is "designed to place the aggrieved party in as good a position as if the other party had properly performed the contract." It is undisputed that Chicago Prime's loss is $178,200. . . .

The Clerk of the Court is directed to enter judgment in favor of the plaintiff Chicago Prime Packers, Inc. and against the defendant Northam Food Trading Co. in the sum of $178,200 plus $27,242.63, representing prejudgment interest calculated at a rate of 5 percent from [the day of delivery] for a total payment of $205,442.63

QUESTIONS FOR ANALYSIS
1. Why did the CISG govern this dispute?
2. How could Northam have averted this problem?

Resolving International Sales Disputes: The Dominance of Arbitration

There are very few cases in the courts ruling upon contract disputes that occur under the CISG because most commercial sales contracts specify arbitration as the required method of dispute resolution. The United Nations encourages the use of arbitration in commercial dealings through the *Convention on the Recognition and Enforcement of Foreign Arbitrable Awards*. If a country has adopted the Convention, as the United States has, then courts are bound to recognize and enforce arbitration decisions that have followed proper procedure unless it is in conflict with the law of the nation of one of the parties or has gone beyond the scope of the matter covered by arbitration. Hence, as with domestic contracts in the United States, the parties to a contract written under the CISG who mandate arbitration have little reason ever to be in court, as it is the duty of the arbitrators to resolve the dispute under the rules of the CISG.

Full Circle

Centuries ago, when merchants could not rely upon public courts for resolution of disputes and commercial law was not well developed, the law merchant developed. It was a voluntary set of rules by which merchants across national boundaries could solve disputes under a common set of rules. It was based upon the way most business was done. Disputes were resolved by a process similar to arbitration—private dispute resolution.

Over many decades, nations adopted commercial law based upon business practices. Public courts were used to resolve some disputes. As international trade has grown, the basic rules of law under which most contracts are formed is much the same whether it is the law of a particular nation, such as the UCC, or the civil code of a nation such as France, or the CISG. The rules do not vary radically from country to country.

Increasingly, merchants have turned to private dispute resolution. As with contracts made in the United States, parties know that arbitration is quicker and cheaper than court litigation. In international dealings, parties worry that they may suffer discrimination, intentional or not, if they litigate disputes in the home courts of the other parties, so neutral arbitrators are again preferred. Courts around the world have come increasingly to enforce arbitration decisions, so parties have confidence in the integrity of the international legal system.

SUMMARY

- To make contract law more consistent with business practices, the Uniform Commercial Code was developed. Article 2 of the UCC governs contracts for the sale of goods. Goods are tangible things that are movable at the time of the identification of the contract. Real estate, services, stocks, bank accounts, patents, and copyrights are not goods under the UCC. Transactions involving those things are under the common law of contracts.
- Under the UCC, merchants are subject to a higher standard of conduct than are nonmerchants. A person is a merchant if she deals, holds herself out as having special knowledge, or employs an agent, broker, or other intermediary who holds himself out as having special knowledge of the goods involved in the transaction. Merchants are required to conduct their activities in good faith and must follow business practices common in the trade.
- The common law governs a transaction unless the UCC modifies or specifically changes the effect of the common law. Generally, when the UCC modifies the common law, the effect is usually to be less demanding than the common law. An acceptance under the UCC, for example, does not have to be unequivocal to form a contract. An indefinite offer can form the basis of a contract (even with open price, quantity, delivery, or payment terms) under the UCC but not under the common law.
- The basic obligation of the seller is to transfer and deliver the goods. The buyer is obligated to accept and pay for them. In performing their obligations, in contract performance and enforcement, the parties are required by the UCC to act in good faith.
- In delivering conforming goods to the buyer, the seller is concerned with the appropriate manner and timeliness of delivery, place of tender, and the quality of tender. The UCC instructs the courts to provide such terms according to the apparent intent of the parties or the trade custom.
- The common law's perfect tender rule requires that the seller's tender of delivery conform in detail to the terms of the contract. The UCC modifies the buyer's common-law right to reject the goods by providing the seller with the right to cure defects within the time frame of the contract.

- The UCC obligates the seller to warrant title to goods being sold. The seller warrants good title, the absence of any interests or liens on the goods, and that the goods are free of any patent, copyright, or trademark infringements.
- A seller may create an express warranty under the UCC by making a statement to the buyer about the goods or by providing the buyer with a description of the goods or a sample or model of the goods.
- The UCC provides an implied warranty of merchantability and an implied warranty of fitness for a particular purpose. The good must conform to the contract description; be fit for the purposes for which it is intended; be of even kind, quality, and quantity; be adequately labeled; and conform to label descriptions. If a seller knows a buyer has a particular purpose for a good, and the buyer relies on the seller's skill or judgment in selecting a good, an implied warranty of fitness for a particular purpose may be created.
- The UCC extends to designated third parties any express warranty made by the seller to a buyer. To be consistent with other third-party beneficiary rules within a state, the UCC provides alternative rules.
- When a buyer or seller breaches a contract for the sale of goods, the UCC provides the nonbreaching party with remedies designed to place them in the same position as if the contract had been performed. The seller may recover for losses suffered due to buyer's failure to accept goods or to pay for goods. Buyer may recover the difference between what had to be paid to obtain substitute goods and the contract price. The seller and the buyer may seek incidental damages for recovery of costs resulting from the breach. The buyer is also allowed to recover consequential damages suffered, usually lost profits.
- The U.N. Convention on Contracts for the International Sale of Goods applies to contracts for commercial sale of goods by parties who have places of business in different countries that have ratified the CISG. Most major nations, including the United States, have ratified it. Such sales are covered by the CISG unless the parties specify that they want some other law to govern the contract.
- The CISG applies only to goods in commercial sales, that is, between merchants. Like the UCC, it does not require contracts to be formal writings, but gives priority to written terms in case of dispute. When terms are unclear, the courts are to look to the intent of the parties and to trade usage.
- In the event of a battle of the forms, under the CISG, when there are differences in material terms, no contract is formed; when changes are to minor terms, they may become incorporated into the contract unless objected to by a party.
- As with commercial contracts in the United States, most international commercial sale contracts include an arbitration clause. Many nations have adopted the Convention on the Recognition and Enforcement of Foreign Arbitrable Awards, so courts will uphold arbitration clauses and enforce arbitration results unless it conflicts with national policy or there was a serious problem with the arbitration process.

Review and Discussion Questions

1. Define the following terms:

sales contracts	fitness for a particular purpose
requirements contract	warranty of title
output contract	trade usage

goods   statute of frauds
merchant
merchantability

2. What is the advantage of the UCC compared to the common law of contracts? Are there disadvantages to the adoption of a statute such as the UCC?

CASE QUESTIONS

3. Cal-Cut had dealt with Idaho Pipe for years. In response to one of its ads, Idaho Pipe requested 30,000 feet of steel pipe from Cal-Cut. After phone conversations, Cal-Cut sent a written offer in August. Idaho Pipe accepted the offer by return mail, changed the delivery date from October 15 to December 15, and sent a check for $20,000 in partial payment, which Cal-Cut deposited. Cal-Cut returned confirmation of the order and did not change the October 15 delivery date, but wrote, "We will work it out" on the contract. Cal-Cut delivered 12,937 feet of pipe before October 5, which Idaho Pipe accepted. Then Cal-Cut refused to deliver any more pipe. The sale had become unprofitable, as the price of pipe had risen quickly. Was this deal enforced? Could Idaho Pipe recover any damages? [*Southern Idaho Pipe & Steel Co. v. Cal-Cut Pipe & Supply, Inc.*, 567 P.2d 1246 (Sup. Ct., Id., 1977)]

4. Polygram, a French company, makes records, tapes, and CDs. Defendant 32-03, a New York distributor, ordered goods from Polygram that were delivered in four shipments with written invoices. The invoices noted that payment was due in sixty days and that claims about problems with the goods must be made within three months after delivery. The companies had done business this way for years. 32-03's objections to the terms of sale arose for the first time in this incident. 32-03 refused to pay, claiming that there was no written contract in violation of the statute of frauds and that it was trade custom in the industry for distributors to be allowed to return any defective goods for credit. Polygram claims that the terms of the agreement were violated and sued for payment. Who was right? [*Polygram v. 32-03 Enterprises*, 697 F.Supp. 132 (E.D.N.Y., 1988)]

5. Marquette agreed to provide all cement that Norcem would need for over two years. The quantity and sales price for the first two shipments were specified in the contract. The third shipment, according to the contract, was to be negotiated for a price "not to exceed $38 per short ton." At the time of the third shipment, Marquette told Norcem the price would be $38; Norcem responded that Marquette's insistence on the maximum price was not in good faith and refused to buy the cement. Marquette sued for breach of contract. Was Marquette right? [*Marquette Co. v. Norcem, Inc.*, 494 N.Y.S.2d 511 (Sup. Ct., App. Div., N.Y., 1985)]

 Check your answer at <u>http://meiners.westbuslaw.com</u>

6. In January, T.W. Oil purchased fuel oil at sea on the tanker Khamsin. After the purchase, T.W. Oil contracted to sell the oil to Consolidated Edison (ConEd). The contract called for delivery between January 24 and 30 and for the oil to have a sulfur content of 0.5 percent. During negotiations with ConEd, T.W. Oil learned that ConEd was authorized to use oils with sulfur contents up to 1.0 percent. The Khamsin arrived on time. However, the oil tested at 0.92 percent sulfur, 0.42 percent higher than specified in the contract. On February 14, ConEd rejected the shipment. T.W. Oil offered ConEd a reduced price. ConEd rejected the lower price offer. T.W. Oil offered to cure by providing a substitute

due to arrive on February 28. ConEd rejected T.W. Oil's offer to cure. Was T.W. Oil's offer to cure properly rejected by ConEd? Was ConEd required to accept the substitute shipment tendered by T.W. Oil? [*T.W. Oil* v. *Consolidated Edison*, 443 N.E.2d 932 (Ct.App., N.Y., 1982)]

7. Community Television Services (CTS) contracted with Dresser Industries to design, construct, and install a 2,000-foot antenna tower in South Dakota for $385,000. The contract contained technical specifications warranting that the tower would withstand winds of 120 mph. During negotiations, Dresser had given CTS a sales brochure that stated:

   "Wind force creates the most critical loads to which a tower is normally subjected. When ice forms on the tower members, thereby increasing the surface area resisting the passage of wind, the load is increased. Properly designed towers will safely withstand the maximum wind velocities and ice loads to which they are likely to be subjected. Dresser . . . can make wind and ice load recommendations to you for your area based on U.S. Weather Bureau data. In the winter, loaded with ice and hammered repeatedly with gale force winds, these towers absorb some of the roughest punishment that towers take anywhere in the country . . . yet continue to give dependable, uninterrupted service."

   The tower was built according to the contract's technical specifications. Six years later, the tower collapsed during an 80-mph blizzard. Is Dresser liable for breach of an express warranty? [*Community Television Services* v. *Dresser Ind.*, 586 F.2d 637 (8th Cir., 1978)]

 Check your answer at http://meiners.westbuslaw.com

8. Hartwig Farms bought seed potatoes from Pacific, which bought them from Tobiason. The seed potatoes were stated to be "blue tag certified," meaning they were certified by the North Dakota State Seed Department not to have more than 1 percent infection with a disease that ruins potatoes. Hartwig planted the seeds, but almost the entire crop turned out to be infected. Hartwig sued for damages from the loss of the crop. Tobiason defended, noting that when the seeds were shipped the invoice had a disclaimer: "Tobiason . . . gives no warranty, express or implied, as to description, variety, quality, or productiveness, and will not in any way be responsible for the crop. All claims must be reported immediately on receipt . . . or no claim will be allowed." Hartwig claimed that this was not a part of the contract, since nothing before the actual shipment of the seeds with the invoice said anything about a disclaimer. Is the disclaimer a part of the contract? [*Hartwig Farms* v. *Pacific Gamble Robinson* v. *Tobiason Potato*, 625 P.2d 171 (Ct. App., Wash., 1981)]

9. Leavitt bought a new motor home. He told the dealer he would be driving in the mountains and wanted to be sure to have sufficient engine and brake power, which he was assured he would. He contended that there was not enough power to go uphill and the brakes overheated going downhill. Despite many warranty repairs, Leavitt concluded that the engine and brakes were not suitable and he sued for breach of implied warranty of fitness for a particular purpose under the UCC. The jury awarded Leavitt $33,730 (the vehicle was worth about $80,000). The judge also awarded Leavitt attorney fees under the Magnuson-Moss Warranty Act. Defendant appealed. Was the award justified under the UCC? [*Leavitt* v. *Monaco Coach Corp.*, 616 N.W.2d 175 (Ct. App., Mich., 2000)]

 Check your answer at http://meiners.westbuslaw.com

10. Roth went to her hairstylist of seven years to have her hair bleached. The stylist proposed using a new product from Roux Laboratories. The stylist had used

other Roux products with good results. However, the new product severely damaged Roth's hair, causing Roth embarrassment and distress until her hair grew back months later. The product's label stated that the product would not cause damage to hair. Roth sued the stylist and Roux, alleging negligence and breach of implied and express warranties. Did the product's performance breach a warranty? [*Roth* v. *Ray-Stel's Hair Stylists*, 470 N.E.2d 137 (App.Ct., Mass., 1984)]

11. ServBest Foods entered into a sales contract with Emessee. The contract called for Emessee to purchase 200,000 pounds of beef trimmings from ServBest at 52.5¢ per pound. ServBest delivered the warehouse receipts and the invoice for the beef trimmings to Emessee. The market price of beef trimmings then fell significantly, providing Emessee with the opportunity to buy the trimmings from another seller at a lower price. Emessee returned the warehouse receipts and invoice to ServBest and canceled the contract. ServBest sold the trimmings for 20.25¢ per pound and sued Emessee for damages for breach of contract plus incidental damages. Should Emessee be required to pay damages in this case? [*ServBest Foods* v. *Emessee Ind.*, 403 N.E.2d 1 (App.Ct., Ill., 1980)]

12. In 1975, NDI contracted to manufacture 1,180 metric tons of ½-inch steel strand for Grand Pre-Stressed at a price of $675 per ton. The strand is used to reinforce concrete. NDI was to deliver the strand over a seven-month period, and Grand agreed to pay for each shipment. Grand accepted deliveries of 221.1 tons and still owed $57,960 for them when it repudiated the contract in May 1976. Of the 958.9 tons of strand that remained for delivery under the contract, NDI had already produced 317.9 tons and later sold them privately to other customers at prices averaging $608.47 per ton. At all times, NDI had sufficient capacity to produce 12,500 tons of strand annually at an average cost of $394.57 per ton. NDI sued Grand for breach of contract and won. Can you calculate the damages under the UCC? [*Nederlandse Draadindustrie NDI B.V.* v. *Grand Pre-Stressed Corp.*, 466 F.Supp. 846 (E.D.N.Y., 1979)]

13. "On August 20, 1983, Elmer and Martha Bosarge purchased from J&J Mobile Homes Sales in Pascagoula a furnished mobile home manufactured by North River Homes, an Alabama corporation. The Bosarges were extremely proud of their new home—described by a J&J salesman as the 'Cadillac of mobile homes.' This 'Cadillac,' which cost the Bosarges a whopping $23,900, turned out to be a jalopy. That is, upon moving into their new home, the Bosarges immediately discovered defect after defect after defect." After arguing with North River for a year, during which time only a few repairs were made, the Bosarges refused to make further monthly payments and sued North River for selling a mobile home of unmerchantable quality. North River countered that the Bosarges could not claim to reject the mobile home when they continued to live in it. Who was right? [*North River Homes* v. *Bosarge*, 594 So.2d 1153 (Sup. Ct., Miss., 1992)]

14. Anhui, a Chinese company, contracted to sell dyed yarn to Hart, an American company. The contract contained a clause requiring arbitration of disputes before the China Council for the Promotion of International Trade in Beijing. When a dispute arose and Hart refused to pay Anhui, it began arbitration proceedings. Hart did not respond but sued Anhui in federal court in the United States. Hart claimed the arbitration clause was not enforceable because arbitration in Beijing would be a hardship and, even if it were not, the dispute was over the validity of the contract itself, an issue of contract law, not a payment dispute. Since that was a legal matter, it could be litigated. What result in federal court? [*Hart Enterprises Intl.* v. *Anhui Provincial Import & Export Corp.*, 888 F.Supp. 587 (S.D., NY, 1995)]

15. A textile mill in Bangladesh bought a large quantity of cotton from a broker in Tennessee. The contract stated that any problems with quality had to be resolved by arbitration at the Liverpool Cotton Association in England. Complaints had to be filed within two months, or the matter would not be heard. The buyer did not realize that the cotton was lower quality than paid for until six months had passed. Could it then sue under the CISG in federal court in Tennessee? [*Quasem Group, Ltd.* v. *W.D. Mask Cotton Co.*, 967 F.Supp. 288 (W.D. Tenn., 1997)]

ETHICS QUESTIONS

16. Joseph Steiner negotiated with representatives of Mobil Oil to operate a service station. During negotiations, Steiner made it clear that he would not operate the service station unless Mobil gave him a 1.4¢ per-gallon discount from the tank wagon price for ten years. However, Mobil's standard dealer contract provided that Mobil could revoke or modify the discount at any time. A Mobil representative sent Steiner a letter granting him a 1.4¢ discount for ten years. Shortly thereafter, Mobil gave Steiner a package of forms that described their agreement. Unknown to Steiner, one of the forms reduced the discount to 0.5¢ per gallon. Without looking at the agreements, Steiner signed the contract modification. What result?

17. Many U.S. retailers include in their contracts with suppliers, domestic and foreign, a requirement that the supplier agrees not to violate any local labor laws or the contract can be terminated. Yet the illegal use of child labor is common in many countries, especially in carpet making in Pakistan and in sewing operations in many countries. The retailers have been criticized as using the codes of conduct for publicity purposes, since enforcement is difficult and rare. Should such codes be used, and if so, how can they be enforced?

PULLING IT  *Together*

Sales and Arbitration

Gateway 2000 sells computers and related products by mail, Internet, and telephone. With each PC, Gateway sent a "Standard Terms and Conditions Agreement" including a "Dispute Resolution" clause, stating that any dispute would be settled by arbitration under the rules of the International Chamber of Commerce (ICC) in Chicago. Several buyers of computers and software from Gateway sued for breach of contract and breach of warranty, contending the company falsely stated that technical support for products was available when in fact, the plaintiffs claimed, it was almost impossible to get technical support by phone. The trial court dismissed the suit, holding that the parties had to go to arbitration. The plaintiffs appealed, contending that the arbitration clause violated UCC §2-302 as an unconscionable contract because ICC rules require payment of $4,000 advance fee when a claim is filed, of which $2,000 is nonrefundable regardless of outcome, and each plaintiff would have to bear the cost of travel to Chicago. These expenses are greater than the value of most of the products purchased. Is the arbitration clause valid under the UCC?

[*Brower* v. *Gateway 2000*, 676 N.Y.S.2d 569 (Sup. Ct., App. Div., N.Y., 1998)]

▨ INTERNET ASSIGNMENT

Midsummer, the air-conditioning unit at Hot Tub Heaven's (HTH) store in a busy strip mall broke. Needing to replace it or lose customers to the heat, HTH bought a new unit from Charlie's Cooling, Inc., signed a sales agreement covering the terms of the sale, and had the unit installed the next day. However, after only three weeks in service, the new unit broke on one of the hottest days in July. Although Charlie's Cooling sent a technician out to repair the unit, it repeatedly broke down over the rest of the summer and interfered with HTH's ability to run its business. HTH's owner eventually got so angry that he demanded the return of his purchase price and compensation for damages caused to his business. When Charlie's Cooling only agreed to a full refund under the terms of the parties' sales agreement limiting its obligations to repair, replacement, and refund, HTH sued.

Can HTH recover damages, or is it limited to a refund by the terms of the sales agreement? What does the Uniform Commercial Code (UCC) provide in this case? Did the remedies in the parties' sales agreement fail of their essential purpose? For answers to these questions, see the Fourth Circuit's decision in the following case: *Figgie International, Incorporated* v. *Destileria Serralles, Incorporated*, #98-1739, *http://www.findlaw.com*.

Chapter 12 | *Negotiable Instruments, Credit, and Bankruptcy*

As students, you know about student loans. Credit has never been as extensive as it is now. What's a little more debt? Some students have used student loans to finance vacations to the Caribbean and help pay for weddings. After all, when you graduate, the income will roll in to cover all that. And, if worse comes to worst, you can just file bankruptcy! So buy that car on time payments and use the credit cards that you are offered. What's the downside?

Credit and its opposite, debt, are contractual relationships. Many such contracts are common-law contracts, but some fall under the UCC. Real property, such as an office building, is usually purchased by using debt. Most companies rely on debt to get operations going or to expand. When in business, most firms extend credit to their customers. Sometimes the promises to pay are negotiable instruments that can be traded, as happens to most mortgages on property.

The downside is that each year over one million individuals and many businesses file for bankruptcy. These are debtors with financial problems that overwhelm them. Their creditors—other individuals and businesses—share the pain by being forced to absorb well over $20 billion a year in unpaid debt.

Just as managing personal finances is important, balancing the cost of carrying debt and minimizing the losses from bad credit is critical. Most businesses operate on thin profit margins, so decisions about borrowing and issuing credit are important to survival. This chapter considers the legal aspects of debt obligations and the financial instruments often used to evidence the granting of credit; it ends with a look at the major parts of the federal bankruptcy code.

NEGOTIABLE INSTRUMENTS

Like much law in the United States, the law of negotiable instruments had its origin in England. Five hundred years ago, the right to payment was a contract right; it could not be sold to another. This inhibited trade because of the difficulty it created for traders who worked on credit. Traders had to wait until they were paid by the buyer before they would have more cash to acquire more goods to sell.

To resolve this problem, laws developed that allowed traders to *assign* a promise to pay to a third party. Typically, a trader would sell a third party, at a discount, his right to payment. The trader could then buy more goods without waiting for the debtor to pay. The third party made her profit by collecting the amount owed from the debtor.

Gradually, the law recognized assignments of promises to pay. Contractual promises to pay became tradable. Negotiable instruments became something that could be bought and sold. Over the years, the law of negotiable instruments became even more responsive to the needs of business, and they are now a part of the commercial law through Article 3 of the UCC.

The Functions of Negotiable Instruments

The *negotiable instrument* began as a written promise or order to pay a certain sum of money. It functions as a substitute for cash. Few businesses today require cash in payment for all customer purchases. Because the law recognizes their validity, negotiable instruments such as checks are accepted as a substitute for cash for the payment of goods and services.

Negotiable instruments also provide a way for credit to be extended to debtors. Suppose Lynex wants to purchase new computers for its management information systems department but needs to borrow money to finance the purchase. The company may borrow the money from a financial institution by signing a negotiable instrument called a promissory note. In that note, Lynex promises to repay the money it borrows to make the purchase.

Types of Negotiable Instruments

UCC §3-104 identifies four types of negotiable instruments: drafts, checks, notes, and certificates of deposit. These instruments can be separated into two categories: orders to pay and promises to pay. Orders to pay, which include drafts and checks, are three-party instruments used instead of cash and as credit devices. Promises to pay, which include notes and certificates of deposit, are two-party instruments used as credit devices.

Orders to Pay: Drafts

A *draft*, or bill of exchange, is an unconditional written order to pay that involves three parties. It is created by one party (called the *drawer*) who orders another party (the *drawee*) to pay a certain sum of money to a third party (the *payee*). In most cases, the draft represents a debt the drawee owes to the payee. A draft may be a *time draft* or a *sight draft*. A time draft calls for a payment at a specified time in the future— for example, "60 days from date" of the draft. A common form of time draft is a *trade acceptance agreement*, an example of which is provided in Exhibit 12.1. A sight draft is payable upon presentation by the seller to the buyer of the goods. The buyer must pay the amount of the draft before receiving the goods.

Sales Draft   A *sales draft*, which is a form of the trade acceptance agreement, is a draft used when a commercial transaction involves the sale of goods. It may be either a time or a sight draft. The draft is drawn by the seller (the drawer). The purchaser of the goods accepts the responsibility of paying for the goods and becomes the drawee by signing and accepting the obligation to pay the payee—which in many cases is the seller/drawer. Normally, the draft states that payment is to be made within a specified time frame, such as "90 days after the date of the draft."

The time delay allows the buyer/drawee to use the draft as a credit device and delay payment to the seller/drawer for the period mentioned (here, 90 days). The seller/drawer may also use the document as a credit device. For instance, the seller may use the draft as collateral on a loan with third parties, since third parties have proof that the seller will be paid "90 days after the date of the draft." Exhibit 12.2 illustrates this process. Note that in the figure the seller/drawer is also the payee.

Orders to Pay: Checks

According to UCC §3-104(2), a check is a "draft drawn on a bank and payable on demand." The check is the most commonly used form of draft. However, unlike a draft—which may be payable at a later date and have a bank, an individual, or a corporation as a drawee—the check must be paid *on demand* and must have a bank as its drawee.

Cashier's Check   A *cashier's check* is one form of check in which the bank is both the drawer and the drawee. The customer gives money to the bank and designates a payee. The bank then writes a check on itself as drawee, with the check payable

Exhibit 12.1

*Sample Trade
Acceptance Document*

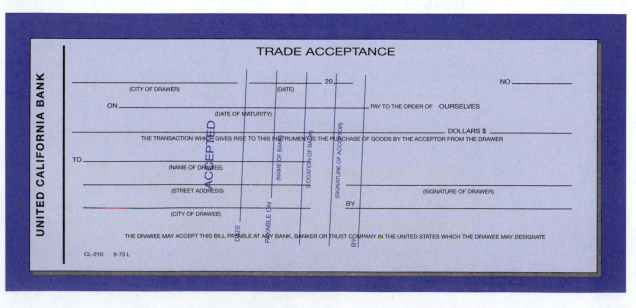

Exhibit 12.2

Sales Draft and Procedure

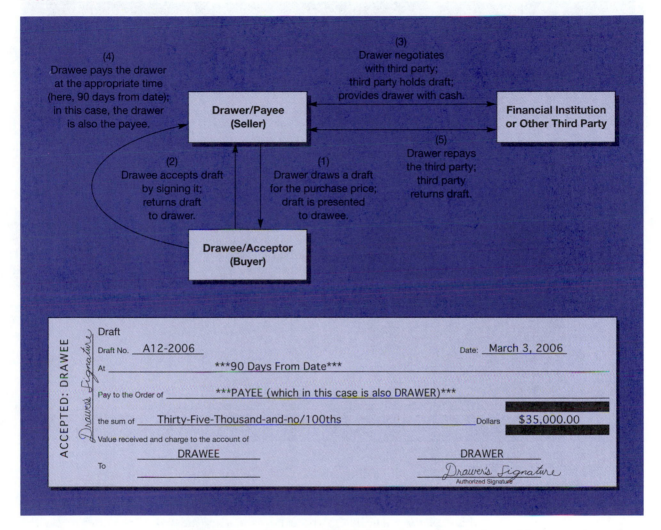

on demand to that payee. Cashier's checks are frequently used in transactions where the seller demands guaranteed payment.

An example is the purchase of real estate where the owner/seller of the property requires that a guarantee of payment occur when title to the property is to pass to the buyer. To meet the owner/seller's payment requirement, a buyer submits to the seller a cashier's check. Because the check is drawn by the bank ordering itself to pay, the seller can be secure that the bank will honor the check when it is presented.

Promises to Pay: Notes

The third classification of commercial paper is *notes*. A note is a promise (not an order) by one party (called the *maker*) to pay a certain sum of money to another party (the *payee*). Usually called *promissory notes*, these instruments involve two parties—the maker and the payee—rather than the three parties (a drawer, a drawee, and a payee) required for a draft or check. An example of a simple promissory note is provided in Exhibit 12.3.

A Sample Note

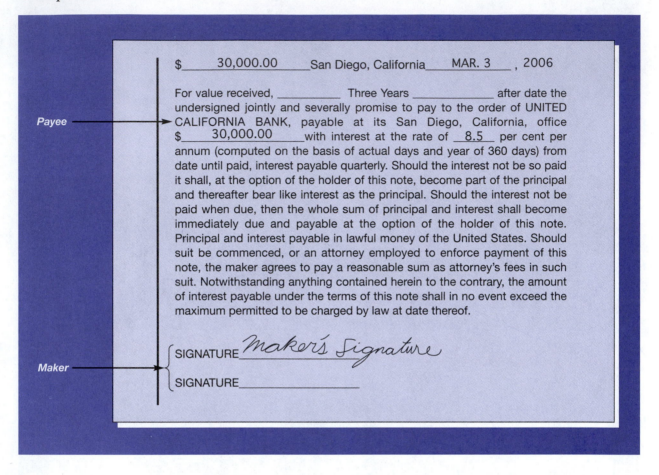

Notes can have different forms, depending upon the transactions. Most notes are promissory notes—a promise by one person to pay money to another. For example, when personal property is used as collateral to back up a loan, the note created is a *collateral note*. The party seeking the loan (the maker) promises to pay the party giving the loan (the payee) according to the loan agreement. If repayment is not made, the payee has certain rights to the personal property to help repay the loan. When real estate is used as collateral to secure the loan, the note is a *real estate mortgage note*. When the maker promises to repay the note in specified installments, the note is an *installment note*. A *balloon note* provides for installment payments but with a required final payment more than double that of the installment payments, or for one final payment of all principal.

Promises to Pay: Certificates of Deposit

The fourth type of commercial paper is a *certificate of deposit*. The UCC states that a certificate of deposit is an "acknowledgment by a bank" that it has received money from a customer with a promise by the bank that it will repay the money received at a date specified or, in some instances, on demand. The bank as maker creates the certificate and acknowledges receipt of the customer's money, promising to repay the customer as payee. Most large certificates of deposit (CDs) are negotiable, which allows them to be sold, used to pay debts, or used as collateral for a loan.

The Concept of Negotiability

Negotiable instruments are very flexible in how they are used in business. Once issued, a negotiable instrument can be transferred to another party. If the instrument is *assigned*, the assignee has the same contract rights and responsibilities as the assignor. If the instrument is transferred by *negotiation*, the transferee takes the instrument free of any of the transferor's contract obligations. This way, the transferee may have better rights than the transferor.

If an instrument is made "to bearer," the party in possession is required only to deliver the instrument to transfer it. Note that *bearer instruments* can be created in different ways. For example, the maker (drawer) may create a bearer instrument by stating: "to bearer," "to the order of bearer," "payable to bearer," "to cash," or "pay to the order of cash." Bearer instruments are risky since mere delivery creates a negotiation or transfer. Suppose a buyer of a car pays the seller by check made out "To the order of cash." Later, the seller loses the check. The check is found by Sam Jones, who uses it to buy goods from April Smith Appliances. The check has been negotiated, since delivery is sufficient for the transfer of a bearer instrument.

Requirements for Negotiable Instruments

To be negotiable, a commercial instrument must meet the requirements of a negotiable instrument as provided by the UCC. Although commercial paper may be *negotiable* or *nonnegotiable*, only negotiable instruments fall under the UCC. If the instrument is nonnegotiable, the common law of contracts applies. The assignee is subject to the assignor's contract responsibilities under the instrument. If the commercial instrument is negotiable, the UCC governs the resolution of the dispute.

The UCC Requirements

According to UCC §3-104, a negotiable instrument must meet certain requirements. It must:

1. be written.
2. be an unconditional order or promise to pay.
3. be signed by the maker or drawer.
4. be payable on demand or at a specified time.
5. be made out "to order" or "to bearer."
6. state a certain sum of money.

The UCC requires commercial instruments to be in writing for practical reasons. Oral promises would be nearly impossible to transfer to third parties. Under UCC §3-105, the writing must be signed and unconditional so the terms of payment are easily determined and not subject to the occurrence of another event or agreement. It must contain a clear statement of an order or promise to pay. UCC §3-106 requires that it must state a specific sum of money. If the instrument stated that payment was to be made in goods, for example, it would be too difficult for third parties to determine its market value. The UCC also requires that the instrument be payable on demand or at a definite time. It must make it clear when payment is to be made and received. Finally, the instrument must be "payable to order" (called *order paper*, under UCC §3-110) or "to bearer" (called *bearer paper*, under UCC §3-111) to ensure that it is freely transferable. With this language (or its equivalent), the parties acknowledge that a third party who currently may be unknown could become the owner of the instrument.

A negotiable instrument may be transferred in two basic ways according to UCC §3-202(1). If the instrument is made "to the order" of the payee, the payee must (1) endorse and (2) deliver the instrument to a third party. Endorsement without delivery cannot bring about a transfer. Therefore, if a check is made "To the order of John Tomlin," and Tomlin endorses the check but keeps it, there has not been a transfer.

Requirements for Holders in Due Course

If an instrument is negotiable under the UCC, it may be freely traded in the market without concern for other contract responsibilities—if the instrument is in the possession of a holder in due course. The person in possession of a negotiable instrument may be a *holder in due course* or an *ordinary holder*. An ordinary holder has the same contract responsibilities as an assignee under nonnegotiable instrument. UCC §3-302 states that to be a holder in due course, the transferee must

1. Give value for the negotiable instrument
2. Take the instrument without knowledge that it is overdue or otherwise defective
3. Take the instrument in good faith

Thus, a transferee may be an ordinary holder who transforms her position to that of a holder in due course upon meeting these three requirements of the UCC. The courts will require the drawer or maker to pay the instrument once it is in the possession of a holder in due course. This is the case even when a hardship may be imposed.

Suppose Pam is negotiating with Tommy to buy the rights to a J-Right Car Wash distributorship. Pam agrees to pay $50,000 by cashier's check to Tommy for the distributorship. After sending the check, Pam learns that Tommy is going bankrupt. She then tries to stop payment on the check. However, Tommy has already transferred the check to a third party, who meets the UCC's requirements for a holder in due course. Tommy declares bankruptcy, so J-Right is worthless. The bank pays the third party upon proper presentation of the check. The third party is a holder in due course and, despite the fact that Tommy defrauded Pam, the third party has no legal obligation to repay Pam. This is why the business community has confidence in negotiable instruments as a substitute for cash.

CREDIT

Not all promises to pay are negotiable instruments. Other payment arrangements are common. Whether a person or a business, a *creditor* is one who lends money to or allows goods or services to be purchased on credit by another party, the *debtor*. Businesses have credit policies that instruct employees about the factors to take into account in deciding whether credit should be granted and the terms that apply to it.

Credit terms include when the bill is to be paid, such as in thirty days for materials or over thirty years for land. Credit terms must specify the interest rate, if any, that applies to the sum owed, the *principal* of the debt, and payment dates. As discussed below, creditors want evidence of debt, such as a signed loan agreement, and may attach terms to debt that increase the chance the debt will be repaid.

While large corporations raise much of their funding by *equity financing*, that is, the sale of stock in the company, which we discuss in Chapter 20 on securities regulation, smaller businesses tend to rely on *debt financing*, which usually means borrowing money evidenced by a contract. The debt incurred by business includes long-term debt (such as financing of a building) and short-term debt (for inventory). Often, creditors will want to see debt backed by something more solid than a promise to repay the money plus interest, so we discuss some of the devices used to strengthen the position of the parties to debt.

Credit Policy

Some businesses, such as banks, are in the credit business. Other businesses extend credit as a part of operations, whether the primary purpose of the business is to provide accounting services or sell bricks. Since many businesses do not demand cash at the time of the sale of their services or products, they have policies for credit standards and terms as well as a collection policy. Credit policy focuses on such characteristics as the following:

1. Capacity (the debtor's ability to pay)
2. Capital (the debtor's financial condition)
3. Character (the debtor's reputation)
4. Collateral (the debtor's assets to secure debt)
5. Conditions (the economic situation affecting debtor's business)

Since few lenders know all there is to know about a party seeking debt, sources are available to provide information about a potential borrower (see Exhibit 12.4). Most creditors use credit reporting agencies that sell reports about individuals and companies. Some consumers' rights with respect to credit reports are specified by the Fair Credit Reporting Act (discussed in Chapter 18). For our discussion here, which focuses on business debt, an important point is that credit reports are not always accurate. Mistakes are made, and information is difficult to collect. Reputations can suffer because of incorrect business and credit information. As the *Dun & Bradstreet* case indicates, it is possible for firms that have suffered reputational injuries to recover

Exhibit 12.4 *Sources of Credit Information*	**Customer Financial Statements.** It is normal practice to require a credit applicant to supply financial information. Individuals normally will be asked to provide financial statements, whereas business applicants may also be asked to provide audited balance sheets and income statements. **Banks.** Banks may provide credit information about a customer. Credit departments of banks often share information about loan payment histories and related credit information about their customers. **Credit Reporting Agencies.** Credit reporting agencies such as Dun & Bradstreet specialize in providing credit reports and credit ratings on companies. Credit histories of individuals can be purchased from reporting agencies such as Experian, Trans Union, and Equifax. **Trade Associations.** A growing number of trade associations provide information about the credit experience of its members. The typical information provided deals with the credit obtained from suppliers and lists the amount of credit and the repayment history.

damages. However, proof of damages in practice is not simple, so firms should be vigilant about the accuracy of their credit information.

Dun & Bradstreet, Inc. v. Greenmoss Builders, Inc.

United States Supreme Court
472 U.S. 749, 105 S.Ct. 2939 (1985)

CASE BACKGROUND   *Dun & Bradstreet (D&B), a credit reporting agency, sold confidential reports to five business subscribers about the financial status of Greenmoss Builders (GB). The reports incorrectly stated that GB had filed for bankruptcy. Learning of the report, GB told D&B that the information was incorrect and asked who had received it. D&B would not reveal the names of the subscribers who had the information but issued a correction notice that GB was not bankrupt.*

GB sued D&B for defamation in Vermont state court, claiming that the false report injured its reputation. At trial, it was shown that the mistake was made by a student working at D&B who thought that the bankruptcy of an employee of GB meant that GB was bankrupt. The report was not checked before the information was sold to subscribers. The jury awarded GB $50,000 compensatory damages and $300,000 punitive damages. The trial judge overturned the jury verdict, ruling that D&B was protected by the First Amendment. The Vermont supreme court reversed, reinstating the jury verdict. D&B appealed to the Supreme Court.

CASE DECISION   Powell, Justice.

* * *

Speech on matters of purely private concern is of less First Amendment concern. . . . In such a case, "there is no threat to the free and robust debate of public issues; there is no potential interference with a meaningful dialogue of ideas. . . ."

* * *

Petitioner's credit report concerns no public issue. It was speech solely in the individual interest of the speaker and its specific business audience. This particular interest warrants no special protection when—as in this case—the speech is wholly false and clearly damaging to the victim's business reputation. Moreover, since the credit report was made available to only five subscribers, who, under the terms of the subscription agreement, could not disseminate it further, it cannot be said that the report involves any "strong interest in the free flow of commercial information." There is simply no credible argument that this type of credit reporting requires special protection to ensure that "debate on public issues will be uninhibited, robust, and wide-open."

In addition, the speech here . . . is solely motivated by the desire for profit, which, we have noted, is a force less likely to be deterred than others. Arguably, the reporting here was also more objectively verifiable than speech deserving of greater protection. In any case, the market provides a powerful incentive to a credit reporting agency to be accurate, since false credit reporting is of no use to creditors. Thus, any incremental "chilling" effect of libel suits would be of decreased significance.

We conclude that permitting recovery of presumed and punitive damages in defamation cases absent a showing of "actual malice" does not violate the First Amendment when the defamatory statements do not involve matters of public concern. Accordingly, we affirm the judgment of the Vermont Supreme Court.

QUESTIONS FOR ANALYSIS

1. In practice, few suits brought against credit reporters such as D&B by companies that had incorrect reports issued about them are successful even when false information was reported. Why would that be?

2. Many states require that for there to be damages, false information must have been intentionally reported. Is this a sensible rule, or should damages be had anytime false information is reported?

Credit Accounts

When a company gives credit to its customers, it usually offers credit terms according to the size of the account and the importance of the customer. Many accounts

Exhibit 12.5	
Common Types of Credit Accounts	**Open Account.** The most common form of credit. Goods and services are sold on an invoice that provides evidence of the transaction. Full payment is expected within a fixed time period. **Installment Account.** Generally used by consumers for the purchase of durable goods such as automobiles. Debtors repay by regular (generally monthly) payments. **Revolving Account.** Similar to the installment account except that the debtor makes a minimum monthly payment, which is generally a fraction of the outstanding balance. More debt can be added to the account over time.

do not charge interest if the debt is paid within a certain time. Exhibit 12.5 lists some basic credit accounts offered by many companies.

In most cases, credit terms are determined by competitive conditions or industry standards. For credit under an *open account*, for example, the terms define the credit period available to the customer and any discounts offered for early payment. A typical industry standard is "net 60 days" from the date of invoice with a discount of 2 percent if paid within ten days of invoice. Consumer credit accounts—installment and revolving accounts—state the interest rate to be paid and the timing of the payments.

Collections Policy

Most bills are paid on time. However, a collections policy is needed for debtors that fail to make timely payments. This usually begins with a letter stating that the account is past due. A telephone call or a second letter may then follow. Depending on the business, letters may be followed by a personal visit.

At times, additional action is necessary to protect the creditor's rights. The alternatives depend on whether the business is an unsecured or a secured creditor. In most transactions, the lender is an *unsecured (general) creditor:* it holds little more than the customer's promise to pay. If the customer proves to be *insolvent*—unable to pay—the business receives nothing. If the customer simply will not pay, legal actions

INTERNATIONAL *Perspective*

The Check Is in the (Foreign) Mail

Your widget company, always looking for new markets, gets a large order for widgets from a company in Kabul, Afghanistan. Odds are the company cannot pay you until after it sells the goods. What if it defaults? Are you going to take it to court in Kabul?

How long it takes a business to pay for goods or services often depends on the state of the economy. When times are good, bills get paid faster. An electric motor company, Baldor, in Fort Smith, Arkansas, was doing well in Mexico until the economy there took a nosedive. The Mexican sellers' market dried up, so the motor sellers were not getting the cash

needed to pay Baldor. To compound problems, the Mexican peso fell in value. It took a year of effort, but most accounts were put back into business. Working with good customers to get their business going again paid off.

Payment also depends on where you are doing business and what the traditional practices are in various countries. For example, a European business survey by the firm Grant Thornton showed that the average length of time for payment in the Netherlands was forty-seven days; in Italy it was almost twice as long, ninety days. The longer the time, the higher the costs of carrying the accounts.

will have to be considered. Next we consider ways to make more formal credit agreements.

CREDIT WITH SECURITY

In contrast to being an unsecured creditor, a business is a *secured creditor* when it has the ability to take the nonpaying customer's property to satisfy the debt. The law provides two avenues through which the creditor can obtain the customer's property (referred to as *security* or *collateral*):

1. By agreement with the debtor
2. By operation of law, and without an agreement between the lender and the borrower

By Agreement

The nature of the credit agreement depends upon whether the debtor's property is *real property* (real estate or other immovable property) or *personal property* (movable goods such as vehicles and supplies). The distinction between real and personal property is important for several reasons. The sale of goods is governed by the Uniform Commercial Code (discussed in Chapter 11). The sale of personal property can take place with relatively little or no formal documentation. On the other hand, real property is governed by contract and property law and requires documentation before a sale can be finalized. The agreement providing security in real property is a *mortgage* and is examined later.

Suretyship

Businesses often need to raise funds (working capital) to operate and expand. Small businesses frequently must provide a *guaranty* or *suretyship* for major debts. If a business has a poor credit history, it may be required to provide a guaranty or suretyship for virtually any borrowing it would like to do.

For most small businesses, such a guaranty may be a pledge of personal assets by the owners. In addition, a third party may provide the guaranty or suretyship. In either case, a promise is made to pay a debt of a business in the event the business does not pay. In this way, a suretyship or guaranty is created, and the credit of the party providing it becomes the security for the debt owned.

ISSUE
Spotter

Helping a Dream?

Your sister has opened her own store, fulfilling her dream. The store looks great and customer traffic seems good, but the up-front costs are high. She is deep in debt and needs more credit to keep the store stocked well. The cash flow looks good and she believes, based on the trend and revenues, that within a year she will be turning a profit. To get more credit at a decent interest rate, she needs help. She asks you and your parents to co-sign for an extension on her line of credit from a bank. She will sign a contract holding herself primarily liable on the debt and liable to you in case anything goes wrong. Is there much of a risk here? What is the downside?

JURIS *prudence?*

So, Do We Write This Off as a Bad Loan?

Clancy and Ken Smith, newly married, bought a car. Since their credit was limited, Clancy's father co-signed the car loan from Trustmark Bank in Laurel, Mississippi. The couple fell behind on the loan, and the bank sent a tow truck to repossess the car. Clancy's parents made the needed payments to cover the loan to get the car back.

After five years, the loan was paid. But then the Smiths received a bill for $9,500. The bank had bought car insurance for them—at three times the normal price—when they let their insurance lapse in violation of the terms of the loan.

The Smiths and Clancy's father sued the bank. The jury awarded the Smiths and Clancy's father $19 million each. "We wanted to send a message to the insurance companies and financial institutions to straighten their act up," the jury foreman said.

Source: *The Wall Street Journal*

Surety Defined   A contract for *suretyship* is a promise by a third party (the *surety*) to be responsible for the borrower's payment (or *performance*) obligations to a creditor. The borrower or debtor is referred to as the *principal*. In addition to being a party providing a suretyship for a fee (or out of kindness), the surety could be an owner or shareholder in the business. A suretyship can be created only by an express contract between the surety and the creditor and, as such, is governed by the principles of contract law. The surety is obligated to pay the creditor if the principal fails to pay the debt (or provided performance) to the creditor. A common form of suretyship is a cosignature on a bank loan.

A *guarantor* provides a guarantee of payment to another and therefore is the same as surety. That is, to guarantee is to assume the obligation of a surety. In some states, the distinction between a guaranty and a surety is that a surety is primarily liable after the debtor, whereas the guarantor is secondarily liable. Generally, one contract binds both the surety and the borrower, and the creditor is not obligated to exhaust legal remedies before demanding payment by the surety. In other states, the guarantor can be obligated to pay only after the creditor has exhausted legal remedies against the borrower and any surety.

Defenses of Sureties   Since suretyship is governed by contract law, the contract defenses available to the principal also are available to the surety. Depending whether the suretyship governs the borrower's performance or payment obligations, contract defenses available include impossibility, illegality, duress, and fraud—but not bankruptcy (because the surety is providing financial protection to the creditor for just such an event). A surety also has a defense that it is released when the creditor releases the borrower without its consent. Similarly, the surety is released if material changes are made to the original contract between the creditor and the debtor without its consent.

When in a bind, small-business owners might take extraordinary financial risks, particularly when they believe in their company's future. When creditors push the business for payment and the future of the firm is in jeopardy, the owners may use personal assets to meet the demands of the creditors. Care should be taken in the use of such personal assets. In the *Hill Roofing* case we see an innocent party suffering a loss for failure to follow the proper procedures regarding a guaranty.

Hill Roofing Co. v. Lowe's Home Centers, Inc.
Court of Appeals of Georgia
265 Ga.App. 822, 595 S.E.2d 638 (2004)

CASE BACKGROUND   *Raymond Hill owned Hill Roofing Company. He had a business charge account at Lowe's. He executed a Personal Guaranty Agreement, guaranteeing the payment of all sums due to Lowe's on Hill Roofing's account. Two years later, Hill sold his company to two employees. He owed no money on the Lowe's account. Two years after that, the new owners had run up a $9,215 bill at Lowe's in the Hill Roofing account and did not pay, so a judgment was entered against the company. Lowe's then sued Hill to pay the money due based on the guaranty agreement.*

Hill testified that when he sold the company he told a Lowe's representative he wanted the account closed. Lowe's testified that it never received any notification of a change in the status of the account. The trial court entered judgment for Lowe's for the amount due, interest, and attorney fees, for a total of $12,949. Hill appealed.

CASE DECISION   Mikell, Judge.

* * *

The agreement provided, in pertinent part, and in bold lettering, as follows:

Where the term of this Guaranty is not limited by applicable law, this Agreement will remain in full force and effect until revoked in the manner set forth below. . . . Any revocation of this Guaranty Agreement shall be in writing and delivered to Vice President—Credit Management, Lowe's Companies, Inc., P.O. Box 1111, North Wilkesboro, NC 28656 via U.S. POSTAL SERVICE . . . certified mail, return receipt requested. . . .

No evidence was introduced to show that Lowe's consented to revocation of the guaranty on any terms other than those specified therein. . . . .

"Under the rules of contract construction, where the language in an agreement is clear and unambiguous, no construction is required or permitted by the trial court." The guaranty was unambiguous, and by his own admission, Hill failed to comply with its provision governing notice of revocation.

Judgment Affirmed.

QUESTIONS FOR ANALYSIS
1. Could Hill have protected himself if, when he sold his company, he inserted a clause into the sale agreement making it clear that the new owners were solely responsible for all debts incurred?
2. Suppose a Lowe's employee testified that Hill had told him that he wanted the account closed, and he said OK, but then did nothing?

Surety's Rights against the Principal   In the event the principal (borrower) does not meet its payment obligations to the creditor and the surety has to satisfy the debt, the principal is obligated to repay the surety. If the borrower could pay the creditor but refuses to do so, the surety is entitled to *exoneration*, a court order requiring the principal to pay. In addition, the surety is entitled to be *subrogated* to the rights of the creditor against the debtor. This generally occurs when the creditor is satisfied but part of that satisfaction came from the surety. In seeking reimbursement from the principal, the surety may assert any rights the creditor could have asserted against the debtor had it not paid the creditor in the absence of the surety, including taking any security interests the creditor obtained from the borrower.

Secured Transactions

The law governing the financing of commercial sales of goods is *Article 9* of the UCC. When a good is sold to a customer (either a person or a business), the UCC provides that the product itself may secure the consumer's obligation to pay. Called a *secured transaction*, it occurs when a buyer wants a good and does not pay cash or have sufficient credit standing to obtain the good on open credit, which would be unsecured debt. By meeting the requirements of the UCC, the seller obtains a *security interest* in the goods sold to the customer to secure payment of all or part of the sales price.

Attachment   To make the security interest enforceable, the seller must create the interest (or legal right) and make sure that the interest is *attached* and *perfected*. According to the UCC, for a security interest to attach, the security agreement must be signed by the customer, the seller must have provided value, and the customer must have legal, transferrable rights in the collateral. If the customer is unable to pay, the seller has rights against the customer that are superior to unsecured creditors, but not necessarily superior to other secured creditors and certain other creditors.

Perfection   To establish superior rights—that is, to *perfect* the security interest— the creditor must give notice to others of the existence of the security interest. The primary way to perfect is to file the financing statement with the secretary of state or other relevant official so it is available for public inspection. This process must be followed unless the goods being sold are consumer goods. Under the UCC, a security interest for consumer goods is perfected without filing. Normally, the financing statement contains little more than the names and addresses of the firm and the customer, a description of the product, and the signature of the customer. The details of the credit transaction, including the amount financed, the payment schedule, interest rate, and other such matters, are left to the security agreement. A seller's retail installment contract is a typical security agreement. Consumer debt is covered in Chapter 18.

Interests in Inventory   As collateral, supplies such as equipment, inventory, and raw materials can be classified as *tangible property*—goods that are movable at the time a security interest attaches (begins). To protect its interests, the lender extending credit to a business obtains a security interest, sometimes called a purchase money security interest. The procedure is nearly the same as the procedure followed by the business when it extends credit to customers buying its product. As in that case, the security interest gives the lender rights against the borrower—rights that are superior to other creditors in the event the borrower fails to meet its debt obligations.

A "Floating Lien" for Inventory   Under the UCC, *inventory* includes goods held for sale as well as raw materials, and work in process. Inventory is constantly changing. This could create a problem for a creditor that provides financing to a business with inventory as collateral. To avoid the need to renew the financing contract every time something is sold or used, the UCC allows a perfected security interest in property acquired after the security agreement is formed. This permits a *floating lien*. The security interest in any specific item of inventory ends upon the item's sale or use, but attaches to new inventory.

Default by the Debtor

A security interest helps to protect the interests of the seller in the event the customer *defaults*, that is, cannot or will not meet its payment obligations. Because the seller has a security interest in the product, it has *priority* to the product over other, unsecured creditors.

The UCC provides that when repossessing a product, "a secured party may proceed without judicial process if this can be done without breach of peace." That is, if you do not make payments on your car, it can be repossessed. In taking possession of such goods, the seller is not obligated to notify other parties who also may have a security interest in the product. The creditor may either keep the product or resell it. If the product is resold, it must be sold in a "commercially reasonable manner." Any proceeds generated in excess of what is owed must be returned to the customer.

Default by a debtor usually affects more than one party. Repossession may or may not be possible, and in searching for funds to repay the debt, creditors commonly argue over who is eligible for whatever funds are available. The UCC, like the bankruptcy code, helps to determine who gets what when a debtor cannot satisfy all creditors. As the *Peerless Packing* case discusses, creditors must follow the rules regarding securing debt or they can be left with nothing.

Peerless Packing Co. v. Malone & Hyde, Inc.

Supreme Court of Appeals of West Virginia
180 W.Va. 267, 376 S.E.2d 161 (1988)

CASE BACKGROUND *Kizer managed a PIC PAC grocery store owned by Malone & Hyde (M&H). He negotiated with M&H to buy the store. The agreement included a price of $200,000 for equipment, $187,000 for inventory, subleasing the store building, and maintaining the name PIC PAC. Kizer provided $50,000 for working capital and gave M&H a promissory note for $387,000, which was secured by a security interest in the present and after-acquired inventory. The lien against the collateral was perfected.*

Kizer continued to receive groceries from the twelve companies that are appellants in this case. The suppliers delivered goods several times a week on open account credit. None of the suppliers obtained purchase money security interests in the inventory they supplied to Kizer. Such a security interest would have given them priority over M&H's security interest in the inventory.

In less than a year, Kizer was in trouble and could not keep up on his payments. He signed a Notice of Default and Transfer of Possession Agreement that transferred all of his rights in the store, equipment, inventory, and the store's bank account ($64,000) to M&H, which released Kizer from any liability on his debts. M&H took ownership and hired Kizer as manager.

M&H (appellee here) notified the twelve grocery suppliers that it was the new owner of the store and that it would not pay any invoices for deliveries made prior to the date M&H assumed ownership. Peerless and the other

suppliers sued M&H on a theory of unjust enrichment. The trial court granted M&H a directed verdict. Plaintiffs appealed.

CASE DECISION Neely, Justice.

* * *

Appellants . . . contend that appellee was unjustly enriched by the transfer because appellee, knowing it was going to foreclose on the store, allowed appellants to continue to deliver goods for a week before appellee took over. . . .

Appellants also argue that . . . the inventory was sold in the ordinary course of the store's continuing business under ownership of appellee and the store's equipment was retained by appellee. Appellants argue that if a foreclosure sale had taken place, there might have been enough money to pay off some or all of the debt to appellants.

Appellee responds that the $64,000 cash represented "identifiable proceeds" from the sale of the inventory and, therefore, under UCC 9-306(2), the cash was collateral for their security interest. . . . Appellee argues that it was entitled to keep the collateral and that it got no more than it was owed by Mr. Kizer. In fact, appellee insists that it "lost" about $130,000 through the transfer. . . .

We agree with the trial court's order and affirm his ruling with regard to appellants' equitable unjust enrichment claim. As the Oregon Supreme Court [held in a case], although the result of disallowing an unjust enrichment claim in such a case may appear harsh, the unsatisfied creditors (appellants in the case before us) could have protected themselves either by demanding cash payment for their goods, or by taking a purchase money security interest in the goods they delivered. . . .

With regard to the $64,000 cash, UCC 9-306(2) provides that a security interest continues in "any identifiable proceeds" from the sale or exchange of collateral. Because this cash was from the store's bank account, it was clearly proceeds from the sale of the collateral, and appellee had a security interest in it as well. . . .

Because appellants were general unsecured creditors, they have no right under Article 9 to object to appellee's retention of the collateral in satisfaction of the debt.

Affirmed.

QUESTIONS FOR ANALYSIS

1. What could the appellants (grocery suppliers) have done to help prevent this situation?

2. The suppliers are saying that M&H's action was unethical. Do courts let companies get away with action such as M&H's in this matter?

Property Exempt from Attachment

As discussed, it is not uncommon for business owners to pledge personal assets as security for the debts of the business (for example, as a surety). If the business is not able to pay, the creditor may have assets pledged as collateral seized and sold to repay the debt. If the debt is not fully paid after the sale, the creditor may sue the owners for the rest of the debt. To protect its interests, the creditor may ask the court for an attachment. After the judgment has been rendered and the owner is unable (or unwilling) to pay, the creditor may ask the court for a writ of execution.

The creditor moves against the owner's *nonexempt property*. That is, most states provide that certain real and personal property are *exempt* from attachment proceedings. In the interest of ensuring that a debtor has housing, for example, states provide a *homestead exemption*, which, depending on the state, allows the debtor to retain the family home entirely or up to a specified amount free from creditors' claims. The same thing is true in bankruptcy. With regard to personal property, state statutes provide limited exemptions for, among other things, furniture, clothing, automobiles, and tools used in the debtor's trade or business.

Real Estate Financing

For most businesses, buying real estate involves a large outlay of money. Normally, much of the purchase price is borrowed. The real estate itself is used to secure the debt obligation and is evidenced by a *mortgage*. In most states, the mortgage is a lien that gives the lien holder the right to sell the property and repay the debt from sale proceeds in the event the borrower defaults. The debtor is the *mortgagor*, and the creditor is the *mortgagee*. Such transactions are governed by state common law and real estate statutes because the UCC does not apply to real estate.

The Mortgage

According to the Statute of Frauds, a mortgage must be in writing. In most states, a concise form such as that shown in Exhibit 12.6 is recognized by statute. In meeting the requirements of such documents, the mortgage contains a description of the

Exhibit 12.6

Sample Mortgage Agreement

Mortgage
(New York Statutory Form)

This mortgage, made the _____ day of _____, 20_____, between _____, [*insert residence*], the mortgagor, and _____ [*insert residence*], the mortgagee.

Witnesseth, that to secure the payment of an indebtedness in the sum of _____ dollars, lawful money of the United States, to be paid on the _____ day of _____, 20 _____, with interest thereon to be computed from _____ at the rate of _____ per centum per annum, and to be paid _____, according to a certain bond or obligation bearing even date herewith, the mortgagor hereby mortgages to the mortgagee [*description*].

And the mortgagor covenants with the mortgagee as follows:

1. That the mortgagor will pay the indebtedness as hereinbefore provided.

2. That the mortgagor will keep the buildings on the premises insured against loss by fire for the benefit of the mortgagee; that he will assign and deliver the policies to the mortgagee; and that he will reimburse the mortgagee for any premiums paid for insurance made by the mortgagee on the mortgagor's default in so insuring the buildings or in so assigning and delivering the policies.

3. That no building on the premises shall be removed or demolished without the consent of the mortgagee.

4. That the whole or said principal sum and interest shall become due at the option of the mortgagee: after default in the payment of any installment of principal or of interests for _____ days; or after default in the payment of any tax, water rate or assessment for _____ days after notice and demand; or after default after notice and demand either in assigning and delivering the policies insuring the buildings against loss by fire or in reimbursing the mortgagee for premiums paid on such insurance, as hereinbefore provided; or after default upon request in furnishing a statement of the amount due on the mortgage and whether any offsets or defenses exist against the mortgage debt, as hereinafter provided.

5. That the holder of this mortgage, in any action to foreclose it, shall be entitled to the appointment of a receiver.

6. That the mortgagor will pay all taxes, assessments or water rates, and in default thereof, the mortgagee may pay the same.

7. That the mortgagor within _____ days upon request in person or within _____ days upon request by mail will furnish a written statement duly acknowledged of the amount due on this mortgage and whether any offsets or defenses exist against the mortgage debt.

8. That notice and demand or request may be in writing and may be served in person or by mail.

9. That the mortgagor warrants the title to the premises. In Witness Whereof, this mortgage has been duly executed by the mortgagor.

property, sets forth any warranties relative to the property, states the debt, and states the mortgagor's duties concerning taxes, insurance, and repairs. To protect the mortgagee's rights against other creditors, the mortgage should be *recorded*. State statutes typically require that the mortgage be placed in a county office, often called the Recorder's Office or the Register of Deeds.

Default by the Mortgagor

If the borrower is unable to pay the mortgage, the mortgagee has the right to foreclose on the property. Foreclosure may be by judicial sale. As in all such situations, if the proceeds of the sale are sufficient to cover the costs of the foreclosure and the debt, any surplus must be returned to the mortgage holder. If the proceeds are not sufficient, the mortgagee can seek to recover the remainder from the debtor by obtaining a *deficiency judgment*, obtained in a separate legal action after the foreclosure. In many states, a mortgagor has the right to redeem the property by paying the debt within the *statutory redemption* period, normally within six months to a year after the default.

Liens

Security obtained by a creditor through the operation of law is called a *lien*. Because it may be obtained by the seller without a specific agreement with the customer, the security may be called a nonconsensual lien. The term *lien* is derived from the French language and means "tie" or "string." The legal meaning for lien is the legal right the seller has to the product now held by a customer. The lien helps to secure payment for goods or services, such as repairs.

The procedures for using liens are determined by state common law and state statutes. The most common liens are the mechanic's lien (applicable to real property), the possessory lien (applicable to personal property), and court-decreed liens. In each case, a creditor may obtain the lien without the debtor's consent by following statutory procedures. An additional remedy, *garnishment*, is a statutory procedure under which a creditor gains the right to attach up to 25 percent of a customer's net wages to be applied to an outstanding debt.

Lean on a Lien?

ISSUE *Spotter*

Your concrete company is offered a chance to get in on a huge construction project at a new shopping center that will last for two years. If it goes as planned, you will be able to more than double the size of your operation, allowing you to compete for more large-scale jobs. The builder will hire you as a subcontractor and the price offered is fair. But the builder will not pay you, or the other subcontractors, until he is paid. So you will have to carry some debt as the project goes along. The contractor points out that the risk to you is minimal since the scale of the project is huge and you are involved in only a small part of the total cost. Besides, he says, if there is a problem in your getting paid, you can slap a lien on the whole project. Would this action give you adequate protection? Is the gamble worth it?

Mechanic's Lien

A *mechanic's lien* is the most common lien on real property. The party that furnished material, labor, or services for the construction or repair of a building or other real property can place a lien on the property for unpaid bills. The creditor must follow the steps the law requires be taken within a certain time. The requirements vary from state to state; some states require preliminary notice to the debtor before the lien is filed. Upon filing the lien, the creditor obtains security for the debt.

If the owner of the real property does not pay the lien, the creditor can move to force the sale of the property to satisfy the debt. Obviously, the debtor must be notified that the property is going to be sold. In some states, such a sale must take place within twelve months of the original filing. If no action is taken within twelve months, the lien expires and cannot be revived.

Possessory Lien

The *possessory lien* or *artisan's lien* is the most common lien on personal property. It provides a security interest for creditors that add value to or care for personal property. This lien offers the right to continue to hold goods on which work has been done, or for which materials have been supplied, until the customer pays. The business doing the work must have the property in its possession, and it must have agreed to provide the work on a cash basis. The lien stays in existence as long as the creditor retains possession, unless the lien is filed according to the requirements of a state's lien and recording statutes. In that way, the creditor gives notice of the existence of the lien to others and protects its interests if the customer is in possession of the property.

If the customer does not pay for the work or supplies, the creditor can force the sale of the property to fulfill payment of the debt. As with the mechanic's lien, the debtor must have prior notice of the sale. Having a valid lien does not always mean payment can be extracted. Businesses often contribute to enterprises that fail, as the *Kesco* case discusses.

Kesco, Inc. v. Brand Banking Company

Court of Appeals of Georgia
603 S.E.2d 49 (2004)

CASE BACKGROUND   *Tumlin Development received a $1.5 million loan from Brand Banking. The promissory note was secured by real property Tumlin intended to develop into a subdivision, Creekside Estates. Tumlin hired Kesco to perform rock-blasting work on the property. Kesco performed $89,000 worth of services. Soon, Tumlin informed Kesco that it could not pay the bill. Kesco filed a materialman's lien on the property. Other subcontractors, who also had not been paid, filed materialman's liens.*

Tumlin attempted to sell some lots in the subdivision to raise cash, but the liens against the property exceeded the purchase price of each lot, so the sales did not go through. The bank, whose mortgage had first priority over other lienholders, stepped in.

The bank could foreclose on the property, thereby receiving payment for its loan and wiping out the lower-priority liens, such as Kesco's. But, in an effort to keep a good reputation with subcontractors in the community, the bank proposed to let Tumlin keep working to sell the lots and use the proceeds to pay each lienholder at least some amount as each lot sold. The lienholders had to remove their liens before each sale to allow the buyers to obtain clear title.

Kesco and the others agreed. Eleven lots were sold, so each lienholder got something. Kesco received about $18,000. Tumlin determined that it could not proceed as it was way over budget. The bank determined that the sales could not cover all debts, so it foreclosed its mortgage. Kesco received no further payments and sued the bank, contending that it breached a contract in which it promised not to foreclose on the property. The trial court held for the bank. Kesco appealed.

CASE DECISION   Blackburn, Presiding Judge.

* * *

It is undisputed that, at all times, the Bank maintained a superior lien on the property and could have destroyed Kesco's lien at any point via foreclosure. It is further undisputed that, at the time that the agreement between the lienholders was reached, it was based on an assumption that all 60 lots in Creekside Estates would successfully be developed and would generate a certain amount of revenue. At the time the Bank foreclosed, Tumlin was operating at a net loss such that the completion of the subdivision was no longer possible and any future sales would not generate enough income to pay off existing lienholders even at their reduced amounts. At no time did the Bank promise not to foreclose under any circumstances; it simply promised to pay certain funds to Kesco if and when properties were successfully developed and sold and Kesco removed its lien. The agreement extended no further.

In light of these facts, we cannot say that the trial court erred in granting summary judgment to the Bank.

Judgment affirmed.

QUESTIONS FOR ANALYSIS

1. Was there anything else Kesco could have done to protect itself?

2. Did the bank profit at the expense of the lien-holders?

Court-Decreed Liens   When a debt is past due, the creditor may sue the debtor. Creditors prefer alternatives to litigation for collections because of the time and expense involved. If it is necessary to use the court system, creditors will find attachment and judgment liens as judicial means to try to protect their interests.

An *attachment lien* is a court-ordered seizure of goods from the customer to prevent the customer from disposing of it during the lawsuit. Under state statute, the requirements imposed on the creditor are specific and limited. To obtain an attachment lien, the business must show that the debtor is likely to dispose of the product. If the court concurs, it issues a *writ of attachment* directing the sheriff to seize the good. It is important for the creditor to follow state attachment procedures closely or it could be liable for damages for wrongful attachment.

If the creditor is successful in an action against the debtor, the court awards a *judgment lien*. No lien is created simply by the rendering of a court judgment. Rather, the creditor must obtain an *abstract of judgment*, which, when prepared, recorded, and indexed creates a lien against the debtor's real property and provides notice to potential purchasers of the property of the existence of the judgment and lien. Normally, a lien holds for ten years.

If the debtor does not pay the judgment, the creditor asks the court to issue a *writ of execution*. The writ is issued by the clerk of the court and directs the sheriff to seize and sell any of the debtor's nonexempt real or personal property within the court's jurisdiction.

BANKRUPTCY

Financial ruin comes to many in the marketplace. Some consumers and businesses engage in fraud, causing financial messes that others pay for, but most bankruptcies are due to bad luck or unintentional mismanagement. A person or a business is not able to pay debts that are due, usually because liabilities exceed assets and at least some creditors will not extend the time for payment, so something must be done to resolve the financial mess. A study by Dun & Bradstreet attributed 93 percent of business failures to "management incompetence." Bankruptcy is not a new issue; the framers of the Constitution thought it such an important issue that they specifically made bankruptcy a matter of federal law.

The *Bankruptcy Reform Act* of 1978, generally called the *bankruptcy code*, has been amended several times, and is the key statute that governs bankruptcy procedure. That is, it states how matters are resolved when debts are greater than assets available. Since over one and one-half million people file for bankruptcy each year, and over 35,000 businesses file bankruptcy, it is a significant issue. We review the major types of bankruptcy and then discuss nonbankruptcy choices for distressed debtors.

Chapter 7

Chapter 7 of the bankruptcy code is the most commonly used alternative, accounting for over one million a year. It means liquidation and fair distribution of the debtor's assets for the creditors. Liquidating bankruptcy under Chapter 7 is available for corporations and other businesses, but, as we will see, only individuals can use Chapter 7 to obtain discharge.

Most Chapter 7 bankruptcies are filed voluntarily by the debtor. A petition is filed with the bankruptcy court, which may be the federal district court or a federal bankruptcy court. The filing is a statement of the financial affairs of the debtor, including a listing of all assets and liabilities, using specific forms. The petition provides the following:

- Statement of the financial affairs of the debtor
- List of all creditors and their addresses, with amounts owed
- List of properties owned by debtor
- Statement of current income and expenses of debtor

The filing of this petition means that an immediate freeze (an automatic stay) is made against all actions against the debtor or a debtor's property by any creditors. A temporary *trustee* is appointed to administer the debtor's estate. The trustee meets with the creditors within about a month to review the accuracy of the information provided by the debtor. The creditors usually approve formal appointment of the temporary trustee as the trustee. In an *involuntary bankruptcy*, creditors file a petition with the court, forcing the declaration of bankruptcy and the beginning of proceedings.

ISSUE Spotter

Credit for the Bankrupt?

Some credit issuers have a policy of offering credit to people who have just gone through bankruptcy. Having had their debts cleared, they are not allowed to file for bankruptcy again for years. Are these folks in fact good credit risks because they cannot file for bankruptcy?

The Bankruptcy Proceeding

A key feature of bankruptcy is the emphasis on creditors' receiving fair treatment. Under the federal system, once bankruptcy has been declared, a creditor cannot improve its position by getting to the debtor's property first. Nor can the debtor improve a favored creditor's position by transferring property to that creditor. It is the trustee's job to assure that no creditor has improved its relative position. Some creditors may have learned of the debtor's financial plight and then gained control of some of the debtor's property. Hence, bankruptcy proceedings hold that such transfers of debtor's property within ninety days of bankruptcy are void.

Role of the Trustee

The trustee's objective is to maximize the amount of the debtor's assets available for distribution to the creditors. However, as noted earlier, some of the debtor's property

Fine Food Does Not Always Pay

A successful Hooters restaurant in Augusta, Georgia, was forced into bankruptcy by creditors seeking their $11.9 million jury verdict against the dining establishment. The eatery had sent unsolicited faxes advertising its bill of fare to over 1,000 potential customers. Federal law prohibits such faxes and penalizes each fax sent.

A Hooters executive said that Congress could not possibly have intended such a large penalty for a company that just sends "a few pieces of paper out of a fax machine."

Source: *New York Times*

---

is *exempt* from bankruptcy. Normally, states exempt the debtor's house, household furnishings, car, and tools of trade. The trustee is required to liquidate all the debtor's nonexempt property. The *liquidation* takes place through a sale at a public auction unless otherwise ordered by the court. After the property has been sold, the proceeds are disbursed among the creditors. All creditors holding a claim against the debtor are entitled to share in the distribution of the sales proceeds.

Priority Classes of Creditors

Bankruptcy law states that certain creditors take priority over other creditors in receiving shares of the debtor's assets to pay for the debts owed them. Standing first in line are *secured creditors*. As discussed previously, these creditors have a written security agreement that describes the property (collateral) that stands behind a particular debt. For a consumer, the most common would be a home mortgage or an automobile loan. In bankruptcy, the secured creditor may request that the court grant permission for it to take possession of the property covered by the debt. The *priority classes* in bankruptcy usually are as follows:

1. Secured creditors
2. Costs of preserving and administering the debtor's estate
3. Unpaid wage claims
4. Certain claims of farmers and fishermen
5. Refund of security deposits
6. Alimony and child support
7. Taxes
8. General (unsecured) creditors who can file a proof of claim

All the creditors of a particular class must be paid before the next-lower-priority creditors can be paid anything. Rarely is enough money received from the sale to pay general creditors what they are owed.

Discharge in Bankruptcy

The final stage of the bankruptcy proceeding for individuals is the *bankruptcy discharge*. Discharge means that the nonexempt assets are liquidated and the proceeds distributed among the creditors, who may not ask for more. The claimants are paid according to their priority, so unsecured credits are rarely paid and even secured creditors may get very little. The books have been cleared. The debtor gets a fresh

INTERNATIONAL   *Perspective*

Bankruptcy Efficiency around the World

Critics of the Bankruptcy Code in the United States assert that the process is too slow and costly. If so, then perhaps the practices of other countries should be studied for ideas on reform. A study sponsored by the World Bank, completed by a group at Harvard University, looked at business bankruptcy practices.

As the table shows in the first column, the authors measured the average time that bankruptcy lawyers estimate is necessary to complete a procedure. In the second column, lawyers estimated the average cost of bankruptcies as a percent of the value of the bankrupt estate—including court costs, lawyer fees, accounting fees, and other direct costs. The last column documents the recovery rate, which calculates how many cents on the dollar claimants (creditors, tax authorities, and employ-

ees) recover from an insolvent firm. The highest scores for meeting these goals went to Finland, Norway, and Singapore.

Country	Time in Years	Cost as Percentage of Estate	Recovery Rate (cents on the dollar)
Singapore	0.8	1	91.3
United Kingdom	1.0	6	85.8
United States	3.0	8	68.2
Mexico	1.8	18	64.5
France	1.9	8	46.6
Indonesia	6.0	18	10.6
India	10.0	8	12.5

Source: *http://rru.worldbank.org/doingbusiness*

start. However, a declaration of bankruptcy remains on a person's credit history for ten years and the debtor may not seek another discharge for six years.

Some debts are not discharged by bankruptcy proceedings. The reason for these exceptions is to discourage the use of bankruptcy to evade certain responsibilities. The following are among the debts not extinguished by bankruptcy:

- Alimony and child support payments
- Back taxes
- Most student loans
- Some debts incurred immediately before filing bankruptcy
- Debts incurred by fraud against the creditors
- Fines owed to the government

Chapter 11

A portion of the bankruptcy code with a very different intent is *Chapter 11*, which applies to businesses that wish to remain in operation and not be liquidated. Many businesses are worth more if they can be kept alive, generating revenue, than if they are liquidated when debts are greater than assets. About 10,000 businesses each year use this option. The difference between the value of a business as a going concern compared with what is collected from selling the assets of the company is known as a "going concern surplus." It is that surplus that the creditors hope to capture by allowing the business to remain in operation so that they have a greater chance of full repayment. There is a risk, of course, that keeping the business in operation will only worsen things, in which case the creditors lose even more. It is a judgment call.

Although Chapter 11 has been used to restructure some multibillion-dollar businesses, in the airline and asbestos industries, most companies that file have assets worth less than $1 million. Well-planned Chapter 11 cases have much better track records and involve fewer legal fees than those done in haste. But many businesses are in dire straits before a reorganization plan is rushed to court to try to salvage operations as the creditors are pressing in.

Reorganization

As with Chapter 7, the filing under Chapter 11 automatically stays further action by any parties involved. An initial hearing with the trustee determines whether the plan should be allowed to proceed or whether some creditors are due immediate payment or return of property. In most cases, the debtor is allowed by the court to continue operating the "reorganized" business. Thus, the debtor acts as trustee of the operation, called a *debtor in possession*, running the business for the benefit of all parties. This means that the debtor now owes an extra duty of care because the debtor's duty is to act in the best interest of all, not just the owners of the business.

Watching over the debtor is the unsecured creditors' committee, composed of several creditors with the largest claims. These creditors are often the largest suppliers to the business. The committee supervises the management of the reorganized business, cooperating with the debtor to try to make a success of the operation. Any unusual actions by the debtor must be reviewed by the committee in advance; if the creditors object, the court will review the matter. As with Chapter 7, creditors must be satisfied by class in order of priority of claims. However, unlike Chapter 7, where discharge of debts is the goal, under Chapter 11, the purpose is to have the business emerge as a profitable venture or to see it sold for its greatest value. But Chapter 11 proceedings means many issues are fought in court, which is costly and adds significant time delays to getting on with business. Judges and trustees end up running companies. The *Kmart* case illustrates the kind of issues that arise, and this is just one of many rulings involving that one company.

In the Matter of Kmart Corporation

United States Court of Appeals, Seventh Circuit
359 F.3d 866 (2004)

CASE BACKGROUND   *Kmart consists of the parent company and 37 affiliates and subsidiaries. When it filed bankruptcy, it requested to pay, in full, the claims of all "critical vendors." The request stated that some suppliers would be unwilling to do business in the future if past debts were not paid. To stay in operation, it needed to continue to receive supplies. If it did not receive supplies, its ability to pay other creditors would be further impaired.*

The bankruptcy judge agreed and granted the order, without notifying the disfavored creditors. The judge held that its decision was in the best interest of the debtors and creditors. Kmart was allowed to determine who were critical vendors. Kmart paid about $300 million to 2,330 suppliers. Another 2,000 vendors were not paid. They and

43,000 additional unsecured creditors got about 10 cents on the dollar, mostly in stock of the reorganized company.

Some of the creditors appealed. The district court reversed the order authorizing payments to critical vendors. Judge Grady concluded that neither the Bankruptcy Code nor the "doctrine of necessity" supported the order. That decision was appealed.

CASE DECISION   Easterbrook, Circuit Judge.

* * *

Appellants insist that, by the time Judge Grady acted, it was too late. Money had changed hands and, we are told, cannot be refunded. But why not?

continues

Reversing preferential transfers is an ordinary feature of bankruptcy practice, often continuing under a confirmed plan of reorganization. . . .

Section 105(a) [of the Bankruptcy Code] allows a bankruptcy court to "issue any order, process, or judgment that is necessary or appropriate to carry out the provisions of" the Code. This does not create discretion to set aside the Code's rules about priority and distribution. . . . this statute does not allow a bankruptcy judge to authorize full payment of any unsecured debt, unless all unsecured creditors in the class are paid in full. . . .

So does the Code contain any grant of authority for debtors to prefer some vendors over others? Many sections require equal treatment or specify the details of priority when assets are insufficient to satisfy all claims. . . . Filing a petition for bankruptcy effectively creates two firms: the debts of the pre-filing entity may be written down so that the post-filing entity may reorganize and continue in business if it has a positive cash flow. Treating pre-filing debts as . . . claims against the post-filing entity would impair the ability of bankruptcy law to prevent old debts from sinking a viable firm. . . .

The foundation of a critical-vendors order is the belief that vendors not paid for prior deliveries will refuse to make new ones. . . . For the premise to hold true, however, it is necessary to show not only that the disfavored creditors *will* be as well off with reorganization as with liquidation—a demonstration never attempted in this proceeding—but also that the sup-posedly critical vendors would have ceased deliveries if old debts were left unpaid while the litigation continued. . . .

Some supposedly critical vendors will continue to do business with the debtor because they must. They may, for example, have long term contracts, and the automatic stay prevents these vendors from walking away as long as the debtor pays for new deliveries. . . .

Doubtless many suppliers fear the prospect of throwing good money after bad. It therefore may be vital to assure them that a debtor will pay for new deliveries on a current basis. Providing that assurance need not, however, entail payment for pre-petition transactions. . . .

Even if [the Code] allows critical-vendors orders in principle, preferential payments to a class of creditors are proper only if the record shows the prospect or benefit to the other creditors. This record does not, so the critical-vendors order cannot stand.

Affirmed.

QUESTIONS FOR ANALYSIS

1. Assuming a vendor has no long-term obligation, would it continue to sell to Kmart if past debts were not paid?

2. Some critics of Chapter 11 contend that firms should be liquidated under Chapter 7, not operate under court supervision. Can you think of the reasons for that argument?

Chapter 13

About one-half million personal bankruptcies are handled under *Chapter 13* each year. There is only a voluntary option under Chapter 13, which is filed like a Chapter 7 bankruptcy, and is available only for individuals. Because a sole proprietorship is a business owned by an individual, it may be handled under the Chapter 13 option.

In this proceeding, the debtor files a plan for payment of creditors over time. This is an installment repayment plan. Unlike in Chapter 7, where the debtor is relieved of all property except that protected by state statute, in Chapter 13, the debtor keeps the estate's property and shares administration of the bankrupt estate with a court-appointed trustee. The trustee collects income from the debtor and makes payments to creditors as called for by the *confirmation plan* that was approved. The trustee does not manage the affairs of the bankrupt; rather, the trustee is there to make sure that payments are made and to approve any changes in the debt and credit position of the debtor.

Unlike Chapter 7, the debts of the bankrupt are not discharged. Chapter 13 is a court-protected change of debt repayment that usually must be accomplished within three years but no more than five years. Long-term, secured debt, such as a house mortgage, is treated differently. If the plan fails to work, it is possible to shift to a Chapter 7 bankruptcy and have the financial decks cleared by discharge.

Nonbankruptcy Alternatives

Because bankruptcy is costly and affects how one is viewed in the business community, financial distress often is handled without going to bankruptcy even though it is available. All nonbankruptcy options are contractual, so they must be agreed to by the parties involved. We discuss here some of the most common alternatives, which can be quicker and cheaper than bankruptcy.

Debt Composition or Extension

A business in difficulty may bargain with its creditors for relief in the form of *composition*, which is an agreement to repay some percentage of the total amount due to relieve the debt, or an *extension*, which allows more time to pay the debt than the original agreement provided. Because such agreements are reached by bargaining, they require good faith on the part of the parties and usually work only when there are a few creditors who can agree among themselves as to the terms being offered. Such agreements and all terms must be approved by all parties. Any unpaid portions of debts are *discharged*. Because this is a contractual agreement, not one governed by the bankruptcy code, the parties can include any debt in the discharge agreement.

Bank Workout

If most of a company's debt is to a bank, it may be possible to rehabilitate the business with a *bank workout*. In a workout, the major creditor agrees to a new debt payment schedule. If the creditor, which would lose the most in bankruptcy and incur bankruptcy proceedings expenses, thinks that the business may be saved or the losses minimized, it may help to deal with other creditors and even arrange new financing.

Assignment

Especially for small businesses facing bankruptcy, *assignment* may be a quicker and cheaper way to accomplish liquidation. It must be agreed to by all creditors. The

JURIS *prudence?*

Home Sweet Home

Paul Bilzerian, a noted "corporate raider," was ordered to jail for contempt of court for allegedly hiding assets. He was being sued by the government, which was trying to collect a $62 million judgment against Bilzerian for securities fraud. Filing for bankruptcy protection against the judgment, Bilzerian claimed only $15,800 in assets, including a watch worth $5.

Fortunately for the destitute Bilzerian, Florida law allows bankrupts to keep their homes. He lived in a 37,000-square-foot residence which has an indoor basketball court, movie theater, nine-car garage, and an elevator. He offered to rent the home for $600,000 a week during the Super Bowl in Tampa.

Source: *St. Petersburg Times*

debtor assigns all nonexempt assets (assets not tied to a specific creditor, such as a mortgage on a building) to an assignee, who acts as a fiduciary for the benefit of the creditors. The assignee liquidates the assets and distributes the proceeds among the creditors on an agreed share basis. The business is terminated; this is not a rehabilitation plan. Creditors voluntarily accept partial payment of the sums they are owed as satisfaction for their debts.

SUMMARY

- Negotiable instruments function either as a substitute for cash or as a credit device. The UCC identifies four types of instruments as negotiable instruments: drafts, checks, notes, and certificates of deposit.
- Negotiable instruments are flexible commercial instruments because of their ability to be transferred. Once issued, a negotiable instrument can be transferred by assignment or by negotiation. If the instrument is assigned, the assignee has the same contract rights and responsibilities as the assignor. If the instrument is transferred by negotiation, the transferee takes the instrument free of the transferor's contract responsibilities.
- To be negotiable, a commercial instrument must meet the general requirements of a negotiable instrument as provided by the UCC. It must be written, be an unconditional order or promise to pay, be signed by the maker or drawer, be payable on demand or at a specified time, be made out "to order" or "to bearer," and state a certain sum of money.
- If an instrument is negotiable under the requirements of the UCC, the instrument may be freely traded in the marketplace without concern for existing contract responsibilities as long as the instrument is in the possession of a holder in due course.
- As a creditor, a business monitors its credit extension and debt collection policies. As a debtor, a business borrows to pay for equipment, inventory, and land and buildings. Creditors are interested in being protected in the event a debtor is unable or unwilling to pay.
- A secured creditor has the right to take specific property of an insolvent debtor to satisfy the debt. The law provides two ways the creditor can obtain a debtor's property (referred to as security or collateral): (1) by agreement with the debtor or (2) by operation of law, and without an agreement between the lender and the borrower.
- A lender may require that a financially strong third party guarantee a loan. Such a guaranty may be a pledge of personal assets by business owners or from a third party. A promise is made to pay a particular debt of the business in the event it does not pay. A suretyship or guaranty is created, and the credit of the party providing it is the security for the debt owed.
- When a product is sold to a customer, Article 9 of the UCC provides that the product itself may secure the customer's obligation to pay. When credit is extended this way, the sale is called a secured transaction. By meeting the requirements of the UCC, the creditor obtains a security interest in the product to secure payment.
- To make a security interest enforceable, the lender must create the interest and make sure the interest is attached and perfected. When a creditor has a security interest in the product, it has priority to the product over some other and unsecured creditors. The lender can sue the debtor to recover the debt or repossess the product and resell it.

- In most credit transactions except mortgages, creditors require that a security agreement and a financing statement be accepted and signed by the borrower. When money is borrowed for the purchase of real estate, the real estate itself secures the obligation and is evidenced by a mortgage. In most states, the mortgage is a lien, giving the holder the right to sell the property and repay the debt from proceeds in the event of default.

- Security obtained by a creditor through the operation of law is called a lien. The procedures for using liens are determined by state law. The most common liens are the mechanic's lien (applicable to real property), the possessory lien (applicable to personal property), and court-decreed liens. In each case, the lender may obtain the lien without the borrower's consent by following statutory procedures.

- The Bankruptcy Reform Act (the bankruptcy code) governs bankruptcy procedure. There are several approaches to bankruptcy, including Chapter 7 (providing for liquidation and fair distribution of the debtor's assets for creditors), Chapter 11 (allowing businesses to reorganize rather than being liquidated), and Chapter 13 (personal bankruptcy for individuals).

- The trustee (or debtor in possession) is the person in charge of the bankruptcy. It is the trustee's objective (under bankruptcy court supervision) to maximize the amount of the debtor's assets available for distribution to the creditors.

- Bankruptcy law states that certain creditors take priority over other creditors in receiving shares of the debtor's assets. Secured creditors take priority over unsecured creditors.

- Alternatives to bankruptcy that can be quicker and cheaper include debt composition, debt extension, bank workouts, and assignments.

REVIEW AND DISCUSSION QUESTIONS

1. Define the following terms:

negotiable instrument	mechanic's lien
draft	suretyship
secured creditor	trustee in bankruptcy
attachment	secured creditors
perfected security interest	composition

2. What are the basic differences between Chapters 7, 11, and 13 bankruptcy?

CASE QUESTIONS

3. Chung was at Belmont Park, a racetrack operated by the New York State Racing Association. He bought a gambling voucher for use in SAMS, which are "automated machines which permit a better to enter his bet by inserting money, vouchers or credit cards into the machines, thereby enabling him to select the number or combination he wishes to purchase. A ticket is issued showing those numbers." The money credited to a voucher can be bet at once or can be used over time to make bets on SAMS. Chung forgot his voucher in a SAMS machine; it had several thousands of dollars credit on it. Someone found the voucher and traded it in for cash. The betting system does not link a person to a voucher, so the thief is unknown. Chung sued, contending that the racetrack should be liable for failing to check the identity and ownership of vouchers prior to their

use. Is the racetrack liable or is Chung out of luck? [*Chung* v. *New York State Racing Assn.*, 42 UCC Rep.Serv.2d 867 (Dist. Ct., City of N.Y., N.Y., 2000)]

 Check your answer at http://meiners.westbuslaw.com

4. Chrysler Credit Corporation (CCC) had a security interest in a Dodge pickup truck that had been purchased by Robert Keeling. After Keeling defaulted on his payments, CCC tried to repossess the vehicle but could not locate it for some time. The truck was found in the storage lot of Highway Tow Service. It had been towed there from an apartment complex at the request of the manager of the complex. CCC requested that Highway deliver the truck to it, but Highway refused, requesting payment of its towing and storage charges. CCC sued to gain possession. Is Highway entitled to an artisan's or possessory lien on the truck? [*Chrysler Credit Corp.* v. *Keeling*, 793 S.W. 2d 222 (Ct.App., Mo., 1990)]

5. McDowell owned and operated Big River Harley Davidson in Wapello, Iowa. As required by law, McDowell took out a retail motor vehicle dealer's surety bond for $35,000 with United Fire & Casualty Insurance. The bond protects retail customers who get stuck when a motor vehicle dealer, because of fraud or some other reason, does not deliver a vehicle that has been paid for. The surety bond was in force when Big River went out of business and McDowell left the state. While in business, Big River sold two Harleys wholesale to Elworth Harley Davidson Sales and Service in Norfolk, Nebraska. Only one of the two Harleys was delivered; the second Harley, for which Elworth paid $12,000, was not delivered. Elworth sued United Fire as surety for the $12,000. Can Elworth recover? [*United Fire & Casualty Co.* v. *Acker*, 541 N.W.2d 517 (Sup. Ct., Iowa, 1995)]

 Check your answer at http://meiners.westbuslaw.com

6. When the real estate development Poinciana Villages was started in 1971, property declarations of covenants stated that to pay for common-area maintenance, every property owner would be liable for paying homeowner dues. If a homeowner did not pay, a lien would be filed that "shall be superior to any mortgage placed on any of the properties." Kearns bought property in Poinciana and created a mortgage on the property in 1989. He defaulted in 1997. The mortgage issuer sued to seize the property for payment, but Poinciana contended that its lien for unpaid homeowner assessments, which Kearns had not made, was superior in priority. The mortgage company argued that its lien against the property, as issuer of the primary mortgage, should have precedence. Who was right? [*Association of Poinciana Villages* v. *Avatar Properties*, 724 So.2d 585 (Ct. App., Fla., 1998)]

7. Moody and three other people bought a business together and executed promissory notes for $8.17 million to be repaid on a certain schedule. For his contribution, Moody owned 20 percent of the business; the other three owned the other 80 percent of the business. Moody was unable to make several payments on schedule. The other owners covered the payments he was supposed to make so that the notes would not go into default. Moody was sued by the other three for his contribution. He asserted that he was the same as a surety. Since they made the payments that were due, he was no longer obligated on those payments. Is that correct? [*Krumme* v. *Moody*, 910 P.2d 993 (Sup. Ct., Ok., 1996)]

 Check your answer at http://meiners.westbuslaw.com

8. Mollinedo's home was damaged by fire. Her insurance company, Sentry, recommended ServiceMaster as a good repair company. An adjuster for Sentry visited the home with the home contractor from ServiceMaster and approved $30,000 worth of work, which ServiceMaster did with Mollinedo's approval. Sentry was suspicious about the origins of the fire and gave the payment of $30,000 to Mollinedo's mortgage company. Mollinedo filed for bankruptcy. ServiceMaster, which got nothing, sued Sentry for breach of contract and unjust enrichment. Did ServiceMaster, which never filed a lien, have a claim? [*ServiceMaster of St. Cloud* v. *GAB Business Services*, 544 N.W.2d 302 (Sup. Ct., Minn., 1996)]

9. The Boggses were declared bankrupt under Chapter 13. Shortly after their discharge, Somerville Bank & Trust contended that the Boggses did not pay off the interest on a loan secured by a mortgage on their principal residence. The bank had not raised the issue until after the bankruptcy court had issued its discharge order covering the indebtedness. The bank attempted to collect the debt as though there had been no discharge. Is the bank entitled to collect the interest? [*Boggs* v. *Somerville Bank & Trust Company*, 51 F.3d 271 (6th Cir., 1995)]

10. Noggle borrowed $1,005.72 from Beneficial Finance Company to finance a small business project. To obtain the loan, he gave Beneficial a security interest in certain specified household goods, a camera, some household appliances, and a Winchester rifle. Beneficial filed a financing statement to perfect its security interest in the property. Shortly thereafter, Noggle filed a voluntary petition in bankruptcy under Chapter 13. During the administration of the case, Noggle claimed the Winchester rifle as exempt household property. Using the federal list of exemptions, is the rifle exempt from the reach of the bankruptcy proceeding? [*Matter of Noggle*, 30 Bankr. 303 (E.D. Mich., 1983)]

11. Lazar was sued for wrongful interference with a contractual relationship. Three weeks after being notified of the lawsuit, he transferred a number of his assets to his daughters, including $180,000 in interest in a mortgage and $104,000 from his solely owned pension fund. The daughters then purchased a sixty-foot yacht upon which Lazar took residence. Shortly thereafter, Lazar lost the suit, resulting in a $2 million judgment against him. When the judgment creditors attempted to execute the judgment, Lazar filed a Chapter 7 bankruptcy petition, having stripped himself of his assets by the transfers to his daughters. Is Lazar entitled to protection under the Bankruptcy Code? [*In re Lazar*, 81 Bankr. 148 (S.D. Fla., 1988)]

 Check your answer at <http://meiners.westbuslaw.com>

12. Strumpf was in default on a loan with a balance of $5,069 owed to Citizens Bank. When Strumpf filed for bankruptcy under Chapter 13, the bank put a hold on his checking account at the bank so that he could not write checks and leave less than $5,069 in the account. Strumpf complained to the bankruptcy court that the bank's action was illegal because it gave the bank a setoff against the debt, rather than preserving the checking account on behalf of all creditors. Could the bank place a hold on the checking account? [*Citizens Bank of Maryland* v. *Strumpf*, 116 S.Ct. 286 (1995)]

13. Bussewitz borrowed money from Citibank and signed a promissory note. Pitassi also signed the promissory note as co-maker of the note. When Bussewitz failed to make payments and defaulted on the note, Citibank, under the terms of the note, declared the entire unpaid balance due and sued both makers. Pitassi

defended that he should not be liable because he signed the note only as a favor to Bussewitz and, furthermore, the note did not state when the first installment payment was due; that term had been left blank. Is Pitassi liable? [*Citibank* v. *Pitassi*, 432 N.Y.S.2d 389 (Sup. Ct., App. Div., N.Y., 1980)]

ETHICS QUESTIONS

14. Consider the following quote regarding the Texas Homestead Act attributed to Hugh Ray, managing partner of the Houston, Texas, firm of Andrew & Kirth: "People should move here from out-of-state, buy up as much land as they could, then go bankrupt. It's a deadbeat's paradise." There are several anecdotes to back up Ray's statement. For example, Craig Hall was a wealthy real estate syndicator in Dallas, Texas, during the oil boom of the late 1970s and early 1980s. When the bottom dropped out of oil in the early 1980s, the bottom also dropped out of the real estate market. Just before filing for bankruptcy, Hall paid off a $1.5 million mortgage, giving him the homestead free and clear under Texas's liberal homestead law. Is this practice, although legal, also ethical? What about the impact on creditors?

15. Should a small business be allowed to seek discharge of debts through bankruptcy when those debts were incurred as a consequence of an automobile accident caused by one of its drivers who was legally drunk at the time of the accident? [See *Matter of Wooten*, 30 Bankr. 357 (N.D. Ala., 1983)]

PULLING IT  *Together*

Contract Remedy in Equity and Liens

The Maretts owned Marett Properties, LLC. They hired Brice Building to work on two commercial real estate buildings that they intended to lease. The Maretts signed guaranties agreeing to be personally liable for Marett Properties' debt to Brice, but the construction contracts were never signed. After some time, Brice had been paid nothing for the $337,800 worth of work he had completed. The two properties were not leased and were unfinished. Because there was no completed contract, Brice sued the Maretts in quantum meruit, an equity claim, and also to enforce their personal guaranty. The Maretts defended that there was a failure to complete a contract and that without a contract, the guaranty was not valid. Does Brice win the case? [*Marett* v. *Brice Building*, 603 S.E.2d 40 (Ct. App., Ga., 2004)]

INTERNET ASSIGNMENT

1. Using any search engine, find the official web site for the National Conference of Commissioners on Uniform State Laws.
2. What is the URL for the Pre-Final Official Draft, as approved, NCCUSL, July 30, 1998 of the UCC Revised Article 9, Secured Transactions?
3. What four states did not make the UCC Revised Article 9 effective July 1, 2001, and when did it become effective in these states?
4. Search your library's online public access catalog and write down the call number for the following title, if available: *The ABCs of the UCC: (Revised) Article 9 Secured Transactions*, by Russell A. Hakes (2000).

Chapter 13 | *Business Organizations*

Three chums from school, who have all worked as employees in various firms for the past five years, decide to join together to start their own firm, a partnership developing real estate. They consult a lawyer in drawing up the paperwork for the new partnership, knowing that legal form is important, whether the enterprise is a real estate partnership or a restaurant. They also know that all the good intentions at the beginning of an operation often face major problems later when issues arise, and this is exactly what happens to their fledgling partnership. The business does not do well, and the chums quickly turn on each other under the stress. One partner does not do much work. Another partner charges personal expenses to the partnership. They cannot agree on how to split the profits. Could they have headed these problems off by forming the right kind of organization at the outset?

Unfortunately, no. While form is important, managing an organization requires a complex set of abilities. Today's students, more than ever before, report that they would like to be their own bosses some day. It is a great goal, but there is no magic key. You are often on your own, since you cannot afford a team of lawyers, accountants, and other experts to guide you. This chapter examines what a manager needs to know to have a chance to succeed, especially in smaller organizations, and gives guidance to piecing together the complex puzzle of business organizations.

There are over 20 million businesses in the United States. Sole proprietorships, often small businesses such as computer repair stores, dry cleaners, and restaurants, account for about three-quarters of the total. Proprietorships take in about 5 percent of all business revenues but 25 percent of all business profits. Corporations are fewer in number—less than 19 percent of the total—but account for 90 percent of all revenues. Partnerships take in 4 percent of business receipts while making up 7 percent of all businesses.

This chapter begins with a discussion of the major forms of business organization, including sole proprietorships, partnerships, corporations, and limited liability companies. Every state has laws concerning some aspects of corporation and partnership formation, operation, and dissolution, but business organizations are primarily created by actions and contracts. The statutory requirements regarding business formation are not burdensome. Each form has advantages and disadvantages. The chapter considers factors that may influence a business's choice of business organization. Finally, we look at alternative forms that may have applications in various circumstances, such as joint ventures, joint stock companies, cooperatives, syndicates, and, increasingly, franchises.

SOLE PROPRIETORSHIPS

A person doing business for himself or herself is a *sole proprietor*; the business organization is a *sole proprietorship*. The sole proprietorship is the oldest and simplest form of business organization. As a proprietor, a person may simply begin to do business without formality in enterprises that do not require a government license or permit (although most states require business names to be registered if a fictitious business name is used). The proprietor generally owns all or most of the business property and is responsible for the control, liabilities, and management of the business.

In a sole proprietorship, legally and practically, *the owner is the business*; capital must come from the owner's own resources or be borrowed. Perhaps the greatest disadvantage of the sole proprietorship is the fact that limited alternatives exist for raising capital. Because the profits of the business are taxed to the owner personally, a tax return in the business's name is not required so long as records of income and expenses are kept. The operational and record-keeping formalities of the business are at the owner's discretion as long as various taxing authorities are satisfied.

PARTNERSHIPS

A *general partnership* is defined as an association of two or more persons to carry on a business as co-owners for a profit. The *partners* or *general partners* share control over the business's operations and profits. Many attorneys, doctors, accountants, and retail stores are organized as partnerships. A "person" in a partnership may be another partnership or a corporation.

At common law, a partnership was not treated as an independent legal entity. As a consequence, a case could not be brought by or against the business. The partners had to sue or be sued individually. State law now provides that, for many purposes, a partnership may be treated as an independent entity. Thus, a partnership may sue or be sued and collect judgments in its own name. The federal courts also provide that, in most circumstances, a partnership is treated as a legal entity.

Partnership law originated in the common law but is now codified in the *Uniform Partnership Act (UPA)*. The UPA has been adopted in every state except Louisiana and governs partnerships and partnership relations. The UPA determines the operation of partnerships when the partnership agreement is silent or where there is no formal agreement among the partners.

Forming a Partnership

A partnership can begin with an oral agreement between two or more persons to do business as partners or with an implied agreement that may be inferred from the conduct of the partners as they do business together. Typically, the parties formalize their relationship by a written agreement likely to cover the following key points:

Basics—name of the partnership, name of the business, place and date of formation; state law that applies to the partnership

Finances—contributions of the partners (which may be money, facilities, or expertise); when payments are due; how additional capital contributions will be handled; the allocation of ownership shares; accounting rules; the distribution of profits; and priority rights in payments

Management—voting rights of partners; appointment of managing partners; and, in some cases, a compensation committee

Dissolution—procedures to be followed in case partnership is terminated; rights of partners to leave partnership; how partnership shares will be valued; limits on transfers of partnership shares; requirement to go to arbitration in case of dispute among partners

In the absence of a specific agreement, the UPA specifies and governs the relationship of the parties. Since the law does not require that a partnership have a name or that it be registered, outsiders might not know of its existence or who is involved.

INTERNATIONAL *Perspective*

Small Is Not So Beautiful in Japan

Each year about 700,000 new businesses are started in the United States. In Japan, adjusting for population, the number of new businesses would run about 190,000 per year, less than one-third the rate in the United States. Attitudes seem very different in the two countries; in the United States, small businesses are looked on with favor and are exempted from compliance with some laws; in Japan, they are discriminated against by government policy and are considered less desirable places to work.

Tetsu Anzai owns a few stores selling CDs with revenues of $12 million a year. He reports that qualified people do not answer his job ads even though unemployment is at the highest level in decades. Worker wariness of small firms reflects government policy.

Government banking regulations favor big businesses. Small firms without large sums of cash to bankroll operations, including paying large deposits to be able to rent office space, are usually out of luck. Since tax rates run as high as 65 percent, it is hard for entrepreneurs to reinvest their earnings. The stock market is of limited help, as regulations make it difficult for newer firms to be able to offer stock.

As the Japanese economy has hit hard times, consideration is being given to rules that would help small businesses stimulate the growth that was for so many years generated by the big firms smiled upon by public policy.

Duty of Partners

A partnership is a relationship based on extraordinary trust and loyalty. Partners owe a *fiduciary duty* to one another. A fiduciary relationship requires that each partner act in good faith for the benefit of the partnership. The partners must place their personal interests below those of the partnership. The Supreme Court stated the duty of partners as follows in *Latta* v. *Kilbourn*, 150 U.S. 524 (1893):

It is well settled that one partner cannot, directly or indirectly, use partnership assets for his own benefit; that he cannot, in conducting the business of a partnership, take any profit clandestinely for himself; that he cannot carry on the business of the partnership for his private advantage; that he cannot carry on another business in competition or rivalry with that of the firm, thereby depriving it of the benefit of his time, skill, and fidelity without being accountable to his copartners for any profit that may accrue to him. . . .

Control of Partners

Unless otherwise specified in the partnership agreement, which can allocate control any way that the partners want, the presumption is that each partner has an equal voice in partnership management. Regardless of the size of the interest in the partnership, each partner has one vote in managerial decisions. Except in the case of major decisions that require consent of all partners—such as decisions to change the nature of the partnership's business, to admit new partners, or to sell the business—a majority vote is controlling. In most large partnerships, the partners usually delegate most management responsibilities to one person or group, often referred to as the managing partner or partners.

Regardless of who runs a partnership, the partners have a duty to one another to disclose all financial aspects of the business and to be completely honest, regardless of personal differences. As the *Lubritz* case discusses, the courts, when resolving disputes, look to the reality of a business arrangement and the promises parties made to each other.

Clark v. Lubritz
Supreme Court of Nevada
113 Nev. 1089, 944 P.2d 861 (1997)

CASE BACKGROUND   *Lubritz and four other physicians orally agreed to form a preferred provider organization called NPP in 1983. Each invested $15,000 initially, and they agreed to share profits or losses equally. The partnership was later incorporated. When NPP hired a manager, he "learned that the physicians were all equal partners, put the same amount in, and were going to be paid or receive the same benefits."*

In 1986, after arguments about policy with other doctors, Lubritz resigned as president and from the board of directors, but continued to perform his professional services. Starting in 1990, the other doctors cut Lubritz's share of the annual profits and paid themselves more. Lubritz discovered this in 1993. The other doctors told him they paid him less because he contributed less to the work of NPP. Lubritz sued.

At trial it was noted that NPP ignored the bylaws of the corporation. "Stocks were not issued, annual shareholders meetings were not held, and the officers and directors were not elected." From 1991 to 1993, the Secretary of State of Nevada revoked NPP's corporate charter for failure to file its annual list of officers and directors as required by state law. Hence, NPP continued to operate as a partnership.

The jury awarded Lubritz $195,942 for breach of contract and breach of fiduciary duty, $200,000 in punitive damages, and $75,000 in attorney's fees. The other doctors appealed.

CASE DECISION   Per Curiam.

* * *

Breach of Contract

The appellants argue that the district court judge erroneously allowed the jury to find a breach of the oral agreement because it is legally impermissible for a business to be conducted as a corporation and a partnership at the same time. They claim that the incorporation of NPP necessarily precludes Lubritz from recovering for breach of contract. We disagree.

. . . Although this court has not yet addressed this issue, courts in other states are of the opinion that "when joint adventurers use the corporate form for convenience in carrying out their project, their mutual rights and liabilities will be determined in furtherance and in harmony with their joint purpose rather than with the form of their operation, and the corporate entity will be recognized or ignored accordingly." . . .

Additionally . . . Nevada corporation law . . . states that when an agreement of the shareholders treats the corporation as a partnership that the business arrangement is still legal and the law will treat the corporation as if it were a partnership. . . .

Based on the foregoing, we hold that the oral agreement was not invalid per se when the parties formed the corporation. Thus, the district court properly allowed the jury to determine whether the parties breached the oral agreement.

* * *

continues

Breach of Fiduciary Duty

The appellants also argue that there was no evidence that they breached a fiduciary duty in not disclosing the unequal distributions to Lubritz.

The fiduciary duty that partners owe one another has been described as follows:

> The fiduciary duty among partners is generally one of full and frank disclosure of all relevant information for just, equitable and open dealings at full value and consideration. Each partner has a right to know all that the others know, and each is required to make full disclosure of all material facts within his knowledge in anything relating to the partnership affairs. The requirement of full disclosure among partners in partnership business cannot be escaped. . . . Each partner must . . . not deceive another partner by concealment of material facts. [59(A) Am.Jur.2d Partnership §425 (1987)]

In addition, a partner's motives or intent do not determine whether his actions violate his fiduciary duty. Therefore, the appellants owed Lubritz a fiduciary duty of full disclosure of material facts relating to the partnership affairs.

In this case, there was sufficient evidence to show that the appellants breached that duty. The evidence clearly indicated that the appellants did not disclose the unequal distribution. Moreover, as discussed more fully above, there is sufficient evidence upon which a jury could determine that the appellants desired to conceal the unequal distribution from Lubritz. Therefore, this court will not disturb the jury's award for breach of fiduciary duty. . . .

Further we conclude that the breach of fiduciary duty arising from the partnership agreement is a separate tort upon which punitive damages may be based.

* * *

The district court's judgment in favor of Lubritz is hereby affirmed.

QUESTIONS FOR ANALYSIS

1. Suppose Lubritz was contributing less work than the other partners. Why should he share equally in profits?
2. Since the original agreement called for equal shares, if the other doctors wanted Lubritz out, how could they have gotten rid of him?

Termination of the Partnership

A change in the relationship of the partners that shows an unwillingness or an inability to continue with business may bring about *termination* of the partnership. By agreement, partners can allow partnership interests to be sold or assigned, usually with approval of existing partners. A complete termination comes about only after the partnership has been dissolved and its affairs have been wound up. The *dissolution* of the partnership occurs when an event takes place that precludes the partners from engaging in any new business. The *winding up* of partnership affairs involves completing any unfinished business and then collecting and distributing the partnership's assets.

Dissolution can come about in several ways. Change in the composition of the partners results in a new partnership and dissolution of the old one. Thus, the withdrawal or death of a partner causes the partnership to be dissolved. Similarly, the partnership is dissolved if a partner is bankrupt. Since it would be expensive and disruptive for partnerships to be terminated and re-formed because of the withdrawal, death, or bankruptcy of one partner, many agreements have provisions to allow the partnership to continue despite such events.

LIMITED PARTNERSHIP

A limited partnership is a special form of a general partnership. Like a general partnership, a *limited partnership* is a business organization made up of two or more persons (*partners*) who have entered into an agreement to carry on a business venture for a profit. Unlike in a general partnership, however, not all partners in a limited partnership have the right to participate in the management of the enterprise.

Forming a Limited Partnership

All states except Louisiana use some form of the *Uniform Limited Partnership Act* or the *Revised Uniform Limited Partnership Act*. Partners must execute a written agreement, called a *certificate of limited partnership*, and file it with the appropriate state official, often the secretary of state. The Uniform Act requires that certificates contain the following information:

1. Name of the business
2. Type or character of the business
3. Address of an agent who is designated to receive legal process
4. Names and addresses of each general and limited partner
5. Contributions (cash, work, and property) of each partner
6. Duration of the limited partnership
7. The rights for personnel changes in the partnership and the continuance of the partnership upon those changes
8. The proportion of the profits or other compensation that each partner is entitled to receive

In addition, the parties to the limited partnership agreement may agree to bind themselves in ways not required by the certificate.

Relationship of the Parties

A limited partnership has at least one *general partner* and one or more *limited partners*. The general partners are treated in the same manner as partners in a general partnership. They have responsibility for managing the business and are personally liable to the partnership's creditors.

Limited partners are investors who may not participate in managing the business. Although they have the right to see the partnership books and to participate in the dissolution of the business, limited partners are not liable for the debts or torts of the limited partnership beyond their capital contributions. Limited partners lose their limited liability and become general partners if they take an active role in managing the business. To avoid an inference of managerial control, limited partners may not take control of the firm, contribute services to the business, or allow their names to appear in the name of the business. As the *Carella* case indicates, limited partners must be careful in reading the details of limited partnerships they join.

Carella v. Scholet

Supreme Court, Appellate Division, Third Department, New York
773 N.Y.S.2d 763 (2004)

CASE BACKGROUND   *The Scholets owned a building on Main Street in Cobleskill, New York, where they ran a furniture store. When they had financial trouble, their accountant suggested that to raise cash they transfer the building to a limited partnership. The partnership would then lease the building back to their furni-* *ture business. The limited partners each contributed $6,750 annually to the building; the Scholets, as general partners, contributed $750. The limited partners took most of the depreciation deduction for the building, a significant tax advantage to them.*

continues

Eventually, the Scholets arranged for the limited partnership to sell the building to the Scholets' son. He took ownership, paid off the old mortgage, and got a new mortgage for himself. The limited partners each received $15 as their proceeds from the liquidation of the partnership. They sued the Scholets for breach of fiduciary duty for selling the building to their son at a bargain rate. The trial court granted summary judgment to the Scholets; the limited partners appealed.

CASE DECISION   Crew III, Judge.

* * *

The gravamen underlining most of the causes of action in the complaint is that the Scholets sold the Main Street building to their son at a price far below market value and, in so doing, engaged in an act of self-dealing in breach of their fiduciary duties to plaintiffs. While it is true, as urged by plaintiffs, that partners are accountable as fiduciaries and owe a duty of good faith and fairness to their partners, the parties to a partnership may include in the partnership articles any agreement they wish, including contemplated and authorized self-dealing, and the agreement as so written controls.

Here, the partnership agreement provided, in relevant part, that:

> The Limited Partners consent to *any* sale or other disposition . . . by the General Partners on behalf of the partnership of any or all of the partnership's assets, now or hereafter acquired, *on such terms and conditions as may be determined by the General Partners* . . . notwithstanding that any party hereto may have an interest therein [emphasis added].

That clear and unambiguous language plainly permitted the sale that is the subject of this litigation, and any cause of action in the complaint predicated upon a breach of fiduciary duties by reason of such self-dealing was properly dismissed. . . .

Affirmed.

QUESTIONS FOR ANALYSIS

1. Suppose the limited partners proved that the Scholets turned down a higher price for the building than they got from their son. Would that make it fraud or breach of fiduciary duty?

2. What could the limited partners have done to protect themselves?

ISSUE *Spotter*

Brotherly Love?

You and your brother start a small business. You rent a space in a mall and start teaching judo and yoga classes. You have customers who pay fees, which you deposit into a joint checking account, from which you pay your bills. After six months, things are going pretty well. But you notice that a chunk of money seems to be missing and your brother is driving a new car. It turns out that he made the down payment out of the joint account. You get into a fight about that. Whose money was it? Did he have the legal right to take it? As you think about things, it occurs to you, the yoga teacher, that one of your brother's judo clients could get injured and sue. Who could be liable for that? What else have you not thought about that you should?

Terminating a Limited Partnership

A limited partnership is terminated in much the same way as a general partnership. Events that affect a general partner and would bring about the dissolution of a general partnership also dissolve a limited partnership. While the bankruptcy of a general partner dissolves a limited partnership, the bankruptcy of a limited partner usually does not.

The business continues to operate while it is winding up, but it may not enter into any new commitments. In the final dispersal of the assets of the limited partnership, creditors' rights precede partners' rights. The limited partners receive their share of the profits and their capital contributions before general partners receive anything, unless the limited partnership agreement holds otherwise.

CORPORATIONS

When most people think of a business, they think of a *corporation*. A corporation is an artificial person, or legal entity, created under state law. The federal government plays little role in corporate law. Most large, well-known businesses—such as Coca-Cola, General Motors, and Microsoft—are corporations. Although businesses have produced and traded goods for thousands of years, the modern corporation developed in the United States during the late 1700s. State governments issued *corporate charters* to selected businesses. Because the charter often granted special privilege, there was intense competition to receive charters. A charter might, for example, give a business the exclusive privilege of operating a toll bridge over a river or having the only bank in a town. In this way, monopoly power was often associated with early corporate charters.

In the late 1800s, the first "liberal" *general incorporation statutes* were enacted. Those statutes established a simple procedure for incorporating a business. Incorporation is now available to businesses regardless of their field of operation, size, or political influence.

Creating a Corporation

Every state has a general incorporation statute that sets the procedure for incorporation. Although that varies across the states, the basic requirements are similar. In general, a corporation's *articles of incorporation* along with an application must be filed with the appropriate state office along with payment of a fee. As Exhibit 13.1 shows, the articles of incorporation usually provide the following:

1. Name and address of the corporation
2. Name and address of the corporation's registered agent
3. Purpose of the business
4. The class(es) of stock to be issued and their par value
5. Names and addresses of the incorporators

After reviewing the corporation's application for completeness, the state issues a *certificate of incorporation*. As a rule, the incorporators wait until the state has issued the certificate before holding their first formal organizational meeting. At that meeting, the incorporators elect a board of directors, enact the corporation's bylaws, and issue the corporation's stock. The *bylaws* are the "rules" that regulate and govern the internal operations of the corporation. The shareholders, directors, and officers of the corporation must follow the bylaws in conducting corporate activities.

Legal Entity Status

Unlike sole proprietorships, the corporation is a *legal entity* with rights and responsibilities separate from the owners. It is recognized under both federal and state law as a "person" and enjoys some of the same rights and privileges accorded U.S. citizens. Corporations are thus entitled to many constitutional protections, including free speech, equal protection under the law, and protections against unreasonable searches and seizures. As a "person," a corporation has the right of access to the courts as an entity that may sue and be sued. However, although the officers and employees of a corporation enjoy the privilege against self-incrimination under the Fifth Amendment, the corporation itself does not.

Exhibit 13.1

Example of Certificate of Incorporation

Certificate of Incorporation
Of
_____ **Corporation**

1. Name. The name of the Corporation is _____ Corporation.

2. Registered Office and Registered Agent. The address of the Corporation's registered office in Delaware is _____ Street in the City of ____ and County of _____, and the name of its registered agent at such address _____.

3. Purposes. The purpose of the Corporation is to engage in any lawful act or activity for which Corporations may be now or hereafter organized under the General Corporation Law of Delaware.

4. Capital Stock (Providing for Two Classes of Stock, One Voting and One Nonvoting). The total number of shares for all classes of stock the Corporation shall have authority to issue is _____, all of which are to be without par value. _____ of such shares shall be Class A voting shares and _____ of such shares shall be Class B nonvoting shares. The Class A shares and the Class B shares shall have identical rights except that the Class B shares shall not entitle the holder thereof to vote on any matter unless specifically required by law.

5. Incorporators. The names and mailing addresses of the incorporators are

Name	Mailing Address
_____	_____
_____	_____
_____	_____

6. Regulatory Provisions. [The Corporations may insert additional provisions for the management of the business and for the conduct of the affairs of the Corporation, and creating, defining, limiting, and regulating the powers of the Corporation, the Directors and the Stockholders, or any class of Stockholders.]

7. Personal Liability. The Stockholders shall be liable for the debts of the Corporation in the proportion that their stock bears to the total outstanding stock of the Corporation.

8. Amendment. The Corporation reserves the right to amend, alter, change or repeal any provision contained in the Certificate of INCORPORATION, in the manner now or hereafter prescribed by statute, and all rights conferred upon Stockholders herein are granted subject to this reservation.

We, the undersigned, being all of the incorporators above named, for the purpose of forming a Corporation pursuant to the General Corporation Law of Delaware, sign and acknowledge this Certificate of Incorporation this _____ day of ____, 20_____.

Acknowledgment

State of _____

County of _____

On this _____ day of _____, 20_____, before me personally came _____, one of the persons who signed the foregoing certificate of incorporation, known to me personally to be such, and acknowledged that the said certificate is his act and deed and that the facts stated therein are true.

_____
Notary Public

[seal]

Close and Public Corporations

Corporations are often referred to as being a *close corporation* or a *closely held corporation* as compared to a *public corporation* or a *publicly held corporation*. A close corporation is one whose shares are held by one shareholder or a small group of shareholders. There are no public investors; that is, the stock is not actively traded, unlike publicly held corporations. Most corporations are closely held; that is, they have a few stockholders and the stock is not traded on a stock exchange. The rules of the Securities and Exchange Commission, as we will see in Chapter 20, help determine such status. Some closely held corporations, such as Cargill and Koch, would be among the largest firms in the world if their stocks were public, so there is no size limit. Publicly held corporations are those with stock traded on a stock exchange and, therefore, are likely to have many shareholders. Some corporations "go public" at the start of operations, which may be quite small, so that outside investors can help bankroll the new business. Whether a corporation is close or public, the basic rules are much the same.

Relationship of the Parties

A corporation consists of three major groups: the shareholders, the board of directors, and the managers. Each shares specific duties and responsibilities to the other groups, to the corporation, and to third parties.

Shareholders

The *shareholders* own the corporation. Evidence of ownership may be in the number of shares shown on a *stock certificate*, but, as a practical matter, most parties just keep electronic records of who owns how many shares. Shareholders have the right to buy any additional stock issued by the corporation before it is offered to the public. Shareholders have a limited right to inspect the corporation's books and records. As a rule, inspection is provided to shareholders if it is for a proper purpose and a request is made in advance. Finally, unless stated to the contrary on the stock certificate or the bylaws, shareholders are not restricted from selling or giving the stock to someone else.

The shareholders are not responsible for managing the corporation. Shareholders elect the board of directors and vote on matters that change the corporation's structure or existence (such as a merger with another firm or an amendment to the corporation's articles of incorporation).

JURIS *prudence?*

Your Honor, I'll Turn Rocks into Gold

Marinov, a Russian immigrant, formed Amrox Corporation. He gave himself one-half of the stock for his secret knowledge and equipment. Four investors bought the rest of the stock for $330,000.

Marinov claimed to have a Ph.D. in physics from Russia and medical degrees from Bulgaria, Sweden, and Germany. He told investors that this education taught him how to turn corundum, which is cheap, into high-quality rubies and sapphires that would be certified by the American Gemological Institute.

Nothing was ever produced, and the investors sued Marinov. The district court ruled for the investors; Marinov appealed. The appeals court upheld the verdict. Marinov told the court that "he is developing a linear accelerator which he wishes to sell to the United Nations." The court found that claim and others "absolutely incredible." Marinov was held to have breached his fiduciary duty to the investors.

Source: *Gizzi* v. *Marinov*, 79 F.3d 1148

Elections take place at shareholder meetings, which are usually held annually. Notice of shareholder meetings must be provided in advance, and a quorum—usually more than half of the total shares—must be represented at the meeting. Most shareholders give third parties their *proxy*—a written authorization to cast their vote so that they do not have to attend the meeting. The proxy is often solicited by the corporation's management.

At the meeting, important corporate business is presented to the shareholders in the form of *resolutions*, which shareholders vote to approve or disapprove. The articles of incorporation establish voting rules. They usually require more than a simple majority for resolutions for actions such as amendments to the articles of incorporation and the bylaws or the dissolution or merger of the corporation.

The shareholder has no legal relationship with creditors of the corporation. A shareholder's obligation to creditors is limited to capital contributions (usually the amount paid to buy stock). A shareholder, however, may become a creditor of the corporation (for example, by supplying needed material or by working for the business) and enjoy the same rights of recovery against the corporation as any other creditor.

Board of Directors

The initial *board of directors*, the governing committee of a corporation, is specified in the articles of incorporation or chosen by the incorporators at the first corporate meeting. Thereafter, the selection of directors is a shareholder responsibility. Once elected, directors serve terms for a time specified in the articles, although the shareholders can remove a director from office *for cause* (generally for a *breach of duty* or *misconduct*).

Legally, the board is the principal of a corporation. That is, on behalf of the corporation it makes corporate policy, such as the sale of corporate assets, entrance into new product lines, major financing decisions, and appointment and compensation of corporate officers. The directors act, usually by majority vote, to exert managerial authority. Directors are under a *duty of care* to conduct themselves on behalf of the corporation as a reasonably prudent person in the conduct of personal business affairs. Honest mistakes in judgment not resulting from negligence do not result in personal liability to the directors. The *business judgment rule* makes directors and managers immune from liability when problems result from honest mistakes in judgment, so long as they had a reasonable basis for their decisions.

Directors are subject to a *fiduciary duty of loyalty*. This requires that directors place the interests of the corporation before their own interests. As a rule, the board has the duty to undertake actions to preserve the corporate entity. That duty would be different, for example, if the corporation became the target of a takeover attempt by another corporation. Then the fiduciary duty of the directors might change from preserving the corporation to maximizing its sales price in the interest of the shareholders.

Corporate directors have great leeway in making decisions. The courts understand that hindsight is better than foresight, so the business judgment rule protects directors against suits by shareholders claiming that the directors missed profit opportunities that they should have taken. However, if directors clearly fail to let shareholders profit from obvious opportunities, then liability may be assigned, as the *Alessi* case discusses.

Alessi v. Beracha
Court of Chancery of Delaware
849 A.2d 939 (2004)

CASE BACKGROUND   *Earthgrains was a Delaware corporation. Many Earthgrains shareholders owned less than 100 shares, which they did not sell because of the high cost of brokerage commissions due to the inconvenience of selling such "odd lots" of shares. In 2001, the Earthgrains board voted to allow small shareholders to sell shares at the market price, which was $25 a share, between May 18 and June 20, for a very small processing fee. Alessi and other small shareholders immediately sold their shares.*

Before, during, and after that stock buy-sell program, Earthgrains was negotiating to sell the company to Sara Lee. In May, the companies agreed to engage in confidential negotiations. In early June, Earthgrains made a presentation to Sara Lee's management. On June 19, Sara Lee provided a draft merger agreement. On July 2, the deal was announced and Sara Lee bought Earthgrains for $40 a share.

Alessi and others sued the members of the board of directors for breach of fiduciary duty for not disclosing that the merger talks were under way. The directors moved to have the suit dismissed, contending that it was in the best interest of the company for the information to be kept confidential until the merger was finalized. The supreme court of Delaware had held that, as a general rule, discussions of possible mergers are confidential. In general, there is no duty to disclose the facts of ongoing merger possibilities.

CASE DECISION   Chandler, Chancellor.

* * *

The rationale for the [Delaware Supreme Court rule regarding confidentiality about mergers] is threefold. First, "the probability of completing a merger benefiting all shareholders may well hinge on secrecy during the negotiation process." Second, "it would be very difficult for those responsible to determine when disclosure should be made." And finally, "Delaware law does not require disclosure of inherently unreliable or speculative information which would tend to confuse stockholders" . . . . I am not convinced that these rationales dictate dismissal of this action.

The first rationale, that secrecy increases shareholder wealth in some cases, is not a justification for maintaining secrecy in all cases. . . . Confidential negotiations are clearly necessary to preserve the benefit of business transactions, and nothing I say here is meant to denigrate their importance or appropriateness. But the secrecy rationale cannot be used in *every* circumstance as a "free pass" to allow fiduciaries to withhold clearly material information from stockholders.

The second rationale, that fiduciaries find nondisclosure of merger negotiations easier than tough decisions about when to disclose, is insufficient to justify the omission of material information in a communication requesting shareholder action. . . .

The third rationale, shareholder confusion, is the least persuasive reason . . . . Casual inquiries or mere expressions of interest need not be disclosed. In addition, . . . shareholders are [not] entitled to a "play-by-play" of the negotiations. . . .

The United States Supreme Court grappled with whether it would adopt a bright-line rule that all merger discussions before agreement on "price and structure" are immaterial. The United States Supreme Court rejected the bright-line rule, concluding:

> We . . . find no valid justification for artificially excluding from the definition of materiality information concerning merger discussions, which would otherwise be considered significant to the trading decision of a reasonable investor, merely because agreement-in-principle as to price and structure has not yet been reached by the parties or their representatives.

The Supreme Court stated that "whether merger discussions in any particular case are material . . . depends on the facts." . . .

Application of these standards leads to only one conclusion: Alessi's compliant should not be dismissed. . . .

Here, it takes a certain blind arrogance to suggest that, as a categorical matter, Earthgrains' discussions with Sara Lee were immaterial to a reasonable shareholder asked to sell his or her shares in Earthgrains. . . .

continues

QUESTIONS FOR ANALYSIS

1. There was no claim that Earthgrains' directors personally profited by the small-lot stock buyback agreement. Why do you think they instituted it?

2. Why, as a general rule, should shareholders be in the dark about possible major actions such as mergers?

Managers

The corporation's board of directors hires *managers* to run the business. The extent of managerial control and the compensation enjoyed by managers are matters of contract and agency between the board and the managers. Once hired, managers have the same broad duties of care and loyalty as the directors.

Terminating the Corporation

The termination of a corporation, like the termination of a partnership, is conducted in two parts: the dissolution phase and the winding-up phase. *Dissolution* may be voluntary or involuntary and marks the end of the corporation. Upon dissolution, the corporation may not take on any new business. A *voluntary dissolution* involves approval of the shareholders and the board of directors. *Involuntary dissolution* usually occurs because of bankruptcy, but it can also occur as a result of fraud in the establishment of the corporation.

When a corporation is dissolved voluntarily, the board of directors is responsible for *winding up* the affairs of the corporation. After the corporation's affairs have been completed, the assets are liquidated. The proceeds of the liquidation are first used to satisfy creditors, with any remainder going to the shareholders.

JURIS *prudence?*

Mad at Each Other? Sue the Insurance Company

Soon after Truck Insurance sold a liability insurance policy to Marmac, an engineering company, Marmac's board members fell to fighting among themselves. Amey, a board member, 40 percent stockholder, and executive vice president, was demoted by the other board members. He sued Marmac and its officers for breach of fiduciary duty, intentional infliction of emotional distress, and other complaints.

Marmac insisted that Truck Insurance pay for the company and its officers' defense against Amey. Truck refused.

The insurance policy covered torts inflicted by Marmac on outsiders; it did not provide coverage for torts board members commit against each other. The jury did not agree, awarding Marmac and its board members $61 million in damages from the insurer.

The Supreme Court of California noted that "the Amey lawsuit sets forth nothing more than a business dispute." The court tossed out the damage award; the board members would have to carry on their fight without their insurer.

Source: *Waller* v. *Truck Insurance Exchange*, 44 Cal.Rptr.2d 370

Professional Corporations

Many professional associations, such as groups of doctors in practice together, used to be partnerships. In recent decades, all states have enacted statutes to allow *professional corporations* (PCs) to be formed. One reason for this is so that the liability of the members of the group, such as the doctors, would be limited to what is invested in the PC. Each doctor is not personally liable for the debts of all others, which would most likely arise from a costly malpractice judgment against one doctor in the group. A doctor who loses a malpractice case does not have limited liability due to the fact that the practice is a PC, but other members of the practice are protected.

In most states, the owners of a PC can only be the professionals involved in the firm itself, that is, the doctors whose practices are tied together to some extent. Stock cannot be sold to outside investors. The tax treatment of PCs is complicated, but tax considerations are why many professionals choose this form of organization.

LIMITED LIABILITY COMPANIES

Compared with partnerships and proprietorships, the corporate form of organization presents entrepreneurs with a disadvantage—*double taxation* of profits—and an advantage—limited personal liability. The profits of corporations are taxed at the corporate level. They must pay federal taxes and, in some states, state taxes. Then, if the remaining profits are paid to the shareholders, the shareholders must pay income taxes on the earnings. This double taxation discourages the use of the corporate form of organization, especially for smaller businesses. But if a business chooses not to incorporate, it gives up the advantage of *limited liability* of the corporate form. This protection means the shareholders can lose the amount they have invested in the company, but are not personally liable for sums beyond that in the event the business collapses.

These concerns have not escaped the attention of state legislatures. To encourage small business ventures in the early 1990s, most states enacted statutes authorizing limited liability companies. A *limited liability company (LLC)* is a business organization that is treated like a corporation for liability purposes but like a partnership for federal tax purposes.

Although limited liability companies have been common in Latin America, Asia, and Europe for some time (for example, the GmbH in Germany), they were not of interest to U.S. entrepreneurs until the Internal Revenue Service ruled that it would treat LLCs like partnerships for federal tax purposes. The profits are taxed only once, as the earnings of the owners or shareholders. As a result, LLC activity increased markedly, and the states enacted statutes allowing the formation of limited liability companies. Most states adopted at least parts of the *Uniform Limited Liability Company Act*.

Method of Creation

As in the case of corporations, state laws provide the procedure to be followed in the creation of an LLC. The organizers file a document referred to as *articles of organization*, which are similar to a corporation's articles of incorporation and contain basic information:

1. Company name (must include "Limited Liability Company" or "LLC")
2. Address of the company or its registered agent
3. Whether the LLC is to be managed by its members or by a manager
4. Names and addresses of company members
5. Date (or event) upon which the company will be dissolved, if any
6. Whether any members are to be liable for company debts

Personal Liability

After reviewing the application, the state issues a certificate allowing the business to operate as an LLC. Most LLC statutes state that no member or manager will be personally liable for the debts of an LLC. However, members may agree by contract to be personally liable for the company's debts.

Relationship of the Parties

An LLC usually is formed by two or more *members* having equal status. (In Texas and Florida, it is possible to form an LLC with just one member.) The members have a *membership interest* in the company, somewhat like owning stock in a corporation or being a limited partner in a limited partnership. There are generally no restrictions on the number of members, but in practice the number is usually under 30. Individuals, corporations, partnerships, and other LLCs may be members. Unless the agreement says otherwise, members may not transfer membership interests without the consent of the other members.

The members sign an *operating agreement*. Similar to the bylaws of a corporation, the agreement provides rules about the operation of the company and the relationships of the members. It establishes the company's method of management, allocation of profits and losses among members, restrictions on the transfer of membership interests, and the process to be followed in dissolving the company. State statutes provide default provisions to cover issues not stated in the agreement.

The LLC agreement may give each member an equal voice in management regardless of ownership percentage. More typically, the agreement provides that members may hire a manager to run the LLC. The manager need not be a member. The right to set management policy can be delegated to a group of members based on the members' percentage ownership or on any other basis to which the members agree.

The Continuity-of-Life Factor

Unlike a corporation, an LLC is not allowed "perpetual" life. This means that a change in the relationship of the LLC members is determined under state law. Although death, bankruptcy, retirement, resignation, or expulsion of any member terminates the membership of a member, like a partnership the LLC itself can continue if all remaining members give their consent. In this way, although the company continues to exist, the relationship of the members has changed—satisfying the IRS regulations regarding continuity of life and the application of partnership taxation. The ability of the members to consent to the continuation of the LLC must be set out in the articles of organization.

Termination

A limited liability company is dissolved and its affairs are wound up usually because of the occurrence of an event specified in the articles of the organization to bring about the dissolution of the company or by the consent of all the members.

In some states, if there is no event or time specified in the articles of organization, the LLC is dissolved by statute thirty years after its formation. When dissolved, the LLC must wind up its affairs, defend itself against legal actions, and dispose of its property. The company may not take on any additional business. After the LLC has wound up its affairs, its assets are liquidated, first to satisfy creditors and then to satisfy the members. Usually, the company files a certificate of cancellation of articles of organization with the appropriate state office.

KEY ORGANIZATIONAL FEATURES

Several factors influence the choice of business organization, including the potential liabilities imposed on the owners, the transferability of ownership interests, the ability of the business organization to continue in the event of the death or withdrawal of one or more of the owners, the capital requirements of the business, and the tax rate applicable to the business organization selected. Exhibit 13.2 summarizes the differences between the major forms of business discussed so far. The following subsections review some of these factors in more detail.

Exhibit 13.2

Comparing Characteristics of Major Forms of Business Organization

	Proprietorship	Partnership	Corporation	Limited Liability Company
Method of Creation	Owner begins business operations	Created by agreement of parties; statutes may apply	Chartered under state statute	Created under statute by agreement of members
Entity Status	Not separate from owner	Separate from owners for some purposes	Legal entity distinct from owners	Separate from owners for some purpose
Liability of Owners	Owner personally liable for debts	Unlimited liability except for limited partner in a limited partnership	Shareholders liable only to the extent of paid-in capital	Members liable to the extent of paid-in capital
Duration	Same as owner	Ended by agreement or by death or withdrawal of a partner, but easily re-created	May have perpetual existence	Company dissolves after fixed time or the occurrence of a specific event
Transferability of Ownership Interests	May be sold at any time; new proprietorship formed	Generally, sale of partnership interest terminates partnership	Shares of stock can be transferred unless restricted by contract	Other members must consent to transfers
Control	Determined by owner	Partners have equal control unless otherwise agreed to; limited partners have no management rights	Shareholders elect board of directors who set policy and appoint officers to manage	Operating agreement specifies management control
Capital	Limited to what owner can raise	Limited to what partners contribute or can borrow	Sale of more shares increases capital; may also borrow	Limited to what members contribute; may also borrow
Taxation	Profits taxed to owner as individual	Profits taxed to each owner as agreed upon or all share equal	Double taxation; profits of corporation and shareholders' share of profits are taxed	If IRS conditions are met, same as a partnership

Limited Liability

Limited liability allows persons to invest in a business without placing their personal wealth at risk. Limited liability can also allow investors to be passive toward the internal management of the business.

Businesses incur debts by contract—for example, by borrowing money and buying supplies on credit—and they may incur liability arising from tort suits, such as for having sold asbestos in the past. Limited liability means that if the sums owed are so large that the organization must go into bankruptcy, the owners—the shareholders—could lose their investments but cannot be held personally liable. No creditor of the business can come after the owners for their personal assets.

Entities with Unlimited Liability

Sole proprietors and general partners have unlimited personal liability for the debts of the business, including its torts. Some states require that creditors exhaust the business partnership property before moving against the personal property of the partners. After those assets are exhausted, however, the creditor may require any of the partners to pay the entire remaining debt.

Entities with Limited Liability

The liability of a limited partner is limited to the capital the partner has contributed to the limited partnership. Like the limited partner, the shareholders of a corporation and the members of a limited liability company risk only their capital investment if the corporation fails. They are not personally liable for the business debts or torts of the firm unless they contract to make themselves personally liable.

In certain circumstances, the court will "pierce the corporate veil" and hold shareholders personally liable. That is, the court disregards the corporate entity by finding that the corporation is a sham and that the owners actually intend to operate the business as a proprietorship or partnership. Although not common, and usually only involving close corporations, the court can impose liability on shareholders in instances of fraud, undercapitalization, or failure to follow corporate formalities. As the following case illustrates, when the court pierces the veil, the corporate form of business organization may not be used to avoid obligations.

Dana v. 313 Freemason

Supreme Court of Virginia
587 S.E.2d 548 (2003)

CASE BACKGROUND *Dana and Hall bought an abandoned apartment building in 1997 at 313 Freemason Street to renovate it as a four-unit condominium. They registered it as a condo with themselves as owners. The next year, after an attorney advised them that "they would have decreased liability if they formed a corporation," they incorporated 313 Freemason and revised the registration of the condo to list the corporation as owner. They were the only shareholders. Although*

313 Freemason was properly incorporated, Dana and Hall remained holders of the mortgage on the building and never separated the finances to include a different account for the corporation.

While they owned the building and worked on renovations, they had constant problems with the roof and fought with the roofing contractor who had replaced it. They notified him that it "contains major structural defects which have caused extensive damage." After they sold the condos, the four new owners sued 313 Freemason, Dana, and Hall, alleging that the roof was defective when the building was sold. The plaintiffs claimed fraud and misrepresentation. Hall and Dana sought to be removed as defendants, contending that only 313 Freemason should be a defendant, as the corporate entity. The trial court held against them and found that they could be held personally liable. They appealed.

CASE DECISION   Koontz, Justice.

* * *

"The proposition is elementary that a corporation is a legal entity separate and distinct from the stockholders or members who compose it." The whole corporate concept would be meaningless if such were not the case. . . .

Stockholder immunity "is a basic provision of statutory and common law and supports a vital economic policy underlying the whole corporate concept. The decision to ignore the separate existence of a corporate entity and impose personal liability upon shareholders for debts of the corporation is an extraordinary act to be taken only when necessary to promote justice."

We have recognized that "no single rule or criterion . . . can be applied to determine whether piercing the corporate veil is justified." Each case must be considered in the context of its own specific circumstances. . . .

The trial court determined as a matter of fact that the formation of Freemason as a corporate entity in 1998 was "to evade any personal liability that Dana and Hall would have for the problems with the roof." The evidence in the record supports that finding. . . .

The record shows that Freemason was never capitalized even in a de minimis amount. The apparent inability of Freemason to satisfy the judgment against it in this case was not the result of poor business decisions, mismanagement, or unexpected liabilities such that an expected profit never materialized. Rather, because of the deliberate acts of the incorporating shareholders, Freemason suffered from nonexistent capitalization from its inception. Despite an obligation to do so, Dana and Hall never took any steps to establish the corporation's warranty reserve. Moreover, the corporation never had any liquid assets because it had no bank accounts. . . .

This Court has been very reluctant to permit corporate veil piercing. We have made it clear that only an extraordinary exception justified disregarding the corporate entity in order to hold individual stockholders personally liable for a judgment against the corporation. The conduct of Dana and Hall in clearly calculating to use the corporate entity of Freemason for an unjust purpose is just such an extraordinary exception. . . .

Affirmed.

QUESTIONS FOR ANALYSIS

1. Suppose the problem with the roof remained the same, but Dana and Hall had kept all monies related to the building in an account for the corporation. Would the result have been the same?

2. Does this type of decision defeat one of the basic advantages of the corporate form of business organization?

Transferability of Ownership Interests

The *transferability of ownership interests* refers to the ability of an owner in a business venture to sell or pass that interest to others. The ability of owners to transfer ownership interests differs among the various forms of business organizations.

Nontraded Entities

The proprietor of a sole proprietorship is, in essence, the business. A decision to sell the business ends the existing proprietorship and means the creation of a new one. Selling proprietorships, partnerships, and other small businesses can be expensive (relative to the value of the business) because such businesses can be hard to price. Often, specialists are required to help determine the market value of the business.

If a partner sells or assigns his interest in a partnership, the partnership continues but the new person does not automatically become a partner. The person is entitled to receive the share of profits the partner would have received, but she gains neither the right to participate in the management of partnership affairs nor continuous access to partnership information as would the partner. As with sole proprietorships, the sale of partnerships or partnership shares often requires specialists to assist in determining the value of the business.

The sale of shares in a close corporation is similar to the sale of a sole proprietorship or an interest in a partnership or an LLC. Because the price of the share is not determined on a stock exchange, the parties themselves, often with the help of a specialist, must determine the market value of the corporation and its shares.

Keeping Things in Order

You have a small company. Whether it is a corporation or a limited liability company, you know there is always a chance that, should something go wrong, you can be sued by a supplier, customer, employee, or someone else for some problem. What steps should you take to ensure that your company will keep limited liability status?

ISSUE
Spotter

Publicly Traded Corporations

The stock of public corporations may be traded on a stock exchange such as the New York Stock Exchange; the transfer of ownership of shares is simple and is done at very low cost. Since the price of the shares is determined by the many buyers and sellers of the stock, no specialists need be hired to estimate the market value. Thus, the transfer of ownership shares in complex corporations such as IBM is far easier than the transfer of ownership in sole proprietorships and partnerships.

Duration

A business's *duration* refers to its ability to continue to operate in the event of the death, retirement, or other incapacity of an owner of the business. The ability of a business to continue under such circumstances can depend on the form of business organization.

Limited Life

A sole proprietorship terminates with the death or incapacity of the proprietor. Similarly, at common law, a partnership is dissolved by the death, retirement, or other incapacity of a partner, but it is not necessarily terminated. To avoid liquidation, partners usually agree in advance to a continuation agreement. The same is true of LLCs.

Perpetual Existence

Unless its articles of incorporation provide for a specified period of duration, a corporation has *perpetual existence*. With perpetual existence, the death or retirement of a shareholder does not bring about the termination of the corporation. In most corporations, the death of a shareholder has no impact on the operations of the business.

On the other hand, in a close corporation or an LLC with few members, the death of a shareholder can have an impact on the business. Although the business need not terminate with the shareholder's death, if the shareholder is also a key officer in the company, it may be difficult for the business to continue. Suppose Midstates Construction is a close corporation with five shareholders and fifty employees, including Mertz, the president. If Mertz dies, the company will not legally be terminated, but in practice it may be "forced" to liquidate because Mertz was the key employee.

OTHER BUSINESS ORGANIZATIONS

In addition to the most common forms of business organization reviewed to this point, other forms are available, including joint ventures, joint stock companies, cooperatives, and syndicates. These alternative business organizations are generally used as vehicles to manage a specific project or business concept.

Joint Ventures

The Supreme Court has defined a *joint venture* as a general partnership for a limited time and purpose. Generally, a joint venture has several characteristics of a general partnership, including the same rights of control, risks of loss, and manner in which profits are taxed. It usually involves two or more persons who agree to join in a specific project and to share in the losses or profits.

A joint venture is not usually considered a legal entity and therefore may not sue or be sued in its own name. In addition, the members of a joint venture usually have limited authority to bind each other to matters not directly related to the project. Joint ventures vary in size and are most popular as an international business organization.

Joint Stock Companies

A *joint stock company* is an organization involving a unique mixture of partnership and corporation characteristics. It resembles the corporate form in that ownership is represented by shares of stock and the company is usually managed by directors and officers and can have perpetual life.

Despite these characteristics, joint stock companies are generally treated like partnerships. They are usually created through an agreement. Their form does not follow the terms of state law. In addition, joint stock company property is held in the names of the shareholders/members who have personal liability for company actions. The company is generally not considered a legal entity and therefore may not sue or be sued in its own name.

Cooperatives

A *cooperative* is an association (that may or may not be incorporated) organized to provide an economic service without profit to its members. Cooperatives are usually formed by people who want to pool their purchasing power. They may obtain lower product prices for their members by buying products in large quantities at a discount.

INTERNATIONAL Perspective

The Difficulty of Starting a Business

How difficult is it to establish a new business? A study sponsored by the World Bank looked at that issue. It presumed a business owned by five citizens wants to become a limited liability company in the largest city of a country. The owners contribute cash equal to ten times average income per capita in the country. It will have fifty employees, does no foreign trade, seeks no special benefits from the government, and rents the place of operation.

As the table shows, the measures considered in the study were: (1) the number of procedures to be completed; (2) the number of days to complete those procedures if done by an experienced attorney; (3) the cost of the procedure as a percent of per capita income (excluding bribes); and (4) the minimum capital required as a percent of per capita income (many countries require capital to be deposited in a bank account prior to doing business). Obviously, the longer and more costly the process of starting a business is, the fewer opportunities there will be for ordinary people to try to fulfill their dreams.

Country	Number of Procedures	Number of Days	Cost (percent of per capita income)	Minimum Capital Required (percent of per capita income)
United States	5	5	0.6	0.0
Canada	2	3	1.0	0.0
Mexico	8	58	16.7	15.5
Brazil	17	152	11.7	0.0
Japan	11	31	10.6	74.9
China	12	41	14.5	1,104.2
India	11	89	49.5	0.0
Egypt	13	43	63.0	815.6
Indonesia	12	151	130.7	125.6

Source: *http://rru.worldbank.org/doingbusiness*

Cooperatives that are not incorporated are usually treated as partnerships; the members are jointly liable for the acts of the cooperative. If the cooperative is formed as a corporation, it must follow state laws governing nonprofit corporations. In contrast to corporate dividends, however, cooperative dividends are provided on the basis of a member's (shareholder's) transactions with (purchases from) the cooperative rather than on the basis of capital contributed.

Syndicates

A *syndicate* is the name given to a group of persons who join together to finance a specific project. Syndicates are commonly used in financing real estate developments, such as a shopping center or office buildings. Although their specific structure varies considerably, such organizations may exist as general partnerships, limited partnerships, or corporations. It is not uncommon for the members of a syndicate simply to own property together with no other formal business organization.

FRANCHISES

Over one-third of retail sales—more than $1 trillion per year—take place in franchise outlets. So, franchises are a major form of business enterprise. Nationwide, there are about 3,000 franchises and more than half a million franchise outlets. Before the 1950s, only automobile manufacturers, soft-drink companies, and oil companies used franchising to market and distribute their goods. In the 1950s and 1960s, however, many of today's most recognized companies began franchising. Among others, they include Holiday Inn, TGI Friday's, The Gap, H&R Block, Baskin-Robbins, and McDonald's.

Generally a *franchise* exists whenever a *franchisee*, in return for payment of a "franchise fee," is granted the right to sell goods or services by a *franchisor* according to a marketing plan. The plan must be substantially associated with the franchisor's trademark, trade name, or trade dress. As a rule, a franchisee operates as an independent business (usually as a corporation) subject to the standards specified by the franchisor. Successful franchises have two characteristics in common: a trademark (conveying authenticity and exclusivity) and a uniform product or service. For example, as consumers travel throughout the country, they recognize the Burger King name and expect the product to taste the same in California as it does in South Carolina.

Types of Franchises

Franchises may be separated into three basic categories: (1) product distributorships—where the franchise has the right to sell the product of the parent company, such as a car dealership; (2) trademark or trade-name licensing—where the franchise has a license to market the company's brands, such as Coca-Cola; and (3) business format franchising—where the franchise follows the business model set out by the parent company, such as McDonald's.

In business format franchising, the franchisor provides the franchisee with everything needed to begin the business, demanding that the franchisee operate the business according to fixed standards and procedures. Business format franchises have been responsible for franchising growth in recent years. Included in this category are franchised restaurants, nonfood retailers, business services, rental companies, and motels.

The Law of Franchising

Federal and state laws are intended to protect investors from crooked or unethical operators. Franchise scams have defrauded investors of hundreds of millions of dollars over the years. In response, federal and state regulations require franchisors to register the franchise and to disclose all relevant information necessary for franchisees to make informed investment decisions.

The FTC Franchise Rule

Federal statutory protections can be found in the Federal Trade Commission's *franchise rule*, which requires the franchisor to give prospective franchisees an *offering circular*, that is, a detailed disclosure document, at least ten days before any money changes hands or before a franchisee is committed to a purchase. The franchise rule's disclosure document must provide the following important information about the business:

- Names, addresses, and telephone numbers of other franchisees
- An audited financial statement of the franchisor and its financial history
- The background and experience of the business's key executives
- The responsibilities that the franchisor and the franchisee will have to each other once the contract is signed
- The number of franchisees and how many have gone out of business

This document enables prospective investors to know about the background of the business. If the information provided is not true, it affords a legal basis for the franchisee to attempt recovery directly from, or for the FTC to bring an action against, the franchisor. See http://www.ftc.gov for more details about franchises and the franchise rule.

State Regulation

California was the first state to regulate franchises. The California act requires franchisors to register with the state and to provide prospective franchisees with a prospectus disclosure document before selling any franchises. The document must detail all important facts about the franchise transaction. California's registration and disclosure law seeks to prevent misrepresentation in the offering of franchises to prospective franchisees and to force the disclosure of information important for making investment decisions. Fourteen states, including Illinois and New York, have enacted similar laws. Some states have more limited business opportunity disclosure laws. In each case, the requirements imposed go beyond those imposed by the FTC franchise rule (see the FTC web site for a list of the states).

Most states have agencies, such as the attorney general, that have the authority to monitor franchises. The power to investigate franchise fraud is usually very broad. If franchise administrators find fraud, they can institute a civil lawsuit seeking damages, injunctions, and fines. In some cases, criminal liability may be imposed.

ISSUE *Spotter*

The Road to Riches?

You are offered a chance to have your own business: a franchise that would be the only one formed in your city for a new business that would deliver auto parts to auto repair shops in the city. The franchise promoter tells you great stories about the operation in other cities. For only $25,000 you can be your own boss and soon be living well—as your own boss! Not an uncommon situation. Facing this wonderful opportunity, what sorts of questions do you need good answers to? Is the information provided via the FTC offering requirements a good guarantee of security?

The Franchise Agreement

The *franchise agreement* sets forth the rights and obligations of the franchisor and franchisee. Key elements that might be included in a business format franchise are shown in Exhibit 13.3. They include, among other things, the rights and limits associated with the use of the franchise trademarks or trade names, the use of the franchise operating manual, the location and designated territory of operation, fee and royalty payments, the advertising commitment, and termination.

Trade Name and Procedure

The agreement grants the franchisee the right to use the franchisor's name and identifying trademarks and trade dress. The franchisee normally must undergo training and will be given the use of the franchisor's confidential operating manual. The franchisor may specify requirements regarding record keeping, advertising, hours of operation, hiring and training practices, and other details of the franchise's operations.

Territorial Rights

The agreement may impose limits on the territorial rights of the franchisee and the franchisor. For example, the franchisor may not be allowed to operate additional outlets in the territory unless the franchisee does not live up to certain perform-ance standards. The franchisee may be limited to operating only one unit within the territory. The agreement also states which party has the responsibility to select the site and to construct the facility.

Franchise Fees and Royalties

Naturally, the initial franchise fee or up-front payment is specified. Once the busi-ness is operating, the franchisor may require a continuing royalty—generally a

Exhibit 13.3

The Franchise Agreement between Franchisor and Franchisee

Franchisor's Duties and Responsibilities

Grants franchisee the right to
- Operate a franchised unit
- Use all of the franchisor's know-how related to the product
- Use trademarks or trade dress of the franchise
- Use franchise for a fixed period of time, perhaps with options for renewal

Furnishes franchisee with
- Manual setting forth the franchise's operating procedures, including employee training
- Specifications regarding the building, accounting, advertising, and other procedures
- Training for how franchisee is to operate the business
- Company image

May provide franchisee with
- Territorial exclusivity
- Source of product supply
- A regional or national advertising program
- Quality control inspections
- Group purchasing power

Franchisee's Duties and Responsibilities

Promises to the franchisor to
- Pay an initial franchise fee
- Pay a continuing royalty fee
- Pay an advertising fund contribution (1–4 percent of sales)
- Conduct the business according to the franchisor's standards
- Take the franchisor's training program
- Keep franchise information confidential
- Prepare franchise's books and records as franchisor requires
- Purchase certain products from franchisor
- Comply with employee hiring and training requirements

May promise the franchisor to
- Build a facility to franchisor specifications
- Sell only the products of the franchisor
- Pay for national advertising
- Purchase supplies only from approved suppliers
- Exercise personal supervision of franchise operations
- Maintain facilities according to franchisor's requirements
- Maintain specified hours of operation
- Consent to periodic inspections

percentage of annual sales. The franchisor may also require payments for advertising. The advertising fees depend on whether the franchisor does local or national advertising on behalf of its franchises. To protect the trade name, most franchise agreements prohibit franchisees from engaging in any advertising or promotional programs not approved by the franchisor.

Despite the various federal and state regulations, most cases of conflict between franchisors and franchisees involve civil litigation over violations of the terms of the agreement. The largest such case was a suit brought against the Meineke muffler chain by 2,500 franchisees who claimed that over a decade Meineke kept $31 million from a common advertising fund the franchisees contributed to that should have been spent on advertising. A federal judge in North Carolina ordered Meineke to pay the franchisees $600 million (damages were tripled under the North Carolina unfair business practices act) for breach of fiduciary duty.

CYBER Law

Offering Franchises on the Internet

The FTC has ruled that franchises can be marketed through the Internet. So long as a franchisor satisfies the disclosure requirements of the Franchise Rule (16 Code of Federal Regulations 436), such as spelled out in the Uniform Franchise Offering Circular (58 Federal Register 69,224), it does not matter if a prospective franchisee gets the offering on paper or on the Internet. The entire transaction can be carried out on the Internet. The FTC and the National Fraud Information Center's Internet Fraud Watch (see http://www.fraud.org) will look for evidence of investment scams run on the Internet.

Termination

Franchise agreements are usually explicit about events that bring about the franchise's termination. Some have a fixed expiration time, such as twenty years. Typical provisions give the franchisor the right to terminate upon the occurrence of events, ranging from the bankruptcy of a franchisee to the failure of a franchisee to submit to inspection by the franchisor. Notice of termination must be given to the franchisee. In some states, franchisors must give the franchisees reasonable time to correct problems. In addition, several states have laws that restrict a franchisor's ability to terminate a franchise unless there is "good cause." Upon termination, the franchisee loses all rights to the franchisor's trade name.

SUMMARY

- The most prominent forms of business organization are the sole proprietorship, partnership, limited partnership, corporation, and limited liability company. Less frequently employed forms include joint ventures, joint stock companies, cooperatives, and syndicates.
- Sole proprietorships automatically come into existence whenever people begin to do business for themselves. Legally, the sole proprietor is the business, responsible for business's debts and torts, liable for its taxes, and in control of its operation and its transfer.
- General partnerships are composed of two or more persons, general partners, who agree to carry on a business for profit. Partnerships may be structured almost

any way desired by the partners. When an agreement does not specify what happens in some instance, such as death of a partner, the law of partnership, codified in the Uniform Partnership Act, determines the result. In general, partners share in the managerial control, debts, tort liability, and profits of the business. They are taxed personally on partnership profits.

- Limited partnerships are governed by state law. They must have at least one general partner. The limited partners are investors who may not share in managerial control of the business. Their liability is limited to the amount they invest unless they try to exercise managerial control and become general partners, who are fully liable.

- Corporations are created under state law and are recognized as legal entities. They have their own legal life, which is potentially perpetual. They are responsible for their own debts and tort liabilities. Shareholders (investors in corporations) are liable only to the amount they invest in the corporation.

- Shareholders vote to elect the board of directors and must vote on major issues such as selling the corporation. The board of directors is the principal of a corporation. It has responsibility for determining how the company is to be operated and for hiring and instructing the management. Managers are agents of the board and respond to the board's instructions.

- A limited liability company (LLC) provides limited liability for its members (investors) and is taxed as a partnership. Members are thus taxed on the income rather than being subject to the double taxation of a corporation and its shareholders. An LLC must restrict the transfer of member interests and is intended to operate for a fixed or definite time period rather than have perpetual life.

- A key factor in the choice of business form is limited liability, which investors in corporations, limited partnerships, and limited liability companies have but proprietors and general partners do not have. Transfer of ownership interests is easiest in corporations with publicly traded stock. In other organizations, the value of interests is often not known, and often restrictions are placed on transfers. A corporation may have perpetual existence as a legal entity, but in practice, other organizations can last for very long times under contracts that control what happens in case of death or retirement of an investor or partner.

- A franchise exists when a franchisee pays a fee and is granted the right to sell a franchisor's goods or services. Marketing is associated with the franchisor's trade name or trademark. The relationship is defined by a franchise agreement that sets forth the rights and duties associated with the use of the franchise marks or names, the use of the franchise operating manual, designated territory of operation, royalty payments, the advertising commitment, and termination.

REVIEW AND DISCUSSION QUESTIONS

1. Define the following terms:

sole proprietorship	limited liability
partnership	joint venture
limited partnership	cooperative
corporation	syndicate
limited liability company	franchise
fiduciary duty	

2. Four people jointly own a summer cottage and use it solely for their personal enjoyment. Is this a partnership? What if they rent the cottage to other people

for part of the year? Suppose a renter dies in the cottage due to a gas leak. Could all owners be liable?

CASE QUESTIONS

3. Dr. Citrin had an agreement that had Dr. Mehta work in Citrin's medical offices to see his patients when he was on vacation. When Citrin was on vacation, Mehta saw a patient and misdiagnosed the problem; the patient died. The heirs of the patient sued Citrin, claiming that Citrin and Mehta were partners. Were they? [*Impastato* v. *DeGirolamo*, 459 N.Y.S.2d 512 (N.Y. Sup.Ct., Special Term, 1983)]

4. Pena and Antennucci were partners in a medical practice. Both were sued by a patient for malpractice committed by Pena. The jury found that Pena had committed malpractice and imposed a judgment of $4 million against Pena and Antennucci. Antennucci contended he should not be liable because he was not involved in the malpractice. Was he right? [*Zuckerman* v. *Antennucci*, 478 N.Y.S.2d 578 (Sup. Ct., N.Y., 1984)]

5. Covalt owned 25 percent and High owned 75 percent of CSI, a corporation that they operated together. They also entered into a partnership to build an office building that they leased to CSI. Covalt resigned from CSI and went to work for a competitor. When the lease on the office building expired, Covalt demanded that High raise CSI's rent in a new lease, from $1,850 to $2,850 per month. High signed CSI to a new lease in the building at the old rent. Covalt sued High for breach of fiduciary duty to the partnership. Who was right? [*Covalt* v. *High*, 675 P.2d 999 (Ct. App., N.M., 1983)]

 Check your answer at http://meiners.westbuslaw.com

6. Bane was a partner in a Chicago law firm before he retired in 1985. The law firm had a retirement plan funded by current income, not by partners' contribution during their working lives. Retired partners were to be given a pension based on their income before retirement. The law firm merged with another law firm. The merger did not work, and the new firm was dissolved in 1988, which left no retirement funds for Bane. Bane sued the managing partners of the law firm, claiming that their mismanagement was responsible for the loss of his pension. Did he win? [*Bane* v. *Ferguson*, 890 F.2d 11 (7th Cir., 1989)]

7. When Dr. Witlin died, his wife inherited his 2.654 percent share of a partnership that owned a hospital. As the partnership agreement called for, the dead partner's share was paid off. The amount paid was based on the financial records of the time of the payment. The other partners did not reveal that they were in the process of selling the hospital, which soon happened and more than tripled the value of the partners' shares. Was Mrs. Witlin due the sale price of the hospital or its value based on financial records at the time of her husband's death? [*Estate* of *Witlin*, 83 Cal.App.3d 167 (Ct. App., Calif., 1978)]

 Check your answer at http://meiners.westbuslaw.com

8. A law firm, organized as a general partnership, signed a ten-year lease for office property with Sheehan, who was a partner in the law firm. Sheehan withdrew from the law firm and assigned his partnership interest to the remaining partners. Nothing was done at that time to change the lease of the office property. Five years later, the law firm defaulted on the lease and filed for bankruptcy.

Sheehan sued all past and present law firm partners for past due rent and other damages from the default on the lease. The trial court held that the personal assets of the original partners who signed the lease were not at stake, only the assets of the bankrupt partnership, and that none of the later joining partners were liable. Is that correct? [*8182 Maryland Assoc. L.P.* v. *Sheehan*, 14 S.W.3d 576 (Sup. Ct., Mo., 2000)]

9. The Haffs were sole shareholders of a restaurant supply wholesale business that often bought supplies from Cosgrove. When Haff ceased operations, it owed Cosgrove $9,000. Cosgrove sued the Haffs personally for the amount owed, contending that the corporate shield should be pierced. The two companies had done business for ten years. Cosgrove testified that it did not know what legal form Haff had. The phone was answered "J. Haff." The invoices sent from Cosgrove were made out to "J.A. Haff & Sons, Inc." Checks came from "J.A. Haff & Sons." The evidence was that Haff followed proper corporate procedures for annual meetings and separate accounts. Was the veil to be pierced? [*Cosgrove Distributors, Inc.* v. *Haff*, 798 N.E.2d 139 (App. Ct., Ill., 2003)]

 Check your answer at <http://meiners.westbuslaw.com>

10. Miner gave Karen Lynn, a corporation, a ten-year lease for retail space in Chicago. Later, Lynn, a subsidiary of another company that was owned by one person, was in default due to unpaid rent and the court issued a default judgment for $22,000. Miner moved to enforce the judgment, but Lynn had no assets. Miner sued Lynn's parent corporation and the owner of that corporation, requesting the court pierce the corporate veil and hold them liable for the debt. Would it do that? [*Miner* v. *Fashion Enterprise, Inc.*, 794 N.E.2d 902 (App. Ct., Ill., 2003)]

11. Beracha, CEO of Campbell, which operated a bread plant in North Carolina, told the employees in a meeting in August that the plant was profitable and their jobs were secure. In December, the employees were told that the plant would be closed in February and their jobs lost. Some employees sued Beracha and the company for negligent misrepresentation. The trial court dismissed the suit; the employees appealed. Do they have a claim? [*Jordan* v. *Earthgrains*, 576 S.E.2d 336 (Ct. App., N.C., 2003)]

 Check your answer at <http://meiners.westbuslaw.com>

12. Morales owned 20.4 percent of the stock in TV Answer, Inc. After a dispute with other director-shareholders who owned 75 percent of the stock, Morales left the board of the company. The directors made a new stock offering to all shareholders except Morales. When Morales contested the legality of being excluded from the offering, he was given three days to pay a $5 million purchase price. He then sued the directors, contending that he was being treated in a discriminatory fashion, which was a breach of the fiduciary duty of the directors to treat all shareholders equally. Was he right? [*Morales* v. *TV Answer*, 19 Del.J.Corp.L. 290 (Ct. Chan., Del., 1993)]

13. Rust and Kelly each contributed half the price of a plot of land they intended to subdivide and sell. Rust gave Kelly his share of the purchase price. When Kelly bought the land, he put the title to it in his name only. Several years later, Rust found out that Kelly had left him off the deed on the property and sued for his share of the purchase price plus interest. Kelly claimed that Rust had abandoned the property, and so he did not owe him anything. Rust claimed they had a joint venture. Was there a joint venture? [*Rust* v. *Kelly*, 741 P.2d 786 (Sup. Ct., Mont., 1987)]

14. Petricca entered into an agreement that gave Pioneer a one-year option to buy land owned by Petricca. Pioneer intended to build a shopping center on the land. Pioneer paid Petricca $11,300 per month in option fees and had the right to buy the land or not. The contract also allowed Petricca an option to form a joint venture with Pioneer to develop the shopping center. A month later, Petricca notified Pioneer it would participate in the joint venture. Pioneer moved forward, but could not get zoning permission for the construction. Pioneer dropped this effort and bought another piece of land to build on. Petricca sued Pioneer for breach of fiduciary duty arising under the existence of a joint venture. Was there a joint venture? [*Petricca Development L.P.* v. *Pioneer Development Co.*, 214 F.3d 216 (1st Cir., 2000)]

15. Domino's Pizza sold two franchises to experienced Domino's managers. The agreement stated that the franchisees agreed to "operate the Store in full compliance with all applicable laws, ordinances and regulations." If not, Domino's had the right to terminate the franchise if problems were not corrected within thirty days of notification. Later, the franchisees' books were a mess, reports were not filed on time, and the franchisees failed to pay city, state, or federal payroll, income, and sales taxes. After six months of the franchisees' not correcting the problems, Domino's gave thirty days' termination notice. The franchisees put the stores up for sale. When prospective buyers asked Domino's about the history of the stores, Domino's told the truth, which led to the sale price falling below what would have been offered if Domino's had not said anything and let the franchisees sell on their own. The franchisees sued Domino's; a jury awarded the franchisees over $2 million damages. Did this decision stand? [*Bennett Enterprises* v. *Domino's Pizza*, 45 F.3d 493 (D.C. Cir., 1995)]

16. Several investors, organized through corporations, owned several Burger King restaurants in Wisconsin. The franchise agreement stated that franchise owners could not own competitor franchises. The investors formed other corporations and then obtained Hardee's franchises. Burger King terminated its franchise agreements with the owners for violating the franchise agreements. The owners argued that since the Burger King and Hardee's franchises were owned by different corporations the agreement had not been breached. Is that correct? [*Deutchland Enterprises* v. *Burger King*, 957 F.2d 449 (7th Cir., 1992)]

ETHICS QUESTIONS

17. Jensen and Cross had a partnership selling insulation to contractors. The business was successful, and the two became wealthy. As the business grew, they discussed the advantages of the corporate form of business. Since their partnership agreement served them well, the change to a corporation was not undertaken. The partners came to fear that some of the workers for the contractors to whom they sold insulation were developing illnesses that may have been caused by long-term exposure to the insulation. By incorporating now, Jensen and Cross hoped to avoid personal liability for the possible injuries to those workers. Was the move to incorporate ethically justifiable even if it was a good business practice?

18. Cook and Smith formed a limited partnership called Trinty Development to develop a shopping center. Adjacent to the shopping center was a ten-acre tract of undeveloped land that came up for sale after the limited partnership had begun its operations. Cook, the general partner, purchased the property from McCade, but only after McCade had refused to sell the property to Trinty. McCade stated

that he did not want to do business with Smith. Cook then sold the property to another developer for a $60,000 profit. If Cook had sold the property to Trinty, Trinty could have profited. Smith has objected to the sale and purchase by Cook. What alternatives did Cook have? With regard to his employment with Trinty, what was the ethical choice? How was Trinty damaged? With regard to Cook's relationship with McCade, what were Cook's alternatives?

PULLING IT Together

Torts and Business Organizations

Three accountants formed a partnership. Deodati was a client of McCreight, one of the partners. Deodati authorized McCreight to buy and sell certificates of deposit on his behalf. McCreight stole Deodati's money, generating fictitious income statements to conceal the fraud. The other partners knew nothing about the fraud. Deodati paid the partnership $3,500 for accounting services. When another partner uncovered the fraud, he notified Deodati, who sued the partnership for his losses. The trial court awarded Deodati $290,000 and imposed joint and several liability against the partnership and the individual partners. The innocent partners then filed for bankruptcy. Deodati sought to prevent them from discharging the debt because it arose from fraud. The trial court held for the innocent partners. Deodati appealed. Are the innocent partners liable?

In the Matter of M.M. Winkler & Associates, 239 F.3d 746 (5th Cir., 2001)

INTERNET ASSIGNMENT

After working on an assembly line for twenty-five years, Jim Howard retired from his job and opened a car parts store. Although he incorporated his business, Jim was a sole shareholder and president who never observed any corporate formalities such as tracking his capital investments, salary, dividends and other distributions, or appointing directors and holding regular meetings. Although Jim knew cars, he ordered too many parts, failed to pay everything that he owed, overcharged his customers, and pocketed the profits. When one of Jim's largest suppliers, Fender Bender Supply, sued Jim and his business for payment of significantly overdue debts, Jim claimed that the business was insolvent and that he could not be held personally liable for the corporation's liabilities.

Is Jim right? Can Fender Bender recover against Jim, his business, or both? Under what legal theory might Fender Bender reach Jim's assets to satisfy the debts? For answers to these questions, see the First Circuit Court of Appeals decision in the following case:

Goya Foods, Inc. v. Lilane Unanue and Kalif Trading, Inc. (#98-1553)
http://www.findlaw.com

Chapter 14 | *Employment Relationships*

The Levine Cancer Institute, like most health-care facilities, is concerned about cost control. One proposal recommends reducing the number of doctors and nurses employed directly by the hospital. It recommends that nurses and doctors be encouraged to form a company to provide professional medical services—their services—to the hospital. The hospital would contract with the company to obtain the services of the nurses and doctors it needed as independent contractors. While hospital administrators believe that the plan could reduce costs, they are concerned about several legal matters. Would the new company be an agent of the hospital? Would the hospital's liability change? By using the new company, is it possible to designate the doctors and nurses as independent contractors rather than as employees and thus reduce potential liability?

Another proposal recommended is to have an outsider do all buying for the hospital, rather than have an employee do the supply purchasing. One manager thinks that, this way, if the buyer makes a mistake in product choice or if a patient is asserted to have been injured due to the use of an inappropriate product, then the buyer will be liable for the mistake instead of the hospital. Is that right?

These are among the subjects discussed in this chapter, which considers the range of employment relationships that are possible, how they are created, and the legal constraints on their formation and functions. We begin by considering agency relationships, which are often part of an employment relationship but can be more limited in purpose.

AGENCY RELATIONSHIPS

According to *Black's Law Dictionary*, an *agency relationship* is

An employment [of an agent] for the purpose of representation in establishing relations between a principal and third parties.

That is, an agency is created when a person or company—the *agent*—agrees to act for or in place of another person or company—the *principal*. The agent is a representative of the principal. An agent may negotiate and legally bind a principal to contracts with third parties as long as he acts within the scope of authority granted by the principal. In dealing with third parties—normally the customers or suppliers of the principal—the agent is granted certain authority to act for the principal. The typical agency relationship is compared with the typical two-party business transaction in Exhibit 14.1.

A principal's purpose for developing agency relationships is to expand business opportunities and use the expertise of an agent. For example, John Elway Ford dealership in Denver employs managers and sales agents to make decisions about ordering cars and selling them to customers. John Elway and his customers enjoy business dealings that would not be possible without the ability to use agency relationships, since Elway personally could not directly run everything needed in a large business.

Exhibit 14.1

A Contract and an Agency Relationship

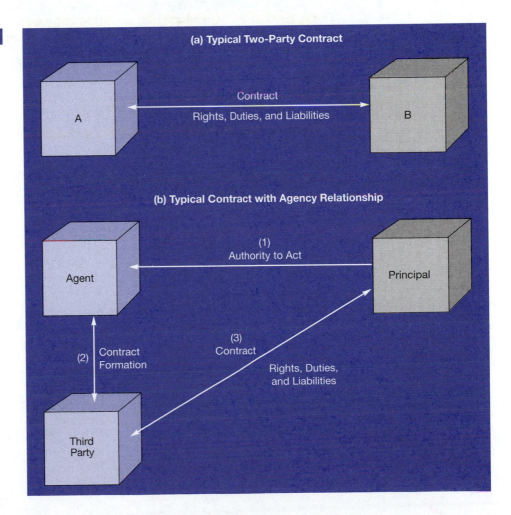

Similarly, the board of directors of a corporation enters into agency relationships with officers of the corporation who are charged with the authority to manage the corporation. The managers represent the directors (the principals of the corporation) and have the authority to bind the principals to contracts. The agency relationship is essential to business.

Creating an Agency

No particular formal procedure is needed to establish an agency relationship. However, the principal must show a desire for the agent to act on her behalf, and the agent must consent to do so. Most agency relationships are created without formal statements such as "I will represent you," but they can be based on a written agreement. An agency can be established by

- Agreement of the parties
- Ratification of the agent's activities by the principal
- Application of the doctrine of estoppel
- Operation of law

Agency by Agreement of the Parties

An agency is normally formed by an agreement of the parties. The principal and agent establish the agency by an oral or a written contract. A written contract is required by law in some cases. Many states require that the agency be in writing when it is to last longer than one year or is for the sale of land. However, most agencies are established by agreements that do not qualify as contracts. The basis of the agency, its own area of law, is that the agent acts for the benefit of the principal and is subject to the principal's control.

One legal document that establishes an agency is the *power of attorney*, which authorizes a person or a company to act as an agent for a principal (see Exhibit 14.2). The power of attorney can be general, or it can provide the agent with limited authority to act for the principal for one deal. The term *power of attorney* describes the document itself and does not mean that the agent (who may be called an attorney-in-fact) is actually an attorney.

Implied or Express Ratification by the Principal

An agency relationship also may be created by the principal's ratification of the agent's activities. This arises when a person who is not an agent—or an agent who is acting beyond her authority—enters into a contract on behalf of a third party (the alleged principal). In such circumstances, the alleged principal is ordinarily under no obligation to be bound by the person's actions. However, the alleged principal may become bound to the contract. Accepting responsibility is a *ratification*. By ratifying the agreement, the alleged principal becomes a real principal, and is bound by the contract as if it had been negotiated by an agent with the authority to enter into the contract.

Suppose you advertised your car for sale for $9,000. A prospective buyer came to look at it while you were gone and offered $8,500, which your roommate accepted, thinking you would be happy to sell it for that. Since your roommate was not your agent, you would not be obligated to go through with the deal. However, you could also ratify the deal by selling for that price.

Exhibit 14.2

General Power of Attorney

POWER OF ATTORNEY

KNOW ALL MEN BY THESE PRESENTS: That I, _____, of _____, have made, constituted and appointed, and by these presents do hereby make, constitute and appoint _____, of _____, by true and lawful attorney for me and in my name, place and stead and for my use and benefit:

(a) To ask, demand, sue for, collect, recover and receive all such sums of money, debts, dues, accounts, legacies, bequests, interests, dividends, annuities and demands whatsoever as are now or shall hereafter become due, owing, payable or belonging to me, and have, use and take all lawful ways and means in my name or otherwise for the recovery thereof, by actions at law or in equity, attachments, or otherwise, and to compromise and agree for the same, and acquittances, releases and other sufficient discharges for the same for me, and in my name to make, seal and deliver;

(b) To bargain, contract, agree for, purchase, receive and take lands, tenements and hereditaments and accept the seisin and possession of all lands and all deeds and other assurances in the law therefore;

(c) To lease, let, demise, bargain, sell, remise, release, convey, mortgage and hypothecate my lands or interests in lands, tenements and hereditaments, upon such terms and conditions, and under such covenants as he shall think fit;

(d) To vote at all meetings of any corporation or corporations and otherwise to act as my representative in respect of any shares now held or which may hereafter be acquired by me therein and for that purpose to sign and execute any proxies or other instruments in my name and on my behalf;

(e) To make deposits and withdrawals and otherwise engage in all banking transactions at any and all banking institution or institutions;

(f) To have access to such safety deposit box as may be leased by me;

(g) To borrow money on the security of the same or surrender the same and receive the surrender value thereof;

(h) To bargain and agree for, buy, sell, mortgage and hypothecate and in any and every way and manner deal in and with goods, wares and merchandise, shares of stock, bonds, choses in action, and other property, in possession or in action, and to make, do and transact all and every kind of business of what nature and kind soever; also for me and in my name and as my act and deed to sign, seal, execute, deliver and acknowledge such deeds, releases of dower, leases and assignments of leases, covenants, indentures, agreements, mortgages, hypothecations, bottomries, charter parties, bills of lading, bills, bonds, checks, notes, receipts, evidences of debt, releases and satisfaction of mortgages, judgments, and other debts, proofs of claims in receiverships and estates and such other instruments in writing of whatever kind or nature as may be necessary or proper in the premises.

GIVING AND GRANTING unto my said attorney, and his substitute or substitutes, full power and authority to do and perform all and every act and thing whatsoever requisite and necessary to be done in and about the premises, as fully to all intents and purposes as I might or could do if personally present, hereby ratifying and confirming all that my said attorney, or his substitute or substitutes, shall lawfully do or cause to be done in the premises.

In WITNESS whereof, I have hereunto set my hand this _____ day of _____, 20_____.

_____   _____

State of California

County of _____

On _____, before me, the undersigned, a Notary Public in and for said State personally appeared _____

known to me to be the person _____ whose name _____ subscribed to the within instrument and acknowledged that _____ executed the same.

(Seal) _____

Notary Public in and for said State

Witness my hand and official seal.

_____

Ratification can be express or implied. An *express ratification* is a principal's clear signal to be bound to the otherwise unauthorized agreement. *Implied ratification* takes place when the principal behaves as if he has the intent of ratifying an unauthorized agreement. It usually occurs when the principal accepts the benefits of the agreement.

Express or implied, a ratification has limits as to what it covers. A principal can ratify only agreements when he knows the important facts. Further, an agreement can be ratified only if the agent purported to act for the principal. The principal must ratify the agreement before the third party involved withdraws. Finally, if the agreement between the agent and the third party was required by law to be in writing, such as a sale of real estate, the ratification must be in writing.

The *StreetScenes* case gives us an example of how implied ratification can come about and the serious consequences it can have.

StreetScenes L.L.C. v. ITC Entertainment Group, Inc.

Court of Appeal, Second District, Division 7, California
103 Cal.App.4th 233, 126 Cal.Rptr.2d 754 (2002)

CASE BACKGROUND   *Clark was brought to ITC Entertainment Group to share and create ideas and to develop projects. Hunt was a partner in StreetScenes, a group of investors. He gave Clark a screenplay he had written for consideration as a movie. Clark told him the script was good and that ITC was interested in making a movie for distribution. Clark said he was an executive producer at ITC and that he could commit the company to distribute the film, which Clark would produce independently.*

Clark was housed in an executive office at ITC, on the same floor as the president. He was provided ITC letterhead and business cards, and he had use of ITC office resources. One visiting Clark at the ITC offices would come away with the impression that Clark was a senior executive.

In Clark's office, StreetScenes agreed it would finance a new company that would produce the film. Clark would head up that company and then use ITC to distribute the movie. Production began, using ITC offices for casting and rehearsals. The budget was soon out of control, with Clark asking StreetScenes for more and more money to complete the project. He assured investors that everything was going fine and that Stevie Wonder would provide music for the film. Eventually, StreetScenes forced the issue and found that many bills had not been paid and the film was a mess.

StreetScenes sued Clark and ITC. ITC asserted that Clark was an independent film producer and they had no responsibility for his actions, as ITC had not approved the notion of distributing the film. Clark was found liable for fraud, but he could not cover the losses. ITC was found liable also for negligent supervision of Clark. The jury awarded StreetScenes $9 million in damages plus $8 million in punitive damages. ITC appealed.

CASE DECISION   Munoz (Aurelio), Judge.

* * *

Ratification is a question of fact. The burden of proving ratification is upon the party asserting its existence. But ratification may be proved by circumstantial as well as direct evidence. Anything which convincingly shows the intention of the principal to adopt or approve the act in question is sufficient. It may also be shown by implication. . . . "where an agent is authorized to do an act, and he transcends his authority, it is the duty of the principal to repudiate the act as soon as he is fully informed of what has been thus done in his name, . . . else he will be bound by the act as having ratified it by implication." . . .

ITC did not repudiate Clark's acts. That in itself was evidence of ratification. . . . The fact that . . . ITC took the "see no evil, hear no evil and speak no evil" defense does not mean there was no evil. [StreetScenes] showed that activities were going on that had to have been noticed at ITC. . . .

Affirmed.

QUESTIONS FOR ANALYSIS

1. ITC said that since it was common in the movie industry for independent producers to have offices located in a distributor's office, its arrangement with Clark was industry practice. Why was that defense not acceptable?

2. What could ITC have done to have protected itself at low cost from this sort of situation?

Agency by Estoppel

Very similar to implied ratification, and legally identical in some states, is an *agency by estoppel*. There, an agency is created by the words or actions of a "principal." Although no formal agency exists, the actions of the principal may lead one to reasonably believe that the presumed agent has the authority to act for the principal. When the agent enters into a contract with a third party for the principal, the principal is bound to the contract and will be *estopped* to deny the existence of the agent's authority.

Agency by Operation of Law

The courts may impose an agency relationship when an emergency exists. Suppose a hurricane is headed for Florida. Unable to talk to the boss, an employee buys $500 worth of plywood to protect the windows and other business property. That purchase is beyond delegated authority. The situation required a decision. The agent, although acting beyond the authority granted by the principal, is provided the authority to do so in emergencies by *operation of law*, and must be compensated.

Classification of Agents

An agent's *authority* is the power to change the principal's legal obligations. That is, when an agent uses authority, say, by making a contract with a third party, new rights and duties are created for the principal. The principal controls this by establishing the extent and the scope of the agent's authority to act on the principal's behalf.

JURIS *prudence?*

Is Slavery an Employment Relationship?

Ruiz, a 60-year-old former schoolteacher from the Philippines, worked as a domestic servant for James Jackson and his wife. She claimed she was paid $300 a year for working 18 hours a day. She said she was hit and slept in a dog bed. She was told she would go to jail and never see her family again if she told anyone.

After she escaped and sued, a Los Angeles jury awarded her $825,000 damages for involuntary servitude and false imprisonment. She was helped by the Coalition to Abolish Slavery & Trafficking, which estimates that 15,000 people a year are brought to the U.S. and kept in such conditions.

Jackson, who knows the law, filed for bankruptcy right before the trial began. When he lost the suit, his employer fired him from his position as vice president for legal affairs for Sony Pictures Entertainment.

Source: *Associated Press*

Agents can have whatever duties they agree to accept, so the classes of agents are nearly unlimited. Some major ones are:

- Universal Agent—someone designated to do all acts that can be legally granted to an agent. The agent is usually given a general power of attorney to do all business transactions on behalf of the principal.
- General Agent—a person authorized to execute all transactions connected with a business, such as a manager who runs all aspects of a hotel. The principal may limit the extent of the general agent's authority to a portion of the business.
- Special Agent—an agent with authority to represent the principal only for a specific transaction, usually for a limited time.
- Agency Coupled with an Interest—when an agent pays for the right to have authority for a business. Suppose you lend someone money to buy a house to use as rental property. The borrower agrees that the rent payments on the property will be sent to you to help pay off the loan. The lender has become the agent of the borrower for the purpose of collecting rent.
- Gratuitous Agent—when a person volunteers with no expectation of being paid for her services, there is a gratuitous agency. The fact that there is no pay does not change the legal consequences of the agency relationship itself.
- Subagents—when a principal authorizes an agent to delegate authority to other agents, the subagents assist the agent. The subagents work for the agent but owe duties to both the agent and the principal.

Acts for the Principal

An agent's ability to transact business for a principal depends upon the scope of authority given to the agent. Authority is determined by statements of the principal, the principal's conduct, or the trade customs in business. An agent can have two general classes of authority: *actual authority* and *apparent authority*. As we just saw in the *StreetScenes* case, the plaintiffs had good reason to believe that Clark had actual authority to act on behalf of ITC. If an agent claims to have authority but in fact has none, the principal is not responsible for the agent's dealings with third parties who have no reason to think the agent has authority.

Actual Authority

Actual authority, sometimes called real authority, is the authority given by the principal to the agent. Actual authority can come from express and implied authority. It confers upon an agent the power and the right to change the principal's legal status.

Express authority consists of oral or written instructions given by the principal to an agent. Suppose the owner of an apartment complex hires a leasing agent and tells the agent to rent apartments at a certain price. The agent would have express authority to rent the apartments as instructed.

Often, when an agent receives express authority, he also receives *implied authority* to do whatever is reasonable to carry out the agency purpose. Suppose a landowner authorizes a real estate agent to find a buyer for some acreage. The landowner does not describe to the agent every step that could be taken. Even though the parties may not discuss the matter, the agent would have implied authority to post a "For Sale" sign on the property, advertise the offer for sale in a newspaper, and take possible buyers to the property. The agent would have implied authority to use normal business practices unless instructed not to by the principal.

Apparent Authority

A principal can be bound by unauthorized acts of an agent who appears to have authority to act. *Apparent authority* arises when the principal creates an appearance of authority in an agent that leads a third party to conclude reasonably that the agent has authority to act for the principal. For example, in *Foley v. Allard*, 405 N.W.2d 503, Allard had an account at an investment company. Since he was a customer, the company let him use its facilities and take calls there. Allard convinced Foley to give him $10,000 to invest for her. He deposited the money into his account at the investment firm and spent it. Foley believed Allard was an employee of the investment firm because her calls to him there were accepted, giving the appearance that he worked there. Even though the firm did not know or approve of Allard's actions, allowing him "to take calls is a manifestation of authority by the principal." Since Allard had apparent authority to act for the investment firm, the firm could be held liable for Foley's losses.

Apparent authority commonly arises when a principal hires a business manager as an agent. As a rule, the general authority to manage a business gives the agent the implied authority to undertake usual business activities.

Duties of the Agency Parties

Once they have created an agency relationship, the parties have duties that govern their conduct. For example, each party is required to act in good faith toward the other and to share information having an important effect on the relationship. In addition, as Exhibit 14.3 summarizes, there are duties that each party owes the other.

Principal's Duties to an Agent

The law of agency emphasizes the duties an agent owes to his principal. This is understandable, since the acts central to the agency relationship are to be performed by the agent. Nevertheless, the principal owes the agent certain duties.

The principal has a *duty to cooperate* with her agent by performing responsibilities defined in the agreement forming the agency. If relevant, the principal must

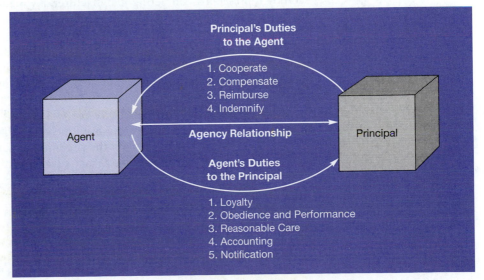

Exhibit 14.3

Duties in an Agency Relationship

Principal's Duties to the Agent
1. Cooperate
2. Compensate
3. Reimburse
4. Indemnify

Agency Relationship

Agent

Principal

Agent's Duties to the Principal
1. Loyalty
2. Obedience and Performance
3. Reasonable Care
4. Accounting
5. Notification

provide a safe working environment and warn the agent of any unreasonable risk associated with the agency. In addition, the principal must not furnish goods of inferior quality to the agent if the agreement calls for the sale of goods of a specific quality.

Unless the agent agreed to work for free, the principal is under a *duty to compensate* her agent. If the agency does not specify the compensation, the principal has a duty to pay for the reasonable value of the services provided. In such circumstances, the agent is paid the "customary" rate for services provided.

A principal has a duty to pay the reasonable expenses incurred by an agent. The principal would be expected, for example, to pay travel and lodging expenses. Hence, the principal is under a *duty to reimburse* authorized payments the agent makes to third parties on behalf of the principal. The agent cannot recover expenses incurred as a result of his misconduct or negligence.

The principal is under a *duty to indemnify*—to pay for damages or to insure the agent against losses suffered while undertaking authorized transactions. Suppose the principal has goods that belong to someone else and directs the agent to sell them. The agent sells the goods, believing they are the property of the principal. Later, if the agent is sued by the legal owner, the principal has a duty to indemnify the agent for losses incurred in the lawsuit.

Agent's Duties to the Principal

The agent's duties to the principal arise because an agent is a *fiduciary* of the principal. That is, the agent occupies a position of trust, honesty, and confidence for the principal. In addition to responsibilities the principal and agent agree upon in establishing the agency relationship, the law automatically imposes certain duties upon an agent.

The *duty of loyalty* requires an agent to place the principal's interests before the agent's personal interests or those of any third party. That is, the agent may not compete with the principal while working for the principal, unless the principal approves. It would be a violation of this duty if the agent also represented another party whose interests were in conflict with those of the principal.

Suppose a sales agent represents an electronics manufacturer and the primary responsibility is to locate potential customers for that manufacturer. If the agent also secretly represents a competing manufacturer, a violation of the duty of loyalty to the first manufacturer has taken place. It would also be a violation of the duty of loyalty if the agent took kickbacks from customers.

An agent must perform instructions provided by the principal. The agent violates this *duty of obedience and performance* by ignoring the principal's instructions and is liable to the principal. However, an agent has no obligation to engage in acts that could lead to personal liability.

An agent is required to exercise *reasonable care* and skill in the performance of duties. The duty is to perform responsibilities with the degree of care that a reasonable person would exercise under the circumstances. An accountant hired to prepare an income tax return who failed to take advantage of a legal tax deduction would violate this duty of reasonable care.

An agent has a *duty to account* for the funds and property of his principal that have been entrusted to him or come into his possession. The agent must be able to show where money or property comes from and goes to. An agent must also avoid mixing personal funds with funds belonging to the principal.

Finally, an agent is under a duty to keep her principal informed of all facts relevant to the agency. Suppose Trapnell hires Amacher as her agent to sell some farmland at a given price. Amacher learns that in the next several months the farmland will likely increase in value because of a new highway to be built nearby. Amacher is under a *duty to inform* Trapnell of this information so that she can decide whether she still wants Amacher to sell according to her original instructions. We see an example of an agent violating duties to a principal in the *Bearden* case.

Bearden v. Wardley Corp.

Court of Appeals of Utah
72 P.3d 144 (2003)

CASE BACKGROUND   *Bearden decided to sell some rental property she owned. She listed the property with real estate agent Gritton, who worked for Wardley Corporation, a real estate brokerage firm. Soon after listing the property, Gritton told Bearden that he wanted to buy the property for $89,000. She agreed and allowed Gritton to take over the property. The contract called for him to pay Bearden $400 a month followed by a one-time balloon payment at the end of five years. Bearden would keep title to the property until the balloon payment was made.*

Unknown to Bearden, when Gritton gave her assorted documents to sign, one was a warranty deed that transferred title to Gritton immediately. He had the signature improperly notarized and then recorded the deed. When he did not keep up on his payments to Bearden, she hired a lawyer to help her. He discovered that Gritton had fraudulently obtained the warranty deed, that he had borrowed money against the property, and that the property was in foreclosure because he had not made payments on the loan. Bearden paid $60,000 to keep the property from being lost.

She sued Gritton and Wardley for breach of contract, fraud, and breach of fiduciary duty. The jury awarded Bearden $75,000 in damages, plus $25,000 punitive damages, plus $50,000 attorney fees, plus costs and interest. Since the judgment was against both Gritton and Wardley, Wardley was stuck with paying the judgment. It appealed.

CASE DECISION   Thorne, Judge.

* * *

Wardley argues that the trial court erred . . . because Bearden did not introduce evidence regarding Wardley's duty to Bearden or the resulting breach. Bearden introduced into evidence a listing contract drafted by Wardley and signed by Gritton, individually and as Wardley's agent. The listing contract provided:

Wardley Better Homes & Gardens and the Agent agree to act as agent for the Seller and will work diligently to locate a Buyer for the Property. As the Seller's agent, they will act consistent with their *fiduciary duties to the Seller of loyalty, full disclosure, confidentiality, and reasonable care.* (Emphasis added.)

Bearden also introduced evidence that it was Wardley's policy to have management or a supervisor review the documents in its transition files and that Wardley had an internal policy that prohibited agents from purchasing properties that an agent listed. From this evidence, the jury could have found that Wardley owed Bearden the fiduciary duties of "loyalty, full disclosure, confidentiality, and reasonable care."

. . . Bearden introduced evidence that (1) Gritton was employed by Wardley, (2) Wardley was aware that Gritton had executed a listing agreement and a real estate purchase agreement with Bearden wherein Gritton acted as buyer and seller's agent and the purchaser of the property, (3) Wardley never questioned Gritton about violating its internal policy against an agent purchasing property listed by that agent, (4) Wardley never asked Gritton to stop representing Bearden, and (5) Wardley never informed Bearden of Gritton's violations of the internal policy. This evidence is sufficient for the jury to find that Wardley breached its duty of care to Bearden. . . .

Affirmed.

QUESTIONS FOR ANALYSIS

1. Since there was no evidence that Wardley participated in Gritton's fraud, why should it be liable?
2. Suppose Gritton had told Wardley he wanted to buy the property he had listed. What should Gritton have done?

Liability for Contracts

The primary purpose of agency relationships is to help principals expand business activities. Agents enter into contracts on behalf of the principal. In large part, the rights and liabilities of the principal and agent are determined by whether the principal is disclosed or undisclosed and by what authority the agent acted.

Principals Are Disclosed

According to the *Restatement (2d) Agency*, a *disclosed principal* is one whose identity is known by the third party at the time a contract is entered into with an agent.

A disclosed principal is liable to a third party for a contract made by an agent who had *actual authority* to act on behalf of the principal. Suppose Cook instructs Chan, her agent, to buy her a car. Chan contracts for a car with a seller who knows that Chan is acting as an agent. Cook is bound by the contract and must honor it. The third-party seller may sue Cook if she fails to perform according to the agreement made for her by Chan.

The principal is also liable if a third party enters into a contract with an agent with *apparent authority*. However, an agent who violates the duty of obedience to the principal is liable to the principal for any losses. To illustrate, suppose Cook did not give Chan authority to buy a car, but Cook's conduct in the past led the seller to believe that Chan has authority. If Chan contracts for a car, Cook is bound by it. However, Chan must indemnify Cook for losses incurred as a result.

Principals Are Undisclosed

An *undisclosed principal* is one whose identity is unknown by the third party. The third party has no knowledge that the agent is acting for another when a contract is made. Thus, the third party is unaware of both the identity of the principal and of the agency relationship. In this situation, the agent is liable to the third party for the principal's nonperformance of the contract.

If the agent had authority to make a contract, the undisclosed principal is bound to the obligations formed with third parties by the agent just as if the identity had been disclosed.

If the agent is found liable to the third party because the principal failed to perform and the third party sues the agent, the agent is entitled to be indemnified by the principal. However, the agent must have been operating within the scope of his authority. If the agent acted outside his authority, the undisclosed principal is under no obligation to accept responsibility for the agent's actions. The *Unisource* case provides an example of an undisclosed principal.

Unisource Worldwide, Inc. v. Barth

Missouri Court of Appeals, Southern District, Division Two
190 S.W.3d 252 (2003)

CASE BACKGROUND   *Unisource sells paper. One of its customers sold its printing business to Ken Barth, who took over the existing business name, Creative Printing & Design. Barth incorporated the business as* Barth Enterprises, which owned Creative Printing. Unisource received a commercial credit application from Barth, as new owner of Creative Printing. Unisource did not know that Barth Enterprises owned Creative

Printing. Barth filled out the credit application and signed "Pres. Ken Barth" as the authorized party who would handle invoices.

Unisource sold paper to Creative Printing on the credit account. There was an unpaid balance of $35,401. A check from Creative Printing signed by Ken Barth bounced. Unisource sued Barth. The trial court held that Barth Enterprises, not Ken Barth, was liable on the account. Barth Enterprises could not pay the amount due. Unisource appealed.

CASE DECISION   Parrish, Judge.

* * *

Plaintiff presents two points on appeal. The first is dispositive. It contends the trial court erred in entering judgment for defendant because defendant was liable to plaintiff as an agent for an undisclosed principal; that defendant, through his agents, obtained credit from plaintiff but did not disclose he was acting as the agent of Barth Enterprises.

The general rule with respect to agent liability provides that one who, as an agent for another, enters into a contract with a third party without disclosing his agent status, or discloses his agent status without disclosing the identity of his principal, can be held liable on the contract at the third party's election. The duty is on the agent to inform the third party of the actual identity of the principal in order to avoid liability; "it is not enough for the agent to disclose or for the third party to know the agent is acting for another." Likewise, the third party's mere ability to discover the name of the principal is insufficient to remove an agent's liability. Also, the fact of incorporation will not relieve an agent of his or her burden of disclosing a corporate principal.

Here . . . the only business name appearing on the credit application was an unregistered fictitious name, in this case, Creative Printing & Design. No reference was made to the corporate principal, Barth Enterprises.

. . . Defendant signed the application in his individual capacity. Absent disclosure of a corporate principal's agency identity, a third party dealing with the agent may consider the transaction to be with the agent and the agent deemed to have intended to pledge his personal responsibility. . . .

Reversed and remanded with directions.

QUESTIONS FOR ANALYSIS

1. Do you think Barth intended to avoid paying his bills from the time he filed the credit application?
2. Barth signed as "Pres." Should that have tipped off Unisource that there was a corporation involved?

INTERNATIONAL *Perspective*

Principals and Agents under a Civil-Law System

Comparing the common-law and civil-law traditions, it becomes apparent that agency relationships differ in important ways. For example, under the common law, an undisclosed principal is bound to contracts with third parties if the agent forming the contract has actual authority to enter into those contracts. The principal is able to hold the third party to the contract. In this situation, the common-law and the civil-law traditions can reach different conclusions. Under civil law, the "principle of lack of communication among parties that have no knowledge of each other's existence" prevails, and the principal is not bound. The principal is not able to hold the third party to the contract unless the third party had knowledge of the principal's existence.

Consider a situation where the principal and the agent have decided to establish their agency relationship on the basis of a written contract. With that contract, the agent has actual authority to act on behalf of the principal. The agent enters into a contract with a third party, and then the agency contract is found to have been invalid. Under the common-law tradition, the principal is not liable to the third party (unless through her actions she had created apparent authority in the agent.) In most countries with a civil-law tradition, the agent's power to perform is independent of the validity of the agency contract. Thus, under civil law, the principal is liable to the third party.

Terminating an Agency

The agency relationship is voluntary. Thus, when a party leaves or when the consent comes to ends, the agency is *terminated*. The agent's authority to act for the principal ends. It may be necessary to give notice of the termination to third parties to end the agent's apparent authority.

Parties may set a specific date for an agency to end. If no time is set, the agency ends when its purpose, such as the sale of real estate, is fulfilled. The parties may agree to end the agency or to extend it beyond its original time and scope of duties. An agency can be ended upon reasonable notice by either the agent or the principal. Such termination is effective even if it is in breach of a contract between the parties, but the breaching party may be liable for contract damages, as we see in the *Rosno* case.

Certain events automatically terminate an agency. Termed *termination by operation of law*, an agency ends without any action by the principal or the agent. For example, if either the principal or the agent dies, the agency ends. It also ends if the subject matter is destroyed (a house for sale burns down).

Professional Business Services Co. v. Rosno

Supreme Court of Nebraska
268 Neb. 99, 680 N.W.2d 176 (2004)

CASE BACKGROUND   *Professional Business Services (PBS) provides tax, accounting, payroll, management, and billing services for health care provider firms. For a number of years, an accounting firm provided most of the accounting work for PBS. Rosno worked for that firm but spent most of his time doing tax work for PBS clients. After five years, Rosno came to work for PBS full time on a year-by-year employment agreement.*

The agreement specified compensation, vacation time, sick leave, retirement benefits, annual bonuses, and a ninety-day termination notice by either party. After three years, Rosno suddenly announced that he was quitting to set up his own firm and that he would take PBS clients with him. Because he said he was going to take PBS clients, PBS fired him immediately and refused to give him ninety-day notice, accrued vacation time, or other benefits. The parties sued each other in complicated litigation. Rosno demanded his pay for the ninety-day termination period; PBS claimed that he could not leave and take clients. The matter reached the Nebraska high court a second time.

CASE DECISION   McCormack, Justice.

* * *

The Restatement (Second) of Agency §387 at 201 provides that "unless otherwise agreed, an agent is sub-

ject to a duty to his principal to act solely for the benefit of the principal in all matters connected with his agency." This general rule forbids the doing of acts in competition with the principal and taking unfair advantage of the agent's position in the use of information or things acquired by him because of his position as an agent.

The Restatement, §393 at 216, further provides that "unless otherwise agreed to, an agent is subject to a duty not to compete with the principal concerning the subject matter of his agency." Comment (e) provides, in relevant part:

> *e. Preparation for competition after termination of agency.*
> After the termination of his agency, in the absence of a restrictive agreement, the agent can properly compete with his principal as to matters for which he has been employed. . . . Even before the termination of the agency, he is entitled to make arrangements to compete, except that he cannot properly use confidential information peculiar to his employer's business and acquired therein. Thus, before the end of his employment, he can properly purchase a rival business and upon termination of employment immediately compete. *He is not, however, entitled to solicit customers for such rival business before the end of his employment* nor can he properly do other similar acts in direct

competition with the employer's business. (Emphasis supplied.)

The trial court found that when Rosno told [PBS] that he was resigning and would take PBS clients with him, Rosno's actions constituted malfeasance. . . . This was in direct contravention of his duty of loyalty to PBS. . . . Accordingly, we affirm the trial court's order declining to award Rosno his salary and vacation and sick leave pay that would have accrued during his 90-day notice period. . . . Finally, we conclude that Rosno is not entitled to a bonus.

QUESTIONS FOR ANALYSIS

1. Suppose Rosno gave his ninety-day notice and then took PBS clients. Would that violate his previous duty as an agent?

2. Could PBS get an injunction to prevent Rosno from competing against them?

EMPLOYEES AND CONTRACTORS

Two important relationships that are similar to agency relationships are the *master-servant* or, in more modern language, *employer-employee* and *employer–independent contractor* relationships. As Exhibit 14.4 shows, while they share common elements with agency, each differs in important ways.

Master-Servant Relationship

Master-servant is an old term still often used in law that describes the employment relationship. The *servant* (employee) is hired by a *master* (employer). Traditionally, servants or employees did manual labor; they were not in a position to act on behalf of the master or employer when dealing with third parties. The master-servant rules apply when an employee is under the direct control of an employer, such as a food service or road maintenance worker. When the employee does not have authority to represent the employer in business dealings, no agency exists, but a master-servant relationship exists. Since employers are presumed to be in control of their employees, employers may be liable for the torts committed by employees in the course of employment.

Employees as Servants and Agents

Many employees now are agents and servants. Some work is under the control of their employers, but, in some capacities, they act as agents, in which case their employers are also principals. Employees often make business decisions that affect their employer. Sales representatives at John Elway's auto dealership who are authorized

Exhibit 14.4	Types of Relationships	Characteristics
Distinguishing Legal Relationships	Principal-Agent	Agent acts on behalf of or for the principal, with a degree of personal discretion.
	Master-Servant (Employer-Employee)	The servant is an employee whose conduct is controlled by the employer. A servant can also be an agent.
	Employer–Independent Contractor	An independent contractor is not an employee, and the employer does not control the details of the independent contractor's performance. The contractor is usually not an agent.

to sell cars within certain price ranges without permission of a supervisor are employees with certain agency powers to act for their employer.

The distinction between agent-principal and master-servant is often blurred. Most employers do not specify to their employees that they are agents in certain matters and employees in others. What matters is what legal authority or responsibility exists when questions arise about the validity of a contract or the responsibility for a tort.

Employment at Will

At common law, employees are presumed to work at will. That is, employers are free to discharge employees for any reason at any time, and employees are free to quit their jobs for any reason at any time. The *employment-at-will* doctrine is limited by contract, statutes, and court-imposed restrictions, as we will see in the next chapter. The *Geary* decision shows that the employment-at-will rule can produce harsh results.

Geary v. United States Steel Corp.

Supreme Court of Pennsylvania
319 A.2d 174 (1974)

CASE BACKGROUND   *George Geary sold oil and gas pipe for U.S. Steel for fourteen years. He determined that a new pipe for high-pressure use "constituted a serious danger to anyone who used it." He told his superiors about the problem and was told to "follow directions." He finally revealed the problem to a vice president, who had the product evaluated and then pulled it from the market. Geary was fired by his supervisor. He sued, requesting damages for loss of reputation, mental anguish, and financial harm. The trial court dismissed Geary's suit. Geary appealed.*

CASE DECISION   Pomeroy, Justice.

* * *

The Pennsylvania law is in accordance with the weight of authority elsewhere. Absent a statutory or contractual provision to the contrary, the law has taken for granted the power of either party to terminate an employment relationship for any or no reason. . . .

In essence, Geary argues that his conduct should be protected because his intentions were good. No doubt most employees who are dismissed from their posts can make the same claim. We doubt that establishing a right to litigate every such case as it arises would operate either in the best interest of the parties or of the public. . . .

Of [great] concern is the possible impact of such suits on the legitimate interest of employers in hiring and retaining the best personnel available. The ever-present threat of suit might well inhibit the making of critical judgments by employers concerning employee qualifications.

The problem extends beyond the question of individual competence, for even an unusually gifted person may be of no use to his employer if he cannot work effectively with fellow employees. Here, for example, Geary's complaint shows that he by-passed his immediate superiors and pressed his views on higher officials, utilizing his close contacts with a company vice president.

The praiseworthiness of Geary's motives does not detract from the company's legitimate interest in preserving its normal operational procedures from disruption. In sum, while we agree that employees should be encouraged to express their educated views on the quality of their employer's products, we are not persuaded that creating a new non-statutory cause of action of the sort proposed by appellant is the best way to achieve this result. On balance, whatever public policy imperatives can be discerned here seem to militate against such a course.

Order affirmed.

QUESTIONS FOR ANALYSIS

1. Is the court correct that, even if employers use poor judgment in cases such as this, to allow litigation about who was right about internal company matters would open the door to endless litigation?

2. Should there be an exception to the at-will rule in a case involving public safety where the employee kept all information confidential, compared to a case in which the employee goes public with negative information?

Employer–Independent Contractor Relationship

The employer–independent contractor relationship differs from the agency and employee-employer relationships in several ways. Consider how *independent contractor* is defined by the *Restatement (2d) Agency*:

> An independent contractor is a person who contracts with another to do something for him but who is not controlled by the other nor subject to the other's right to control with respect to his physical conduct in the performance of the undertaking.

As this definition implies, the independent contractor is distinguished by the extent of control the employer retains over work performance. The more control the employee retains, the more likely the employee will be characterized as an independent contractor. As a rule, the employer is not liable for the torts of an independent contractor.

Contractors as Agents

Some independent contractors are also agents. Contractors authorized to enter into contracts for the principal are agents. This often includes attorneys, auctioneers, and other such persons who conduct business on behalf of the principal. Some contractors do not have authority to enter into contracts for the principal and so are not agents. This would usually include building contractors and others hired to perform certain tasks for an employer.

TORT LIABILITY FOR EMPLOYERS AND PRINCIPALS

Besides creating contractual liability, agents and employees can create tort liability. The principal or employer is liable for the tort of an agent or employee if the tort was authorized by the principal or, more commonly, if the tort occurred within the scope of employment. If the agent or employee commits an unauthorized tort outside the scope of employment, the agent or employee is liable to the third party for damages incurred, and the principal or employer is usually not liable.

Principal's Liability

It is obvious that a principal or employer is liable for torts committed by an agent or an employee following orders. If Mike, the building contractor, tells Marty, his bricklayer, to skimp on concrete and use low-quality bricks, and that causes a building to collapse, Mike, the principal, is liable in tort for injuries suffered as a result of the shoddy work done by Marty.

Vicarious Liability

Under the rule of *vicarious liability*, a principal or employer can be liable for the unauthorized intentional or negligent torts of agents and employees who were acting within the scope of employment. Courts consider many factors in determining whether an act was within the scope of employment. Some of the most important are whether

1. The act was of the same general nature as those authorized by the principal
2. The agent was authorized to be where he was at the time the act occurred
3. The agent was serving the principal's interests at the time of the act

The rule of law imposing vicarious liability upon an innocent principal is known as *respondeat superior* (let the master answer). This doctrine has been justified on the grounds that the principal is in a better position to protect the public from such torts, by controlling the actions of its agents, and to compensate those injured. This rule also means that employers may be liable for torts of employees that can be attributed to negligent hiring or supervision.

This is one of the most difficult areas of agency and employment law. The line between when an employer may or may not be liable for torts or criminal acts committed by employees, agents, or independent contractors is difficult to draw. The *Read* case is one such case.

Read v. Scott Fetzer Company

Supreme Court of Texas
990 S.W.2d 732 (1998)

CASE BACKGROUND *Fetzer does business as The Kirby Company. It sells vacuum cleaners only to independent distributors who are governed by a uniform distributor agreement. Each distributor establishes a door-to-door sales force by recruiting salespeople, called dealers, for in-home demonstrations, delivery, sales, and service of Kirby systems.*

Sena, a Kirby distributor and owner of Sena Kirby Company of San Antonio, recruited Carter to be a dealer. Carter signed an independent contractor agreement to be a dealer. Soon after he was hired, Carter sexually assaulted a customer, Read, in her home. Read sued Kirby and Sena for negligence. The jury found Sena and Read each 10 percent negligent, and Kirby 80 percent negligent, and found Kirby grossly negligent. It imposed $160,000 in actual damages and $800,000 in punitive damages. The appeals court affirmed the judgment but reversed the punitive damage award. Kirby appealed.

CASE DECISION Gonzalez, Justice.

* * *

In applying for employment, Carter listed three references and three prior places of employment. Had

Sena checked, he would have found that women at Carter's previous places of employment had complained of Carter's sexually inappropriate behavior. Sena also would have found that Carter had been arrested and received deferred adjudication on a charge of indecency with a child. . . . Sena did not check. . . .

[In an earlier case] we held that a general contractor, like Kirby, has a duty to exercise reasonably the control it retains over the independent contractor's work. Here, by requiring its distributors to sell vacuum cleaners only through in-home demonstration, Kirby has retained control of that portion of the distributor's work. Kirby must therefore exercise this retained control reasonably.

In concluding that Kirby must act reasonably, we require no more and no less than is required of other general contractors in similar situations. We recognized the direct liability of a general contractor for failure to reasonably exercise the control it retained over an independent contractor when we adopted Section 414 of the Restatement (2d) of Torts. Through its contract with Sena, Kirby retains control of specific details of the work by requiring the "in-home" sales of its vacuum cleaners.

Kirby argues that it owes no duty because it has successfully divorced itself from the independent dealers. Kirby notes that it has no contract with the dealers, only with the distributors. Moreover, Kirby's contract with its distributors provides that: "[Kirby] shall exercise no control over the selection of Distributors . . . Dealers. . . . The full cost and responsibility for recruiting, hiring, firing, terminating and compensating independent contractors and employees of Distributor shall be borne by Distributor."

Kirby also relies heavily on the fact that Read stipulated that Carter was an independent contractor. The stipulation provided that "an independent contractor is a person who, in pursuit of an independent business, undertakes to do specific work for another person, *using his own means and methods* without submitting himself to the control of such other persons with respect to the details of the work, and who represents the will of such other person only as to the result of his work and not as to the means by which it is accomplished."

We do not question Carter's status as an independent contractor, but this status is not a defense to Read's claim. As previously noted, it is undisputed that Kirby directed its distributors that its Kirby vacuum cleaners be marketed solely through in-home demonstration. It was Kirby's retention of control over this detail that gave rise to the duty to exercise that control reasonably. That Kirby's agreement with the distributors allowed the distributors to independently contract with dealers does not excuse Kirby from the duty to act reasonably with regard to the detail—required in-home sales—over which it did retain control. . . .

Sena testified that although he had not done a background check on Carter, he would have if Kirby had directed him to. There was evidence that Sena would have learned about Carter's past problems if he had performed a background check. Sena testified that he would not have hired Carter as a Kirby dealer if he had learned about Carter's history. . . .

Sending a sexual predator into a home poses a foreseeable risk of harm to those in the home. Kirby dealers, required to do in-house demonstration, gain access to that home by virtue of the Kirby name. A person of ordinary intelligence should anticipate that an unsuitable dealer would pose a risk of harm. We hold that there is more than a scintilla of evidence that the risk of harm created by Kirby's in-home sales requirement was foreseeable. . . .

Affirmed.

QUESTIONS FOR ANALYSIS

1. There are millions of people with criminal records. Does this sort of decision create a further disincentive for employers to hire people with problems on their records?

2. Is the result here any different than if Carter had been an employee of Kirby?

ISSUE *Spotter*

Use of Company Cars

Your organization provides company cars for many sales reps so that they can present the proper image for the organization. Occasionally, accidents happen. The company has insurance for the cars, but that rate goes up every time there is an accident. Should an accident be severe, there could be liability in the millions. Sometimes employees are in accidents when they are running personnel errands in the company cars. What is a sensible way to handle this liability that the employer faces?

Determining Liability

Whether a person acts as an agent or employee or as an independent contractor can be important in determining tort or contract liability. An employer-principal is liable for contracts made on her behalf by a person acting as her agent but is not likely to be liable for torts involving the same person when acting as an independent contractor.

Suppose Burns is a sales representative for Reno's Pizza. She negligently injures a pedestrian while driving a company car between sales calls. She is clearly acting

JURIS *prudence?*

Who, Him? Must Be an Independent Contractor

Armando Martinez worked for Harjeet Singh at Singh's Donuts R' More shop in Sacramento. If Martinez is recognized as Singh's employee, Singh would be required to pay payroll taxes, such as for workers' compensation and social security. Singh was not paying these taxes.

After Martinez was shot by gunmen who robbed Singh's store, Singh dragged him outside and told police Martinez was a customer. Singh then told an insurance agent that Martinez was a friend who had dropped by to watch him make doughnuts. Singh was fined $1,000 for falsifying information at a crime scene but was also sued by Martinez, who was, in fact, his employee.

Source: *Sacramento Bee*

---

within the scope of her employment. Her employer would be liable for the pedestrian's injuries. However, if Burns has the accident while going to visit a friend, Reno's may or may not be liable, depending on the extent to which Burns has deviated from the principal's business. The point at which the principal gains or loses liability varies among jurisdictions. Traditionally, an agent who departs from her employment to the point of abandonment is not within the scope of employment.

Suppose Cristina hires Jaime, an attorney, to make a deal on her behalf. Jaime makes a deal with Ahmad on Cristina's behalf. Cristina is responsible for that contract. If Ahmad trips over a loose rug in Jaime's office and hits his head, Cristina is not liable for the tort because Jaime is an independent contractor. However, if Jaime worked for Cristina as an in-house attorney at Cristina's offices, Cristina could be liable for the tort because Jaime would be an employee, not an independent contractor.

Suppose Cristina pays Anthony $40,000 to build an addition to her office. Anthony is an independent contractor, not an agent, so Cristina is unlikely to be liable for any contracts he signs related to the construction work and is not liable if he hits Jaime on the head with a brick at the construction site.

When such cases arise, the courts have certain guidelines they look to rather than the words the parties themselves may attach to their relationship. The *Santiago* decision outlines the major issues that courts consider in such cases.

Santiago v. Phoenix Newspapers, Inc.

Supreme Court of Arizona
794 P.2d 138 (1990)

CASE BACKGROUND *Frausto delivered the Arizona Republic for Phoenix Newspapers (PNI). He worked under a "Delivery Agent Agreement" that stated that he was an independent contractor. He could work as he pleased, but he had to deliver the papers himself at least 75 percent of the time, and if the papers were not delivered properly and on time, he could be dismissed. He picked up the papers at a distribution point each morning and delivered them to a list of addresses provided by PNI.*

The number of people on his route varied over time, but he was paid a set amount.

Frausto was delivering papers when his car hit a motorcycle driven by Santiago, who sued PNI for negligence, claiming that Frausto was PNI's agent. The trial court and appeals court held that Frausto was an independent contractor and not an agent and, thus, that Santiago could sue only Frausto and not PNI. Santiago appealed, contending that Frausto was an employee or agent of PNI and that vicarious liability in tort could be imposed on PNI for Frausto's alleged negligence.

CASE DECISION   Grant, Chief Judge, Court of Appeals.

* * *

We reject PNI's argument that the language of the employment contract is determinative. Contract language does not determine the relationship of the parties, rather the "objective nature of the relationship is determined upon an analysis of the totality of the facts and circumstances of each case." . . .

The fundamental criterion is the extent of control the principal exercises or may exercise over the agent. . . .

In determining whether an employer-employee relationship exists, the fact finder must evaluate a number of criteria. They include: . . .

1. The extent of control exercised by the master over the details of the work

Such control may be manifested in a variety of ways. A worker who must comply with another's instructions about when, where, and how to work is an employee. . . . In deciding whether a worker is an employee we look to the totality of the circumstances and the indicia of control. In this case, PNI designated the time for pick-up and delivery, the area covered, the manner in which the papers were delivered, i.e., bagged and banded, and the persons to whom delivery was made. . . .

2. The distinct nature of the worker's business

Whether the worker's tasks are efforts to promote his own independent enterprise or to further his employer's business will aid the fact finder in ascertaining the existence of an employer-employee relationship. . . . As far as the nature of the worker's business, Frausto had no delivery business distinct from that of his responsibilities to PNI. Unlike the drivers in [another case], Frausto had an individual relationship and contract with the newspaper company. Furthermore, he did not purchase the papers and then sell them at a profit or loss. Payments were made directly to PNI and any complaints or requests for delivery changes went through PNI. If Frausto missed a customer, a PNI employee would deliver a paper.

3. Specialization or skilled occupation

The jury is more likely to find a master-servant relationship where the work does not require the services of one highly educated or skilled. PNI argues that its agents must drive, follow directions, and be diligent in order to perform the job for which they are paid. However, these skills are required in differing degrees for virtually any job. Frausto's services were not specialized and required no particular training. In addition, an agreement that work cannot be delegated indicates a master-servant relationship. In this case, Frausto could delegate work but only up to twenty-five percent of the days.

4. Materials and place of work

If an employer supplies tools, and employment is over a specific area or over a fixed route, a master-servant relationship is indicated. In this case, PNI supplied the product but did not supply the bags, rubber bands, or transportation necessary to complete the deliveries satisfactorily. However, PNI did designate the route to be covered.

5. Duration of employment

Whether the employer seeks a worker's services as a one-time, discrete job or as part of a continuous working relationship may indicate that the employer-employee relationship exists. The shorter in time the relationship, the less likely the worker will subject himself to control over job details. In addition, the employer's right to terminate may indicate control and therefore an employer-employee relationship. The "right to fire" is considered one of the most effective methods of control. In this case, the contract provided for a six-month term, renewable as long as the carrier performed satisfactorily. Frausto could be terminated without cause in 28 days and with cause immediately. The definition of cause in the contract was defined only as a failure to provide "satisfactory" service. A jury could reasonably infer that an employer-employee relationship existed since PNI retained significant latitude to fire Frausto inasmuch as the "satisfactory service" provision provides no effective standards. In addition, the jury could also infer that PNI provided health insurance to encourage a long-term relationship and disability insurance to protect itself in case of injury to the carrier, both of which support the existence of an employer-employee relationship.

6. Method of payment

PNI paid Frausto each week, but argues that because Frausto was not paid by the hour, he was an independent contractor. Santiago responds that payment was not made by the "job" because Frausto's

continues

responsibilities changed without any adjustment to his pay or contract. . . .

7. Relation of work done to the employer's regular business

A court is more likely to find a worker an employee if the work is part of the employer's regular business. . . . PNI is hard-pressed to detach the business of delivering news from that of reporting and printing it, especially when it retains an individual relationship with each carrier.

8. Belief of the parties

As stated above, Frausto believed that he was an employee, despite contract language to the contrary. Even if he believed he was an independent contractor, that would not preclude a finding of vicarious liability. As the *Restatement* explains: "It is not determinative that the parties believe or disbelieve that the relation of master and servant exists, except insofar as such belief indicates an assumption of control by the one and submission of control by the other." . . .

Whether an employer-employee relationship exists may not be determined as a matter of law in either side's favor, because reasonable minds may disagree on the nature of the employment relationship. . . . Vacated and remanded.

QUESTIONS FOR ANALYSIS

1. Why should employers not be liable for the torts of independent contractors they hire when they may be liable for people they hire who are classified as employees?

2. Suppose PNI sold Frausto papers that Frausto then sold to customers on delivery routes run by his employees. Would Frausto and his employees be employees or agents of PNI?

For many businesses, whether workers are classified as employees or as independent contractors can have significant tax consequences. Under both state and federal tax laws, an employer must pay employment and insurance taxes on employees—but not on independent contractors. By hiring independent contractors, businesses can avoid thousands of dollars in taxes and paperwork each year for each employee so classified. Both the Internal Revenue Service (IRS) and state tax agencies have begun looking more closely at such practices.

ISSUE *Spotter*

Contract Medical Personnel?

The opening of this chapter raised the question of the advisability of using contract health professionals, a practice that many organizations have considered in recent years. If you manage a health care provider organization, should you consider hiring personnel, such as nurses and doctors, as independent contractors, rather than employees? Hospitals get sued as part of medical malpractice suits. If medical personnel were independent contractors and were accused of malpractice, would they bear the cost of litigation and spare the hospital those expenses?

SUMMARY

- An agency relationship is created when an agent agrees to act on behalf of and to be subject to the control of the principal. As the principal's representative, the agent may bind the principal to contracts with third parties. By using agents, a principal can expand business activities.
- No formal procedure exists for the creation of an agency relationship. There must, however, be an affirmative response on the part of the parties, with the principal manifesting a desire that the agent act on her behalf.

- Agency relationships can be established by agreement of the parties, ratification of the agent's activities by the principal, application of the doctrine of estoppel, or operation of law.
- Agents' authority can range from the extensive powers of a universal agent, the broad business powers of a general agent, to the more limited powers of a special agent, a gratuitous agent or a subagent.
- The agent's ability to act on behalf of the principal depends on the scope of authority granted by the principal. An agent can have actual authority and apparent authority.
- The agent has actual authority if the principal has given the agent authority to act. For such actions, the principal is generally liable for the contracts entered into on her behalf and for the torts the agent may commit in the process.
- Once an agency is created, the parties have the duty to share information and to act in good faith. The principal owes the agent the duties to cooperate, compensate, reimburse, and indemnify. The agent owes the principal the duties of loyalty, obedience and performance, reasonable care, accounting, and notification.
- The agent has apparent authority if the principal created the appearance of authority in the agent. While the principal is generally liable for the torts and the contracts of an agent with apparent authority, the agent may be obliged to indemnify the principal for losses incurred.
- Agency relationships may terminate through the activities of the parties or by operation of the law. Once an agency relationship is terminated, the agent's authority to act for the principal ceases. It may be necessary to notify third parties to end the agent's apparent authority.
- Agency is distinguishable from master-servant (employer-employee) and employer–independent contractor relationships. Servants and independent contractors do not have authority to represent the employer in business dealings unless they are also authorized to be agents. An employer is liable for the torts of a servant and an agent in the course of business, but not of the independent contractor.

REVIEW AND DISCUSSION QUESTIONS

1. Define the following terms:

agency relationship	undisclosed principal
agent	servant
principal	employment at will
power of attorney	independent contractor
actual authority	vicarious liability
apparent authority	respondeat superior
fiduciary	

2. An agent embezzles funds from his principal and uses the funds to buy a car. What duties has the agent violated? Who is entitled to ownership of the car?

CASE QUESTIONS

3. Barbara Patridge was sued by a lender for failure to pay a loan that was due. Her husband had obtained the loan and admitted his liability, but he signed her

name to the loan without her knowledge. Later, when one payment had been sent to the lender, Barbara attached a letter that said, "Enclosed is a check for $100 as payment toward the outstanding balance on our account. We apologize for the delay as Bill has been in the hospital. I think we've been delinquent in providing you with a plan for repayment. . . . we will make payments to you to show good faith that we wish to satisfy our debt with you. . . ." Was she a principal who could be held liable for the debt? [*Southern Oregon Production Credit* v. *Patridge*, 691 P.2d 135 (Ct. App., Ore., 1984)]

4. Linda Steele, dba (doing business as) The Travel Haus, sold Ben Douglas a vacation package to Hawaii. She had heard that the company she was buying the trip from, Total Hawaii, was having some problems, but she sold Douglas a Total Hawaii package anyway. She sent Douglas's check to Total Hawaii, which went bankrupt, taking Douglas's money with it. Douglas sued Steele for the amount paid; Steele countered that she was only an agent for Total Hawaii and was not liable. Legally, what kind of agent was she? Was she liable? [*Douglas* v. *Steele*, 816 P.2d 586 (Ct. App., Okla., 1991)]

5. Hunter Mining hired Hubco Data to install and customize computer equipment peculiar to Hunter's needs. Before the job was done, Hubco went out of business. Hunter sued MAI, the company that made the computer products that Hubco sold to Hunter, for breach of contract. Hubco was a licensed distributor of MAI when it sold Hunter the computer package. Was MAI liable for Hubco's failure? [*Hunter Mining* v. *Management Assistance, Inc.*, 763 P.2d 350 (Sup. Ct., Nev., 1988)]

 Check your answer at http://meiners.westbuslaw.com

6. Zimmerman, a real estate salesman, asked Robertson whether she was interested in selling her property. Robertson said she might be. Zimmerman came to Robertson's with an offer by Velten to buy the property. After some negotiations, both sides signed a contract for sale. Zimmerman told Robertson he was being paid a commission by Velten. Before the deal on the property was to close, Robertson asked for a copy of the agreement between Zimmerman and Velten, but they refused. Robertson refused to go through with the deal. Velten sued, claiming there was a valid contract. Robertson said that Zimmerman violated his fiduciary duty to her to disclose his interests. Is the deal valid? [*Velten* v. *Robertson*, 671 P.2d 1011 (Ct. App., Colo., 1983)]

7. Guardsmark, a private security company, hired Toufik Kadah as a security guard. His record was fine until one day he was accused of sexually assaulting Eveilia Plancarte, a janitor at the office building where Kadah worked. No one witnessed the event, but one woman saw Plancarte running away hysterically. Plancarte sued Kadah for assault, battery, false imprisonment, and mental distress, and sued Guardsmark based on respondeat superior as the attack occurred while Kadah was on duty. Guardsmark paid for Kadah's attorney. Did that payment imply Guardsmark's ratification of Kadah's wrongful actions? [*Plancarte* v. *Guardsmark, LLC*, 13 Cal.Rptr.3d 315 (Ct. App., Calif., 2004)]

 Check your answer at http://meiners.westbuslaw.com

8. Ruppert owned a construction supply business in Sparks, Nevada. He sold the company to White Cap. The sales agreement contained a clause that Ruppert would not go into competition in Sparks and that he would serve as district manager. One of the employees, Harmon, was unhappy with White Cap's management. He told Ruppert he was going to quit and start a competing company,

which he did. Ruppert did not reveal his conversation with Harmon to White Cap. White Cap sued Ruppert for breach of fiduciary duties for failure to tell White Cap about Harmon's plans. Was that a breach of his duty? [*White Cap Industries* v. *Ruppert*, 67 P.3d 318 (Sup. Ct., Nev., 2003)]

9. Finlay worked as a hearing aid salesman for Robbins (dba Beltone Utah). Finlay did not like the terms of his employment, quit, and went into competition, selling another brand of hearing aids. Some of his customers had been customers of his while he had worked for Robbins. Robbins sued Finlay, claiming that he breached his duty as an agent not to take customers away from his principal. Was Robbins correct? [*Robbins* v. *Finlay*, 645 P.2d 623 (S. Ct., Utah, 1982)]

 Check your answer at http://meiners.westbuslaw.com

10. Two stockbrokers, in clear violation of the rules of their employer, sold worthless stocks to unsuspecting customers. There was no question that the brokers did not have actual or implied authority to sell the stock. The customers who lost money sued the brokerage firm, contending it was liable for their losses because the brokers had apparent authority. Did they? [*Badger* v. *Paulson Investment Co.*, 803 P.2d 1178 (Sup. Ct., Ore., 1991)]

11. Picard was a security guard for National Detective Agency. In violation of company rules, he had his own trained German shepherd dog with him while on duty. Meyers, a passerby, stopped to talk to Picard about the dog, which was in the back of a marked company car. Picard said he could show Meyers how well the dog was trained. When he took the dog from the car, it attacked and injured Meyers. Meyers sued National Detective, which argued that Picard's actions were outside the scope of his employment because he was clearly violating company policy. Could the employer be liable? [*Meyers* v. *National Detective Agency*, 281 A.2d 435 (Ct. App., D.C., 1971)]

 Check your answer at http://meiners.westbuslaw.com

12. Schropp bought a new Mercedes Benz from Crown Eurocars. After the sale, he complained repeatedly to Cohen, Crown's sales manager, about spots on the finish of the car. After leaving the car at the dealership several times to have the problem fixed, it appeared that nothing had been done. Schropp sued Cohen and Crown for fraud for lying to him about supposed efforts to fix the car. The jury found both Cohen and Crown liable and awarded Schropp $500 in compensatory damages. The jury also found that Crown, but not Cohen, acted with malice and awarded Schropp $200,000 in punitive damages from Crown. Could the principal, Crown, be found to have acted with malice if Cohen, its agent who dealt with Schropp, did not act with malice? [*Schropp* v. *Crown Eurocars*, 654 So.2d 1158 (S.Ct., Fla., 1995)]

13. L.M. sued the Southeastern Spanish District Council of the Assemblies of God, the General Council of the Assemblies of God, Iglesia Cristiana La Casa Del Senor (the Church), and its former pastor, Ali Pacheco, contending that Pacheco had sexually assaulted her in 1991 when she was a minor. She contended the Church was liable based on negligent supervision and respondeat superior. The District and Council settled with L.M., leaving the Church and Pacheco as defendants. The jury found the Church liable for Pacheco's criminal act on the grounds of respondeat superior and negligent supervision. The Church appealed. Could it be liable? [*Iglesia Cristiana La Casa Del Senor, Inc.*, v. *L.M.*, 783 So.2d 353 (Ct. App., Fla., 2001)]

14. While working for Lubrizol Corporation, Occhionero was injured by a fellow employee, Edmundson, who assaulted Occhionero. Occhionero sued Lubrizol for intentional tort and on the basis of respondeat superior—"the legal theory that an employer is derivatively responsible for the torts of his employee committed within the scope of employment." The trial court dismissed the suit; Occhionero appealed. Could Lubrizol be liable? [*Occhionero* v. *Edmundson*, 2001 WL 314821 (Ct. App., Ohio, 2001)]

15. Heard was responsible for an injury accident while he was delivering pizzas for a pizza franchise owned by Lee. Lee's liability was determined by Heard's employment status. Heard's agreement with Lee stated that Heard was an independent contractor and required Heard to provide his own car and insurance. Heard was paid a 10 percent commission for each pizza delivered. He was to pay his own taxes and provide his own workers' compensation coverage. He delivered pizzas to customers as directed by Lee and returned all monies collected. He could be terminated for any reason on one-day notice. Was he an employee or an independent contractor? [*Toyota* v. *Superior Court*, 220 Cal.App.3d 864 (Ct. App., Cal., 1990)]

ETHICS QUESTION

16. Clarence has been released from prison after a six-year term for armed robbery and assault. Having "paid his debt to society" for his crimes, he is now looking for work. You are advertising to hire workers for furniture-moving crews. Normally two people work together all the time, so you know Clarence would be accompanied by another employee when on the job. However, you know of recent cases in which employers have been held liable for employees having gone astray during the job and committed crimes. Since Clarence would be in people's homes, it is not impossible that this could happen. Should you not hire Clarence because of this worry?

PULLING IT Together

Contracts, Torts, and Agency

Elliott contracted with the Army to install a freezer at Fort Bliss, Texas. The contract required Elliott to install the freezer and provided that Elliott was "fully responsible for the actions of all employees and contracted representatives" and that Elliott would indemnify the Army for damages "and injury to person or property proximately caused by action or inaction attributable" to Elliott. Elliott subcontracted with Lingle to install the unit, which was done. Later, the Army hired IAS to do some construction work. When IAS employee Diaz was installing a sink, a panel from the Elliott freezer, installed by Lingle, fell and injured Diaz, who sued Elliott for negligence. The trial court dismissed the suit, but the appeals court reversed; Elliott petitioned the Texas high court for review. What controls here—contract law, tort law, or agency law?

Elliott-Williams Co., Inc. v *Diaz*, 9 S.W.3d 801 (Sup. Ct., Tx., 1999)

INTERNET ASSIGNMENT

For over twenty-five years, the Dupont Shoe Company has catered to women clients who prefer conservative and professional shoes. However, one of its hotshot new buyers just went to a shoe trade show and purchased a truckload of loud, brassy high-heeled shoes and sandals from a newcomer called Trendy Footwear, Inc. On the purchase agreement, the buyer signed as "John F. Marsh, on behalf of the Dupont Shoe Company." He also requested that the shoes be delivered to Dupont's corporate headquarters. When the shoes arrived, Dupont called Trendy in an attempt to return the shoes for a full refund, claiming that Marsh had no authority to order them. When Trendy refused, Dupont refused to pay, and Trendy was forced to file an action on its account.

Will Dupont have to pay for the shoes? Can Trendy prove that Marsh was an agent for his disclosed principal Dupont? Is Marshall personally liable on the contract? To answer these questions, see the following case from the Sixth Circuit:

Soberay Machine & Equipment Company, Inc. v. MRF Limited, Inc.
http://www.findlaw.com

THE REGULATORY ENVIRONMENT OF BUSINESS

PART 3

Decades ago, business was almost entirely governed by private relationships based upon common-law principles. Now the legal environment is much more complex. Federal regulation has expanded, often in bursts, over the past century. Regulation is now so common that businesses actively participate in the political process that determines the extent of regulations and how they are enforced.

Why did these laws come about? A century ago, there was concern about the monopoly power of large corporations. After much political agitation, antitrust laws were passed. During the Great Depression, workers believed that they were denied the right to band together to promote their interests. Labor's political influence grew, and the National Labor Relations Act emerged. The 1960s saw social problems, such as race discrimination, that were not being resolved. The civil rights movement helped to promote attitudes that limits on discrimination must be put in place. Pollution became a major issue in the early 1970s, when most of the environmental statutes emerged. Today, as international trade expands, businesses must manage complexities in the law that were not imagined in times past.

Chapter 15 | *Employment Law*

Thirty years ago, anyone hired by IBM believed they had a job for life. The company had grown for years and found ways even to care for employees who were not quality performers. But "Big Blue," once the biggest firm in the computer world, was cut down by tough new competitors and job security went out the window as the company cut back and changed in order to survive in the world of global competition that arose from firms that did not even exist a few years ago.

Like other firms in today's rapidly changing economy, IBM must deal with drug problems, family leave issues, and a generation of workers that understand the lack of job security but are more likely to challenge decisions to fire employees. The strict chain of command that existed in most firms is being changed by a labor market that is more diverse, in terms of race, sex, ethnicity, and by employee expectations that employers will accept more flexible working arrangements. Changes in the law reflect the changes in society. Managing people is more complex than in the days when most workers had assembly line jobs that changed slowly.

In this chapter we look at how statutes passed by legislatures and interpreted by courts have affected the nature of the employment relationship. We start by considering limits on the traditional rule of employment at will and then look at other parts of modern employment law and practice, such as substance abuse policy, employee handbooks, and a number of other rules imposed on employers. The last part of the chapter looks at labor law, which is the law that mostly concerns labor unions but also can affect nonunion workers.

LIMITING EMPLOYMENT AT WILL

As we discussed in Chapter 14, at common law employees are presumed to work at will. As one court said, this means that employees may be fired "for good cause, for no cause, or even for a cause morally wrong, without being thereby guilty of legal wrong" (335 N.W.2d 834, 837). Over the years, limits have been put on the traditional rule because of public policy exceptions, by limits by contract, and because of many statutes that impose specific requirements on many employers.

Public Policy Exceptions

State supreme courts and legislatures have chipped away at the employment-at-will doctrine. There are *public policy exceptions* to at-will discharges for acts that public policy encourages or for refusal to do an act that public policy condemns. In most states, employees may not be fired for the following:

1. Refusing to commit an illegal act (such as falsifying reports required by a government agency or committing perjury at trial)
2. Performing a public duty (such as reporting for jury duty when called)
3. Exercising a public right (such as filing a claim for workers' compensation or filing for bankruptcy)

An increasing number of states have a fourth public policy exception—the *whistle-blower* exception. This occurs when an employee reports an employer's illegal act. The general test of when this applies is that the whistle-blowing is primarily for the public good—to help law enforcement or to expose unsafe conditions—rather than for private gain. This exception is more likely to apply to public-sector employees than to private-sector employees. For example, a government employee who was punished for revealing bribes being taken by her supervisors could be due a reward for having taken that action, if her charges are shown to be true.

When a firm dismisses an employee in violation of a public policy exception to the right of at-will discharge, the employee may sue for *wrongful discharge* or *retaliatory discharge*, which are torts. Most courts limit the public policy exceptions to cases in which there is a clear constitutional or statutory basis. That is, the wrongful discharge suits exist because the state wants to enforce and protect certain public goals, such as reporting for jury duty and reporting health violations, not because there is a desire to control the employment relationship.

For example, in *Fox* v. *MCI Communications*, 931 P.2d 857, the supreme court of Utah held that firing an employee to punish him for reporting alleged violations of the law (slamming long-distance phone accounts) was not in violation of public policy. On the other hand, the Washington supreme court, in *Gardner* v. *Loomis Armored*, 913 P.2d 377, held that it violated public policy for an armored car company to fire an employee who, in violation of company policy, abandoned his vehicle to save a person from a life-threatening hostage situation during a bank robbery. It must be emphasized that such cases are uncommon. The at-will doctrine dominates.

Contractual Limits to At Will

By definition, an *employment contract* exists when a worker is paid for work by an employer. Employment at will presumes that the contract may be terminated by either party at any time, unless the contract includes terms that would indicate otherwise.

JURIS *prudence?*

Don't Rat Out Your Boss

Vernon Blake worked for the Alabama Department of Transportation (ALDOT) for twenty-one years. He was the computer system administrator. Among his duties was "to confirm and document" computer abuse. He thought he was doing that when he created a log to show that his supervisor was spending significant time at work playing computer games and surfing the web.

When this information was reported, his supervisor was given a private reprimand and Blake was fired. He says ALDOT "silenced the whistleblower." Displaying managerial excellence, his superiors also ordered all games removed from ALDOT computers.

Source: *http://www.ALDOTwaste.com*

Many cases are brought claiming breach of employment contract. They generally can be summarized into three categories:

1. An *express contract* exists when the employer and employee agree on employment for a certain time or that job security is provided. The terms of the contract must be considered if the employee is fired. Suppose a company sends an employee to Mexico City on a three-year assignment. The person moves there and a month later is told the job no longer exists. In such cases, there is probably an express contract. Dismissing the employee without just cause—e.g., evidence of incompetence or proof of financial crisis—could be a breach of contract.

2. An *implied contract*, based on written or oral statements, may restrict the grounds for termination or require specific procedures to be followed in a dismissal. Evidence includes the policies and past practices of the employer. More and more, courts expect employers to behave consistently in such matters, not just follow procedure when the mood strikes.

   For example, the supreme court of Connecticut found an implied contract was breached in *Coelho* v. *Posi-Seal International*, 544 A.2d 170. An employee was fired without good cause, despite statements by the company president that he had job security and that the president supported him in conflicts with other employees. The court stated that "there was sufficient evidence to permit the jury to find that the parties had an implied agreement that, so long as he performed his job properly, the plaintiff would not be terminated. . . ." Employers must be cautious about the statements they make to employees, as what they say may be held as part of an employment contract.

3. Similarly, contracts contain an implied covenant of *good faith and fair dealing* that can be extended to employment contracts. The Montana supreme court took that position in *Flanigan* v. *Prudential Federal Savings & Loan*, 720 P.2d 257, when it upheld a jury verdict of $1.5 million for a bank employee dismissed after twenty-eight years of service. No good cause for the discharge was provided; it was found to be a breach of the implied covenant of good faith in employment dealings. Similarly, some successful suits have been brought against employers who misrepresented employment conditions in order to attract an employee, only to soon fire them with no good reason.

Employee Handbooks

Many employers issue *employee handbooks* or *manuals* to explain company policies, benefits, and procedures. The handbooks often discuss grounds for discipline and dismissal. Some explain policy about how such matters will be handled; some assert that employees will be dismissed only for "good cause" and that certain dismissal safeguards exist, such as review by a committee or managerial supervisor. Courts can hold that such handbooks create express or implied contracts that limit the presumption of employment at will.

As the Supreme Court of California noted in *Foley* v. *Interactive Data*, 765 P.2d 373, "breach of written 'termination guidelines' implying self-imposed limitations on employer's power to discharge at will may be sufficient to state a cause of action for breach of employment contract." That is, in California and other states, the courts will look to employment practices, including statements in a handbook, as limits on dismissal at will.

Even if the handbook states that employment is at will, if other provisions of the handbook or company practice indicate otherwise, the employer may have to show that dismissal was for good cause and that proper procedure was followed. Hence, managers should be sure that handbooks and policies are procedures actually followed by the company, or suits for damages for wrongful dismissal may be filed.

Despite cases that have been brought under theories of wrongful discharge that limit employment at will, or that personnel policies in employee handbooks limit the right of employers to dismiss employees, unless an employer has taken specific steps to limit the right to fire employees, the likelihood of a successful claim by an employee is relatively small, as indicated in the *Guz* case.

Guz v. Bechtel National, Inc.

Supreme Court of California
24 Cal.4th 317, 8 p.3d 1089, 100 Cal.Rptr.2d 352 (2000)

CASE BACKGROUND *Guz worked for Bechtel (BNI) for twenty-two years. He had a good employment record. Bechtel's personnel policy stated that its employees were at will. It also stated that employees could be terminated for unsatisfactory performance or because of a reduction in workload or a reorganization. Management decided to cut the budget for Guz's division. Guz and others were fired. This occurred at a time of good work and profits for the company. The duties Guz performed were shifted to other employees. Guz applied for other open positions at BNI, but he was rejected without reason.*

Guz sued, alleging breach of an implied contract to be terminated only for good cause and for breach of the implied covenant of good faith and fair dealing. The trial court dismissed the suit, holding that Guz was an at-will employee. The appeals court reversed, holding that "Guz's longevity, promotions, raises, and favorable performance reviews, together with Bechtel's written progressive discipline policy and Bechtel officials' statements of company practices, raised a triable issue that Guz had an implied-in-fact contract to be dismissed only for good cause." Bechtel appealed.

CASE DECISION Baxter, Judge.

* * *

While the statutory presumption of at-will employment is strong, it is subject to several limitations. For instance, as we have observed, "the employment relationship is fundamentally contractual." . . .

Among the many available options, the parties may agree that the employer's termination rights will vary with the particular circumstances. The parties may define for themselves what cause or causes will permit an employee's termination and may specify the procedures under which termination shall occur. The agreement may restrict the employer's termination rights to a greater degree in some situations, while leaving the employer freer to act as it sees fit in others.

The contractual understanding need not be express, but may be *implied in fact*, arising from the parties' *conduct* evidencing their actual mutual intent to create such enforceable limitations. . . . These factors might include "the personnel policies or practices of the employer, the employee's longevity of service, actions

continues

or communications by the employer reflecting assurances of continued employment, and the practices of the industry in which the employee is engaged." . . .

We did not suggest, however, that every vague combination of . . . factors, shaken together in a bag, necessarily allows a finding that the employee had a right to be discharged only for good cause, as determined in court.

On the contrary, "courts seek to enforce the *actual* understanding" of the parties to an employment agreement. Whether that understanding arises from express mutual words of agreement, or from the parties' conduct evidencing a similar meeting of minds, the exact terms to which the parties have assented deserve equally precise scrutiny. . . .

We see *no* triable evidence of an implied agreement between Guz and Bechtel on *additional, different, or broader* terms of employment security. As Bechtel suggests, the personnel documents themselves did not restrict Bechtel's freedom to reorganize, reduce, and consolidate its workforce for whatever reasons it wished. Thus, contrary to the Court of Appeals' holding, Bechtel had the absolute right to eliminate Guz's work unit and to transfer the unit's responsibilities to another company entity, even if the decision was influenced by dissatisfaction with the eliminated unit's performance, and even if the personnel documents entitled an individual employee to progressive discipline procedures before being fired for poor performance.

* * *

Guz insists his own undisputed long and successful service at Bechtel constitutes strong evidence of an implied contract for permanent employment except upon good cause. Guz argues that by retaining him for over twenty years, and by providing him with steady raises, promotions, commendations, and good performance reviews during his tenure, Bechtel engaged in "actions . . . reflecting assurances of continued employment." . . .

An employee's *mere* passage of time in the employer's service, even where marked with tangible indicia that the employer approves the employee's work, cannot *alone* form an implied-in-fact contract that the employee is no longer at will. Absent other evidence of the employer's intent, longevity, raises and

promotions are their own rewards for the employee's continuing valued service; they do not, *in and of themselves*, additionally constitute a contractual guarantee of future employment security. A rule granting such contract rights on the basis of successful longevity alone would discourage the retention and promotion of employees. . . .

Guz points to the deposition testimony of Johnstone, BNI's president, who stated his understanding that Bechtel terminated workers only with "good reason" or for "lack of [available] work." But there is no evidence that Bechtel employees were aware of such an unwritten policy, and it flies in the face of Bechtel's general disclaimer. This brief and vague statement, by a single Bechtel official, that Bechtel sought to avoid arbitrary firings is insufficient as a matter of law to permit a finding that the company, by an unwritten practice or policy on which employees reasonably relied, had contracted away its right to discharge Guz at will.

In sum, if there is any significant evidence that Guz had an implied contract against termination at will, that evidence flows exclusively from Bechtel's written personnel documents. It follows that there is no triable issue of an implied contract on terms *broader than the specific provisions of those documents*. . . .

Bechtel's written personnel documents—which, as we have seen, are the sole source of any contractual limits on Bechtel's rights to terminate Guz—imposed no restrictions upon the company's prerogatives to eliminate jobs or work units, for any or no reason, even if this would lead to the release of existing employees such as Guz.

* * *

The judgment of the Court of Appeals is reversed.

QUESTIONS FOR ANALYSIS

1. Is there an incentive for employers to make it very clear to employees that they are strictly at will and there is no assurances of continued employment?

2. Is there an employment contract? Guz had to follow the requirements of his employer; what consideration did the employer give?

SUBSTANCE ABUSE

Some abused substances, such as cocaine, are illegal; others, like Valium, are legal but can be obtained illegally. The most common abused substance, alcohol, is usually legal. The National Institute of Mental Health reports that 13.6 percent of all adults have experienced alcohol addiction or abuse at one time or another. About 8 percent of the working population are alcoholics. Add to this the estimated 5 percent to 10 percent of the adult population who abuse or are addicted to illegal drugs or improperly dispensed drugs such as Valium, and it means that as many as one in six working-age people has a substance abuse problem. This issue provides an example of how employers may change the employment relationship in response to a problem.

Issues for Business

Substance abuse directly affects employers because it can mean reduced productivity and higher medical insurance costs, costing employers over $100 billion per year. The National Institute on Alcoholism and Alcohol Abuse estimates that health-care (insurance) costs for families with an alcoholic are double the average. The huge cost of substance abuse does not include the costs that arise from another widely used, highly addictive legal drug, nicotine, which also reduces productivity and increases medical expenses.

The oil spill caused by the wreck of the Exxon *Valdez* off the Alaska coast in 1989 raised issues beyond environmental liability. The captain was found guilty of operating the ship under the influence of alcohol, which was, of course, in violation of company policy. While he suffered a small legal penalty for his action, Exxon suffered over $4 billion in costs. The company subsequently announced that all known alcohol and other drug abusers, even after treatment, would not be allowed to return to critical duties such as piloting a ship or operating a refinery. Such workers would be given less sensitive—and less productive—assignments.

The U.S. Chamber of Commerce reports that workers under the influence of alcohol or other drugs are 3.6 times more likely to suffer an injury or cause one to someone else. The Federal Railroad Administration found that over ten years, forty-eight railroad accidents that killed thirty-seven people and caused millions of dollars in damages were caused by alcohol or other drug-impaired workers. The National Transportation Safety Board found alcohol or other drugs a factor in one-third of accidents involving truck drivers killed in highway accidents.

ISSUE
Spotter

Can You Be Too Encouraging to Employees?

Your company is an at-will employer that has a handbook that makes clear the legal status of employees. But no one likes to think he or she is always on the verge of being fired, or there will be little reason for loyalty. To encourage employee retention, it is not uncommon for supervisors to approach employees whose personal problems have begun to affect their job performance to say that the company "wants you to stay" and "will provide help for you." Does this kind of supportive talk set the company up for a suit for violation of an implied contract if the employee is later fired? Would it be better to say nothing if it is clear there are problems? How are such matters best handled?

Legal Issues in Drug Testing

The discussion here largely concerns nonunionized places of employment because companies that are unionized cannot impose a drug-testing program unless approved by the union in collective bargaining. Further, a substance abuser may have certain rights under disabilities laws, an issue discussed in the next chapter.

Drug-Free Workplace Act

The *Drug-Free Workplace Act* requires all companies with more than $25,000 worth of business with the federal government (which includes all companies of any size) to certify that they will provide a "drug-free" workplace. The main requirements are that the employer

1. Publish and distribute a statement notifying employees that the use, distribution, or possession of drugs in the workplace is prohibited.
2. Specify what action will be taken against employees who violate the policy, which may range from completion of a rehabilitation program to dismissal.
3. Establish a drug-free awareness program and make a serious effort to make it work.
4. Notify employees that as a condition of employment, the employer must be notified of any drug-related convictions that occur in the workplace and the employer must notify the federal government.

Employers failing to comply may lose their business with the federal government. In practice, this statute has been simple to deal with and is not regarded as having a significant effect in fighting substance abuse.

Federal Requirements

Federal employees in certain positions, such as drug agents, are required to participate in drug-testing programs. The Omnibus Transportation Employee Testing Act requires employers who operate aircraft, public transportation, or commercial motor vehicles to test their employees for use of alcohol and illegal drugs. The tests include preemployment testing, random testing during employment, and testing after any accident. Confidentiality of test results is maintained, and the laboratory procedures used are highly accurate.

State Standards

Some state legislatures have enacted statutes concerning drug testing, so one must be aware of local requirements. Iowa allows employees to be tested if:

1. The employer has "probable cause" to believe that the employee's job performance is impaired by drug use.
2. The employee poses a safety danger to persons or property.
3. The drug test is sent to a state-approved laboratory.

There may be no disciplinary action for a first drug offense if the employee completes the treatment that is recommended upon evaluation.

Minnesota allows testing of job applicants if a job offer is extended, if all applicants in the same job classes are required to be tested, and if those who fail the test are notified. Like Connecticut, Minnesota allows random drug testing of current employees only for those in safety-sensitive positions. Vermont, Montana, and Rhode Island, among others, allow testing of employees only if there is "reasonable suspicion" or "probable cause" to believe that alcohol or other drug use is impairing job performance.

Maryland and Nebraska do not restrict the conditions under which drug tests may be required. However, they do provide quality and procedural safeguards for the tests to ensure that records are kept properly and that there is a chance for independent verification of test results.

Utah holds employers immune from liability for action taken by employees dismissed for drug usage or by applicants rejected because they failed a drug test, so long as the employer has a written policy, informs employees of positive tests, and maintains proper documentation of tests.

Not using a state-certified lab for drug tests can cause employers problems. An employee won a wrongful discharge suit against his employers, in *Garner* v. *Rentenbach Constructors*, 501 S.E.2d 83, when he was fired for failing a drug test that was improperly processed at a laboratory not on the list of labs approved by the state of North Carolina.

Employer Substance Abuse Policy

Court cases give guidance as to what private employers can do in the area of substance abuse. Because the elements listed here may not be treated the same in all states, managers are advised to seek counsel or employ an experienced drug-testing firm.

1. Preemployment screening of job applicants for substance abuse is usually legal.
2. Testing of employees on an annual basis or as a part of occasional physical examinations is generally legal. However, physical examinations must be voluntary or directly related to the ability to perform the job. These tests are upheld when a job is safety sensitive, when the policy is announced, and when it is applied consistently.
3. Random drug tests, when announced in advance as a condition of employment, are upheld for jobs where safety is an issue, such as for truck drivers and pipeline welders. Drug tests for employees not in sensitive positions, such as a vegetable stocker at a grocery store, are more likely to be subject to challenge.
4. Drug tests after accidents have been upheld, again because the public safety issues generally outweigh the employee's right to privacy.
5. Substance tests given because of "reasonable suspicion" of improper usage are most likely to be upheld when there is an announced policy of such tests and when safety is an issue. Testing an employee because someone reported that the employee was seen in the company of drug users is less likely to be upheld unless the person is in a position of sensitivity or safety.

In all cases, a *substance abuse policy* should be clear and ensure that the testing is not discriminatory or done carelessly. The policy should state why the tests are done, what is being tested for, what will be done with the results, and what will be the consequences of the test results. To eliminate the chance of a false test result, employees should be given an opportunity to have a second, high-quality test if they challenge the results of a positive test result.

WORKER SAFETY AND HEALTH

Concern about worker safety and health dates to the 1800s. Federal regulations of coal mines were first enacted in the late 1800s. Early legislation concentrated on issues of job safety—accidents, injuries, and deaths. Between 1890 and 1920, most states enacted job safety laws, although many of the laws were weak and poorly enforced. Over the years, laws have imposed more requirements on employers to provide certain levels of safety and health protection.

Occupational Safety and Health Act

In 1970, the National Safety Council reported that 14,000 workers died and two million workers suffered serious injuries on the job every year. Occupational illnesses, such as exposure to toxic substances, cause additional deaths. Congress enacted the Occupational Safety and Health Act of 1970 (OSHAct), which created the *Occupational Safety and Health Administration (OSHA)*, a federal administrative agency. The Act states that employers must provide employees a workplace "free from recognized hazards that are causing or are likely to cause death or serious physical harm" and that employers must "comply with occupational safety and health standards" issued by OSHA under the statute. See http://www.osha.gov.

Inspections

OSHA inspectors routinely visit workplaces as well as respond to workers' calls of concern. The Supreme Court reviewed the issue of workplace inspection by government agents in *Marshall* v. *Barlow's, Inc.*, 436 U.S. 307. The Court held that the Fourth Amendment prohibits warrantless searches. But because OSHA inspectors routinely obtain administrative warrants that do not require a showing of probable cause, unlike such a requirement for obtaining a criminal search warrant, the warrant requirement is not difficult.

Most workplace inspections include a look at health and safety records, interviews with employers, and a walk-around inspection of the facility. Company representatives and employees have the right to accompany the inspector. OSHA concentrates inspection efforts in industries where health and safety problems are the worst—such as construction, petrochemicals, and heavy manufacturing. The Occupational Safety and Health Review Commission reviews challenges to citations issued for safety and health violations. Appeals from Commission decisions go to the federal courts of appeals.

Employee Rights

It is unlawful for an employer to punish an employee for participating in an OSHA inspection or exercising any right guaranteed by the OSHAct. In particular, employees have the right to refuse work assignments they believe might pose a serious threat to their safety or health.

The Supreme Court reviewed such an incident in *Whirlpool Corp.* v. *Marshall*, 100 S.Ct. 883. Two employees refused to work on a screen twenty feet above the plant floor. The safety of the screen was at issue, since one employee had fallen through it and been killed and there had been other close calls. When the employees refused to go on the screen, they were sent home, lost pay, and had a reprimand placed in their file. OSHA sued the employer on behalf of the workers, asking that their records be cleared and that they be paid the lost wages. The Supreme Court supported the workers, holding that the OSHA rule that allows employees to refuse to obey orders that pose a serious risk was within the intent of Congress when the law was passed.

Penalties

Based on inspections by compliance officers, citations may be issued for violations of OSHA rules or for failure to meet the general standard of a workplace free of preventable hazards that could cause injury or death. Penalties may be imposed under Section 17 of OSHAct for the following:

- A willful or repeated violation—up to $70,000 per violation
- A serious violation—up to $7,000 per violation
- A nonserious violation—up to $7,000 per violation
- Failure to correct a violation—up to $7,000 per day—or for knowingly making false statements in OSHA records
- A willful violation resulting in the death of an employee may result in criminal penalties being imposed: first conviction—up to $10,000 and six months in jail; subsequent convictions—up to $20,000 and one year in jail

Since fines are often multiplied because of violations that continue over time, the total fine can be high. For example, Bridgestone/Firestone was fined $7.5 million for willful safety violations related to the death of a worker at an Oklahoma City plant.

Workers and Toxic Substances

Most OSHA standards concern safety and include specifications for machine design and placement, stairway design, and height of fire extinguishers. Health standards have been issued, some of which have had a major impact. Protection from exposure to asbestos was one of the first health standards developed; compliance costs billions of dollars. Other standards have been issued for exposure to vinyl chloride, coke-oven emissions, and other industrial carcinogens.

OSHA must issue standards that "most adequately assure, to the extent feasible, . . . that no employee will suffer material impairment of health or functional capacity even if such employee has regular exposure to the hazard . . . for the period of his working life." Every health standard that OSHA has issued has been attacked by industry and labor. Supreme Court decisions that resulted from those attacks significantly influence OSHA's health standard–setting process.

Risks and Benefits

In the "benzene case"—*Industrial Union* v. *American Petroleum Institute*, 100 S.Ct. 2844—the Supreme Court held that before OSHA sets a standard for worker exposure to a toxic substance it must have scientific evidence that current exposure levels "pose a significant health risk in the workplace" and that the proposed standard is "reasonably necessary or appropriate to provide safe or healthful employment." In the "cotton dust" case—*American Textile Manufacturers* v. *Donovan*, 101 S.Ct. 2478—the Court held that cost-benefit analysis is not required to justify a standard; standards need only be technologically feasible. Thus, costs of complying with a health or safety standard may outweigh the estimated benefits.

Hazard Communication Standard

Besides exposure limits for some specific toxic substances, the *hazard communication standard (HazCom)* covers employees exposed to hazardous chemicals. Chemical producers and users must conduct a "hazard determination" of each chemical they produce or use. Information about chemical hazards must be updated as new evidence becomes available. Where hazardous chemicals are used, employers must have:

1. A written hazard communication program that includes
   • A list of hazardous chemicals in the workplace.
   • The manner in which safety data sheets, chemical labels, and worker training about chemical safety will be handled.
   • A description of how employees will be trained for nonroutine tasks, such as chemical spills or explosions.
2. Labels for hazardous chemical containers that identify the chemical, hazard warnings, and the name and address of the producer or seller.
3. Material safety data sheets provided by chemical distributors with every container. The data sheets identify the chemical, its characteristics, its physical (such as fire) and health hazards, its primary route of entry (such as skin contact), safe exposure limits, cancer dangers, precautions for safe handling and use, proper control measures in the workplace, emergency procedures, date of issue, and identity of who can provide more information.
4. Programs to inform employees of the HazCom requirements and to train employees to detect hazards, to know the consequences of the chemicals, to protect themselves, and to take certain actions in an emergency.

WORKERS' COMPENSATION

In 1910, states first enacted *workers' compensation laws* to require employers to pay insurance premiums for injury and death benefits for employees. The benefits are paid regardless of the cause of a work-related injury; that is, workers' comp is no-fault insurance. Workers' compensation benefits are set by state law. In exchange for paying premiums, employers become immune from employee damage suits (torts) arising from on-the-job accidents. The objectives are to:

1. Provide sure, prompt, and reasonable income and medical benefits to work-accident victims or income benefits to their dependents, regardless of fault.
2. Provide a certain remedy and reduce court costs and time delays associated with tort litigation.
3. Prevent public and private charities from incurring the financial strains that would accompany uncompensated accidents.
4. Reduce payment of fees to lawyers and expert witnesses.
5. Encourage employer interest in safety and rehabilitation of workers through an insurance scheme that bases rates on the accident rating of the employer.
6. Promote open discussion of the causes of accidents rather than encourage concealment of fault, thus helping to reduce accidents and health hazards.

Compensation Claims

Most workers are covered by workers' compensation laws. To have a claim, workers must generally show that they have (1) a personal injury, (2) as a result of an accident or occupational disease, (3) that arose out of and in the course of employment. The negligence or fault of the employer in causing the injury is not an issue. Coverage is broad. Compensable injuries can include mental and nervous disorders and heart attacks that occur on the job.

Most courts are strict in interpreting state statutes that clearly state that the liability coverage of workers' compensation "shall be exclusive in place of any and all other liability to such employees . . . entitled to damages in any action at law or otherwise on account of any injury or death." The actions of the employer, employee, or third person become relevant only if there was intentional infliction of harm, that is, an intentional tort. The employee may then file a civil action for damages outside the workers' compensation system. As we noted earlier, employers are forbidden by public policy from punishing employees who seek compensation by filing claims.

Benefits and Incentives

Workers' compensation usually has five benefit categories: death, total disability, permanent partial disability, temporary partial disability, and medical expenses. Most states do not restrict the amount or length of medical benefits. While some injuries require only medical assistance, others take the worker out of the workplace for a recovery period, sometimes for life. Workers usually receive about two-thirds of their gross wages as disability income up to a state-imposed weekly maximum, as low as $400 in some states to over $1,000.

Premiums Tied to Safety

Generally, workers' compensation provides employers with financial incentives to invest in safety at the worksite. Insurance premiums are based on injury claims records. Hence, firms with the lowest number of injuries, and therefore the fewest claims, will have the lowest premiums. For example, in North Carolina, the average workers' compensation premium is $2 per $100 of wages paid, but the rate falls to as low as 23¢ per $100 for lawyers and rises to as high as $52 per $100 for painters who work on high metal structures. Nationally, premiums average $2.70 per $100 wages. California, at $6.30, is the highest in the country.

A Flawed System?

Employers complain that workers' compensation insurance is too expensive. Employers pay premiums of nearly $100 billion per year. Despite rising premiums, many compensation systems have run in the red. One reason for the expense appears to be that too many awards are given for permanent partial disability, which results in lifetime payment awards, when the worker is in fact not permanently disabled. Fraud and dubious claims plague many state workers' compensation systems.

On the other side, consider the amounts paid for losses suffered from injuries that are usually fixed by a schedule. Suppose a worker loses an arm but is able to return to work. Medical expenses and lost work time aside, how much is an arm worth? Some workers' comp systems would say less than $100,000. It is likely that

ISSUE *Spotter*

Reducing Risks and Improving Looks

To prevent workers from being injured, which reduces the likelihood of an OSHA safety violation, as well as the number of workers' compensation claims, you would like to impose a dress code for employees that covers both safety and looks. You believe such a code would also improve professionalism in the workplace. Can you do what you want in this regard? Does a new dress code change the nature of the work contract you have with the workers? Do you need the workers to agree to the new dress code?

if a jury determined the worth of the loss of a foot for a lifetime, where an employer had been negligent, the award would be much larger. It is unlikely that employers would prefer to operate under the tort system rather than under this system of awards determined by statute.

JURIS *prudence?*

Watch Out for the Glazed Ones!

David Howard was snacking on donuts and coffee while driving a truck in Oklahoma. He stated that he choked on a donut bite, which caused him to sneeze, which caused pain in his lower back. After chiropractors could not solve the problem, Howard had surgery to remove a herniated disk.

Howard applied for disability benefits, testifying that eating donuts and drinking coffee is customary in the truck-driving business. The trucking company argued that sneezing is a "personal internal weakness not related to his employment."

A Missouri workers' compensation administrative law judge sided with Howard and awarded him $18,542 in permanent partial disability benefits. The award was upheld by the Missouri Labor and Industrial Relations Commission. A dissenting commissioner said that he had "serious doubts" about a "donut disability."

Source: *National Law Journal*

GENERAL REGULATION OF LABOR MARKETS

Besides the major laws already discussed, a variety of other laws restrict the labor market. Immigration laws limit who is allowed to work in the country. The minimum wage law sets a lower limit on what employees may be paid. States restrict entry into occupations by licensing requirements. Employers must warn employees of pending plant closings and must provide family-leave opportunities. Employee pensions are also subject to federal regulation.

Restrictions on Immigration

The United States is a nation of immigrants and is the most popular destination for peoples from many countries. Millions of undocumented immigrants work in the country, with large concentrations in California, Arizona, New Mexico, Texas, and Florida. The *Immigration Reform and Control Act* sets standards for employees and employers. To be hired legally in the United States, a person must present certain documents to show identity and authorization to work. Such documentary proof is required even if a person is a U.S. citizen. For more details, see http://www.ins. usdoj.gov.

Since violations of the law can mean criminal penalties, employers must be sure to meet the basic requirements. Employers must collect evidence of citizenship or of legal work status for all new employees. The following documents are proof of personal identity and of employment eligibility:

* U.S. passport
* Unexpired employment authorization card
* Unexpired temporary resident card
* Foreign passport with employment authorization
* Alien registration card with photograph

Combinations of other documents, such as driver's license, school ID card, original Social Security card, or birth certificate, may provide proof to satisfy Immigration and Naturalization Service of identity and employment eligibility requirements.

Federal Minimum Wage Requirements

Federal *minimum wage* requirements were initiated in 1938 as a part of the Fair Labor Standards Act. Over the years, the minimum wage has averaged about 50 percent of the average manufacturing wage. The minimum wage was set at $5.15 an hour as of 1997. Employers must also pay Social Security (FICA) tax (7.65 percent), workers' compensation insurance, and unemployment insurance. These rules apply to almost all nonsupervisory employees in the private sector. About ten states have minimum wage rates higher than the federal rate.

Supporters of the minimum wage contend that the law requires employers to pay a fair wage to employees and will not allow workers to be paid so little that they have trouble buying the necessities of life. Critics argue that the law results in lower demand for workers in the minimum wage category—usually young people, often minorities, with little education or job experience. The result is high unemployment among persons in those groups who never get the chance to work to develop skills that will command higher wages.

Occupational Licensure and Regulation

Entry into many occupations is controlled by various regulations or *licensing requirements*. In such occupations, a person cannot simply set up and begin to operate a business. Rather, permission from the regulating agency is required. Such permission usually requires some demonstration of competency or payment of a high entry fee. The expressed purpose of these labor restrictions is to protect the consumer. The restrictions are supposed to help guarantee that businesses will provide service of a certain quality and that fewer unscrupulous people will operate in the professions.

Regulation Set by State Law

Although entry controls for a few occupations are set at the federal level, most restrictions are set at the state level. In most states, a person must receive a license or certificate from the state to practice as a lawyer, doctor, dentist, nurse, veterinarian, optometrist, optician, barber, cosmetologist, or architect. In various states, an individual must be licensed to be a dog groomer, beekeeper, industrial psychologist, building contractor, electrician, plumber, or massage parlor operator. Usually, a state commission determines the entry criteria for a person to be licensed to practice. In most cases, there is a formal education requirement; in some cases, an apprenticeship period is required or a test of knowledge about the profession must be passed.

Family and Medical Leave

The *Family and Medical Leave Act (FMLA)* applies to private employers with fifty or more employees and applies to all governmental units. Employers must grant workers up to twelve weeks of unpaid leave after childbirth or adoption; to care for a seriously ill child, spouse, or parent; or in case of an employee's own serious illness. While on leave, the employees' health-care benefits must remain in force. When

INTERNATIONAL *Perspective*

Flexibility in Labor Markets

The ability of labor markets to respond to changing conditions in a rapidly changing global economy means flexibility is more important than ever. A group of researchers from Harvard, Yale, and the World Bank looked at labor laws in more than 20 nations to see how they compare.

The authors constructed a number of measures. In all indexes, the lower the score, the greater the flexibility in the labor market. The higher the score, the great the regulatory barriers faced by an employer. The first measure, the Difficulty of Hiring Index, includes the ability to hire part-time labor and use other nontraditional labor terms. The second measure, the Difficulty of Firing Index, includes the difficulties and expense of terminating a worker no longer needed. The third measure, the Rigidity of Employment Index, is a general measure that includes the first two measures and other factors, such as the ability to change the number of hours a worker provides. The fourth column, Firing Costs, is the average number of weeks of wages incurred by an employer in severance pay and other costs that are incurred in the dismissal process. Notice that many poor countries have the most restrictions on labor markets. How beneficial are the regulations in helping the lives of ordinary workers?

Country	Difficulty of Hiring Index	Difficulty of Firing Index	Rigidity of Employment Index	Firing Costs (weeks of wages)
United States	0	10	3	8
Singapore	0	0	0	4
Denmark	0	10	17	39
Canada	11	0	4	28
Haiti	11	20	24	26
Mexico	67	90	72	83
Pakistan	78	30	49	90
Ukraine	33	80	64	94

Source: *http://rru.worldbank.org/doingbusiness*

the employees return from such leave, they must be returned to the same job or a comparable position. Employers in violation of the law, and individual managers who make improper decisions, are subject to suit by the employee, as we see in the *Russell* case, which discusses the grounds for an FMLA case.

Russell v. North Broward Hospital
United States Court of Appeals, Eleventh Circuit
346 F.3d 1335 (2003)

CASE BACKGROUND *Russell worked for several years at North Broward Hospital as an account representative. She had been reprimanded for absences and was on notice that she could be fired if she missed more work. Russell fell at work, breaking her elbow and injuring her ankle. After treatment, her doctor told her she could return to work but could not use her injured arm. After that, the time she worked varied from day to day, as she complained of too much pain to be able to work. She missed several days without calling in to say she would not be coming in. She was fired, and she sued for violation of* the Family and Medical Leave Act (FMLA). The jury held for the hospital. Russell appealed.

CASE DECISION Carnes, Circuit Judge.

* * *

The two types of claims available to employees under the FMLA are interference and retaliation claims. In an interference claim the employee must show only that he or she "was entitled to the benefit denied." In contrast, with a retaliation claim the employee "faces the increased burden of showing that his employer's actions were motivated by an impermissible retaliatory or discriminatory animus." Russell, wanting to take advantage of the lesser burden for interference claims, has briefed this case as though she had brought an interference claim. The Hospital will have none of it, though, and protests that Russell pleaded and tried a retaliation claim, not an interference claim.

We need not decide which of those two legal theories Russell pursued in the district court, because it does not matter. Interference and retaliation claims both require the employee to establish a "serious health condition," and as we will explain, Russell has failed to do that. As a result, she has not established her entitlement to a benefit even under the more employee-friendly interference theory. . . .

The FMLA provides that "an eligible employee shall be entitled to a total of 12 workweeks of leave during any 12-month period . . . because of a serious health condition that makes the employee unable to perform the functions of the position of such employee." 29 U.S.C. §§2612(a)(1)(D). Employees who take leave to which they are entitled under that provision must be reinstated to the position they held before the leave; they cannot be fired for taking the leave.

The FMLA defines a "serious health condition" as "an illness, injury, impairment, or physical or mental condition that involves—(A) inpatient care in a hospital, hospice, or residential medical care facility; or (B) continuing treatment by a health care provider." The first part of that definition is not relevant to this case because Russell's absences did not involve inpatient care. The second part of the "serious health condition" definition, the one involving "continuing treatment by a health care provider" is at issue.

The FMLA does not define "continuing treatment by a health care provider," but the Department of Labor has issued a regulation defining that phrase, in relevant part, as follows:

(2) *Continuing Treatment* by a health care provider. A serious health condition involving continuing treatment by a health care provider includes any one or more of the following:

(i) *A period of incapacity* (*i.e.*, inability to work, attend school or perform other regular daily activities due to the serious health condition, treatment therefor, or recovery therefrom) of *more than three consecutive calendar days*, and any subsequent treatment or period of incapacity relating to the same condition, that also involves:

(A) Treatment two or more times by a health care provider, by a nurse or physician's assistant under direct supervision of a health care provider, or by a provider of health care services (*e.g.*, physical therapist) under orders of, or on referral by, a health care provider; or

(B) Treatment by a health care provider on at least one occasion which results in a regimen of continuing treatment under the supervision of the health care provider. . . . 29 C.F.R. §§825.114(a)(2). . . .

If we interpret §§825.114 as requiring full days of incapacity, as we do, the requirement will ensure that "serious health conditions" are in fact serious, and are ones that result in an extended period of incapacity, as Congress intended. This interpretation adds certainty to the law by reading the regulation to set forth an objective, bright-line rule defining the period of incapacity necessary to invoke the protections of the FMLA. . . .

To summarize our conclusions, we hold that 29 C.F.R. §§825.114, the Department of Labor's regulation requiring that an employee be incapacitated for more than three consecutive calendar days in order to have a qualifying "serious health condition," is valid. And it is properly understood to require more than three consecutive full days of incapacity; consecutive partial days are not enough. Accordingly, the district court correctly entered judgment for the Hospital, in accordance with the jury's verdict, and correctly denied Russell's motion for judgment as a matter of law or, in the alternative, for a new trial. All of the other issues Russell raises in her brief are either not preserved or are meritless.

Affirmed.

QUESTIONS FOR ANALYSIS

1. If Russell was in too much pain to work, why would the hospital want her to come in?

2. The court follows the definitions of "serious health condition" from a Department of Labor regulation. Congress did not define the term. Does the court have to follow the Department of Labor definition?

FMLA coverage may be denied, on a case-by-case basis, to "key" employees. This may only include employees among the 10 percent highest paid whose leave would cause "substantial and grievous economic injury to the operations of the employer." Also not covered are employees who have not worked for at least one year and who have not worked at least 1,250 hours in the past year. Employees are required to notify employers at least thirty days in advance for foreseeable leave, such as for birth, adoption, or planned medical treatment.

Warning Employees of Plant Closings

The *Worker Adjustment and Retraining Notification Act (WARN)* requires employers with 100 or more full-time employees to give advance notice of a plant closing or mass layoff if 50 or more employees will be affected. The notice must be given direct-ly to each affected employee sixty days in advance of the closing or layoff. Notices must also be sent to collective bargaining agents, local elected officials, and state labor department officials. Such notices must be given for permanent terminations and reduction in work time of 50 percent or more for six months or longer.

Employees who do not receive proper notice of plant closing or mass layoff may sue for up to sixty days' back pay and fringe benefits, interest, and attorney's fees. If the local government has not been properly notified, it may sue the company for up to $500 per day for each day there was no notice. If a firm fails to comply with WARN, it may not be ordered to not cut its labor force. In several states—including Connecticut, Maine, Massachusetts, and Wisconsin—state plant closing requirements go beyond the federal requirements. This statute has not generated much litigation.

Employee Retirement Plans

The most important legislation regulating private employee retirement plans is the *Employee Retirement Income Security Act (ERISA)*. The main objective of ERISA is to guarantee the expectations of retirement plan participants and to promote the growth of private pension plans. ERISA was prompted by horror stories about employees who made years of contributions to retirement funds only to receive noth-ing. For example, the closing of Studebaker in 1963 left more than 8,500 employ-ees without retirement benefits.

ERISA is directed at most employee benefit plans, including medical, surgical, or hospital benefits; sickness, accident, or disability benefits; death benefits; unem-ployment benefits; vacation benefits; apprenticeship or training benefits; day-care centers; scholarship funds; prepaid legal services; retirement income programs; and deferred income programs.

Vesting Requirements

The law establishes *vesting* requirements. It guarantees that plan participants will receive some retirement benefits after a certain length of employment. All plans must be adequately funded to meet their expected liabilities. A termination insurance pro-gram is to be provided in case of the failure of a plan. The law provides standards of conduct for trustees and fiduciaries of employee benefit plans.

The major problem addressed by ERISA was that of the loss of all benefits by employees who had many years of service with a company and then either quit or were fired. The law makes all full-time employees over the age of twenty-five with one year of service eligible for participation in employee benefit plans.

Mandatory vesting (when the employee becomes the owner of the retirement proceeds) was established by ERISA. It provides the employee with three options: (1) to have 100 percent vesting after ten years of employment; (2) to have 25 per-cent vesting after five years, then 5 percent vesting a year for five years, then 10 percent vesting a year for five years, to achieve 100 percent vesting in fifteen years; and (3) vesting under the rule of forty-five vesting. Under the rule of forty-five, if the age and years of service of an employee total forty-five or if an employee has ten years' service, there must be at least 50 percent vesting. Each added year of employment provides 10 percent more vesting so that an employee will be fully vested within fifteen years.

MAJOR LABOR RELATIONS ACTS

The federal labor code, generally called the *National Labor Relations Act (NLRA)*, was enacted by Congress in three major phases: the Wagner Act in 1935, the Taft-Hartley Act in 1947, and the Landrum-Griffin Act in 1959. The only major labor law passed before the NLRA was the Norris–La Guardia Act of 1932. While much of labor law deals with unions, the laws are broader than that and the rules can apply to all workers. We first review the major acts and then discuss the key aspects of labor law in practice.

Norris–La Guardia Act

Before passage of the *Norris–La Guardia Act* in 1932 there was little federal legislation that specifically addressed labor issues. Some courts held union activities to be criminal conspiracies, while others upheld similar activities as legal. The most common tactic of employers was to plead for an injunction to stop strikes and other union activities as a violation of antitrust law. The Norris–La Guardia Act ended such court intervention. The Act declared that every worker should "have full freedom of association, self-organization, and designation of representatives of his own choosing, to negotiate terms and conditions of his employment."

Injunctions Prohibited

Norris–La Guardia prohibits federal courts from issuing injunctions in nonviolent *labor disputes*. For example, to protest the Russian invasion of Afghanistan, the union at the port of Jacksonville (Florida) told the workers to refuse to load goods onto ships that were bound for the Soviet Union; the goods sat on the dock. The shippers said that the issue was a political dispute concerning Russian foreign policy, not a labor dispute, and wanted a court order to force the workers to go back to work. The Supreme Court held, in *Jacksonville Bulk Terminals*, 102 S.Ct. 2672, that since the Act prohibits court involvement in "any labor dispute," the courts could not intervene in this dispute even though the motive was political. Hence, management must deal with the union or begin administrative proceedings involving the National Labor Relations Board (discussed later).

Specific acts not subject to court intervention include *striking*, belonging to a union, paying strike or unemployment benefits to labor dispute participants, publicizing a labor dispute, picketing, peacefully assembling, and advising others to do any of these acts without violence or fraud. The Act also prohibits employers from requiring employees to sign *yellow-dog contracts*. Under such contracts, employees agreed not to join a union; if they did, they were fired.

Wagner Act of 1935

The basic goal of the *Wagner Act* of 1935 (the first phase of the *National Labor Relations Act*, or *NLRA*) was to ensure workers the right to "self-organization, to form, join, or assist labor organizations, to bargain collectively through representatives of their own choosing, and to engage in other concerted activities for the purpose of collective bargaining or other mutual aid or protection. . . ." The *National Labor Relations Board (NLRB)* was created to monitor unfair labor practices and assure that union representation elections are fair. The NLRB does not regulate the substance of bargaining—the actual terms and conditions of employment—between employers and employees; its concern is mostly about proper procedure and review of claims that the NLRA has been violated.

The Taft-Hartley Act of 1947

The *Taft-Hartley Act* of 1947 (the Labor-Management Relations Act), which amended the NLRA, marked a change in federal policy from actively encouraging labor union formation to a more balanced approach. Employers could also file charges with the NLRB for unfair labor practices. The Act prohibits unions from the following activities:

1. Coercing employees to support the union
2. Refusing to bargain in good faith with employers about wages and working conditions
3. Carrying out certain kinds of strikes, such as secondary boycotts, charging "excessive" union initiation fees or dues, or engaging in featherbedding (making employers pay for work not performed)
4. Going on strike during a thirty-day "cooling-off" period or during a sixty-day period ordered by the president

The Landrum-Griffin Act of 1959

The *Landrum-Griffin Act* of 1959 (Labor-Management Reporting and Disclosure Act), which amended the NLRA, increased regulation of internal union affairs. Senate investigations revealed the improper use of union funds by union leaders and election fraud. The Act is intended to assure that union members are protected from improper actions by union leaders.

Monitoring Leadership

Union finances are subject to federal review, and a report is to be available to union members so that they know how their dues are used. Union officials who betray the trust of their office are subject to prosecution. Penalties exist to reduce employer wrongdoing, such as bribing union officials or attempting to hold off union activities by other illegal means. Employers must report annually to the Secretary of Labor about expenditures to attempt to influence collective bargaining activities.

Union Member Bill of Rights

A "bill of rights" for union members is included in the Landrum-Griffin Act. The Act ensures members the right to nominate candidates for union offices, maintains fair election procedures (such as the use of secret ballots in union elections), and allows members to participate in union business, subject to "reasonable" union rules. Union dues and fees are to be set by majority vote of the members. If a union member is to be disciplined by the union, procedural safeguards protect the member's rights, and punishment may not be inflicted on members who challenge union leadership or its actions. Members must be given copies of their collective bargaining agreement and be made aware of their rights under the Act.

The Supreme Court applied this law in *Sheet Metal Workers'* v. *Lynn*, 109 S.Ct. 639. In that case, the head of a local union was removed from his position by union leadership after he spoke out against proposals recommended by the leadership. The Court held that removal from office in retaliation for the statements made violated the free speech rights about union policy guaranteed by the Landrum-Griffin Act.

THE NATIONAL LABOR RELATIONS BOARD

The NLRB is an administrative agency charged with overseeing the National Labor Relations Act. NLRB leadership includes five board members, a general counsel, regional directors, and administrative law judges. Board members are appointed by the president with the consent of the Senate for five-year terms. The board reviews unfair labor practice case decisions by regional directors and administrative law judges. The general counsel oversees the investigation and prosecution of unfair labor practice charges and represents the NLRB in court. The NLRB has regional and field offices throughout the country. See http://www.nlrb.gov.

The NLRB has jurisdiction over all employers and all employees where a labor dispute affects interstate commerce. Certain classes of employees are not covered by the NLRA—federal, state, and municipal employees (the public sector), supervisors, managers, independent contractors, domestic servants, and agricultural laborers. Airline and railroad employees are covered by the Railway Labor Act, which is similar to the NLRA.

Unfair Labor Practice Complaints

In general, *unfair labor practices* are actions by employers or unions that impair the goals of the NLRA. Such practices include employer interference with employee rights guaranteed by the Act; employer-formed or -dominated "company unions"; discrimination by employers on account of union activity in hiring, firing, or other matters of employment; discrimination by employers against employees who testify or file charges before the NLRB; and failure by employers to bargain collectively with the union selected by employees.

More than 50,000 charges are filed each year with the NLRB. Most are charges of unfair labor practice. Charges filed against employers outnumber charges filed against unions about two to one. Each case must be filed by a private party, such as a worker, a union, or an employer.

Most casework is done in the field through the regional offices and involves the following process. Charges of unfair labor practices are filed at field offices that do investigations. If the investigation shows the case has merit, the regional director files a *complaint*. About two-thirds of the charges filed do not lead to a complaint being filed; they are either dismissed by the regional director or withdrawn by the complaining party when informed of their likely lack of success. Of the charges that do lead to a complaint, most are settled before a hearing takes place.

Hearing Complaints

An administrative law judge (ALJ), an employee of the NLRB, presides over complaints that are to be resolved at an administrative hearing. After taking evidence and receiving briefs, the ALJ issues a decision and order. The order either sets out the appropriate remedy or recommends that the complaint be dismissed. Unless one of the parties involved files an *exception*, the decision is final.

If an exception to the decision is filed, the appeal is heard in Washington by a panel of three NLRB members if the case is routine, or by the entire board if the case is considered important. Board members hear no evidence and see no witnesses; in that sense they are similar to an appellate court. The board issues decisions in about 1,600 cases a year.

If one of the parties refuses to accept the board's decision, the case will be referred to the U.S. Court of Appeals for enforcement or review of the order. Most decisions of the board that are referred to the Court of Appeals are upheld. In rare instances, the case may be taken for final review by the U.S. Supreme Court.

Pivotal Role of NLRB

The NLRA gives the NLRB great leeway to make policy and remedies regarding unfair labor practices. For example, in *ABF Freight System* v. *NLRB*, 114 S.Ct. 835, an employee contested his dismissal as a violation of a collective bargaining agreement. The worker lied to his employer about the incident for which he was fired; he also lied under oath to the ALJ, which was perjury. The ALJ upheld his dismissal. The NLRB reinstated the worker with back pay, declaring that the lies were less important than other issues in the case. The Court upheld the decision of the NLRB because Congress gave it broad authority in labor disputes. Its determinations are not to be reversed unless they are arbitrary, capricious, or manifestly contrary to the NLRA.

Because of the board's powers to determine much of the substance of labor law in practice, appointment to the NLRB is politically sensitive. Presidents sympathetic to labor unions because of political support appoint "pro-labor" members; presidents who are more sympathetic to the interests of employers appoint "pro-management" members. As the composition of the NLRB changes, its rulings tend to swing in one direction or another.

Remedies

If the NLRB finds that an employer has committed an unfair labor practice, the remedies it may impose include

- Posting a notice in the workplace
- Issuing a cease and desist order
- Providing back pay for lost wages
- Reinstating dismissed workers
- Issuing an order to bargain with the union

UNIONIZATION

A major responsibility of the NLRB is to determine whether employees want to be represented by a union. The NLRA focuses on the right of employees to "self-organization, to form, join, or assist labor organizations." To ensure that the employees' right of self-organization can be exercised effectively, the NLRB has rules governing employer and union conduct.

Unionization Process

If employees are not represented by a union, a move to unionize might come about by some interested employees who contact a union for assistance, or by a union organ-

German Workers and Employers Belong to Unions

The competitive nature of the U.S economy has always limited the strength of employee unions. If a union representing workers at one firm gets a generous package that makes the firm less cost competitive than other firms in the industry, the firm and its employees both lose. In Germany, competition among firms has been limited because the majority of workers belong to trade unions and most employers belong to industry associations.

Since all autoworkers belong to the same union and automakers belong to the same industry association, one collective bargaining agreement traditionally covered all employees and all firms, so that wages and conditions were the same at all firms. German workers have enjoyed higher wages and shorter work hours than in any major nation in the world. But the high costs made German products less price competitive in the international market, putting pressure on the system.

German companies have begun to build more plants in lower-cost countries, including the United States. Persistent high unemployment in Germany also put pressure on the system to become more flexible and allow more workers to find employment. Increased flexibility has been demanded by German auto producers, or more jobs will leave the country.

izer who contacts employees to determine whether interest exists. The union starts an organization drive. An employee committee is formed and with the help of the organizer calls informational meetings and distributes information.

Representation Elections

If a union organizer collects *authorization cards* signed by 30 percent or more of the employees asking for an election to be held to determine whether the union should be their agent in collective bargaining (the cards are kept secret from the employer), the organizer turns the cards over to the NLRB and requests a *representation election*. The election determines whether a majority of employees in a *bargaining unit* want the union as their agent. A bargaining unit may be all workers at a company, the workers at one plant, or workers in certain skills at one or more work sites, such as nurses at a hospital or at several hospitals. Managers may not be in the bargaining unit. Unions win less than half of the representation elections. As employers have become more sophisticated in responding to union challenges, the trend has been against unions.

Before the NLRB-monitored election, a campaign is held. The union tells the workers of the benefits of unionization and management tells the workers the benefits the company provides without a union. The company is prohibited from threatening those who favor unionization, nor may it promise, say, a 10 percent pay raise if the workers defeat the union. The company can argue about real problems it sees from unionization. For example, if the union tells workers it will get them a 25 percent raise, the company may give its understanding of the consequences of such an event.

The NLRB and the courts protect the interests of the employees in having access to union information and the employers in controlling business interests without interference. As a rule, the NLRB and the courts do not permit access to company property by outside organizers. Like any other private property, the owner can control who comes on the property.

Union Certification

NLRB agents supervise the election, which is often held at the workplace. After the election, the NLRB certifies the results. If more than 50 percent of the employees vote for the union, then *union certification* is granted by the NLRB. The union is declared the *exclusive bargaining agent* for all employees in the bargaining unit and must be recognized as such by the company. All employees in the bargaining unit, even those who do not want the union, are bound by the recognition of the union as the exclusive bargaining agent. (Exhibit 15.1 illustrates the unionization process.)

On the other side of the coin, sixty to ninety days before the expiration of a collective bargaining agreement, 30 percent of the workers can call for an election to attempt to *decertify* a union, that is, to get a majority of employees to vote to remove the union as bargaining agent. The number of such elections has increased over the years.

Exhibit 15.1

Unionization Process

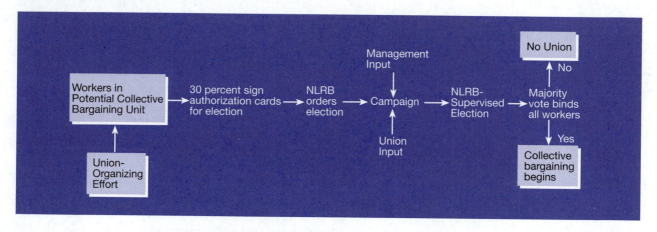

Agency Shops

When a union is selected to be the collective bargaining agent, the workers who join the union must pay *union dues*. What about the workers who do not want to be union members?

The NLRA prohibits *closed shops*, where an employee must be a union member before going to work at a unionized worksite. It also prohibits *union shops*—worksites where being a member of the union is a condition of employment. *Agency shops*—places of employment where a majority of employees have voted to be represented by a union in a collective bargaining agreement—are legal. In an agency shop, employees who belong to the union pay union dues, while employees who do not want to join the union pay *agency fees*. That is, nonunion employees are represented by the union and have fees deducted from their paychecks that go to cover the costs of union services, including collective bargaining and enforcing the bargain. Agency fees are a little lower than union dues.

Political Action

The use of agency fees to support union political activities not directly related to the union's duties as a bargaining representative raises concerns about the constitutional rights of employees who are forced to provide financial support for political action. That is, unions devote significant sums to support favored political candidates. That money comes from union dues and may also come from agency fees. A number of Supreme Court cases have been heard on this issue. In *Chicago Teachers Union*, 106 S.Ct. 1066, the Court listed four requirements regarding agency fees paid by nonunion workers to unions at unionized workplaces. There must be

1. An adequate explanation of the basis for the fee
2. A reasonably prompt explanation of the basis for the fee
3. An opportunity to challenge the fee before an impartial decision maker
4. An escrow account for the amounts in dispute while challenges are pending

In the *Beck* decision, 108 S.Ct. 2641, the Supreme Court found that 79 percent of the agency fees paid by Beck and other non-union AT&T employees represented by a union went to political action. The Court ordered the union to cut its agency fees, refund the excess fees collected from nonunion workers, and keep clear records about union expenditures by category. Justice Brennan noted that unions are not "free to exact dues equivalents from nonmembers in any amount they please, no matter how unrelated those fees may be to collective-bargaining activities."

In practice, the Supreme Court decisions have been difficult to enforce. About two million workers are represented by unions but do not belong to the unions, and so pay agency fees. Most agency fees, like union dues, go to support political action and other union activities not related to the expenses of collective bargaining at a workplace. Unions generally ignore the *Beck* ruling, forcing employees to go to the expense of litigation to enforce their rights.

Right-to-Work Laws

A feature of the Taft-Hartley Act that is still politically controversial is the provision that allows states to pass *right-to-work* laws that prohibit agency shops. In right-to-work states, if a majority of the employees vote for union representation and pay union dues, the union is the collective bargaining agent for all employees. However, no employees can be required to pay agency fees even though their wages and working conditions are determined by the collective bargaining agreement. Since some employees receive the benefits of the union without paying union dues or agency fees, unions claim they are free riders. Right-to-work laws, in effect in twenty-two Southern and Western states, clearly retard the effectiveness of unions in such states.

COLLECTIVE BARGAINING

Once employees choose a bargaining representative, that representative—the union—becomes the legal representative of the employees. The employer must bargain with the union. *Collective bargaining* refers to the process by which the employer and the union, on behalf of all employees in a collective bargaining unit, negotiate a contract, setting forth the terms and conditions of employment for a given time period. Collective bargaining is more than the initial contract negotiation; it is the entire process of contract administration resulting in a continuous relationship between an employer and the employee representative.

Good-Faith Bargaining

The NLRA defines the duty to bargain in good faith as follows:

> To bargain collectively is the performance of the mutual obligation of the employer and the representative of the employees to meet at reasonable times and confer in good faith with respect to wages, hours, and other terms and conditions of employment, or the negotiation of an agreement, or any question arising thereunder, and the execution of a written contract incorporating any agreement reached if requested by either party, but such obligation does not compel either party to agree to a proposal or require the making of a concession. . . .

Essentially, *good faith* means an obligation to meet and be willing to present proposals and explain reasons, to listen to and consider the proposals of the other party, and to search for some common ground that can serve as the basis for an agreement—but with no legal requirement that agreement be reached.

So long as no unfair labor practices are used by the employer or the union, even if there is bitterness, the use of legal labor practices is not a failure to bargain in good faith. The Supreme Court has indicated that the NLRB and the courts should not become too involved in the details of the bargaining process, since Congress did not intend for direct intervention in the substance of labor bargains. Rather, Congress took the position that the parties should be free to reach an agreement of their own making.

JURIS *prudence?*

Not All Notes Are Created Equal

The sixteen violinists of the Beethoven Orchestra in Bonn, Germany, sued to have terms of their collective bargaining agreement overturned on grounds of unfairness. They contend that they should be paid more than other orchestra members because they usually play the most notes in any symphony that is performed.

The violinists noted that some instruments, such as the oboe, usually play very few notes. Furthermore, the violinists contend, it is unfair for musicians who play a solo performance to receive a bonus for that since they do not necessarily play any more notes than do the violinists.

The orchestra director called the suit "ridiculous" and "absurd," but the matter was referred to a labor judge for consideration.

Source: *The Guardian* (U.K.)

Actions Not in Good Faith

Certain actions are recognized as a failure to bargain in good faith. For example, in *NLRB* v. *Katz*, 82 S.Ct. 1107, the Supreme Court said that an employer cannot change the terms of an existing agreement with a union without bargaining with the union. To increase or decrease employment terms—wages or benefits—without consulting the union may be held to be a bad-faith attempt to convince the workers that they do not need the union or to create confusion in bargaining. In remedying bad-faith bargaining, the NLRB is limited to issuing a cease and desist order; it cannot insert terms into a collective bargaining agreement.

Mandatory Subjects of Bargaining

The NLRA states that bargaining in good faith must occur with respect to "wages, hours, and other terms and conditions of employment." These are *mandatory subjects* about which employers and unions must bargain in good faith. However, either party may insist on its position and back that up with a strike or a lockout.

Employers and unions are free to bargain over any topics they agree to discuss. Among the topics that may be placed on the bargaining table because they have been determined by the NLRB or the courts to be subject to mandatory bargaining are the following:

- Pay rate
- Insurance plans
- Holidays
- Overtime pay
- Vacations
- Retirement plans
- Work hours
- Individual merit raises
- Breaks and lunch periods
- Safety practices
- Seniority rights
- Discipline procedures
- Termination procedures
- Layoff procedures
- Recall rights
- Union dues collection
- Grievance procedures
- Arbitration procedures
- No-strike clauses
- Drug testing

There is no requirement that every such issue be covered in a collective bargaining contract, only that the employer must consider demands about such issues raised by the union. In case the employer and the union cannot reach an agreement, an arbitrator may be called in to help get the talks going, or either party may request help from the Federal Mediation and Conciliation Service. These mediators have no authority to impose a settlement but often help the parties reach an agreement.

Arbitration Clauses

Under *grievance arbitration* clauses and arbitration procedures defined in collective bargaining agreements, disputes between employers and unions are to be resolved by an internal grievance procedure. If the results are not satisfactory, disputes are heard by an outside labor arbitrator. If an arbitration decision is violated, the aggrieved party may then go to federal court for enforcement.

Almost all collective bargaining agreements contain such dispute-resolution clauses. The federal courts encourage the use of the grievance arbitration process. This helps prevent the federal court system from being clogged with thousands of disputes.

We Want Higher Wages and Mauve Carpeting

Collective bargaining agreements can include any subject relevant to the workplace that the parties agree upon or that federal labor regulators say must be included in negotiations. Unions representing federal government workers have convinced labor regulators to declare that the interior design schemes are subject to negotiation.

A fight between the Federal Aviation Administration and the National Air Traffic Controllers Association over the inte-rior colors of the control towers at Denver International Airport lasted six years. Hundreds of hours of testimony were taken, and numerous hearings were held. The Federal Labor Relations Authority finally ruled that if the controllers do not like the paint, wallpaper, and tiles used in the newly opened airport, the FAA would have to have the control towers repainted, repapered, and retiled because the FAA failed to consult sufficiently with the union about the interior decoration choices made during construction.

Source: *The Washington Post*

Concerted Activities

For productive collective bargaining, an employer and a union must be able to back up their positions. A union can do so with a strike, an employer can lock out the workers, or each side may use some other activity that puts pressure on the other party to settle. To promote productive collective bargaining, Congress provided that certain activities would be protected so that the parties could back up bargaining demands.

Protected Activities

The NLRA protects the rights of employees, individually or in groups, to engage in *concerted activities* for mutual aid or protection. Protected concerted activity includes most union organizing efforts. It also involves actions by employees, unionized or not, such as a refusal to work because of unreasonable hazards or other working conditions that endanger health or safety.

That point was made clear by the Supreme Court in *NLRB* v. *Washington Aluminum Co.*, 82 S.Ct. 1099. Seven employees, who did not belong to a union, left work without permission because the furnace at their plant was broken; it was eleven degrees outside and freezing in the plant. The company fired the workers, claiming they had to make specific demands to which the company could respond rather than just walk out. The Court held that action taken by the employees to protect themselves from terrible working conditions is a concerted activity protected by the NLRA. Because the decision to walk out was reasonable given the conditions, the workers could not be fired.

Unprotected Activities

If workers engage in threats or acts of violence, they will not be protected by the law. The Supreme Court has held that employers may fire employees for insubordination, disobedience, or disloyalty unless the reason for such activity involves protected concerted activity. That is, a worker may not be fired for engaging in a union organizing activity that the employer thinks is disloyal.

Strikes and Boycotts

A *primary boycott*—a strike by a union against an employer whose collective bargaining agreement is in question—is clearly legal. The law restricts *secondary boycotts*, which occur when a union uses economic pressure to try to force others to stop doing business with an employer not directly involved in a primary labor dispute. The following secondary boycotts are illegal:

- A strike against an employer other than the one involved in the primary labor dispute, such as a strike against the steel companies that sell steel to the automakers if a strike is going on against the automakers.
- Refusal to handle goods or perform services for a secondary employer, such as refusing to carry steel from the steel companies to the automakers during a strike against the automakers.
- Threats, coercion, or restraints against any person engaging in commerce—usually an employee—in an effort to spread the dispute beyond the primary employer. For example, in a strike against the food manufacturer Hormel, the union picketed local banks, some of which did business with Hormel, others of which did not. The NLRB ruled that the union could not picket any of the banks, since they were not directly involved with Hormel products. The picketing was an unfair labor practice, an illegal secondary boycott.

Public Support

One way to make a strike more effective is to get cooperation from the employer's customers. A union may request other firms or the public not to buy certain products. That is a right of free speech, just as is the right to picket a store peacefully to give customers information about certain products sold at the store that the union would like the public to stop buying. For example, the Supreme Court decision *Edward J. DeBartolo Corp.* v. *Florida Gulf Coast Building & Construction Trades Council*, 485 U.S. 568, held that it was legal for the union to distribute leaflets at a shopping mall urging customers not to shop there because of a labor dispute between the union and a construction company building a store at the mall.

Employer Economic Responses

Although employers may not retaliate against employees for engaging in protected activities, they have the right to use economic pressure. As previously noted, an employer may lock out the employees, that is, refuse to let employees work until the dispute with the union is settled.

Lockouts are legal if evidence of bad intent is not shown, such as trying to break the union. A *lockout* is usually defensive—in response to a strike, to prevent a sit-down strike in the plant, or to prevent some other activity that would be destructive to the plant or its materials. So long as the lockout is seen as promoting the settlement of the collective bargaining process, it should be upheld as legal.

Replacement Workers

A tactic successfully used by companies in recent years is the hiring of nonunion workers to replace striking workers. Once a collective bargaining agreement expires, if the union and the employer have not agreed to a new contract and the union calls for a strike, the employer may hire new workers and keep using existing workers who will cross the picket line (crossovers). In some cases, a strike has gone on so long and there were enough replacement workers and crossovers that the union disappeared or lost substantial strength by the time a new agreement was signed. This is illustrated by the *TWA* case, where deregulation of airlines forced firms to be much more cost-conscious than they had been. As companies have become more adept at hiring replacement workers during strikes, the economic power of unions has declined, and the unions often settle for about what the company offers.

Trans World Airlines v. Independent Federation of Flight Attendants

United States Supreme Court
489 U.S. 426, 109 S.Ct. 1225 (1989)

CASE BACKGROUND   *TWA and the flight attendants union began bargaining in March 1984 on a new collective bargaining agreement to replace the contract that expired in July 1984. By March 1986 a new agreement had not been reached. The attendants were working under the terms of the old contract, and a strike was called. TWA announced that it would stay in operation and would hire permanent replacements for striking attendants but that it welcomed attendants who crossed the picket line to continue working. One-quarter of the 5,000 attendants continued to work, and TWA hired 2,350 new attendants. When the strike was settled after seventy-two days with a new contract, TWA recalled only 197 of the striking attendants. By May 1988, only 1,100 strikers had been recalled—all with full seniority.*

The union sued, claiming that (1) it was an unfair labor practice to hire new attendants and (2) even if hiring the new attendants was legal, the striking attendants had to be hired back because they had more seniority than the newly hired attendants. The District Court upheld TWA's policy; the Court of Appeals reversed in favor of the union. The Supreme Court reviewed the matter.

CASE DECISION   O'Connor, Justice.

* * *

In virtually every strike situation there will be some employees who disagree with their union's decision to strike and who cannot be required to abide by that decision. It is the inevitable effect of an employer's use of the economic weapons available during a period of self-help that these differences will be exacerbated and that poststrike resentments may be created. Thus, for example, the employer's right to hire permanent replacements in order to continue operations will inevitably also have the effect of dividing striking employees

between those who, fearful of permanently losing their jobs, return to work and those who remain stalwart in the strike.

While the employer and union in many circumstances may reach a back-to-work agreement that would displace crossovers and new hires or an employer may unilaterally decide to permit such displacement, nothing in the NLRA or the federal common law we have developed under that statute requires such a result. That such agreements are typically one mark of a successful strike is yet another indication that crossovers opted not to gamble; if the strike was successful the advantage gained by declining to strike disappears.

* * *

The decision to guarantee to crossovers the same protections lawfully applied to new hires was a simple decision to apply the preexisting seniority terms of the collective bargaining agreement uniformly to all working employees. That this decision had the effect of encouraging prestrike workers to remain on the job during the strike or to abandon the strike and return to work before all vacancies were filled was an effect of the exercise of TWA's peaceful economic power, a power that the company was legally free to deploy once the parties had exhausted the private dispute resolution mechanisms. . . . Accordingly, the judgment of the Court of Appeals is Reversed.

QUESTIONS FOR ANALYSIS
1. If the collective bargaining agreement provides for preference based on seniority, as was the case here, why would the senior attendants who had been on strike not have preference in hiring?
2. Can employers use this tactic to "break" a union?

SUMMARY

- Most workers are employed at will. There are public policy and statutory exceptions to the rule of employment at will, but most aspects of job rights are determined by written, verbal, or implied contracts, which can include the terms established in a firm's employee handbook. Companies can be open to charges of unjust dismissal if they do not follow promised procedures.

- Most companies have policies regarding testing for substance abuse and steps that must be taken by an employee if abuse is detected. Generally, companies are free to require drug tests of job applicants and of employees in positions that impact health, safety, or large sums of money. Companies may wish to control substance abuse to reduce medical expenses, improve worker productivity, and reduce accidents.

- OSHA may impose work safety and health regulations. If a company fails to meet minimal safety standards, workers have the right to walk off the job to protect their health. OSHA regulations must be justified by documented health or safety needs, but there is no requirement that they be cost effective. OSHA HazMat rules regard worker handling of hazardous chemicals.

- Most employers must pay for workers' compensation insurance to ensure that injured employees, regardless of fault, have medical expenses covered and receive partial compensation for lost wages. Workers' compensation prohibits tort suits except in cases of intentional infliction of injury.

- Labor regulations require employers to collect evidence that all new employees are U.S. citizens or are noncitizens with a legal work status. Employers must also comply with federal minimum wage requirements. Employers of more than 100 employees must notify employees at least sixty days in advance of any plant closings or layoffs that will affect 50 or more employees. Employers with 50 or more employees must allow employees to take up to twelve weeks unpaid leave for family or medical reasons.

- The Employee Retirement Income Security Act gives employees the right to their pension benefits after a certain time of service and provides federal inspection and guarantee of the solvency of pension funds.

- Under the Norris–La Guardia Act, federal courts may not issue injunctions against unions in labor disputes. Employers must bargain with unions according to the terms of the collective bargaining agreement rather than seek relief in federal court.

- The National Labor Relations Act (NLRA) originated with the Wagner Act in 1935. It gives employees the right to organize unions and to bargain collectively through representatives of their choosing. It is illegal for an employer to interfere with employees in the exercise of those rights, and employee actions may not interfere with the employer's interest in plant safety, efficiency, and discipline. The Act created the National Labor Relations Board (NLRB), which is responsible for resolving unfair labor practice complaints and supervising matters of union representation.

- The Landrum-Griffin Act, a part of the NLRA, regulates internal union affairs. The law is intended to make union procedures and elections democratic. It covers the election of union leadership, protects the right of union members to speak out about union matters, and assures union members the right to see the books of the union, which are audited by the Department of Labor.

- If more than 30 percent of the workers at a workplace petition for a union representation election, the NLRB holds an election to determine whether a majority of the workers want union representation. Workers can also vote to end union representation. The employer and the union debate the pros and cons of union representation before workers vote.

- When a majority of the workers at a workplace vote for union representation, all workers are covered by the collective bargaining agreement settled by management and the union, and all workers must follow the procedures established for handling complaints. Workers who are not union members must follow the rules set by the collective bargaining contract.

- Workers who work at a unionized workplace must either join the union and pay dues or, if they do not want to join the union, pay agency fees to the union. Agency fees should not include money used for union political purposes; they are to cover the cost of union representation. In the twenty-one right-to-work states (which are allowed under the Taft-Hartley Act), workers at unionized workplaces cannot be forced to pay agency fees, making unions less effective in such states.

REVIEW AND DISCUSSION QUESTIONS

1. Define the following terms and phrases:

whistle-blower	agency shop
employee handbooks	agency fees
substance abuse policy	right-to-work laws
workers' compensation laws	collective bargaining
licensing requirements	mandatory subjects (of bargaining)
vesting	concerted activities
yellow-dog contracts	secondary boycott
authorization cards	lockout
union certification	

2. Do firms have the right to test all job applicants and refuse to hire applicants who test positive for drug use even if the job in question has no safety or sensitivity concerns?

CASE QUESTIONS

3. Barbara Reynolds and Jason Stephens were at-will truck driver employees of Ozark Motor Lines. They were fired when they refused to begin a trip from Memphis to Chicago without having adequate time to inspect the truck as required by safety provisions of the Tennessee Motor Carriers Act. The jury found this to be wrongful dismissal because Ozark violated statutory public policy. Was this upheld on appeal? [*Reynolds* v. *Ozark Motor Lines*, 887 S.W.2d 822 (Tenn. Sup.Ct., 1994)]

4. While Jackson was working for a newspaper publisher, she injured her wrist. She sought medical treatment and was unable to perform some of her duties. Two months later, her supervisor began to criticize her performance. Jackson's physical therapist contacted her supervisor to recommend that she not perform repetitive duties. A month later, it was discovered that Jackson had actually broken her wrist. Because of the delay in treating the break, major surgery was required, and she filed for workers' compensation benefits. Jackson was fired. She sued, contending she was fired for filing a workers' compensation claim.

The trial court dismissed the suit; Jackson appealed to the Nebraska high court. Does she have grounds for suit? [*Jackson* v. *Morris Communications*, 657 N.W.2d 634 (Sup. Ct., Neb., 2003)]

5. When Norton was hired in 1978, he signed an "Employment Agreement" that stated that his employment could be terminated at any time. Several years later, his employer issued a "Work Rule Policy & Handbook" that established policy for discipline and dismissal. Steps for notifying an employee about unsatisfactory performance were described. Norton was fired in 1989 because his boss was unhappy with sales in the office that Norton ran. Norton sued for violation of his employment contract because the company did not follow the steps in the handbook. A jury awarded him $305,000 in back pay for breach of contract. Was the award upheld on appeal, or was Norton an at-will employee? [*Norton* v. *Caremark, Inc.*, 20 F.3d 330 (8th Cir., 1994)]

 Check your answer at http://meiners.westbuslaw.com

6. Scholz began working for Montgomery Ward in 1970. She told the manager she did not want to work on Sunday and was told that that was fine. Over the years, when she was asked to work on Sunday, she refused, and the matter was dropped. In 1982, Scholz and other employees signed a sheet agreeing to the terms of a new employee manual that stated that all were employees at will and that the company could change the terms and conditions of employment at any time. In 1983, Scholz was told to work Sunday or be fired; she refused and was fired. Her work record was excellent otherwise. She sued for breach of contract, contending she had been told by the manager she did not have to work on Sunday. Was that correct? [*Scholz* v. *Montgomery Ward*, 468 N.W.2d 845 (Mich. Sup. Ct., 1991)]

7. Rowan worked as a cashier for TSC. She believed that her manager, Snider, and other employees were embezzling money from TSC. When Rowan expressed her concern to Snider, he reacted violently by twisting her arm and pushing her against the desk. Rowan reported the matter to Snider's supervisor, Carter, who told her to "keep her mouth shut." Rowan sued Snider for assault and was awarded $1,500 in damages. She also reported the assault to the police and charges were filed against Snider. Another TSC manager told Rowan to drop the criminal charges. She refused and was fired. A month later, Snider was convicted of criminal assault and battery. Rowan then sued TSC for wrongful termination in violation of public policy. The federal district court certified a question to the Virginia supreme court asking if the public policy exception to the employment-at-will doctrine applied in this case. Do you think it does? [*Rowan* v. *Tractor Supply Co.*, 559 S.E.2d 709 (Sup. Ct., Va., 2002)]

 Check your answer at http://meiners.westbuslaw.com

8. Tanks was a bus driver for the Greater Cleveland Rapid Transit Authority (GCRTA). The GCRTA had a published substance abuse policy to protect public safety that required drivers to be tested after accidents. Tanks ran into a pole. As required, she submitted blood, saliva, and urine samples, which tested positive for cocaine. Under the terms of the policy, Tanks was fired. She sued, claiming that the drug test was an unreasonable search in violation of the Fourth Amendment to the Constitution. Did she have a case? [*Tanks* v. *GCRTA*, 930 F.2d 475 (6th Cir., 1991)]

9. A group of Boeing workers sued for injuries and disabilities from their four-year exposure to toxic chemicals. There was evidence that Boeing had known

of the problem but did nothing about it. Boeing asserted that the employees could collect, if anything, under workers' compensation; the employees sued for intentional tort. Could they bring such an action? [*Birklid* v. *Boeing*, 904 P.2d 278 (Wash. Sup. Ct., 1995)]

 Check your answer at http://meiners.westbuslaw.com

10. Fifteen-year-old Joshua Zimmerman was on his third day on the job at a car wash run by Valdak in North Dakota. Valdak used an industrial centrifuge extractor to spin-dry towels for use at the car wash. The extractor had a warning: "NEVER INSERT HANDS IN BASKET IF IT IS SPINNING EVEN SLIGHTLY." It had an interlocking device to prevent the lid from being opened while it was spinning, but the interlock did not work all the time and was not working when Joshua reached inside for towels and had his arm severed at the elbow (the arm was reattached by surgeons). OSHA cited Valdak for a willful violation and fined it $28,000. Valdak appealed. Did the finding of willfulness stand? [*Valdak* v. *OSHA*, 73 F.3d 1466 (8th Cir., 1996)]

11. Guess had worked at a Sharp manufacturing facility for four years when a co-worker cut his hand and Guess got some of the co-worker's blood on her hand. She believed the worker to be suffering from AIDS because he "looked and acted gay," was often sick, and had gay friends. At the time of the incident, she was "hysterical," convinced that she would become HIV positive due to the blood exposure. Subsequent AIDS tests on Guess are negative, but she suffers from depression, will not associate with other people, and will not have sex with her husband. She applies for workers' compensation. At trial, her doctor testifies that Guess suffered permanent impairment and could no longer work on an assembly line. Her fear is real and limits her functioning. The trial court awarded Guess 38 percent permanent partial disability. Sharp appealed. Who wins? [*Guess* v. *Sharp Mfg. Co. of America*, 114 S.W.3d 480 (Sup. Ct., Tenn., 2003)]

 Check your answer at http://meiners.westbuslaw.com

12. Nastasi drove a propane gas delivery truck for Synergy Gas. He had been very active in getting a union certified as the bargaining agent for fellow employees. The unionization fight was bitter, and the company was cited by the NLRB for five unfair labor practices. Soon after the unionization fight, Nastasi was in a serious accident in his truck. Synergy fired him, claiming that it fired all drivers in serious accidents because of the danger involved in driving such trucks. The union protested that the firing was because of Nastasi's union leadership. The NLRB ordered Nastasi reinstated to his job; Synergy appealed. What was the result? [*Synergy Gas* v. *NLRB*, 19 F.3d 649 (D.C. Cir., 1994)]

13. During a campaign for a company's production facility to become unionized, the management showed a movie to employees that dramatized some supposed risks of unionization. The union complained this was an unfair labor practice, and the NLRB agreed. The company claimed this was protected by freedom of speech and was not an unfair labor practice. What was the result when the case was appealed to the federal court of appeals? [*Luxuray of New York* v. *NLRB*, 447 F.2d 112 (2d Cir., 1971)]

14. During a campaign to get the printing department workers at a large company to become represented by the same union that represented most workers at

the company, the printing department's manager told the workers that if they unionized they could end up getting paid less because they would be paid by the hour instead of by the month and that their work could be organized such that they would be needed for fewer hours. The manager also said the workers could lose the flexible arrangements they enjoyed for breaks and lunch. The union lost a close vote and filed a claim of unfair labor practice by the employer. Was the employer engaging in unfair practices? [*NLRB* v. *Lenkurt Electric Co.*, 438 F.2d 1102 (9th Cir., 1971)]

15. During a unionization campaign, a company told workers that no materials related to the union effort could be posted on employee bulletin boards. A supervisor told a union supporter that "if we got a union in there, we'd be in the unemployment line." The union claimed these were unfair labor practices. The NLRB agreed; did the court? [*Guardian Industries* v. *NLRB*, 49 F.3d 317 (7th Cir., 1995)]

16. Mead operates a large paper mill where most workers are represented by a union. When Mead and the union negotiated a new agreement, they fought over the company's "flex" plans that gave all personnel broader responsibilities and a wage increase. The new agreement included the flex plans, but the union was not happy. Workers wore T-shirts, buttons, and decals that said "Hey Mead—Flex This," "Just Say No—Mead," and other sayings in reference to the fight. After a year, Mead issued an order banning such shirts, buttons, and decals from company property. Mead said this was needed to maintain discipline and to not send negative messages to the public. The union protested that this violated their right to come together for mutual aid and protection. The NLRB sided with the union; did the court? [*NLRB* v. *Mead Corp.*, 73 F.3d 74 (6th Cir., 1996)]

17. WinCo operates a grocery store in Chico, California. It sits on a ten-acre parcel of land. Except for allowing Girl Scouts to sell cookies on the premises, WinCo has allowed no other solicitors. Union organizers came on the premises and passed out handbills purported to be from "Mothers Against WinCo" urging shoppers not to patronize the store. WinCo kicked the organizers off the premises. The union complained, and the NLRB held that WinCo violated the NLRA when it prohibited non-employee union representatives from giving handbills to customers. WinCo petitioned for review of the NLRB order. Was the NLRB correct? [*Waremart Foods* v. *NLRB*, 354 F.3d 870 (D.C. Cir., 2004)]

ETHICS QUESTION

18. Contemplating the opening of a factory, you discover that it appears to be a toss-up between building a plant that uses cheaper machinery and 200 workers who will earn an average of $6 an hour and building a plant that uses more expensive, sophisticated machinery and 70 workers likely to earn about $15 an hour. Is it more responsible to build one kind of factory than another? What if you know that the first kind of factory will probably never be unionized but the second kind of factory is more likely to be unionized?

PULLING IT *Together*

Torts, Business Organizations, and Employment Law

Sisters Morrison and Gugle opened a store together. Their business was incorporated; each owned half of the stock. Gugle was president; Morrison was secretary-treasurer. Both were employees of the corporation. Trouble developed between the two; Gugle suspected Morrison of taking company money. Gugle sent Morrison a letter offering to buy her out of the business and gave her three days to decide.

Morrison did not respond. Gugle fired her and denied her access to company property and records. Gugle asked the bank to move all company money to an account over which she would have sole control due to concern over missing money. Morrison sued Gugle for wrongful termination and defamation. The trial court directed a verdict for Gugle. Morrison appealed. Does employment law or corporation law or tort law control this matter?

Morrison v. *Gugle*, 755 N.E.2d 404 (Ct. App., Ohio, 2001)

INTERNET ASSIGNMENT

http://www.nlrb.gov
http://www.dol.gov
http://www.osha.gov

1. What is the policy stated in the National Labor Relations Act (Wagner Act), 29 U.S.C. §151 *et seq.*?
2. What is the URL for decisions and orders (vol. 272+) of the National Labor Relations Board?
3. What is the finding stated in the Fair Labor Standards Act (1938), 29 U.S.C. §201 *et seq.*?
4. What is the URL for the Fair Labor Standards Act (FLSA) Advisor? Hint: Wage and Home Division.
5. What is the finding stated in the Occupational Safety and Health Act (OSHA) (1970), 29 U.S.C. §§553, 651 *et seq.*?
6. According to the OSHA web site, what are the three forms of anthrax infection?

Chapter 16 | *Employment Discrimination*

The owner of an Iowa electronics company made sexual advances to an employee after she posed nude in a nationally distributed magazine. Was he guilty of violating the law that limits sex discrimination in employment? "John Doe" worked as an engineer at Boeing aircraft. After six years, he, under physician supervision, decided to become "Jane Doe." Prior to sex-transformation surgery, he began to live the social role of a woman. Boeing fired "John/Jane Doe" for using the women's restroom and dressing as a woman despite company orders not to do so prior to sex-change surgery. Was Boeing guilty of disability discrimination?

These cases illustrate the wide range of employment issues that arise today. Years ago, neither of these cases would have emerged, but now the law restricts employment practices with respect to discrimination based on personal characteristics. In this chapter, we focus on the Civil Rights Act of 1964—the primary basis of modern employment discrimination law; the statutes that have been added over the years; and the cases that have helped to define the rights and duties of employees and employers in dealing with race, sex, color, religion, national origin, age, and disability. (The answer to the first question—Was he guilty of sex discrimination?—is yes; the answer to the second question—Was Boeing guilty of disability discrimination?—is no.)

ORIGINS OF DISCRIMINATION LAW

Discrimination in employment based on personal characteristics such as sex, race, religion, national origin, or disability occurs everywhere. For example, in Asian nations, female executives are much more uncommon than in the United States. In France, despite being 8 percent of the residents, Muslims have no high-ranking jobs in the government. But here we focus on discrimination in the United States and how the law deals with that.

Statistical differences exist in employment based on sex and race. For example, the unemployment rate for African Americans is twice the unemployment rate for whites. Of those working, about one in four African Americans has a white-collar job, compared to one in two working whites. White male wageworkers earn an average of one-third more than African American and Hispanic male wageworkers. Men traditionally dominate many higher-paying professions, such as medicine, law, and management, while women are traditionally concentrated in lower-paying professions such as nursing, paralegal, and clerical. White male wageworkers earn an average of 30 percent more than female wageworkers.

Much of the difference between men and women and between racial and ethnic groups may be unintentional and attributable to employment patterns. Some of the "wage gap" is attributed to differences in education, training, family demands, and years of experience in the workforce. Professor June O'Neill and other scholars have estimated that the wage gap for younger men and women with similar education, experience, and life situations has nearly disappeared. Still, some disparity is probably due to stereotyped assumptions about productivity and to preferences for associating in the workplace with "one's own kind."

The Civil Rights Movements

Historically, employers could hire and fire at will, subject to the limits we covered in the last chapter. Employers could discriminate because of race, sex, or any other personal characteristics. Similarly, labor unions could impose discriminatory membership rules. Employers and unions were largely free to conduct their affairs with few legal restrictions. The situation was worsened by federal and state laws (Jim Crow laws) that supported segregation and labor market discrimination.

The drive for civil rights in employment and other aspects of life became a national movement in the early 1960s. Rising public concern provided support for the first federal employment discrimination statute in 1963, the Equal Pay Act, followed by the Civil Rights Act of 1964, which is the cornerstone of federal employment discrimination law.

Equal Pay Act of 1963

The *Equal Pay Act of 1963* was the first federal law to address employment discrimination. It prohibits pay discrimination on the basis of sex. The Act holds it illegal to pay men and women employees different wages when a job requires equal skill, effort, responsibility, and the same working conditions. Job titles are not relevant; job content is reviewed. The Equal Pay Act allows differences in wages if they are due to "(i) a seniority system; (ii) a merit system; (iii) a system which measures earnings by quantity or quality of production; or (iv) a differential based on any factor other than sex." Pay differentials on the basis of sex are to be eliminated by raising the pay of the women employees, not by lowering the pay of the men employees.

To help enforce the Act, employers are required to keep records of each employee's hours, wages, and other relevant information. Government investigators may examine the records, which must be kept for several years. If a firm is found in violation, the most likely result will be an order to pay employees who have suffered discrimination an amount equal to the wages they should have received. If employees hire an attorney to bring the suit and they win, they will be awarded reasonable attorney's fees and court costs. Some discrimination suits are brought based on this statute, but most potential suits are also covered by the next statute.

TITLE VII OF THE 1964 CIVIL RIGHTS ACT

The most important source of antidiscrimination in employment law is *Title VII of the Civil Rights Act of 1964*. The Act was amended in 1972 by the *Equal Employment Opportunity Act* to give the *Equal Employment Opportunity Commission (EEOC)* the power to enforce the Act, by the *Pregnancy Discrimination Act* in 1978, and by the *Civil Rights Act of 1991*. Title VII makes it illegal for an employer of fifteen or more workers

> (1) to fail or refuse to hire or to discharge any individual, or otherwise to discriminate against any individual with respect to his compensation, terms, conditions, or privileges of employment; or
> (2) to limit, segregate, or classify his employees or applicants for employment in any way which would deprive or tend to deprive any individual of employment opportunities or otherwise adversely affect his status as an employee because of such individual's race, color, religion, sex, or national origin.

Protected Classes

Title VII applies to employers, employment agencies, and labor unions in the private and public sectors. In general, it forbids *discrimination* in all aspects of employment on the basis of *race, color, religion, sex, or national origin*. The Supreme Court has stated that law firms and other partnership organizations are covered by the law, but the law does not apply to business relationships or to the selection of independent contractors.

Title VII requires *equal employment opportunity* regardless of race, color, religion, sex, or national origin. Congress sought to protect certain classes of people who had a history of discriminatory treatment in employment relationships. Race, color, national origin, religion, and sex are the characteristics that determine *protected classes* for purposes of Title VII coverage.

Race

The courts have little difficulty in determining racial class. Federal law recognizes five major racial groupings: black, white, Native American, Hispanic, and Asian.

Contrary to some claims that have been made, whites are protected under Title VII. That was made clear by the Supreme Court in *McDonald* v. *Santa Fe Trail Transportation*, 96 S.Ct. 2574. In *McDonald*, an African American employee and a white employee had stolen property from their employer. The African American employee was reprimanded but allowed to keep his job, while the white employee was fired. The Court stated:

Title VII prohibits racial discrimination against the white petitioners. . . . While Santa Fe may decide that participation in a theft of cargo may render an employee unqualified for employment, this criteria must be applied alike to members of all races.

Reverse discrimination—preferential treatment to members of protected classes—is illegal, but if minorities or women are *underrepresented* in a certain job category, it is legal for an employer to see that more minorities or women are hired to increase their share of the jobs. Affirmative action programs (discussed later) designed to remedy discrimination against minorities or women may be adopted and not violate the rule against reverse discrimination.

Color

Under Title VII, the term *color* refers generally to discrimination claims based on shade of skin. About 3 percent of discrimination cases are in this category, many brought by dark-skinned blacks against light-skinned blacks.

National Origin

According to the Supreme Court in *Espinoza* v. *Farah Manufacturing*, 94 S.Ct. 334, the term *national origin* is to be given its ordinary meaning:

[The term national origin] refers to the country where a person is born or . . . the country from which his or her ancestors came.

Discrimination has been held to exist where a person has a physical, cultural, or speech characteristic of a national origin group. It is also discrimination to require that English be spoken at all times in the workplace. However, if business necessity requires that English be spoken, such as for reasons of safety or productivity, it may be a legitimate job requirement. Employment discrimination can take place when an employer allows ethnic slurs to occur and does not take steps to prevent such actions.

This protection is not provided to noncitizens (aliens) employed or seeking employment in this country. However, while an employer may discriminate against aliens, the employer may not discriminate on the basis of different origins. For example, an employer may not accept aliens from Italy but reject all aliens from Mexico.

Religion

Title VII does not define the term *religion* but states that "religion includes all aspects of religious observances and practice." The courts have defined the term broadly. According to the Court in *United States* v. *Seeger*, 380 U.S. 163:

[All that is required is a] sincere and meaningful belief occupying in the life of its possessor a place parallel to that filled by the God of those [religions generally recognized].

The employer is required to provide *reasonable accommodation* for an employee's religious practices. The employer may discriminate, however, if the accommodation will impose an *undue hardship* on the conduct of business. The Court has stated that undue hardship is created by accommodations that would cost an employer more than a minimal amount. For example, if an employer has a strict dress code so that the company gives a certain "look" to the public, the code need not be modified to allow certain employees to wear religious garb, such as a headdress. But if an employer does not have a strict code, then it could not tell an employee not to wear religious garb.

Further, an employer need not make other employees change their work schedule to accommodate the religious holiday preferences of an employee. But if such accommodation can be made at no cost other than giving employees the opportunity to switch work days, then only a minimal cost is incurred.

A religious institution, such as a seminary training ministers or mullahs, may legally hire only members of a particular religion for jobs in which that is critical. For example, Baylor University, a Baptist school, may wish to hire only Baptists to teach in its theological seminary to train ministers. But it could not require that math instructors be Baptist since there is no specific religious purpose in teaching math, unlike teaching religion.

JURIS *prudence?*

A New Protected Class?

Curt Storey sued Burns International Security Services for wrongful discharge. He claimed he was fired for refusing to remove Confederate flags from his lunchbox and pickup truck.

A lifelong resident of Pennsylvania, Storey claims protection to display such items because he is a "Confederate Southern American." Title VII does not recognize loyalty to the Confederacy as a protected class.

Source: *Observer-Reporter* (Washington, Penn.)

Sex

The limits on sex discrimination were included with little legislative history to provide ideas about how Congress intended to define sex discrimination. Thus, the courts must take the lead in defining the limits of the term.

The courts hold that the term *sex* should be given its ordinary meaning. Thus, Title VII prohibits sex discrimination simply on the basis of whether a person is male or female. Hence, the courts have held that discrimination on the basis of sexual preference or sexual identity is not protected by Title VII, although the law in several states prohibits discrimination on the basis of sexual orientation. Title VII does not prohibit discrimination on the basis of marital status, as long as an employer applies employment rules evenly to employees of both sexes. However, many states prohibit discrimination on the basis of marital status.

Pregnancy Discrimination Title VII was amended by the *Pregnancy Discrimination Act.* It states that an employer may not discriminate against women because of pregnancy, childbirth, or related medical conditions. Women affected by these conditions "shall be treated the same for all employment-related purposes, including receipt of benefits under fringe benefit programs." Examples of pregnancy discrimination include:

- Denying a woman a job, assignment, or promotion because she is pregnant or has children
- Requiring a pregnant woman to go on leave when she is able to do her job
- Treating maternity leave different from other leaves for temporary disabilities

CYBER
Law

Your E-Mail Is Your Boss's E-mail

In general, e-mail that is sent at work on company computers is available for company inspection. Whether the employee is told or not, employers have the right to monitor employee e-mail. A class-action suit by Epson employees against their employer for routinely reading employee e-mail was dismissed by the court because there was no right-of-privacy issue.

A sports writer for a Chicago newspaper was told by his employer to quit sending unwanted e-mails to a female co-worker. When he did not quit sending her e-mail, the employer transferred the writer to another department. A federal court held that the paper was within its rights to do so; he could not complain about the interference with his e-mail, nor could he claim sex discrimination. The employer "was obviously trying to make the best of a difficult situation." See *Greenslade* v. *Chicago Sun-Times, Inc.*, 112 F.3d 853.

Why do employers care so much about e-mail transmissions at work? Chevron paid $2.2 million to settle sexual harassment claims of women employees for dirty jokes that were transmitted around the office on the e-mail system.

• Discriminating in fringe benefits, such as health insurance, to discourage women of childbearing age from working

Sexual Harassment A sexually hostile work environment is a form of sex discrimination that violates Title VII. *Sexual harassment* is defined by the EEOC in the *Code of Federal Regulations* as unwelcome sexual advances, requests for sexual favors, and other verbal or physical conduct of a sexual nature . . . when

(1) submission to such conduct is made either explicitly or implicitly a term or condition of an individual's employment,
(2) submission to or rejection of such conduct by an individual is used as a basis for employment decisions affecting such individual, or
(3) such conduct has the purpose or effect of unreasonably interfering with an individual's work performance or creating an intimidating, hostile, or offensive working environment.

In practice, sexual harassment has been put in two major categories. The first is *quid pro quo* or "this for that," where there is a promise of reward, such as promotion or pay raise, for providing sexual favors being demanded or there is a threat of punishment for not going along with sexual requests. The second form is a *hostile environment* created at work by others. An abusive work environment is created by words or acts related to a person's sex. Examples are

• Discussing sexual activities
• Commenting on physical attributes
• Unnecessary touching or gestures
• Using crude, demeaning, or offensive language
• Displaying sexually suggestive pictures

Trivial and isolated incidents usually are not sufficient grounds for a sexual harassment suit. The courts look to factors such as how often such conduct occurred; whether the harassment was by a supervisor who could control progress, pay, and working conditions; or by a co-worker; whether there was talk or actual touching, and whether more than one person was involved. The Supreme Court offered guidance in the *Harris* case about what constitutes a hostile work environment in general.

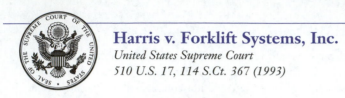

Harris v. Forklift Systems, Inc.
United States Supreme Court
510 U.S. 17, 114 S.Ct. 367 (1993)

CASE BACKGROUND   *Harris worked as a rental manager for two years for Forklift Systems. Her boss, Hardy, often insulted her in front of others and made her the target of sexual slurs and suggestions. He said, "We need a man as the rental manager," and "You're a woman, what do you know?" He told her she was "a dumb-ass woman," and that they should "go to the Holiday Inn to negotiate her raise." Hardy would ask Harris and other women employees to get coins from his front pants pocket, throw things on the ground and ask women to pick them up, and make sexual comments about their clothing.*

Harris complained to Hardy about his comments. Hardy said that he was only kidding. Soon after, while Harris was arranging a deal with a customer, Hardy asked her, "What did you do, promise the guy sex Saturday night?" Harris quit and sued, claiming that Hardy's conduct created a hostile work environment for her. The district and appeals courts ruled against her. She appealed.

CASE DECISION   O'Connor, Justice.

* * *

When the workplace is permeated with "discriminatory intimidation, ridicule, and insult" that is "sufficiently severe or pervasive to alter the conditions of the victim's employment and create an abusive working environment," Title VII is violated.

This standard . . . takes a middle path between making actionable any conduct that is merely offensive and requiring the conduct to cause a tangible psychological injury. . . . Conduct that is not severe or pervasive enough to create an objectively hostile or abuse work environment—an environment that a reasonable person would find hostile or abusive—is beyond Title VII's purview. Likewise, if the victim does not subjectively perceive the environment to be abusive, the conduct has not actually altered the conditions of the victim's employment, and there is no Title VII violation.

But Title VII comes into play before the harassing conduct leads to a nervous breakdown. A discriminatorily abusive work environment, even one that does not seriously affect employees' psychological well-being, can and often will detract from employees' job performance, discourage employees from remaining on the job, or keep them from advancing in their careers. Moreover, even without regard to these tangible effects, the very fact that the discriminatory conduct was so severe or pervasive that it created a work environment abusive to employees because of their race, gender, religion, or national origin offends Title VII's broad rule of workplace equality. . . .

This is not, and by its nature cannot be, a mathematically precise test. We need not answer today all the potential questions it raises. . . . But we can say that whether an environment is "hostile" or "abusive" can be determined only by looking at all the circumstances. These may include the frequency of the discriminatory conduct; its severity; whether it is physically threatening or humiliating, or a mere offensive utterance; and whether it unreasonably interferes with an employee's work performance. The effect on the employee's psychological well-being is, of course, relevant to determining whether the plaintiff actually found the environment abusive. But while psychological harm, like any other relevant factor, may be taken into account, no single factor is required.

* * *

We therefore reverse the judgment of the Court of Appeals, and remand the case for further proceedings consistent with this opinion.

QUESTIONS FOR ANALYSIS
1. The Court held that the actions must be severe enough to create a hostile work environment to a reasonable person. If this issue were left to a jury, might not some people on the jury, especially men, be likely to think that Harris overreacted?
2. Two concurring opinions indicated that another standard that might be focused on is whether the abusive actions are sufficient to affect work performance. Would that provide better guidance?

The Supreme Court further clarified the law in *Oncale* v. *Sundowner Offshore Services*, 118 S.Ct. 998. In that case, a male worker sued his employer because he suffered verbal and physical abuse, of a sexual nature, by other male workers. The Court held that same-sex harassment is prohibited by Title VII. The law:

> does not reach genuine but innocuous differences in the ways men and women routinely interact with members of the same sex and of the opposite sex. The prohibition of harassment on the basis of sex requires neither asexuality nor androgyny in the workplace; it forbids only behavior so objectively offensive as to alter the 'conditions' of the victim's employment. . . . the objective severity of harassment should be judged from the perspective of a reasonable person in the plaintiff's position, considering 'all the circumstances.' . . . Common sense, and an appropriate sensitivity to social context, will enable courts and juries to distinguish between simple teasing or roughhousing among members of the same sex, and conduct which a reasonable person in the plaintiff's position would find severely hostile or abusive.

Age Discrimination

Enacted in 1967 and amended several times, the *Age Discrimination in Employment Act (ADEA)* prohibits discrimination in employment against persons over age forty. All employers, private and public, who have twenty or more employees must comply with this statute. The ADEA generally parallels Title VII in its prohibitions, exceptions, remedies, and enforcement. So, while the ADEA is a separate statute, we presume it acts the same way as Title VII unless specifically noted. The law prohibits employment discrimination, such as failing or refusing to hire or promote because of age, terminating employees because of age, or other discrimination in the terms and conditions of employment.

Often the courts must, as in cases of race or sex discrimination, look to see whether age discrimination can be inferred by studying practices at the place of employment. The following are examples of age discrimination:

- Forcing retirement because of age
- Assigning older workers to duties that limit their ability to compete for higher-level jobs in the organization
- Requiring older workers to pass physical examinations as a condition of continued employment
- Indicating an age preference in advertisements for employees, such as "young, dynamic person wanted"
- Choosing to promote a younger worker rather than an older worker because the older worker may be retiring in several years
- Cutting health-care benefits for workers over age sixty-five because they are eligible for Medicare

The *Reeves* case discusses how juries are to evaluate evidence in cases of intentional discrimination. As in other cases, the Court wishes for the fact finders to view all the circumstances of a situation involving a claim of discrimination and the standard of proof that must be met.

Reeves v. Sanderson Plumbing Products, Inc.
Supreme Court of the United States
530 U.S. 133, 120 S.Ct. 2097 (2000)

CASE BACKGROUND   *Reeves, fifty-seven, and Oswalt, in his thirties, were supervisors in a department known as the Hinge Room, which was managed by Caldwell, forty-five. Reeves helped handle recording attendance of employees. Caldwell told Chesnut, director of manufacturing, that production was down because employees' attendance was not good, but the records did not indicate an attendance problem. Chesnut ordered an audit, which found problems with attendance records. On his recommendation, Caldwell and Reeves were fired. Reeves sued for age discrimination.*

At trial, respondent contended that the dismissal was justified because Reeves had failed to maintain accurate attendance records. Reeves, petitioner, contended that was a pretext for age discrimination, providing evidence that his record keeping was acceptable and that Chesnut had shown age-based hostility toward him. The jury found for Reeves. The appeals court reversed, holding that Reeves had not presented sufficient evidence to show that he was fired because of his age. Reeves (petitioner) appealed.

CASE DECISION   Justice O'Connor delivered the opinion of the Court.

* * *

In this case, the evidence supporting respondent's explanation for petitioner's discharge consisted primarily of testimony by Chesnut and Sanderson and documentation of petitioner's alleged "shoddy record keeping." . . .

Petitioner, however, made a substantial showing that respondent's explanation was false. First, petitioner offered evidence that he properly maintained the attendance records. Most of the timekeeping errors cited by respondent involved employees who were not marked late but who were recorded as having arrived at the plant at 7 a.m. for the 7 a.m. shift. . . . But both petitioner and Oswalt testified that the company's automated timeclock often failed to scan employees' timecards, so that the timesheets would not record any time of arrival. . . .

Petitioner similarly cast doubt on whether he was responsible for any failure to discipline late and absent employees. Petitioner testified that his job only included reviewing the daily and weekly attendance reports, and that disciplinary writeups were based on the monthly reports, which were reviewed by Caldwell.

* * *

The ultimate question is whether the employer intentionally discriminated, and proof that "the employer's proffered reason is unpersuasive, or even obviously contrived, does not necessarily establish that the plaintiff's proffered reason. . . is correct." In other words, "it is not enough . . . to *dis*believe the employer; the factfinder must *believe* the plaintiff's explanation of intentional discrimination."

In reaching this conclusion, however, we reasoned that it is *permissible* for the trier of fact to infer the ultimate fact of discrimination from the falsity of the employer's explanation. . . .

Proof that the defendant's explanation is unworthy of credence is simply one form of circumstantial evidence that is probative of intentional discrimination, and it may be quite persuasive. In appropriate circumstances, the trier of fact can reasonably infer from the falsity of the explanation that the employer is dissembling to cover up a discriminatory purpose. Such an inference is consistent with the general principle of evidence law that the factfinder is entitled to consider a party's dishonesty about a material fact as "affirmative evidence of guilt." Moreover, once the employer's justification has been eliminated, discrimination may well be the most likely alternative explanation, especially since the employer is in the best position to put forth the actual reason for its decision. . . .

In this case, in addition to establishing a prima facie case of discrimination and creating a jury issue as to the falsity of the employer's explanation, petitioner introduced additional evidence that Chesnut was motivated by age-based animus and was principally responsible for petitioner's firing. Petitioner testified that Chesnut had told him that he "was so old he must have come over on the Mayflower" and, on one occasion when petitioner was having difficulty starting a machine, that he "was too damn old to do his job." According to petitioner, Chesnut would regularly "cuss at me and shake his finger in my face." Oswalt, roughly 24 years younger than petitioner, corroborated that there was an "obvious difference" in how Chesnut treated them. . . .

Given that petitioner established a prima facie case of discrimination, introduced enough evidence for the jury to reject respondent's explanation, and produced additional evidence of age-based animus, there was sufficient evidence for the jury to find that respondent had intentionally discriminated. The District Court was therefore correct to submit the case to the jury, and the Court of Appeals erred in overturning its verdict.

For these reasons, the judgment of the Court of Appeals is reversed.

1. Do nasty comments about one's age create a hostile environment that may, by itself, be a violation of the age discrimination law?

2. Do you think juries will be more sympathetic to employees than to employers, thereby creating a bias in the testimony they are likely to believe?

Procedure

The first step for a person claiming to be the victim of a discriminatory act (under Title VII or the ADEA) is to file a charge with a federal, state, or local equal employment opportunity (EEO) office (see http://www.eeoc.gov). For example, a person in Illinois who believes he has a Title VII claim would file a complaint with the Illinois Department of Human Rights or the federal EEOC office; all states, and many cities, have offices that handle EEO matters. Charges must be filed with the EEOC within 300 days of an alleged discriminatory act.

When a charge is filed, the EEOC notifies the employer, and the EEOC investigates the complaint to determine if there is reasonable cause to believe the complaint. The employer is asked to come to a fact-finding conference. The EEOC agent hears statements from both parties. Many complaints are settled at this stage by a conciliation agreement. If there is no settlement, the EEOC finishes the investigation and informs both parties of the result. As Exhibit 16.1 shows, the EEOC may find no merit to the complaint. If it does find merit, it issues a right-to-sue letter to the employee, giving him the right to bring an action against the employer in federal court. In about two percent of the complaints, the EEOC itself sues the employer on behalf of the complaining employee(s).

The average response time on the nearly 100,000 complaints filed each year is about a year. EEOC offices sort complaints by priority, based on their initial evaluation. Top priority cases, when discrimination appears likely, get the most attention.

Exhibit 16.1

Usual Steps in a Discrimination Complaint to EEOC

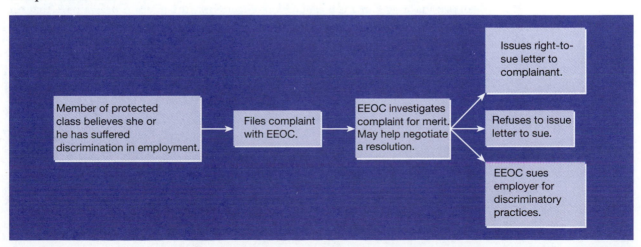

Second-category cases include complaints that may have merit but require added investigation for a determination. Complaints that appear to lack a legitimate claim may be dismissed immediately.

Types of Discrimination Claims

The courts have struck down employment practices that impose *differential standards* on employees on the basis of race, sex, or age. For example, it would be illegal to give men positions as traveling sales representatives but not give such positions to women, even though the employer's reason may be concern about the possible dangers that traveling women face.

While it is obvious that it is illegal to pay women lower salaries for the same work as performed by men, when the assignments and the years of service are the same, illegal *compensation differentials* also take into account differences in fringe benefits. That is, it is illegal to base health or retirement benefits on race, sex, or age.

Everyone understands that the most obvious forms *of segregation* in the workplace are illegal. Segregation today tends to be subtle and cases are not common. It is illegal to assign employees to customers based on race, such as to send Hispanic employees to serve only Hispanic customers and Asian American employees to serve Asian American customers.

Title VII cases have concerned unequal treatment in hiring, promotion, compensation, and discharge decisions. It is also illegal to make life so miserable on the job that the employee is "forced" to quit, as we saw in the *Harris* case. To make the working conditions intolerable is illegal *harassment*. If the employee quits because of harassment, it is a *constructive discharge*, which is treated the same as if the employee had been fired illegally.

Employers can legally differentiate among employees, but the law restrict the grounds for treating employees differently. Although there are many different ways that discrimination may appear, when the line has been crossed, there are two primary types of discrimination claims under Title VII. In general, a plaintiff can make a case by proving either disparate treatment or disparate impact by the employer. These two major categories cover cases of intentional discrimination and unintentional discrimination.

Disparate Treatment

To recover for illegal discrimination, whether for race, color, religion, sex, or national origin, or age, in a claim of *disparate treatment*, the plaintiff must prove that the employer *intentionally* discriminated. That is, a member of a protected class claims an employer treated the plaintiff differently than other employees because of the plaintiff's personal characteristics.

Plaintiff Must Establish a Prima Facie Case The Supreme Court established a four-part test in the *McDonnell-Douglas* decision, 93 S.Ct. 1817, that the plaintiff in a disparate treatment case must meet to provide a *prima facie discrimination case*. Exhibit 16.2 lists the four steps that must be met for a case to go forward. This test holds for all aspects of employment—hiring, promotion, compensation, conditions, discipline, and termination. In *Swierkiewicz v. Sorema*, 122 S.Ct. 992, the Supreme Court made clear that only a "short and plain statement of the claim" is needed. Once the plaintiff meets the McDonnell-Douglas test, the burden shifts to the defendant to overcome the presumption of discrimination.

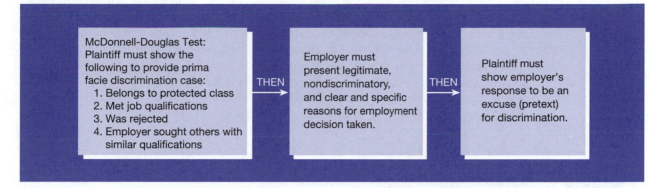

Exhibit 16.2

Initial Steps in Disparate Treatment Cases

McDonnell-Douglas Test: Plaintiff must show the following to provide prima facie discrimination case:
1. Belongs to protected class
2. Met job qualifications
3. Was rejected
4. Employer sought others with similar qualifications

THEN

Employer must present legitimate, nondiscriminatory, and clear and specific reasons for employment decision taken.

THEN

Plaintiff must show employer's response to be an excuse (pretext) for discrimination.

Burden Shifts to Defendant   After a plaintiff shows a prima facie case of employment discrimination, the plaintiff wins unless the employer provides a successful defense. That is, the burden shifts to the defendant to present evidence that the claim is untrue or that there was a legal reason for the employment decision. The employer must show a legitimate, nondiscriminatory, clear, and reasonably specific reason for its decision to overcome the presumption of discrimination. The courts prefer clear standards for employment decisions rather than vague claims that amount to "I felt like it." Legitimate reasons include, as we will see, such factors as seniority, education, and experience.

JURIS *prudence?*

Modify Your Body in Private

Cloutier worked for Costco for four years. While she was there, she kept adding to her collection of body piercings, tattoos, cuttings, and scars. She is a card-carrying member of the Church of Body Modification (see its web site at *http://www.uscobm.com*). Costco's dress code requires such personal decorations to be covered or removed. When Cloutier refused to hide or remove some new facial piercings, she was fired.

The EEOC tried to negotiate a compromise, but Cloutier refused to cover her piercings. She sued Costco for $2 million, claiming religious discrimination. The federal court held that while it would presume her religious beliefs were sincere, Costco has the right to a dress code so that customers see the workers as "reasonably professional in appearance."

Source: *Cloutier v. Costco*, 311 F.Supp.2d 190 (2004).

Burden Shifts to Plaintiff to Establish Defense   After the employer offers legitimate reasons for the employment decision, the burden shifts back to the plaintiff to show that the defendant had an illegal motive. As we saw in the *Reeves* case, a plaintiff must show that the rationales offered by the employer are just *pretexts* or unacceptable excuses for disparate treatment. Such evidence can take many forms, such as showing inconsistency in decisions made by the employer, giving different reasons at different times for the decision, and presenting statistical evidence of discrimination based on sex or race. While discrimination is clear in some cases, it often requires a review of the entire situation and testimony from witnesses, as we saw in the *Reeves* case.

In the *Ellerth* case, the Supreme Court made clear how important it is for an employer to have clear, effective policy and procedures to reduce the likelihood of discrimination cases. Going to the roots of the employment relationship, agency law, the Court notes that without policies that can be shown to be meaningful, an employer is likely to have a more difficult defense and be more likely to incur vacarious liability for the actions of employees who engage in discriminatory behavior. It also means there is a greater likelihood of punitive damages being imposed if the employer loses, because it is less likely to be able show good-faith efforts to prevent discrimination.

Burlington Industries v. Ellerth

Supreme Court of the United States
524 U.S. 742, 118 S.Ct. 2257 (1998)

CASE BACKGROUND   *Ellerth worked for fifteen months in sales at Burlington. One of her supervisors was Slowik, a midlevel manager with authority to hire, promote, and fire employees, subject to higher approval, but not in a policymaking position. Ellerth quit, claiming she was subject to sexually offensive remarks by Slowik and that his comments could be taken as threats to deny her job benefits. She refused his advances, did not suffer retaliation, and was promoted once. She did not tell anyone at Burlington about the problem until after she quit and filed suit. The district court granted Burlington summary judgment. The appeals court reversed. Burlington appealed.*

CASE DECISION   Justice Kennedy delivered the opinion of the court.

* * *

A trier of fact could find in Slowik's remarks numerous threats to retaliate against Ellerth if she denied some sexual liberties. The threats, however, were not carried out or fulfilled. Cases based on threats which are carried out are referred to often as *quid pro quo* cases, as distinct from bothersome attentions or sexual remarks that are sufficiently severe or pervasive to create a hostile work environment. The terms *quid pro quo* and hostile work environment are helpful, perhaps, in making a rough demarcation between cases in which threats are carried out and those where they are not or are absent altogether, but beyond this are of limited utility. . . .

We do not suggest the terms *quid pro quo* and hostile work environment are irrelevant to Title VII litigation. To the extent they illustrate the distinction between cases involving a threat which is carried out and offensive conduct in general, the terms are relevant when there is a threshold question whether a plaintiff can prove discrimination in violation of Title VII. When a plaintiff proves that a tangible employment action resulted from a refusal to submit to a supervisor's sexual demands, he or she establishes that the employment decision itself constitutes a change in the terms and conditions of employment that is actionable under Title VII. For any sexual harassment preceding the employment decision to be actionable, however, the conduct must be severe or pervasive. Because Ellerth's claim involves only unfulfilled threats, it should be categorized as a hostile work environment claim which requires a showing of severe or pervasive conduct. . . .

When we assume discrimination can be proved, however, the factors we discuss below, and not the categories *quid pro quo* and hostile work environment, will be controlling on the issue of vicarious liability. That is the question we must resolve.

We must decide, then, whether an employer has vicarious liability when a supervisor creates a hostile work environment by making explicit threats to alter a subordinate's terms or conditions of employment, based on sex, but does not fulfill the threat. We turn to principles of agency law, for the term "employer" is defined under Title VII to include "agents." . . .

Section 219(1) of the Restatement (Second) of Agency sets out a central principle of agency law:

> A master is subject to liability for the torts of his servants committed while acting in the scope of their employment.

An employer may be liable for both negligent and intentional torts committed by an employee within the scope of his or her employment. Sexual harassment under Title VII presupposes intentional conduct. While early decisions absolved employers of liability for the intentional torts of their employees, the law now imposes liability where the employee's "purpose, however misguided, is wholly or in part to further the master's business." In applying scope of employment principles to intentional torts, however, it is accepted that "it is less likely that a willful tort will properly be held to be in the course of employment and that the liability of the master for such torts will naturally be more limited." . . .

Scope of employment does not define the only basis for employer liability under agency principles. In limited circumstances, agency principles impose liability on employers even where employees commit torts outside the scope of employment. . . .

Although a supervisor's sexual harassment is outside the scope of employment because the conduct was for personal motives, an employer can be liable, nonetheless, where its own negligence is a cause of the harassment. An employer is negligent with respect to sexual harassment if it knew or should have known about the conduct and failed to stop it. Negligence sets a minimum standard for employer liability under Title VII; but Ellerth seeks to invoke the more stringent standard of vicarious liability. . . .

At the outset, we can identify a class of cases where, beyond question, more than the mere existence of the employment relation aids in commission of the harassment: when a supervisor takes a tangible employment action against the subordinate. . . .

A tangible employment action constitutes a significant change in employment status, such as hiring, firing, failing to promote, reassignment with significantly different responsibilities, or a decision causing a significant change in benefits. . . .

In order to accommodate the agency principles of vicarious liability for harm caused by misuse of supervisory authority, as well as Title VII's equally basic policies of encouraging forethought by employers and saving action by objecting employees, we adopt the following holding in this case and in *Faragher* v. *Boca Raton,*

524 U.S. 775, 118 S.Ct. 2275, 141 L.Ed.2d 662 (1998), also decided today. An employer is subject to vicarious liability to a victimized employee for an actionable hostile environment created by a supervisor with immediate (or successively higher) authority over the employee. When no tangible employment action is taken, a defending employer may raise an affirmative defense to liability or damages, subject to proof by a preponderance of the evidence. The defense comprises two necessary elements: (a) that the employer exercised reasonable care to prevent and correct promptly any sexually harassing behavior, and (b) that the plaintiff employee unreasonably failed to take advantage of any preventive or corrective opportunities provided by the employer or to avoid harm otherwise. While proof that an employer had promulgated an antiharassment policy with complaint procedure is not necessary in every instance as a matter of law, the need for a stated policy suitable to the employment circumstances may appropriately be addressed in any case when litigating the first element of the defense. And while proof that an employee failed to fulfill the corresponding obligation of reasonable care to avoid harm is not limited to showing any unreasonable failure to use any complaint procedure provided by the employer, a demonstration of such failure will normally suffice to satisfy the employer's burden under the second element of the defense. No affirmative defense is available, however, when the supervisor's harassment culminates in a tangible employment action, such as discharge, demotion, or undesirable reassignment. . . .

Given our explanation that the labels *quid pro quo* and hostile work environment are not controlling for purposes of establishing employer liability, Ellerth should have an adequate opportunity to prove she has a claim for which Burlington is liable.

Although Ellerth has not alleged she suffered a tangible employment action at the hands of Slowik, which would deprive Burlington of the availability of the affirmative defense, this is not dispositive. In light of our decision, Burlington is still subject to vicarious liability for Slowik's activity, but Burlington should have an opportunity to assert and prove the affirmative defense to liability.

For these reasons, we will affirm the judgment of the Court of Appeals, reversing the grant of summary judgment against Ellerth. On remand, the District Court will have the opportunity to decide whether it would be appropriate to allow Ellerth to amend her pleading or supplement her discovery.

continues

The judgment of the Court of Appeals is affirmed.

QUESTIONS FOR ANALYSIS

1. The dissent in this case argued that it opens the barn door to cases that employers cannot defend themselves against—such as this case, where the company had a policy against discrimination that was apparently violated but the injured employee did not take advantage of company policy. Is that likely to happen?

2. What steps should an antidiscrimination policy include?

In 2004, Justice Ginsburg repeated the key point of the *Ellerth* case in *Pennsylvania State Police* v. *Suders*, 124 S.Ct. 2342. Suders claimed she was subject to sexual harassment by her supervisors, which caused her to resign. She sued, claiming constructive discharge based on hostile environment. The employer responded that it had an affirmative defense. It should not be held vicariously liable for the supervisors' conduct because Suders did not take advantage of the internal anti-harassment procedures before she quit.

The Court held that when harassment is "so intolerable as to cause a resignation" the employee need not "remain on the job while seeking redress." In such cases, constructive discharge is the same as being fired for an illegal reason. It is possible for an employer to establish an affirmative defense that it had a proper anti-harassment procedure in such a case, but it will be difficult.

Disparate Impact

Liability for employment discrimination may be based on a claim of *disparate impact* or adverse impact, which means that the employer used a decision rule that caused discrimination in some aspect of employment based on protected class status. The discrimination may have been *unintentional*, but the effect of the employer's action was to limit employment opportunities for a person or group of persons based on race, color, religion, sex, or national origin. In practice, few age discrimination suits fall into the disparate impact category.

These cases involve employment practices that appear to be neutral but in fact have a disproportionately adverse impact on an employee or group of employees who are members of a protected class. Proof of intent to discriminate is not required, but the plaintiff must prove that the employment practice adversely impacts employment opportunities for members of a protected class. Hence, the key issues are

1. Does an employer have rules or practices that affect members of a protected group differently from other workers?
2. Are the rules or practices justified by business necessity or because they relate to valid job requirements?

ISSUE
Spotter

Effective Sexual Harassment Policy

As the Supreme Court made clear in the *Ellerth* case, a critical part of a defense for an employer to avoid liability in a suit for sexual harassment is an effective in-house procedure to try to prevent such behavior and then deal with it, should it arise. What steps would be reasonable to take to implement such a policy in an organization?

For example, employment procedure often requires that applicants have a high school diploma, achieve a minimum score on a specified test, or meet some other standard. If it is asserted that the employer's hiring or promotion practices have a discriminatory impact on an applicant, the employer must show that the applicant was rejected not because of race, color, religion, sex, or national origin but because the qualification requirements of the job were not met. The impact of employment rules must be neutral—that is, the rules must not have a disparate impact on a protected class. Congress reemphasized this point in the 1991 Civil Rights Act.

The relationship between the use of such rules and Title VII was established in *Griggs* v. *Duke Power*, a landmark case that determined that neutral employment criteria will be judged by their impact, not by the good or bad faith involved in their implementation.

Griggs v. Duke Power Company
United States Supreme Court
401 U.S. 424, 91 S.Ct. 849 (1971)

CASE BACKGROUND   *Duke Power was a segregated company before the 1964 Civil Rights Act. African Americans were hired only to work in certain low-level jobs; all higher-level jobs were held by whites. When Title VII took effect, Duke Power allowed all persons to compete for all jobs. Except for jobs already held by African Americans, the company required a high school diploma and certain scores on two aptitude tests. These job requirements, while neutral on their face, were claimed to have a discriminatory impact against African American applicants. At that time, 34 percent of the white men in North Carolina had high school diplomas, while only 12 percent of African American men had them; and 58 percent of the whites passed the aptitude tests, but only 6 percent of the African Americans passed.*

The district court ruled in favor of Duke Power, saying that the purpose of the standards was not to discriminate but to achieve a workforce of a certain quality. The court of appeals agreed, saying that there was no discriminatory motive. Griggs appealed to the Supreme Court.

CASE DECISION   Burger, Chief Justice.

* * *

The objective of Congress in the enactment of Title VII . . . was to achieve equality of employment opportunities and remove barriers that have operated in the past to favor an identifiable group of white employees over other employees. Under the Act, practices, procedures, or tests neutral on their face, and even neutral in terms of intent, cannot be maintained if they operate to "freeze" the status quo of prior discriminatory employment practices.

* * *

On the record before us, neither the high school completion requirement nor the general intelligence test is shown to bear a demonstrable relationship to successful performance of the jobs for which it was used. Both were adopted . . . without meaningful study of their relationship to job-performance ability. Rather, a vice president of the Company testified, the requirements were instituted on the Company's judgment that they generally would improve the overall quality of the work force.

The evidence, however, shows that employees who have not completed high school or taken the tests have continued to perform satisfactorily and make progress in departments for which the high school and test criteria are now used. The promotion record of present employees who would not be able to meet the new criteria thus suggests the possibility that the requirements may not be needed even for the limited purpose of preserving the avowed policy of advancement within the Company. . . .

Congress directed the thrust of the Act to the consequences of employment practices, not simply the motivation. More than that, Congress has placed on the employer the burden of showing that any given requirement must have a manifest relationship to the employment in question. . . .

Nothing in the Act precludes the use of testing or measuring procedures; obviously they are useful.

continues

What Congress has forbidden is giving these devices and mechanisms controlling force unless they are demonstrably a reasonable measure of job performance. Congress has not commanded that the less qualified be preferred over the better qualified simply because of minority origins. Far from disparaging job qualifications as such, Congress has made such qualifications the controlling factor, so that race, religion, nationality, and sex become irrelevant. What Congress has commanded is that any test used must measure the person for the job and not the person in the abstract.

The judgment of the Court of Appeals is . . . reversed.

QUESTIONS FOR ANALYSIS

1. Does this decision reduce the incentives for people to achieve higher levels of education?

2. Suppose an employer knows of a valid aptitude test that is related to job performance but is one on which African Americans do less well than they do on another, similar test. May the employer use the test that discriminates more against African Americans than would an alternative test?

Defenses under Title VII

As we saw in cases of disparate treatment, the employer must present a legitimate, nondiscriminatory, and clear and specific reason for the employment action taken. Certain business practices are specifically protected by Title VII. Other defenses are more general and have been determined by the courts as they have evaluated cases and considered the evidence presented.

Business Necessity

If employment practices can be shown to discriminate against some employees, the 1991 Civil Rights Act states that the burden is on the employer to prove that the challenged practices are justified as a *business necessity* and are *job related*. Business necessity is evaluated with reference to the ability of the employee to perform a certain job. Written tests, no matter how objective, must meet this business necessity test.

Experience and skill requirements, frequently measured by seniority, are often accepted as necessary. For example, to be a skilled bricklayer generally requires experience gained only by long practice. To require such experience for certain positions is not a violation of Title VII. Similarly, if a job requires certain abilities of strength and agility, tests for such ability are legitimate.

Selection criteria for professional, managerial, and other "white-collar" positions must also meet the business necessity test. When objective standards (such as two years' brick-laying experience) cannot be used, subjective evaluations such as impressions made by job interviews, references, and job performance evaluation are generally recognized as necessary in hiring and promoting professional personnel. Similarly, positions may have an education requirement. As in *Griggs*, educational requirements for manual or semiskilled jobs are less likely to be held necessary. However, for jobs such as teachers, police officers, laboratory technicians, airline pilots, and engineers, education requirements are usually valid.

Professionally Developed Ability Tests

Tests are often used by employers to determine whether applicants for a job possess the necessary skills and attributes. According to Title VII:

Dealing with Discrimination Complaints

Companies need internal policies to deal with discrimination and harassment complaints raised by employees. Having a policy is not very hard, but dealing with incidents that arise can be difficult. When a complaint of sexual harassment or racial discrimination arises, what steps would you think important in handling the matter in an effective way?

> It shall not be an unlawful employment practice for an employer to give and to act upon the results of any professionally developed ability test provided that such test, its administration, or action upon the results is not designed, intended, or used to discriminate because of race, color, religion, sex, or national origin.

As stated by the Supreme Court in *Griggs*, such tests must be shown to predict the work ability required for the job. Employers are usually required to supply statistical validation of the tests. Expert testimony from educational and industrial psychologists is often used to interpret the results.

Bona Fide Seniority or Merit Systems

Employers often use differential treatment based on seniority or merit. Title VII requires the courts to uphold *bona fide seniority* or *merit systems*. Seniority is usually the length of time an employee has been with an employer and can be used to determine such things as eligibility for pension plans, length of vacations, security from layoffs, preference for rehire and promotion, and amount of sick leave. According to Title VII:

> It shall not be an unlawful employment practice for an employer to apply different . . . terms, conditions, or privileges of employment pursuant to a bona fide seniority or merit system . . . provided that such differences are not the result of an intention to discriminate because of race, color, religion, sex, or national origin. . . .

The effects of seniority systems come under attack most often in cases involving layoffs on the basis of seniority. Many employers hold that in the event of a cutback in the workforce, workers with the most seniority have the most job protection—last hired, first fired. This means that minorities may suffer a greater share of the layoffs in a workforce cutback because they have less seniority than white workers who were hired when discrimination was practiced. The Supreme Court recognizes this fact, but seniority rights are protected by statute.

The Bona Fide Occupational Qualification (BFOQ)

Another defense is a *bona fide occupational qualification (BFOQ)*. Title VII states that discrimination is permitted in instances in which sex, religion, or national origin (but not race) is a BFOQ "reasonably necessary to the normal operation of that particular business." The employer has the burden of persuasion to establish the necessity of the BFOQ.

The EEOC has given this defense a narrow interpretation. Just because certain jobs have been traditionally filled by men does not mean that a legitimate defense exists for not hiring women for such positions. Simply because people were used to seeing and may have preferred female flight attendants did not mean that airlines could refuse to hire male flight attendants. No BFOQ on the basis of race is allowed. For example, an employer cannot assert that the business must have a white person for a particular job.

Generally, the increased cost of hiring members of the opposite sex may not be used to justify discrimination. The fact that separate bathroom facilities will have to be constructed is not a BFOQ.

A BFOQ exists where hiring on the basis of a personal characteristic is needed to keep the "authenticity" of a position. For example, a topless bar can argue that the cocktail servers should be female, since customers expect that as a part of the service. Male clothing is expected to be modeled by a male model. In some medical care situations, hospitals may restrict the sex of attendants for the comfort of patients or to protect sexual privacy.

Age Discrimination Defenses

The ADEA specifies defenses that employers rely on when defending age discrimination suits. These are much like the defenses in Title VII cases, but some are more specific to issues that arise because of age:

1. Good cause. Employers may fire or discipline an employee for unsatisfactory performance or for violating work rules. Good-faith business decisions are not prohibited.
2. Bona fide occupational qualification. Employers may discriminate on the basis of age "where age is a bona fide occupational qualification reasonably necessary to the normal operation of the particular business." The courts are skeptical of this justification, but mandatory retirement for public safety employees, such as police officers, prison guards, and firefighters, has been allowed.
3. Reasonable factors other than age. The ADEA states that employers may use criteria that happen to discriminate against older employees "where the differentiation is based on reasonable factors other than age." Employers may not fire older workers to hire new workers at lower wages. Rather, replacements must be made because the employee's performance has deteriorated. Age should be irrelevant to performance evaluations.
4. Seniority. As with Title VII, the ADEA states that employers may "observe the terms of a bona fide seniority system that is not intended to evade the purposes of" the ADEA. Hence, if a company has a reduction in force (RIF) and a protected worker loses a job instead of a younger worker who happens to have more seniority, there is no violation. An announced rule in a RIF, such as seniority (last-in, first-out) decides who will be terminated, means less chance of violating the law.
5. Bona fide employee benefit plans. The ADEA was amended by the *Older Workers Benefit Protection Act*, which states that an employer may "observe the terms of a bona fide employee benefit plan . . . that is a voluntary early retirement incentive plan consistent with the relevant purpose . . . of this Act." That is, employers are not supposed to force "involuntary retirement," but if early retirement incentive plan (ERIP) benefits are so generous that an employee chooses to retire, the employee cannot claim to have been forced to retire. Employers may ask employees to sign "knowing and voluntary waivers" of age discrimination claims when they agree to retire early in response to an ERIP. The ADEA also exempts senior executives in high-level policy positions who are at least age sixty-five and are entitled to a company pension.

Remedies

Title VII states that when an employer is found to have committed an unlawful discriminatory employment practice:

> the court may enjoin the . . . practice, and order such affirmative action as may be appropriate, which may include, but is not limited to, reinstatement or hiring of employees, with or without back pay . . . or any other equitable relief as the court deems appropriate.

Courts have used their statutory powers to order offending employers to reinstate employees with back pay, promote employees, give artificial seniority to existing or new employees, and implement an affirmative action program. Relying on the Act's reference to "equitable relief," the courts have broad and flexible powers to provide the most appropriate relief.

The 1991 Civil Rights Act amended Title VII so that the kinds of damages that may be sought by a plaintiff are the same in most discrimination suits. Compensation may go beyond back wages, such as payment for therapy or medical treatment related to the discrimination or for pain and suffering.

Punitive damages as a remedy are authorized by the 1991 Act if the employer acted "with malice or with reckless indifference" to plaintiff's rights. When punitive damages are requested, companies with fewer than 15 employees are exempt; companies with 15 to 100 employees may be sued for up to $50,000; between 101 and 200 employees, $100,000; between 201 and 500 employees, $200,000; and more than 500 employees, $300,000.

In addition, the court is empowered "in such circumstances as [it] may deem just" to appoint an attorney for a poor plaintiff. Ordinarily, a winning plaintiff is awarded attorney's fees. A winning employer may be awarded attorney's fees only if the court determines that the plaintiff's action was frivolous, unreasonable, or without foundation.

AFFIRMATIVE ACTION

An *affirmative action program* is a deliberate effort by an employer to remedy discriminatory practices in the hiring, training, and promotion of protected class members when a particular class is underrepresented in the employer's workforce. Such programs have been adopted based only on race or sex—not on color, religion, national origin, or age.

After finding that members of a protected class are underrepresented in the company's workforce, an employer may voluntarily start an affirmative action program to ensure that the company provides more opportunities for women or minorities in certain job categories. An involuntary program may be imposed by the courts as a remedy to correct past discriminatory employment practices by the company or, in the special case of government contractors, by the federal government as a requirement to enter into a government contract. This is probably the most controversial part of employment discrimination law.

Executive Order 11246

As the chief executive officer of the United States, the president has the authority to determine certain conditions for government business that are issued in *executive orders* by the president. Referred to as *government contractors*, businesses must abide by the executive orders when they contract with the government. In 1965, President

Johnson issued Executive Order 11246, a requirement that government contractors adopt *affirmative action*.

Enforced by the Office of Federal Contract Compliance Programs (OFCCP), the order requires companies with federal contracts totaling $10,000 per year to take affirmative action. Those with $50,000 in contracts and fifty or more employees must have a written affirmative action plan, which requires a contractor to conduct a *workforce analysis* for each job within the organization. Jobs are studied by rank, salary, and the percent of those employed on the basis of race and sex.

The contractor must do an *underutilization analysis*, comparing the percent of minorities and women in the community in each job category with the percent employed by the contractor. If underutilization is found—say because 19 percent of the lab technicians are women compared with 41 percent of the lab technicians available in the community—the contractor must establish an affirmative action plan to increase the number of women in these positions.

The program may require efforts to hire more women or to invest in training women to improve their qualifications for certain jobs. If these efforts fail because the employer was not serious, a numerical goal may be set, such as to double the number of female lab technicians in three years. In recent years, this has not been common. Hiring and promotion quotas that are set are reviewed periodically to see if adequate progress is being made. In the event that progress is not being made, federal contracts may be canceled.

INTERNATIONAL *Perspective*

Employment Discrimination in Europe and Japan

Europeans often are portrayed as more sophisticated than Americans with regard to social legislation. However, in many respects they are years behind the United States in their treatment of minorities and women in the labor force. Most European countries and Japan have antidiscrimination statutes on the books, but the laws are not nearly as strict as the U.S. laws.

Employees in Europe can be forced to retire between ages fifty-five and sixty-five, depending on the country. Europeans over age forty-five who lose their jobs have a harder time finding employment again than do their counterparts in the United States.

The first sexual harassment case in Japan was not decided until 1992. A woman who was harassed by her boss for two years was fired for complaining. She was awarded $12,500

in damages. While not unusual by American standards, the case was a landmark in Japan.

Minority immigrants are treated as second-class citizens in most countries. In general, it is much harder for a non-citizen, especially a member of a racial minority, to obtain work and citizenship in Japan and most of Europe than it is in the United States.

Where affirmative action exists, it tends to be weak or even overtly discriminatory in favor of male-citizen workers who already dominate the labor force. Women are kept out of many higher-level jobs and are not paid as much as men for equal work—especially in Japan.

European countries and Japan appear to treat women better in certain respects, such as by mandating generous maternity benefits, but one effect of those laws is to encourage employers not to hire women because of the high cost of the benefits to which women are entitled if they have children.

Affirmative Action as a Remedy

Title VII provides that in the event an employer is found to have engaged in illegal discrimination, "the court may . . . order such affirmative action as may be appropriate." Courts may require an offending employer to begin an affirmative action program. The court could require the employer to hire qualified employees in the protected class to make up for past discriminatory activities. The action may be oriented at new employee recruitment, or it could be using more resources to training current minority or women employees to become qualified candidates for promotion into positions in which they are underrepresented.

In recent years, as the worst vestiges of overt discrimination have been reduced, court-ordered affirmative action programs have become less common than voluntary affirmative action programs. Most employers adopt a program before one is forced upon them. The Supreme Court has approved mandated programs where a pattern of intentional discrimination makes it clear that a strong remedy is required under the flexible powers granted courts by the Civil Rights Act. In *U.S. v. Paradise*, 107 S.Ct. 1053, the Court upheld a court-ordered hiring and promotion goal program for the Alabama Department of Public Safety, which had failed to hire African American troopers for years after passage of Title VII. Consistent with the state population, the Court upheld an ordered goal that 25 percent of all employees at all ranks should be qualified African Americans.

Voluntary Affirmative Action

Employers may voluntarily implement an affirmative action program. They may do so to be sure they are in compliance with Executive Order 11246. Employers often implement a program after determining that a protected class is underrepresented in its workforce in certain job categories. An affirmative action program allows an employer to correct for underrepresentation. The Supreme Court examined a voluntary affirmative action program in the *Johnson* decision.

Johnson v. Transportation Agency, Santa Clara Co., Calif.
United States Supreme Court
480 U.S. 616, 107 S.Ct. 1442 (1987)

CASE BACKGROUND *The Transportation Agency voluntarily adopted an affirmative action plan for hiring and promoting employees. Women were significantly underrepresented in some job categories. To achieve a better balance in the workforce, the sex of qualified applicants would be given consideration. No specific goals were set for the number of positions to be occupied by women, but annual goals were adjusted each year based on experience.*

The agency announced a vacancy for the position of road dispatcher in the skilled craft job category. Johnson, a man, and Diane Joyce applied and were rated the top two applicants for the position. Johnson scored a 75 on the interview test, Joyce a 73. After taking into account Joyce's sex, she was picked over Johnson, who then sued, claiming that he had been discriminated against on the basis of sex.

The district court held the affirmative action plan illegal because it had no ending point or clear goals. The

Court of Appeals reversed, finding that the plan was legal. Johnson appealed.

CASE DECISION Brennan, Justice.

* * *

As the Agency Plan recognized, women were most egregiously underrepresented in the Skilled Craft job category, since none of the 238 positions was occupied by a woman. In mid-1980, when Joyce was selected for the road dispatcher position, the Agency was still in the process of refining its short-term goals for Skilled Craft Workers in accordance with the directive of the Plan. This process did not reach fruition until 1982, when the Agency established a short-term goal for that year of three women for the 55 expected openings in that job category—a modest goal of about 6% for that category.

continues

We reject petitioner's argument that . . . it was inappropriate for the Director to take into account affirmative action considerations in filling the road dispatcher position. The Agency's Plan emphasized that the long-term goals were not to be taken as guides for actual hiring decisions, but that supervisors were to consider a host of practical factors in seeking to meet affirmative action objectives, including the fact that in some job categories women were not qualified in numbers comparable to their representation in the labor force.

By contrast, had the Plan simply calculated imbalances in all categories according to the proportion of women in the area labor pool, and then directed that hiring be governed solely by those figures, its validity fairly could be called into question. This is because analysis of a more specialized labor pool normally is necessary in determining underrepresentation in some positions. If a plan failed to take distinctions in qualifications into account in providing guidance for actual employment decisions, it would dictate mere blind hiring by the numbers, for it would hold supervisors to "achievement of a particular percentage of minority employment or membership . . . regardless of circumstances such as economic conditions or the number of qualified minority applicants . . ."

* * *

Affirmed.

QUESTIONS FOR ANALYSIS
1. Why might a company or organization undertake a voluntary affirmative action program?
2. In the absence of its affirmative action program, could the agency have hired Joyce over Johnson?

DISABILITY DISCRIMINATION

The *Rehabilitation Act* of 1973 provides protection for disabled persons seeking employment with, or currently employed by, employers that receive federal funds. The Act tends to follow the steps in Title VII employment discrimination suits. Section 503 of the Act is most important. It holds that all companies with federal contracts of $2,500 or more have a duty to ensure the disabled an opportunity in the workplace by providing reasonable accommodations.

The *Americans with Disabilities Act (ADA)* of 1990 expands the rights of persons with disabilities in employment and supplements access rights to public accommodations, such as hotels, restaurants, theaters, public transportation, telecommunications, and retail stores. The ADA expands the rights of people with mental and physical disabilities beyond those provided by the Rehabilitation Act. Besides encompassing the Rehabilitation Act, the ADA incorporates most remedies and procedures set out in Title VII. The ADA applies to all employers with fifteen or more employees.

Definition of Disabled

The Rehabilitation Act and the ADA define *a person with disabilities* as

> any person who (i) has a physical or mental impairment which substantially limits one or more of such person's major life activities, (ii) has a record of such an impairment, or (iii) is regarded as having such an impairment.

The Supreme Court has recognized regulations by the Department of Health and Human Services as a guide to determining what is a disability. The regulations define "major life activities" as "functions such as caring for one's self, performing manual tasks, walking, seeing, hearing, speaking, breathing, learning, and working." Examples of disabilities covered by the statutes include people:

- With a history of alcohol or other drug abuse
- With a severe disfigurement

- Who have had a heart attack
- Who must use a wheelchair
- Who are hearing- or vision-impaired

Even if a person is not actually impaired, if other people think the person is impaired, the person is considered disabled. For example, former cancer patients have found that some people are afraid to hire them because they think cancer is contagious. As a result, even though no impairment exists and even though doctors may say there is no disease present, bias against the person who had the disease makes the person disabled for purposes of this law.

Unlike Title VII discrimination suits, where there are some very clear standards, ADA cases involve more individual evaluation of circumstances of what constitutes disability in relationship to particular employment. In the *Williams* case the Supreme Court provided some clarification of standards.

Toyota Motor Manufacturing, Kentucky, Inc. v. Williams

Supreme Court of the United States
534 U.S. 184, 122 S.Ct. 681 (2002)

CASE BACKGROUND   *Williams began work at a Toyota assembly plant in 1990. Using power tools eventually caused pain in her hands, wrists, and arms. She was diagnosed with carpal tunnel syndrome and tendonitis, which restricted her from lifting more than twenty pounds or from constant repetitive motions using her wrists or elbows. For two years she was assigned to modified jobs. Then she was assigned to an inspection team where she looked for flaws in paint jobs. After two years, the company announced that the inspection teams would rotate through all four parts of the inspection process. This required Williams to do more lifting and motions than did paint inspection only, causing her to suffer neck and shoulder pain. Refusing to do all four inspection jobs, she was fired. She sued for disability discrimination, contending that Toyota failed to reasonably accommodate her disability.*

She "based her claim that she was 'disabled' under the ADA on the ground that her physical impairments substantially limited her in (1) manual tasks; (2) housework; (3) gardening; (4) playing with her children; (5) lifting; and (6) working, all of which, she argued, constituted major life activities under the Act." The trial court dismissed her suit but the Sixth Circuit Court of Appeals reversed, concluding that she was disabled and due accommodation. Toyota appealed.

CASE DECISION   O'Connor, Justice.

* * *

To qualify as disabled . . . a claimant must initially prove that he or she has a physical or mental impairment. The. . . regulations issued by the Department of Health and Human Services, define "physical impairment," the type of impairment relevant to this case, to mean "any physiological disorder or condition, cosmetic disfigurement, or anatomical loss affection one or more of the following body systems: neurological; musculoskeletal; special sense organs; respiratory, including speech organs; cardiovascular; reproductive, digestive, genito-urinary; hemic and lymphatic; skin; and endocrine." . . .

Merely having an impairment does not make one disabled for purposes of the ADA. Claimants also need to demonstrate that the impairment limits a major life activity. The . . . regulations provide a list of examples of "major life activities," that includes "walking, seeing, hearing," and, as relevant here, "performing manual tasks."

To qualify as disabled, a claimant must further show that the limitation on the major life activity is "substantial."

* * *

The parties do not dispute that respondent's medical conditions, which include carpal tunnel syndrome, myotendinitis, and thoracic outlet compression, amount to physical impairments. The relevant question, therefore, is whether the Sixth Circuit correctly analyzed

continues

whether these impairments substantially limited respondent in the major life activity of performing manual tasks. Answering this requires us to address an issue about which the EEOC regulations are silent: what a plaintiff must demonstrate to establish a substantial limitation in the specific major life activity of performing manual tasks.

Our consideration of this issue is guided first and foremost by the words of the disability definition itself. "Substantially" in the phrase "substantially limits" suggests "considerable" or "to a large degree."

. . . The word "substantial" thus clearly precludes impairments that interfere in only a minor way with the performance of manual tasks from qualifying as disabilities. . . .

"Major" in the phrase "major life activities" means important. "Major life activities" thus refers to those activities that are of central importance to daily life. In order for performing manual tasks to fit into this category—a category that includes such basic abilities as walking, seeing, and hearing—the manual tasks in question must be central to daily life. If each of these tasks included in the major life activity of performing manual tasks does not independently qualify as a major life activity, then together they must do so. . . .

We therefore hold that to be substantially limited in performing manual tasks, an individual must have an impairment that prevents or severely restricts the individual from doing activities that are of central importance to most people's daily lives. The impairment's impact must also be permanent or long-term.

It is insufficient for individuals attempting to prove disability status under this test to merely submit evidence of a medical diagnosis of an impairment. Instead, The ADA requires those "claiming the Act's protection . . . to prove a disability by offering evidence that the extent of the limitation [caused by their impairment] in terms of their own experience . . . is substantial." . . .

When addressing the major life activity of performing manual tasks, the central inquiry must be whether the claimant is unable to perform the variety of tasks central to most people's daily lives, not whether the claimant is not to perform the tasks associated with their specific job. . . .

Even more critically, the manual tasks unique to any particular job are not necessarily important parts of most people's lives. As a result, occupation-specific tasks may have only limited relevance to the manual task inquiry. In this case, "repetitive work with hands and arms extended at or about shoulder levels for extended periods of time," the manual task on which the Court of Appeals relied, is not an important part of most people's daily lives. The court, therefore, should not have considered respondent's inability to do such manual work in her specialized assembly line job as sufficient proof that she was substantially limited in performing manual tasks. . . .

The record also indicates that her medical conditions caused her to avoid sweeping, to quit dancing, to occasionally seek help dressing, and to reduce how often she plays with her children, gardens, and drives long distances. But these changes in her life did not amount to such severe restrictions in the activities that are of central importance to most people's daily lives that they establish a manual-task disability as a matter of law. . . .

Accordingly, we reverse the Court of Appeals' judgment. . . .

QUESTIONS FOR ANALYSIS

1. Since it was clear that Williams physically could no longer do the same job, why was she not disabled?

2. Since Toyota had previously given her other job duties that relieved her pain, why did the company still have such an obligation?

Compliance with the Statutes

The Rehabilitation Act is enforced primarily by complaints to the Department of Labor, which may bring suit on behalf of people with disabilities. Only a small number of suits have been filed. Suits under the ADA arise the same way that discrimination suits brought under Title VII come about—by filing complaints with the EEOC. The suits proceed much the same way as do Title VII suits.

Reasonable Accommodation

Employers are obliged to make *reasonable accommodations* for persons with disabilities. Employers are expected to incur expenses in making a position or workstation available to qualified disabled applicants and employees. Exactly where the line is drawn is not clear. Ford does not have to redesign its assembly line at high cost so that a worker in a wheelchair could work on the assembly line, because that would impose an *undue hardship* on business operations. However, when a workstation can be redesigned for several thousand dollars to accommodate a person with a disability, that must be done. The Department of Labor estimates that in most cases, the cost of accommodation is under $500. However, firms are also expected to provide special equipment and training for the disabled and allow modified work schedules.

EEOC Guidance

The EEOC has issued *ADA Enforcement Guidance: Preemployment Disability-Related Questions and Medical Examinations*. The guidelines note that the ADA prohibits employers from asking disability-related questions or requiring medical exams before a job is offered. Hence, employers cannot ask questions about the nature or severity of a disability. The following are examples of questions that are illegal to ask during a job interview:

- Do you have AIDS?
- Have you ever been treated for mental health problems?
- Have you ever filed for workers' compensation benefits?
- Do you have a disability that would interfere with ability to perform the job?
- How many sick days were you out last year?
- Have you ever been unable to handle work-related stress?
- Have you ever been treated for drug addiction or drug abuse?

In the case of drugs, past addiction is treated as a disability, but current use of illegal drugs is not, so applicants may be asked about current use and may be given a drug test. However, current alcoholism is a protected disability, and applicants may not be asked questions about drinking habits, although it is permissible to ask whether an applicant has been arrested for driving under the influence of alcohol.

If a disability is obvious or if an applicant volunteers a disability, some questions may be asked about the need for reasonable accommodation. For example, if an applicant discloses that she needs to take breaks to take diabetes medication, the employer may ask how often such breaks are needed and how long they would be. Employers may make clear the requirements needed to perform a job, and if it is

ISSUE
Spotter

Accommodating Disabilities

The Americans with Disabilities Act does not give "bright lines" for exactly what accommodation is reasonable for employees with disabilities. Proper accommodation is a case-by-case determination. The key terms are "reasonable" and "undue hardship." What would be the guidelines you would set for an organization in developing an accommodation policy?

dubious that someone could perform a job function, an applicant may be asked to demonstrate how he or she could accomplish the task.

Once a job offer has been made, an employer may ask for documentation of a disability and may ask more questions about the reasonable accommodation needed for the employee. If a physical exam is given to new employees, similar exams must be given to all employees in the same job categories and the results must be kept confidential. Such exams can be given so long as they are related to the ability to do the job, and not because an employer is trying to screen out employees with potential health problems.

Juris *prudence?*

Get the Women Out of My Classes

Winston was fired after nineteen years as an English teacher in the Maine Technical College System. While complaints had been made of sexual misconduct, he was dismissed after a sexual harassment complaint was filed after he kissed a female student "after a sexually suggestive conversation."

Winston sued, "claiming that he was terminated because of his 'mental handicap of sexual addiction.'" His expert witness testified that this disorder, which had led to his seeking the services of prostitutes, was a permanent condition but that Winston could perform his job as a teacher.

The supreme court of Maine tossed out the complaint, noting that the ADA specifically excludes "sexual behavior disorders" from the term *disability*.

Source: *Winston* v. *Maine Tech. College Sys.*, 631 A.2d 70

Violations by Employers

As in the case of discrimination based on race, sex, or age, the law is broken if a qualified person is denied an opportunity primarily because of disability. However, in the case of disabilities, besides not discriminating, an employer must also make reasonable accommodations—go the extra step to make adjustments for disabilities. In this sense, there is an affirmative action requirement, but it is not one tied to specific goals. This requirement works on a case-by-case basis. Employment situations that have been in violation of the law include

- Using standardized employment tests that tend to screen out people with disabilities
- Refusing to hire applicants because they have a history of alcohol abuse rather than because they are currently alcohol abusers
- Rejecting a job applicant because he or she is HIV-positive
- Asking job applicants if they have disabilities rather than asking if they have the ability to perform the job
- Limiting advancement opportunities for employees because of their disabilities
- Not hiring a person with a disability because the workplace does not have a bathroom that can accommodate wheelchairs

The first judgment under the ADA occurred in 1993. AIC Security Investigation fired an executive who was suffering from terminal brain cancer but was still able to work. The EEOC pursued the case on the executive's behalf, and the jury awarded the man more than $500,000 in damages plus back pay. Since the 1991 Civil Rights Act restricts damages in employment discrimination cases such as this one to $200,000 plus back pay, the jury verdict had to be reduced. The case delivered a clear message that as employment rights of persons with disabilities expand, employers must adjust. About 18,000 complaints are filed with the EEOC annually.

SUMMARY

- Title VII of the Civil Rights Act and the Age Discrimination in Employment Act require employers not to discriminate on the basis of sex, race, color, religion, national origin, or age. This applies to all aspects of the employment process—hiring, promotion, discipline, benefits, and firing. The laws are enforced by the EEOC and private party suits.
- Sex discrimination specifically includes discrimination with respect to childbearing plans, pregnancy, and related medical conditions. Sexual harassment now poses a legal challenge for managers, who must take steps to inform employees of the seriousness and the consequences of harassment and establish internal procedures to allow claims to be investigated with an assurance of confidentiality.
- Key tests that the courts use to look for discrimination are *disparate treatment*, where, everything else being equal, employment decisions are illegally motivated by discrimination based on race, sex, national origin, religion, or age; and *disparate impact*, where the effect of hiring or promotion standards is to discriminate, even if unintentionally, on the basis of protected class status.
- When employers are sued under the discrimination laws, they must present a preponderance of evidence that the practices they engage in are not discriminatory. The practices must be related to legitimate business necessity. Practices that when properly designed are allowed to stand include professionally developed ability tests, bona fide seniority and merit systems, and bona fide occupational qualifications that provide a rationale for personnel decisions.
- An affirmative action plan may be adopted by an employer and a union in a collective bargaining agreement, or it may be adopted voluntarily by an employer. Strategically, adopting such a plan voluntarily might reduce the likelihood of a more rigid program being imposed on the company in the event of a lawsuit or government investigation of discrimination charges.
- Employers may have affirmative action plans imposed on them by court order as a remedy for discrimination. Federal contractors must have affirmative action plans in place. These plans are designed to increase minority or female representation in certain job categories. This may be done by setting goals to be met within certain time frames.
- The Rehabilitation Act of 1973 and the Americans with Disabilities Act of 1990 require employers to take positive steps to make accommodations for disabled workers. Court decisions have broadened the definition of a disabled person to include alcohol and other drug addicts as well as persons with serious diseases such as AIDS. Employers must balance the interests and safety of other employees and customers against the rights of the disabled employees to gain or retain meaningful employment.

REVIEW AND DISCUSSION QUESTIONS

1. Define the following terms and phrases:

discrimination
equal employment opportunity
protected classes
color
national origin
hostile environment
constructive discharge

disparate treatment
prima facie discrimination case
disparate impact
bona fide occupational qualification
affirmative action
reasonable accommodations

2. Would a dress code that required men to wear three-piece suits but stated only that women had to "look professional" be discriminatory against the male employees? What differences would be considered discriminatory?

CASE QUESTIONS

3. Wise was fired for getting into a fight with another employee during lunch at the company lunchroom. She kicked and scratched the other employee and used abusive language. She claimed sex discrimination under Title VII because male employees who had been in fights had not been fired. Was this sex discrimination? [*Wise* v. *Mead Corp.*, 614 F.Supp. 1131 (1985)]

4. Parr applied for a position as an insurance representative for which he was well qualified and had experience. The manager who interviewed Parr told him he would probably be hired and also told him the company did not sell insurance to African Americans. Parr told the employment service that set up the interview of the manager's remarks and told the service that he was married to an African American woman. The employment service told the insurance company of Parr's interracial marriage, at which point they declined to hire him. Was that a violation of Title VII? [*Parr* v. *Woodmen of the World Life Insurance Co.*, 791 F.2d 888 (11th Cir., 1986)]

 Check your answer at http://meiners.westbuslaw.com

5. Houldsworth worked for the City of Temple Terrace, Florida, from 1987 to 1996. During 1993 to 1994, she had an affair with a city manager who was her supervisor's manager. Her job evaluations began to fall after her affair ended. She complained to the human relations office that she believed the decline in her evaluations was because she had terminated her affair. The city manager learned that there had been an affair and told Houldsworth's former boyfriend to seek alternative employment. He soon left for another job. Houldsworth's evaluations continued to deteriorate, and she quit after a year. She sued for constructive discharge. The trial court dismissed her suit; she appealed. Does she have a suit? [*Pipkins* v. *City of Temple Terrace*, 247 F.3d 169 (11th Cir., 2001)]

6. Friedman applied for employment at a pharmaceutical warehouse. He was offered a position and told that, as a condition of employment, he would have to be vaccinated against the mumps. He refused to be vaccinated because the vaccine is grown in chicken embryos. He said that it would violate his system of beliefs as a vegan, which prohibits the use of any animal-related product. The employment offer was withdrawn; he sued for discrimination based on religion. The district court dismissed the case, holding that veganism is not a religion. Friedman

appealed. Does he have a case? [*Friedman* v. *So. Cal. Permanente Medical Group*, 102 Cal.App.4th 39 (Ct. App., Calif., 2002)]

 Check your answer at http://meiners.westbuslaw.com

7. Lack sued his former employer, Wal-Mart, and supervisor, Bragg, for sexual harassment. He contended that Bragg made "inappropriate and demeaning statements . . . of a sexual nature" and told vulgar jokes in front of Lack and others. When Lack complained, he suffered retaliation as Bragg made "his work scheduled more burdensome and inconvenient." Wal-Mart ignored the problem. Other employees testified as to Bragg's behavior. The jury found for Lack and awarded him $80,000 in damages. Wal-Mart appealed. Did Lack have a case? [*Lack* v. *Wal-Mart Stores, Inc.*, 240 F.3d 255 (4th Cir., 2001)]

8. Breeden worked for a school district in Nevada. She attended a meeting with two male workers. One of the men made a sexist joke to the other male, but it was not directed at Breeden, who complained to her supervisor about the incident. Breeden filed a sexual harassment complaint with the EEOC. Soon after, she was transferred to another position, a move that she had known for some time might occur. She added a charge of retaliation to her complaint. The district court dismissed the case. The court of appeals reversed for Breeden. The school district appealed to the Supreme Court. Does Breeden have a good case? [*Clark County School District* v. *Breeden*, 121 S.Ct. 1508 (Sup. Ct., 2001)]

 Check your answer at http://meiners.westbuslaw.com

9. Rawlinson applied for a position as a correctional counselor—a prison guard—with the Alabama prison system. The primary duty was to maintain security and control the inmates by supervising their activities. The Alabama Board of Corrections rejected her application because she failed to meet the minimum 120-pound weight requirement set by Alabama law. The law also imposed a minimum five-foot, two-inch height requirement on applicants. Did the Alabama statute violate Title VII? What if the requirements were imposed for the protection of prison guards? [*Dothard* v. *Rawlinson*, 97 S.Ct. 2720 (1977)]

10. The Jackson, Michigan, Board of Education had a rule that in the event of a cutback in teachers, the layoffs would be proportional on the basis of race. That way, students would be guaranteed more minority teachers as role models. This was done because more of the older teachers were white; if the layoff was based on seniority only, more minority teachers would be laid off proportional to the white teachers. The district court and court of appeals agreed with the school board, saying the rule helped to remedy past discrimination. What did the Supreme Court say? [*Wygant* v. *Jackson Board of Education*, 106 S.Ct. 1842 (1986)]

 Check your answer at http://meiners.westbuslaw.com

11. Grosjean worked for First Energy since 1970. In 1997 he was promoted to a supervisory position. Two years later, when he was 54, his boss, Dressner, who was 41, removed Grosjean from his position, stating that he was not performing adequately. Grosjean kept the same pay, but had less status. The position was given to Riley, who was 51. Grosjean sued for age discrimination for being denied promotion to his supervisory position. The trial court dismissed the suit. Grosjean appealed. Does he have a case? [*Grosjean* v. *First Energy*, 349 F.3d 332 (6th Cir., 2003)]

12. Medina Rene, who is openly gay, worked for the MGM Grand Hotel in Las Vegas for two years. During his employment, he contends that his male supervisor

and co-workers subjected him to a hostile work environment on a daily basis. He was subject to crude jokes, name-calling, and unwelcome physical touching. He sued the hotel for sexual harassment, noting that the reason for the harassment was his sexual orientation. The district court dismissed the suit, holding that his claim of sexual orientation discrimination is not recognized under Title VII. Rene appealed. Does he have a case? [*Rene* v. *MGM Grand Hotel, Inc.*, 305 F.3d 1061 (9th Cir., 2002)]

13. Chenoweth was an experienced nurse, age forty-one. She worked for Hillsborough County, Florida, as a manager, reviewing files of hospital patients for whom the county is financially responsible. She could do some of the work at home, but she drove to hospitals to review records. She suffered a seizure and was diagnosed as having epilepsy. Her physician prescribed a medicine for her and told her not to drive at all until she had gone six months without a seizure. Since she could not drive, she proposed to the county that she work at home two days a week and that she not have to drive to hospitals to check records. The county agreed she could work at home some, but did not agree to the other request. She sued for disability discrimination. The trial court granted summary judgment for her employer; she appealed. Does she have a suit for ADA violation? [*Chenoweth* v. *Hillsborough County*, 250 F.3d 1328 (11th Cir., 2001)]

14. J. B. Hunt Transport would not hire truck drivers who used prescription medications with side effects that might impair their driving ability. The EEOC sued Hunt, contending that this practice violated the Americans with Disabilities Act because Hunt discriminated against those with perceived disabilities. The district court held for Hunt; the EEOC appealed. [*EEOC* v. *J.B. Hunt Transport, Inc.*, 321 F.3d 69 (2nd Cir., 2003)]

15. A Vermont ski resort hired a cleaning woman who wore dentures. The woman had a good work record, and she had a neat and clean appearance, but she quit wearing her dentures because they hurt. The resort manager told her she had to wear her dentures or she would be dismissed, which she was because her appearance hurt their high-class image. She sued for disability discrimination under Vermont's Fair Employment Practices Act, which contains language nearly identical to that in the ADA. Is she protected? [*Hodgdon* v. *Mt. Mansfield Co.*, 624 A.2d 1122 (Sup. Ct., Vt., 1992)]

16. Bolton worked in a grocery warehouse for two years when he suffered a work-related injury that required medical leave. Under company policy, an employee on medical leave could not return until the company doctor certified that the employee was fit to resume work. When Bolton wanted to return, the doctor declared him unable to perform his work in the warehouse, which refused to rehire him. Bolton sued, claiming disability discrimination. Did he have a case? [*Bolton* v. *Scrivner, Inc.*, 36 F.3d 939, (10th Cir., 1994)]

17. Sullivan worked successfully in a number of retail sales positions for more than a decade. During that time he battled alcoholism with varying degrees of success. Neiman Marcus fired him after he worked there for six months. A subordinate employee complained about Sullivan being drunk at work and being abusive when he was drinking. The supervisor searched Sullivan's desk and found an empty bottle of vodka. The company decided to fire Sullivan, but held off informing him, as he reported that was he taking leave for alcohol treatment. When his treatment ended, he was fired for violating company rules regarding alcohol use on the job. He sued. The district court held for the employer; Sullivan appealed. Does he have a claim? [*Sullivan* v. *Neiman Marcus Group*, 358 F.3d 110 (1st Cir., 2004)]

ETHICS QUESTION

18. You are a supervisor at a company that does not have an affirmative action program. In looking to hire a new person for a certain position, the person who best fits the job criteria is a white male age thirty. Two other candidates are also well qualified for the position but just slightly less so than the top candidate. One of the other candidates is African American; the third is a white woman age sixty-three. You believe that, in general, there is societal discrimination against minorities and older people. Should you give a little extra credit to the candidates who are in protected classes, given that you can justify whatever choice you make? How would you decide between the African American man and the older white woman? Should you take into account that the man supports a wife and three children, whereas the woman has an employed husband and no children?

PULLING IT  *Together*

Labor Law and Employment Discrimination

Ravenscroft worked for Westvaco for twenty years before he was fired for sexual harassment of a co-worker. His actions were found to have violated the company policy that forbids "sexual harassment of any sort." Ravenscroft challenged his discharge through his union. The collective bargaining agreement stated that the union could challenge discharges by arbitration. The arbitrator found that Ravenscroft had harassed the woman who had complained, and had violated company policy, but ordered him reinstated to his job. The company sued in federal court, contending that the arbitrator exceeded the scope of his authority by substituting his judgment for that of management and that reinstatement violated public policy because it prevented the company from carrying out its duty to eliminate sexual harassment in the workplace. The district court agreed that the reinstatement violated public policy and held for Westvaco. The union appealed. Who prevailed? Does labor law or discrimination law prevail?

Westvaco v. *United Paperworkers International Union, AFL-CIO,* 171 F.3d 971 (4th Cir. 1999)

INTERNET ASSIGNMENT

http://www.law.cornell.edu

Provide a brief summary of each of the following discrimination-related statutes.

1. Civil Rights Act of 1964 (42 U.S.C. Chapter 21)
2. Equal Pay Act of 1963 (29 U.S.C. Section 206)
3. Americans with Disabilities Act of 1990 (42 U.S.C. Chapter 126)
4. Age Discrimination in Employment Act (29 U.S.C. Sections 621–634)

Hint: The Legal Information Institute has overviews of many legal topics.

Chapter 17 | *Environmental Law*

S ome years ago, the Environmental Protection Agency (EPA) and Amoco Corporation cooperated on a four-year project to study pollution control effectiveness. The EPA listened to company experts; the company revealed operation details to EPA. The study showed that EPA regulations required Amoco to spend $41 million a year to trap air pollution from one refinery system, when the same control, using a better technology, could be achieved for $11 million. The regulations did not allow the cheaper control methods. The study also showed that no controls were required on another part of the refinery that emitted five times as much pollution as the pollution being controlled at a cost of $41 million. EPA was as frustrated as Amoco by the results, but both were trapped by inflexible regulations that are slow to change.

More than $100 billion per year is spent on pollution controls in the United States; this figure represents the largest share of any major nation's income. Because pollution controls are so costly, there has often been a fight between industry and regulators. Some expensive pollution controls achieve little, while some major sources of pollution go largely uncontrolled. Whether recognition of this will translate into more cost-effective pollution controls that deliver better environmental quality at a lower price remains to be seen.

This chapter reviews the major federal laws providing environmental protection, but it begins with a discussion of common-law rules that regulate environmental quality, such as the application of nuisance law. The chapter then discusses the creation of the EPA and the most important environmental statutes, including the Clean Air Act, the Clean Water Act, the Resource Conservation and Recovery Act, the Superfund, and the Endangered Species Act.

ENVIRONMENTAL REGULATION

During the 1960s, the environment became a major issue. Books such as Rachel Carson's *Silent Spring*, which discussed problems such as the effects of heavy pesticide use on birds, brought attention to environmental concerns. Since that time there has been strong support for federal legislation to improve environmental quality. Whether the legislation has been effective in reducing pollution or is cost-effective in getting the most protection for the money spent is beyond the scope of what we study here.

Federal control of the environment essentially began in 1970. Before then, some pollution laws were on the books, but they meant little in practice. Since 1970, an explosion of federal legislation has affected most aspects of the environment. Exhibit 17.1 lists only a fraction of the environmental statutes on the books now, but those statutes are the ones that have the greatest effects.

Exhibit 17.1

Federal Regulation of Environmental Pollution

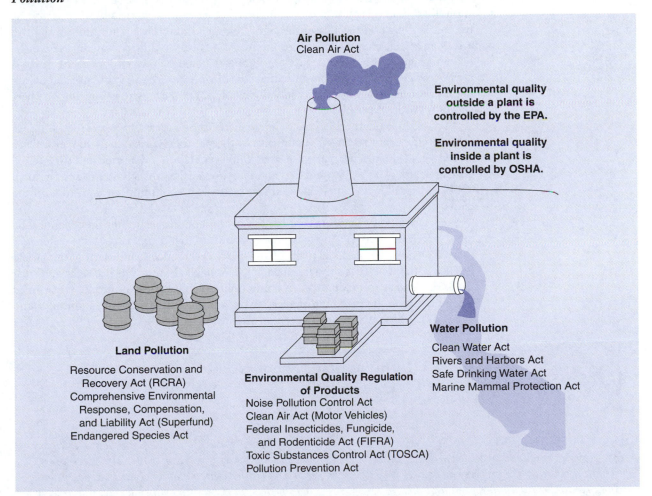

Air Pollution
Clean Air Act

Environmental quality outside a plant is controlled by the EPA.

Environmental quality inside a plant is controlled by OSHA.

Land Pollution

Resource Conservation and Recovery Act (RCRA)
Comprehensive Environmental Response, Compensation, and Liability Act (Superfund)
Endangered Species Act

Environmental Quality Regulation of Products

Noise Pollution Control Act
Clean Air Act (Motor Vehicles)
Federal Insecticides, Fungicide, and Rodenticide Act (FIFRA)
Toxic Substances Control Act (TOSCA)
Pollution Prevention Act

Water Pollution

Clean Water Act
Rivers and Harbors Act
Safe Drinking Water Act
Marine Mammal Protection Act

To implement and enforce federal environmental mandates, Congress created the EPA in 1970. Today, the EPA is one of the largest federal agencies, with almost 18,000 employees and a budget of about $8 billion. Add to that the state environmental agencies that are required to help enforce the federal and state environmental laws. The EPA has primary responsibility for four major external environmental problems: air pollution, water pollution, land pollution, and pollution associated with certain products (see http://www.epa.gov). The rest of the chapter reviews the key features of the major federal mandates, but before we get to the regulations, let's review an important contribution of the common law, historically and today, that helps to protect environmental quality.

POLLUTION AND THE COMMON LAW

Before 1970, pollution was a problem handled by the states. State statutes dealt with some of the worst problems, such as automobile emissions in California, but citizens primarily relied on the common law, especially nuisance and trespass.

Nuisance, Trespass, and Pollution

As we saw when we studied property and torts, nuisances may be public or private. A public nuisance is an unreasonable interference with a right held in common by the public. In a pollution case, the right held in common is a community's right to a reasonably clean and safe environment. As a rule, a public nuisance case will be brought against the polluter in a community's name by a city or state attorney. A *private nuisance* is a substantial and unreasonable interference with the use and enjoyment of the land of another. It generally involves a polluter who is injuring one person or a group of people.

For example, in the 1907 case *Georgia* v. *Tennessee Copper Company*, 206 U.S. 230, the Supreme Court reviewed a complaint by the state of Georgia that a copper smelter in Tennessee was discharging gases that killed vegetation in Georgia and threatened human health. The Court held that an injunction against the smelter to shut it down could be issued if the smelter could not control the pollution enough to stop the damage.

A *trespass* is an unauthorized breach of the boundaries of another's land. The main difference between trespass and nuisance is that a trespass occurs whenever there is physical invasion of a plaintiff's property. A nuisance requires proof that interference with property is substantial and unreasonable. In practice, nuisance and trespass are difficult to distinguish in many pollution cases. For example, when toxic gases float onto the property of another person, there may be both a nuisance and a trespass. Those issues were raised in the *Stevenson* case.

Stevenson v. E.I. DuPont De Nemours and Co.
United States Court of Appeals, Fifth Circuit
327 F.3d 400 (2003)

CASE BACKGROUND   *The Stevensons bought twenty-eight acres of land in Victoria, Texas, in 1970. They built a house on the property and raised horses. Barium, cerium, chromium, copper, lead, manganese,* *and zinc were emitted by the DuPont plant located one and one-half miles from their home. The Stevensons sued DuPont for contamination of their person, property, and livestock on the theories of negligence, nuisance, and* *trespass. DuPont did not deny that some emissions were deposited on the Stevensons' property. The minerals were found in soil samples from the property. The Stevensons claimed that the emissions caused the paint on the house to peel and the window screens to erode.*

The jury found that DuPont was not negligent and that its actions did not constitute a nuisance. The jury denied recovery for physical pain and mental anguish and for injury to the animals. However, the jury found that a trespass had occurred and that the value of the property had been reduced by $168,000. DuPont appealed.

CASE DECISION   DeMoss, Circuit Judge.

* * *

DuPont argues that a trespass traditionally required a direct and physical invasion by tangible matter onto another person's property, while a cause of action for nuisance requires a showing of indirect invasion and intangible intrusion. . . .

DuPont's arguments . . . fail because this Court is required to apply the law of Texas as it currently stands. The Texas Supreme Court set for the following definition of trespass . . . "To constitute trespass there must be some physical entry upon the land by some 'thing.'" Research shows no Texas cases adopting a "direct and tangible" requirement to prove trespass. Because the only showing necessary is entry over land by some "thing," Texas law would permit recovery for airborne particulates. . . .

The evidence presented at trial supports a finding of trespass on the Plaintiffs' properties. Testimony showed that the emissions from DuPont's factory were most heavily concentrated over Plaintiffs' property and that their property showed evidence of heavy metal contamination that was most likely airborne in nature. Accordingly, the jury could reasonably infer that a trespass was committed, and the jury's findings is affirmed. . . .

Texas law is very clear that the proper measure of damages for permanent trespass is "the difference in the market value of the land immediately before and immediately after the trespass." Here, the jury was presented with testimony about only one value for the property. No evidence was presented to show the value of the land before the trespass began. As such, the jury could not reasonably have awarded the damages it did in this case. . . .

We hold that the damages award, therefore, should be vacated and the case remanded for a new trial on damages.

QUESTIONS FOR ANALYSIS
1. Why did the Stevensons not recover for injury to their health from breathing the metals?
2. How can they establish the value of the damage to their property?

Negligence, Strict Liability, and Pollution

Both *negligence* and *strict liability for abnormally dangerous activities* may apply in pollution cases. Tort liability may be due to negligence—failure to use reasonable care to prevent pollution from causing a foreseeable injury. Strict liability for abnormally dangerous activities applies to businesses that produce toxic chemicals or emit toxic pollutants. In imposing strict liability, the courts emphasize the risks created by the toxic pollutant and the location of the business relative to where people live. The doctrine is simple; it requires proof that the discharge of the pollutant was abnormally dangerous and that the pollutant was the cause of the plaintiff's injury. Courts have found crop dusting, the leakage of chemicals into groundwater, the storing of flammable liquids in quantity in a populated area, and the emitting of noxious gases by factories all to be abnormally dangerous.

Water Rights and Pollution

There is no common-law right to pollute water. Most states rely on *riparian water law*, although the western states have a variety of other water rights. Riparian water law holds that people who live along rivers and other bodies of water have the right to use the water in reasonable amounts but must allow the water to flow downstream in usable form. People have no right to pollute the water so that it is not usable downstream. Hence, along with nuisance and other common-law rights, enforcement of riparian water rights has long been a basis for suing polluters. The *Whalen* decision illustrates how the law works to protect water quality in the absence of any regulation. Note the court's classic statement about how rights are to be protected.

Whalen v. Union Bag & Paper Co.

Court of Appeals of New York
208 N.Y. 1, 101 N.E. 805 (1913)

CASE BACKGROUND   *Whalen owned a farm on a creek in New York. He used water from the creek to water plants and livestock. Union Bag built a pulp mill upstream, employing about 500 people. The mill polluted the creek so that Whalen could not use the water.*

Whalen sued Union Bag for damages and requested that the court issue an injunction to stop the pollution. The trial court [special term] awarded damages of $312 per year and issued an injunction to take effect in one year. Either the pollution stopped or the mill was to be shut down. The appellate court eliminated the injunction and reduced damages to $100 per year. Whalen appealed to the highest court in New York.

CASE DECISION   Werner, Justice.

* * *

The setting aside of the injunction was apparently induced by a consideration of the great loss likely to be inflicted on the defendant by the granting of the injunction as compared with the small injury done to the plaintiff's land by that portion of the pollution which was regarded as attributable to the defendant. Such a balancing of injuries cannot be justified by the circumstances of this case.

. . . Although the damage to the plaintiff may be slight as compared with the defendant's expense of abating the condition, that is not a good reason for refusing an injunction. Neither courts of equity nor law can be guided by such a rule, for if followed to its logical conclusion it would deprive the poor litigant of his little property by giving it to those already rich. It is always to be remembered in such cases that "denying the injunction puts the hardship on the party in whose favor the legal right exists, instead of on the wrongdoer." . . .

The fact that the appellant has expended a large sum of money in the construction of its plant, and that it conducts its business in a careful manner and without malice, can make no difference in its rights to the stream. Before locating the plant the owners were bound to know that every riparian proprietor is entitled to have the waters of the stream that washes his land come to it without obstruction, diversion, or corruption, subject only to the reasonable use of the water, by those similarly entitled, for such domestic purposes as are inseparable from and necessary for the free use of their land; they were bound also to know the character of their proposed business, and to take notice of the size, course, and capacity of the stream, and to determine for themselves at their own peril whether they should be able to conduct their business upon a stream of the size and character of Brandywine creek without injury to their neighbors; and the magnitude of their investment and their freedom from malice furnish no reason why they should escape the consequences of their own folly. . . .

The judgment of the Appellate Division, insofar as it denied the injunction, should be reversed and the judgment of the special term in that respect reinstated, with costs to the appellant.

QUESTIONS FOR ANALYSIS

1. If the common law was this tough, why would we need federal regulation of water pollution?

2. Should damages be the only resort in such cases? Assuming that the real loss to Whalen was $312 per year, why should he be able to get an injunction that would put hundreds of people out of work?

This decision contrasts sharply with a famous decision years later by the same court, *Boomer* v. *Atlantic Cement Company*, 257 N.E.2d 870 (1970). The air pollution, noise, and vibration from a cement plant created a nuisance for nearby homes. The court refused to issue an injunction, instead only awarding damages to the homeowners. The court reasoned that the value of the cement plant was higher than the cost suffered by the homeowners, so no injunction should be issued. Unlike in the *Whalen* case, where no price tag was put on rights and where costs and benefits were not compared, the *Boomer* court compared costs and benefits and made the economically "efficient" decision rather than simply order the nuisance to be stopped. This kind of decision played a large role in the push for federal regulation of pollution.

CLEAN AIR ACT

The *Clean Air Act of 1970*, which had major amendments in 1977 and 1990, established federal authority to control air pollution. In the words of the Supreme Court, Congress intended to "take a stick to the states" with this law. The Act requires the EPA to set pollution standards and, through forced cooperation of the states, to enforce the standards across the country.

National Ambient Air Quality Standards

The key regulatory program to achieve air quality is the *National Ambient Air Quality Standards (NAAQS)*. The EPA determines NAAQS for air pollutants that, in its judgment, "arise or contribute to air pollution which may reasonably be anticipated to endanger public health and welfare." The NAAQS set limits for how much of a pollutant is allowed to be found in the air outside (ambient air) as its quality is measured at hundreds of sites around the country.

The primary factors for a pollutant's NAAQS are the public health effects. Secondary factors are its considerations of public welfare effects (impact on plants, animals, soil, and constructed surfaces). The EPA has national standards for sulfur dioxide, particulates, ozone, carbon monoxide, nitrogen oxide, and lead. Exhibit 17.2 summarizes the principal characteristics, health effects, and sources of those major air pollutants.

State Implementation Plans

When EPA sets limits for the NAAQS, each state develops a *State Implementation Plan (SIP)*. The SIPs define the control efforts to be used in each state to achieve the national standards. In theory, if each emission source in a state met its pollution control requirements, the state's air quality would meet the national standards. The Act requires that regulated emission sources meet pollution control requirements as set by the SIP by a certain date.

The Clean Air Act, like some of the other major pollution statutes, places the primary enforcement burden on the states. The EPA is the oversight agency that sets the limits of what the states may do and sets the minimum regulations they must impose. Whenever the EPA changes air pollution standards, states must revise their SIPs, which are then reviewed by the EPA. If a state does not submit an adequate plan, the EPA writes one for it. All SIPs must include

Exhibit 17.2

Major Air Pollutants
Subject to NAAQS

Pollutant	Characteristics	Sources	Health Effects
Sulfur Dioxide (SO_2)	Colorless gas with pungent odor; oxidizes to form sulfur trioxide, which forms acid rain	Power and industrial plants that burn sulfur-containing fossil fuels; smelting of sulfur-bearing ores	Causes and aggravates respiratory ailments, inducing asthma, chronic bronchitis, emphysema
Particulates (PM)	Any particle dispersed in the atmosphere, such as dust, ash, and various chemicals	Wind erosion; stationary sources that burn solid fuels; agricultural operations	Chest discomfort; throat and eye irritation
Ozone (O_3)	A gas formed from hydrocarbon vapors and nitrogen oxides in sunlight; smog	Mostly from vehicle exhaust, refineries, and chemical plants	Aggravates respiratory ailments; causes eye irritation
Carbon Monoxide (CO)	Colorless, odorless gas	Motor vehicle exhaust and other carbon-containing materials; natural sources	Reduces oxygen-carrying capacity of blood; impairs heart function, visual perception, and alertness
Nitrogen Oxide (NO_x)	Brownish gas with pungent odor; component in photochemical oxidants	Motor vehicle exhaust; power plants	Aggravates respiratory ailments
Lead (Pb)	Heavy metallic chemical element; often occurs as lead oxide or dust	Nonferrous metal smelters; motor vehicle exhaust	Can cause mental and physical disabilities (lead poisoning)

- Enforceable emission limits
- Schedules and timetables for compliance
- Measures for monitoring air quality and emissions from pollution sources
- Adequate funding, personnel, and authority for implementing and enforcing the SIP

The Permit System

The Clean Air Act sets rules for the construction of new industrial plants or major renovation of existing facilities. The standards imposed on plant owners depend on the air quality of the area in which a plant is built. One set of rules applies if the plant is built in a "clean air area," and another set applies if a plant is built in a "dirty air area." In either case, the plant owner is required to obtain a preconstruction permit from the EPA or the state agency that enforces the Act.

Clean Air Areas

Areas with clean air—air of better quality than required by the NAAQS—are called *attainment areas* or *prevention of significant deterioration (PSD) areas*. PSD areas include national parks, wilderness areas, and other areas where the air quality is better than the national standards. Because of the sensitive nature of those areas, only a slight increase in pollution is allowed from new construction. That slight increase is called the *maximum allowable increase*. Any activity, including the construction or expansion of a plant, that will cause the maximum allowable increase to be exceeded is prohibited in a PSD area.

New construction is allowed in PSD areas if two basic requirements are met. First, the owner must agree to install the *best available control technology (BACT)*— as determined by the EPA—on the new plant to control its air pollution. Second, the owner must show that the pollution from its plant will not cause the maximum allowable increase in the area to be exceeded. The maximum allowable increase in the various forms of air pollution depends upon the classification of an area and the effect a particular pollutant would have on the air there. Some PSD classes, such as wilderness areas, are subject to much stricter controls than are less sensitive PSD areas.

Dirty Air Areas

Dirty air areas are called *nonattainment areas*, meaning that they have not met the NAAQS. Businesses wanting to build in nonattainment areas are required to meet even more restrictive rules than are imposed in PSD areas. The *emissions offset policy* imposes three requirements on owners of new or expanded plants:

1. A new plant's pollution must be controlled to the maximum degree possible. The plant must use the *lowest achievable emissions rate (LAER) technology*. LAER is a cleaner (and more expensive) technology than the BACT requirement in PSD areas. Generally, the EPA designates the LAER as the cleanest emission technology in use by any similar plant in the country.
2. New plant owners must certify that any other plants they have in the area meet SIP requirements. If a business cannot prove compliance, the EPA will not allow the new plant to be built.
3. A new plant can be built in a nonattainment area only if the air pollution from the new plant is *offset* by reductions in the same pollutants from other plants in the area. The offset from other plants must match the air pollution from the new plant more than one for one. That is, when the new plant is operating, the area must enjoy an overall air quality improvement.

To illustrate, suppose Polo Automotive wants to build a new plant in Detroit, a nonattainment area for sulfur dioxide. Polo must obtain a preconstruction permit from the EPA. The EPA will require Polo to show that it will apply the LAER technology and that any other plants it owns in the area are in compliance with Michigan's SIP. Polo must also obtain an emissions offset by reducing pollution in other plants by buying them and closing them or by paying for their pollution controls. That is, if Polo's new plant will add ten units of pollution to the air, Polo must reduce pollution elsewhere in the area by more than ten units. When the plant begins operation, air quality in the area should improve.

Whether a plant is an attainment area or a nonattainment area, a facility that will produce emissions must go through the permit process at the state level to show that it is using the correct kind of pollution-reducing technology. The EPA has the power to override the state environmental agency if it finds that the state is not complying with EPA policy. Hence, EPA can prevent industrial expansion by denying air pollution permits, as the *Alaska Department of Environmental Conservation* case explains.

Alaska Department of Environmental Conservation v. Environmental Protection Agency

Supreme Court of the United States
124 S.Ct. 983 (2004)

CASE BACKGROUND *Cominco operates a zinc mine in northwest Alaska. It is defined, under the Clean Air Act, as a major emitting facility due to its diesel electric generators. It has a Prevention of Significant Deterioration (PSD) permit to operate using best available control technology (BACT) since it is in an attainment area. After years of operation, it applied to add another generator so it could increase zinc output. It offered to use an emission control technology on all existing generators and the new generator, which would cut nitrogen oxide pollutants by 30 percent.*

The Alaska Department of Environmental Conservation (ADEC) approved the use of that technology as BACT, even though another technology, called selective catalytic reduction (SCR), would cut emissions by 90 percent. That technology was much more expensive and, ADEC ruled, was economically not possible for Cominco to use. ADEC granted a PSD permit to Cominco using the 30 percent reduction technology. EPA objected, contending that the SCR technology was BACT and should be required. EPA prohibited ADEC from issuing a PSD permit and prohibited Cominco from adding another generator. ADEC and Cominco appealed, but the appeals court upheld the EPA decision. ADEC and Cominco appealed to the Supreme Court.

CASE DECISION Ginsburg, Justice.

* * *

Centrally at issue in this case is the question whether EPA's oversight role, described by Congress in CAA . . . extends to ensuring that a state permitting authority's BACT determination is reasonable in light of the statutory guidelines. . . . Congress armed EPA with authority to issue orders stopping construction when "a State is not acting in compliance with any [CAA] requirement or prohibition . . . relating to the construction of new sources or the modification of existing sources," or when "construction or modification of a major emitting facility . . . does not conform to the requirements of [the PSD program]."

The federal Act enumerates several "preconstruction requirements" for the PSD program. Absent these, "no major emitting facility . . . may be constructed." One express preconstruction requirement is inclusion of a BACT determination in a facility's PSD permit. . . .

BACT's statutory definition requires selection of an emission control technology that results in the "maximum" reduction of a pollutant "achievable for a facility" in view of "energy, environmental, and economic impacts, and other costs. . . .

We emphasize that today's disposition does not impede ADEC from revisiting the BACT determination in question. In letters and orders throughout the permitting process, EPA repeatedly commented that it was open to ADEC to prepare "an appropriate record" supporting its selection of [the 30 percent reducing technology] as BACT.

In sum, we conclude that EPA has supervisory authority over the reasonableness of state permitting authorities' BACT determinations and may issue a stop construction order [under the CAA] if a BACT selection is not reasonable. We further conclude that, in exercising that authority, the Agency did not act arbitrarily or capriciously in finding that ADEC's BACT decision in this instance lacked evidentiary support. EPA's orders, therefore, were neither arbitrary nor capricious. The judgment of the Court of Appeals is accordingly

Affirmed.

QUESTIONS FOR ANALYSIS

1. Why does Congress delegate to EPA the final authority on appropriate pollution control technology, rather than to the states?

2. Why did the Court need to state that the EPA determination on this matter was neither arbitrary nor capricious?

Mobile Sources of Pollution

Since the Clean Air Act was passed, some major air pollutants, such as lead, have nearly disappeared from the atmosphere. Large reductions have occurred in particulates and carbon monoxide. But ozone (at lower levels of the atmosphere) has changed little. It is mostly produced by the imperfect burning of petroleum products. Since motor vehicles are the primary source, the law has tightened controls on cars and trucks. While vehicles produce fewer hydrocarbons that help form ozone than they did when the Clean Air Act was passed, many more miles are driven by more vehicles today, keeping ozone emissions up.

The level of ozone allowed is determined by the NAAQS, but the law also imposes direct controls on certain emission sources. Tailpipe exhaust standards for cars, trucks, and buses have become tougher. Where ozone pollution is especially bad, as in most major cities, SIPs impose tougher vehicle emission inspections, vapor recovery systems at gas stations, reformulated gasoline, and alternative fuel sources.

The law allows states to impose emissions standards that go beyond the federal requirements. California has set tougher auto emissions standards and requirements for cleaner-burning gasoline and has forced use of alternative-fuel and electric-powered cars. The regulations are supposed to cut auto pollution 50 percent more than do the federal standards. New York, New Jersey, Pennsylvania, Massachusetts, Virginia, Maryland, Delaware, New Hampshire, Maine, Rhode Island, and Vermont have adopted the California standards, which means that some California standards will become the national standard.

Toxic Pollutants

As amended in 1990, the Clean Air Act lists 191 substances declared to be hazardous air pollutants. The EPA must set *maximum emission rates (MERs)* for each pollutant. The general goal is a 90 percent reduction in emissions for the pollutants that had been uncontrolled and a 75 percent reduction in cancer caused by air pollution. If the EPA determines that a pollutant is a threat to public health or the environment, tighter control standards are to be imposed without regard to such economic factors as cost or technological feasibility. Tough standards for many pollutants, such as emissions from dry-cleaning establishments and commercial bakeries, are being issued by the EPA.

Acid Rain

The main sources of *acid rain* are sulfur dioxide and nitrous oxides, which mostly come from burning coal or oil to produce electricity. These chemicals become sulfuric and nitric acid, returning to earth in rain or other precipitation. While the extent of the problem caused by acid rain is not established, it is clear that much of it occurs in the Northeast, as winds carry acids from electricity plants, mostly in the Midwest and the Appalachian region, especially from those burning soft coal. The 1990 amendments to the Clean Air Act require that about half of the sulfur dioxide and nitrous oxide emissions that were produced in 1990 be eliminated. As with other environmental laws, stated goals are often different from actual results.

INTERNATIONAL *Perspective*

Industrialization Brings Environmental Problems to China

The pollution that afflicts the poorest people—breathing smoke-filled air from cooking fires in their living huts and drinking contaminated water—is reduced when industrialization occurs and economic conditions improve. But then the pollutants from rising industrial production create problems.

As the economy of China has grown rapidly in the past two decades, environmental damage has increased rapidly. The government of China understands the magnitude of the problem and has laws and agencies to deal with pollution. On the books, the structure looks much like the EPA. In practice, there is little enforcement.

At least 70 percent of the water in major rivers is rated as "severely polluted." The China National Environmental Monitoring Center reports that no major city has good air quality. Waters around coastal cities are badly polluted. The State Oceanographic Administration Marine Environment Protection Department warns that marine ecological systems near Shanghai and other major cities are "dangerously close to collapse."

Rules that have weak enforcement mean little. When a fertilizer plant dumped large quantities of ammonia and nitrate into a river, killing 450,000 pounds of fish and poisoning drinking water for downstream cities, nothing much happened. An official from the State Environmental Protection Administration said that there is no authority to shut down the worst offenders: "We can only fine them, and such a small amount at that. They basically decide it's a cost that doesn't matter."

Sources: *China Daily News* and *The Wall Street Journal*

Enforcement

The EPA has primary authority to enforce the Clean Air Act and other environmental statutes, but state environmental agencies also are involved because they carry out a large part of the regulatory mission. Citizens, including environmental groups, have rights to bring *citizen suits* to enforce environmental statutes when government agencies fail to do so. Like most regulations, the environmental statutes list the penalties that may be imposed on violators.

In recent years, more environmental offenses have been prosecuted as criminal matters, which means more than 100 criminal indictments per year. Business facilities may be banned from receiving any federal contracts because of environmental crime convictions. EPA and state environmental agencies collect hundreds of millions of dollars per year in fines.

Carrot-and-Stick Approach

Enforcement uses a carrot-and-stick approach. The U.S. Sentencing Guidelines punishment for environmental crimes holds that the penalties imposed on a company and its executives should take into account several factors. Punishment is reduced for companies that

- Cooperate with the government in investigations
- Voluntarily report illegal actions
- Educate their workforce about environmental standards
- Assist those who suffer from environmental wrongdoing
- Have a strong internal environmental compliance program

CLEAN WATER ACT

Federal statutory control over water pollution goes back to the Rivers and Harbors Act of 1886 and 1899. But like the Federal Water Pollution Control Act of 1948, there was little effective federal control over water pollution. Primary responsibility was left with the states. By 1970, marine life in Lake Erie was almost gone, and many rivers were unfit for drinking water or recreation.

The Clean Water Act (CWA) was passed in 1972 and was substantially amended in 1977 and 1986. The objective of the Clean Water Act is to "restore and maintain the chemical, physical, and biological integrity of the Nation's waters." The Act has five main elements:

1. National *effluent* (pollution) standards set by the EPA for each industry
2. Water quality standards set by the states under EPA approval
3. A *discharge permit* program that uses water quality standards to enforce pollution limits
4. Special provisions for toxic chemicals and oil spills
5. Construction grants and loans from the federal government for *publicly owned treatment works (POTWs)*, such as sewage treatment plants

The CWA makes it unlawful for any person—an individual, business, or governmental body—to dump pollutants into navigable waters without a *permit.* Although the Act does not define the phrase "navigable waters," it is broadly interpreted for regulatory purposes. Except for isolated small bodies of water, all waters are considered to be under EPA jurisdiction, and National Pollution Discharge Elimination System (NPDES) permits are required not only for dumping waste water into water, but even for moving water from one place to another. However, as the Supreme Court discusses in the *South Florida Water Management District* case, there may be a move in the direction of treating water systems on the basis of their hydrology or ecological system, rather than as a system of independent bodies of water that are unrelated.

South Florida Water Management District v. Miccosukee Tribe of Indians

Supreme Court of the United States
124 S.Ct. 1537 (2004)

CASE BACKGROUND   *The South Florida Water Management District (District) manages the Everglades. It balances the need for water in urban areas, the intrusion of salt water, and the need to restore the environment of the Everglades. To do this, it uses canals and pumps waters from one area to another. One pump station, S-9, moves water from a canal that carries urban and agricultural waters into an undeveloped wetland. Without such pumping, the water would flow back into and flood populated areas.*

The Miccosukee Tribe sued the District, claiming that S-9 must have an NPDES permit because some of the water it pumps contains a lot of phosphorus from agricultural operations. The District responded that S-9's operations did not discharge pollutants under the Clean Water Act, so that a permit was not required. The district court held for the Tribe, requiring the District to obtain an NPDES permit for the pumping operations. The District appealed.*

CASE DECISION   O'Connor, Justice.

* * *

continues

Congress enacted the Clean Water Act (Act) in 1972. Its stated objective was "to restore and maintain the chemical, physical, and biological integrity of the Nation's waters." To serve those ends, the Act prohibits "the discharge of any pollutant by any person" unless done in compliance with some provision of the Act. The provision relevant to this case establishes the National Pollutant Discharge Elimination System, or "NPDES." Generally speaking, the NPDES requires discharges to obtain permits that place limits on the type and quantity of pollutants that can be released into the Nation's waters. The Act defines the phrase "discharge of a pollutant" to mean "any addition of any pollutant to navigable waters from any point source." A "point source," in turn, is defined as "any discernible, confined, and discrete conveyance," such as a pipe, ditch, channel, or tunnel, "from which pollutants are or may be discharged." . . .

The District argued that the NPDES program applies to a point source "only when a pollutant originates from the point source," and not when pollutants originating elsewhere merely pass through the point source. . . . Although the Government rejects the District's legal position, it and the Tribe agree with the factual proposition that S-9 does not itself add any pollutants to the water it [pumps into other waters]. . . .

A point source is, by definition, a "discernible, confined, and discrete *conveyance*." That definition makes plain that a point source need not be the original source of the pollutant; it need only convey the pollutant to "navigable waters," which are, in turn, defined as "the waters of the United States." Tellingly, the examples of "point sources" listed by the Act include pipes, ditches, tunnels, and conduits, objects that do not themselves generate pollutants but merely transport them. . . . That definition includes within its reach point sources that do not themselves generate pollutants. . . .

Because the Act requires NPDES permits only when there is an addition of a pollutant "to navigable waters," the Government's approach would lead to the conclusion that such permits are *not* required when water from one navigable water body is discharged, unaltered, into another navigable water body. That would be true even if one water body were polluted and the other pristine, and the two would not otherwise mix. Under this "unitary waters" approach, the S-9 pump station would not need an NPDES permit.

The "unitary waters" argument focuses on the Act's definition of a pollutant discharge as "any addition of any pollutant to navigable waters from any point source." The Government contends that the absence of the word "any" prior to the phrase "navigable waters" signals Congress' understanding that NPDES permits would not be required for pollution caused by the engineered transfer of one "navigable water" into another. . . .

In the courts below, as here, the District contended that the [water areas and canals] are not distinct water bodies at all, but instead are two hydrologically indistinguishable parts of a single water body. The Government agrees with the District on this point, claiming that [the waters] "can appropriately be viewed [under the CWA] as parts of a single body of water." . . .

Because Everglades soil is extremely porous, water flows easily between ground and surface waters, so much so that "ground and surface waters are essentially the same thing." . . .

After reviewing the full record, it is possible that the District Court will conclude that [the canals and water bodies] are not meaningfully distinct water bodies. If it does so, then the S-9 pump station will not need an NPDES permit. In addition, the Government's broader "unitary waters" argument is open to the District on remand. . . .

Vacated and remanded.

QUESTIONS FOR ANALYSIS

1. If the Everglades were considered to be a unitary body of water, rather than a system of independent canals, lakes, and such, how might that interpretation change the application of the Clean Water Act?

2. What would you suspect "navigable" body of water means?

Cleaning the nation's waters has been much more expensive and has taken longer than was anticipated when the Clean Water Act was passed in 1972. At that time, Congress said that the discharge of pollutants into any waters would be eliminated by 1985. That was an impossible goal. As it stands, discharges have probably dropped to about half of what they were when the Act was passed. But since pollutants that are easiest to eliminate have been attacked first, the cost of removing more pollutants will be much higher.

Point Source Pollution

The water pollution that is easiest to identify comes out of a pipe. We can see it, measure it, and, given technical knowledge, treat the discharge. Control of such *point source pollution* has been the primary focus of federal law since 1972. Sewage from homes and from some industrial sources (point sources) is often treated at publicly owned treatment works (POTWs). Billions are spent every year to improve existing POTWs (sewage treatment plants) and to put new ones in place in small towns that have minimal systems. Since most effluents treated at POTWs are not toxic, the *sludge*—the glop that is removed during sewage treatment—is often used for fertilizer. The treated water is pumped back into rivers or lakes. Exhibit 17.3 illustrates primary water effluent sources.

Under the Clean Water Act, states must designate all surface water as to intended use. If the use is drinking water, treated water dumped into a bay, lake, or river must be quite pure; if the body of water is designated for recreation, the treated water must be clean enough not to contaminate swimmers or fish.

Industrial Permits

Industrial wastewater discharges from production processes are subject to a permit process. As we have seen already, the EPA and state environmental agencies, under the National Pollutant Discharge Elimination System (NPDES), require industrial polluters to list the amount and type of their discharges. The polluters are issued permits to release various pollutants in certain quantities.

Exhibit 17.3

Primary Sources of Water Effluents

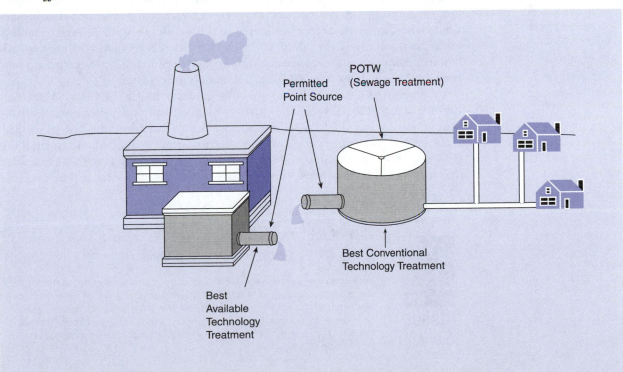

Control Technology   Each firm in an industry must meet the effluent limits set by the EPA for each chemical dumped into a wastewater. The list of controlled substances is expanding, and the degree to which the substances must be controlled grows gradually tighter. Conventional pollutants, like human waste, are controlled by the *best conventional technology (BCT)*. Congress ordered the EPA to consider cost-effectiveness when setting such standards.

Cost considerations are not as important for toxic or unconventional pollutants, which are subject to tighter control, called *best available technology (BAT)*—defined by the EPA as the "very best control and treatment measures that have been or are capable of being achieved." Hence, as better technology is invented to control pollutants, polluters must use it to reduce their pollution. Regardless of the kind of pollutants, if a polluter is located on a particularly sensitive waterway, even more stringent controls may be ordered.

When a new plant is built or a new source of pollution is created by a producer, it is subject to even tighter controls—called *new source performance standards (NSPS)*. The law says that the standard is "the greatest degree of effluent reduction . . . achievable through application of the best available demonstrated control technology, processes, operating methods, and other alternatives, including, where practicable, standards permitting no discharge of pollutants." Using BAT controls for the pollution produced is not enough; the entire production process must use the best technology that exists to minimize pollution output.

Enforcement

Since point source water pollution control is based on a permit system, it is the key to enforcement. Under the NPDES, the states have primary responsibility for enforcing the permit system, subject to EPA monitoring and approval.

Operating without a permit or discharging more pollution than is allowed under a permit violates the law. Firms that have pollution permits must monitor their own performance and file *discharge monitoring reports (DMRs)*, available for public inspection. Hence, firms must report violations of the amount they are allowed to pollute under their permits. Lying about violations is more serious than admitting to violations. Serious violations can lead to criminal prosecution. Every year, prison sentences are handed down for violators who dump toxic wastes.

Citizen suits against polluters are quite common under the Clean Water Act, running at least 200 per year. The citizen, which is usually an environmental organization, must notify the EPA and the alleged permit violator of the "intent to sue." If the EPA takes charge of the situation, the citizen suit is blocked. However, if the EPA does not act diligently and the violations continue, the private suit to force enforcement of the law may proceed. If the plaintiff wins a citizen suit, the loser pays for attorneys' fees.

ISSUE
Spotter

Does Obeying EPA Regulations Make You Safe from Environmental Litigation?

Your company's production facility produces certain water pollutants that are treated according to EPA standards. You have all the EPA permits that are required. Does this mean the treated water you pump into the river near the plant has no legal consequence? Are there legal problems that you could face even if EPA has no complaints about your operations? How can you be sure?

Nonpoint Source Pollution

About half of all waterborne pollution is from nonpoint sources—it is runoff from construction sites, logging and mining operations, streets, and agriculture. Pollutants are washed by rain into streams and lakes and seep into groundwater. Much *nonpoint source pollution* has only recently come under federal control efforts. The complexity of the problem requires multiple solutions.

Because runoff from streets usually occurs during rainstorms, when sewage treatment plants do not have the capacity to treat all runoff water, holding tanks may have to be built to allow the water to be treated later. Since a lot of pollution is due to air pollution that settles on the ground or is washed from the atmosphere by rain, tighter air pollution rules result in less nonpoint source water pollution.

The consequences of groundwater pollution that comes from agricultural fertilizers and sprays are considered by various agencies under statutes in addition to the Clean Water Act. These include the Safe Drinking Water Act; the Federal Insecticide, Fungicide, and Rodenticide Act; the Toxic Substances Control Act; and other laws that deal one way or another with pollution that shows up in water from nonpoint sources. Although regulations to reduce runoff from construction sites, mining and logging operations, and agriculture have been gradually tightened, runoff pollution remains a problem that is difficult to resolve technologically or politically.

Wetlands

In years past, *wetlands* were thought of as nuisances to be drained and filled. Wetlands destruction was subsidized by agencies such as the Army Corps of Engineers. Now that the environmental value of wetlands is better known, there have been moves to protect them. Developers and others are now forced to protect wetlands instead of being encouraged to destroy them. The EPA defines wetlands as

> Those areas that are inundated or saturated by surface or groundwater at a frequency and duration sufficient to support, and that under normal circumstances do support, a prevalence of vegetation typically adapted for life in saturated soil conditions. Wetlands generally include swamps, marshes, bogs, and similar areas.

This definition includes mangrove swamps of coastal saltwater shrubs in the South; prairie potholes in the Dakotas and Minnesota, where shallow depressions that hold water during part of the year are visited by migrating birds; and playa lakes in the Southwest that are rarely flooded basins. Wetlands can be small holes or large areas and may contain one plant or dozens of important species. What is covered by the law is not yet fixed, as we saw in the *Army Corps* case.

Permit System

Under the CWA, anyone wanting to change a wetland must receive a §404 permit from the Army Corps of Engineers. The EPA may block an Army Corps permit to prevent environmental damage. About 10,000 permits are issued each year to allow dredging or filling of wetlands. Often, a permit to dredge wetlands will include a requirement that other land will be restored to wetland status in exchange. Another 75,000 permits are issued each year for activities that "cause only minimal adverse environmental effects" to wetlands. Hence, businesses involved in construction or other activities that disturb earth must make sure that wetlands requirements have been met.

Wetlands Takings

The wetlands permit system can result in prohibitions on building or modifying land that was purchased with the expectation that certain uses were allowed. Some landowners have discovered their land to be worthless because they cannot get a permit for the land to be modified. Several cases, such as *Loveladies Harbor* v. *U.S.*, 28 F.3d 1171 (1994), have resulted in decisions that the government must pay for land it forces out of circulation for wetlands protection.

In *Loveladies*, a New Jersey coastal development that had been under construction for thirty years was halted when the Army Corps prohibited any further construction. Fifty acres of wetlands fell from $2.66 million in value to nearly nothing. The Federal Circuit Court of Appeals ordered the government to pay the developer for the land as a taking for public benefit. If such compensation requirements increase, controls on wetlands may be slowed, since Congress allocates little money for the purchase of such lands.

LAND POLLUTION

Millions of tons of hazardous waste are disposed of each year. Some of that waste is stored in drums and deposited in clay-lined dumps, injected deep underground between layers of rock, or illegally abandoned in vacant lots, lagoons, and landfills. Some storage methods fail as containers corrode and rain washes the wastes from storage sites. Hazardous waste can make its way into lakes, streams, and groundwater.

To reduce the amount of toxic substances that are dumped into the environment and to limit exposure to chemicals that are toxic to people or animals, controls are imposed on the production, distribution, use, and disposal of toxic chemicals. Careless disposal of chemicals in the past means that billions are now being spent to clean up waste sites. As Exhibit 17.4 indicates, managers must be aware of the liability that can arise from use of chemicals today and from ownership of property that may contain toxic wastes.

Exhibit 17.4

Regulation of Hazardous Substance

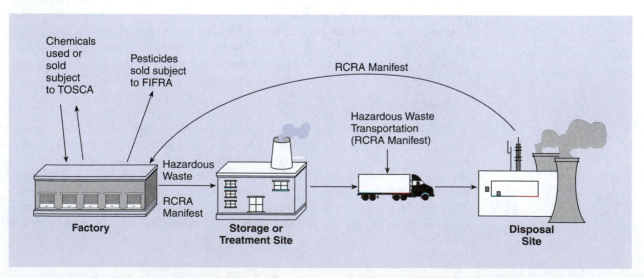

Toxic Substances Control Act

More than 70,000 chemicals are in commercial use. Under the *Toxic Substances Control Act (TOSCA)* passed in 1976, the EPA controls and keeps track of chemicals. Because chemicals can cause health hazards, accurate information about their possible effects is vital.

When a producer wants to sell a new chemical, it must notify the EPA, which studies the substance and its proposed uses to determine environmental hazards. Producers may be required to run tests for toxicity and other effects so that the EPA can determine whether any restrictions should be placed on the chemical. Restrictions may be nothing more than labeling requirements; some chemicals are allowed in restricted uses, and some are banned.

Biotechnology—the manipulation of biological processes to produce chemicals or living organisms for commercial use—is subject to TOSCA. Since the results may be eligible for patents, this is a field with valuable products worth tens of billions of dollars. Genetic engineering produces such things as enzymes that can purify water and consume the oil in oil spills. The EPA monitors efforts to use natural organisms in new ways and to use genetically altered microorganisms.

Pesticides

Pesticides are used to prevent, kill, or disable pests, including undesirable plants, insects, rodents, fungi, and molds. Most pesticides are toxic, and some are extremely toxic to people and the environment. Congress originally passed the *Federal Insecticide, Fungicide, and Rodenticide Act (FIFRA)* in 1947 and has amended it several times since.

The EPA has registered more than 20,000 products under FIFRA. Registration means that before a pesticide is sold, the EPA has examined scientific data about the product's effects and the label on the product is accurate as to proper use and precautions. Registration is approved for five years at a time for pesticides that meet these conditions:

1. The product does what the producers claim it will do.
2. The registration materials are accurate, and the label is accurate as to proper product use.
3. The product, when used properly, will not have "unreasonable adverse effects on the environment."

FIFRA requires that the economic and environmental costs and benefits of each product be considered. The EPA tries to determine what risk might be posed by a pesticide, such as groundwater contamination or skin irritation, so that it can limit how the product is used and who may use it. Since some products pose a danger to certain species, the EPA may restrict use to locations that minimize exposure for those who could be harmed. Working with the Food and Drug Administration, the EPA sets usage requirements to take into account the residues that remain in food products to ensure that consumers are not exposed to unsafe levels of pesticides.

Resource Conservation and Recovery Act

TOSCA and FIFRA are primarily concerned with controlling toxic substances before they get to the market. How toxic substances are handled once they are in the market or when they are being disposed of is the concern of the *Resource Conservation and Recovery Act (RCRA)* passed in 1976 and amended in 1984.

"Out of sight, out of mind" was standard procedure for the disposal of many hazardous wastes before we came to know about the environmental consequences of improper disposal. RCRA requires that the 500,000 generators of about 200 million tons of hazardous waste each year comply with an EPA regulatory program—over the transportation, storage, treatment, and disposal of hazardous waste—that reduces dangers to health and the environment.

Hazardous Waste

RCRA requires the EPA to identify and maintain a list of hazardous wastes. The Act defines *hazardous waste* as follows:

> . . . [a] solid waste . . . which because of its quantity, concentration, or physical, chemical, or infectious characteristics may—
> (a) cause, or significantly contribute to, an increase in mortality or an increase in serious irreversible, or incapacitating reversible, illness; or,
> (b) pose a substantial present or potential hazard to human health or the environment when improperly treated, stored, transported, or disposed of, or otherwise managed.

The characteristics of hazardous waste are ignitability (such as gasoline); corrosivity (such as acids); reactivity (unstable chemicals); and toxicity (ingredients that threaten groundwater). Wastes like that, such as batteries and unused pesticides, may be stored or disposed of only at sites whose owners or operators have obtained a permit from the EPA. To get the permit, the owners of the *treatment, storage, and disposal (TSD) sites* agree to meet all regulations regarding the handling of hazardous wastes.

Regulation of TSD Sites

RCRA requires the EPA to regulate TSD sites. Certain hazardous wastes must be treated prior to disposal. A treatment facility is where there is a change in the physical, chemical, or biological character of any hazardous waste to make it less hazardous, to recover energy or materials from it, or to otherwise process it. A storage facility is where waste is held, such as in storage tanks, until it can be disposed of or treated. A disposal facility is where hazardous wastes are placed into water or land, such as sealed landfills.

The Manifest System

RCRA forces compliance by generators, transporters, and TSD-site owners by a *manifest system*. The producer of a hazardous waste must complete a *manifest*—a form that states the nature of the hazardous waste and identifies its origin, shipping route, and final destination. The waste must be packaged in appropriate and properly labeled containers.

Generators must give transporters of hazardous waste a copy of the manifest. Transporters, such as trucking companies, must sign the manifest and, upon delivery, provide a copy to the owner of the TSD site, who must return a copy of the manifest to the generator, thereby closing the circle. If a generator is not informed of the proper deposit of the waste, it notifies the EPA. This reporting system provides regulators with the ability to track hazardous waste through its generation, transportation, and disposal phases.

JURIS *prudence?*

Hot Cargo!

American Shippers sent a truck to pick up a load from a Denver exporter to haul to Los Angeles for shipment to Taiwan. The goods were loaded on the truck but not shipped because the exporter went bankrupt.

The trucking company wanted to get rid of its load, which contained radioactive smoke-detector circuit boards. It called the EPA, which said the problem was the responsibility of the Colorado Health Department. The Health Department wanted $40,000 to dispose of the load. So the trucking com-

pany let the goods sit in a truck until going bankrupt seven years later.

Two years after the bankruptcy, the new owner of the trucking company looked for help. The Department of Energy took two years to respond to a request for help from the governor of Colorado and said it could do nothing. The Nuclear Regulatory Commission said it could not help—but suggested that the EPA be contacted.

Source: *Denver Post*

Superfund

RCRA helps prevent improper disposal of hazardous wastes today, but dumping practices in the past have left many sites contaminated with toxic materials. Cleaning these dump sites is costing tens of billions of dollars and taking decades to accomplish. The EPA evaluated thousands of waste sites and identified 1,327 that needed action; these sites were placed on the *National Priority List (NPL)*. Sites on the NPL are scattered throughout the country. Many sites are still in process. Most cleanups involve digging up and removing contaminated soil for treatment, such as burning, and restoration of the land to something like its natural state. This takes an average of ten years.

Congress enacted the Comprehensive *Environmental Response, Compensation, and Liability Act (CERCLA)* in 1980. Called the *Superfund*, the Act provides the authority to clean up abandoned hazardous sites. Congress amended the Superfund program in 1986 with the *Superfund Amendments and Reauthorization Act (SARA)*, which imposes a tax on the petroleum and chemical industries. The $1 billion to $2 billion per year in revenues go to Superfund cleanups. However, private parties are incurring substantial costs. The Congressional Budget Office estimated that cleanup costs could total $500 billion over eighty years, not counting the cost of cleaning up contaminated federal lands, which could be even higher. Because of the nearly endless possible costs of the program, Congress has effectively put a limit on the number of NPL sites.

Responsible Parties

An abandoned dump site might contain hazardous wastes contributed by many waste generators. In addition, the dump site may have been operated by different parties over the years. Under the law, there may be multiple *potentially responsible parties (PRPs)*. CERCLA defines PRPs who can be held liable for both cleanup costs and damages to natural resources:

1. Current owners of a hazardous waste site
2. Prior owners of a site at the time of hazardous waste disposal

3. Any hazardous waste generator who arranged for disposal at the site
4. Any transporter of hazardous waste who selected the site for disposal

The parties may be held *strictly and jointly and severally liable* for these costs; that is, each party can be liable for the entire cleanup cost regardless of the size of its contribution to the hazardous waste at the site. As a result, each party has a strong incentive to identify other PRPs, which often results in lengthy, expensive litigation.

Practical Problems

The EPA may begin a cleanup if there is a threat to public health or the environment if cleanup is delayed. Later, the government can try to recover expenses by suing PRPs, if they can be located. More commonly, the EPA orders private parties to pay to clean up the site under EPA supervision. This generates a lot of expensive litigation. Studies have shown that more Superfund money goes to litigation and engineering studies than to actual cleanup.

So, an important issue when buying property is if it contains toxic wastes that may have been buried years ago or, when buying a business, whether the business was involved in handling toxic materials. If so, the new owner may be held responsible for cleanup costs. Some new owners have been handed cleanup bills for more than the property is worth, even though the new owners did not generate the waste. If they cannot find other PRPs capable of paying the bill, the new owners are stuck. As a result, property buyers often have an *environmental audit* performed for property they intend to purchase.

Because of the nearly unlimited liability for unknown cleanup costs, useful property sits abandoned. The Cleveland *Plain Dealer* built a new plant for the newspaper on farmland out of the city. The abandoned urban site it had originally chosen was found to have chemicals in the soil from years before. Such old sites are referred to as *brownfields*. Since the newspaper could not risk Superfund liability, it moved out of town rather than help restore downtown Cleveland. Bringing brownfields back into use may be helped by the Brownfields Revitalization Act of 2002. It limits the liability to purchasers of contaminated sites for previous improper dumping of toxic wastes on the land.

JURIS *prudence?*

Honor Your Local Superfund Site

The Department of Interior declared the Fresno, California, municipal landfill to be a historical landmark listed on the National Register because it pioneered certain methods of disposal. Upon being informed that the landfill was on the National Priority List of Superfund sites, the Department decided to rescind the honor.

Source: *New York Times*

SPECIES PROTECTION

Most environmental laws are written with primary concern for the effect of pollutants on human health. But some laws address environmental protection for wildlife or, more broadly, for all species. The most important of these laws is the *Endangered*

Exhibit 17.5	Endangered and Threatened Species in the United States by Category (2004)			
Types of Endangered and Threatened Species	Mammals	78	Flowering Plants	713
	Birds	91	Conifers and Cycads	3
	Reptiles	36	Ferns and Allies	26
	Amphibians	21	Lichens	2
	Fishes	114	Plant Total:	746
	Clams	70		
	Snails	32		
	Insects	44		
	Spiders	12		
	Crustaceans	21		
	Animal Total:	519		

Source: Fish and Wildlife Service

Species Act (ESA), enacted in 1973 and amended several times. In some respects, the ESA is the toughest environmental statute of all.

The Act recognizes the value of species habitat. It authorizes designation of critical habitat—areas needed to preserve endangered species—and calls for recovery plans for listed species. The Department of the Interior has estimated that a recovery program for the 1,265 recognized threatened and endangered species in the United States (see http://endangered.fws.gov) would cost billions of dollars. Funding from Congress has often been a few hundred million dollars per year.

Habitat Protection

The ESA authorizes the Secretary of the Interior to declare species of animal or plant life "endangered" and to establish the "critical habitat" of such species. An *endangered species* is defined as "any species which is in danger of extinction throughout all or a significant portion of its range." When a species is *listed* as endangered or threatened by the Interior Department, the Act imposes obligations on private and public parties. Under the ESA, no person may "take, import, or conduct commercial activity with respect to any endangered species." In most disputes involving an endangered species, parties generally agree that the species deserves protection; the conflict centers on how protection is provided.

Since Congress does not allocate enough money to accomplish the goals of the ESA, its primary use is to block or alter activity when an endangered species is present. This first came to attention in the 1978 Supreme Court decision *Tennessee Valley Authority v. Hill*, 437 U.S. 153. The Court prohibited completion of the Tellico Dam on the Little Tennessee River. Even though the federal government had spent $100 million on the dam, the Court ordered work on the dam stopped because it would destroy the habitat of a tiny fish, the snail darter. The Act says that no project may "result in the destruction or modification of habitat of such [endangered] species."

The northern spotted owl, which is on the threatened species list, brought more attention to the ESA. In 1991, a federal court ordered logging stopped on most federal lands in Washington, Oregon, and northern California until the Forest Service could devise a plan to protect the forest habitat of the northern spotted owl. The cost of the resulting restrictions on logging has been estimated to be at least $20 billion. There were conflicting cases regarding the extent of the application of the ESA to the habitat of species. The Supreme Court addressed that issue in the *Sweet Home* decision.

Babbitt v. Sweet Home Chapter of Communities for a Great Oregon
United States Supreme Court
515 U.S. 2407, 115 S.Ct. 2407 (1995)

CASE BACKGROUND   *Private landowners and loggers sued the Secretary of the Interior and the Fish and Wildlife Service (FWS). They challenged the Secretary's definition of the word "harm" in regulations issued to enforce the protection of species:*

> *Harm . . . means an act which actually kills or injures wildlife. Such act may include significant habitat modification or degradation where it actually kills or injures the wildlife by significantly impairing essential behavioral patterns, including breeding, feeding, or sheltering.*

Under this regulation, the FWS controls contact with the habitat of the northern spotted owl (a threatened species) in the Pacific Northwest and of the red-cockaded woodpecker (an endangered species) in the Southeast. The plaintiffs contended that the "harm" regulation went beyond what Congress intended in the ESA and injured them economically by limiting their right to log timber. The court of appeals agreed, holding that the statute did not intend to give such broad meaning to the word "harm." The Secretary and FWS appealed.

CASE DECISION   Stevens, Justice.

* * *

We assume respondents have no desire to harm either the red-cockaded woodpecker or the spotted owl; they merely wish to continue logging activities that would be entirely proper if not prohibited by the ESA. On the other hand, we must assume arguendo that those activities will have the effect, even though unintended, of detrimentally changing the natural habitat of both listed species or that, as a consequence, members of those species will be killed or injured. . . . The Secretary . . . submits that the . . . prohibition on takings, which Congress defined to include "harm," places on respondents a duty to avoid harm that habitat alter-

ation will cause the birds unless respondents first obtain a permit. . . .

The fact that Congress in 1982 authorized the Secretary to issue permits for takings that [the ESA] would otherwise prohibit, "if such taking is incidental to, and not the purpose of, the carrying out of an otherwise lawful activity," strongly suggests that Congress understood [the ESA] to prohibit indirect as well as deliberate takings. The permit process requires the applicant to prepare a "conservation plan" that specifies how he intends to "minimize and mitigate" the "impact" of his activity on endangered and threatened species, making clear that Congress had in mind foreseeable rather than merely accidental effects on listed species. . . .

When it enacted the ESA, Congress delegated broad administrative and interpretive power to the Secretary. . . . When Congress has entrusted the Secretary with broad discretion, we are especially reluctant to substitute our views of wise policy for his, . . . the Secretary reasonably construed the intent of Congress when he defined "harm" to include "significant habitat modification or degradation that actually kills or injures wildlife." . . .

The judgment of the Court of Appeals is reversed.

QUESTIONS FOR ANALYSIS

1. If the habitat of a bird is modified because it must move its nest from one tree to another, can that be considered "significant habitat modification" that "injures wildlife"?

2. Plaintiffs argued that the ESA gave the Secretary the authority to buy habitat for endangered species and that should be required rather than force private lands to be taken out of production, thereby imposing the cost on the landowner rather than on taxpayers. Is that a reasonable alternative?

Controversy and Uncertainty

Endangered species protection joins wetlands in being one of the most controversial environmental issues. There is no clear legal definition of *endangered* or *species* or *habitat*. The legal requirements for adding a species to the list are minimal. Because listing a species can lead to very tight controls on private property use, landowners

Picking a Sweet Spot

Your firm develops resort spots. Nice pieces of land are found for developing a hotel and a golf course and other facilities. Sometimes houses are also built for permanent residents. The plots of land purchased run between 100 and 600 acres. In considering land for development, what environmental issues should be considered before buying the property?

ISSUE
Spotter

fear having their land removed from any use other than uncompensated habitat protection. In response, Congress has encouraged a limit on ESA listings while pondering alternatives. Of all species listed, habitats have been defined for only a fraction. The Fish and Wildlife Service devotes most of its resources to protecting the most "popular" species, such as the manatee and the grizzly bear. Creatures like the Alabama cave fish and the red hills salamander are largely ignored. When resources are limited, how does one decide which species are most deserving of protection?

Exhibit 17.6

Threatened and Endangered Species

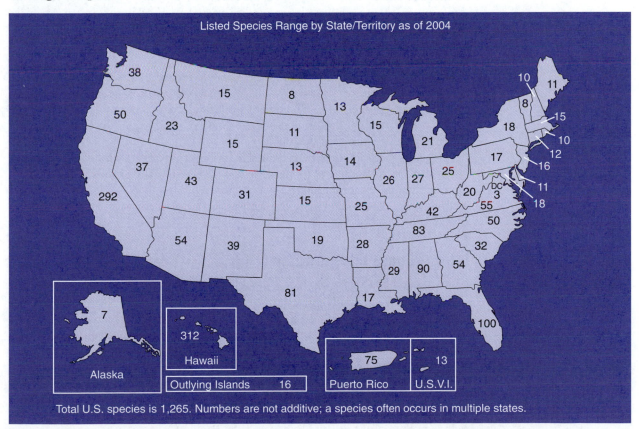

Listed Species Range by State/Territory as of 2004

Total U.S. species is 1,265. Numbers are not additive; a species often occurs in multiple states.

Source: Fish and Wildlife Service

GLOBAL ENVIRONMENTAL ISSUES

Some of the biggest environmental issues—the ozone layer, global climate change, habitat destruction, and the marine environment—must be dealt with on an international scale. Even if the United States did not contribute to global environmental problems, the consequences would still be borne here, so the United States must work with other countries to decide what to do about such issues. The ozone issue provides a good example of an international legal solution to an environmental problem.

The Ozone

While too much ozone (O_3) in the air we breathe is a problem caused largely by vehicle exhaust and is a localized problem, ozone depletion at high levels in the atmosphere is caused by chemicals called chlorofluorocarbons (CFCs), known popularly by such brand names as Freon. CFCs were widely used as refrigerants in air-conditioning systems, in making computer chips, and in some plastics products. In the stratosphere, CFCs are presumed to eat away at the ozone layer, which protects life on earth from ultraviolet radiation. The effect on humans would be an increase in skin cancer, more eye cataracts, and injury to the immune system.

Evidence of a "hole" in the ozone layer over Antarctica by 1985 convinced industry and the government that CFCs could pose a serious problem. Since there were estimates that the ozone loss could cause tens of thousands of deaths per year from skin cancers, the possibility of tort liability existed. In the United States, the makers of CFCs—DuPont, Allied Chemical, Pennwalt, Kaiser, and Racon—which produced one-third of the world supply, agreed with the EPA that CFC production had to be eliminated.

The producers agreed to support the *Montreal Protocol* of 1987, which the United States signed. Under the protocol, an international treaty, nations that produced CFCs agreed to cut production by 50 percent by 1998. The protocol was revised by the London treaty of 1990, requiring production of CFCs and halon (the best firefighting chemical) to be eliminated by 2000.

A solution was achieved that resulted in producers giving up a multibillion-dollar-per-year market. Producers' cooperation was hastened by the promise from the government that the existing producers would have a monopoly over the product during its final years. The total cost to the world's economy of the CFC phaseout is estimated to be $200 billion.

International Cooperation

CFC production was largely in the United States, Japan, and European nations, countries that could essentially force the decision on this issue. Other international environmental issues require more cooperation from less-developed nations, since those nations will bear more of the effects of changes in policies that would reduce environmental problems.

The Montreal Protocol provided a fund, set up by wealthier nations, to pay poorer nations to sign the agreement to ban CFCs. That is, the United States paid for environmental cooperation from other nations. Similarly, the United States helps to pay the cost of water treatment plants in Mexico located near the U.S. border to reduce pollution of the Rio Grande and the Pacific Ocean.

High-Tech Toxic Trash

The National Safety Council estimates that more than a billion pounds of lead, two million pounds of cadmium, and 400,000 pounds of mercury from discarded personal computers (PCs) will have piled up in landfills. The metals could leach into groundwater.

Facing the same problem in Europe, the EU adopted the Waste Electrical and Electronic Equipment (WEEE) Directive. It requires firms doing business in Europe to be responsible for the cleanup of obsolete equipment. The Electronics Industry Alliance notes that over $50 billion worth of electronics products sold each year in Europe, many from the United States and Japan, are covered by the directive. Companies will be responsible for collection, transportation, treatment, and recycling of all electronics products.

WEEE also requires toxic chemicals to be phased out of use in electronics products. Since the rule may violate World Trade Organization rules, the phaseout is not to take effect until 2007 to allow more time for study and innovation. As often happens when one large buyer of products sets such rules, it is expected that the EU regulations could become the global standard.

There is little doubt that if the United States and other nations are concerned about species preservation and other environmental issues, they must pay less-developed nations to protect species and to cover the costs of some pollution controls.

Global Warming

Greenhouse gases that many scientists link to global warming are the basis of the current major environmental issue. A treaty drafted in Kyoto, Japan, in 1997 contains assertions by most developed nations that they will take steps to substantially reduce gas (such as carbon dioxide) emissions by 2008–2012. The Clinton administration signed the treaty in 1998 but did not submit it to Congress for ratification because it would not have passed. The Bush administration dropped the treaty and proposed an alternative plan. Many other nations assert a commitment to greenhouse gas reduction but as yet have introduced only minor changes as politicians around the world try to determine how to make such a high-cost policy politically acceptable. Most of the reductions in greenhouse gas emissions would not occur before 2008, and there is no enforcement mechanism.

POLLUTION PREVENTION

Most environmental legislation has been concerned with cleaning up pollution and setting limits on how much pollution can be dumped into the air, water, and land. The *Pollution Prevention Act* of 1990 provides a framework for thinking about the environment as we plan for the future. It focuses on waste management and says that priority should be given to reducing sources of pollution.

The Act emphasizes the reduction of industrial hazardous wastes and encourages making changes in equipment and technology; redesigning products to minimize environmental damages that arise from the production process and the consequences of the product; substituting raw materials; and improving maintenance, training, and inventory control. The EPA is required to address industrial pollution prevention by the following measures:

- Identify measurable goals
- Improve measurement, data collection, and access to data
- Assess existing and proposed programs and identify barriers
- Offer grants to states for technical assistance programs
- Require companies to disclose amounts of toxic chemicals they release
- Use federal procurement to encourage source reduction

Businesses can integrate pollution prevention into all aspects of operations. Increasingly, companies are making environmental management a part of routine goals as they encourage a commitment to managing pollution control rather than responding to specific rules on a case-by-case basis.

SUMMARY

- Before passage of federal environmental laws, environmental protection relied on common-law remedies, including private and public nuisance actions, trespass, negligence, strict liability for hazardous activities, and riparian water rights. Actions could result in damages or an injunction ordering the offender to cease damaging activities. The EPA is the key regulator of the environment. It works with environmental agencies in all states to enforce federal requirements.
- The Clean Air Act sets air quality standards for several major pollutants: sulfur dioxide, particulates, ozone, carbon monoxide, nitrogen oxide, and lead. These standards are constantly tightened. New polluters must use the best pollution control technology available. In some areas, if a business is to produce any new air pollution, it must buy pollution rights from existing polluters, who are paid either to quit polluting or to install better pollution control equipment.
- The Clean Water Act focuses on point source pollution, which comes out of pipes from factories or sewer systems. Point sources must have permits that allow them to discharge certain amounts of pollution into water bodies. States must declare what standards according to the use—drinking versus swimming quality—all bodies of water in the state will meet. Nonpoint source pollution—runoff from farms, streets, construction sites, mining, and logging—is just beginning to be addressed.
- Wetlands are lands saturated with water at least part of the year. Prior to building on or disturbing a wetland, developers must obtain a permit from the Army Corps of Engineers. The EPA has final say on wetlands use.
- The Toxic Substances Control Act and the Federal Insecticide, Fungicide, and Rodenticide Act require EPA review and approval of toxic substances before they are sold. The EPA may restrict product usage and keep track of evidence of harm from such products.
- The Resource Conservation and Recovery Act requires comprehensive paperwork (manifests) to follow the production, distribution, and disposal of hazardous substances. Hazardous waste treatment, storage, and disposal facilities are subject to strict licensing and regulatory control.
- The Superfund program provides federal support to clean up abandoned hazardous waste sites. Any parties who contribute to the disposal of the wastes, even if legal at the time, may be held liable for part or all of the cleanup costs. Land purchasers should consider an environmental audit to check for possibilities of hazardous wastes, wetlands, or endangered species.

- The Endangered Species Act can block any economic activity, without compromise, if the activity can harm the habitat of an endangered species. Compromises that demonstrate habitat protection may allow a project to go forward as approved by the Fish and Wildlife Service.
- Some environmental controls are imposed by international agreements. The Montreal Protocol required the production of chlorofluorocarbons (CFCs) and halon—chemicals used in refrigeration systems, plastics production, and fire-fighting chemicals—to be eliminated. Protection of biological diversity and reduction of greenhouse gases are other international issues that require the United States and other advanced nations to pay for environmental protection in poor nations.
- The Pollution Prevention Act of 1990 encourages businesses and government agencies to think about environmental issues in all phases of operations. Integration of environmental concerns into regular managerial controls is becoming a necessity.

REVIEW AND DISCUSSION QUESTIONS

1. Define the following terms:

riparian water law	point source pollution
National Ambient Air Quality Standards	nonpoint source pollution
prevention of significant deterioration areas	wetlands
bubble concept	manifest system
acid rain	Superfund
citizen suits	endangered species

2. Were common-law actions—such as nuisance, trespass, and strict liability—against pollution too weak? That is, was federal statutory intervention needed to prevent serious environmental damage?

CASE QUESTIONS

3. A land developer started a retirement village in an area known for its large cattle feedlots. Later, after much of the village is built and sold, the developer brings an environmental nuisance action against the largest feedlot owner in the area. The developer claims that the feedlot is polluting the air with terrible odors, causing discomfort to the residents of the village, and reducing the sale value of the remaining lots. What factors will the court consider in determining whether the feedlot is a nuisance? Assume the court finds the feedlot to be a nuisance. What should be the remedy? Could the feedlot be a nuisance in one location and entirely acceptable in another? [*Spur Industries* v. *Del Webb Development Co.*, 108 Ariz. 178, 494 P.2d 700 (Sup. Ct., Ariz., 1972)]

4. For ten years, a company dumped millions of gallons of chemical wastes on its property in Tennessee. The state shut down the site. Residents around the property sued the company, claiming that their drinking water was contaminated. What basis for suit did they have, and could they win? [*Sterling* v. *Velsicol Chemical Corp.*, 647 F. Supp. 303 (W.D. Tenn., 1986)]

Check your answer at http://meiners.westbuslaw.com

5. The EPA set emission standards for vinyl chloride, a toxic substance that is carcinogenic to humans. The Clean Air Act says such standards must be "at the level which . . . provides an ample margin of safety to protect the public health." The exact threat from vinyl chloride was not known. The EPA said that the proper emissions requirement is the lowest level attainable by best available control technology. The Natural Resources Defense Council sued, contending that since there was uncertainty about the danger, the EPA had to prohibit all emissions. Which position was held correct? [*NRDC* v. *EPA*, 824 F.2d 1146 (D.C. Cir., 1987)]

6. As required by the Clean Water Act, the EPA issued standards for discharges from hundreds of sources. Despite the standards, the EPA issues on a case-by-case basis variances to some water polluters, allowing them to exceed the discharge standards. The Natural Resource Defense Council sued to oppose such variances; the Chemical Manufacturers Association defended the variances. Who won? [*Chemical Manufacturers Assn.* v. *NRDC*, 470 U.S. 116, 105 S.Ct. 1102 (1985)]

 Check your answer at <u>http://meiners.westbuslaw.com</u>

7. James City County, Virginia, planned to build a dam and reservoir across a creek in the county to improve the local water supply. The Army Corps of Engineers granted the building permit, but the EPA rejected it. The county appealed to federal district court, claiming that the project was the most practical method for improving water for county residents. The court ordered the building permit to be issued. The EPA said that it could reject the permit solely on environmental grounds; it did not have to consider the community's need for water. What did the court of appeals say? [*James City County, Virginia*, v. *EPA*, 12 F.3d 1330 (4th Cir., 1993)]

8. The City of Cochran, Georgia, operated a wastewater treatment facility under an NPDES (Clean Water Act) permit. Treatment water is dumped into Jordan Creek, a tributary of the Ocmulgee River in the Altamaha River basin. For five years, the city regularly exceeded the effluent limitations in its NPDES permit. The Altamaha Riverkeeper (ARK), a nonprofit environmental organization founded to protect and restore the Altamaha River, sued Cochran under the citizen suit provision of the Clean Water Act. ARK sought injunctive relief against the pollution as well as civil penalties and attorney fees. ARK moved for partial summary judgment. Does the citizen group have the right to bring such a suit? [*Altamaha Riverkeepers* v. *City of Cochran*, 162 F.Supp.2d 1368 (M.D. Ga., 2001)]

 Check your answer at <u>http://meiners.westbuslaw.com</u>

9. Congress gave the EPA the power in RCRA to regulate "solid wastes." The EPA declared that this includes materials that are being recycled. This was challenged as incorrect, that Congress meant the regulation of materials being discarded or disposed of, not materials being reused. Which position is correct? [*American Mining Congress* v. *EPA*, 824 F.2d 1177 (D.C. Cir., 1987)]

10. The city of Chicago dumped ash from a solid waste incinerator in a waste disposal facility that did not meet RCRA standards for treatment and disposal of hazardous waste. The EPA approved Chicago's action, but an environmental group objected that failure to meet RCRA standards violated the statute. Could EPA exempt Chicago from the RCRA? [*Chicago* v. *Environmental Defense Fund*, 114 S.Ct. 1588 (1994)]

11. A South Carolina company ran a hazardous waste disposal and recycling operation. Several companies sent their hazardous wastes to the site. The facility was improperly managed: waste was dumped on the ground, chemicals were mixed, and records were not kept about what was there. The EPA cleaned up the site under Superfund and sued the companies that sent their waste to the site (since the owners of the site could not pay the bill). The companies responded that they were not liable under CERCLA because there was no evidence that the particular waste they sent had been improperly disposed of. Were they right? [*U.S. v. S.C. Recycling and Disposal*, 653 F.Supp. 984 (Dist. S.C., 1984)]

12. Georgoulis was sole shareholder and president of TICI, which owned White Farm Equipment (WFE) from 1980 to 1985. During those years, WFE dumped its hazardous waste in a dump in Iowa owned by another company. The EPA declared the dump to be a Superfund site. It claimed Georgoulis was a responsible party and should have to contribute personally to the cleanup costs. The court found that Georgoulis did not "have any personal knowledge of the disposal practices at the dumpsite, or was in any way directly involved in waste disposal matters. However . . . Georgoulis had authority to control, and did in fact exert direct control over many significant aspects of the ongoing operations and management of WFE." Could Georgoulis be liable? [*U.S. v. TIC Investment Corp.*, 68 F.3d 1082 (8th Cir., 1995)]

13. Rankin contracted to buy some land in Hammond, Indiana, from SCM Corporation for $500,000. SCM delivered good title but gave no warranty as to the quality of the land. Rankin discovered hazardous waste on the land which could lead to a costly cleanup. Could Rankin rely on CERCLA to get out of the contract to buy? [*HM Holdings v. Rankin*, 70 F.3d 933 (7th Cir., 1995)]

ETHICS QUESTIONS

14. You are an executive with a leading manufacturing company, and one aspect of your business pollutes heavily. You know that you can build a plant in a third world country to handle that aspect without pollution control. This would mean that for the same amount of production, you would add ten times as much pollution to the world's environment as you do now, but it would be more profitable for the company. Can you legally move the plant? Should you?

15. A chemical company is owned by a family that is concerned about the impact of pollution. Recently the family has become concerned about the company's hazardous waste disposal site. Investigators have determined that the site is located over the town's underground water supply. Fortunately, they also determined that the site poses no current threat to the water supply. To be safe, the family would like to move the site. However, because the move would be very expensive, they would like to share the cost with the town's residents. Should this expense be shared by the community?

INTERNET ASSIGNMENT

The Environmental Protection Agency is a primary source of information related to the environment.

PULLING IT  *Together*

Environmental and Administrative Law

The Clean Air Act (CAA) requires the EPA to issue National Ambient Air Quality Standards (NAAQS) for pollutants for which air quality criteria have been issued. The EPA issued revised ozone and particulate matter NAAQS, which were challenged by several private parties, such as the makers of diesel engines for trucks, and several states. The appeals court set aside the new standards, holding that Congress violated the Constitution by delegating legislative power to the EPA. The court also held that the EPA must consider the costs of implementing NAAQS. The EPA appealed to the Supreme Court. Did the EPA exceed its administrative authority by issuing such clean air regulations?

[*Whitman* v. *American Trucking Associations, Inc.*, 531 U.S. 457, 121 S.Ct. 903 (Sup. Ct., 2001)]

1. What is the URL for the EPA's summary of the Clean Air Act (CAA)?
2. What title of the *Code of Federal Regulations (CFR)* addresses the protection of the environment?

The Pace Virtual Environmental Law Library is a good starting point for environmental law research.

3. What is the URL for the Index of International Environmental Law Treaties in Force in the United States?
4. What is the text of the proposed Environmental Constitutional Amendment (XXVIII)?

An example of an established site that offers quick and easy access to environmental information is clay.net: Environmental Professional's Homepage

5. What are the first three quick links offered by the *easy-on, easy-off* ramp at clay.net?
   http://www.epa.gov
   http://www.pace.edu/lawschool
   http://www.clay.net

Chapter 18 | *Consumer Protection*

People suffering from AIDS and other deadly diseases are willing to try new drugs before the drugs are fully tested because they see no advantage in waiting. However, under Food and Drug Administration supervision, drug manufacturers engage in years of tests on animals and limited tests on humans before marketing drugs so that the public is protected from defective drugs and manufacturers can reduce expensive liability suits for selling drugs with undesirable side effects.

Abbott Laboratories was working on a drug (HIVIG) for HIV-infected people. The National Institutes of Health and various private groups wanted Abbott to begin tests on people in 1992. Abbott was concerned that the drug could increase the risk that a baby born to a mother who used the drug would be more likely to become AIDS-infected. Abbott refused to go ahead with human tests unless it was granted immunity from liability for such side effects. The American Civil Liberties Union sued, claiming Abbott had a duty to test the drug. Abbott walked away from all rights to the drug, giving up its investment. The government ordered the drug turned over to a small company that had little to lose if liability problems arose.

Drug regulation, like other forms of consumer protection covered in this chapter, such as credit regulation, affects liability and the decisions made by consumers and producers. Regulations can protect consumers but can also prevent parties from entering into contracts to which they might otherwise agree. Should the government prohibit voluntary agreements among informed, consenting parties? As we discuss various regulations, consider whether producers such as drug makers should be allowed to avoid government regulation and deal directly with consumers.

THE FDA: FOOD AND DRUG REGULATION

The Food and Drug Administration (FDA), an agency of the federal government, is charged with monitoring food and drug safety (see http://www.fda.gov). About one-third of its nearly $2 billion budget is devoted to food safety, sanitation, and processing. One-third of the budget is devoted to the study of the quality of marketed drugs and new-drug evaluations. The rest of the budget supports the study of biological products, veterinary products, medical devices, radiological products, cosmetics, and the National Center for Toxicological Research. Besides a large research staff, every year, more than 1,000 FDA inspectors inspect thousands of establishments and their products that have annual sales of over $1.5 trillion, which amounts to 20 percent of all consumer expenditures.

Food Safety

The control of safety in commercial food, drink, drugs, and cosmetics affects a large sector of the economy. It began with the Pure Food and Drug Act of 1906. For years the primary concern was food safety. This was triggered by several events:

- More soldiers in the American army during the Spanish-American War were reputed to have died from impure food than from enemy bullets.
- Upton Sinclair's *The Jungle*, while failing to stir the public to support socialism as Sinclair had hoped, caused concern about food safety with its graphic description of food processing.
- The chief chemist of the U.S. Department of Agriculture studied the safety of certain food preservatives and determined that some were harmful to human health.

The 1906 Act concerned sanitation and misbranding of food and drug products. The Bureau of Chemistry of the Department of Agriculture performed food analyses for identification of misbranded or impure foods. The Bureau of Chemistry of the Department of Agriculture administered the Food and Drug Act until the FDA was created as a separate unit in 1927.

FDA Powers Expanded in the 1930s

After a drug disaster in which many people were poisoned by a nonprescription medicine, Congress passed the *Federal Food, Drug, and Cosmetic Act* in 1938. The Act greatly expanded the regulatory reach of the FDA by providing the agency with the power not only to extend the standards for foods beyond canned goods but also to prohibit false advertising of drugs, classify unsafe food, add new enforcement powers, form inspection systems, and set the safe levels of additives in foods.

The burden of responsibility is placed on manufacturers to assure that no damage to health comes from the substances present in their food. This responsibility was emphasized by the Supreme Court in the *Park* decision, which addresses the issue of the responsibilities of corporate executives for compliance with the Food, Drug, and Cosmetic Act.

United States v. Park
Supreme Court of the United States
421 U.S. 658, 95 S.Ct. 1903 (1975)

CASE BACKGROUND   *Park was chief executive officer of Acme Markets, a grocery store chain with 874 retail outlets. Acme and Park were charged with violations of the Food, Drug, and Cosmetic Act, because food in Acme warehouses was found on several inspections to be contaminated by rodents.*

Acme and Park were convicted in district court of violating the law. Park appealed, and his conviction was overturned. The court of appeals held that Park could not be held responsible. The government appealed.

CASE DECISION   Burger, Chief Justice.

* * *

The rationale of interpretation given the Act . . . as holding criminally accountable the persons whose failure to exercise the authority and supervisory responsibility reposed in them by the business organization resulted in the violation complained of, has been confirmed in our . . . cases. Thus, the Court has reaffirmed the proposition that "the public interest in the purity of its food is so great as to warrant the imposition of the highest standard of care on distributors." In order to make "distributors of food the strictest censors of their merchandise," the Act punishes "neglect where the law requires care, or inaction where it imposes a duty. The accused, if he does not will the violation, usually is in a position to prevent it with no more care than society might reasonably expect and no more

exertion than it might reasonably exact from one who assumed his responsibilities." . . .

Thus . . . in providing sanctions which reach and touch the individuals who execute the corporate mission—and this is by no means necessarily confined to a single corporate agent or employee—the Act imposes not only a positive duty to seek out and remedy violations when they occur but also, and primarily, a duty to implement measures that will insure that violations will not occur. The requirements of foresight and vigilance imposed on responsible corporate agents are beyond question demanding, and perhaps onerous, but they are no more stringent than the public has a right to expect of those who voluntarily assume positions of authority in business enterprises whose services and products affect the health and well-being of the public that supports them.

* * *

Reversed.

QUESTIONS FOR ANALYSIS
1. Suppose Park did not know of the inspection reports issued by the FDA inspectors because his subordinates did not pass them along to him. Should he still be responsible?
2. Who in corporate leadership could be held responsible under this Supreme Court interpretation of leadership responsibility?

Food Quality Protection

The Food Additives Amendment, known as the *Delaney Clause*, was added to the Food, Drug, and Cosmetic Act in 1958. It gave the FDA authority to set the safe-use level of food additives. It was so strict (a "zero risk" standard) that it was replaced by the more flexible Food Quality Protection Act of 1996. The FDA is to ensure that there is a "reasonable certainty of no harm" (meaning no more than a one-in-a-million lifetime chance of cancer) from any source that affects foods, raw or processed, whether added directly, such as food coloring, or indirectly, such as pesticide residues. The Food Quality Protection Act expanded FDA jurisdiction to thousands of pesticides used in food production.

Nutrition Labeling

The FDA began issuing regulations for *nutrition labeling* in 1973. The *Nutrition Labeling and Education Act* of 1990 required the FDA to issue new nutrition labeling regulations in 1994. These requirements apply to more than 250,000 products. The Department of Agriculture, which regulates meat and poultry, works with the FDA to have regulations for those foods that are consistent with the FDA rules. The intent is to prevent misleading product claims and to help consumers make informed purchases.

Nutrients by Serving Size

FDA regulations list over 100 categories of food, from soup to nuts, whose nutrients must be listed by standard serving size. The following must be listed per serving portion on nutrition labels:

- Total calories and calories from fat
- Total fat and saturated fat
- Carbohydrates (sugar and starch separately)
- Cholesterol
- Calcium
- Fiber
- Iron
- Sodium
- Protein
- Vitamins A and C

Producers may list other nutrients, such as potassium, other essential vitamins and minerals, and polyunsaturated fat. Vitamins that are so common—thiamin, riboflavin, and niacin—that there is no shortage in American diets do not have to be listed.

Standards for Health Claims

Since many consumers know little about the details of nutrition, labels must meet standards for words commonly used so that consumers can learn more about what they are buying. For example, "fresh" refers to raw food that has not been processed, frozen, or preserved; "low fat" means 3 or fewer grams of fat per serving and per 100 grams of the food; "low calorie" means fewer than 40 calories per serving and per 100 grams of food; and "light" or "lite" may be used on foods that have one-third fewer calories than comparable products.

Further, health claims that are not well established, such as the claim that fiber reduces heart disease and cancer, may not be made unless sufficiently documented by the seller. The food/health claims that may be noted on labels involve the health connection between calcium and the prevention of osteoporosis (weak bones), sodium (salt) and high blood pressure, fat and heart disease, and fat and cancer.

Drug Safety

Until 1938, drug control was to protect the public against quacks, false claims, mislabeling, and the sale of dangerous drugs. The Food, Drug, and Cosmetic Act

INTERNATIONAL *Perspective*

Exporting Drug Regulation

The FDA has a major effect on drug production around the world. Many nations adopt FDA regulations as a part of their drug standards. In many countries, the domestic market is not regulated—many drugs sold would be illegal in the United States—but the export market is regulated to FDA standards. This is intended to make pharmaceutical producers competitive in world markets. Since countries do not want a reputation for producing low-quality drugs, they require their exporters to meet U.S. standards.

Another reason countries adopt FDA standards is that foreign drug producers must be licensed and inspected by the FDA to be eligible to export drugs to the United States. FDA inspectors visit foreign plants to assure that U.S. standards are met.

European nations do not have drug regulations as stringent as those of the FDA. Introducing a new drug to the market often happens years sooner in Europe, where the long testing period prescribed by the FDA may not be required. Some drugs that require prescriptions in the United States may be bought over the counter in Europe. Furthermore, the European Union recognizes the inspections conducted by each member country. That is, a Ministry of Health inspection and approval in the United Kingdom qualifies a British producer to export drugs to other EU countries.

The American system probably better reduces risk from defective drugs, but it also keeps lifesaving, pain-reducing, and disease-curing drugs off the market for a longer time than does Europe's system. The result of differences in regulatory standards is that some drug research has grown more rapidly in Europe (and Japan) than in the United States.

provided federal regulators with new powers in 1938 and has been added to since then. The Act prohibits the sale of any drug until the FDA approves the application submitted by the manufacturer. The applicant must submit evidence that the drug is *safe* for its intended use. This prevents the sale of untested drugs in a market that generates well over $100 billion per year in sales.

A critical issue for a seller is whether or not its product is classified as a drug. This has become a major issue for the nutrition supplement industry. Its sales, in the tens of billions of dollars a year, are largely unregulated. If a dietary supplement seller goes too far in its claims, then the FDA may classify the product as a drug, which makes it subject to significant regulations, as the court discusses in the *Whitaker* case.

Whitaker v. Thompson

United States Court of Appeals, District of Columbia Circuit
353 F.3d 947 (2004)

CASE BACKGROUND *Whitaker intended to market "saw palmetto," an extract from the pulp and seed of the dwarf American palm. The label would read: "Consumption of 320 mg daily of Saw Palmetto extract may improve urine flow, reduce nocturia, and reduce voiding urgency associated with mild benign prostatic hyperplasia (BPH)." BPH is classified as a disease. It is a non-cancerous enlargement of the prostate that affects about half of all men over age fifty.*

The FDA rejected Whitaker's petition that this label was a "health claim"—that is, a claim that a product will promote good health and prevent disease. The FDA held that the label is a "drug claim"—a claim that a product would "treat" a disease. As a drug claim, the product would have to undergo extensive testing before marketing. Health claims are under few controls.

Whitaker challenged the FDA's application of the Federal Food, Drug, and Cosmetic Act (FFDCA). The district court dismissed Whitaker's suit; he appealed.

CASE DECISION Williams, Senior Circuit Judge.

* * *

The FFDCA definition of "drug" includes "articles intended for use in the diagnosis, cure, mitigation, treatment, or prevention of disease," which would seem by its plain terms to cover the marketing of a substance intended to mitigate the symptoms associated with BPH. But that apparent simplicity is undermined by language added in 1990 by the Nutrition Labeling and Education Act (NLEA), which created a separate procedure authorizing "health claims" for food (or for dietary supplements classified as food). The general purpose of the NLEA appears to have been to allow the dissemination—subject to a regulatory approval process—of certain dietary and health information on food products without requiring that those products be regulated as drugs. Specifically, the NLEA amended the FFDCA to authorize the sale of dietary supplements pursuant to "health claims.". . .

Congress has given definitions [for health claims and drug claims] that at least partially overlap. And it has given little guidance as to how the FDA should sort out claims that seem to fit both definitions. . . .

The FDA gave several reasons for classifying claims regarding cure, mitigation, or treatment of an existing disease ("treatment claims") as drug claims and for exempting only health claims that concern reducing the risk of contracting a disease ("prevention claims"). The

agency reasoned that the legislative history of the NLEA demonstrated an understanding that the health claim provision was intended for claims of prevention rather than ones of treatment. The agency noted statements in the legislative history indicating that the purpose of the health claims provision was to promote long-term health maintenance and prevention of disease, but found nothing suggesting that legislators enacting this provision contemplated treatment of a person's existing disease with dietary supplements. . . .

The FDA invoked policy concerns to support a distinction between treatment and prevention claims. It argued that, because the health of diseased populations is particularly vulnerable, greater regulation may be justified for products intended for their consumption. Moreover, it argued that treatment claims for symptoms of a disease might lull people with those symptoms into a "false sense of security," leading them to delay a visit to a doctor that might result, for example, in a diagnosis of prostate cancer rather than BPH. . . .

Given our finding that the statute is ambiguous on the critical question of how to classify a claim that meets the statutory definitions both of a drug claim *and* of a health claim, the legislative history and statutory context invoked by FDA are enough to render its interpretation reasonable. . . .

Affirmed.

QUESTIONS FOR ANALYSIS

1. Does the fact that Whitaker cannot make claims about saw palmetto without government approval violate his right to free speech?
2. Is there a clear logical line between health claims and drug claims, as you read the brief definitions above?

Designation of Prescription Drugs

Before the 1938 Act, no drugs were designated as *prescription drugs*—that is, drugs that may be used only with the permission of a physician. Drugs were either legal or illegal. Since 1938, the FDA has determined which drugs will be prescription drugs—that is, sold by pharmacies only with a physician's permission.

Drug Effectiveness

The *Kefauver Amendment* of 1962 requires the FDA to approve drugs based on their proven effectiveness—not just on their safety. The FDA must approve testing of drugs on humans and may specify the details of the testing. The FDA has strict regulations concerning testing and adoption of new drugs. It now costs almost $1 billion and takes years to develop a new drug and to clear all FDA rules before marketing the product. As a result of the high cost, drug companies are spending twice what they did a decade ago on research and development, but produce only half as many new drugs each year.

Liability for Problems

Does FDA approval of a drug reduce the liability of the producers if the drug creates problems? The courts give weight to the protection offered by the regulatory process. The number of liability suits from consumers injured by side effects of a drug is reduced because some effects are not preventable given the state of technology. But FDA approval is only evidence of safety, not a shield against liability.

What if a drug was improperly administered? The drug companies are not likely to be liable, assuming they have given proper dosage instructions. If a physician ignores the instructions and changes the recommended dosage, resulting in an injury, the drug manufacturer is shielded from liability by the *learned intermediary doctrine*. That is, the learned intermediary—the doctor—would be liable for misuse of the product.

Enforcement Activities

Besides deciding when drugs will be allowed to be marketed, the FDA can force existing products, including food, cosmetics, and medical devices, to be removed from the market if their claims appear to be misleading or if new information becomes available that indicates the product was not as safe as previously thought. The FDA forces hundreds of products off the market each year and seizes thousands of import shipments.

For example, most silicone breast implants were ordered off the market by the FDA when questions were raised about the long-term health consequences of the product. The FDA seized shipments of Citrus Hill Fresh Choice orange juice because the juice was made from concentrate and not "fresh" from oranges. The agency ordered vegetable oil manufacturers to remove "no cholesterol" from the labels of their product. The no-cholesterol claim was not false, but the FDA said it was misleading, since many consumers think cholesterol is the same as fat, which is not the case.

While enforcement has become tougher, the FDA has been allowing quicker approval for drugs that show some promise in life-threatening diseases such as AIDS. Rather than require the full, lengthy review process before the drugs are allowed to be sold to informed patients, the FDA allows the drugs to be carefully distributed.

ISSUE *Spotter*

How Much Can You Hype Health Supplements?

Your store sells "health foods" and many "health supplements," such as vitamins and herbs. It is common for new claims to be made about products. Several years ago, shark cartilage (ground up shark bones) was touted as preventing cancer. Many products grow popular at first, then fall by the wayside when the alleged benefits become less clear. For example, if the media is reporting that eating seaweed from the coast of Brazil is believed to prevent senility, can you repeat such a claim? Do you have the right to advertise a product for having such a benefit? Can you get in trouble for going too far to promote a product?

THE FTC AND CONSUMER PROTECTION

The Federal Trade Commission (FTC) was established in 1915 to help enforce the antitrust laws (Chapter 19), but the FTC also devotes substantial resources to its Bureau of Consumer Protection, which handles a wide range of matters such as deceptive business advertising and marketing practices (see http://www.ftc.gov). Some responsibilities are specifically ordered by Congress, such as enforcement of the Magnuson-Moss Warranty Act and the consumer credit statutes. But most consumer protection efforts evolve as the FTC decides what Congress meant when it amended the FTC Act in the 1930s and said, in Section 5, that "unfair and deceptive acts or practices in or affecting commerce are hereby declared unlawful."

Based on its experience, and in response to concerns expressed by Congress, the FTC investigates a wide range of practices said to be *unfair and deceptive*. The FTC staff proposes complaints to the five commissioners, who decide by majority vote whether to issue a complaint. The complaint begins formal legal proceedings against a business engaged in practices the commission would like to see ended or modified.

Many complaints are settled by a *consent decree* agreed upon by the parties charged in an FTC complaint. Consent decrees contain the terms of a settlement and frequently include prohibition of certain practices, redress for consumers, and payment of civil penalties. Some cases result in administrative trials at the FTC. If the accused party or the FTC attorneys are not satisfied with the decision of the administrative law judge, they may appeal to the commissioners for review. An accused party who is not satisfied with the decision of the commissioners may appeal to a federal court of appeals.

Unfair and Deceptive Acts or Practices

Congress ordered the FTC to fight "unfair and deceptive acts or practices." The lack of a clear legal definition for those terms means that the FTC has considerable leeway in deciding what cases to bring—what advertising is deceptive and what sales practices are unfair. The key term has always been *deceptive*. Essentially, things held to be deceptive are also unfair, a term we define below.

Policy Statement on Deception

To give the FTC staff guidance, the commissioners adopted a *deception policy statement* that summarizes a three-part test for deciding whether a particular act or practice is deceptive. There is *deception* if the following are true:

1. There is a misrepresentation or omission of information in a communication to consumers.
2. The deception is likely to mislead a reasonable consumer.
3. The deception is material; that is, it is likely to be misleading to the detriment of consumers.

Some points help make clear the elements of deception. First, not all omissions are deceptive. Omissions (failure to reveal information) are not deceptive if there is no affirmative misrepresentation (false statement) or practice that takes advantage of consumer misunderstanding. Second, to decide whether a representation (claim or statement) or omission is deceptive, the FTC looks at what has been presented to consumers. The words in an advertisement are examined in the context of the entire ad, and consideration is given to evidence about what consumers think the ad means. Third, a reasonable consumer is an "ordinary person" in the target audience of the ad. For example, ads directed at children or ill people are held to a tougher standard. Fourth, the representation or omission must be likely to affect a consumer's product choice. Fifth, no proof of injury to consumers (usually financial loss) is needed if there is evidence that such injury is likely to occur, given the practice in question. Here are some examples.

Telemarketing Fraud   The FTC obtained an injunction against five telemarketing firms for making misrepresentations in the sale of water purifiers and home security systems. The FTC charged that the companies mailed postcards telling consumers they had won valuable awards, including $5,000 worth of merchandise. In fact, the awards consisted only of certificates that required payment of large sums of money to get the goods. The telemarketers also made charges against consumers' credit cards without permission and billed customers for goods never sent.

Note that telemarketers are subject to the Telephone Consumer Protection Act and the Telemarketing and Consumer Fraud and Abuse Prevention Act, which resulted in the FTC's Telemarketing Sales Rule. These laws allow consumers to sue telemarketers if they make telemarketing calls in violation of consumer instructions to be removed from call lists. Some states have statutes that strengthen federal requirements.

Oil- and Gas-Well "Investments"   Several companies were involved in oil- and gas-well lease scams. They persuaded more than 8,000 people to invest $5,000 to $10,000 each in application fees to participate in a lottery for oil and gas rights on federal lands. The FTC obtained $47 million in refunds. Not only were the promoters sued, so were all the companies that worked with them in the scheme, such as insurance companies, banks, and accounting firms.

JURIS *prudence?*

Protecting Consumers

A group that calls itself Common Good annually lists the most useless warning labels that are put on products, supposedly to help consumers. Winners include labels on:
- A bottle of drain cleaner: "If you do not understand, or cannot read, all directions, cautions and warnings, do not use this product."
- A snow sled: "Beware: sled may develop high speed under certain snow conditions."
- A 12-inch rack for storing CDs: "Do not use as a ladder."
- A fishing lure with a three-prong hook on the end: "Harmful if swallowed."
- A smoke detector: "Do not use the Silence Feature in emergency situations."

Source: *http://www.cgood.org*

Work-at-Home Opportunities   A federal appeals court upheld a $16 million judgment against a company and its officers in *FTC* v. *Febre*, 128 F.3d 530, for deceptive practices in four work-at-home "opportunities." This included mailing postcards, which supposedly could earn up to $15,000 per day. Almost 200,000 consumers had paid the promoters over $13 million, which was ordered rebated to the consumers, plus $3 million in damages.

Invention-Promotion Scams The FTC sued twelve companies that raked in $90 million by claiming that they were consultants who help people make deals for valuable new inventions. "Project Mousetrap" discovered that people paid between $10,000 and $20,000 each to get "expert advice" in licensing and marketing such things as a toothbrush with bristles at both ends and a device that collects the shavings scratched off lottery tickets. While the operations were closed, only $250,000 remained for consumer redress.

Unfairness

Section 5 of the FTC Act says that "unfair or deceptive acts or practices in or affecting commerce, are declared unlawful." The word *unfairness* is usually added to a charge of deception. The FTC has given operational meaning to unfair acts or practices in business by issuing a policy statement that gives a consumer injury standard:

1. It causes substantial harm to consumers.
2. Consumers cannot reasonably avoid injury.
3. The injury is harmful in its net effects.

The first major consumer unfairness case that did not involve a claim of deception was the *Orkin* case (which was supervised by one of the authors of this text while working for the FTC). The decision to bring the case was based on the belief that the unfairness seemed much like fraud or breach of contract, both of which are common-law standards the courts have long enforced.

Orkin Exterminating Company v. Federal Trade Commission

United States Court of Appeals, Eleventh Circuit
849 F.2d 1354 (1988)

CASE BACKGROUND *Beginning in 1966, Orkin Exterminating offered customers a "continuous protection guarantee" if they had their houses treated for termites. The contract said that by paying a set annual fee, customers were guaranteed free retreatment if termites reappeared for as long as they owned their house.*

By 1975, Orkin realized that the promise was a mistake. The fee was too low to cover the costs. Orkin then notified over 200,000 customers that the fee was being raised $25. If the customers did not pay the higher fee, the guarantee was lost. The new fee was consistent with market prices but differed from what the contract stated. Most customers paid the higher fees. The FTC found the fee increase to be unfair and ordered Orkin to roll back its prices to the original levels. Orkin appealed to the U.S. Court of Appeals.

CASE DECISION Clark, Circuit Judge.

* * *

The Commission's conclusion was simply that it was an "unfair" practice to breach over 200,000 contracts. We think this was a reasonable application of the Commission's unfairness standard.

There remains . . . the question whether this case represents a significant departure from prior Commission precedent. We note what has been written in a recent law review article:

> Some of the oldest "unfairness" decisions involve sellers' refusals to live up to the terms of their contract. The Commission has often challenged sellers for traditional breaches of contract: failure to fill orders, delivery of inferior merchandise, refusal to return goods taken for repair, or refusal to return promised deposits. Recent trade regulation rules have focused

continues

on similar issues. These actions have attracted little controversy. Breach of contract has long been condemned as a matter of law, economics, and public policy.

Orkin claims the statements in this article are erroneous, for each of the cases cited therein involved some sort of deceptive practice. We think it important to remember, however, that section 5 by its very terms makes deceptive and unfair practices distinct lines of inquiry which the Commission may pursue. As is suggested above, while a practice may be both deceptive and unfair, it may be unfair without being deceptive. . . .

This case may be "unprecedented" to the extent it concerns non-deceptive contract breaches. But given the extraordinary level of consumer injury which Orkin has caused and the fact that deceptiveness is often not a component of the unfairness inquiry, we think the limitation of the Commission's section 5 authority urged by Orkin would be inconsistent with the broad mandate conferred upon the Commission by Congress. Thus, because the Commission's decision fully and clearly comports with the standard set forth in its Policy Statement, we conclude that the Commission acted within its section 5 authority.

* * *

Affirmed.

QUESTIONS FOR ANALYSIS

1. Assuming that Orkin breached its contracts with 200,000 consumers, why not let the consumers sue Orkin rather than have the FTC get involved?

2. Does the ability to bring suits for a practice being "unfair" open the door to almost everything being challenged, since we all have different ideas of what is unfair?

Regulating Advertising Claims

About $200 billion is spent on advertising each year. The *advertising substantiation program* requires advertisers and advertising agencies to have a reasonable basis before they make claims. When advertisers claim that "studies show" or "tests prove," they must actually have evidence that provides a reasonable basis for the claims. The FTC considers the following factors to determine what is a reasonable basis:

• The product
• The type of claim
• The consequences of a false claim and the benefits of a truthful claim
• The cost of developing substantiation for the claim
• The amount of substantiation that experts believe is reasonable

What Advertising Is Deceptive?

Years ago, the FTC commissioners said: "Perhaps a few misguided souls believe . . . that all 'Danish pastry' is made in Denmark. Is it therefore an actionable deception to advertise 'Danish pastry' when it is made in this country? Of course not." The point is that some people may misunderstand certain advertisements, but that does not mean that the FTC will be concerned. For example, if a hair dye is advertised as "permanent" and someone thinks it means that their hair will be the color of the dye forever, no deception is involved. Most consumers know what is meant, and those who do not understand do not incur significant injury.

Some ads that reach a small number of people, such as pamphlets handed out door-to-door, may deceive many who read it because the claims are false and likely to deceive. Other ads may reach a large number of people, deceive very few, yet be held to be deceptive. For instance, if a small number of consumers lose a lot of money because they believe a deceptive claim, the FTC may act because of the seriousness of the injury. Note that most states have laws similar to the FTC Act that allow state attorneys general to file suit in deceptive advertising cases.

Examples of Deceptive Ad Cases

Gateway Educational Products settled FTC charges that the claims about the ability of its "Hooked on Phonics" program to teach reading, including those with learning disabilities, were unsubstantiated. The FTC contended that consumer testimonials did not represent typical experiences. Experts on reading disability said that phonics instruction may not help people with dyslexia or other reading disabilities. The producer promised to stop the challenged claims and to make no other claims without substantiation.

The FTC helps enforce FDA definitions of food terms. The FTC sued Häagen-Dazs about the fat and calorie claims on its frozen yogurt products: "And each with just 1 gram of fat and 100 calories." In fact, the products contained up to twelve grams of fat per serving (compared to the FDA definition of low fat as three grams or less) and up to 230 calories per serving. The company agreed to meet FDA standards for labeling food products and not to misrepresent the amount of fat or calories.

The FTC sued Bee-Sweet for this claim about its bee-pollen products: "Studies performed by doctors around the world have shown bee pollen to be effective in treating illnesses from allergies to arthritis, anorexia to overweight, fatigue to arteriosclerosis." Because there was no scientific evidence to back up the claims, the company agreed to stop making such claims and to inform product distributors about the settlement with the FTC.

Quaker State agreed to stop running unsubstantiated ads for Slick 50, an engine treatment. Similarly, Ashland Oil agreed to end a major ad campaign that touted Valvoline TM8 Engine Treatment. The ads claimed, without substantiation, that the additive would reduce wear on some engine parts by as much as 75 percent.

Most deceptive advertising cases are settled in a similar manner—the advertiser agrees to stop making false claims. In some cases, a civil penalty is imposed, but

---

INTERNATIONAL *Perspective*

Foreign Advertising Regulation

Advertising is subject to different controls around the world. Most countries impose fewer regulations on ads than is the case in the United States. In Europe, ad regulations tend to be tightest in northern Europe and loosest in the Mediterranean countries.

Britain has an Office of Fair Trading that operates somewhat like the FTC with respect to ad regulation. The general standard is that an ad is illegal if it misrepresents a product, whereas in the United States it may be illegal if it simply misleads. For an ad to misrepresent a product, there must be an estimation that consumers suffer damages because they have not been told the truth in the ad. For example, a

soup ad in the United States was held illegal by the FTC because the soup was photographed to look as though it had more chunky bits in it than a random bowl of the soup really would have. In most of Europe and Japan, that ad would not be illegal because, while it misleads, it does not injure consumers.

Beer ads in Japan promote the "extra strong" alcohol content, a practice that would be illegal in the United States under the alcohol advertising rules of the Bureau of Alcohol, Tobacco, and Firearms. As the chairman of a Japanese advertising firm explained, "When you come to Japan, you have to do as the Japanese do, especially in advertising."

large sums are not common. In rare instances, the FTC orders a company to engage in corrective advertising to make up for past false claims.

False Advertising and the Lanham Act

Another way that false advertising claims may be struck down, and one that can yield far more expensive results than most FTC advertising cases, is when a private party brings a suit under the *Lanham Act*. Section 43 of the Act states:

> Any person who, or in connection with any goods or services, or any container for goods, uses in commerce any word, term, name, symbol, or device . . . or any false designation "of origin, false or misleading description of fact, or any false or mislead-ing representation" of fact, which (1) is likely to cause confusion, or to cause mistake, or to deceive as to the affiliation, connection, or association of such person with another person, or as to the origin, sponsorship, or approval of his or her goods, serv-ices, or commercial activities by another person, or (2) in commercial advertising or promotion, misrepresents the nature, characteristics, qualities, or geographic origin of his or her or another person's goods, services, or commercial activities, shall be liable in a civil action by any person who believes that he or she is or is likely to be damaged by such act.

When private cases claiming misleading advertising are brought under the Lanham Act, the courts generally consider the meaning of "deceptive" the same as does the FTC. Most cases result in injunctions against further false advertising claims, much like most FTC advertising cases. But plaintiffs also may recover damages, as in *U-Haul International* v. *Jartran*, 793 F.2d 1034, where the appeals court upheld an award of $40 million. The Act allows injured parties (the plaintiff who is a com-petitor) to collect double the value of the profits that the defendant earned from false advertising by luring business away. Similarly, many states have laws, such as the Business and Professions Code of California, that prohibit false and misleading advertising. Competitors or consumers injured by such advertising may sue.

ISSUE
Spotter

How Aggressive Can You Be in Advertising Tactics?

Different advertising tactics seem to work for various products and in dif-ferent markets. Some small firms, to get noticed, directly take on the big firms in the industry by calling their products by name and saying that the small firm has a better product or service. If you really believe your product is better for the price, how explicit can you be in comparing it to your competitor without violating false advertising rules? How much risk is there in calling your competitor names to draw attention to yourself?

Trade Regulation Rules

Under Section 18 of the FTC Act, the Commission may issue *trade regulation rules* that set boundaries for practices when problems are common. Because many trade regulation rules are on the books—most dealing with narrow areas—here we con-sider only a few major rules.

As with most regulations, a proposed rule must be published in the *Federal Register* so that interested parties may comment on it before it is finalized. When the rule is finalized, it becomes part of the Code of Federal Regulations. It gives the FTC

Regulating Cyberspace Advertising

The FTC has prosecuted dozens of cases involving alleged online scams and false advertising. One company paid $195,000 in consumer redress in response to an FTC challenge to its claims for "self-improvement" products. In another case, the FTC charged that Fortuna Alliance collected more than $6 million based on false claims that "investors" could easily earn large sums in what amounted to a pyramid scheme. The FTC seized Fortuna's assets and obtained a court order that a notice of the FTC's action be placed on Fortuna's web site.

The FTC pushed for Congress to pass the Children's On-line Privacy Protection Act, which requires the FTC to adopt rules requiring web sites that appeal to children (under age thirteen) to provide parents with notice of information that is being collected and how the web site uses the information. Such sites must obtain "verifiable parental consent" regarding the collection, distribution, and use of their children's information, and parents must be able to withdraw consent.

grounds for charging that violators of the rule are committing an unfair and deceptive act, since firms in an industry are required to know about rules that apply to them. Rules may limit certain contracts, as in the case of the rule that allows buyers to cancel contracts they agreed to in certain door-to-door sales.

The Insulation R-Value Rule

The FTC's Trade Regulation Rule Concerning the Labeling and Advertising of Home Insulation (the *R-value Rule*) was written because of problems consumers had understanding insulation claims. By standardizing R-values, the FTC requires insulation manufacturers and installers to use the same terminology and measures of R-values.

The rule provides a standard to evaluate home insulation products. If a company claims that it provides R-19-value insulation and it has not, there is a standard to measure the R-value. For example, the FTC sued Sears for violating the R-value Rule. Sears advertised the thickness and price of an insulation product but failed to disclose the R-value. In the settlement, Sears agreed to pay a civil penalty, to comply with the rule in the future, and to pay for advertisements to educate consumers about home insulation and R-values.

The Mail-Order Rule

One of the best-known trade regulation rules is the *Mail-Order Rule*. If a company sells merchandise by mail, it must ship goods in the time stated in its ads. Shipping dates must be stated on the offers (such as "Allow five weeks for shipment") or shipment must be within thirty days of receipt of an order. If the goods cannot be shipped on time, customers must be sent a notice allowing them to cancel the order or to agree to a new shipping date. The rule gives the FTC a simple basis for issuing complaints against companies that fail to live up to the terms of their offers.

The Used Car Rule

The FTC *Used Car Rule* requires dealers to give consumers clear information on who pays for repairs after a sale. A Buyer's Guide must be put in the window of used cars offered for sale. The guide must contain

1. A statement of the terms of any warranty offered with the car
2. A prominent statement of whether the dealer is selling the car "as is" and, if so, that the consumer must pay for any repairs needed after buying the car
3. A warning that oral promises are difficult to enforce, with a suggestion to get all promises in writing
4. A suggestion that the consumer ask for an independent inspection of the car

Magnuson-Moss Warranty Act

An amendment to the FTC Act gave the FTC power to set guidelines for consumer products warranties. Compliance with the *Magnuson-Moss Warranty Act* does not appear to have been very costly.

Required Written Warranty Information

The law requires *written warranties* to include information about the following:

* The parts of the product or the types of problems the warranty covers and, if necessary for clarity, the parts or problems it does not cover
* The time period of coverage
* What will be done to correct problems and what will not be done
* How the customer can get warranty service
* How state law may affect warranty

Full or Limited Warranty

Products that cost more than $10 and have warranties must state clearly whether the warranty is full or limited. A *full warranty* meets these five standards:

1. Warranty service is provided to anyone who owns the product during the warranty period.

JURIS *prudence?*

Born in the USA . . .

New Balance Athletic Shoe was sued for "making false and misleading advertising and labeling claims that its athletic shoes are 'Made in the USA.'" The FTC wanted to prohibit New Balance from making "Made in the USA" claims "unless all, or virtually all, of the components and labor are of U.S. origin."

The company responded that its shoes are assembled in the United States and about 70 percent of the components are from the United States. Since rubber is not grown in the United States, it has to be imported, thereby, according to the FTC, preventing New Balance from saying that its shoes are "Made in the USA."

New Balance pressed the issue. Different agencies use different rules for what constitutes "Made in the USA." NAFTA holds that 55 percent of the labor and components must be from Canada, Mexico, or the United States. The Department of Transportation says that 75 percent of an automobile must be from the United States. Customs says that only 50 percent must be from the United States.

The FTC dropped the case against New Balance and reviewed the matter. The agency floated a rule of 75 percent parts and labor to mean "Made in the USA." That resulted in protests from unions and domestic producers. The FTC then said 90 percent.

Source: *Federal Trade Commission* and *The Wall Street Journal*

2. Warranty service is provided free of charge, including such costs as returning or removing and reinstalling the product when necessary.
3. At the consumer's choice, a replacement or a full refund will be provided if the product cannot be repaired after reasonable efforts.
4. Warranty service is provided without requiring that consumers return a warranty registration card.
5. Implied warranties are not limited.

If any of these conditions are not met, the warranty is a *limited warranty* and must be so stated. To comply with the FTC's Rule of Disclosure of Written Consumer Product Warranty Terms and Conditions, warranties must be clear, simple, and useful. If a company writes an unclear warranty in fine print to discourage or confuse consumers, it will be subject to FTC attack, especially if consumers have difficulties enforcing the warranty. State courts have made similar determinations in cases brought under contract law. Fine print is not held in favor.

CONSUMER CREDIT PROTECTION

Congress first involved the federal government in the direct regulation of consumer credit with the *Consumer Credit Protection Act (CCPA)* of 1968. At that time there was about $100 billion worth of consumer credit outstanding; now the figure is over $1.5 trillion. The CCPA is an umbrella law containing several credit-related laws. The laws provide rights for consumers and put requirements on creditors, including the following:

- Creditors must disclose all relevant terms in credit transactions (truth in lending).
- Procedures for correcting inaccurate and disputed bills and charges must be provided (fair credit billing).
- Credit-reporting agencies must provide accurate information in consumer reports (fair credit reporting).
- Creditors may not use certain personal characteristics (such as sex or race) in determining a person's creditworthiness (equal credit opportunity).
- Abusive debt collection techniques are prohibited (fair debt collection practices).

Truth-in-Lending Act

As Exhibit 18.1 shows, the first law to come under the CCPA was the *Truth-in-Lending Act (TILA)*, which requires creditors in consumer transactions to disclose basic information about the cost and terms of credit to the consumer-borrower. By standardizing credit terms and methods of calculation, it helps people to shop for the most favorable credit terms.

Finance Charge Disclosures

Until TILA was passed, creditors quoted interest in many ways. For example, an 8 percent "add-on interest rate" is the same as a 15 percent "simple interest rate." This is because an add-on rate calculates interest on the initial amount of the loan regardless of the outstanding principal. The simple interest rate calculates interest only on the outstanding principal. Both methods are legitimate, but standardized terms let consumers make better comparisons.

Exhibit 18.1

The Major Elements of Consumer Credit Legislation

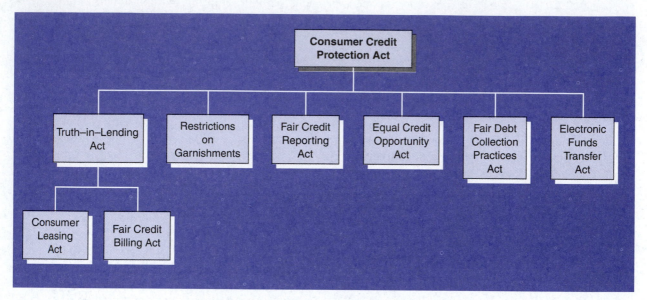

TILA does not control interest rates; it requires standardized loan terms. TILA covers only consumer credit transactions, since the debtor must be a "natural person," not a business organization. Since the creditor must be in the credit business, TILA does not apply to transactions such as loans to friends. The law does not apply if the credit transaction does not include a finance charge, unless the consumer repays the creditor in more than four installments. Finally, the Act does not apply to consumer credit transactions for more than $25,000, except real estate purchases.

Credit Cost Disclosure

Transactions covered by TILA must disclose the credit costs in dollars (the *finance charge*) and the interest rate of that finance charge (the *annual percentage rate*, or *APR*). These items must be disclosed prominently in the agreement. *Regulation Z*, written by the Federal Reserve Board to implement the Truth-in-Lending Act, specifies items that must be listed if part of the finance charge:

1. Service, activity, carrying, and transaction charges
2. Loan fees and points
3. Charges for credit life and credit accident and health insurance
4. In non–real-estate transactions, the fees for credit reports and appraisals

Certain other items, such as licenses and fees imposed by law, are not part of the finance charge if they are itemized and disclosed to the consumer in the transaction. Exhibit 18.2 shows the disclosure required in the sale of a car on credit.

Enforcement and Penalties

TILA provides for both civil and criminal penalties. The creditor can avoid liability for a violation, such as a failure to specify all finance charges, if the violation is

Exhibit 18.2

Sample Credit Sale
Disclosure Form

Big Wheel Auto   **Alice Green**

ANNUAL PERCENTAGE RATE	FINANCE CHARGE	Amount Financed	Total of Payments	Total Sale Price
The cost of your credit as a yearly rate.	The dollar amount the credit will cost you.	The amount of credit provided to you or on your behalf.	The amount you will have paid after you have made all payments as scheduled.	The total cost of your purchase on credit, including your down-payment of $ 1500—
14.84%	$ 1496.80	$ 6107.50	$ 7604.30	$ 9129.30

You have the right to receive at this time an itemization of the Amount Financed.
☐ I want an itemization. ☒ I do not want an itemization.

Your payment schedule will be:

Number of payments	Amount of Payments	When Payments Are Due
36	$211.23	Monthly, beginning 6-1-06

Insurance:
Credit life insurance and credit disability insurance are not required to obtain credit, and will not be provided unless you sign and agree to pay the additional cost.

Type	Premium	Signature	
Credit Life	$120—	I want credit life insurance.	*alice Green* Signature
Credit Disability		I want credit disability insurance.	Signature
Credit Life and Disability		I want credit life and disability insurance.	Signature

Security: You are giving a security interest in:
☒ the goods being purchased.
☐ _____.

Filing Fees $_____   Non-filing insurance $_____

Late Charge: If a payment is late, you will be charged $10.

Prepayment: If you pay off early, you
☐ may   ☐ will not   ☐ have to pay a penalty.
☒ may   ☐ will not   ☐ be entitled to a refund of part of the finance charge.

See your contract documents for any additional information about nonpayment, default, any required repayment in full before the scheduled date, and prepayment refunds and penalties.

I have received a copy of this statement.

alice Green _____   5-1-06
Signature   Date

_____
e means an estimate

corrected within fifteen days from the time it is discovered by the creditor and before the consumer gives written notification of error.

Consumers may sue creditors who violate TILA disclosure rules for twice the amount of the finance charge—up to $1,000—court costs, and attorney's fees. A creditor who willfully or knowingly gives inaccurate information or fails to make proper disclosures is subject to criminal liability.

Consumer Leasing Act

The *Consumer Leasing Act* does for consumer leases, such as for automobiles, what the Truth-in-Lending Act does for consumer credit. That is, it provides standard terms for leases. The Act applies to leases of personal property for personal or household purposes, not for business use. The lease must be longer than four months and have an obligation of less than $25,000. Apartment leases are not covered by the Act because the property leased is real, not personal. Most car rentals are not covered because the term of the agreement is too short.

Disclosure Requirements

The Consumer Leasing Act specifies information that must be given. The required disclosures include the following:

- Number, amount, and period of the payments and the payment total
- Express warranties offered by the leasing party or the manufacturer of the leased property
- Identification of the party responsible for maintaining the leased property
- Whether the consumer has an option to buy the leased property and, if so, the terms of that option
- What happens if the consumer terminates the lease before the lease expires

Fair Credit Billing Act

TILA includes the *Fair Credit Billing Act (FCBA)*. Before the Act, some consumers complained they were unable to get creditors to correct inaccurate or unauthorized charges that appeared on their bills. Another problem was that credit cards were sent to people who did not request them. Some cards were lost or stolen, and consumers who never requested the cards were billed for unauthorized purchases. The FCBA addresses these problems:

1. In case of a *billing error* a consumer must notify the creditor in writing within sixty days of the billing of a disputed charge. The creditor must answer the complaint within thirty days of receipt and has ninety days to resolve the problem and notify the consumer.
2. It prohibits the mailing of unsolicited credit cards.
3. It establishes procedures to report lost or stolen credit cards. Liability for unauthorized charges is $50.

Enforcement

Most billing disputes are resolved through the procedures established by the FCBA. Dissatisfied consumers can also sue for civil penalties for FCBA violations. In successful actions, creditors are liable for twice the amount of the finance charge, plus attorney's fees and court costs.

The FTC is a major FCBA enforcement agency, with jurisdiction over department stores, gasoline retailers, and non–bank-card issuers, such as American Express. Other federal agencies enforce the credit statutes for other credit-granting institutions. Most banks are regulated by the Federal Reserve Board.

INTERNATIONAL *Perspective*

Differences in Legal Protection of Consumer Rights

While the United States has many statutes dealing with consumer credit rights, how does that number compare to that of other countries? The World Bank sponsored research on consumer credit markets around the world, which is summarized in the chart here. The second column following the list of countries addresses whether the country has a public credit registry, that is, a database usually run by the central bank that collects information on the standing of debtors and makes the information available to creditors. The third column, "Registry Index," is a measure of the quality of information in the public credit registry—the higher the number, the better and more useful the information. The fourth column, "Credit Bureaus?" lists which countries have credit bureaus.

Some countries, such as the United States, have no public registry and so rely on private credit bureaus. For those countries, column five lists the coverage of debtors per 1,000 people by credit bureaus. The higher the number, the more comprehensive the database. Finally, the study constructed a Creditor Rights Index on a 0 to 4 scale, with higher scores indicating countries where creditors have stronger legal rights, especially in the case of bankruptcy. The index is given in the last column in the chart.

Country	Public Registry?	Registry Index	Credit Bureaus?	Coverage	Creditor Rights Index
United States	No	0	Yes	810	1
Canada	No	0	Yes	806	1
Japan	No	0	Yes	777	2
United Kingdom	No	0	Yes	652	4
China	Yes	56	No	0	2
Germany	Yes	44	Yes	693	3
France	Yes	53	No	0	0

Source: *http://rru.worldbank.org/doingbusiness*

Fair Credit Reporting Act

The *Fair Credit Reporting Act (FCRA)* regulates *credit bureaus* (consumer reporting agencies). It focuses on confidentiality and accuracy in *consumer credit reports*. No limit is placed on the information that consumer reporting agencies may include in their files (such as information on political beliefs or sexual practices), so long as the information is accurate.

Agencies may sell consumer reports only for business needs, such as to evaluate an applicant for credit, insurance, or employment. Any other use requires a court order or the consumer's permission.

Consumer Rights

The FCRA gives consumers the right to see information reported about them to a creditor that results in credit being denied. Further, credit bureaus must

- Respond to consumer complaints about inaccurate information within thirty days
- Tell consumers, on request, who has asked for copies of their credit history in the past year

- Provide a toll-free consumer service number
- Get the consumer's permission before giving a report to an employer or before releasing a report containing medical information

When a consumer tells a reporting agency about incorrect information, the information must be deleted or changed or a statement from the consumer about the problem must be put in the file.

To settle a lawsuit with the FTC and various states, the big three consumer credit reporting agencies—Experian, Equifax, and Trans Union—agreed to allow consumers to have copies of their credit reports for free or at very low cost so that they can check them for accuracy.

Enforcement and Penalties

The FTC has responsibility for enforcing the FCRA. The Act provides civil remedies to injured consumers, who may recover actual damages when noncompliance is negligent. When the credit agency is in willful noncompliance, the consumer may recover actual damages and a punitive penalty. In one suit, TRW was ordered to pay $290,000 in damages—of which $275,000 was punitive damages—for ignoring a consumer's attempt to correct errors in his credit report.

Equal Credit Opportunity Act

The *Equal Credit Opportunity Act (ECOA)* was added to the CCPA to prohibit *credit discrimination* on the basis of race, sex, color, religion, national origin, marital status, receipt of public benefits, the good-faith exercise of the applicant's rights under any part of the CCPA, or age (provided the applicant is old enough to sign a contract). Creditors are prohibited from using such criteria (known as *prohibited bases*) in determining creditworthiness.

Unlawful Credit Discrimination

The guiding law for ECOA compliance is simple:

> A creditor shall not discriminate against an applicant on a prohibited basis regarding any aspect of a credit transaction.

Because this provision is broad, *Regulation B*, issued by the Federal Reserve Board, provides rules explaining what is unlawful discrimination. These include

- A creditor may not make statements related to a prohibited basis to discourage a person from applying for credit.
- A creditor may not use information concerning the likelihood that the applicant may have children or that the applicant is likely, for that reason, to have reduced or irregular income.
- Credit history must, at the applicant's request, consider not only the applicant's direct history but also the applicant's indirect credit history (for example, accounts that the applicant was liable for and accounts listed in the name of a spouse or former spouse that reflect his or her credit history).
- A creditor may not request information about a spouse or former spouse of the applicant unless (a) the spouse will use the account or will be liable for the debt; (b) the applicant is relying on the spouse's income or on alimony or child

support from the former spouse; or (c) the applicant lives in a community property state.

A violation of ECOA exists if a creditor used a factor prohibited by the Act. The consumer can sue the creditor for ECOA violations. If successful, the creditor is liable to the consumer for actual damages, punitive damages up to $10,000, attorney's fees, and court costs, whether the discrimination was intentional or not.

ECOA Notification Requirements

When a consumer's credit application is denied or accepted at less-favorable terms, the creditor must provide *written notification* containing the following:

1. The basic provisions of ECOA
2. Name and address of the federal agency regulating the creditor
3. Either a statement of the reasons for the action taken or a disclosure of the applicant's right to receive a statement of reasons

The first and second requirements tell rejected applicants that it is against the law to discriminate on a prohibited basis and point them to the federal agencies that enforce the Act. The third requirement is the most significant. By knowing why they were rejected, applicants can reapply when their situation changes, or they can correct any misinformation. By knowing the reasons for credit denial, applicants can better understand how credit decisions are made.

Fair Debt Collection Practices Act

Creditors have the right to collect debts they are owed. If not repaid, under state law they may go to court and ask for an order to *garnish* (set aside a portion of) the wages of the debtor to pay the debt, but that is a costly process. If unsuccessful in collecting a debt, a creditor can sell the debt to a *debt collection agency*—or pay the agency a commission for the funds it collects. Agencies handle about $100 billion in claims each year.

To collect accounts, debt collectors advise consumers by telephone or letter of the outstanding debt and urge them to pay. Sometimes, consumers are subjected to phone calls in the middle of the night, obscene language, and other harassment and abusive tactics. The *Fair Debt Collection Practices Act (FDCPA)* helps reduce unfair, deceptive, and abusive collection techniques used by some debt collectors.

JURIS *prudence?*

Watch Who You Nickle and Dime

Wendy Ehringer bounced a check for $15.02. She got a notice from a debt collector (ACS) demanding the $15.02 plus $40 in fees, so she sent a money order for $55.02. Months later, she received notice of a lawsuit. Her payment was late, ACS claimed, so she was being sued for 18 cents—the interest on the original amount she owed because her payment arrived two days late—plus $311.26 in attorney fees.

Ehringer, a paralegal, knew her rights under the FDCPA and countersued. The court threw out ACS's claim and awarded Ehringer $500 damages plus $7,000 for attorney's fees.

Source: *Seattle Times*

Restrictions Imposed

The FDCPA regulates the conduct of about 5,000 independent debt collection agencies that collect billions of dollars each year from consumers. In *Heintz* v. *Jenkins*, 115 S.Ct. 1489, the Supreme Court held that the FDCPA "applies to attorneys who regularly engage in consumer-debt collection activity." The law does not apply to creditors attempting to collect their own debts, such as a department store trying to collect from a customer. The Act makes abusive debt collection practices illegal and contains a list of required actions.

Harassing, deceptive, and unfair debt collection practices—including threats of violence or arrest, obscene language, the publication of a list of delinquent consumers, and harassing phone calls—are prohibited. Debt collectors may not discuss the debts with other people, including the debtor's employer. The Act prohibits the use of false or misleading representations in collecting a debt.

ISSUE
Spotter

How Should You Handle Unpaid Accounts?

Your company sells furniture mostly to low-income people who buy on credit provided by your company. You know that the default rate, which is pretty high in your business, can determine whether the store is profitable or not. Should you sell or assign the debt to a debt collector or handle the collection internally? What difference is there legally? Are there advantages of going one way or another?

What Must Be Communicated

The FDCPA requires the debt collector to send certain information to the consumer within five days of the initial communication:

- Amount of debt
- Name of the creditor to whom the debt is owed
- A statement that unless the consumer disputes the validity of the debt within thirty days, the debt collector will assume the debt is valid
- A statement that the debt collector must show proof of the debt if the consumer advises the debt collector within thirty days of the notification that the consumer disputes the debt

Contact with the consumer must end when the collector learns that the consumer is represented by an attorney or when the consumer requests in writing that contact end. The debt collector then waits for payment or sues to collect the debt. Most cases that arise under the FDCPA concern improper language in debt collection letters. As the *Chuway* case shows, debt collectors must be precise in their language.

Chuway v. National Action Financial Services, Inc.

United States Court of Appeals, Seventh Circuit
362 F.3d 944 (2004)

CASE BACKGROUND   *National Action, a debt collector, mailed Chuway, a debtor, a letter which identified a creditor (a credit card company) and stated that the "balance" on the debt was $367.52. The letter said that the creditor "has assigned your delinquent account to our agency for collection. Please remit the balance listed above in the return envelope provided. To obtain your most current balance information, please call 1-800-916-9006. Our friendly and experienced representatives will be glad to assist you and answer any questions you have."*

Chuway sued National Action for violating the FDCPA because the communication was not proper under the Act. The district court granted summary judgment for National Action because the letter stated "the amount of the debt" and so did not violate the statute. Chuway appealed.

CASE DECISION   Posner, Circuit Judge.

* * *

Here . . . the *entire* debt that the defendant was hired to collect was the $367.42 listed as the "balance."

So if the letter had stopped after the "Please remit" sentence, the defendant would be in the clear. But the letter didn't stop there. It went on to instruct the recipient on how to obtain "your most current balance information." If this means that the defendant was dunning her for something more than $367.42, it's in trouble because the "something more" is not quantified. . . . The credit card company, which is to say the creditor, not the debt collector, may charge the plaintiff interest on the $367.42 between when the debt accrued and when the plaintiff finally pays and may add the interest accruing in the interim to the plaintiff's current bal-

ance. But that would not be a part of "the amount of the debt" for which the *defendant* was dunning her. . . .

It is not enough that the dunning letter state the amount of the debt that is due. It must state it clearly enough that the recipient is likely to understand it. Otherwise the collection agency could write the letter in Hittite and have a secure defense. . . .

If the debt collector is trying to collect only the amount due on the date the letter is sent, then he complies with the Act by stating the "balance" due, stating that the creditor "as assigned your delinquent account to our agency for collection," and asking the recipient to remit the balance listed—and stopping there, without talk of the "current" balance. If, instead, the debt collector is trying to collect the listed balance plus the running interest on it or other charges, he should use the safe-harbor language [established in an earlier case]: "As of the date of this letter, you owe $____ [the exact amount due]. Because of interest, alter charges, and other charges that may vary from day to day, the amount due on the day you pay may be greater. Hence, if you pay the amount shown above, an adjustment may be necessary after we receive your check, in which event we will inform you before depositing the check for collection. For further information, write the undersigned or call 1-800-[phone number]."

Reversed and remanded.

QUESTIONS FOR ANALYSIS

1. How could Chuway afford to sue National Action over such a small sum of money?

2. Why did National Action not use the language the court cited as providing a safe harbor because the words meet the specific requirements of the FDCPA?

Enforcement

Consumers subjected to collection abuses enforce compliance by suing. A collector who violates the FDCPA is liable for actual damages caused as well as any additional damages (not over $1,000). Consumers bringing action in good faith will have their attorney's fees and court costs paid by the collector. The FTC can sue collectors that violate the act, as can state attorneys general in states with similar laws.

When debt collection practices go overboard, the debtor may, of course, sue in tort, as well as for violations of the FDCPA. In a case in El Paso, Texas, a jury awarded debtors $11 million in damages against Household Credit Services, their creditor, and Allied Adjustment Bureau, a collection agency used by Household Credit. Attempting to collect a $2,000 debt, death threats and numerous other violations of the debtor's rights were made. Damages under the FDCPA were a tiny fraction of the jury tort verdict.

Electronic Fund Transfer Act

Various *electronic fund transfer* services are available to consumers:

*   Automated teller machines (ATMs) that let consumers perform banking transactions at any time
*   Pay-by-phone or e-mail systems, permitting consumers to call the bank or manage their account online to order payments or funds transferred
*   Direct deposits of wages into a bank account or automatic payments that deduct money from the consumer's account, such as for automobile car loan payments
*   Point-of-sale transfers (debit cards), which allow consumers to transfer money from their bank account to a merchant.

As electronic innovations developed, Congress became concerned about the rights and liabilities of the consumers, financial institutions, and retailers who use electronic fund transfer systems. The *Electronic Fund Transfer Act* was passed and required the Federal Reserve Board to write *Regulation E* to implement the Act.

Liability for Stolen Cards

One important protection provided by the Act is the liability limit when a consumer's ATM card is stolen and an unauthorized user drains the account. Unlike the Fair Credit Billing Act's $50 limit on liability for lost or stolen credit cards, the Electronic Fund Transfer Act's limit on liability is potentially greater.

Regulation E provides that the consumer's liability is no more than $50 if the financial institution is notified within two days after the consumer learns of the theft. The consumer's liability becomes $500 as long as the financial institution is notified within sixty days. If the consumer does not report the theft within sixty days after receiving the first statement containing unauthorized transfers, the consumer is liable for all amounts after that.

Liability for Mistakes

The Act makes financial institutions liable to consumers for damages caused by failure to make electronic transfers. However, liability is limited to actual damages proved, such as costs incurred by a consumer, such as if a car is repossessed for failure to make a required payment.

Consumers are to receive a monthly statement from financial institutions. Consumers have sixty days to report errors. When a consumer reports an error, the institution must resolve the dispute within forty-five days. If an investigation takes more than ten business days to complete, the institution must recredit the disputed amount to the consumer's account; the consumer has use of the funds until the complaint is resolved. Failure to undertake a good-faith investigation of an alleged error makes the institution liable for triple the consumer's actual damages.

SUMMARY

- The Food, Drug, and Cosmetic Act, enforced by the FDA, imposes liability on companies and persons involved in the production and distribution of food and drug products. The primary concern for food is safety. The FDA is helped by the U.S. Department of Agriculture and various state agencies in food inspection to ensure sanitation.

- Food additives must be approved by the FDA before being sold to the public. Nutrition labels on processed foods must list by standard consumer portions fat, carbohydrates, cholesterol, and other nutrients, as well as certain vitamins and minerals and total calories.

- The FDA determines when drugs are safe and effective for sale and whether drugs will be sold by prescription only or over the counter. Food, drugs, cosmetics, and medical devices that the FDA determines to be unsafe may be ordered off the market or seized.

- The FTC has broad authority to attack unfair or deceptive business practices. The consumer protection mission includes the advertising substantiation program, which requires advertisers to be able to demonstrate the truth of product claims.

- The FTC issues trade regulation rules to govern business practices that have raised problems. The rules fix standards that businesses must meet, which makes prosecution for rule violations quite simple.

- The Truth-in-Lending Act, which applies to most consumer loans, requires that lenders meet requirements on how the details of loan amounts, interest charges, and other items are calculated and stated to the borrower. There is no defense for certain violations of this statute. The Consumer Leasing Act sets similar standards for consumer leases.

- The Fair Credit Billing Act details the rights of consumers to resolve billing errors. Creditors must follow requirements on how long they have to respond to the consumer and what they must do to resolve the dispute. As under other parts of the credit statutes, violations mean double damages, plus attorney's fees, for the plaintiff.

- Credit bureaus sell lenders the credit history about consumers seeking credit. The Fair Credit Reporting Act specifies consumers' rights to challenge the accuracy of reports issued by these bureaus. Credit bureaus must respond to inquiries from consumers about errors in credit reports.

- Under the Equal Credit Opportunity Act, creditors may not consider the following factors in determining who will be granted credit: race, sex, age, color, religion, national origin, marital status, receipt of public benefits, or the exercise of legal rights. Specific regulations govern how lenders must comply with this statute.

- Debt collectors may not abuse the rights of debtors granted by the Fair Debt Collection Practices Act. They may not make abusive phone calls, threats, or claims of legal action not actually under way or use other forms of harassment. A debt collector informed by any debtor that no further contact is desired may not contact the debtor except for notice of legal action.

- Consumer rights and responsibilities for credit cards and ATM cards that have been stolen are spelled out in the law. To limit liability for unauthorized charges, the consumer must notify the card issuer of the theft of the card.

REVIEW AND DISCUSSION QUESTIONS

1. Define the following terms:

   learned intermediary doctrine   trade regulation rules
   consent decree   full warranty
   deception   limited warranty
   unfairness   consumer credit reports
   advertising substantiation program   debt collection agency

2. What incentives do FDA administrators have to approve new drugs for sale? Do they have an incentive to hurry the process or to be very careful?

3. If consumers think agencies such as the FTC prevent unfair and deceptive practices, will they become less careful in watching out for themselves, thereby encouraging more bad business practices?

CASE QUESTIONS

4. Laetrile is a drug not approved by the FDA for sale. Some people believe it helps fight certain types of cancer. People who had cancer would travel to Mexico to be treated with Laetrile. Some people with cancer sued the FDA, saying they had a constitutional right to privacy that was being denied by the FDA's refusal to let them have access to Laetrile. A court of appeals held that it is not reasonable to apply the FDA's drug safety and effectiveness standards to dying cancer patients. The Supreme Court reviewed the case. What was the result? [*U.S. v. Rutherford*, 99 S.Ct. 2470 (1979)]

5. Heath took Ortho-Novum oral contraceptive from 1967 to 1974, when, at age twenty-eight, she suffered kidney failure that eventually required a kidney transplant. She sued, claiming the kidney failure was caused by Ortho-Novum, which did not adequately warn physicians to monitor blood pressure or watch for signs of kidney problems. Ortho defended that it was in compliance with FDA regulations in marketing the product and in the literature that accompanied the drug; hence, it should not be subject to common-law strict liability or negligence. Could the case go to the jury, or did federal regulation of the drug remove common-law liability? [*Ortho Pharmaceutical* v. *Heath*, 722 P.2d 410 (Colo. Sup. Ct., 1986)]

 Check your answer at http://meiners.westbuslaw.com

6. Buckingham Productions sold various diet plans, such as the Rotation Diet and the Freedom Diet. It claimed that dieters could eat almost anything they wanted for four days each week and lose weight if during the other three days they followed a low-calorie diet and took the company's vitamin supplements. The company reported that the average monthly weight loss was eight to twenty pounds for women and twelve to twenty-five pounds for men. What government agency would likely sue the company and on what grounds, and what would be the likely result?

7. A store constantly has big signs in its windows and puts ads in the newspapers that take different approaches. For a month the store will advertise "Gigantic Savings of 75%" and similar claims. The next month it will advertise "Going-Out-of-Business Clearance Sale." The next month it will advertise "Distress Sale

Prices—Everything Must Go." In fact, the store is not going out of business, and most of its prices are always the same. The prices are competitive, but not 75 percent off normal retail. Is this deceptive advertising?

 Check your answer at http://meiners.westbuslaw.com

8. BASF and Old World Trading compete in the private-label antifreeze market. Old World advertised that its antifreeze met industry specifications, such as those of GM and Ford. BASF sued under the Lanham Act for false advertising and showed that Old World did not meet industry standards. During the years in question, Old World's market share rose from 4 percent to 15 percent. The district court awarded BASF $2.5 million for lost profits it would have earned if Old World had not taken so much of the market. Old World appealed, claiming that it was not liable for such damages. Was the trial court right? [*BASF* v. *Old World Trading*, 41 F.3d 1081 (7th Cir., 1994)]

9. Procter & Gamble sold a detergent, Ace con Blanqueador, in Puerto Rico. It advertised that "Mas blanco no se puede" (Whiter is not possible). Clorox, a bleach maker, sued Procter & Gamble, contending that the ad was false and misleading in violation of the Lanham Act. The district court dismissed the suit; Clorox appealed. Did it have a suit for false advertising against its competitor under the Lanham Act? [*Clorox Company Puerto Rico* v. *Procter & Gamble Commercial Co.*, 228 F.3d 24 (1st Cir., 2000)]

 Check your answer at http://meiners.westbuslaw.com

10. A requirement of the Truth-in-Lending Act and Regulation Z is that each borrower receive two copies of the Notice of Right to Cancel. The lender gave Jacquelyn Elsner and her husband Max each one copy of the notice, along with other materials on the loan document they both signed. The Elsners later moved to cancel the loan agreement because they did not *each* receive two copies of the notice, which was a simple oversight by the lender. Is the loan good, or can the Elsners walk away because of a technical violation of the Act? [*Elsner* v. *Albrecht*, 460 N.W.2d 232 (Ct.App., Mich., 1990)]

11. Virginia Miller's husband had an American Express card, and Virginia Miller had a supplementary card on that account, which had a different number on the card and her name on it. The supplementary card carried an annual fee, and Miller was liable for all charges. Upon her husband's death, American Express canceled Miller's card, saying that Miller could apply for a new card. Miller did and was given a new American Express card and account. She sued American Express for violation of the Equal Credit Opportunity Act based on marital status. Did she have a case? [*Miller* v. *American Express*, 688 F.2d 1235 (9th Cir., 1982)]

12. Fairbanks Capital acquired 12,800 mostly delinquent mortgages from a mortgage company, including a mortgage owned by the Schlossers. Identifying itself as a debt collector, Fairbanks sent the Schlossers a letter asserting that their mortgage was in default. In fact, the Schlossers were not in default and sued Fairbanks for failure to notify the debtors of their right to contest the debt as required by the Fair Debt Collections Practices Act (FDCPA). The district court held that since the Schlossers were not in default, there was no debt to collect, so the FDCPA did not apply. The Schlossers appealed. Do they have a case? [*Schlosser* v. *Fairbanks Capital Corp.*, 323 F.3d 534 (7th Cir., 2003)]

13. Pfennig sued Household Credit Services for violations of the Truth in Lending Act. She contended that she was extended credit but was then charged a fee of

$29 a month when she went over the $2,000 limit on her credit card. The fee was not listed in the finance charges disclosed on her monthly statements, but was listed as a new purchase on which additional finance charges were calculated. Does she have a case? [*Pfennig* v. *Household Credit Services, Inc.*, 295 F.3d 522 (6th Cir., 2002)]

14. Sarah Grendahl moved in with Lavon Phillips and was planning to marry him. Mary Grendahl, Sarah's mother, believed Phillips was lying about his background, so she hired a private investigator to check him out. Using consumer reports, the investigator determined that Phillips had been convicted for writing bad checks, sued for paternity in one state, and was delinquent in child support in another state. When Phillips learned that the truth about his background had been revealed, he sued Mary Grendahl, the detective agency, and the consumer reporting agency for violating the Fair Credit Reporting Act. Does he have a case? [*Phillips* v. *Grendahl*, 312 F.3d 357 (8th Cir., 2002)]

15. King borrowed $500 from Cashland in an unsecured loan. The agreement included this clause: "I agree that Cashland, Inc. may contact any person(s) on my original application and on this application. I waive any privacy claims against Cashland, Inc." His application included his sister and a friend as references and gave the name of his employer. King's check to repay the loan bounced, so Cashland began collection efforts. It called King forty times and used abusive language. Cashland also called his sister and friend and told them King would be arrested; King's landlord and employer were also contacted by letter and fax about the debt. King sued Cashland for invasion of privacy and for violation of the FDCPA. The trial court dismissed the suit; King appealed. Did he waive his privacy rights? [*King* v. *Cashland, Inc.*, 2000 WL 1232768 (Ct. App., Ohio, 2000)]

ETHICS QUESTION

16. The FDA, FTC, or some other agency is proposing a regulation that would hurt the sales of one of the products your company produces. The agency believes that there is a long-run consumer health issue that it should address. You estimate the regulation will cost your company $20 million a year in sales and $2 million a year in profits. The three other firms in the industry that make a similar product will likewise be hurt. Your Washington representative tells you that if all four firms are willing to spend $5 million in lobbying efforts it can get Congress to kill the proposed regulation. All other firms agree to help foot the bill. This kind of lobbying is common. Should you pay to help get the regulation killed?

PULLING IT *Together*

Consumer Protection and Business Organization

Kossol was a major operating partner in Continental Food Network, which sold food plans to consumers. Consumers signed contracts to pay thousands of dollars for a plan that was supposed to provide them a certain quantity of food over several years and give them a "free" freezer. In fact the freezers were sold for triple their market value and the food was not the quantity or quality claimed. The Consumer Protection Division of the Attorney General Office of Maryland sued to have the operation shut down and ordered $6 million in restitution paid to customers, plus $265,000 in penalties paid to the state. Kossol was held jointly and severally liable for the payments. He appealed, contending that the business could be held liable, but that he could not be held liable personally. Assuming there was consumer fraud, would liability go against the business only, or does it also go against the owners?

[*State of Maryland Central Collection Unit* v. *Kossol*, 771 A.2d 501 (Ct. Sp. App., Md., 2001)]

Chapter 19 | *Antitrust Law*

Because of the downturn in housing construction, your building supply company is suffering. Trying to stay in business, you have cut prices to the bone, leaving no profit for yourself. Your competitors are doing the same thing. In fact, you know that some are selling certain supplies at less than cost, just to keep some cash flowing in. If this continues, some, if not all, suppliers in your area will be out of business.

Stability would be better if you and the other suppliers agreed not to sell supplies at a loss. Housing construction is always boom-and-bust, you think. If all the suppliers just hold on for a while, everyone can stay in business and be ready to serve clients when things pick up again. Your clients will be better served at that time than if a number of suppliers go broke now and only a few competitors remain in business to serve the market when things pick up.

What happens if you discuss this idea—not selling supplies at a loss—with your competitors to try to get an agreement? What kind of agreement among competitors will not cause antitrust-law violations?

The antitrust statutes written by Congress do not tell us whether that would be legal. Instead, the courts must interpret the very general language in the statutes to determine what activities are prohibited and what activities are allowed. Antitrust law, therefore, refers to the antitrust statutes, the interpretation of the statutes by the courts, and the enforcement policies of administrative agencies, especially the Department of Justice and the Federal Trade Commission. This chapter reviews the antitrust statutes and looks at how antitrust law is applied to both horizontal and vertical business arrangements.

ANTITRUST STATUTES

The growth of large corporations in the late nineteenth century led to calls for constraints on business. The result was the passage of federal antitrust legislation: the Sherman Act, the Clayton Act, and the Federal Trade Commission (FTC) Act. The key parts of these broadly written statutes are excerpted in Appendix H. Except for some actions that are clearly illegal under the statutes, it has been left largely to the federal agencies and courts to determine how the laws will be applied in practice.

The Sherman Act

The *Sherman Antitrust Act* was passed by Congress in 1890 in response to the unpopularity of large business organizations. The most famous was the Standard Oil Trust, John D. Rockefeller's company, which had about 90 percent of the oil sales in the country. The word *antitrust* comes from Standard Oil. The sponsors of the Act saw it as a way to reduce concerns that some industries were dominated by a few large firms. The major sections of the Sherman Act are so broad that one could find almost any business activity to be illegal:

> Sec. 1: Every contract, combination in the form of trust or otherwise, or conspiracy, in *restraint of trade* or commerce among the several States, or with foreign nations, is hereby declared to be illegal.
>
> Sec. 2: Every person who shall *monopolize*, or *attempt to monopolize*, or combine or conspire with any other person or persons, to monopolize any part of the trade or commerce among the several States, or with foreign nations, shall be deemed guilty of a felony.

The Clayton Act

Enacted in 1914, the *Clayton Act* was meant to add to the Sherman Act. The Clayton Act is intended to stop a business practice early in its use to prevent a firm from becoming a *monopoly* by making practices that "substantially lessen competition or tend to create a monopoly" illegal.

Under the antitrust laws, what is a monopoly? There is no exact answer. In general, a monopoly exists in a market when one firm or only a few dominate the sales of a product or service. As we will see in this chapter, the fact that a company obtains such a position is not necessarily illegal. The laws focus more on certain actions that show an effort to eliminate competition. The Clayton Act holds some specific actions to be illegal. The most important sections of the Act are

> Sec. 2: It shall be unlawful for any person engaged in commerce . . . to discriminate in price between different purchasers of commodities of like grade and quality . . . where the effect of such discrimination may be substantially to lessen competition or tend to create a monopoly in any line of commerce . . . [This section was added by the Robinson-Patman Act of 1936 and restricts price discrimination in the sale of goods. As we will see, this means when a producer sells the same good at different prices to different buyers.]
>
> Sec. 3: It shall be unlawful for any person engaged in commerce . . . to lease or make a sale . . . on the condition . . . that the lessee or purchaser thereof shall not use or deal in the goods . . . or other commodities of a competitor . . . where the

effect . . . may be to substantially lessen competition or tend to create a monopoly. . . . [This is a restriction on tying sales, where the sale of one good is tied to the sale of another good, and exclusive dealing, when a company is forbidden from dealing with other possible buyers or sellers.]

   Sec. 7: No corporation . . . shall acquire the whole or any part of the assets of another corporation engaged also in commerce, where . . . the effect of such acquisition may be substantially to lessen competition, or to tend to create a monopoly. [This restricts mergers of competitors, such as Wendy's and Burger King.]

   Sec. 8: No person at the same time shall be a director in any two or more corporations . . . if such corporations are or shall have been . . . competitors, so that the elimination of competition by agreement between them would constitute a violation of . . . the antitrust laws. [This restricts interlocking directorates, such as the same people sitting on the boards of directors of both Ford and GM.]

The Federal Trade Commission Act

In addition to the Clayton Act, in 1914 Congress enacted the *Federal Trade Commission Act*. It established the FTC as an agency to investigate and enforce violations of the antitrust laws. Although most of the Act provides for the structure, powers, and procedures of the FTC, it also provides a major addition to antitrust law:

   Sec. 5: Unfair methods of competition in or affecting commerce, and unfair or deceptive acts or practices in commerce, are hereby declared unlawful.

The *unfair methods of competition* referred to in the FTC Act have been interpreted by the courts as any business activity that may tend to create a monopoly by unfairly eliminating or excluding competitors from the marketplace.

Exemptions

Not all business activities are subject to the antitrust laws. In some cases, successful lobbying of Congress resulted in statutory exemptions from the antitrust laws. The following activities and businesses are provided exemptions:

- The Clayton Act exempts some activities of nonprofit organizations and of agricultural, fishing, and some other cooperatives.
- The Export Trading Company Act allows sellers of exports to receive limited antitrust immunity. For example, a group of domestic producers may be allowed to join together to improve their ability to sell their products in other countries.
- The "Parker doctrine," or *state action doctrine*, allows state governments to restrict competition in industries such as public utilities (e.g., cable television), professional services (e.g., nursing), and public transportation (e.g., taxicabs). However, the Supreme Court has held that for the doctrine to protect parties from antitrust actions, the state must play "a substantial role in determining the specifics of the economic policy." That is, the state must have intended to restrict competition and perhaps fix prices.
- The McCarran-Ferguson Act exempts the insurance industry from federal antitrust laws so long as the states regulate insurance.

- Under the Noerr-Pennington doctrine, lobbying to influence a legislature is not illegal. This is because the First Amendment gives persons the right to petition their government, even if the purpose is anticompetitive.
- Most labor unions activities are exempt. The National Labor Relations Act protects collective bargaining to set conditions of employment.

Enforcement

Individuals and businesses have the right to sue for the violations of the antitrust laws. The Antitrust Division of the Justice Department brings criminal antitrust suits. For a civil lawsuit under the Sherman Act or Clayton Act, a choice must be made as to whether the Justice Department or the FTC will bring the case. The agencies have agreed to divide the cases by industry, but may consult to decide which agency will handle a particular case. State attorneys general may also bring antitrust cases under federal or state law.

Sherman Act

Violations of the Sherman Act carry the most severe penalties of the antitrust statutes. Most of the criminal cases involve price-fixing or bid rigging by competitors.

- Violations of Sections 1 and 2 of the Sherman Act can be *criminal felonies*. Individuals found guilty of violating the Act face up to ten years in prison, a fine of $1 million, or both. Corporations found guilty can be fined up to $100 million. Criminal cases are brought by the Antitrust Division of the Department of Justice. Some years, fines totaling over $1 billion have been collected.
- Private parties or the government can seek injunctive relief under the Act in a civil proceeding. An *injunction* is an order to a defendant (the party who may have violated the Act) to stop the illegal acts.
- Private parties harmed by a violation of the Sherman Act can sue for *treble damages*; if they win, they get three times their actual money damages, plus court costs and attorney's fees.

Clayton Act

The Department of Justice or private parties may bring civil proceedings under the Clayton Act, but the normal procedure has been for the FTC, which shares jurisdiction with the Justice Department, to issue cease and desist orders, prohibiting further violation. The FTC has the authority to investigate suspect business dealings, hold hearings (rather than trials), and issue administrative orders approved in federal court that require parties to stop or change certain business acts. When these orders are ignored there may be criminal penalties.

FTC Act

Violation of this statute carries a variety of penalties, ranging from an order preventing a planned merger to substantial civil penalties. It is much easier for the FTC to bring administrative actions against a company than for the Justice Department to bring a criminal suit under the Sherman Act, so the agencies decide which route is most appropriate to take in each case.

Remedies Available

Whether an antitrust suit is brought by a private plaintiff or by the government, the courts can provide a number of remedies, besides monetary damages, including the following:

- Restrain a company or individuals from certain conduct
- Force a company to sell part of its assets (break up the company)
- Force a company to let others use its patents or facilities (licensing)
- Cancel or modify existing business contracts

For a firm to recover damages under the antitrust laws, the harm suffered by the plaintiff must be the kind of harm that the antitrust laws are meant to avoid. A firm that loses profits because a new competitor enters its market cannot sue for damages, because increased competition is favored by antitrust law. Only plaintiffs suffering injuries caused by *anti*competitive behaviors of defendants can recover damages under antitrust law.

Per Se Rule and the Rule of Reason

As we will see as we look at antitrust cases, one question the courts must address is whether, as a matter of policy, a certain business practice will be held to be per se illegal or whether a rule of reason is appropriate.

A *per se rule* means that some business agreements or activities will automatically be held to be illegal. The classic example of a per se violation of antitrust law is a group of competitors agreeing on the prices they will charge for their goods so as to eliminate price competition. In discussing per se illegality, the Supreme Court in *Northern Pacific Railway Co.* v. *United States*, 356 U.S. 1, stated that there are certain activities that

> because of their pernicious effect on competition and lack of any redeeming virtue are conclusively presumed to be unreasonable and therefore illegal without elaborate inquiry as to the precise harm they have caused or business excuse for their use.

A *rule of reason*, in contrast, means that the court looks at the facts surrounding business practice before deciding whether it helps or hurts competition. The court considers such factors as the business reasons for the restraint, the restraining business's position in its industry, and the structure of the industry.

If the court concludes that the business practice promotes competition, the court dismisses the case. But if the court finds that the practice on net reduces competition, the court rules that it violates the antitrust laws.

MONOPOLIZATION

The Sherman Act and Clayton Act are concerned with monopolization of markets but provide little guidance as to what behavior crosses the line of illegal monopoly practices. Therefore, antitrust law has been built on many court cases over the years. The courts usually consider the structure of a market and the nature of the behavior that is attacked. The concern is to protect competition in a given market, not just to protect individual competitors who complain about another competitor's behavior. In the *Spanish Broadcasting* case we see a discussion of the factors that courts consider in a monopolization case brought under the Sherman Act.

Spanish Broadcasting System of Florida v. Clear Channel Communications

United States Court of Appeals, Eleventh Circuit
376 F.3d 1065 (2004)

CASE BACKGROUND *Spanish Broadcasting System (SBS) owns fourteen Spanish-language stations, including five stations in top-ten markets. Hispanic Broadcasting Corporation (HBC) owns fifty-five Spanish-language stations and is in all top-ten markets. Clear Channel (CC) owns the largest English-language radio network in the United States, with 1,200 stations, and it owns 26 percent of HBC.*

SBS sued CC and HBC, claiming they conspired to drive SBS out of the Spanish-language radio market by practices that violate the Sherman Act. SBS claimed that the two stations discouraged advertisers from placing ads with SBS and induced SBS employees to quit to join HBC. SBS contended that the stations made it difficult for SBS to enter new markets by bidding up prices and taking away business opportunities, and interfered with SBS's ability to raise money in capital markets. The district court dismissed the suit, holding that SBS did not meet the standards necessary to maintain an antitrust suit under the Sherman Act; SBS appealed.

CASE DECISION Barkett, Circuit Judge.

* * *

Because the Sherman Act contains only general language, courts have played an extremely important role in shaping the reach of the Act and the requirements for stating a cause of action under each section. Critically, under both sections, an antitrust plaintiff must show harm to competition in general, rather than merely damage to an individual competitor. . . . This case turns in large part on whether SBS has met its obligation to allege facts that would support a showing of this harm to competition, rather than merely to itself. . . .

SBS alleged that the practices [described above] constituted an agreement between CC and HBC to restrain trade in violation of Section One of the Sherman Act as well as attempted monopolization by both CC and HBC of the major Spanish-language radio markets in violation of Section Two of the Act. . . .

Section One of the Sherman Act . . . prohibits combinations and conspiracies that restrain interstate or foreign trade. This provision applies both to agreements between companies that directly compete with one another, called "horizontal" agreements, and to agreements between businesses operating at different levels of the same product's production chain or distribution chain, known as "vertical" agreements. In addition, although some restraints on trade remain illegal per se, such as certain agreements to fix prices, most asserted antitrust violations now require "the finder of fact [to] decide whether the questioned practice imposes an *unreasonable* restraint on competition, taking into account a variety of factors, including specific information about the relevant business, its condition before and after the restraint was imposed, and the restraint's history, nature, and effect." Section One claims that do not allege per se antitrust violations are analyzed under this "rule of reason," and the claims fail if the restraint on trade is reasonable. Both parties accept that the rule of reason applies to the Section One claims raised by SBS in this case. . . .

Even if we were to assume that CC and HBC acted in concert for purposes of Section One, however, we would still affirm here, given that SBS failed to allege sufficient anticompetitive effect, a critical component of any antitrust claim. . . .

Anticompetitive effects are measured by their impact on the market rather than by their impact on competitors. . . . In order to prove this anticompetitive effect on the market, the plaintiff "may either prove that the defendants' behavior had an actual detrimental effect on competition, or that the behavior had the potential for genuine adverse effects on competition."

In an attempt to meet this burden, SBS focuses upon the harm it allegedly suffered at the hands of HBC and CC, such as weakened stock prices, restricted access to capital markets, loss of employees, damaged reputation, and loss of advertising revenue. None of these allegations assert damage to competition itself rather than damage to SBS, one competitor in the Spanish-language advertising market. As the district court indicated, the amended complaint contains no allegations at all about a factual connection between the conduct alleged and overall impact on the advertising market. . . .

continues

We find that although SBS may have alleged "unfair" competitive practices, it did not adequately allege actual harm to competition. . . .

Although damage to a critical competitor *may* also damage competition in general, SBS bears the burden of drawing that implication with specific factual allegations. It has not done so here. . . .

SBS has not described how the defendants' alleged behavior would be likely to harm competition. In fact, as the district court noted, SBS has expanded considerably over the past few years, has a share of the New York, Chicago, and Miami markets somewhat comparable to that of HBC, and was itself engaged in merger talks with HBC. By its own admission, advertisers continue to shift larger portions of their budget toward the Spanish-language market as that market grows. . . . Given these alleged facts, and in the absence of specific allegations detailing the threat to the Spanish-language advertising market, SBS did not state a claim for relief against CC or HBC under Section One, and the district did not err in dismissing the Section One claims of the First Amended Complaint. . . .

Section Two makes it a crime to monopolize, to attempt to monopolize, or to conspire to monopolize any part of interstate or foreign trade. This provision covers behavior by a single business as well as coordinated action taken by several businesses.

The . . . complaint alleged only attempted monopolization, which involves three distinct elements: "(1) the defendant has engaged in predatory or anticompetitive conduct with (2) a specific intend to monopolize and (3) a dangerous probability of achieving monopoly power."

Like claims under Section One, Section Two claims require harm to competition that must occur within a "relevant," that is, a distinct market, with a specific set of geographical boundaries and a narrow delineation of the products at issue. . . . SBS explained that it considered the relevant market to be advertising purchased

in the top ten Spanish-language markets and that HBC earned 51 percent of the advertising revenue in that market. . . .

There is no question that CC does not participate in the Spanish-language radio market. Thus, CC cannot attempt to monopolize that market. SBS attempts to overcome this hurdle by pointing out that CC owns 26 percent of HBC, implying that this either makes CC an effective participant in the relevant market or at least gives CC sufficient control over HBC to permit attempted monopolization. We reject this contention. Absent allegations of significant control over the policies of a subsidiary, a minority ownership share does not convert a parent corporation into a competitor. . . . To be a competitor at the level of the subsidiary, the parent must have substantial control over the affairs and policies of the subsidiary.

As with Section One claims, conduct that injures individual firms rather than competition in the market as a whole does not violate Section Two. The Supreme Court has explained that "even an act of pure malice by one business competitor against another does not, without more, state a claim under the federal antitrust laws." . . .

Because SBS has not alleged any harm to competition in the market, nor explained how any of the actions taken by HBC could lead to monopolization of that market, SBS has not alleged anticompetitive conduct and thus has not stated a claim against HBC under Section Two. . . .

Affirmed.

QUESTIONS FOR ANALYSIS

1. The court focused on damage to competition in the market. What is the relevant product market that was under consideration?
2. If it is true that HBC lured away SBS employees, which weakened SBS's ability to compete, why was the court not concerned?

Mergers

Mergers are a source of monopolization concern. If competitor companies in a market merge, will competition be significantly injured? A *merger* involves two or more firms coming together to form a new firm. The combination can be created by one firm's acquiring all or part of the stock or the assets of another firm. A merger is termed a *horizontal merger* when the two firms were competitors before they merged (e.g., Exxon and Mobil). One of the most famous merger decisions, *Standard Oil*, established the rule of reason as the approach the courts use in judging merger activities.

Standard Oil Co. of New Jersey v. United States
United States Supreme Court
221 U.S. 1, 31 S.Ct. 502 (1911)

CASE BACKGROUND   *Claiming violations of Sections 1 and 2 of the Sherman Act, the Department of Justice sued seventy-one corporations and partnerships and seven individuals, including John D. Rockefeller, for conspiring "to restrain the trade and commerce in petroleum [in the United States] and to monopolize the said commerce." The conspiracy was traced back to 1870, when Rockefeller began to merge his company, Standard Oil of Ohio, with other oil companies and agreed with others to control all aspects of the petroleum business. Over the years, the companies were joined together in the Standard Oil Trust, which controlled as much as 90 percent of the production, shipping, refining, and selling of petroleum products. This allowed the trust to fix the price of oil and to monopolize interstate commerce in these products.*

The government requested, and the lower court ordered, that the trust be broken up so that companies would operate independently and compete with each other. After reviewing the complex background of this case, the Court explained the application of Sections 1 and 2 of the Sherman Act.

CASE DECISION   White, Chief Justice.

* * *

Having by the 1st section forbidden all means of monopolizing trade, that is, unduly restraining it by means of every contract, combination, etc., the 2d section seeks, if possible, to make the prohibitions of the act all the more complete and perfect by embracing all attempts to reach the end prohibited by the 1st section, that is, restraints of trade, by any attempt to monopolize, or monopolization thereof.

* * *

Because the unification of power and control over petroleum and its products which was the inevitable result of the combining in the Trust . . . of the stocks of so many other corporations, aggregating so vast a capital, gives rise, in and of itself, in the absence of countervailing circumstances, to say the least, to the prima facie presumption of intent and purpose to maintain the dominancy over the oil industry, not as a result of normal methods of industrial development, but by new means of combination which were resorted to in order that greater power might be added than would otherwise have arisen had normal methods been followed, the whole with the purpose of excluding others from the trade, and thus centralizing in the combination a perpetual control of the movements of petroleum and its products in the channels of interstate commerce.

* * *

To meet the situation with which we are confronted the application of remedies two-fold in character becomes essential: 1st. To forbid the doing in the future of acts like those which we have found to have been done in the past which would be violative of the statute. 2d. The exertion of such measure of relief as will effectually dissolve the combination found to exist in violation of the statute, and thus neutralize the extension and continually operating force which the possession of the power unlawfully obtained has brought and will continue to bring about.

Our conclusion is that the decree below was right and should be affirmed. . . .

QUESTIONS FOR ANALYSIS

1. Justice Harlan, who dissented in part, said the court should not use a rule of reason; all contracts in restraint of trade should be per se illegal. Is that practical?

2. Standard Oil controlled 90 percent of the market, yet the price of oil dropped consistently, thereby benefiting consumers. Should the court have taken this into account?

Before two firms merge, the Hart-Scott-Rodino Antitrust Improvements Act (HSR) requires the firms to notify the Antitrust Division of the Department of Justice or the Federal Trade Commission at least one month before the planned merger. The *premerger notification* requires payment of a filing fee.

Of the thousands of HSR notices filed each year, about 100 to 150 are subject to detailed examination by antitrust authorities, which may put the merger on hold while it is studied. The result may be that the merging firms agree to sell certain assets to allow the merger to go forward. For example, in several mergers of gasoline producers, the merged company was required to sell gas stations in some parts of the country where it would have had too much market power. Very few merger cases go to the courts for review. Most that are opposed, such as the proposed merger of Staples and Office Depot, are called off.

Determining Market Power

To help businesses and regulators assess the antitrust implications of a merger, over the years the Department of Justice has issued *merger guidelines*. Revised by Justice and the FTC in 1982, 1992, and 2000, the guidelines discuss factors that will be considered in determining whether a merger will likely be challenged (http://www.ftc.gov). Many of the factors considered important by the Supreme Court in merger cases over the years have been incorporated into the guidelines, which place particular importance on the notion of *market power:*

> The unifying theme of the Guidelines is that mergers should not be permitted to create or enhance *market power* or to facilitate its exercise. . . . The ability of one or more firms profitably to maintain prices above competitive levels for a significant period of time is termed *market power*.

Product and Geographic Markets

To assess a firm's market power in antitrust cases, the courts determine the *market share* held by the firms involved in the merger. A firm's market share refers to the percentage of the relevant market controlled by the firm.

Recall that the Clayton Act states that the legality of a merger between two firms rests on whether "in any line of commerce in any section of the country, the effect of such acquisition may be substantially to lessen competition, or tend to create a monopoly." The phrase "in any line of commerce" refers to the particular *product market* in which the firms operate. For example, banks may be both in the credit market and the checking account market. The phrase "in any section of the country" has reference to a *geographic market*. The relevant area may be one city or may be the nation. Therefore, in determining the *relevant market*, the courts and antitrust authorities take into account the appropriate product and geographic markets.

After determining the relevant market, a firm's market share can be determined by dividing the firm's sales by total sales within that market. In a merger case, the court will often consider whether the combined market share of the merging firms will exceed some maximum market share and will, therefore, "substantially . . . lessen competition" within the relevant market. The determination of the product and geographic markets can be very complex.

Potential Competition

Ordinarily one thinks of competitors as offering similar products in the same market area. If the companies do not compete in this sense, should the courts be concerned about a merger? The Supreme Court has stated that the *potential competition*

JURIS *prudence?*

Didn't We Just Sue Them Eighty Years Ago?

Kodak lost an antitrust case in 1915 that found the company "had monopolized the amateur camera, film, and photo-finishing industries" by anticompetitive practices. The matter was resolved in 1921 when Kodak signed a consent decree. The company sold some of its assets and agreed not to sell "private-label" film, that is, film under any name besides Kodak.

Years later, in 1995, Kodak was arguing to a federal court that it should be freed from the 1921 decree and allowed to sell private-label film. The government opposed releasing Kodak from the decree, arguing that Kodak may still be benefiting from "its illegal monopoly ninety years ago." The court found, however, that the film market is competitive. Kodak has 36 percent of world sales, followed by Fuji at 34 percent, Konica at 16 percent, Agfa at 10 percent, and 3M at 4 percent. Since Kodak "lacks market power" in the film market, it was released from the 1921 decree.

Source: *U.S. v. Kodak*, 63 F.3d 95 (1995)

(the possibility that two companies will become *competitors*) may be enough to stop a merger.

For example, in *United States* v. *El Paso Natural Gas*, 376 U.S. 651, a gas pipeline company with a large share of the natural gas market in California wanted to merge with a pipeline company that operated in the Northwest. The Court blocked the merger because the possibility that the northwestern company could move into California served as a check on El Paso's operations in California. The Court wanted El Paso to have the threat of strong potential competition that would be eliminated by the merger.

The idea of potential competition was also used in *FTC* v. *Procter & Gamble Co.*, 386 U.S. 568, in which Procter & Gamble, a large household products maker, wanted to merge with Clorox, the leading maker of liquid bleach. After finding that bleach was the relevant product market, the Supreme Court held that even though Procter & Gamble did not make bleach, it could not merge with Clorox, because Procter & Gamble could make bleach in the future. The Court wanted Clorox to face the threat of potential competition by a company like Procter & Gamble.

When Mergers Are Allowed

The Supreme Court has noted that if one of the firms involved in a merger is facing bankruptcy or other circumstances that threaten the firm, the Court will look more favorably upon the merger. This is called the *failing firm defense*. That defense was created by the courts. To use the defense, the merging firms must establish that

1. The firm being acquired is not likely to survive without the merger.
2. Either the firm has no other prospective buyers or, if there are other buyers, the acquiring firm will affect competition the least.
3. Other alternatives for saving the firm have been tried but not succeeded.

The merger guidelines also note that a major defense to a merger is the demonstration that it will enhance efficiency in the market, benefiting consumers by a better allocation of resources.

Considering Business Realities

The courts weigh economic evidence and, as a result, like the FTC and Justice Department, often find that mergers are not harmful to consumers. One defense used recently is the *power-buyer defense*. Under this defense, a merger that increases concentration to high levels can be defended by showing that the firm's customers are sophisticated and powerful buyers. If the court finds that powerful buyers have sufficient bargaining power to ensure that the merged firm will be unable to charge monopoly prices, the merger might be allowed.

For example, in *United States* v. *Baker Hughes*, 908 F.2d 981, the D.C. Circuit Court of Appeals denied the government's attempt to stop a merger of manufacturers of hardrock hydraulic underground drilling rigs. Even though this industry had few sellers, the court found that the sophisticated and powerful buyers of such drilling rigs—oil companies—had sufficient bargaining power to ensure that the merged firm would be unable to charge monopoly prices for its rigs.

CYBER *Law*

B2B Antitrust Concerns

Selling goods on the Internet has increased competition—retailers located anywhere have the potential to reach customers they could not have reached before. There are few antitrust issues in that regard. However, the growing use of the Internet for large buyers, such as Ford and Boeing, to obtain supplies in highly competitive markets has raised some concerns.

Many buyers use reverse auctions. The bidders post the lowest price at which they are willing to sell to the buyer who has announced how much of what is needed by when. The bidders see each others' bids and can change their bids up to the last second of the auction. The result

has been some substantial reductions in prices, and competition is very strong.

The FTC and the Department of Justice have stressed the need for competitors to use effective firewalls to prevent them from learning each other's sensitive information. Another issue has been the open nature of such bidding—where all bidders see each other's bids. The open records can increase the ability to collude, since all buyers or sellers can know what everyone else is bidding, and thereby know if someone is willing to sell for less than the colluders' agreed-upon price. Such information was much harder for colluders to obtain when bids were all sealed.

HORIZONTAL RESTRAINTS OF TRADE

When businesses at the same level of operation (such as retailers of a common product or producers of a raw material) come together (integrate) in some manner—through contract, merger, or conspiracy—they risk being accused of restraining trade. A *horizontal restraint of trade* occurs when the businesses involved operate at the same level of the market and generally in the same market. It is easy to visualize a horizontal arrangement among competitors by examining the diagram in Exhibit 19.1. For example, think of three manufacturers of lightbulbs who agree to charge the same price for bulbs or to split the market on a geographical basis.

The diagram could also show an arrangement among wholesalers or among retailers of a certain product. A collection of rival firms that come together by some form of agreement in an attempt to restrain trade by restricting output and raising prices is called a *cartel*. The most famous cartel of our day is the Organization of Petroleum Exporting Countries *(OPEC)*, the group of oil-producing nations that banded together

Horizontal Business Relationships

for the express purpose of controlling the output of oil and raising its price. Since that cartel consists of sovereign nations, American antitrust laws do not affect it. When private firms in the United States attempt to cartelize an industry, however, they are subject to antitrust law.

When firms selling the same product agree to fix prices, they are in a conspiracy and the agreement will almost certainly violate the Sherman Act. One question the Supreme Court must decide as a matter of policy is whether price-fixing is *per se illegal* or whether a *rule of reason* may be applied.

Price-Fixing

Many antitrust cases have concerned price-fixing. When firms sell the same product and agree to fix the price, they have formed a conspiracy that will likely violate the Sherman Act. Price-fixing has usually been held to be the worst violation of the antitrust laws. In a 1927 case, *U.S. v. Trenton Potteries*, 276 US 392, the Supreme Court held that when competitors get together to fix prices, there is a violation of the Sherman Act, whether the prices they set are reasonable or not. The Court decision held that agreements to set prices "may well be held to be in themselves unreasonable or unlawful restraints, without the necessity of minute inquiry whether a particular price is reasonable or unreasonable." That is, most price-fixing is a horizontal arrangement that is *per se* illegal. In the *Freeman* case we see a modern application of this principle.

Freeman v. San Diego Association of Realtors

United States Court of Appeals, Ninth Circuit
322 F.3d 1133 (2003)

CASE BACKGROUND   *In most cities, a Multiple Listing Service (MLS) is used by real estate agents to share information about properties on the market via a computerized database. Agents subscribe to the MLS to list the properties they represent, as well as to see information about other properties on the market.*

Before 1992, there were twelve such MLS associations in San Diego, California. The associations bought data services from four different database operators. Eleven of the MLS associations decided to combine so that all subscribing agents would have access to all San Diego properties; the combined database would also cost less to

maintain than separate databases. The new entity, owned by the eleven MLS associations, was called Sandicor. The eleven associations continued to sign up agents and collect subscription fees, but Sandicor set the rules. No price-cutting was allowed. When the MLSes compared costs, they discovered that the largest MLS spent $10 per month per subscriber, while two small ones spent $50 per month per subscriber. The fee for all was set at $44 per subscribing agent, paid to Sandicor. That price was less than the $50 cost per subscriber that the small operators incurred, so the lower-cost MLSes agreed to cover the losses that the smaller MLS associations incurred.

continues

Freeman and other San Diego real estate agents who subscribed to MLS sued. They contended that Sandicor's central database was beneficial and efficient, but that the price of Sandicor's services was inflated. A service that had cost $10 a month at some MLSes was now $44. Plantiffs contended that Sandicor was charging excessive service fees to the MLS members who ran Sandicor, and who passed on the higher prices to subscribing agents, allowing Sandicor to profit millions from excessive fees. Freeman offered Sandicor the opportunity to market the MLS information to subscribers through a new service center at lower prices than the existing associations charged, but Sandicor refused. Freeman sued for Sherman Act violations for a conspiracy in restraint of trade by fixing prices, a violation of Section 1. The district court dismissed the suite; plaintiffs appealed.

CASE DECISION   Kozinski, Circuit Judge.

* * *

No antitrust violation is more abominated than the agreement to fix prices. With few exceptions, price-fixing agreements are unlawful *per se* under the Sherman Act and . . . no showing of so-called competitive abuses or evils which those agreements were designed to eliminate or alleviate may be interposed as a defense." The dispositive question generally is not whether any price-fixing was justified, but simply whether it occurred. . . .

Sandicor charges subscribers for their use of the MLS; its MLS fee includes the support services provided by the associations. The support fee Sandicor in turns pays the associations for support services was fixed at a level more than twice what it cost the most efficient association to provide them. . . .

Were we to grant immunity from Section 1 merely because defendants nominally sell services through another entity rather than to consumers directly, we would risk opening a major loophole for . . . retailer collusion. . . . Sandicor charges MLS subscribers $44 per month; an association collects this fee from each subscriber and hands it over to Sandicor, which then returns $22.50 to the association as the support fee. . . . Defendants can't turn a horizontal agreement to fix prices into something innocuous just by changing the way they keep their books. . . .

Reversed and remanded.

QUESTIONS FOR ANALYSIS

1. Sandicor claimed that the quality of its data was better because all associations contributed data, and the subscribers got superior service. Why did that argument not matter?

2. Sandicor claimed that it helped competition because the smallest, highest-cost associations were kept in business because they were subsidized by the larger ones. Why was that argument rejected?

While the courts take a hard line against collusion for the purpose of rigging prices, any one company has the right to charge whatever price it wishes for its products or services. The courts also recognize that certain organizations, such as joint ventures, may help markets to work better. In some cases, a joint venture helps to set market prices, and if a court finds that a good reason exists for this, it will allow the practice to stand.

Consider the problem faced by the thousands of artists and owners of music copyrights who have the right to earn royalties when their music is played by thousands of radio stations and other commercial music users. Because the artists could not possibly contract with every user of their music, they join organizations such as Broadcast Music, Inc. (BMI), or the American Society of Composers, Authors and Publishers (ASCAP), which issue "blanket licenses" that set the fees to be paid by any commercial users of the music. In *Broadcast Music, Inc. v. CBS*, 441 U.S. 1, the Court held that blanket licensing in such situations is not illegal price-fixing because there is no other way for this market to work. Since the market works better than it would if BMI and ASCAP did not exist, the "price-fixing" is not illegal. But, in general, price-fixing is rarely found to be legal.

Exchanges of Information

One problem in antitrust law is deciding whether the trading of information among businesses helps or restrains the competitive process. Some business information is collected and shared by the government, but many exchanges are done by private organizations, such as trade associations of firms in the same industry. If a business knows its competitors' sales, production, planned or actual capacities, cost accounting, quality standards, and research developments, is competition enhanced or is the information likely to be used to restrain trade?

Information Sharing

The Supreme Court considered the issue of the sharing of information by competitors in *U.S. v. United States Gypsum Co.*, 438 U.S. 422. Six major producers of gypsum called each other to determine the price being offered on gypsum products to various customers. That is, a buyer would tell Company B that Company A had offered to sell gypsum board at a certain price. Company B would call Company A to confirm the offer to make sure the buyer was telling the truth. The gypsum companies defended the practice as a good-faith effort to meet competition.

The Court said that a rule of reason may be applied, but the practice was not defensible. In an industry with few producers, an exchange of price information by competitors would most likely help to set prices and so could not be justified. The Court did not apply a per se rule against such price information exchanges. Instead, it warned that such exchanges would be examined closely and would be allowed in limited circumstances.

We see an example of illegal information sharing by competitors in the *Todd* case.

Todd v. Exxon Corporation

United States Court of Appeals, Second Circuit
273 F.3d 191 (2001)

CASE BACKGROUND   *Fourteen large companies in the oil industry organized a system to conduct surveys of the salaries they each paid to managerial, professional, and technical (MPT) employees. They used a "Job Match Survey" to be sure that the jobs at each company were compared properly. Representatives of each company met regularly to discuss job classifications and other data issues. A consultant then analyzed, refined, and distributed the data to the fourteen firms. The firms used the data in setting the salaries of MPT employees.*

Todd and other employees sued, contending that the sharing of information was done to hold down MPT salaries. Plaintiffs contended this violated Section 1 of the Sherman Act. They did not claim that the companies conspired to fix wages, but that the sharing of information *allowed the employers to control wages more effectively than they could have without such information. The district court dismissed the suit. Plaintiffs appealed.*

CASE DECISION   Sotomayor, Circuit Judge.

* * *

Traditional "hard-core" price-fixing remains *per se* unlawful. . . . If the plaintiff in this case could allege that defendants actually formed an agreement to fix MPT salaries, this *per se* rule would likely apply. Furthermore, even in the absence of direct "smoking gun" evidence, a horizontal price-fixing agreement may be inferred on the basis of conscious parallelism, when such interdependent conduct is accompanied by

continues

circumstantial evidence and plus factors such as defendants' use of facilitating practices. Information exchange is an example of a facilitating practice that can help support an inference of a price-fixing agreement. . . .

The [Supreme Court has explained]: "The exchange of price data and other information among competitors does not invariably have anticompetitive effects; indeed such practices can in certain circumstances increase economic efficiency and render markets more, rather than less, competitive." . . .

Plaintiff argues that the relevant market in this case is the market for "the services of experienced, salaried, non-union, managerial, professional, and technical (MPT) employees in the oil and petrochemical industry, in the continental United States and various submarkets therof." If the market is defined in this way, defendants would have a substantial market share of 80–90 percent. . . .

The traditional horizontal conspiracy case involves an agreement among sellers with the purpose of raising prices to supracompetitive levels. The Sherman Act, however, also applies to abuse of market power on the buyer side—often taking the form of monopsony or oligopsony. Plaintiff is correct to point out that a horizontal conspiracy among buyers to stifle competition is as unlawful as one among sellers. . . . There is thus no reason to doubt that a . . . data exchange claim—a close cousin of traditional price-fixing—can be brought against a group of buyers. . . .

If . . . the plaintiff in this case could prove that (1) defendants engaged in information exchanges that would be deemed anticompetitive . . . and (2) such activities did in fact have an anticompetitive effect on the market for MPT labor in the oil and petrochemical industry, we would not deny relief. . . . On remand, therefore, the court should consider whether plaintiff has demonstrated anticompetitive effects as part of the court's assessment of defendants' market power. . . .

Another important factor to consider in evaluating an information exchange is whether the data are made publicly available. Public dissemination is a primary way for data exchange to realize its procompetitive potential. . . . Access to information may better equip buyers to compare products, rendering the market more efficient while diminishing the anticompetitive effects of the exchange. A court is therefore more likely to approve a data exchange where the information is made public.

In the instant case, dissemination of the information to the employees could have helped mitigate any anticompetitive effects of the exchange and possibly enhanced market efficiency by making employees more sensitive to salary increases. No such dissemination occurred, however. The information was not disclosed to the public nor to the employees whose salaries were the subject of the exchange. . . .

Remanded.

QUESTIONS FOR ANALYSIS

1. Wage information is often gathered and published. Why is it normally legal?

2. The district court held that the oil companies did not control the MPT market, but that contention was rejected by the appeals court. Why might that court see it differently?

Conspiracy to Restrict Information

Although the courts have indicated that it is generally legal to share price information in an open manner and it is illegal to share information secretly among competitors or for the purpose of constructing a common price list for competitors, it may also be illegal to band together to restrict certain nonprice information.

In the Supreme Court decision *FTC v. Indiana Federation of Dentists*, 476 U.S. 447, the Court held that the FTC justifiably attacked the policy of an Indiana dentists' organization requiring members to withhold X rays from dental insurance companies. Insurance companies sometimes required dentists to submit patient X rays to help evaluate patients' claims for insurance benefits. The X rays helped the companies eliminate insurance fraud and make sure that dentists did not prescribe dental work not required. The FTC attack on this policy was upheld under a rule of reason analysis that showed the dentists' policy to be a conspiracy in restraint of trade. The Court noted that no procompetitive reason for the anti–X-ray-sharing rule was found.

We're Lawyers, and We're Here to Help You

Nineteen lawyers teamed together to bring a class-action antitrust suit on behalf of consumers against three gasoline retailers in Dothan, Alabama. In a trial that lasted six weeks in federal court, the jury found that there was a conspiracy to fix gasoline prices. Damages were found to be $1. However, under the law, the guilty party is also responsible for attorney's fees. The judge granted the attorneys $2 million in legal fees for their diligent efforts.

Source: *Associated Press*

Territorial Restrictions

A horizontal market division occurs when firms competing at the same level of business reach an agreement to divide the market on geographic or other terms. The effect of the agreement is to eliminate competition among those firms. Firms competing in a national market, for example, may reach an agreement to divide the market into regional markets, with each firm being assigned one region. Each firm can then exercise monopoly power within its region.

Agreements intended to provide horizontal customer or *territorial allocations* are often held to violate antitrust law. When the agreement does not involve price-fixing by the firms participating in the agreement, the case may be considered under a rule of reason; that is, each challenged agreement will be evaluated in light of its effect on consumer welfare. This has not been a common basis for antitrust cases in recent years.

ISSUE
Spotter

Share and Share Alike

Your customers, retail housing construction supply firms, tell you that the price your pipe production company is asking for PVC pipe is too high and that they will be taking their business elsewhere. The profit margins are thin, and you are not interested in cutting prices unless it is absolutely necessary to retain business. When you go to the annual PVC pipe makers convention, how might you legally find out what your competitors are charging? What type of action would be most likely to get you into trouble with the antitrust authorities?

VERTICAL RESTRAINT OF TRADE

Until now, we have considered antitrust law mostly as it applies to horizontal restraints of trade. We now turn to antitrust issues such as vertical restraint of trade, exclusionary practices, and price discrimination. *Vertical restraint of trade* concerns relationships between buyers and sellers, such as between the manufacturer and its wholesalers or the wholesalers and retailers. A key subject of this part of the chapter is how firms deal with each other along the business chain. We look at how producers', distributors', and retailers' dealings are controlled by antitrust law.

Vertical business arrangements govern relationships in the different stages of the production, distribution, and sale of the same product, as we see in Exhibit 19.2. For example, think of a manufacturer that imposes resale restrictions on the retailers. The producer tells the retailer the price it must set at retail (the resale price), the area in which there may be resales, or who the retailer's customers may be. Since these arrangements may restrain competition, they may be challenged as being contrary to the goals of antitrust law.

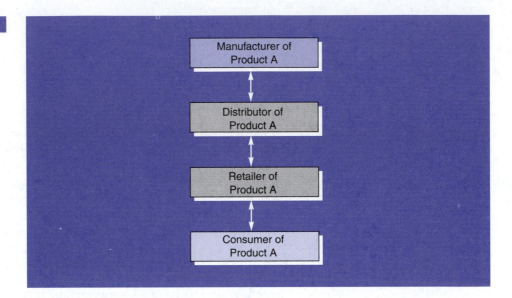

A company that does more than one function internally, such as manufacturing and distribution, is not constrained by the antitrust laws. However, a group of firms doing business at different levels in a given product are prohibited from engaging in certain practices.

Vertical Price-Fixing

Vertical price-fixing arrangements involve agreements between a manufacturer, its wholesalers, its distributors or other suppliers, and the retailers that sell the product to consumers. As a rule, these are intended to control the price at which the product is sold to consumers. In many cases, it has been the retailers that approach the manufacturer and request a price agreement. In other instances, the manufacturer requires the wholesaler (supplier) to control the price being charged by retailers. Agreements can call for the retailer to fix minimum prices or maximum prices.

Resale Price Maintenance

Resale price maintenance (RPM) is an agreement between a manufacturer, a supplier, and retailers of a product under which the retailers agree to sell the product at not less than a minimum price. One purpose of these arrangements is to prevent retailers from cutting the price of a brand-name product. Although manufacturers contend that such arrangements make product distribution more efficient, such arrangements can be illegal restraint of trade.

Dr. Miles *Case*   In 1911 the Supreme Court pronounced a basic rule about RPM. It stated that once a producer or supplier sells a product to a retailer, it cannot control the price the retailer will charge consumers. In *Dr. Miles Medical Co.* v. *John D. Park & Sons Co.*, 220 U.S. 373, a producer of patented medicines sold its products to wholesalers and told them the price they must charge to retailers and, then, the price retailers must charge customers. Any wholesaler or retailer who would not follow the pricing scheme set by Dr. Miles would be cut off from further sales. The court held that a manufacturer can, of course, sell its product for whatever it wants, but it cannot "fix prices for future sales." That is, it cannot set prices further down the sales chain.

Pros and Cons of Resale Price Maintenance   RPM has been the subject of political wrangling in Congress and of debate by lawyers and economists since the time of *Dr. Miles*. The groups favoring the ability to control resale prices have been the producers of quality, well-known products and small retailers. Opponents have been mass retailers and producers of lesser-known products.

Because small retailers favor RPM, they are more likely to have the same prices as the mass merchandisers. That is, most small retail stores cannot match Wal-Mart prices, so they would like to see all retailers forced to offer goods at the same prices. As we will see later in the chapter, this was one reason for passage of the Robinson-Patman Act. Even in the absence of competition from discount retailers, if the retailers are strong enough, they band together to demand that the producer impose RPM so that retailers will not compete with each other by price-cutting. RPM thus prevents cheating by members of the retail cartel.

Producers of well-known, established products (such as Sony televisions) may favor RPM because it allows retailers to earn higher profits from the sale of their products. These higher retail profits, in turn, encourage retailers to advertise the products more to customers and to give good service.

Mass retailers oppose RPM because they have grown large by slashing retail prices and taking customers away from smaller stores. The mass retailers often offer little point-of-sale service; their concern is selling a large volume of products at lower markup. Similarly, the producers of lesser-known brands want to compete on the basis of price, so they like the chance to be on the mass retailers' shelves with the best-known products. They have not incurred the high costs of establishing a good reputation, so their prices are lower even if the quality is good. If the result is that fewer full-service stores can afford to stay in business, RPM advocates claim that consumers and well-established brands may be worse off by the disappearance of the information and service that would be provided under an RPM arrangement.

Vertical Maximum Price-Fixing

While *Dr. Miles* is still good law in that producers may not completely control prices down the distribution chain, the Supreme Court has overruled a previous case that prohibited maximum price-fixing in vertical relationships.

In *State Oil Co.* v. *Khan*, 118 S.Ct. 275 (1997), a gasoline distributor controlled the maximum gasoline sales markup that its gasoline station dealers could charge customers. One gas station owner wanted to charge more for retail gasoline than the distributor would allow and sued, claiming this was illegal price-fixing. The Supreme Court upheld the maximum-price controls, noting that low prices benefit consumers regardless of how the prices are set. A rule of reason will be applied in such cases.

Vertical Nonprice Restraints

Manufacturers frequently impose nonprice restraints on their distributors and retailers. Such vertical arrangements often take the form of territorial or customer restrictions on the sale of the manufacturer's products. Coca-Cola and PepsiCo, for example, set *territorial restrictions* on their bottlers. Each bottler is permitted to sell and deliver the product within its designated territory. Delivery outside that territory—that is, delivery in competition with another bottler—is grounds for loss of the franchise agreement.

Customer restrictions may be imposed on distributors and retailers when the manufacturer sells directly to a certain customers. A construction materials manufacturer, for example, may deal directly with large commercial accounts but allow distributors to deal with smaller accounts. The courts apply the rule of reason in such cases.

Territorial Restraints and the Rule of Reason

In most territorial restraint cases, the plaintiff is a retailer or distributor that has been terminated by a manufacturer changing its product distribution strategy. The manufacturer often eliminates some distributors so that the remaining distributors have the necessary territorial or customer base to be successful.

Sharp Electronics is the Supreme Court's major holding on this issue. It reduces the likely success of distributors who sue manufacturers who refuse to sell to them. The decision encouraged some manufacturers to limit the distribution of their products to wholesalers and retailers that follow the marketing strategies of the parent company. Unless a conspiracy can be shown to exist or unless direct price-fixing is involved, manufacturers have significant control in selecting dealers to distribute their products.

Business Electronics Corp. v. Sharp Electronics Corp.

United States Supreme Court
485 U.S. 717, 108 S.Ct. 1515 (1988)

CASE BACKGROUND   *Sharp appointed Business Electronics and Hartwell as its retailers in Houston. Sharp published a list of suggested retail prices, but dealers were not contractually bound to follow those prices. Business Electronics sold Sharp calculators below Sharp's suggested minimum prices and below Hartwell's prices. Hartwell told Sharp that it would quit selling Sharp products unless Business Electronics was terminated as a Sharp dealer. Sharp terminated Business Electronics, which then sued Sharp for conspiracy under Section 1 of the Sherman Act. The district court held Sharp to be guilty of a per se violation of the Sherman Act. The court of appeals reversed, applying the rule of reason. Business Electronics appealed to the Supreme Court.*

CASE DECISION   Scalia, Justice.

* * *

Without an agreement with the remaining dealer on price, the manufacturer both retains its incentive to cheat on any manufacturer-level cartel (since lower prices can still be passed on to consumers) and cannot as easily be used to organize and hold together a retailer-level cartel. . . .

Any agreement between a manufacturer and a dealer to terminate another dealer who happens to have charged lower prices can be alleged to have been directed against the terminated dealer's "price cutting." In the vast majority of cases, it will be extremely difficult for the manufacturer to convince a jury that its motivation was to ensure adequate services, since price cutting and some measure of service cutting usually go hand in hand. Accordingly, a manufacturer that agrees to give one dealer an exclusive territory and terminates another dealer pursuant to that agreement, or even a manufacturer that agrees with one dealer to terminate another for failure to provide contractually obligated services, exposes itself to the highly plausible claim that its real motivation was to terminate a price cutter. Moreover, even vertical restraints that do not result in dealer termination, such as the initial granting of an exclusive territory or the requirement that certain services be provided, can be attacked as designed to allow existing dealers to charge higher prices. Manufacturers would be likely to forgo legitimate and competitively useful conduct rather than risk treble damages and perhaps even criminal penalties. . . .

As the above discussion indicates, all vertical restraints . . . have the potential to allow dealers to increase "prices" and can be characterized as intended to achieve just that. In fact, vertical nonprice restraints . . . reduce intrabrand price competition to the point where the dealer's profit margin permits provision of the desired services. . . . "The manufacturer often will want to ensure that its distributors earn sufficient profit to pay for programs such as hiring and training additional salesmen or demonstrating the technical features of the product, and will want to see that 'free-riders' do not interfere."

* * *

In sum, economic analysis supports the view, and no precedent opposes it, that a vertical restraint is not illegal per se unless it includes some agreement on price or price levels. Accordingly, the judgment of the [appeals court] is Affirmed.

QUESTIONS FOR ANALYSIS
1. Why was this case not treated as an RPM? In what way was this case different from an RPM case?
2. Does this decision mean that producers will have more control over retailers, or does it mean that more terms of trade will be settled by contract than was the case before?

Sharp indicates that retail dealers and manufacturers are free to discuss ways in which the profitability of both parties will be improved by business practices so long as there is no clear evidence of collusion in fixing retail prices. If several retailers sell the same brand of product in an area, the manufacturer may work with the retailers to encourage practices that strengthen consumer satisfaction with its brand. If a manufacturer wants retailers to invest in service departments and other extras, discount dealers, who will not incur the costs of such extras, will likely be dropped from the list of retailers as a consequence. The courts are more concerned with interbrand competition than intrabrand competition.

Exclusionary Practices

A principal concern of the antitrust laws is the extent to which firms with market power can control the markets in which they do business. Various business practices are designed to make it more difficult for competitors to challenge the market dominance of the firm using such tactics. Such practices, which include tying arrangements, exclusive-dealing agreements, and boycotts, can come under antitrust attack if the courts find them to be anticompetitive. Section 3 of the Clayton Act applies to tying arrangements and exclusive-dealing agreements involving goods, while Section 1 of the Sherman Act, which covers goods and services, governs the antitrust aspects of group boycotts.

Tying Arrangements

In *Northern Pacific Railway Company* v. *United States*, 356 U.S. 1, the Supreme Court defined a *tying arrangement* or *tie-in sale* as

> an agreement by a party to sell one product [the tying product] but only on the condition that the buyer also purchases a different [complementary or tied] product, or at least agrees that he will not purchase that product from any other supplier.

The Supreme Court holds that where monopoly power exists, tying arrangements violate the antitrust laws; the arrangement extends a firm's market power over the tying product into the market for the tied product. The courts apply either Section 1 of the Sherman Act—viewing tying arrangements as an unreasonable restraint of trade—or Section 3 of the Clayton Act—viewing tying arrangements as a sales contract that may substantially lessen competition or tend to create a monopoly.

The practice of tying products together is found in other, generally legal, business practices. A grocery store, for example, that offers Brand A flour at half price when a buyer purchases a bag of Brand A sugar is conducting a legal tie-in sale because Brand A and the grocery store have no monopoly power over either product.

Rule of Reason Applied to Tie-In Cases   The Supreme Court has held that tie-ins meet a rule of reason test so long as competitive alternatives exist. That is, if a tie-in creates a monopoly when there are no or few good alternatives, it is likely illegal; but if products or services are tied together when there are competitors, the tie-in will likely pass the rule of reason test, as the Court held in *U.S. Steel Corp.* v. *Fortner Enterprises*, 429 U.S. 610.

U.S. Steel produced mobile homes. Fortner needed $2 million to develop land on which to place mobile homes that he promised to buy from U.S. Steel if it would loan him the money. U.S. Steel made the loan. Later, Fortner's venture failed, and he claimed the contract with U.S. Steel violated antitrust law because there was a tie-in between the purchase of homes and the financing. The mobile homes were the product tied to U.S. Steel's alleged power over the credit market. The Court rejected that argument, holding that U.S. Steel, while large, had no monopoly power over credit or over mobile homes, which are in highly competitive markets. Since the tie-in did not exploit any monopoly power, the actions of U.S. Steel did not violate the antitrust law under a rule of reason analysis.

INTERNATIONAL *Perspective*

Merging of EU and U.S. Antitrust Law

As large firms are increasingly global in operations, the laws of other nations take on more importance. When General Electric and Honeywell planned to merge, the merger was approved by U.S. antitrust authorities but was prohibited by the European Union's antitrust watchdog, the European Commission (EC). Since portions of the proposed company would be unable to operate in Europe, the merger was called off.

While the EC has been tougher on mergers than has the Department of Justice or the FTC, the EC changed its rules on exclusive dealings, territorial restrictions, and resale price maintenance to become more like the United States. Previously, firms operating in Europe often had to adopt distribution practices significantly different from the ones used in the United States, but now it is possible to have more similar practices in both markets.

Dropping rigid rules that prohibited certain business practices, the EC will, like U.S. authorities, look more at evidence about market power that is anticompetitive, rather than simply declare whole classes of practices to be illegal. However, since rules are now less black-and-white, it will mean more careful evaluation of marketing strategies by firms moving into Europe.

Vertical Restraint Guidelines

The Department of Justice's *Vertical Restraint Guidelines* claim that the Supreme Court is likely to impose a per se rule of illegality only when three conditions are met:

1. The seller has market power in the tying product.
2. Tied and tying products are separate.
3. There is evidence of substantial adverse effect in the tied product market.

In other situations, the rule of reason approach is to be employed. The Justice Department said that in such cases, the following test would hold:

> The use of tying will not be challenged if the party imposing the tie has a market share of 30 percent or less in the market for the tying product. This presumption can be overcome only by a showing that the tying agreement unreasonably restrained competition in the market for the tied product.

The Supreme Court found an illegal tie-in arrangement in *Eastman Kodak Co.* v. *Image Technical Services* (504 U.S. 451). Kodak, a maker of complex equipment, refused to sell replacement parts for its machines to independent companies that offered repair and maintenance service on the machines. Kodak required buyers of its machines to use its repair personnel in order to obtain Kodak replacement parts. Independent repair companies lost business and some went out of business. The Court held that Kodak used its market power over the machines to extend the power to replacement parts. That would not be allowed unless Kodak could show that the practice promoted competition in the market for the machinery.

Boycotts

A *boycott* occurs when a group conspires to prevent the carrying on of business or to harm a business. It can be promoted by any group—consumers, union members, retailers, wholesalers, or suppliers—who, when acting together, can inflict economic damage on a business. The boycott is used to force compliance with a price-fixing scheme or some other restraint of trade. Boycott cases usually fall under the per se rule against price-fixing.

Unlike other vertical restrictions where one manufacturer negotiates with individual dealers about terms of trade for its goods, boycotts involve either all manufacturers getting together to tell dealers what they must do, or all dealers getting together to tell manufacturers what they must do. In 1990, the Supreme Court reiterated that when horizontal competitors use a boycott to force a change in the nature of a vertical relationship, there is a per se violation of the law.

FTC v. Superior Court Trial Lawyers Association

United States Supreme Court
493 U.S. 411, 110 S.Ct. 768 (1990)

CASE BACKGROUND *Under the Criminal Justice Act (CJA), a group of about 100 lawyers in private practice regularly acted as court-appointed attorneys for criminal defendants in the District of Columbia. The attorneys belonged to the Superior Court Trial Lawyers Association (SCTLA), a private organization. Their fees*

continues

for legal work ($30 per hour for court time, $20 per hour for out-of-court time) were paid by the District of Columbia on behalf of their clients. The average annual income for the attorneys from this work was $45,000 in 1982 (about $85,000 in 2005 dollars). The SCTLA demanded that the District of Columbia double its fees. When this did not happen, the SCTLA organized a boycott. The attorneys boycotted the criminal courts of the District, which nearly brought the system to a stop. After two weeks, the District raised attorney fees to $35 per hour for all work and promised to double the original fees as demanded as soon as possible.

The FTC charged the SCTLA with a conspiracy to fix prices and to conduct a boycott that constituted unfair methods of competition. The Commission ruled that the boycott was illegal per se. The court of appeals reversed the FTC, holding that the boycott was a political expression protected by the First Amendment. The Supreme Court reviewed the decision.

CASE DECISION   Stevens, Justice.

* * *

Prior to the boycott CJA lawyers were in competition with one another, each deciding independently whether and how often to offer to provide services to the District at CJA rates. The agreement among the CJA lawyers was designed to obtain higher prices for their services and was implemented by a concerted refusal to serve an important customer in the market for legal services and, indeed, the only customer in the market for the particular services that CJA regulars offered. "This constriction of supply is the essence of 'price-fixing,' whether it be accomplished by agreeing upon a price, which will decrease the quantity demanded, or by agreeing upon an output, which will increase the price offered." The horizontal arrangement among these competitors was unquestionably a "naked restraint" on price and output.

* * *

The *per se* rules in antitrust law serve purposes analagous to *per se* restrictions upon, for example, stunt flying in congested areas or speeding. Laws prohibiting stunt flying or setting speed limits are justified by the State's interest in protecting human life and property. . . .

So it is with boycotts and price-fixing. Every such horizontal arrangement among competitors poses some threat to the free market. . . .

Of course, some boycotts and some price-fixing agreements are more pernicious than others; some are only partly successful, and some may not succeed when they are buttressed by other causative factors, such as political influence. But an assumption that, absent proof of market power, the boycott disclosed by this record was totally harmless—when overwhelming testimony demonstrated that it almost produced a crisis in the administration of criminal justice in the District and when it achieved its economic goal—is flatly inconsistent with the clear course of our antitrust jurisprudence. Conspirators need not achieve the dimensions of a monopoly, or even a degree of market power any greater than that already disclosed by this record, to warrant condemnation under the antitrust laws.

* * *

The judgment of the Court of Appeals is accordingly reversed insofar as that court held the *per se* rules inapplicable to the lawyers' boycott.

QUESTIONS FOR ANALYSIS

1. The lawyers claimed that their freedom of speech was repressed by the antitrust laws—that is, that their First Amendment rights to gather for political expression were hurt. Is there merit to this argument?

2. Is there a difference between horizontal and vertical price-fixing?

THE ROBINSON-PATMAN ACT

The Robinson-Patman Act, enacted in 1936, amends the Clayton Act. Section 2(a) states that "it shall be unlawful for any person engaged in commerce . . . to discriminate in price between different purchasers of commodities of like grade and quality . . . where the effect of such discrimination may be substantially to lessen competition or tend to create a monopoly in any line of commerce." Thus, a seller is said to engage in *price discrimination* when the same product is sold to different buyers at different prices.

Section 2(a) is perhaps the most controversial part of antitrust law, as the reason for its passage was to limit the ability of chain stores to offer merchandise at a price lower than their single-store competitors. The intent of the Act is to deny consumers the benefits from lower prices that result from mass merchandising. As a consequence, the Department of Justice and the FTC have been reluctant to enforce the Act. Most cases brought under the Robinson-Patman Act are private actions.

Price Discrimination

Many cases brought under the Robinson-Patman Act concern a firm charging different prices in different markets or bulk sale discounts given to larger volume retailers. To illustrate, suppose that two sellers—Allen's Wholesale and Ceplo Distributors—sell the same product in competition with each other in San Francisco. Allen's also sells the product in Oakland, but Ceplo does not. If Allen's reduces its price levels in San Francisco but not in Oakland, that price cut may violate the Robinson-Patman Act. Allen's is engaging in price discrimination—charging different prices in different markets to the detriment of a competitor, which in this case is Ceplo.

Predatory Pricing

The business practice just described is sometimes called *predatory pricing*. That is, Allen's attempts to undercut Ceplo in San Francisco and sells the product for a higher price in other markets in which it does not compete with Ceplo. Presumably, Allen's intends to drive Ceplo from the San Francisco market and then raise prices there when Ceplo goes out of business.

Firms can file suits alleging predatory pricing under both the Robinson-Patman Act and Section 2 of the Sherman Act. However, because it is difficult to distinguish predatory prices from prices driven low by competition, the Supreme Court today is reluctant to rule in favor of plaintiffs alleging predation.

To win, a plaintiff must present strong evidence showing that

1. The defendant priced below cost.
2. The defendant's below-cost prices created a genuine prospect that the defendant would monopolize the market.
3. The defendant would enjoy its monopoly at least long enough to recoup the losses it suffered during the price war.

The Court puts this heavy burden on predatory-pricing plaintiffs because it understands that firms might otherwise sue their price-cutting rivals for no reason other than to keep these rivals from lowering prices to competitive levels. As the Court said in *Brooke Group* (113 S.Ct. 2578), "It would be ironic indeed if the standards for predatory pricing liability were so low that antitrust suits themselves became a tool for keeping prices high."

Volume Discounts Legal?

The Robinson-Patman Act is also concerned with sales discounts given to large-volume retailers. To illustrate, suppose Allen's and Ceplo both buy the same product from Central Distributors for the purpose of selling it retail. Because Allen's is a larger-volume retailer, Central gives Allen's a price discount on its larger bulk purchases. The price discount gives Allen's a competitive advantage over Ceplo in the sale of the product to customers in the area. The alleged injury to competition is the price discount given to Allen's, the larger purchaser. This type of action generates numerous private actions against producers who discriminate in pricing to wholesalers or retailers.

Who Do You Sell What to, and for How Much?

ISSUE
Spotter

Your company sells appliances. You handle the selling of refrigerators to retailers. Your Big Box model has a wholesale price of $629, plus actual shipping cost. Home Depot calls and wants to buy 20,000 Big Box units over ten months. Bob's Home Store calls and wants to buy ten Big Box units over ten months. Home Depot wants a discount because of the size of its order. Can you give them a discount? What about Bob's? How might Robinson-Patman apply?

Defenses

A key defense for firms charged with violating the Robinson-Patman Act is to show a *cost justification* for different prices charged in different markets or to different buyers. An obvious cost-justification defense is a difference in transportation costs—it costs more to deliver a refrigerator three hundred miles than fifty miles. Similarly, on a per unit basis, it is cheaper to deliver one thousand refrigerators than it is to deliver five refrigerators. The major problem with using the cost-justification defense is that it is virtually an accounting impossibility to assign specific costs of production to individual products. As a consequence, the cost-justification defense is rarely successful by itself.

The other defense that may be used is that of *meeting competition*. That is, a firm cuts its price in response to a competitor's cutting its price first. The problem with this defense can be that the original price cut will be held illegal under Robinson-Patman, which will mean that subsequent price cuts may also be illegal, at least at some point. Competitors must show that the meeting-competition price cut was done in good faith, not in an effort to injure competitors but to stay competitive. In the *Texaco* decision, the Supreme Court reaffirmed that price discrimination may violate Robison-Patman.

Texaco v. Hasbrouck

United States Supreme Court
496 U.S. 543 110 S.Ct. 2535 (1990)

CASE BACKGROUND   *Texaco sold gasoline to Hasbrouck (Rick's Texaco) and other independent Texaco gas stations. Texaco also sold gasoline to Gull and Dompier at lower prices. Gull sold the gasoline under the Gull name. Dompier sold the gasoline under the Texaco brand name. Because Gull and Dompier paid less for their gasoline, they sold it for less at retail and grew rapidly. Sales at Rick's Texaco and the other independent*

Texaco stations dropped from 76 percent to 49 percent of Texaco retail sales in the area.

Dompier used his own tanker trucks to pick up gasoline from Texaco's plant. The independent dealers asked Texaco if they could hire their own tanker trucks to pick up the gasoline and pay the same price as Dompier and Gull. Texaco said no.

Hasbrouck and other independent Texaco station owners sued Texaco for violating Section 2(a) of the Robinson-Patman Act, alleging that Texaco's discounts to Dompier and Gull were illegal. The trial court awarded treble damages to Hasbrouck, and the court of appeals affirmed. Texaco appealed, claiming that the lower prices charged to Dompier and Gull were legal "functional" discounts, that is, "discounts given to a purchaser based on its role in the supplier's distribution system that reflect the cost of the services performed by the purchaser for the supplier."

CASE DECISION   Stevens, Justice.

* * *

The Robinson-Patman Act contains no express reference to functional discounts. It does contain two affirmative decisions that provide protection for two categories of discounts—those that are justified by savings in the seller's cost of manufacture, delivery or sale, and those that represent a good faith response to the equally low prices of a competitor. As the case comes to us, neither of those defenses is available to Texaco.

In order to establish a violation of the Act, respondents had the burden of proving four facts: (1) that Texaco's sales to Gull and Dompier were made in interstate commerce; (2) that the gasoline sold to them was of the same grade and quality as that sold to respondents; (3) that Texaco discriminated in price as between Gull and Dompier on the one hand and Hasbrouck on the other; and (4) that the discrimination had a prohibited effect on competition. Moreover, for Hasbrouck to recover damages, he had the burden of proving the extent of his actual injuries.

The first two elements of Hasbrouck's case are not disputed in this Court, and we do not understand Texaco to be challenging the sufficiency of Hasbrouck's proof of damages. Texaco does argue, however, (1) that although it charged different prices, it did not "discriminate in price" within the meaning of the Act, and (2) that, at least to the extent that Gull and Dompier acted as wholesalers, the price differentials did not injure competition. We consider the two arguments separately.

Texaco's first argument would create a blanket exemption for all functional discounts. Indeed, carried to its logical conclusion, it would exempt all price differentials except those given to competing purchasers. . . . We remain persuaded that the argument is fore-

closed by the text of the Act itself. In the context of a statute that plainly reveals a concern with competitive consequences at different levels of distribution, and carefully defines specific affirmative defenses, it would be anomalous to assume that the Congress intended the term "discriminate" to have such a limited meaning. . . .

Since we have already decided that a price discrimination within the meaning of §2(a) "is merely a price difference," we must reject Texaco's first argument.

* * *

[In its second argument, Texaco asserts that the price differentials did not injure competition.] A supplier need not satisfy the rigorous requirements of the cost justification defense in order to prove that a particular functional discount is reasonable and accordingly did not cause any substantial lessening of competition between a wholesaler's customers and the supplier's direct customers. The record in this case, however, adequately supports the finding that Texaco violated the Act.

. . . A price differential "that merely accords due recognition and reimbursement for actual marketing functions" is not illegal. In this case, however, both the District Court and the Court of Appeals concluded that even without viewing the evidence in the light most favorable to Hasbrouck, there was no substantial evidence indicating that the discounts to Gull and Dompier constituted a reasonable reimbursement for the value to Texaco of their actual marketing functions. Indeed, Dompier was separately compensated for its hauling function, and neither Gull nor Dompier maintained any significant storage facilities.

* * *

The judgment is Affirmed.

QUESTIONS FOR ANALYSIS

1. Suppose Texaco could show that the result of its pricing decision was to make the retail gasoline market more competitive in Spokane, thereby helping consumers. Would that be a defense?

2. Texaco claimed that Dompier and Gull were wholesale distributors, while Hasbrouck was a retailer. Texaco justified the price difference because it was selling to wholesalers versus selling to retailers. Is this a plausible defense?

SUMMARY

- The three most important antitrust statutes—the Sherman Act of 1890, the Clayton Act of 1914, and the FTC Act of 1914—were enacted in response to concern about the economic power of the large industrial corporations and trusts that emerged during the late nineteenth century. Before the enactment of the statutes, common-law precedent was relied on to combat certain restraints of trade, but the government had little authority to intervene.

- Congress exempts labor unions and others from the antitrust laws. The state action doctrine allows states to regulate business in such a way as to fix prices or otherwise monopolize a market.

- Violations of the antitrust laws can expose defendants to criminal penalties, which can include prison sentences, as well as civil penalties. Defendants who lose antitrust suits in which damages are found must pay treble damages. The antitrust laws are enforced by the Antitrust Division of the Justice Department, the Federal Trade Commission, and private parties. Only the Justice Department can bring criminal charges for alleged antitrust violations.

- Most antitrust matters are determined by a rule of reason analysis, where the courts weigh the pros and cons of business practices alleged to be anticompetitive. Some practices, such as price-fixing by competitors, are so clearly anticompetitive that they are declared to be per se illegal.

- Horizontal restraints of trade occur when business competitors at the same level of business, such as producers of similar products, agree to act together.

- Mergers of competitor companies are likely to be challenged only if the merger would significantly reduce competition in a market. The market is defined along both territory and product lines.

- Independent companies in the same industry are usually not allowed to agree to segregate the market geographically, by type of customer, or in any other arrangement that reduces competition.

- Horizontal price-fixing occurs when competitors agree to act together to set prices for their products or services. This can happen at any level of operation and is usually per se illegal.

- There is no defense for companies in the same industry that get together, by any means, to agree on product prices in the markets in which they operate. Prices may not be fixed at any level by competitors unless there are special circumstances that make the arrangement procompetitive, which is rare.

- Companies in an industry may share price and other market information through a trade association so long as the information is not used to control the market and the information is available to the public.

- Vertical relationships are between sellers and buyers at different levels of business, such as between manufacturer and distributor. Vertical restraints of trade occur when a firm at one level of business controls the practices of a firm at another level, such as a distributor telling a retailer what price to charge its customers for its products.

- Vertical price-fixing, or resale price maintenance, where the producer tells the retailers of its products the minimum prices at which to sell the products, is per se illegal. Suggested retail prices are legal but may not be enforced by a threat to cut off a retailer who will not adhere to them.

- Vertical nonprice restraints, such as granting exclusive territory to dealers, are viewed under a rule of reason. Manufacturers are given wide latitude in picking dealers and deciding the terms under which they will retain them. The producer may not conspire with a dealer against another dealer.

- Tie-in sales, where the sale of one product is tied to the sale of another, are judged under a rule of reason. For such a sale to be illegal, it must be shown that monopoly power in one product existed and was extended to the other product.
- When any organized group at one level of business (such as hardware store owners) gets together to agree to a joint action (such as refusal to deal) against one or more businesses at another level of business (such as a particular hardware supplier), such action is a boycott, which is usually per se illegal.
- The Robinson-Patman Act holds that price discrimination—selling the same product to different buyers at different prices—must be justified by differences in the cost of selling to the different buyers or because the price difference was required to meet competition. This is one of the most troublesome areas of law for producers, since hundreds of private lawsuits are filed each year by unhappy buyers (usually retailers) claiming they were discriminated against. The courts are not sympathetic to such cases, but they pose expensive problems that can be avoided by careful planning with legal counsel.

REVIEW AND DISCUSSION QUESTIONS

1. Define the following terms:

per se rule	territorial allocations
rule of reason	vertical restraint of trade
horizontal restraint of trade	resale price maintenance
market share	tying arrangement
potential competition	boycott
failing firm defense	price discrimination
horizontal price-fixing	

2. Why was the Sherman Act written in such broad language? Is it possible that Congress wrote the legislation in an unclear manner to give the courts broad leeway in attacking monopolistic business practices? Would it have been better for Congress to have specified more of the terms of antitrust violations?

3. The courts use a rule of reason in looking at territorial restrictions. Why should there be any concern about territorial restrictions? So long as there is competition between brands, is not that more important than intrabrand competition by the sellers of a product in a given geographic market? That is, can you think of cases in which intrabrand competition might be more important than interbrand competition?

CASE QUESTIONS

4. Many professional engineers belong to a trade association called the National Society of Professional Engineers that governs the nontechnical aspects of the practice of engineering. The canon of ethics adopted by the society held that engineers could not bid against one another for a particular job. The society claimed that this rule was to prevent engineers from engaging in price-cutting to get engineering jobs, which could then give them incentives to cut corners on the quality of work to save time and resources. Such a practice could lead

591 PART 3 THE REGULATORY ENVIRONMENT OF BUSINESS

to inferior work that could endanger the public. The Justice Department sued, claiming that this was a violation of Section 1 of the Sherman Act. The government claimed that the ethical rule reduced price competition and gave an unfair advantage to engineers with well-established reputations. Who wins? [*National Society of Professional Engineers* v. *United States*, 98 S.Ct. 1355 (1978)]

5. Professional basketball players and their union sued the National Basketball Association (NBA) for various practices, such as the draft of college players and its salary-cap system. They claimed that this violated the antitrust law by restricting opportunities for professional basketball players. Could such practices survive a rule of reason analysis? [*NBA* v. *Williams*, 45 F.3d 684 (2nd Cir., 1995)]

 Check your answer at <http://meiners.westbuslaw.com>

6. Certified registered nurse anesthetists (CRNAs) sued a hospital and its doctors, claiming a violation of Section 1 of the Sherman Act, based on the hospital's staffing decision to terminate its contract with the CRNAs and instead use a group of physician anesthesiologists, a competitor, that would provide anesthesia services for the hospital at lower cost. The district court dismissed the case. Was that the correct decision? [*BCB Anesthesia Care* v. *Passavant Memorial Area Hospital*, 36 F.3d 664 (7th Cir., 1994)]

7. Several companies operated downhill ski facilities in Aspen, Colorado. They all sold a joint ticket that allowed skiers to ski at all facilities; the receipts were later divided according to various use rates. Eventually, one firm owned all the ski areas but one. This firm stopped issuing the joint ticket and instead issued a ticket good for all of its ski areas. The firm that owned only one ski facility saw its market share fall from 20 percent to 11 percent over a four-year period. It sued, claiming that the larger firm violated Section 2 of the Sherman Act by attempting to monopolize skiing by ending the joint ticket arrangement. Is the sale of the joint ticket a violation of the antitrust law? [*Aspen Skiing Company* v. *Aspen Highlands Skiing Corporation*, 472 U.S. 585, 105 S.Ct. 2847 (1985)]

 Check your answer at <http://meiners.westbuslaw.com>

8. For years the American Medical Association (AMA) stated that chiropractors were unscientific cult members. The Principles of Medical Ethics of the AMA said that a "physician should practice a method of healing founded on a scientific basis; and she should not voluntarily associate with anyone who violates this principle." This was the basis of medical discrimination against chiropractic until the AMA dropped these statements in 1980. Five chiropractors sued the AMA after 1980, claiming that the effect of the past actions had "lingering effects" that injured their business in the medical market and that this was an illegal boycott. What result? [*Wilk* v. *AMA*, 895 F.2d 352 (7th Cir., 1990)]

9. Raymond Syufy bought all of Las Vegas's first-run movie theaters. The government sued Syufy for monopolization. While admitting that he had a substantial share of the market, Syufy defended his mergers by pointing out the following facts: first, movie prices in Las Vegas were no higher than movie prices in comparable cities; second, no sooner did Syufy acquire all of Las Vegas's first-run theaters than other competitors successfully entered the market; and third, movie studios (for example, Paramount Pictures) are such powerful firms with an interest in avoiding theater monopolization that they can be relied upon to ensure that Syufy does not abuse his market dominance. Evaluate Syufy's arguments. [*United States* v. *Syufy*, 903 F.2d 659 (9th Cir., 1990)]

 Check your answer at <http://meiners.westbuslaw.com>

10. Compcare, an HMO (health maintenance organization), sued Marshfield Clinic for monopolizing the HMO market. HMOs charge their members fixed annual fees. The HMO negotiates with each physician it has under contract the amount it will pay for each medical procedure performed. The idea is that HMOs can bargain with physicians for lower fees and then pass the savings on to HMO members. Compcare objected that Marshfield Clinic signed up so many physicians that there were too few physicians left in the region for Compcare to use. Marshfield defended by pointing out that all of its HMO physicians remained free to treat patients from other HMOs. What result? [*Blue Cross & Blue Shield United of Wisconsin* v. *Marshfield Clinic*, 65 F.3d 1406 (7th Cir., 1995)]

11. Dr. Johnson joined the obstetrics practice of Dr. Fadel. She soon became unhappy with the arrangement, contending she was not being given enough patients. She wanted to set up her own practice, so she met with the physician recruiter at the hospital used by their patients. Johnson claimed the recruiter promised her an $800,000 line of credit and guaranteed annual income of at least $200,000 a year. The hospital board voted not to make her such an offer. Fadel fired her; she moved to another city and sued for conspiracy to restrain trade in violation of the Sherman Act. The district court dismissed the suit; Johnson appealed. Did she have grounds for suit? [*Johnson* v. *University Health Services, Inc.*, 161 F.3d 1334 (11th Cir., 1998)]

 Check your answer at http://meiners.westbuslaw.com

12. Coca-Cola required independent food distributors (IFDs) that sold its fountain syrup to sign a loyalty agreement that they would not sell any Pepsi products so long as they were selling Coke products. Pepsi sued, contending that the loyalty agreement was monopolization and attempted monopolization of the IFD market. Is this monopolization, or are there adequate alternatives in the relevant markets? [*Pepsico* v. *Coca-Cola Co.*, 315 F.3d 102 (2nd Cir., 2002)]

13. Tanaka was recruited out of high school to play college soccer at the University of Southern California. Unhappy there, she asked if she could transfer to another school and was told she could. Wanting to stay in Los Angeles, she decided to transfer to UCLA. USC invoked the NCAA rule that limits transfers within a conference and would require her to sit out her first year at UCLA and lose one year of athletic eligibility. She sued USC and the NCAA for restraint of trade in violation of the Sherman Act. The district court ruled against Tanaka, holding that the matter was "noncommercial" so it was exempt from antitrust. Tanaka appealed. Did she have grounds for an antitrust claim? [*Tanaka* v. *University of Southern California*, 252 F.3d 1059 (9th Cir., 2001)]

14. A maker of hamburger patty machines requires its dealers to also purchase its hamburger patty paper. A dealer that did not like this requirement was cut off by the manufacturer. The dealer sued, claiming that his was an illegal tie-in sale. The dealer was awarded $300,000 damages for the value of its lost sales, which were trebled. Was this the correct decision? [*Roy B. Taylor Sales* v. *Hollymatic Corp.*, 28 F.3d 1379 (5th Cir., 1994)]

15. The Utah Pie Company made and sold frozen pies in the Salt Lake City area. It was very successful and soon had two-thirds of the frozen-pie market in that area. In response to the loss of their market shares, three large pie makers—Carnation, Pet, and Continental—cut their prices in the Salt Lake area but not elsewhere. As a result, their sales picked back up and Utah Pie's fell to 45 percent of the market. The result was lower frozen-pie prices for consumers in that market. Utah Pie sued the other three companies for violating what part of the antitrust law? Did it win? [*Utah Pie Co.* v. *Continental Baking Co.*, 87 S.Ct. 1326 (1967)]

ETHICS QUESTIONS

16. The largest American filmmakers—Paramount, MCA, Metro-Goldwyn, and United Artists—formed a joint venture called United International Pictures to distribute films in Europe and other parts of the world. This venture would clearly be an illegal horizontal restraint of trade in the United States but was sanctioned in Europe by the EU despite complaints by European filmmakers who had seen the American company grab a quarter of the market since 1989. Should American companies engage in business practices outside the United States that are legal in other countries but would be illegal at home?

17. Your firm produces electric blenders. A certain popular model has a suggested retail price of $30. Your firm sells it wholesale for $18. Smaller stores tend to sell the blender at the suggested retail price. One large discount chain begins to sell the blender for $26 and asks you to cut the price to them to $17.50. Because of that chain's large sales, your production and profits are up. You will earn even higher profits if you cut the price to them to $17.50—a possible violation of the Robinson-Patman Act. Should you cut the price for the chain? What if the chain says that it will cut its retail price to $25.50 if you cut the price to $17.50?

PULLING IT Together

Antitrust and Intellectual Property

Xerox, a maker of high-volume copiers, refused to sell parts to its copiers and diagnostic software for the copiers to independent service organizations (ISOs). The ISOs had competed with Xerox in repair service on copiers; being unable to obtain the parts or software meant that they could not be competitive against Xerox in copier repairs. The ISOs sued, contending that the Sherman Act was violated since Xerox's failure to sell the parts and software to the ISOs eliminated much of the competition for repair services. Xerox contended that since its parts were patented, it had the right to decide who could buy its parts and copyrighted software. Do the patents and copyrights provide a defense for Xerox against the antitrust claim?

[*In re Independent Service Organizations Antitrust Litigation*, 203 F.3d 1322 (Fed. Cir., 2000)]

INTERNET ASSIGNMENT

http://www.sskrplaw.com/nfl

For recent important cases, the Internet may provide access to essential documents such as briefs, motions, and press releases. However, such information, as with much Internet data, may prove to be short-lasting and incomplete. In 2004, Maurice Clarett, a running back from Ohio State, filed suit against the National Football League, attempting to be included in the 2004 NFL Draft. Can you still access relevant data at the web site for the law firm that represented him? Search the Internet for subsequent related events (later court decisions, appeals to higher courts, etc.) that may not be included on the law firm's web site.

Chapter 20 | *Securities Regulation*

Martha Stewart, once worth a billion dollars, went to prison for securities law violations. Other people who made massive sums of money, and must have felt like they were on top of the world, also came to grief in securities scandals. Careers and fortunes evaporated for some who crossed the securities line and were prosecuted by the government and sued by private investors. Innocent investors saw billions of dollars evaporate when companies such as WorldCom and Enron collapsed when the companies' complex schemes that hid the truth of their declining value came undone. Thousands of employees lost their jobs and, in some cases, pensions were destroyed, leaving the victims with very little to show for years of good work.

Since securities markets handle trillions of dollars in assets, perhaps there should be little surprise that there are cases involving huge sums of money put at risk. When that happens, confidence in securities is shaken. The Securities and Exchange Commission (SEC) is important as the primary regulator of U.S. securities markets. Other nations look to the SEC for leadership in how to regulate, but not damage the quality of, the major sources of support for financing business operations. This chapter looks at the workings and legal control of some of the key elements of the securities industry.

THE ELEMENTS OF SECURITIES

Securities are the financial backbone of the U.S. economy, so the efficient operation of the securities market is critical to economic growth. Business operations, especially larger companies, rely on securities for financing operations. Those securities are the major form of investment for pension funds, so the financial future of most people is tied to securities.

Corporate Finance

A *security* is almost always one of two things. First, it may be *debt* of certain forms—primarily money borrowed by a corporation—usually a note or bond that can be traded. Second, it may be *equity*—the most famous being common stocks traded on the New York Stock Exchange and other stock exchanges. Securities provide *capital* for business operations—the money needed to get a business started or increased in size. Securities are represented by pieces of paper, or records in computers, that represent value in something real. This chapter opens with a look at the elements of debt and equity.

Debt

When bonds are sold, there is often an *issue* of a certain amount. For example, if General Motors issues 10,000 bonds that are each worth $10,000, the company raises $100 million to help pay for expansion of a factory. The bond issue means that GM has incurred debt that is to be repaid to the holders or owners of the bonds. The bonds are usually traded on the securities market, so they are securities. *Debt financing* may also be obtained by borrowing money from large lenders, such as banks and insurance companies. In that case, as we discussed in Chapter 12, a note may be issued to represent the debt. Since that note may be sold to other parties, it can also be a security. A debt instrument issued by a corporation, such as a bond, specifies:

1. Amount of the debt
2. Length of the debt period
3. Debt repayment method
4. Rate of interest charged to the sum borrowed

Most purchases and sales are handled by professional bond traders, such as Merrill Lynch, which earns a commission for handling the sale of bonds or later trades by bond owners.

Equity

Equity financing is raising funds through the sale of company stock. It is called equity financing because a purchaser of shares of stock gains an ownership, or equitable, interest in the corporation. Shareholders have a claim on a portion of the future profits (if any) of the corporation. Unlike with debt financing, a company has no liability to repay shareholders the amount they have invested. For example, when Google sold stock for the first time to the public, it sold 19.6 million shares at $85 a share, which raised $1.67 billion cash to finance Google operations. Each share represents a right to a tiny fraction of the future profits of the corporation.

Investors buy shares in the corporation if they think the profits will be sufficient to provide them a competitive rate of return on their investment. The officers of the corporation are under an obligation to make reasonable efforts to earn a profit. As in the case of bonds, unless prohibited by contract, stock can be traded, usually through a stock exchange.

Origins of Securities Regulation

Concern with fraud in the sale of securities to the public led to state laws regulating the sale of securities. The first securities statute was enacted by the state of Kansas in 1911. State securities laws are called *blue sky laws*. That comes from a Supreme Court opinion describing the purpose of state securities laws as attempting to prevent "speculative schemes which would have no more basis than so many feet of blue sky." Promoters had gone door-to-door selling worthless securities to unsuspecting Kansas investors. Later—after their money and the promoters were gone—the buyers found that the securities had nothing more backing them than the blue sky.

Beginnings of Federal Regulation

Federal regulation of securities began during a time of economic catastrophe. The stock market crashed in 1929. The crash was followed by the Great Depression. Over one-quarter of all jobs disappeared, and national income fell by one-third. Many people blamed the depression on the stock market crash. In fact, the market was correctly forecasting the coming depression. Nevertheless, there was a common belief that manipulators on Wall Street needed to be controlled and, indeed, there had been abusive practices. Congress enacted a number of statutes.

Most important are the Securities Act of 1933 and the Securities Exchange Act of 1934. The 1933 Act regulates the public offerings of securities when they are first sold. The Act requires that investors be given material information about new securities and prevents misrepresentation in the sale of securities. The 1934 Act regulates trading in existing securities. The Act imposes disclosure requirements on corporations that have issued publicly held securities. It also regulates securities markets and professionals.

The Securities and Exchange Commission

The *Securities and Exchange Commission (SEC)* is the agency charged with the responsibility for the enforcement and administration of the federal securities laws (see http://www.sec.gov). The SEC has five members appointed by the president for five-year terms. One is appointed as chairman. The SEC's staff is composed of attorneys, accountants, financial analysts and examiners, and other professionals. The staff is divided into divisions and offices—including regional offices around the country.

WHAT IS A SECURITY?

Although Congress often provides vague guidance to regulators—forcing the courts and the regulatory agencies to define the terms and the scope of the legislation—this was not the case in defining the term *security* in the 1933 Act. Congress provided a detailed definition. According to the 1933 Act, *security* includes any note, stock, treasury stock, bond, debenture, evidence of indebtedness, certificate of interest or participation in any profit-sharing agreement, collateral-trust certificate, preorganization certificate or subscription, transferable share, investment contract, voting-trust certificate, certificate of deposit for a security, fractional undivided interest in oil, gas, or other mineral rights, or, in general, any interest or instrument commonly known as a "security," or any certificate of interest of participation in, temporary or interim certificate for, receipt for, guarantee of, or warrant or right to subscribe to or purchase, any of the foregoing.

Despite this detailed definition of a security, both the courts and the SEC look to the economic realities of an investment transaction to determine whether it is a security. That is, just because something is called a stock does not mean it is a security that falls within the jurisdiction of the federal security laws. Similarly, other things with names not included in the list written by Congress are securities.

Supreme Court's *Howey* Test

If an investment instrument is a security, it must comply with the legal requirements imposed on securities issuers. Note that investors have incentives to sue to have the court declare that an investment instrument is a security. If an investment instrument is a security, investors have a higher degree of legal protection than that given to investments not qualifying as securities. In *Howey*, the Supreme Court established a test to determine when an investment is a security for the purposes of federal regulation.

Securities and Exchange Commission v. W. J. Howey Company
United States Supreme Court
328 U.S. 293, 66 S.Ct. 1100 (1946)

CASE BACKGROUND *Howey owned hundreds of acres of orange trees in central Florida. Half the land was offered for sale to the public. Buyers were offered title to land and a service contract under which Howey would harvest and sell the oranges grown on each parcel. Most land buyers lived outside Florida and bought the service contract.*

The SEC sued Howey, claiming that the sale of the land and service contracts was a security that should have been registered with the SEC before being offered for sale to the public. The district court and the court of appeals found for Howey. The SEC appealed to the Supreme Court.

CASE DECISION Murphy, Justice.

* * *

An investment contract for purposes of the Securities Act means a contract, transaction or scheme whereby a person invests his money in a common enter-

prise and is led to expect profits solely from the efforts of the promoter of a third party, it being immaterial whether the shares in the enterprise are evidenced by formal certificates or by nominal interests in the physical assets employed in the enterprise.

* * *

The transactions in this case clearly involve investment contracts as so defined. The [sellers] are offering something more than fee simple interest in land, something different from a farm or orchard coupled with management services. They are offering an opportunity to contribute money and to share in the profits of a large citrus fruit enterprise. . . . They are offering this opportunity to persons who reside in distant localities and who lack the equipment and experience requisite to the cultivation, harvesting and marketing of the citrus products. Such persons have no desire to occupy the land or to develop it themselves;

continues

they are attracted solely by the prospects of a return on their investment. . . .

Thus all the elements of a profit-seeking business venture are present here. The investors provide the capital and share in the earnings and profits; the promoters manage, control and operate the enterprise. It follows that the arrangements whereby the investors' interests are made manifest involve investment contracts, regardless of the legal terminology in which such contracts are clothed. The investment contracts in this instance take the form of land sales contracts, warranty deeds and service contracts which respondents offer to prospective investors. And [sellers'] failure to abide by the statutory and administrative rules in making such offerings, even though the failure results from a bona fide mistake as to the law, cannot be sanctioned under the Act. . . .

Reversed.

QUESTIONS FOR ANALYSIS

1. Suppose Howey had sold the land to investors but had not offered to manage the orange trees. Would the land still have been a security?

2. Justice Frankfurter, in a dissenting opinion, noted that 20 percent of the buyers did not sign a management contract. Such signing was voluntary and not required to make a land purchase. Did the Supreme Court majority violate their own test for what makes a security?

The test developed by the Court in *Howey* is still the critical test. It holds that for an investment to be classified as a security for the purpose of federal regulation, it must contain four basic elements:

1. The investment of money
2. In a common enterprise
3. With an expectation of profits
4. Generated by the efforts of persons other than the investors

The Four Elements

The first element, *the investment of money*, requires that an investor turn over money to someone else for an investment. The second element, *in a common enterprise*, means that the investment is not the property of an investor, such as an investor's house. Rather, an investor's capital has been pooled with other investors' money so that each investor owns an undivided interest in the investment. An investor who owns Ford stock, for example, does not have the right to go to a Ford factory and demand a truck or other property equal in value to the money the investor invested in the company. An investor has a claim only to a share of future earnings as established in the securities contract. Even though stock owners (or shareholders) own a portion of the company, they own an *undivided interest* in the company. That is, the shareholders cannot divide company property among themselves unless they agree to liquidate (sell) the company.

The third and fourth elements, *the expectation that profits will be generated by the efforts of persons other than the investor*, require that an investor not have direct control over the work that makes the investment a success or failure. That is, a board of directors controls the future of the organization. They hire managers to run the company. The shareholders do not have direct control. If an investment meets this definition, it is a security, and must be registered with the SEC before it is sold to the public.

Securities Exempt from Regulation

Some new securities that are being sold to the public are exempt from regulation. The most important securities exempted by both the 1933 and the 1934 Acts are debts issued or guaranteed by a government—federal, state, or local. The 1933 Act also provides an exemption for securities issued by banks, religious and charitable organizations, insurance policies, and annuity contracts. Since most of these securities are subject to control by other federal agencies, such as the Federal Reserve System, there is another regulatory scheme to protect investors.

In general, an exempted security is not subject to the registration requirements of the federal statutes. However, the security may be subject to the Acts' antifraud and civil liability provisions.

What Are You Selling?

ISSUE
Spotter

Your family cattle business, like many, has had a hard time making a profit. Your idea is to let city folks buy a piece of a cattle herd. You will sell young cows to investors for the going market price. Your family will keep possession of the cattle, raise them, and then market them. After costs are deducted, such as food and transport, you will split any profit (per cow) 50-50 with its buyer. Since there are about 800 cattle in the herd at any time, that is the maximum number of cows you will sell. Investors may buy as many cows as they wish up to the maximum, and they are welcome to come visit the herd. Assuming everything is done honestly, could there be any securities issues here?

OFFERING TO INVESTORS

The 1933 Act, sometimes called the "truth in securities" law, requires that before a security is sold, the sellers *disclose* to prospective investors all material information about a security, its issuers, and the intended use of the funds raised. *Material information* is all relevant information that an investor would want to know about a company—its background, its executives, and its plan of operation. Disclosure is accomplished by filing a registration statement with the SEC.

Registration of securities provides investors with sufficient information about important facts that a company is proposing to sell. With that information, investors can make an informed decision about the merits of new securities before buying them.

The Registration Statement

The *registration statement* for a new security offering has two parts. The first part is the *prospectus*—a document providing the legal offering of the sale of the security. The second part is detailed information required by the SEC.

The Prospectus

A prospectus (called Schedule A) condenses the longer registration statement provided to the SEC and helps investors evaluate a security. The first version of the prospectus is called a *red herring* (because of the red ink used on the first page). It is used by securities brokers to interest potential investors in a forthcoming offering. Every prospectus provides material information about

- The security issuer's finances and business
- The purpose of the offering

- The plans for the funds collected
- The risks involved in the business venture
- The promoters' managerial experience and financial compensation
- Financial statements certified by independent public accountants

Regulation S-K

The second part of the registration statement has more detailed information than the prospectus. The SEC spells out the requirements in *Regulation S-K*. More history on the financial background and past experience of the issuers is required. There is also more information about the proposed business and the issuers. This information may be used by investment analysts who want to see more detail. The disclosure document is available for public inspection.

Review by the SEC

The SEC does not rule on the *merits* of an offering (that is, give an opinion about the likelihood of success of a proposed business), but it can require issuers to make high-risk factors clear in the prospectus so as to put buyers on notice. The registration becomes effective twenty days after it is filed, but if the SEC issues a *deficiency letter*, the issuer needs time to amend the filing to provide more detail in the registration materials. The SEC can issue a *stop order* to prohibit sale of securities until the registration statement is amended to satisfy the examiners, but this is not common.

The Costs of Registration

The registration process is expensive. The prospective issuer must hire professionals, including a securities attorney, a certified public accountant, and a printer for the prospectus. There is also the expense of hiring an *underwriter* (an investment banker, such as Morgan Stanley) that will market the securities.

Stock underwriting fees may be less than 1 percent of the value of a large stock offering sold to the public, but the fee may be as high as 10 percent for a small offering by an unknown company. To avoid such costs, one may consider selling through a transaction that makes the security exempt from the registration process.

Exemptions from Registration

Some securities, such as government bonds, are exempt from the securities laws. All other securities are subject to the securities laws, but they may qualify for an *exemption from registration*. Only the initial sale of the securities is exempt from registration; the securities are not exempt from other parts of the securities laws.

Private Placement

The 1933 Act provides that registration is not necessary for new securities not offered to the public. In some years, more money has been raised through *private placement* securities than through public offerings. The primary users of the exemption are those placing large blocks of securities with institutional investors—most often pension funds or insurance companies. For example, IBM might sell $250 million in new bonds directly to Prudential Insurance rather than offering the bonds to the general public.

Securities Offerings on the Web

CYBER *Law*

There is no technological reason why new securities offerings cannot be posted on the Web, and some have been. The Capital Markets Efficiency Act of 1996, which preempts state registration of offers to "qualified purchasers," provides an opportunity for such offerings to develop. They are much cheaper than the traditional offers presented on paper. But such offerings have been slow to come about.

Outdated state laws tend to block Web offerings for categories not specifically covered by the Act. Such offerors must still comply with state-law paper requirements. Offerings covered by the law are private placements or fall under the accredited investor category. These are not easy to use by unknown firms trying to get their securities placed with low overhead cost. Since few people are used to looking at the Web for new securities offerings, especially those with such a limited set of buyers, such efforts have not been all that successful. But, as with other areas of e-commerce, this more cost-effective offering method should become more common.

Regulation D To explain what qualifies as a private placement exemption, the SEC adopted *Regulation D* to spell out the elements:

- *Accredited investors* are presumed sophisticated and wealthy enough to evaluate investment opportunities without an SEC-approved prospectus. Only accredited investors may participate in private placement offerings of securities. Institutions, such as banks and insurance companies, are accredited investors. Individual investors must have an annual income of at least $200,000 or a net worth of at least $1 million. Other investors are unaccredited.
- Placements up to $5 million in securities can involve up to thirty-five unaccredited investors (and any number of accredited investors). Unaccredited investors must be provided information similar to that provided in a registration statement.
- Securities offerings of over $5 million may be made only to accredited investors to keep the private placement exemption.

The rules about private placements are complex. Even though the offerings may be exempt from registration, there is usually a reporting requirement to the SEC about the offers, and the law requires that investors be given information (called a private-placement memorandum) similar to what they would have received in a prospectus. Also, restrictions are placed on the resale of securities bought by investors in private placements, which can reduce their value.

Rule 144A Private placements are most common for large security issues—mostly bonds—that are sold to institutional investors. Rule 144A exempts U.S. and foreign security issuers from registration requirements for the sale of bonds and stocks to institutions with a portfolio of at least $100 million in securities. Further, securities issued to such large institutions may be traded among similar institutions without registration or disclosure requirements. About one-third of all offerings have been sold under this registration exemption.

REGULATION OF SECURITIES TRADING

While the 1933 Act imposes *disclosure requirements* on corporations issuing new securities, the 1934 Act imposes disclosure requirements on securities that are publicly traded. A security registered under the 1933 Act must be registered with the SEC under the 1934 Act. Even if exempt from registration under the 1933 Act, a security must be registered under the 1934 Act if it is listed on a *securities exchange* (New York Stock Exchange, etc.) or if it is traded *over the counter (OTC)* and the company has $5 million or more in assets and 500 or more shareholders.

Any company that has issued securities that are traded is a *publicly held company* and is subject to reporting requirements. A company that has fewer than 500 shareholders and does not allow its securities to be openly traded is called a *private company*. Its financial information is not available to the public. A company can go from being publicly held to private by buying up its stock so that it is held by fewer than 500 shareholders. A number of multibillion-dollar corporations are in this category, such as RJR-Nabisco, which went private when its $25 billion in stock was all purchased by an investment group.

Disclosure requirements apply to more than 10,000 publicly held companies, most of which have securities traded in the OTC market. These companies must file reports on their securities. The most important report is the *10-K annual report*, an extensive audited financial statement similar in content to the information provided in the registration process under the 1933 Act. Companies must also file *quarterly 10-Q reports* with unaudited financial information and *8-K reports* whenever significant financial developments occur. The purpose of these reports is to ensure disclosure of financial information to investors.

JURIS *prudence?*

Triple Your Money Overnight!

Ade Ogunjobi filed papers with the SEC to announce that he was offering to buy all of the stock in GM, GE, AOL Time Warner, AT&T, Hughes Electronics, and Marriott, which together were worth about $600 billion. He was offering three times the current value of the shares in the form of shares in his company, Toks, which had zero value. Ogunjobi asserted in the filing that the tripling in value would occur due to "synergies" and would allow "aggressive expansions of Toks Inc. into other industry sectors." The SEC accepted the filing, but response by investors to the offering was not good.

Source: *Chicago Tribune*

Regulation FD

The SEC adopted *Regulation Fair Disclosure (Reg FD)* to create a more "level playing field." It requires public companies to release material information to the public rather than to reveal such information selectively. The primary purpose of Reg FD is to restrict the traditional practice of firms having executives give private briefings to big investors and favored securities analysts. Such meetings may occur, so that analysts can better understand company operations, but any material information provided at such meetings must also be released to the public. All securities traders are to have the same access to information, not just those who attend private briefings.

Firms are not required to provide more information; the regulation simply requires open disclosure of material information that is revealed to anyone outside the company. Public disclosure of material information can be made by filing Form 8-K or by distributing the information in a way "reasonably designed to provide broad, non-exclusionary distribution of information to the public," such as by press release or on a company web site.

Proxies and Tender Offers

Most shares of stock, besides representing a claim on a share of the future profits of a company, carry voting rights used to elect boards of directors and to determine major issues facing the company. Shares of stock carry extra value because of voting rights, especially when major events such as a takeover occur. The SEC ensures that fair voting procedures are followed.

Proxies

A *proxy* is permission given by a shareholder to someone else to vote his shares in the manner he instructs. Since it is not practical for many stock owners to attend corporate meetings at which shareholders vote to approve major decisions, such as to merge with another company, or elect the board of directors, shareholders are sent proxies to be voted on their behalf. Firms must provide shareholders with proxy statements—information about major proposed changes in the business. SEC regulations spell out the form and timing that proxy solicitations must take.

While most proxies are routine, such as voting for boards of directors or amendments to company bylaws, proxy fights can be used in a struggle over the future of the organization. For example, a proxy fight was waged over the issue of whether Compaq Computer should be merged with Hewlett-Packard. The board of directors was successful in getting approval, but the vote was close on the issue. Shareholders were offered the chance to stay with two independent companies or go with a different strategy of merging into one company.

Tender Offers

When one company attempts to take over another, it often uses *a tender offer*. Stock owners in the target company are offered stock in the acquiring company or cash in exchange for their stock. If successful, the acquiring company obtains enough stock to control the target company. Tender offers must be registered with the SEC, and certain procedures must be followed.

SECURITIES FRAUD

Disclosure requirements do not prevent the sale or trading of securities in risky or poorly managed companies. Rather, the Acts help ensure the adequate and accurate disclosure of material facts concerning the securities of a publicly traded company. Failure to follow the disclosure requirements may result in suits for *securities fraud*. Some securities fraud cases arise from false and misleading information in the registration materials, but most arise from information during later disclosure, such as public statements by corporate representatives.

Basis for Securities Fraud

Because obligations are created in the sale of a security, an investor can rely on common-law fraud standards for protection. Investors who think they have suffered a loss due to fraud and want to sue for damages often have difficulty establishing all elements of common-law fraud. Thus, injured investors generally rely on the antifraud provisions of the 1933 and 1934 Acts that hold that specific acts cause statutory fraud.

Section 11 of the 1933 Act imposes civil liability for *misleading statements* or *material omissions* in securities registration material. Any person who buys a security covered by a registration statement that contains false or misleading information, or that omits information that was important to a decision to purchase, may sue to recover losses incurred in that purchase.

Rule 10b-5

Section 10(b) of the 1934 Act makes it illegal for any person "to use or employ, in connection with the purchase or sale of any security registered on a national securities exchange or any security not so registered, any manipulative or deceptive device or contrivance in contravention of such rules and regulations as the Commission may prescribe. . . ." It provides the broadest base for bringing a securities fraud action, and it has come to be used in litigation more than any other part of the Act.

The SEC adopted *Rule 10b-5* to enforce Section 10(b) of the 1934 Act. The rule is broad in scope:

> It shall be unlawful for any person, directly or indirectly, by the use of any means or instrumentality of interstate commerce, or of the mails, or of any facility of any national securities exchange,
>
> 1. To employ any device, scheme, or artifice to defraud;
> 2. To make any untrue statement of a material fact or to omit to state a material fact necessary in order to make the statements made, in the light of the circumstances under which they were made, not misleading; or
> 3. To engage in any act, practice, or course of business which operates or would operate as a fraud or deceit upon any person, in connection with the purchase or sale of any security.

The rule applies to all securities, registered or not. Since the rule does not state specific offenses, it has been left to the SEC and the courts to decide how strict the standards will be.

Liability for Securities Law Violations

The law allows investors who lose in the purchase or sale of securities because of omission of material information or misleading statements to sue parties connected with the preparation of disclosure documents or other important information about the securities. This includes directors of the company; the chief executive, financial, and accounting officers of the company; and accountants, lawyers, and other experts who helped prepare disclosure material. All parties are held to high standards of professional care, which is one reason for the high cost of preparing disclosure materials.

SEC Action

The SEC may also sue those alleged to be violating securities law. Most SEC actions are remedial, such as an injunction ordering someone not to do something again or to direct a company to issue corrected financial statements. Since the SEC action is public, the parties involved are exposed to publicity. Injury to reputation in financial dealings can be costly as people are likely to shy away from future dealings. Further, SEC action may lead to private suits to recover losses attributed to the error in information.

The SEC can also recommend that the Department of Justice bring criminal charges against violators. To warrant a criminal action, the offender must have engaged in fraud related to securities. Penalties may involve fines and imprisonment.

Liability for Misstatements

Securities law imposes liability for *misstatements* or *omissions* about the financial status of a business that has issued securities. Misleading information that would reasonably affect investment decisions by securities owners includes misinformation about the present financial status or the future prospects of the enterprise that would affect the price of the security. For example, overly optimistic statements by executives can cause expectations of higher profits, leading investors to bid up the price of the stock. When the statements are found to be false, the stock price falls, imposing losses on those who bought the stock on the basis of the positive statements. This is one of the most common grounds for private suits seeking damages based on a claim of securities fraud.

Directors and senior managers of businesses know they may be responsible for the consequences of misstatements they make that cause the price of the securities issued by their company to rise or fall. Under the law of securities fraud, if investors lose money because of things not said (omissions) or because of misstatements that investors reasonably rely on, then there was *material misinformation* that caused the loss. The Supreme Court made that point clear in the *Basic* case.

Basic Inc. v. Levinson
United States Supreme Court
485 U.S. 224, 108 S.Ct. 978 (1988)

CASE BACKGROUND *Basic, a publicly traded company, began talks with Combustion in 1976 about the possibility of a merger. Basic made public statements denying that it was engaged in merger negotiations. In 1978, the Basic board endorsed Combustion's offer of $46 per share for Basic's common stock.*

Basic and its directors were sued by shareholders who had sold their stock before the merger announcement but after Basic's first statement in 1977 that there were no merger negotiations. The shareholders received less than $46 per share, which they claim was caused by false and misleading statements of Basic and its directors in violation of Section 10(b) of the 1934 Securities Exchange Act and of Rule 10b-5. That is, they sold their stock at lower prices than they would have received had the company told the truth about the merger talks. The Supreme Court

had to decide if any misstatements were material and would result in liability.

CASE DECISION Blackmun, Justice.

* * *

The Supreme Court . . . has defined a standard of materiality under the security laws, concluding . . . that "an omitted fact is material if there is a substantial likelihood that a reasonable shareholder would consider it important. . . ." We now expressly adopt that standard of materiality for the §10(b) and Rule 10b-5 context. . . .

In order to prevail on a Rule 10b-5 claim, a plaintiff must show that the statements were *misleading* as to a *material* fact. It is not enough that a statement is

continues

false or incomplete, if the misrepresented fact is otherwise insignificant. . . .

Materiality depends on the significance the reasonable investor would place on the withheld or misrepresented information. The fact-specific inquiry we endorse here is consistent with the approach a number of courts have taken in assessing the materiality of merger negotiations.

* * *

We turn to the question of reliance and the fraud-on-the-market theory. Succinctly put:

> The fraud on the market theory is based on the hypothesis that, in an open and developed securities market, the price of a company's stock is determined by the available material information regarding the company and its businesses. . . . Misleading statements will therefore defraud purchasers of stock even if the purchasers do not directly rely on the misstatements. . . . The causal connection between the defendants' fraud and the plaintiffs' purchase of stock in such a case is no less significant than in a case of direct reliance on misrepresentations.

. . . We previously have dispensed with a requirement of positive proof of reliance, where a duty to disclose material information had been breached, concluding that the necessary nexus between the plaintiffs' injury and the defendant's wrongful conduct had been established. Similarly, we did not require proof that material omissions or misstatements in a proxy statement decisively affected voting, because the proxy solicitation itself, rather than the defect in the solicitation materials, served as an essential link in the transaction.

* * *

The Court of Appeals found that Basic "made public, material misrepresentations and Levinson sold Basic stock in an impersonal, efficient market. Thus the class, as defined by the district court, has established the threshold facts for proving their loss." The court acknowledged that Basic may rebut proof of the elements giving rise to the presumption, or show that the misrepresentation in fact did not lead to a distortion of price or that an individual plaintiff traded or would have traded despite his knowing the statement was false.

* * *

CASE NOTE Defendants can rebut a claim of material misrepresentation by showing that the omission or misrepresentation was not material or did not affect the security price or that the plaintiff did not rely on the information in making a decision to buy or sell the security.

QUESTIONS FOR ANALYSIS

1. Since rumors about mergers usually come out, should executives always admit when they are engaged in merger talks? What problems could that cause?

2. How can security holders who were ignorant of what was going on later get involved in such litigation?

Safe Harbor

The Securities Litigation Reform Act of 1995 amended the securities law to protect companies from liability for predictions about profits and the likely success of its products so long as forecasts are accompanied by "meaningful cautionary statements identifying important factors that could cause actual results to differ materially from those in the forward-looking statement." This is called a *safe harbor* because it gives greater immunity from suit for corporate forecasts that turned out after the fact not to be accurate.

Federal Exclusivity

The Securities Litigation Uniform Standards Act of 1998 requires securities suits involving nationally traded securities to be brought exclusively in federal court under federal law. The 1998 Act prohibits the pursuit of a class action under the law of any state if the suit alleges: (a) an untrue statement or omission of a material fact in connection with the purchase or sale of a covered security; or (b) that the defendant used or employed any deceptive device or contrivance in connection with the purchase or sale of a covered security.

JURIS *prudence?*

Pay Is OK, but the Food Is Terrible

Randall Hutchens was in federal prison for trying to cheat the IRS out of $300,000. A former investment adviser, he spent his time filing shareholder-fraud cases against companies in California small claims court, where the damages are limited to $5,000.

Rather than contest the claims, at least seventeen companies paid settlements between $500 and $5,000, allowing Hutchens to collect over $30,000. His claims were bogus, especially since he never actually owned the stock involved. But the cost of hiring a California attorney to look into the securities fraud claims, based on alleged misinformation, was high enough that many companies just offered settlements.

Given that the prison provided Hutchens all the material he needed, his only expense was the small court filing fee.

Source: *The Wall Street Journal*

Sarbanes-Oxley Act Requirements

Congress added new requirements to the securities law in 2002 with the Sarbanes-Oxley Act. It requires that the Chief Executive Officer (CEO) and Chief Financial Officer (CFO) of large companies that have publicly traded stock personally certify that financial reports made to the SEC comply with SEC rules and that the information in the reports is accurate. Knowingly making a misstatement is a criminal offense with fines up to $5 million and up to twenty years in prison. The law also provides protection for corporate whistleblowers who report securities violations and provides them a statutory basis for suing their employer if they suffer retaliation.

INSIDER TRADING

Rule 10b-5 is used to prohibit *insider trading*—the buying or selling of stock by persons who have access to information affecting the value of the stock that has not yet been revealed to the public. As the Supreme Court has noted, misappropriation of private information gives insiders an unfair advantage in the market over investors who do not have the information. It is illegal for an insider to trade on inside information until the information has been released to the public and the stock price has had time to adjust to the new information.

Executives are the ones most likely to be affected by the rule, as they have valuable information concerning the financial well-being of the company before the release of the information to the public. The SEC brings over forty such cases each year.

In Rule 10-b5-1, the SEC defines insider trading to include trading "on the basis of" material, nonpublic information, which means that "the person making the purchase or sale was aware of the material, nonpublic information when the person made the purchase or sale." To be aware of the information means "having knowledge: conscious; cognizant." Executives in a firm, who almost always are aware of material, nonpublic information, may trade stock in their company and not be liable for insider trading if they contracted at an earlier date to have another person buy or sell the security at a specific time or on a "program" basis, that is, make trades at specific time intervals.

SEC Prosecution

The SEC may prosecute insiders if they trade in the stock before the public has a chance to act on the information. For example, suppose an attorney working for

General Electric found out that GE would announce the sale of $1 billion worth of jet engines to Boeing in two days. Knowing that this good news would make GE stock rise, the attorney buys some GE stock before the announcement. This is insider trading for which the attorney could be sued for all profits earned from the stock transaction.

Supreme Court Interpretation

The Supreme Court started to clarify the rules about insider trading in a 1980 case. A printer at a company that printed financial documents read some confidential information. The printer (Chiarella) traded in the stock of the company involved and made $30,000 in profits because of his access to inside information. The SEC charged Chiarella with securities fraud, but the Supreme Court reversed the lower court conviction.

In *Chiarella* v. *United States*, 445 U.S. 222, the Court said that Chiarella was not a corporate insider who owed a *fiduciary duty* to the shareholders of his company. He was an outsider who was lucky enough to learn inside information. He could be responsible only if his position had a requirement that he could not use such information. He may have had an unfair advantage over other stock traders, but it did not constitute securities fraud.

In the 1983 case, *Dirks* v. *SEC*, 463 U.S. 646, the Supreme Court held that not all breaches of fiduciary duty in a securities transaction mean there is securities fraud. There must also be "manipulation or deception" and, in insider-trading cases, there must be "inherent unfairness involved where one takes advantage of information intended to be available only for a corporate purpose and not for the personal benefit of anyone." An example of how the court applies the law against insider trading is seen in the *Ginsburg* case.

U.S. Securities and Exchange Commission v. Ginsburg

United States Court of Appeals, Eleventh Circuit
262 F.3d 1292 (2004)

CASE BACKGROUND   *Scott Ginsburg was CEO of Evergreen Media, which owned radio stations. He met with the CEO of EZ Communication to discuss "strategic alternatives." Two days later, Ginsburg called his brother, Mark. The next day Mark bought 3,800 shares of EZ stock. Ginsburg also talked to his father, Jordan, who immediately bought 20,000 shares of EZ. The next day, Evergreen and EZ began discussing a merger under a confidentiality agreement. Cell phone calls were then made from Scott to Mark and Jordan. The calls were followed by immediate large purchases of EZ stock. When EZ's stock rose 30 percent, Mark made a profit of $413,000 and Jordan made $664,000.*

The SEC brought a civil action against Ginsburg for securities violations for communicating material, nonpublic information to his brother and father. The jury found that Ginsburg violated the rule against insider trading

and ordered him to pay $1 million in penalties. The trial judge set aside the verdict, holding that the evidence was insufficient to find that Ginsburg had tipped off his brother and father. The SEC appealed.

CASE DECISION   Carnes, Circuit Judge.

* * *

The SEC must prove violations . . . by a preponderance of the evidence, and may use direct or circumstantial evidence to do so. . . .

The district court stated that "the phone records are insufficient to compel an inference that Scott Ginsburg conveyed material, nonpublic information to Mark," but that is not the issue. The SEC did not have the burden of putting in evidence that compelled the inference Ginsburg conveyed nonpublic information to Mark. All it was required to do was put in evidence that reasonably permitted that inference. It did that. The call/trade pattern occurrences coupled with the jury's right to disbelieve the innocent explanations of the calls and trades are enough to support the verdict. . . .

Ginsburg contends that the SEC did not provide sufficient evidence to permit a reasonable jury to find that the information tipped was material and nonpublic, as required by Rule 10b-5. "An omitted fact is material if there is a substantial likelihood a reasonable shareholder would consider it important in deciding how to vote." Materiality is proved by showing a "substantial likelihood that the disclosure of the omitted fact would have been viewed by the reasonable investor as having significantly altered the 'total mix' of information made available."

The insider information in this case meets the materiality standard. In *Basic Inc.* v. *Levinson*, the Supreme Court held that preliminary merger talks can be material well before any agreement is reached. The materiality of an uncertain prospective event "depends at any given time upon a balancing of both the indicated probability that the event will occur and the anticipated magnitude of the event in light of the totality of the company activity." The Court explained that "a factfinder will need to look to indicia of interest in the transaction at the highest corporate levels," and consider factors such as "board resolutions, instructions to investment bankers, and actual negotiations between principals or their intermediaries." The determination of materiality "requires delicate assessments of the inferences a 'reasonable shareholder' would draw from a given set of facts and the significance of those inferences to him, and these assessments are peculiarly ones for the trier of fact." . . .

The jury could recognize as material . . . nonpublic information about a private meeting between executives and the specific share price they discussed confidentially. . . .

The district court's grant of judgment as a matter of law is reversed and the case is remanded with instructions that the court reinstate the civil penalty of $1,000,000, and enjoin Scott Ginsburg from future violations of the securities laws and regulations.

QUESTIONS FOR ANALYSIS

1. The Ginsburgs denied that the phone conversations were about a likely merger between Evergreen and EZ, and there is no recording of the conversations, so how could Ginsburg be found liable for insider trading for passing on private information?

2. Why was this a civil case and not a criminal case?

INTERNATIONAL *Perspective*

European Approaches to Insider Trading

The U.K. passed insider trading legislation in 1980 and brings about the same number of suits as the SEC does in the United States, given the size of the two nations.

After a scandal involving high-ranking government officials, France adopted insider trading rules in 1989, giving the Commission des Operacions de Bourse stronger powers than it had under older statutes. However, there have been only a few administrative sanctions.

Italy enacted its first insider trading law in 1991. While the terms of the statute appear to be stringent, in practice, enforcement is minimal, and the law has significant loopholes. There were only two convictions in ten years, and in 2001 false accounting was reduced to a misdemeanor.

Germany did not pass a law against insider trading until 1994. The law is enforced by a new agency, the Bundesaufsichtsamt für den Wertpapierhandel, which obtained its first conviction in 1995.

Compared to the United States, where the SEC convicts an average of more than fifty defendants a year for insider trading, European nations still show minimal concern. *The Wall Street Journal* reports that the head of the German Association for Shareholder Protection says that the organization gives evidence of abuses to the authorities, but "more than 95 percent end up not being investigated. The cases are often too complicated for prosecutors to handle. They've not been trained in these matters."

Insider Trading Sanctions Act

The *Insider Trading Sanctions Act* of 1984 gave the SEC a statutory basis for prosecuting insider trading. The law does not define insider trading, but it gives the SEC authority to bring enforcement actions, as in the *Ginsburg* case, against violators who trade in securities while in possession of material, nonpublic information. The courts may order violators to pay treble damages based on a measure of the illegal profit gained or the loss avoided by the insider trading. Those convicted of violations may also have to pay back illegal profits to those who suffered the losses, which effectively means quadruple damages. In addition, criminal penalties may be assessed.

This law was strengthened by the *Insider Trading and Securities Fraud Enforcement Act* of 1988, which increased the maximum fine to $1 million for persons convicted of violating the law against insider trading and set the maximum prison term at ten years per violation. The fine against corporations was raised to $2.5 million per violation, and the SEC is authorized to pay bounties (up to 10 percent of the penalty the government receives) to informants who give leads that produce insider trading convictions.

ISSUE Spotter

Can You Exploit the Gossip?

Riding the elevator 42 floors in a New York City building, you overhear two people from the headquarters of a company located in the building discussing the fact that tomorrow they will announce that their company will be bought by another company. Price is not discussed, but you know that in such cases the stock of the company being purchased often rises 20 to 30 percent when the announcement is made. You can immediately buy stock in that company and probably profit nicely from the information you overheard. Could you be accused of insider trading? Is there a breach of fiduciary duty if you trade?

THE INVESTMENT COMPANY ACT

The *Investment Company Act (ICA)* of 1940 gives the SEC control over the structure of investment companies. It requires investment companies to register as such with the SEC, which then makes the companies subject to regulations of their activities and holds them liable to the SEC and to private parties for violations of the ICA.

Investment Companies

An *investment company* invests and trades in securities. The ICA defines three types of investment companies: face-amount certificate companies, which issue debt securities paying a fixed return; unit investment trusts, offering a fixed portfolio of securities; and management companies, the most important type of investment company.

Mutual Funds

The most common management (investment) company is the *open-end company*, or *mutual fund*. In 1980, $52 billion was invested in mutual funds. That has risen into the trillions. Most mutual funds are open-end companies that offer no specific number of shares and can expand as long as people invest with them. The money from these shares is invested in a portfolio of securities. The price of the shares is determined by the value of the portfolio divided by the number of shares sold to the public.

There are *load* and *no-load* mutual funds. The former are sold through a securities dealer and have a sales commission (load) of some percentage of the price. No-load funds are sold directly to the public through the mail or Internet with no sales commission. All funds charge an annual expense fee that covers costs of operation. The fee usually runs about 1 percent per year.

Investment companies that do not offer securities to the public but are involved in internal investing (such as banks and insurance companies) are exempt from the regulations imposed on investment companies that deal with the public.

Regulation of Investment Companies

Investment companies must register with the SEC, stating their investment policy and providing financial information. Annual reports and other information must be provided on a continuing basis. Capital requirements, including how much debt such companies may have, are set by the SEC. Payment of dividends to investors must equal at least 90 percent of the taxable ordinary income of the investment company. A company must invest in only those activities that it said it would in its sales literature and policy statements.

Registration and Disclosure

Since investment companies sell securities, such as shares in mutual funds, to buy securities for investment purposes, their securities must be registered with the SEC. Hence, companies under the ICA are subject to the *registration and disclosure* requirements of the SEC for publicly traded securities. The sales literature used by mutual fund companies to promote their investment strategies to the public must be filed with the SEC for review. In general, no share of stock in an investment company may be sold for more than its current net asset value plus a maximum sales charge (load) of 8.5 percent.

Limiting Conflicts of Interest

To reduce possible *conflicts of interest*, there are restrictions on who may be on the board of directors of an investment company. At least 40 percent of the members of the board must be outsiders—persons with no direct business relationship with the company or its officers. The outsiders on the board are responsible for approving contracts with the investment advisers who are hired to manage the investment fund offered. Further, investment companies may not use the funds invested for deals with any persons affiliated with the company. All deals are to be "arm's length."

To reduce conflicts of interest, in 2001 Merrill Lynch became the first major brokerage firm to announce that it was prohibiting its research analysts from trading in the securities of the firms they cover. That is, a Merrill Lynch analyst who covers Intel may not buy and sell that company's stock while making recommendations about the stock to clients of Merrill Lynch.

Investment Advisers

Investment companies hire *investment advisers* to manage operations. Registered investment advisers manage pension funds and the portfolios held by insurance companies and banks. According to the ICA, investment advisers are "deemed to have a fiduciary duty with respect to the receipt of compensation for services" rendered to investment companies. The standard fee paid to advisers to manage an investment company fund is about 0.5 percent of the net assets of the funds each year.

THE INVESTMENT ADVISERS ACT

The *Investment Advisers Act (IAA)* defines *investment adviser* as a "person who, for compensation, engages in the business of advising others . . . as to the advisability of investing in, purchasing or selling securities." Investment advisers direct the investment strategies of mutual funds.

Brokers and Dealers

The IAA regulates *brokers* (persons who make transactions in securities for the account of others), *dealers* (persons who buy and sell securities for their own account), and *advisers* (persons who charge fees for investment advice). They are all *securities professionals* and must be registered with the SEC. Violations of SEC rules can lead to suspension or loss of the right to do business in the industry, as happens hundreds of times a year.

Professional Responsibility to Clients

Primary concerns of the SEC in regulating securities professionals are obligations to clients and conflicts of interest. The Supreme Court has held that broker-dealers must make known to their customers any possible conflicts or other information that is material to investment decisions. Professionals violate their duty when they charge excessive markups on securities above their market value to unsuspecting customers. Markups over 5 percent are difficult to justify, and those over 10 percent are not allowed under SEC guidelines.

Illegal practices include *churning*, when a broker who has control of a client's account buys and sells an excessive amount of stock to make money from the commissions earned on the transactions. Also illegal is *scalping*, when a professional buys stock for personal benefit, then urges investors to buy the stock so that the price will rise to the benefit of the professional.

Another concern of the SEC focuses on ensuring investors *adequate information* about available securities to make informed investment decisions. Generally, professionals violate the antifraud provisions of the regulations when they recommend securities without making adequate information available.

STOCK MARKET REGULATION

The volume and value of stock transactions have grown rapidly. They are more than thirty times higher than they were in 1970. Since trillions of dollars are changing hands on the New York Stock Exchange and the other securities markets, investors want to be assured that proper safeguards are in place.

Self-Regulation of Securities Markets

The 1934 Securities Exchange Act allows private associations of securities professionals to set rules for professionals dealing in securities markets. Congress gave the SEC the power to monitor these *self-regulating organizations*, which include the stock exchanges, such as the *New York Stock Exchange (NYSE)*, the American Stock Exchange (AMEX), the regional exchanges, and the over-the-counter (OTC) markets, the most important of which is the NASDAQ.

Rules for Exchange Members

The stock exchanges have rules of conduct for their members. Rules govern the operation of an exchange, how securities are listed, obligations of issuers of securities, who may handle certain transactions, and how prices are set and reported. Other rules include how investors' accounts are to be managed and the qualifications of dealers and brokers. Governing the OTC market is the *National Association of Securities Dealers (NASD)*, which sets rules of behavior for its traders similar to the rules of the NYSE for its members.

Liability and Penalties

Punishment for violating rules can include suspension or expulsion from the exchange. If an exchange knows that a member is violating the rules or the law and ignores such a violation, causing investors to lose money, it can be held liable for the losses. The potential liability and SEC pressure have given the exchanges an incentive to watch securities professionals for bad behavior.

Regulations of Securities Transactions

The SEC, with the NASD, regulates securities professionals who handle the actual trading of securities. To reduce problems, floor trading by professionals is limited to registered experts, as is off-floor trading. The difference between these two types of trading is that one is done on the floor of a securities exchange, while the other is done elsewhere, such as OTC. In either case, the professional securities dealers may not trade for their own advantage ahead of their customers.

Regulations also cover *specialist firms*. These firms generally do not deal directly with the public; rather, they handle transactions for brokers. Brokers may leave customers' orders with specialists to be filled. For example, if a stock is selling for $21 a share and a stock owner is willing to sell at $22 dollars, the order may be left to be filled should the price rise to $22. SEC rules prohibit specialists from dealing for their own benefit in the orders they execute. Since they are first to learn of price changes, they could buy and sell the stock left with them to take advantage of changes in stock prices.

Arbitration of Disputes

When investors establish accounts with investment firms or stockbrokers, they usually sign a standard form that states that disputes must be arbitrated, not litigated. SEC rules govern the arbitration process, which is the primary dispute resolution mechanism for brokers and investors. Although arbitration records are secret, the decisions are made public so that people have a better understanding about the process.

Supreme Court Support

The Supreme Court has upheld the arbitration agreements. It will be an unusual case when an investor will be allowed to litigate a dispute with a broker. The Court has held that the arbitration agreements apply to security fraud claims against brokers and that there is a "strong endorsement of the federal statutes favoring this method of resolving disputes."

Arbitration is generally much less expensive than litigation. Most of the thousands of arbitration cases filed annually are resolved in favor of the client. For example, an American Arbitration Association panel ordered Prudential Securities to pay $1.4 million in damages, including $600,000 in punitive damages, for allowing its San Diego office to engage in excessive trading in an account of a retired couple. Three officers of the San Diego office were ordered to pay damages from $100,000 to $300,000.

SUMMARY

- Securities include any (1) investment of money (2) in a common enterprise in which there is (3) an expectation of profits (4) from the efforts of persons other than the investors. This definition from the *Howey* case includes any investment device that meets these general criteria.
- Registration of new securities requires public disclosure of financial and managerial information and of future business plans with the SEC. Since the disclosure is complicated and mistakes can lead to serious legal consequences, skilled counsel is required.
- Securities that are sold under a private placement exemption do not have to be registered with the SEC prior to sale. Most securities sold this way are large bond issues sold directly to institutional investors, such as insurance companies. Some smaller stock offerings are sold in limited numbers to accredited (wealthy and sophisticated) investors to avoid the cost of registration. These securities are subject to SEC regulation after their sale.
- Companies that have publicly traded securities must file financial disclosure information with the SEC, including quarterly and annual reports. Production of these reports is costly and exposes a company's finances to the public, including competitors.
- Takeover attempts and proxy battles for control of a company are subject to SEC regulations, as are certain voting rights of shareholders.
- All securities are subject to the law concerning securities fraud, which arises from the common law of fraud. They are also subject to the securities statutes that are expressed by the SEC in Rule 10b-5, which applies to a wide range of activities related to the handling of securities.
- Liability may be imposed on securities issuers or corporate officials for misstatements in corporate documents, including statements to the media. Material information that misleads investors about a company and that causes profits in a security to be lost may be the basis of legal action. Executives and those who work with sensitive financial matters must address company matters with a high degree of care.

- Insider trading can lead to criminal and civil prosecution under securities law as well as private liability. Liability is imposed when insiders violate a fiduciary duty. If one is in a position of trust that provides access to valuable information, one may not exploit the information for personal gain, since one has a duty to protect the information and use it for the benefit of those to whom the duty is owed—the shareholders.
- Securities professionals (brokers, dealers, and financial advisers) are regulated by the SEC and must meet certain financial requirements. Those who give investment advice only through an investment newsletter are not subject to regulation.
- Firms that trade securities for investors (brokerage firms), firms that make investments for investors (investment companies, such as mutual funds), and the stock exchanges are regulated by the SEC. Self-regulatory organizations impose rules on industry members that are subject to SEC approval. Violations of regulatory requirements are subject to civil and criminal penalties.

REVIEW AND DISCUSSION QUESTIONS

1. Define the following terms:

security	proxies
debt	tender offer
equity ownership	securities fraud
Howey test	misstatements
material information	insider trading
registration statement	investment company
exemption from registration	mutual fund
disclosure requirements	investment adviser

2. What is the difference in the legal protection for purchasers of registered versus unregistered securities?
3. It is generally known that the information required by the SEC to be disclosed by various statutes is "stale" by the time it is available to the SEC. Does this necessarily mean that it has no value to investors?

CASE QUESTIONS

4. A developer announced that a new apartment building was to be constructed. To have first chance at a unit in the building, you would have to deposit $250 per room. Each room was called a share of stock in the building. If you wanted a six-room apartment, you had to buy six shares of stock and later pay the sale price or rental rate. The stock price was to be refunded at the time you sold your apartment or quit renting and left the building. You could not sell the stock directly to another person. Is this stock a security? [*United Housing Foundation* v. *Forman*, 421 U.S. 837, 95 S.Ct. 2051 (1975)]

 Check your answer at http://meiners.westbuslaw.com

5. PTL (Praise the Lord, or People That Love) was a nonprofit ministry run by James Bakker. Bakker and his wife Tammy had a TV show on which they discussed, among other things, the availability of "Lifetime Partnerships" in PTL

that cost from $500 to $10,000. About 153,000 people bought the partnerships, contributing $158 million to the construction of Heritage USA, a Christian retreat center for families. According to the level contributed, purchasers were promised a short annual stay at a hotel at Heritage USA. Contributors were told that the number of partnerships sold was limited. However, the partnerships were oversold, and much of the money was spent on other facilities and lavish living. Was the sale of the partnerships securities fraud? [*Teague v. Bakker*, 35 F.3d 978 (4th Cir., 1994)]

6. For ten years, a certified public accounting firm audited the books of an investment company to prepare disclosure documents required by the SEC. The head of the firm was stealing investors' funds and rigging the books, and the accountants never found out. One day the head of the firm disappeared, leaving behind a mess and many unhappy investors. The investors sued the accounting firm to recover the money they lost, claiming that the firm was liable for securities fraud. Who won? [*Ernst & Ernst v. Hochfelder*, 425 U.S. 185, 96 S.Ct. 1375 (1976)]

 Check your answer at http://meiners.westbuslaw.com

7. Novell merged with WordPerfect by issuing Novell stock in exchange for WordPerfect stock. After the merge, Novell's stock fell 7 percent. Grossman sued in a class-action suit alleging false and misleading statements and omissions from Novell, in the filing with the SEC related to the merger, that caused the stock price to be artificially inflated before the fall. Grossman cited statements from the company that the merger was "perhaps the smoothest of mergers in recent history" and that WordPerfect was "gaining market share . . . from less than 20 percent in 1992 to more than 40% today [1994]," and that the merger created a "compelling set of opportunities." Did the case have merit? [*Grossman v. Novell, Inc.*, 120 F.3d 1112 (10th Cir., 1997)]

8. Plains Resources' executives reported that the company found an unusually large natural gas field. As a result, the company's stock was bid up from $7.63 to $29 a share in a few months. Insiders were told that initial estimates were too high. They sold more than 30,000 shares of stock. Information about the lower estimates was then released, driving the price down to about $15. Shareholders sued, claiming that the executives traded on insider information and misled investors by not revealing bad information about the gas find more quickly. Was that securities fraud? [*Rubinstein v. Collins*, 20 F.3d 160 (5th Cir., 1994)]

 Check your answer at http://meiners.westbuslaw.com

9. SG ran "StockGeneration," a web site offering the chance to buy shares in "virtual companies" listed on SG's "virtual stock exchange." SG arbitrarily set the buy and sell prices of each stock in the imaginary companies biweekly and allowed investors to buy and sell any quantity at posted prices. Millions of dollars had been collected by SG, and participants had trouble redeeming their shares. SG suspended operations and the SEC sued, contending that the sale of shares in a company that was claimed to be a "game without any risk" that had an average increase in value of 10 percent per month was in fact a sale of an unregistered security in violation of the Securities Exchange Act. The district court dismissed the complaint, holding that the shares were clearly marked and defined as a game lacking a business context. The SEC appealed. Were these unregistered securities? [*SEC v. SG Ltd.*, 265 F.3d 42 (1st Cir., 2001)]

10. Fleming, a publicly held company, and several officers of the company, were sued by various stockholders for securities fraud for filing documents that were

materially false and misleading. The stockholders contended that information in various reports failed to discuss litigation lost by Fleming that resulted in a damage award of $200 million, which saw the company's stock fall by about 25 percent. The stock price recovered some after part of the trial verdict was set aside and Fleming settled the case by paying $20 million. Stockholders contended that failure to fully reveal the risks of that litigation caused losses to investors in Fleming stock. The district court dismissed the suit because the plaintiffs failed to show that Fleming made deliberate and materially misleading statements or omissions. Stockholders appealed; did they have a case? [*City of Philadelphia* v. *Fleming Companies, Inc.*, 264 F.3d 1245 (10th Cir., 2001)]

 Check your answer at http://meiners.westbuslaw.com

11. FIG was a registered broker-dealer and a member of the NASD. In hundreds of transactions, FIG sold securities to its customers at markups from 11.11 percent to 186.46 percent above its cost for such securities. The securities were not risky; the only issue was the markup on sale to investors. The NASD claimed that this was securities fraud; it levied heavy fines on the company and placed restrictions on its trading activities. The SEC upheld that disciplinary action. FIG appealed, claiming that the SEC rule that markups over 5 percent are generally not allowed is arbitrary and capricious. Who wins? [*First Independence Group* v. *SEC*, 37 F.3d 30 (2d Cir., 1994)]

12. Several investors sued Merrill Lynch for securities fraud by charging excessive markups (that is, inflated prices and fees) and by failing to disclose either the prevailing market price of the bonds or the amount of the markups, which ran 4 percent to 10 percent on municipal bonds. The district court dismissed the case, holding that Rule 10b-5 was not violated because Merrill Lynch had no duty to disclose the markups. Did that decision hold on appeal? [*Grandon* v. *Merrill Lynch & Co., Inc.*, 147 F.3d 184 (2d Cir., 1998)]

ETHICS QUESTION

13. You started the Triangular Frisbee Company as a small operation. When the product went over big, you decided to seek outside funding to build a larger company. Your lawyer explained to you the costs of SEC registration and securities disclosure in the case of a public stock offering. Your lawyer also explained that you could avoid this by organizing as a corporation on the Caribbean island nation of Torlaga and selling stock in the corporation from there. U.S. investors would simply buy your stock through a Torlaga stockbroker. This would be much cheaper and quicker than U.S. registration. What are the pros and cons of this arrangement? Is it ethical to avoid compliance with American laws in this manner?

INTERNET ASSIGNMENT

1. What is the primary mission of the U.S. Securities and Exchange Commission (http://www.sec.gov)?
2. What are the laws that govern the securities industry? Give the URL to which the SEC refers.
3. What is the EDGAR database?

PULLING IT Together

Securities and Constitutional Law

Lowe was a registered investment adviser when he was convicted of stealing clients' funds. The SEC ordered Lowe not to operate as an investment adviser nor to associate with investment advisers. He then began to publish and sell an investment newsletter. It sold for $900 a year and attracted 19,000 subscribers in its first year of operation. The newsletter contained commentary about securities markets, investment strategies, and specific recommendations for buying, selling, or holding stocks. Subscribers could call a "hot line" for current market tips.

The SEC sued Lowe, claiming that the sale of investment advice violated the Investment Advisers Act because of his previous conviction and sentence. The court of appeals agreed with the SEC. Lowe appealed to the Supreme Court, contending that the First Amendment allowed him to publish and sell the investment newsletter. Was he right?

[*Lowe* v. *SEC*, 472 U.S. 181, 105 S.Ct., 2557 (1985)]

Chapter 21 | *The International Legal Environment of Business*

Seawinds Limited was a Hong Kong corporation with its principal place of business in California. The shipping company owned three container ships that operated between the Far East and the United States. Hoping to expand, the company entered into shipping contracts with companies from Hong Kong, Singapore, Great Britain, the Netherlands, and the United States. Its expectations were not met and it sued the shippers for delivering only a small amount of goods for shipment, an alleged breach of contract. The contract specified that all disputes were to be brought before the Hong Kong courts and subject to the law of Hong Kong. However, the law of Hong Kong—compared to U.S. law—would not likely be favorable to Seawinds.

Was Seawinds obligated to bring the lawsuit in Hong Kong? Did all aspects of the dispute require the application of Hong Kong law? Was it possible to try some disputes in U.S. courts under U.S. law?

These are some of the issues that are the focus of this chapter on the international legal environment of business. We begin with a discussion of the nature of the international business environment. Then we consider the various ways that the U.S. government works to restrict imports and stimulate exports. The business organizations that may be considered before becoming involved in an international venture are then looked at. The constraints imposed by the Foreign Corrupt Practices Act are next considered. Finally, the chapter discusses the nature of international contracting, insurance against loss, and procedures for the resolution of international disputes.

INTERNATIONAL LAW AND BUSINESS

Technical improvements in transportation and communications have changed the nature of business substantially. The percentage of U.S. gross domestic product involved in international trade has tripled in recent decades. Most businesses are affected by events originating in other countries. Crop failures in Argentina, political unrest in the Middle East, currency devaluations in Mexico, and shipping strikes in England can all have a significant impact on U.S. businesses.

The International Business Environment

International business includes all business transactions that involve entities from two or more countries. In addition to the movement of goods across countries, international business involves the movement of services, capital, and personnel by multinational enterprises.

The *international business environment* includes business activities that are affected by international business conditions and world events. For example, U.S. businesses that operate only in the domestic market often find themselves in direct competition with foreign manufacturers. Initially, the main source of foreign competition was from imported products. However, foreign competitors now build factories in the United States to compete more effectively.

A major difference between domestic and international businesses is the special *financial*, *political*, and *regulatory risks* in international enterprises. They arise from a variety of sources, including differences between countries in currencies, language, customs, legal systems, social philosophies, and government policies.

Origins of International Law

Before the development of the modern international procedures we will focus on, nations and merchants involved in international commerce developed rules for trade. Early trade customs centered around the law of the sea. They provided, among other things, for rights of shipping in foreign ports, salvage rights, fishing rights, and freedom of passage.

International commercial codes date back as far as 1400 B.C. to Egyptian merchants involved in international trade. Merchants from other countries developed similar codes to provide some legal certainty in international transactions. The Greek and Roman civilizations both had well-developed codes of practice for international trade.

During the Middle Ages, principles embodied in the *lex mercatoria* (law merchant) arose from trading customs to govern commercial transactions throughout Europe. The law merchant conduct created a workable legal structure for the protection and encouragement of international transactions. The international commerce codes in use today are partly derived from codes reaching back many centuries.

Sources of International Law

The main sources of international commercial law are the laws of individual countries, the laws defined by trade agreements between countries, and the rules enacted by a worldwide or regional organization—such as the United Nations or the European Union (EU). There is, however, no international system of courts generally accepted for resolving international conflicts between businesses. An overview of some international and U.S. organizations affecting the international legal environment is provided in Exhibit 21.1.

International Trade Agreements

Most countries seek to improve their economic relations through trade agreements. The intent is to improve the investment and trade climates among countries. For example, most industrialized countries have tax agreements to prevent double taxation of individuals and businesses. Two particularly important trade agreements for U.S. businesses are the *North American Free Trade Agreement (NAFTA)* and the General Agreement on Tariffs and Trade, which created the World Trade Organization.

North American Free Trade Agreement

NAFTA was signed by the governments of Canada, the United States, and Mexico in 1992. After being ratified in each of those countries, it went into effect in 1994. NAFTA reduces or eliminates tariffs and trade barriers on most North American trade. Although some tariffs were eliminated immediately, most tariffs are being phased out through 2009. The industries most affected by NAFTA are agriculture, automobiles, pharmaceuticals, and textiles. In the end, the agreement creates a huge free trade area with over 400 million consumers.

NAFTA also provides for greater Mexican protection of U.S. and Canadian intellectual property. It calls for greater protection of the environment and ensures that the managers of U.S. companies do not use access to Mexico as a way to avoid U.S. environmental laws. NAFTA uses special panels to resolve disputes involving unfair trade practices, investment restrictions, and environmental issues. The activity spurred by NAFTA has generated interest to expand the reach of NAFTA to include other Latin American countries.

World Trade Organization

After World War II, the *General Agreement on Tariffs and Trade (GATT)* worked to reduce trade barriers. GATT focused on trade restrictions (import quotas and tariffs). It published tariff schedules to which countries agreed. Tariff schedules were developed in trade negotiations, or *rounds*. In the most recent round (called the Uruguay Round), 124 nations participated.

GATT was replaced by the *World Trade Organization (WTO)*, one of the significant developments of the last round. Since 1995, the WTO has overseen the trade agreement and has worked to set up a dispute resolution system using three-person arbitration panels. The panels follow strict schedules for making decisions. WTO member nations agreed they should not veto WTO decisions.

The WTO trade agreement eventually will lower world tariffs by 40 percent. The United States, Japan, Canada, countries of the European Union, and other industrialized nations agreed to eliminate tariffs completely among themselves in ten industries:

Beer	Medical equipment
Construction equipment	Paper
Distilled spirits	Pharmaceuticals
Farm machinery	Steel
Furniture	Toys

Exhibit 21.1

Selected Organizations Affecting the International Legal Environment

World Organizations

• United Nations (http://www.un.org)	Created as a peacekeeping body, the U.N. works to encourage international cooperation in a variety of areas. It has several departments that encourage world trade.
• World Bank (http://www.worldbank.org)	Promotes private foreign investment through loans and guarantees; also provides technical and managerial assistance on large capital projects.
• International Monetary Fund (IMF) (http://www.imf.org)	Responsible for promoting international trade by working to promote the stabilityof currency exchange rates.
• World Trade Organization (WTO) (http://www.wto.org)	Promotes international trade by working to reduce trade barriers and to establish uniform tariff schedules.
• Commission on International Trade Law (http://www.un.org.law)	Promotes uniformity in laws; discourages legal obstacles to trade.
• World Intellectual Property Organization (http://www.wipo.org)	Promotes protection of intellectual property worldwide and promotes uniformity in laws.
• International Court of Justice (http://www.icj-cij.org)	Principal court of the United Nations. Located in the Netherlands, it has jurisdiction over all cases brought to it, but only countries (not private parties) have standing.

United States Organizations

• International Trade Administration (ITA) (http://www.ita.doc.gov)	Part of the Department of Commerce. Developed to promote trade and to help American companies sell their products overseas. Provides companies with data, foreign license requirements, and other information.
• International Trade Commission (ITC) (http://www.usitc.gov)	Independent agency responsible for recommending trade restrictions to the President. Examines the impact of a subsidized foreign import on domestic industry.
• Court of International Trade (http://www.uscourts.gov)	Has jurisdiction to review findings of the ITC or ITA. Has jurisdiction over lawsuits against the United States regarding imports, tariffs, duties, or embargoes.
• Bureau of Export Administration (BEA) (http://www.bxa.doc.gov)	Part of the Department of Commerce. Responsible for maintaining the Commodity Control List—goods subject to export controls.
• United States Export-Import Bank (Ex-Im Bank) (http://www.exim.gov)	Provides loans and loan guarantees to foreign purchasers of goods exported from the United States. Mostly involved in heavy capital equipment projects and aircraft sales.
• Overseas Private Investment Corporation (OPIC) (http://www.opic.gov)	Provides insurance for U.S. projects that would be rejected by private insurers—largely projects in developing countries. Coverage protects against currency exchange problems, expropriation or confiscation, and war.
• United States Trade Representative (USTR) (http://www.ustr.gov)	Appointed by the president. Has authority to negotiate trade agreements on the behalf of the United States to reduce trade barriers, including the WTO.

As we saw in Chapter 9, the WTO also helps to provide worldwide protection for intellectual property. The WTO countries also agree to reduce or eliminate governmental subsidies on business research, civil aviation, and agriculture. Only in the film and television programming area was the United States not able to gain reductions in trade barriers by the Europeans. France wanted to maintain the barrier because of its concerns about the domination of American films, music, and videos in Europe.

U.S. IMPORT POLICY

Countries have long imposed restrictions on the import and export of certain products and services. In addition, regulations are often enacted to encourage international business activity by domestic industries.

Taxes on Imports

Restrictions on imports generally are imposed to generate revenue for the government and to protect a country's domestic industries from foreign competition. Import licensing procedures, quotas, testing requirements, safety and manufacturing standards, government procurement policies, and complicated customs procedures are all ways to regulate imports.

Tariff Classes

A *tariff* is a duty or tax imposed by a government on an imported good. Tariffs can be classified into two categories: *specific tariffs*, which impose a fixed tax or duty on each unit of a product, and *ad valorem tariffs*, which impose a tax as a percentage of the price of the product. Domestic producers often argue that without a tariff, foreign products will force them out of the market. Workers will lose their jobs and the country will grow dependent on foreign businesses for products. Those arguing against tariffs assert that only through free trade will countries exploit their comparative advantage and help consumers by lowering prices on many goods.

In the United States, the duty imposed is published in the *tariff schedules*, which are applied by the Customs Service to all products entering U.S. ports. Customs officials classify products and determine the tariff rates when products enter the country. Any tariff must be paid before the good enters the country.

Each year, importers file hundreds of requests with Customs for determination of the classification of goods. The Supreme Court stated, in *U.S. v. Mead Corp.*, 121 S.Ct. 2164, that Customs is entitled to significant deference by the courts when it interprets the tariff laws passed by Congress.

An appeal of a Customs Service tariff determination goes first to the U.S. Court of International Trade and from there to the U.S. Court of Appeals for the Federal Circuit. Since classification greatly affects the tariff that is imposed on imports, companies argue to be classified in the most favorable category. The *Russ Berrie* case is typical of the many appeals heard by those courts.

Russ Berrie & Company v. U.S.
United States Court of Appeals, Federal Circuit
381 F.3d 1334 (2004)

CASE BACKGROUND *Berrie imported inexpensive lapel pins and earring sets with Halloween and Christmas themes, such as a witch, Santa Claus, and a snowman. Berrie proposed that the goods would be classified as "festive articles" under heading 9505, which are duty-free. Customs classified the goods as "imitation jewelry" under heading 7117, subject to an 11 percent ad valorem tariff.*

Berrie appealed and the Court of International Trade held in its favor, ruling that U.S. Customs' "rulings lacked thoroughness and valid reasoning." The Court held that heading 9505 should apply. Customs appealed.

CASE DECISION Friedman, Senior Circuit Judge.

* * *

The imported merchandise is . . . classifiable under heading 7117 as "imitation jewelry." . . .

Heading 9505 applies to "festive, carnival, or other entertainment articles," which include "articles for Christmas festivities and parts and accessories thereof." . . .

The imported articles in this case fit comfortably within that standard. . . . The imported pins and earrings are . . . classifiable under heading 9505. . . .

Our function . . . is to apply the Customs classification standards as Congress has written them. . . .

Where, as here, the imported objects are . . . classifiable under more than one heading, the Schedules' General Rules of Interpretation determine the outcome. . . .

Rule 3 states in pertinent part that "when . . . goods are . . . classifiable under two or more headings, the heading which provides the most specific description shall be preferred.". . .

Under this reasoning, the "imitation jewelry" heading is more specific than the "festive articles" heading because it covers a narrower set of terms. . . .

The judgment of the Court of International Trade is reversed, and the case is remanded to that court with instructions to uphold Customs' classification of the imported merchandise under heading 7117.

QUESTIONS FOR ANALYSIS
1. Why would tariffs for one category be zero and for another category be 11 percent?
2. Would you expect Customs to usually apply the highest tariff rate that might fit?

Harmonized Tariff Schedules

The United States uses a *harmonized tariff schedule*, developed by countries for the purpose of standardizing the ways in which goods are classified by customs officials worldwide. Each country uses the same codes to classify goods traded. The process streamlines trade by reducing language and usage differences between countries, but different countries may impose different tariffs.

Bans on Certain Products

Importing certain products may violate regulations. For example, some explosives and weapons cannot be imported. Illegal products, such as narcotics, violate domestic laws and cannot legally be imported. Products made from endangered species are prohibited. Other items may not meet safety regulations or pollution requirements and cannot be imported.

Foreign vehicles that do not meet with U.S. safety or pollution regulations will not be cleared for importation. For example, Bill Gates, the chairman of Microsoft, tried to import a new Porsche 959 from Germany. It was the first Porsche of that model sold in the United States. The car was not allowed by customs officials to enter the country because that model Porsche had not been crash tested to show it met U.S. standards.

Import Controls

Congress has given the Department of Commerce, through its *International Trade Administration (ITA)* and the *International Trade Commission (ITC)*, the ability to restrict imports. These agencies are concerned with foreign companies that sell their products at prices lower in the U.S. market than in their home market (called dumping) or receive a subsidy from their government to lower costs of production so they can produce more goods to sell in other countries.

Antidumping Orders

Under both the WTO and U.S. law, *dumping* "is the business practice of charging a lower price in the export market than in the home market, after taking into consideration important differences in the sale (such as credit terms and transportation) and the goods being sold."

The law provides that if it is determined that goods from a country are being dumped and domestic industries are losing sales as a result, an antidumping order may be issued. Under an order, the incoming goods will be subject to an antidumping duty (tax). The amount of the duty is determined by comparing the market price in the home market with the price charged in the United States. The difference between the two prices determines the tariff to be applied to the price of the product.

Similarly, if the Commerce Department determines that a government is "providing, directly or indirectly, a subsidy with respect to the manufacture, production, or exportation of a class or kind of merchandise imported, or sold for importation into the U.S.," and the ITC determines that this injures U.S. producers, duties (tariffs) are imposed in an amount equal to the net subsidy.

Duty orders generally remain in place until the importer can show three consecutive years of "fair market value" sales and Commerce is convinced that there is little chance of "less than fair market value" sales in the United States in the future. Hundreds of antidumping requests are filed each year by companies hoping to impose taxes on their competitors' imports. After a decision is made by the Department of Commerce, the decision may be appealed to the Court of International Trade and then to the Court of Appeals for the Federal Circuit. We see an example in the *Huaiyin Foreign Trade Corp.* case.

Huaiyin Foreign Trade Corp v. U.S.

United States Court of Appeals, Federal Circuit
322 F.3d 1369 (2003)

CASE BACKGROUND   *Crawfish processors in the United States filed an antidumping petition with the Department of Commerce, claiming that freshwater crawfish tail meat from the People's Republic of China (PRC) was sold in the United States at less than fair market value. Commerce investigated. It sent questionnaires to various PRC freshwater crawfish tail meat exporters and producers.*

Commerce determined that most crawfish producers in the PRC were controlled by the government and were not market companies selling crawfish at market prices. Government-controlled processors are called NME (nonmarket economy). Commerce imposed a dumping duty of 201.63 percent for all crawfish tail meat from NME processors and a duty of 91.5 percent for crawfish producers able to show they were not controlled by the government.

One exporter, Huaiyin, was accidentally classified as not under government control and so received the duty rate of 91.5 percent. U.S. competitors noticed that classification and complained that Huaiyin was under government control. Commerce then issued a Final Determination that changed the rate that applied the higher duty to Huaiyin. That decision was upheld by the Court of International Trade. Huaiyin appealed.

CASE DECISION Clevenger, Circuit Judge.

* * *

As required by statute, we will sustain the agency's determinations unless they are "unsupported by substantial evidence on the record, or otherwise not in accordance with law." . . .

First, Huaiyin had no entitlement to the lower duty margin. . . . Only entities able to demonstrate their independence from the PRC government were entitled to an individual rate as if they were part of a market economy. Based on the responses and evidence it received from participating companies during its investigation,

the Department calculated company-specific rates from only eight entities. Beyond those eight specifically-named entities, the Department instructed Customs to apply the PRC-wide higher dumping duty margin of 201.63 percent to all exporters not specifically identified in the *Final Determinations*. Since Huaiyin concedes that it neither participated in the initial investigation nor provided any evidence that it was independent from the PRC, it necessarily fell within the ambit of the NME presumption and the Department justifiably determined that the PRC controlled its export activities. Subject to the presumption, Huaiyin received the default PRC-wide dumping duty margin; it could not and did not receive a lower rate. . . .

Affirmed.

QUESTIONS FOR ANALYSIS

1. Antidumping cases have steadily risen over the years. What might contribute to that increase?
2. When the United States imposes dumping duties on the sale of imports to the country, how are other countries likely to respond?

When a dumping duty is imposed by the United States, or any other government, there may also be an appeal to the World Trade Organization, which hears hundreds of complaints each year. It does not have the power to force nations to change restrictions on imports, but it can allow other nations to retaliate without violating international trade treaties.

Foreign Trade Zones and Duty-Free Ports

Foreign trade zones are areas where businesses can import goods without paying tariffs. The zone is a secured area where goods may be processed, assembled, or warehoused. Tariffs are imposed only on the finished product (generally much less than those imposed on individual parts) and only when the product leaves the zone for sale in the domestic market. Products exported from the zone to other countries are generally not subject to tariffs.

Duty-free ports are ports of entry that do not assess duties or tariffs on products. Duty-free ports encourage the importation and sale of international goods within the country. Hong Kong is well known for such practices. Benefits to a country are the encouragement of trade with other countries and the attraction of businesses and tourists to the country to purchase products free of duties and other fees.

Export Regulation and Promotion

Most governments encourage the export of domestic products. They hope to stimulate employment and bring in foreign exchange from export sales. When the value of imports exceeds the value of exports, the country is said to be running a *trade deficit*. However, for reasons of national defense and foreign policy, governments may restrict exports of certain products.

Where to Produce?

Your company makes electric scooters sold in the North American market. You import the motors from China, the tires come from Brazil, the frame from the United States, and other parts come from suppliers around the world. Where might you consider building the scooters? What are the tradeoffs?

Federal Government Efforts

The Commerce Department is the major export-promotion agency. Primary responsibility for export promotion within Commerce falls upon the ITA. The ITA manages the U.S. Foreign Commercial Service, which has commercial officers at major cities around the world and export counselors in district offices around the United States. At its overseas offices, referred to as Commercial Consulates, it supplies U.S. product information, arranges business meetings with local firms, accompanies U.S. company representatives to meetings, and gathers local market information. The Commercial Consulates, for example, might assist a U.S. company in finding a foreign agent to distribute its products. They also lead trade missions overseas each year and participate in hundreds of trade expositions.

The *Export Trading Company Act* allows U.S. companies to form trading companies similar to those in Japan. A large Japanese trading company will handle as many as 20,000 different products. This allows the trading companies to provide customers with better prices and quality control. Although the Export Trading Company Act provides an antitrust exemption, the exemption is too weak to encourage the development of large trading companies in the United States. Primarily small, single-product trading companies have been established under the Act.

Export Restrictions

Despite the desire to increase exports, the U.S. government imposes some restrictions on exports. The sale of a certain good may (1) injure domestic industry (for example, exporting a raw material in short supply), (2) jeopardize national security (for example, selling military hardware to the wrong country), or (3) conflict with national policy (for example, selling goods to a country that supports terrorist activities). Restrictions are implemented through licensing requirements in the *Export Administration Act*.

Congress delegated the power to enforce export licenses to the Secretary of Commerce. It can do so only according to strict standards. The standards reflect the tension between a desire to control exports of strategic goods for security reasons and the desire to encourage exports to reduce the trade deficit.

Licensing Agreements   The Export Administration Act gives Commerce the ability to require the following export licenses, depending on the good being exported:

1. A *validated license*, authorizing a specific export (such as for military goods and advanced computers), issued upon application by the exporter
2. A *qualified general license*, authorizing multiple exports, issued upon application by the exporter

JURIS *prudence?*

A Bargain—Only $29.35 for a Razor Blade!

Finance professors Zdanowicz and Pak from Florida International University question whether the trade deficit numbers are not inflated as a result of global money laundering via fake import/export invoices.

They found ordinary telephones from Hong Kong "priced" at $2,400 each, salad dressing at $720 per bottle, smoke detectors at $653 each, and razor blades from Panama at $29.35 apiece. Similarly, they found underpriced export invoices: radial tires shipped to Colombia at $3.03 each, pianos to France at $38 each, and snowplows to Jamaica (!) at $267.70.

The professors' explanation is that the funds are transferred as the invoices assert, but the transferring is done for the purpose of money laundering to avoid paying income taxes. By making inflated payments to itself in another country, a business avoids taxes, and the transfer of funds is counted as a business expense. The professors estimate that the cost to the U.S. Treasury is about $40 billion a year in lost revenue. The Treasury "expressed interest" in the issue.

Source: *Forbes*

---

3. A *general license*, authorizing exports, without application by the exporter, and that applies to most U.S. goods intended for export
4. Other special licenses that help implement the Act

Commerce maintains a list—the *Commodity Control List*—of the goods subject to such licenses. The restrictions imposed depend upon the country to which goods are to be sent and the reason for the export restriction. Goods not on the list are subject to a general license, which requires little more than filing a Shipper's Export Declaration with Commerce.

Application to Reexported U.S. Goods   Commerce's export licensing requirements also apply to the *reexport* of U.S. goods. That is, an export license is needed to ship U.S.-origin controlled goods from, say, India to Iran. The intent is to prohibit the shipment of sensitive goods from the United States first to a "safe" country and then to a controlled country. In this way, the Export Administration Act reaches beyond U.S. boundaries.

Penalty Provisions   Penalties for violations of Commerce's licensing provisions include criminal and civil penalties. For example, McDonnell Douglas, an aircraft maker, paid a $2.1 million fine for improper sale of sensitive equipment to China. Since the company reported the violation, there were no criminal penalties. An exporter who "knowingly" violates the Act can be fined up to $50,000 or five times the value of the exports involved, whichever is greater, and receive up to five years in prison. An exporter who "willfully" violates the Act can be fined more and receive up to ten years in prison. Penalties also can result in the suspension or revocation of an individual's or a business's authority to export.

BUSINESS STRUCTURES IN FOREIGN MARKETS

Businesses have two basic ways of selling products in foreign markets. They can either export products manufactured in this country to the foreign country or manufacture products in the foreign country for distribution there.

Exporting Manufactured Products

Companies first entering international business usually export products manufactured domestically. Exporting requires relatively little investment on the part of the business and has fewer risks than foreign manufacturing.

Businesses may export indirectly or directly. *Indirect exporting* means using an exporter who sells the product in foreign markets for a U.S. manufacturer. The manufacturer may sell through a foreign agent who specializes in marketing particular products overseas. *Direct exporting* means developing an organization within a business that is responsible for exports.

Foreign Manufacturing

Foreign manufacturing is motivated by a desire to reduce costs and expand. Costs reduced by foreign manufacturing may include shipping, labor expenses, and raw materials. Operating in another country may also help secure long-term contracts to supply goods to producers in that country. In addition, foreign manufacturing may be a way to avoid import restrictions or tariffs imposed by the host country.

Several leading Japanese companies decided to open manufacturing facilities in the United States. They feared that Congress might impose high tariffs on Japanese products. Since products made by a Japanese business located in the United States are made in America, they are not subject to duties. Businesses considering foreign manufacturing have several options, including

- A wholly owned foreign subsidiary
- A joint venture
- A licensing agreement
- A franchise agreement
- Contract manufacturing

INTERNATIONAL *Perspective*

Controlling International Pirates

One of the most significant challenges facing a manager is deciding how to react to foreign manufacturers who pirate (copy) a company's product and then sell the product as authentic at lower prices than the real thing. Pirates cost U.S. industry more than $100 billion in lost sales every year.

Microsoft knows that pirates make copies of its Windows programs. After one three-month investigation, Microsoft led police to an apartment building in Taipei, Taiwan.

Police uncovered a sophisticated software pirating operation. In addition to finding the diskettes, they found flawless copies of the operation and installation manuals and of the hologram sticker intended to foil pirates. The number of copies on order at this one operation represented a lost revenue of $150 million to Microsoft, which sued the pirating company. In addition, the U.S. International Trade Commission issued a warning against Taiwan that Taiwan try to reduce pirating. If it fails, the United States could impose high tariffs on Taiwanese products entering the United States.

Wholly Owned Subsidiary

By doing foreign manufacturing through a *wholly owned subsidiary*, a business owns the operation. A business may buy an existing facility or build a new one. *Situations* exist, however, in which complete ownership is not possible. Many countries impose limits on the percentage of ownership in a local enterprise by foreigners.

Joint Venture

A *joint venture* means sharing ownership with foreign partners. For example, one party may supply the facilities, and the other party the technological skills required for the operation. Although a joint venture requires less investment by the company than does a wholly owned subsidiary, it can mean loss of managerial control.

Licensing Agreement

A *licensing agreement* is a contract. One business—the *licensor*—grants another business—the *licensee*—access to its patents and other technologies. The licensor is usually granted a royalty on sales. Allowing the licensee to use the business's trademark could help establish a worldwide reputation. However, the licensing company needs to make sure that the agreement is enforceable in the licensee's country or the technology and trademark may be easily stolen.

Franchise Agreement

Franchising is a popular vehicle for establishing a foreign market presence. Franchising is a form of licensing. The franchisor (the supplier) grants the franchisee (the foreign dealer) the right to sell products or services in exchange for a fee. The most visible franchises are the fast-food restaurants: McDonald's, Pizza Hut, Coca-Cola, and KFC have made major inroads with franchises in China. The franchising company must work to make sure that the quality (and thus the reputation) of its products is maintained at overseas franchises.

Contract Manufacturing

Companies may contract for the production of certain products in foreign facilities. U.S. retailers, for example, contract for the production of clothing and shoes in Malaysia, India, and China, where labor costs are low. Contract manufacturing has the advantage of requiring limited investment in production facilities.

Nike has made contract manufacturing an important part of its operations. The company does not own the manufacturing plants that produce its shoes. When demand for the products slows, it can end a manufacturing contract. The company does not have to worry about making payments on a plant that is not producing.

FOREIGN CORRUPT PRACTICES ACT

Governments in many countries are involved in business activity. Government permission often is required before business transactions can be completed, which increases the likelihood of bribery. Corruption is a global problem, but is more common in less-developed nations.

In the United States, the *Foreign Corrupt Practices Act (FCPA)* prohibits U.S. companies and their agents from bribing foreign officials (http://www.state.gov/e/eb/cba/gc). The law was enacted in 1977 after exposure of cases in which U.S. corporations bribed foreign officials for favors. A study by the Securities and Exchange Commission found that the practice was widespread: more than 400 companies (117 of which were Fortune 500 companies) admitted to making substantial bribes to foreign officials.

Corruption

In many countries, corruption is so common that normal business is nearly impossible. It is a major barrier to economic development. There are measures of risk of investment around the world. One measure comes from Transparency International (TI) (see http://www.transparency.org), an organization in Berlin founded by a former World Bank director who was frustrated at the inability of countries to grow because of corruption. Exhibit 21.2 shows some of TI's Corruption Perception Index, which is based on numerous surveys. A score of 10 would indicate a corruption-free country.

Exhibit 21.2

Corruption Perception Index

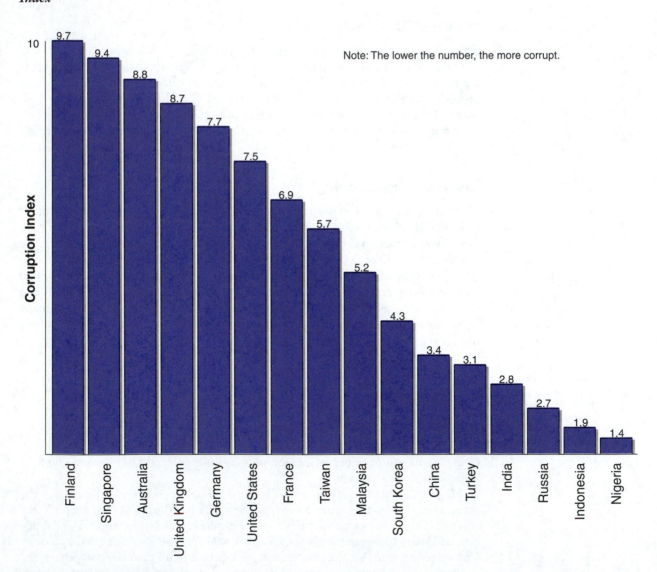

Note: The lower the number, the more corrupt.

Source: *Transparency International.*

International Antibribery Movement

Recently, many nations signed a convention against corruption. All agreed to present legislation to their national legislatures that would make bribery a crime. In 1998, the U.S. Senate ratified the Convention on Combating Bribery of Foreign Officials in International Business Transactions (http://www.oecd.org/home). Other nations have not been quick to act, and, in some cases, enforcement remains another issue.

Antibribery Provisions

The antibribery provisions of the FCPA prohibit U.S. companies from "corruptly" paying or offering to pay a foreign official to gain assistance in obtaining or retaining business. The Act also prohibits payments to a person, such as a foreign agent, when the U.S. company knows that payment will go toward bribing a foreign official.

The Act recognizes that some payments are necessary and routine. An exception exists for a "facilitating or expediting payment . . . the purpose of which is to expedite or secure the performance of a routine government action." Such "routine actions" normally include bribes for services such as processing visas and providing utilities or transportation services. Guess wrong, and the consequences could be serious. The basic test in determining whether a bribe is permissible focuses not on the person to whom payment is made, but on the purpose of the payment. This is complicated by the fact that such payments are often made by local agents without the knowledge of the U.S. manager.

Who Knows What?

The most controversial part of the antibribery law is the "knowing" requirement. Congress stated that "simple negligence" or "mere foolishness" should not be the basis for liability. The FCPA provides that the knowing requirement covers "any instance where any reasonable person would have realized the existence of the circumstances or result and the [individual] has consciously chosen not to ask about what he had reason to believe he would discover." For example, managers should be concerned about foreign agents who work on a commission basis. The government is particularly suspicious that large commissions may be a cover for the agent to make bribes.

Accounting Requirements

The FCPA requires companies to "make and keep books, records, and accounts which, in reasonable detail, accurately and fairly reflect the transactions and dispositions of [their] assets." The law also requires companies to "devise and maintain a system of internal accounting controls sufficient to provide reasonable assurances" that all transactions are authorized and that access to assets can be tracked. The accounting provisions were included in the Act in response to a study by the Securities and Exchange Commission that showed that many corporations maintained "slush funds" that were "off the books" to make bribes to foreign officials. The Act requires a "paper trail" that improves corporate accountability.

Penalties

The Department of Justice is responsible for criminal enforcement of the FCPA. A violation leads to fines up to $100,000 and imprisonment for up to five years for individuals. Corporations convicted of violations can incur fines of up to $2 million per violation. The *King* case is an example of an FCPA action.

United States v. King

United States Court of Appeals, Eighth Circuit
351 F.3d 859 (2003)

CASE BACKGROUND   *The FBI investigated the dealings of Owl Securities and Investments (OSI), a Kansas City company that was raising funds for a large land development project in Costa Rica. The investigation focused on King, one of OSI's largest investors. The FBI obtained the cooperation of OSI executives, including Kingsley, OSI's president, who tape-recorded conversations.*

King was convicted of planning to bribe senior Costa Rican officials to obtain the rights to the land to be developed. He was fined $60,000 and sentenced to 30 months in prison. He appealed.

CASE DECISION   Beam, Circuit Judge.

* * *

Viewing the evidence in the light most favorable to the verdict, there was ample evidence in the record to support the jury's conviction. The tape recordings, alone, support the jury's verdict. [Footnote, quoting King: "I think we could pay the top people enough, that the rest of the people won't bother us any. That's what I'm hoping this million and a half dollars does. I'm hoping it pays for enough top people."] There was sufficient evidence to prove King's knowledge of the proposed payment long before Kingsley became an informant for the government. Moreover, the recordings show King's knowing participation in, approval of, and subsequent actions in furtherance of the conspiracy to offer the bribe. In addition, the testimony of six witnesses conducted over a five-day period, and the remaining exhibits, support the jury's conviction of King for conspiracy and substantive violations under the FCPA. . . .

Affirmed.

QUESTIONS OF ANALYSIS

1. King contended that since Kingsley was a co-conspirator, his testimony should not be allowed as it could not be considered reliable. Is it?

2. Is it fair that King got prison time and Kingsley did not because he cooperated with the FBI?

INTERNATIONAL CONTRACTS

As in domestic business agreements, the basis for any international agreement is a contract. As we saw in Chapter 11, many sales of goods are under the CISG, but many contracts are not. Such contracts can differ from domestic contracts in complexity and use of unusual provisions. The distance between the parties often complicates contract negotiation, substance, and performance. The differing languages, currencies, legal systems, and business customs of parties can affect the nature of the contract and influence the way it is written.

Cultural Aspects

Sensitivity to cultural differences is important in international contracting. In Japan, for example, *meishi*, or business cards, are exchanged formally at a first meeting, while in the United States, business cards may be exchanged casually at any time. In many countries, including China, hours may go by before the details of the business are mentioned. This is different from the U.S. approach, where the parties usually get right to the point.

The attitude toward relationships is another difference. Many countries have a cultural expectation that a relationship will be long-term. As a result, the negotiation process may be long, since it is necessary for the parties to know one another before entering into a relationship. Contracts based on long-term expectations are often relatively short, with few contingencies expressly provided. The idea is that problems can be worked out as they arise, with the parties trying to maintain the relationship.

Language itself should not be a barrier to an international contract. However, it is important that the terms of the contract are clearly defined in a language that all parties understand. Interpreters can be an integral part of the negotiations and the final draft of the contract where parties are not fluent in a common language.

Financial Aspects

To manage the financial risks that may arise in international contracts, care must be taken in specifying the method of payment. In addition, the parties may be concerned about removing profits from the countries in which they conduct their business.

Exchange Markets

In an international transaction, the seller often receives another country's currency. A business may want to exchange that currency into dollars, but the exchange is not always simple. Exchange risk is the potential loss or profit that occurs between the time currency is acquired and the time it is exchanged for another currency. Suppose, for example, that U.S. Wine, Inc., buys French wines. The contract calls for the payment of three million Euros in 180 days. When the contract is signed, the exchange rate is 1.00 Euros to the dollar, or $3,000,000. Suppose that U.S. Wine waits 180 days before paying and the exchange rate falls to .85 Euros to the dollar. U.S. Wine now must pay $3,530,000. Change in the exchange rate costs the company $530,000. To avoid such difficulties, businesses may require payment in dollars rather than in the currency of the other country.

Financial Instruments Used in International Contracts

International contracts often use special international financial devices. These assure later payment or allow for the arrangement of credit when buyers are otherwise unable to come up with the cash necessary for the transaction. One device commonly used is the letter of credit.

A *letter of credit* is an agreement or assurance by the bank of the buyer to pay a specified amount to the seller upon receipt of certain documents that prove that the goods have been shipped and that contractual obligations of the seller have been fulfilled. The usual documentation required includes a certificate of origin, an export license, a certificate of inspection, a bill of lading, a commercial invoice, and an insurance policy. Once the bank has received the required documentation, it releases payment to the seller. Exhibit 21.3 illustrates the route taken by a letter of credit and the documentation in an international business transaction between an Italian seller and an American buyer, each using its own bank.

Letters of credit can be either revocable or irrevocable. As the label attached to each implies, a *revocable letter of credit* may be withdrawn, while an *irrevocable letter of credit* may not be withdrawn before the specific date stated on it. Exhibit 21.4 is an example of an irrevocable letter of credit.

*Letter of Credit
in an International
Transaction*

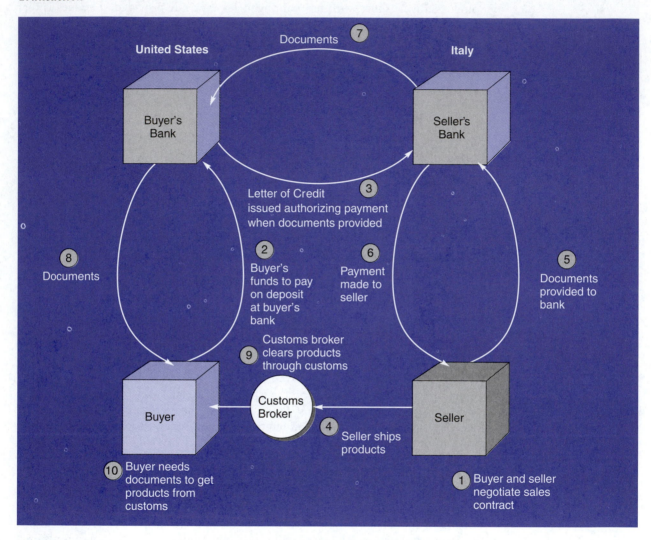

Repatriation of Monetary Profits

Repatriation is the ability of a business to return money earned in a foreign country to its home country. Some countries restrict the amounts of currencies that can be taken out of the country. The usual reason for restrictions on repatriation is a desire that money earned in the country be put back into the local economy.

Key Clauses in International Contracts

The contract is the foundation of any business venture. As with domestic contracts, care should be taken that the intent of the parties is fully represented by the contract. International contracts should be in writing, even if they only state the positions and goals of the parties. The following clauses are generally considered critical in international deals.

Exhibit 21.4

Example of an Irrevocable Letter of Credit

LETTER OF CREDIT—CONFIRMED, IRREVOCABLE

Western Reserve Bank   Letter of Credit #59723
Chicago, Illinois   Issued on August 1, 2006

To: Exotica Company   From: Tiramisu Import Company
Dallas, Texas   Rome, Italy

Gentlemen:

We are instructed by Commercial Bank of Italy, Rome, Italy, to inform you that they have opened their irrevocable credit in favor of Tiramisu Import Company, Rome, Italy, for the sum in U.S. dollars not exceeding a total of about $55,000.00 (Fifty-five Thousand and 00/100 Dollars), available by your drafts on us, to be accompanied by:

1. Full Set On Board Negotiable Ocean Bills of Lading, stating: "Freight Prepaid" and made out to the order of Commercial Bank of Italy.

2. Insurance Policy or Certificate covering Marine and War Risk.

3. Packing List.

4. Commercial Invoice in triplicate:
    Covering 200 Pcs. 1025 Electric Espresso Coffee Machines
    200 Pcs. 750 Stove Top Espresso Coffee Makers
    350 Pcs. 420 Electric Pasta Makers

Total Value $54,702.75 C.I.F. Rome, Italy

Import Lic. No. 3792 Expires October 24, 2006

5. Shipper's Export Declaration.
    Partial Shipment Permitted. Transshipment Not Permitted.
    Merchandise must be shipped in SS Mercaso.

All documents must indicate Letter of Credit No. 59723, Import License No. 3792, expires October 24, 2006.

All drafts must be marked "Drawn under Letter of Credit No. 59723, issued by Western Reserve Bank. Drafts must be presented to this company not later than October 1, 2006."

This credit is subject to the Uniform Customs and Practices for Documentary Credits (1984 Revision) International Chamber of Commerce Publication No. 400.

We confirm the credit and thereby undertake that all drafts drawn and presented as above specified will be duly honored by us.

By
International Credit Department

Payment Clauses

The *payment clause* states the manner in which payment is to be received and the currency in which it is made. Since some nations restrict currencies from leaving the country, payments have special effects on the receiver of the currency that must be addressed. Problems with inflation and currency exchange risks, especially in unstable economies or in long-term agreements, should also be covered.

Choice of Language Clause

Even when parties speak the same language, complex contractual terms may exceed the understanding of one of the parties when the contract is made in another country. A word or phrase in one language or country may not be readily translatable to another. Technical terms should be defined. A contract should have a *choice of language clause*, which sets out the official language by which the contract is to be interpreted, as seen in Exhibit 21.5.

Exhibit 21.5

Choice of Language Clauses

Example of Choice of Language Clause with Arbitration Provision
This Agreement is signed in two (2) originals in the English language, which shall be regarded as the authoritative and official text. Any matters referred to arbitration will also be in the English language, which will be the official language used in arbitration.

Example of Choice of Language with Translation Provision
This Agreement is signed in two (2) originals in the French language, which shall be regarded as the authoritative and official text. Parties hereto agree to provide an official translation of this Agreement in the English language. This translation will be ratified by both parties, and it may be relied upon as being an accurate representation of the official form.

Force Majeure Clause

Force majeure is a French term meaning a "superior or irresistible force." Thus, it protects contracting parties from problems beyond their control. Traditionally, this clause was used to protect the parties from the consequences of a natural disaster that interfered with performance. The clause also protects the parties against political upheavals. An illustration of a typical force majeure clause is given in Exhibit 21.6. You may want to see if insurance can cover such risks.

Forum Selection and Choice-of-Law Clauses

To reduce uncertainties in the event of a dispute, companies often put *forum selection* and *choice-of-law clauses* in their contracts. (Examples are given in Exhibit 21.7.) The forum may be in one place (Paris), and the law to be applied may be from another place (California).

By selecting the court or place of arbitration in which disputes must be resolved and law that is to be applied, the possibility that the parties will go "forum shopping"—looking for the most favorable forum for the resolution of a dispute—is reduced.

Loss of Investment

Political upheavals, unstable monetary systems, and changes in laws are some of the risks encountered in other countries. In addition, businesses must be concerned about the loss of investment by nationalization, expropriation, and confiscation.

Nationalization

Nationalization is when a country takes over, or nationalizes, a foreign investment or, at times, an entire industry in a country. The compensation paid by the government is often less than the true value of the business. Nationalization has been seen in Iran, Saudi Arabia, and Venezuela. England has nationalized certain industries on and off over the years.

Exhibit 21.6

Example of Force Majeure Clause

The parties hereto shall not be liable for failure of performance hereunder if occasioned by war, declared or undeclared, fire, flood, interruption of transportation, inflation beyond the expected rate, embargo, accident, explosion, inability to procure or shortage of supply of materials, equipment, or production facilities, prohibition of import or export of goods covered hereby, governmental orders, regulations, restrictions, priorities or rationing by strike or lockout or other labor troubles interfering with production or transportation of such goods or with the supplies of raw materials entering into their production or any other cause beyond the control of the parties.

Exhibit 21.7

Forum Selection and Choice-of-Law Clauses

All claims and disputes arising out of or in relation to this contract shall be litigated before the courts of the city of Paris, France.

This contract shall be governed by the laws of the state of California, the country of the United States of America.

Expropriation

Expropriation, like nationalization, is the action of a country in taking foreign property in accordance with international law. Most countries agree that for a valid expropriation there must be adequate compensation provided. International law recognizes a country's right to expropriate the property of foreigners within its jurisdiction, so long as payment is made. If a takeover is unlawful, it is a *confiscation*.

Making the Deal Stick

ISSUE *Spotter*

You have worked for a long time to attract the client and finally won an order for your company to supply financial services to Glorious, a large Chinese company headquartered in Shanghai. Glorious sends you an agreement drawn up by its attorney. Chinese law governs in all respects. Are you sure you want to sign? What changes in the agreement would be high on your list?

Insuring against Risk of Loss

An all-risk insurance policy can provide financial relief in the event of nationalization or if other problems occur. Short-term private insurance usually lasts from three to five years and is available for most investments. Risks such as currency blockages, embargoes, and a government's arbitrary decision to recall letters of credit may be insured by such major insurers as Lloyds of London. In addition, sellers may obtain rejection insurance in the event that a buyer rejects a product for reasonable cause, such as spoilage at sea.

Some countries have government agencies to assist in insuring exporters from risk of loss. In the United States, for example, the *Overseas Private Investment Corporation (OPIC)* insures investors willing to invest in less-developed countries friendly to the United States. OPIC offers investors insurance against expropriation, currency inconvertibility, and damage from wars or revolutions.

INTERNATIONAL DISPUTE RESOLUTION

World trade is in the trillions of dollars and growing rapidly. With that much commerce, disputes will arise. They may be due to unanticipated events, difficulties in performance, or changes in the political climate of a country that affect a contract. Whatever the problem, parties to international contracts need help to try to resolve disputes and enforce their rights.

Litigation

Disputes often end up either in the court system at home or within the opposing party's country. Litigation is complicated because evidence, witnesses, and documents central to resolving the dispute are often located in two or more countries. In some instances, these difficulties may be overcome by treaties or conventions between the two countries. These may allow for proper notice of the suit to the foreign party, appropriate service of process, issues of standing, methods for documentation certification, and procedures for taking evidence.

If the action is commenced in a foreign court, the U.S. participant often encounters a judicial system very different from that in this country. Courts in some countries are influenced more by political pressures than are U.S. courts. In addition, some courts will not enforce contract provisions that may be enforceable in the United States.

JURIS *prudence?*

You Yanks Are Too Old for Us Hip Brits

Garland Denty worked for Smith Kline (a U.S. company) in Philadelphia, where he was Director of Manufacturing Operations/Technical Services, International. The firm merged with Beecham and became SmithKline Beecham, a British corporation.

Denty was told he was to be promoted to Vice President of Technical Services/Plant Operations and transferred to England. But the company reversed its decision and told

Denty he would not get the job because he was too old (at age fifty-two). Denty sued for age discrimination.

The federal court tossed out Denty's suit. The Age Discrimination in Employment Act does not apply to employment decisions affecting U.S. employees that are made by foreign-owned companies regarding employment outside the United States.

Source: *Denty* v. *SmithKline Beecham*, 907 F.Supp. 879

Arbitration

Judicial forums are not very effective in resolving many international commercial disagreements. Cost considerations, jurisdictional barriers, the length of time to litigate, legal uncertainties, and the inability of judicial systems to fashion appropriate relief encouraged the use of alternative dispute resolution techniques, especially *arbitration*.

Attempts to standardize arbitral rules and procedures have resulted in the creation of organizations such as the United Nations Commission on International Trade Law, the International Chamber of Commerce, and other arbitration organizations around the world. These organizations have rules to address issues concerning arbitration proceedings and awards. In many countries, including the United States, the enforcement of arbitral awards is facilitated by the United Nations Convention on the Recognition and Enforcement of Foreign Arbitral Awards. Federal district courts have jurisdiction to hear motions to confirm or challenge an international arbitration award involving a U.S. business.

The International Court of Justice

Contrary to common belief, there are no "international courts" to handle business disputes. Certain disputes may be taken to the *International Court of Justice (ICJ)*. It is headquartered at The Hague, Netherlands, and is a part of the United Nations.

The ICJ has fifteen judges representing all of the world's major legal systems, with no two judges from the same country.

Only nations have standing to go before the ICJ. Individuals and businesses have no standing to initiate a suit. Hence, countries, not the parties to a dispute, have complete discretion in deciding whether to pursue a claim. Suppose a country where an investor does business violates the law and damages the investor. The country in which the investor is a citizen has discretion to pursue or not to pursue the investor's claim by bringing suit against the other nation. This is rarely used.

Doctrine of Sovereign Immunity

In international law, the *doctrine of sovereign immunity* allows a court to give up its right to jurisdiction over foreign enterprises or countries. The doctrine is based on traditional notions that a sovereign should not be subject to litigation in a foreign court. As a result, investors may not be able to obtain relief in their country's court system.

Some countries restrict the doctrine's application in commercial circumstances. If a foreign nation does not do this when it enters into a contract with a private party, then there is no recourse to U.S. courts in case of breach. The *Foreign Sovereign Immunities Act* provides a uniform rule for the determination of sovereign immunity in legal actions in this country's courts. The Act provides the following:

> Under international law, [countries] are not immune from the jurisdiction of foreign courts insofar as their commercial activities are concerned, and their commercial property may be levied upon for the satisfaction of judgments rendered against them in connection with their commercial activities.

Doing business with foreign partners can result in special problems that are not as common in domestic business. Issues of jurisdiction, the effect of statutes and treaties, and the ability to obtain a judgment, and collect on one, are not unique to international business, but are major concerns that should not be ignored in the rush to grab what may look like easy money.

SUMMARY

- In contrast to the domestic market, the international market is characterized by additional financial, political, and regulatory risks. Those risks arise from differences among countries in currencies, language, business customs, legal and social philosophies, and national economic goals.
- The principal sources of international trade law are the laws of individual countries, the laws arising from trade agreements between countries, and the rules enacted by worldwide or regional trade organizations.
- To reduce trade barriers, most nations participated in the General Agreement on Tariffs and Trade (GATT), which resulted in the World Trade Organization, which now oversees some trade disputes.
- Most countries have import and export regulations. Import restrictions include import licensing requirements, import quotas, safety standards, government procurement policies, and customs procedures. To standardize tariff schedules and their application, most countries have adopted the harmonized tariff schedule to classify goods.

- The United States imposes prohibitions on the export of certain technologies that could be used by hostile nations or terrorists. The exportation of weapons and computers is monitored by the government.
- The most common international business arrangements are wholly owned subsidiaries, joint ventures, licensing agreements, franchise agreements, and contract manufacturing. The choice of business organization is influenced by the laws of a country, the purposes of the commercial venture, the financial resources of the parties, and the degree of managerial control desired by the company.
- The Foreign Corrupt Practices Act (FCPA) prohibits U.S. companies and their agents from bribing foreign officials. The FCPA makes the bribery of foreign officials a criminal offense and requires U.S. companies to establish internal accounting mechanisms to prevent such bribery. It is a criminal offense to make payments to foreign officials for the purpose of gaining business favor in a foreign country.
- To create an effective international contract, a business should consider differences in business customs, attitudes toward the contractual relationship, and language. Specific clauses in international contracts worthy of special consideration are the payment, choice of language, force majeure, and forum selection and choice-of-law clauses.
- Business in foreign countries may face special risks. Political upheavals, unstable monetary systems, dramatic changes in laws, and other problems associated with doing business with a developing country must be considered. Losses may occur through nationalization, expropriation, or confiscation of the foreign investment.
- Although most international trade occurs without incident, disputes sometimes arise concerning contract performance. Various national and international institutions may assist a business in effective dispute resolution. Those institutions include judicial litigation in country court systems and arbitration. The doctrine of sovereign immunity may create bars to recovery through the judicial system.

REVIEW AND DISCUSSION QUESTIONS

1. Define the following terms:

   tariff   foreign trade zone
   harmonized tariff schedule   letter of credit
   dumping   force majeure
   countervailing duty laws

2. Compare the merits of arbitration and judicial litigation as methods of dispute resolution in international trade.

CASE QUESTIONS

3. Dart (an American) planned to sell and ship to (then communist-controlled) Czechoslovakia wafer polishers used in making integrated circuits. Because the polishers were U.S.-origin goods, Dart told the importer to check at the Department of Commerce to see whether an export license would be required

for the technically advanced equipment. The importer falsely told Dart that no license was required. The goods were seized by customs agents at the Los Angeles airport. Commerce charged Dart with attempting to violate the law by shipping without a license, threatening fines of $150,000 and a suspension of export privileges for fifteen years. Can you make an argument that Dart "knew or should have known" that such goods were subject to an export license? Is there another way that Dart could have handled the inquiry at Commerce? [*Dart* v. *U.S.*, 848 F.2d 217 (D. C. Cir., 1988)]

4. A Houston corporation contracted for a German corporation to tow a drilling rig from Louisiana to an area off Italy, where the Houston company was to drill wells. The contract provided that: "Any dispute arising must be treated before the London Court of Justice." While on its way to Italy, the rig was damaged by a severe storm. The German tug towed the rig to Tampa, Florida, the nearest port. The Houston company sued in the U.S. District Court at Tampa, seeking $3.5 million damages from the German company. Is the use of the American court proper in this situation? What effect would the contract clause have on the lawsuit? [*M/S Bremen* v. *Zapata Off-Shore Co.*, 92 S.Ct. 1907 (1972)]

5. Seawinds, a shipping company, was incorporated in Hong Kong with its principal place of business in California. It contracted with Nedlloyd Lines, a shipping company in the Netherlands, to "establish a joint venture company to carry on a transportation operation." The agreement had the following choice-of-law provision:

   This agreement shall be governed by and construed in accordance with Hong Kong law and each party hereby irrevocably submits to the non-exclusive jurisdiction and service of process of the Hong Kong courts.

   Later, Seawinds sued in California state court, asserting that Nedlloyd had breached its duties under the contract by engaging in activities that led to the cancellation of charter hires essential to the joint venture's business and by making and then reneging on commitments to contribute additional capital. Nedlloyd responded that Seawinds had failed to state causes of action because Hong Kong law was to be applied. If the case is brought in California court, which law should be applied: that of Hong Kong or that of California? Does California have a substantial relationship to the parties or their transaction? Is there a reasonable basis for the selection of Hong Kong law by the parties in their original agreement? [*Nedlloyd Lines B.V.* v. *Superior Court* (Seawinds Limited), 834 P.2d 1148 (Sup.Ct., Cal., 1992)]

 Check your answer at <u>*http://meiners.westbuslaw.com*</u>

6. Nettie Effron, a Florida resident, bought a sixteen-day cruise of the Brazilian coast from Sun Line Cruises. The cruise was on the Stella Solaris, owned by Sun Line Greece. The cruise ticket stated that "any action against the carrier must be brought only before the courts of Athens, Greece, to the jurisdiction of which the Passenger submits himself formally excluding the jurisdiction of all and other court or courts of any other country." Effron was injured when she fell while on the ship. She sued for damages in federal court in New York. Sun Line moved to have the case dismissed because of the forum selection clause in the ticket. The district court refused to dismiss; Sun Line appealed. What result? [*Effron* v. *Sun Line Cruises*, 67 F.3d 7 (2nd Cir., 1995)]

7. Farr, a U.S. company, contracted to buy sugar from CAV, a Cuban company owned by U.S. citizens. Because the government of Cuba nationalized its sugar

industry, including CAV, it demanded that payments for sugar already shipped must be made to the Banco Nacional de Cuba. At CAV's insistence that it was the rightful owner of the sugar and that the nationalization violated international law, Farr paid CAV. Banco Nacional sued to collect payment from Farr for the sugar delivered. The case went to the Supreme Court, where Banco Nacional was held to be correct. On what theory did the Supreme Court base this opinion? [*Banco Nacional de Cuba* v. *Sabbatino*, 84 S.Ct. 923 (1964)]

 Check your answer at http://meiners.westbuslaw.com

8. The *F/V Cape Cod*, a commercial fishing vessel and the only asset of R&M, sank in 1994; during the accident, DiMercurio, a fisherman, was injured. He sued the company for his injuries and was awarded $350,000. R&M, having no assets, assigned DiMercurio all rights it had against Sphere Drake, a London-based insurer of the boat. DiMercurio took his claim to Sphere Drake but it denied the demand and invoked the arbitration process specified in the policy, which called for arbitration of all coverage disputes in London. DeMercurio then sued, contesting the validity of the arbitration provision. The district court held for Sphere Drake. DiMercurio appealed. Does he have a valid claim? [*DiMercurio* v. *Sphere Drake Insurance PLC*, 202 F.3d 71 (1st Cir., 2000)]

9. Chisholm & Company and the Bank of Jamaica agreed that Chisholm was to arrange lines of credit from a number of banks and to obtain ExIm Bank credit insurance. The Bank of Jamaica then "went around" Chisholm and dealt with ExIm Bank directly. It excluded Chisholm from receiving any benefit from the credit insurance that ExIm Bank provided. Chisholm sued the Bank of Jamaica. In its defense, the bank asserted that its actions were protected by sovereign immunity and the act of state doctrine. Were the bank's assertions correct? [*Chisholm & Company* v. *Bank of Jamaica*, 643 F.Supp. 1393 (S.D. Fla., 1986)]

 Check your answer at http://meiners.westbuslaw.com

10. Vance provides security services. The company was hired by Saudi Arabis to help with security for Princess Anud, a wife of King Fahad, while she was undergoing medical treatment in California. Security was supervised by the Saudi military. Vance hired Butters as a part-time, at-will security agent in the team guarding the Saudi royal family. Vance recommended she serve a full rotation in the command post at the family's California residence. The Saudi officer in charge of security rejected that recommendation, saying it would violate Islamic law for a woman to be in a command position and that the Princess only wanted to speak to male officers when she called the command post. Butters quit and sued Vance for sex discrimination. The district court entered summary judgment for Vance. Butters appealed; does she have grounds? [*Butters* v. *Vance International, Inc.*, 225 F.3d 462 (4th Cir., 2000)]

11. Robinson worked for the Shields Agency as a security guard at a building in New York owned by the government of Malaysia. While the building was being renovated, Robinson slipped and fell on some "white substance" that had been spilled on the floor. Contending that he suffered permanent injuries in the fall, he sued the Malaysian government in tort for his injuries. The district court dismissed the suit, holding that the government was immune due to the Foreign Sovereign Immunities Act. Robinson appealed. Does the Act bar his suit? [*Robinson* v. *Government of Malaysia*, 269 F.3d 133 (2nd Cir., 2001)]

 Check your answer at http://meiners.westbuslaw.com

ETHICS QUESTIONS

12. In some circumstances, cultural expectations and business customs of a country may run counter to a person's ethical beliefs. What factors should people take into consideration when such a conflict arises and they are charged with making a business work within the cultural setting?

13. In some countries, it is expected that businesses will pay off officials. Suppose it makes the difference between getting the contract and not getting the contract? If a payoff is not made, because of the Foreign Corrupt Practices Act, a foreign competitor that will make the bribe will get the deal. The American company that loses the deal would have to close a factory, putting 500 people out of work. The law aside, can you justify a bribe in that instance?

PULLING IT  *Together*

International Contracts and Arbitration

NAFT, a New York company, had Smoothline, a Hong Kong company, produce telephones that NAFT resold to various companies. This was done on the basis of an oral agreement. After a while, Smoothline hired Welback, another Hong Kong company, to make phones as a subcontractor to be paid directly by NAFT. NAFT agreed to allow Welback to do the work but, at that point, NAFT and Smoothline had signed a contract that included an arbitration clause requiring arbitration of disputes to occur in New York before the American Arbitration Association. Later, when more phones were ordered, Smoothline hired another Hong Kong company, Greatsino, to help produce phones for NAFT. When the defect rate in the phones began to rise, NAFT cut its payments to all companies and complained about the quality. Smoothline and Greatsino sued NAFT in the Princely District Court in Liechtenstein for breach of contract. NAFT petitioned the Federal Court in New York to enjoin the proceedings in Liechtenstein and to compel arbitration. The court held that since Greatsino was brought in as a subcontractor after the contract was signed, the arbitration clause did not apply to the work it performed and NAFT appealed. Was it correct?

[*Smoothline Ltd.* v. *North American Foreign Trading Corp.*, 249 F.3d 147 (2nd Cir., 2001)]

INTERNET ASSIGNMENT

http://www.hg.org
http://www.llrx.com
http://www.wto.org
http://www.oecd.org/home

1. Find the URL for a legal guide to Australia by the Law Library of Congress.
2. Find the URL for Nicholas Pengelley's *Update to Researching Australian Law*.
3. Find the URL for the text of the Agreement Establishing the World Trade Organization.
4. According to the Organisation for Economic Co-operation and Development, what does the acronym PPP represent?

Legal Research and the Internet

Note: URLs are subject to change.

LEGAL INFORMATION

There are five good starting points for finding free legal information on the Internet. FindLaw (*http://www.findlaw.com*) has become the legal information portal for the masses lacking access to Westlaw or Lexis. The Legal Information Institute (LII) at Cornell (*http://www.law.cornell.edu*) also attempts to provide legal information to the world. WashLaw WEB (*http://www.washlaw.edu*) provides a myriad of links through its no-nonsense menu. The Indiana University Law School Virtual Law Library (*http://www.law.indiana.edu/v-lib/index.html*) provides a searchable index. Hieros Gamos (*http://www.hg.org*) is a good starting point for foreign and international legal research.

Google is the search engine of choice for most users. For other options, and a comparison of available features, consult the Search Engine Showdown (*http://notess.com/search*), maintained by Greg Notess. Obviously, it helps to know and use the advanced search techniques of whichever search engine you choose. Also, it helps to be familiar with the area of law you are researching. For topical legal research (including business organizations), Kathy Biehl and Tara Calishain, authors of *The Lawyer's Guide to Internet Research* (2000), pp. 220–221, recommend the following three sites: FindLaw Legal Subjects (*http://www.findlaw.com/01topics/index.html*), the Internet Law Library's Laws of All Jurisdictions (arranged by subject) (*http://www.lawguru.com/ilawlib/90.htm*), and Legal Materials Organized by Topic (*http://www.law.cornell.edu/topics/index.html*). LSU Libraries provide an Internet Searching page (*http://www.lib.lsu.edu/general/internet_search.html*) with the following: search tips; links to meta-search engines, unmediated engines and mediated subject guides; and subject-specific search engines. As an alternative to the automated search engines, the Open Directory Project (*http://www.dmoz.org*) offers "the largest, most comprehensive human-edited directory of the Web."

In addition to LII, Washburn, and Indiana University, it is essential that as a student you become familiar with your institution's library web site. Almost every law school library and university has a web site with links to pertinent reference sources. In addition to providing access to the library's online catalog, the library or its consortium may allow affiliated students to access legal databases, full text journal databases, indexes to legal journals, and general reference databases. In addition, libraries are increasingly accommodating e-mail reference questions and virtual reference sessions. Many of these services are available to affiliated users remotely via the Internet. Public patrons may be able to access some of these services in the library itself and, in some instances, electronic citators (such as KeyCite and Shepard's), traditionally available only to Westlaw or Lexis subscribers.

Although there are a number of commercial sites where you can access free legal information, FindLaw has become the dominant provider of legal information to the public. Among its services, FindLaw provides links to official court sites. LexisOne (*http://www.lexisone.com*) offers selected case law, forms, and legal news to registered users. Yahoo! (*http://dir.yahoo.com/Government/Law*) offers another alternative index to free legal information. For legal newspapers via the Internet, visit Law.com (*http://www.law.com*).

For a fee, Westlaw (*http://www.westlaw.com*) and Lexis (*http://www.lexis.com*) directly market their services to the public via the Internet. Several of their value-added services, such as citators (used to ensure that the cited law is still "good"), case digesting services, and annotated codes are notably absent from other free or less expensive legal databases.

In the United States, primary sources of law consist of cases, legislation (statutes), and administrative regulations. The Internet is a potential source for each type of law, though not every statute or case can be found for free on the Internet. Courts (e.g., the U.S. Supreme Court, federal appellate courts, and some federal district courts) have been releasing their opinions via the Internet in vendor-neutral formats since 1994. Government agencies such as the Library of Congress and the Government Printing Office have made available via the Internet (for free) such sources as federal legislative materials (since the 104th Congress), the *Federal Register*, and the *Code of Federal Regulations*. Secondary sources such as encyclopedias, treatises, and the *American Law Reports* are not likely to be found for free on the Web. Only a fraction of published law review articles will be available for free on the Internet, although recent international or technological law review articles may be available. One may search FindLaw's American Law Sources On-Line (*http://www.lawsource.com/also/usa.cgi?usj*), or the USC Law School's List of General Law Reviews (*http://lawweb.usc.edu/library/resources/journals.html*) to see if a given law review article is available in full-text via the Internet. The savvy legal researcher realizes that consulting a relevant secondary source at the outset, even one not available via the Internet, may save time and effort in the long run.

Supreme Court opinions are available at FindLaw (1893–current) and LII (May 1990–current, plus selected previous opinions). The U.S. Supreme Court also has its own web site (*http://www.supremecourtus.gov*). Federal appellate courts began to place their opinions on the Internet in the early 1990s. For an interactive map of the U.S. federal appellate courts, visit the Emory Law Library's Federal Courts Finder (*http://www.law.emory.edu/FEDCTS*). Federal district court opinions may or may not be available; try searching FindLaw's index (*http://www.findlaw.com/10fedgov/judicial/district_courts.html*). For coverage of state courts, a good starting point is Courts.net (*http://www.courts.net*) or FindLaw (*http://guide.lp.findlaw.com/11stategov*).

The House of Representatives is now a reliable source for a fairly current, free version of the *United States Code* (*U.S.C.*). Currently, the U.S. Code is also available for free from a nonprofit source (LII) and a commercial source (FindLaw). It is important to weigh the need for authenticity and currency against the associated costs and risk. For example, a student researching paper topics may be satisfied with any of the three free versions of the *U.S. Code*, whereas an attorney may prefer to use a fee-based source of the Code, either to find annotations for additional research or to be advised of legislative developments that have impacted a given Code section since its release via the Internet.

The Thomas database (*http://thomas.loc.gov*) of the Library of Congress allows users to access federal legislative information such as Bill Summary & Status (93rd Congress-current), Bill Text (101st–current), Public Laws By Law Number (93rd–current), *Congressional Record* (101st–current), *Congressional Record Index* (104th–current), Roll Call Votes (101st–current), Committee Reports (104th–current), and House and Senate Committee information. The Government Printing Office's GPO Access database also hosts *Public Laws* (1994–current) and the *Congressional Record* (1994–current). For state law sources, consult the Center for Information Law and Policy's *State Web Locator* (*http://www.infoctr.edu/swl*).

Administrative law resources are readily available via the Internet. The GPO Access database (*http://www.access.gpo.gov*) provides access to the *Federal Register* (1994–current), the *Code of Federal Regulations*, the *LSA* (*List of CFR Sections Affected*), the *United States Government Manual*, and other administrative law databases. Most, if not all, federal administrative agencies have web pages that allow access to pertinent statutory and regulatory sources, as well as agency-specific information. The government has established a portal (*http://firstgov.gov*) that includes an A-Z agency link.

The CILP's *Federal Web Locator* (*http://www.infoctr.edu/fwl*), which had been providing federal agency information since 1994 may be a casualty of the new federal government portal. Availability of state administrative law sources via the Internet varies; the web site of the National Association of Secretaries of State (*http://www.nass.org/acr/internet.html*) provides comprehensive links to state administrative materials, where available.

Researching a new topic? Visit LLRX.com (*http://www.llrx.com*) to see if there are any pertinent research guides. For example, *Update to A Guide to the U.S. Federal Legal System: Web-Based Publicly Accessible Sources* (*http://www.llrx.com/features/us_fed2.htm*) will help one access the wealth of federal legal information available via the Internet.

BUSINESS INFORMATION

Academic institutions once again offer the starting point for effective business research via the Internet. Most business school web sites offer a hybrid of proprietary information accessible only to currently affiliated members of their communities as well as an assortment of generally accessible web sites. Two academic institutions that offer selected business web sites are the Jackson Library at Stanford University (*http://wesley.stanford.edu/library/articles/business_sites/business_sites.html*) and the Lippincott Library of the Wharton School at the University of Pennsylvania (*http://gethelp.library.upenn.edu/guides/business/businesswebsites.html*). Ohio State University provides the Virtual Finance Library (*http://fisher.osu.edu/fin/cerns.htm*), which provides, among other information, a Finance Site List for researchers. Another important academic resource for financial research is Ohio State University's *Financial Data Finder*. OSU Libraries also provide The Gateway to Information for business (*http://www.lib.ohio-state.edu/gateway/bib/business.html*) and economics (*http://www.lib.ohio-state.edu/gateway/bib/economics.html*), which provide annotated links to some publicly accessible databases in addition to the many proprietary databases to which OSU subscribes either independently or as a member of the OhioLINK consortium. Thus, as previously mentioned, it is imperative that as a business researcher, you become familiar with the online subscription databases to which you have access via affiliation with an institutional, or even a public, library.

The Library of Congress provides access to business and economics links via its BE*Online+* service (*http://www.loc.gov/rr/business/beonline*). The Securities and Exchange Commission's EDGAR database (*http://www.sec.gov*) is another key governmental source for finding information (registration statements and periodic reports) of large public companies. Another nonprofit source of business information links is the Librarian's Index to the Internet (*http://lii.org/search/file/business*).

Companies, big and small, have web pages offering their mission statements, product descriptions, annual reports, and official plant locations. Larger companies, such as IBM (*http://www.ibm.com*), also post press releases and messages from company executives. Corporate web sites, while primarily marketing tools, may shed light on corporate America's reaction to and opinions regarding specific government policy measures or rules of law. Many corporate sites provide an e-mail address for a company official. To find a company's web site, use a standard search engine, or use Yahoo!, which has compiled a searchable list of thousands of companies.

The commercial providers of business information via the Internet include BRINT.com, The BizTech Network (*http://www.brint.com*). This site claims to be "The Premier Business and Technology Knowledge Portal and Global Community Network for the New World of Business." It features a searchable news section, an e-business and e-commerce section, featured articles and books, a knowledge management section, and a new economy business technology section. CEOExpress (*http://www.ceoexpress.com*), "designed by a busy executive for busy executives," provides links to daily news and information, as well as business research. Hoovers Online (*http://www.hoovers.com*), "The Business Network," features sections about companies, IPOs, free newsletters, small businesses, business links, and a portfolio tool. As a testament to the commercialization of the Web, the original URL for Dr. Ed Yardeni's Economics Network (*http://www.yardeni.com*) now redirects searchers to the Prudential Financial page. In a presumably similar fashion, at a recent conference, Internet expert Gary Price said he "sold his name" to a company named Vivísimo.

NEWS INFORMATION

Keeping abreast of recent news developments is easy via the Internet. For breaking news, visit ABC News (*http://abcnews.go.com*), CBS News (*http://cbsnews.com*), CNN Interactive (*http://www.cnn.com*), or Fox News (*http://www.foxnews.com*). In addition to news updates via web browsers, almost all newspapers have a web site with at least some free content. However, you have to pay for full access to *The Wall Street Journal* (*http://www.wsj.cm*). The *New York Times* (*http://www.nyt.com*) requires registration but is still free as of this writing. Articles from the archives are $2.50 each. Other choices for current news include the *Boston Globe* (*http://www.boston.com/globe*) and the *Chicago Tribune* (*http://www.chicagotribune.com*). The *Washington Post* (*http://www.washingtonpost.com*) includes a searchable database of the previous two weeks' issues. The *Los Angeles Times* (*http://www.latimes.com*) archives the past week of the print version. Newspapers.com (*http://www.newspapers.com*) is the place to see if one's local newspaper has a web presence.

KEEPING CURRENT

Two excellent sources for keeping up to date with Internet developments are the Virtual Chase (*http://www.virtualchase.com/index.shtml*) and Resource Shelf (*http://www.resourceshelf.com*). News aggregators and weblogs (blogs) (employing the RSS format) are becoming increasingly popular. There are established web sites that have incorporated blogging (*http://law.case.edu/faculty/friedman/raw*), as well as standalone weblogs devoted to specific topics (see *http://www.bloglines.com*). As with all information sources, particularly those available via the Internet, it is important to be cognizant of the authenticity, currency, and reliability of your sources.

Case Analysis and Legal Research

The legal environment of business is often a student's first encounter with the law and the legal process. Legal citations, the organization of legal materials, and opinion analysis can be bewildering at first. This appendix provides a general explanation and overview of the important ingredients in legal research and analysis.

READING A LEGAL OPINION

In resolving disputes, courts often report their decisions in written opinions. Decisions of appellate courts are most frequently reported. Usually only important decisions at the trial court level are reported. Through a written opinion, a judge explains the legal basis for the decision reached. Published opinions provide legal precedents in the common law.

An opinion can exceed one hundred pages and involve several complex issues. To assist in the analysis of an opinion, law students often prepare a summary of the opinion, called a case *brief*—essentially a digest or abstract of the opinion setting forth its most essential parts. Attorneys often write case briefs in researching a legal problem, particularly when a case involves a complicated situation or the dispute requires the court to consider several legal questions in reaching a resolution.

To brief an opinion, there is no formal or standard procedure. Here, we provide a basic approach to assist in briefing the opinions excerpted in this text. It is an effective way to study legal opinions.

Before you brief an opinion, read it carefully. Then separate the opinion into its five fundamental parts by asking yourself questions about those parts:

(1) A Statement of the Significant Facts
   Who is the plaintiff? The defendant?
   Who did what to whom?
   What relief is being sought from the court?
(2) A Statement of the Relevant Procedural Details
   Who prevailed in the lower court?
   Which party is appealing?
(3) A Statement of the Legal Issue in the Dispute
   What are the specific legal questions the court is being asked to address?
(4) A Statement of the Court's Decision
   How does the court respond to the question(s) posed to it?
   Does the plaintiff or the defendant prevail on the appeal?
(5) An Explanation of the Court's Reasoning
   Which is the legal basis for the court's decision?

This basic procedure is illustrated and described in the following opinion. Before examining the brief, read the actual opinion of the court (in the right-hand column). In the left-hand column is a commentary on the case opinion. Although an understanding of the law and legal terms used in the opinion is not essential to an understanding of the briefing process, most legal terms used in the opinion are defined in the glossary at the back of this text. As in the text, this opinion has been shortened by inserting * * * or . . . where material has been deleted. The essence is retained in the material that remains.

Dallas Parks v. George Steinbrenner and New York Yankees, Inc.

New York Supreme Court, Appellate Division, First Department

520 N.Y.2d 374 (1987)

BRIEF AND EXPLANATION. Begin by summarizing the essential facts in the opinion. In the text, the facts are summarized for you in the **Case Background** section provided with each opinion.

1. FACTS. Dallas Parks, the plaintiff, alleges that he was defamed by the defendant, George Steinbrenner, owner of the New York Yankees. The alleged defamation occurred when the defendant issued a press release criticizing Parks's abilities as an umpire. The plaintiff seeks damages on the grounds that the press release falsely attacked his abilities as an umpire.

> The procedural history summarizes how the lower court(s) ruled on the dispute. In the text, the procedural history is summarized in the **Case Background** section.

2. PROCEDURAL HISTORY. The defendant argued that the press release represented a constitutionally protected expression of opinion. The Special Term (the lower court) disagreed, finding that although the press release expressed an opinion, it was not backed up by an adequate statement of the facts to support that opinion. The defendant appealed to the New York Supreme Court.

> The legal issue in the opinion is the question the parties are asking the court to resolve. In some opinions, the opinion states exactly what the issue is that the court is being asked to resolve. In the text, the issue is generally found in our summary of the lower court's decision or from the stated contentions of the parties. In analyzing an opinion in the text, state the issue in your own words to aid your understanding of the opinion.

Before Carro, J. P., and Kassal, Ellerin, Wallach, JJ.

MEMORANDUM DECISION. This action for defamation brings into play one of the most colorful of American traditions—the razzing of the umpire.

The plaintiff, Dallas Parks, served as an American League baseball umpire from 1979 through 1982. He alleges that he was defamed by George Steinbrenner, principal owner of the New York Yankees, when Steinbrenner on August 29, 1982, issued a press release, excerpts of which were published in newspapers throughout the United States, criticizing Parks's abilities as an umpire. The press release, which was issued after the Yankees had played a two-game series with the Toronto Blue Jays in Toronto, Canada, on August 27th and 28th, at which Parks officiated, reads as follows:

> Judging on his last two days' performance, my people tell me that he is not a capable umpire. He is a member of one of the finest crews umpiring in the American League today, but obviously he doesn't measure up.
>
> We are making no excuse for the team's play this season, but this weekend our team has had several key injuries and for umpire Dallas Parks to throw two of our players out of ballgames in two days on plays he misjudges is "ludicrous."
>
> This man, in my opinion, has had it in for the Yankees ever since I labeled him and several of the umpires as "scabs" because they worked the American League games in 1979 during the umpires' strike.
>
> Parks must learn that the word scab is a commonly used phrase. It is in no way meant as a personal insult. However, because he worked during the strike for baseball management does not mean he should be protected by them and annually given a job he is not capable of handling.

3. ISSUE. Does the press release constitute a constitutionally protected statement of pure opinion?

> After stating the issue, state the court's decision, both procedural (e.g., judgment for the defendant) and substantive (a yes or no response to the issue presented).

continues

4. THE COURT'S DECISION. Yes, the press release is a constitutionally protected expression of pure opinion. Judgment for the defendant; the Special Term's decision is reversed.

> The court's rationale is the heart of the opinion. The court will generally discuss the relevant law surrounding the question presented to it. Then the court will apply that law to the facts of the dispute before it. In reaching its decision, the court will explain its rationale—why and how it reached the conclusion that the facts in this dispute do or do not fall within the existing law. In the text, the court's rationale is presented in excerpts from the actual opinions in the **Case Decision** section.

5. COURT'S RATIONALE. A statement of pure opinion is a statement that is accompanied by the facts upon which it is based, or it does not imply that it is based on undisclosed facts.

Statements that constitute pure opinion whether false or libelous may not serve as the basis for an action for defamation.

In determining whether a statement is fact or opinion, consideration is given to what an average person hearing or reading the statement will take it to mean, the circumstances surrounding its use, and the way it is written.

The press release must be evaluated within the broader social context of baseball. It is an American tradition to verbally abuse umpires. In this context, the average reader would perceive the release as opinion and not fact. The release is the kind of statement that generally accompanies a voicing of displeasure at an umpire's calls.

The statement by the defendant represents the view of an owner of a baseball team that is doing poorly and who has chosen to vent his frustration by baiting the umpire.

There is no indication that defendant's opinions are based on some other undisclosed facts unknown to the reader.

This less than complimentary critical assessment appears to have been the "final straw" in the rhubarb that had long simmered between the umpire and the owner and resulted in commencement of the instant action, against Steinbrenner and the Yankees, wherein plaintiff seeks damages for defamation on the ground that the press release falsely impugned his ability, competence, conduct and fairness as a baseball umpire.

In subsequently moving to dismiss the complaint for failure to state a cause of action, defendants argued that the press release represented a nonactionable constitutionally protected expression of opinion. While Special Term [lower court] found that the statement was "clearly expressed as an opinion," it nevertheless held that the complaint sufficiently pleaded a cause of action in defamation because the press release did not set forth an adequate statement of fact contained in the statement—i.e., that Parks expelled two Yankee players from the game—did "not in anyway support the opinions proffered" that plaintiff was incompetent and biased and, further, that no factual basis was set forth for the conclusory assertion that plaintiff misjudged plays.

We disagree with Special Term's assessment of the press release in question and find that it constituted a constitutionally protected expression of pure opinion.

In all defamation cases, the threshold issue which must be determined, as a matter of law, is whether the complained of statements constitute fact or opinion. If they fall within the ambit of "pure opinion," then even if false and libelous, and no matter how perjorative or pernicious they may be, such statements are safeguarded and may not serve as the basis for an action in defamation. A non-actionable "pure opinion" is defined as a statement of opinion which either is accompanied by a recitation of the facts upon which it is based, or, if not so accompanied, does not imply that it is based upon undisclosed facts. Alternatively, when a defamatory statement of opinion implies that it is based upon undisclosed detrimental facts which justify the opinion but are unknown to those reading or hearing it, it is a "mixed opinion" and actionable. Similarly actionable as a "mixed opinion" is a defamatory opinion which is ostensibly accompanied by a recitation of the underlying facts upon which the opinion is based, but those underlying facts are either falsely misrepresented or grossly distorted.

Determining whether particular statements, or particular words, express fact or opinion is ofttimes an exercise beset by the uncertainties engendered by the imprecision and varying nuance inherent in language. While mechanistic rules and rigid sets of criteria have been eschewed as inappropriate vehicles for the sensitive process of separating fact from opinion, reference to various general criteria has been found helpful in resolving the issue. Predominant among these is that the determination is to be made on the basis of what the average person hearing or reading the communication would take it to mean, and what significance is to be accorded the purpose of the words, the circumstances surrounding their use and the manner, tone and style with which they are used. An approach which was favorably commented upon in the *Steinhilber* case is that set forth by Judge Starr in his plurality opinion in *Ollman* v. *Evans* which enunciates four factors which should generally be considered in differentiating between fact and opinion. They are summarized . . . as follows:

(1) an assessment of whether the specific language in issue has a precise meaning which is readily understood or whether it is indefinite and ambiguous;

(2) a determination of whether the statement is capable of being objectively characterized as true or false;

(3) an examination of the full context of the communication in which the statement appears; and

(4) a consideration of the broader social context or setting surrounding the communication including the existence of any applicable customs or conventions which might signal to readers or listeners that what is being read or heard is likely to be opinion, not fact.

These factors have particular relevance to the statement here in issue which must be evaluated within the broader social context of a baseball club owner versus an umpire, and special attention should be accorded to whether there exist any customs and conventions regarding the status of an umpire in the great American pastime which would signal to readers that what is being read is likely to be opinion not fact.

* * *

From the late nineteenth century on, the baseball umpire has come to expect not only verbal abuse, but in many cases, physical attack as well, as part of the "robust debate" ingrained in the profession. . . .

Judges, too, have expressed their acceptance of this American tradition. In dismissing a minor league general manager's defamation action on other grounds, a federal court noted that harsh insults, especially those directed at an umpire, are accepted commonplace occurrences in baseball.

* * *

When Steinbrenner's remarks are viewed in this context, it is clear that they would be perceived by the average reader as a statement of opinion, and not fact. The negative characterizations of the plaintiff umpire as "not capable," that "he doesn't measure up," that he "misjudges" plays and that his decision to "throw two of our players out of ball games" was "ludicrous" are readily understood to be the kind of "rhetorical hyperbole" that generally accompany the communication of displeasure at an umpire's "calls." While the subjective and emotional character of such sentiments is commonly recognized and construed as "opinion" rather than fact, that view is expressly emphasized upon a reading of the entire press release with its qualifying phrases of "my people tell me" immediately evident that the statement represents the view of the owner of an embattled baseball team who is obviously chafing at "the team's (poor) play this season," which has been exacerbated by a weekend of injuries and ejections of players, and who is venting his frustrations in the venerated American tradition of "baiting the umpire." Indeed, even if the assertions in the statement implying that plaintiff was incompetent and biased in performing his duties were to be viewed as statements of fact, it is questionable whether they could be construed as defamatory, i.e., exposing the plaintiff to public contempt, ridicule, aversion and disgrace and inducing an evil opinion of him in the minds of right thinking persons—in light of the generally "critical" attitudes which baseball umpires, in any event, ordinarily inspire in both the game's fans and its participants.

Although acknowledging that the statement in issue was "clearly expressed as opinion," Special Term held that it was actionable because the accompanying underlying facts were found by Special Term not to adequately support the opinions proffered. That one may dispute the conclusions drawn from the specified facts is not, however, the test. So long as the opinion is accompanied by a recitation of the facts upon which it is based it is deemed a "pure opinion" and is afforded complete immunity even though the facts do not support the opinion. The rationale for this broad protection of an expression of opinion accompanied by a recitation of the facts upon which it is based is that the reader has the opportunity to assess the basis upon which the opinion was reached in order to draw his or her own conclusions concerning its validity.

* * *

The reverence which the First Amendment accords to ideas has properly resulted in the determination that, "however pernicious an opinion may seem, we depend for its correction not on the conscience of judges and juries but on the competition of other ideas." Those competing ideas about baseball's arbiters will undoubtedly continue to abound aplenty both on the playing

continues

fields and in the sports columns, albeit not in the courtroom.

Accordingly, the Order, Supreme Court, Bronx County (Alfred J. Callahan, J.), entered May 9, 1986, which denied the defendants' motion to dismiss the complaint and supplemental complaint for failure to state a cause of action, should be reversed, on the law, and the complaint dismissed, without costs.

FINDING THE LAW

There are several important sources of law in the United States, including the U.S. Constitution; case law established by the written opinions of judges; statutes enacted by legislative bodies; regulatory agency orders, opinions, and regulations; treatises; law reviews; and Restatements of Law. At one time or another, we reference these sources in explaining the laws making up the legal environment of business. This section provides a guide to reading a citation to a source of law. If you decide to study an aspect of the legal environment in more detail, this section provides guidance in locating appropriate material.

Case Law

The published judicial opinions of all federal courts and the appellate state courts are available in court reporters. As a rule, opinions appear in hardback volumes of the reporters about a year after a court has delivered its decision. The opinions are available more quickly in paperback volumes published shortly after the case is decided, even more quickly through computer research services (such as Westlaw and Lexis), and in the form of "slip opinions," copies of a decision as soon as it is made public by the court.

Supreme Court decisions are published in *United States Reporter* (U.S.), *Supreme Court Reporter* (S.Ct.), *Lawyers' Edition of Supreme Court Reports* (L.Ed.), and *U.S. Law Week*. A citation reads as follows: *Arnett* v. *Kennedy*, 416 U.S. 134, 94 S.Ct. 1633 (1974). This tells us that Arnett appealed a decision of a lower court to the U.S. Supreme Court. In 1974, the Supreme Court decided the case (which was argued in 1973), and its decision is reported in volume 416 of *United States Reporter* beginning on page 134 and in volume 94 of *Supreme Court Reporter* beginning on page 1633. A reference to a point cited on a particular page in that opinion might read 416 U.S. 134, 137, which means that the case begins on page 134 and the particular point referenced is on page 137. Decisions of U.S. Circuit Courts of Appeals are reported in *Federal Reporter* (F.), now in its third series (F.3d). The following is an example of a citation: *Easton Publishing Co.* v. *Federal Communications Commission*, 175 F.2d 344 (1949). The decision in this case can be found in volume 175 of *Federal Reporter* (second series), page 344. The decision was issued by the court in 1949.

Opinions of U.S. district courts that the judges decide to publish are reported in *Federal Supplement* (F.Supp.) now in its second (2d) series. An example is *Amalgamated Meat Cutters* v. *Connally*, 337 F.Supp. 737 (S.D.N.Y.1971). The decision can be found in volume 337 of *Federal Supplement* beginning on page 737. The case was decided by the federal district court in the southern district of New York in 1971.

State appellate court decisions are reported in regional reporters published by West Publishing Company. Decisions of the state supreme courts and courts of appeals for Arkansas, Kentucky, Missouri, Tennessee, and Texas, for example, are reported in *South Western Reporter* (S.W.). As shown in Exhibit A.1, other state court opinions are reported in *Atlantic Reporter* (A.), *North Eastern Reporter* (N.E.), *North Western Reporter* (N.W.), *Pacific Reporter* (P.), *South Eastern Reporter* (S.E.), and *Southern Reporter* (S.), all of which are in the second series (2d). Because they handle so many cases, California and New York have individual reporters, *New*

York Supplement and *California Reporter*. Some states publish their own reporters in addition to the West series.

STATUTORY LAW

Statutes—laws passed by Congress—are published in the *United States Code* (U.S.C.) and printed by the U.S. Government Printing Office. The U.S.C. contains the text of all laws passed by Congress and signed by the president. A reference to this source might read 40 U.S.C. §13.1 (volume 40, *United States Code*, section 13.1).

A very popular source of statutory law is the *United States Code Annotated* (U.S.C.A.). In the U.S.C.A., each section of a statute contains helpful annotations that provide references to the legislative history of the section and to court decisions using and interpreting it. A reference to this source might read 14 U.S.C.A. §45.3 (volume 14, *United States Code Annotated*, section 45.3). In both the U.S.C. and the U.S.C.A., the laws are organized and integrated into a pattern that makes them relatively easy to find and to read.

The U.S. Government Printing Office also publishes *Statutes at Large*, a chronological list of all laws enacted by Congress. This list is not often used unless it is necessary to look up a law that has just been passed by Congress but that is not yet reported in the U.S.C. or U.S.C.A. A full citation might read: Voting Rights Act of 1965, Pub.L. No. 89—110, 79 Stat. 437, 42 U.S.C. §§1971, 1973. The Voting Rights Act of 1965 was the 110th *Public Law* enacted by the 89th Congress and appears in volume 79 of *Statutes at Large*, page 437. In addition, it appears in volume 42 of the U.S.C., sections 1971 and 1973. Also, remember that there is often a difference between the number of the section in the statute as written by Congress and the number of the section in the Code. For example, the "National Environmental Policy Act of 1969, §102, 42 U.S.C. §4332" means that section 102 of the statute as passed by Congress is found in section 4332 of volume 42 of the U.S.C.

Regulatory Law

Regulations—rules passed by agencies subsequent to a congressional statute—are published in the *Code of Federal Regulations* (C.F.R.). These regulations are intended to implement a particular statute enacted by Congress. The C.F.R., revised annually, is organized by subject matter and contains the text of regulations in effect as of the date of publication. A citation reading 7 C.F.R. §912.65 refers to Title 7 of the *Code of Federal Regulations*, section 912.65. Different titles refer to different government agencies.

To keep up-to-date on new and proposed regulations, one needs to consult the *Federal Register* (Fed.Reg.). Printed five days a week by the U.S. Government Printing Office, the *Federal Register* lists all proposed regulations and all new and amended regulations. A citation might read 46 Fed.Reg. 26,501 (1981). This refers to volume 46 of the *Federal Register*, published in 1981, page 26,501, which has to do with a new environmental standard.

Agency Orders and Opinions

Agency orders and opinions are official regulatory materials that go beyond the regulations. Orders may be issued by the top officials (e.g., the commissioners) of a regulatory agency, while opinions are generally issued by an agency's administrative law judge in adjudicatory hearings (discussed in Chapter 6). While agencies usually have official publications, the easiest way to find agency materials is to look in commercial reporters published by private companies such as Commerce Clearing House, Bureau of National Affairs, and Prentice-Hall. Each reporter covers a single topic, such as environmental law or federal tax law. The reporters are up-to-date and contain new regulations, orders, opinions, court decisions, and other materials of interest to anyone following regulations in a certain area. These reporters, which are usually large loose-leaf binders, cover hundreds of topics, such as chemical regulations, hazardous materials, transportation, noise regulations, collective bargaining negotiations, securities regulations, patents, and antitrust laws.

Treatises, Law Reviews, and Restatements of the Law

Important secondary sources of law are legal treatises, law reviews, and Restatements of Law. Treatises generally cover one area or topic of law, summarizing the principles and rules dealing with the topic. An example of a treatise is W. Jaeger, *Williston on Contracts* (3d ed. 1957).

Law reviews, published by law schools and edited by law students, contain articles written by legal scholars, judges, law students, and practitioners on virtually all aspects of the law. An example of a legal citation to a law review is Mark J. Roe, "Corporate Strategic Reaction to Mass Tort," 72 *Virginia Law Review* 1 (1986), which means that the article "Corporate Strategic Reaction to Mass Tort" written by Mark J. Roe can be found in volume 72 of *Virginia Law Review* beginning on page 1.

Like a treatise, a Restatement is limited in its coverage to a single area of law. Restatements are the consequence of intensive study on a specific topic by legal scholars, culminating in a written statement of the law. That statement will include rules stated in bold type—often referred to as "black-letter law"—along with explanatory comments. The rules presented are usually synthesized from opinions of the courts in all jurisdictions. An example is *Restatement (Second) of Torts*.

Application to Environmental Law

In addition to all the general sources just discussed, helpful special sources of the law are available in any given area of law. In environmental law, there are, of course, the federal statutes in the *U.S. Code* and *U.S. Code Annotated*. In addition, a good single source for environmental statutes is *West's Selected Environmental Statutes—Educational Edition*, which contains the most important statutes and is updated annually to account for new laws and amendments to existing laws.

The federal regulations are found in *Title 40* of the *Code of Federal Regulations*. Because there are so many environmental regulations, the number of volumes (twenty-nine at last count) was second only to the number of volumes needed for IRS tax regulations (twenty-one). As regulations are proposed and then finalized (before they are entered in the *Code of Federal Regulation*), they are published in the *Federal Register*.

Reading the Federal Register is a task few enjoy, and it is not an efficient way to keep up on regulatory developments. To keep up on new legal events, one can consult the Bureau of National Affair's (BNA's) *Environmental Reporter*. Each week it has a "Current Developments" section. Indeed, the BNA publishes a *Daily Environmental Reporter* to keep on top of environmental stories on all fronts—state, federal, and international legal developments, as well as news events. Other publications, such as *Inside EPA* published by Inside Washington Publishers, monitors news inside the EPA and news affecting the EPA, such as what is being rumored in the White House or in Congress about the EPA. Such publications are a mixture of facts and rumors, often supplied by personnel in the agency.

Environmental law opinions appear in the various reporters, such as the *Federal Supplement*, but because it is hard to sort through all of the opinions that appear in the reporters to find the ones on environmental law, it is better to consult a reporter such as *Environmental Law Reporter* published monthly by the Environmental Law Institute. That reporter contains summaries of pending litigation, new cases, settlement agreements, and unpublished decisions, all in the environmental area.

Numerous environmental law treatises exist, published by different companies. They include *The Law of Environmental Protection* by Sheldon Novick, published by Clark Boardman. West Publishing Company's *Environmental Law* by William Rodgers is a well-known hornbook. An introductory level book is *A Practical Guide to Environmental Law* by David Sive and Frank Friedman, published by ALI-ABA, which also recently published *The Environmental Law Manual*, a collection of articles by experts on different areas of environmental law.

There are dozens of environmental journals and magazines. The Environmental Law Institute publishes *Environmental Forum*, devoted to recent policy developments. The American Bar Association Section of Natural Resources, Energy and Environmental Law publishes *Natural Resources & Environment*, which contains technical but short articles about new developments. The EPA publishes the easily readable *EPA Journal*. A number of law journals are devoted to environmental law, including *Ecology Law Quarterly*, *Columbia Journal of Environmental Law*, and *Harvard Environmental Law Journal*.

Each year, the Environmental Law Institute and the American Bar Association host environmental law conferences at which leading experts talk about recent developments and forthcoming events. The conferences usually publish the papers presented. Many law schools and state bar associations hold environmental law conferences either regularly or on special occasions. There is no lack of materials—it's just a matter of tracking them down!

The Constitution of the United States of America

Preamble

We the People of the United States, in Order to form a more perfect Union, establish Justice, insure domestic Tranquility, provide for the common defence, promote the general Welfare, and secure the Blessings of Liberty to ourselves and our Posterity, do ordain and establish this Constitution for the United States of America.

Article I

Section 1. All legislative Powers herein granted shall be vested in a Congress of the United States, which shall consist of a Senate and House of Representatives.

Section 2. The House of Representatives shall be composed of Members chosen every second Year by the People of the several States, and the Electors in each State shall have the Qualifications requisite for Electors of the most numerous Branch of the State Legislature.

No Person shall be a Representative who shall not have attained to the Age of twenty five Years, and been seven Years a Citizen of the United States, and who shall not, when elected, be an Inhabitant of that State in which he shall be chosen.

Representatives and direct Taxes shall be apportioned among the several States which may be included within this Union, according to their respective Numbers, which shall be determined by adding to the whole Number of free Persons, including those bound to Service for a Term of Years, and excluding Indians not taxed, three fifths of all other Persons. The actual Enumeration shall be made within three Years after the first Meeting of the Congress of the United States, and within every subsequent Term of ten Years, in such Manner as they shall by Law direct. The number of Representatives shall not exceed one for every thirty Thousand, but each State shall have at Least one Representative; and until such enumeration shall be made, the State of New Hampshire shall be entitled to chuse three, Massachusetts eight, Rhode Island and Providence Plantations one, Connecticut five, New York six, New Jersey four, Pennsylvania eight, Delaware one, Maryland six, Virginia ten, North Carolina five, South Carolina five, and Georgia three.

When vacancies happen in the Representation from any State, the Executive Authority thereof shall issue Writs of Election to fill such vacancies.

The House of Representatives shall chuse their Speaker and other Officers; and shall have the sole Power of Impeachment.

Section 3. The Senate of the United States shall be composed of two Senators from each State, chosen by the Legislature thereof, for six Years; and each Senator shall have one Vote.

Immediately after they shall be assembled in Consequence of the first Election, they shall be divided as equally as may be into three Classes. The Seats of the Senators of the first Class shall be vacated at the Expiration of the second Year, of the second Class at the Expiration of the fourth Year, and of the third Class at the Expiration of the sixth Year, so that one third may be chosen every second Year; and if Vacancies happen by Resignation, or otherwise, during the Recess of the Legislature of any State, the Executive thereof may make temporary Appointments until the next Meeting of the Legislature, which shall then fill such Vacancies.

No Person shall be a Senator who shall not have attained to the Age of thirty Years, and been nine Years a Citizen of the United States, and who shall not, when elected, be an Inhabitant of that State for which he shall be chosen.

The Vice President of the United States shall be President of the Senate, but shall have no Vote, unless they be equally divided.

The Senate shall chuse their other Officers, and also a President pro tempore, in the Absence of the Vice President, or when he shall exercise the Office of President of the United States.

The Senate shall have the sole power to try all Impeachments. When sitting for that Purpose, they shall be on Oath or Affirmation. When the President of the United States is tried, the Chief Justice shall preside: And no Person shall be convicted without the Concurrence of two thirds of the Members present.

Judgment in Cases of Impeachment shall not extend further than to removal from Office, and disqualification to hold and enjoy any Office of honor, Trust or Profit under the United States: but the Party convicted shall nevertheless be liable and subject to Indictment, Trial, Judgment and Punishment, according to Law.

Section 4. The Times, Places and Manner of holding Elections for Senators and Representatives, shall be prescribed in each State by the Legislature thereof: but the Congress may at any time by Law make or alter such Regulations, except as to the Places of chusing Senators.

The Congress shall assemble at least once in every Year, and such Meeting shall be on the first Monday in December, unless they shall by Law appoint a different Day.

Section 5. Each House shall be the Judge of the Elections, Returns and Qualifications of its own Members, and a Majority of each shall constitute a Quorum to do Business; but a smaller Number may adjourn from day to day, and may be authorized to compel the Attendance of absent Members, in such Manner, and under such Penalties as each House may provide.

Each House may determine the Rules of its Proceedings, punish its Members for disorderly Behaviour, and, with the Concurrence of two thirds, expel a Member.

Each House shall keep a Journal of its Proceedings, and from time to time publish the same, excepting such Parts as may in their Judgment require Secrecy; and the Yeas and Nays of the Members of either House on any question shall, at the Desire of one fifth of those Present, be entered on the Journal.

Neither House, during the Session of Congress, shall, without the Consent of the other, adjourn for more than three days, nor to any other Place than that in which the two Houses shall be sitting.

Section 6. The Senators and Representatives shall receive a Compensation for their Services, to be ascertained by Law, and paid out of the Treasury of the United States. They shall in all Cases, except Treason, Felony and Breach of the Peace, be privileged from Arrest during their Attendance at the Session of their respective Houses, and in going to and returning from the same; and for any Speech or Debate in either House, they shall not be questioned in any other Place.

No Senator or Representative shall, during the Time for which he was elected, be appointed to any civil Office under the Authority of the United States, which shall have been created, or the Emoluments whereof shall have been encreased during such time; and no Person holding any Office under the United States, shall be a Member of either House during his Continuance in Office.

Section 7. All Bills for raising Revenue shall originate in the House of Representatives; but the Senate may propose or concur with Amendments as on other Bills.

Every Bill which shall have passed the House of Representatives and the Senate, shall, before it become a Law, be presented to the President of the United States; If he approve he shall sign it, but if not he shall return it, with his Objections to that House in which it shall have originated, who shall enter the Objections at large on their Journal, and proceed to reconsider it. If after such Reconsideration two thirds of that House shall agree to pass the Bill, it shall be sent, together with the Objections, to the other House, by which it shall likewise be reconsidered, and if approved by two thirds of that House, it shall become a Law. But in all such Cases the Votes of both Houses shall be determined by Yeas and Nays, and the Names of the Persons voting for and against the Bill shall be entered on the Journal of each House respectively. If any Bill shall not be returned by the President within ten Days (Sundays excepted) after it shall have been presented to him, the Same shall be a Law, in like Manner as if he had signed it, unless the Congress by their Adjournment prevent its Return, in which Case it shall not be a Law.

Every Order, Resolution, or Vote to which the Concurrence of the Senate and House of Representatives may be necessary (except on a question of Adjournment) shall be presented to the President of the United States; and before the Same shall take Effect, shall be approved by him, or being disapproved by him, shall be repassed by two thirds of the Senate and House of Representatives, according to the Rules and Limitations prescribed in the Case of a Bill.

Section 8. The Congress shall have Power to lay and collect Taxes, Duties, Imposts and Excises, to pay the Debts and provide for the common Defence and general Welfare of the United States; but all Duties, Imposts and Excises shall be uniform throughout the United States;

To borrow Money on the credit of the United States;

To regulate Commerce with foreign Nations, and among the several States, and with the Indian Tribes;

To establish an uniform Rule of Naturalization, and uniform Laws on the subject of Bankruptcies throughout the United States;

To coin Money, regulate the Value thereof, and of foreign Coin, and fix the Standard of Weights and Measures;

To provide for the Punishment of counterfeiting the Securities and current Coin of the United States;

To establish Post Offices and post Roads;

To promote the Progress of Science and useful Arts, by securing for limited Times to Authors and Inventors the exclusive Right to their respective Writings and Discoveries;

To constitute Tribunals inferior to the supreme Court;

To define and punish Piracies and Felonies committed on the high Seas, and Offenses against the Law of Nations;

To declare War, grant Letters of Marque and Reprisal, and make Rules concerning Captures on Land and Water;

To raise and support Armies, but no Appropriation of Money to that Use shall be for a longer Term than two Years;

To provide and maintain a Navy;

To make Rules for the Government and Regulation of the land and naval Forces;

To provide for calling forth the Militia to execute the Laws of the Union, suppress Insurrections and repel Invasions;

To provide for organizing, arming, and disciplining, the Militia, and for governing such Part of them as may be employed in the Service of the United States, reserving to the States respectively, the Appointment of the Officers, and the Authority of training the Militia according to the discipline prescribed by Congress;

To exercise exclusive Legislation in all Cases whatsoever, over such District (not exceeding ten Miles square) as may, by Cession of particular States, and the Acceptance of Congress, become the Seat of the Government of the United States, and to exercise like Authority over all Places purchased by the Consent of the Legislature of the State in which the Same shall be, for the Erection of Forts, Magazines, Arsenals, dock-Yards, and other needful Buildings;—And

To make all Laws which shall be necessary and proper for carrying into Execution the foregoing Powers, and all other Powers vested by this Constitution in the Government of the United States, or in any Department or Officer thereof.

Section 9. The Migration or Importation of such Persons as any of the States now existing shall think proper to admit, shall not be prohibited by the Congress prior to the Year one thousand eight hundred and eight, but a Tax or Duty may be imposed on such Importation, not exceeding ten dollars for each Person.

The Privilege of the Writ of Habeas Corpus shall not be suspended, unless when in Cases of Rebellion or Invasion the public Safety may require it.

No Bill of Attainder or ex post facto Law shall be passed.

No Capitation, or other direct, Tax shall be laid, unless in Proportion to the Census or Enumeration herein before directed to be taken.

No Tax or Duty shall be laid on Articles exported from any State.

No Preference shall be given by any Regulation of Commerce or Revenue to the Ports of one State over those of another; nor shall Vessels bound to, or from, one State, be obliged to enter, clear, or pay Duties in another.

No Money shall be drawn from the Treasury, but in Consequence of Appropriations made by Laws; and a regular Statement and Account of the Receipts and Expenditures of all public Money shall be published from time to time.

No Title of Nobility shall be granted by the United States: And no Person holding any Office of Profit or Trust under them, shall, without the Consent of the Congress, accept of any present, Emolument, Office, or Title, of any kind whatever, from any King, Prince, or foreign State.

Section 10. No State shall enter into any Treaty, Alliance, or Confederation; grant Letters of Marque and Reprisal; coin Money; emit Bills of Credit; make any Thing but gold and silver Coin a Tender in Payment of Debts; pass any Bill of Attainder, ex post facto Law, or Law impairing the Obligation of Contracts, or grant any Title of Nobility.

No State shall, without the Consent of the Congress, lay any Imposts or Duties on Imports or Exports, except what may be absolutely necessary for executing its inspection Laws: and the net Produce of all Duties and Imposts, laid by any State on Imports or Exports, shall be for the Use of the Treasury of the United States; and all such Laws shall be subject to the Revision and Controul of the Congress.

No State shall, without the Consent of Congress, lay any Duty of Tonnage, keep Troops, or Ships of War in time of Peace, enter into any Agreement or Compact with another State, or with a foreign Power, or engage in War, unless actually invaded, or in such imminent Danger as will not admit of delay.

Article II

Section 1. The executive Power shall be vested in a President of the United States of America. He shall hold his Office during the Term of four Years, and, together with the Vice President, chosen for the same Term, be elected, as follows:

Each State shall appoint, in such Manner as the Legislature thereof may direct, a Number of Electors, equal to the whole Number of Senators and Representatives to which the State may be entitled in the Congress: but no Senator or Representative, or Person holding an Office of Trust or Profit under the United States, shall be appointed an Elector.

The Electors shall meet in their respective States, and vote by Ballot for two Persons, of whom one at least shall not be an Inhabitant of the same State with themselves. And they shall make a List of all the Persons voted for, and of the Number of Votes for each; which List they shall sign and certify, and transmit sealed to the Seat of the Government of the United States, directed to the President of the Senate. The President of the Senate shall, in the Presence of the Senate and House of Representatives, open all the Certificates, and the Votes shall then be counted. The Person having the greatest Number of Votes shall be the President, if such Number be a Majority of the whole Number of Electors appointed; and if there be more than one who have such Majority, and have an equal Number of Votes, then the House of Representatives shall immediately chuse by Ballot one of them for President; and if no Person have a Majority, then from the five highest on the List the said House shall in like Manner chuse the President. But in chusing the President, the Votes shall be taken by States, the Representation from each State having one Vote; a quorum for this Purpose shall consist of a Member or Members from two thirds of the States, and a Majority of all the States shall be necessary to a Choice. In every Case, after the Choice of the President, the Person having the greatest Number of Votes of the Electors shall be the Vice President. But if there should remain two or more who have equal Votes, the Senate shall chuse from them by Ballot the Vice President.

The Congress may determine the Time of chusing the Electors, and the Day on which they shall give their Votes; which Day shall be the same throughout the United States.

No Person except a natural born Citizen, or a Citizen of the United States, at the time of the Adoption of this Constitution, shall be eligible to the Office of President; neither shall any Person be eligible to that Office who shall not have attained to the Age of thirty five Years, and been fourteen Years a Resident within the United States.

In Case of the Removal of the President from Office, or of his Death, Resignation, or Inability to discharge the Powers and Duties of the said Office, the Same shall devolve on the Vice President, and the Congress may by Law provide for the Case of Removal, Death, Resignation or Inability, both of the President and Vice President, declaring what Officer shall then act as President, and such Officer shall act accordingly, until the Disability be removed, or a President shall be elected.

The President shall, at stated Times, receive for his Services, a Compensation, which shall neither be encreased nor diminished during the Period for which he shall have been elected, and he shall not receive within that Period any other Emolument from the United States, or any of them.

Before he enter on the Execution of his Office, he shall take the following Oath or Affirmation:—"I do solemnly swear (or affirm) that I will faithfully execute the Office of President of the United States, and will to the best of my Ability, preserve, protect and defend the Constitution of the United States."

Section 2. The President shall be Commander in Chief of the Army and Navy of the United States, and of the Militia of the several States, when called into the actual Service of the United States; he may require the Opinion, in writing, of the principal Officer in each of the executive Departments, upon any Subject relating to the Duties of their respective Offices, and he shall have Power to grant Reprieves and Pardons for Offences against the United States, except in Cases of Impeachment.

He shall have Power, by and with the Advice and Consent of the Senate, to make Treaties, providing two thirds of the Senators present concur; and he shall nominate, and by and with the Advice and Consent of the Senate, shall appoint Ambassadors, other public Ministers and Consuls, Judges of the supreme Court, and all other Officers of the United States, whose Appointments are not herein otherwise provided for, and which shall be established by Law:

but the Congress may by Law vest the Appointment of such inferior Officers, as they think proper, in the President alone, in the Courts of Law, or in the Heads of Departments.

The President shall have Power to fill up all Vacancies that may happen during the Recess of the Senate, by granting Commissions which shall expire at the End of their next Session.

Section 3. He shall from time to time give to the Congress Information of the State of the Union, and recommend to their Consideration such Measures as he shall judge necessary and expedient; he may, on extraordinary Occasions, convene both Houses, or either of them, and in Case of Disagreement between them, with Respect to the Time of Adjournment, he may adjourn them to such Time as he shall think proper; he shall receive Ambassadors and other public Ministers; he shall take Care that the Laws be faithfully executed, and shall Commission all the Officers of the United States.

Section 4. The President, Vice President and all civil Officers of the United States, shall be removed from Office on Impeachment for, and Conviction of, Treason, Bribery, or other high Crimes and Misdemeanors.

Article III

Section 1. The judicial Power of the United States, shall be vested in one supreme Court, and in such inferior Courts as the Congress may from time to time ordain and establish. The Judges, both of the supreme and inferior Courts, shall hold their Offices during good Behaviour, and shall, at stated Times, receive for their Services, a Compensation, which shall not be diminished during their Continuance in Office.

Section 2. The judicial Power shall extend to all Cases, in Law and Equity, arising under this Constitution, the Laws of the United States, and Treaties made, or which shall be made, under their Authority;—to all Cases affecting Ambassadors, other public Ministers and Consuls;—to all Cases of admiralty and maritime Jurisdiction;—to Controversies to which the United States shall be a Party;—to Controversies between two or more States;—between a State and Citizens of another State;—between Citizens of different States;—between Citizens of the same State claiming Lands under Grants of different States, and between a State, or the Citizens thereof, and foreign States, Citizens or Subjects.

In all Cases affecting Ambassadors, other public Ministers and Consuls, and those in which a State shall be Party, the supreme Court shall have original Jurisdiction. In all the other Cases before mentioned, the supreme Court shall have appellate Jurisdiction, both as to Law and Fact, with such Exceptions, and under such Regulations as the Congress shall make.

The Trial of all Crimes, except in Cases of Impeachment, shall be by Jury; and such Trial shall be held in the State where the said Crimes shall have been committed; but when not committed within any State, the Trial shall be at such Place or Places as the Congress may by Law have directed.

Section 3. Treason against the United States, shall consist only in levying War against them, or in adhering to their Enemies, giving them Aid and Comfort. No Person shall be convicted of Treason unless on the Testimony of two Witnesses to the same overt Act, or on Confession in open Court.

The Congress shall have Power to declare the Punishment of Treason, but no Attainder of Treason shall work Corruption of Blood, or Forfeiture except during the Life of the Person attainted.

Article IV

Section 1. Full Faith and Credit shall be given in each State to the public Acts, Records, and judicial Proceedings of every other State. And the Congress may by general Laws prescribe the Manner in which such Acts, Records and Proceedings shall be proved, and the Effect thereof.

Section 2. The Citizens of each State shall be entitled to all Privileges and Immunities of Citizens in the several States.

A Person charged in any State with Treason, Felony, or other Crime, who shall flee from Justice, and be found in another State, shall on Demand of the executive Authority of the State from which he fled, be delivered up, to be removed to the State having Jurisdiction of the Crime.

No Person held to Service or Labour in one State, under the Laws thereof, escaping into another, shall, in Consequence of any Law or Regulation therein, be discharged from such Service or Labour, but shall be delivered up on Claim of the Party to whom such Service or Labour may be due.

Section 3. New States may be admitted by the Congress into this Union; but no new State shall be formed or erected within the Jurisdiction of any other State; nor any State be formed by the Junction of two or more States, or Parts of States, without the Consent of the Legislatures of the States concerned as well as of the Congress.

The Congress shall have Power to dispose of and make all needful Rules and Regulations respecting the Territory or other Property belonging to the United States; and nothing in this Constitution shall be so construed as to Prejudice any Claims of the United States, or of any particular State.

Section 4. The United States shall guarantee to every State in this Union a Republican Form of the Government, and shall protect each of them against Invasion; and on Application of the Legislature, or of the Executive (when the Legislature cannot be convened) against domestic Violence.

Article V

The Congress, whenever two thirds of both Houses shall deem it necessary, shall propose Amendments to this Constitution, or, on the Application of the Legislatures of two thirds of the several States, shall call a Convention for proposing Amendments, which, in either Case, shall be valid to all Intents and Purposes, as Part of this Constitution, when ratified by the Legislatures of three fourths of the several States, or by Conventions in three fourths thereof, as the one or the other Mode of Ratification may be proposed by the Congress; Provided that no Amendment which may be made prior to the Year One thousand eight hundred and eight shall in any Manner affect the first and fourth Clauses in the Ninth Section of the first Article; and that no State, without its Consent, shall be deprived of its equal Suffrage in the Senate.

Article VI

All Debts contracted and Engagements entered into, before the Adoption of this Constitution, shall be as valid against the United States under this Constitution, as under the Confederation.

This Constitution, and the Laws of the United States which shall be made in Pursuance thereof; and all Treaties made, or which shall be made, under the Authority of the United States, shall be the supreme Law of the Land; and the Judges in every State shall be bound thereby, any Thing in the Constitution or Laws of any State to the Contrary notwithstanding.

The Senators and Representatives before mentioned, and the Members of the several State Legislatures, and all executive and judicial Officers, both of the United States and of the several States, shall be bound by Oath or Affirmation, to support this Constitution; but no religious Test shall ever be required as a Qualification to any Office or public Trust under the United States.

Article VII

The Ratification of the Conventions of nine States, shall be sufficient for the Establishment of this Constitution between the States so ratifying the Same.

Amendment I [1791]

Congress shall make no law respecting an establishment of religion, or prohibiting the free exercise thereof; or abridging the freedom of speech, or the press; or the right of the people peaceably to assemble, and to petition the Government for a redress of grievances.

Amendment II [1791]

A well regulated Militia, being necessary to the security of a free State, the right of the people to keep and bear Arms, shall not be infringed.

Amendment III [1791]

No Soldier shall, in time of peace be quartered in any house, without the consent of the Owner, nor in time of war, but in a manner to be prescribed by law.

Amendment IV [1791]

The right of the people to be secure in their persons, houses, papers, and effects, against unreasonable searches and seizures, shall not be violated, and no Warrants shall issue, but upon probable cause, supported by Oath or affirmation, and particularly describing the place to be searched, and the persons or things to be seized.

Amendment V [1791]

No person shall be held to answer for a capital, or otherwise infamous crime, unless on a presentment or indictment of a Grand Jury, except in cases arising in the land or naval forces, or in the Militia, when in actual service in time of War or public danger; nor shall any person be subject for the same offence to be twice put in jeopardy of life or limb; nor shall be compelled in any criminal case to be a witness against himself, nor be deprived of life, liberty, or property, without due process of law; nor shall private property be taken for public use, without just compensation.

Amendment VI [1791]

In all criminal prosecutions, the accused shall enjoy the right to a speedy and public trial, by an impartial jury of the State and district wherein the crime shall have been committed, which district shall have been previously ascertained by law, and to be informed of the nature and cause of the accusation; to be confronted with the Witnesses against him; to have compulsory process for obtaining witnesses in his favor, and to have the Assistance of counsel for his defence.

Amendment VII [1791]

In Suits at common law, where the value in controversy shall exceed twenty dollars, the right of trial by jury shall be preserved, and no fact tried by a jury, shall be otherwise re-examined in any Court of the United States, than according to the rules of the common law.

Amendment VIII [1791]

Excessive bail shall not be required, nor excessive fines imposed, nor cruel and unusual punishments inflicted.

Amendment IX [1791]

The enumeration in the Constitution, of certain rights, shall not be construed to deny or disparage others retained by the people.

Amendment X [1791]

The powers not delegated to the United States by the Constitution, nor prohibited by it to the States, are reserved to the States respectively, or to the people.

Amendment XI [1798]

The Judicial power of the United States shall not be construed to extend to any suit in law or equity, commenced or prosecuted against one of the United States by Citizens of another State, or by Citizens or Subjects of any Foreign State.

Amendment XII [1804]

The Electors shall meet in their respective states and vote by ballot for President and Vice-President, one of whom, at least, shall not be an inhabitant of the same state with themselves; they shall name in their ballots the person voted for as President, and in distinct ballots the person voted for as Vice-President, and they shall make distinct lists of all persons voted for as President, and of all persons voted for as Vice-President, and of the number of votes for each, which lists they shall sign and certify, and transmit sealed to the seat of the government of the United States, directed to the President of the Senate;—The President of the Senate shall, in the presence of the Senate and House of Representatives, open all the certificates and the votes shall then be counted;—The person having the greatest number of votes for President, shall be the President, if such number be a majority of the whole number of Electors appointed; and if no person have such majority, then from the persons having the highest numbers not exceeding three on the list of those voted for as President, the House of Representatives shall choose immediately, by ballot, the President. But in choosing the President, the votes shall be taken by states, the representation from each state having one vote; a quorum for this purpose shall consist of a member or members from two-thirds of the states, and a majority of all the states shall be necessary to a choice. And if the House of Representatives shall not choose a President whenever the right of choice shall devolve upon them, before the fourth day of March next following, then the Vice-President shall act as President, as in the case of the death or other constitutional disability of the President. The person having the greatest number of votes as Vice-President, shall be the Vice-President, if such number be a majority of the whole number of Electors appointed, and if no person have a majority, then from the two highest numbers on the list, the Senate shall choose the Vice-President; a quorum for the purpose shall consist of two-thirds of the whole number of Senators, and a majority of the whole number shall be necessary to a choice. But no person constitutionally ineligible to the office of President shall be eligible to that of the Vice-President of the United States.

Amendment XIII [1865]

Section 1. Neither slavery nor involuntary servitude, except as a punishment for crime whereof the party shall have been duly convicted, shall exist within the United States, or any place subject to their jurisdiction.

Section 2. Congress shall have power to enforce this article by appropriate legislation.

Amendment XIV [1868]

Section 1. All persons born or naturalized in the United States, and subject to the jurisdiction thereof, are citizens of the United States and of the State wherein they reside. No State shall make or enforce any law which shall abridge the privileges or immunities of citizens of the United States; nor shall any State deprive any person of life, liberty, or property, without due process of law; nor deny to any person within its jurisdiction the equal protection of the laws.

Section 2. Representatives shall be appointed among the several States according to their respective numbers, counting the whole number of persons in each State, excluding Indians not taxed. But when the right to vote at any election for the choice of electors for President and Vice President of the United States, Representatives in Congress, the Executive and Judicial officers of a State, or the members of the Legislature thereof, is denied to any of the male inhabitants of such State, being twenty-one years of age, and citizens of the United States, or in any way abridged, except for participation in rebellion, or other crime, the basis of representation therein shall be reduced in the proportion which the number of such male citizens shall bear to the whole number of male citizens twenty-one years of age in such State.

Section 3. No person shall be a Senator or Representative in Congress, or elector of President and Vice President, or hold any office, civil or military, under the United States, or under any State, who, having previously taken an oath, as a member of Congress, or as an officer of the United States, or as a member of any State legislature, or as an executive or judicial officer of any State, to support the Constitution of the United States, shall have engaged in insurrection or rebellion against the same, or given aid or comfort to the enemies thereof. But Congress may by a vote of two-thirds of each House, remove such disability.

Section 4. The validity of the public debt of the United States, authorized by law, including debts incurred for payment of pensions and bounties for services in suppressing insurrection or rebellion, shall not be questioned. But neither the United States nor any State shall assume or pay any debt or obligation incurred in aid of insurrection or rebellion against the United States, or any claim for the loss or emancipation of any slave; but all such debts, obligations and claims shall be held illegal and void.

Section 5. The Congress shall have power to enforce, by appropriate legislation, the provisions of this article.

Amendment XV [1870]

Section 1. The right of citizens of the United States to vote shall not be denied or abridged by the United States or by any State on account of race, color, or previous condition of servitude.

Section 2. The Congress shall have power to enforce this article by appropriate legislation.

Amendment XVI [1913]

The Congress shall have power to lay and collect taxes on incomes, from whatever source derived, without apportionment among the several States, and without regard to any census or enumeration.

Amendment XVII [1913]

The Senate of the United States shall be composed of two Senators from each State, elected by the people thereof, for six years; and each Senator shall have one vote. The electors in each State shall have the qualifications requisite for electors of the most numerous branch of the State legislatures.

When vacancies happen in the representation of any State in the Senate, the executive authority of each State shall issue writs of election to fill such vacancies; Provided, That the legislature of any State may empower the executive thereof to make temporary appointments until the people fill the vacancies by election as the legislature may direct.

This amendment shall not be so construed as to affect the election or term of any Senator chosen before it becomes valid as part of the Constitution.

Amendment XVIII [1919]

Section 1. After one year from the ratification of this article the manufacture, sale, or transportation of intoxicating liquors within, the importation thereof into, or the exportation thereof from the United States and all territory subject to the jurisdiction thereof for beverage purposes is hereby prohibited.

Section 2. The Congress and the several States shall have concurrent power to enforce this article by appropriate legislation.

Section 3. This article shall be inoperative unless it shall have been ratified as an amendment to the Constitution by the legislatures of the several States, as provided in the Constitution, within seven years from the date of the submission hereof to the States by the Congress.

Amendment XIX [1920]

The right of citizens of the United States to vote shall not be denied or abridged by the United States or by any State on account of sex.

Congress shall have power to enforce this article by appropriate legislation.

Amendment XX [1933]

Section 1. The terms of the President and Vice President shall end at noon on the 20th day of January, and the terms of Senators and Representatives at noon on the 3d day of January, of the years in which such terms would have ended if this article had not been ratified; and the terms of their successors shall then begin.

Section 2. The Congress shall assemble at least once every year, and such meeting shall begin at noon on the 3d day of January, unless they shall by law appoint a different day.

Section 3. If, at the time fixed for the beginning of the term of the President, the President elect shall have died, the Vice President elect shall become President. If a President shall not have been chosen before the time fixed for the beginning of his term, or if the President elect shall have failed to qualify, then the Vice President elect shall act as President until a President shall have qualified; and the Congress may by law provide for the case wherein neither a President elect nor a Vice President elect shall have qualified, declaring who shall then act as President, or the manner in which one who is to act shall be selected, and such person shall act accordingly until a President or Vice President shall have qualified.

Section 4. The Congress may by law provide for the case of the death of any of the persons from whom the House of Representatives may choose a President whenever the right of choice shall have devolved upon them, and for the case of the death of any of the persons from whom the Senate may choose a Vice President whenever the right of choice shall have devolved upon them.

Section 5. Sections 1 and 2 shall take effect on the 15th day of October following the ratification of this article.

Section 6. This article shall be inoperative unless it shall have been ratified as an amendment to the Constitution by the legislatures of three-fourths of the several States within seven years from the date of its submission.

Amendment XXI [1933]

Section 1. The eighteenth article of amendment to the Constitution of the United States is hereby repealed.

Section 2. The transportation or importation into any State, Territory, or possession of the United States for delivery or use therein of intoxicating liquors, in violation of the laws thereof, is hereby prohibited.

Section 3. This article shall be inoperative unless it shall have been ratified as an amendment to the Constitution by conventions in the several States, as provided in the Constitution, within seven years from the date of the submission hereof to the States by the Congress.

Amendment XXII [1951]

Section 1. No person shall be elected to the office of the President more than twice, and no person who has held the office of President, or acted as President, for more than two years of a term to which some other person was elected President shall be elected to the office of the President more than once. But this Article shall not apply to any person holding the office of President when this Article was proposed by the Congress, and shall not prevent any person who may be holding the office of President, or acting as President, during the term within which this Article becomes operative from holding the office of President or acting as President during the remainder of such term.

Section 2. This article shall be inoperative unless it shall have been ratified as an amendment to the Constitution by the legislatures of three-fourths of the several States within seven years from the date of its submission to the States by the Congress.

Amendment XXIII [1961]

Section 1. The District constituting the seat of Government of the United States shall appoint in such manner as the Congress may direct:

A number of electors of President and Vice President equal to the whole number of Senators and Representatives in Congress to which the District would be entitled if it were a State, but in no event more than the least populous State; they shall be in addition to those appointed by the States, but they shall be considered, for the purposes of the election of President and Vice President, to be electors appointed by a State; and they shall meet in the District and perform such duties as provided by the twelfth article of amendment.

Section 2. The Congress shall have power to enforce this article by appropriate legislation.

Amendment XXIV [1964]

Section 1. The right of citizens of the United States to vote in any primary or other election for President or Vice President, for electors for President or Vice President, or for Senator or Representative in Congress, shall not be denied or abridged by the United States or any State by reason of failure to pay any poll tax or other tax.

Section 2. The Congress shall have power to enforce this article by appropriate legislation.

Amendment XXV [1967]

Section 1. In case of the removal of the President from office or of his death or resignation, the Vice President shall become President.

Section 2. Whenever there is a vacancy in the office of the Vice President, the President shall nominate a Vice President who shall take office upon confirmation by a majority vote of both Houses of Congress.

Section 3. Whenever the President transmits to the President pro tempore of the Senate and the Speaker of the House of Representatives his written declaration that he is unable to discharge the powers and duties of his office, and until he transmits to them a written declaration to the contrary, such powers and duties shall be discharged by the Vice President as Acting President.

Section 4. Whenever the Vice President and a majority of either the principal officers of the executive departments or of such other body as Congress may by law provide, transmit to the President pro tempore of the Senate and the Speaker of the House of Representatives their written declaration that the President is unable to discharge the powers and duties of his office, the Vice President shall immediately assume the powers and duties of the office as Acting President.

Thereafter, when the President transmits to the President pro tempore of the Senate and the Speaker of the House of Representatives his written declaration that no inability exists, he shall resume the powers and duties of his office unless the Vice President and a majority of either the principal officers of the executive department or of such other body as Congress may by law provide, transmit within four days to the President pro tempore of the Senate and the Speaker of the House of Representatives their written declaration that the President is unable to discharge the powers and duties of his office. Thereupon Congress shall decide the issue, assembling within forty-eight hours for that purpose if not in session. If the Congress, within twenty-one days after receipt of the latter written declaration, or, if Congress is not in session, within twenty-one days after Congress is required to assemble, determines by two-thirds vote of both Houses that the President is unable to discharge the powers and duties of his office, the Vice President shall continue to discharge the same as Acting President; otherwise, the President shall resume the powers and duties of his office.

Amendment XXVI [1971]

Section 1. The right of citizens of the United States, who are eighteen years of age or older, to vote shall not be denied or abridged by the United States or by any State on account of age.

Section 2. The Congress shall have power to enforce this article by appropriate legislation.

Amendment XXVII [1992]

No law varying the compensation for the services of the senators and representatives shall take effect, until an election of representatives shall have intervened.

The Uniform Commercial Code (Excerpts)

Article 1. General Provisions

Section 1—101. Short Title.
This Act shall be known and may be cited as Uniform Commercial Code.

Section 1—102. **Purposes; Rules of Construction; Variation by Agreement.**
(1) This Act shall be liberally construed and applied to promote its underlying purposes and policies.
(2) Underlying purposes and policies of this Act are
    (a) to simplify, clarify and modernize the law governing commercial transactions;
    (b) to permit the continued expansion of commercial practices through custom, usage, and agreement of the parties;
    (c) to make uniform the law among the various jurisdictions.
(3) The effect of provisions of this Act may be varied by agreement, except as otherwise provided in this Act and except that the obligations of good faith, diligence, reasonableness and care prescribed by this Act may not be disclaimed by agreement but the parties may by agreement determine the standards by which the performance of such obligations is to be measured if such standards are not manifestly unreasonable.
(4) The presence in certain provisions of this Act of the words **"unless otherwise agreed"** or words of similar import does not imply that the effect of other provisions may not be varied by agreement under subsection (3).
(5) In this Act unless the context otherwise requires
    (a) words in the singular number include the plural, and in the plural include the singular;
    (b) words of the masculine gender include the feminine and the neuter, and when the sense so indicates words of the neuter gender may refer to any gender.

Section 1—103. **Supplementary General Principles of Law Applicable.**
Unless displaced by the particular provisions of this Act, the principles of law and equity, including the law merchant and the law relative to capacity to contract, principal and agent, estoppel, fraud, misrepresentation, duress, coercion, mistake, bankruptcy, or other validating or invalidating cause shall supplement its provisions.

Section 1—106. **Remedies to Be Liberally Administered.**
(1) The remedies provided by this Act shall be liberally administered to the end that the aggrieved party may be put in as good a position as if the other party had fully performed but neither consequential or special nor penal damages may be had except as specifically provided in this Act or by other rule of law.
(2) Any right or obligation declared by this Act is enforceable by action unless the provision declaring it specifies a different and limited effect.

Section 1—201. **General Definitions.**

Subject to additional definitions contained in the subsequent Articles of this Act which are applicable to specific Articles or Parts thereof, and unless the context otherwise requires, in this Act:

(1) **"Action"** in the sense of a judicial proceeding includes recoupment, counterclaim, set-off, suit in equity and any other proceedings in which rights are determined.

(2) **"Aggrieved Party"** means a party entitled to resort to a remedy.

(3) **"Agreement"** means the bargain of the parties in fact as found in their language or by implication from other circumstances including course of dealing or usage of trade or course of performance as provided in this Act (Sections 1—205 and 1—206). Whether an agreement has legal consequences is determined by the provisions of this Act, if applicable; otherwise by the law of contracts (Section 1—103). (Compare "Contract".)

(4) **"Bank"** means any person engaged in the business of Banking.

(5) **"Bearer"** means the person in possession of an instrument, document of title, or certificated security payable to bearer or indorsed in blank.

(6) **"Bill of lading"** means a document evidencing the receipt of goods for shipment issued by a person engaged in the business of transporting or forwarding goods, and includes an airbill. "Airbill" means a document serving for air transportation as a bill of lading does for marine or rail transportation, and includes an air consignment note or air waybill.

(7) **"Branch"** includes a separately incorporated foreign branch of a bank.

(8) **"Burden of establishing"** a fact means the burden of persuading the triers of fact that the existence of the fact is more probable than its nonexistence.

(9) **"Buyer in ordinary course of business"** means a person who in good faith and without knowledge that the sale to him is in violation of the ownership rights or security interest of a third party in the goods buys in ordinary course from a person in the business of selling goods of that kind but does not include a pawnbroker. All persons who sell minerals or the like (including oil and gas) at wellhead or minehead shall be deemed to be persons in the business of selling goods of that kind. "Buying" may be for cash or by exchange of other property or on secured or unsecured credit and includes receiving goods or documents of title under a preexisting contract for sale but does not include a transfer in bulk or as security for or in total or partial satisfaction of a money debt.

(10) **"Conspicuous"**: A term of clause is conspicuous when it is so written that a reasonable person against whom it is to operate ought to have noticed it. A printed heading in capitals (as: Non-Negotiable Bill of Lading) is conspicuous. Language in the body of a form is "conspicuous" if it is in larger or other contrasting type or color. But in a telegram any stated term is "conspicuous". Whether a term or clause is "conspicuous" or not is for decision by the court.

(11) **"Contract"** means the total legal obligation which results from the parties' agreement as affected by this Act and any other applicable rules of law. (Compare "Agreement".)

(12) **"Creditor"** includes a general creditor, a secured creditor, a lien creditor and any representative of creditors, including an assignee for the benefit of creditors, a trustee in Bankruptcy, a receiver in equity and an executor or administrator of an insolvent debtor's or assignor's estate.

(13) **"Defendant"** includes a person in the position of defendant in a cross-action or counterclaim.

(14) **"Delivery"** with respect to instruments, documents of title, chattel paper, or certificated securities means voluntary transfer of possession.

(15) **"Document of title"** includes bill of lading, dock warrant, dock receipt, warehouse receipt, or order for the delivery of goods, and also any other document which in the regular course of business or financing is treated as adequately evidencing that the person in possession of

it is entitled to receive, hold and dispose of the document and the goods it covers. To be a document of title a document must purport to be issued by or addressed to a bailee and purport to cover goods in the bailee's possession which are either identified or are fungible portions of an identified mass.

(16) **"Fault"** means wrongful act, omission or breach.

(17) **"Fungible"** with respect to goods or securities means goods or securities of which any unit is, by nature or usage of trade, the equivalent of any other like unit. Goods which are not fungible shall be deemed fungible for the purposes of this Act to the extent that under a particular agreement or document unlike units are treated as equivalents.

(18) **"Genuine"** means free of forgery or counterfeiting.

(19) **"Good faith"** means honesty in fact in the conduct or transaction concerned.

(20) **"Holder"** with respect to a negotiable instrument, means the person in possession if the instrument is payable to bearer or, in the case of an instrument payable to an identified person, if the identified person is in possession. "Holder" with respect to a document of title means the person in possession if the goods are deliverable to bearer or to the order of the person in possession.

(21) To **"honor"** is to pay or to accept and pay, or where a credit so engages to purchase or discount a draft complying with the terms of the credit.

(22) **"Insolvency proceedings"** includes any assignment for the benefit of creditors or other proceedings intended to liquidate or rehabilitate the estate of the person involved.

(23) A person is **"insolvent"** who either has ceased to pay his debts in the ordinary course of business or cannot pay his debts as they become due or is insolvent within the meaning of the federal bankruptcy law.

(24) **"Money"** means a medium of exchange authorized or adopted by a domestic or foreign government and includes a monetary unit of account established by an intergovernmental organization or by agreement between two or more nations.

(25) A person has **"notice"** of a fact when
    (a) he has actual knowledge of it; or
    (b) he has received a notice or notification of it; or
    (c) from all the facts and circumstances known to him at the time in question he has reason to know that it exists.
    A person **"knows"** or has **"knowledge"** of a fact when he has actual knowledge of it. "Discover" or "learn" or a word or phrase of similar import refers to knowledge rather than to reason to know. The time and circumstances under which a notice or notification may cease to be effective are not determined by this Act.

(26) A person **"notifies"** or "gives" a notice or notification to another by taking such steps as may be reasonably required to inform the other in ordinary course whether or not such other actually comes to know of it. A person "receives" a notice or notification when
    (a) it comes to his attention; or
    (b) it is duly delivered at the place of business through which the contract was made or at any other place held out by him as the place for receipt of such communications.

(27) Notice, knowledge, or a notice or notification received by an organization is effective for a particular transaction from the time when it is brought to the attention of the individual conducting that transaction, and in any event from the time when it would have been brought to his attention if the organization had exercised due diligence. An organization exercises due diligence if it maintains reasonable routines for communicating significant information to the person conducting the transaction and there is reasonable compliance with the routines. Due diligence does not require an individual acting for the organization to communicate information unless such communication is part of his regular duties or unless he has reason to know of the transaction and that the transaction would be materially affected by the information.

(28) **"Organization"** includes a corporation, government or governmental subdivision or agency, business trust, estate, trust, partnership or association, two or more persons having a joint or common interest, or any other legal or commercial entity.

(29) **"Party"**, as distinct from **"Third Party"**, means a person who has engaged in a transaction or made an agreement within this Act.

(30) **"Person"** includes an individual or an organization (Section 1—102).

(31) **"Presumption"** or **"presumed"** means that the trier of fact must find the existence of the fact presumed unless and until evidence is introduced which would support a finding of its non-existence.

(32) **"Purchase"** includes taking by sale, discount, negotiation, mortgage, pledge, lien, issue or reissue, gift, or any other voluntary transaction creating an interest in property.

(33) **"Purchaser"** means a person who takes by purchase.

(34) **"Remedy"** means any remedial right to which an aggrieved party is entitled with or without resort to a tribunal.

(35) **"Representative"** includes an agent, an officer of a corporation or association, and a trustee, executor or administrator of an estate, or any other person empowered to act for another.

(36) **"Rights"** includes remedies.

(37) **"Security interest"** means an interest in personal property or fixtures which secures payment or performance of an obligation. The retention or reservation of title by a seller of goods notwithstanding shipment or delivery to the buyer (Section 2—401) is limited in effect to a reservation of a "security interest". The term also includes any interest of a buyer of accounts or chattel paper which is subject to Article 9. The special property interest of a buyer of goods on identification of those goods to a contract for sale under Section 2—401 is not a "security interest", but a buyer may also acquire a "security interest" by complying with Article 9. Unless a consignment is intended as security, reservation of title thereunder is not a "security interest", but a consignment in any event is subject to the provisions on consignment sales (Section 2—326).

Whether a transaction creates a lease or security interest is determined by the facts of each case; however, a transaction creates a security interest if the consideration the lessee is to pay the lessor for the right to possession and use of the goods is an obligation for the term of the lease not subject to termination by the lessee, and

(a) the original term of the lease is equal to or greater than the remaining economic life of the goods,

(b) the lessee is bound to renew the lease for the remaining economic life of the goods or is bound to become the owner of the goods,

(c) the lessee has an option to renew the lease for the remaining economic life of the goods for no additional consideration or nominal additional consideration upon compliance with the lease agreement, or

(d) the lessee has an option to become the owner of the goods for no additional consideration or nominal additional consideration upon compliance with the lease agreement.

A transaction does not create a security interest merely because it provides that

(a) the present value of the consideration the lessee is obligated to pay the lessor for the right to possession and use of the goods is substantially equal to or is greater than the fair market value of the goods at the time the lease is entered into,

(b) the lessee assumes risk of loss of the goods, or agrees to pay taxes, insurance, filing, recording, or registration fees, or service or maintenance costs with respect to the goods,

(c) the lessee has an option to renew the lease or to become the owner of the goods,

(d) the lessee has an option to renew the lease for a fixed rent that is equal to or greater than the reasonably predictable fair market rent for the use of the goods for the term of the renewal at the time the option is to be performed, or

(e) the lessee has an option to become the owner of the goods for a fixed price that is equal to or greater than the reasonably predictable fair market value of the goods at the time the option is to be performed.

For purposes of this subsection (37):

(x) Additional consideration is not nominal if (i) when the option to renew the lease is granted to the lessee the rent is stated to be the fair market rent for the use of the goods for the term of the renewal determined at the time the option is to be performed, or (ii) when the option to become the owner of the goods is granted to the lessee the price is stated to be the fair market value of the goods determined at the time the option is to be performed. Additional consideration is nominal if it is less than the lessee's reasonably predictable cost of performing under the lease agreement if the option is not exercised;

(y) **"Reasonably predictable"** and **"remaining economic life of the goods"** are to be determined with reference to the facts and circumstances at the time the transaction is entered into; and

(z) **"Present Value"** means the amount as of a date certain of one or more sums payable in the future, discounted to the date certain. The discount is determined by the interest rate specified by the parties if the rate is not manifestly unreasonable at the time the transaction is entered into; otherwise, the discount is determined by a commercially reasonable rate that takes into account the facts and circumstances of each case at the time the transaction was entered into.

(38) **"Send"** in connection with any writing or notice means to deposit in the mail or deliver for transmission by any other usual means of communication with postage or cost of transmission provided for and properly addressed and in the case of an instrument to an address specified thereon or otherwise agreed, or if there be none to any address reasonable under the circumstances. The receipt of any writing or notice within the time at which it would have arrived if properly sent has the effect of a proper sending.

(39) **"Signed"** includes any symbol executed or adopted by a party with present intention to authenticate a writing.

(40) **"Surety"** includes guarantor.

(41) **"Telegram"** includes a message transmitted by radio, teletype, cable, any mechanical method of transmission, or the like.

(42) **"Term"** means that portion of an agreement which relates to a particular matter.

(43) **"Unauthorized"** signature means one made without actual, implied, or apparent authority and includes a forgery.

(44) **"Value"**. Except as otherwise provided with respect to negotiable instruments and bank collections (Sections 3—303, 4—208 and 4—209) a person gives "value" for rights if he acquires them

(a) in return for a binding commitment to extend credit or for the extension of immediately available credit whether or not drawn upon and whether or not a charge-back is provided for in the event of difficulties in collection; or

(b) as security for or in total or partial satisfaction of a preexisting claim; or

(c) by accepting delivery pursuant to a preexisting contract for purchase; or

(d) generally, in return for any consideration sufficient to support a simple contract.

(45) **"Warehouse receipt"** means a receipt issued by a person engaged in the business of storing goods for hire.

(46) **"Written"** or **"writing"** includes printing, typewriting or any other intentional reduction to tangible form.

Section 1—202. **Prima Facie Evidence by Third-Party Documents.**

A document in due form purporting to be a bill of lading, policy or certificate of insurance, official weigher's or inspector's certificate, consular invoice, or any other document authorized or required by the contract to be issued by a third party shall be prima facie evidence of its own authenticity and genuineness and of the facts stated in the document by the third party.

Section 1—203. **Obligation of good faith.**

Every contract or duty within this Act imposes an obligation of good faith in its performance or enforcement.

Section 1—204. **Time; Reasonable Time; "Seasonably".**

(1) Whenever this Act requires any action to be taken within a reasonable time, any time which is not manifestly unreasonable may be fixed by agreement.

(2) What is a reasonable time for taking any action depends on the nature, purpose, and circumstances of such action.

(3) An action is taken **"seasonably"** when it is taken at or within the time agreed or if no time is agreed at or within a reasonable time.

Section 1—205. **Course of Dealing and Usage of Trade.**

(1) A course of dealing is a sequence of previous conduct between the parties to a particular transaction which is fairly to be regarded as establishing a common basis of understanding for interpreting their expressions and other conduct.

(2) A usage of trade is any practice or method of dealing having such regularity of observance in a place, vocation or trade as to justify an expectation that it will be observed with respect to the transaction in question. The existence and scope of such a usage are to be proved as facts. If it is established that such a usage is embodied in a written trade code or similar writing the interpretation of the writing is for the court.

(3) A course of dealing between parties and any usage of trade in the vocation or trade in which they are engaged or of which they are or should be aware give particular meaning to and supplement or qualify terms of an agreement.

(4) The express terms of an agreement and an applicable course of dealing or usage of trade shall be construed wherever reasonable as consistent with each other; but when such construction is unreasonable express terms control both course of dealing and usage of trade and course of dealing controls usage of trade.

(5) An applicable usage of trade in the place where any part of performance is to occur shall be used in interpreting the agreement as to that part of the performance.

(6) Evidence of a relevant usage of trade offered by one party is not admissible unless and until he has given the other party such notice as the court finds sufficient to prevent unfair surprise to the latter.

Section 1—206. **Statute of Frauds for Kinds of Personal Property Not Otherwise Covered.**

(1) Except in the cases described in subsection (2) of this section a contract for the sale of personal property is not enforceable by way of action or defense beyond five thousand dollars in amount or value of remedy unless there is some writing which indicates that a contract for sale has been made between the parties at a defined or stated price, reasonably identifies the subject matter, and is signed by the party against whom enforcement is sought or by his authorized agent.

(2) Subsection (1) of this section does not apply to contracts for the sale of goods (Section 2—201 nor of securities (Section 8—319) nor to security agreement (Section 9—203).

Article 2. Sales

Part 1 **Short Title, General Construction and Subject Matter**

Section 2—101. **Short Title.**
This Article shall be known and may be cited as Uniform Commercial Code—Sales.

Section 2—102. **Scope; Certain Security and Other Transactions Excluded From This Article.**
Unless the context otherwise requires, this Article applies to transactions in goods; it does not apply to any transaction which although in the form of an unconditional contract to sell or present sale is intended to operate only as a security transaction nor does this Article impair or repeal any statute regulating sales to consumers, farmers or other specified classes of buyers.

Section 2—103. **Definitions and Index of Definitions.**
(1) In this Article unless the context otherwise requires
    (a) "Buyer" means a person who buys or contracts to buy goods.
    (b) "Good faith" in the case of a merchant means honesty in fact and the observance of reasonable commercial standards of fair dealing in the trade.
    (c) "Receipt" of goods means taking physical possession of them.
    (d) "Seller" means a person who sells or contracts to sell goods.

Section 2—104. **Definitions: "Merchant"; "Between Merchants"; "Financing Agency".**
(1) "Merchant" means a person who deals in goods of the kind or otherwise by his occupation holds himself out as having knowledge or skill peculiar to the practices or goods involved in the transaction or to whom such knowledge or skill may be attributed by his employment of an agent or broker or other intermediary who by his occupation holds himself out as having such knowledge or skill.
(2) "Financing agency" means a bank, finance company or other person who in the ordinary course of business makes advances against goods or documents of title or who by arrangement with either the seller or the buyer intervenes in ordinary course to make or collect payment due or claimed under the contract for sale, as by purchasing or paying the seller's draft or making advances against it or by merely taking it for collection whether or not documents of title accompany the draft. "Financing agency" includes also a bank or other person who similarly intervenes between persons who are in the position of seller and buyer in respect to the goods (Section 2—707).
(3) "Between merchants" means in any transaction with respect to which both parties are chargeable with the knowledge or skill of merchants.

Section 2—105. **Definitions: Transferability; "Goods"; "Future" Goods; "Lot"; "Commercial Unit".**
(1) "Goods" means all things (including specially manufactured goods) which are movable at the time of identification to the contract for sale other than the money in which the price is to be paid, investment securities (Article 8) and things in action. "Goods" also includes the unborn young of animals and growing crops and other identified things attached to realty as described in the section on goods to be severed from realty (Section 2—107).
(2) Goods must be both existing and identified before any interest in them can pass. Goods which are not both existing and identified are "future" goods. A purported present sale of future goods or of any interest therein operates as a contract to sell.
(3) There may be a sale of a part interest in existing identified goods.
(4) An undivided share in an identified bulk of fungible goods is sufficiently identified to be sold although the quantity of the bulk is not determined. Any agreed proportion of such a bulk or any quantity thereof agreed upon by number, weight or other measure may to the

extent of the seller's interest in the bulk be sold to the buyer who then becomes an owner in common.

(5) "Lot" means a parcel or a single article which is the subject matter of a separate sale or delivery, whether or not it is sufficient to perform the contract.

(6) "Commercial unit" means such a unit of goods as by commercial usage is a single whole for purposes of sale and division of which materially impairs its character or value on the market or in use. A commercial unit may be a single article (as a machine) or a set of articles (as a suite of furniture or an assortment of sizes) or a quantity (as a bale, gross, or carload) or any other unit treated in use or in the relevant market as a single whole.

Section 2—106. Definitions: "Contract"; "Agreement"; "Contract for Sale"; "Sale"; "Present Sale"; "Conforming" to Contract; "Termination"; "Cancellation".

(1) In this Article unless the context otherwise requires "contract" and "agreement" are limited to those relating to the present or future sale of goods. "Contract for sale" includes both a present sale of goods and a contract to sell goods at a future time. A "sale" consists in the passing of title from the seller to the buyer for a price (Section 2—401). A "present sale" means a sale which is accomplished by the making of the contract.

(2) Goods or conduct including any part of a performance are "conforming" or conform to the contract when they are in accordance with the obligations under the contract.

(3) "Termination" occurs when either party pursuant to a power created by agreement or law puts an end to the contract otherwise than for its breach. On "termination" all obligations which are still executory on both sides are discharged but any right based on prior breach or performance survives.

(4) "Cancellation" occurs when either party puts an end to the contract for breach by the other and its effect is the same as that of "termination" except that the cancelling party also retains any remedy for breach of the whole contract or any unperformed balance.

Part 2 Form, Formation and Readjustment of Contract

Section 2—201. Formal Requirements; Statute of Frauds.

(1) Except as otherwise provided in this section a contract for the sale of goods for the price of $500 or more is not enforceable by way of action or defense unless there is some writing sufficient to indicate that a contract for sale has been made between the parties and signed by the party against whom enforcement is sought or by his authorized agent or broker. A writing is not insufficient because it omits or incorrectly states a term agreed upon but the contract is not enforceable under this paragraph beyond the quantity of goods shown in such writing.

(2) Between merchants if within a reasonable time a writing in confirmation of the contract and sufficient against the sender is received and the party receiving it has reason to know its contents, it satisfies the requirements of subsection (1) against such party unless written notice of objection to its contents is given within ten days after it is received.

(3) A contract which does not satisfy the requirements of subsection (1) but which is valid in other respects is enforceable

(a) if the goods are to be specially manufactured for the buyer and are not suitable for sale to others in the ordinary course of the seller's business and the seller, before notice of repudiation is received and under circumstances which reasonably indicate that the goods are for the buyer, has made either a substantial beginning of their manufacture or commitments for their procurement; or

(b) if the party against whom enforcement is sought admits in his pleading, testimony or otherwise in court that a contract for sale was made, but the contract is not enforceable under this provision beyond the quantity of goods admitted; or

(c) with respect to goods for which payment has been made and accepted or which have been received and accepted (Sec. 2—606).

Section 2—202. Final Written Expression: Parol or Extrinsic Evidence.

Terms with respect to which the confirmatory memoranda of the parties agree or which are otherwise set forth in a writing intended by the parties as a final expression of their agreement with respect to such terms as are included therein may not be contradicted by evidence of any prior agreement or of a contemporaneous oral agreement but may be explained or supplemented

(a) by course of dealing or usage of trade (Section 1—205) or by course of performance (Section 2—208); and

(b) by evidence of consistent additional terms unless the court finds the writing to have been intended also as a complete and exclusive statement of the terms of the agreement.

Section 2—203. Seals Inoperative.

The affixing of a seal to a writing evidencing a contract for sale or an offer to buy or sell goods does not constitute the writing a sealed instrument and the law with respect to sealed instruments does not apply to such a contract or offer.

Section 2—204. Formation in General.

(1) A contract for sale of goods may be made in any manner sufficient to show agreement, including conduct by both parties which recognizes the existence of such a contract.

(2) An agreement sufficient to constitute a contract for sale may be found even though the moment of its making is undetermined.

(3) Even though one or more terms are left open a contract for sale does not fail for indefiniteness if the parties have intended to make a contract and there is a reasonably certain basis for giving an appropriate remedy.

Section 2—205. Firm Offers.

An offer by a merchant to buy or sell goods in a signed writing which by its terms gives assurance that it will be held open is not revocable, for lack of consideration, during the time stated or if no time is stated for a reasonable time, but in no event may such period of irrevocability exceed three months; but any such term of assurance on a form supplied by the offeree must be separately signed by the offeror.

Section 2—206. Offer and Acceptance in Formation of Contract.

(1) Unless otherwise unambiguously indicated by the language or circumstances

(a) an offer to make a contract shall be construed as inviting acceptance in any manner and by any medium reasonable in the circumstances;

(b) an order or other offer to buy goods for prompt or current shipment shall be construed as inviting acceptance either by a prompt promise to ship or by the prompt or current shipment of conforming or nonconforming goods, but such a shipment of nonconforming goods does not constitute an acceptance if the seller seasonably notifies the buyer that the shipment is offered only as an accommodation to the buyer.

(2) Where the beginning of a requested performance is a reasonable mode of acceptance an offeror who is not notified of acceptance within a reasonable time may treat the offer as having lapsed before acceptance.

Section 2—207. Additional Terms in Acceptance or Confirmation.

(1) A definite and seasonable expression of acceptance or a written confirmation which is sent within a reasonable time operates as an acceptance even though it states terms additional to or different from those offered or agreed upon, unless acceptance is expressly made conditional on assent to the additional or different terms.

(2) The additional terms are to be construed as proposals for addition to the contract. Between merchants such terms become part of the contract unless:

(a) the offer expressly limits acceptance to the terms of the offer;

(b) they materially alter it; or

(c) notification of objection to them has already been given or is given within a reasonable time after notice of them is received.

(3) Conduct by both parties which recognizes the existence of a contract is sufficient to establish a contract for sale although the writings of the parties do not otherwise establish a contract. In such case the terms of the particular contract consist of those terms on which the writings of the parties agree, together with any supplementary terms incorporated under any other provisions of this Act.

Section 2—208. **Course of Performance or Practical Construction.**

(1) Where the contract for sale involves repeated occasions for performance by either party with knowledge of the nature of the performance and opportunity for objection to it by the other, any course of performance accepted or acquiesced in without objection shall be relevant to determine the meaning of the agreement.

(2) The express terms of the agreement and any such course of performance, as well as any course of dealing and usage of trade, shall be construed whenever reasonable as consistent with each other; but when such construction is unreasonable, express terms shall control course of performance and course of performance shall control both course of dealing and usage of trade (Section 1—205).

(3) Subject to the provisions of the next section on modification and waiver, such course of performance shall be relevant to show a waiver or modification of any term inconsistent with such course of performance.

Section 2—209. **Modification, Rescission and Waiver.**

(1) An agreement modifying a contract within this Article needs no consideration to be binding.

(2) A signed agreement which excludes modification or rescission except by a signed writing cannot be otherwise modified or rescinded, but except as between merchants such a requirement on a form supplied by the merchant must be separately signed by the other party.

(3) The requirements of the statute of frauds section of this Article (Section 2—201) must be satisfied if the contract as modified is within its provisions.

(4) Although an attempt at modification or rescission does not satisfy the requirements of subsection (2) or (3) it can operate as a waiver.

(5) A party who has made a waiver affecting an executory portion of the contract may retract the waiver by reasonable notification received by the other party that strict performance will be required of any term waived, unless the retraction would be unjust in view of a material change of position in reliance on the waiver.

Section 2—210. **Delegation of Performance; Assignment of Rights.**

(1) A party may perform his duty through a delegate unless otherwise agreed or unless the other party has a substantial interest in having his original promisor perform or control the acts required by the contract. No delegation of performance relieves the party delegating of any duty to perform or any liability for breach.

(2) Unless otherwise agreed all rights of either seller or buyer can be assigned except where the assignment would materially change the duty of the other party, or increase materially the burden or risk imposed on him by his contract, or impair materially his chance of obtaining return performance. A right to damages for breach of the whole contract or a right arising out of the assignor's due performance of his entire obligation can be assigned despite agreement otherwise.

(3) Unless the circumstances indicate the contrary a prohibition of assignment of "the contract" is to be construed as barring only the delegation to the assignee of the assignor's performance.

(4) An assignment of "the contract" or of "all my rights under the contract" or an assignment in similar general terms is an assignment of rights and unless the language or the

circumstances (as in an assignment for security) indicate the contrary, it is a delegation of performance of the duties of the assignor and its acceptance by the assignee constitutes a promise by him to perform those duties. This promise is enforceable by either the assignor or the other party to the original contract.

(5) The other party may treat any assignment which delegates performance as creating reasonable grounds for insecurity and may without prejudice to his rights against the assignor demand assurances from the assignee (Section 2—609).

Part 3 General Obligation and Construction of Contract

Section 2—301. General Obligations of Parties.
The obligation of the seller is to transfer and deliver and that of the buyer is to accept and pay in accordance with the contract.

Section 2—302. Unconscionable Contract or Clause.
(1) If the court as a matter of law finds the contract or any clause of the contract to have been unconscionable at the time it was made the court may refuse to enforce the contract, or it may enforce the remainder of the contract without the unconscionable clause, or it may so limit the application of any unconscionable clause as to avoid any unconscionable result.
(2) When it is claimed or appears to the court that the contract or any clause thereof may be unconscionable the parties shall be afforded a reasonable opportunity to present evidence as to its commercial setting, purpose and effect to aid the court in making the determination.

Section 2—303. Allocations or Division of Risks.
Where this Article allocates a risk or a burden as between the parties "unless otherwise agreed", the agreement may not only shift the allocation but may also divide the risk or burden.

Section 2—304. Price Payable in Money, Goods, Realty, or Otherwise.
(1) The price can be made payable in money or otherwise. If it is payable in whole or in part in goods each party is a seller of the goods which he is to transfer.
(2) Even though all or part of the price is payable in an interest in realty the transfer of the goods and the seller's obligations with reference to them are subject to this Article, but not the transfer of the interest in realty or the transferor's obligations in connection therewith.

Section 2—305. Open Price Term.
(1) The parties if they so intend can conclude a contract for sale even though the price is not settled. In such a case the price is a reasonable price at the time for delivery if
    (a) nothing is said as to price; or
    (b) the price is left to be agreed by the parties and they fail to agree; or
    (c) the price is to be fixed in terms of some agreed market or other standard as set or
    recorded by a third person or agency and it is not so set or recorded.
(2) A price to be fixed by the seller or by the buyer means a price for him to fix in good faith.
(3) When a price left to be fixed otherwise than by agreement of the parties fails to be fixed through fault of one party the other may at his option treat the contract as cancelled or himself fix a reasonable price.
(4) Where, however, the parties intend not to be bound unless the price be fixed or agreed and it is not fixed or agreed there is no contract. In such a case the buyer must return any goods already received or if unable so to do must pay their reasonable value at the time of delivery and the seller must return any portion of the price paid on account.

Section 2—306. Output, Requirements, and Exclusive Dealings.
(1) A term which measures the quantity by the output of the seller or the requirements of the buyer means such actual output or requirements as may occur in good faith, except that no quantity unreasonably disproportionate to any stated estimate or in the absence of a stated

estimate to any normal or otherwise comparable prior output or requirements may be tendered or demanded.

(2) A lawful agreement by either the seller or the buyer for exclusive dealing in the kind of goods concerned imposes unless otherwise agreed an obligation by the seller to use best efforts to supply the goods and by the buyer to use best efforts to promote their sale.

Section 2—307. **Delivery in Single Lot or Several Lots.**

Unless otherwise agreed all goods called for by a contract for sale must be tendered in a single delivery and payment is due only on such tender but where the circumstances give either party the right to make or demand delivery in lots the price if it can be apportioned may be demanded for each lot.

Section 2—308. **Absence of Specified Place for Delivery.**

Unless otherwise agreed

(a) the place for delivery of goods is the seller's place of business or if he has none his residence; but

(b) in a contract for sale of identified goods which to the knowledge of the parties at the time of contracting are in some other place, that place is the place for their delivery; and

(c) documents of title may be delivered through customary banking channels.

Section 2—309. **Absence of Specific Time Provisions; Notice of Termination.**

(1) The time for shipment or delivery or any other action under a contract if not provided in this Article or agreed upon shall be a reasonable time.

(2) Where the contract provides for successive performances but is indefinite in duration it is valid for a reasonable time but unless otherwise agreed may be terminated at any time by either party.

(3) Termination of a contract by one party except on the happening of an agreed event requires that reasonable notification be received by the other party and an agreement dispensing with notification is invalid if its operation would be unconscionable.

Section 2—310. **Open Time for Payment or Running of Credit; Authority to Ship Under Reservation.**

Unless otherwise agreed

(a) payment is due at the time and place at which the buyer is to receive the goods even though the place of shipment is the place of delivery; and

(b) if the seller is authorized to send the goods he may ship them under reservation, and may tender the documents of title, but the buyer may inspect the goods after their arrival before payment is due unless such inspection is inconsistent with the terms of the contract (Section 2—513); and

(c) if delivery is authorized and made by way of documents of title otherwise than by subsection (b) then payment is due at the time and place at which the buyer is to receive the documents regardless of where the goods are to be received; and

(d) where the seller is required or authorized to ship the goods on credit the credit period runs from the time of shipment but post-dating the invoice or delaying its dispatch will correspondingly delay the starting of the credit period.

Section 2—311. **Options and Cooperation Respecting Performance.**

(1) An agreement for sale which is otherwise sufficiently definite (subsection (3) of Section 2—204) to be a contract is not made invalid by the fact that it leaves particulars of performance to be specified by one of the parties. Any such specification must be made in good faith and within limits set by commercial reasonableness.

(2) Unless otherwise agreed specifications relating to assortment of the goods are at the buyer's option and except as otherwise provided in subsections (1)(c) and (3) of Section 2—319 specifications or arrangements relating to shipment are at the seller's option.

(3) Where such specification would materially affect the other party's performance but is not seasonably made or where one party's cooperation is necessary to the agreed performance of the other but is not seasonably forthcoming, the other party in addition to all other remedies

(a) is excused for any resulting delay in his own performance; and

(b) may also either proceed to perform in any reasonable manner or after the time for a material part of his own performance treat the failure to specify or to cooperate as a breach by failure to deliver or accept the goods.

Section 2—312. **Warranty of Title and Against Infringement; Buyer's Obligation Against Infringement.**

(1) Subject to subsection

(2) there is in a contract for sale a warranty by the seller that

(a) the title conveyed shall be good, and its transfer rightful; and

(b) the goods shall be delivered free from any security interest or other lien or encumbrance of which the buyer at the time of contracting has no knowledge.

(2) A warranty under subsection (1) will be excluded or modified only by specific language or by circumstances which give the buyer reason to know that the person selling does not claim title in himself or that he is purporting to sell only such right or title as he or a third person may have.

(3) Unless otherwise agreed a seller who is a merchant regularly dealing in goods of the kind warrants that the goods shall be delivered free of the rightful claim of any third person by way of infringement or the like but a buyer who furnishes specifications to the seller must hold the seller harmless against any such claim which arises out of compliance with the specifications.

Section 2—313. Express Warranties by Affirmation, Promise, Description, Sample.

(1) Express warranties by the seller are created as follows:

(a) Any affirmation of fact or promise made by the seller to the buyer which relates to the goods and becomes part of the basis of the bargain creates an express warranty that the goods shall conform to the affirmation or promise.

(b) description of the goods which is made part of the basis of the bargain creates an express warranty that the goods shall conform to the description.

(c) Any sample or model which is made part of the basis of the bargain creates an express warranty that the whole of the goods shall conform to the sample or model.

(2) It is not necessary to the creation of an express warranty that the seller use formal words such as "warrant" or "guarantee" or that he have a specific intention to make a warranty, but an affirmation merely of the value of the goods or a statement purporting to be merely the seller's opinion or commendation of the goods does not create a warranty.

Section 2—314. **Implied Warranty: Merchantability; Usage of Trade.**

(1) Unless excluded or modified (Section 2—316), a warranty that the goods shall be merchantable is implied in a contract for their sale if the seller is a merchant with respect to goods of that kind. Under this section the serving for value of food or drink to be consumed either on the premises or elsewhere is a sale.

(2) Goods to be merchantable must be at least such as

(a) pass without objection in the trade under the contract description; and

(b) in the case of fungible goods, are of fair average quality within the description; and

(c) are fit for the ordinary purposes for which such goods are used; and

(d) run, within the variations permitted by the agreement, of even kind, quality and quantity within each unit and among all units involved; and

(e) are adequately contained, packaged, and labeled as the agreement may require; and

(f) conform to the promises or affirmations of fact made on the container or label if any.

(3) Unless excluded or modified (Section 2—316) other implied warranties may arise from course of dealing or usage of trade.

Section 2—315. **Implied Warranty: Fitness for Particular Purpose.**

Where the seller at the time of contracting has reason to know any particular purpose for which the goods are required and that the buyer is relying on the seller's skill or judgment to select or furnish suitable goods, there is unless excluded or modified under the next section an implied warranty that the goods shall be fit for such purpose.

Section 2—316. **Exclusion or Modification of Warranties.**

(1) Words or conduct relevant to the creation of an express warranty and words or conduct tending to negate or limit warranty shall be construed wherever reasonable as consistent with each other; but subject to the provisions of this Article on parol or extrinsic evidence (Section 2—202) negation or limitation is inoperative to the extent that such construction is unreasonable.

(2) Subject to subsection (3), to exclude or modify the implied warranty of merchantability or any part of it the language must mention merchantability and in case of a writing must be conspicuous, and to exclude or modify any implied warranty of fitness the exclusion must be by a writing and conspicuous. Language to exclude all implied warranties of fitness is sufficient if it states, for example, that "There are no warranties which extend beyond the description on the face hereof."

(3) Notwithstanding subsection (2)

   (a) unless the circumstances indicate otherwise, all implied warranties are excluded by expressions like "as is", "with all faults" or other language which in common understanding calls the buyer's attention to the exclusion of warranties and makes plain that there is no implied warranty; and

   (b) when the buyer before entering into the contract has examined the goods or the sample or model as fully as he desired or has refused to examine the goods there is no implied warranty with regard to defects which an examination ought in the circumstances to have revealed to him; and

   (c) an implied warranty can also be excluded or modified by course of dealing or course of performance or usage of trade.

(4) Remedies for breach of warranty can be limited in accordance with the provisions of this Article on liquidation or limitation of damages and on contractual modification of remedy (Sections 2—718 and 2—719).

Section 2—317. **Cumulation and Conflict of Warranties Express or Implied.**

Warranties whether express or implied shall be construed as consistent with each other and as cumulative, but if such construction is unreasonable the intention of the parties shall determine which warranty is dominant. In ascertaining that intention the following rules apply:

   (a) Exact or technical specifications displace an inconsistent sample or model or general language of description.

   (b) A sample from an existing bulk displaces inconsistent general language of description.

   (c) Express warranties displace inconsistent implied warranties other than an implied warranty of fitness for a particular purpose.

Section 2—318. **Third Party Beneficiaries of Warranties Express or Implied.**

Note: If this Act is introduced in the Congress of the United States this section should be omitted. (States to select one alternative.)

Alternative A

A seller's warranty whether express or implied extends to any natural person who is in the family or household of his buyer or who is a guest in his home if it is reasonable to expect that such person may use, consume or be affected by the goods and who is injured in person by breach of the warranty. A seller may not exclude or limit the operation of this section.

Alternative B

A seller's warranty whether express or implied extends to any natural person who may reasonably be expected to use, consume or be affected by the goods and who is injured in person by breach of the warranty. A seller may not exclude or limit the operation of this section.

Alternative C

A seller's warranty whether express or implied extends to any person who may reasonably be expected to use, consume or be affected by the goods and who is injured by breach of the warranty. A seller may not exclude or limit the operation of this section with respect to injury to the person of an individual to whom the warranty extends. As amended 1966.

Section 2—319. **F.O.B. and F.A.S. Terms.**

(1) Unless otherwise agreed the term F.O.B. (which means "free on board") at a named place, even though used only in connection with the stated price, is a delivery term under which
> (a) when the term is F.O.B. the place of shipment, the seller must at that place ship the goods in the manner provided in this Article (Section 2—504) and bear the expense and risk of putting them into the possession of the carrier; or
> (b) when the term is F.O.B. the place of destination, the seller must at his own expense and risk transport the goods to that place and there tender delivery of them in the manner provided in this Article (Section 2—503);
> (c) when under either (a) or (b) the term is also F.O.B. vessel, car or other vehicle, the seller must in addition at his own expense and risk load the goods on board. If the term is F.O.B. vessel the buyer must name the vessel and in an appropriate case the seller must comply with the provisions of this Article on the form of bill of lading (Section 2—323).

(2) Unless otherwise agreed the term F.A.S. vessel (which means "free alongside") at a named port, even though used only in connection with the stated price, is a delivery term under which the seller must
> (a) at his own expense and risk deliver the goods alongside the vessel in the manner usual in that port or on a dock designated and provided by the buyer; and
> (b) obtain and tender a receipt for the goods in exchange for which the carrier is under a duty to issue a bill of lading.

(3) Unless otherwise agreed in any case falling within subsection (1)(a) or (c) or subsection (2) the buyer must seasonably give any needed instructions for making delivery, including when the term is F.A.S. or F.O.B. the loading berth of the vessel and in an appropriate case its name and sailing date. The seller may treat the failure of needed instructions as a failure of cooperation under this Article (Section 2—311). He may also at his option move the goods in any reasonable manner preparatory to delivery or shipment.

(4) Under the term F.O.B. vessel or F.A.S. unless otherwise agreed the buyer must make payment against tender of the required documents and the seller may not tender nor the buyer demand delivery of the goods in substitution for the documents.

Section 2—320. **C.I.F. and C. & F. Terms.**

(1) The term C.I.F. means that the price includes in a lump sum the cost of the goods and the insurance and freight to the named destination. The term C. & F. or C.F. means that the price so includes cost and freight to the named destination.

(2) Unless otherwise agreed and even though used only in connection with the stated price and destination, the term C.I.F. destination or its equivalent requires the seller at his own expense and risk to
> (a) put the goods into the possession of a carrier at the port for shipment and obtain a negotiable bill or bills of lading covering the entire transportation to the named destination; and

(b) load the goods and obtain a receipt from the carrier (which may be contained in the bill of lading) showing that the freight has been paid or provided for; and

(c) obtain a policy or certificate of insurance, including any war risk insurance, of a kind and on terms then current at the port of shipment in the usual amount, in the currency of the contract, shown to cover the same goods covered by the bill of lading and providing for payment of loss to the order of the buyer or for the account of whom it may concern; but the seller may add to the price the amount of the premium for any such war risk insurance;

(d) prepare an invoice of the goods and procure any other documents required to effect shipment or to comply with the contract; and

(e) forward and tender with commercial promptness all the documents in due form and with any indorsement necessary to perfect the buyer's rights.

(3) Unless otherwise agreed the term C. & F. or its equivalent has the same effect and imposes upon the seller the same obligations and risks as a C.I.F. term except the obligation as to insurance.

(4) Under the term C.I.F. or C. & F. unless otherwise agreed the buyer must make payment against tender of the required documents and the seller may not tender nor the buyer demand delivery of the goods in substitution for the documents.

Section 2—321. C.I.F. or C. & F.: "Net Landed Weights"; "Payment on Arrival"; Warranty of Condition on Arrival.

Under a contract containing a term C.I.F. or C. & F.

(1) Where the price is based on or is to be adjusted according to "net landed weights", "delivered weights", "out turn" quantity or quality or the like, unless otherwise agreed the seller must reasonably estimate the price. The payment due on tender of the documents called for by the contract is the amount so estimated, but after final adjustment of the price a settlement must be made with commercial promptness.

(2) An agreement described in subsection (1) or any warranty of quality or condition of the goods on arrival places upon the seller the risk of ordinary deterioration, shrinkage and the like in transportation but has no effect on the place or time of identification to the contract for sale or delivery or on the passing of the risk of loss.

(3) Unless otherwise agreed where the contract provides for payment on or after arrival of the goods the seller must before payment allow such preliminary inspection as is feasible; but if the goods are lost delivery of the documents and payment are due when the goods should have arrived.

Section 2—322. Delivery "Ex-Ship".

(1) Unless otherwise agreed a term for delivery of goods "ex-ship" (which means from the carrying vessel) or in equivalent language is not restricted to a particular ship and requires delivery from a ship which has reached a place at the named port of destination where goods of the kind are usually discharged.

(2) Under such a term unless otherwise agreed

(a) the seller must discharge all liens arising out of the carriage and furnish the buyer with a direction which puts the carrier under a duty to deliver the goods; and

(b) the risk of loss does not pass to the buyer until the goods leave the ship's tackle or are otherwise properly unloaded.

Section 2—323. Form of Bill of Lading Required in Overseas Shipment; "Overseas".

(1) Where the contract contemplates overseas shipment and contains a term C.I.F. or C. & F. or F.O.B. vessel, the seller unless otherwise agreed must obtain a negotiable bill of lading stating that the goods have been loaded in board or, in the case of a term C.I.F. or C. & F., received for shipment.

(2) Where in a case within subsection (1) a bill of lading has been issued in a set of parts, unless otherwise agreed if the documents are not to be sent from abroad the buyer may demand tender of the full set; otherwise only one part of the bill of lading need be tendered. Even if the agreement expressly requires a full set

(a) due tender of a single part is acceptable within the provisions of this Article on cure of improper delivery (subsection (1) of Section 2—508); and

(b) even though the full set is demanded, if the documents are sent from abroad the person tendering an incomplete set may nevertheless require payment upon furnishing an indemnity which the buyer in good faith deems adequate.

(3) A shipment by water or by air or a contract contemplating such shipment is "overseas" insofar as by usage of trade or agreement it is subject to the commercial, financing or shipping practices characteristic of international deep water commerce.

Section 2—324. **"No Arrival, No Sale" Term.**

Under a term, "no sale no arrival" or terms of like meaning, unless otherwise agreed,

(a) the seller must properly ship conforming goods and if they arrive by any means he must tender them on arrival but he assumes no obligation that the goods will arrive unless he has caused the nonarrival; and

(b) where without fault of the seller the goods are in part lost or have so deteriorated as no longer to conform to the contract or arrive after the contract time, the buyer may proceed as if there had been casualty to identified goods (Section 2—613).

Section 2—325. **"Letter of Credit" Term; "Confirmed Credit".**

(1) Failure of the buyer seasonably to furnish an agreed letter of credit is a breach of the contract for sale.

(2) The delivery to seller of a proper letter of credit suspends the buyer's obligation to pay. If the letter of credit is dishonored, the seller may on seasonable notification to the buyer require payment directly from him.

(3) Unless otherwise agreed the term "letter of credit" or "banker's credit" in a contract for sale means an irrevocable credit issued by a financing agency of good repute and, where the shipment is overseas, of good international repute. The term "confirmed credit" means that the credit must also carry the direct obligation of such an agency which does business in the seller's financial market.

Part 4 **Title, Creditors and Good Faith Purchasers**

Section 2—401. **Passing of Title; Reservation for Security; Limited Application of This Section.**

Each provision of this Article with regard to the rights, obligations and remedies of the seller, the buyer, purchasers or other third parties applies irrespective of title to the goods except where the provision refers to such title. Insofar as situations are not covered by the other provisions of this Article and matters concerning title became material the following rules apply:

(1) Title to goods cannot pass under a contract for sale prior to their identification to the contract (Section 2—501), and unless otherwise explicitly agreed the buyer acquires by their identification a special property as limited by this Act. Any retention or reservation by the seller of the title (property) in goods shipped or delivered to the buyer is limited in effect to a reservation of a security interest. Subject to these provisions and to the provisions of the Article on Secured Transactions (Article 9), title to goods passes from the seller to the buyer in any manner and on any conditions explicitly agreed on by the parties.

(2) Unless otherwise explicitly agreed title passes to the buyer at the time and place at which the seller completes his performance with reference to the physical delivery of the goods, despite any reservation of a security interest and even though a document of title is to be delivered at a different time or place; and in particular and despite any reservation of a security interest by the bill of lading

(a) if the contract requires or authorizes the seller to send the goods to the buyer but does not require him to deliver them at destination, title passes to the buyer at the time and place of shipment; but

(b) if the contract requires delivery at destination, title passes on tender there.

(3) Unless otherwise explicitly agreed where delivery is to be made without moving the goods,

(a) if the seller is to deliver a document of title, title passes at the time when and the place where he delivers such documents; or

(b) if the goods are at the time of contracting already identified and no documents are to be delivered, title passes at the time and place of contracting.

(4) A rejection or other refusal by the buyer to receive or retain the goods, whether or not justified, or a justified revocation of acceptance revests title to the goods in the seller. Such revesting occurs by operation of law and is not a "sale".

Part 5 **Performance**

Section 2—503. **Manner of Seller's Tender of Delivery.**

(1) Tender of delivery requires that the seller put and hold conforming goods at the buyer's disposition and give the buyer any notification reasonably necessary to enable him to take delivery. The manner, time, and place for tender are determined by the agreement and this Article, and in particular

(a) tender must be at a reasonable hour, and if it is of goods they must be kept available for the period reasonably necessary to enable the buyer to take possession; but

(b) unless otherwise agreed the buyer must furnish facilities reasonably suited to the receipt of the goods.

(2) Where the case is within the next section respecting shipment tender requires that the seller comply with its provisions.

(3) Where the seller is required to deliver at a particular destination tender requires that he comply with subsection (1) and also in any appropriate case tender documents as described in subsections (4) and (5) of this section.

(4) Where goods are in the possession of a bailee and are to be delivered without being moved

(a) tender requires that the seller either tender a negotiable document of title covering such goods or procure acknowledgment by the bailee of the buyer's right to possession of the goods; but

(b) tender to the buyer of a non-negotiable document of title or of a written direction to the bailee to deliver is sufficient tender unless the buyer seasonably objects, and receipt by the bailee of notification of the buyer's rights fixes those rights as against the bailee and all third persons; but risk of loss of the goods and of any failure by the bailee to honor the non-negotiable document of title or to obey the direction remains on the seller until the buyer has had a reasonable time to present the document or direction, and a refusal by the bailee to honor the document or to obey the direction defeats the tender.

(5) Where the contract requires the seller to deliver documents

(a) he must tender all such documents in correct form, except as provided in this Article with respect to bills of lading in a set (subsection (2) of Section 2—323); and

(b) tender through customary banking channels is sufficient and dishonor of a draft accompanying the documents constitutes non-acceptance or rejection.

Section 2—504. **Shipment by Seller.**

Where the seller is required or authorized to send the goods to the buyer and the contract does not require him to deliver them at a particular destination, then unless otherwise agreed he must

(a) put the goods in the possession of such a carrier and make such a contract for their transportation as may be reasonable having regard to the nature of the goods and other circumstances of the case; and

(b) obtain and promptly deliver or tender in due form any document necessary to enable the buyer to obtain possession of the goods or otherwise required by the agreement or by usage of trade; and

(c) promptly notify the buyer of the shipment.

Failure to notify the buyer under paragraph (c) or to make a proper contract under paragraph (a) is a ground for rejection only if material delay or loss ensues.

Section 2—507. **Effect of Seller's Tender; Delivery on Condition.**

(1) Tender of delivery is a condition to the buyer's duty to accept the goods and, unless otherwise agreed, to his duty to pay for them. Tender entitles the seller to acceptance of the goods and to payment according to the contract.

(2) Where payment is due and demanded on the delivery to the buyer of goods or documents of title, his right as against the seller to retain or dispose of them is conditional upon his making the payment due.

Section 2—508. **Cure by Seller of Improper Tender or Delivery; Replacement.**

(1) Where any tender or delivery by the seller is rejected because non-conforming and the time for performance has not yet expired, the seller may seasonably notify the buyer of his intention to cure and may then within the contract time make a conforming delivery.

(2) Where the buyer rejects a non-conforming tender which the seller had reasonable grounds to believe would be acceptable with or without money allowance the seller may if he seasonably notifies the buyer have a further reasonable time to substitute a conforming tender.

Section 2—511. **Tender of Payment by Buyer; Payment by Check.**

(1) Unless otherwise agreed tender of payment is a condition to the seller's duty to tender and complete any delivery.

(2) Tender of payment is sufficient when made by any means or in any manner current in the ordinary course of business unless the seller demands payment in legal tender and gives any extension of time reasonably necessary to procure it.

(3) Subject to the provisions of this Act on the effect of an instrument on an obligation (Section 3—802), payment by check is conditional and is defeated as between the parties by dishonor of the check on due presentment.

Section 2—512. **Payment by Buyer Before Inspection.**

(1) Where the contract requires payment before inspection non-conformity of the goods does not excuse the buyer from so making payment unless

(a) the non-conformity appears without inspection; or

(b) despite tender of the required documents the circumstances would justify injunction against honor under the provisions of this Act (Section 5—114).

(2) Payment pursuant to subsection (1) does not constitute an acceptance of goods or impair the buyer's right to inspect or any of his remedies.

Section 2—513. **Buyer's Right to Inspection of Goods.**

(1) Unless otherwise agreed and subject to subsection (3), where goods are tendered or delivered or identified to the contract for sale, the buyer has a right before payment or acceptance to inspect them at any reasonable place and time and in any reasonable manner. When the seller is required or authorized to send the goods to the buyer, the inspection may be after their arrival.

(2) Expenses of inspection must be borne by the buyer but may be recovered from the seller if the goods do not conform and are rejected.

(3) Unless otherwise agreed and subject to the provisions of this Article on C.I.F. contracts (subsection (3) of Section 2—321), the buyer is not entitled to inspect the goods before payment of the price when the contract provides

(a) for delivery "C.O.D." or on other like terms; or

(b) for payment against documents of title, except where such payment is due only after the goods are to become available for inspection.

(4) A place or method of inspection fixed by the parties is presumed to be exclusive but unless otherwise expressly agreed it does not postpone identification or shift the place for delivery or for passing the risk of loss. If compliance becomes impossible, inspection shall be as provided in this section unless the place or method fixed was clearly intended as an indispensable condition failure of which avoids the contract.

Part 6 Breach, Repudiation and Excuse

Section 2—601. Buyer's Rights on Improper Delivery.

Subject to the provisions of this Article on breach in installment contracts (Section 2—612) and unless otherwise agreed under the sections on contractual limitations of remedy (Sections 2—718 and 2—719), if the goods or the tender of delivery fail in any respect to conform to the contract, the buyer may

    (a) reject the whole; or

    (b) accept the whole; or

    (c) accept any commercial unit or units and reject the rest.

Section 2—602. Manner and Effect of Rightful Rejection.

(1) Rejection of goods must be within a reasonable time after their delivery or tender. It is ineffective unless the buyer seasonably notifies the seller.

(2) Subject to the provisions of the two following sections on rejected goods (Sections 2—603 and 2—604),

    (a) after rejection any exercise of ownership by the buyer with respect to any commercial unit is wrongful as against the seller; and

    (b) if the buyer has before rejection taken physical possession of goods in which he does not have a security interest under the provisions of this Article (subsection (3) of Section 2—711), he is under a duty after rejection to hold them with reasonable care at the seller's disposition for a time sufficient to permit the seller to remove them; but

    (c) the buyer has no further obligations with regard to goods rightfully rejected.

(3) The seller's rights with respect to goods wrongfully rejected are governed by the provisions of this Article on Seller's remedies in general (Section 2—703).

Section 2—606. What Constitutes Acceptance of Goods.

(1) Acceptance of goods occurs when the buyer

    (a) after a reasonable opportunity to inspect the goods signifies to the seller that the goods are conforming or that he will take or retain them in spite of their non-conformity; or

    (b) fails to make an effective rejection (subsection (1) of Section 2—602), but such acceptance does not occur until the buyer has had a reasonable opportunity to inspect them; or

    (c) does any act inconsistent with the seller's ownership; but if such act is wrongful as against the seller it is an acceptance only if ratified by him.

(2) Acceptance of a part of any commercial unit is acceptance of that entire unit.

Section 2—607. Effect of Acceptance; Notice of Breach; Burden of Establishing Breach After Acceptance; Notice of Claim or Litigation to Person Answerable Over.

(1) The buyer must pay at the contract rate for any goods accepted.

(2) Acceptance of goods by the buyer precludes rejection of the goods accepted and if made with knowledge of a non-conformity cannot be revoked because of it unless the acceptance was on the reasonable assumption that the non-conformity would be seasonably cured but acceptance does not of itself impair any other remedy provided by this Article for non-conformity.

(3) Where a tender has been accepted

    (a) the buyer must within a reasonable time after he discovers or should have discovered any breach notify the seller of breach or be barred from any remedy; and

(b) if the claim is one for infringement or the like (subsection (3) of Section 2—312) and the buyer is sued as a result of such a breach he must so notify the seller within a reasonable time after he receives notice of the litigation or be barred from any remedy over for liability established by the litigation.

(4) The burden is on the buyer to establish any breach with respect to the goods accepted.

(5) Where the buyer is sued for breach of a warranty or other obligation for which his seller is answerable over

(a) he may give his seller written notice of the litigation. If the notice states that the seller may come in and defend and that if the seller does not do so he will be bound in any action against him by his buyer by any determination of fact common to the two litigations, then unless the seller after seasonable receipt of the notice does come in and defend he is so bound.

(b) if the claim is one for infringement or the like (subsection (3) of Section 2—312) the original seller may demand in writing that his buyer turn over to him control of the litigation including settlement or else be barred from any remedy over and if he also agrees to bear all expense and to satisfy any adverse judgment, then unless the buyer after seasonable receipt of the demand does turn over control the buyer is so barred.

(6) The provisions of subsections (3), (4) and (5) apply to any obligation of a buyer to hold the seller harmless against infringement or the like (subsection (3) of Section 2—312).

Section 2—608. **Revocation of Acceptance in Whole or in Part.**

(1) The buyer may revoke his acceptance of a lot or commercial unit whose non-conformity substantially impairs its value to him if he has accepted it

(a) on the reasonable assumption that its non-conformity would be cured and it has not been seasonably cured; or

(b) without discovery of such non-conformity if his acceptance was reasonably induced either by the difficulty of discovery before acceptance or by the seller's assurances.

(2) Revocation of acceptance must occur within a reasonable time after the buyer discovers or should have discovered the ground for it and before any substantial change in condition of the goods which is not caused by their own defects. It is not effective until the buyer notifies the seller of it.

(3) A buyer who so revokes has the same rights and duties with regard to the goods involved as if he had rejected them.

Section 2—609. **Right to Adequate Assurance of Performance.**

(1) A contract for sale imposes an obligation on each party that the other's expectation of receiving due performance will not be impaired. When reasonable grounds for insecurity arise with respect to the performance of either party the other may in writing demand adequate assurance of due performance and until he receives such assurance may if commercially reasonable suspend any performance for which he has not already received the agreed return.

(2) Between merchants the reasonableness of grounds for insecurity and the adequacy of any assurance offered shall be determined according to commercial standards.

(3) Acceptance of any improper delivery or payment does not prejudice the party's right to demand adequate assurance of future performance.

(4) After receipt of a justified demand failure to provide within a reasonable time not exceeding thirty days such assurance of due performance as is adequate under the circumstances of the particular case is a repudiation of the contract.

Section 2—612. **"Installment Contract"; Breach.**

(1) An "installment contract" is one which requires or authorizes the delivery of goods in separate lots to be separately accepted, even though the contract contains a clause "each delivery is a separate contract" or its equivalent.

(2) The buyer may reject any installment which is non-conforming if the non-conformity substantially impairs the value of that installment and cannot be cured or if the non-conformity is a defect in the required documents; but if the non-conformity does not fall within subsection (3) and the seller gives adequate assurance of its cure the buyer must accept that installment.

(3) Whenever non-conformity or default with respect to one or more installments substantially impairs the value of the whole contract there is a breach of the whole. But the aggrieved party reinstates the contract if he accepts a non-conforming installment without seasonably notifying of cancellation or if he brings an action with respect only to past installments or demands performance as to future installments.

Part 7 **Remedies**

Section 2—701. **Remedies for Breach of Collateral Contracts Not Impaired.**
Remedies for breach of any obligation or promise collateral or ancillary to a contract for sale are not impaired by the provisions of this Article.

Section 2—702. **Seller's Remedies on Discovery of Buyer's Insolvency.**
(1) Where the seller discovers the buyer to be insolvent he may refuse delivery except for cash including payment for all goods theretofore delivered under the contract, and stop delivery under this Article (Section 2—705).

(2) Where the seller discovers that the buyer has received goods on credit while insolvent he may reclaim the goods upon demand made within ten days after the receipt, but if misrepresentation of solvency has been made to the particular seller in writing within three months before delivery the ten day limitation does not apply. Except as provided in this subsection the seller may not base a right to reclaim goods on the buyer's fraudulent or innocent misrepresentation of solvency or of intent to pay.

(3) The seller's right to reclaim under subsection (2) is subject to the rights of a buyer in ordinary course or other good faith purchaser under this Article (Section 2—403). Successful reclamation of goods excludes all other remedies with respect to them.

Section 2—703. **Seller's Remedies in General.**
Where the buyer wrongfully rejects or revokes acceptance of goods or fails to make a payment due on or before delivery or repudiates with respect to a part or the whole, then with respect to any goods directly affected and, if the breach is of the whole contract (Section 2—612), then also with respect to the whole undelivered balance, the aggrieved seller may

(a) withhold delivery of such goods;
(b) stop delivery by any bailee as hereafter provided (Section 2—705);
(c) proceed under the next section respecting goods still unidentified to the contract;
(d) resell and recover damages as hereafter provided (Section 2—706);
(e) recover damages for non-acceptance (Section 2—708) or in a proper case the price (Section 2—709);
(f) cancel.

Section 2—708. **Seller's Damages for Non-Acceptance or Repudiation.**
(1) Subject to subsection (2) and to the provisions of this Article with respect to proof of market price (Section 2—723), the measure of damages for non-acceptance or repudiation by the buyer is the difference between the market price at the time and place for tender and the unpaid contract price together with any incidental damages provided in this Article (Section 2—710), but less expenses saved in consequence of the buyer's breach.

(2) If the measure of damages provided in subsection (1) is inadequate to put the seller in as good a position as performance would have done then the measure of damages is the profit (including reasonable overhead) which the seller would have made from full performance by

the buyer, together with any incidental damages provided in this Article (Section 2—710), due allowance for costs reasonably incurred and due credit for payments or proceeds of resale.

Section 2—709. **Action for the Price.**

(1) When the buyer fails to pay the price as it becomes due the seller may recover, together with any incidental damages under the next section, the price

(a) of goods accepted or of conforming goods lost or damaged within a commercially reasonable time after risk of their loss has passed to the buyer; and

(b) of goods identified to the contract if the seller is unable after reasonable effort to resell them at a reasonable price or the circumstances reasonably indicate that such effort will be unavailing.

(2) Where the seller sues for the price he must hold for the buyer any goods which have been identified to the contract and are still in his control except that if resale becomes possible he may resell them at any time prior to the collection of the judgment. The net proceeds of any such resale must be credited to the buyer and payment of the judgment entitles him to any goods not resold.

(3) After the buyer has wrongfully rejected or revoked acceptance of the goods or has failed to make a payment due or has repudiated (Section 2—610), a seller who is held not entitled to the price under this section shall nevertheless be awarded damages for non-acceptance under the preceding section.

Section 2—710. **Seller's Incidental Damages.**

Incidental damages to an aggrieved seller include any commercially reasonable charges, expenses or commissions incurred in stopping delivery; in the transportation, care and custody of goods after the buyer's breach, in connection with return or resale of the goods or otherwise resulting from the breach.

Section 2—711. **Buyer's Remedies in General; Buyer's Security Interest in Rejected Goods.**

(1) Where the seller fails to make delivery or repudiates or the buyer rightfully rejects or justifiably revokes acceptance then with respect to any goods involved, and with respect to the whole if the breach goes to the whole contract (Section 2—612), the buyer may cancel and whether or not he has done so may in addition to recovering so much of the price as has been paid

(a) "cover" and have damages under the next section as to all the goods affected whether or not they have been identified to the contract; or

(b) recover damages for non-delivery as provided in this Article (Section 2—713).

(2) Where the seller fails to deliver or repudiates the buyer may also

(a) if the goods have been identified recover them as provided in this Article (Section 2—502); or

(b) in a proper case obtain specific performance or replevy the goods as provided in this Article (Section 2—716).

(3) On rightful rejection or justifiable revocation of acceptance a buyer has a security interest in goods in his possession or control for any payments made on their price and any expenses reasonably incurred in their inspection, receipt, transportation, care and custody and may hold such goods and resell them in like manner as an aggrieved seller (Section 2—706).

Section 2—712. **"Cover"; Buyer's Procurement of Substitute Goods.**

(1) After a breach within the preceding section the buyer may "cover" by making in good faith and without unreasonable delay any reasonable purchase of or contract to purchase goods in substitution for those due from the seller.

(2) The buyer may recover from the seller as damages the difference between the cost of cover and the contract price together with any incidental or consequential damages as hereinafter defined (Section 2—715), but less expenses saved in consequence of the seller's breach.

(3) Failure of the buyer to effect cover within this section does not bar him from any other remedy.

Section 2—713. **Buyer's Damages for Non-Delivery or Repudiation.**

(1) Subject to the provisions of this Article with respect to proof of market price (Section 2—723), the measure of damages for non-delivery or repudiation by the seller is the difference between the market price at the time when the buyer learned of the breach and the contract price together with any incidental and consequential damages provided in this Article (Section 2—715), but less expenses saved in consequence of the seller's breach.

(2) Market price is to be determined as of the place for tender or, in cases of rejection after arrival or revocation of acceptance, as of the place of arrival.

Section 2—714. **Buyer's Damages for Breach in Regard to Accepted Goods.**

(1) Where the buyer has accepted goods and given notification (subsection (3) of Section 2—607) he may recover as damages for any non-conformity of tender the loss resulting in the ordinary course of events from the seller's breach as determined in any manner which is reasonable.

(2) The measure of damages for breach of warranty is the difference at the time and place of acceptance between the value of the goods accepted and the value they would have had if they had been as warranted, unless special circumstances show proximate damages of a different amount.

(3) In a proper case any incidental and consequential damages under the next section may also be recovered.

Section 2—715. **Buyer's Incidental and Consequential Damages.**

(1) Incidental damages resulting from the seller's breach include expenses reasonably incurred in inspection, receipt, transportation and care and custody of goods rightfully rejected, any commercially reasonable charges, expenses or commissions in connection with effecting cover and any other reasonable expense incident to the delay or other breach.

(2) Consequential damages resulting from the seller's breach include

(a) any loss resulting from general or particular requirements and needs of which the seller at the time of contracting had reason to know and which could not reasonably be prevented by cover or otherwise; and

(b) injury to person or property proximately resulting from any breach of warranty.

Section 2—718. **Liquidation or Limitation of Damages; Deposits.**

(1) Damages for breach by either party may be liquidated in the agreement but only at an amount which is reasonable in the light of the anticipated or actual harm caused by the breach, the difficulties of proof of loss, and the inconvenience or nonfeasibility of otherwise obtaining an adequate remedy. A term fixing unreasonably large liquidated damages is void as a penalty.

(2) Where the seller justifiably withholds delivery of goods because of the buyer's breach, the buyer is entitled to restitution of any amount by which the sum of his payments exceeds

(a) the amount to which the seller is entitled by virtue of terms liquidating the seller's damages in accordance with subsection (1), or

(b) in the absence of such terms, twenty per cent of the value of the total performance for which the buyer is obligated under the contract or $500, whichever is smaller.

(3) The buyer's right to restitution under subsection (2) is subject to offset to the extent that the seller establishes

(a) a right to recover damages under the provisions of this Article other than subsection (1), and

(b) the amount or value of any benefits received by the buyer directly or indirectly by reason of the contract.

(4) Where a seller has received payment in goods their reasonable value or the proceeds of their resale shall be treated as payments for the purposes of subsection (2); but if the seller

has notice of the buyer's breach before reselling goods received in part performance, his resale is subject to the conditions laid down in this Article on resale by an aggrieved seller (Section 2—706).

Section 2—719. **Contractual Modification or Limitation of Remedy.**
(1) Subject to the provisions of subsections (2) and (3) of this section and of the preceding section on liquidation and limitation of damages,

(a) the agreement may provide for remedies in addition to or in substitution for those provided in this Article and may limit or alter the measure of damages recoverable under this Article, as by limiting the buyer's remedies to return of the goods and repayment of the price or to repair and replacement of non-conforming goods or parts; and

(b) resort to a remedy as provided is optional unless the remedy is expressly agreed to be exclusive, in which case it is the sole remedy.

(2) Where circumstances cause an exclusive or limited remedy to fail of its essential purpose, remedy may be had as provided in this Act.

(3) Consequential damages may be limited or excluded unless the limitation or exclusion is unconscionable. Limitation of consequential damages for injury to the person in the case of consumer goods is prima facie unconscionable but limitation of damages where the loss is commercial is not.

Section 2—725. **Statute of Limitations in Contracts for Sale.**
(1) An action for breach of any contract for sale must be commenced within four years after the cause of action has accrued. By the original agreement the parties may reduce the period of limitation to not less than one year but may not extend it.

(2) A cause of action accrues when the breach occurs, regardless of the aggrieved party's lack of knowledge of the breach. A breach of warranty occurs when tender of delivery is made, except that where a warranty explicitly extends to future performance of the goods and discovery of the breach must await the time of such performance the cause of action accrues when the breach is or should have been discovered.

(3) Where an action commenced within the time limited by subsection (1) is so terminated as to leave available a remedy by another action for the same breach such other action may be commenced after the expiration of the time limited and within six months after the termination of the first action unless the termination resulted from voluntary discontinuance or from dismissal for failure or neglect to prosecute.

(4) This section does not alter the law on tolling of the statute of limitations nor does it apply to causes of action which have accrued before this Act becomes effective.

Article 3. Negotiable Instruments

Part 1 **General Provisions and Definitions**

Section 3—104. **Form of Negotiable Instruments; "Draft"; "Check"; "Certificate of Deposit"; "Note".**
(1) Any writing to be a negotiable instrument within this Article must

(a) be signed by the maker or drawer; and

(b) contain an unconditional promise or order to pay a sum certain in money and no other promise, order, obligation or power given by the maker or drawer except as authorized by this Article; and

(c) be payable on demand or at a definite time; and

(d) be payable to order or to bearer.

(2) A writing which complies with the requirements of this section is

(a) a "draft" ("bill of exchange") if it is an order;

(b) a "check" if it is a draft drawn on a bank and payable on demand;

(c) a "certificate of deposit" if it is an acknowledgment by a bank receipt of money with an engagement to repay it;

(d) a "note" if it is a promise other than a certificate of deposit.

(3) As used in other Articles of this Act, and as the context may require, the terms "draft", "check", "certificate of deposit" and "note" may refer to instruments which are not negotiable within this Article as well as to instruments which are so negotiable.

Section 3—105. **When Promise or Order Unconditional.**

(1) A promise or order otherwise unconditional is not made conditional by the fact that the instrument

(a) is subject to implied or constructive conditions; or

(b) states its consideration, whether performed or promised, or the transaction which gave rise to the instrument, or that the promise or order is made or the instrument matures in accordance with or "as per" such transaction; or

(c) refers to or states that it arises out of a separate agreement or refers to a separate agreement for rights as to prepayment or acceleration; or

(d) states that it is drawn under a letter of credit; or

(e) states that it is secured, whether by mortgage, reservation of title or otherwise; or

(f) indicates a particular account to be debited or any other fund or source from which reimbursement is expected; or

(g) is limited to payment out of a particular fund or the proceeds of a particular source, if the instrument is issued by a government or governmental agency or unit; or

(h) is limited to payment out of the entire assets of a partnership, unincorporated association, trust or estate by or on behalf of which the instrument is issued.

(2) A promise or order is not unconditional if the instrument

(a) states that it is subject to or governed by any other agreement; or

(b) states that it is to be paid only out of a particular fund or source except as provided in this section.

Section 3—106. **Sum Certain.**

(1) The sum payable is a sum certain even though it is to be paid

(a) with stated interest or by stated installments; or

(b) with stated different rates of interest before and after default or a specified date; or

(c) with a stated discount or addition if paid before or after the date fixed for payment; or

(d) with exchange or less exchange, whether at a fixed rate or at the current rate; or

(e) with costs of collection or an attorney's fee or both upon default.

(2) Nothing in this section shall validate any term which is otherwise illegal.

Section 3—107. **Money.**

(1) An instrument is payable in money if the medium of exchange in which it is payable is money at the time the instrument is made. An instrument payable in "currency" or "current funds" is payable in money.

(2) A promise or order to pay a sum stated in a foreign currency is for a sum certain in money and, unless a different medium of payment is specified in the instrument, may be satisfied by payment of that number of dollars which the stated foreign currency will purchase at the buying sight rate for that currency on the day on which the instrument is payable or, if payable on demand, on the day of demand. If such an instrument specifies a foreign currency as the medium of payment the instrument is payable in that currency.

Section 3—108. **Payable on Demand.**

Instruments payable on demand include those payable at sight or on presentation and those in which no time for payment is stated.

Section 3—109. **Definite Time.**

(1) An instrument is payable at a definite time if by its terms it is payable

(a) on or before a stated date or at a fixed period after a stated date; or

(b) at a fixed period after sight; or

(c) at a definite time subject to any acceleration; or

(d) at a definite time subject to extension at the option of the holder, or to extension to a further definite time at the option of the maker or acceptor or automatically upon or after a specified act or event.

(2) An instrument which by its terms is otherwise payable only upon an act or event uncertain as to time of occurrence is not payable at a definite time even though the act or event has occurred.

Section 3—110. **Payable to Order.**

(1) An instrument is payable to order when by its terms it is payable to the order or assigns of any person therein specified with reasonable certainty, or to him or his order, or when it is conspicuously designated on its face as "exchange" or the like and names a payee. It may be payable to the order of

(a) the maker or drawer; or

(b) the drawee; or

(c) a payee who is not maker, drawer or drawee; or

(d) two or more payees together or in the alternative; or

(e) an estate, trust or fund, in which case it is payable to the order of the representative of such estate, trust or fund or his successors; or

(f) an office, or an officer by his title as such in which case it is payable to the principal but the incumbent of the office or his successors may act as if he or they were the holder; or

(g) a partnership or unincorporated association, in which case it is payable to the partnership or association and may be indorsed or transferred by any person thereto authorized.

(2) An instrument not payable to order is not made so payable by such words as "payable upon return of this instrument properly indorsed."

(3) An instrument made payable both to order and to bearer is payable to order unless the bearer words are handwritten or typewritten.

Section 3—111. **Payable to Bearer.**

An instrument is payable to bearer when by its terms it is payable to

(a) bearer or the order of bearer; or

(b) a specified person or bearer; or

(c) "cash" or the order of "cash", or any other indication which does not purport to designate a specific payee.

Part 2 **Negotiation, Transfer, and Indorsement**

Section 3—201. **Negotiation.**

1. (a) "Negotiation" means a transfer of possession, whether voluntary or involuntary, of an instrument by a person other than the issuer to a person who thereby becomes its holder.

2. (b) Except for negotiation by a remitter, if an instrument is payable to an identified person, negotiation requires transfer of possession of the instrument and its indorsement by the holder. If an instrument is payable to bearer, it may be negotiated by transfer of possession alone.

Section 3—202. **Negotiation Subject to Rescission.**

1. (a) Negotiation is effective even if obtained (i) from an infant, a corporation exceeding its powers, or a person without capacity, (ii) by fraud, duress, or mistake, or (iii) in breach of duty or as part of an illegal transaction.

2. (b) To the extent permitted by other law, negotiation may be rescinded or may be subject to other remedies, but those remedies may not be asserted against a subsequent holder in due course or a person paying the instrument in good faith and without knowledge of facts that are a basis for rescission or other remedy.

Section 3—203. **Transfer of Instrument; Rights Acquired by Transfer.**

1. (a) An instrument is transferred when it is delivered by a person other than its issuer for the purpose of giving to the person receiving delivery the right to enforce the instrument.

2. (b) Transfer of an instrument, whether or not the transfer is a negotiation, vests in the transferee any right of the transferor to enforce the instrument, including any right as a holder in due course, but the transferee cannot acquire rights of a holder in due course by a transfer, directly or indirectly, from a holder in due course if the transferee engaged in fraud or illegality affecting the instrument.

3. (c) Unless otherwise agreed, if an instrument is transferred for value and the transferee does not become a holder because of lack of indorsement by the transferor, the transferee has a specifically enforceable right to the unqualified indorsement of the transferor, but negotiation of the instrument does not occur until the indorsement is made.

4. (d) If a transferor purports to transfer less than the entire instrument, negotiation of the instrument does not occur. The transferee obtains no rights under this Article and has only the rights of a partial assignee.

Section 3—204. **Indorsement.**

1. (a) "Indorsement" means a signature, other than that of a signer as maker, drawer, or acceptor, that alone or accompanied by other words is made on an instrument for the purpose of (i) negotiating the instrument, (ii) restricting payment of the instrument, or (iii) incurring indorser's liability on the instrument, but regardless of the intent of the signer, a signature and its accompanying words is an indorsement unless the accompanying words, terms of the instrument, place of the signature, or other circumstances unambiguously indicate that the signature was made for a purpose other than indorsement. For the purpose of determining whether a signature is made on an instrument, a paper affixed to the instrument is a part of the instrument.

2. (b) "Indorser" means a person who makes an indorsement.

3. (c) For the purpose of determining whether the transferee of an instrument is a holder, an indorsement that transfers a security interest in the instrument is effective as an unqualified indorsement of the instrument.

4. (d) If an instrument is payable to a holder under a name that is not the name of the holder, indorsement may be made by the holder in the name stated in the instrument or in the holder's name or both, but signature in both names may be required by a person paying or taking the instrument for value or collection.

Article 9. Secured Transactions; Sales of Accounts and Chattel Paper

Part 1 **Short Title, Applicability, and Definitions**

Section 9—105. **Definitions and Index of Definitions.**

(1) In this Article unless the context otherwise requires:

1. (a) **"Account debtor"** means the person who is obligated on an account, chattel paper, or general intangible;

2. (b) **"Chattel paper"** means a writing or writings which evidence both a monetary obligation and a security interest in or a lease of specific goods, but a charter or other contract involving the use or hire of a vessel is not chattel paper. When a transaction is evidenced

both by such a security agreement or a lease and by an instrument or a series of instruments, the group of writings taken together constitutes chattel paper;

3. (c) **"Collateral"** means the property subject to a security interest, and includes accounts and chattel paper which have been sold;

4. (d) **"Debtor"** means the person who owes payment or other performance of the obligation secured, whether or not he owns or has rights in the collateral, and includes the seller of accounts or chattel paper. Where the debtor and the owner of the collateral are not the same person, the term **"debtor"** means the owner of the collateral in any provision of the Article dealing with the collateral, the obligor in any provision dealing with the obligation, and may include both where the context so requires;

5. (e) **"Deposit account"** means a demand, time, savings, passbook, or like account maintained with a bank, savings and loan association, credit union or like organization, other than an account evidenced by a certificate of deposit;

6. (f) **"Document"** means document of title as defined in the general definitions of Article 1 (Section 1—201), and a receipt of the kind described in subsection (2) of Section 7—201;

7. (g) **"Encumbrance"** includes real estate mortgages and other liens on real estate and all other rights in real estate that are not ownership interests;

8. (h) **"Goods"** includes all things which are movable at the time the security interest attaches or which are fixtures (Section 9—313), but does not include money, documents, instruments, accounts, chattel paper, general intangibles, or minerals or the like (including oil and gas) before extraction. "Goods" also includes standing timber which is to be cut and removed under a conveyance or contract for sale, the unborn young of animals, and growing crops;

9. (i) **"Instrument"** means a negotiable instrument (defined in Section 3—104), or a certificated security (defined in Section 8—102) or any other writing which evidences a right to the payment of money and is not itself a security agreement or lease and is of a type which is in ordinary course of business transferred by delivery with any necessary indorsement or assignment;

10. (j) **"Mortgage"** means a consensual interest created by a real estate mortgage, a trust deed on real estate, or the like;

11. (k) An advance is made **"pursuant to commitment"** if the secured party has bound himself to make it, whether or not a subsequent event of default or other event not within his control has relieved or may relieve him from his obligation;

12. (l) **"Security agreement"** means an agreement which creates or provides for a security interest;

13. (m) **"Secured party"** means a lender, seller or other person in whose favor there is a security interest, including a person to whom accounts or chattel paper have been sold. When the holders of obligations issued under an indenture of trust, equipment trust agreement or the like are represented by a trustee or other person, the representative is the secured party;

14. (n) **"Transmitting utility"** means any person primarily engaged in the railroad, street railway or trolley bus business, the electric or electronics communications transmission business, the transmission of goods by pipeline, or the transmission or the production and transmission of electricity, steam, gas or water, or the provision of sewer service.

Section 9—106. Definitions: "Account"; "General Intangibles".

"Account" means any right to payment for goods sold or leased or for services rendered which is not evidenced by an instrument or chattel paper, whether or not it has been earned by performance. **"General intangibles"** means any personal property (including things in action) other than goods, accounts, chattel paper, documents, instruments, and money. All rights to payment earned or unearned under a charter or other contract involving the use or hire of a vessel and all rights incident to the charter or contract are accounts.

Section 9—107. **Definitions: "Purchase Money Security Interest".**
A security interest is a "purchase money security interest" to the extent that it is
1. (a) taken or retained by the seller of the collateral to secure all or part of its price; or
2. (b) taken by a person who by making advances or incurring an obligation gives value to enable the debtor to acquire rights in or the use of collateral if such value is in fact so used.

Part 2 **Validity of Security Agreement and Rights of Parties Thereto**

Section 9—201. **General Validity of Security Agreement.**
Except as otherwise provided by this Act a security agreement is effective according to its terms between the parties, against purchasers of the collateral and against creditors. Nothing in this Article validates any charge or practice illegal under any statute or regulation thereunder governing usury, small loans, retail installment sales, or the like, or extends the application of any such statute or regulation to any transaction not otherwise subject thereto.

Part 3 **Rights of Third Parties; Perfected and Unperfected Security Interests; Rules of Priority**

Section 9—306. **"Proceeds"; Secured Party's Rights on Disposition of Collateral.**
(1) "Proceeds" includes whatever is received upon the sale, exchange, collection or other disposition of collateral or proceeds. Insurance payable by reason of loss or damage to the collateral is proceeds, except to the extent that it is payable to a person other than a party to the security agreement. Money, checks, deposit accounts, and the like are "cash proceeds". All other proceeds are "non-cash proceeds".
(2) Except where this Article otherwise provides, a security interest continues in collateral notwithstanding sale, exchange or other disposition thereof unless the disposition was authorized by the secured party in the security agreement or otherwise, and also continues in any identifiable proceeds including collections received by the debtor.
(3) The security interest in proceeds is a continuously perfected security interest if the interest in the original collateral was perfected but it ceases to be a perfected security interest and becomes unperfected ten days after receipt of the proceeds by the debtor unless
1. (a) a filed financing statement covers the original collateral and the proceeds are collateral in which a security interest may be perfected by filing in the office or offices where the financing statement has been filed and, if the proceeds are acquired with cash proceeds, the description of collateral in the financing statement indicates the types of property constituting the proceeds; or
2. (b) a filed financing statement covers the original collateral and the proceeds are identifiable cash proceeds; or
3. (c) the security interest in the proceeds is perfected before the expiration of the ten day period.
Except as provided in this section, a security interest in proceeds can be perfected only by the methods or under the circumstances permitted in this Article for original collateral of the same type.
(4) In the event of insolvency proceedings instituted by or against a debtor, a secured party with a perfected security interest in proceeds has a perfected security interest only in the following proceeds:
4. (a) in identifiable noncash proceeds and in separate deposit accounts containing only proceeds;
5. (b) in identifiable cash proceeds in the form of money which is neither commingled with other money nor deposited in a deposit account prior to the insolvency proceedings;
6. (c) in identifiable cash proceeds in the form of checks and the like which are not deposited in a deposit account prior to the insolvency proceedings; and

7. (d) in all cash and deposit accounts of the debtor in which proceeds have been commingled with other funds, but the perfected security interest under this paragraph (d) is
8. (i) subject to any right to set-off; and
9. (ii) limited to an amount not greater than the amount of any cash proceeds received by the debtor within ten days before the institution of the insolvency proceedings less the sum of (I) the payments to the secured party on account of cash proceeds received by the debtor during such period and (II) the cash proceeds received by the debtor during such period to which the secured party is entitled under paragraphs (a) through (c) of this subsection (4).
(5) If a sale of goods results in an account or chattel paper which is transferred by the seller to a secured party, and if the goods are returned to or are repossessed by the seller or the secured party, the following rules determine priorities:
10. (a) If the goods were collateral at the time of sale, for an indebtedness of the seller which is still unpaid, the original security interest attaches again to the goods and continues as a perfected security interest if it was perfected at the time when the goods were sold. If the security interest was originally perfected by a filing which is still effective, nothing further is required to continue the perfected status; in any other case, the secured party must take possession of the returned or repossessed goods or must file.
11. (b) An unpaid transferee of the chattel paper has a security interest in the goods against the transferor. Such security interest is prior to a security interest asserted under paragraph (a) to the extent that the transferee of the chattel paper was entitled to priority under Section 9—308.
12. (c) An unpaid transferee of the account has a security interest in the goods against the transferor. Such security interest is subordinate to a security interest asserted under paragraph (a).
13. (d) A security interest of an unpaid transferee asserted under paragraph (b) or (c) must be perfected for protection against creditors of the transferor and purchasers of the returned or repossessed goods.

National Labor Relations Act (Excerpts)

* * *

Rights of Employees

Section 7. Employees shall have the right to self-organization, to form, join, or assist labor organizations, to bargain collectively through representatives of their own choosing, and to engage in other concerted activities for the purpose of collective bargaining or other mutual aid or protection, and shall also have the right to refrain from any or all of such activities requiring membership in a labor organization as a condition of employment as authorized in section 8(a)(3).

Unfair Labor Practices

Section 8. (a) It shall be an unfair labor practice for an employer—

(1) to interfere with, restrain, or coerce employees in the exercise of the rights guaranteed in section 7;

(2) to dominate or interfere with the formation or administration of any labor organization or contribute financial or other support to it: *Provided*, That . . . an employer shall not be prohibited from permitting employees to confer with him during working hours without loss of time or pay;

(3) by discrimination in regard to hire or tenure of employment or any term or condition of employment to encourage or discourage membership in any labor organization. . . .

(4) to discharge or otherwise discriminate against an employee because he has filed charges or given testimony under this Act;

(5) to refuse to bargain collectively with the representatives of his employees, subject to the provisions of section 9(a).

    (b) It shall be an unfair labor practice for a labor organization or its agents—

(1) to restrain or coerce (A) employees in the exercise of the rights guaranteed in section 7: *Provided*, That this paragraph shall not impair the right of a labor organization to prescribe its own rules with respect to the acquisition or retention of membership therein; or (B) an employer in the selection of his representatives for the purposes of collective bargaining or the adjustment of grievances;

(2) to cause or attempt to cause an employer to discriminate against an employee . . . or to discriminate against an employee with respect to whom membership in such organization has been denied or terminated on some ground other than his failure to tender the periodic dues and the initiation fees uniformly required as a condition of acquiring or retaining membership;

(3) to refuse to bargain collectively with an employer, provided it is the representative of his employees subject to the provisions of section 9(a);

(4) (i) to engage in, or to induce or encourage any individual employed by any person engaged in commerce or in an industry affecting commerce to engage in, a strike or a refusal in the course of his employment to use, manufacture, process, transport, or otherwise handle or work on any goods, articles, materials, or commodities or to perform any services; or (ii) to threaten, coerce, or restrain any person engaged in commerce or in an industry affecting commerce, where in either case an object thereof is—

(A) forcing or requiring any employer or self-employed person to join any labor or employer organization or to enter into any agreement which is prohibited by section 8(e);

(B) forcing or requiring any person to cease using, selling, handling, transporting, or otherwise dealing in the products of any other producer, processor, or manufacturer, or to cease doing business with any other person, or forcing or requiring any other employer to recognize or bargain with a labor organization as the representative of his employees unless such labor organization has been certified as the representative of such employees under the provisions of section 9: Provided, That nothing contained in this clause (B) shall be construed to make unlawful, where not otherwise unlawful, any primary strike or primary picketing;

(C) forcing or requiring any employer to recognize or bargain with a particular labor organization as the representative of his employees if another labor organization has been certified as the representative of such employees under the provisions of section 9;

(D) forcing or requiring any employer to assign particular work to employees in a particular labor organization or in a particular trade, craft, or class rather than to employees in another labor organization or in another trade, craft, or class, unless such employer is failing to conform to an order or certification of the Board determining the bargaining representative for employees performing such work:

Provided, That nothing contained in this subsection (b) shall be construed to make unlawful a refusal by any person to enter upon the premises of any employer (other than his own employer), if the employees of such employer are engaged in a strike ratified or approved by a representative of such employees whom such employer is required to recognize under this Act: *Provided further*, that for the purposes of this paragraph (4) only, nothing contained in such paragraph shall be construed to prohibit publicity, other than picketing, for the purpose of truthfully advising the public, including consumers and members of a labor organization, that a product or products are produced by an employer with whom the labor organization has a primary dispute and are distributed by another employer, as long as such publicity does not have an effect of inducing any individual employed by any person other than the primary employer in the course of his employment to refuse to pick up, deliver, or transport any goods, or not to perform any services, at the establishment of the employer engaged in such distribution:

(5) to require of employees covered by an agreement authorized under subsection (a)(3) the payment, as a condition precedent to becoming a member of such organization, of a fee in an amount which the Board finds excessive or discriminatory under all the circumstances. In making such a finding, the Board shall consider, among other relevant factors, the practices and customs of labor organizations in the particular industry, and the wages currently paid to the employees affected;

(6) to cause or attempt to cause an employer to pay or deliver or agree to pay or deliver any money or other thing of value, in the nature of an exaction, for services which are not performed or not to be performed; and

(7) to picket or cause to be picketed, or threaten to picket or cause to be picketed, any employer where an object thereof is forcing or requiring an employer to recognize or bargain with a labor organization as the representative of his employees, or forcing or requiring the employees of an employer to accept or select such labor organization as their collective bargaining

representative, unless such labor organization is currently certified as the representative of such employees:

(A) where the employer has lawfully recognized in accordance with this Act any other labor organization and a question concerning representation may not appropriately be raised under section 9(c) of this Act;

(B) where within the preceding twelve months a valid election under section 9(c) of this Act has been conducted, or

(C) where such picketing has been conducted without a petition under section 9(c) being filed within a reasonable period of time not to exceed thirty days from the commencement of such picketing. . . .

Nothing in this paragraph (7) shall be construed to permit any act which would otherwise be an unfair labor practice under this section 8(b).

(c) The expressing of any views, argument, or opinion, or the dissemination thereof, whether in written, printed, graphic, or visual form, shall not constitute or be evidence of an unfair labor practice under any of the provisions of this Act, if such expression contains no threat of reprisal or force or promise of benefit.

(d) For the purposes of this section, to bargain collectively is the performance of the mutual obligation of the employer and the representative of the employees to meet at reasonable times and confer in good faith with respect to wages, hours, and other terms and conditions of employment, or the negotiation of an agreement, or any question arising thereunder, and the execution of a written contract incorporating any agreement reached if requested by either party, but such obligation does not compel either party to agree to a proposal or require the making of a concession. . . .

(e) It shall be an unfair labor practice for any labor organization and any employer to enter into any contract or agreement, express or implied, whereby such employer ceases or refrains or agrees to cease or refrain from handling, using, selling, transporting, or otherwise dealing in any of the products of any other employer, or to cease doing business with any other person, and any contract or agreement entered into heretofore or hereafter containing such an agreement shall be to such extent unenforceable and void. . . .

Representatives and Elections

Section 9. (a) Representatives designated or selected for the purposes of collective bargaining by the majority of the employees in a unit appropriate for such purposes, shall be the exclusive representative of all the employees in such unit for the purposes of collective bargaining in respect to rates of pay, wages, hours of employment, or other conditions of employment: *Provided*, That any individual employee or a group of employees shall have the right at any time to present grievances to their employer and to have such grievances adjusted, without the intervention of the bargaining representative, as long as the adjustment is not inconsistent with the terms of a collective-bargaining contract or agreement then in effect: *Provided further*, That the bargaining representative has been given opportunity to be present at such adjustment.

(b) The Board shall decide in each case whether, in order to assure to employees the fullest freedom in exercising the rights guaranteed by this Act, the unit appropriate for the purposes of collective bargaining shall be the employer unit, craft unit, plant unit, or subdivision thereof. . . .

(c) (1)Whenever a petition shall have been filed, in accordance with such regulations as may be prescribed by the Board—

(A) by an employee or group of employees or an individual or labor organization acting in their behalf, alleging that a substantial number of employees (i) wish to be represented for collective bargaining and that their employer declines to recognize their representative as the representative defined in section 9(a), or (ii) assert that the individual or labor organization, which has been certified or is being currently recognized by their employer as the bargaining representative, is no longer a representative as defined in section 9(a); or

(B) by an employer, alleging that one or more individual or labor organizations have presented to him a claim to be recognized as the representative defined in section 9(a); the Board shall investigate such petition and if it has reasonable cause to believe that a question of representation affecting commerce exists shall provide for an appropriate hearing upon due notice. Such hearing may be conducted by an officer or employee of the regional office, who shall not make any recommendations with respect thereto. If the Board finds upon the record of such hearing that such a question of representation exists, it shall direct an election by secret ballot and shall certify the results thereof.

(2) In determining whether or not a question of representation affecting commerce exists, the same regulations and rules of decision shall apply irrespective of the identity of the persons filing the petition or the kind of relief sought and in no case shall the Board deny a labor organization a place on the ballot by reason of an order with respect to such labor organization or its predecessor not issued in conformity with section 10(c).

(3) No election shall be directed in any bargaining unit or any subdivision within which, in the preceding twelve-month period, a valid election shall have been held. Employees engaged in an economic strike who are not entitled to reinstatement shall be eligible to vote under such regulations as the Board shall find are consistent with the purposes and provisions of this Act in any election conducted within twelve months after the commencement of the strike. In any election where none of the choices on the ballot receives a majority, a run-off shall be conducted, the ballot providing for a selection between the two choices receiving the largest and second largest number of valid votes cast in the election.

(4) Nothing in this section shall be construed to prohibit the waiving of hearings by stipulation for the purpose of a consent election in conformity with regulations and rules of decision of the Board.

(5) In determining whether a unit is appropriate for the purposes specified in subsection (b) the extent to which the employees have organized shall not be controlling.

(d) Whenever an order of the Board made pursuant to section 10(c) is based in whole or in part upon facts certified following an investigation pursuant to subsection (c) of this section and there is a petition for the enforcement or review of such order, such certification and the record of such investigation shall be included in the transcript of the entire record required to be filed under section 10(e) or 10(f), and thereupon the decree of the court enforcing, modifying, or setting aside in whole or in part the order of the Board shall be made and entered upon the pleadings, testimony, and proceedings set forth in such transcript.

(e) (1) Upon the filing with the Board, by 30 per centum or more of the employees in a bargaining unit covered by an agreement between their employer and a labor organization made pursuant to section 8(a)(3), of a petition alleging they desire that such authority be rescinded, the Board shall take a secret ballot of the employees in such unit, and shall certify the results thereof to such labor organization and to the employer.

(2) No election shall be conducted pursuant to this subsection in any bargaining unit or any subdivision within which, in the preceding twelve-month period, a valid election shall have been held.

* * *

Title VII of Civil Rights Act of 1964 (Excerpts)

Definitions

Section 701. (j) The term "religion" includes all aspects of religious observance and practice, as well as belief, unless an employer demonstrates that he is unable to reasonably accommodate to an employee's or prospective employee's religious observance or practice without undue hardship on the conduct of the employer's business.

(k) The terms "because of sex" or "on the basis of sex" include, but are not limited to, because of or on the basis of pregnancy, childbirth or related medical conditions; and women affected by pregnancy, childbirth, or related medical conditions shall be treated the same for all employment-related purposes, including receipt of benefits under fringe benefit programs, as other persons not so affected but similar in their ability or inability to work, and nothing in Section 703(h) of this title shall be interpreted to permit otherwise. This subsection shall not require an employer to pay for health insurance benefits for abortion, except where the life of the mother would be endangered if the fetus were carried to term, or except where medical complications have arisen from an abortion: *Provided*, That nothing herein shall preclude an employer from providing abortion benefits or otherwise effect bargaining agreements in regard to abortion.

Discrimination Because of Race, Color, Religion, Sex, or National Origin

Section 703. (a) It shall be unlawful employment practice for an employer—
(1) to fail or refuse to hire or to discharge any individual, or otherwise to discriminate against any individual with respect to his compensation, terms, conditions, or privileges of employment, because of such individual's race, color, religion, sex, or national origin; or
(2) to limit, segregate, or classify his employees or applicants for employment in any way which would deprive or tend to deprive any individual of employment opportunities or otherwise adversely affect his status as an employee, because of such individual's race, color, religion, sex, or national origin.

(b) It shall be unlawful employment practice for an employment agency to fail or refuse to refer for employment, or otherwise to discriminate against, an individual because of his race, color, religion, sex, or national origin, or to classify or refer for employment any individual on the basis of his race, color, religion, sex, or national origin.

(c) It shall be an unlawful employment practice for a labor organization—
(1) to exclude or to expel from its membership, or otherwise to discriminate against, any individual because of his race, color, religion, sex, or national origin;
(2) to limit, segregate, or classify its membership or applicants for membership or to classify or fail or refuse to refer for employment any individual, in any way which would deprive or tend to deprive any individual of employment opportunities, or would limit such employ-

ment opportunities or otherwise adversely affect his status as an employee or as an applicant for employment, because of such individual's race, color, religion, sex, or national origin; or (3) to cause or attempt to cause an employer to discriminate against an individual in violation of this section.

(d) It shall be an unlawful employment practice for any employer, labor organization, or joint labor-management committee controlling apprenticeship or other training or retraining, including on-the-job training programs to discriminate against any individual because of his race, color, religion, sex, or national origin in admission to, or employment in, any program established to provide apprenticeship or other training.

(e) Notwithstanding any other provision of this title, (1) it shall not be an unlawful employment practice for an employer to hire and employ employees, for an employment agency to classify, or refer for employment any individual, or for any employer, labor organization, or joint labor-management committee controlling apprenticeship or other training or retraining programs to admit or employ any individual in any such program, on the basis of his religion, sex, or national origin in those certain instances where religion, sex, or national origin is a bona fide occupational qualification reasonably necessary to the normal operation of that particular business or enterprise, and (2) it shall not be an unlawful employment practice for a school, college, university, or other educational institution or institution of learning to hire and employ employees of a particular religion if such school, college, university, or other educational institution or institution of learning is, in whole or in substantial part, owned, supported, controlled, or managed by a particular religion or by a particular religious corporation, association, or society, or if the curriculum of such school, college, university, or other educational institution or institution of learning is directed toward the propagation of a particular religion.

* * *

(h) Notwithstanding any other provision of this title, it shall not be an unlawful employment practice for an employer to apply different standards of compensation, or different terms, conditions, or privileges of employment pursuant to a bona fide seniority or merit system, or a system which measures earnings by quantity or quality of production or to employees who work in different locations, provided that such differences are not the results of an intention to discriminate because of race, color, religion, sex, or national origin; nor shall it be an unlawful employment practice for an employer to give and to act upon the results of any professionally developed ability test provided that such test, its administration or action upon the results is not designed, intended, or used to discriminate because of race, color, religion, sex, or national origin. It shall not be an unlawful employment practice under this title for any employer to differentiate upon the basis of sex in determining the amount of wages or compensation paid or to be paid to employees of such employer if such differentiation is authorized by the provision of Section 6(d) of the Fair Labor Standards Act of 1938 as amended (29 U.S.C. 206(d)).

(i) Nothing contained in this title shall apply to any business or enterprise on or near an Indian reservation with respect to any publicly announced employment practice of such business or enterprise under which a preferential treatment is given to any individual because he is an Indian living on or near a reservation.

(j) Nothing contained in this title shall be interpreted to require any employer, employment agency, labor organization, or joint labor-management committee subject to this title to grant preferential treatment to any individual or to any group because of the race, color, religion, sex, or national origin of such individual or group on account of an imbalance which may exist with respect to the total number or percentage of persons of any race, color, religion, sex, or national origin employed by any employer, referred or classified for employment by any employment agency or labor organization, admitted to membership or classified by any labor organization, or admitted to, or employed in, any apprenticeship or other training program, in comparison with the total number or percentage of persons of such race, color, religion, sex, or national origin in any community, State, section, or other area, or in the available work force in any community, State, section, or other area.

Other Unlawful Employment Practices

Section 704. (a) It shall be an unlawful employment practice for an employer to discriminate against any of his employees or applicants for employment, for an employment agency, or joint labor-management committee controlling apprenticeship or other training or retraining, including on-the-job training programs, to discriminate against any individual, or for a labor organization to discriminate against any member thereof or applicant for membership, because he has opposed any practice, made an unlawful employment practice by this title, or because he has made a charge, testified, assisted, or participated in any manner in an investigation, proceeding, or hearing under this title.

(b) It shall be an unlawful employment practice for an employer, labor organization, employment agency, or joint labor-management committee controlling apprenticeship or other training or retraining, including on-the-job training programs, to print or cause to be printed or published any notice or advertisement relating to employment by such an employer or membership in or any classification or referral for employment by such a labor organization, or relating to any classification or referral for employment by such an employment agency, or relating to admission to, or employment in, any program established to provide apprenticeship or other training by such a joint labor-management committee indicating any preference, limitation, specification, or discrimination, based on race, color, religion, sex, or national origin, except that such a notice or advertisement may indicate a preference, limitation, specification, or discrimination based on religion, sex, or national origin when religion, sex, or national origin is a bona fide occupational qualification for employment.

Americans with Disabilities Act (Excerpts)

Title I—Employment Section 101. Definitions.

(8) Qualified individual with a disability. The term "qualified individual with a disability" means an individual with a disability who, with or without reasonable accommodation, can perform the essential functions of the employment position that such individual holds or desires. For the purposes of this title, consideration shall be given to the employer's judgment as to what functions of a job are essential, and if an employer has prepared a written description before advertising or interviewing applicants for the job, this description shall be considered evidence of the essential functions of the job.

(9) Reasonable Accommodation. The term "reasonable accommodation" may include—

(A) making existing facilities used by employees readily accessible to and usable by individuals with disabilities; and

(B) job restructuring, part-time or modified work schedules, reassignment to a vacant position, acquisition or modification of equipment or devices, appropriate adjustment or modifications of examinations, training materials or policies, the provision of qualified readers or interpreters, and other similar accommodations for individuals with disabilities.

(10) Undue Hardship.

(A) In general: The term "undue hardship" means an action requiring significant difficulty or expense, when considered in light of the factors set forth in subparagraph (B).

(B) Factors to be considered: In determining whether an accommodation would impose an undue hardship on a covered entity, factors to be considered include—

(i) the nature and cost of accommodation needed under this Act;

(ii) the overall financial resources of the facility or facilities involved in the provision of the reasonable accommodation; the number of persons employed at such facility; the effect on expenses and resources, or the impact otherwise of such accommodation upon the operation of the facility;

(iii) the overall financial resources of the covered entity; the overall size of the business of a covered entity with respect to the number of its employees; the number, type, and location of its facilities; and

(iv) the type of operation or operations of the covered entity, including the composition, structure, and functions of the workforce of such entity; the geographic separateness, administrative, or fiscal relationship of the facility or facilities in question to the covered entity.

Section 102. Discrimination.

(a) General Rule. No covered entity shall discriminate against a qualified individual with a disability because of the disability of such individual in regard to job application procedures, the hiring, advancement, or discharge of employees, employee compensation, job training, and other terms, conditions, and privileges of employment.

(b) Construction. As used in subsection (a), the term "discriminate" includes—

(1) limiting, segregating, or classifying a job applicant or employee in a way that adversely affects the opportunities or status of such applicant or employee because of the disability of such applicant or employee;

(2) participating in a contractual or other arrangement or relationship that has the effect of subjecting a covered entity's qualified applicant or employee with a disability to the discrimination prohibited by this title (such relationship includes a relationship with an employment or referral agency, labor union, an organization providing fringe benefits to an employee of the covered entity, or an organization providing training and apprenticeship programs);

(3) utilizing standards, criteria, or methods of administration—

(A) that have the effect of discrimination on the basis of disability; or

(B) that perpetuate the discrimination of others who are subject to common administrative control;

(4) excluding or otherwise denying equal jobs or benefits to a qualified individual because of the known disability of an individual with whom the qualified individual is known to have a relationship or association;

(5) (A) not making reasonable accommodations to the known physical or mental limitations of an otherwise qualified individual with a disability who is an applicant or employee, unless such covered entity can demonstrate that the accommodation would impose an undue hardship on the operation of the business of such covered entity; or

(B) denying employment opportunities to a job applicant or employee who is an otherwise qualified individual with a disability, if such denial is based on the need of such covered entity to make reasonable accommodation to the physical or mental impairments of the employee or applicant;

(6) using qualification standards, employment tests or other selection criteria that screen out or tend to screen out an individual with a disability or a class of individuals with disabilities unless the standard, test or other selection criteria, as used by the covered entity, is shown to be job-related for the position in question and is consistent with business necessity; and

(7) failing to select and administer tests concerning employment in the most effective manner to ensure that, when such test is administered to a job applicant or employee who has a disability that impairs sensory, manual, or speaking skills, such test results accurately reflect the skills, aptitude, or whatever other factor of such applicant or employee that such test purports to measure, rather than reflecting the impaired sensory, manual, or speaking skills of such employee or applicant (except where such skills are the factors that the test purports to measure).

Section 104. Illegal Use of Drugs and Alcohol.

(b) Rules of Construction. Nothing in subsection (a) shall be construed to exclude as a qualified individual with a disability an individual who—

(1) has successfully completed a supervised drug rehabilitation program and is no longer engaging in the illegal use of drugs, or has otherwise been rehabilitated successfully and is no longer engaging in such use;

(2) is participating in a supervised rehabilitation program and is no longer engaging in such use; or

(3) is erroneously regarded as engaging in such use, but is not engaging in such use; except that it shall not be a violation of this Act for a covered entity to adopt or administer reasonable policies or procedures, including but not limited to drug testing, designed to ensure that an individual described in paragraph (1) or (2) is no longer engaging in the illegal use of drugs.

The Antitrust Statutes (Excerpts)

Sherman Act
Restraints of Trade Prohibited

Section 1—Trusts, etc., in restraint of trade illegal; penalty. Every contract, combination in the form of trust or otherwise, or conspiracy, in restraint of trade or commerce among the several States, or with foreign nations, is declared to be illegal. Every person who shall make any contract or engage in any combination or conspiracy declared by sections 1 to 7 of this title to be illegal shall be deemed guilty of a felony, and, on conviction thereof, shall be punished by fine not exceeding $10,000,000 if a corporation, or if any other person, $350,000, or by imprisonment not exceeding three years, or both said punishments, in the discretion of the court.

Section 2—Monopolizing trade a felony; penalty. Every person who shall monopolize, or attempt to monopolize, or combine or conspire with any other person or persons, to monopolize any part of the trade or commerce among the several States, or with foreign nations, shall be deemed guilty of a felony, and, on conviction thereof, shall be punished by fine not exceeding $10,000,000 if a corporation, or, if any other person, $350,000, or by imprisonment not exceeding three years, or by both said punishments, in the discretion of the court.

Clayton Act
Refusals to Deal

Section 3—Sale, etc., on agreement not to use goods of competitor. It shall be unlawful for any person engaged in commerce, in the course of such commerce, to lease or make a sale or contract for sale of goods, wares, merchandise, machinery, supplies, or other commodities, whether patented or unpatented, for use, consumption, or resale within the United States or any Territory thereof or the District of Columbia or any insular possession or other place under the jurisdiction of the United States, or fix a price charged thereof, or discount from, or rebate upon, such price, on the condition, agreement, or understanding that the lessee or purchaser thereof shall not use or deal in the goods, wares, merchandise, machinery, supplies, or other commodities of a competitor or competitors of the lessor or seller, where the effect of such lease, sale, or contract for sale or such condition, agreement or understanding may be to substantially lessen competition or tend to create a monopoly in any line of commerce.

Private Suits

Section 4—Suits by persons injured; amount of recovery. Any person who shall be injured in this business or property by reason of anything forbidden in the antitrust laws may sue therefor in any district court of the United States in the district in which the defendant resides or is found or has an agent, without respect to the amount in controversy, and shall recover threefold the damages by him sustained, and the cost of suit, including a reasonable attorney's fee. . . .

Mergers

Section 7—Acquisition by one corporation of stock of another. No corporation engaged in commerce shall acquire, directly or indirectly, the whole or any part of the stock or other share capital and no corporation subject to the jurisdiction of the Federal Trade Commission shall acquire the whole or any part of the assets of another corporation engaged also in commerce, where in any line of commerce in any section of the country, the effect of such acquisition may be substantially to lessen competition, or to tend to create a monopoly.

No corporation shall acquire, directly or indirectly, the whole or any part of the stock or other share capital and no corporation subject to the jurisdiction of the Federal Trade Commission shall acquire the whole or any part of the assets of one or more corporations engaged in commerce, where in any line of commerce in any section of the country, the effect of such acquisition, of such stocks or assets, or of the use of such stock by the voting or granting of proxies or otherwise, may be substantially to lessen competition, or to tend to create a monopoly.

This section shall not apply to corporations purchasing such stock solely for investment and not using the same by voting or otherwise to bring about, or in attempting to bring about, the substantial lessening of competition. Nor shall anything contained in this section prevent a corporation engaged in commerce from causing the formation of subsidiary corporations for the actual carrying on of their immediate lawful business, or the natural and legitimate branches or extensions thereof, or from owning and holding all or part of the stock of such subsidiary corporations, when the effect of such formation is not to substantially lessen competition.

Interlocking Directorates

Section 8—Interlocking directorates and officers. No person at the same time shall be a director in any two or more corporations, any one of which has capital, surplus, and undivided profits aggregating more than $1,000,000, engaged in whole or in part in commerce, other than banks, banking associations, trust companies, and common carriers subject to the Act to regulate commerce approved February fourth, eighteen hundred and eighty-seven, if such corporations are or shall have been theretofore, by virtue of their business and location or operation, competitors, so that the elimination of competition by agreement between them would constitute a violation of any of the provisions of any of the antitrust laws. The eligibility of a director under the foregoing provision shall be determined by the aggregate amount of the capital, surplus, and undivided profits, exclusive of dividends declared but not paid to stockholders, at the end of the fiscal year of said corporation next preceding the election of directors, and when a director has been elected in accordance with the provisions of this Act it shall be lawful for him to continue as such for one year thereafter.

Federal Trade Commission Act
Unfair Methods of Competition Prohibited

Section 5—Unfair methods of competition unlawful; prevention by Commission— declaration. Declaration of unlawfulness; power to prohibit unfair practices.

(a) (1) Unfair methods of competition in or affecting commerce, and unfair or deceptive acts or practices in or affecting commerce, are declared unlawful. . . .

(b) Any person, partnership, or corporation who violates an order of the Commission to cease and desist after it has become final, and while such order is in effect, shall forfeit and pay to the United States a civil penalty of not more than $5,000 for each violation, which shall accrue to the United States and may be recovered in a civil action brought by the Attorney General of the United States. Each separate violation of such an order shall be a separate offense, except that in the case of a violation through continuing failure or neglect to obey a final order of the Commission each day of continuance of such failure or neglect shall be deemed a separate offense.

Robinson-Patman Act (an Amendment to the Clayton Act)
Price Discrimination; Cost Justification; Changing Conditions

Section 2—Discrimination in price, services, or facilities.
(a) Price; selection of customers.

It shall be unlawful for any person engaged in commerce, in the course of such commerce, either directly or indirectly, to discriminate in price between different purchases of commodities of like grade and quality, where either or any of the purchasers involved in such discrimination are in commerce, where such commodities are sold for use, consumption, or resale within the United States or any Territory thereof or the District of Columbia or any insular possession or other place under the jurisdiction of the United States, and where the effect of such discrimination may be substantially to lessen competition or tend to create a monopoly in any line of commerce, or to injure, destroy, or prevent competition with any person who either grants or knowingly receives the benefit of such discrimination, or with customers of either of them: *Provided*, That nothing herein contained shall prevent differentials which make only due allowance for differences in the cost of manufacture, sale, or delivery resulting from the differing methods or quantities in which such commodities are to such purchasers sold or delivered: *Provided, however*, That the Federal Trade Commission may, after due investigation and hearing to all interested parties, fix and establish quantity limits, and revise the same as it finds necessary as to particular commodities or classes of commodities, where it finds that available purchasers in greater quantities are so few as to render differentials on account thereof unjustly discriminatory or promotive of monopoly in any line of commerce; and the foregoing shall then not be construed to permit differentials based on differences in quantities greater than those so fixed and established: *And provided further*, That nothing herein contained shall prevent persons engaged in selling goods, wares, or merchandise in commerce from selecting their own customers in bona fide transactions and not in restraint of trade: *And provided further*, That nothing herein contained shall prevent price changes from time to time where in response to changing conditions affecting the market for or the marketability of the goods concerned, such as but not limited to actual or imminent deterioration of perishable goods, obsolescence of seasonal goods, distress sales under court process, or sales in good faith in discontinuance of business in the goods concerned.

Meeting Competition

(b) Burden of rebutting prima-facie case of discrimination.

Upon proof being made, at any hearing on a complaint under this section, that there has been discrimination in price or services or facilities furnished, the burden of rebutting the prima-facie case thus made by showing justification shall be upon the person charged with a violation of this section, and unless justification shall be affirmatively shown, the Commission is authorized to issue an order terminating the discrimination: *Provided, however,* That nothing herein contained shall prevent a seller rebutting the prima-facie case thus made by showing that his lower price or the furnishing of services or facilities to any purchaser or purchasers was made in good faith to meet an equally low price of a competitor, or the services or facilities furnished by a competitor.

Brokerage Payments

(c) Payment or acceptance of commission, brokerage or other compensation.

It shall be unlawful for any person engaged in commerce, in the course of such commerce, to pay or grant, or to receive or accept, anything of value as a commission, brokerage, or other compensation, or any allowance of discount in lieu thereof, except for services rendered in connection with the sale or purchase of goods, wares, or merchandise, either to the other party to such transaction or to an agent, representative, or other intermediary therein where such intermediary is acting in fact for or in behalf, or is subject to the direct or indirect control, of any party to such transaction other than the person by whom such compensation is so granted or paid.

Promotional Allowances

(d) Payment for services or facilities for processing or sale.

It shall be unlawful for any person engaged in commerce to pay or contract for the payment of anything of value to or for the benefit of a customer of such person in the course of such commerce as compensation or in consideration for any services or facilities furnished by or through such customer in connection with the processing, handling, sale, or offering for sale of any products or commodities manufactured, sold, or offered for sale by such person, unless such payment of consideration is available on proportionally equal terms to all other customers competing in the distribution of such products or commodities.

Promotional Services

(e) Furnishing services or facilities for processing, handling, etc.

It shall be unlawful for any person to discriminate in favor of one purchaser against another purchaser or purchasers of a commodity bought for resale, with or without processing, or by contracting to furnish or furnishing, or by contributing to the furnishing of, any services or facilities connected with the processing, handling, sale, or offering for sale of such commodity so purchased upon terms not accorded to all purchasers on proportionally equal terms.

Buyer Discrimination

(f) Knowingly inducing or receiving discriminatory price.

It shall be unlawful for any person engaged in commerce, in the course of such commerce, knowingly to induce or receive a discrimination in price which is prohibited by this section.

Predatory Practices

Section 3—Discrimination in rebates, discounts, or advertising service charges; underselling in particular localities; penalties. It shall be unlawful for any person engaged in commerce, in the course of such commerce, to be a party to, or assist in, any transaction of sale, or contract to sell, which discriminates to his knowledge against competitors of the purchaser, in that, any discount, rebate, allowance, or advertising service charge is granted to the purchaser over and above any discount, rebate, allowance, or advertising service charge available at the time of such transaction to said competitors in respect of a sale of goods of like grade, quality, and quantity; to sell, or contract to sell, goods in any part of the United States at prices lower than those exacted by said person elsewhere in the United States for the purpose of destroying competition, or eliminating a competitor in such part of the United States; or, to sell, or contract to sell, goods at unreasonably lower prices for the purpose of destroying competition or eliminating a competitor.

Securities Statutes (Excerpts)

Securities Act of 1933

Definitions

Section 2. When used in this title, unless the context requires—

(1) The term "security" means any note, stock, treasury stock, bond, debenture, evidence of indebtedness, certificate of interest or participation in any profit-sharing agreement, collateral-trust certificate, preorganization certificate or subscription, transferable share, investment contract, voting-trust certificate, certificate of deposit for a security, fractional undivided interest in oil, gas, or other mineral rights, any put, call, straddle, option, or privilege on any security, certificate of deposit, or group or index of securities (including any interest therein or based on the value thereof), or any put, call, straddle, option, or privilege entered into on a national securities exchange relating to foreign currency, or, in general, any interest or participation in, temporary or interim certificate for, receipt for, guarantee of, or warrant or right to subscribe to or purchase, any of the foregoing.

Exempted Securities

Section 3. (a) Except as hereinafter expressly provided the provisions of this title shall not apply to any of the following classes of securities:

* * *

(2) Any security issued or guaranteed by the United States or any territory thereof, or by the District of Columbia, or by any State of the United States, or by any political subdivision of a State or Territory, or by any public instrumentality of one or more States or Territories, or by any person controlled or supervised by and acting as an instrumentality of the Government of the United States pursuant to authority granted by the Congress of the United States; or any certificate of deposit for any of the foregoing; or any security issued or guaranteed by any bank; or any security issued by or representing an interest in or a direct obligation of a Federal Reserve Bank. . . .

(3) Any note, draft, bill of exchange, or banker's acceptance which arises out of a current transaction or the proceeds of which have been or are to be used for current transactions, and which has a maturity at the time of issuance of not exceeding nine months, exclusive of days of grace, or any renewal thereof the maturity of which is likewise limited;

(4) Any security issued by a person organized and operated exclusively for religious, educational, benevolent, fraternal, charitable, or reformatory purposes and not for pecuniary profit, and no part of the net earnings of which inures to the benefit of any person, private stockholder, or individual; . . .

Exempted Transactions

Section 4. The provisions of section 5 shall not apply to—

(1) transactions by any person other than an issuer, underwriter, or dealer.

(2) transactions by an issuer not involving any public offering.

(3) transactions by a dealer (including an underwriter no longer acting as an underwriter in respect of the security involved in such transactions), except—

(A) transactions taking place prior to the expiration of forty days after the first date upon which the security was bona fide offered to the public by the issuer or by or through an underwriter,

(B) transactions in a security as to which a registration statement has been filed taking place prior to the expiration of forty days after the effective date of such registration statement or prior to the expiration of forty days after the first date upon which the security was bona fide offered to the public by the issuer or by or through an underwriter after such effective date, whichever is later (excluding in the computation of such forty days any time during which a stop order issued under section 8 is in effect as to the security), or such shorter period as the Commission may specify by rules and regulations or order, and

(C) transactions as to the securities constituting the whole or a part of an unsold allotment to or subscription by such dealer as a participant in the distribution of such securities by the issuer or by or through an underwriter.

With respect to transactions referred to in clause (B), if securities of the issuer have not previously been sold pursuant to an earlier effective registration statement the applicable period, instead of forty days, shall be ninety days, or such shorter period as the Commission may specify by rules and regulations or order.

(4) brokers' transactions, executed upon customers' orders on any exchange or in the over-the-counter market but not the solicitation of such orders.

(6) transactions involving offers or sales by an issuer solely to one or more accredited investors, if the aggregate offering price of an issue of securities offered in reliance on this paragraph does not exceed the amount allowed under section 3(b) of this title, if there is no advertising or public solicitation in connection with the transaction by the issuer or anyone acting on the issuer's behalf, and if the issuer files such notice with the Commission as the Commission shall prescribe.

Prohibitions Relating to Interstate Commerce and the Mails

Section 5. (a) Unless a registration statement is in effect as to a security, it shall be unlawful for any person, directly or indirectly—

(1) to make use of any means or instruments of transportation or communication in interstate commerce or of the mails to sell such security through the use or medium of any prospectus or otherwise; or

(2) to carry or cause to be carried through the mails or in interstate commerce, by any means or instruments of transportation, any such security for the purpose of sale or for delivery after sale.

(b) It shall be unlawful for any person, directly or indirectly—

(1) to make use of any means or instruments of transportation or communication in interstate commerce or of the mails to carry or transmit any prospectus relating to any security with respect to which a registration statement has been filed under this title, unless such prospectus meets the requirements of section 10, or

(2) to carry or to cause to be carried through the mails or in interstate commerce any such security for the purpose of sale or for delivery after sale, unless accompanied or preceded by a prospectus that meets the requirements of subsection (a) of section 10.

(c) It shall be unlawful for any person, directly, or indirectly, to make use of any means or instruments of transportation or communication in interstate commerce or of the mails to offer to sell or offer to buy through the use or medium of any prospectus or otherwise any security, unless a registration statement has been filed as to such security, or while the registration statement is the subject of a refusal order or stop order or (prior to the effective date of the registration statement) any public proceeding of examination under section 8.

Securities Exchange Act of 1934

Definitions and Application of Title

Section 3. (a) When used in this title, unless the context otherwise requires—

* * *

(4) The term "broker" means any person engaged in the business of effecting transactions in securities for the account of others, but does not include a bank.

(5) The term "dealer" means any person engaged in the business of buying and selling securities for his own account, through a broker or otherwise, but does not include a bank, or any person insofar as he buys or sells securities for his own account, either individually or in some fiduciary capacity, but not as part of a regular business.

* * *

(7) The term "director" means any director of a corporation or any person performing similar functions with respect to any organization, whether incorporated or unincorporated.

(8) The term "issuer" means any person who issues or proposes to issue any security; except that with respect to certificates of deposit for securities, voting-trust certificates, or collateral-trust certificates, or with respect to certificates of interest or shares in an unincorporated investment trust not having a board of directors or the fixed, restricted management, or unit type, the term "issuer" means the person or persons performing the acts and assuming the duties of depositor or manager pursuant to the provisions of the trust or other agreement or instrument under which such securities are issued; and except that with respect to equipment-trust certificates or like securities, the term "issuer" means the person by whom the equipment or property is, or is to be, used.

(9) The term "person" means a natural person, company, government, or political subdivision, agency, or instrumentality of a government.

Regulation of the Use of Manipulative and Deceptive Devices

Section 10. It shall be unlawful for any person, directly or indirectly, by the use of any means or instrumentality of interstate commerce or of the mails, or of any facility of any national securities exchange—

(a) To effect a short sale, or to use or employ any stop-loss order in connection with the purchase or sale, of any security registered on a national securities exchange, in contravention of such rules and regulations as the Commission may prescribe as necessary or appropriate in the public interest or for the protection of investors.

(b) To use or employ, in connection with the purchase or sale of any security registered on a national securities exchange or any security not so registered, any manipulative or deceptive device or contrivance in contravention of such rules and regulations as the

Commission may prescribe as necessary or appropriate in the public interest or for the protection of investors.

Sarbanes-Oxley Act of 2002

(Public Company Accounting Reform and Corporate Responsibility Act)
Title 15, Ch. 98, United States Code
Sec. 7241.—Corporate responsibility for financial reports
(a) Regulations required

The Commission shall, by rule, require, for each company filing periodic reports under section 78m(a) or 78o(d) of this title, that the principal executive officer or officers and the principal financial officer or officers, or persons performing similar functions, certify in each annual or quarterly report filed or submitted under either such section of this title that—

(1) the signing officer has reviewed the report;

(2) based on the officer's knowledge, the report does not contain any untrue statement of a material fact or omit to state a material fact necessary in order to make the statements made, in light of the circumstances under which such statements were made, not misleading;

(3) based on such officer's knowledge, the financial statements, and other financial information included in the report, fairly present in all material respects the financial condition and results of operations of the issuer as of, and for, the periods presented in the report;

(4) the signing officers—

(A) are responsible for establishing and maintaining internal controls;

(B) have designed such internal controls to ensure that material information relating to the issuer and its consolidated subsidiaries is made known to such officers by others within those entities, particularly during the period in which the periodic reports are being prepared;

(C) have evaluated the effectiveness of the issuer's internal controls as of a date within 90 days prior to the report; and

(D) have presented in the report their conclusions about the effectiveness of their internal controls based on their evaluation as of that date;

(5) the signing officers have disclosed to the issuer's auditors and the audit committee of the board of directors (or persons fulfilling the equivalent function)—

(A) all significant deficiencies in the design or operation of internal controls which could adversely affect the issuer's ability to record, process, summarize, and report financial data and have identified for the issuer's auditors any material weaknesses in internal controls; and

(B) any fraud, whether or not material, that involves management or other employees who have a significant role in the issuer's internal controls; and

(6) the signing officers have indicated in the report whether or not there were significant changes in internal controls or in other factors that could significantly affect internal controls subsequent to the date of their evaluation, including any corrective actions with regard to significant deficiencies and material weaknesses.

Glossary

Abnormally dangerous activity *see* ultrahazardous activity.

Absolute liability liability for an act or activity that causes harm or injury even though the alleged wrongdoer was not at fault.

Absolute privilege a defense in a defamation suit affirming that the defendant had an unconditional right to make the statements in question and be free from litigation. This most often applies to statements made by members of a legislature as part of the deliberation process.

Acceptance the offeree's notification or expression to the offeror that he agrees to be bound by the terms of the offeror's proposal, thereby creating a contract. The trend is to allow acceptance by any means that reasonably notifies the offeror of the acceptance.

Accord in a debtor/creditor relationship, an agreement between the parties to settle a dispute for some partial payment. The creditor has a right of action against the debtor.

Accord and satisfaction in a debtor/creditor relationship, an agreement between the parties to settle a dispute, and subsequent payment. The agreement is an accord because the creditor has a right of action against the debtor. Accord and satisfaction is complete when payment has been tendered.

Account receivable a debt that arises in the course of business that is not supported by negotiable paper; for example, the charge accounts at a department store.

Actual authority power of an agent to bind a principal; the power is from an express or an implied agreement between principal and agent.

Adjudication the legal process of resolving a dispute.

Adjudicatory hearing in administrative law, a formal process involving a regulatory agency and the private parties involved in a complaint; procedures are more informal than a court trial, but protect due process rights.

Administrative agency a governmental bureau established by Congress (or the president) to execute certain functions of Congress. Agencies transact government business and may write and enforce regulations under the authority of Congress or the president.

Administrative law rules and regulations established by administrative agencies to execute the functions given them by Congress or the president; also the law that governs how agencies must operate.

Administrative law judge a person appointed to conduct an administrative hearing about a regulatory matter. Usually attorneys who work for the administrative agency, such as the Federal Trade Commission, serve in this capacity. They run a trial-like proceeding and issue a decision in the matter based on the facts determined at the hearing.

Adversary system of justice a legal system in which the parties to a dispute present their own arguments and are responsible for asserting their legal rights.

Adverse possession (easement by prescription) a method by which one obtains the right to property by following specific rules under which a non-owner may be declared to be the lawful owner. This normally requires open possession of the property and restraining others from use of the property for a period of time required by state law, and may require payment of property taxes.

Affirm in a court of appeals, or supreme court, a decision to declare that a judgment entered by a lower court is valid and will stand as decided.

Affirmative action employment programs, often mandated by federal law, to remedy discriminatory employment practices affecting racial minorities and women. Programs seek to remedy past patterns of discrimination and discrimination that results from facially neutral employment practices.

Affirmative defense defendant's response to plaintiff's claim that attacks the plaintiff's legal right to bring the action rather than attacking the truth of the claim. An example of an affirmative defense is the running of the statute of limitations.

Agency a relationship between two persons, by explicit or implicit agreement, where one (the agent) may act on behalf of the other (the principal) and bind the principal by words and actions.

Agency by estoppel an agency created by operation of law that arises when the principal, by failing to properly supervise the agent, allows the agent to exercise too many powers, thereby allowing others to be justified in thinking that the agent possesses the powers the agent claimed to have.

Agency coupled with an interest when an agent has an interest in the subject matter that is relevant to the agency relationship; this is often an interest in a specific piece of property.

Agency order in administrative law, a statement by a regulatory agency, under its powers granted by Congress and subject to procedural requirements, to inform parties subject to the rules what they must do to comply with a rule they are violating.

Agency regulation in administrative law, a rule issued by a regulatory agency, under its powers granted by Congress and subject to procedural requirements that detail the legal obligations of affected parties.

Agency shop in labor law, a unionized workplace where employees who are not union members must pay agency fees to the union for being the sole bargaining agent for all employees; illegal in states that have right-to-work laws.

Agent a person authorized to act for or to represent another, called the principal.

Agreement a "meeting of the minds"; a mutual understanding between the parties as to the substance of a contract.

Agreement (U.C.C.) means the bargain of the parties in fact as found in their language or by implication from other circumstances including course of dealing or usage of trade or course of performance as provided in the U.C.C.

Alternative dispute resolution a process by which the parties to a dispute resolve it through a mechanism other than litigation in court. Alternative dispute resolution includes arbitration, negotiation, and mediation.

Ambient air under the Clean Air Act, ambient air is the air outside of buildings or other enclosures.

Amicus curiae a party not directly involved in the litigation but who participates as a friend of the court, usually by submitting briefs in favor of one position at the appellate level.

Amount in controversy the damages claimed or the relief demanded by the injured party in a dispute.

Answer the response of a defendant to the plaintiff's complaint, denying in part or in whole the charges made by the plaintiff.

Anticipatory breach the assertion by a party to a contract that she will not perform a future obligation as required by the contract.

Antitrust federal and state statutes to protect commerce from certain restraints of trade, such as price fixing and monopolization.

Apparent authority that authority a reasonable person would assume an agent possesses in light of the principal's conduct.

Appeal requesting removal from a court of a decided or an adjudicated case to a court of appellate jurisdiction for the purpose of obtaining a review of the decision.

Appellant the party, either the plaintiff or the defendant, who invokes the appellate jurisdiction of a superior court.

Appellate courts courts that have jurisdiction to review cases decided in trial courts to ensure that the law was properly applied to a case in question

Appellate jurisdiction the power of a court to revise or correct the proceedings in a case already acted upon by a lower court or administrative agency.

Appellee the party against whom an appeal is taken.

Arbiter in an arbitration proceeding, the person granted the authority to decide a controversy.

Arbitrary and capricious a judgment or decision, by an administrative agency or judge, which is without basis in fact or in law. Such a decision is often referred to as being without a rational basis.

Arbitration a means of settling disputes between parties when they submit the matter to a neutral third party of their choosing, who resolves the dispute by issuing a binding award. A popular alternative to the court system for resolving disputes due to lower cost and greater speed.

Articles of incorporation under state law, a document that every new corporation must file providing information about the name, address, and purpose of the corporation, as well as a statement about the stock that may be issued and the names of the principal officers.

Artificial seniority in employment discrimination law, a remedy that may be granted giving minority or women workers extra years of work credit to make up for past acts of discrimination by their employer.

Artisan's lien a possessory lien given as security for payment to a person who has made improvements to another person's property. The statutory right of an artisan to keep possession of the object that she has worked on until paid for the work.

Assault any word or action intended to cause another to be in fear of immediate physical harm.

Assault and battery intentionally causing another to anticipate immediate physical harm through some threat and then carrying out the threatened activity.

Assignment a transfer of one's interest in property or a contract to another person.

Assumption of risk common-law doctrine under which a plaintiff may not recover for the injuries or damages that result from an activity in which the plaintiff willingly participated. A defense used by the defendant in a negligence case when the plaintiff had knowledge of the danger, voluntarily exposed himself to the danger, and was injured.

Attachment the legal process of seizing another's property in accordance with a writ or judicial order for the purpose of security satisfaction of a judgment to be rendered.

Attachment (U.C.C.) when the requirements of a security interest (agreement, value, and conveyable rights in the collateral) exist, the security agreement becomes enforceable between parties and is said to attach.

Attainment areas   under the Clean Air Act, areas that meet federal standards for major pollutants; they are designated "prevention of significant deterioration areas," because they are not allowed to become more polluted.

Authorization card   a card signed by an employee at a worksite targeted for possible unionization; the card authorizes the union to request that an election be held to determine if all workers will be represented by the union.

Award   the decision that settles an arbitration proceeding. It is normally the determination of a single arbiter, but can be the decision of a panel of arbitrators that heard the dispute. The decision may be in writing, but need not give a rationale.

Back pay   compensation for past economic losses (lost wages and fringe benefits) caused by an employer's discriminatory employment practices, such as limiting promotion opportunities for older workers.

Balance of payments   an official accounting that records a country's foreign transactions; exports are recorded as credits and imports as debits.

Bankruptcy   a proceeding under the law that is initiated by an insolvent individual or business (a voluntary bankruptcy), or by creditors (an involuntary bankruptcy) seeking to have the insolvent's assets distributed among the creditors and to then discharge the insolvent from further obligation or to reorganize the insolvent's debt structure.

Bankruptcy trustee   in bankruptcy proceedings the person given authority to manage the assets of the bankrupt for the benefit of the creditors.

Bargaining agent   the union recognized and certified by the National Labor Relations Board, upon election by a majority of the workers, to be the exclusive representative of employees in a bargaining unit (worksite) to determine working conditions and wages.

Battery   the intentional unallowed touching of another. The "touching" may involve a mere touch that is offensive, or an act of violence that causes serious injury.

Bearer   (U.C.C.) the person in possession of an instrument, document of title, or certificated security payable to bearer or indorsed in blank.

Bearer instrument   an instrument payable to bearer (the person in possession); it must specify that it is payable to bearer, to cash, or to a specific bearer.

Beyond a reasonable doubt   in criminal law, the general rule that for a judge or jury to find a defendant guilty there can be no significant doubt that the defendant violated a criminal statute.

Bilateral contract   a contract formed by the mutual exchange of promises of the parties.

Bill of exchange   an unconditional order in writing, addressed by one person to another, signed by the person giving it, requiring the person to whom it is addressed to pay on demand or at a fixed or determinable future date a certain sum of money. Same as a draft under the U.C.C.

Bill of lading   (U.C.C.) a document evidencing the receipt of goods for shipment issued by one engaged in the business of transporting goods; includes an airbill.

Blue Sky laws   name given to state laws that regulate the offer and sale of securities.

Board of directors   the principals of a corporation, elected by shareholders, responsible for governing the business, especially as to major decisions; directors appoint corporate officers and agents to act on their behalf in running the business day to day. Boards are usually composed of inside directors, such as the president of the company, and outside or independent directors, who have no employment relationship with the company.

Bona fide occupational qualification (BFOQ)   employment in particular jobs may not be limited to persons of a particular sex or religion unless the employer can show that sex or religion is an actual qualification for performing the job. Not permitted on the basis of race.

Bond   an evidence of debt carrying a specified amount (principal), schedule of interest payments, and a date for redemption of the face value of the bond.

Bondholders   creditors of a business, whose evidence of debt is a bond issued by the business.

Boycott   an effort to organize a group to not deal with some party, such as a group of retailers refusing to buy products from manufacturers who do certain things not liked by the retailers, or a group of labor unions agreeing not to handle any products made by a certain company.

Breach of contract   failure, without a legal excuse, of a promisor to perform the terms agreed to in a contract.

Bribery   the offering, giving, receiving, or soliciting of something of value for the purpose of influencing the action of an official in the discharge of public or legal duties.

Brief   an appellate brief is a written document, prepared by an attorney, to be the basis for an appeal of a case to an appellate court. It contains the points of law the attorney wants to establish, with the arguments and authorities to support that view.

Bubble concept   under the Clean Air Act, when a polluting facility or a geographic area is treated as a single pollution source, in which one may build additional polluting facilities so long as total pollution is lowered within the "bubble."

Business judgment rule   a principle of corporate law under which a court will not challenge the business decisions of a corporate officer or director made with ordinary care and in good faith.

Business necessity   justification for an otherwise prohibited discriminatory employment practice based on employer's proof that (1) the otherwise prohibited employment practice is essential for the safety and efficiency of the business, and (2) no reasonable alternative with a lesser impact exists.

Business tort a noncontractual breach of a legal duty by a business resulting in damages or injury to another; includes certain torts that can only occur in business situations.

Bylaws in corporation law, the rules that regulate and govern the internal operations of a corporation with respect to directors, shareholders, and officers rights and duties.

Cartel a combination of independent producers in an industry attempting to limit competition by acting together to fix prices, divide markets, or restrict entry into the industry.

Cashier's check a bank's check, drawn on itself, and signed by the cashier of the bank or other bank official, obligating the bank to pay the payee a certain sum of money on demand.

Cause in fact an act or omission without which an event would not have occurred. Courts express this in the form of a rule commonly referred to as the "but for" rule: the injury to a person would not have happened but for the conduct of the wrongdoer.

Cause of action the facts that give rise to a person's legal right of redress against another.

Caveat emptor Latin for "let the buyer beware."

Cease and desist order an order by an administrative agency or a court prohibiting a firm from conducting activities that the agency or court deems illegal.

Certificate of deposit a written bank document that provides evidence of a deposit made at a bank, for a certain time, that pays a certain rate of interest that is promised to be paid to the depositor or to another party as ordered.

Certificate of incorporation *see* corporate charter.

Certification mark in trademark law, any symbol, name, or word used to identify the location or other aspect of the origin of a product.

Challenge for cause challenge by an attorney to a prospective juror for which some cause or reason is asserted.

Charter *see* corporate charter.

Chattel in property law, an article of personal property, but not real property. These are things that are movable.

Check a draft or order drawn upon a bank, and payable on demand, signed by the maker or drawer, that is an unconditional promise to pay a certain sum of money to the order of the payee named on the instrument. It normally must say "pay to the order of" on the face of the check.

Citizen-suit provisions in regulatory law, a right provided by Congress for private citizens to bring a suit before a federal court to force compliance with the law passed by Congress; in some instances, the cost of the suit is borne by the government or the defendant if the private party wins the case.

Civil law (1) laws, written or unwritten, that specify the duties that exist between and among people, as opposed to criminal matters. (2) Codified or statutory law, used in many Western European countries and Japan, as distinguished from the common or judge-made law used in England and the United States.

Close corporation (or closely held corporation) a corporation that has stock that is not allowed to be widely held; the number of shareholders is limited and usually, unlike in a publicly held corporation, the shareholders are active in oversight of the firm.

Closed shop a worksite where one must be a union member before obtaining work.

Closing argument oral presentation to the jury by the attorneys after the plaintiff and defendant have stated their cases and before the judge charges the jury.

Collateral property pledged as a secondary security for the satisfaction of a debt in the event the debtor does not repay as expected.

Collective bargaining the process by which a union and an employer arrive at and enforce agreements regarding employment of workers represented by a union.

Collective mark a trademark or service mark used by the members of a cooperative association to identify the goods and services they produce.

Commerce clause that part of the U. S. Constitution that gives Congress the power to regulate interstate commerce; the basis of much federal regulation.

Commercial speech expressions made by businesses about commercial matters or about political matters; the First Amendment protects most truthful speech in this category.

Common law law developed by American and English courts by decisions in cases. Unlike statutes, it is not passed by a legislative body and is not a specific set of rules; rather, it must be interpreted from the many decisions that have been written over time.

Common stock the shares of ownership in a corporation having the lowest priority with regard to payment of dividends and distribution of the corporation's assets upon dissolution.

Community property property owned in common by husband and wife.

Comparative negligence a defense to negligence whereby the plaintiff's damages are reduced by the proportion his fault bears to the total injury he has suffered.

Compensatory damages a sum awarded to an injured party that is equivalent to her actual damages or injuries sustained. The rationale is to restore the injured party to the position she was in before the injury.

Complaint the initial pleading by the plaintiff in a civil action that informs the defendant of the material facts on which the plaintiff bases the lawsuit.

Compliance program under the federal Sentencing Guidelines, a company that maintains a compliance program with regulations that apply to the company will be subject to less punishment in case of violations of the law than if there is no good-faith effort to have internal procedures to help ensure that the law is followed within the organization.

Concentration in antitrust law, the percent of market share (usually sales volume) that one or more firms control in a given product or geographic market; used as a measure of the degree of competition within a market.

Concentration ratio fraction of total market sales made by a specified number of an industry's largest firms. Four-firm and eight-firm concentration ratios are the most frequently used.

Concerted activity in labor law, actions by employees, such as a strike or other mutual activity that furthers their employment interests, protected by the National Labor Relations Act.

Concurrent jurisdiction when two different courts are each empowered to deal with the subject matter at issue in a dispute.

Concurring opinion at the appellate court level, an opinion filed by one or more of the justices in which the justices agree with the majority opinion but state separate views or reasons for the decision.

Condition a provision in a contract providing that upon the occurrence of some event the obligations of the parties will be set in motion, suspended, or terminated.

Condition precedent in a contract, a condition that must be met before the other party's obligations arise.

Condition subsequent in a contract, a condition which, if met, discharges the obligations of the other party.

Conditional privilege a defense in defamation cases affirming that the defendant published in good faith or as part of a duty to publish; it protects the defendant in a case that may otherwise be actionable.

Confiscation the act whereby a sovereign takes private property without a proper public purpose or just compensation.

Conflict of laws body of law establishing the circumstances in which a state or federal court shall apply the laws of another state, rather than the laws of the state in which it is sitting, to decide a case before it.

Conglomerate merger a merger between two companies that do not compete with or purchase from each other.

Consent a voluntary agreement, implied or expressed, to submit to a proposition or act of another.

Consent decree a judgment entered by consent of the parties and approval of a court, whereby the defendant agrees to stop alleged illegal activity without admitting guilt or wrongdoing. Often used to settle complaints by regulatory agencies.

Consideration in a contract, the thing of value bargained for in exchange for a promise; the inducement or motivation to a contract; the element that keeps the contract from being gratuitous and, therefore, makes it legally binding on the parties.

Consignment the act or process of depositing goods to be sold in the custody of a third party.

Constitution the fundamental law of a nation; a written document establishing the powers of the government and its basic structure; the controlling authority over all other law.

Constructive notice information or understanding that is equivalent to a formal notice of facts that a person using proper diligence would be expected to know.

Consumer expectation test in tort law, as applied to products, the level of safe performance an ordinary consumer could expect from a product under the circumstances.

Consumer reports often called credit reports; files maintained by companies concerning consumers' credit history and evidence of income and debt; sold for legitimate business purposes.

Contempt of court any act that obstructs a court in the administration of justice, or that is calculated to lessen the court's authority.

Contract a legal relationship consisting of the rights and duties of contracting parties; a promise or set of promises constituting an agreement between the parties that gives each a legal duty to the other and also the right to seek a remedy for the breach of those duties. The elements of a contract include agreement, consideration, legal capacity, lawful subject matter, and genuine consent.

Contract (U.C.C.) the total legal obligation which results from the parties' agreement as affected by the U.C.C. and any other applicable rules of law.

Contract clause the statement in the constitution that "No State shall . . . pass any . . . Law impairing the Obligation of Contracts. . . ." Arises primary when a state attempts to reduce its obligations created by contracts with private parties.

Contractual capacity the mental capacity required by law for a party entering into a contract to be bound by that contract. Generally, minors, intoxicated persons, and the insane lack capacity to contract.

Contributory negligence as a complete defense to negligence, an act or a failure to act that produces a lack of reasonable care on the part of the plaintiff that is the proximate cause of the injury incurred.

Conversion the unauthorized taking of property, permanently or temporarily, that deprives its rightful owner of its lawful use.

Cooperative two or more persons or enterprises that act through a common agent to achieve a common objective.

Copyright a grant to an author or a publisher of an exclusive right to print, reprint, publish, copy, and sell literary work, musical compositions, works of art, and motion pictures for the life of the author plus an additional fifty years.

Corporate charter a certificate issued by a state government recognizing the existence of a corporation as a legal entity; it is issued automatically upon filing the information required by state law and payment of a fee.

Corporate social responsibility the belief that businesses have a duty to society that goes beyond obeying the law and maximizing profits.

Corporation a business organized under the laws of a state that allow an artificial legal being to exist for purposes of doing business in its name.

Cost-benefit analysis computing the costs of an activity compared to the estimated monetary value of the benefits from the activity.

Cost justification in antitrust law, a defense available in price discrimination (Robinson-Patman) cases to show that a buyer was offered a good at a lower price than another buyer because of differences in the costs of serving the two customers.

Counterclaim a claim a defendant asserts against the plaintiff.

Counterfeiting to imitate, forge, or copy, without authority, and to pass off as original with an intent to deceive. This may be done for money, securities, copyrights, patents, trademarks, and other protected property.

Counteroffer an offeree's response to an offeror rejecting the offeror's original offer and at the same time making a new offer.

Court of appeals courts with the power to review cases decided in trial courts; in the federal court system and in about half the states, these are intermediate courts between trial courts and supreme courts.

Court of original jurisdiction *see* original jurisdiction.

Covenant an agreement between two or more parties in which one or more of the parties pledges that some duty or obligation is or is not to be done.

Covenant in property law, an agreement by two or more parties, in writing, that places certain restrictions on the use of property or obligates the owner of the property to take specific actions with respect to the land. These obligations normally go with the property as it passes from owner to owner over time.

Covenant not to compete part of an agreement in the sale of a business for the seller not to compete with the buyer for a given time in a given market; in employment law, it is an agreement, not enforceable in all states, for an employee not to go to work for a competitor for a certain time after leaving current employment.

Craft union a union organized on the basis of a specified set of skills or occupations.

Credit rating an opinion as to the reliability of a person in paying debts.

Credit report a report made by a consumer reporting agency concerning the financial condition and credit character of a person or business.

Creditor a person to whom a debt is owed by a debtor.

Crime a violation of the law that is punishable by the state or nation. Crimes are classified as felonies and misdemeanors.

Criminal law governs or defines legal wrongs, or crimes, committed against society. Wrongdoers are punished for violating the rules of society. A person found guilty of a criminal offense is usually fined or imprisoned.

Cross complaint during the pleadings, a claim the defendant asserts against the plaintiff. *See* also counterclaim.

Cross examination examination by the attorney representing the adverse party after the other party has examined her witness.

Cruel and unusual punishment punishment that is disproportionate to the offense and is a shock to the moral sense of the community; prohibited by the Eighth Amendment.

Damages money compensation sought or awarded as a remedy for a breach of contract or for tortious acts.

Debt a sum of money due by an express agreement.

Debt collection agency a business that is paid to or buys the right to collect the debts owed by consumers to a business.

Debt securities an obligation of a corporation, usually in the form of a bond, issued for a certain value at a certain rate of interest to be repaid at a certain time.

Debtor a person who owes a debt to a creditor.

Debtor in possession in bankruptcy law, the debtor in Chapter 11 bankruptcy who remains in control of a business or assets, or the trustee appointed to control a business or assets.

Deception in consumer protection law, a claim, practice, or omission likely to mislead a reasonable consumer and cause the consumer to suffer a loss.

Decertification a process by which employees vote to withdraw their consent to union representation; an election is conducted by the National Labor Relations Board.

Deed a conveyance of realty; a writing signed by a grantor, whereby title to realty is transferred from one to another.

Defamation an intentional false communication, either published or publicly spoken, that injures another's reputation or good name.

Default the omission or failure to perform a contractual duty to fulfill a promise or discharge an obligation to pay interest or principal on a debt when due. Under the U.C.C., when default occurs may be defined by the parties to the agreement.

Default judgment judgment entered against a party who failed to appear in court to defend against a claim brought by another party.

Defendant the party against whom an action or lawsuit is brought.

Defense that offered and alleged by a defendant as a reason in law or fact why the plaintiff should not recover, or recover less than what she seeks.

Delaney clause the portion of the Food, Drug and Cosmetic Act that any food additive that is found to cause cancer in animals may not be marketed.

Delegation the legal transfer of power and authority to another to perform duties.

Delegation of powers the constitutional right of Congress to authorize government agencies to perform certain legal duties.

Demurrer an older term for a motion to dismiss a claim for failure to state a cause of action. *See* motion to dismiss.

Deposition sworn testimony—written or oral—of a person taken outside the court.

Design defect in products liability litigation, a claim that a consumer suffered an injury because a safer product design was not used.

Detrimental reliance *see* promissory estoppel.

Direct examination the initial examination of a witness by the party on whose behalf the witness has been called.

Directed verdict verdict granted by the court on the grounds that the jury could reasonably reach only one conclusion on the basis of the evidence presented during the trial.

Directors *see* board of directors.

Disability under the Americans with Disabilities Act, a physical or mental condition that affects a major life activity that limits the ability of a person to perform a particular job function.

Discharge the termination of one's obligation. Under contract law, discharge occurs either when the parties have performed their obligations in the contract, or when events, the conduct of the parties, or the operation of law releases parties from performing.

Disclosure requirements in securities law, the revealing of financial and other information relevant to investors considering buying securities; the requirement that sufficient information be provided prospective investors so that they can make an informed evaluation of a security.

Discovery the process by which the parties to a lawsuit gather information from each other to reduce the scope of what will be presented in court; process is determined by rules of procedure and may be limited by the court hearing the case.

Discrimination illegal treatment of a person or group (intentional or unintentional) based on race, color, national origin, religion, sex, disability or age. This includes the failure to remedy the effects of past discrimination.

Disparagement a false communication that injures a person in his business or profession.

Disparate impact in employment discrimination law, when an apparently neutral rule regarding hiring or treatment of employees works to discriminate against a protected class of employees.

Disparate treatment differential treatment of employees or applicants on the basis of their race, color, religion, sex, national origin, or age (for example, when applicants of a particular race are required to pass tests not required of other applicants).

Dissenting opinion an opinion written by one or more appellate judges or justices explaining why they disagree with the decision of the majority of the court in a given case.

Dissolution the process of terminating or winding up a corporation or partnership that changes the nature of the organization, or ends it completely. This may come about involuntarily, such as through forced bankruptcy, or may be voluntary, as when a board of directors approves the end of the life of a company.

Diversity jurisdiction when parties to a suit are from different jurisdictions (states or nations), it may create a basis for having a case heard in federal court.

Diversity of citizenship an action in which the plaintiff and the defendant are citizens of different states.

Dividend a distribution to corporate shareholders in proportion to the number of shares held.

Draft a written order signed by a party (the drawer), instructing another party (the drawee, usually a bank) to pay a certain sum of money, on demand, to a third party (the payee).

Due care the degree of care that a reasonable person can be expected to exercise to avoid harm reasonably foreseeable if such care is not taken.

Due process constitutional limitation requiring that a person has a right not to be deprived of life, liberty, or property without a fair and just hearing.

Duress when coercion or threats are used to get another person to act in a way, such as sign a contract, that the person would not otherwise agree to.

Easement the right to use the property of another in a particular manner. Most commonly, this is a right of access to cross one piece of property to reach another piece of property or the right to have utilities go across, on, or under property. It is a right that is said to run with the land.

Effluent charge a fee, fine, or tax imposed on a polluting activity.

Electronic fund transfer monetary transactions made electronically (telephone, computer).

Embezzlement statutory offense when a person fraudulently appropriates for her own use the property or money entrusted to her by another.

Eminent domain the power of the government to take private property for public use for fair compensation.

Emission offset under the Clean Air Act, a requirement that for a polluting facility to be built or expanded, the owner must reduce certain pollutants by as much or more than the new pollution to be generated; this may be done by paying other polluters to reduce emissions.

Emotional distress a tort action for damages to compensate a person for mental injury suffered due to another's actions.

Employee handbooks manuals issued by employers to inform employees of their duties and rights as employees; often used as evidence of an employment contract that must be followed by both parties.

Employment-at-will a doctrine under the common law providing that unless otherwise explicitly stated an employment contract was for an indefinite term and could be terminated at any time by either party without notice.

Enabling statute legislative enactment granting power to an administrative agency.

En banc legal proceedings before or by the court as a whole rather than before or by a single judge, or a panel of judges.

Endangered species in environmental law, a list of animals and plants declared by the government to be in danger of becoming extinct; violators may be prosecuted for killing endangered animals or plants or injuring their habitat.

Environmental Impact Statement statements required by National Environmental Protection Act of agencies when they make recommendations concerning proposed legislation or other federal activity that significantly affects the quality of the environment.

Equal protection clause Section 1 of the Fourteenth Amendment to the Constitution, providing that states treat all persons subject to state laws in a similar manner. "No State shall . . . deny to any person within its jurisdiction the equal protection of the laws."

Equitable remedy the means by which a court enforces a right adjudicated in equity or prevents or redresses the violation of such a right. Remedies include specific performance, injunction, recission, reformation and declaratory judgment.

Equity (1) in securities law, an ownership claim on a business interest; usually a security with no repayment terms; (2) a legal system that operates alongside the "law," and is concerned with achieving justice in cases when courts of law are incompetent to act.

Error of law a determination by an appeals court that a lower court, usually a trial court, made a mistake in applying the law to the facts that were established at trial.

Estoppel a principle that provides that a person is barred from denying or alleging certain facts because of that person's previous conduct, allegation, or denial.

Ethics the duties which a member of society owes to other members.

Evidence in procedural law, the legal matters—oral, written or physical testimony—that may be presented at a trial or at other legal proceeding for use in resolving a dispute.

Excessive fine an excessive penalty that is held to violate the Eighth Amendment. This occurs when a fine or penalty, such as a prison term, is too large relative to the legal violation that occurred.

Excise tax a tax on the sale of a good. A specific tax is a fixed tax per unit of the good sold. An ad valorem tax is a fixed percentage of the value of the good. *See* tariff.

Exclusionary rule under the Fourth Amendment, as interpreted by the courts, evidence that has been gathered in violation of the search-and-seizure rules cannot be used against a defendant at trial.

Exclusive dealing contract an agreement between two firms to deal only with each other for certain products or services.

Exclusive jurisdiction the power of a court over a particular subject matter as provided by statute to the exclusion of other courts.

Exculpatory contract a contract that releases one of the parties from liability for their wrongdoings.

Executed contract a contract that has been fully performed by the parties.

Executive order under powers granted by the Constitution, or by Congress in legislation, an order by the president to establish or enforce a legal requirement.

Executory contract a contract that has not been performed by the parties.

Exemplary damages *see* punitive damages.

Exemptions from registration in securities law, provisions that allow certain securities to be sold without meeting the usual registration requirements with the Securities and Exchange Commission; does not exempt the securities from other aspects of securities laws.

Exhaustion of administrative remedies a doctrine providing that in instances when a statute provides an administrative remedy, relief must be sought through all appropriate agency channels before a court can act to consider other relief.

Ex parte Latin for "by one party."

Expert witness a witness with professional training or skill in helping evaluate evidence in a case.

Export products manufactured in one country, and then shipped and sold in another.

Express authority in agency law, when an agent has clear authority, verbal or written, to act on behalf of a principal for certain matters.

Express contract a contract that is oral or written, as opposed to being implied from the conduct of the parties (*see* implied contract).

Express warranty a promise, in addition to an underlying sales agreement, that goes beyond the terms of the sales agreement and under which the promisor assures the description, performance, or quality of the goods.

Expropriation the taking of a privately owned property by a government. Governments are required to, but at times do not pay compensation for such takings.

Ex rel (Ex relatione) Latin for "on the relation or information."

Externalities effects, good or bad, on parties not directly involved in the production or use of a product. Pollution is an example of a bad effect, or negative externality.

Failing firm defense in antitrust law, a rule that firms may be allowed to merge that would not be allowed to do so otherwise because one of the firms is in danger of going out of business anyway.

Failure to warn in products liability cases, when a producer is found liable in tort for not warning consumers of dangers the producer knew existed or should have known existed.

Fair use the right of persons other than the owner of copyrighted material to use it in a reasonable manner without the consent of the owner; factors include the purpose of the use, the extent of the use, and the economic effect of the use.

False imprisonment (false arrest) the intentional detention or restraint of an individual by another.

Featherbedding a practice, under a union rule, in which the number of employees used, or the amount of time taken, to perform a job is unnecessarily high.

Federal question a question in a case in which one of the parties, usually the plaintiff, is asserting a right based on a federal law.

Fee simple in property law, an absolute ownership interest in an estate (real property) without restrictions; the strongest form of property ownership.

Fellow-servant rule a rule that precludes an injured employee from recovering from his employer when the injury results from the negligent conduct of a fellow employee.

Felony a serious class of crime (such as rape, murder, or robbery) that may be punishable by death or imprisonment in excess of one year.

Fiduciary a person having a duty, generally created by his own undertaking, to act in good faith for the benefit of another in matters related to that undertaking. A fiduciary duty is the highest standard of duty implied by law.

Firm offer (U.C.C.) a signed writing by a merchant promising to keep an offer open. In contrast to an option, a firm offer does not require consideration to make the offer irrevocable.

Floating lien a security interest retained in collateral even when the collateral changes in character, classification, or location. An inventory loan in which the lender receives a security interest or general claim on a company's inventory. Under the U.C.C., such security is not only in inventory or accounts

of the debtor at the time of the original loan, but also in after-acquired inventory or accounts.

Foreign exchange rate the price of a country's currency stated in terms of the currency of another country.

Foreseeable dangers in tort law, the duty to reasonably anticipate when an injury is likely to result from certain acts or failure to act to protect others.

Forgery the false making, or the material altering, of a document with the intent to defraud.

Forum non conveniens a rule that allows a court, in equity, to decline jurisdiction over a case when it believes that the matter would be better resolved in another forum. Usually this is invoked when most of the parties and witnesses to a case are in another location, making it more convenient for the trial to be held there rather than where the case was filed.

Franchise a contract between a parent company (franchisor) and an operating company (franchisee) to allow the franchisee to run a business with the brand name of the parent company, so long as the terms of the contract concerning methods of operation are followed.

Fraud an intentional misrepresentation of a material fact designed to induce the person receiving the miscommunication to rely upon it to her detriment, so that a loss is suffered.

Free trade when all goods and services can be freely imported and exported without special taxes or restrictions being imposed.

Free trade zone areas where foreign merchandise may be brought without formal customs entry and payment of duty for most legal purposes including storage, grading, sampling, manufacturing, cleaning, or packaging. Duties are paid when the products enter the domestic market.

Fringe benefits medical, accident, and life insurance; retirement benefits; profit sharing; bonus plans; leave; and other terms and conditions of employment other than wage or salary compensation.

Frustration a doctrine in contract law that allows a party to be relieved of a duty to perform because the purpose of the contract no longer exists. Circumstances occurred after the contract was formed that make performance irrelevant or impossible.

Full warranty defined by the Magnuson-Moss Warranty Act as an unlimited warranty for repairs or product replacement for problems that arise with a product within the warranty period.

Garnishment a legal process by which a creditor appropriates a debtor's wages, or property in the hands of a third party.

General agent a person serving as an agent who is authorized to act for the principal in all matters relating to a particular business or employment relationship.

General creditor a lender with no lien or security to assist in the payment of his debt or claim.

General jurisdiction a power of a court to hear all controversies that may be brought before it.

General partner a partner in a limited partnership or any partner in a general partnership who accepts, or has imposed by law, personal liability for all debts of the partnership.

General verdict a verdict whereby the jury finds either for the plaintiff or the defendant in general terms.

Geographic market in antitrust law, the area in the country in which a business has market power.

Golden parachute a severance agreement a manager of a corporation negotiates in return for withdrawing opposition to a tender offer.

Good faith (U.C.C.) honesty in fact in the conduct or transaction in question.

Goodwill an intangible property that is generally considered to be the expected continued business that will come due to the existing reputation of a firm.

Gratuitous agent an agent who volunteers services without an agreement or expectation of compensation, but whose voluntary consent creates the rights and liabilities of the agency relationship.

Grievance in labor law, a complaint filed by an employer or a union regarding failure to comply with terms of a collective bargaining agreement or to negotiate in good faith; also a dispute resolution procedure that workers must follow if represented by a union.

Guarantor one who makes a guaranty. Person who becomes secondarily liable for another's debt; in contrast to a surety who is primarily liable with the debtor. One who promises to answer for the debt in case of default.

Guaranty a collateral agreement for performance of another's undertaking. An agreement in which the guarantor agrees to satisfy the debt of a debtor, only if the debtor fails to repay the debt (secondary liability).

Guardian a person appointed to act on behalf of a person lacking ability to perform legal acts, to acquire legal rights, or incur legal liabilities.

Hazardous waste a substance that may cause or contribute to an increase in mortality or pose a hazard to human health or the environment when improperly treated.

Hearsay evidence not derived from the personal knowledge of the witness, but from what the witness has heard others say. Hearsay evidence is allowed only in special cases.

Hispanic legally, a person of Mexican, Puerto Rican, Cuban, Central or South American or other Spanish culture or origin, regardless of race.

Holder in due course (U.C.C.) a holder of an instrument who took it for value in good faith, and without any notice of any claim against the instrument; the holder is free of any claims against the instrument.

Horizontal business arrangement an agreement among firms operating at the same level of business in the same market.

Horizontal merger a merger between two companies that compete in the same product market.

Horizontal price fixing price fixing among competitors; an agreement among competitors to charge noncompetitive prices.

Horizontal restraint of trade anticompetitive action by businesses at the same level of operation. Rival firms that come together by agreement in an attempt to restrain trade by restricting output and raising prices is called a *cartel*.

Hot cargo agreement an agreement between an employer and a union when the employer agrees to refrain from handling, using, selling, transporting or dealing in any products of an employer the union has labeled as unfair or "hot."

Howey test the rule established by the Supreme Court to determine what a security is under the federal securities law: an investment of money, in a common enterprise, with the expectation that profits will be generated by the efforts of others.

Hung jury a jury so divided in opinion that it cannot agree upon a verdict.

Identification (U.C.C.) the process of specifying the actual goods that are covered by a contract.

Implied authority in agency law, when the right of an agent to act on behalf of a principal is inferred from past actions or from the current position of the agent.

Implied contract a contract formed on the basis of the conduct of the parties.

Implied warranty an unwritten, unexpressed promise or guarantee that a court infers to exist and that accompanies a good.

Import a product manufactured in another country, then shipped to and sold in this country.

Impossibility of performance a doctrine used to discharge the obligations of parties to a contract when an event—such a law being passed that makes the contract illegal or the subject matter of the contract is destroyed (called objective impossibility)—makes performance "impossible" for one or both parties.

Impracticability an interpretation of the doctrine of impossibility in contracts that allows a party to a contract to be relieved of the duty to perform when the basis of the contract no longer exists due to unforseen events.

Independent contractor one who provides service in the course of an occupation and who follows the employer's direction as to the result of the work, but does the work according to her own methods, unlike a servant or employee, who is subject to detailed control in the performance of work.

Indictment a formal written charge issued by a grand jury asserting that the named person has committed a crime.

Infringement in patent, copyright, and trademark law, the unauthorized use or imitation of another's recognized right to the property involved.

Injunction an order issued by a court that restrains a person or business from doing some act or orders the person to do something. May be permanent or temporary.

In personam jurisdiction the power the court has over the person(s) involved in the action.

In rem jurisdiction an action taken by a court against the property of the defendant.

Insider an officer or other person who has information not yet available to the general public concerning the future profits or losses of a corporation.

Insider trading the buying or selling of securities of a firm by persons who have information about the firm not yet available to the public and who expect to make a profit through those transactions.

Insolvency the financial state of a person or business when debts and liabilities exceed the value of assets.

Intangible asset property that is a "right" such as a patent, copyright or trademark, or one that is lacking physical evidence, such as goodwill in a firm.

Intangible property property that has no value because of its physical being but is evidence of value, such as securities, promissory notes, copyrights, patents, and certain contracts.

Intellectual property property recognized at law that arises from mental processes, such as inventions and works of art.

Intentional misrepresentation *see* fraud.

Intentional tort a wrong committed upon the person or property of another where the actor is expressly or impliedly judged to have intended to commit the act that led to the injury.

Interbrand competition competition among various brands of a particular product.

Interference with business relationship a tort in which a defendant commits an intentional and unjustified interference with a plaintiff's valid business dealings that inflicts monetary damage.

Interference with contractual relationship a tort in which there is a valid contract and the defendant knew of the contract but intentionally caused a breach of the contract, resulting in damages to the plaintiff.

Interference with prospective advantage (or with a business relationship) a tort where there is an intentional and unjustified intervention with a relationship that a party had been developing with others in an effort to obtain new business or more business.

International law those laws governing the legal relations between nations.

Interpretative rules statements issued by administrative agencies that explain how the agency understands its statutory authority to operate; these may be advisory or binding.

Interrogatories in the discovery process, a set of written questions for a witness or a party for which written answers are prepared with assistance of counsel and signed under oath.

Interstate commerce the carrying on of commercial activity that affects business in more than one state.

Intervening conduct in tort, an independent cause that comes between the original wrongful act and the injury that relieves liability that would otherwise exist for the original act; a legal break in the causal connection.

Intraband competition competition among retailers in the sales of a particular brand of product.

Invasion of privacy in tort, the encroachment on the right of a person to their solitude, the appropriation of a person's reputation for commercial purposes, or the public disclosure of facts that the person had a legal right to keep private.

Investigatory hearing in administrative law, when an agency uses rulemaking authority granted by Congress to gather information, on the public record, needed to determine the desirability of proposed rules.

Investment advisers Under securities law, a "person who, for compensation, engages in the business of advising others . . . as to the advisability of investing in, purchasing or selling securities. . . ." This includes securities brokers and dealers.

Investment company any corporation in business to own and hold the stock of other corporations.

Involuntary bankruptcy a bankruptcy proceeding against an insolvent debtor that is initiated by creditors.

Jeopardy a person is said to be in jeopardy when she is charged with a crime before a court. The constitutional doctrine of *double jeopardy* prohibits a person from being prosecuted twice in the same court for the same offense.

Joint and several liability liability that a person or business either shares with other tortfeasors or bears individually.

Joint liability liability that is owed to a third party by two or more other parties together.

Joint stock company a partnership in which the capital is divided, or agreed to be divided, into shares so as to be transferable without the express consent of the other partners.

Joint venture the participation of two companies jointly in a third enterprise. Generally, both companies contribute assets and share risks.

Judgment the official decision of a court of law upon the rights and claims of the parties to an action litigated in and submitted to the court for its determination.

Judgment lien a lien binding the real estate of a judgment debtor, in favor of the judgment holder, and giving the latter a right to levy on the property for the satisfaction of his judgment to the exclusion of others.

Judgment notwithstanding the verdict judgment entered by the court for a party following a jury verdict for the other party.

Judicial review authority of a court to reexamine a dispute considered and decided previously by a lower court or by an administrative agency.

Junior creditor a creditor whose claim against a debtor arose at a later date than that of the claim held by another creditor with the same or superior priority. A creditor whose claim ranks below other creditors with regard to priority to the debtors property.

Jurisdiction the right of a court or other body to hear a case and render a judgment.

Jurisdiction over the person power of a court to lawfully bind a party involved in a dispute before it.

Jurisdiction over the subject power of a court to lawfully affect the thing or issue in dispute.

Jurisprudence the science or philosophy of law.

Jury a body of people selected to hear the evidence in a case presented in court and who are given the power to apply the law to the facts established at trial in determining which party prevails in the matter in dispute, whether civil or criminal.

Just compensation clause the portion of the Fifth Amendment that states "nor shall private property be taken for public use, without just compensation." The requirement that when the government uses its power to force a private party to give up a property interest, fair market value should be paid.

Kefauver amendment the portion of the Food, Drug and Cosmetic Act that requires the Food and Drug Administration to approve drugs only after their safety and effectiveness have been established.

Laissez faire French for "let do"; a policy implying the absence of government intervention in a market economy.

Landlord the owner of real property (an estate) that has been leased to another party, the tenant.

Law enforceable rules of conduct set forth by a government to be followed by the citizens of the society.

Law merchant in commercial law, the rules devised by merchants in Europe over several centuries to govern their trade; many of these rules were formally adopted into law.

Leading question a question by an attorney in a trial that instructs the witness how to answer or provides the desired answer.

Lease an agreement, usually a contract, that gives the right to a party to take exclusive possession of property for a specific time for a certain payment. This normally creates a landlord and tenant relationship.

Leasehold refers to the real property, an estate, that is under the lawful control of a tenant for the term of the lease agreed to with the landlord.

Legal capacity the right to be able to enter into legal matters that may be restricted by age, mental ability, or other requirements established at common law or by statute.

Legal cause *see* proximate cause.

Legal detriment when a promisee gives up the right to retain control of something he was entitled to keep, or to give up the right to do something, in exchange for a promise by the other party to the contract.

Legal entity the existence of a thing, other than a natural person, that has legal existence so that it can function in a legal capacity, such as a corporation doing business.

Legal ethics practice and customs among members of the legal profession, involving their moral and professional duties toward one another, clients, and the courts.

Legislative history the history of a statute consisting of the legislative committee reports and transcripts of debates in the legislature. Often used by a court in interpreting the terms and provisions of a statute.

Letter of credit a written document in which the party issuing the document—usually a bank—promises to pay third parties in accordance with the terms of the document.

Levy a seizure; the process by which a state official is empowered by writ or other court directive to seize or control a judgment debtor's property to satisfy a judgment.

Liability a general term referring to possible or actual responsibility; when one is bound by law or equity to be accountable for some act; in product liability, it is in reference to the obligation to pay for damages for which the manufacturer has been held responsible.

Libel a defamation that is in the form of a printing, a writing, pictures, or a broadcast on radio or television.

Lien a claim or encumbrance on property for payment of some debt, obligation or duty. Qualified right that a creditor has in or over specific property of a debtor as security for the debt or for performance of some act. Right to retain property for payment of a debt.

Lien creditor a creditor who has acquired a lien on certain property by attachment, levy or other judicial means.

Life estate in property law, when a life tenant (the beneficiary of the arrangement) has the right to occupy a piece of property for life or earn income from a piece of property for life, after which control of the property passes to the designated owner.

Limited liability the fact that shareholders of a corporation are not liable for the debts of the corporation beyond the amount of money they have invested in the corporation.

Limited or special jurisdiction power of a court to hear a particular cause which can be exercised only under the limitations and circumstances prescribed by statute.

Limited partner a partner in a limited partnership whose liability for partnership debts is limited to the amount of his contribution to the partnership.

Limited partnership a business organization consisting of one or more general partners who manage and contribute assets to the business and who are personally liable for the debts of the business, and one or more limited partners who contribute assets only and are liable only up to the amount of that contribution.

Limited warranty under the Magnuson-Moss Warranty Act, any product sold with less than a full warranty has what is defined as a limited warranty, the terms of which must be explained in writing.

Liquidated damages amounts specified in a contract to be paid in the event of a breach. They represent a reasonable estimation by the parties of the damages that will occur in the event of breach.

Liquidated debt a debt for a known or determinable amount of money that can not be disputed by either the debtor or the creditor.

Liquidation the sale of the assets of a debtor, the proceeds from which are distributed to the creditors, with any remaining balance going to the debtor.

Lockout refusal by an employer to allow employees to work.

Long-arm statute a state statute permitting courts to obtain personal jurisdiction over nonresidents as long as the requirements of the statute are met.

Majority opinion when an appeals court issues an opinion in a case, which affirms or reverses the decision of the lower court, a majority of the judges join in an opinion that expresses the legal rationale for the decision of the court. If all judges agree, it is a unanimous opinion.

Malice the intentional doing of a wrongful act, without a legal excuse, with the intent to inflict injury.

Mandatory subjects of bargaining under the National Labor Relations Act, all terms and conditions of employment that must be discussed by employers and unions or an unfair labor practice occurs.

Manifest system in environmental and occupational safety law, the requirement that certain chemicals have documentation concerning their production, distribution, and disposal to ensure proper handling and disposal of toxic substances.

Margin requirement the fraction of a price of a stock that must be paid in cash, while putting up the stock as security against a loan for the balance.

Market failure failure of an unregulated market to achieve socially optimal results. Sources include monopolies and externalities.

Market power in antitrust law, the ability to raise prices significantly above the competitive level without losing much business.

Market share the percentage of a market, by sales volume of a product nationally or in a geographic area, that is controlled by a firm.

Market share liability when plaintiff is unable to determine which manufacturer of a product caused her injury, the court may assign liability to all firms in the industry on the basis of their shares of the product market.

Master a principal who hires another to perform services and who has the right to control the conduct of that person in the performance of the service; more commonly, an employer.

Material breach *see* breach of contract.

Material fact information that is substantially relevant to the consideration of a contract or to securities or to the decision made in a trial.

Maturity the due date of a financial instrument.

Mechanic's lien a claim under state law to secure priority of payments for the value of work performed and materials supplied in building on or improving land and buildings.

Mediation a form of alternative dispute resolution when a third party is hired by parties to a dispute with the intent to persuade them to settle their dispute.

Meeting competition in antitrust law, a defense in price discrimination (Robinson-Patman) cases, when a firm shows that prices were cut to meet the prices of competitors.

Meeting of minds a key element of a contract; it means that there has been agreement by both parties to the substance of the agreement.

Mens rea Latin for "the state of mind" of the actor.

Mental distress *see* emotional distress.

Merchantability in commercial law, the notion that goods are "reasonably fit for the ordinary purposes for which such goods are used."

Merger a contract through which one firm acquires the assets and liabilities of another firm.

Merit regulations state securities law provision that in some states allows a securities commissioner to decide if a proposed security offering is "too risky" to be sold to the public in that state.

Mineral rights (or subsurface rights) in property law, an interest in minerals in land, usually underground, that is separate from ownership of the surface of the land. There is a right to take the minerals from the land or to receive a royalty from the sale of minerals.

Minimum contacts a due process doctrine that requires an out-of-state defendant in a civil suit to have sufficient contacts in a state to make the party subject to the jurisdiction of the state courts.

Minitrial a voluntary form of alternate dispute resolution in which attorneys for both sides make a presentation to a neutral third party, who plays the role of judge. The person who hears the matter gives an opinion that is often the basis of a settlement negotiated without a trial in court.

Minorities persons classified as black (not of Hispanic origin), Hispanic, Asian, Pacific Islander, American Indian, or Alaskan native.

Misappropriation an unauthorized taking of another's property that denies the rightful owner the full use and benefit of the property.

Misdemeanor a lessor crime that is neither a felony nor treason, punishable by a fine and/or imprisonment in other than state or federal penitentiaries.

Misrepresentation words or conduct by a person to another that, under the circumstances, amount to a false statement.

Misstatements in securities law, liability may be imposed on those responsible for issuing information about securities that misleads a reasonable investor in investment decisions to her detriment.

Mistrial a trial that cannot stand in law because the court lacks jurisdiction, because of juror misconduct, or because of disregard for some other procedural requirement.

Mitigation of damages doctrine that imposes a duty upon an injured party to exercise reasonable diligence in attempting to minimize damages after being injured.

Mobile source under the Clean Air Act, a pollution source such as automobiles, trucks, and airplanes.

Modify in an appeals court, to change some detail of a lower court holding, but to leave the primary finding in place. For example, the decision of the lower court is likely to be affirmed, but the legal reasoning for the decision is amended.

Monetary damages *see* damages.

Monopoly a market structure in which the output of an industry is controlled by a single seller or a group of sellers making joint decisions regarding production and price.

Moral principles social rules that categorize different actions as right or wrong.

Morals generally accepted standards of right and wrong in a society.

Mortgage an interest in real property created by a written instrument providing security for the payment of a debt. In many states, a mortgage is a lien; it is a pledge or security of particular property to help insure payment of a debt or other obligation.

Mortgagee party who holds or receives a mortgage; the creditor.

Mortgagor one who, having all or part of title to real property, pledges the property in writing for a particular purpose, such as to secure a debt; the party who mortgages property; the debtor.

Motion the formal way an attorney submits a proposed measure for the consideration and action of the court.

Motion to dismiss a request that a complaint be dismissed because it does not state a claim for which the law provides a remedy, or is in some other way legally deficient.

Mutual consent *see* consent.

National Ambient Air Quality Standards federal standards under the Clean Air Act that set the maximum concentration levels in the atmosphere for several air pollutants.

National Priority List contaminated sites, as determined by the Environmental Protection Agency under the Superfund law, that must be cleaned up and returned to nearly original condition.

National Uniform Effluent Standards federal standards under the Clean Water Act that set the water pollution effluent standards for every industry that discharges liquid wastes into the nation's waterways.

Natural monopoly an industry characterized by economies of scale so large that one business can supply the entire market most efficiently.

Necessary and proper clause the part of the U.S. Constitution that gives Congress the authority to use various powers to execute its functions under the Constitution.

Negligence the failure to do something that a reasonable person, guided by the ordinary considerations that regulate human affairs, would do, or the doing of something that a reasonable person would not do.

Negotiable instrument a signed, written unconditional promise to pay, to the bearer of the instrument or to order of a certain party, a specific sum of money on demand or on a certain date.

Negotiation the deliberation over the terms and conditions of a proposed agreement, or a form of alternative dispute resolution to resolve a dispute and avoid litigation.

Negotiation (U.C.C.) the transfer of an instrument to another party who becomes the holder; the act of putting into circulation a check or promissory note.

Nominal damages a damage award whereby a court recognizes that the plaintiff has suffered a breach of duty but has not suffered any actual financial loss or injury as a result. Plaintiff's recovery for such breaches is often as little as one dollar.

Nonattainment area under the Clean Air Act, an area in which the air quality for certain pollutants fails to meet the national ambient air quality standards.

Nonpoint sources under the Clean Water Act, sources of pollution that are diverse, such as urban and agricultural runoff from rainstorms.

Novation an agreement between the parties to a contract to discharge one of the parties and create a new contract with another party to be responsible for the discharged party's obligations.

Nuisance an unreasonable and substantial interference with the use and enjoyment of another's land (*private nuisance*); an unreasonable or substantial interference with a right held in common by members of the general public (*public nuisance*).

Occupational licensure requirements at the state level that for one to practice a certain profession one must meet certain educational or experience guidelines, pass an entry examination, and show evidence of continuing education accomplishments.

Offer a proposal to do or refrain from doing some specified thing by a party called the offeror to another called the offeree. The proposal creates in the offeree a legal power to bind the offeror to the terms of the proposal by accepting the offer.

Offeree the party to whom an offer is made.

Offeror the party making an offer to another party to enter into a contract.

Open account credit extended by a seller to a buyer that permits buyer to make purchases without security.

Opening argument oral presentations made to the jury by the attorneys before the parties present their cases.

Oral argument presentations made in an appeals court or supreme court, usually by attorneys, in support of or objecting to the decision of a lower court as part of the appeals process.

Ordinary care *see* due care.

Original jurisdiction power of a court to take a lawsuit at its beginning, try it, and pass judgment upon the law and facts.

Out-of-court settlement an agreement by the parties in a case to resolve the matter before a determination by the court.

Over-the-counter market a stock market for securities generally not sold in large daily volumes so that they are not listed on a stock exchange, such as the New York Stock Exchange; a securities market created by stockbrokers who relay information to a central location about offers to buy or sell certain amounts of a stock.

Parol in French and Latin, "spoken" or "oral."

Parol evidence rule a rule that prohibits the introduction into a lawsuit of oral evidence that contradicts the terms of a written contract intended to be the final and complete expression of the agreement between the parties.

Partnership a business owned by two or more persons that is not organized as a corporation.

Par value stock stock that has been assigned a specific value by the corporation's board of directors.

Patent a grant from the government conveying and securing for an inventor the exclusive right to make, use, and sell an invention for twenty years from the time of application.

Per curiam opinion Latin for "by the court." A per curiam opinion expresses the view of the court as a whole in contrast to an opinion authored by one member of the court.

Perfect tender rule at common law, seller's offer of delivery must conform to every detail of contract with buyer; under the U.C.C., parties may agree to limit the operation of this rule or the seller may cure a defective tender if the time for performance has not ended, the seller notifies the buyer quickly of intent to cure defect, or the seller repairs or replaces defective goods within performance time limits.

Perfection of security interest in a secured transaction, the process by which a security interest is protected against competing claims to the collateral. It usually requires the secured party to give notice of the interest by filing it in the appropriate government office, usually the secretary of state.

Performance in contract law, the fulfilling of obligations or promises according to the terms agreed to or specified by parties to a contract. Complete performance of those obligations or promises by both parties discharges the contract.

Periodic disclosure in securities law, requirements that issuers of most publicly held securities file monthly, quarterly, and annual reports with the Securities and Exchange Commission.

Permanent injunction *see* injunction.

Per se Latin for "in itself" or "taken alone"; as in the per se rule in antitrust, whereby the facts alone are enough to lead to conviction of the defendants.

Personal property physical, movable property other than real estate.

Personal service in the pleadings stage, personal service of the complaint is accomplished by physically delivering it to the defendant.

Piercing the corporate veil a court's act of ignoring the legal existence of a corporation and holding the corporation's officers personally liable for their wrongful acts done in the name of the corporation.

Plaintiff the party who initiates a lawsuit.

Pleadings statements of the plaintiff and the defendant that detail their facts, allegations, and defenses, which create the issues of the lawsuit.

Point source under the Clean Water Act, any definitive place of discharge of a water pollutant such as pipes, ditches, or channels.

Police power a general power of the states to enact laws to protect public safety, health, and order so long as due process and equal protection are not violated.

Political speech in constitutional law, speech that concerns political, as opposed to commercial, matters; given a high level of protection by the First Amendment.

Pollution the release of substances into the air, water, or land that cause physical change.

Possessory lien (artisan's lien) a lien in which the creditor has the right to the possession of specific property until a debt is satisfied or an obligation is performed.

Potential competition in antitrust law, consideration given to the degree of competitiveness that exists in a market because of the possibility that firms not now in the market will enter it and compete with existing producers.

Power of attorney a document authorizing another person to act as one's agent or attorney with respect to the matters stated in the document.

Precedent a decision in a case that is used to guide decisions in later cases with similar fact situations.

Predatory pricing in antitrust law, pricing below an accepted measure of cost (such as average variable cost) to drive competitors from the market in the short run to reduce competition in the long run.

Pre-existing duty in common-law contracts, the rule that when a party promises to do something she was already obligated to do, there is not sufficient consideration to support a new contract.

Preferred stock class of stock that has priority over common stock both as to payment of dividends and to distribution of the corporation's assets upon dissolutionment.

Premises liability an intentional tort or a tort based on negligence when the owner or party with responsibility for maintaining certain property fails to provide adequate safety for visitors to the property against criminal attacks or accidents.

Preponderance of the evidence in civil trials, the burden of persuasion to win a verdict requires that the plaintiff prove its claim by having the majority or bulk of the evidence on its side.

Presumption means the trier of fact must find the existence of the fact presumed unless and until evidence is introduced which would support a finding of its nonexistence.

Prevention of significant deterioration area under the Clean Air Act, an area where the air quality is better than required by the national ambient air standards, such as national parks and wilderness areas. Air quality is not allowed to fall.

Price discrimination in antitrust law, charging different prices to different customers for the same product without a cost justification for the price difference.

Prima facie Latin for "at first sight." Something presumed to be true until disproved by contrary evidence.

Primary boycott in labor law, a union action that tries to convince people not to deal with an employer with which the union has a grievance.

Principal in an agency relationship, a person who, by explicit or implicit agreement, authorizes an agent to act on his behalf and perform acts that will be binding on the principal.

Principal (credit transactions) an amount of money borrowed or invested. The capital sum of a debt or obligation, distinguished from interest or other additions to it.

Principal (suretyship) the person primarily liable, for whose performance of her obligation the surety has become bound.

Private law a classification of law, generally denoting laws that affect relationships between people.

Private nuisance in tort law, when an activity reduces the right of one person, or a small number of persons, to enjoy property without unreasonable interference.

Private property right an individual economic interest supported by the law.

Privilege in tort law, the ability to act contrary to another's legal right without that party having legal redress for the consequences of that act; usually raised as a defense.

Privity a legal relationship between parties, such as between parties to a contract.

Privity of contract the immediate relationship that exists between the parties to a contract.

Probable cause reasonable ground to believe the existence of facts warranting the undertaking of certain actions, such as the arrest or search of a person.

Procedural law the rules of the court system that deal with the manner in which lawsuits are initiated and go forward. Court systems generally have rules regarding pleadings, process, evidence, and practice.

Product abuse (product misuse) a defense in a product liability suit where the producer or seller accused of marketing a defective product that caused an injury can show that the user of the product abused or misused the product in such a way as to be the primary cause of the injury that occurred.

Product liability a general category of cases in which the producer or seller of products may be held responsible to buyers, users, or innocent third parties who suffer injuries due to defects in the goods.

Product market in antitrust law, the product market includes all products that can be reasonably substituted by consumers for the product of the business under investigation.

Professional corporation in most states, a category of corporations that may be used by those providing a personal service that require a license, such as physicians, dentists, architects, and accountants. The primary reason to adopt this status are tax benefits.

Program trading the trading of stock on stock exchanges through the use of computers programmed to buy and sell at specified prices and other conditions.

Promise a statement or declaration that binds the party making it (the promisor) to do or refrain from doing a particular act or thing. The party to whom the declaration is made (the promisee) has a right to demand or expect the performance of the act or thing.

Promissee party to whom a promise is made.

Promisor party who makes a promise.

Promissory estoppel a doctrine that allows promises to be enforced in the absence of consideration if a promise is made which the promisor reasonably expects will induce action or forbearance on the part of the promisee and, which in fact, does cause such action or forbearance to the detriment of the promisee.

Promissory note an unconditional promise, in writing, to pay a certain sum at a specific time, or on demand, to a person named on the instrument or to the bearer of the instrument; such notes are negotiable.

Promulgation an administrative order that causes an agency law or regulation to become known and obligatory.

Proprietorship a business owned by a person that is not organized as a corporation.

Prospectus under securities law, a pamphlet that must be produced for distribution to prospective buyers of securities that contains information about the background of the security being offered.

Protected class under Title VII of the Civil Rights Act of 1964, those groups the law seeks to protect, including groups based on race, sex, national origin, religion, and color.

Protective order a decree by a court to protect a person or a legal entity against harassment by another person or to protect certain documents, such as trade secrets, against discovery in the litigation process.

Proximate cause in tort law, the action of the defendant that produces the plaintiff's injuries, without which the injury or damage in question would not have existed.

Proxy giving another person the right to vote on one's behalf; in stock votes, when a person gives another the right to vote in a certain manner, such as for candidates for board of directors.

Public corporation (publicly held corporation) while this can refer to a corporation established by the government for a specific purpose, it generally means a private corporation that has stock that is actively and openly traded.

Public law a classification of law, generally denoting laws that affect relationships between people and their governments.

Public nuisance in tort law, when an activity reduces the right of the public in general to enjoy property without unreasonable interference.

Punitive damages compensation awarded to a plaintiff beyond actual damages; awarded to punish the defendant for doing a particularly offensive act.

Purchase money security interest a secured interest created when a buyer uses the money of a lender to make a purchase and gives the lender a security interest in the property purchased.

Quantum meruit a concept in equity that a party should not be unjustly enriched by not paying for goods or services received that do not clearly fall under a contract; it is the recovery a plaintiff is allowed to be granted under an implied contract to pay for the reasonable value of services provided.

Quasi-contract a contract imposed by law, in the absence of an actual contract, to prevent unjust enrichment. A contract implied in law.

Quasi in rem jurisdiction a proceeding brought against the defendant personally, but when the defendant's interest in property serves as the basis of the court's jurisdiction.

Quid pro quo what for what, or something for something; the giving of something valuable for something valuable, such as consideration in a contract. Also refers to sexual discrimination when sexual favors are exchanged for employment favors.

Ratification in contract law, the act of accepting responsibility for a previous act that would not constitute an enforceable contractual obligation but for the ratification. Ratification causes the obligation to be binding as if it were valid and enforceable in the first place.

Real property land, the products of land (such as timber), and property that cannot be moved (such as houses).

Reasonable accommodation in employment discrimination law, the requirement that employers take steps that are not very costly to make employment possible for persons with disabilities.

Reasonable care the degree of care that a person of ordinary prudence would use in the same or similar circumstances or in the same line of business.

Reasonable person the standard which one must observe to avoid liability for negligence; often includes the duty to foresee harm that could result from certain actions.

Rebuttal during the trial stage, when evidence is given by one party to refute evidence introduced by the other party.

Recission in contract law, agreement of the parties to cancel a contract without performance; as a remedy, the cancellation of a contract by a court, the effect being as if the contract had never been made.

Red herring in securities law, a prospectus that has not yet been approved by the Securities Exchange Commission. It has a red border on its front to signal to interested parties that it is not yet approved for final distribution; used as an advertising device.

Reformation when a court orders a correction to a contract so that its true intention will be met; it is a remedy in equity that allows a court to correct mistakes the parties did not intend or to correct fraud that occurred.

Registration statements in securities law, the financial information that must be filed with the Securities and Exchange Commission for review prior to the sale of securities to the public.

Regulation Z a rule issued by the Federal Reserve Board to implement the Truth-in-Lending Act requiring systematic disclosure of the costs associated with credit transactions.

Rejoinder during the trial stage, the defendant's answer to the plaintiff's rebuttal.

Reliance when the tort of fraud or deceit occurs, the plaintiff must show that she relied on the false information that was provided, and that such reliance was reasonable under the circumstances.

Remand the act of an appellate court in sending a case back to trial court ordering it to take action according to its decision. The order usually requires a new trial or limited hearings on specified subject matter.

Remedy the legal means by which a right is enforced or the violation of a right is prevented or compensated.

Removal jurisdiction the power to remove a case from one court system to another.

Repatriation the process used to transfer assets or earnings from a host nation to another nation.

Reply during the pleading stage, plaintiff's response to the defendant's answer to the plaintiff's original complaint.

Representation election in labor law, when at least 30 percent of workers in a current or proposed bargaining unit sign a request to have an election to determine if all workers in that workplace will be represented by a particular union.

Repudiation a rejection, disclaimer, or renunciation of a contract before performance is due, but which does not operate as an anticipatory breach unless the promisee elects to treat the rejection as a breach and brings a suit for damages.

Request for admission a statement of facts about a case that the other party to a case is asked to admit are facts so that they need not be proved at trial.

Res Latin for "a thing" or "things."

Resale price maintenance when a manufacturer or wholesaler sets the price of a good at the next level, such as at the retail level; if the price set is not charged by the retailer, the manufacturer or wholesaler will no longer sell the good to the retailer.

Rescission to cancel or nullify a contract; it is the unmaking of a contract, as if it never existed. It may occur because both parties agree to avoid the contract or because one party gives the other party grounds for canceling the contract, such as by an act that would create grounds for not fulfilling the obligations.

Res ispa loquitor Latin for "the thing speaks for itself;" given the facts presented, it is clear that the defendant's actions were negligent and were the proximate cause of the injury incurred.

Res judicata a rule that prohibits the same dispute between two parties from being relitigated by a court after final judgment has been entered and all appeals exhausted.

Respondeat superior doctrine of vicarious liability under which an employer is held liable for the wrongful acts of his employees committed within the scope of their employment.

Respondent the party, plaintiff or defendant, who won in a lower court but must now respond to the appeal of the case by the losing party, the appellant.

Restatement of Law a series of books sponsored by the American Law institutes that explain the current state of the law in different areas (contracts, property, agency, torts, etc.) and the direction the law is moving. As the books are authored by leading scholars in the fields, they are often looked to for authority on points of law by courts in interpreting the law as it applies to a case.

Restitution a remedy in equity to restore a person to his original position had there been no loss or injury, or the position he would have enjoyed had there been no breach of contract.

Restraint of trade any contract, agreement, or combination that eliminates or restricts competition.

Reverse a decision by an appellate court that overturns or vacates the judgment of a lower court.

Reverse discrimination when discrimination is employed against majority groups so as to favor certain minority groups, often in affirmative action programs.

Revocation the recall of some power, authority, or thing granted; in contract law, the withdrawal by the offeree of an offer that had been valid until withdrawn.

Right-to-work law state laws that prohibit unions from forcing employees who do not want to pay union dues or agency fees to pay such dues or fees even if the employees are represented by the union under a collective bargaining agreement.

Riparian at common law, relating to the bank of a river or stream; the owner of land bounded by a river or body of water has the right to reasonably use the water next to the land or that passes over the land.

Rule making in administrative law, the procedures that agencies must follow when issuing rules to interpret or enforce the statutory authority they were granted by Congress.

Rule of reason in antitrust law, the court considers all facts and decides whether what was done was reasonable and did not harm competition in net; compare to the per se rule.

Sales contract under the U.C.C. "the passing of title from the seller to the buyer for a price."

Sanctions the penalty imposed, or threatened to be imposed, by a court on a party to litigation that is not complying with some aspect of the process, such as refusing to provide documents requested by the opposing party and approved by the court.

Satisfaction the performance of a substituted obligation in return for the discharge of the original obligation.

Scienter Latin for "knowingly;" usually meaning that the defendant knew that the act in question was illegal.

Second lien a lien that ranks after a first lien on the same property (such as a second mortgage) and is entitled to satisfaction out of the proceeds of the sale of the property after the first lien is satisfied.

Secondary boycott a union's refusal to handle products of or work for a secondary company with whom the union has no dispute; purpose is to force that company to stop doing business with another company with which the union has a dispute.

Secured creditors a person who has loaned money to another and has a legally recognized interest in the property of the debtor until fulfillment of the terms of the debt agreement.

Secured transaction any transaction, regardless of form, intended to create a security interest in personal property, including goods, documents, and other intangible property.

Securities debt or equity instruments that, in securities law, are evidence of a contribution of money by a group of investors into a common enterprise that will be operated for profit by professional managers.

Securities fraud in securities law, the statutory basis for charging anyone involved in the issuance or trading of securities with fraud, which is usually due to misleading issuance of information or failure to disclose material information that causes investors to suffer losses.

Security interest interest in property obtained under a security agreement. An interest in property that allows the property to be sold on default to satisfy the obligation for which the security interest is given. A mortgage grants a security interest in real property.

Self-defense generally, a legal excuse for the use of force to resist an attack on one's person, or to defend another person who is under attack, or property that is under attack. This defense may apply in common-law cases and in criminal cases.

Self-incrimination the rule that a witness is not bound to give testimony that would incriminate him with respect to a criminal act.

Seniority in employment, a system that recognizes length of service in deciding promotions, layoffs, and other job actions, where preference is given to the worker with more years of employment and/or more time in a particular position.

Separation of powers governments at the state and federal level in the United States are divided into the legislative, executive, and judicial branches, which each have certain duties and powers. This division of authority was designed to restrain the power of any one branch.

Service mark under trademark law, any symbol, word, or name used in the sale of goods to distinguish the services available from a particular source; service marks apply to services; trademarks apply to goods.

Service of process in the pleadings stage, the delivery of the complaint to the defendant either to her personally or, in most jurisdictions, by leaving it with a responsible person at her place of residence.

Servitude a burden that rests on one estate for the benefit of another. Servitudes on land may impose obligations on the owner of land to permit something to be done on the property by another, or it may be a restriction on the use of property that would normally be permitted.

Sexual harassment discrimination in employment in violation of Title VII of the 1964 Civil Rights Act that may be evidenced by sexual advances, requests for sexual favors, and other conduct of a sexual nature.

Shareholder the owner of one or more shares of stock in a corporation.

Shelf registration a Securities and Exchange Commission rule that allows certain companies to file a single registration statement for the future sale of securities. This registration allows the company to react quickly to favorable market conditions.

Short-swing profits profits made by an insider on the purchase and sale of stock of a corporation within a six-month period.

Sight draft a draft payable upon proper presentment.

Sine qua non rule *see* cause in fact.

Slander an oral defamation of one's reputation or good name.

Sole proprietorship *see* proprietorship.

Sophisticated purchaser in tort law, a defense that when a manufacturer sells a product to a sophisticated buyer, such as another manufacturer, the purchaser is responsible for instructing its employees about the dangers in using the product.

Sovereign a person, body, or nation in which independent and supreme authority is vested.

Sovereign immunity the doctrine under which a nonsovereign party is precluded from engaging in a legal action against a sovereign party, unless the sovereign gives its consent.

Special agent one employed as an agent to conduct a specific transaction or business act for a principal; while there may be more than one action involved, it is not expected to be a continuous relationship.

Special damages in contract law, damages not contemplated by the parties at the time the contract is made. To be recoverable, they must flow directly and immediately from the breach of contract, and must be reasonably foreseeable.

Specific performance an equitable remedy, whereby the court orders a party to a contract to perform his duties under the contract. Usually granted when money damages are inadequate as a remedy and the subject matter of the contract is unique.

Standing the right to sue in a particular court.

Stare decisis the use of precedent by courts; the use of prior decisions to guide decision making in cases before the courts.

State implementation plans under the Clean Air Act, a requirement that each state prepare, under Environmental Protection Agency supervision, a plan to control certain air pollutants by certain dates to meet national air quality standards.

Stationary sources under the Clean Air Act, a nonmoving source of pollution such as a factory or an electrical power plant.

Statute a law enacted by a legislative body.

Statute of frauds a statutory requirement that certain types of contracts be in writing to be enforceable.

Statute of limitations a statute setting maximum time periods, from the occurrence of an event, during which certain actions can be brought or rights enforced. If an action is not filed before the expiration of that time period, the statute bars the use of the courts for recovery.

Statutory law laws enacted by a legislative body.

Stock equity securities that evidence an ownership interest in a corporation.

Strict liability a legal theory that imposes responsibility for damages regardless of the existence of negligence; in tort law, any good sold that has a defect that causes injury leads to the imposition of liability.

Strike a work stoppage by employees for the purpose of coercing their employer to give in to their demands.

Subagent one authorized by an agent to help perform agency duties for a principal. When an agent has authority to appoint a subagent; he is subject to control by both the agent and the principal.

Subpoena an order by a court or other legal authority empowered to require a person to appear to give testimony about a certain civil or criminal matter. A subpoena duces tecum orders the production of documents.

Subrogation the substitution of one party in place of another with respect to a lawful claim, so that the party substituted succeeds to the rights of the other in relation to the debt or claim and its rights and remedies.

Subsidy a government monetary grant to a favored industry.

Substantial factor test a standard adopted in several states in place of proximate cause; a jury may hold a defendant liable in tort if it finds that defendant's conduct was a major cause of the injury in question.

Substantial performance a doctrine that recognizes that a party that performs a contract, but with a slight deviation from the contract's terms, is entitled to the contract price less any damages caused by the deviation.

Substantive law law that defines the rights and duties of persons to each other, as opposed to procedural law, which is law that defines the manner in which rights and duties may be enforced.

Substantive rules administrative rulings based on statutory authority granted an agency by Congress; the rules have the same legal force as statutes passed by Congress.

Substituted service a form of service other than personal service, such as service by mail or by publication in a newspaper.

Summary judgment a judgment entered by a trial court as a matter of law when no genuine issue of law is found to exist.

Summary jury trial a form of alternate dispute resolution in which both parties give a brief presentation of their argument in a courtlike setting in which a mock jury may be used; the decision of the jury need not be binding, but often helps the parties negotiate a settlement based on the information learned from the proceedings.

Summons process through which a court notifies and compels a defendant to a lawsuit to appear and answer a complaint.

Supreme courts in the federal and state court systems the highest court of appeal or the court of last resort; such courts are established by the federal and state constitutions.

Sunset laws a statute that requires periodic review for the continued existence of an administrative agency; the legislature must take positive steps to allow the agency to continue to exist by a certain date.

Superfund in environmental law, the Comprehensive Environmental Response, Compensation, and Liability Act (CERCLA) is called Superfund; it concerns requirements about when hazardous waste sites must be cleaned up and who is liable for the costs.

Superseding cause the act of a third party, or an outside force, that intervenes to prevent a defendant from being liable for harm to another due to negligence.

Surety one who undertakes to pay money or otherwise act in the event that her principal fails to pay or act as promised. A surety is usually bound with her principal by the same contract, executed at the same time and for the same consideration. Under the U.C.C., this includes a guarantor. However, liability of guarantor, depending on state law, is secondary and collateral, whereas liability of surety is primary and direct.

Suretyship the relationship among three parties in which one party (the surety) guarantees payment of a debtor's debt owed to a creditor or acts as a co-debtor.

Syndicates a business association made of parties for the purpose of carrying out some particular business transaction in which the members are mutually interested.

Takings clause *see* just compensation clause.

Tangible property property that has physical form and substance, such as real estate and goods.

Tariff a tax imposed on imported goods by the government to encourage domestic industry, or to raise revenues. *See* excise tax.

Tax incentive a government taxing policy intended to encourage a particular activity.

Temporary injunction *see* injunction.

Tenancy in common an ownership interest in which each tenant (owner) has an undivided interest in property. More than one party owns the property in joint possession, but there are separate titles so that when an owner dies, her interest passes to her heirs.

Tenant one who possesses (rents) real property for a period of time, usually under a lease. The property or estate is normally owned by the landlord.

Tender offer an offer open to current stockholders to buy a stock at a certain price; offer may be contingent upon receiving a certain amount of stock before any purchase is completed or may be an open offer; a method used to obtain enough stock to control a corporation.

Termination in contract law, the ending of an offer or contract, usually without liability.

Territorial allocation in antitrust law, the boundaries specified by contract or other agreement in which a wholesaler or retailer may sell a product.

Territorial jurisdiction territory over which a court has jurisdiction. The authority of any court is generally limited to its territorial boundaries. *See* long-arm statute.

Tie-in sale in antitrust law, the requirement that if one product or service is purchased then another product or service must also be purchased, even if it is not desired by the customer.

Title generally, the legal right of ownership; under the U.C.C., title is determined by rules regarding identification of goods, the risk of loss of goods, and insurable interest in the goods.

Tort an injury or wrong committed with or without force to another person or to his property; a civil wrong that is a breach of a legal duty owed by the person who commits the tort to the victim of the tort.

Tortfeasor an individual or business that commits a tort.

Toxic pollutants a pollutant that may cause an increase in mortality or serious illness.

Trade acceptance a draft drawn by a seller that is presented for acceptance to the buyer when goods are purchased; it is a negotiable instrument that the seller can use to raise funds.

Trade dress intellectual property protected by trademark law and the Lanham Act that concerns the total appearance and image of products and of service establishments, including shape, size, graphics and color.

Trademark a distinctive design, logo, mark, or word that a business can register with a government agency for its exclusive use in identifying its product or itself in the marketplace.

Trade name a word or symbol that has become sufficiently associated with a product over a period of time that it has lost its primary meaning and has acquired a secondary meaning; once so established, the company has a right to bring a legal action against those who infringe on the protection provided the trade name.

Trade regulation rules administrative rulings by the Federal Trade Commission or other agencies that hold certain practices to be illegal or create standards that must be met by sellers of certain products or services.

Trade secret in tort law, valuable, confidential data, usually in the form of formulas, processes, and other forms of information not patented, or not patentable, that are developed and owned by a business.

Treble damages a money damage award allowable under some statutes that is determined by multiplying the jury's actual damage award by three.

Trespass an unauthorized intrusion upon the property rights of another.

Trespass to personal property an unlawful interference with the rights of another person to possess their personal property, such as movable objects.

Trial a judicial examination of a dispute between two or more parties under the appropriate laws by a court or other appropriate tribunal that has jurisdiction.

Trial de novo Latin for "a new" trial, or retrial at an appellate court in which the entire case is examined as though no trial had occurred.

Trustee a person who has legal title in some property (such as the property of a bankrupt business) held in trust for the benefit of another person (the beneficiary).

Tying arrangements an agreement between a buyer and a seller in which the buyer of a specific product is obligated to purchase another good. *See* tie-in sale.

Ultrahazardous activity in tort law, a rule that when an activity "necessarily involves a risk of serious harm," such as the use of explosives or toxic chemicals, strict liability will be imposed when any harm is caused to other persons or property.

Unconscionable contract a contract, or a clause in a contract, that is grossly unfair to one of the parties because of stronger bargaining powers of the other party; usually held to be void as against public policy.

Underwriter a professional firm that handles the marketing of a security to the public; it either buys all of a new security offering and then sells it to the public, or takes a commission on the securities it actually sells.

Undisclosed principal when the identity of a principal is unknown to a third party, so that the third party is unaware that the agent being dealt with is representing the agency.

Undue influence the misuse of one's position of confidence or relationship with another individual to overcome that person's free will, thereby taking advantage of that person to affect decisions.

Unenforceable contract a contract that was once valid but, because of a subsequent illegality, will not be enforced by the courts.

Unfair labor practice in labor law, a wide range of actions that violate the right of workers to organize and engage in collective activities or violate the rights of employers to be free from practices defined as illegal under the National Labor Relations Act.

Unfair methods of competition under the Federal Trade Commission Act, a range of business practices found to violate the public interest; they may be based on fraud, deception, or a violation of public policy because competition is injured.

Unfairness in consumer protection law, a charge under Section 5 of the Federal Trade Commission Act that a business practice causes harm to consumers that the business cannot reasonably avoid.

Uniform Commerical Code (U.C.C.) a statute passed in similar form by the states that sets many rules of commercial sales agreements and negotiable debt instruments.

Unilateral contract an offer or promise of an offeror that is binding only after completed performance by the offeree. The offeree's completed performance serves as acceptance of the offer and performance of the contract.

Union an association of workers that is authorized to represent them in bargaining with their employers.

Union certification in labor law, when a majority of the workers at a workplace vote to have a union be their collective bargaining agent, the National Labor Relations Board certifies the legal standing of the union for that purpose.

Union shop a place of employment where one must be a union member before obtaining employment or must become a union member after obtaining employment.

Universal agent one serving as an agent who is authorized to conduct every transaction that can be lawfully delegated by a principal to an agent.

Unknown hazard in products liability, a claim that tort liability should be assigned to a producer for injuries suffered by a consumer due to a defect or hazard in a product that was not known by the producer at the time the product was made.

Unliquidated debt a disputed debt; a debt that has not been reduced to some specific amount.

Unsecured creditor a party owed money but who has no collateral, lien, or other security to secure the debt or claim in the event of default by the debtor.

Usury laws statutes that prohibit finance charges (interest and other forms of compensation for loaning money) above a certain level for debt.

Valid contract a contract in which all of the elements of a contract are present and, therefore, is enforceable at law by the parties.

Venue the geographic area in which an action is tried and from which the jury is selected.

Verdict from a Latin term meaning a true declaration. It is the formal finding of a jury in a case, determining which party prevails and, depending on the case, awarding damages or imposing a criminal penalty.

Vertical merger a merger of two business firms, one of which is the supplier of the other.

Vertical price-fixing an agreement between a supplier and a distributor, relating to the price at which the distributor will resell the supplier's product.

Vertical restraint of trade in antitrust law, contracts or combinations which reduce or eliminate competition among firms in the production, distribution, and sale of some good.

Vesting under the Employee Retirement Income Security Act, the requirement that pension benefits become the property of workers after a specific number of years of service to an employer.

Vicarious liability liability that arises from the actions of another person who is in a legal relationship with the party upon whom liability is being imposed.

Void contract a contract that does not exist at law; a contract having no legal force or binding effect.

Voidable contract a contract that is valid, but which may be legally voided at the option of one of the parties.

Voidable preference a preference given to one creditor over another by a bankrupt person or business, usually manifested by a payment to that creditor just prior to the bankruptcy declaration, that may be set aside by the trustee in bankruptcy.

Voir dire literally, to "speak the truth." In the trial stage, preliminary examination of a juror in which the attorneys and the court attempt to determine bias, incompetency, and interest.

Voluntary bankruptcy a bankruptcy proceeding that is initiated by the debtor.

Waiver an express or implied relinquishment of a legal right.

Warrant a judicial authorization for the performance of an act that would otherwise be illegal.

Warranty an assurance or guaranty, either express in the form of a statement by a seller of goods, or implied by law, having reference to and ensuring the character, quality, or fitness of purpose of the goods.

Warranty of title in general, the duty of a seller to provide good title or legal right of ownership of goods to the buyer;

under the U.C.C., specific warranty rights are provided when title to goods pass.

Wetlands in environmental law, land covered by water at least a part of the year; exact coverage by various environmental statutes is still unresolved.

Whistle-blower an employee who alerts the authorities to the fact that her employer is undertaking an activity that is contrary to the law.

Winding up process of settling the accounts and liquidating the assets of a partnership or corporation for the purpose of dissolving the concern.

Worker's compensation laws state statutes that provide for awards to workers or their dependents if a worker incurs an injury or an illness in the course of employment. Under such laws, the worker is freed from bringing a legal action to prove negligence by the employer.

Writ a mandatory precept issued by a court of justice.

Writ of certiorari an order by an appellate court used when the court has discretion whether or not to hear an appeal from a lower court. If appeal is granted, the writ orders the lower court to certify the record and send it to the higher court which then has the discretion to hear the appeal. If the writ is denied, the judgment of the lower court stands.

Writ of execution a writ to put into force the judgment of a court.

Written brief *see* brief.

Yellow-dog contract an agreement between an employer and an employee under which the employee agrees not to join a union and that if he joins a union there is a breach of contract and the employee is dismissed.

Zoning when the land in an area, usually a city, is divided into categories according to the kinds of structures that may be built, the purposes of the use of the land, and other regulations that may apply to different parcels of property.

INDEX